The Moral of the Story

For Craig and my parents

Immorality may be fun, but it isn't fun enough to take the place of 100 percent virtue and three square meals a day.

—Noel Coward, *Design for Living*

The Moral of the Story

AN INTRODUCTION TO ETHICS

Fifth Edition

NINA ROSENSTAND

San Diego Mesa College

Boston   Burr Ridge, IL   Dubuque, IA   Madison, WI   New York
San Francisco   St. Louis   Bangkok   Bogotá   Caracas   Kuala Lumpur
Lisbon   London   Madrid   Mexico City   Milan   Montreal   New Delhi
Santiago   Seoul   Singapore   Sydney   Taipei   Toronto

Higher Education

THE MORAL OF THE STORY

Published by McGraw-Hill, an imprint unit of The McGraw-Hill Companies, Inc., 1221 Avenue of the Americas, New York, NY, 10020. Copyright © 2006 by The McGraw-Hill Companies, Inc. All rights reserved. No part of this publication may be reproduced or distributed in any form or by any means, or stored in a database or retrieval system, without the prior written consent of The McGraw-Hill Companies, Inc., including, but not limited to, in any network or other electronic storage or transmission, or broadcast for distance learning.

This book is printed on acid-free paper.

1 2 3 4 5 6 7 8 9 0 DOC/DOC 0 9 8 7 6 5

ISBN 0-07-296335-2

Editor in Chief: Emily Barrosse
Publisher: Lyn Uhl
Senior Sponsoring Editor: Jon-David Hague
Senior Marketing Manager: Zina Craft
Editorial Coordinator: Allison Rona
Editorial Assistant: Liliana Almendarez-Wang
Production Editor: Leslie LaDow
Manuscript Editor: Joan Pendleton
Senior Design Manager: Violeta Díaz
Cover Designer: Lisa Buckley

Art Editor: Ayelet Arbel
Photo Research: Natalia Peschiera and
    Connie Gardener
Senior Production Supervisor: Richard DeVitto
Lead Media Project Manager: Marc Mattson
Composition: 10.5/12.5 Berkeley Book by
    Thompson Type
Printing: 45# New Era Matte by
    R. R. Donnelley, Crawfordsville, IN

Cover image by Karen Barbour

Credits: The credits section for this book begins on page 700 and is considered an extension of the copyright page.

Library of Congress Cataloging-in-Publication Data

Rosenstand, Nina.
    The moral of the story : an introduction to ethics / Nina Rosenstand. — 5th ed.
        p.   cm.
    Includes bibliographical references and index.
    ISBN 0-07-296335-2 (alk. paper)
    1. Ethics—Textbooks.   I. Title.
    BJ1012.R59   2005
    171—dc22   2005040885

The Internet addresses listed in the text were accurate at the time of publication. The inclusion of a website does not indicate an endorsement by the authors or McGraw-Hill, and McGraw-Hill does not guarantee the accuracy of the information presented at these sites.

www.mhhe.com

Contents

PART 3
How Should I Be? Theories of Virtue   369

Preface

*W*hen a new edition of a textbook is being prepared, choices have to be made: which elements to keep, and which to update or let go? Inevitably, even with an eye toward the timeless, classical questions, a new edition becomes a slice of time, reflecting the social and political ambiance of the time it was written. The fourth edition of this book was written in the shadow of September 11. Writing the present, fifth edition is taking place during what has become known as the War on Terror, with two post-9/11 wars, in Afghanistan and in Iraq. This means that some themes have stood out for me as important, such as the added concept of *courage* (Chapter 11) and the expanded issue of *terrorism and just war* (Chapter 13). Other sections of the book have remained untouched or are slightly revised. A number of new narratives have been added, films as well as novels.

The general concept of *The Moral of the Story* remains the same: that discussions about moral issues can be facilitated using stories as examples, as a form of ethics lab where solutions can be tried out under controlled conditions. The book is written primarily for such college courses as Introduction to Ethics; Moral Philosophy; and Introduction to Philosophy: Values. Many textbooks in value theory or ethics choose to focus on problems of social importance, such as abortion, euthanasia, and capital punishment. This book reflects my own teaching experience that it is better for students to be introduced to basic ethical theory before they are plunged into discussions involving moral judgments. Consequently, *The Moral of the Story* provides an overview of influential classical and contemporary approaches to ethical theory. However, without practical application of the theories there can be no complete understanding of the problems raised, so each chapter includes examples that illustrate and explore the issues. As in previous editions, each chapter concludes with a section of examples — summaries and excerpts — taken from the world of fiction, particularly films.

Within the last few decades, narrative theory has carved out a niche in American and European philosophy as well as in other academic disciplines. It is no longer unusual for ethicists and other thinkers to include works of fiction in their courses as well as in their professional papers, not only as examples of problem solving but also as illustrations of an epistemological phenomenon: Humans are, in Alasdair MacIntyre's words, storytelling animals, and we humans seem to choose the narrative form as our favorite way to structure meaning as we attempt to make sense of our reality. The narrative trend is making itself felt in other fields as well: the medical profession is looking to stories that teach about doctor-patient relationships; psychotherapists recommend that patients watch films to achieve an understanding of their own situation, and have patients write stories with themselves as the lead character. The court system is making use of films and novels to reach young people in trouble with the law. It seems that new fields are constantly being added to the list of professions that are discovering, or rediscovering, the potential of stories.

Organization

Like the previous editions, the fifth edition of *The Moral of the Story* is divided into three major sections. Part 1 introduces the topic of ethics and places the phenomenon of storytelling within the context of moral education and discussion. Part 2 examines the conduct theories of ethical relativism, psychological and ethical egoism, altruism, utilitarianism, and Kantian deontology, and explores the concepts of personhood, rights, and justice. Part 3 focuses on the subject of virtue theory and contains chapters on Socrates and Plato, Aristotle, contemporary virtue theories in America, theories of authenticity in the Continental tradition, and gender theory. The virtues of courage, compassion, and gratitude are examined in detail, and the book concludes with a more detailed discussion of four moral issues, applying both ethics of conduct and virtue ethics: media ethics, just war, animal rights, and capital punishment. Each chapter concludes with a set of study questions, a section of Primary Readings with excerpts from classical and contemporary texts, and a section of Narratives, a collection of stories that illustrate the moral issues raised in the chapter. The Primary Readings are selected for their value as discussion topics; they don't necessarily reflect my own views, and I have made no attempt to select readings that cover all possible angles, because of space limitations. The Narratives will be described in more detail below.

Major Changes to the Fifth Edition

Chapter 1 has been revised and expanded in light of the cultural changes since 9/11, but also, in a more traditional way, with a discussion of more logical fallacies. Chapter 2 now contains a new box on ethical wills, and a favorite section of mine about "bargain" and "quest" stories from way back in the first edition has been revised and reinstated. New examples have been added to Chapters 3 and 4, and Chapter 4 now has a discussion about free will and determinism. In Chapter 5, utilitarianism has been applied to the highly controversial issue of wartime torture; Chapter 7 has updated examples, including an updated stem cell research discussion; Chapter 8 has been expanded with information about the transitional years from Antiquity to Christianity, and Chapter 9 contains additional information about Aristotle and his school. In Chapter 10 a box discussing personal identity has been added; Chapter 11 (formerly Chapter 12) has been expanded with an entirely new section on the virtue of courage and a section on soft universalism and the political climate of today; Chapter 12 (formerly Chapter 11) has a new discussion of women in combat and a section reflecting the debate about same-sex marriage; and Chapter 13 has an expanded section on media ethics in light of both the CBS scandal of 2004 and the terrorist beheadings in Iraq, another expanded section on terrorism and just war, and updates on the death penalty debate.

New Primary Readings include an excerpt from Dwight Furrow's critique of ethical relativism and absolutism in "Of Cave Dwellers and Spirits: The Trouble with Moral Absolutes"; an excerpt from "The Rings of Tolkien and Plato: Lessons in Power, Choice, and Morality," by Erik Katz, from the book *The Lord of the Rings and Philosophy: One Book to Rule them All;* an excerpt from Senator John McCain's *Why Courage Matters;* an excerpt from Harriet Taylor Mill's "Enfranchisement of Women"; an excerpt from "Ethics as a Vehicle for Media Quality" by Andrew Belsey and Ruth Chadwick; and an excerpt from the *Ethics* July 2004 Symposium on Terrorism, War, and Justice: David Rodin's "Terrorism Without Intention." In addition, you will find excerpts from Tom Sorell's retentionist paper, "Two Ideals and the Death Penalty," and Mark Fuhrman's abolitionist argument in *Death and Justice: An Exposé of Oklahoma's Death Row Machine.*

New Narratives include the films *Big Fish, Lord of the Rings, Runaway Jury, Mississippi Burning, Minority Report, Pay It Forward, Tom Horn, Band of Brothers* episode 3, *Mona Lisa Smile,* and *The Life of David Gale,* and the novels *The Poisonwood Bible* and *How to Be Good.*

In addition, in response to reader suggestions, the Primary Readings and Narratives are now integrated in the chapter text through references: the titles of readings and stories, with brief descriptions, are cited within the appropriate chapter context.

Using the Narratives

The Narratives have been chosen from a wide variety of sources ranging from epic prose, poems, and novels to films. I wish to emphasize that from a literary and artistic point of view summaries and excerpts do not do the originals justice; a story worth experiencing, be it a novel, short story, or film, can't be reduced to a mere plot outline or fragment and still retain all of its essence. As Martha Nussbaum says, the form is an inherent part of the story content. Usually, there is more to the story than the bare bones of a moral problem, and in writing these summaries I have had to disregard much of the richness of story and character development. Nevertheless, I have chosen the summary or excerpt format in order to discuss a number of different stories and genres as they relate to specific issues in ethics. Because I believe it is important to show that there is a cross-cultural, historic tradition of exploring moral problems through telling a story, I have opted for a broad selection of Narratives. Each chapter has several Narratives, but it is not my intention that the instructor should feel obligated to cover all of them in one course; rather, they should be regarded as options that can be alternated from semester to semester—a method I like to use for the sake of variety. There are, of course, other ways than summaries in which stories and ethical theory can be brought together; one might, for instance, select one or two short stories or films in their original format for class discussion. I hope that instructors will indeed select a few stories—novels, short stories, or videos—for their classes to experience firsthand. However, the Narratives are written so that firsthand experience should not be necessary to a discussion of the problem presented by the story. The summaries and excerpts give readers just enough information to enable them to discuss the moral problem presented. I hope that some readers will become inspired to seek out the originals on their own.

Because space is limited, I have not been able to include more than a sampling of stories, and I readily admit that my choices are subjective ones; I personally find them interesting as illustrations and effective in a classroom context where students come from many different cultural backgrounds. Because I am a naturalized U.S. citizen, originally a native of Denmark, I have chosen to include a few references to the Scandinavian literary tradition. I am fully aware that others might choose other stories or even choose different ethical problems to illustrate, and I am grateful to the many users of the previous four editions, instructors as well as students, who have let me know about their favorite stories and how they thought this selection of stories might be expanded and improved. The new Narratives reflect some of these suggestions.

A new feature which I hope many instructors and students will avail themselves of is the McGraw-Hill website (http://www.mhhe.com/moralofthestory); one of the features of this website is access to Narratives from previous editions. Here you will be able to find the summaries of films such as *Hero, Tombstone, Working Girl, The Searchers,* the *Star Trek* television episode "Justice," and all the other stories that were a part of one or more editions of *The Moral of the Story* but had to be excluded from new editions because of space concerns. I welcome e-mails from students and instructors who use this book, with comments and suggestions for new stories as well as additional philosophical perspectives: nrosenst@sdccd.edu.

Acknowledgments

*A*s always I want to thank my students in the classes Introduction to Philosophy: Values, Philosophy of Women, Issues in Social Philosophy, Reflections on Human Nature, Human Nature and Society, and Philosophy and Literature for their enthusiastic cooperation in suggesting good stories and discussing drafts of the stories and study questions in this edition with me—an invaluable help in fine-tuning the summaries and questions. A special thank you to Tim Novak and Mack Tompkins III for sharing their research with me.

I also want to thank the production team at McGraw-Hill Higher Education for a smooth and enjoyable production experience: in particular my manuscript editor, Joan Pendleton, who aside from being a superb professional is also a personal friend—working with her is always a joy; and my editor Jon-David Hague, who keeps the overall goal in mind while listening with understanding to his authors' tales of woe, who is so good at thinking "outside the box," and who is also a good friend. My sincere thanks to my production editor Leslie LaDow, editorial coordinator Allison Rona, and editorial assistant Liliana Almendarez. I am proud to have yet another *Moral of the Story* cover created by artist Karen Barbour, with an image I find particularly evocative: It indicates that, contrary to some people's impression, you can live in a garden spot and still get some reading done!

I also want to thank the following reviewers for their excellent suggestions and critique, as well as their kind words about the fourth edition:

- Michael W. Blazek, Oklahoma State University
- Tom Caldwell, Lake Land College
- Nancy J. Matchett, University of Denver
- Chris Ann Moore, Honolulu Community College
- Debra K. Wicks, Pittsburgh Technical Institute

My colleagues at the Social Sciences and Behavioral and Multicultural Studies Department at San Diego Mesa College, which includes professors, adjuncts, and professors emeritus of philosophy, history, political science, and geography, are a wonderful support group—many of us come from different professional fields and have different outlooks on many things, but we all cherish the ambience of professional integrity in our workplace and find time to discuss ethics-related issues on a regular basis: Thank you to my colleagues from the Social Sciences Department as well as other departments: Madeline Hinkes, Jonathan McCleod, Mary Lou Locke, Don Abbott, Mark Trembly, Richard Hammes, John Crocitti, Hal Throckmorton, Terry Valverde, Charles Zappia, John Avohr, Sudata Debchaudhury, Sam Farahani, Chuck Corum, Arelene Wolinski, Pat Pidgeon, Tony Pettina, Michael Mussachia, Melissa Campbell, Joseph Binter, Scott Marcus, Madeleine Hinkes, Sondra Frisch, Angela Oberbauer, Dean of The Humanities Institute David Snyder, Dean of Learning Resources and Instructional Support William Craft, and all my colleagues on the Women's Studies Advisory Committee. In particular I want to extend my gratitude and appreciation to my fellow philosophers Dwight Furrow and Michael Kuttnauer for continual support and for a series of inspired meetings, which I hope will continue for many years. I don't know of any other department meetings that have gone more than an hour over the scheduled time because there were so many interesting new issues in ethics to talk about!

Other colleagues and friends who have been most helpful in assisting me either directly or indirectly through our discussions of ethics and stories, are Harold Weiss, Northampton Community College; Stephen George, Brigham Young University, Idaho; John Berteaux, previously of San Diego State University and now of Monterey State University; Lawrence Hinman, University of San Diego and the Ethics Consortium of Southern and Baja California; Virginia Lewis, University of San Diego; Peter Kemp, the Danish Institute of Pedagogy and leader of the Ethics and Law Institute, Copenhagen; Hans Hertel, University of Copenhagen; Maxine Sheets-Johnstone, independent scholar; and Steen Wackerhausen, University of Aarhus.

I'm grateful to Jerry Krase, Professor Emeritus, Brooklyn College, for a great radio conversation and subsequent e-mails with information and good cheer, and to Linda MacDonald Glenn, University of Vermont School of Nursing and Allied Health Care, for sharing her insights with me, as well as consistently positive personal e-mails. A heartfelt thank you to Annette Farnaes and the other members of The Book Club for friendship and good company, and for excellent book suggestions, including *How to Be Good.* Also, thank you, Claire, from Eddie Brandt's Saturday Matinee movie memorabilia store, for opening up the memorabilia section of the store to help me out on a a day when the section was closed, finding film stills for this edition. Likewise, I greatly appreciate the help I received from Hollywood Book and Poster World in locating and copying a great many of the film stills I needed for this edition, including a last-minute still, received within 24 hours.

In addition, I would like to thank Kathleen Brooks, host of the 2003–2004 Internet radio show "Ethics from Bedroom to Boardroom," for many a good talk on ethical issues and for inviting me on her show as a monthly co-host.

Also, many thanks to Mikkel Krause, Ole Brink, Marianne Skovlund, Katrine Nyland Sørensen, Kirsten Palmer, and Karen Secher of Denmark's Public Radio *P1 Morgen,* and Niels Lindvig of Denmark Public Radio's *Orientering,* for inviting me on their shows and asking me such good, thought-provoking questions about social, moral, and political issues regarding the United States.

A special appreciation goes to my good friends Mark Fuhrman and Rebecca Mack, 1510 KGA, for our lively ongoing debates over the years, on and off the air, on the phone and in person, about the death penalty, other moral issues, and the intersection of ethics, politics, and the law.

As usual, other friends have contributed to the new edition through their steadfast friendship, great suggestions, and good companionship, whether it be locally, by phone, e-mail, or during vacations back in my country of origin, Denmark: Betty Owens, Randi McKenzie, Phil Martin, Ned Huthmacher, Rich Curilla, J. R. Edmondson, Christa Blichmann and Søren Faartoft, Niels Foss, Frank Thompson and Claire McCullough, Søren Hyldgaard, Jan Niebuhr, Søren and Jytte Hansen, Astrid and Ellen Hansen, Stine and Mikkel Faartoft, Susanne and Maurice Schwer, Natalie and Sophia Schwer. In addition, I would like to express my gratitude to someone who was immensely influential in introducing me to literary theory: renowned Danish literary critic and editor Torben Brostrøm.

The first and second editions wouldn't have been possible without my first editor at Mayfield Publishing Company, my good friend Jim Bull. And the previous editions wouldn't have been possible without the help and suggestions from the following friends and colleagues: Helmut Wautischer, Sonoma State University; Eugene Troxell and Peter Atterton, San Diego State University; Betsy Decyk, Daniel Guerriere, and G. A. Spangler, California State University, Long Beach. In addition, I am grateful to Richard Taylor for his correspondence, to the late Philip Hallie for his inspiration, and to his late wife Dorrit Hallie; to Russell Means for sharing his views on American Indian traditions; to Leonard Maltin for his time and advice while I was working on the first edition; to Sue Savage-Rumbaugh for her time and comments on a draft of the second edition; to Carol Enns, College of the Sequoias; John Hasenjaeger, Clackamas Community College; John Osborne, Butte College; Thomas Wren, Loyola University, Chicago; Børge Pontoppidan, Barcelona; Marianne Ammitzbøll, Copenhagen. In addition, my eternal thanks to two people who were irreplaceable to me, and whose moral demands on themselves were without compromise: my late father-in-law Herbert Covner, and my late uncle Palle Hansen. Also, I wish to express my gratitude to the late James Rachels for his inspiration, and for his correspondence; it was a shock to learn of his passing, and I will always regret that we never met in person—I didn't realize that time was short.

I am very privileged to be able to thank both my parents, Gladys and Finn Rosenstand, for their continued help, encouragement, and love, and a faith in my writing skills from the day I wrote my first essay in elementary school. Throughout five editions of this book, and three additional books, they have been looking out for articles, books, and interesting stories for me. They deserve credit for teaching me to appreciate a good story, as well as the moral of a story. When most other kids watched TV, my father read aloud the classics, from Hans Christian Andersen to Kipling to Jules Romain, and my mother introduced me to science fiction, another abiding love. It is also a privilege to be able to thank Rowdie, again, for her loyal, brave heart and intelligent mind and her priceless company. But most of all my husband, Craig R. Covner, deserves my gratitude for being who he is, a companion, a friend, and a clear-headed critic when I need one—and someone who loves good movies as much as I do. Especially in the turbulent times since 9/11 it has been a relief beyond words to have a companion who shares one's core values as well as one's general worldview, on ethics as well as politics. With a line from one of our favorite movies, "Political arguments don't flavor folks' supper."

Part 1

The Story as a Tool of Ethics

Chapter One

Thinking About Values

The Best of Times, the Worst of Times?

*C*harles Dickens's *A Tale of Two Cities* from 1859 begins with this passage:

> It was the best of times, it was the worst of times,
> it was the age of wisdom, it was the age of foolishness,
> it was the epoch of belief, it was the epoch of incredulity,
> it was the season of Light, it was the season of Darkness,
> it was the spring of hope, it was the winter of despair,
> we had everything before us, we had nothing before us,
> we were all going direct to Heaven, we were all going direct
> the other way—in short, the period was so far like the present
> period, that some of its noisiest authorities insisted on its
> being received, for good or for evil, in the superlative degree
> of comparison only.

Dickens was referring to the era of the French Revolution, but, as many have pointed out, his words apply to just about any particular time period one cares to scrutinize. And yet—aren't these words a particularly good fit for the years immediately following September 11, 2001? The memories of people helping people on 9/11, and stories of wartime heroism in the war in Afghanistan and the war in Iraq, show us that heroism and self-sacrifice are to be found not just in tales of times past. They are part of today's moral landscape too—but so are atrocities that prior to 9/11 had seemed unimaginable to most people expecting a steady progression of what we call civilization. 9/11 was in itself a gruesome example of innocent civilians being targeted deliberately to create terror and to make a political statement. In Iraq and Pakistan, American civilians as well as people of other nationalities have been beheaded by terrorists, with live video to prove it. While the Abu Ghraib prisoner abuse scandal didn't rise to the level of atrocity of the beheadings, it was still a shock for most Americans to see U.S. military reservists posing for pictures with Iraqi prisoners of war in humiliating situations after the fall of Saddam Hussein's regime.

A Normal Life?

One would think that such concerns would make peacetime worries seem trivial; prior to September 11 we used to worry about racial profiling, road rage, and school shootings. For a short few months in the fall of 2001 the focus changed; in the months after 9/11 politicians and "talking heads" predicted that nothing would ever be the same for us—we had been attacked on American soil, and from now on we would always feel on the alert, looking forward with unity and resolve, and backward with perhaps some nostalgia for the late twentieth century, when a nation could be consumed with curiosity about which character shot another character in a TV series, who was voted off an island on a reality show, or whether a famous ex-football player killed his ex-wife and her friend. Some would say "Such luxury—being able to devote time and mental energy to such matters!" In what was termed the *new normalcy,* the war on terrorism rose to occupy our minds and the airwaves.

And yet—as I am working on this new edition, it almost looks as if life has gone back to normal, focusing on people and issues as if we were in peacetime. How different is the everyday life *you* live now from your life prior to September 11? If you were directly affected by 9/11, or if you are a member of the armed forces, or have loved ones in the military, you know that these are different times. If not, the War on Terror may seem rather remote and unreal to you. The media have spent a lot of time on a court case involving a young husband on trial for killing his wife, pregnant in the eighth month. We have spent time discussing the fate of Martha Stewart, going to prison for lying to the court about her financial dispositions. Many people have become encouraged, or appalled, at the possibility of same-sex marriage becoming a legal option. We have been disturbed by the Enron scandal and by the scandal of the Catholic Church covering up child abuse crimes committed by a number of priests over a period of thirty years. Politically, the unity and cohesion we experienced after 9/11, illustrated by bumper stickers such as "United We Stand," has eroded and fragmented into something like politics as usual. However, for many of us this is only a surface normalcy: The fact that we *thought* we were secure prior to 9/11, as illusory as it may have been, and that we now *know* we are not, provides a new context for our entire cultural and ethical debate, and you will find this new context reflected in many of the discussions in this text.

A "50-50" Nation?

Since the 2000 election, this nation has experienced a division between "conservatives" and "liberals"—what has become known as the "50-50 nation," a division in the population that we have not seen since the days of the Vietnam War. The presidential election of 2004 illustrated this division, with a twist: Republican President George W. Bush was reelected with a 51 percent majority, while Democratic presidential candidate John Kerry lost by 48 percent—not quite 50–50, but close enough for many voters to feel alienated from "the other half" of the country. The Kerry states, or "blue states" as they became known due to the color-coding of the election maps on TV, were primarily coastal: the West Coast, and upper East Coast states in particular, as well as some states around the Great Lakes. The "red," or Bush, states covered the entire middle of the country. And if you took a look at a map displaying election results according to *counties* instead of states, the picture was even more interesting, because the "blue" counties were primarily large cities and university centers, while the "red" counties were everywhere else: smaller towns and rural areas. This division indicates that it was not just a matter of political preferences: It might even be a matter of different worldviews. As an aside, one should not forget that "50–50" can be

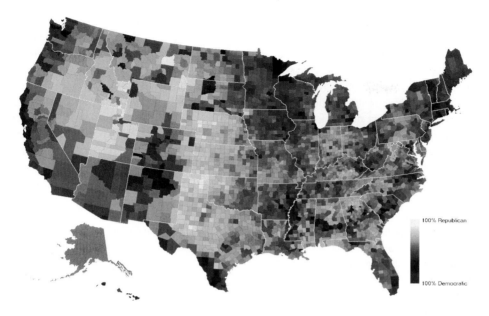

After the 2004 presidential election, it became popular to refer to the states that voted Democratic as "blue states" and the Republican states as "red states" because of the election map colors displayed on TV. However, the county election map shows that each state, too, was divided, between large cities and the rest of the state. Here the "blue" counties are shown in dark gray, while the "red" counties are light gray.

rather misleading, inasmuch as not everybody is registered to vote, and not all registered voters actually choose to go to the polls. Nor is everybody either a Democrat or a Republican—other parties are on the ballot too, and there is a steadily growing number of Independents (who "declare not to state" a party) who may have some Republican and some Democratic viewpoints. For some, the ultimate reason for re-electing Bush lay in the question of the war on terrorism and the war in Iraq: The all-important issue was to continue the course of action that was begun during the first three years after 9/11. Many Kerry-voters felt that it was time to move on and deal with issues of terror through the United Nations and the World Court. In other words, it became clear that there is a dramatic difference in how we view ourselves as a moral nation vis-à-vis the world.

But there were additional issues. Some found it extremely important to elect a president who would support certain *values,* so in a sense we can be viewed as residents of two American moral cultures: the culture of liberal values and the culture of conservative values. Some call it a culture war. It isn't uncommon for some of us to identify so deeply with one that we downright refuse to accept the legitimacy or even rationality of the other. As we strive to become a nation of successful diversity, we sometimes forget that *moral and political diversity* also deserves a place alongside diversity of gender, race, religion, economic background, sexual orientation, and so forth. In other words, people have a right to have a wide variety of opinions, and we have little chance of being able to talk with each other if we keep thinking that everybody who doesn't agree with us is stupid, ignorant, or evil.

On the other hand, an acceptance of the fact that people disagree on moral issues doesn't have to lead to a moral relativism, or an assumption that there is always "another side" to everything. Despite our moral differences in this culture, most "reasonable" people are going to agree on some basic values: In my experience, the majority of Americans are in favor of justice and equality, and against murder, child abuse, racism, sexism, slavery, animal torture, and so forth. In Chapter 3 you'll find a discussion of ethical relativism, and in Chapter 11 you'll find a further discussion of the search for common values in a politically divided culture.

Good and Evil

For many people the topic of morals involves the concepts of *good* and *evil,* and the choices we make in one direction or the other. Certainly, in the post–September 11 world it has become more customary to use the term *evil* to describe an attitude that disregards the humanity and dignity of another person. So what do the professionals say—the ethicists who make a living teaching theories of moral values and writing papers, monographs, and textbooks? Interestingly, most contemporary ethicists tend to talk about issues such as selfishness and unselfishness, informed consent, weighing moral principles against overall consequences of one's actions, group right versus individual rights, and so forth. We hear discussions about the concepts of moral *right and wrong* and the principles by which we determine such concepts. What we rarely hear mentioned by any contemporary ethicists are the concepts that most people associate with moral issues: *good and evil.* Exceptions would be American philosophers such as Philip Hallie and Richard Taylor and the British philosopher Mary Midgley. Why are so few philosophers these days interested in talking about good and evil, when it used to be one of the key topics in centuries past? For one thing, there is an underlying assumption that good and evil are *religious* concepts, and as we shall see, the philosophical discussions about ethics and values these days tend to steer clear of the religious connection to ethics. For another, talking about good and evil generally implies that we *pass judgment* on what is good and what evil—which means that we take sides, we no longer analyze concepts in some lofty realm of objectivity, we engage ourselves in seeking good and shunning evil. This also means that we condemn those who are labeled evil and praise those we call good. In other words, we engage in what some would call *moralizing,* and most ethicists have for decades tried to avoid just that, with some exceptions. However, since September 11 the concept of evil has been part of our political vocabulary, spearheaded by President Bush, who labeled nations supporting terrorism as an *axis of evil* and referred to the terrorists of 9/11 and others as *evildoers.* A precedent was created when President Reagan labeled the Soviet Union "The Evil Empire" in the 1980s. While this terminology, to some critics, is far too close to a religious vocabulary for comfort, for other Americans there is great relief and, indeed, comfort in being able to use a word with the weight of tradition behind it to describe something most of us consider dreadful acts committed by people with no consideration for human decency.

But what exactly do we call evil? Is evil a force that exists outside human beings—is there a source of evil such as the devil, some satanic eternal power that tempts and preys on human souls? Or is it rather a force within the human mind, disregarding the needs and interests of other human beings just to accomplish a goal? Or might it perhaps be a *lack of something* in the human mind—a blind spot where the rest of us have a sense of community, belonging, empathy for others? In that case, might we explain the acts of "evildoers" as those of sick individuals? But wouldn't that entail that they can't be *blamed* for what they do, because we don't usually blame people for their illnesses? These are questions that involve religion, psychology, and ethics, and there is to this day no consensus among scholars as to how "evil" should be interpreted. Some see terrorists, serial killers, and child molesters as evil, but we may not agree on what makes them evil—a childhood deprived of love, a genetic predisposition, a selfish choice that involves disregard for other people's humanity, a brainwashing by an ideology that distinguishes between "real" people and throwaway people, an outside superhuman evil force that chooses a human vehicle? When news of the Abu Ghraib prison scandal hit, many people were reminded of the Stanford prison experiment in 1971: A group of experimental subjects—ordinary male college students—were divided into "prisoners" and "prison guards," and before long the "prison guards" began treating the "prisoners" with abusive cruelty, believing that such behavior was somehow warranted to maintain authority. The German film *The Experiment* is a chilling reenactment of the experiment. Some see such an event as proof that human nature is fundamentally bad—it doesn't take much for the veneer of civilization to wear thin, and our true, evil nature surfaces. For others, all this means is that there are all kinds of reasons why people do what they do; some of what we call evil is based on a moral choice, and some of it is an outcome of environmental pressures or brain anomalies. For the German philosopher Immanuel Kant, whom you'll meet in Chapter 6, there is no doubt what evil is: It is the self-serving choice individuals make freely even when they know full well the moral law they ought to be following.

So what do we label "good"? There is hardly a word with a broader meaning in the English language—we can talk about food tasting good, test results being good, a feeling being good, but also, of course, of actions being good and persons being good, and we mean something different in all these examples. In Box 1.1 you'll find a discussion of moral and nonmoral values, and "good" fits right into that discussion: It is a value term because it expresses approval, but it can be an approval that has to do with moral issues (such as actions and a person's character) or it can be unrelated to moral issues, such as judging the result of a quiz, or a medical test, or something we approve of because of its aesthetic qualities (it looks good, tastes good, sounds good, etc.). If we assume that we're mostly interested in the moral value of "good," we have only narrowed it down somewhat, because now we have to define what, in our context and in our culture, is considered a morally good act. It could be acting according to the rules of one's culture's religion; it could be acting with compassion or with foresight as to the overall consequences of one's actions, or it could be simply doing one's

In *The Lord of the Rings* (2001–2003) the concept of evil is symbolized by the Ring. Here the hobbit Smeagol (Andy Serkis) finds the Ring on his birthday (top). Many years later the effects of evil are clearly visible: Smeagol has become Gollum (bottom), a solitary creature whose mind is focused exclusively on the Ring.

duty. A "good person" could be someone who is simply nice by nature, but it could also be someone who struggles to do the right thing, perhaps even against his or her nature. Or it could be simply someone we approve of, based on our cultural rules. But

Box 1.1   MORAL AND NONMORAL VALUES

What is a *value?* Most often the word refers to a moral value, a judgment of somebody's behavior according to whether or not it corresponds to certain moral rules (for example, "Tiffany is a wonderful person; she always stays after the party to help with the dishes"). However, some value judgments have nothing to do with moral issues, and so they are called *nonmoral,* which is not the same as *immoral* (breaking moral rules) or *amoral* (not having any moral standards). Such nonmoral value judgments can include statements about taste (such as "The new gallery downtown has a collection of exquisite watercolors"; "I really dislike Bob's new haircut"; and "Finn makes a great jambalaya"), as well as statements about being correct or incorrect about facts (such as "Lois did really well on her last math test" and "You're wrong; last Saturday we didn't go to the movies; that was last Sunday"). Like moral value judgments, nonmoral value judgments generally refer to something being right or wrong, good or bad; but, unlike moral value judgments, they don't refer to morally right or wrong behavior.

there is also something called being "too good," like a Goody Two-Shoes, so perhaps being morally above reproach isn't always good? The Narrative at the end of the this chapter called "How to Be Good" is a modern and rather cynical take on this subject.

Morals, Ethics, and Values

In the late twentieth century the number of college classes in introductory ethics and value theory swelled. When they hear I teach ethics, people who are unfamiliar with how college classes in the subject are taught say, "Good! Our college students really need that!" This response always makes me pause: What do they think I teach? Right from wrong? Of course, we do have discussions about right and wrong, and we can, from time to time, even reach agreement about some moral responses being *preferable* to other moral responses. If students haven't acquired a sense of values by the time they're in college, I fear it's too late: Psychologists say a child must develop a sense of values *by the age of seven* in order to become an adult with a conscience. If the child hasn't learned by the second grade that other people can feel pain and pleasure, and that one should try not to harm others, that lesson will probably never be truly learned. (Box 1.2 explores the topic of a moral center in the brain.) Fortunately this doesn't mean everyone must be taught the *same* moral lessons by the age of seven—as long as we have *some* moral background to draw on later, as a sounding board for further ethical reflections, we can come from morally widely diverse homes and still become morally dependable people. A child growing up in a criminal, *Sopranos*-type of family will certainly have acquired a set of morals by the age of seven—but it isn't necessarily the same set of morals as those acquired by a child in a liberal, secular, humanist family or in a Seventh-Day Adventist family. The point is that all these children will have their "moral center" activated and can expand their moral universe. A child who has never been taught *any* moral lessons may be a sociopath of the future; a person who has no comprehension of how other people feel, no empathy.

Box 1.2   A MORAL CENTER IN THE BRAIN

In 1999, researchers led by Antonio Damasio at the University of Iowa found that an area in the brain, the prefrontal cortex, plays a pivotal role in our development of a moral sense. People who have undergone a normal psychological and moral development (1) know there is a difference between right and wrong, and (2) can act on that knowledge. Adults who have had their prefrontal cortex damaged in an accident still know the difference between right and wrong, but somehow it doesn't translate into action: They can't make decisions based on that knowledge or act on such decisions. Two patients investigated by the Iowa team had suffered damage to their prefrontal cortex before they were sixteen months of age, and—in spite of having apparently recovered from their injuries, having normal intellectual capacities, and having been reared in stable, middle-class homes—both developed severely antisocial behavior as adolescents and adults: recklessness, inability to care about others, including their own babies, abuse of others, and criminal tendencies. They seemed to recognize moral issues intellectually but were unable to act on them because they had no sense of the consequences of their actions.

So now that we know where our morals are located in the brain, can we say we understand everything about the issues of morals, ethics, and values? Can we perhaps say that a person whose moral center is damaged shouldn't be held accountable for what she or he does? This is where sweeping generalizations can become dangerous: It may be that some people are genuinely unaware of the moral consequences of their actions—but it may be a dubious legal trend to assume that every criminal must have a damaged prefrontal cortex. For if we do so, we create an easy excuse and throw out the possibility of people actually making decisions *deliberately*—decisions that go against the values of society. Indeed, we should be careful not to assume that neuroscience can tell us everything we need to know about who we are. Brain research can pinpoint where our thoughts and feelings originate and what affects them chemically, but it can't tell us whether one moral answer is better than another; we need the actual human thought process for that.

Dilbert by Scott Adams

© 2001. DILBERT reprinted by permission of United Feature Syndicate, Inc.

Lately, research has pointed to the existence of an actual moral center in the brain. If this center is damaged, the individual seems to have a hard time acting on moral deliberations or even understanding moral issues. Obviously, this *Dilbert* cartoon takes a dim view of whether people in management have a functioning moral center.

Should elementary schools teach values, then? It may be just a little too late, if indeed a child's moral sense is developed by the age of seven, but at least there is a chance it might help; and for children whose parents have done a minimal job of teaching them respect for others, school will probably be the only place they'll learn it. Some elementary schools are developing such programs. Problems occur, however, when schools begin to teach values with which not all parents agree. We live in a multicultural society, and although some parents might like certain topics to be on the school agenda, others certainly would not. Some parents want their children to have early access to sex education, whereas others consider it unthinkable as a school subject. There is nothing in the concept of values that implies we all have to subscribe to exactly the same ones, no matter how strongly we may feel about our own. So, beyond teaching basic values such as common courtesy, perhaps the best schools can do is make students aware of values and value differences and let students learn to argue effectively for their own values, as well as to question them. Schools, in other words, should focus on *ethics* in addition to *morality.*

So what is the difference between *ethics* and *morality*? *Ethics* comes from Greek (*ethos,* character) and *morality* from Latin (*mores,* character, custom, or habit). Today, in English as well as in many other Western languages, both words refer to some form of proper conduct. Although we, in our everyday lives, don't distinguish clearly between morals and ethics, there is a subtle difference: Some people think the word *morality* has negative connotations, and in fact it does carry two different sets of associations for most of us. The positive ones are guidance, goodness, humanitarianism, and so forth. Among the negative associations are repression, bigotry, persecution— in a word, *moralizing.* Suppose the introductory ethics course on your campus was labeled "Introduction to Morals." You would, in all likelihood, expect something different than you would from a course called "Introduction to Ethics" or "Introduction to Values." The word *morality* has a slightly different connotation than do the terms *ethics* and *values:* That is because *morality* usually refers to *the moral rules we follow,* the values that we have. *Ethics* is generally defined as *theories about these rules;* ethics questions and justifies the rules we live by, and, if ethics can find no rational justification for those rules, it may ask us to abandon them. Morality is the stuff our social life is made of—even our personal life—and ethics is the ordering, the questioning, the awareness, the investigation of what we believe: Are we justified in believing it? Is it consistent? Should we remain open to other beliefs or not?

How, then, do we define *values*? In the 1980s and 1990s a frequent media topic was *family values*—from a conservative point of view, it meant adhering to traditional morals with respect for family life and marriage. Some liberals, in contrast, chose to view family values as any public policy that would help families stay together, financially and emotionally. It was quite a surprise to many in the media when the notion of *moral values* popped up in the 2004 presidential election. The implication was that moral values equal traditional values—in particular, respect for the institution of marriage (as opposed to support for same-sex marriage, one of the key political issues in 2004). Liberal commentators pointed out that having moral values can also mean respecting cultural and sexual diversity—although one liberal writer, Michael Kinsley, wrote that he was sick and tired of trying to turn his liberal views into "values" and said, "When I want values, I go to Wal-Mart." This tongue-in-cheek remark is a double-entendre, of course: "Values" can mean an awful lot of things, from cheap buys to morals. You may remember a commercial for a clothing company where a professor complains to a female student that her generation has no values, and she responds by telling him how value-conscious she is in her purchases! In our everyday language, something we value is something we believe is set apart from other things that we don't value or value less. When do we first begin to value something? As babies, we live in a world that is divided into what we like and what we don't like—a world of plus and minus, of yes and no. According to some psychoanalysts, we never really get over this early stage, and some people simply divide their world into what they like or approve of and what they don't like or disapprove of. However, most of us add an element to that, a justification for our preferences or aversions.

If values have to do with people's likes and dislikes, why are they not studied only in the discipline of psychology? Why is philosophy involved with what values we have, what moral rules we follow, and what ethical justifications we give? Psychology can tell us only what people believe in and possibly why they believe it; it can't make a statement about whether people are *justified* in believing it. Philosophy's job, at least in this connection, is to *question* our values; it forces us to give reasons, and preferably good reasons, for why we approve of one thing and disapprove of something else. We might approve or disapprove of something that is a matter of taste; in that case we talk about the values of *aesthetics*. However, the primary field in which philosophers voice their approval or disapproval is the field of morality. And when we are evaluating issues in morality, we are practicing ethics.

In today's complex society it is not considered enough for an adult person merely to divide the world into likes and dislikes; we are exposed to so many different values that we are expected to have reasons for our moral preferences. In other words, it is not enough just to have moral rules; we should, as moral, mature persons, be

Dilbert by Scott Adams

© 1997. DILBERT reprinted by permission of United Feature Syndicate, Inc.

Ethicists point out that having a system of values isn't enough for a person to be morally mature—one must also engage in thinking about those values and critically examine them from time to time. Cartoonist Scott Adams obviously agrees.

able to justify our viewpoints with ethical arguments or, at the very least, ask ourselves why we feel this way or that about a certain issue. Ethics, therefore, is much more than a topic in a curriculum. As moral adults, we are required to think about ethics all the time.

Most people, in fact, do just that, even in their teens, because it is also considered a sign of maturity to question authority, at least to a certain extent. If a very young adult is told to be home at 11 P.M., she or he will usually ask, "Why can't I stay out till midnight?" When we have to make up our minds about whether to study over the weekend or go hiking, we usually try to come up with as many pros and cons as we can. When someone we have put our trust in betrays that trust, we want to know why. All of these questions are practical applications of ethics: They question the rules of morality and the breaking of those rules. Although formal training in ethical questions can make us better at judging moral issues, we are, as adult human beings, already quite experienced just because we already have asked, "Why?" a number of times in our lives.

Why Be Moral?

Do we know *why* humans all over the world have an interest in establishing and following moral rules? An age-old answer is, Because the moral rules are decrees from God (or the gods). Philosophy has several answers, and, interestingly enough, some of them are mutually exclusive. Philosophy has traditionally looked for the origin of morality in the realm of *reason:* Somehow, applying rules for decent behavior makes sense, so rationality becomes a prerequisite for moral behavior. Some philosophers, however, reject the idea of morality being a matter of the head—they claim it is the *heart* that is involved, and the head just rationalizes whatever it is the heart wants. If this is the case, no amount of rational argumentation will persuade people who listen just to their heart and to their gut feelings. For those who adhere to this theory, there is no such thing as a "morally superior" point of view. All viewpoints are just subjective emotions. A new breed of thinkers, including the American philosopher Martha Nussbaum, holds the theory that our moral values do indeed have a strong connection to our emotions, but that doesn't mean the values or our moral decisions reflecting them can't be rational. According to this theory, there is a rational element within our emotional life that makes some emotional reactions reasonable and morally relevant, while others may not be: Being angry because someone has mistreated us is justified and may pave the way for an understanding of justice, but being angry for no appropriate reason is not morally acceptable. We return to Nussbaum later in this chapter.

There also are those who believe that morality is a built-in, fail-safe *biological* trait: We can't help being moral because otherwise our species would perish. Genetically, we have an interest, in a limited sense, in looking after one another: It is to our own advantage and that of our descendants.

Some philosophers go further in stressing the advantageous nature of morality. Morality, they say, is nothing but playing it safe when you can't get away with doing what you want; it derives from *fear of being caught.* We stick to the straight and narrow because we are afraid of what may happen if we don't: We'll go to jail, or lose our friends, or go to hell, or endure some other nasty prospect. If we ean get away with something, however, we will do it—that is human nature. This view, a variety of *egoism,* will be discussed shortly.

Some of these attempts at explaining the nature of morality will be discussed in Part 2, where we examine the ongoing human endeavor to answer the question, *What should I do?* When faced with a moral problem that requires our immediate attention, we often realize that deep down we know what we ought to do, but we just don't feel like doing it—perhaps we feel very much like doing the exact opposite. We may, for example, believe it is our duty to be with our family for Thanksgiving, but we would rather accept an invitation to go to a mountain cabin with some good friends. Or we know we ought to work Friday afternoon, but the weather is so nice . . . or we feel attracted to someone who already has a partner, so we know we ought to get out of the way, but. . . . This conflict between what we ought to do and what we want to do—between duty and inclination—is perhaps the most common form of a moral dilemma; some people think it is the *only* form of moral conflict. There may be another kind, however, one in which we have to choose between two things we should do but don't want to do—or perhaps we don't mind doing them, but one just happens to preclude the other. We may be caught between a rock and a hard place when we need to study for a final on the same night that our boss wants us to help take inventory at our part-time job. Tell the boss that school is more important, and chances are she won't agree. Tell the professor that work is more important, and he may be completely unsympathetic. Clearly, we need to do both, but we can do only one. We may even find ourselves in a situation in which we have to decide whether to give up our car to a carjacker or to put up a fight. We don't really want to do either, but we have to make a choice; if we dawdle, the carjacker will take that to mean we have chosen to refuse to give up the car, and we may be harmed. Such moral dilemmas fill our lives and can be either fascinating or extremely anxiety-provoking. Can moral theories help us decide what to do when we really need some good advice? That is the whole point; indeed, theories of moral conduct set out to do just that by giving us a basic value by which to measure the situation. What are you most concerned with? Your own happiness? Overall consequences down the line? Doing the right thing? Keeping a promise? Obeying the law? And what do you think your priorities *ought* to be? In Part 2 of this book we look at various answers to these moral problems.

Debating Moral Issues

Every functional society on earth has had a "philosophy" of what one should do or be in order to be considered a good person. Sometimes this moral code is expressed orally in stories and songs, and sometimes it is expressed in writing. When it is expressed as a set of rules with explanations justifying the rules, we may call it a *code of ethics.* In order for it to become a philosophical discipline, we must add the practice of examining and questioning the rules. In the Western intellectual tradition, Greek philosophers were the first to focus on ethics as a subject worth studying; Socrates asked the all-important question, *How should one live?* From then on, and for over two thousand years, ethics has been one of the major branches of philosophical inquiry in the Western tradition, and contemporary philosophers around the world continue to dedicate curriculum hours, journals, papers, and conferences to its study. Other key areas of philosophy are logic (defining the rules for proper thinking), metaphysics (theories of the nature of reality), aesthetics (theories of beauty and art), and epistemology, also known as theory of knowledge (theories of how the human mind can obtain knowledge and whether the knowledge we obtain can ever be *certain*).

Cultures developing independently of the Western tradition have experienced a similar fascination for the subject of acting and living right. Socrates' version remains unique among ancient thinkers because he encouraged critical thinking instead of emphasizing being an obedient citizen. In China, Confucius expressed his philosophy of proper moral conduct as a matter of obedience to authorities and, above all, respect for one's elders at approximately the same time at which Socrates was teaching students critical thinking in the public square in Athens. In Africa, tribal thinkers developed a strong sense of morality in terms of individuals' sense of responsibility to the community and the community's understanding of its responsibility to each individual—a philosophy that has become known to the West in recent years through the proverb, "It takes a village to raise a child." Among American Indian tribes, the philosophy of harmony between humans and their environment—animate as well as inanimate nature—has been part of the moral code.

Do we have any guidelines for whether one viewpoint is *morally better* than another? How would we know which one is superior? Centuries ago the answer would have been plain: Religion would have provided the answer. We would have looked for help with moral problems in religious texts or in the advice of religious leaders; indeed, many people continue to find comfort in the belief that the answers are there. More and more people in the Western part of the world, however, live a secularized life; and, although they may ask their God for guidance, they by no means believe that all of the answers are to be found in their religious tradition. Often, people find that our society today is more complex than that presented in their religious texts. For agnostics and atheists there can be no turning to religion for unquestioned moral guidance because they view religion itself as an unknown or nonexistent factor. Agnostics claim that they do not know whether there is a God or that it is impossible to know. Atheists claim that there is no God. Both the agnostic and the atheist may find that religion suggests solutions to their problems, but such solutions are accepted not because they come from religion but because they somehow make sense.

For a philosophical inquiry the requirement that a solution make sense is particularly important; although religion may play a significant role in the development of moral values for many people, a philosophical investigation of moral issues must involve more than faith in a religious authority. Regardless of one's religious belief or lack thereof, such an investigation must involve reasoning because, for one thing, philosophy teaches that one must examine issues without solely relying on the word of authority. For another thing, a rational argument can be a way for people to reach an understanding in spite of having different viewpoints on religion. Accordingly, a good way to communicate about ethics for both believers and nonbelievers is to approach the issue through the language of *reason*.

When we reach a conclusion based on rational premises, we are presenting an *argument*. Such arguments can be *inductive,* or they can be *deductive*. An inductive argument is a conclusion based on a gathering of evidence, but there is no certainty that the conclusion is true, only that it is likely. A deductive argument, on the other hand, is an argument where the conclusion does follow with certainty from the premises.

Logical fallacies invalidate a moral viewpoint just as they do any other kind of viewpoint. Have you heard someone claim that because she has been cheated by two auto mechanics, no auto mechanics can be trusted? That's the fallacy of *hasty generalization.* Have you heard someone who is an expert in one field claim to be an authority in another—or people referring to some vague "expert opinion" in defense of their own views? That is the fallacy of *appeal to authority.* When someone tries to prove a point just by rephrasing it, such as "I'm right, because I'm never wrong," that is the fallacy of *begging the question,* a circular definition assuming that what you are trying to prove is a fact. How about a bully arguing that if you don't give him your seat/purse/car, he will harm you? That's the *ad baculum* (Latin for "by the stick") fallacy, the fallacy of using physical threats. And if someone says, "Well, you know you can't believe what Fred says—after all, he's from out of town," that's an *ad hominem* ("to the man") fallacy, which assumes that who a person is determines the correctness or incorrectness of what he or she says. And a politician declaring "If we continue to allow women to have abortions, then pretty soon nobody will give birth, and the human race will die out" offers a *slippery slope* argument, which assumes that drastic consequences will follow a certain policy. Closely related is the *straw man* fallacy, inventing a viewpoint so radical that hardly anyone holds it, so you can knock it down: "Gun advocates want to allow criminals and children to own weapons, so we should work toward a gun ban." And if you claim that we either have to respect all individual rights or curtail people's rights in order to achieve security, one or the other, then you are *bifurcating*—you are creating a *false dichotomy* (unless, of course, we're really talking about a situation with no third possibility, such as being pregnant—you can't be a little bit pregnant; it's either/or).

Another fallacy is the famed *red herring,* familiar to every fan of mystery and detective stories. A "red herring" is placed on the path to confuse the bloodhound. In other words, it is a deflection away from the truth. In an everyday setting, this can be accomplished by changing the subject when it gets too uncomfortable ("Why did you get an F on your test, Bob?" "Mom, have I ever told you you're prettier than all my friends' moms?"). The notoriety of the red herring fallacy in court cases is well known, from introducing the race issue in the O. J. Simpson criminal trial to attacking a rape victim's sexual history in order to deflect attention away from the defendant. A fallacy most of us who make our living teaching are very familiar with is the fallacy of *ad misericordiam,* appeal to pity. "Please, can I get an extension on my paper? My backpack was stolen, my cat ran away, my grandma is in the hospital, and I've got these really killer hangnails." Or is it hangovers, perhaps? We've heard them all, all the bad excuses. But an excuse becomes an *ad misericordiam* fallacy only if it is nothing but an excuse. Sometimes a person truly deserves special consideration because of individual hardship, of course. These and other logical fallacies are rampant in media discussions, and part of proper moral reasoning consists in watching out for the use of such flawed arguments, in one's own statements as well as in those of others.

But is logic all there is to a good moral argument? Some philosophers would say yes: The force of a moral viewpoint derives from its compelling logic. But increasingly, other voices are adding that a good moral argument is compelling not just because of its logic but because it also makes sense *emotionally.* If we have no feeling of moral approval or outrage, then do we really *care* about whether something is morally right or wrong? If we don't *feel* that it's wrong to harm a child, then how is logic going to persuade us? A classic answer has been an appeal to the logic of the Golden Rule: You wouldn't want someone to harm *you,* would you? But say some, that's an appeal to how you'd *feel* in the same situation. An appeal to pure feeling isn't going to be enough, because feelings can be manipulated, and appeals to emotions don't solve conflicts if we don't share those emotions; but combined with the logic of reasoning emotions can form the foundation of a forceful moral argument, according to some modern thinkers.

Martha Nussbaum: Stories Have Value

All cultures tell stories, and all cultures have codes for proper behavior. Very often those codes are taught through stories, but stories can also be used to *question* moral rules and to examine morally ambiguous situations. A fundamental premise of this book is that stories sometimes can serve as shortcuts to understanding and solving moral problems. Many literature professors may be inclined to tell us that people don't read anymore, that the novel is dead, or that nobody appreciates good literature these days. I myself am rather disappointed when students are unfamiliar with the classics of literature or have grown to hate them through high school manglings. However, it just isn't true that people don't read novels—best-sellers are flourishing like never before. And an element has been added to our appreciation of good stories: *movies.* The American film industry has been in existence for over a hundred years, and it should be no surprise to anyone that as much as films can provide simple entertainment, they can also give us in-depth, unforgettable views of human life, including moral issues. This book makes use of that treasure trove of movie stories as well as novels, short stories, epic poems, television shows, and plays as illustrations of moral problems and solutions.

After each chapter in this book you will find a small selection of stories titled *Narratives* (summaries and/or excerpts) that illustrate the moral theory discussed in the chapter. Some examples can be seen as arguments in favor of the type of theory in question, and some can be viewed as arguments against it.

In most cases the ending is important to the moral significance of a story, and whenever that is the case, I include that ending. In cases in which the ending is not significant to the moral drama, I have done my best to avoid giving it away because I don't want to be a spoiler. Using stories here has two purposes. One is to supply a foundation for further debate about the application of the moral theories presented in the chapter; the other is to inspire you to experience these stories in their original form, through print or video, since they are, of course, richer and more interesting than any outline can show.

"We Have Never Lived Enough"

For the greater part of the twentieth century most Western philosophers had a tacit agreement that stories were best left in the nursery, but times have changed: There is now a growing interest in the cultural and philosophical importance of story-telling, in technological as well as pretechnological cultures, and stories are becoming shortcuts to understanding ourselves on an individual as well as a cultural level. One of the most influential voices speaking for narratives as a way to communicate about values is Martha Nussbaum (b. 1947), a philosopher and professor of law and ethics; her main interest is not the intellectual value of storytelling as much as the emotional force of narratives.

Nussbaum believes there was a time when philosophers understood the value of narratives. The Greek thinker Aristotle (whom she greatly admires) believed that experiencing a drama unfold teaches the viewer basic important lessons about having the proper feelings at the proper time—lessons about life and virtue in general. As modern Western philosophy took shape, however, the idea of emotions seemed increasingly irrelevant. There are signs today that philosophy is making a turn-around, that it is allowing itself to take a closer look at emotions as a legitimate subject for research. Nussbaum contributes to this turnaround with her books *Love's Knowledge* (1990), *Upheavals of Thought: The Intelligence of Emotions* (2001), and *Hiding from Humanity* (2004). She points out that emotions weren't excluded from philosophy because they did not yield *knowledge;* in other words, it is not because of any lack of *cognitive value* that philosophers have refused to investigate emotions. There is actually much cognitive value in emotions, for emotions are, on the whole, quite *reasonable* when we look at them in context. When do we feel anger? When we believe that someone has deliberately injured us or someone we care about—in other words, when we feel the situation warrants it. Feelings such as disappointment, elation, grief, and even love are all responses to certain situations. They develop according to some inner logic; they don't strike at random. How do we know? Because if we realize that we were wrong about the situation, our anger slowly disappears. Perhaps love is not that easy to analyze—people in love don't seem to respond all that logically to situations that ought to change their feelings of love. (The person you love is seeing someone else, and what do you do? Continue to be helplessly in love.) But even love responds to such challenges in a way; we probably realize that our feelings are, somehow, out of place.

Why, then, have so many philosophers refused to deal seriously with emotions? Not because emotions lack cognitive value, but because they show we react to situations outside our control: When we are emotional, we are not *self-sufficient,* and most philosophers have, according to Nussbaum, preferred to investigate a more autonomous part of the human character, our reason. (Of course some philosophers and psychoanalysts have pointed out that reason is not immune to outside influence, either, but Nussbaum is addressing the trends in traditional philosophy before the

Martha Nussbaum (b. 1947), American philosopher. The author of *Love's Knowledge, Upheavals of Thought,* and *Hiding from Humanity,* she suggests that novels are supremely well suited to explore moral problems. Through novels we have the chance to live more than our own lives and to understand human problems from someone else's point of view. Since others can read the same novels, we can share such knowledge and reach a mutual understanding.

twentieth century, when the idea of reason being affected by the Unconscious was not yet commonly accepted.)

For Nussbaum, emotions provide access to values, to human relationships, and to understanding ourselves, so they must be investigated. And where do they manifest themselves most clearly? In narratives. Stories are actually emotions put into a structure. When we are children and adolescents we learn how to manipulate objects and relate to others; we learn cognitive skills and practical skills, and among the skills we learn are when to feel certain kinds of emotions. The prime teacher of emotions is the story. This means, of course, that different societies may tell different stories teaching different lessons, so we must retain a certain amount of social awareness and social criticism when reading stories from any culture, including our own. People in their formative years are not just empty vessels into which stories are poured. Nussbaum maintains there is no rule saying that people must accept everything their culture teaches them; so those who don't approve of the stories being told or who think the stories haven't been told right, will begin to tell their own stories. As important as emotions are, alongside our reason, in shaping our moral values, Nussbaum has of late found it necessary to specify that two particular emotions should not be considered conducive to moral understanding: *disgust* and *shame.* Here Nussbaum enters the political arena by claiming that some emotions are more morally and politically appropriate than others. When we say we are disgusted with something or someone, we set ourselves on a pedestal as being better and purer, says Nussbaum, and that to her is an unrealistic assessment that does nothing more than create an us-versus-them environment.

To understand emotions we must read stories, but that ought to come easily to us, Nussbaum believes, since we already enjoy doing just that. She does stress, however, that we have to read the entire story, not just rely on a synopsis. There is an integral relationship between the form and the content of a story. As she says in her book *Love's Knowledge,* we can't skip "the emotive appeal, the absorbing plottedness, the variety and indeterminacy of good fiction" without losing the heart of the experience. So in a sense Nussbaum does not specifically advocate *using stories to illustrate moral problems,* as we will be doing in this book. Instead, she supports reading stories as a way of *sharing basic experiences of values* and using philosophy as a tool for analyzing this experience. For her, the story comes first, and then the analysis can follow. In the Primary Readings section, you'll find an excerpt from *Love's Knowledge*.

Why use stories, though? Why can't we approach moral issues by more traditional avenues, such as examples that are "made to order" by philosophers? Because, says Nussbaum, they lack precisely the rich texture that makes the story an experience we can relate to. Besides, such examples are formulated in such a way that the conclusion is obvious. Novels tend to be quite open-ended, a feature that Nussbaum believes is valuable. Novels preserve "mystery and indeterminacy," just like real life.

Why not just rely on your own experiences to learn about life? Some of them must certainly contain both mystery and indeterminacy. To some extent we do that already; we draw on our own experience as much as we possibly can when judging concrete and abstract cases. But the trouble is, one human life is just not enough for understanding the myriad ways of being. As Nussbaum says,

> We have never lived enough. Our experience is, without fiction, too confined and too parochial. Literature extends it, making us reflect and feel about what might otherwise be too distant for feeling. . . . All living is interpreting; all action requires seeing the world *as* something. So in this sense no life is "raw" and . . . throughout our living we are, in a sense, makers of fictions. The point is that in the activity of literary imagining we are led to imagine and describe with greater precision, focusing our attention on each word, feeling each event more keenly—whereas much of actual life goes by without that heightened awareness, and is thus, in a certain sense, not fully or thoroughly lived.

Furthermore, it is much harder to talk about events in your own life than it is to discuss events in a story. We may not want to share our deepest feelings, or we may not be able to express them. But if we talk with friends about a passage in a favorite book or film, we can share both an emotional and a moral experience. One final word about Nussbaum's theory: It is important that we remember that she has no wish to replace the traditional rational approach to moral issues with an emotional approach—to her, emotions can be relevant in moral decision making, but that doesn't make reason irrelevant. But we have a fuller understanding of being human, and making moral decisions, if we allow our focus to include relevant emotions as well as reason. At the end of the chapter you'll find two narratives which, each in their own way, illustrate Nussbaum's theory of storytelling as a key to understanding ourselves and each other and of emotion as having a rational component: *Big Fish* tells of a man who sees his own life as a story—perhaps excessively—and *Smoke Signals* shows the character development of an angry young man who learns that the cause of his anger against his father was only in his own head.

Study Questions

1. In your opinion, should children learn values in elementary school? Explain why or why not, and craft an argument for and against the idea as it might be presented by a teacher and a parent.

2. Give three examples of statements about moral issues, illustrating three logical fallacies.

3. Do you remember a story that has made a moral choice easier for you? Explain.

4. Comment on Nussbaum's statement, "We have never lived enough. Our experience is, without fiction, too confined and too parochial. Literature expands it, making us reflect and feel about what might otherwise be too distant for feeling." What does she mean? Do you agree? Why or why not?

5. Consider the multicultural challenge of storytelling. Do you remember any story that has enhanced your understanding of another culture? Do you remember any story from your own culture that expresses a moral you find unacceptable? Do you know any story from another culture whose moral you find unacceptable? Is it possible to find some common ground? Explain.

Primary Reading and Narratives

The Primary Reading is from *Love's Knowledge* by Martha Nussbaum, explaining why fictional stories are better at teaching moral lessons than real-life stories and little made-to-order philosophical examples. The first Narrative is an excerpt from Nick Hornby's novel *How to Be Good,* about a wife and a husband in a marital as well as a moral crisis situation; the second Narrative is the film *Smoke Signals,* about two young American Indian males, Victor and Thomas, who understand their reality in very different ways—one through stereotypes, the other through stories—and Victor's journey from anger toward his father to a rational reassessment of his feelings. The third Narrative is the film *Big Fish,* also about a father-son relationship, seen in light of what some would call storytelling, and others simply lying!

Primary Reading

Love's Knowledge

MARTHA NUSSBAUM

Excerpt, 1990.

In this excerpt, Nussbaum argues that novels, short stories, and dramas are very well suited to providing an emotional lesson in moral issues because of the brevity of human life: We just can't experience everything ourselves, so fiction provides a shortcut to understanding the range of human emotions. She also explains why such philosophical examples as those you will encounter in this book (such as Kant's example of the killer at the door looking for your friend) aren't good enough to teach the same lesson. You may want to consider why Nussbaum's argument omits the mention of movies—is it deliberate? or an oversight?

Not only novels prove appropriate, because (again, with reference only to these particular issues and this conception) many serious dramas will be pertinent as well, and some biographies and histories—so long as these are written in a style that gives sufficient attention to particularity and emotion, and so long as they involve their readers in relevant activities of searching and feeling, especially feeling concerning their own possibilities as well as those of the characters. [. . .]

But the philosopher is likely to be less troubled by these questions of literary genre than by a prior question: namely, why a literary work at all? Why can't we investigate everything we want to investigate by using complex examples of the sort that moral philosophers are very good at inventing? In reply, we must insist that the philosopher who asks this question cannot have been convinced by the argument so far about the intimate connection between literary form and ethical content. Schematic philosophers' examples almost always lack the particularity, the emotive appeal, the absorbing plottedness, the variety and indeterminacy, of good fiction; they lack, too, good fiction's way of making the reader a participant and a friend; and we have argued that it is precisely in virtue of these structural characteristics that fiction can play the role it does in our reflective lives. As [novelist Henry] James says, "The picture of the exposed and entangled state is what is required." If the examples do have these features, they will, themselves, be works of literature. Sometimes a very brief fiction will prove a sufficient vehicle for the investigation of what we are at that moment investigating; sometimes, as in "Flawed Crystals" (where our question concerns what is likely to happen in the course of a relatively long and complex life), we need the length and complexity of a novel. In neither case, however, would schematic examples prove sufficient as a substitute. (This does not mean that they will be totally dismissed; for they have other sorts of usefulness, especially in connection with other ethical views.)

We can add that examples, setting things up schematically, signal to the readers what they should notice and find relevant. They hand them the ethically salient description. This means that much of the ethical work is already done, the result "cooked." The novels are more open-ended, showing the reader what it is to search for the appropriate description and why that search matters. (And yet they are not so open-ended as to give no shape to the reader's thought.) By showing the mystery and indeterminacy of "our actual adventure," they characterize life more richly and truly—indeed, more precisely—than an example lacking those features ever could; and they engender in the reader a type of ethical work more appropriate for life.

But why not life itself? Why can't we investigate whatever we want to investigate by living and reflecting on our lives? Why, if it is the Aristotelian ethical conception we wish to scrutinize, can't we do that without literary texts, without texts at all—or, rather, with the texts of our own lives set before us? Here, we must first say that of course we do this as well, both apart from our reading of the novels and (as [French novelist Marcel] Proust insists) in the process of reading. In a sense Proust is right to see the literary text as an "optical instrument" through which the reader becomes a reader of his or her own heart. But, why do we need, in that case, such optical instruments?

One obvious answer was suggested already by Aristotle: we have never lived enough. Our experience is, without fiction, too confined and too parochial. Literature extends it, making us reflect and feel about what might otherwise be too distant for feeling. The importance of this for both morals and politics cannot be underestimated. *The Princess Casamassima* [1886, a novel by Henry James]—justly, in my view—depicts the imagination of the novel-reader as a type that is very valuable in the political (as well as the private) life, sympathetic to a wide range of concerns, averse to certain denials of humanity. It cultivates these sympathies in its readers.

We can clarify and extend this point by emphasizing that novels do not function, inside this account, as pieces of "raw" life: they are a close and careful interpretative description. All living is interpreting; all action requires seeing the world *as* something. So in this sense no life is "raw," and (as James and Proust insist) throughout our living we are, in a sense, makers of fictions. The point is that in the activity of literary imagining we are led to imagine and describe with greater precision, focusing our attention on each word, feeling each event more keenly—whereas much of actual life goes by without that heightened awareness, and is thus, in a certain sense, not fully or thoroughly lived. Neither James nor Proust thinks of ordinary life as normative, and the Aristotelian conception concurs: too much of it is obtuse, routinized, incompletely sentient. So literature is an extension of life not only horizontally, bringing the reader into contact with events or locations or persons or problems he or she has not otherwise met, but also, so to speak, vertically, giving the reader experience that is deeper, sharper, and more precise than much of what takes place in life.

Study Questions

1. Is Nussbaum right that philosophical examples don't work as well as fictional stories when it comes to conveying a moral point? Why or why not?

2. What does she mean by "no life is 'raw'"?

3. Should her theory include the use of films? Why or why not?

Narrative

How to Be Good

NICK HORNSBY

Novel, 2001. Excerpt and summary.

The novel with the very moralistic-sounding title "How to Be Good" would work in many chapters in this book, because it deals with selfishness and altruism, with authenticity, and with character, but I've chosen to place it here, because it also deals with learning moral lessons from stories—novels and films. As moralizing as the title sounds, the story isn't about finding moral answers, but *seeking* them—in a series of musings that are both funny and extremely cynical.

David and Katie are a middle-class couple living in British suburbia, year 2000. They have been married for twenty-four years, and now they're thinking about getting a divorce—at least Katie is. She has just had an affair with Stephen, but she's not really in love with him—she just wants somebody who is different from her husband. David writes a column for a small newspaper about things that make him angry and has been working on a novel for years. It's not going anywhere. Katie is a medical doctor with a full schedule, they have two young children, and it seems to her that what he contributes to the household is mostly sarcasm and cynicism. But when he is confronted with the fact that his wife has been unfaithful to him, he takes on the blame—to the extent that, overnight, David changes his life: He becomes repentant, not really about what he hasn't done for his family, but about what he hasn't done for the world. Soon, David is giving all of his children's toys away, including their computer—because some other children are deprived of toys. He takes all the cash out of Katie's purse one evening when they are on their way home from the theater, and gives it to a homeless person. He contemplates giving the family roast lunch to the homeless (but Katie and the kids suggest he give them the lasagna instead). He strikes up a friendship with a homeless faith healer, Dr. GoodNews, invites him to come and live with them (without consulting Katie), and together the men embark upon projects that will make people do something for other, less fortunate fellow human beings. One of the projects is for their neighbors and themselves to take in a homeless young person who will live in the typical middle-class spare bedroom until able to get back on his or her feet (and Katie tries to point out that that's what they've already done—since GoodNews is living with them). The project is three-fourths a disaster: Only half their neighbors are willing to join the project, and out of those six families, three of them are ripped off by the homeless kids they housed—the remaining three are a success. Katie realizes that while she can think of no good (meaning, selfless) arguments why David is wrong, his enthusiasm for helping others is ruining her life.

In this first excerpt, the young homeless people have just moved in:

> We don't get to bed until after midnight, but David's much too hyper to sleep.
> "Is five any good, do you think?"
> It's amazing," I tell him, and I mean it, because I had anticipated nobody, nothing, a dismal and humiliating failure and the end of the story.
> "Really?"
> "Did you honestly think you could get ten people to volunteer?"
> "I didn't know. All I can say is that when I was going through it in my head, I couldn't think of any arguments against it."
> That's it. That's the whole David/GoodNews thing, right there: "I couldn't think of any argument against it." My problem exactly. I want to destroy David's whole save-the-world-and-love-everyone campaign, but I want to do it using his logic and philosophy and language, not the language of some moaning, spoiled smug, couldn't-care-less, survival-of-the-fittest tabloid newspaper columnist. And of course it's not possible, because David's fluent in his language, and I'm a beginner. It's as if I'm trying to argue with Plato in Greek.
> "What arguments are there?" he says. "I mean, these people are—"
> "I know, I know. You don't have to argue with me. But that's not the point, is it?"
> "Isn't it?"

There are never any arguments against anything you want to do. People are hungry, give them food if you've got it. Kids have nothing to play with, give them toys if you've got too many. I can never think of anything to say to you. But that doesn't mean I agree with you."

"But it has to."

"That isn't how the world works."

"Why not? OK, I know why not. Because people are selfish and scared and . . . and brainwashed into thinking that they have no alternatives. But they have. They have."

And what am I supposed to say now? That people have a right to be selfish if they want to? That they don't have any alternatives? And what's the Greek for "Please shut up and leave me alone?"

A few days later David and Katie leave the children with GoodNews and their other homeless houseguest, the teenager Monkey, and go to the movies, where they see *Erin Brockovich,* the famous 1990s film about the American whistleblower. Here Katie begins to understand what it is she finds so offensive about David's newfound helpfulness:

One night we leave our guests in charge of the children (Imaginary conversation with my parents, or Social Services: "Who's in charge of your children?" "Oh, GoodNews and Monkey") and we go to the local cinema. We see a Julia Roberts film: she plays a struggling single mother who gets a job at a law firm and discovers that a water company is poisoning people, and she goes on a campaign to get compensation for them. Her relationship with a sexy bearded man suffers, and she becomes a bad, neglectful mother, but she is Fighting the Good Fight, and the water company is bad bad bad, and she only has two children and one boyfriend and there are hundreds of sick people, so it's OK. It's not a particularly good film, but I love it simply because it is a film, in color, with a story that doesn't involve spacecraft or insects or noise, and I drink it down in one, like I drank the Stoppard play. David loves it because he thinks it is about him.

"Well?" he says afterward.

"Well what?"

"Do you see?"

"Do you see what?"

"If you're going to do this stuff, it comes at a cost."

"There was no cost. Not in the film. Everyone lived happily ever after. Apart from the sick people, perhaps."

"Her boyfriend left her."

"She made it up with him." I point out.

"But weren't you on her side?"

And he used to have such a complicated, interesting mind. "No. I was on the side of the water company. Of course I was on her side. I wasn't given much choice. Are you trying to say that you're Julia Roberts?"

"No, but—"

"Because you're not."

We stop while he gives a kid fifty pence, and then continue in silence for a little while.

"Why not?"

"David, I'm not going to waste an awful lot of time on this."

"Why not?"

"Why aren't I going to waste time explaining why you're not Julia Roberts?"

"Yes. This is important. Tell me the difference between what I'm doing and what she was doing."

"What are you doing? Explain it to me."

"You explain to me what she was doing first. And then we'll see what the differences are."

"You're going to drive me mad."

"Ok, I'm sorry. The point is that she and I want to do something about things. A water company is poisoning people. Bad. She wants justice for the people affected. Kids are sleeping out on the street. Bad. I want to help them."

"Why you?"

"Why her?"

"It was a film, David."

"Based on a true story."

"Let me ask you something: is this worth wrecking your family for?"

"I don't intend to wreck my family."

"I know you don't intend to wreck your family. But two of us are very unhappy. And I don't know how much more I can take."

"I'm sorry."

"That's all you can say?"

"What else is there to say? You're threatening to leave me because I'm trying to do something for people who can't do much for themselves. And I—"

"That's not true, David. I'm threatening to leave you because you're becoming unbearable."

"What can't you bear?"

"Any of it. The . . . the sanctimony. The smugness. The—"

"People are dying out there, Katie, I'm sorry if you think that I'm being smug."

"I cannot bring myself to say any more.

After a while Katie has reached her boiling point, and moves out—but only at night. Early in the morning she comes back and cooks breakfast, so her kids won't know she isn't sleeping at home anymore. But living in a studio apartment at a friend's place makes her think about her life in terms of *Star Wars: The Empire Strikes Back:*

The only scenes I can stand in any of the Star Wars films are the quiet scenes in the second one, *The Empire Strikes Back.* Or rather, it used to be the second one, before the fourth one became the first one, thus making the second one the third one. A couple of years ago Tom used to watch his Star Wars videos over and over again, in sequence, and at first I preferred *The Empire Strikes Back* simply because it offered some respite from all the roaring and banging and whizzing. But later I came to appreciate its . . . I don't know what you'd call it. Message? Moral? Do Star Wars films have messages? Anyway, something in it began to chime somewhere in me, and I wanted to be Luke Skywalker, off somewhere on my own, learning to be a Jedi. I wanted a break from the war. I wanted someone wise to teach me how to do the things I needed to know to survive the rest of my life. And I know it's pathetic that it should have been a children's science-fiction film telling me this—it should have been George Eliot, or Wordsworth, or Virginia Woolf. But then, that's precisely the point, isn't it? There is no time or energy for Virginia Woolf, which means that I am forced to look for meaning and comfort in my son's Star Wars videos. I have to be Luke Skywalker because I don't know who else to be.

When Monkey and his pals moved into the street, I became acutely aware of the need to think; it seemed as though life were unsustainable without thought, in fact. I couldn't work out who was right and who was wrong, my house was full of people I didn't know . . . I was going mad, really. So I had to do this didn't I? And of course it's selfish and indulgent and bad, but it seemed at the time as though I couldn't work out how to be good without being bad. Anyone would understand. God, the Archbishop of Canterbury, Ann Landers, anyone. Wouldn't they? And it doesn't mean I love my children less, and it doesn't mean I love my husband less (I don't think, although that's one of the things I need to think about) . . .

We can't get into all the soul-searching moments of this bitterly humorous book, but much of it deals with confrontations about keeping and breaking promises, staying true to oneself, finding a "oneself" that one might be able to stay true to, and all the while working on having an everyday life that is still fulfilling, even if it doesn't have much excitement.

Study Questions

1. Should Katie have shown more backbone and thrown GoodNews out early on? Or should she have been more of a support to David by accepting GoodNews's presence?

2. Who is more right, Katie or David? Should we focus on the nearest duty of taking care of our loved ones and ourselves, or is the plight of the world as important as, or more important than, our own needs? Is it selfish to want to have a good life? (You may want to return to this question after having read Chapter 4.)

3. What did Katie learn from *Erin Brockovich?* And from *Star Wars?*

4. Katie finds wisdom in movies and novels. Can we find wisdom in this novel? In that case, what might it be? (Remember Nussbaum's admonishment that we have never lived enough, and we need novels to broaden our horizon.)

5. Toward the end of the novel, it becomes clear that both David and Katie are haunted by a certain sense of emptiness in their lives, a lack of passion, not just for each other but for life itself. Would that explain their behavior? Why or why not? Might goodness have something to do with a passion for life, according to the author?

6. This novel is pre–September 11. Do you think it would make a difference that we, as well as the United Kingdom, have been nations at war with terrorism ever since? Are family problems generally affected by the greater political picture, or not?

Narrative

Smoke Signals

SHERMAN ALEXIE (SCREENWRITER)

CHRIS EYRE (DIRECTOR)

Film, 1998. Summary. Based on the short story collection by Sherman Alexie,
The Lone Ranger and Tonto Fistfight in Heaven.

Thomas and Victor are young Coeur d'Alene Indians living on the reservation in Idaho in the late 1990s. They grew up together and share the story of one fateful night when they were babies. On that night Thomas's parents' house burned down, with Thomas, his parents, and Victor inside. Someone saved Victor, and Thomas's parents threw their baby to safety out the second-story window while they themselves burned to death. Thomas was caught in midair by Victor's father, Arnold. Since then, Thomas has lived with his grandmother.

Not much happens on the reservation; everyone knows one another, and the height of excitement seems to be playing basketball at the gym. One of the young Indians remarks, "Sometimes it is a good day to die—other times it is a good day to play basketball." Sometimes they watch Westerns on TV and discuss whether the cowboys always win or whether the Indians sometimes win. Thomas remarks, with a grin, that there is nothing more pathetic than Indians on TV—except Indians watching Indians on TV!

Thomas is a seer and a storyteller; everything he has experienced in his short life turns into stories—and his stories contain a considerable amount of pure fantasy too. This irritates Victor, who wants him just to tell the truth. Much about Thomas irritates Victor: Thomas braids his long hair very tightly; Victor wears his long hair free-flowing. Thomas always wears a dark three-piece suit, whereas Victor wears blue jeans and T-shirts. And Victor cultivates a warrior's inscrutable face, whereas Thomas has a ready smile for everyone. What irritates Victor most is Thomas's stories about Victor's father, Arnold. Victor knows him as a man who got drunk and beat him and his mother. Thomas sees Arnold as his hero, a magic man—the man who not only saved his life but also took him to a breakfast at Denny's in Spokane once. They met on the footbridge across the Spokane Falls, and somehow Thomas has associated Arnold with that spot ever since; it has become a power place to him. And Arnold was a storyteller, like Thomas—with a love for a *good* story rather than a *true* story. But Arnold is no longer around for Thomas to tell new stories about—he left his family in anger when Victor was a child.

Their quiet life is interrupted by a phone call from Phoenix: A woman named Suzy calls Victor's mother, with the news that Arnold is dead. He lived in a trailer close to her, and his things are still there, including his truck. Someone needs to get him and his belongings. Victor is reluctant to go because he harbors immense resentment toward his father for leaving him, but Thomas puts up the money for the ticket from his piggy bank under one condition: that he gets to go to Phoenix too.

On the bus, Thomas and Victor have a variety of encounters with the world of the whites, not all of them pleasant. For instance, a pair of rednecks take their seats and force

In *Smoke Signals* (1998) Victor (Adam Beach, left) and Thomas (Evan Adams) from the Coeur d'Alene Indian reservation in Idaho are on their way to pick up the ashes of Victor's father Arnold in Arizona. Thomas irritates Victor because he wears his hair in tight braids, wears a three-piece suit—and was rescued as a baby by Arnold, while Victor believes his own father didn't care about him.

them to move. But Victor is not very pleasant, either. He calls a young girl a liar for embellishing on her one life story: her near chance of going to the Olympics. And he gets on Thomas's case for not knowing how to be an Indian: He must have watched *Dances with Wolves* two hundred times, says Victor, and he still doesn't know how to act like he's come home from the buffalo hunt. Thomas protests that their people weren't buffalo hunters but fishermen. Victor replies that there is nothing glorious about coming home from fishing—the movie wasn't called "Dances with Salmon"!—and we get a sense that perhaps it is Victor, not Thomas, who feels uncomfortable about his role and his culture.

After days of traveling nonstop they finally arrive in Phoenix and walk to the desert hideout of Arnold and Suzy. She turns out to be a hospital administrator and much younger than Arnold, but for years she has had a close relationship with him—"We kept each other's secrets," she says. The three of them share her frybread, traditional American Indian fare, and Thomas tells a wonderful story of how Victor's mother fed a hundred Indians with only fifty frybreads—which turns out to be not quite true, although it is a good story. Suzy has heard about Victor and Thomas and all the basketball games Arnold played with Victor. And she has heard the true story about the night of the fire. What had haunted Arnold for all those years was that he set the fire by accident in a drunken stupor. But now that Victor hears the truth, he also hears something he dares not believe: that it was Arnold who ran back into the burning house to save him. For years, Victor has resented Thomas for being the one saved by Arnold. And now he has to revise all his resentments. Coming face-to-face with the loss of his father, Victor grieves in the traditional Indian way: He cuts his long hair.

The next morning, Victor and Thomas leave in Arnold's truck, taking with them only Arnold's ashes and his basketball. Victor is in a panicked, angry rush to get home, but there is yet another trial ahead for him. Late that night, on a dark desert road, he and Thomas crash the truck, barely avoiding ramming into two cars that had collided moments before the boys' arrival. The driver of the car that caused the accident, a white man, is drunk and obnoxious, and his wife is desperately apologetic. But down in the ravine is an injured woman, and the nearest town is twenty miles away. Victor's truck is disabled, but he doesn't hesitate for a moment: He must run for help. And he starts out running into the night, with the long stride of his ancestor warriors. He runs until his side hurts and his vision blurs, and by dawn he collapses. But he is close enough to a town to be seen by a road repair crew, and he gets the message about the injured motorist through.

As Victor and the motorist—who would have died if it hadn't been for his heroic run—are recovering in the hospital, Thomas is standing by, and we can tell that he has the material for many future stories. One woman says they are heroes, coming to the rescue just like the Lone Ranger and Tonto—and the boys answer that they're more like Tonto and Tonto. One snag develops, though: The man who caused the accident has filed false charges against the boys for assault and causing the accident, and Victor and Thomas are taken to the police station. All the old fear and resentment of the white power structure descend on the boys, who feel they won't be believed—but not everyone outside the reservation is like the drunken white driver. His wife, for one, has issued a statement against her husband, and the two women who were in the other car side with the boys, too. And the police chief is a man of good sense and sends the boys on their way.

Six days after leaving Idaho, Victor and Thomas are back with Arnold's ashes. The one who has undergone the most profound change is Victor; he now understands that his dad never planned to leave and that he just hadn't gotten around to going home yet. Now he understands the ghosts his father lived with year after year. So he barely picks on Thomas anymore and even offers him the deepest gesture he can think of: He shares his father's ashes with him. At last, Victor gets to scatter Arnold's ashes where both he and Thomas feel Arnold's spirit belongs: over the Spokane Falls. Meanwhile, in a voice-over, Thomas leaves us with thoughts about forgiving our fathers: "How do we forgive our fathers? Maybe in a dream? . . . Do we forgive our fathers for leaving us too often when we were little, or scaring us with unexpected rage or making us nervous because there never seems to be any rage at all? . . . Shall we forgive them for their excesses of warmth, or coldness, shall we forgive them for pushing, or leaning, for shutting doors, for speaking through walls, or being silent? . . . If we forgive our fathers, what is left?"

Study Questions

1. What do you think made Victor come to terms with his father's disappearance and death? How has Victor changed? Why didn't Thomas change as much?

2. Thomas can make any mundane situation into an interesting, magical time by telling stories about it—but the stories are not always true. Is this morally acceptable? Why or why not?

3. Apply Martha Nussbaum's theory of the rationality of emotions to Victor's situation: Was Victor's anger at his father rational? Why or why not? How can we tell? (Clue: What happened to Victor's anger when he learned the truth about this father?)

4. Why do Western movies play such a big role in Thomas's and Victor's lives? Do you think it is a positive or a negative role?

5. What is funny about the boys' remark that they are more like Tonto and Tonto?

Narrative

Big Fish

JOHN AUGUST (SCREENWRITER)

TIM BURTON (DIRECTOR)

Film, 2003. Based on the novel by Daniel Wallace.

Here you have another story about a son and his father, and about storytelling—but with a different focus, because this time it is the father who is the teller of stories. In the film's introduction we hear the core story of the father's life: There was a big old fish in the river that couldn't be caught no matter what kind of bait was used. But on the day when his son was born, Ed caught the fish, by using as bait his own wedding ring—because, as it turned out, the fish was female. And, as Ed Bloom adds, this time to his new daughter-in-law on his son's wedding day, sometimes the only way to catch an uncatchable woman is to offer her a wedding ring! His son Will winces: He's heard the story hundreds of times; he hates it—because it is fake, but also because it reduces him to a mere footnote in his father's life. And since that wedding day three year's earlier, the father and son have not spoken to each other. But now Ed is dying of cancer, the chemo treatment is being stopped, and Will and his wife Josephine travel back to the United States from her home country of France to be with him and Will's mother Sandra. Will tells us, as the narrator, that it is impossible to separate fact from fiction in his father's life—most of the stories he has been telling over the years have never happened. But while he is approaching the final hours with his dad, the childhood stories emerge—stories Ed told his son of his own childhood, such as the one with the witch who lived in the neighborhood: Her glass eye would show the manner of death of anyone who peered into it. Two of Ed's friends

In *Big Fish* (2003) Ed Bloom (here played as a young man by Ewan McGregor) tells a lot of stories about his life, and his son Will doesn't believe any of them. One of his stories tells of his arrival in the magical town of Spectre, where he meets the little girl Jenny (here eight years old, played by Hailey Anne Nelson). Later, Will discovers that there may have been something to the stories after all.

looked, and saw their deaths—Ed looked, too, and saw, but he never shared his vision with anyone.

When Will sees his father, Ed is concerned, because "This is not the way I go"—but he doesn't want to elaborate. When Will confronts him and wants to know the "true version of things," he evades the issue and falls back on telling stories of his life. In his childhood, he read about goldfish—how they adjust their growth to their environment, so the bigger the pond, the bigger the fish. He decided to become a big fish, which entailed leaving his little town. But he was not alone—he had make friends with a giant who terrorized the town. So already, Ed was a giant-slayer, but in a peaceful way, because he pacified the giant, who only wanted more to eat. During their travels they split up temporarily, and Ed found himself in a strange place, a small town where everybody was happy and apparently nothing happened. Grass grew like a lawn down Main Street, and everybody was clad in white. The town was Spectre. Mysteriously, the townsfolk told him he was too soon, but in town he met with three people who would mean very much to him in the future: The poet Winslow, who arrived and got stuck in Spectre; Jenny, who was a little precocious girl; and a naked woman at night in the river—a woman who appeared in different guises for different people, but in reality was a fish. And no one could catch her. Ed made an effort and escaped from town because he didn't want to get stuck there too.

While Will is reminiscing, Old Ed is bonding with his daughter-in-law Josephine, telling her another scary story—which turns out to be a joke! Josephine sees into the heart of the old man, loves his spirit, and is tolerant of his stories, far more so than Will is.

She asks Ed to tell about how he met his wife Sandra, Will's mother, still a beautiful woman—and that is the primary story of Ed's life. Here we, the audience, get to hear the story straight from Ed—this is not a flashback told by Will: On a visit to Calloway's circus Ed not only gets the giant, Carl, a job but also falls in love, with a girl who disappears. Calloway knows her parents, and Ed offers to work for free, as long as Calloway tells him about the girl. And so he does, for months, for little tidbits of information, until Calloway finally tells him her name, Sandra, and where she goes to college (after Ed finds out that Calloway is really a werewolf). He promptly looks her up, only to find out that she's engaged to one of his school friends—one of those who saw his death in the eye of the witch. Ed starts courting Sandra anyway, and awakens the wrath of her fiancé who beats Ed up—which prompts Sandra to end the engagement. And shortly after, her fiance really dies, the way he had seen in the eye of the witch. But Sandra and Ed are in for more trouble, because he is being drafted and sent to Vietnam. Through a series of unlikely adventures involving a pair of conjoined, singing, beautiful Vietnamese twins, he returns to Sandra, who, in the meantime, had received the official note that he was missing in action.

Josephine finds the story beautiful—Will is disgusted because it's all fake, and his wife now advises him to have a talk with his dad. Initially the talk goes nowhere: Will asks his father for once in his life, to tell him the truth, to be himself, to let his son know who he is—and Ed answers that he has always been himself. But some window of understanding is opening for Will; during a cleanup in the garage the family comes upon papers that fit into the puzzle of Ed's life: The MIA note is there—and Will always thought that was a fake story. And a mechanical hand—which his father supposedly sold as a traveling salesman. But there is also a trust, for a woman in Spectre, Jennifer; and now Will thinks he has found his father's real secret life. He travels to Spectre, a real small town, and seeks out the woman, a middle-aged single woman in a nice house. Did she have an affair with his father? No, Ed took care of her, and the town, and her house, because he wanted to—they were his friends from his first visit, but he professed his undying love for Sandra when Jennifer shyly told him she'd like him to stay. And, she says, his son was real to him—not her, not Spectre. And Jennifer became a recluse, and a witch (and we realize that the witch with the glass eye really was Jennifer, although it doesn't fit with the time line).

So now Will has learned that some of his father's stores were true and that he really was important to his dad—but when he comes home, there is no one there. Ed has had a stroke and is in intensive care. Will chooses to stay and watch over his dad while the others go home to rest up; Sandra has one last moment with her beloved Ed while he is asleep. The old doctor who has known the family forever asks Will if he wants to hear the story of when he was born. It's not the one with the fish—it's a simple story of an easy birth. And Will likes it.

After Will has been sitting by his father's bedside for a while, Ed surprisingly wakes up; he has lost almost all his capacity to speak, but Will understands that he is desperate because his death is wrong—this is not the way it happens according to the vision! Ed never told his story to Will, but now Will understands his dad well enough to tell the story to *him*. The exact way Ed dies I will leave as a mystery for you to experience when you see the film, as Ed would have wanted it—suffice it to say that Will fulfills his father's dream of dying the right way and tells the story right. And then, in a final confirmation, we're present at the funeral, where Ed's friends show up—Jennifer and the doctor, but also all those elusive characters Will used to think were made up: the Vietnamese singer twins, Calloway the circus manager, Carl the giant, Winslow the poet, and other story characters. They're not completely the way Ed had described them (as you should see for yourself) but they were real after all. Flash forward to a few years later: We see Will's little son tell his friends one of Ed's stories. And Will concludes, "A man tells his stories so many times that he becomes his stories—they live on after him and in that way he becomes immortal." Now does that mean that all the stories Ed told were true? Or is it rather that Will understood the poetic truth beneath his father's tall tales? I'll let you decide that for yourself.

Study Questions

1. Let's repeat that question: Was everything that Ed told true? Or has Will discovered the poetic truth behind the improbable stories? Explain.

2. Is it morally right for Will to play along with his father's death fantasy, or should he have insisted on realism, as he did before? Explain.

3. What might Nussbaum say to this story? Do we understand life better after having read/seen it? Does Will understand life better after hearing his dad's stories?

4. Do you have a family member who constantly tells stories about himself or herself? Do you feel you understand that person better now, or did you have a good understanding prior to reading this?

5. What is the difference between a tall tale and a lie? Is one morally acceptable, while the other isn't? Why or why not? You may want to take up this subject again after reading Chapter 6.

Chapter Two

Learning Moral Lessons from Stories

We may think that the most powerful moral lessons are learned from events in our childhood (when we are caught doing something we aren't supposed to do, or when we *aren't* caught), but chances are the most powerful lessons we carry with us are lessons we learn from the *stories* we have read or that were read to us.

Didactic Stories

Many of you may recognize this typical, unpleasant event from childhood: Your authority figure takes you aside to tell you Aesop's fable "The Boy Who Cried Wolf." A lad was tending sheep at the outskirts of town, and he thought it might be fun to give the village a scare, so he cried, "The wolf is here! The wolf is here!" And the villagers came running, but there was no wolf. The boy tricked the town again and again, until that fateful day when the wolf really did come. The boy cried for his life, "The wolf is here!" but nobody believed him anymore. The wolf ate the sheep and the shepherd too. At least this is the way the story was told to me when I was five years old.

Why are children told such a gruesome story? Because adults deem it necessary to teach children a moral lesson. Even a child understands the message: "The shepherd boy lied and suffered the consequences. You don't want to be like him, do you?" It is a powerful lesson. Indeed, the appeal of the story seems to go beyond European and American traditions: I have a colleague from India who tells me that when she was a little girl in Calcutta, she was told the story of the boy who cried tiger.

When discussing stories that have made a moral impact on them, several of my students have brought up another story with a grim point: "The Wooden Spoon" (or, in another version, "The Woven Basket"). Old Grandpa lives on the farm with his son and the son's family. The old man makes a terrible noise when he slurps his soup, because he has no teeth left. At the dinner table, the son irritably tells him to go sit in the corner with his soup because he isn't fit for human company anymore. The grandson hears everything, and after dinner he goes out in the woodshed and picks up some wood. When his father sees him whittling, he asks what he's making. The boy answers, "This is going to be a spoon for you, Dad, for when you get old and have to sit in the corner and eat your soup." Next time dinner is served, the son brings his old father back to the table to eat with the family. (The version called "The Woven Basket" is about Grandma, who is sent to the old folks' home in a basket, as tradition requires; the young granddaughter weaves a basket and tells her mother, "This is for you, when you grow old, Mother." And Grandma is brought back from the old folks' home.) This story mirrors the terrifying moral lesson of the epitaph I've

"The Boy Who Cried Wolf" embodies one of the most effective early moral lessons in many people's lives: If we make a habit out of lying, the chances are that we will not be believed when we are finally telling the truth.

seen in old Boston cemeteries: "Remember, friend, as you pass by/As you are now so once was I/As I am now so you shall be/Prepare thyself to follow me." In addition, it is a lesson in the Golden Rule: Would you yourself like to be treated the way you are actually treating others?

Stories that are told to teach a moral lesson are called *didactic* stories. These instructional stories may well be as old as humanity. When giving a keynote address about stories in ethics at a philosophical retreat in Denmark some years ago, I asked the audience, a mixed group of several hundred people ranging from their teens to their eighties, if they had been told the story of "The Boy Who Cried Wolf" when they were kids; a forest of hands went up, young smooth hands alongside gnarled old hands, and all of a sudden it seemed to me that I was looking down the corridor of time, from these living generations backwards to the other generations long gone, each one of them telling their children about the lying shepherd boy—in all likelihood a story so old that it predates Aesop's version.

The New Interest in Stories

The interest in using stories (narratives) to explore moral problems is increasing today, for stories can serve as a laboratory in which moral solutions can be tried out before any decisions are made. Here are some examples of how stories are being used as moral laboratories today.

- Many psychologists are advocating a method they call "bibliotherapy" to facilitate communication between parents and children. Through reading stories with their children, parents may find it easier to explain difficult issues because together, through the fictional universe, they can explore issues and emotions that might be more difficult to approach on either an abstract or a highly personal level. For example, it's hard to explain death to children—either as a concept or as a real event in a family. Perhaps a story about the death of a pet could help focus the discussion. Of course, this may be just an easy way out for parents who don't have a clue how to relate to their children, but ideally the sharing of stories is a positive way to make the child understand about arrivals of new siblings, a move to a new home, deaths in the family, and other traumatic events. (It may sound like a brand-new idea, but in the next section you will see that this is in effect how myths and fairy tales used to work in traditional societies.)

- Medical students in many parts of this country are now exposed not only to case studies that involve medical ethics but also to stories of fiction, such as Leo Tolstoy's "The Death of Iván Ilyich" (1886) and the 1994 film *Philadelphia,* that deal with medical problems. The students seem to feel better equipped to deal with "real" problems because of this exploratory background. Why? Because no matter how many case histories she examines or how many colleagues she talks to, a medical student may not be able to understand a patient from the inside quite as well as when a great writer tells the story from the patient's point of view. The New York University School of Medicine's Literature, Arts, and Medicine Database is a website dedicated to listing films and works of literature that may be of help as a resource for medical personnel, such as *And the Band Played On, Awakenings, Gattaca, Lorenzo's Oil, The English Patient,* Christy Brown's *My Left Foot,* Camus's *The Plague,* and Jane Austen's *Emma.* The Literature and Medicine program in Maine has since 1997 gathered health care professionals around the concept that reading and discussing literature can improve their professional skills and help them understand their patients and clients.

- Patients have been encouraged to use movies as a sort of treatment. In the February 2000 issue of *Psychology Today* magazine, an article titled "Reel Therapy" explored the psychological benefits that may come from watching the right movie at the right time. The story noted that doctors assign certain films to help patients come to terms with their situation or discover a new side to themselves. Unfortunately, it gave some readers the impression that watching a movie would solve their problems. Have emotional injuries in need of healing? Rent *The Horse Whisperer.* Hopelessly cynical about modern life? Then see *Shakespeare in Love.* It doesn't quite work that way in real life, and not in this book, either! If we want to delve into moral issues in depth, we have to get beyond the sound bites and

Watch two "FEEL GOOD" movies a day until your symptoms subside.

Psychologists are beginning to tap the therapeutic potential of movies—but of course merely watching movies will not solve one's emotional or moral problems.

quick fixes. Good stories can help us begin to explore an issue—but they can't be a substitute for insight or discussion.

- The criminal justice system is experimenting with the use of stories. A website, "Picturing Justice, the On-line Journal of Law and Popular Culture," specializes in discussing films that relate to legal issues. Examples range from the classics *Notorious* and *Twelve Angry Men* to *Amistad, The Life of David Gale,* and the comedies *Legally Blonde* and *My Cousin Vinnie.* What is interesting is that the didactic value of such films to the legal community is no longer something that just happens by accident after someone goes to the movies and sees a connection to real-life cases—it is now something that is an accepted and established form of learning. But it goes further than scholars and lawyers talking movies among themselves: In a county in Massachusetts, the court is running a reading class as part of a rehabilitation program for certain inmates. They are each asked to read an American classic, such as Hemingway's *Old Man and the Sea,* and then they discuss the book in group sessions under the guidance of a literature professor. The mere exposure to the story of the old man and the giant fish caused several of these men (all male inmates) to rethink their own lives, because they had learned to see the story as a metaphor for some universal human problems. In Italy a judge sentenced a juvenile delinquent to read four novels in two months, in the hope that his moral outlook on life might be improved. In Winona, Minnesota, an eighteen-year-old was ordered to watch *Saving Private Ryan* as part of his sentence for vandalizing a park honoring veterans, because he had told the judge he didn't know what a veteran was. According to an Associated Press story, the young man thought the movie was "pretty cool."

- Psychotherapists are having patients tell about their own lives as if they were stories or asking them to select a famous fairy tale as a model or template of the way they see their own lives. The idea of telling one's own story as a form of therapy and moral education is something we will look at in detail at the end of the chapter.

- Stories have been found to have great potential for promoting cross-cultural or multicultural understanding. They can highlight cultural differences in a way that presents them as exciting and worth exploring, while emphasizing the fundamental human similarities underneath the surface differences.

- Last on this list, but not least: Some philosophers are beginning to look to stories as a way not only to explain difficult theories to their freshman students but also to explore the philosophical richness of literature and films in itself. Philosophers have for a long time been suspicious of using stories as illustrations of moral problems for several reasons. Some have felt that using stories would cause readers to be concerned with *specific* cases rather than with seeing the general picture. Others have worried that telling stories might manipulate readers' emotions instead of appealing to their reason: Such stories would perhaps lead people to *do* the right thing, but they wouldn't lead people to *think* about moral issues, because a story is not a logical argument but rather a persuasion—a story is not logic but rhetoric.

There is a difference, however, between stories that moralize and stories that discuss moral problems. In the past, philosophers seem to have assumed that stories illustrating moral problems are always of the moralizing kind. Now a different attitude seems to be growing among ethics scholars; they recognize that stories need not be moralizing in order to illustrate a moral point. Such stories may express a moral point of view, and then that point of view can be open for discussion. Or a story may have an open-ended conclusion, one in which the moral issues are not resolved. Even moralizing stories may have their proper role to play from time to time, and stories are an excellent way to illustrate how difficult a moral problem can be. As noted in Chapter 1, the field of philosophy is also slowly warming up to the old idea that feelings are not irrelevant in moral discussions. The psychologist Carol Gilligan argues for the legitimacy of emotions in moral decision making. As you know, Martha Nussbaum points out that emotions are not a matter of something uncontrollable, like hunger, but instead involve decision making and rational choices. Another philosopher, Philip Hallie, states that without feelings for the victims of evildoing, we can't hope to understand what a moral sense is all about. Jonathan Bennett, another contemporary philosopher, insists that although certain moral principles may be admirable, others may be warped: The Nazi exterminators (members of the National Socialist German Worker's Party, 1920–1945) had firm moral principles, but they were principles most people don't approve of today. Without sympathy for other people, our principles may go astray. One of the ways in which we can engage both our sympathy and our moral principles is through stories.

Some of the stories in this book are didactic (they teach a lesson), and some of them are more open-ended. It seems that, usually, we prefer learning from stories that were *not* written especially to teach a lesson. This may be one of the secrets of literature: We may forgive a good story for preaching a little, but we can't forgive a bad story for preaching. In other words, we are most accepting of a moral lesson if it is not too obvious, if it appears only between the lines and is subordinate to the plot and the characters. The stories that are most effective in teaching lessons may be those that are not obviously intended to do so. Examples of extreme didactic films would be the classic *The Birth of a Nation* (the Civil War seen from the Southern viewpoint) and *Reefer Madness,* a film generally viewed today as a propaganda film against the use of marijuana. Stories with more dimensions to them, and thus more interesting to a modern audience, might be films such as *Monster's Ball* and *Mystic River* or the anti-drug films *Drugstore Cowboy* and *Requiem for a Dream* (see Chapter 10).

Of course, real-life events and discussions of these events are essential to our understanding of moral issues, but using stories is an alternate way of talking about these issues, because a story can serve as a slice of life that we are invited to share in.

The Value of Stories

The philosopher Alasdair MacIntyre finds the telling of stories so important for humans that he calls us "storytelling animals." There are many reasons for telling stories, for reading and writing novels and short stories, and for making and watching films. It seems that in early, pretechnological cultures the purpose of storytelling was twofold: On the *human* side, the purpose was to knit the tribe firmly together by setting up the rules and boundaries that would establish a group identity. Besides, storytelling helped to pass the time on rainy days, and it kept the children occupied for a while. On the *cosmic* side, the purpose was to establish the story of the beginning of time, when everything was created, so if a symbolic re-creation seemed necessary (and it did, periodically), one could tell and enact the "beginning" stories and in that way "renew" the cosmos. Storytelling has never been more important than it was in those ancient times, for in telling the story people helped re-create the universe, put the sun in its right place, and make sure that the seasons followed one another in the proper order.

The strength of storytelling is no less apparent in many religions. Periodically (usually once a year), believers remind themselves of an important time in the history of their religion: the creation of the world, the creation of the religion itself, or the establishment of the believers' identity through a religious event. Usually a story is told about this event, and even if it is supposed to be a reminder rather than a re-creation, it is still a sacred and powerful vehicle.

In ancient times the storytellers were the primary teachers of morals. Of course, parents have always had a hand in moral education, but in pretechnological cultures (what used to be called "primitive" cultures), those who knew the legends were the ones who, in effect, represented the social institutions of religion, school, and government. The myths surrounding the origin of the world, of society, of food items, and of love and death and the stories of the important men and women in the tribe's past provided rules for the tribe to live by—moral structures that could be used in everyday life to make decisions about crops, marriages, warfare, and so forth. The way to teach children how to become good members of the tribe was to tell the old stories.

In our technological world we no longer have such a body of ready-made prescriptions for moral conduct—at least we don't think we do. In fact, however, we still tell stories, we still listen to stories, and we still take moral lessons from them. Some people read the Bible, the Torah, the Koran, or other religious books and seek comfort in their stories of human frailty and perseverance. Some people keep their childhood comic book collections and dive into the old stories from time to time for some basic moral reinforcement (see the rabbit outwit the fox; see the bad guy get blasted; see Robin Hood be vindicated once again). Some people read biographies of remarkable men and women and are inspired by the stories of courage and bravery. Adults may not read fairy tales anymore, but we read novels—classics, best-sellers, or science fiction. And if we don't read novels, we go to the movies or watch TV. Wherever we turn we find *stories*—some are real and some fictional, some are too outdated or too radical for us to relate to, but we find at least some stories that have served as our moral guideposts. Even if you are not a great reader or movie-goer, you probably can recall at least one story that has moved you.

Stories Past and Present

Fact, Fiction, or Both?

In the secular world we usually tell stories of two kinds: those that we believe to be historically true and those that we know never took place but that have their own special truth to them, a *poetic* truth. The fairy tale "Little Red Riding Hood" is not a historical account, but children may enjoy it if they are old enough to deal with their fear of the wolf, who comes to a gruesome end. Parents enjoy telling it, because they can smuggle home a lesson: Don't talk to strangers, and watch out for "wolves" in disguise. Box 2.1 looks at reality TV—which purports to be fact, not fiction.

What about accounts that we don't know to be either historical or poetic? The story of Zorro, for example, is not a historical account, although there may have been an outlaw in Old California who vaguely resembled the Zorro character. Some readers feel cheated if they find out that a story is more legend than history, but others find it all the more fascinating because it is a mixture of what we think happened and what we wish had happened. It may not tell us much about history, but it tells us a lot about people, including ourselves, who *wish* that Zorro were real.

Even stories that we believe to be factual, such as the story of the battle of the Alamo or the sinking of the *Titanic,* are not usually simple reports of facts; such stories must have a beginning, a middle, and an ending, and most often we choose the beginning and the ending according to what we feel makes the most *sense.* In actual life, the stream of events goes on, usually with little indication that here begins something new or here a story comes to an end—except in the case of someone's birth or death. Even in the latter case, the story goes on without the person who has died. So even "true" stories have an element of *poetic creativity,* in that we choose what to include in the story, what is *relevant* to the story (not every meal or visit to the bathroom is important in order for us to understand the life and times of Gandhi, or James Dean, or Princess Diana), and where to begin and end the story. Even eyewitness accounts, often regarded as the one true record of events, are full of creativity. Two persons observing the same event will very likely come up with slightly different versions

Box 2.1   REALITY SHOWS: WHERE DID THE STORY GO?

While the academic interest in stories has been on the increase, some story aficionados worry that the public interest in stories may be on the wane, considering the popularity of computer games without a story line and, in particular, the growing popularity of *reality shows:* TV shows such as *Survivor* and *The Bachelor* have scored top ratings, but that's not all: The public's interest in the lives of "public figures," whether they be celebrities, criminals, or just ordinary people caught up in some media circus, has also been on the rise. Some media analysts claim there is a decreasing interest in made-up stories these days, and an increased interest in real stories. There are two things we can say about that: For one thing, "reality shows" aren't really real—sorry to burst that bubble. As much as they feature "real people," they are scripted to a great extent and heavily edited in terms of content and structure; and this means that even if they don't have a clear plot structure laid out beforehand, they are still narratives—stories that interest us. For another, perhaps there is a reason why the stories of "real people" attract attention these days. We only have to think of the media attention given to the abduction of Elizabeth Smart, the disappearance and murder of Laci Peterson, the Martha Stewart trial, the murder of Danielle van Dam, the Jessica Lynch rescue and homecoming—not to mention the circus around the O. J. Simpson trial and its aftermath. Some of these cases involve money, some involve violence and murder, most—if not all—involve women and girls; and, as we shall see in a later chapter, there are even philosophical theories why we all of a sudden care so much about these strangers. The positive spin, as we shall see in Chapter 4, is that we ex-

tend the feelings we have for friends and relatives to these strangers, for a while. The negative spin, which I will suggest here, is that our world, presented to us by the media, has started to seem overwhelming to us. Our brains have evolved, through hundreds of thousands of years, into tribal brains, focusing on interacting intimately with a group of people probably no bigger than about 100 members, mostly relatives and neighbors. That meant close interaction, with lots of talk and gossip about those relatives and neighbors. But most of us no longer live in such communities—we don't know our neighbors, and we have little connection to our relatives. But we still have the need for tribal gossip and concern—so we turn to those new neighbors of ours, the TV people. And the more "real" they seem, the more we (or some of us) feel engaged in their destinies. Some people would say, "Then get a life!" But this *is* our life in the modern world, for better or worse. The upside is that our horizon literally expands, through the stories of others, factual as well as fictional, introducing moral issues we would never have related to or even imagined in previous times. We have all now been educated in the unethical: insider trading, child molestations by priests, religious fanatics kidnapping children and brainwashing them, red herrings introduced in court cases to confuse juries, and so forth. The downside is, of course, that this expanded interest may be nothing but a thirst for titillation, a ghoulish rubbernecking taken to an extreme. How much should we engage ourselves in other people's problems, and to what extent should the media report them? We return to such issues in Chapter 13.

of it; they notice different things because they are standing in different spots and because they are different people with different interests in life. If eyewitnesses are asked to tell about an event long past, some of their memories will be sharper than others, some will mirror exactly what they saw, and some will mirror what they felt or what they feel now, which turns their stories into personal interpretations of the event. At best, any account of a past event can only approximate what happened. We can never truly reproduce the event.

Religious legends reveal the same tension between fact and fiction. If believers suspect that events described in the legends never happened or that they happened in a different and more "everyday" way than is described in the religious text, they may experience a general disappointment with their religion, feeling that it is based on stories that have no foundation in fact. Other believers, however, may see the stories as being rich with poetry and telling human truths that are on a higher, more spiritual level. Aristotle, who was intensely interested in the relationship between history and poetry, said that history may deal with facts, but poetry deals with Truth.

Traditional Stories

Myths   We don't know anything about the first stories ever told, but if we are to judge from ancient myths and legends, there is a good chance that they served as reminders of proper conduct. The Cherokees tell of Grandmother Spider's way of making clay pots, and it seems to be (among other things) a lesson for Cherokee women in how to make pots the correct way. Myths in general have two main purposes: to strengthen the social bonding among people and to fortify the individual psychologically. *Traditional myths* work on both levels at once by presenting stories of gods, goddesses, and culture heroes who tell their society about the ideal social behavior and individuals about the proper role models to follow. In a sense, traditional myths are a successful combination of *ethics of conduct* and *virtue ethics* (see Parts 2 and 3). The philosopher Peter Muntz calls myths "concrete universals," stories that in a very concrete form tell about the human condition and give us courage to deal with the troubles that being human usually entails.

The myth of the loss of immortality told by the Trobriand people of New Guinea is such a story. It tells us that once humans could rejuvenate themselves; they could shed their skins and become young again. A grandmother took her granddaughter to the river and then went off by herself to shed her skin. When she came back, the granddaughter didn't recognize her (she appeared to be a young girl) and shooed her away. Upset, the grandmother went back and put her old skin on again. The granddaughter told her that she had chased a young girl, an impostor, away. The grandmother said, "Just because you refused to recognize me, nobody will be able to be young again. We shall all die of old age now." Aside from the fact that the story unfairly places the immense burden of causing humanity to die on an ignorant young girl—myths often blame a major disaster on a small event, as when Eve eats the fruit from the Tree of Knowledge—the lesson is that we humans are mortal and there is nothing we can do about it. The story also seems to say that humans, far from being victims, are very important beings since they can cause such a cosmic calamity as the loss of immortality!

Fairy Tales   Another ancient category of stories with moral lessons is the *fairy tale.* The fairy tales collected by the Grimm brothers in early-nineteenth-century Germany reflect what is probably a very old tradition of stories with morals, and they are not just for children; the stories were told originally to both young and old. The Trobriand people distinguish between three different kinds of stories. First, there are the "myths," which are sacred stories about the beginning of the world and of society. They must be taken very seriously. Second, there are the "true legends," semihistorical accounts of heroes in the past and their travels. They are supposed to be taken at face value, for the most part. Last, there are the "fairy tales," stories to be told in the rainy season, usually with some point of teaching the young about the customs of the people but also with the intent of pure entertainment. They are recognized as never having happened.

Most cultures acknowledge that there is a difference between stories in which the good get rewarded and the bad get punished and stories of everyday life. The fairy tale has been described by psychoanalysts as pure wishful thinking, but many fairy tales involve gruesome events that are hardly wish fulfillments, because they often happen to characters who don't "deserve" them. Such events do serve a purpose, though, in making the punishment of the bad characters seem justified.

In spite of its enormous popularity, the tale of Little Red Riding Hood seems to be a product of the literary elite and not of folklore, but that doesn't detract from its didactic power. "Hansel and Gretel" is a folklore classic with much the same lesson: Don't go with strangers, and don't let them feed you candy! There are also more obscure Grimm stories, such as "The Maiden Without Hands," in which a pious girl's tears fall on her hands and prevent the Devil from taking her, so her father, tricked by the Devil, chops her hands off; but she cries on the stumps, so the Devil leaves her alone, and an angel gives her silver hands. When she is finally reunited with her beloved, she even gets her own hands back. What is the lesson here? That purity and piety carry their own reward? There are, of course, stories that teach a different lesson: In "The Juniper Tree," the stepmother kills, cooks, and serves the baby brother up for dinner. His father loves the stew but doesn't know he is eating his own son. The boy's older sister Marjory (who knows about the evil deed) gathers his bones and buries them under the big tree in the yard where their mother also lies buried; in the tree is a bird (the boy's spirit) who takes on the task of punishment and reward. Marjory receives a pair of red shoes; the stepmother, in her envy, wants something too. She gets a millstone, which falls on her head. The baby brother comes alive again, after which the father, the sister, and the brother go in and finish their dinner. What do we have here? An untrustworthy, evil (step)mother and a drastic revenge. Some psychoanalysts today maintain that the real value of such stories—which, they say, children should not be protected from but rather exposed to—is that children can get rid of their aggressions toward their parents through the stories. (As we shall see in an upcoming section, Aristotle would have agreed with this psychoanalytic point of view.) In addition, the child is exposed to evil but at the same time acquires a dose of hopeful strength and learns that evil can be dealt with. In other words, the most horrible, gruesome, bloody fairy tales may be the ones with the most positive message for the impressionable reader: Yes, there are terrible things out there, but with fortitude we can vanquish them.

Parables   For two thousand years, Christians have found moral support in parables such as those of the Good Samaritan and the prodigal son.

The *parable* is an allegorical story for adults; it is supposed to be understood as a story about ourselves and what we ought to do. Although the purpose of the fairy tale seems to be primarily to entertain and secondarily to teach a moral lesson, the purpose of the parable is *primarily* to teach a moral and religious lesson. Christianity is not the only religion with parables; the Islamic, Hebrew, and Buddhist traditions contain such stories.

What fascinated the early readers of Jesus of Nazareth's parables was that they were so hard to live up to—not just because it was hard to be good but also because the moral demands of Jesus himself usually ran counter to what society demanded of its citizens or what it viewed as proper moral conduct. What was so difficult for Jesus' contemporaries to understand? He demanded not only that we be compassionate toward all in need but also that we consider *every* person a fellow human being, not just those from our own village, country, or culture, and especially not just those who show compassion toward us.

The parable of the prodigal son (Luke 15:11–32) has been one such lesson that people with ordinary common sense and good manners find hard to follow. The "bad" son who has squandered his inheritance comes home and is sorry. The father makes a fuss over the bad son and slaughters the fattened calf for him. The good son, who has stayed with his father, is upset, for he has never received any recognition of his stability from his father, and yet now it seems that the bad son is more important. And he is, to Jesus, for he has been on a longer journey than the good son: all the way to perdition and back. Christians, therefore, ask themselves if that means we should go on a binge and then repent rather than never go on a binge at all. The answer may be that the story is supposed to be judged from the point of view not of the good or the bad brother but of the father. Indeed, the secret to many of the parables is to find out whose viewpoint they express. The parable of the Good Samaritan (Luke 10:30–34) is about a victim of highway robbery and mugging. As he lies wounded at the roadside, he is ignored by several upstanding citizens but is helped by a social outcast, the Samaritan. (The story is outlined in Chapter 11.) This parable is told from the wounded man's point of view ("who is my neighbor"), not from the point of view of the Samaritan.

A Story of Sacrifice: Abraham and Isaac   Although it is not classified as a parable, the Old Testament story of Abraham being told to sacrifice his son Isaac (Genesis 22:1–19) has had the same kind of effect on its listeners. It is one of the hardest stories for a religion that believes in a loving God, be it from a Jewish or Christian point of view, to explain. Abraham and his wife Sarah are childless until they have Isaac very late in their lives, through God's intervention. God tells Abraham that his descendants will be as numerous as the stars in the sky and the grains of sand in the desert. When Isaac is a half-grown boy, however, God tells Abraham to take Isaac up the mountain and sacrifice him like a sheep. Abraham leads Isaac away, heavyhearted but obedient to God. He ties Isaac to the sacrificial stone and is about to stab him the ritual way when God's voice stops him, saying the request was just a test of Abraham's piety. God supplies a ram for Abraham to sacrifice instead.

The implications of this story have confounded believers and nonbelievers for two thousand years. A God who commands such a thing must be a cruel God, critics say,

The Trial of Abraham's Faith (plate by Gustave Doré, 1866). Abraham, having received the command from God to sacrifice his only son, Isaac, dutifully takes Isaac up the mountain to the place of sacrifice. Isaac, unaware that it is he himself who is to be the victim, is carrying the firewood that Abraham will use to light the sacrificial fire.

cruel and with a strange sense of humor. The philosopher Søren Kierkegaard sees the story as an illustration of the *limitations of ethics:* Ethically speaking, what Abraham was about to do was wrong; he had no business killing his son, because that is not how people are supposed to behave. But for Abraham, as for any believer, there is a law that is higher than the moral laws of society, and that is the law of *faith*—not faith that God will save his child, but faith that it really *is* God who is requiring him to sacrifice Isaac and that we can't know God's purpose. Kierkegaard saw Abraham's ordeal as a test of his faith in God rather than of his morals, and a "leap of faith" is, for the Lutheran Kierkegaard, a matter between the individual and God and nobody else. The opinion of society does not enter into the picture at all. Other interpretations of the story see no split between morality and faith, but view it as an illustration of God's absolute demands on his people. Yet others see it as justification for sacrificing everything one holds dear if a higher law demands it. With this last interpretation it really is irrelevant that God stopped Abraham at the last moment. For all Christians, the parallel to a later time when God did not stop himself from sacrificing his own son to save the world is a close one. (See Box 2.2 for Franz Kafka's interpretation of this parable.)

A recent critique of the old story has been suggested by anthropologist Carol Delaney in her book *Abraham on Trial: The Social Legacy of Biblical Myth.* Delaney asks, Why should faith in God be illustrated best by a father's willingness to sacrifice his son? Why couldn't the test of faith instead be measured by a parent's willingness to protect his or her child, not sacrifice it? The story has been told as if Abraham is the sole parent, with sole rights and responsibilities, and the biblical writers obviously didn't see Isaac's mother Sarah as someone with a right to her opinion about the matter. Delaney isn't criticizing the male-dominated ways of the Old Testament so much as asking why nobody since then, of all the commentators in Judeo-Christian history, has thought to ask whether Sarah might have had something relevant to say about the murder of her son as a proof of faith in God. Delaney actually echoes Kierkegaard's idea here that Abraham's willingness to kill Isaac would be completely *immoral,* but she doesn't agree with his further step that morals and faith are different things altogether.

Fables and Counterfables   In the eighteenth and nineteenth centuries adults finally began to notice that children were not just small and inadequate adults, and children's literature was invented as a literary genre. The gory fairy tale was toned down to suit the nursery, and another kind of story, which had previously been enjoyed by adults, was introduced to children: the *fable.* Aesop's and La Fontaine's fables became very popular as moral lessons for children. "The Mouse and the Lion" taught that you had better not disregard someone unimportant, for he or she might be of help to you some day, and "The Sour Grapes" taught that if someone claims something is not worth having, it may be because he or she can't have it. The main reason adults told these fables to children was, of course, that the grown-ups wanted their children to become good citizens, and the stories seemed an efficient way to press home the point. These early stories for children said, in essence, "Behave, or else"; they provided little opportunity for children's imagination to take flight. An important exception is the work of Hans Christian Andersen (1805–1875), who, throughout his fairy tales and stories, insisted that children's imaginations should be left unfettered by the sour realism of grown-ups. In fact, Andersen's stories have a true poetic quality and carry multiple meanings; they are not really children's stories at all. Children can enjoy them, to be sure, but they will enjoy them much more when they are older and capable of reading between the lines. For Andersen, it was not just the imagination

Box 2.2   KAFKA'S ABRAHAM

The Austrian-Czech novelist Franz Kafka (1883–1924) interprets the story of Abraham and Isaac in ways that are rather different from the traditional one. For one thing, he says, there was no need for any "leap of faith" in order for Abraham to accept the word of God, because if Abraham were to prove himself, then something precious to him had to be put on the line. If Abraham had so much—riches, a son, and a prophecy that he would become the father of the Jewish people—then he could be tested only by the threat of having something taken away from him. This is logical, says Kafka; it requires no leap of faith at all. What *would* require a leap of faith is if Abraham had been a different sort of person. Suppose he truly wanted to please God by performing the sacrifice but was a person of low self-esteem? He really wants to do what is right, like Cervantes' Don Quixote, but he can't quite believe that he can be the one God was speaking to because he believes he is unworthy. He is afraid that if he proceeds with the sacrifice, it will turn out that the command was just a joke, and he will be a laughingstock, like Quixote, who always tried to do the heroic thing but ended up fighting windmills. For this Abraham, being laughed at would make him even more unworthy of being called by God. It would be as though a worthy person had been called, but this grungy, unworthy Abraham showed up instead, foolishly believing himself to be the worthy one. Now this, says Kafka, would indeed require a leap of faith.

of the children that was in danger of being stifled by adults, it was the imagination of the adults themselves that was also in danger of withering away. Andersen's moral lesson is one of openness. He tells us to listen to the world and not just respond to it with preconceived notions; if we do, we will encounter only what we expect, and we will never again see the magic and splendor of the world the way children do.

Few of us who heard Hans Christian Andersen's story "The Fir Tree" as children paid much attention to the lesson it taught. Way out in the woods a little Christmas tree is growing. It is a pretty little tree, and it ought to be happy just being a little tree in the woods, but every time a rabbit jumps over it, it wishes that it were already fully grown because it's not much fun to be little. Season after season this happens—the little tree wants to grow and be a mighty pine so that it can be cut down and travel to foreign lands and see exciting things. The wind and the sun whisper, "Be happy you're young! Be happy you're here in the forest with your friends. Don't wish for time to hurry." Finally the tree becomes a young adult. It is cut down for Christmas, purchased, and taken to a nice, middle-class home. It experiences a wonderful Christmas Eve, but that is it for the little Christmas tree. It keeps expecting other wonderful things to happen, but it has no future; and, finally, stuck in the attic with brown, drooping branches, it realizes that the wind and the sun were right—it should have been happy to be young and surrounded by its friends in the woods. The moral lesson is obvious: that we often don't appreciate something until it is lost to us, and then we realize that we should have been more appreciative while it was still ours.

Other stories with moral lessons were being written for children during this same time period. Didactic stories took up the thread of the fables and taught children how to behave: to obey their parents, to be kind to animals, to finish their porridge, and to not make fun of people who looked different. Although today the lessons of these stories may seem, for the most part, quite inoffensive, the stories themselves often reveal sexism, racism, and a general naive belief that the writer had all the wisdom in the world. These "moral stories" not only present a moral problem but also *moralize*. This tendency to teach moral lessons enraged Mark Twain to the extent that he wrote a parody called "About Magnanimous-Incident Literature" (to which *Mad* magazine and the *Naked Gun* films are indebted). Twain's parody gives us the "true" ending to the little moral stories. In one story, the scruffy little homeless dog that the kindly village doctor cures comes back the next day with another scruffy little dog to be cured, and the doctor praises God for the chance to heal another unfortunate creature. End of moral story; here comes Twain: The next day there are four scruffy dogs outside the doctor's office, and the following week there are hundreds of howling mutts waiting to be treated. The original mutt is going crazy from all this helpfulness and bites the doctor, who wishes he had shot it in the first place.

Stories with Role Models

What kind of people do we like to hear stories about? And after the story, do we go out and do the same thing as the hero in the book or the movie?

When we talk about fictional characters who somehow teach a moral lesson, we are talking about *role models.* Cartoon characters such as Superman and Spiderman may have certain qualities that we identify with and would like to emulate. But if we include Batman, we encounter an interesting twist: Batman is not a wholesome character; he has a psychological problem (which was, to some extent, explored in the recent films). Not all heroic characters are completely virtuous. If we look at fictional heroes in Western popular literature, from King Arthur, Lancelot, and Robin Hood to D'Artagnan and Scarlett O'Hara, we see that most of these people are morally flawed. The tendency in the twentieth century had been to depict them as being as morally flawed as possible, something that may reflect a certain sense of cynicism. A talk-show guest once announced that she had learned her moral lessons exclusively from soap operas, and we know that soap characters are by no means morally without reproach.

This is not a new phenomenon; in the medieval churches of Europe, peasant congregations were spellbound by murals depicting biblical scenes that sometimes covered the entire inside of the church. The murals kept them occupied during the long hours while the priest spoke in Latin, which the peasants did not understand. The moral lesson of this artwork was obvious, but it was expressed through depictions not of good people so much as of *bad* people; scenes illustrating people going to hell are usually much more vivid and artistically interesting than are scenes of people going to heaven. Perhaps the artists thought it was more fun to depict horrors than bland happiness. It does seem to be a human trait that we dwell on stories with a dark element, rather than on those with happy endings. Yet these stories can certainly teach a moral lesson. We must conclude, therefore, that not all moral lessons involve role models to be emulated; rather, a considerable number of moral lessons are negative rather than positive: *Don't.* Sometimes characters who show themselves to be morally flawed become our heroes not because they are good but because they are like us, or worse. If these "bad good people" see the folly of their ways in the end, we especially take them to our hearts. (For example, in Jane Austen's novel *Pride and Prejudice,* Elizabeth Bennet, realizing that her own biases have blinded her to the vices of Mr. Wickham and the virtues of Mr. Darcy, says, "Till this moment, I never knew myself.") Perhaps we do this because we hope that we will be loved too, even if we make mistakes. It seems that, on the whole, we have the heroes we deserve, as it has sometimes been said. A cautious time has cautious heroes; a violent time has violent heroes. During the time that we accept them as our heroes, we let their images guide our actions; when their day is done, we can still learn from them—they can teach us about the way we once were.

Some stories are moral investigations of a flawed character, such as Joseph Conrad's *Lord Jim* (see the Narrative in Chapter 9), who makes a fatal, cowardly decision in his youth and tries to live it down for the rest of his life. In Victor Hugo's *Les Misérables,* Jean Valjean morally rises above the crimes of his youth only to be haunted by them until the end of his life. Fyodor Dostoyevsky's *Crime and Punishment* examines the philosophical deliberations of Raskolnikov as he imagines the right of the extraordinary individual to do whatever he wants, including committing murder. Gustave Flaubert's *Madame Bovary* (outlined in Chapter 4) traces Emma's deterioration through boredom and through fantasies (brought on by reading novels!). A work by the Danish author J. P. Jacobsen, *Marie Grubbe,* in some ways parallels *Madame Bovary.* It investigates the downfall of a noble lady through three marriages: to a nobleman, to a soldier, and finally to a drunk. The cause of her deterioration seems to be the same as Emma's: sensualism and boredom. The last time we encounter Marie, she is tending the ferry that runs between two small towns, in order to support her drunkard husband. The irony of the story is that in this squalor Marie finally finds the happiness that eluded her when she was a "fine lady."

Stories such as these are not written with the intention of sending their readers out on any heroic errands. They are, primarily, explorations of fascinating human characters. They also serve as moral evaluations by asking whether the characters redeem themselves somehow, even in their degradation. At times a character's redeeming act or quality goes against mainstream morality, as in the story of Marie Grubbe, and then the story forces us to ask which value is the ultimate moral value. Do we agree with society that Marie's life was wasted, full of missed opportunities? Or do we agree with the author that life, and morality, have many faces and that there is some intrinsic value in staying true to yourself, no matter how much this sentiment may differ from the public ethos? If such characters serve as a warning not to emulate them, we call them *negative role models.* We meet this concept again in Chapter 10.

Some Fantastic Tales for Grown-Ups

The stories that have affected Western culture are too numerous to count, but a few stand out as *archetypes,* models that we seem to return to over and over again. In this section we will look at three themes that keep showing up in the world of fiction: *the bargain, the good twin and the bad twin,* and *the quest.*

The Bargain   There is a certain genre of stories that continually fascinates the adult imagination: the story in which someone bargains with fate (or with gods or devils) to gain some advantage—or doesn't literally bargain, but simply puts his life and happiness on the line to obtain what he wants most. Why do such stories continue to intrigue us? Perhaps it is because we recognize the single-mindedness of some individuals, and their success, and wonder what price they may have to pay (perhaps even hoping that they have to pay a price). Or perhaps it is because we, in desperate situations, also try to bargain with fate: If you let me live, I'll give up smoking/be kinder to my spouse/stop gambling/stop eating junk food, and so on. If you let me pass the test I promise I'll be a good student from now on. If you let me win the battle I promise you I will sacrifice the first living thing that approaches me when I come home. This is the bargain in the biblical horror story of Jephtha's Daughter. Jephtha thinks he will be met by his dog, but it is his virgin daughter who comes to greet him. What does he do? Does he resolve to cheat God and save his daughter? No, he gives her a month to grieve for her virginity, and then he sacrifices her. (In this case, God does not step in to prevent it as he did for Abraham.) Sometimes, like Jephtha, we keep our bargains with fate, but most often we don't. Stories in which a bargain has been made with the devil, however, usually cast him as a reliable businessman: He keeps his end of the deal, and he expects you to keep yours.

The grandmother of all devil bargains is the story of Dr. Faust, the main character in Johann Wolfgang von Goethe's masterpiece, *Faust*. There was, in Wüttemberg, Germany, in the sixteenth century, an actual man named Johann Faust; he was an astrologer and magician at a time when science, astrology, and magic were only just beginning to be separated, conceptually and practically. "Alchemists" were undertaking experiments based in part on scientific evidence and in part on magical formulae; such practices usually were outlawed as heresy by the Catholic Church. The Spanish Inquisition disposed of many an early scientist for being a heretic well into the seventeenth century. Even before *Faust*, though, stories appeared with the same motif: the necromancer (sorcerer) who sells his soul. These stories have been fused with the legend of Faust because of this frequent representation in literature. Around 1589 (some fifty years after the death of the actual Dr. Faust) Marlowe wrote the *Tragical History of Dr. Faustus,* but it was Goethe's version (1780–1833) that became the ultimate metaphor for the scientist who will do anything, including sell his soul, for pure knowledge (in Faust's case, to secure the formula for turning base metals into gold). (Later in this chapter you'll find an early story by Goethe, *The Sorrows of Young Werther,* about a young man who dies from unrequited love—the novel that made Goethe instantly famous.) The story of Faust was made into an American tale by Stephen Vincent Benét, "The Devil and Daniel Webster," but with a twist: Webster outwits the devil. (This is actually a whole subgenre by itself—the outwitting of the devil.) In the 1940s, Nobel Prize winner Thomas Mann modernized the original story in his novel *Dr. Faustus,* which explores the mind-set of a man of the times; in Mann's book the obsession is not science, but art.

Through the Faust story runs a moralizing thread: *Faust does wrong in selling his soul.* There are folklore and fairy tale stories that are in complete accordance with this view. One traveling story, a story that has traveled from country to country in different versions, is the tale of the boy who wanted to play the fiddle like no one else, and the devil taught him to play so sweetly that the fish would jump out of the river to listen, the birds would stop singing, and all the girls the boy ever wanted would flock to him. The trouble was that every time he wanted to put the fiddle down, he couldn't. In other words, The devil made him do it, and he played himself to death. Some musicians might say it was worth it.

The Faustian theme also has been explored in films from time to time, as in *Angel Heart,* in which a character realized something he had forgotten—that he sold his soul—and there is no help or redemption for him in the end. At the end of this chapter you will find a summary of the film *Pulp Fiction.* One of the study questions hints at a possible interpretation—did the gangster boss sell his soul to the devil?

The Good Twin and the Bad Twin   A story that is closely related to that of Dr. Faust, but with an added element, is Robert Louis Stevenson's 1886 story of *Dr. Jekyll and Mr. Hyde.* As with Goethe's story, Stevenson's is loosely based on a real person—in this case a nineteenth-century British scientist. The kindly Dr. Jekyll becomes the evil Mr. Hyde by drinking his own invention, a personality-changing drug intended, the story goes, to distill goodness from evil in the human character. Jekyll, who is not so kindly after all given that he throws away his life and *respectability* (a notion nineteenth-century readers found particularly problematic) for the sake of finding knowledge, parallels Dr. Faust in this obsession—but here the story departs from the Faustian pattern. Not only is the devil absent (he is manifested only in the "well-deserved" death of Jekyll/Hyde), but also another theme is introduced: the *double character.* After all, Jekyll and Hyde are the same man, and the symbolism is easy to read: We all have a beast "hyding" in us, an alter ego, and we must not let it loose no matter how much we would like to. The reason Jekyll keeps returning to his Hyde persona is because it feels good, it amuses him; he gets to do things that Victorian England frowned upon, like going out on the town. Of course, he exceeds even the tolerance of any time period when he tortures and kills. The moral lesson is broad and completely in tune with nineteenth-century Victorian mores, as well as with most of the Christian tradition: Keep your inner beast in check, and don't give in to your physical desires.

When we look at the theme of twin souls, we generally have two versions: One person with two personalities, such as Jekyll and Hyde, or two persons who are inextricably linked, but very different, such as good and evil twins, a theme that we will return to below. A famous story from the early twentieth century of one person with two "natures" is Herman Hesse's *Steppenwolf,* the tale of Harry Haller, a middle-aged, middle-class man who is contemplating suicide at fifty because he sees nothing positive in life any longer—and his dual nature, the Steppenwolf, a sarcastic, lonely being still thirsty for the outrageous experience. Another story (which you will meet in Chapter 8) is the popular film *Shrek:* The haughty, beautiful Princess Fiona has a deep secret; at night she is transformed into a green-skinned ogre. One hundred years prior to *Shrek,* Hans Christian Andersen wrote his story of "The Swamp King's Daughter," a serious, symbolic tale of the daughter of a beautiful Egyptian princess and the vicious king of the swamp: In daylight she is a beautiful, but evil woman; but at night she is a sweet, gentle, compassionate soul trapped in the body of a giant toad. The dual-nature stories are easily interpreted as the battle between our "angel" side and our "devil" side—or, as the Christian tradition has generally viewed it, our spirit and our flesh. But as Herman Hesse says, "The division into wolf and man, flesh and spirit, by means of which Harry tries to make his destiny more comprehensible to himself is a very great simplification. . . . Harry consists of a hundred or a thousand selves, not of two. His life oscillates, as everyone's does, not merely between two poles, such as the body and the spirit, the saint and the sinner, but between thousands and thousands."

The stories of twins are sometimes harder to interpret, but interestingly, they often work along the same symbolic lines: One twin (or sibling or friend) generally represents "good," or the spiritual life, while the other twin represents "evil," or the world of physical desires, as with the story of Cal and Aron in *East of Eden*. And often the author's purpose is to describe two sides of any one of us, just as the dual-nature stories do. Where the story gets interesting, such as in Steinbeck's novel, is when the good twin suddenly seems to have an evil streak, and the "bad" twin reveals a higher moral nature, and we begin to doubt the stereotypes. But of course life rarely imitates fiction, except for one California court case in the 1990s where a woman actually hired a hit man to kill her twin sister because she wanted to take over her life—because her sister was admired for her goodness and kindness. The plot was foiled, and the "good" sister testified against her "evil" sister in court and got her convicted.

The Quest   The first quest story that we know of is that of Gilgamesh, the king of Uruk. Gilgamesh loses his only friend, Enkidu, to a withering disease. This brings home to Gilgamesh the fact that all humans are mortal, and he is seized by a terrible fear. So he sets out to find the secret of immortality. This story has been told by Sumerians since at least approximately 1500 B.C.E. Gilgamesh goes to the ends of the earth and finds the oldest living humans, Utnapishtim and his wife, who survived the big flood by the grace of the gods (they were safe in a wooden box that floated the waters—an *ark*). Utnapishtim's rescue, however, was a one-time deal, and Gilgamesh must look elsewhere for his own rescue from death. In the end he finds the plant that gives immortality, picks it, and drops it in the water. Gilgamesh must go under the sea where the monster snake lives; into its gaping maw he must crawl to get the weed—but he can't retrieve it. Gilgamesh had immortality for a while, but then he lost it, for it is the fate of humans to be mortal.

Gilgamesh's quest was a failure, but it was heroic nevertheless, because it embodied a human longing to live forever, as well as the acknowledgment that we can't, even if we are the king of Uruk. The quest motif is one of the most moving in the history of literature and film, precisely because even if the hero doesn't find what he or she sets out to find, the search itself remains the most important part of the story. The quest forces the hero to mature and makes him or her realize the true importance, or lack of importance, of the quest's object.

Myths and legends abound with quest stories. The Navajo goddess Grandmother Spider searches for the sun in the early days when the land is in darkness. She finds it and steals a piece and puts it into her clay pot to bring home. In the Greek legend of Jason and the Golden Fleece, Jason and his argonauts go on a quest for a sheepskin made of gold. Egyptian legend tells of the goddess Isis, who searches for the remains of her husband, Osiris, who was murdered. Some searchers even go to the underworld to find what they are looking for: Ulysses goes to the realm of the dead to speak with the wise Teresias. Orpheus goes to the underworld to try to retrieve his beloved wife, Eurydice, from the dead. The Native American Modoc culture hero Kumokum goes to the land of the dead in search of his daughter. Ishtar, the all-powerful goddess of the Middle East, finds that her powers are limited when her young lover, Tammuz, dies, and she goes to the underworld to buy him back. The earth goddess Demeter goes to the kingdom of the dead to get back her daughter, Persephone, who has been abducted by the king of the dead.

These stories confirm what we know: that we would go to the ends of the earth and the land of the dead if it could bring back those we love. We also know that it would be to no avail; Gilgamesh's lesson is one that every human learns.

Some quests are of a happier nature. In the African folktale about the girl Wanjiru, Wanjiru's family sacrifices her so that the rains will come, but a young warrior goes to the underworld to fetch her back. He carries her on his back to the world of the living and hides her until she is strong again; then he displays her at the great dance. Her family is now ashamed of the way they treated her, and the warrior and Wanjiru are married.

One of Grimm's fairy tales has an unusual quest story: the quest for the feeling of fear and trembling. In "The Youth Who Could Not Shiver and Shake," the protagonist goes through the most frightful horrors but still can't seem to shiver and shake properly, until his young bride throws a bucket of minnows at him: Now he knows what it feels like to shiver and shake! There is more to this story than just a joke, for without this feeling of fear we are not complete humans. This quest, like the quest for love, is a search for something that will make the character a whole person. Indeed, most modern literature and films somehow involve a quest for oneself, a search for self-identity through encounters with the Other.

Two quest motifs have, each in its own right, come to epitomize the *search*. One is *Moby Dick,* and the other is the legend of the Holy Grail.

Herman Melville's *Moby Dick* (1851) has become the American model for the quest, but with a special angle: The searcher is mad, and the quest is meaningless, except to Captain Ahab himself. In many stories, although the object of the quest may be out of reach, it usually is something to which the reader can relate. In the case of *Moby Dick,* though, the reader identifies not with the searcher, but with an observer, Ishmael. The quest itself is seen as pointless, and quite mad. Eventually, Captain Ahab finds his white whale but he and the rest of the crew die, except for Ishmael, who alone "survived to tell thee."

Hollywood came up with a modern version of the whale search for a society that reveres whales but dislikes sharks. In *Jaws,* the symbolism is stronger than in the Melville story; the gigantic shark is a more obvious representation of inhuman evil. However, the sense of ambiguity present in *Moby Dick* is missing in *Jaws.* The Melville story makes us wonder if Ahab's quest was worth the passion and trouble; in *Jaws* we know the quest was ill-advised.

In a sense, there is one Hollywood story that is much more closely related to *Moby Dick* than *Jaws*. In one of its most superb productions, John Ford's film *The Searchers,* Hollywood created a folklore version of the mad quest. As the title indicates, in the movie it is the search, more than the object of the search, that matters. For eight years Ethan and Marty look all over the western United States for Ethan's niece Debbie, who was captured by the Comanche Indians. Marty is the observer we identify with, the "Ishmael" of the story. Marty tries to reason with Ethan, who is obsessed with revenge rather than rescue. Ethan finds his "white whale," the Comanche chief responsible for murdering Ethan's family and kidnapping Debbie, but he realizes, in the knick of time, that his motives were misguided. Ethan is redeemed and returned to sanity through human love. However, he has traveled too far on the road to obsession and human loneliness and is doomed to wander alone.

The search for the Holy Grail, part of Arthurian legend, is a quest that succeeds only symbolically, if at all. Several years after the glorious time of the Round Table, Arthur's knights become obsessed with finding the cup from the Last Supper of Christ, the Grail. They each go through trials to find the cup, but only Galahad (or sometimes Percival) succeeds in seeing the Grail, and even he is denied any further access. Since the time that the tale was first told, the quest for the Grail has become a symbol of the search for a profound truth, a holy revelation, for the meaning of life, if you will. (Box 2.3 looks at some grail quests in film.) Even when the search is unsuccessful and even futile, as it is for Cervantes' Don Quixote, who searches far and wide for the "impossible dream," the search itself nevertheless lends the searcher a cloak of heroism, no less than it did for Gilgamesh. The grail theme can encompass any kind of quest, not just a search for a cup or an item. One of the surprise best-sellers in recent years was Dan Brown's *The DaVinci Code,* a story set in the contemporary world and featuring a hunt for the truth behind the legend of the Holy Grail. To many readers' surprise—even shock—the grail turns out to be not a cup, but—a person! A woman who, according to the speculative theory, gave birth to a child of Jesus Christ: Mary Magdalene. She, and the bloodline, are the Holy Grail or, in French, not the *San Greal* but the *Sang Real. The DaVinci Code* spawned a veritable cottage industry of TV specials and interpretive books, but in fact the theory had been floated decades earlier in the controversial book *Holy Blood, Holy Grail* by Baignet, Leigh, and Lincoln. While the plot captures the imagination of many, it remains speculation without solid evidence, according to most historians.

If the Holy Grail is a symbol of the search for ideal truth, the Philosopher's Stone has become a symbol of the search for material riches. Some scholars believe that the Holy Grail and the Philosopher's Stone are one and the same thing. Originally, the Philosopher's Stone was a fantasy of the alchemists, the pseudoscientists of medieval Europe (it also was the dream of Dr. Faust). These people had one specific goal: to find the chemical substance that would turn base metals into gold. This elusive substance became known as the Philosopher's Stone. It achieved a symbolic meaning as the agent that could transform life into a higher, spiritual existence, but on the whole the tie-in to gold proved to be the more vigorous one. Although there are few stories directly related to the Philosopher's Stone, there are plenty of stories about *treasure hunting.* The

Box 2.3   THE HOLY GRAIL IN THE MOVIES

The grail theme has been explored in films such as *Quest for Fire,* the hominid adventure story with gibberish dialogue by Anthony Burgess, and in out-and-out adventure stories such as *Raiders of the Lost Ark. Indiana Jones and the Last Crusade* is about the hunt for the Grail itself. The science fiction classic *2001: A Space Odyssey* is a grail quest for the ultimate mystery, the black, ancient monolith. *The Fisher King* is another film that uses the grail motif. It presents a realistic portrayal of homelessness and teaches the lesson that anything is worthy of being the object of a quest if that quest is undertaken in the spirit of love. In other films, from *Stanley and Livingstone* to *The Mountains of the Moon,* people traverse the jungles of Africa seeking out other people, the source of the Nile, or a better understanding of themselves and their role in the scheme of things.

Stories that involve a search for an antidote may incorporate both the grail element and an element of catharsis (a spiritual cleansing). Finding the grail is the cure for the ailment, but it also may serve as a liberating, spiritual healing process. Perhaps the one grail movie trilogy that is most familiar to younger moviegoers of the early twenty-first century is in fact a reversed grail story, because it has to do not with *finding* a special object, but with *getting rid of it:* Tolkien's *Lord of the Rings.* The Ring that Frodo has to take to Mordor in order to destroy it is the source of evil, and a great temptation for everyone, including Frodo. As in the Holy Grail legend, it is only Galahad who is of sufficient spiritual purity to even have a vision of the Grail, so Frodo is the only one whose heart is pure enough to undertake the journey (although, as many fans of the trilogy will want to point out, without the unselfish courage of Sam Gangee, his friend, the Ring would never have been destroyed). In Chapter 4 we take a closer look at *Lord of the Rings.*

ultimate model for such stories is *Treasure Island* by Robert Louis Stevenson, but any story involving the search for hidden wealth can be viewed as a version of the legend of the Philosopher's Stone—the search for the item that will change your life and make you rich. The first Harry Potter book even uses the theme as its primary plot.

The quest can thus be for something sublime, something ideal, or not of this world, or it can be for something as down-to-earth as money. Regardless of whether the story takes the high path or the low path, the quest as a story type seems to be very enduring.

Contemporary Story Genres

Sometimes the moral lesson in a story is hard to find; we may be blind to it, or it may be somewhat dated, having evolved in another era. There is a scene in Aldous Huxley's novel *Brave New World* (1932) in which the young "savage," John, who has grown up on a nature reservation unaffected by the modern era of eugenics, total sexual liberty, and test-tube babies, introduces his friend, the scientist Helmholtz, to Shakespeare. He reads from *Romeo and Juliet,* certain that the moral drama of the young lovers who can't have each other will move his modern friend. Helmholtz, however, doubles up laughing, because he can't for the life of him see that there is a problem: If

In *Indiana Jones and the Last Crusade* (1989), the archaeologists Indiana Jones (Harrison Ford) and his father (Sean Connery) search for the ultimate treasure in the Christian tradition: the Holy Grail, presumably the cup used by Jesus Christ at the Last Supper. Here Jones and Jones are barely escaping with their lives from a fire in a Nazi stronghold.

Romeo and Juliet want each other, why don't they just have sex and let it go at that, instead of making such an embarrassing fuss about it? He is blind to the social and moral structures of the past, and the savage is very upset that ethical communication seems impossible in a new era that has done away with family relationships, birth, siblings, and spouses and that refuses to recognize the phenomenon of death.

In a similar way, stories depicting unwanted pregnancies struck a deep chord in times past but haven't had the same resonance since the advent of legal abortion and safe birth control. Old Hollywood films about the trials of two lovers who can't get a divorce from their spouses also sometimes require us to stretch a bit in order to empathize with the characters. Stories praising the glory of war, which were quite successful until the early twentieth century, have not done well with the majority of modern readers and viewers for quite some time now.

Wartime Stories: Duty and Honor   Wartime stories with moral lessons were common in past eras when it seemed that each generation of young men was expected to be initiated into manhood through some local armed conflict. But the idea of war as a natural arena for the exercise of masculine virtues received a serious blow in World War I, with its murky reasons for fighting and its wholesale slaughter of entire squadrons—young men from the same family or village or the same university, dying side by side in the trenches from mustard gas and machine gun fire, and leaving villages and colleges empty of an entire generation of male youth. The soldier on the white horse with a feather plume in his helmet, dying gloriously for his country, became one of the images left behind in the nineteenth century, giving way to twentieth-century bitterness. For many people the entire idea of glory in war has become nothing but propaganda, invented by the leaders in order to inspire their legions to march unquestioningly off to the front as cannon fodder.

However, the image of the warrior as stalwart and honorable is so deeply imbedded in most human cultures that it shouldn't be dismissed as merely the result of the manipulation of gullible people by poets, propagandists, monarchs, and generals. It seems to resonate with something deep in us that identifies us as social beings, with a loyalty to our own people, for better or worse. Some would say it is a specifically *male* resonance; others see it as a class identification, which should be uprooted in a global community—but many see it as a part of a natural love for where we grew up and who we grew up with, regardless of class and gender, and not infrequently a love for the principles we have been taught.

For some pacifists, any story of war is a distasteful reminder of human nature at its worst—but even for many pacifists, a wartime story can be meaningful in its focus, not on the glory of war, but on humans under pressure, displaying devotion to duty and their comrades. And as many otherwise peace-loving people discovered (or rediscovered) in the wake of September 11, it is possible to think of a war as *just,* and a war-time story not just as a sad testimony to the blind aggression of humanity but also as a tribute to brave people righteously responding to an attack. The classic definition of a just war (see Chapter 13) is that a war can't be fought for territory, or for glory, but strictly for defending one's country or preventing future genuine threats. This means a war can be fought only if no other option seems reasonable or practical. A story about a just war must show that war is the last moral option and that the goal is peace. In addition, it must demonstrate a clear vision of who is right and who is wrong.

World War II, which until September 2001, many considered to be the last war that had a clear moral focus and an identifiable good and evil side, spawned thousands of novels and films telling the story of good triumphing over evil. Some films attempt factually to depict actual wartime events, such as *The Longest Day, A Bridge Too Far, Enola Gay,* and *Hamburger Hill.* Others spin fictional elements and characters into a story with a message about the experience of war, such as *Twelve O'Clock High, Memphis Belle, Midnight Clear, Saving Private Ryan, The Thin Red Line,* and the acclaimed HBO series *Band of Brothers.* We will have to see what kinds of stories of human nature and human character will be told by novelists and filmmakers about September 11 and its aftermath, the war on terrorism.

The Moral Universe of Westerns: Hard Choices   Stories of the American West, called *Westerns,* have served as moral lessons for both the American public and a worldwide audience for more than a hundred years. All nations seem to go through periods when they "rediscover" their past, but the American West as a historical period is both recent and very short: from 1865 to about 1885—from the end of the

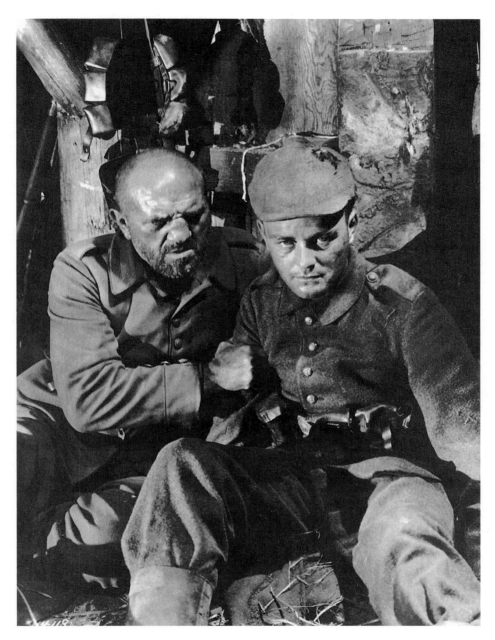

In *All Quiet on the Western Front* (Universal Studios, 1930, based on Erich Maria Remarque's 1929 novel), Katczinsky (Louis Wolheim) is the old "trench hog" and Paul Baumer (Lew Ayres), the young idealist who is about to get his lesson in the realities of war. The West's image of war changed with World War I. No more shining swords and prancing horses—there was nothing glorious about dying in the trenches of the European battlefields, and few soldiers understood the purpose of the prolonged fighting. However, the virtues of friendship, courage, and loyalty seemed all the more important as a twentieth-century war ethic. (From the collection of C. R. Covner.)

Civil War to the end of the open cattle range, which resulted from the advent of barbed wire and the bad winters of the 1880s. There have probably been more stories told about the Old West than could ever have happened. Even when the Old West was still alive, those in the East were reading dime novels that glamorized the West; the first Western films were shot outside New York City in the early 1900s. The process of creating a legend about the recent past was very rapid and even involved actual cowboys and gunfighters who moved from the plains and deserts to Hollywood to lend a hand.

Making entertainment out of recent history was one way to draw people to the theaters. If that were all, though, the Western never would have endured as long as it has. Part of its allure seems to have been its exoticism; the West is, still, a unique landscape. And then there is wishful thinking: Perhaps the Old West was never the way it appears in movies, but we wish it had been. An even greater appeal is the *moral potential* of a Western. For Western aficionados, it is almost like watching a ritual. The story usually is one we are familiar with, even if we are seeing it for the first time: There have to be good guys and bad guys, and horses, and they have to do a lot of riding back and forth among rocks in a gorgeous landscape. Then there is usually a good girl and sometimes also a bad girl. And there is a threat, either from Indians or the railroad or rustlers or (in later Westerns) big business, which is warded off by the strength and wit of Our Hero, sometimes even reluctantly (he often has to be dragged into the fight). When the problem is solved, the hero rarely settles down but rides off into the sunset so that he doesn't get entangled in the peace and prosperity of the society he helped stabilize. In later Westerns, the good guys are Indians or blacks or a gang of outlaws and the bad guys are the army or other Indians or the law; the stable society becomes a negative rather than a positive image. Traditionally, though, the general pattern is the same: The power of the individual (the Good) rises above the threat of a larger force (the Evil). Sometimes the individual paves the way for civilization, but in the process makes himself superfluous, as in what may be the best Western ever made, *The Searchers* (see p. 55). Sometimes the individual accomplished his moral triumph in spite of the community that lets him down, as in another classic, *High Noon* (see Chapter 6). And sometimes the individual stands up for what he believes in but is sacrificed by the community who rejects his values, as in the underrated little masterpiece *The Life of Tom Horn* (see Chapter 11).

Why do people watch Westerns if they already know what will happen? Because the movie experience (or TV experience) itself is a *moral event.* People take part in the story by watching it, and they feel that when the problems on the screen are solved, the general problems of life are, in some symbolic way, put to rest at the same time. The moviegoer may not even be aware of this psychological process.

One might think that if the Western had a moral message, it would seem pretty dated, and sometimes even offensive, to modern audiences. After all, the first generation of Westerns left the overall impression that it was fine to kill Indians, that women were weak and had to be protected, that blacks were nonexistent, that the land was there only to be developed, that animal life and suffering were irrelevant, and so on. However, the values of the Western movie changed with the changing times. There were still good guys and bad guys, but in each period they reflected the

The 1985 Western *Silverado* (Columbia Pictures) abandoned the 1970s trend of depicting the Old West in decline and gave its audience a story in a vigorous frontier setting with a happy ending. For this reason, the film is sometimes referred to as a "retro-Western." Many of the themes incorporated in *Silverado* are anything but "retro," however; for example, with this film the Western genre entered a new era of racial awareness. Here the four buddies (Danny Glover, Kevin Costner, Scott Glenn, and Kevin Kline) ride out to save the town of Silverado from corruption.

problems of the contemporary world, at least in a symbolic sense. In the 1950s the Western began to reflect a growing unease with the stereotype of townspeople conquering the wilderness; the sixties saw an increasing sympathy for the outlaw. The Western of the seventies was influenced by the Vietnam War and began to address problems of discrimination, overdevelopment, and pollution. In the eighties the Western seemed to have nothing more to say, but in the nineties it acquired a voice once again; current Westerns often deal with cross-cultural and cross-racial issues in the American melting pot. (See Box 2.4 for an overview of how the messages of Westerns have changed.) The Western, being the one narrative genre that is truly American, shows an amazing potential for being able to introduce many kinds of social and moral problems in a single framework in which people have to make big, moral decisions in a land where they are dwarfed by rocks, mountains, and deserts. These stories of momentous decisions appeal not just to Americans but to people all over the world. This makes the Western much more than just a movie genre. It has become a transcultural story told in a universal moral language.

Box 2.4   THE CHANGING MESSAGES OF WESTERNS

Western films have from the early days managed to integrate modern problems into the period plot, sometimes without much respect for the historical context. The Vietnam War era had its "Vietnam Westerns" in which massacred Indians symbolized the Vietnamese and the army symbolized the U.S. Army in Vietnam (*Soldier Blue, Little Big Man*). Post-Watergate Westerns showed corrupt politicians and greedy railroad tycoons (*Young Guns I and II*). Westerns of the 1990s explored the issue of violence and killing; contrary to most classic Westerns, in which violence was part of the formula, the new Western asked about its justification. *Tombstone* and *Wyatt Earp* both examine the effects of violence on a township and on the individual (Earp) who tries to put an end to it, and *Unforgiven* probably makes the strongest antiviolence statement of all newer Westerns, reflecting on the loss of humanity in the life of a gunfighter.

With the return of the Western, there has been a growing sensitivity not only to historical accuracy but also to a multiethnic presence in the Old West. African Americans have found a heroic identity in the Western landscape (*Silver-ado, Lonesome Dove*), and American Indians have emerged from old stereotypes such as devils or angels to become real people with their own language and their own problems and jokes (*Dances with Wolves, The Last of the Mohicans, Geronimo*). Strong female characters in Westerns are still rare, although there have been a few of them over the years in the films *Johnny Guitar, Rio Bravo,* and *High Noon*, the television movie *Lonesome Dove,* and the television series *Dr. Quinn, Medicine Woman. The Ballad of Little Jo,* about a woman passing herself off as a man to get by in life; *Open Range,* featuring a female character who, in her determination, is as strong as the male "hero"; and in particular the film *Missing,* with its female lead trying to rescue her abducted little sister, all help to dispel the impression that Westerns are exclusively about men and for men. On the television front we have the miniseries *Buffalo Girls,* with Anjelica Huston and Melanie Griffith in the powerful lead roles: a somber, sensitive look at the final days of the Old West, moving from the romantic hardship of the open country to the phony romance of Buffalo Bill's traveling circus.

Science Fiction: What Future Do We Want?   Like the Western, science fiction was born as a literary genre in the nineteenth century. The French author Jules Verne astounded the world with his fantasies of men on the moon and journeys to the center of the earth and the bottom of the sea. Even Hans Christian Andersen predicted, in one of his lesser known stories, that in "thousands of years" Americans would be flying in machines to Europe to visit the Old World. Verne's stories contained an element that has blossomed in modern science fiction: a *moral awareness.* His stories reveal an awareness of the possible repercussions of the inventions, as well as a general political consciousness, which makes his books much more than mere entertainment. In England, the works of H. G. Wells combined science fantasy and social comment in the same way.

In the twentieth century, science fiction became a major genre of entertainment, from pulp magazines and comic books to serious novels and films of high quality. Their subjects range from the pure fantasy of magical universes to hard-core thought experiments of exploratory science. (A *thought experiment* is a mental exercise in which a researcher sets up an imaginary scenario and follows it to its logical conclusion in order to explore what might happen if the scenario came true.) Although science fiction need not always involve ethical issues, it has proved to be one of the most suitable genres for exploring them, especially such problems as we believe may lurk in our future.

In a category by itself is the end-of-civilization type of science fiction, sometimes referred to as "cyberpunk." The civilized world is destroyed by a nuclear war or a giant meteor strike or pollution or the advent of hostile aliens or an epidemic disease. Although this type of story affords the author a chance to present lots of scenes of gruesome death or terrible disaster, the most serious problems usually occur in the relationships among the survivors. Will they degenerate into a "war of everybody against everybody," as the philosopher Thomas Hobbes would say, or will the human spirit of compassion for one's fellow beings triumph? This form also allows us to discuss how the characters got into such dire situations in the first place. If it is through human folly or neglect, such as global war or pollution, the stories can serve as powerful moral *caveats,* or warnings. This mistrust of what the future might bring has no greater expression than in the subtitle of the *X-Files* movie from 1998, *Fight the Future.* Other dreadful-future scenarios that have appeared recently and feature either threats from Above (aliens or meteorites) or Within (our own government, stupidity, or greed) include *Independence Day, Starship Troopers, Deep Impact, Armageddon,* and *The Postman.* For all these films that belong to the "fight the future" genre, the point is that humans are capable of surviving if only we can realize the threat in time and work together.

In the weeks after September 11, *Variety* magazine reported, screenwriters and directors met with representatives from the U.S. Army to brainstorm possible terrorist scenarios, a series of "what-ifs" to improve the preparedness of the army. No longer are action movies, sci-fi movies, and disaster movies to be considered merely lowbrow entertainment; as some of us who occasionally enjoy watching such films have known for years, to be forewarned is to be forearmed: If we can imagine an *Independence Day* or a *Die Hard* scenario, then perhaps we can prevent a similar scenario from happening or be ready for it when it does. The screenwriter of *Die Hard* attended the army's anti-terrorism conference; so did the director of *Delta Force One.* In addition, David Brin, the author of *The Postman* (a fine novel that became a not-so-fine movie), suggested in an interview in the fall of 2001 that we all have to become members of a new class of amateur warriors, vigilant in our everyday life, watching out for each other and any unusual activity, and bringing our cellphones with us wherever we go. In a sense, the cyberpunk nightmare future has arrived, even if the world still looks the same by and large, except for the New York skyline. And perhaps those of us who have been encouraged by the movies to anticipate that future will adjust faster and imagine alternative ways to maintain our "new normalcy" even under trying conditions.

Interestingly enough, there is a "counterfable" to the end-of-the-world scenario. It is the story of the Happy Future—not a future without problems, but a future in which some of today's pressing problems have been solved. Such stories present a world without nuclear threat, without racism or sexism, without nationalistic chauvinism—a world in which science has acquired a humanistic face and politics on earth, as well as in space, is conducted with a democratic spirit and common sense. The original *Star Trek* television series pioneered this hopeful fantasy of the future. The sequel, *Star Trek: The Next Generation,* showed that the Happy Future scenario was as welcome as ever, not in a naive sense but as a vision of a maturing humanity that, free from the fears, deprivations, and resentments of the modern age, may be able to turn its energy toward new frontiers and challenges.

Another great series of science fiction stories that has also proved to have staying power is the *Star Wars* franchise. But in the *Star Wars* universe we find no Federation of civilized planets as in *Star Trek;* on the contrary, the evil forces are organized into an evil Empire, and the heroes, the Jedi Knights, are guerrillas battling the overwhelming military power—and its bureaucracy. Scholars and journalists have spent time analyzing this interesting opposition of space-opera scenarios—a benevolent Federation and an evil Empire—and some have pronounced *Star Trek* to be the fantasy of liberals preferring big government, and *Star Wars* the fantasy of conservatives fighting for individual freedoms in the face of the bureaucracy.

Be that as it may, both series have created enduring stories that, in many ways, have become part of our American mythology, and both occasionally approach the question of what it really means to be human: Who (or what) counts as a person? In *Star Trek* we have the half-human, half-Vulcan Mr. Spock, the android Data, and the hologram The Doctor, all on the edge of humanity, all counting as persons and yet having their personhood placed in doubt time and time again. In *Star Wars* we have a multitude of characters who are considered persons, but not human, such as Chewbacca the Wookie, the 'droids, Yoda, and Jar-Jar Binks. The question of who counts as a person is especially popular in science fiction novels: Several sci-fi authors have specialized in this issue, among them Cordwainer Smith, Octavia Butler, Rebecca Ore, Ursula K. Le Guin, and C. H. Cherry. In stories about genetically altered chimps and other animals who do the dirty work for humans (Smith), humans adopted by aliens (Butler, Ore), and lone human envoys to alien societies (Le Guin and Cherry), we are invited to explore (1) what makes us human and (2) how we treat those we think don't qualify. In Chapter 7 we take a closer look at the issue of personhood and discuss the films *Blade Runner* and *Gattaca,* about challenges to the concepts of personhood and rights.

The *golem* may be the oldest character in the science fiction genre. It comes from the Eastern European Jewish tradition, in which it was said that a man might create an artificial person out of clay, a golem, but if he weren't careful to keep this creature in check with certain magical acts and formulas, the clay man would grow and eventually take over and kill him. One story tells of a rabbi creating a golem to help the Jews protest false accusations of blood-sacrificing of Christians during Passover. This particular golem helped the Jewish people for years by exposing Christian plots to plant dead bodies of Christians in Jewish homes. But the golem became too strong and powerful for the rabbi to handle, so in the end the rabbi had to turn him back into the clay from which he had been created. In another version of the story, the rabbi turned the golem back into clay because his job was done and there was no reason to keep him around anymore. (And the character *Gollum* in *Lord of the Rings*

The Day After Tomorrow tells a story of instant global weather disaster, brought about by global warming. Here New York City is being hit by a gigantic tsunami, right before the big chill sets in and plunges the East into a new ice age. Critics praised the special effects, but weren't kind to the plot or the science behind it.

wasn't named by accident—he is, in effect, a creation of the Ring, originally a hobbit transformed by its evil power.) In the early nineteenth century, Mary Wollstonecraft Shelley created a similar artificial person, the monster of Frankenstein. Shelley's theme was the same as that of the golem story: human arrogance and invention run wild. In a strange sense we might say that the golem story is very traditional: If you exceed your boundaries, your creation will come back to haunt you. In a broader sense, though, the story teaches us to evaluate our actions from a moral perspective. In the movies, the artificial monster has taken on a number of guises, from the maniacal computer HAL in *2001: A Space Odyssey* to the Arnold Schwarzenegger character in the *Terminator* movies.

In any event, the artificial person serves well not just as a topic for discussion about what to do if artificial beings become viable in our society but also as a figurative image of ourselves. (Box 2.5 discusses the human qualities of the artificial person.) The artificial person makes us realize what it is to be human and what we ought to be like to be *more* human; it provides an excursion into our own descriptive and normative concepts of humanity and provokes us to explore how we should treat the *Other*. (In philosophy the person who is different from oneself is often referred to as the Other. The term signifies that one is facing something or someone that one is fundamentally unfamiliar with. It can mean a stranger, a person of the other sex or of another race, or it can mean other people or beings as such, as opposed to oneself and one's own experiences. Sometimes it signifies someone complementary to oneself, but it may also mean that the Other is not as complete, worthy, or important as oneself and one's own kind.)

Mystery and Crime: The Fight Against Evil   As some surveys have found, we modern humans have developed a deep sense of vulnerability—even prior to 9/11, at a time when the crime rate was dropping, people still felt that everyday life was full of

Box 2.5   THE NONHUMAN WHO WANTS TO BECOME HUMAN

Artificial persons in fiction and films often yearn to become human. Frankenstein's monster suffers from this yearning, but he is not allowed to become what he wishes to be. Data, the android in *Star Trek: The Next Generation,* does not have the capability to feel human emotions, but he is intellectually curious about what causes humans to act passionately or maliciously. He longs to be human the way a child longs to grow up. The replicants in *Blade Runner* are ready to kill for a chance to become full-dimensional humans. And the robot Sonny in *I, Robot* awakens to consciousness and becomes the visionary liberator of all of his kind—the artificial beings created as servants without rights. The artificial human in *Terminator 2* displays definite human characteristics; he bonds with a small boy and sacrifices himself for the sake of humankind. Just as the monster side of the artificial person is symbolized by the golem, the wanting-to-be-human side is epitomized by Pinocchio, the wooden puppet who wants to become a real boy. As the story of Pinocchio teaches, you don't become a "real" boy by doing the bad-boy things. If you do the bad-boy things (have fun and skip school), you become what bad boys become: an ass. *Pinocchio* is for all intents and purposes a very moralistic fable.

dangers. Perhaps that accounts for the perennial popularity of detective stories. Cop shows and murder mysteries give us some semblance of a feeling that something can actually be done to control the forces we feel are threatening us.

More than in any other genre, the attention centers on the issue of *good and evil*—not in an abstract sense but as personified on the streets. We may generalize somewhat and say that science fiction deals with desirable versus undesirable futures, Westerns deal with hard choices, and war movies deal with questions of duty, but crime stories above all specialize in questions of good and evil—and what to do about evil. Sometimes we follow the story to its ending with a lot of hope: Something can be done. At other times, it seems like forces of good are trying to empty the ocean with a slotted spoon. What makes this genre so compelling is that evil acquires a face: the face of the bad guy (male or female). And when that person is caught, sentenced, or killed, the greater formless threat of Evil seems to have been vanquished for a while too. Even when the bad guy wins, as he has so often in recent movies, we still have a sense that the fight against evil is not fruitless or without merit. As such, this genre has an inside angle on moral narratives: Regardless of whether the good guys or the bad guys win, or whether you can tell the difference between the good guys and bad guys (as in some movies from the 1970s), or whether the good guys are really bad guys (as in stories of corrupt cops), there is a subtext of a moral discussion going on: What is good? What is evil? And what can be done about it?

The first acknowledged detective story with a "whodunit" focus, "The Murders in the Rue Morgue," was written by Edgar Allan Poe in 1841. Sir Arthur Conan Doyle followed shortly after with his stories about the sleuth Sherlock Holmes. In France, Georges Simenon created the police detective Maigret in 1931. Major heroic

In the popular television series *CSI: Crime Scene Investigation,* the CSI team assists the Las Vegas Police Department in crime scene investigations, usually providing the decisive pieces of evidence. A real forensic scientist will usually tell you that the job is far less glamorous than depicted in the series, but television viewers do get an education in the language and science of forensics. Here Catherine Willows (Marg Helgenberger) and Gil Grissom (William Petersen), both CSI Level Three, are ready to take on a case.

fictional detectives—mostly private investigators—in the literary tradition include characters such as Mike Hammer, Sam Spade, Dick Tracy, Lord Peter Wimsey, Philip Marlowe, Paul Drake (from *Perry Mason*), Nero Wolfe, Miss Marple, and lately Easy Rawlins. At the movies, we've followed the puzzle-solving efforts of police detectives and private eyes from Nick and Nora Charles (*The Thin Man* films) to Dirty Harry to the detectives of *L.A. Confidential, Mulholland Falls,* the *Die Hard* and *Lethal Weapon* films, *48 Hours,* and *Devil in a Blue Dress.* Television has given us cop shows such as *Dragnet, Adam 12, Columbo, Barney Miller, Hill Street Blues, NYPD Blue, Law and Order, Homicide,* and *CSI.* A borderline mystery/sci-fi series that reached almost mythic proportions in the late 1990s was *The X-Files,* with its two-person team of FBI agents attempting to solve crimes that, in some cases, were "out of this world." Mulder (the believer) and Scully (the skeptic) revealed conspiracies within conspiracies, only to have their results sealed by yet another cover-up; the driving force behind Mulder's idealism was that "the truth is out there." The show *CSI: Crime Scene Investigation* has in some sense taken over where *The X-Files* left off, in popularity and influence on our popular culture: With its highly glamorized stories of forensic crime scene research, the network show has educated an entire TV-watching nation to the point that it has become commonplace among laypeople (including jurors!) to expect that DNA, hair, and fiber will be found at each crime scene and will point unequivocally to a suspect—and that is of course not always the case.

Like Westerns and science fiction, the mystery genre reflects changing mores: For the longest time, law enforcement officers were depicted as the good guys and criminals as the bad guys. (See Box 2.6 for a discussion of the changing sympathies in mystery films.) And if the law wasn't the hero, at least the detective was. As modern cynicism increased, it became common for novels and films to depict the criminal as an "antihero" and the establishment as the evil power. Lately, the patterns have merged into the good cop/detective/FBI agent fighting a two-front battle against both the bad guys on the streets and the bad guys in administration or the Internal Affairs Division. An example of this is the acclaimed film (and novel) *L.A. Confidential,* in which the truly bad guy is not the mobster or a street gang member but a high-ranking police officer. This story model—which is used so often that it has almost become a cliché—reflects something interesting: We the audience don't particularly like to see the criminal given the hero treatment anymore, and we don't automatically buy in to the idea that perps are poor misguided souls who would have been upstanding citizens if they'd had a decent childhood. On the other hand, today's audience doesn't believe that law enforcement officers are all knights in shining armor, either. We do still want to believe, however, that somebody competent and committed is out there fighting crime. So the story model of the cop fighting criminals *and* superiors strikes a realistic, as well as a hopeful, chord for a modern audience.

A special category within the crime genre has been created by the HBO series *The Sopranos,* about a middle-class New Jersey family—who happens to be part of the Mafia. Mafia and middle-class morals collide in Tony Soprano's attempt to raise a decent family and provide for them, to the point where he, like so many others these days, is seeing a therapist for his anxiety attacks. At one point she asks him about his values, as someone who raises children in a criminal environment, and he snaps at her in anger, pointing to the greater crimes of big business polluting the environment. Does the end justify the means? Can one be a good person in one area of one's life, and a bad one in another? *The Sopranos* just raises the questions—the series leaves it up to us to ponder whether there are any easy answers.

Stories to Live and Die By

In 1774 *The Sorrows of Young Werther,* a novel, was published in Germany. The author was twenty-four-year-old Johann Wolfgang von Goethe, who would later write the definitive version of *Faust.* In the novel—incidentally, one of the first modern novels as we know it, with a story line involving the emotional development of a main character during the course of a happy or unhappy encounter—young Werther suffers so dramatically from unrequited love that he takes his own life (see the Narrative at the end of the chapter). In the wake of the book's publication, Germany, and later all of Europe, witnessed a rash of suicides being committed or attempted by young readers of *Werther.* Why did they do it? Goethe certainly never intended his book to be a suicide manual. This is one of the first examples in mod-

Box 2.6 THE GOOD GUYS AND THE BAD GUYS

Does it make a big difference in crime stories whether we are supposed to sympathize with the criminal? As is the case with Westerns, there are several types of crime stories. There are classic stories in the Agatha Christie mode (in which we usually approve of the apprehension of the criminal). Then there is the mobster genre, in which we may sympathize with some of the bad guys, such as *Bonnie and Clyde, The Godfather I* and *II, Dillinger, Goodfellas, Bugsy, Miller's Crossing, Casino,* and the enormously popular HBO series *The Sopranos.* The last decades of the twentieth century saw an increasing number of films that express some ambivalence toward crime fighting. The hunter often becomes the hunted, the cop be-comes a criminal, the line between good and bad is blurred. Hollywood's recent response to such films? It has returned to a defense of law enforcement, with mobsters and other criminals clearly the bad guys once again and the good guys fighting both the underworld and the corruption of the authorities. This was the focus of the 1987 movie *The Untouchables.* Another response has been a wholesale tossing around of preconceived notions about right and wrong, as in *Pulp Fiction* (see the Narrative at the end of this chapter), where tales of characters helping each other, killing each other, and sparing each other make a fast, bloody, and—for many viewers—fascinating mix.

ern times of a work of fiction inspiring its readers to take drastic action. This book, along with other works of literature, art, and philosophy, ushered in the new Age of Romanticism, when the ideal person was perceived as an *emotional* rather than a *rational* being, and men, as well as women, acted on their emotions, often in public. The decision of young Werther was seen as a romantic option and had a powerful emotional effect; even some famous poets of the day chose to end their lives, and the rest of Europe woke up to the dangers, and the thrill, of literature.

Since then, scholars of literature have discussed why Goethe's book had such an effect; it was not the first tragic story printed, and poems and songs of unrequited love had been common since the Middle Ages. Several factors seem to have been involved. First, mass printing and distribution of literature were now under way. Second, the era known as the Enlightenment was coming to an end, and its effects were beginning to be felt. There was a focus on the rights and capacities of the individual, including the right (for boys) to receive an education. This meant that the common man, as well as many women, was now able to read. Third, the theme of the story, Werther's emotions, seemed to strike a chord in the young readers who were moving away from the idealization of reason, which had been central to the lives of their parents and grandparents, to an idealization of emotions—so we are talking about a kind of generational rebellion. All in all, you might say that this was a book that appeared at exactly the right time. And its fame landed Goethe a job with the royal court at twenty-six years of age. But for the rest of his long life, he was disturbed at the effect his book had had on its young readers.

The aftermath of *Werther* was not the first time in Western culture that the topic of the effects of an artistic work had arisen: In ancient Greece, Plato and Aristotle had debated whether art was a good or a bad psychological influence. Plato claimed

In *L.A. Confidential* (Warner Bros., 1997), the bad guys are not always the only crooks on the street. The twist-and-turn plot sees the two antagonists, Detective Ed Exley (Guy Pearce, *middle front*) and Detective Bud White (Russell Crowe, *middle rear*), put aside their differences to find the mastermind behind a series of murders. Here the detectives are flanked by Captain Dudley Smith (James Cromwell, *left*) and celebrity cop Jack Vincennes (Kevin Spacey, *right*).

that art, especially drama, was bad for people because it inspired violent emotions; people watching a play with a violent theme would be inspired to commit violence themselves. For Plato the ideal life was spent in complete balance and harmony; if the balance was upset, that life would be less perfect. Reason helped keep a person in balance; if emotions took over, reason would be diminished, and imbalance would occur. And since art helped stir emotions, then art was dangerous. At the end of this chapter, you'll find an excerpt from Plato's *Republic* expressing this theory. Aristotle believed that art, and especially drama, was good for people because it allowed them to act out their emotions vicariously; a good play would thus cleanse the spectator of disturbing emotions, and he or she could return home a calmer person: The exposure to strong feelings and to a considerable amount of stage violence would have a *cathartic* effect. Aristotle claimed that feeling pity and fear for the victim of the tragedy cleanses us by making us understand that tragedy could happen to anyone, including ourselves. In his book on tragedy, *Poetics* (see the excerpt at the end of the chapter), Aristotle makes it clear that the best tragic plays are those in which misfortune happens not to a very good person but to an ordinary person who made a monumental error in judgment. And since most of us are ordinary persons, the play

The HBO television series *The Sopranos* features two families, sometimes at odds with each other: the family of Tony Soprano, and the "Family"—his mobster pals. Tony believes he is raising his two children with good values, while at the same time he is upholding an entirely different set of values in his professional life. Here Tony (James Gandolfini) and Silvio Dante (Steven van Zandt) are contemplating applying mobster values.

becomes a moral learning experience—a moral laboratory in which we can see our inner urges acted out and learn from the tragic consequences. (Box 2.7 explores the debate between reason and emotion.)

One might wonder what kind of plays the ancient Greeks watched at the time of Plato and Aristotle that led to such different evaluations of the experience of drama from these two thinkers. For one thing, Greek drama had been around for only a couple of generations. It seems to have begun in the form of religious pageants at the annual festival of Dionysus in Athens and developed rapidly into a contest among playwrights of tragedies, comedies, and satyr plays (wild farces with sexual themes), with much prestige for the winners. More than fifteen thousand spectators might see one performance of any play at the theater in Athens. The oldest surviving Greek play is *The Persians* by Aeschylus (ca. 472 B.C.E.); by that time, the emphasis on religious themes in the plays had already waned, and stories depicting the human condition (with some divine intervention) became popular.

Just what was it about drama that Plato found so dangerous and Aristotle so uplifting? One of the stories in the Narratives section is a Greek tragedy, Euripides' *Medea,* in which a woman kills her children to get revenge on her estranged husband. Another, perhaps the most famous, example of Greek tragedy is the story of

Box 2.7   REASON OR EMOTION? APOLLO VERSUS DIONYSUS

Goethe's novel *The Sorrows of Young Werther* came as a harbinger of a cultural sea change between the dominant worldview of the eighteenth century, the Age of Reason, and the new age that was dawning, the Age of Romanticism. Goethe himself embraced the philosophy of the Age of Reason—the belief that reason, not emotion, is the true problem solver—but others took their cue from *Werther* and let the age of emotions roll in. Interestingly, these shifts of focus between rationality and emotion have happened at other times. In some ways one can say such a shift took place on a small scale between the 1950s and the late 1960s. And much earlier that same transformation had swept through a society in which intellectuals—perhaps purely by chance—had also been debating about the dangers and value of stories: Plato's and Aristotle's Greece.

The Greek theater was only a couple of generations old by the time Plato warned against its emotional pull, yet it had already developed a rich tradition of annual plays and prizes, all in honor of a god imported from the Middle East,

Dionysus. The older gods such as Zeus, Athena, and Apollo, were still worshiped, especially in Athens, but a religious battle was brewing during the lifetime of Plato and Aristotle for the souls of all Greeks: Whereas the old gods, in particular Apollo and Athena, symbolized reason and self-control (a principle that is predominant in Socrates' and Plato's way of thinking), Dionysus was the god of wine and excess. You may know him under his Roman name, Bacchus. This philosophical battle between self-control and emotional abandon was won by Plato: His writings have endured, with their praise of reason, while nobody is a true worshiper of Dionysus anymore. Within the ancient Greek world itself, however, one can say that Dionysus won: The theater flourished, with the moral support of Aristotle, who himself was from the north where they worshiped Dionysus. And today the ultimate legacy of the Dionysian religion, movies and television shows, are being produced and enjoyed all over the world.

Oedipus Rex by Sophocles. At Oedipus's birth, his parents, the king and queen of Thebes, are told that their baby son will grow up to kill his father and marry his mother, so in order to thwart the fates, they have him placed on the ground in the mountains for the animals to dispose of. But his life is saved by a passing shepherd who takes him to the court of the king and queen of Corinth to be raised as their son. As a young adult, Oedipus inquires about his future—and is told by the oracle that he is destined to kill his father and marry his mother. He flees his homeland, fearing that he might harm his beloved parents (who never told him that he was adopted). At a crossroads he meets a man who won't give way to him, so Oedipus fights and kills him. Later he marries the widowed queen of the land and becomes king. But after years of happily married life, Oedipus and his wife learn the truth: that he did indeed fulfill the prophecy and kill his natural father—the unknown man at the crossroads—and marry his natural mother. His wife/mother commits suicide, and Oedipus gouges out his eyes in grief and shame.

Other stories watched avidly by the Athenian audiences include *The Bacchae*, a lesser known story by Euripides in which a mother, in a religious frenzy, tears her own son's head off, believing him to be a mountain lion; and Aeschylus's tragedy *Agamemnon,* about the king who leads the Greeks into the battle of Troy, only to lose his life on his homecoming at the hands of his wife and her lover.

The common denominators in these tragedies were strong family passions, speculations on the nature of fate, and a considerable amount of bloodshed. In the excerpt from *Poetics* (at the end of the chapter), Aristotle points out that the quality of the tragedy is far superior if the producers don't rely on (in modern terminology) special effects but on the elements of the story itself: If it is well written, the audience will be shocked to the bone by the mere telling of the story—no stagecraft can make it more effective.

The debate is still with us, although it now takes a somewhat different form. We now must consider whether violence in movies and on television inspires people (and especially children) to commit violence or whether it allows them to act out their aggressions in a safe environment. Psychologists who believe that violent fairy tales can be good for children clearly belong to the Aristotelian tradition, although they may not support the excessive violence portrayed in movies and on TV. Examples of people enacting situations from fictional stories with terrible results include the scene from the 1993 film *The Program,* deleted from presently available videotapes, of football players daring each other to lie in the middle of rushing traffic; inspired by the film, some teenagers tried the stunt and died. Another example is the small boy who, after watching an episode of *Beavis and Butt-head* about arson, set fire to the trailer he and his family were living in. (The producers of *Beavis and Butt-head* promptly prohibited any reference to fire in future shows.) Video and computer games have come under increasing scrutiny for the very same reasons: Children and immature adult players may be influenced by the violence of the games. Generally, this phenomenon falls outside the scope of this discussion because we are talking about the influence of stories; however, games such as *Grand Theft Auto: San Andreas* and *Halo 2* contain plots and have been cited as possible inspiration for violent crimes.

Movies that have acquired a reputation for inspiring copycats are *The Burning Bed* (an abused wife kills her husband), *The Getaway* (robbers observe the schedule of money transports), *Stand By Me* (kids knock down mailboxes), *Taxi Driver* (said to have inspired John Hinckley in his attempt to assassinate President Reagan in order to impress Jodie Foster, who starred in the film), *Heat* (a bank robbery in L.A.), and *Set It Off* (a film about female bank robbers that served as a blueprint for a gang of two adult women and three teen girls who robbed banks in the state of Washington in 1998. After they were caught, a copy of the *Set It Off* video was found at their home, so there was no doubt as to the source of inspiration). The 1994 film *Natural Born Killers* may have inspired both a bank robbery and the massacre of high school students in Littleton, Colorado, in 1999. The Columbine High massacre has also been linked to the film *The Basketball Diaries.* In Los Angeles, a sixteen-year-old boy and two male cousins who stabbed the boy's mother to death told detectives that they had been inspired by *Scream* and *Scream 2.* In Michigan, a group of teens tried to make a *Blair Witch Project*–type horror video by kidnapping a young woman. In Oceanside, California, in 2003, two boys killed their mother and then attempted to dispose of her body by dismembering her—only weeks after a *Sopranos* episode aired where Tony Soprano kills, dismembers, and disposes of another mobster, Ralph.

Even if we might feel tempted to do something we've seen in a film, most of us refrain because our common sense, experience, or conscience tells us it is not a smart thing to do. We believe we have a choice; we have the free will to decide whether or not to do things. Thus the question is, Should society play it safe and make sure that nobody has access to violent or suggestive stories because a few will imitate the action? In other words, should we allow censorship? Or should we let people take responsibility for what they watch and for what their children watch? Should we trust them to be their children's guides rather than hand the job over to the government?

Plato believed in censorship in his ideal state because he didn't trust people to know what was good or bad for them. Was Plato correct in saying that it can be dangerous to be exposed to emotion-stirring dramas? It seems so, under certain circumstances; but are these circumstances enough to justify censorship's being imposed on all viewers, even those who would never let their balance be disturbed?

On the other hand, is Aristotle right that it is beneficial overall to a mind under a lot of tension to be exposed to violent fictional dramas? Given that television sets in American homes are on several hours a day on the average and that a great many shows during those hours will bring violence into the home, television is not necessarily a good prescription for a modern stressed-out person seeking relaxation. We should remember that the drama Aristotle recommended as beneficial was not available twenty-four hours a day, as it is on a TV set; Greek dramas were originally performed once a year in connection with religious festivals, and Aristotle's philosophy in general advocates *moderation* in all things. If he could have taken part in the modern debate, he most certainly would have advised against overdoing the exposure to violence on TV and in movies. At the end of the chapter in the Primary Readings section, you will find an excerpt from one of Plato's works, one of Aristotle's—and an excerpt from a novel by contemporary philosopher Umberto Eco, *The Name of the Rose,* in which he pits the tradition of Plato against the words of Aristotle. Plato advised against the use of fiction, and Aristotle advocated enjoying fiction in moderation—comedy as well as tragedy. According to Eco, the Western world would have been a happier place, had Aristotle's views prevailed! (For more on Plato and Aristotle, see Box 2.8.)

Of course, children and adults are exposed to violence not just on TV and on film; fictional violence is on the increase in comic books, in video games and computer games, and in the lyrics to music often favored by teens. The framework for this chapter, however, is the influence of stories, so I've chosen to focus on violence in movies and television.

Whether we agree with Plato or with Aristotle, the fact remains that stories—both in written and in visual form—affect us. Some societies have reacted by banning certain works or by conducting what to me is one of the foulest displays of cultural censorship: book burning. Other societies support the right of their citizens to decide for themselves what they wish to read or view.

Most influential works were never intended as moral guidebooks for the public except in the broadest sense. Goethe didn't write his *Werther* in order to convince

Box 2.8   SOCRATES, PLATO, AND ARISTOTLE

Plato (427?–347 B.C.E.) was a student of Socrates, the man who is sometimes called the father of Western philosophy. He studied with Socrates in Athens for over twenty years, and after Socrates' execution (see Chapter 8) he left Athens in anger and grief. A few years later he returned and became a teacher in his own right. While running his own school of philosophy he wrote numerous books, *Dialogues,* about the teachings of Socrates. Among his students was a young man from the province of Stagira, Aristotle (384–322 B.C.E.). Deeply influenced by Plato, Aristotle nevertheless developed his own approach to philosophy. For that and other reasons, Aristotle was not chosen as leader of the school when Plato died, so he left Athens for other jobs, including tutoring the young prince Alexander of Macedonia (Alexander the Great). But like Plato after his exile, Aristotle also returned to Athens, opened up his own school, and began a short but immensely influential career of teaching and writing about philosophy and science. We talk about Socrates and Plato in detail in Chapter 8 and about Aristotle in Chapter 9.

dozens of young, lovesick Germans to kill themselves—quite possibly, he intended for young Germans to examine their lives and loves more closely. Few authors would want their readers to imitate the actions of their fictional characters, although most would like to think their story has at least been food for thought. The many readers of Dante's *Divine Comedy* probably do not expect the afterlife to be designed according to that author's specifications, but many a reader who has traveled through Dante's circles of hell probably has been motivated to rethink the general course of his or her life.

Stories considered good learning tools in twenty-first-century America will in all likelihood be different from didactic stories in Hitler's Germany, in eighteenth-century France, in tribal Native America of the nineteenth century, and in Greece in the fifth century B.C.E. It is a separate and very interesting question whether there is such a thing as universally morally commendable stories; we take a look at the subject of ethical relativism in Chapter 3 and return to the subject of intercultural values in stories at the end of this chapter. Box 2.9 examines the idea of a "wrong" moral lesson.

Is it appropriate to talk about the impact of stories as if they take place in a vacuum, with vacuous people as receptacles? Of course not. Children, as well as adults, all have a certain background that helps us process the stories we are exposed to, and this is where the influence of parents becomes important: If parents and children usually communicate about the stories the children are exposed to—or if parents are the ones telling their children the stories—the children hopefully acquire a critical stance from the stories they will hear and watch as adults. This critical stance lowers the risk of their running out mindlessly to emulate some action that may look "cool" on the screen. It lowers the risk both that we take stories too seriously and that we don't take them seriously enough. Indeed, we don't even have to agree on which stories are morally valuable and which ones are misguided, or even nefarious propaganda. Many Americans find Michael Moore's films *Bowling for Columbine* and *Fahrenheit 9/11* to be

Box 2.9   TEACHING WRONG LESSONS

What about films that not only inspire confused souls to take the wrong kind of action, but that directly *teach* lessons that are offensive to a large section of society? Censorship and Hollywood is a story that goes back to the mid-1930s and the Hays Office, a group of self-proclaimed moral watchdogs who eliminated most direct references to sex in the movies until well into the 1950s. For many people, the "wrong" moral lesson is often associated with permissive sexual behavior, and this approach may well become a Hollywood issue once again, as the moral debate progresses in the twenty-first century. But there are other kinds of lessons generally deemed "wrong" by our modern society: Should films advocate violence? Should they advocate insensitivity toward the pain and suffering of other people (or animals), as some comedies have done lately? In many cases what counts as violence and insensitivity, and even sexual permissiveness, is in the eye of the beholder, but there is today a general consensus that promoting racial and ethnic stereotypes is not a positive lesson for a film to teach, especially if its target audience is children. According to many viewers, one such film is the animated *Shark Tale*. Like many animated films, it is a story about animals—in this case, fish—but of course it isn't a true-to-life depiction of life under the sea. The characters are meant to serve as moral metaphors for human lives, as in all animated films. And this is precisely what worried many viewers when the film premiered—for it seemed to relish in presenting negatively stereotyped characters, precisely the kind of attitude parents and teachers try to prevent from developing in our children. Brooklyn College Professor Emeritus Jerome Krase wrote in a letter to the *New York Times,* "Promoting negative ethnic and racial stereotypes can make children wary of strangers who share the surface characteristics of media stereotypes. There is also nothing cheerful about inserting into the beautiful minds of children the idea that people who have Italian names, or use colloquial speech are also organized criminals." Critics are usually not calling for censorship, but for a higher level of reflection and self-disciplining by the film makers, since it is likely that most such movie "missteps" are not intended to be deliberately offensive—they are in all likelihood just put in production by people who didn't bother to think twice.

valuable and brave statements addressing troubling political aspects of our contemporary life, while others find them to be offensive, overly partisan, and creative propaganda rather than a compilation of facts. Some of us find John McCain's true stories of courage in *Why Courage Matters* (see Chapter 11) to be orally fortifying, while others find them to be preachy. But either way, we relate to stories as having the potential for expressing moral values. So in the final analysis, those of us who, like me, love stories and like to use them as moral lessons should remember to approach any story cautiously. Do stories create moral saints? No. Do they create moral sinners? No, not without cooperation from their audience. We must process the stories we are exposed to and ask questions such as, *Do we understand its lesson? Do we want its lesson? Would we want the children in our lives to learn from the story?* And if we say no, rather than trying to ban the story we should perhaps encourage others to acquire that same critical distance. Even if the story may not have a valuable lesson to teach children, it may still be an interesting story for adults!

Seeing Your Life as a Story

Have you ever been in a situation where someone you have just met asks you to talk about yourself? You may have found yourself answering, "Oh, there isn't much to tell," and then immediately felt that this was a poor answer—especially if you were trying to make a good impression. And perhaps later, when alone, you thought of all kinds of things to say about yourself. This is a common experience, and the good thing about it is that it serves as a wake-up call: That time around you were caught by surprise, but next time you will have a story to tell, because we all do. It is sometimes said that we could all write one good novel, the novel of our life—although the saying assumes a lot in terms of our ability as storytellers. Most of us aren't very good at telling our own story and must develop a talent for shaping it and adjusting it to our audiences. Talking about ourselves makes us realize that, as much as we may try to be completely accurate, it's not possible. We simply can't remember everything that has happened to us; we also realize that even if we could remember, it would not all be equally interesting. So *selectivity* is part of the secret of effective storytelling. And we select different things to tell depending on the audience. If you are telling your story to a new boyfriend or girlfriend, you will emphasize certain things in your life, but if you are describing yourself in front of a panel of strangers during a job interview, you will most definitely emphasize other things. And if you are updating your parents about recent events in your life, you will probably choose quite a different story to tell.

Another feature of telling one's own story is a result of being alive: The story is *incomplete*. We are always in the middle of it; we may be closer to the beginning than to the end or closer to the end than the beginning, but we never view our own story from the same point of view as that of an author telling a story—because our story is not finished yet. We don't know how it will end.

FOR BETTER OR FOR WORSE by Lynn Johnston

© Lynn Johnston Productions Inc. Distributed by United Features Syndicate, Inc.

In this *For Better or Worse* comic strip, life is viewed as a story, written perhaps by fate, perhaps by God, but definitely with an individual's input. What do you think is meant by "writing our own story"? Is it the same as *telling* our own story, or is there a difference?

A third feature is that, contrary to what we might think, the telling of our own story is to a great extent *fictional,* put together with *poetic creativity.* We may try to remember to be objective, but telling a story generally involves not only a beginning, a middle, and an ending but also a movement from one situation to the next. We don't just say, "And then this happened, and then that happened"; we say, "And *because* this happened, *then* that happened." We assume causality—and since we rarely know all factors involved, we make use of interpretations and make assumptions. (And then, of course, we may be outright lying, but that is a different story!)

So if telling one's own story is such an unreliable enterprise, why bother? Because it is good for us; it helps us find out where we have been and where we are going. As you read at the beginning of this chapter, storytelling is now part of many therapy sessions, and it involves not only listening to stories but also telling them, mostly about oneself. If we see our past as a story, we might be able to identify things to be proud of and things to improve upon. In other words, we may get a better grip on our identity. And when we realize that we are also part of other people's stories, and they are part of ours, then we begin to see ourselves as part of a much bigger story, that of our community and culture.

Searching for Meaning

The psychoanalyst Erik Erikson believed that if we are lucky enough to have become psychologically mature, we will have developed *ego integrity,* and we will stop asking useless questions such as "Why did I do that? Why didn't I do such and such?" We will learn to accept the events in our lives, those we are responsible for and those that just happened to us, as facts with which we must contend. Knowing individuals who have attained this peace of mind may help us along the way.

One challenge to our ego integrity occurs when something happens in our life that we didn't expect and that we find grossly unfair. A man works hard and saves his money so he can enjoy his later years, and then he dies six months after retiring. Parents give up everything they have so that their daughter can go to college, and she ends up on skid row because of drug abuse. A young child who receives a "routine" blood transfusion is infected with AIDS.

Is there a good way to deal with such calamities? One approach that has provided comfort to many people over the ages has been to view such an event as an act of God or of Fate: It had to happen, we don't know why, but to God it makes sense. Now, we see "through a glass darkly" (1 Corinthians 13:12) but later, in heaven, we will see why it happened. Another source of comfort for some is to view it as *karma:* It is the consequence of something you did earlier or in a previous life. In other words, it is your own fault, and it will do you no good to rage about it or blame someone else. The best you can do is to realize it and try to create good karma for next time around.

A popular modern Western way of approaching the problem is to assign guilt, or blame. We say the retiree brought on his death himself; he never exercised, and his cholesterol level was too high. The parents of the girl who became a drug addict must have done a terrible job of raising her. And the parents of the child who contracted AIDS should have been more careful about checking up on the hospital. Our accusations are sometimes justified, but they can also be unnecessarily cruel. Sometimes, common sense will tell us, people really can't be blamed for what happens to them or to those they love. But it is reassuring to bystanders to blame the victim—it's a way of believing that if they're careful to avoid the victim's mistakes, they'll escape disaster. Although it may be true in some cases that a person's conduct contributed to what happened to him or her, that is far from being a universal pattern. In any case, we have no right to infer *guilt* from *causality;* in other words, just because someone's conscious or unconscious conduct led to some problem, we can't automatically conclude that he or she is guilty of some *moral wrongdoing.* Such an attitude often reflects a double standard: If it happens to strangers, they must have done something "wrong"; if it happens to me or to one of my heroes, we are just unfortunate victims. This double standard has frequently been applied to the AIDS crisis; some people see AIDS as punishment for immoral behavior—unless it strikes someone close to them.

An alternate way of dealing with life's crises is to see them in the light of *stories.* Humans—at least modern humans in the Western world—seem to have a need for history and their own lives to make sense; we need to understand *why* something happened. Even people in traditional cultures with little written history have the same concern about a life well spent. In such cultures the models are usually the myths and legends of that culture: Do as the cultural hero did, and you will have lived well. In our pluralistic culture the emphasis is much more on doing something *new*— blazing a trail, inventing something, writing a paper about an idea nobody has thought of before. We like our children to be different from their friends, to be individuals. Martha Nussbaum says that stories teach us to deal emotionally with the unexpected. Of course, the unexpected situation in our own life is not likely to be the same as the one in our favorite story—then it wouldn't be unexpected. But we can react to the unexpected in the same way our favorite characters do, and in this way we may be able to rise to the occasion. Persons from a traditional culture might find such efforts at being ready for the unexpected, as well as efforts at being different, incomprehensible, for what makes persons good in their culture is precisely that they do the *same* as their ancestors. The urge to act well, however, is the same for members of both modern and traditional cultures. In order to live an accomplished life you must follow a pattern ("Do like the ancestors" or "Do something new"), and others will deem it a good thing if you succeed. *Havamal,* "The Word of the High One," the ancient Norse poem of rules for living, says that "Cattle die, kindred die, every man is mortal. But the good name never dies, of one who has done well." This doesn't just mean that good people will be remembered—it means that *we pass judgment* on people according to how they handled themselves in life.

When things go our way, we don't ask about the meaning of life. We find that the whole development makes sense. The mythologist Joseph Campbell compares it to being at a fun party: You don't stop and ask yourself what you are doing there. But at a boring party you might ask yourself that question. Similarly, when things go wrong in someone's life, he or she may question the meaning of life—because somehow, life doesn't make sense anymore. An unexpected element interrupts our life's story, and we lose the thread—we experience an *identity crisis* (an expression introduced by Erikson). So how can stories help?

When we change direction in life, we change our future; we don't know what it may be, but we can assume that if we decide to have a child or switch majors or move to another city, our future will at least contain elements different from what it would have otherwise. But when we change direction in our life we also change our past, because we now see it in a different light, *redescribing* and *reinterpreting* it. When our viewpoint shifts and we interpret our past in the light of the present, we rewrite our own story and sometimes even the story of our community and our culture. When I decide to major in pre-med instead of business because of my sister's illness, I rewrite my story from then on. If my uncle dies just after retiring, I rewrite his story, and it *does* become a moral lesson; I tell myself I will try not to do what he did or try to avoid what life did to him, or at least to make every day count. (In this way I rewrite my own story as well.) If I lose my money because of bad investments, I may rewrite the story in a number of ways: I was victimized, but now I'm smarter; or I was too concerned with money, but now I'm smarter. (Of course, we are not always smarter, but it makes us feel better to think so.) At any rate, we rewrite our past so it will make sense to us in the present and give a new, meaningful direction to our future. It is when we feel incapable of finding a new story line in our life—when the change has been so dramatic, there seems to be no new purpose lurking among the rubble—that the identity crisis may be hard to shake. In that case, it takes courage to choose to view the world and human life the way the British philosopher Bertrand Russell described it as a collection of atoms brought together at random, with no rhyme nor reason other than the rules of science and biology. But even this is a story: It is a story of natural forces and how each human fits into the greater whole of biology—rather a romantic notion. In the face of meaninglessness, we also might choose, with certain existential philosophers, to say that life is its own meaning. In this case the force and will of life in any shape or form become a story we can relate to when no other stories present themselves. We may, of course, choose to say that we just don't know. We would like to think that there is some story, some purpose, but we don't know what it is or whether there is one at all. In the Primary Readings you'll find an excerpt from a self-help book by Tristine Rainer, teaching readers how to tell their own story.

When we tell our own story and the story of our culture, it is most often an attempt to see the overall pattern, or impose one, to find some sense behind chaotic events. But we tell personal and cultural stories to try to improve ourselves and perhaps to make up for cultural errors or wrongdoing of the past. This level of storytelling doesn't just *describe* the situation, it also *prescribes* what we ought to be doing next. This *normative* element contains what may be the deepest moral dimension of the so-called true stories of oneself and one's culture: looking forward to the future, trying to shape it into an ideal image, and reshaping the past so that it appears to lead toward the ideal. (Fictional stories that warn against an unwanted future are part of this moral effort.) Do we have any guarantees that such stories, told to make the future better, actually match reality at all? An actress says she has had a drug problem, but now she is clean and wants to teach others about the dangers of drugs. A schoolteacher tells her class that their culture has elements of discrimination and persecution in its past but that this will never happen again if they will all work together. A politician tells of the hardships we have endured and of the great things we can accomplish if we stand together and vote for him. Or a couple get together again after having broken up and tell each other how they were both wrong and how this time it is going to be different. In some cases these projections are, of course, just wishful thinking, and the future may not comply. But well-told stories have a power all their own: *They can make the future happen.* So while we listen to, and create, great stories that can change our lives and the life of our culture, we should remember to retain our critical sense and our sense of moral responsibility: Do our stories prescribe a future that we would actually want to have happen?

A trend has developed lately that literally addresses the future, attempting to change it through stories: the phenomenon of ethical wills. An increasing number of people choose to leave to their heirs not only their material, but also their spiritual goods. People write long or short essays, or create videos or audiotapes, all for the purpose of leaving some kind of statement to their children and grandchildren—and perhaps to the world in general—about their values. And the way these values are expressed is generally by telling one's story, specifying the moral of one's own story. To be sure, it isn't the first time in history such ethical wills have been written—in 1050 a Jewish father wrote such a letter in which he gave his son advice about how to live a good life. But especially after September 11 the ethical will phenomenon has flourished. Box 2.10 explores some questions raised by ethical will workshops.

Living in the Narrative Zone

We humans are temporal beings. We live in the present, but we are always reaching back to the past and forward to the future, in a constant state of tension between memory and anticipation. We live our own story, which has its own beginning and its own end, although we can't describe them. Furthermore, we live the stories of our culture; we identify with them or criticize them or rewrite them. We seek moral lessons in our own stories and in the stories of our culture. We also just like to hear stories, watch stories, and tell stories; and when we do, the time period we experience multiplies. We are still living our own life, but there is a new element: *narrative time,* a concept introduced by the French philosopher Paul Ricoeur. Narrative time is the compressed time of a novel or a movie, the time it takes for the story to unfold. So while it may take us three days to read a book, its narrative time may span generations. Two hours at the movies, and we may have lived through years of narrative time, following the lives of the characters from youth to old age. In this way we share multiple experiences with fictional characters and expand our moral horizons, as Nussbaum suggested in Chapter 1.

There is a story, "Mantage," by the science fiction writer Richard Matheson about a man who wanted his life to be the way things are in the movies, because he thought his life was extremely dull. His wish was granted, and this is what happened: He found that time had sped up, and before he knew it he had fallen in love, was married and had kids; now he found himself making money, living in style, and having love affairs, but when he looked at his watch, only an hour had passed. He

Box 2.10   ETHICAL WILLS

In an iterview with the *Christian Science Monitor,* workshop leader Susan Turnbull characterizes what she calls "personal legacy letters," or ethical wills, as a way of capturing "the spark of your soul." In her workshops she suggests starting out with questions such as these:

- What do you want your loved ones to know about your family history?

- What is your vision for your heirs' use of their inheritance?

- Have you made mistakes for which you want to ask forgiveness? Or is there forgiveness you want to offer?

- Why have you made certain decisions about your estate, such as donating a portion of it to charity?

- How does your use of money reflect your most important values?

- What are some values and life lessons you'd like to share regarding education, the workplace, marriage, and parenting?

- What have your friendships meant to you over the years?

Workshop leaders suggest updating one's ethical will every five years, reflecting new life experiences. While most people might think that the writing of an ethical will is an exercise that should be postponed until the end of one's life, it may also be a useful way to do an overview of what one's life story is all about—and there is no age restriction on such an exercise; there can be moral wisdom in the life experience of a twenty-five-year old as well as in that of an older person.

found that he was living out his life in abbreviated chunks of time, the same as in a movie. After two hours he was old and dying, and the last thing he saw before his eyes was the letters DNE EHT—"The End" to the audience watching him. As the saying goes, when the gods want to punish us, they give us what we wish for.

Obviously this is not what the man truly wished for—he wanted a life with an exciting story line, not a life lived in the time it takes for a film audience to watch a movie. We readers and viewers are luckier, because we can have the best of both worlds. We can retain our own real-life time while we share in the accelerated, telescoped time of books and movies. When we open a book or sit down in a movie theater, we enter what we might call the *Narrative Zone,* where we can live other lives vicariously, acquire skills and experiences that we might never know of otherwise.

We may be emotionally cleansed by experiencing the strong feelings in a story, as Aristotle suggested. We may get an idea of what it feels like to be a member of the other gender or another race, of another time and place, or of another species entirely—and these experiences may help us decide how to live once we leave the Narrative Zone. Nothing else provokes our empathy as effectively as a good story: We weep and rejoice with our friends in the novel or in the movie, even if we know that it is only make-believe. They are not wasted tears or smiles, for they are, ultimately, the building blocks of our character.

If we happen to read the story of the Good Samaritan, there is a chance that we will stop to help the victim should we happen to see a mugging in progress. There is also a chance that the "victim" will end up mugging us, but that doesn't mean we should not have read the story or that we should not have come to the victim's aid; it means that life doesn't always conform to the stories we read, and we shouldn't think it does.

So sometimes we get hurt when we are inspired by stories, and sometimes we are inspired by the wrong stories. The essayist and science fiction writer Ursula K. Le Guin compares our existence as readers and listeners to the hoop snake that bites its own tail: It hurts, but *now you can roll!* What is the moral? If the hoop snake doesn't make a hoop, it won't move, and it will be as though it never lived. So we must take chances—we mustn't shy away from taking part in the listening process, in becoming engaged in the story—and we mustn't shy away from becoming engaged in our own story. For Le Guin, telling stories and listening to stories is a kind of life affirmation and an incentive to live life to the fullest.

All of the stories in this book are examples of how natural it is for humans to think in terms of stories when we want to discuss a moral problem. At this point, though, I would like to repeat something I mentioned earlier. These summaries of stories are by no means a sufficient substitute for reading the stories or watching the films yourself; the outlines merely provide a basis for discussing the specific problems explored in the stories in light of the theories presented in this book. Without actually reading the book or viewing the movie, the essential experience of being in the Narrative Zone—of sharing the narrative time with the work of fiction—is lost, or at least thoroughly diluted, and the emotional impact is at best a weak approximation of the original narrative experience. So do yourself a favor: If a certain narrative appeals to you, then read the original book or watch the original film. In this way you will add another set of "parallel lives" to your own life experience. Besides, it's not a bad idea to let the characters in films and novels make some of our mistakes for us, as long as we don't forget to make ourselves the central character in some stories of our own now and again.

Throughout this book you will see examples of stories' being the bearers of moral values. Of course, we have not even scratched the surface of the treasure of stories available to us, and I hope that our discussion will inspire you to experience and evaluate other narratives in light of the theories of ethics you'll encounter in this book.

Study Questions

1. Name three didactic stories, describe their plots, and explain their moral lessons. Do you agree with these lessons? Why or why not?

2. Discuss the phenomenon of Goethe's novel about Werther, who commits suicide because of unrequited love: What were the effects of the publication? Why did this phenomenon happen? Do you think something similar could happen today, inspired by a film, a novel, or some other medium of fiction? If yes, what should be done to prevent it, if anything? If no, why not?

3. Compare and contrast Plato's and Aristotle's views on whether watching a dramatic play (or, today, perhaps a film) has a positive influence. Compare their viewpoints to the current discussion on the subject of violence in films and on

television. In your opinion, is one viewpoint more correct than the other? Why or why not?

4. Pick a sequence from your life and tell it as a story. Review it afterward: Did it give you any new insight?

Primary Readings and Narratives

This chapter concludes with four Primary Readings from the classical philosophical tradition and three Narratives. In a section from Plato's *Republic* you will read, in his own words, his argument why drama is bad for the mind; next, you will read Aristotle's argument that drama can be beneficial; the section is taken from his *Poetics*. The third Primary Reading is an excerpt from a novel, Umberto Eco's *The Name of the Rose,* in which Eco gives us an idea of how he thinks the lost part of Aristotle's *Poetics* might have read. The last Primary Reading is from Tristine Rainer's self-help book, *Your Life as Story,* a practical guide to writing one's autobiography.

Two of the narratives are dramas. They were written more than two thousand years apart, but they are both intended to be spoken by actors and experienced by an audience, and they both contain violence and human tragedy: an excerpt from Euripides' play *Medea* and a summary of a scene from Quentin Tarantino's movie *Pulp Fiction.* The third narrative represents other aspects of the discussions in Chapter 2: an excerpt from Goethe's *The Sorrows of Young Werther.*

 Primary Reading

Republic

PLATO

*Excerpt from Book X, **Republic,** fourth century B.C.E. Translated by F. M. Cornford.*

In this excerpt from Plato's dialogue *Republic,* Socrates (left) is having a conversation with Plato's brother Glaucon about the nature of art and of drama in particular. Glaucon is supplying the "Quite so"s, and Socrates is supplying the rest of the conversation.

Drama, we say, represents the acts and fortunes of human beings. It is wholly concerned with what they do, voluntarily or against their will, and how they fare, with the consequences which they regard as happy or otherwise, and with their feelings of joy and sorrow in all these experiences. That is all, is it not?

Yes.

And in all these experiences has a man an undivided mind? Is there not an internal conflict which sets him at odds with himself in his conduct, much as we were saying that the conflict of visual impressions leads him to make contradictory judgments? However, I need not ask that question; for, now I come to think of it, we have already agreed that innumerable conflicts of this sort are constantly occurring in the mind. But there is a further point to be considered now. We have said that a man of high character will bear any stroke of fortune, such as the loss of a son or of anything else he holds dear, with more equanimity than most people. We may now ask: will he feel no pain, or is that impossible? Will he not rather observe due measure in his grief?

Yes, that is near the truth.

Now tell me: will he be more likely to struggle with his grief and resist it when he is under the eyes of his fellows or when he is alone?

He will be far more restrained in the presence of others.

Yes; when he is by himself he will not be ashamed to do and say much that he would not like anyone to see or hear.

Quite so.

What encourages him to resist his grief is the lawful authority of reason, while the impulse to give way comes from the feeling itself; and, as we said, the presence of contradictory impulses proves that two distinct elements in his nature must be involved. One of them is law-abiding, prepared to listen to the authority which declares that it is best to bear misfortune as quietly as possible without resentment, for several reasons: it is never certain that misfortune may not be a blessing; nothing is gained by chafing at it; nothing human is matter for great concern; and, finally, grief hinders us from calling in the help we most urgently need. By this I mean reflection on what has happened, letting reason decide on the best move in the game of life that the fall of the dice permits. Instead of behaving like a child who goes on shrieking after a fall and hugging the wounded part, we should accustom the mind to set itself at once to raise up the fallen and cure the hurt, banishing lamentation with a healing touch.

Certainly that is the right way to deal with misfortune.

And if, as we think, the part of us which is ready to act upon these reflections is the highest, that other part which impels us to dwell upon our sufferings and can never have enough of grieving over them is unreasonable, craven, and faint-hearted.

Yes.

Now this fretful temper gives scope for a great diversity of dramatic representation; whereas the calm and wise character in its unvarying constancy is not easy to represent, nor when represented is it readily understood, especially by a promiscuous gathering in a theater, since it is foreign to their own habit of mind. Obviously, then, this steadfast disposition does not naturally attract the dramatic poet, and his skill is not designed to find favour with it. If he is to have a popular success, he must address himself to the fretful type with its rich variety of material for representation.

Obviously.

We have, then, a fair case against the poet and we may set him down as the counterpart of the painter, whom he resembles in two ways: his creations are poor things by the standard of truth and reality, and his appeal is not to the highest part of the soul, but to one which is equally inferior. So we shall be justified in not admitting him into a well-ordered commonwealth, because he stimulates and strengthens an element which threatens to undermine the reason. As a country may be given over into the power of its worst citizens while the better sort are ruined, so, we shall say, the dramatic poet sets up a vicious form of government in the individual soul: he gratifies that senseless part which cannot distinguish great and small, but regards the same things as now one, now the other; and he is an image-maker whose images are phantoms far removed from reality.

Quite true. . . .

But, I continued, the heaviest count in our indictment is still to come. Dramatic poetry has a most formidable power of corrupting even men of high character, with a few exceptions.

Formidable indeed, if it can do that.

Let me put the case for you to judge. When we listen to some hero in Homer or on the tragic stage moaning over his sorrows in a long tirade, or to a chorus beating their breasts as they chant a lament, you know how the best of us enjoy giving ourselves up to follow the performance with eager sympathy. The more a poet can move our feelings in this way, the better we think him. And yet when the sorrow is our own, we pride ourselves on being able to bear it quietly like a man, condemning the behaviour we admired in the theatre as womanish. Can it be right that the spectacle of a man behaving as one would scorn and blush to behave oneself should be admired and enjoyed, instead of filling us with disgust?

No, it really does not seem reasonable.

It does not, if you reflect that the poet ministers to the satisfaction of that very part of our nature whose instinctive hunger to have its fill of tears and lamentations is forcibly restrained in the case of our own misfortunes. Meanwhile the noblest part of us, insufficiently schooled by reason or habit, has relaxed its watch over these querulous feelings, with the excuse that the sufferings we are contemplating are not our own and it is no shame to us to admire and pity a man with some pretensions to a noble character, though his grief may be excessive. The enjoyment itself seems a clear gain, which we cannot bring ourselves to forfeit by disdaining the whole poem. Few, I believe, are capable of reflecting that to enter into another's feelings must have an effect on our own: the emotions of pity our sympathy has strengthened will not be easy to restrain when we are suffering ourselves.

That is very true.

Does not the same principle apply to humour as well as to pathos? You are doing the same thing if, in listening at a comic performance or in ordinary life to buffooneries which you would be ashamed to indulge in yourself, you thoroughly enjoy them instead of being disgusted with their ribaldry. There is in you an impulse to play the clown, which you have held in restraint from a reasonable fear of being set down as a buffoon; but now you have given it rein, and by encouraging its impudence at the theatre you may be unconsciously carried away into playing the comedian in your private life. Similar effects are produced by poetic representation of love and anger and all those desires and feelings of pleasure or pain which accompany our every action. It waters the growth of passions which should be allowed to wither away and sets them up in control, although the goodness and happiness of our lives depend on their being held in subjection.

I cannot but agree with you.

If so, Glaucon, when you meet with admirers of Homer who tell you that he has been the educator of Hellas and that on questions of human conduct and culture he deserves to be constantly studied as a guide by whom to regulate your whole life, it is well to give a friendly hearing to such people, as entirely well-meaning according to their lights, and you may acknowledge Homer to be the first and greatest of the tragic poets; but you must be quite sure that we can admit into our commonwealth only the poetry which celebrates the praises of the gods and of good men. If you go further and admit the honeyed muse in epic or in lyric verse, then pleasure and pain will usurp the sovereignty of law and of the principles always recognized by common consent as the best.

Quite true.

Study Questions

1. Is Plato right that a well-balanced, emotionally stable character is rarely the main focus of a fictional drama? Can you think of any dramatic story involving an even-tempered person as the main character (or one of the main characters)? I have often asked my students this question, and I'll let you be the judge of some of my students' suggestions: How about Verbal Kint from *The Usual Suspects*? Hannibal Lecter from *The Silence of the Lambs*? Mr. Spock from *Star Trek*? James Bond? Sherlock Holmes? The butler from *The Remains of the Day*? Are these characters even-tempered, emotionally balanced, in other words, unflappable? And if so, are they still interesting as lead characters? Can you think of a female lead character who would fit the description?

2. Do you agree with Plato that having your emotions stirred on behalf of a character in a story undermines your ability to control your own emotions?

3. In your opinion, should we always be able to control our emotions? Why or why not? Consider this: In 1997 Ennis Cosby, the son of comedian and cultural activist Bill Cosby, was murdered. His killer was later caught, tried, and sentenced to life without the possibility of parole. When Cosby was interviewed by the media immediately after his son's murder, he made it clear that he was not going to grieve in front of the cameras. His grief was very deep and very real, but he stressed that the family's grieving would be done behind closed doors. How do you think Socrates would have evaluated this statement?

4. Relate Plato's viewpoint to the current debate about violence in entertainment.

5. In Plato's view, what is the danger in watching comedies? Do you agree? Why or why not?

Primary Reading

Poetics

ARISTOTLE

Excerpts from Chapters 6, 13, and 14, Poetics, *fourth century* B.C.E. **Translated by**
Ingram Bywater.

In these two excerpts from Aristotle's *Poetics* he has just explained that delight in poetry
(fiction in general) is natural for humans because fiction is imitation of life, and so we
learn about life from fiction—and to Aristotle, knowledge is always a good thing. Here
he proceeds to tell us what makes a good tragic story.

A tragedy, then, is the imitation of an action that is serious and also, as having magnitude, complete in itself; in language with pleasurable accessories, each kind brought in
separately in the parts of the work; in a dramatic, not in a narrative form; with incidents
arousing pity and fear, wherewith to accomplish its catharsis of such emotions. . . .

We assume that, for the finest form of Tragedy, the Plot must not be simple but complex; and further, that it must imitate actions arousing fear and pity, since that is the distinctive function of this kind of imitation. It follows, therefore, that there are three forms
of Plot to be avoided. (1) A good man must not be seen passing from happiness to misery, or (2) a bad man from misery to happiness. The first situation is not fear inspiring or
piteous, but simply odious to us. The second is the most untragic that can be; it has not
one of the requisites of Tragedy; it does not appeal either to the human feeling in us, or
to our pity, or to our fears. Nor, on the other hand, should (3) an extremely bad man be
seen falling from happiness into misery. Such a story may arouse the human feeling in us,
but it will not move us to either pity or fear; pity is occasioned by undeserved misfortune,
and fear by that of one like ourselves; so that there will be nothing either piteous or fear-
inspiring in the situation. There remains, then, the intermediate kind of personage, a man
not pre-eminently virtuous and just, whose misfortune, however, is brought upon him
not by vice and depravity but by some error of judgment, of the number of those in the
enjoyment of great reputation and prosperity; e.g. Oedipus, Thyestes, and the men of
note of similar families. The perfect Plot, accordingly, must have a single, and not (as some
tell us) a double issue; the change in the hero's fortunes must be not from misery to happiness, but on the contrary from happiness to misery; and the cause of it must lie not in
any depravity, but in some great error on his part; the man himself being either such as
we have described, or better, not worse, than that. Fact also confirms our theory. Though
the poets began by accepting any tragic story that came to hand, in these days the finest
tragedies are always on the story of some few houses, on that of Alcmeon, Oedipus,
Orestes, Meleager, Thyestes, Telephus, or any others that may have been involved, as either agents or sufferers, in some deed of horror. The theoretically best tragedy, then, has
a Plot of this description. The critics, therefore, are wrong who blame Euripides for taking this line in his tragedies, and giving many of them an unhappy ending. It is, as we

have said, the right line to take. The best proof of this: on the stage, and in the public performances, such plays, properly worked out, are seen to be the most truly tragic; and Euripides, even if his execution be faulty in every other point, is seen to be nevertheless the most tragic certainly of the dramatists. After this comes the construction of Plot which some rank first, one with a double story (like the *Odyssey*) and an opposite issue for the good and the bad personages. It is ranked as first only through the weakness of the audiences; the poets merely follow their public, writing as its wishes dictate. But the pleasure here is not that of Tragedy. It belongs rather to Comedy, where the bitterest enemies in the piece (e.g. Orestes and Aegisthus) walk off good friends at the end, with no slaying of any one by any one.

The tragic fear and pity may be aroused by the Spectacle; but they may also be aroused by the very structure and incidents of the play—which is the better way and shows the better poet. The Plot in fact should be so framed that, even without seeing the things take place, he who simply hears the account of them shall be filled with horror and pity at the incidents; which is just the effect that the mere recital of the story in *Oedipus* would have on one. To produce this same effect by means of the Spectacle is less artistic, and requires extraneous aid. Those, however, who make use of the Spectacle to put before us that which is merely monstrous and not productive of fear, are wholly out of touch with Tragedy; not every kind of pleasure should be required of a tragedy, but only its own proper pleasure.

The tragic pleasure is that of pity and fear, and the poet has to produce it by a work of imitation; it is clear, therefore, that the causes should be included in the incidents of his story. Let us see, then, what kinds of incident strike one as horrible, or rather as piteous. In a deed of this description the parties must necessarily be either friends, or enemies, or indifferent to one another. Now when enemy does it on enemy, there is nothing to move us to pity either in his doing or in his meditating the deed, except so far as the actual pain of the sufferer is concerned; and the same is true when the parties are indifferent to one another. Whenever the tragic deed, however, is done within the family—when murder or the like is done or meditated by brother on brother, by son on father, by mother on son, or son on mother—these are the situations the poet should seek after.

Study Questions

1. Would you agree with Aristotle that the best kind of dramatic fiction involves an ordinary man who experiences misfortune because of an error in judgment? Think of modern films and novels that might fit this pattern (involving ordinary men *and* women). How about *American Beauty*? Brecht's *Mother Courage*? *Million Dollar Baby*? (These are some suggestions from my students.)

2. What is "catharsis of emotions"? Do you agree with Aristotle that it can be obtained by experiencing dramatic fiction?

3. As we have seen, Plato disapproves of a dramatic story, whereas Aristotle approves of it. In view of the fact that Plato wrote in quite a dramatic way about the downfall of Socrates (see Chapter 8), do you think Aristotle would have viewed Plato's story as an example of cathartic literature?

4. Aristotle says a good tragedy shouldn't need any "Spectacle" if the story is enough to make people shudder with fear and pity. In the *Poetics* he defines it as the actual, physical appearance of actors on the stage, but as you see in this excerpt he also specifies that the Spectacle is unnecessary if the audience can imagine the situation through a good narration on stage. We could perhaps take that to mean a good dramatic performance doesn't need any exaggerated display or special effects to get its point across. Can you think of movies that have been extremely vivid even with very few special effects, because they rely on our minds to fill in the gaps with our own visions of horror? Are there movies whose impact has been completely dependent on special effects? Does that detract from the story?

Primary Reading

The Name of the Rose

U M B E R T O   E C O

Novel, 1980. Excerpt. Translated by William Weaver.

Usually we do not present a work of fiction as a Primary Reading, but this exception relates to the Aristotle text you have just read. Aristotle's *Poetics* consisted of two books, one on tragedy, and the other on comedy, but the latter has been lost since before the Middle Ages. We know, however, that Aristotle admired the theater, and that book would probably have paralleled his book on tragedy, outlining the proper plot type for a good comedy and so forth. The Italian philosopher and novelist Umberto Eco's novel *The Name of the Rose*, a murder mystery set in the High Middle Ages, features the resurfacing of a copy of Aristotle's book on comedy, and speculates that if a work by Aristotle had been available in those days that legitimized comedy and laughter, Western culture might have developed differently. It was made into a movie with Sean Connery as the monk/detective William of Baskerville—a literary reference that isn't lost on anyone who is a fan of Arthur Conan Doyle's Sherlock Holmes stories, because one of the most famous stories of the British private detective is the one called *The Hound of the Baskervilles*. Here William of Baskerville is visiting the monastery where serial killings are taking place, accompanied by his trusty young helper Adsel, the narrator of the story. William is getting close to solving the crimes and reads here from the long-lost book by Aristotle on comedy (written by Eco to resemble Aristotle's style, because the book, as you know, has never been found). After the quote from Aristotle, William has a passionate discussion with the blind librarian Jorge about the effects of laughter, and it becomes clear that Jorge is responsible for hiding the book from the other monks—among other things.

In the first book we dealt with tragedy and saw how, by arousing pity and fear, it produces catharsis, the purification of those feelings. As we promised, we will now deal with comedy (as well as with satire and mime) and see how, in inspiring the pleasure of the ridiculous, it arrives at the purification of that passion. That such passion is most worthy of consideration we have already said in the book on the soul, inasmuch as— alone among the animals—man is capable of laughter. We will then define the type of actions of which comedy is the mimesis, then we will examine the means by which comedy excites laughter, and these means and actions and speech. We will show how the ridiculousness of actions is born from the likening of the best to the worst and vice versa, from arousing surprise through deceit, from the impossible, from violation of the laws of nature, from the irrelevant and the inconsequent, from the debasing of the characters, from the use of comical and vulgar pantomime, from disharmony, from the choice of the least worthy things. We will then show how the ridiculousness of speech is born from the misunderstandings of similar words for different things and different words for similar things, from garrulity and repetition, from play on words, from diminutives, from errors of pronunciation, and from barbarisms. [. . .]

"But now tell me," William was saying, "Why? Why did you want to shield this book more than so many others? Why did you hide—though not at the price of crime— treatises on necromancy, pages that may have blasphemed against the name of God, while for these pages you damned your brothers and have damned yourself? There are many other books that speak of comedy, many others that praise laughter. Why did this one fill you with such fear?"

"Because it was by the Philosopher. Every book by that man has destroyed a part of the learning that Christianity had accumulated over the centuries. [. . .]

"But what frightened you in this discussion of laughter? You cannot eliminate laughter by eliminating the book."

"No, to be sure. But laughter is weakness, corruption, the foolishness of our flesh. It is the peasant's entertainment, the drunkard's license; even the church in her wisdom has granted the moment of feast, carnival, fair, this diurnal pollution that releases humors and distracts from other desires and other ambitions. . . . Still, laughter remains base, a defense for the simple, a mystery desecrated for the plebeians. The apostle also said as much: it is better to marry than to burn. Rather than rebel against God's established order, laugh and enjoy your foul parodies of order, at the end of the meal, after you have drained jugs and flasks. Elect the king of fools, lose yourselves in the liturgy of the ass and the pig, play at performing your saturnalia head down. . . . But here, here"—now Jorge struck the table with his finger, near the book William was holding open—"here the function of laughter is reversed, it is elevated to art, the doors of the world of the learned are opened to it, it becomes the object of philosophy, and of perfidious theology. [. . .] That laughter is proper to man is a sign of our limitation, sinners that we are. But from this book many corrupt minds like yours would draw the extreme syllogism, whereby laughter is man's end! Laughter, for a few moments, distracts the villein from fear. But law is imposed by fear, whose true name is fear of God. This book could strike the Luciferine spark that would set a new fire to the whole world, and laughter would be defined as the new art, unknown even to Prometheus, for canceling fear. To the villein who laughs, at that moment, dying does not matter: but then, when the license is past, the liturgy again imposes on him, according to the divine plan, the fear of death. And from this book there could be born the new destructive aim to destroy death through redemption from fear.

Study Questions

1. Compare the real Aristotle text on tragedy and Eco's pastiche (attempt at writing something similar). Has Eco done a good job, in your view?

2. Compare Plato's view on comedy and laughter with what Eco believes to have been Aristotle's view. Which comes close to your opinion? Explain why. (Also, whom do you think Eco would side with: Plato or Aristotle?)

3. Is Jorge right that law is imposed by fear of God, and laughter is a distraction from fear, so laughter is dangerous? Compare Jorge's and Plato's comments on laughter. (Remember that Jorge is a fictional character.)

4. Could Eco be right that if Aristotle's book had survived, it might have changed the course of Western culture? Why or why not?

Primary Reading

Your Life as Story

TRISTINE RAINER

Book, 1997. Excerpt.

Rainer's book is a practical guide to writing one's autobiography and includes chapters such as "The Nine Essential Elements of Story Structure," "Genres of the Self," "Truth in Autobiographic Writing," and "Finishing the Unfinished Story." She suggests looking for patterns in your life and the lives of others as a stargazer looks for constellations. Her book is more than a guide to writing a best-selling story about yourself—it is intended as a guide to make you understand yourself better. In this selection she gives the first lesson in finding the story of your life.

What is a story anyway? We all know intuitively. As children we gobble them up and never feel too full for more. Myths are stories, fairy tales and folktales are stories; so are novels, movies, and sitcoms. But you can't touch, taste, smell, hear, or see a story—only the images and words it assumes. To say what a story is, is like trying to get your hands around a ghost shape.

Though they are intangible, stories are powerful and their power seems to come from another realm. They appear to be a way in which the sacred enters our lives. Myths, stories to explain how and why we are here, begot religion. The morality tales of Moses, Jesus, Mohammed, and Buddha—stories that tell us what to value and how to live— have determined the course of world history for more than nineteen centuries. Stories remembered within a community or family transport the beliefs and values of past generations into the future. The individual stories of our own lives tell us who we are and infuse our personal existence with excitement, meaning, and mystery.

Myths, parables, family stories, and the innumerable media stories of our popular culture are offered to us already embodied in the words or images of others. However, the stories of our own lives require active searching—learning to look through our memories in a new way. To find story in your life, you must engage imagination with memory; you must invent a line of continuity—not from nothing, but from the raw materials of your life. It's like reading a pattern in DNA or figuring out the possible anagrams in a word. To find story in your life, you have to know what you are looking for. Fortunately, though you can't see a story, if you learn what its features are, when you look you will recognize one—and then many.

So what are the features of a story? A story isn't just a plot, a series of interconnected events. A story is a meaningful narrative with a beginning, a middle, and a conclusion. You started out at point A, the beginning, and because of what you did and what happened to you in the middle, point B, you ended up at point C, the conclusion. At point C you were a different person than you were at A, not just because you were older, but because you saw things differently.

In its simplest form a story is: what you wanted, how you struggled, and what you realized out of that struggle. A story is a series of interrelated events that you made happen and that happened to you, and the consequence. The consequence is a change in you. In an autobiographic story, change may occur in other characters, but it must also occur in you, because you are the protagonist. The change may come from an event (you married, you got old), but it is also a moral change. You had a realization, a shift in values or perception.

In other words, within the story you made a "character arc," you had a change in character. Gradually, because of what happened to you in life and the minirealizations you had along the way, you went from "there" to "here" as a person. What you believed, what you valued, and how you acted toward others changed, even if only slightly. You track this character arc in an autobiographic story by including your feelings, reactions to the events you experienced, and your realizations. You give the events of your life significance because of what they meant to you and how you changed from your engagement with them. An autobiographic story is not just an account of events; it is the charting of your emotional, moral, and psychological course, which gives meaning to those events.

It is worth taking some time to think about the inner course you wish to trace before you start putting down everything you can remember about your past. It is worth considering what story you want your life to tell. Why? Why not just write down everything you can remember, like so many people do? Because it won't be alive, it won't tap into the power of myth, it won't participate in the kind of truth that we read narratives for.

Study Questions

1. What does Rainer mean by a "moral change" in a story?

2. What is a "character arc"?

3. Write three pages of autobiography (the story of your life so far) using Rainer's method. Have a friend who knows you well critique it: Did you mention points in your life he or she would recognize? Are there important events you chose to omit?

Does he or she recognize your self-image? Write a new version using your friend's critique, and compare the two.

4. In the first season of the television series *The Sopranos,* young Chris, a mobster as well as an aspiring screenwriter, is experiencing an existential crisis. Feeling that nobody takes him seriously enough, he shoots a deli manager in the foot because he doesn't get preferential treatment. Afterward he agonizes that his life seems disjointed and meaningless, because he has no "character arc." He proceeds to try to establish a reputation as a tough mobster. Is this what Rainer means by a character arc? If you are a *Sopranos* fan, what do you think the screenwriter had in mind by having Chris talk about character arcs?

 ## Narrative

Medea

EURIPIDES

From a fifth-century-B.C.E. play. Summary and Excerpts. Translated by Moses Hadas.

The Greek dramatist Euripides (ca. 485–406 B.C.E.) was considered an eccentric and an intellectual radical. Nineteen of his eighty-eight plays have survived into modern times. In fifth-century B.C.E. Athens, the annual festival held for Dionysus had developed into an established tradition of competitions among playwrights of tragedies, satyr plays, and comedies. Although the tragedies were originally supposed to deal with the life, death, and resurrection of the god Dionysus (Bacchus) and stories of the gods in general, they quickly developed into stories about human failings and revenge. The tragedy *Medea,* written in 451 B.C.E., is unusual in that it doesn't follow the established tragic pattern of the triumph of divine justice; but Euripides rarely followed the established patterns of tragedies. He won only four first prizes at the festivals in his lifetime, but after his death his plays became immensely popular. Toward the end of his life he left Athens; he died in Macedonia (where Aristotle was born in 384 B.C.E., twenty-two years later). In the preceding excerpt from Aristotle's *Poetics,* you may have noticed that Aristotle specifically praises Euripides and his unique style.

Greek mythology tells of Jason and his Argonauts, who captured the Golden Fleece from the king of Colchis and brought it back to Corinth in triumph. That is a heroic story, one of Greece's legends of the golden age. Jason was helped in his quest by the daughter of the king of Colchis, Medea, who betrayed her father, her brother, and her country in order to help Jason, the man she loved. So Medea followed him to Corinth. That was the old myth—and Euripides tells us "the rest of the story."

Years have passed, and Medea is in a deep depression. She won't eat, she can't sleep, she weeps incessantly. Jason has tired of her—she is no longer young, and Jason has fallen in love with another woman, the young blonde princess of Corinth. He has taken her as his second wife without so much as asking Medea's permission. Now the king, the princess's father, is about to banish Medea from the kingdom, together with her and Jason's two sons, because he fears that this woman, an unpredictable foreigner, may take revenge on his daughter. But Medea cannot go home because she caused her brother's death and betrayed her father in helping Jason. She forsook everything for him, including her ties to her homeland, and, without a homeland, one was barely considered a person in the ancient Greek world.

> It's all over, my friends; I would gladly die. Life has lost its savor. The man who was everything to me, well he knows it, has turned out to be the basest of men. Of all creatures that feel and think, we women are the unhappiest species. In the first place, we must pay a great dowry to a husband who will be the tyrant of our bodies (that's a further aggravation of the evil); and there is another fearful hazard: whether we shall get a good man or a bad. For separations bring disgrace on the woman and it is not possible to renounce one's husband. Then, landed among strange habits and regulations unheard of in her own home, a woman needs second sight to know how best to handle her bedmate. And if we manage this well and have a husband who does not find the yoke of intercourse too galling, ours is a life to be envied. Otherwise, one is better dead. When the man wearies of the company of his wife, he goes outdoors and relieves the disgust of his heart [having recourse to some friend or the companions of his own age], but we women have only one person to turn to.
>
> They say that we have a safe life at home, whereas men must go to war. Nonsense! I had rather fight three battles than bear one child. But be that as it may, you and I are not in the same case. You have your city here, your paternal homes; you know the delights of life and association with your loved ones. But I, homeless and forsaken, carried off from a foreign land, am being wronged by a husband, with neither mother nor brother nor kinsman with whom I might find refuge from the storms of misfortune. One little boon I crave of you, if I discover any ways and means of punishing my husband for these wrongs: your silence. Woman in most respects is a timid creature, with no heart for strife and aghast at the sight of steel; but wronged in love, there is no heart more murderous than hers.

But Medea has a plan, and the old king has seen it coming with a sure instinct: Medea plots to poison both the princess and the king. She has one last, horrible argument with Jason, who comes to make sure she won't be destitute, because he has heard that she has been expelled from the country:

> Rotten, heart-rotten, that is the word for you. Words, words, magnificent words. In reality a craven. You come to me, you come, my worst enemy! This isn't bravery, you know, this isn't valor, to come and face your victims. No! it's the ugliest sore on the face of humanity, Shamelessness. But I thank you for coming. It will lighten the weight on my heart to tell your wickedness, and it will hurt you to hear it. I shall begin my tale at the very beginning.
>
> I saved your life, as all know who embarked with you on the Argo, when you were sent to master with the yoke the fire-breathing bulls and to sow with dragon's teeth that acre of death. The dragon, too, with wreathed coils, that kept safe watch over the Golden Fleece and never slept—I slew it and raised for you the light of life again. Then, forsaking my father and my own dear ones, I came to Iolcus where Pelias reigned, came with you, more than fond and less than wise. On Pelias too I brought death, the most painful

death there is, at the hands of his own children. Thus I have removed every danger from your path.

And after all those benefits at my hands, you basest of men, you have betrayed me and made a new marriage, though I have borne you children. If you were still childless, I could have understood this love of yours for a new wife. Gone now is all reliance on pledges. You puzzle me. Do you believe that the gods of the old days are no longer in office? Do you think that men are now living under a new dispensation? For surely you know that you have broken all your oaths to me. Ah my hand, which you so often grasped, and oh my knees, how all for nothing have we been defiled by this false man, who has disappointed all our hopes.

Jason and Medea part with bitter words, and now Medea is in luck: King Aegeus of Athens pays her a visit and hears of her marital problems and banishment. He finds Jason despicable and admires Medea for her righteous anger. He himself is looking for a wife to bear him children and offers Medea a refuge as his wife as soon as she is "done with her business."

Medea now pretends to be submissive when Jason comes back and asks that the children be allowed to take gifts to his young bride. The enormity of what she is about to do is beginning to envelop her, and she finds it hard to control herself. After Jason leaves, she hands the gifts to the two young boys and can't stop weeping—because she not only plans to kill the princess, she also plans to *kill her own children,* to hurt Jason the only way she knows how:

O the pain of it! Why do your eyes look at me, my children? Why smile at me that last smile? Ah! What can I do? My heart is water, women, at the sight of my children's bright faces. I could never do it. Goodbye to my former plans. I shall take my children away with me. Why should I hurt their father by *their* misfortunes, only to reap a double harvest of sorrow myself? No! I cannot do it. Goodbye to my plans.

And yet . . . what is the matter with me? Do I want to make myself a laughing-stock by letting my enemies off scot-free? I must go through with it. What a coward heart is mine, to admit those soft pleas. Come, my children, into the palace. Those that may not attend my sacrifices can see to it that they are absent. I shall not let my hand be unnerved.

Ah! Ah! Stop, my heart. Do not you commit this crime. Leave them alone, unhappy one, spare the children. Even if they live far from us, they will bring you joy. No! by the unforgetting dead in hell, it cannot be! I shall not leave my children for my enemies to insult. (In any case they must die. And if die they must, *I* shall slay them, who gave them birth.) My schemes are crowned with success. She shall not escape. Already the diadem is on her head; wrapped in the robe the royal bride is dying. I know it well. And now I am setting out on a most sorrowful road (and shall send these on one still more sorrowful). I wish to speak to my children. Give your mother your hands, my children, give her your hands to kiss.

O dear, dear hand. O dear, dear mouth, dear shapes, dear noble faces, happiness be yours, but not here. Your father has stolen this world from you. How sweet to touch! The softness of their skin, the sweetness of their breath, my babies! Away, away, I cannot bear to see you any longer.

[CHILDREN *retire within.*]

My misery overwhelms me. O I *do* realize how terrible is the crime I am about, but passion overrules my resolutions, passion that causes most of the misery in the world.

She sends the children away, and after a while, a messenger tells the gruesome details: The princess put on the golden diadem, Medea's gift, and instantly the poison began to work:

> The golden diadem on her head emitted a strange flow of devouring fire, while the fine robes, the gifts of your children, were eating up the poor girl's white flesh. All aflame, she jumps from her seat and flees, shaking her head and hair this way and that, trying to throw off the crown. But the golden band held firmly, and after she had shaken her hair more violently, the fire began to blaze twice as fiercely. Overcome by the agony she falls on the ground, and none but her father could have recognized her. The position of her eyes could not be distinguished, nor the beauty of her face. The blood, clotted with fire, dripped from the crown of her head, and the flesh melted from her bones, like resin from a pine tree, as the poisons ate their unseen way. It was a fearful sight. All were afraid to touch the corpse, taught by what had happened to her.

The princess's old father rushed to the scene and took her in his arms, and that was how the poison spread to him; within minutes he, too, was dead.

The news galvanizes Medea into action: Now she feels she must kill her children so nobody will take their revenge on them, and she rationalizes,

> No flinching now, no thinking of the children, the darling children, that call you mother. This day, this one short day, forget your children. You have all the future to mourn them. Aye, to mourn. Though you mean to kill them, at least you loved them. Oh! I am a most unhappy woman.

From inside the room, we hear the cries for help as she stabs her two sons to death.

Jason returns, devastated at the turn of events. Medea gloats because now she knows she's "got under his skin." To the end, they quarrel over whose fault it is and who is to blame for the children's death. Jason didn't seem to care much for his sons while they were alive, but now that they are dead he loves them with all his heart. He invokes the power of the gods to avenge his children—but the gods don't help him. No divine lightning bolt strikes Medea down—she leaves him to become the wife of Aegeus.

Study Questions

1. This tragedy seemed nothing short of immoral to many critics in Athens because Medea gets away with quadruple murder. Can we defend Medea's actions in any way? Is Jason free of blame? What do you think Euripides intended the "moral of the story" to be?

2. How would Plato evaluate *Medea*—as a moral learning tool or a dangerous temptation to be irrational? How would Aristotle evaluate it? Does it meet his criteria for a well-written tragedy? (Tragedy has to happen to an ordinary person as the result of some grave error in judgment of theirs and preferably should happen between family members.) In other words, if Aristotle is right and a good tragedy is the story of an ordinary person—not good, not bad—who makes a major mistake and suffers for it

for the rest of his/her life, then who is the main character in *Medea*? From whose viewpoint is the story told? Medea's—or Jason's?

3. Sadly, the phenomenon of parents killing their children is not unusual at all; it may be done in anger, or for insurance purposes, for convenience, or out of some peculiar sense of responsibility ("I won't allow my children to become fatherless/motherless when I kill myself, so I'll take them with me"). Rarely is it done for revenge, as in the case of Medea. Susan Smith, who in 1994 strapped her two little boys in a car and let it roll into a lake, killing both of them, wanted to be unencumbered so her former boyfriend would come back to her—apparently it didn't occur to her that she could just have left them in the loving care of their father, her ex-husband. Andrea Yates, who drowned her five children in 2001, was diagnosed as suffering from severe postpartum depression and said she heard voices telling her to take their lives. But one recent case seems like a true Medea scenario: Susan Eubanks killed her four sons in 1998 specifically to get back at their fathers. Now remember that in the play, Medea isn't punished; she leaves for a new life as the queen of Athens. How do you feel about that, considering that Smith and Yates are serving life sentences, and Eubanks is on death row?

Narrative

The Sorrows of Young Werther

JOHANN WOLFGANG VON GOETHE

Novel, 1774. Excerpt. Translated by Elizabeth Mayer and Louise Bogan.

The hypnotic power of Goethe's book about young lovesick Werther may be hard to imagine today, but the fact remains that many young readers in Europe took their own lives after suffering along with Werther. Goethe presented the story as though he had found Werther's letters to a friend and then told about the final days in narrative form. From May to December, Werther undergoes all the highs and lows of falling in love, but in the end his beloved Lotte marries someone else. Shortly after writing this letter to his friend Wilhelm, Werther takes his pistol and shoots himself in the head.

December 4

I beg you—you see I am done for; I cannot bear it any longer. Today I sat near her as she played the clavichord, all sorts of tunes and with so much expression. So much! So much! What could I do? Her little sister sat on my knee and dressed her doll. Tears came into my eyes. I bowed my head and caught sight of her wedding ring. The tears ran down my cheek—and suddenly Lotte began to play the heavenly old melody. All at once my soul was touched by a feeling of consolation, by a memory of the past, of the other occasions when I had heard the song, of the dark intervals of vexation between, of shattered hopes, and then—I walked up and down the room, my heart almost suffocated by the rush of emotions. "For God's sake," I said, in a vehement outburst, "for God's sake, stop!" She paused and looked at me steadily. "Werther," she said with a smile that went deep to my heart, "Werther, you are very sick. You dislike the things you once liked. Go! I beg you, calm yourself!" I tore myself from her sight, and—God! You see my misery and will put an end to it.

Study Questions

1. Evaluate Werther's reaction from your own point of view: Is suicide because of rejection a realistic scenario? Is it emotionally understandable? Is it morally defensible? Explain your viewpoint.

2. Apply Plato's and Aristotle's views to this excerpt.

3. Can you think of stories (movies or other media) that have had a similar effect on the audience in recent years? If so, do you think something should be done to prevent such influence in the future? Explain your viewpoint.

4. Goethe gives the story credibility by pretending that he found these letters of Werther's (although he of course made the whole story up, including the character of Werther himself). The format of letting a story unfold within a frame of a letter, or an ancient manuscript in the loft, or a videotape, lives on in the best of health, because it is such a good way to lend credence to the story. Recently a hugely popular film used this format to make it look like a documentary: *The Blair Witch Project.* Can you think of other stories—novels or films—that use the same trick?

Narrative

Pulp Fiction

QUENTIN TARANTINO (DIRECTOR AND SCREENWRITER)

Screenplay, 1996. Film, 1994. Summary and Excerpt.

In this summary (with a short excerpt)* we focus on one aspect of a complex story. *Pulp Fiction,* which shocked its first audiences with its graphic violence and strong language, has now acquired the status of an instant classic, often referred to in educational contexts precisely because of its casual attitude toward death and violence—up to a point. Here we look at the point where violence suddenly seems to have lost its appeal for one of the main characters, Jules.

Author's note of caution: Please be advised that the excerpt from the screenplay (Jules's monologue) contains some profanity. Additional profanity has been omitted from the excerpt. The entire screenplay of *Pulp Fiction* uses vernacular speech laden with what many readers will consider vulgarities. In the film it may be said to serve an artistic purpose, giving the audience an immediate understanding of the underworld in which the story takes place and often providing a deliberate counterpoint to intellectual dialogue; however, excerpts from the screenplay may strike some readers as being offensive. I suggest that the issue of offensive language, in films as well as in everyday life, be part of the class discussion after reading the narrative, as indicated in study question 4.

Pulp Fiction (Miramax, 1994) appears to many people to glorify violence, but educators have discerned a deeper intention: a strong statement against violence. Here Honey Bunny (Amanda Plummer) and Pumpkin (Tim Roth) are preparing to rob the customers and staff of the diner.

Jules and Vincent have had a rough morning. Hit men for a mobster, they have just murdered two young men, with Jules quoting a passage supposedly from Ezekiel, but heavily embroidered with Jules's own words of doom, to them before he kills them, as he usually does; it is his style. Completing the job, they retrieve a briefcase for their boss. What Jules and Vincent don't know is that another man is hiding in the bathroom. When he bursts out, emptying his Magnum at the two hit men, they fire back, and he dies—but neither Jules nor Vincent is hurt. Vincent wants to label it a stroke of good luck and get out of there, but Jules is profoundly shocked and sees it as something else: divine intervention.

Marvin, a young friend of Jules's who has helped him set up the hit, follows them out of the bloodstained apartment into their car; while Vincent is discussing the incident of the bullets that missed, his gun accidentally goes off and shoots the young man in the face. Terribly upset, Jules worries that they are now driving on the highway with a bloody car and a dead body—his concern is not for the untimely death of Marvin.

Later they are having breakfast in a coffee shop, coming down from the morning's events. Jules is still contemplating what he thinks of as a miracle, the fact that he wasn't killed, and he announces that he now considers himself retired from "the Life."

Something else is going on in the coffee shop. A young couple, Pumpkin and Honey Bunny, are now rising up out of a booth, pointing guns at the patrons and the waitresses:

They are going to rob the place. Vincent has gone to the restroom and is unaware of the developments, but Jules witnesses the entire holdup. The young couple take the money from the cash register and move in to rob the patrons. When Pumpkin points his gun at Jules, he gives up his wallet but flatly refuses to hand over the briefcase. He lets Pumpkin look inside (we don't get to see the contents, only its mysterious glow), but that is as far as it goes. When Pumpkin points his gun at Jules, Jules quickly twists his arm, and now Pumpkin is the one staring into the gun. The girl attempts to help her lover but realizes that Jules will shoot if she moves. Now Vincent comes back to the table and takes in the situation. Together, Jules and Vincent keep the young couple under control, and Jules tells them that under normal circumstances they would both be dead now—but today he is in a "transitional period" and doesn't want to kill them. He instructs Pumpkin to go into the loot bag, fish out Jules's wallet, take out the cash, $1,500, and just go away. And he tells Pumpkin:

> Wanna know what I'm buying? . . . Your life. I'm giving you that money so I don't hafta kill your ass. . . . You read the Bible? . . . There's a passage I got memorized: Ezekiel 25:17. "The path of the righteous man is beset on all sides by the inequities of the selfish and the tyranny of evil men. Blessed is he who, in the name of charity and good will, shepherds the weak through the valley of the darkness. For he is truly his brother's keeper and the finder of lost children. And I will strike down upon thee with great vengeance and furious anger those who attempt to poison and destroy my brothers. And you will know I am the Lord when I lay my vengeance upon you." I been sayin' that shit for years. And if you ever heard it, it means your ass. I never really questioned what it meant. I thought it was just a coldblooded thing to say. . . . But I saw some shit this morning made me think twice. Now I'm thinkin'. It could mean you're the evil man. And I'm the righteous man. And Mr. .45 here he's the shepherd protecting my righteous ass in the valley of darkness. Or it could be you're the righteous man and I'm the shepherd and it's the world that's evil and selfish. I'd like that. But that shit ain't the truth. The truth is you're weak. And I'm the tyranny of evil men. But I'm tryin'. I'm tryin' real hard to be a shepherd.

Jules lowers his gun and puts it on the table; Pumpkin looks at him, at Honey Bunny, at the $1,500 in his hand, and then he grabs the trash bag full of cash and wallets, and he and Honey Bunny walk out the door.

Study Questions

1. What does Jules mean by suggesting that he might be the "righteous man"? What does he mean by suggesting that he might be the shepherd?

2. What does Jules mean by saying that he is giving Honey Bunny and Pumpkin the money so he won't have to kill them?

3. What do you think is the point of talking about being "righteous" and "being evil," given that the scene we are witnessing is a confrontation between robbers and hit men?

4. If you have seen the film, you will know that the dialogue is laden with profanity (as is evident in the excerpt from Jules's monologue). Do you think the foul language serves a purpose in this context? Why or why not? You might want to discuss the issue of profanity in contemporary speech styles.

5. Do you believe this particular film might inspire more violence (as Plato would believe), or do you think that, in some way, it might serve as a "cleansing" experience (as Aristotle might say) or perhaps as a warning against wholesale cultural acceptance of violence?

6. You may have wondered what the briefcase contains. It is not revealed in the film, but rumor has it that it contains the soul of the gangster boss. Would such an interpretation make a difference to the story? Explain.

Part 2

What Should
I Do?

THEORIES OF
CONDUCT

Chapter Three

Ethical Relativism

*O*n occasion we are forced to face this fact: Not everybody shares our idea of what constitutes decent behavior. You may wait at the movie theater for a friend who never shows up because she is on the phone with another friend and it doesn't occur to her that it is important to keep her date with you. Such actions usually can be dismissed as merely bad manners or callousness; still, you probably will not want to make plans with that person again. *Moral differences* can run deeper than that, however. Suppose you are dating someone to whom you feel very attracted. During dinner at a nice restaurant, your friend casually mentions that he or she supports a candidate or cause that you strongly oppose on moral grounds. The fact that your friend has a different idea about what constitutes moral behavior will probably affect the way you feel about him or her.

We regularly read and hear about actions that are morally unacceptable to us. A young foreign girl is killed by her brother because she is pregnant and unmarried or perhaps merely going out with an American boy. To the Western mind the brother's act is an unfathomable crime. But the brother believes he is only doing his duty, as unpleasant as it may be; he is upholding the family honor, which the sister has tainted by her act of unspeakable immorality (according to the traditional code of his culture—hence the term *honor-killing*). The world is full of stories about people who feel duty-bound to do things others find repugnant. People in some cultures feel it is their moral obligation, or moral right, to dispose of their elderly citizens when they become unproductive. Pretechnological cultures, in particular, have a tradition during times when food is scarce of exposing their oldest members to the elements and leaving them to die. Often the decision rests with these older people, who feel morally obliged to remove themselves from the tribe when they believe it is time. Some cultures feel a moral right or duty to dispose of infants in the same way—usually cultures with no safe medical access to contraception. Other cultures believe it is a sin to seek medical assistance—they believe life should be left in the hands of God. Some people believe it is a sin to destroy any life, even by inadvertently stepping on an insect. Some people think they have a moral duty to defend themselves, their loved ones, and their country from any threat; others think it is their moral duty to refrain from resorting to violence under any circumstances.

In the days following the terrorist attacks of September 11, I was asked by many of my students how anyone could be so utterly devoid of morals that they would choose civilian targets, with no concern for the lives they were destroying. If ever there was a situation that brought home the challenge of dealing with moral differences, this was the one. As we have since learned, the al Qaeda code of ethics identified their actions as morally justified and even mandated. Since then, we have witnessed a number of what most of us would label atrocities by al Qaeda, directed against Americans and other nations, such as the beheadings of civilians in Iraq and the bombings of a night club in Bali and commuter trains in Madrid. In the great majority of cases the victims have been civilians; and while Muslim leaders generally have denounced these terrorist acts and pointed out that civilians are not a legitimate target, Osama bin Laden and other al Qaeda leaders have pointed out in interviews that their moral code doesn't recognize the difference between combatants and noncombatants, between soldiers and civilians. (This difference is greatly emphasized in the Western concept of just war, which you can read about in Chapter 13.) So is each culture right in its own way, or is there some universal moral standard that al Qaeda just isn't living up to? Or perhaps one that the West isn't living up to? The question was easier in the days when different cultural moral codes weren't costing lives, very publicly and on a regular basis, and it felt right and enlightened to be tolerant of quaint customs from far away; but now the credo of ethical relativism—there is no universal moral code, only different cultural morals—is up against the impression, shared by many who see the war against terrorism as stretching into the indefinite future, that we are fighting for the survival of our own culture and our own moral standards. It ups the ante and brings the discussion of ethical relativism to the forefront—no longer an enjoyable if abstract philosophical discussion but rather a passionate matter of standing up for what one believes in.

How to Deal with Moral Differences

How do we approach this phenomenon of moral differences? There are at least four major paths to choose.

1. Moral Nihilism, Skepticism, and Subjectivism We may choose to believe that there are no morally right or wrong viewpoints—that the whole moral issue is a cultural game, and neither your opinion nor mine matters in the end, for there is no ultimate right or wrong. This view is called *moral nihilism,* and at various times in our lives, especially if we are facing personal disappointment, we may be inclined to take this approach. This is a difficult position to uphold, however, because it is so extreme. It is hard to remember, every minute of the day, that we don't believe there is any difference between right and wrong. If we see somebody steal our car, we are inclined to want the thief stopped, regardless of how much our jaded intellect tells us that no one is more right or wrong than anyone else. If we watch a child or an animal being abused, we feel like stepping in, even if we tell ourselves that there is no such thing as right or wrong. In other words, there seems to be something in most of us—instinct, or socialization, or reason, or compassion, or maybe something else altogether—that surfaces even when we try to persuade ourselves that moral values are but an illusion.

Related to the attitude of moral nihilism is *moral skepticism,* which holds that we can't know whether there are any moral truths, and *moral subjectivism,* which holds that moral views are merely inner states in a person and that they can't be compared to the inner states of another person, so a moral viewpoint is valid only for the person who holds it. Both skepticism and subjectivism are more common than nihilism, but they seem to be equally difficult to adhere to in the long run, because at crucial times we all act *as if* there are valid moral truths that we share with others—we criticize a friend for being late, a politician for being a racist or sexist, a colleague for the way she raises her children. We praise a stranger for coming to our aid when we are stuck on the freeway, we praise our kids when they come home on time—so it seems that even if we believe ourselves to be nihilists, skeptics, or subjectivists, we still expect to share some values with others of our own culture.

Although moral subjectivism generally seems a more flexible and appealing theory than categorical moral nihilism or moral skepticism—to the point that some thinkers choose to treat subjectivism as a subcategory of ethical relativism—the three theories have something in common that makes all of them less than successful: *They have no conflict-solving capacity.* How would you persuade the car thief to leave your car alone on moral grounds if you are a nihilist? A skeptic? Or a subjectivist? In each case, you have given up on the idea of finding common moral ground. The best you can do is tell the car thief that he is behaving in an illegal fashion; you can't claim that you have a moral argument that he ought to listen to. Box 3.1 introduces the basic concepts of philosophy of law.

2. Ethical Relativism We may choose to believe that there is no universal moral truth—that each culture has its own set of rules that are valid for that culture, and we have no right to interfere, just as they have no right to interfere with our rules. This attitude, known as *ethical relativism,* is not as radical as skepticism because it allows that moral truths exist but holds that they are relative to their time and place. Ethical relativism is viewed as an attitude of tolerance and as an antidote to the efforts of cultures who try their best to impose their set of moral rules on other cultures. Can ethical relativism solve conflicts? Yes, quite effectively. You may not like the solution, but ethical relativism says that whatever the majority deems to be the moral rule is the proper rule to follow. This theory is discussed in detail in the next section.

3. Soft Universalism We may believe that deep down, in spite of all their differences, people of different cultures can still agree on certain moral basics. We may think it is a

BOBO'S PROGRESS © 2001 Dan Wright. Reprinted by permission of King Features Syndicate.

In this cartoon Lenny, the moral nihilist, is being challenged by Bobo. How does Bobo restore Lenny's sense of justice? Do you think it would convince a moral nihilist? Why or why not?

Box 3.1   MORALITY AND THE LAW

The relationship between morals and legislation is ancient. From the Code of Hammurabi (developed by Babylonians in approximately 2000 B.C.E.) to the legislation of today, some laws have reflected the moral climate of the time. Not all laws have done so, though some scholars argue that because laws tell us what we ought to do or ought not to do, all laws have a moral element to them; if nothing else, they promote the idea that it is morally good to uphold the law. However, sometimes the law does not seem to be morally right. When times change, what seemed right before may not seem right anymore, and if the legislative power is sensitive to that fact, the law will change. Sometimes it takes a civil war for such laws to be changed; sometimes it takes an act of defiance; sometimes it takes only a simple vote. We can't, therefore, conclude that all laws are morally just, because experience tells us this is not so. Some laws may not even have an obvious moral element. A traffic law that allows us to turn right on red hardly addresses a moral issue.

Legislators, though, are naturally interested in the public's opinion of right and wrong, because, in general, this opinion will be represented by the laws of the country. Not all moral issues are relevant for legislators, however; whether you go home for Thanksgiving may be an important moral issue in your family, but it is hardly the business of anyone else, let alone the state legislature. Philosophy of law generally speaks of two viewpoints concerning the relationship between ethics and the law. The viewpoint of *naturalism* (or *natural law*) holds that the law reflects, or ought to reflect, a set of universal moral standards; some naturalists consider these standards given by God,

and some see them as part of human nature. The other viewpoint is referred to as *legal positivism* and holds that the law is based on consensus among legislators; in other words, there is no ultimate moral foundation for our laws; they are relative and merely reflect shifting opinions over time.

There is thus an affinity between legal positivism and *ethical relativism,* because the ethical relativist sees moral codes as representing independent cultural traditions. The *hard universalist,* on the other hand, argues that only one moral code should prevail—which means that the naturalist is generally also a hard universalist. The *soft universalist* looks for common denominators underlying the moral differences, such as concern for the life and well-being of oneself, one's family and friends, and will suggest that some laws are clearly culture-relative, while other laws reflect deeper, universal human concerns.

If we look at the relationship between the moral codes and the laws of various societies we find that they differ dramatically: One society's legislation may reflect the belief that the law should not dictate people's moral choices as long as no harm is caused. Another society's laws may be anchored solidly in the moral code of that society, usually derived from the society's religion. The first type of society reflects a popular Western twentieth-century viewpoint; an example of the latter would be a Muslim society such as Iran where a code of law inspired by Islam, the *Sharia,* is enforced. Over time, societies have opted for various combinations of the law, morals, and religion, with a close connection between the three being very common until the twentieth century.

matter of biology—that people everywhere have basically the same human nature. Or we may view this agreement as a process of acculturation, whereby people adjust to the normal way of doing things in their culture. If the native peoples of harsh climates put their unwanted babies out in the wild to perish, it need not mean that they are cruel but rather that they want to give the babies they already have a chance to survive, and they know that having another mouth to feed will kill them all. In this way we find common ground in the fact that we, and they, do care for the children we are able to raise. If we believe that somehow, under the surface of antagonism and contradiction, we can still find a few things we can agree on, even if we choose to act on them in different ways, then we believe in the existence of a few universal moral truths. I call this attitude *soft universalism*—*universalism* because it perceives that there are some universal moral rules; *soft* because it is not as radical as hard universalism, or absolutism.* Can soft universalism solve conflicts? Perhaps it can do so better than any other approach, because the main goal of soft universalism is to seek common ground beneath the variety of opinions and mores.

   4. Hard Universalism *Hard universalism* (sometimes called *moral absolutism*) is the attitude that most often is supported in ethical theories. It is an attitude toward morals in everyday life to which many people relate very well. Hard universalism holds that there is one universal moral code. It is the viewpoint expressed by those who are on a quest for the code ("I know there must be one set of true moral rules, but I would not presume to have found it myself"), by those who make judgments based on its analysis ("After much deliberation I have come to the conclusion that this moral code represents the ultimate values"), and by those who put forth the simple sentiment that moral truth is not open for discussion ("I'm right and you're wrong, and you'd better shape up!"). Whereas moral nihilism, with its claim that there are no moral truths, represents one end of the spectrum in terms of dealing with moral differences, hard universalism represents the other extreme: It does not acknowledge the possibility or legitimacy of more than one set of moral codes. Can hard universalism/moral absolutism solve moral conflicts? Yes, in a variety of ways: If you accept someone telling you that you must be wrong because you don't agree with him or her, then that conflict is solved right there; more frequently, an absolutist will try to show you, on the basis of reasoning and evidence, that his or her moral conclusion is better than yours. Appeals to evidence and reasoning are the common problem-solving approaches among most absolutist philosophers, not appeals to force or fallacious arguments such as "I'm right because I'm right." Being a hard universalist thus doesn't equal inflexibility or dogmatism as much as a firm moral conviction—although such a conviction can of course also be dogmatic.

   The first set of viewpoints will not be discussed much in this book. The second one, *ethical relativism,* has greatly influenced moral attitudes in the West since the early twentieth century and is the main topic of this chapter. The third, *soft universalism,* and fourth, *hard universalism,* will be discussed in the subsequent chapters of Part 2.

The Lessons of Anthropology

In the nineteenth century, cultural anthropology came into its own as a scientific discipline and reminded the West that "out there" were other societies vastly different

---

*Some readers have asked me if I am the originator of the term *soft universalism,* and I have to confess that I simply don't know; I have used it for the past 15–20 years. I may have read it in someone else's book many years ago, or I may have simply constructed it in contrast to hard universalism, as may be the case with other philosophers—it's a handy, straightforward term. If anyone remembers encountering the term *soft universalism* prior to the publication of the first edition of *The Moral of the Story* in 1994, please let me know! I would like to be able to give credit where credit is due.

from those of Victorian Europe. Anthropological scholars set out to examine other cultures, and the facts they brought back were astounding to the nineteenth-century Western mind-set: There were cultures that didn't understand the male's role in procreation but thought that babies somehow ripened in the woman with the help of spirits. There were people who would devour the bodies of enemies killed in war in order to share their fighting spirit. There were cultures that believed in animal gods, cultures that felt it appropriate for women to bare their breasts, cultures that felt it utterly inappropriate to let your in-laws watch you eat, and so on. It was easy to draw the conclusion that there were cultures out there whose moral codes differed substantially from those of the West.

This conclusion, the first step in what has become known as ethical relativism, was not new to the Western mind-set. Because people had always traveled and returned with tales of faraway lands, it was common knowledge that other cultures did things differently. Explorers in earlier centuries brought home tales of mermaids, giants, and other fantasies. Some stories were truer than others. There really were, for instance, peoples out there who had a different dress ethic and work ethic. The Arabian messenger Ibn Fadlan traveled north into Russia in 922 and watched a Viking burial; he wrote with disgust about how different and primitive the Viking customs were (his story was the theme of the film *The 13th Warrior*), so not all such reports come from Western travelers commenting about non-Western ways. But what we're most familiar with is of course the tales about non-Western, exotic lands. The lifestyle of the South Sea islanders became a collective fantasy for Europeans of the eighteenth and nineteenth centuries; imagine not wearing any clothes, not having to work all the time, living in perpetual summertime, and not having any sexual restrictions! Depending on their ethical predisposition, Europeans considered such peoples to be either the luckiest ones on this earth or the most sinful, subhuman, and depraved. Reports of cultural diversity were also supplied by Christian missionaries over the centuries; they confronted more or less reluctant cultures with their message of conversion.

The idea of cultural diversity even in early historic times is well documented. The Greek historian Herodotus (485–430 B.C.E.) tells in his *Histories* of the Persian king Darius the Great, who from the borders of his vast empire, which at the time stretched from the Greek holdings in the West to India in the East, had heard tales of funerary practices that intrigued him. The Greeks were at that time in the habit of cremating their dead; Darius learned that a tribe in India, the Callatians, would eat their dead. In Darius's Persia, burials were the norm. Herodotus wrote:

> Everyone without exception believes in his own native customs, and the religion he was brought up in, to be the best . . . [Darius] summoned the Greeks who happened to be present at his court, and asked them what it would take to eat the dead bodies of their fathers. They replied that they would not do it for any money in the world. Later, in the presence of the Greeks, and through an interpreter, so that they could understand what was said, he asked some Indians, of the tribe called Callatia, who do in fact eat their parents' dead bodies, what they would take to burn them. They uttered a cry of horror and forbade him to mention such a dreadful thing. One can see by this what custom can do, and Pindar [a Greek poet] was right when he called it "king of all."

It was not so strange that King Darius might have heard of peoples living as far apart as the Greeks and the Callatian tribe of northern India, because they were in fact his neighbors. At the time of its greatest expansion, Persia (today, Iran) covered a territory stretching from Greece in the west to today's Pakistan in the east. Until the time of Alexander the Great, this was the greatest empire in the ancient Western world.

Usually, the sound bite condensing Herodotus's observation is "Custom is king"—we all prefer what we are used to.

When anthropologists point out that moral codes vary enormously from culture to culture, they are describing the situation as they see it. As long as those anthropologists make no judgments about whether it is *good* for humanity to have different moral codes or whether those codes represent the moral truths of each culture, they are espousing a descriptive theory usually referred to as *cultural relativism*. Let us look at an example. An anthropologist acquaintance of mine came back from a field trip to Tibet and told me the following story: In the little Tibetan village where he had been "adopted" by a local family and was doing his fieldwork, the children worked hard and had very little leisure time. The concept of competition was totally alien to them. One day my friend thought he would give them a treat, and he arranged for a race. All the kids lined up, puzzled and excited, to listen to his directions: Run from one end of the compound to the other and back again, and whoever comes in first wins. The race was on, and the children ran like mad to beat each other and "win." As one beaming kid came in first, the anthropologist handed over a prize—some little trinket or piece of candy. There was dead silence among the kids, who just looked at each other. Finally one of the children asked, "Why are you giving a gift to our friend who won?" The anthropologist realized that because the children had no idea of competition, they had no knowledge that winning often is connected with a prize. To them, this new idea of "winning" was great all by itself, and there was no need to add anything else; indeed, the prize made them feel very uncomfortable. (My friend said it also made him feel very stupid.)

What the anthropologist was doing by telling this story was relating an example of cultural relativism—describing how customs differ from culture to culture. Suppose, though, he had added, "and I realized that they were right in their own way." (In other words, suppose he had made a *judgment* about the validity of the tribal way of life.) In that case, he would have moved into the area of *ethical relativism.* Cultural relativism is a *descriptive* theory which states that different cultures have different moral codes. Ethical relativism is a *normative* theory which states there is no universal moral code and that each culture's codes are right and valid for that culture. It is a subtle difference, but philosophically it is an important one. (See Box 3.2 for an introduction to descriptive and normative ethics.) The cultural relativist sees the cultural differences and describes them: There are many moral codes in the world. The ethical relativist sees the cultural differences and makes a judgment: We can never find a common code, and what seems right for one culture is right *for that culture.*

The anthropologist Ruth Benedict (1887–1948) was a student of the cultural anthropologist Franz Boas, who had already declared that cultures around the world should not be judged by the standards of Western civilization and that moral standards are not universal, but relative to each culture. Sharing her teacher's viewpoint, Benedict did most of her writing toward the end of the era in which one could still speak of "uncontaminated" societies—cultures that hadn't yet been massively exposed to Western civilization. The term *primitive* still was used for some cultures, and Benedict used it too, but she was quick to point out that the attitude that Western civilization was at the top of the ladder of cultural evolution was—or should be—outdated. In a famous paper, "Anthropology and the Abnormal," from 1934, she says that "modern civilization becomes not a necessary pinnacle of human achievement but one entry in a long series of possible adjustments." With this emphasis she established herself as an advocate of cultural and moral *tolerance,* implying that Western civilization has no right to impose its codes of conduct on other cultures. Ethical relativism has remained popular ever since as a tool of cultural tolerance.

In the same paper, Benedict tells of a number of cultural phenomena that may seem morally odd, to say the least. In the Primary Readings you'll find an excerpt focusing on the custom of extreme paranoia on an island in Melanesia. Here in the chapter text, one example will have to suffice: Among the Kwakiutl Indians of the Pacific Northwest in times past, it was customary to view death, even natural death, as an affront that should be retaliated against in one way or another. In one tribe, a chief's sister and her daughter had drowned on a trip to Victoria. The chief gathered a war party. They set out, found seven men and two children asleep, and killed them. This made them all feel much better.

What intrigued Benedict about this story was not so much that the chief and the members of the war party viewed their actions as morally good, but that most of the tribespeople felt the same way. In other words, it was *normal* in the tribe to feel this

Box 3.2   DESCRIPTIVE AND NORMATIVE ETHICS

The terms *descriptive* and *normative* are important terms for any ethical theory, not just relativism. When we talk about a theory being *descriptive,* we mean that the theory merely describes what it sees as fact, such as, In the United States it is, in general, not considered immoral to eat meat. In other words, a descriptive theory describes what people actually do or think. A *normative* theory adds a *moral judgment,* evaluation, or justification, such as, It is okay to eat meat because it is nourishing, or a criticism, such as, Eating meat *should* be considered immoral. In addition to descriptive ethics and normative ethics, there is a third ethical approach, *metaethics.* Metaethics does not describe or evaluate but analyzes the *meaning* of the moral terms we use. Some typical questions would be, But what do you mean by immoral? What do you mean by meat—beef, horse, or snake, perhaps? Most ethical systems involve judgments, criticisms, evaluations, and justifications,

and are thus normative, but many systems also require an awareness of the terms used to justify the theory. Any time a moral debate moves into a discussion about the meaning of terms, it moves into the area of metaethics. A current example would be the debate about terrorism: At the level of descriptive ethics, one would establish the existence and frequency of terrorist plots and assaults; at the normative level, one would usually condemn such assaults, or perhaps question their justification; at the metaethical level one would engage in a discussion about the meaning of such words as *terrorism, justification, patriotism, appeasement, pacifism, courage,* and others. In fact, it is hard to engage in a meaningful debate about a concept such as terrorism without engaging in all three levels. In Chapter 13 you'll find examples of discussions about terrorism involving metaethics as well as normative and descriptive ethics.

way. Benedict concludes, "The concept of the normal is properly a variant of the concept of the good. It is that which society has approved."

Two things are worth mentioning here. First, Benedict is taking a giant leap from expressing *cultural* relativism to expressing *ethical* relativism. She moves from a description of the people's behavior to the statement that it is normal and thus good for them to behave this way—in their own cultural context. Second, Benedict is saying that normalcy is culturally defined; in other words, cultures, especially isolated cultures, often seem to develop some behaviors to an extreme. (For Benedict the range of possible human behavior is enormous, extending from paranoia to helpfulness and generosity.) Those individuals who somehow can't conform (and they will always be the minority, because most people are very pliable) become the abnormals in that culture.

Is the behavior of the Northwest Coast people totally alien to us? Benedict thinks not, because it constitutes *abnormal* behavior in our own society, not *unthinkable* behavior. We might illustrate her idea with some examples. The postal worker who has been fired and who shows up the next day with a shotgun and kills a number of his coworkers is "crazy" to us, but he actually is following the same logic as the chief: His world has been torn apart by powers over which he has no control, and he is retaliating against the affront. The driver who cuts you off on the freeway because she had a fight with her husband is doing the same thing; so was the little girl who ripped a button off your coat in grade school because someone else ripped

Ruth Benedict (1887–1948), American anthropologist and defender of ethical relativism. Her best-known work is *Patterns of Culture* (1934).

a button off her coat. There is no question of vengeance, because neither the driver nor the little girl was looking to punish a guilty party. The seven men and two children had nothing to do with the deaths of the chief's relatives, and the chief never said they did. It is not a matter of seeking out the cause of the problem, of gaining retribution; rather, it is an experience of healing a wound by wounding someone else. (What if the strangers who were killed had been American or Canadian loggers who had grown up in a culture that believes it is proper to find and punish whoever is guilty? Then we'd see retribution.) Perhaps we all take it out on someone innocent from time to time; some of us probably do it more often than others. The difference is that we've chosen to call what the Northwest Coast people did *abnormal*, whereas they, in the context of their tribal civilization, considered their actions to be normal. How do such choices evolve? Usually it is a matter of habits developing over time. If there is such a thing as a "normal" way for humans to behave, it is to adjust to the pattern of normalcy that prevails in their particular culture. Today, sociologists would call this process *acculturation.*

Although Benedict obviously wants her readers to approach other cultures with more tolerance for customs alien to them, her choice of examples may seem odd to a modern, culturally sensitive reader: Is Benedict, in giving this account of a tribe of American Indians, actually helping to cement the old notions popular in white Western culture of the "savage Indian"? If so, she is not furthering any mutual intercultural understanding. There are two things to say here: (1) Benedict herself might answer with something like, "If you read this account as a criticism of Indian customs, then it is just because you are seeing it through the eyes of a prejudiced Westerner. The whole point is to recognize cultural differences as being equally meaningful within their cultural contexts." We should not shy away from noticing differences—but we should not judge them either. (2) As readers looking at the disadvantages as well as the advantages of ethical relativism, we must conclude that relativism does not have as its goal any mutual *understanding*—merely noninterference. Trying to achieve an understanding requires us to find some common ground, and relativism does not allow for any intercultural common ground. We return to the question of common ground later in this chapter.

For Benedict there is no sense in imposing Western morals on another culture, because Western morals are just one aspect of the range of possible human behavior that we have chosen to elaborate; they are no better or no worse than anyone else's morals. Whatever is normal for us we think of as good, and we have no right to claim that our choice is better than any other culture's. A novel which in many ways advocates this approach to other cultures is Barbara Kingsolver's *The Poisonwood Bible,* and you will find an excerpt from it in the Narratives section of this chapter.

Problems with Ethical Relativism

Given the overwhelming intolerance for other cultures and customs that is displayed from time to time by Western civilization (a stance some refer to as "cultural imperialism"), many people find something very appealing and refreshing about ethical relativism. And we shouldn't forget to see it in its proper historical perspective: It served as an antidote to nineteenth-century "Eurocentrism" and Western colonialism, in which the notion of Western religious and moral superiority (in addition to the technological superiority of the West) had been considered an obvious truth. Ethical relativism broke away from this self-congratulatory attitude and became the inspiration for a shift toward cultural tolerance in the early part of the twentieth century, an attitude that continues in today's United States, with its plurality of cultural and ethnic heritages. Increasingly, throughout the twentieth century, it seemed of doubtful virtue among American intellectuals to impose a particular brand of acculturation on another group that believed it was doing just fine with its own set of moral rules. So many cultures in the nineteenth century had suffered precisely because of this attitude, from American Indians to Asian Indians, and many non-European cultures in between. For many Americans, the fundamental acceptance of the fact that other cultures had a right to be different was so ingrained that when a young American male was caned by the authorities in Singapore in the 1990s for spraying graffiti on cars, the overall reaction was that if he chose to live in Singapore, he should not break its rules, and ought to be punished according to its rules—a modern "When in Rome, do as the Romans do" attitude. And it cuts both ways: When people from elsewhere visit the United States, we expect from them that they respect our ways of life: A young single mother from Denmark visited her American boyfriend with her baby in New York City some years back and did what she was used to doing in Denmark: The couple had dinner in a New York restaurant at ground level, and she put the baby carriage outside *with the baby in it* and got a table by the window so she could watch the baby. When she was arrested for reckless child endangerment, she was puzzled: "But we do this all the time at home!" she said. I can attest to that personally, having grown up in Denmark. Indeed, babies (in their carriages) and dogs on their leashes are left outside stores and restaurants all the time, in the summer, at least in the smaller towns. But not in New York City! What has become known as the *cultural differences argument* didn't cut it with the judge—her lawyer's argument that she should have a right to do what she used to was dismissed, and she was sent back to Denmark with her baby, presumably never to come back.

So it appears that we have taken the method of problem solving suggested by ethical relativism to heart. And yet—even prior to September 11—some people (who

Calvin and Hobbes   by Bill Watterson

Bill Watterson's comic strip, *Calvin and Hobbes* had a knack for putting its finger on tricky philosophical issues, especially in the fields of ethics and metaphysics. Here Hobbes, the stuffed tiger that only Calvin can see move, speculates that the demand for tolerance in ethical relativism may not be all that much of an advantage.

weren't necessarily hard universalists, either) questioned the noninterference ethics of relativism. What if the culture in question sells children into the sex trade? What if it refuses women the right to vote and own property? And, post–September 11, what if other cultures believe that Americans are fair targets for terrorism everywhere? Are these beliefs and customs just a matter of their moral choices, which should be respected, or do we have a moral right—perhaps even a moral obligation—to step in and effect changes? This is the big issue that is challenging ethical relativism at the beginning of the twenty-first century.

Six Problems with Ethical Relativism

Even if we grant that ethical relativism provided a positive lesson in the early twentieth century, suggesting the suspension of Western judgmental attitudes toward other cultures, there are serious problems within the theory. Here we look at six problems, all of them logical consequences of the basic idea of ethical relativism that there is no universal moral code. (Box 3.3 is a general overview of examining and testing theories.)

    1. No Criticism or Praise of Other Cultures Does this mean that it is always wrong to criticize another culture or group for what it does? If we are to follow the idea of ethical relativism to its logical conclusion, yes. We have no right to criticize other cultures, period. But on occasion things happen in other cultures that we feel, either by instinct or through rational argument, we *should* criticize in order to maintain our own moral integrity. Curiously enough, at the time Benedict wrote her article (1934), one of the most offensive social "experiments" in history was being conducted in the Western world. Europe was being overtaken by the Nazis, whose

Box 3.3 HOW TO TEST A THEORY

What we are doing in this text is following standard philosophical procedure. We test a theory by pounding at it with hypothetical and actual situations until we see whether it still makes sense. It is not unlike the procedure of testing a presidential candidate. When the going gets tough and all the nasty (but usually reasonable and relevant) questions are asked, we see what kind of character the candidate has. Is he or she arrogant? Weak? Capable of a sense of humor? Vindictive? Intelligent? Stupid? Lying? Truthful? Honest? Strong? What is the breaking point of the candidate? In the same way, we seek the breaking point of a theory. As you will see, almost every theory

does have a breaking point, but this does not always disqualify the theory (that is, render it invalid). If the breaking point comes late in the discussion and only when the theory is attacked by an extremely unlikely hypothesis or by trifles, this speaks well for the theory and encourages acceptance or perhaps only a minor rewrite of the theory. Some theories, however, break early in the discussion and can be discarded. Ethical relativism is a theory with a fairly late breaking point; in other words, there are some good things to be said for the theory, which is a good reason not to discard it altogether.

extreme racism was not kept secret, even though the existence of the death camps of later years was not generally known until after the war. A true ethical relativist would have had to stick to her guns and maintain that other countries had no right to criticize what was going on in Germany and Austria in the 1930s and 1940s. (As it happens, this pretty much mirrored the actual attitude of the rest of the world at the time.) Benedict, however, mentions nothing about this issue in her paper.

People often say, in retrospect, that someone should have protested against or intervened in a particular situation while there was still time. Indeed, this was one of the arguments for going into Iraq in 2003: that Saddam Hussein had the makings of a Middle Eastern Hitler and needed to be stopped while there was still time. In the case of the war in Afghanistan, the relativist might have approved, provided the goal was stopping terrorists from attacking other nations, such as our own, but not if the goal was to put an end to the Taliban regime. In the war in Iraq, the issue is even more complex: If the goal was exclusively to find and destroy WMDs, weapons of mass destruction (which were not found by the time of this writing, at least not in large quantities), the relativist might find the invasion acceptable, because it would stop aggression toward other countries. However, if the goal was primarily a regime change, toppling Saddam Hussein and creating a democracy, the relativist would not approve, regardless of how much the living conditions would improve for Iraqis, in the short or the long run, because it would be interfering with the internal affairs of a sovereign country. To put it graphically, if Saddam Hussein tortured Iraqis and attempted genocide on certain groups, that would be an internal matter for the Iraqis themselves to deal with. In the eyes of the relativist we are against genocide only because it happens to be against the norms of our own culture; for another culture, genocide may be right.

For most people, however, even those believing they ought to be tolerant, there are moral limits to tolerance, and any theory that doesn't recognize this is just not a good theory. Most Western people, as tolerant as they might like to be, would prefer to see certain things come to an end: In China there are reports of female infanticide, a result of a strict one-child-per-family policy; in several cultures, primarily on the African continent, female genital mutilation is practiced, usually on young girls of seven to eight years of age. A report issued by the United Nations in 2000 suggests that many of these countries have recently outlawed female genital mutilation, but the practice still exists. At the end of this chapter you will find a summary of a novel that deals with this issue: Alice Walker's *Possessing the Secret of Joy.* In Sudan in 2000 the government issued a decree that women could no longer study at the universities, nor use their education in Sudanese society, because it was seen as impermissible by the Sudanese reading of the Koran. Professional women found themselves reduced to making a living doing manual labor.

In Afghanistan from 1996 to 2001, a brief period of time that must have seemed like an eternity to those victimized by the policy, the Taliban government deprived all women of their rights to freedom of movement, education, work, health care, and other essentials. Women were forced to wear a head-to-toe garment, the burka, which allowed only a limited vision through an embroidered net covering their eyes. *Beneath the Veil* (2001), a documentary secretly filmed by a British-Afghani journalist, Saira Shah, and a follow-up, *Unholy War,* told the world of women being beaten in the streets by the Taliban police for showing any skin and for wearing white socks or squeaky shoes, in an apparent attempt to eliminate the presence of women in public. Women and men were summarily executed in the football stadium, to the cheers of the all-male crowd. Hearing of such conditions, can one morally remain a relativist, holding that each culture must be left in peace to explore its own values? Many ethical relativists have felt that a line must be drawn between mere cultural preferences and assaults on human rights—but that means giving up on ethical relativism. However, when issues such as equal rights for women are raised in the United Nations, representatives of those cultures that do not recognize rights for women often respond with indignation, asserting that the West is merely doing what it has always done, trying to superimpose its cultural and moral values on other peoples in the old tradition of cultural imperialism. Although ethical relativism wanted to put an end to the wholesale export of Western values, the theorists have reached a critical point: Many people may agree with relativists that there is no need or excuse for the West to try to dictate every aspect of what other nations should think or do, but in extreme situations many of us would like to reserve the right to speak up for people in other parts of the world who can't (or aren't allowed to) speak up for themselves. We want to believe that we have the right to complain about governments that do not respect human rights and that abuse a part of their population; and, in fact, pressure on such governments has at times yielded results. South Africa is not the bastion of segregation it used to be, and the concept of human rights is not alien to the Russian media or Russian leaders any longer.

Not only are we prevented from criticizing another culture's doings if we accept the teachings of relativism, but we also cannot praise and learn from that culture. If we find that the social system of Scandinavia is more humane and functions better than any other in the world, the conclusion based on relativism has to be that this is because it is right for them, but we still can't assume that it is right for us. If we happen to admire the work ethic of Japan, we can't learn from it and adapt it to our own culture, nor can Jainism's teachings of nonviolence have anything to say to us. In short, ethical relativism, when taken to its logical conclusion, precludes learning from other cultures because there can be no "good" or "bad" that is common to all cultures. Curiously, this doesn't mean that all ethical relativists would actually *forbid* us to learn from other cultures or to criticize others—on the contrary, ethical relativists think of themselves as very tolerant and open-minded. The problem is in the logic of the theory itself: When it is applied to real-life situations as a moral principle, it reveals itself to have certain limitations.

2. Majority Rule The isolation of moral values to the conventions of specific cultural groups has another curious effect: It forces us to bow to *majority rule*. Remember that ethical relativism does not say there are *no* moral rules—only that the rules of each society are proper and valid for that society. What if you live in a society and don't agree with the rules? Then you must, ipso facto, be wrong, because we know that the rules that are morally good in a society are those rules that are in effect. If you disagree with those rules, you must be wrong. This makes it impossible to disagree with any rules that exist, and therefore civil disobedience is out of the question. In Iran, if you disagree with the fundamentalist Islamic rules of punishment, then you are wrong. It is, in fact, right and proper in Iran to amputate the hand of a thief. If you are an American and disagree with the general attitude against euthanasia and doctors who help patients commit suicide, then you are wrong, and the attitude of the majority is right—not because the attitude has been subjected to moral analysis but simply because it happens to be the attitude of the majority. It does not work, either, to point to a historical precedent and say that things were not always done as they are now, because ethical relativism cuts through time as well as space. There are no universal values among different time periods, any more than there are common values among different cultures of the same era. In other words, that was then and this is now. For an intellectual tradition such as ours, which prides itself on valuing minority opinions and promotes the idea of moral progress, the idea that the attitude of the majority is always right simply is unacceptable.

3. Professed or Actual Morality? There is a further problem with the idea that a group's morality is determined by the majority or that a certain kind of behavior is normal, for what is "normal"? Is it the *professed* morality of the group or the *actual* morality? Imagine the following situation. The majority of a cultural group, when asked about their moral viewpoints, claim that they believe infidelity is wrong; however, in that particular society, infidelity is common practice. Does that mean the morality of the culture is what the majority say they ought to do or what they actually do? We might simply decide that it must be the *normative* rules that define the morality and not the actual behavior; however, Ruth Benedict assumed morality to be the same as majority *behavior*. If Benedict had implied that morality is the same as what people think they *ought* to do, then all our example would amount to would be to show that most people have a hard time living up to their own moral standards, which is hardly a novel observation. However, Benedict's theory of ethical relativism clearly states that "moral" is the same as "normal," meaning how the majority *actually* behave.

4. What Is a "Majority"? Ethical relativism involves a practical problem as well. Suppose the question of doctor-assisted suicide had been determined by a referendum and the law against it overturned in your state. (The only state in the nation that allowed euthanasia in 2004 was Oregon.) The majority now believe it is right for doctors to help terminally ill patients die. It was morally wrong the week before, but today it is morally right. By next year people may have changed their minds, and it will become morally wrong again. There is something very disconcerting about moral rightness being as arbitrary as that and depending on a vote, especially since so few people actually vote in elections. So who exactly is the majority? Most of the people? the registered voters? or the actual voters? And what about the individual states? They obviously are part of a larger unit, the United States, and the moral standards of this larger unit would define the morals of each singular state. But not all laws and customs are the same from state to state, and what is considered morally wrong by the majority in one state may well be considered morally acceptable by the majority in another (such as abortion or doctor-assisted suicide). Therefore, might we instead want to allow for morally autonomous subgroups in which the majority within each group defines the moral rules, even if they are at odds with the larger cultural group? If we have large minority subgroups *within* a state and their moral values differ from those of the majority, should such groups constitute morally autonomous units that should not be criticized? (See Box 3.4.)

5. What Is a "Culture"?   Question 4 leads right into question 5, because ethical relativists have not explained exactly what they mean by a culture either. How can we know if something is the norm within a culture if it isn't clear what a culture is? What sets one culture off from other cultures? Is the United States one culture (as most foreigners believe)? or is it a collective of many smaller cultures, as many Americans see it? Is Europe one culture? Is Africa? Asia? Central or South America? Iraq contains at least three cultures, but it is one country. From the outside, perhaps, but once you see the regional differences, you'll know it's not so easy to focus on common denominators rather than on the differences.

What unifies a culture? It used to be *geography*: People living within the same area moved around only rarely and acquired the same general characteristics. But now people move all over the globe, join societies across borders as never before, and subscribe to newsletters and newsgroups on the Internet. Is it *ethnicity*? Historically people have tended to stick with others of their own ethnic background, but that seems to be partly a geographical limitation and partly a *cultural* choice (and culture is what we are trying to define). People who were brought up not to be bigoted choose partners, friends, and neighbors from outside their own ethnic group all the time, yet they still feel they are choosing within their culture. In my ethnically and racially diverse college classes, it always strikes me that, as diverse as we are, we generally have much more in common than we have with some people in our own families and neighborhoods, because the world of academia is our "culture"—our common experiences with classes and grades, studying and research, exams, and so forth create a cultural identity in itself. Is it *race*? When people were less mobile, people within a region generally formed a culture, and there was ethnic and racial cohesion in the group. But now we are (at least in the United States) moving toward a mixed-race society, and biologists and sociologists are beginning to question the very concept of race and to interpret it as an eighteenth-century invention. Therefore, the category of race can hardly be a firm foundation for a definition of culture. Is it *religion*? Places with one dominant (or one permitted) religion seem to be obvious candidates for a culture, but what about places in which people

Box 3.4 MORAL SUBJECTIVISM AND ETHICAL RELATIVISM: A COMPARISON

Sometimes the theory of moral subjectivism is listed as a subcategory of ethical relativism. You may recall that we placed it under the general heading of *moral nihilism* at the beginning of this chapter, because such theories deny that there can be any agreement about moral values based on something other than personal opinion. Ethical relativism is not a morally nihilistic theory because it holds that there are very strong reasons for agreeing about values within a culture precisely because they are values shared by that culture. However, there is definitely something "relative" about moral subjectivism, so we might say that it represents the transposition of "each culture is right in its own way" to "each person is right in his or her own way." This theory is an extremely tolerant theory, a "live and let live" attitude in which no one has the right to impose his or her moral viewpoints, including a preference for tolerance, on anyone else. It has its own severe flaws, however: For one thing, it cannot solve moral conflicts because there is no common value denominator to resort to. This means we can't hope to learn from other people's advice or even their mistakes because their values and situations will always differ slightly from ours. And because the theory can't solve moral conflicts, we have no moral weapon against what we personally consider unacceptable. How would you argue against Hitler's Holocaust from a subjectivist viewpoint? Against slavery? Child abuse? Female circumcision and other enforced mutilation rituals? The only thing you might say is that you *feel* these actions are wrong—but others can also feel and think any way they like. For most people this way of thinking is so excessively tolerant that it borders on an obscene lack of social responsibility.

Furthermore, as appealing as moral subjectivism may seem when we have just escaped the confines of the moral regulations of our childhood, it simply isn't intuitively sound. We may think we can "live and let live," but in actual fact we react *as if* there is a basic appeal to conflict-solving values. If you are a subjectivist and you see an adult at the supermarket repeatedly hitting a small crying child, are you going to be content telling yourself that you wouldn't do such a thing but that the adult in question is entitled to feel he or she is doing the right thing? Or would you try to appeal to some common value system by stepping in? Moral subjectivism is not only counterintuitive and impractical but also downright dangerous as a moral theory because it provides no social cohesion and no protection against the whims of those in power, whose "feelings" may be as legitimate as yours but whose ability to carry them out is far greater.

To summarize, the criticism of moral subjectivism is different from the criticism of ethical relativism in the following ways: (1) moral subjectivism cannot solve conflicts, but ethical relativism can (through majority rule), and (2) ethical relativism is problematic because it implies a moral majority rule, but moral subjectivism does not (because each person is right in his or her own way). What the two theories have in common is the relativity of moral values: The moral subjectivist has no right to call anyone else's values wrong or evil, and neither does the ethical relativist (when judging *other* cultures). So the challenge to both moral subjectivism and ethical relativism is the experience of something that is so egregiously against "common decency" or "our sense of humanity" that we must speak up, regardless of our modern tradition of tolerance toward others' life choices. Finding a universal foundation for criticism of traditions of female circumcision or ritual animal torture or child sacrifice is equally impossible from a basis of either moral subjectivism or ethical relativism.

tend to dress the same, see the same movies, buy the same groceries, and drive the same cars but have different religions? Is it (as anthropologists might suggest) how we view *family relations*? Those categories also are not so stable anymore. And if we resort to vague categories of habits, worldviews, tastes, and so forth, all we end up with is a classification of people according to some criteria, whereas other criteria may cut across those same groups. If an ethical relativist insists that as long as we can identify some form of cultural cohesion, then that group should not be interfered with in its moral practices, we run into horrible problems.

Some ethnic groups in the United States differ from the majority in their views about male–female relationships, about using for food animals that others consider pets, about contraception and abortion, about the rights of fathers to punish their families. How large do such groups have to be in order to be considered morally right in their own ways? If we are generous and tolerant relativists, perhaps we'll say that any large ethnic group should be considered morally autonomous. But would that mean the Mafia could be considered such a subgroup? or neighborhood gangs? Would society then have to accept a plurality of "laws," each governing the sub-groups, with no higher means of control? The relativist might accept that one set of laws—federal ones, for instance—would be above all other laws, but it would still be an extremely complicated matter, with possible contradictions arising between what the national law says and what the gang law says. Could we eventually end up in a situation in which acts such as looting are morally right for some because of their subgroup affiliation but not for others? In the Narratives section you'll find an excerpt from a science fiction novel, *Sideshow,* by Sheri S. Tepper, which very effec-tively explains some of the problems inherent in a moral philosophy that reveres cul-tural diversity simply because of diversity itself.

6. Can Tolerance Be a Universal Value? One of the best qualities of ethical relativism is its tolerance, although we've now seen that it can lead to problems. However, there is something problematic about the very claim of tolerance coming from a relativist, for is someone who believes in ethical relativism allowed to claim that tolerance is something everyone should have? In other words, can a relativist say that tolerance is *universally good*? If all values are culture-relative, then this con-dition must apply to tolerance as well. Tolerance may be good for us, but who is to say if it is good for other groups! This notion severely undermines the whole pur-pose of tolerance, which is not usually considered a one-way street. And what if the highest moral dictum of a certain culture is to superimpose its values on other cul-tures? Does relativism teach that we must respect a moral system that doesn't respect the morals of others? Western cultures of the past—and, some would say, even the present—have exported their own moral systems; the Communist bloc of the twen-tieth century sought expansion along those same principles; today, Muslim extrem-ism in some parts of the world also seeks this kind of expansion, combined with political ambitions. One could say, as some ethical relativists have attempted, that as long as they keep their moral (and perhaps even political and religious) expansion-ism within their own borders, they have a right to think whatever they want—but the problem is that the moral focus of certain cultures is precisely to export itself to other places. Not only does ethical relativism not have a right to claim that tolerance is universally good, since it also claims that there are no universal values, but it also can't even give a practical answer as to how to deal with moral, religious, and political expansionism.

Refuting Ethical Relativism

The "Flat Earth" Argument

Now we have seen why many people believe that ethical relativism doesn't have enough to offer to be adopted 100 percent; it is a theory with immense theoretical and practical problems. For some critics, the *logic* of the key argument proposed by ethical relativism is faulty. Let us assume that the culture "up north" believes that abortion is morally wrong, whereas the culture "down south" believes it to be morally permissible. The relativist concludes that because there is a disagreement between the two groups, neither can be right in an absolute sense. But surely, the critics say, that is not so; some things are simply true or false. We may have had a disagreement in the past about whether the earth is round or flat. (Indeed, the Flat Earth Society today is upholding that tradition by claiming that all space reports and photos from space missions are fraudulent and were concocted in a movie studio.) However, that doesn't mean there is no correct answer; the idea that the earth is round is a verifiable fact. We may be able to verify that some moral codes are objectively right and others are wrong.

The trouble with this critique is that it is easy to verify that the earth is round; all we have to do is look at how things gradually disappear over a flat horizon. But how exactly would you go about verifying that abortion is objectively right or wrong? That would bring us into a much bigger discussion of the very nature of moral truths, which would be no help at all in determining whether ethical relativism is right. The flat earth example is, of course, not supposed to be taken that far. All it shows is that you can't conclude, on the basis of there being a disagreement, that both parties are wrong. It is never as easy to find out who is right in a discussion of moral issues as it is to settle questions of geography.

The Problem of Induction

Some critics believe that the very foundation of the ethical relativism theory is wrong; they believe it simply is not true that there is no universal moral code. If relativists were asked how they know that there is no universal moral code, they would answer that they looked around and found none or possibly that, given the diversity of human nature, there never will be one. This begs the question, though, because we might reasonably suggest that they should look around a bit longer and refrain from making absolute statements about the future. Blanket statements bring on their own undoing, because any theory based on collecting evidence faces a classic problem: *the problem of induction.*

Induction is one of two major scientific methods; the other is deduction. In deductive thinking we start with an axiom that we believe is true, and we apply this axiom to establish the validity of other axioms, or we apply the theory to specific cases. In inductive thinking we gather empirical evidence in order to reach a comprehensive theory. Ethical relativism is an example of inductive thinking; it bases its general theory that there are no universal moral codes on evidence from particular cultures. The problem of induction is that we never can be sure that we have looked hard enough to gather all possible evidence.

As an example of the problem of induction we're going to look at a phenomenon that is well known to anyone watching court cases on TV or just about any crime show from *CSI* to *Law and Order* and crime scene documentaries: the gathering of evidence at a murder scene. The detectives gather evidence according to a preliminary hypothesis: that this is a homicide, not a suicide or a natural death. (And if they can't determine this from the start, they keep all interpretations open.) They gather what looks to them like evidence, usually casting a wide net, and this evidence goes to the district attorney, who decides whether to file a case. In other words, the detectives reach a theory of the identity of the killer based on the evidence they gather—they don't gather evidence based on a theory of who-dun-it, or at least this is the way it is supposed to work. (That theory would have been *de*duction. It would also shape a biased investigation. In other words, Sherlock Holmes was great at, not deduction, but *induction*!) So, theoretically, the evidence is presented in court, and the jury decides whether it points to guilt or whether there is reasonable doubt. But what if a piece of evidence was overlooked? Blood spatter in a corner—or a fingerprint or a hair, or blood, or semen, belonging to someone other than the defendant? Or something that, to a forensic scientist decades down the line, would be hard evidence but has no significance for today's scientists? Something like DNA prior to the mid-1980s? Or an eyewitness who left town without knowing she saw something important? These are factors that can't be completely controlled. And then there are the ones that *can* be controlled—such as a forensic scientist deliberately skewing the test results in favor of the prosecution. Either way, we are looking at a real problem of induction: Because we are dealing with empirical science—gathering evidence and building a theory—we can't be 100 percent certain when we have gathered enough material. Induction is a fine method and yields magnificent scientific results. We couldn't do without it—but it is not 100 percent accurate. Fortunately, in natural science as in court cases, even in murder cases, we don't have to be mathematically 100 percent certain in order to have a working theory or to be legally and morally certain: Circumstantial evidence, if there is a lot of it, and nothing points elsewhere, is the accepted standard for finding someone guilty. Anything can be doubted—but not everything can be the subject of *reasonable* doubt. But as the Innocence Project, headed by Barry Scheck, has shown, there are people on death row who are, in fact, innocent of the crimes they are convicted of, because of the problem of induction: Evidence was overlooked or not available at the time, such as DNA tests, or (in a few nefarious cases) exculpatory evidence was not introduced in court. In Chapter 13 we take a closer look at the death penalty and such problems.

Now what does this have to do with ethical relativism? Everything—because the method of investigation used by the relativist to claim there are no universal moral codes is the method of induction. The Greeks and the Callatians—different codes. The Northwest Coast Indians, the Tibetan noncompetitive people, all point to the absence of a universal moral code. So can we know, with 100 percent certainty, on the basis of collected evidence, that there are no universal codes? No. We have to leave it open; perhaps some day a universal code will appear—or perhaps we will find that it had been there all the time, and we just didn't see it.

Soft Universalism

The clue to toppling ethical relativism actually lies very close, and perhaps that is why ethical relativists haven't seen it. Remember King Darius, who tried to get the Greeks to eat their dead and the Callatians to burn theirs? You may have asked yourself why any group would want to eat its dead. You may have wanted to ask Ruth Benedict why the Northwest Coast Indians were so aggressive (she doesn't say). We all may wonder why some peoples approve of infanticide or of dismemberment as punishment. As soon as we ask why, though, we have left the realm of ethical relativism. Relativists don't ask why; they just look at different customs and pronounce them fine for those who hold them. In asking why, we are looking for an explanation, one we can understand from our own point of view. In other words, we are expecting, or hoping, that there is some point at which that other culture will cease to seem so strange. And very often we reach that point. For instance, disposing of the dead through cannibalism is not at all uncommon, and it usually is done for the sake of honoring the dead or sharing in their spiritual strength. It would seem, then, that the Greeks and Callatians had something in common after all: The Greeks burned their dead because they wanted to honor their spirits, and the Callatians ate their dead for the same reason. Some nomad tribes of the Sahara consider it bad manners to eat in front of their in-laws. American couples rarely talk about sexual matters in the presence of their in-laws for the same reason—it is considered bad manners. These cultures share some common values: Both value good family relationships, and both express embarrassment when a transgression occurs.

The idea that all cultures have at least some values in common, even if they are buried beneath layers of different behavior patterns, is what I called *soft universalism* at the beginning of this chapter. The idea is not new; it was suggested by the Scottish philosopher David Hume in the eighteenth century. Hume believed that all people share a fellow-feeling, a compassion, that may show itself in different ways but that is present in all cultures nevertheless.

The philosopher James Rachels suggests that at least three values are universal:

1. A policy of caring for enough infants to ensure the continuation of the group
2. A rule against lying
3. A rule against murder

We may be horrified to learn about the custom of killing female babies in the old Eskimo (Inuit) culture, Rachels says, but we gain a better understanding when we learn that female babies were killed only because a high death rate among male hunters led to a surplus of females in the community. Why would it be a bad thing for an Inuit tribe to have more women than men? Certainly not because the women were unproductive—in addition to raising children and cooking, they were the ones manufacturing tools and clothing from the animals brought home by the hunters—but because male hunters were the sole providers of food (the Inuit diet is primarily meat). Therefore, a shortage of men in relation to the number of women would mean a shortage of food. Another important fact is that babies were killed only during hard times and only if adoptive parents couldn't be found. In such times, if the babies had been kept alive, the lives of the older children would have been in jeopardy. In other words, the Inuit killed some infants in order to protect the children they already had. Their culture valued what ours values: caring for the babies we already have.

Why do all cultures have a rule against lying? Because if you can't expect a fellow citizen to tell the truth most of the time, there is no use attempting to communicate, and without communication human society would grind to a halt. This doesn't mean, obviously, that humans never lie to one another, but only that, on the whole, the acceptable attitude is one of truthfulness.

The rule against murder derives from similar reasoning: If we can't expect our fellow citizens not to kill us, we will not want to venture outdoors, we will stop trusting in people, and society will fall apart (not, as some might think, because everyone will be killed off, but because of general mistrust and lack of communication). Rachels believes that even under chaotic circumstances small groups of friends and relatives would band together, and within these groups the nonmurder rule would be upheld.

The only trouble with the last two rules is that they seem to apply to "fellow citizens" only. As a member of society, you are expected not to lie to or murder members of your own social group, but there is really nothing preventing you from being morally free to lie through your teeth to an outsider or to an enemy government. You may even be free to prey on and murder members of other tribes, gangs, or countries. A scandal in the discipline of anthropology illustrates this phenomenon in a way that is quite significant: The renowned anthropologist Margaret Mead (1901–1978), who was a student of Franz Boas and Ruth Benedict, and like them an ethical relativist, wrote a book about the sexuality of young South Sea islanders, *Coming of Age in Samoa* (1928), which became a best-seller. But in the 1980s it became clear that she had been the victim of a hoax: Her native contacts in Samoa had strung her along to see how many whopping lies she'd swallow before she became suspicious—but she was young and gullible. It appears that with some additional research Mead could have discovered this for herself, but she never did. So even though the Samoans certainly had an overall rule against lying within their culture (which we know because one of Mead's contacts felt she ought to 'fess up when she was in her eighties), it didn't necessarily extend to the inexperienced young anthropologist.

Besides, is it true that we are expected to tell the truth? Many would challenge this idea across the board of world cultures. In some cultures it is considered good manners to lie, to play down one's own accomplishments (such as the Chinese tradition of berating one's own cooking skills), not to tell the whole truth about a friend's appearance if she or he asks your opinion, to lie about sexual relationships to protect those involved (the notion of chivalry is sometimes invoked). In folklore there is even a tradition of telling "whoppers," and American Western folklore contains many prime examples of "tall tales." The frontiersman David ("Davy") Crockett was elected to Congress in 1827 not just because he was a likable and conscientious man but because

James Rachels (1941–2003), American philosopher and advocate of human and animal rights. He was the author of *Elements of Moral Philosophy* (1968), *The End of Life: Euthanasia and Morality* (1986), *Created from Animals: The Moral Implications of Darwinism* (1990), and *Can Ethics Provide Answers?* (1997). He completed his last two books only shortly before he died: *The Truth About the World* and *Problems from Philosophy,* both with the publication date 2005.

he told better whoppers than his opponent (and had the grace to freely admit that he had been lying). So although it may not be true that a rule against lying is universal, if we characterize it as a rule against malicious deception we are closer to what Rachels means: Without that trust, your network of communications will break down.

Another problem with Rachels's three rules lies in the fact that, whatever rules may apply to a given culture, the *leaders* of those cultures, who should embody the cultural standards, are often the ones who break those rules. If it was to a leader's advantage to bend or break a rule, he or she might even consider it a duty to the throne to do so. Only in the twentieth century did the concept of rulers' not being above the law become solidified (to the extent that some leaders have to deal with civil lawsuits during their time-limited reign rather than face charges afterward). Even the near-universal ban on incest, which might well qualify as a fourth universal value, has traditionally been broken by leaders such as the pharaohs of ancient Egypt, who would marry their own siblings, and the royal families of Europe in previous centuries, who sometimes matched up first cousins because nobody else with "blue blood" was available.

Rachels has not provided us with any rules that apply universally, only with rules that all responsible people seem to be required to stick to *within their own societies*. Rachels has, however, provided all we need to show that ethical relativism is wrong in its assumption that cultures have nothing in common; we don't have to find a universal moral rule, just a universal pattern of behavior. Because Rachels believes that there are at least three such patterns—care of infants, not lying, and not murdering—we can call him a *descriptive soft universalist:* He describes what he thinks is the case, that we actually have some codes of behavior in common. But even if you can't find any codes in common, you might still be a *normative soft universalist.* In that case you believe we *ought* to have some code of behavior in common and that we ought to work toward establishing or finding such a code. You can, of course, be both a descriptive and a normative soft universalist. In that case you believe human beings around the world do have a few basic moral codes in common; but you also believe that in order to move toward a world community in which we can respect one another's differences while striving to work together to solve problems, we ought to find some common ground and set up a basic moral code for humanity to live by, a code such as the concept of human rights.

In the end, the soft universalist may point out that since the relativist's position is logically impossible in that he or she wants universal tolerance but can't have it because of not believing in universal values, so ethical relativism is in fact disingenuous, because it doesn't take itself seriously as a theory—it is an armchair exercise. In a clash of cultures where your own culture is under attack—do you choose to defend it just because it's yours? No, you defend it because you believe its values are good. And if you choose not to defend it, is it because you think nobody is right? Probably not—it is probably because you think the "other culture" has a point. And if you find yourself on trial in another country and (truly) consider yourself not guilty, would you want to be acquitted because of your cultural affiliation? Anything that leads to an acquittal will probably be welcome, but in the end, wouldn't you rather be cleared because you are *not guilty?* These basic situations reveal to the soft universalist that even if we may think we profess to ethical relativism, it can't be upheld when push comes to shove—in effect, like moral nihilism, moral skepticism, and moral subjectivism, it involves an internal contradiction, because as a matter of fact nobody really believes that each culture is right in its own way, and there are no common denominators. The bottom line for the soft universalist is the fact that *we are all mortal human beings,* with the same physical limitations and the same capacities for language, relationships, and pleasure and pain. Unless we're sociopaths, we all want what's best for our loved ones; we all want to live, unless by dying we serve some greater good (some take that further than others). We dread illness, cherish our good memories, and enjoy the company of our friends. We tell stories, and believe that ethics is indispensable to social life. How could we *not* have more in common than what divides us culturally? At the end of the chapter, you'll find an excerpt from Dwight Furrow's paper "Of Cave Dwellers and Spirits: The Trouble with Moral Absolutes," in which he seeks a middle ground between relativism and absolutism.

Ethical Relativism and Multiculturalism

With the increasingly pluralistic character of modern Western society comes an increasing belief that all cultural traditions and all perspectives represented in the public deserve to be heard—at universities, in politics, in the media, and elsewhere. Sometimes this is referred to as "multiculturalism," sometimes as "cultural diversity."

Let us consider multiculturalism and its goals. America used to be called a melting pot, meaning that there was room for anybody from anywhere, that all would be welcomed, and that after a while all individual cultural differences would subside in favor of the new culture of the United States. To many Americans (those from many different ethnic backgrounds, in fact) this continues to represent a beautiful image as well as an accurate description of what America is all about. For many people around the world this is what America seems to be. For others, however, the idea of the melting pot is a travesty, an illusion, and an insult. America may have embraced immigrants from countries such as England, Sweden, Ireland, and Germany, but many other people still feel as though they are living on the fringes of American society; they have not been accepted the way others have been. For such people, who feel that they and their ancestors were excluded from the melting pot because they were too different or simply unwanted, there is no such thing as a *common* American culture, only a *dominant* American culture; and they claim that what has been taught and practiced until recently has been *monoculturalism* (sometimes referred to as *Eurocentrism*). Today there is an understanding even among those from the "dominant culture" that this damages the very concept of an American culture. The question is what to do about it.

Some proponents of multiculturalism believe that what we must do is begin to listen to one another. I call this *inclusive multiculturalism* (also referred to as *pluralism*). The general idea is to integrate everyone—by law, if necessary—into all aspects of our society; to break through the "glass ceilings" that prevent people of color (women and men) as well as white women from reaching top positions; to become sensitized to what others might perceive as slurs (what one scholar calls *micro-inequities,* those little jabs that can hurt so deeply); and, if we are on the receiving end of such slurs, to learn to speak up for ourselves. An increased awareness of the multicolored pattern of our society will, the thinking goes, result in better working relationships, less of a sense that one cultural tradition dominates the country and that everyone who doesn't share it must be left out, and more tolerance and understanding among the groups. In the Primary Readings you'll find a text that illustrates this issue as it has been perceived in the United Kingdom: Bhikhu Parekh's "The Concept of Multicultural Education." This awareness is supposed to begin in schools, where children should learn about as many cultural groups in American society as possible. Adding multicultural awareness to the curriculum means there will be less time for some subjects that are usually taught, but proponents of inclusive multiculturalism believe that a growing cultural understanding is worth the price. Today, a new image is frequently offered as an alternative to the old image of the melting pot: the *salad bowl.* A metaphor for inclusive multiculturalism, the salad image implies that each group retains its original "flavor" but that the groups also relate to one another; together they make a sum that is greater than its parts. The metaphor can be stretched only so far, though: Critics who believe that inclusive multiculturalism is not doing enough to foster cultural identity can always turn the image around and ask, Who supplies the salad dressing? The "dominant culture"! (Box 3.5 examines how some advocates of cultural diversity apply what appears to be an ad hominem fallacy.)

For a while in the 1980s and 1990s a certain approach was attempted in some schools, but its popularity seems to have declined over the last decade: The method of *exclusive multiculturalism* (also called *particularism*) was intended to help children from minority cultures retain or regain their self-esteem, under the assumption that self-esteem is fragile for such children (which in itself might be a questionable assumption). To counteract this supposed lack of self-esteem, children from each ethnic group were isolated so they could be taught about the cultural advances of their particular group. Many parents as well as students felt uncomfortable about this approach, claiming that it led to a new form of segregation. And indeed, problems with the method of exclusive multiculturalism haven't quite been worked out to everyone's

Box 3.5   CULTURAL DIVERSITY OR CULTURAL ADVERSITY?

The idea that moral viewpoints acquire their importance from the groups that utter them rather than from their content is, to some philosophers, a misguided attitude. In the old days of Western culture, the dominant viewpoint was the one held by some—but not all—white males, and for most white males as well as for others that was enough to make the viewpoint "correct." Churches and political groups occasionally take the same attitude: The identity of the group is enough justification for the correctness of its views. Today we also see this same viewpoint applied socially by certain groups: If you are a member of an oppressed group, your viewpoint on right and wrong is valuable just because you are a member of that group, and if you are not, then your viewpoint is irrelevant. This form of relativism, which grants the importance of a viewpoint on the basis of gen-

der, race, and class, may be as misplaced as one that denies the importance of certain groups just because they are who they are. Such an attitude, the argument goes, reflects the logical fallacy of the *ad hominem argument:* You are right or wrong because of who you are, not because of what you say. In Jim Garrison's words from Oliver Stone's film *JFK,* "I always wondered in court why it is because a woman is a prostitute, she has to have bad eyesight" (meaning some people think that just because someone is a prostitute, we can't trust her testimony). Whether this attitude is assumed by those in power or by those who are dispossessed, it is equally faulty as a moral principle, according to the rules of critical thinking. Can you imagine situations in which a person's identity alone would determine whether he or she was right or wrong?

satisfaction: In a future society where mixed race and ethnicity are the rule rather than the exception, must a child then choose a primary racial or ethnic affiliation? And where would students of Euro-American ancestry be placed, regardless of whether they have majority or minority status—surely not in separate groups learning about the illustrious achievements of exclusively Euro-Americans? That would end up looking like white supremacy.

All in all, it seems that the inclusive approach to multiculturalism has become the standard method in primary and secondary schools. Since the early 1990s I have tried to keep track of the progress of an inclusive approach to American history in high schools, and in the fall of 2001, for the first time, more students in one of my classes (Introduction to Philosophy: Values) had been taught American history in high school according to inclusive multicultural principles than through history books reflecting a monocultural approach.

How might multiculturalism affect our attitude toward basic values in ethics? That depends greatly on what we believe those values to be. If we think our values can't be disputed, that they are somehow determined by God or by Nature, then we will find it hard to accept other and different viewpoints. As we will see, such absolutism ("hard universalism") usually does not allow for any tolerance of other basic ideas.

If we adopt the attitude of ethical relativism, the result may surprise us, because ethical relativism doesn't automatically support multiculturalism. Ethical relativism states that there is no universal moral code—that each culture will do what is right for it, and no other culture has any business interfering. This may work when cultures are separate and isolated from one another because the moral code in that case is defined as the code of the *dominant population*. Remember problem 2, "majority rule"? One of the problems with ethical relativism is precisely that it implies the moral rule of the majority. However, in our pluralistic society, this won't work because the "dominant culture" (white society) is increasingly reproached for displaying cultural insensitivity. Can ethical relativism function, therefore, in a country as diverse as ours, where we often find opposing values ("Looting is antisocial" versus "Looting is a righteous act for the dispossessed," for example) within the same neighborhood? Because a multicultural ethic asks us not to think in terms of one dominant set of rules, some might opt for an attitude of total *moral nihilism* instead: No values are better than any other values because no values are objectively correct. Such nihilism might well result in the breakdown of the fabric of a society, and possibly in a greater cohesion within subgroups, with different groups battling one another. Rather than describe these battles as gang wars, we might call this phenomenon *Balkanization*—when groups have nothing or very little in common except hatred for what the other groups stand for. It seems as though ethical relativism is not the answer to our new ethical problems of multiculturalism.

Suppose we look to soft universalism for the answer? If we are soft universalists we hope to be able to agree with others on some basic issues, but not on all issues. In the case of multiculturalism we may be able to agree on the promotion of general equality, tolerance, and cohesion in the nation (in other words, the will and ability to live together); we *have* to agree that what we want is a functioning society we all share in. If we don't agree on this, multiculturalism is a lost cause, and so is the whole idea of a United States. According to soft universalism, values can't be allowed to differ dramatically, so we wouldn't end up with acts such as looting being morally right for some and not for others, nor would the killing of family members for the sake of honor be acceptable in one neighborhood and not in another. These questions of common values in the context of a multicultural society are particularly burning, for without some values in common we simply won't have a society.

Is it possible to have one overall culture and several subcultural affiliations at the same time? In other words, can we have loyalties to our ancient ethnic roots and also be Americans (or Canadians, or Italians, or Brazilians, or whatever the case may be)? A few generations ago, immigrant parents made sure their children learned English and had American first names, encouraging them to blend in as quickly as possible so that their future as American citizens would have as few obstacles as possible—an obvious ethnic identity being considered an obstacle. A generation of children lost the language of their parents, and in many cases their family history, too. But over the past twenty-five years or so, people have been involved in looking for their roots, to a great extent inspired by Alex Haley's novel and television series *Roots* (1977), about an African American family's history. This trend has involved a renewed interest in teaching the new generation of children the language of their grandparents as a second language. One's cultural identity has been to a great extent perceived as formed through the original nationality of one's immigrant ancestors: one is "Irish-American," "Polish-American," "Chinese-American," and so forth—to the extent that the nationality to

Box 3.6   AN AMERICAN CULTURE?

When discussing the mores and habits of other cultures with my classes, I often hear students claim that there is no American culture—and if common denominators do exist, they are considered negative: brashness, ignorance or mistrust of other cultures, materialism, and so on. To many students, the fact that we are a very diverse society means that we have no shared culture; many consider themselves hyphenated Americans: Irish-Americans, African-Americans, Italian-Americans, Arab-Americans, and so forth. And yet in the weeks and months following the terrorist attacks of September 2001, many Americans, including many of my students, discovered that they had an American identity after all, and the loss of American lives felt like a personal loss. But the feelings of September 11 have receded for many, and as I am writing this, there is a great rift in the American populace. While the patriotism that surged after 9/11 hasn't gone away, it has taken on political colors. For some, pride in being an American is best expressed in being critical of the administration that took us into Iraq; for others, patriotic pride is linked to the concept that as a nation in war, we ought to present a united front. A commercial a few years ago lined up a number of people of different races and with different accents, all proudly proclaiming "I am an American." But what does that mean, other than citizenship?

If you agree that an American cultural identity exists, how would you characterize it? Is it founded in our Constitution? Is it a matter of a general outlook on life? Is it the fact that we, as

a matter of course, question authority? Does it have to do with common cultural experiences, common holidays and food rituals (such as Thanksgiving), a love of traveling within our country, and perhaps also with an image of ourselves that has been invented by the movies?

Or perhaps it is the very freedom to define oneself that other cultures seem to have only to a lesser degree? Many Americans don't realize what it means to be an American until they travel abroad and experience other cultures—or perhaps tangle with legal systems that do not presume one to be innocent until proven guilty! Rather (as in the Napoleonic Law of France), you are presumed guilty until you can prove yourself innocent.

In the event of a common threat from abroad, one's cultural identity seems to loom larger, in the form of an appreciation for everyday things we used to take for granted and for the rights this society grants us—even the right to disagree about this whole issue. The philosopher and novelist Ayn Rand (see Chapter 4), an immigrant from the Soviet Union, called America the only truly moral culture in the world. Some naturalized Americans believe they are better at identifying what it means to be an American than many natural-born citizens do, being appreciative of the Bill of Rights and the quintessential American quality of always being ready to reexamine an issue and "make things right"—even when it involves profound self-criticism.

the left of the hyphen has seemed, to some, to outweigh the second identity: American. This is what has spawned the expression "hyphenated American"—someone who sees himself or herself as having a composite heritage and perhaps also a split cultural identity. Does this mean you have to identify with some ancient ethnic heritage because there really isn't any American cultural identity per se? Box 3.6 explores what it might mean to have an American identity. In the aftermath of the terrorist at-

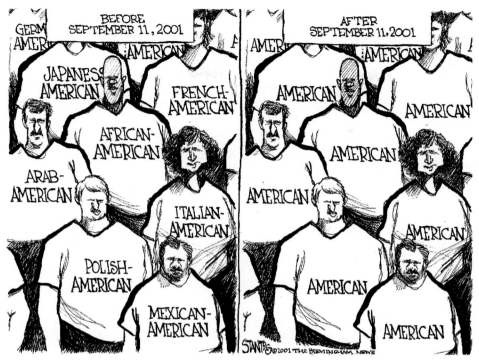

©2001 Scott Stantis. Reprinted by permission of Copley News Service

For many Americans, September 11 brought about a reevaluation of what it means to have a national and ethnic identity. Does this cartoon reflect your post-9/11 feelings about your nationality and ethnicity? Why or why not? Have we reverted to the first panel? Should we?

tacks of 2001, a new generation may have found, on its own, an answer to what it means to be an American. It doesn't mean disregarding one's ethnicity or ancient national roots—but it does mean that to many the common denominator of being American outweighs the individual differences.

Study Questions

1. Describe the four major approaches to moral differences outlined at the beginning of this chapter. Which one comes closest to your own viewpoint? Explain.

2. Discuss Ruth Benedict's claim that what is normal for a culture is what is moral in that culture. Discuss the advantages and problems associated with the theory of ethical relativism.

3. Discuss James Rachels's three suggested universal values: Are they truly universal? Why or why not? Can you think of other universal values not mentioned?

4. Can one have both an ethnic and a national identity? Explain.

Primary Readings and Narratives

The first Primary Reading is an excerpt from Ruth Benedict's famous paper "Anthropology and the Abnormal." The second is an excerpt from Dwight Furrow's paper, "Of Cave Dwellers and Spirits: The Problem with Moral Absolutes," where he seeks an alternative approach to both moral relativism and absolutism. The third excerpt comes from Bhikhu Parekh's "The Concept of a Multicultural Education," in which he argues that a monocultural education is harmful to children. The Narratives include a summary with excerpts from Barbara Kingsolver's *The Poisonwood Bible,* a novel pitting a Christian missionary and his family against traditional African customs, written as a critique of absolutist ethics; next, you'll find a summary of Alice Walker's novel *Possessing the Secret of Joy,* which indirectly—but powerfully—criticizes ethical relativism's tolerance toward the tribal practice of female circumcision; a summary of and excerpt from Sheri Tepper's novel *Sideshow* about excessive respect for traditions; and a summary of Spike Lee's film *Do the Right Thing,* which explores multiracial tensions and relationships in a Brooklyn neighborhood.

 Primary Reading

Anthropology and the Abnormal

RUTH BENEDICT

1934. Excerpt.

In her famous paper, Benedict talks about a Melanesian culture displaying extreme fears of poisoning. In addition, you'll read in her own words her view that morality is merely what is considered normal in a given society.

> The most spectacular illustrations of the extent to which normality may be culturally defined are those cultures where an abnormality of our culture is the cornerstone of their social structure. It is not possible to do justice to these possibilities in a short discussion. A recent study of an island of northwest Melanesia by Fortune describes a society built upon traits which we regard as beyond the border of paranoia. In this tribe the exogamic groups look upon each other as prime manipulators of black magic, so that one marries always into an enemy group which remains for life one's deadly and unappeasable foes. They look upon a good garden crop as a confession of theft, for everyone is engaged in making magic to induce into his garden the productiveness of his neighbors'; therefore no secrecy in the island is so rigidly insisted upon as the secrecy of a man's harvesting of his yams. Their polite phrase at the acceptance of a gift is, "And if you now poison me, how shall I repay you this present?" Their preoccupation with poisoning is constant; no woman ever leaves her cooking pot for a moment untended. Even the great affinal economic exchanges that are characteristic of this Melanesian culture area are quite altered

in Dobu since they are incompatible with this fear and distrust that pervades the culture. They go farther and people the whole world outside of their own quarters with such malignant spirits that all-night feasts and ceremonials simply do not occur here. They have even rigorous religiously enforced customs that forbid the sharing of seed even in one family group. Anyone else's food is deadly poison to you, so that communality of stores is out of the question. For some months before harvest the whole society is on the verge of starvation, but if one falls to the temptation and eats up one's seed yams, one is an outcast and a beachcomber for life. There is no coming back. It involves, as a matter of course, divorce and the breaking of all social ties.

Now in this society where no one may work with another and no one may share with another, Fortune describes the individual who was regarded by all his fellows as crazy. He was not one of those who periodically ran amok and, beside himself and frothing at the mouth, fell with a knife upon anyone he could reach. Such behavior they did not regard as putting anyone outside the pale. . . . But there was one man of sunny, kindly disposition who liked work and liked to be helpful. The compulsion was too strong for him to repress it in favor of the opposite tendencies of his culture. Men and women never spoke of him without laughing; he was silly and simple and definitely crazy. Nevertheless, to the ethnologist used to a culture that has, in Christianity, made his type the model of all virtue, he seemed a pleasant fellow.

These illustrations, which it has been possible to indicate only in the briefest manner, force upon us the fact that normality is culturally defined. An adult shaped to the drives and standards of either of these cultures, if he were transported into our civilization, would fall into our categories of abnormality. He would be faced with the psychic dilemmas of the socially unavailable. In his own culture, however, he is the pillar of society, the end result of socially inculcated mores, and the problem of personal instability in his case simply does not arise.

No one civilization can possibly utilize in its mores the whole potential range of human behavior. Just as there are great numbers of possible phonetic articulations, and the possibility of language depends on a selection and standardization of a few of these in order that speech communication may be possible at all, so the possibility of organized behavior of every sort, from the fashions of local dress and houses to the dicta of a people's ethics and religion, depends upon a similar selection among the possible behavior traits. In the field of recognized economic obligations or sex [taboos] this selection is as nonrational and subconscious a process as it is in the field of phonetics. It is a process which goes on in the group for long periods of time and is historically conditioned by innumerable accidents of isolation or of contact of peoples. In any comprehensive study of psychology, the selection that different cultures have made in the course of history within the great circumference of potential behavior is of great significance.

Every society, beginning with some slight inclination in one direction or another, carries its preference farther and farther, integrating itself more and more completely upon its chosen basis, and discarding those types of behavior that are uncongenial. Most of those organizations of personality that seem to us most incontrovertibly abnormal have been used by different civilizations in the very foundations of their institutional life. Conversely the most valued traits of our normal individuals have been looked on in differently organized cultures as aberrant. Normality, in short, within a very wide range, is culturally defined. It is primarily a term for the socially elaborated segment of human behavior in any culture; and abnormality, a term for the segment that that particular civilization does not use. The very eyes with which we see the problem are conditioned by the long traditional habits of our own society. . . .

. . . Mankind has always preferred to say, "It is morally good," rather than "it is habitual." . . . But historically the two phrases are synonymous. . . . The concept of the normal is properly a variant of the concept of good. It is that which society has approved. . . . Western civilization allows and culturally honors gratifications of the ego which according to any absolute category would be regarded as abnormal. The portrayal of unbridled and arrogant egoists as family men, as officers of the law, and in business has been a favorite topic of novelists, and they are familiar in every community. Such individuals are probably mentally warped to a greater degree than many inmates of our institutions who are nevertheless socially unavailable. They are extreme types of those personality configurations which our civilization fosters. . . .

The relativity of normality is important in what may some day come to be a true social engineering. Our picture of our own civilization is no longer in this generation in terms of a changeless and divinely derived set of categorical imperatives. We must face the problems our changed perspective has put upon us. In this matter of mental ailments, we must face the fact that even our normality is man-made, and is of our own seeking. Just as we have been handicapped in dealing with ethical problems so long as we held to an absolute definition of morality, so too in dealing with the problems of abnormality we are handicapped so long as we identify our local normalities with the universal sanities. I have taken illustrations from different cultures, because the conclusions are most inescapable from the contrasts as they are presented in unlike social groups. But the major problem is not a consequence of the variability of the normal from culture to culture, but its variability from era to era. This variability in time we cannot escape if we would, and it is not beyond the bounds of possibility that we may be able to face this inevitable change with full understanding and deal with it rationally. No society has yet achieved self-conscious and critical analysis of its own normalities and attempted rationally to deal with its own social process of creating new normalities within its next generation. But the fact that it is unachieved is not therefore proof of its impossibility. It is a faint indication of how momentous it could be in human society.

Study Questions

1. Is it important for Benedict to discover why the members of the tribe on the Melanesian island are afraid of poisoning? Why or why not? Would it make a difference in terms of ethical relativism if we knew the origin of the fear?

2. Is she right in her statement that "the concept of the normal is properly a variant of the concept of good"? Why or why not?

3. Does Benedict's cultural approach facilitate intercultural understanding? Why or why not?

4. Benedict is now viewed as one of the first spokespersons for ethical relativism, although her aim in this paper was to explore the concept of the abnormal. Her paper

ends with these rarely quoted words, exploring the possibility of intercultural standards of normalcy: "It is as it is in ethics: all our local conventions of moral behavior and of immoral are without absolute validity, and yet it is quite possible that a modicum of what is considered right and what wrong could be disentangled that is shared by the whole human race." Does this statement contradict the general view of Benedict as being an ethical relativist? Does it undermine the philosophy of ethical relativism? Is she contradicting herself? Why or why not?

Primary Reading

Of Cave Dwellers and Spirits: The Problem with Moral Absolutes

DWIGHT FURROW

Essay, 2004. Excerpt.

In this paper, American philosopher Dwight Furrow argues that students and others who find that moral absolutes are not a satisfactory response to today's problems go too far in the other direction when they embrace moral relativism instead. Furrow distinguishes between two forms of moral relativism—what you in this text have been introduced to as (1) moral subjectivism and (2) ethical relativism—and explains that the fact that few, if any, truly universal values have been found does not mean that all values are relative. In this section he explains why we often take recourse in what is legal, rather than what is moral. Toward the end of the excerpt he shares a vision of hope: that when push comes to shove, we respond to the needs of other human beings, regardless of theories of moral absolutism or relativism. (The reference to moral conscience in a cave refers to Plato's Myth/Allegory of the Cave, which you will find in Chapter 8.)

Our current cultural debate over values is often framed as a disagreement between those who prefer clear, unambiguous answers to moral questions, anchored in firm, unchanging moral principles, and those who think what is right depends on where you were raised. I have been arguing that neither side of this debate can support its position, and thus they contribute little but noise to our attempts to live and act well. Perhaps the deeper issue is whether either of these unsupportable positions causes any real harm. Does it make any practical difference whether one is a relativist or an absolutist? As I noted above, the exigencies of life force relativists, against their inclinations, to make reasonably consistent moral judgments. Aside from a tendency toward misplaced tolerance, which though incurring the liabilities of naiveté nevertheless enjoys the benefits of trust, there are few consequences to being a relativist. Unfortunately, the search for moral absolutes is not so benign. In fact, moral absolutism is positively pernicious. Far from providing a moral anchor, the fruitless search for evaporating absolutes encourages the abdication of moral responsibility.

The baleful effects of this long search for absolutes underlie one of our most persistent popular moral attitudes—the idea that if an action is legal it is right. Recent accounting scandals attest to the ubiquity of the belief that the perfume of legal casuistry masks the stench of corruption. Yet, a legal code is an unwieldy instrument for dealing with moral questions. It is inefficient and insensitive at best, coercive and tyrannical at worst, and ceding moral authority to government officials is inimical to American ideals. Ironically, the search for universality and objectivity, with its unrealistic demands, encourages this transfer of moral liability, for it eviscerates the only moral resources available to individuals in our current situation.

Contemporary society places increasingly abstract moral demands on us, as we try to cope with the unfamiliar, the unexpected, and the unintended. We routinely interact with others whose lives seem opaque; we use technology that promises to utterly transform human existence in ways that even our most prescient prognosticators cannot foresee; and each of us occupies multiple, incompatible social roles with conflicting norms and expectations. There is seldom a straightforward answer to the question of what moral burdens an individual must accept. Yet, in these circumstances, the task of sustaining a moral point of view, nevertheless, falls by default squarely on the shoulders of individuals who must use their own critical judgment while bootstrapping moral feelings by cobbling together communities of interest or accident and sustaining relationships across time and distance.

It is not surprising, in this atmosphere of ambiguity and uncertainty, that many struggle unsuccessfully to hone their basic moral impulses. We acquire the capacity for compassion and the disposition toward honesty, loyalty, and justice in face-to-face meetings where issues of dependence and support have palpable consequences and emotional weight. Unfortunately, in the face of increasingly abstract demands, where consequences are less obvious and relationships less secure, our moral feelings become confused and attenuated—less compulsive, and ultimately less trustworthy. Though we look for moral authorities to replace these impulses, there are too many and they are in conflict. Only the law with its explicit sanctions and reasonably sure consequences provides guidance. Thus, we cede moral authority to the lawmakers and their lawyers. . . .

Hence, the ambivalence our students, and much of the rest of culture, feel toward ethics. This ambivalence arises not from the lack of moral authority but from the presence of too many moral authorities and an unachievable, arid ideal of objectivity that cannot be met, which thus encourages the ceding of responsibility to any half-baked authority that promises stability. Contemporary citizens hesitate to judge, not because they lack civilizing contact with tradition or because they stupidly think all judgments are equivalent but because our traditions don't help much in seeing through the fog of our present circumstances. . . .

After centuries of horror, we should now know that what keeps us on the rails is neither regulations nor theories but simply the sense that others call upon us to respond. Moral conscience has never had to wait for the word magic of philosophers or social scientists—it arises unbidden and often incoherent. Yet, as imperfect as it is, moral conscience is all we have, though it is too dynamic and idiosyncratic to rest on moral absolutes, since it flourishes only in caves where spirits fear to tread.

Study Questions:

1. Is Furrow right that there are more damaging consequences if one is an absolutist than if one is a relativist? Explain.

2. Think of examples from the news in recent years where a legal solution has been sought to a moral problem. Do these solutions seem satisfactory, or do we still need to solve the issues at the level of ethics?

3. Is Furrow right that moral conscience, in the end, boils down to what David Hume called a "fellow-feeling" (see Chapter 4), a response to others in need? Does that remove the need for universal principles?

4. Would you call Furrow a soft universalist? Why or why not? (He doesn't use that term about his own philosophy.)

Primary Reading

The Concept of Multicultural Education

BHIKHU PAREKH

Essay, 1986. Excerpt.

Bhikhu Parekh is professor of political theory at the University of Hull (UK) and deputy chair of the Commission for Racial Equality. In this excerpt Parekh addresses the lack of multicultural sensitivity in English schools. In England the reference to "blacks" covers both people of African descent and people from India, Bangladesh, and Pakistan.

Let us now briefly explore the impact of this type of mono-cultural education (whether in Britain or elsewhere) on the child and how it measures up to the objectives the school claims to achieve.

First, it is unlikely to awaken his curiosity about other societies and cultures either because he is not exposed to them at all or because they are presented in uncomplimentary terms, or both. Thus our curriculum on religious studies is hardly likely to inspire him to enquire how some non-Christian religions manage to do without the idea of God as the creator of the universe, or have very different views of prophets, or conceive human destiny and come to terms with death and suffering in very different ways. A child exposed to no other religion but his own grows up asking only those questions that it encourages him to ask. And since he asks only those questions that his religion answers, he finds its answers satisfactory. In other words, he never gets out of its framework, and never feels disturbed or perplexed enough to explore other religions. What is true of religious studies is equally true of history, geography, literature, social studies and so on, none of which is likely to stimulate his curiosity about other civilizations and societies.

Second, mono-cultural education is unlikely to develop the faculty of imagination. Imagination represents the ability to conceive alternatives; that is, it is the capacity to recognize that things can be done, societies can be organized and activities can be performed in several different ways, of which the most familiar is but one and not necessarily the best. Imagination does not develop in a vacuum. It is only when one is exposed to different societies and cultures that one's imagination is stimulated and the consciousness of alternatives becomes an inseparable part of one's ways of thinking. One cannot then think of anything, be it an activity, a form of enquiry, a culture or a society without at the same time realizing that it can be conceptualized or thought about or conducted in several different ways. And this awareness of alternatives radically alters one's perspective to the way it is organized in one's own environment. One cannot avoid asking *why* it is organized in a particular manner in one's society, and *if* this way of organizing it is better than others. Mono-cultural education blots out the awareness of alternatives and restricts imagination. It cannot avoid encouraging the illusion that the limits of one's world are the limits of the world itself, and that the conventional way of doing things is the only natural way.

Third, mono-cultural education stunts the growth of the critical faculty. A child taught to look at the world from the narrow perspective of his own culture and not exposed to any other is bound to reject all that cannot be accommodated within the narrow categories of his own way of looking at the world. He judges other cultures and societies by the norms and standards derived from his own, and predictably finds them odd and even worthless. And since he judges his society in terms of its own norms, he can never take a genuinely critical attitude to it. Further, as we saw, mono-cultural education blunts imagination, and therefore the child lacks the sharp awareness of alternatives that alone can give a cutting edge to his critical faculties. Unable to criticize his society and unable to appreciate alternatives, he can hardly avoid admiring its "glory" and the "genius" and greatness of his "race," and remains vulnerable to the deadly vice of narcissism.

Fourth, mono-cultural education tends to breed arrogance and insensitivity. The child who is not encouraged to study other cultures and societies or to study them with sympathy and imagination cannot develop a respect for them. Imprisoned within the framework of his own culture, he cannot understand and appreciate differences nor accept diversity of values, beliefs, dress, food, ways of life and views of the world as an integral part of the human condition. He does not welcome, let alone rejoice in, diversity. Naturally he feels threatened by it and does not know how to cope with it. He approaches the world on his own terms, expecting it to adjust to him and seeing no reason why he should adjust to it. This leads to arrogance and double standards and, what is but a converse of it, an attitude of hypocrisy. When he visits other countries, he sees no need to learn their languages and adjust to their customs, whereas he expects others visiting his own to speak his language and accept its customs. . . .

Fifth, mono-cultural education provides a fertile ground for racism. Since a pupil knows very little about other societies and cultures, he can only respond to them in terms of superficial generalizations and stereotypes. These, in turn, are not haphazard products of individual imagination but culturally derived. A culture not informed by a sensitive appreciation of others cannot but judge them in terms of its own norms. It sets itself up as an absolute, that is, as the only universally valid point of reference, and evaluates others in terms of their approximation to it. The greater the degree to which they resemble it, the more civilized or developed they are supposed to be. And conversely the more they diverge from it, the more uncivilized they are judged to be. This is indeed how the Victorians built up a hierarchy of human societies. They placed the African societies at the bottom, the Asians a little higher, the Mediterranean still higher, and so on until they got to the English whom they regarded as representing the highest stage of human development. . . .

We have so far considered the impact of mono-cultural education on white children. We may now briefly consider its impact on their black peers. The latter obviously suffer from the same consequences as the former. In addition they also suffer from other sets of consequences.

The white children raised on a mono-cultural diet look at their black peers through the prism of the stereotypes they have acquired from their education. They find it difficult to accept them as equals, relax in their presence, appreciate their desire to retain their distinct cultural identity, and generally treat them with a mixture of contempt and pity. For their part, the black children either reciprocate the hostility, or bend over backwards to conform to their white peers' expectations and in so doing alienate their parents and less conformist peers. Like the white children, some white teachers have grown up on a mono-cultural diet and share their cultural arrogance and insensitivity. Consciously or unconsciously they approach their black pupils with the familiar stereo-types; they expect little of them, tend not to stretch them to their fullest, and fail to provide them with necessary educational and emotional support and encouragement. Not surprisingly many black children tend to under-achieve, rarely feel relaxed at school, lack trust in their teachers and go through the school with a cartload of frustrations and resentment.

When constantly fed on an ethnocentric curriculum that presents their communities and cultures in a highly biased and unflattering manner, black children can hardly avoid developing a deep sense of inferiority and worthlessness. They feel that they belong to a "race" which is culturally deficient and scarred by grave defects of character and intelligence; and that their ancestors have contributed "nothing" to the growth of human civilization, invented nothing of which others should take note, composed nothing which others could read with profit, built no empires, left behind nothing that is worth preserving or even cherishing, and indeed had lived such a fragile and primitive life that, but for the white colonizers, they would have by now become extinct. The impact of all this on the self-respect and identity of a black child and on his relations with his parents, brothers, elders and indeed with the members of his community in general is shattering. Lacking a sense of worth, he develops self-pity and self-hatred. He resents his parents for what they are and what they have done to him. He feels they have nothing worthwhile to teach or transmit to him; and that diminishes his respect for them, and consequently their authority over him. With their authority diminished, the parents feel compelled to rely on physical force to maintain a modicum of order in the family. . . .

The black child raised on a mono-cultural diet in an English school experiences profound self-alienation. His colour and his affections bind him to his people; the culture he is in the process of acquiring distances him from them. His birth and his destiny, his past and his future, point in wholly different and incompatible directions. His present is nothing but a battleground between his present and his future, and he is not quite sure which will eventually win. He feels suspended between two worlds; he half-wishes to leave one but he cannot, and it would not let go of him either; he half-wishes to embrace the other, but fears that he cannot and that it will not accept him either. . . .

What is, perhaps clumsily, called multi-cultural education is ultimately nothing more than this. It is essentially an attempt to release a child from the confines of the ethnocentric straitjacket and to awaken him to the existence of other cultures, societies and ways of life and thought. It is intended to de-condition the child as much as possible in order that he can go out into the world as free from biases and prejudices as possible and able and willing to explore its rich diversity. Multi-cultural education is therefore an education in freedom—freedom *from* inherited biases and narrow feelings and sentiments, as well as freedom *to* explore other cultures and perspectives and make one's own choices in full awareness of available and practicable alternatives. Multi-cultural education is therefore not a departure from, nor incompatible with, but a further refinement of, the liberal idea of education. It does not cut off a child from his own culture; rather it enables him to enrich, refine and take a broader view of it without losing his roots in it.

Study Questions

1. Discuss the five consequences of monocultural education outlined by Parekh: Is he right? Why or why not?

2. Does Parekh advocate inclusive or exclusive multiculturalism?

3. Do you think Parekh's arguments are equally valid for the American and for the British educational system?

4. Parekh is concerned about raising the cultural sensitivity of the dominant, white British culture. How does he himself fare in terms of *gender* sensitivity? (A clue: How does he refer to the schoolchildren?) Is this a relevant issue? Why or why not?

Narrative

The Poisonwood Bible

BARBARA KINGSOLVER

Novel, 1998. Summary and Excerpts.

The Poisonwood Bible is a story whose message of cultural tolerance has deeply affected readers. In some ways it can be said to support an ethical-relativist philosophy, but in others it seems to support soft universalism. Since this is a work of fiction and not a philosophical treatise, the author shouldn't be judged according to whether she presents a unified theory or not: It will be up to you to decide whether she is, at heart, an ethical relativist or a soft universalist; the quality of the story is what counts. (I think we can exclude the possibility of hard universalism right from the start.)

In 1959 Orleanna Price, a housewife from Georgia, travels with her husband and four daughters to the Congo in Africa so that her husband can fulfill his dream of bringing Christ to the natives. We follow their individual destinies all the way into the 1980s, see-

American author Barbara Kingsolver (b. 1955) has a deep interest in multiethnic issues. In 1963 her father worked as a medical doctor in Zaire (then Congo), and he brought his family along to the Caribbean in 1967 on another medical assignment. Kingsolver is the author of *The Bean Trees* (1988), *The Poisonwood Bible* (1998), and *Prodigal Summer* (2001), among other novels.

ing the consequences unfold of Nathan Price's decision to take his family to Africa. The book is structured with biblical overtones, beginning with a Genesis section, and ending with an Exodus section, but we learn fairly early in the story that this is no story of happy missionaries bringing salvation to the heathens. It is instead the story of the clash between cultures, the culture of the (presumably hard universalist) Christian missionary, and his wife and daughters who have grown up in an American world, meeting a culture where just about *everything* is different: the concepts of right and wrong, good and bad, what's food and what's not food, what's clean and unclean, what's near and far—and eventually, what is home and what is not home. All five women react in their own way, and with their own voice. Nathan Price's voice is not heard except through the reflections of the women, but he is the catalyst of the changes in their lives. Orleanna, a religious, faithful wife who initially just wants to stand by her husband in his work, eventually finds that the affront to the Africans and their culture perpetuated by her husband's cultural and moral arrogance will require a lifetime of atonement from her. Rachel, the eldest daughter, becomes the voice of longing for her lost American culture of affluence and convenience. Leah, once her father's strongest supporter, finds her love and life's work in the politics of revolutionary Africa and lives an African life perpetually apologizing for her whiteness; her twin sister Adah comes to terms with a physical disability afflicting her since childhood, seeing herself in light of another culture. And the baby sister Ruth May—well, you'll have to read the book to find out about Ruth May.

In the first excerpt Leah tells us of the cultural differences she is experiencing in the Congolese village; the young teacher Anatole, who has been educated in the big city, tries to mediate between the village chief and Price. In the second excerpt Leah relates an incident where the village chief calls her father on his sincerity in having elections, and his religious sincerity, and in the final excerpt she sums up her life experiences as a white American in Africa, with Anatole by her side.

>   Anatole leaned forward and announced, "our chief, Tata Ndu, is concerned about the moral decline of this village."
>
>   Father said, "Indeed he should be, because so few villagers are going to church."
>
>   "No, Reverend. Because so *many* villagers are going to church."
>
>   Well, that stupefied us all for a special moment in time. But Father leaned forward, fixing to rise to the challenge. Whenever he sees an argument coming, man oh man, does he get jazzed up.

"Brother Anatole, I fail to see how the church can mean anything but joy, for the few here who choose Christi-*an*-ity over *ignorance* and *darkness!*"

Anatole sighed, "I understand your difficulty, Reverend. Tata Ndu has asked me to explain this. His concern is with the important gods and ancestors of this village, who have always been honored in certain sacred ways. Tata Ndu worries that the people who go to your church are neglecting their duties."

"Neglecting their duties to false idolatry, you mean to say."

Anatole sighed again. "This may be difficult for you to understand. The people of your congregation are mostly what we call in Kikongo the *lensuka*. People who have shamed themselves or had very bad luck or something like that. Tata Boanda, for example. He has had terrible luck with his wives. The first one can't get any proper children, and the second one has a baby now who keeps dying before birth and coming back into her womb, over and over. No one can help this family anymore. The Boandas were very careful to worship their personal gods at home, making the proper sacrifices of food and doing everything in order. But still their gods have abandoned them for some reason. This is what they feel. Their luck could not get any more bad, you see? So they are interested to try making sacrifices to your Jesus."

Father looked like he was choking on a bone. I thought: Is there a doctor in the house? But Anatole went right on merrily ahead, apparently unaware he was fixing to kill my father of a heart attack.

"Tata Ndu is happy for you to draw the bad-luck people away," he said. "So the village's spirit protectors will not notice them so much. But he worries you are trying to lure too many of the others into following corrupt ways. He fears a disaster will come if we anger the gods."

"*Corrupt,* did you say," Father stated, rather than asked, after locating where the cat had put his tongue.

"Yes, Reverend Price."

"Corrupt *ways*. Tata *Ndu* feels that bringing the Christian word to these people is leading them to corrupt *ways*."

. . .

Father was poised to go on with the story when suddenly Tata Ndu stood right straight up, cutting him off in the middle of hammering home his message. We all stared. Tata Ndu held up his hand and declared in his deep, big-man's voice, giving each syllable the exact same size and weight: "Now it is time for the people to have an election."

"What?" I said out loud.

But Father, who's accustomed to knowing everything before it happens, took this right in stride. He replied patiently, "Well, now, that's good. Elections are a fine and civilized thing. In America we hold elections every four years to decide on new leaders." He waited while Anatole translated that. Maybe Father was dropping the hint that it was time for the villagers to reconsider the whole proposition of Tata Ndu.

Tata Ndu replied with equal patience, "*A yi bandu,* if you do not mind, Tata Price, we will make our election now. *Ici, maintenant.*" He spoke in a careful combination of languages that was understood by everyone present. This was some kind of joke, I thought. Ordinarily Tata Ndu had no more use for our style of elections than Anatole did.

"With all due *respect,*" my father said, "this is not the time or the place for that kind of business. Why don't you sit down now, and announce your plans after I've finished with the sermon? Church is not the place to vote anyone in or out of public office."

"Church is the place for it," said Tata Ndu. "*Ici, maintenant,* we are making a vote for Jesus Christ in the office of personal God, Kilanga village."

Father did not move for several seconds.

Tata Nadu looked at him quizzically. "Forgive me, I wonder if I have paralyzed you?"

Father found his voice at last. "You have not."

"*A bu,* we will begin, *Beto tutakwe Kusala.*" There was a sudden colorful bustle through the church as women in their bright *pagnes* began to move about. I felt a chill run down my spine. This had been planned in advance. The women shook pebbles out of calabash bowls into the folds of their skirts and moved between the benches, firmly placing one pebble into each out-stretched hand. This time women and children were also getting to vote, apparently. Tata Mwanza's father came forward to set up the clay voting bowls in front of the altar. One of the voting bowls was for Jesus, the other was against. The emblems were a cross and a bottle of *nsamba,* a new palm wine. Anyone ought to know that was not a fair match.

Father tried to interrupt the proceedings by loudly explaining that Jesus is exempt from popular elections. But people were excited, having just recently gotten the hang of the democratic process. The citizens of Kilanga were ready to cast their stones. They shuffled up to the alter in single file, just exactly as if they were finally coming forward to be saved. And Father stepped up to meet them as if he also believed this was the heavenly roll call. But the line of people just divided around him like water around a boulder in the creek, and went on ahead to make their votes. The effect of it wasn't very dignified, so Father retreated back to his pulpit made of wired-together palm fronds and raised up one hand, intending I guess to pronounce the benediction. But the voting was all over with before he could really get a word in sideways. Tata Ndu's assistant chiefs began counting the pebbles right away. They arranged them in clusters of five in a line on the floor, one side matched up against the other, for all to see.

"*C'est juste,*" Tata Ndu said while they counted. "We can all see with our own eyes it was fair."

My father's face was red. "This is *blasphemy*!" He spread his hands wide as if casting out demons only he could see, and shouted, "There is nothing fair here!"

Tata Ndu turned directly to Father and spoke to him in surprisingly careful English, rolling his r's, placing every syllable like a stone in a hand. "Tata Price, white men have brought us many programs to improve our thinking," he said. "The program of Jesus and the program of elections. You say these things are good. You cannot say now they are *not* good."

A shouting match broke out in the church, mostly in agreement with Tata Ndu. Almost exactly at the same time, two men yelled, "*Ku nianga, ngeye uyele kutala!*"

Anatole, who'd sat down in his chair a little distance from the pulpit, leaned over and said quietly to Father, "They say you thatched your roof and now you must not run out of your house if it rains."

Father ignored this parable. "Matters of the spirit are not decided at the marketplace," he shouted sternly. Anatole translated.

"*A bu, kwe?* Where, then?" asked Tata Nguza, standing up boldly. In his opinion he said, a white man who has never even killed a bushbuck for his family was not the expert on which god can protect our village.

When Anatole translated that one, Father looked taken aback. Where we come from, it's hard to see the connection.

Father spoke slowly, as if to a half-wit, "Elections are good, and Christianity is good. Both are good." We in his family recognized the danger in his extremely calm speech, and the rising color creeping toward his hairline. "You are right. In America we honor both these traditions. But we make our decisions about them in different houses."

"Then you may do so in America," said Tata Ndu. "I will not say you are unwise. But in Kilanga we can use the same house for many things."

Father blew up. "Man, you understand *nothing!* You are applying the logic of children in a display of childish ignorance." He slammed his fist down on the pulpit, which caused all the dried-up palm fronds to shift suddenly sideways and begin falling forward, one at a time. Father kicked them angrily out of the way and strode toward Tata Ndu, but stopped a few feet short of his mark. Tata Ndu is much heavier than my father, with very large arms, and at that moment seemed more imposing in general.

Father pointed his finger like a gun at Tata Ndu, then swung it around to accuse the whole congregation. "You haven't even learned to run your own pitiful country! Your children are dying of a hundred different diseases! You don't have a pot to piss in! And you're presuming you can take or leave the benevolence of our Lord Jesus Christ!"

If anyone had been near enough to get punched right then, my father would have displayed un-Christian behavior. It was hard to believe I'd ever wanted to be near to him myself. If I had a prayer left in me, it was that this red-faced man shaking with rage would never lay a hand on me again.

Tata Ndu seemed calm and unsurprised by anything that had happened. "Á, Tata Price," he said, in his deep, sighing voice. "You believe we are *muwana,* your children, who knew nothing until you came here. Tata Price, I am an old man who learned from other old men. I could tell you the name of the great chief who instructed my father, and all the ones before him, but you would have to know how to sit down and listen. There are one hundred twenty-two. Since the time of our *mankulu* we have made our laws without help from white men."

He turned toward the congregation with the air of a preacher himself. Nobody was snoozing now, either. "Our way was to share a fire until it burned down, *ayi?* To speak to each other until every person was satisfied. Younger men listened to older men. Now the *Beelezi* tell us the vote of a young, careless man counts the same as the vote of an elder."

In the hazy heat Tata Ndu paused to take off his hat, turn it carefully in his hands, then replace it above the high dome of his forehead. No one breathed. "White men tell us: *Vote, Bantu!* They tell us: You do not all have to agree, *ce n'est pas nécessaire!* If two men vote yes and one says no, the matter is finished. *Á bu,* even a child can see how that will end. It takes three stones in the fire to hold up the pot. Take one away, leave the other two, and what? The pot will spill into the fire."

We all understood Tata Ndu's parable. His glasses and tall hat did not seem ridiculous. They seemed like the clothes of a chief.

"But that is the white man's law, *n'est-ce pas?*" he asked. "Two stones are enough. *Il-nous faut seulement la majorité.*"

It's true, that was what we believed: the majority rules. How could we argue? I looked down at my fist, which still clutched my pebble. I hadn't voted, nor Mother either. How could we, with Father staring right at us? The only one of us who'd had the nerve was Ruth May, who marched right up and voted for Jesus so hard her pebble struck the cross and bounced. But I guess we all made our choices, one way or the other.

Tata Ndu turned to Father and spoke almost kindly. "Jesus is a white man, so he will understand the law of *la majorité,* Tata Price. *Wenda mbote.*

Jesus Christ lost, eleven to fifty-six.

. . .

We are still the children we were, with plans we keep secret, even from ourselves. Anatole's, I think, is to outlive Mobutu and come back here when we can stand on this soil and say "home" without the taste of gold-leaf chandeliers and starvation burning bitter on the backs of our tongues. And mine, I think, is to leave my house one day unmarked by whiteness and walk on a compassionate earth with Ruth May beside me, bearing me no grudge. Maybe I'll never get over my grappling for balance, never stop believing life is going to be *fair,* the minute we can clear up all these mistakes of the temporarily misguided. Like the malaria I've never shaken off, it's in my blood. I anticipate rewards for goodness, and wait for the ax of punishment to fall upon evil, in spite of years I've rocked in this cradle of rewarded evils and murdered goodness. Just when I start to feel jaded to life as it is, I'll suddenly wake up in a fever, look out at the world, and gasp at how much has gone wrong that I need to fix. I suppose I loved my father too much to escape being molded to at least some part of his vision.

But the practice of speaking a rich, tonal language to my neighbors has softened his voice in my ear. I hear the undertones now that shimmer under the surface of the words *right* and *wrong.* We used to be baffled by Kikongo words with so many different meanings: *bängala,* for *most precious* and *most insufferable* and also *poisonwood.* That one word brought down Father's sermons every time, as he ended them all with the shout "Tata Jesus is *bängala!*"

Study Questions

1. The title itself is a take on mistakes committed by a hard universalist who doesn't try to understand different cultural nuances: Nathan Price tries to tell the local population that "the word of Jesus is beloved," which in the tribal tongue translates as "*Tata* Jesus is *bängala.*" The problem is that, in the context, it comes across as "Jesus is poisonwood." What do you think the author is saying with such a title?

2. What is the significance of Tata Ndu's being trilingual and telling Price that he comes from 122 generations of wise men? What is his message about the three stones and the cooking pot? Could this political philosophy work for a large nation? Why or why not?

3. According to the excerpts, is this text primarily ethical relativist, or soft universalist? If you have read the entire book, do you find these excerpts a fair choice in representing the book's viewpoint?

4. Read the next narrative, *Possessing the Secret of Joy,* and compare its message with that of *The Poisonwood Bible:* What if the tradition Leah had been subjected to had been *female genital mutilation*? Would you still expect a message of cultural tolerance? Why or why not? Would you draw the line at tolerating certain cultural practices? Explain.

Narrative

Possessing the Secret of Joy

ALICE WALKER

Novel, 1992. Summary and Excerpt.

If you have read or seen *The Color Purple,* you will recognize some of the main characters in this moving and shocking novel: Olivia, Adam, and Tashi (Olivia and Adam are the children of Celie, the key character in *The Color Purple,* and Tashi is their best friend in the African village where Olivia and Adam's adoptive parents are missionaries). However, *Possessing the Secret of Joy* is a story that stands on its own, making a powerful argument against the ancient practice of female genital mutilation.* The novel weaves its way through the life of the storyteller Tashi. She is now an American, but originally she was of the Olinka tribe in Africa, a tribe Walker invented as a symbol for all African tribes. In real time and flashbacks, we are introduced to the nightmare of Tashi's life: the death of her older sister Dura, at first a vague memory, but in the end a reality so horrible that, to Tashi, it may be worth killing for.

Tashi has always been afraid of bleeding to death, and she has always had a terrifying dream of a dark tower where she is being kept prisoner, unable to move. Her adult life is in complete disarray. Her husband, Adam, and her best friend, Olivia, try to understand and support her as well as they can, but Tashi has periods of mental instability and moments of great, uncontrollable rage. She sees psychiatrists, and she spends time at a mental institution. But in the course of the book she tells her own story with increasing insight, and we realize that her mental condition is a result of two traumatic events: a terrible experience when she was a child and another when she was a young adult.

Tashi grew up in the Olinka village, the daughter of a Christian woman. Always a sensitive girl, Tashi was never the same after the death of her sister. As a young woman, Tashi left for America with the missionary family and became an American citizen. She and Adam were lovers, and Tashi loved her American life, but, even so, she decided as a young adult to return to Africa for a ceremony. She wanted to be "bathed" like the rest of the women in her tribe. Because of her Christian beliefs, her mother had kept her away from

---

*Female genital mutilation (sometimes referred to by Walker and others as female circumcision) is a process that can involve cutting the clitoris, removing it, or completely cutting away the inner and outer labia and sewing up the young girl with an aperture only big enough to allow for menstrual flow. The procedure is widespread in Africa and the Middle East and occurs illegally in the United States among some immigrant groups from these areas. The purpose of the procedure is not hygiene; it is strictly a cultural and religious ritual. Sexual pleasure becomes all but impossible, and a husband is assured of a virgin wife who is also going to remain faithful. In addition, health problems and chronic pain are often a consequence of the procedure. Most critics of the procedure see it as an affront to human rights and a tool for the subjugation and domination of women. Defenders of the practice argue that Western critics have no right to superimpose Western values on other cultures. As such, female genital mutilation presents a challenge to ethical relativism, which argues that nobody has the right to criticize the moral and traditional practices of another culture. World attention has been focused on this practice since the mid-1990s.

Alice Walker (b. 1944), American novelist, author of *The Color Purple, The Temple of My Familiar, Possessing the Secret of Joy,* and *The Same River Twice.* Walker's fiction incorporates many of the cultural strands contributing to the lives of American people of color and relates the African American experience to that of the African. Walker focuses particularly on the life experiences of women who are African and African American.

this ritual in childhood when most young girls were "bathed," but Tashi, at this point in her life, felt that as a political and sentimental gesture of solidarity with her people, and in particular their charismatic political leader, she ought to undergo the ritual—without completely realizing its ramifications. She sought out the *tsunga* (medicine woman), M'Lissa, who performs the rituals. "Bathing" is a euphemism for female genital mutilation, and, from that day on, Tashi has experienced daily pain and health problems, in addition to a loss of sexual sensitivity. While still recuperating in M'Lissa's custody, Tashi is found by Adam, who has been frantically searching for her. She returns to the United States, marries him, and has a baby, Benny, under extremely painful conditions because of the mutilation. As a result, Benny is born with a mental disability. Increasingly, Tashi experiences bouts of anxiety and rage. With the help of psychiatrists she has begun to remember the death, the *murder,* of her sister: Tashi was hiding outside the hut where her sister died, screaming and bleeding to death—from a botched procedure. And who performed the ritual? The same *tsunga,* M'Lissa, with the help of Tashi and Dura's own mother.

By the time we read this, we also know that Tashi is now, in real time, on trial in Africa for murder—the murder of M'Lissa. Did she do it? We won't know until the very end of the story. But we learn that after many years of marriage to Adam, with increasing problems due to psychological instability, Tashi has chosen to return to Africa to confront M'Lissa, who by now is a nationally renowned person, symbolizing the Olinka tradition. M'Lissa welcomes Tashi and reveals to her that she now expects Tashi to kill her, because that will elevate M'Lissa to the position of a saint. She also reveals that she finds Tashi naive beyond belief to have come back for the mutilation when she didn't have to—something M'Lissa would never have done herself. Even so, M'Lissa didn't try to stop her but performed the operation just because she was asked to do it, and it was her traditional job. And M'Lissa now recalls Tashi's sister who died—she had abandoned the bleeding little girl because her crying was too much for M'Lissa to bear.

Is M'Lissa the great evil figure in the story? Responsible for the death of Dura and the loss of Tashi's own spirit—Tashi calls it her own death—she is certainly a villain. But she herself is also a victim: Her own procedure was botched, with lameness resulting. She is a tool for the culture, passing the terror along to future generations of young girls as it was passed on to her. Tashi realizes that the true culprit is not the mutilator but the older men of the tribal society who want the mutilations done, who argue that God thinks of woman as unclean if she isn't "circumcised"—the ones who think of an "uncircumcised" woman as "loose" and immoral, as someone who needs to be kept under control. But still, Tashi can't help blaming M'Lissa:

> It is what you told me. Remember? The uncircumcised woman is loose, you said, like a shoe that all, no matter what their size, might wear. This is unseemly, you said. Unclean. A proper woman must be cut and sewn to fit only her husband, whose pleasure depends on an opening it might take months, even years, to enlarge. Men love and enjoy the struggle, you said. For the woman . . . But you never said anything about the woman, did you, M'Lissa? About the pleasure she might have. Or the suffering.

At the end of the story we learn the source of Tashi's nightmare about the dark tower, the truth about M'Lissa's death, and Tashi's own fate at the hands of the jury. And the secret of joy? On a very concrete level, the secret of sexual joy is to have an intact, unmutilated body and an unmutilated sense of self, of freedom. On a deeper level, the secret of joy itself is something we each have to find. Tashi's loved ones suggest that the secret is *resistance*.

Alice Walker's novel was received with alarm by many people who were unaware of the practice of female genital mutilation and welcomed by many others as a strong statement against excessive cultural tolerance. Walker was also criticized by some for betraying her African heritage in denouncing a traditional tribal practice as something that should not be tolerated in today's world.

Study Questions

1. Explain how this story can be viewed as an attack on ethical relativism. How might an ethical relativist respond to Walker's attack?

2. In view of the theme of female genital mutilation, do you find ethical relativism to be an appealing or a problematic moral theory? Explain.

3. Can we understand why Tashi went back as an adult to have the operation performed? Is this a realistic idea? Why or why not?

4. In your opinion, is Walker doing the right thing, exposing the practice of female genital mutilation as immoral, or should she show loyalty and solidarity with her African heritage by defending the practice? Is this a true dichotomy (an either-or situation), or is there another alternative?

5. M'Lissa asks Tashi what an American looks like, and Tashi answers, "An American, I said, sighing, but understanding my love for my adopted country perhaps for the first time: an American looks like a wounded person whose wound is hidden from others and sometimes from herself. An American looks like me." What does Tashi mean? Do you agree with her? Why or why not?

6. Now that you have been introduced to both Kingsolver's and Walker's novel, you may want to compare and contrast them. What do they have in common? What are the differences? Which viewpoint (in favor of or against ethical relativism) do you find most compelling? Explain.

Narrative

Sideshow

SHERI S. TEPPER

Novel, 1992. Summary and Excerpt.

Sheri S. Tepper's *Sideshow* is a philosophical debate about misdirected tolerance; it is a philosophical story clad in a science fiction cloak. The planet Elsewhere is the only place left in the galaxy that is not infected with the virus of the Hobbs Land Gods, a virus that, to the people of Elsewhere, is blasphemous; it abolishes war and enmity and cultural differences and creates a new kind of being by fusing humans and other sentient beings into *Fauna sapiens*. Elsewhere is populated by humans who prefer to remain as they are, worship their gods, keep their slaves, sacrifice their children, and keep their men and women prisoners in their home the way they have always done, all in the name of holy diversity. Enforcers make sure that citizens of each country on the planet stay within their own borders (tourism is acceptable, but not emigration), that no one smuggles artifacts from a technologically higher culture to a lower culture, and that all rules pertaining to each country are strictly adhered to. Occasionally an Enforcer will let his or her human side show and will prevent some particularly gruesome tradition from taking place, such as the sacrifice of a child, but on the whole such interference is considered a criminal act.

Nela and Bertran are two young humans from our own time period who have been catapulted to the future by a time travel device and now find themselves on Elsewhere. They have their own problems: Nela and Bertran are Siamese (conjoined) twins, joined at the side, who share too many organs to be separated surgically. Conjoined twins are always genetically identical, and yet Nela is a girl and Bertran is a boy. How could that be? This is a result of socialization, not biology. Nela and Bertran's mother wanted a girl, and their father wanted a boy, but the twins were born androgynous (with both male and female sexual organs). So their parents' choice was to change them both surgically to be distinctly female and male and raise them accordingly. The twins have always dreamed of being separated, although they know it is an impossibility. They befriend two Enforcers, Fringe (a woman) and Danivon (a man), and take a tour of Elsewhere. The twins tell the Enforcers about political and social conditions on Earth, of militarism, slavery, oppression of men and of women, and also of democracies and freedom-loving countries. They are told that equivalent societies to all of them can be found somewhere on Elsewhere.

> "And this is the diversity you are sworn to preserve?" asked Nela.
>
> "There are one thousand and three provinces," said Fringe. "We have mentioned only a tiny few of them. On Elsewhere, mankind is free to be whatever he can, or will."
>
> The twins thought about this for a time before Bertran asked, "Let us suppose one of the women of the Thrasis wishes to escape. Or one of the—what did you call them? The Murrey?—one of the Murrey from Derbeck? Let us suppose a civilian from Frick grows weary of being ruled by soldiers. What recourse do they have?"
>
> "I don't understand," said Danivon. "Recourse?"
>
> "Are they free to leave?"

"Of course not," said Fringe. "Persons must stay in their own place, in the diversity to which they were born. . . ."

"I'd call it a people zoo," [Nela] said. "Just like the zoos on Earth of long ago, with all the people in habitats."

Later the Enforcers apprehend a child killer, and Nela and Bertran congratulate them on a job well done; however, the twins have misunderstood the Enforcers' mission:

"Our job is to protect diversity," [Danivon] said through gritted teeth, "the very diversity that is the essence of humanity! In that diversity children are always being killed for any number of reasons. If the killing is proper to that place, then it is proper. But this old man took children across borders! He interfered in the affairs of a province! Here on Elsewhere, we let one another alone."

As it happens, Fringe begins to doubt the Enforcer code herself when, on a river flowing from the country of Choire, where only children with perfect pitch (for the choir practices) are kept alive, they encounter a child in a basket. The child has been "exposed" by Choire parents, perhaps because they want a newborn child instead, or perhaps because the child is musically defective or doesn't get along with its parents. . . .

Following the extended finger, Fringe saw. A basket floated out in midstream, bobbing on the wavelets, carrying a child some three or four years old who held tight to the closely woven rim and cried silently, mouth open, eyes and nose streaming.

"You said babies . . . ," said Fringe to Jory [another traveler], surprised and offended at this event following so soon upon her catechism.

Jory corrected her, "I said children."

. . . The basket bobbed on the river waves. The child looked up, saw them, stretched out its arms, and cried across the water. "P'ease . . . p'ease . . ." The river flow swept the basket on past, the child's voice still rising in a wail of fright. "Oh, oh, pick Onny up, p'ease. Pick Onny up. . . ." Where the basket bobbed, something large and many-toothed raised itself from the water and gulped hugely.

Fringe turned blind eyes away from the water, shutting out the sight, driving out the memory of it. Such things were. Diversity implied both pleasure and pain, both justice and injustice, both life and death. That's the way things were.

Eventually, Fringe and Danivon join forces with rebels trying to make changes in the diversity enclaves, and now things shift rapidly; a gateway in time and space opens, and the lives of the people of Elsewhere are about to be transformed forever. The conjoined twins Nela and Bertran face their ultimate wish and challenge, that of separation, but it comes at a terrible price. And the ultimate goal for all the turmoil and suffering? "The Ultimate Destiny of Man is to stop being only man." The Hobbs Land Gods are taking over, and *Fauna sapiens* is spreading across the galaxy. (But to find out how it happens, you must read this wonderful novel yourself.)

Study Questions

1. Identify the elements in this excerpt that correspond to the debate about ethical relativism.

2. What is Fringe the Enforcer's problem?

3. What is Tepper trying to convey in this story?

4. There is an additional element to the theme of ethical relativism: gender theory. Nela and Bertran are conjoined twins, which means they are genetically identical, in their case born androgynous. Yet one is raised as a girl and the other as a boy to satisfy their parents' hopes and expectations. What do you think Tepper is trying to say with this subplot?

5. Is this an argument against cultural tolerance? Judging from the excerpt, does Tepper come across as a hard universalist or a soft universalist?

Narrative

Do the Right Thing

SPIKE LEE (SCREENWRITER AND DIRECTOR)

Film, 1989. Summary.

In a book dealing with the question of what one should do, I couldn't possibly pass up a film with the title *Do the Right Thing*. The question was, where to place it? The film can perhaps be seen as an argument for ethical relativism, or at least for cultural tolerance, but perhaps not. I will leave that up to you.

It is a very hot summer morning in Bedford-Stuyvesant, a predominantly African American part of Brooklyn. Sal, an Italian, and his two sons are opening their pizzeria on one corner; a Korean family is opening up their grocery store on the other. The police (all white) are cruising the streets. Most of the black population is out of work. A young, mentally disabled man, Smiley, is trying to sell photos of Martin Luther King, Jr., and Malcolm X. A young black man, Mookie (played by Spike Lee), is delivering pizza in the neighborhood, and "Da Mayor," an old black man, is patrolling the streets, being friendly to everybody although not everybody takes kindly to him. He calls Mookie over and admonishes him always to "do the right thing."

As the day gets hotter, tempers flare. Sal likes the neighborhood and his customers (who all grew up on his pizzas). His younger son, Vito, is a good friend of Mookie. His older son, Pino, however, wants out; all he perceives is that his family members are not welcome in the African American community, and he thinks they should associate with their own kind in their Italian neighborhood. But Mookie points out to Pino that although he may think he does not like blacks, all his heroes are African American. In Sal's pizzeria, one of his customers, Buggin' Out, notices that Sal's wall is full of pictures of famous Italians and Italian Americans and asks why there are no brothers on the wall. When the question becomes a demand, Sal loses his temper and has Mookie throw him out. Radio Raheem, a young man with a big boom box, has a loudness contest with a group of Puerto Ricans and their own boom box. Mookie becomes upset when his sister comes to visit the pizza place and Sal appears to have a crush on her. So Mookie quarrels with his sister and

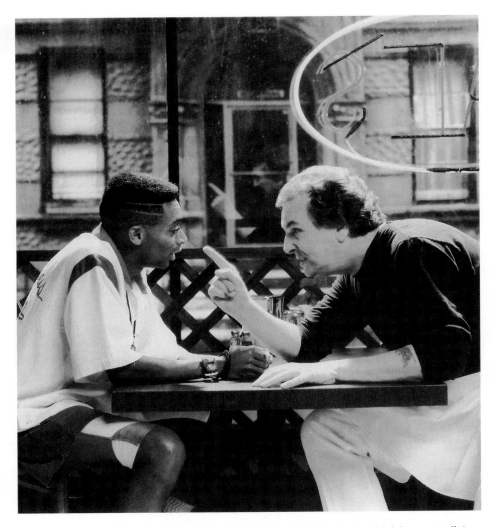

In *Do the Right Thing* (Universal City Studios, 1989) Mookie (Spike Lee) and Sal (Danny Aiello) are discussing neighborhood issues in Sal's pizza restaurant. On this hot day, tensions run high between ethnic groups: the Italians, the blacks, the Koreans, and the all-white police force.

later with his Puerto Rican girlfriend, Tina, too. Quarrels break out at the slightest provocation, such as scuffed running shoes, loud radios, and lack of a certain brand of beer at the grocery store: Blacks, Puerto Ricans, Italians, Koreans—just about everyone has a short temper and a ready vocabulary of epithets. Da Mayor is trying to smooth things out and eventually becomes a hero: He saves a little boy from being run over. The only one who thinks to thank him is Mother Sister, a woman in the neighborhood who apparently has disliked him for years.

The sun sets, but tempers are still hot. Sal and his sons are closing the pizzeria for the night, but Buggin' Out (who has been trying to organize a "Boycott Sal's Pizzeria" campaign), Radio Raheem, and Smiley turn up. Buggin' Out demands pictures of African Americans on the wall, and Raheem is upset that Sal told him to turn his radio down earlier. Everybody starts screaming, and Sal snaps, smashing Raheem's radio with a bat. A fight ensues and spills into the street; Raheem is holding Sal by the throat. The police arrive and pull Raheem off Sal, but the choke hold they apply kills Raheem. In shock, the fighting crowd freezes—until Mookie, as if surfacing from a dream, grabs a trash can and hurls it through Sal's window. The crowd bursts into the restaurant, looting and smashing things, and Smiley lights a match: The place goes up in flames. As the place is burning, he pins one of his pictures of Martin Luther King, Jr., and Malcolm X on the wall next to the photos of Italian Americans.

Next, the crowd turns on the Korean grocery store, but the young Korean store owner cries, "I'm black! You—me—we're the same!" Some laugh, but this quiets down tempers, and the store is safe.

The next day is another hot one. There is no solution to any of the problems in the neighborhood. Da Mayor is the only person who resolved anything; during the riot he managed to overcome the animosity of Mother Sister. Mookie vows only to spend more time with his and Tina's little boy.

The end of the movie? Two quotes appear on the screen, one from Martin Luther King, Jr., and the other from Malcolm X. King says that violence never solves any problems. Malcolm X says that, in general, violence is evil, but not in self-defense—in that case it is not even violence, but, rather, intelligence.

Study Questions

1. What do you think Spike Lee intended us to conclude?

2. *Did* Mookie do the right thing? Did anybody?

3. What did the Korean store owner mean when he said he was black too?

4. Is this film advocating inclusive or exclusive multiculturalism?

5. Can there be different moral rules for different ethnic and cultural groups? Should there be?

6. Does Spike Lee present his characters as stereotypes? Why or why not?

Chapter Four

Myself or Others?

We usually assume that moral behavior, or "being ethical," has to do with not being overly concerned with oneself. In other words, selfishness is assumed to be an unacceptable attitude. Even among scholars, though, there is disagreement about what constitutes ethical behavior. Since very early in Western intellectual history the viewpoint that humans aren't built to look out for other people's interests has surfaced regularly. Some scholars even hold that proper moral conduct consists of "looking out for Number One," period. These viewpoints are known as *psychological egoism* and *ethical egoism,* respectively. Both psychological egoism and ethical egoism are examples of absolutist theories; they hold that only one code is the norm for ethical behavior. (See Box 4.1 for an explanation of the difference between *egoism* and *egotism.*)

Psychological Egoism

On September 11, some three thousand people perished in the terrorist attacks on New York and Washington, D.C., but an estimated twenty thousand people survived, many rescued—by civilian strangers, firefighters, and police. One blind man was saved by his guide dog, which led him to safety down seventy-eight flights of stairs—from above where the second plane hit the World Trade Center's north tower. As we see in Chapter 11, the film *Schindler's List* makes the point, familiar to anyone raised in the Jewish tradition, that whoever saves a life saves a world. Many thousands of worlds were saved that day, some of them through extraordinarily heroic actions. But other worlds perished in the rescue attempts: Three hundred New York firefighters and police officers were among the dead, having rushed into the Trade Center towers before they fell. While everyone else was heading down the stairs, they were running up.

Police officer Walwyn Stuart arrived at the WTC subway station after the first plane had hit, and he herded arriving passengers back on the trains. Then he ordered the trains to leave and stopped all incoming trains. Because of Officer Stuart, apparently not a single person was trapped in the subway at Ground Zero. Then he ran upstairs to do what he could in the burning tower; he never came out. Two men carried a woman in a wheelchair—a complete stranger to them—down sixty flights of stairs to safety. A military man crawled through burning debris to free another man who was trapped in the burning section of the Pentagon. I think most of us wouldn't hesitate to call these people heroes.

And so it is disturbing for many of us that one moral theory would calmly dismiss all these acts as expressions of fundamentally selfish human nature: *psychological egoism.* Similarly, ask a psychological egoist about the fundamental motivation of

Box 4.1   EGOISM OR EGOTISM?

The terms *egoism* and *egotism* are part of our everyday speech, and people often use them interchangeably, but do they really mean the same thing? No: *Egoists* are people who think in terms of their own advantage, generally by disregarding the interests of others. *Egotists* are people who have a very high self-opinion and whose language often consists of self-praise; praise an egotist for a good result on a test or for looking nice, and you might receive responses such as "Of course I did well—I always do, because I'm very smart" or "Nice? I look great!" An egoist need not fall into this pattern, although he or she might, of course, be an egotist as well.

the suicidal hijackers, and the answer will be the same: As much as the terrorists themselves may have felt they were dying selflessly for a cause, they were being utterly selfish, according to psychological egoism. Indeed, we don't even have to inquire into their motivation—for the psychological egoist, it is a given that everyone is selfish all the time, because it is built into our nature as human beings. We simply cannot avoid being selfish.

Cases such as those of Officer Stuart and so many others on that day, and other stories coming out of the wars in Afghanistan and Iraq, stories that seem to exemplify selflessness, are precious to most people, because they show us what we might be capable of. We like to believe that humans have a built-in measure of courage that allows us to rise to the occasion and give up our lives, or at least our comfort, for others. Of course, few people perform heroic deeds with the *intent* of getting killed, but if they lose their lives in the process, we only seem to admire them more. In December of 2004, Southeast Asia experienced what may be the greatest natural disaster in human memory when a tsunami caused by an undersea earthquake hit the coastal areas of numerous nations including Thailand, Sri Lanka, Indonesia, and the eastern coastal areas of Africa. The death toll exceeded 250,000, with entire villages being swept away. Nations around the world responded, slowly at first; but within weeks the amounts pledged rose above $2 billion, including large amounts donated by private individuals and organizations. But on the ground in the affected areas, individuals also rose to the occasion and put their own sense of safety and comfort aside: Many people who had survived the wall of water unharmed stayed behind to help others who had been injured, sometimes putting their own lives in danger. (There are those who feel that losing one's life for someone else is stupid, useless, or even morally wrong. Such people may feel more comfortable with the theory of *ethical egoism.*)

If we ask a person who has performed (and survived) a heroic deed why he or she did it, the answer is almost predictable: "I just had to do it" or perhaps "I didn't think about it, I just did it." We take such comments as a sign that we are in the presence of a person with extraordinary moral character. But there are other ways of interpreting the words and actions of heroes. The theory of psychological egoism states that whatever it may look like and whatever we may think it is, no human action is done for

Box 4.2   SELFISH VERSUS SELF-INTERESTED

Psychological egoism is generally described as a theory which states that everyone is selfish at all times. But what does the word *selfish* mean? Some psychological egoists (people who believe everyone is selfish) sometimes emphasize that there is nothing bad or morally deficient about being selfish; all it means, they say, is that we are "self-ish," we are focused on our own survival, which doesn't necessarily imply that we are disregarding other people's interests. However, we use the word in a different sense in our everyday language. According to Webster's dictionary, *selfish* means "devoted unduly to self; influenced by a view to private advantage," so if we concede that Webster's reflects the common use of the word, we can't deny that *selfish* is a morally disparaging term; it isn't value-neutral, and it certainly isn't a compliment.

Sometimes psychological egoists use the term *selfish,* and sometimes the term used is *self-interested.* There is no consensus among psychological egoists about which term to use. It makes quite a difference which term you choose, but in the end, it may not make the theory of psychological egoism any more plausible. If you say (1), "All acts are selfish," you imply that all of us are always looking for self-gratification and have no feeling for the interests of others. However, if you say (2), "All acts are self-interested," you imply that all of us are always thinking about what is best for us. Is statement 1 true? It may be true that we are always looking out for ourselves in some way, but it is certainly not true that we are always looking for self-gratification; many a moment in a lifetime is spent agonizing over doing what we want versus doing what we ought to do, and often we end up choosing duty over desire. So what if the psychological egoist says, "Doing my duty is better in the long run for me, even if I don't feel like doing it, so I guess I'm self-interested" (statement 2)? But is statement 2 true? Many philosophers over the years have gleefully pointed out that it isn't—we are hardly concerned with what is good for us, at least not all the time. Many people smoke, drink to excess, and take drugs even though they know it is not in their own best interest. So couldn't psychological egoism state that "all acts are either selfish or self-interested"? It could, but it generally doesn't; part of the appeal of psychological egoism is that it is a very simple theory, and putting a dichotomy (an either-or) into the theory makes it much more complicated.

any reason other than for the sake of the agent. In short, we are all selfish, or at least we are all self-interested.

The term *psychological egoism* is applied to the theory because it is a psychological theory, a theory about how humans behave. A psychological egoist believes that humans are always looking out for themselves in some way or other, and it is impossible for them to behave any other way. As such, psychological egoism is a descriptive theory; it doesn't make any statements about whether this is a *good* way to behave. What does it take for a person to be labeled a psychological egoist? It's not necessary that he or she be a selfish person, only that he or she hold to the theory that all people look after themselves. As we see later, it is entirely possible for someone to be kind and caring and still be a psychological egoist. (See Box 4.2 for an explanation of the difference between *selfish* and *self-interested.*) Suppose, though, that someone insists

Box 4.3   "OUGHT IMPLIES CAN"

Sometimes a philosophical text will state that "ought implies can." In the civil code of the Roman Empire (27 B.C.E.–395 C.E.) this principle was clearly stated, and Roman citizens knew that *impossibilium nulla est obligatio* (nobody has a duty to do what is not possible). Many philosophical and legal schools of thought today are still based on this idea, and one of these is psychological egoism. "Ought implies can" means that we can't have an obligation (ought) to do something unless it is actually possible for us to do it (can). I can't make it a moral obligation for you to swim across San Francisco Bay to show your support for the Save the Whales program if you can't swim (but I might try to make it an obligation for you to donate a dollar, because most people can afford that). I can't make it a moral obligation for you to take home a pet from the pound if you are allergic to animals (but I might insist that you have an obligation to help in other ways). You can't tell me that I ought to be unselfish if in fact I was born selfish and can't be any other way because it is part of my human nature. This is the point that psychological egoism wants to make: It is irrational to keep wanting humans to look out for each other when, as a matter of fact, we aren't built that way.

that everyone *ought to* look after themselves. Then he or she is an *ethical egoist.* We discuss the theory of ethical egoism later in this chapter.

All People Look After Themselves

In Plato's *Republic* we find a discussion about morality and selfishness. In the Primary Readings section you will find an excerpt of this discussion. Plato's brother Glaucon is trying to make Socrates give some good reasons why it is better to be just than to be unjust. Glaucon insists that all people by nature look after themselves, and whenever we can get away with something, we will do it, regardless of how unjust it may be to others. Unfortunately, we may receive the same treatment from others, which is highly unpleasant, so for the sake of peace and security we agree to treat each other decently—not because we want to, but because we are playing it safe. Morality is just a result of our looking out for ourselves. (See Box 4.3 for an explanation of psychological egoism in terms of "ought implies can.")

What Glaucon is suggesting here about the origin of society is a first in Western thought. His theory is an example of what has become known as a *social contract theory,* a type of theory that became particularly influential much later, in the eighteenth century. A social contract theory assumes that humans used to live in a presocial setting (without rules, regulations, or cooperation) and then, for various reasons, got together and agreed on setting up a society. Generally, social contract theories assume that humans decide to build a society with rules (1) for the sake of the common good or (2) for the sake of self-protection. Glaucon's theory belongs to the second category because he claims (for the sake of argument) that humans primarily look after themselves.

If an invisibility ring can provide a perfect outlet for selfishness, will we all grab the chance, like Plato's brother Glaucon speculates, or will we fight temptation? Will we even all be tempted? In *The Lord of the Rings* (2001–2003), Frodo volunteers to take the Ring of power to Mount Doom and destroy it; but even Frodo, as good-hearted as he is, is tempted by the Ring's power, and within his small person a great battle is being fought.

To illustrate his point, Glaucon tells the story of a man called Gyges, a shepherd in ancient Lydia. Gyges was caught in a storm and an earthquake, which left a large hole in the ground. He explored the chasm and found a hollow bronze horse with the corpse of a giant inside. The giant was wearing only a gold ring on his finger. Gyges took the ring and left and later, wearing the ring, attended a meeting of shepherds. During the meeting Gyges happened to twist the ring, and he realized from the reaction of the other shepherds that he had become invisible. Twisting the ring back, he reappeared. Realizing the advantages gained by being invisible, Gyges arranged to be one of the elected messengers who report to the king about his sheep. Gyges went to town, seduced the queen, and conspired with her to kill the king. He then took over the kingdom, sired a dynasty, and became the ancestor of King Croesus.

Glaucon's question is, Suppose we had two such rings? Let us imagine giving one to a decent person and one to a scoundrel. We know that the scoundrel will abuse the ring for personal gain, but how about the decent person? To Glaucon it is the same thing; their human natures are identical. Decent persons will do "unjust" things just as quickly as scoundrels if they know they can get away with it; furthermore, if they *don't* take advantage of such situations, they are just stupid. In the end, who will be happier, the unjust person who schemes and gets away with everything or the just person who never tries to get away with anything but is so good that people think there must be something wrong with him? Why, the unjust person, of course.

This little story may be the first in the literary tradition to explore a theme that has remained popular to this day—and that may be one reason it seems timeless, but it could also be that the moral problem it represents hasn't changed, either. *Arabian Nights* is full of stories about invisibility cloaks, magic rings, and owners making creative uses of them, sometimes to gain a personal advantage and sometimes to spy on and vanquish the bad guys; in 1897 H. G. Wells wrote *The Invisible Man,* which has been made into a movie numerous times and inspired the film *Hollow Man* (2000). J. R. R. Tolkien's trilogy *The Lord of the Rings* (1954–56) features an invisibility ring. Usually the moral problem stated is, If you could become invisible, what would you do? Would you still be a morally decent or even halfway decent person? or would you use your power selfishly if you knew you could get away with it? Harry Potter may have his magic cloak, but most of us don't. Interestingly, in cases where people have been under the impression that they enjoy total anonymity, such as in the days of extensive illegal downloading of music from the Internet, few of those people seemed to have any qualms about breaking the law—which plays right into Glaucon's hands. But does this mean that *everyone* would react the same way, with a cloak of anonymity? Let us return to *Lord of the Rings* for a while. Here we have an invisibility ring, like Gyges'—and yet there are important differences: Gyges finds a ring that gives him powers; he uses them to his own advantage and ends up becoming the ancestor of an illustrious royal family. Many people would say, Good for him! But Sauron's ring in Tolkien's trilogy is of a different make: The people (of all species) who are tempted by the ring are marked for life, and the purpose of the entire quest of the ring is to destroy it, rather than use it. The invisibility given by Tolkien's ring is not one that allows much anonymity, either, because the bearer is visible to Sauron's forces and Sauron himself. Frodo does his utmost to fight the temptation to use the ring and see the quest through, having seen what happens to one's soul if one allows oneself to be absorbed by the ring's evil: One becomes like Gollum, who used to be a hobbit like Frodo (see the illustration in Chapter 1). In the Primary Readings you'll find an excerpt from a text that analyzes the similarities and differences between Frodo and Gyges, "The Rings of Tolkien and Plato: Lessons in Power, Choice, and Morality," by Erik Katz, and in the Narratives section you will find an overview of the main characters in the famous trilogy.

With few exceptions, the invisible person succumbs to temptation and meets a terrible end, as punishment for having a weak or evil character. So most invisible-person stories are *didactic* stories (see Chapter 2), designed to teach a moral lesson: If you let your selfish nature rule, you will surely be punished—if not by others, then by fate. But what is the lesson of Glaucon's story? Is he seriously implying that it is foolish and unnatural to be good if you can get away with being bad? No; he is acting as the devil's advocate in order to make Socrates defend justice as something that is good

The English philosopher Thomas Hobbes was one of the first modern materialists, claiming that all of human psychology consists of the attraction and repulsion of physical particles. As such, the natural human approach to life is one of self-preservation, and the natural life of humans outside the regulations of society (the state of nature) is for Hobbes a filthy and frightening war of everyone against everyone.

in itself. However, Glaucon does imply that what he is describing is in fact the opinion of most people. He may have been right; a good two thousand years later Thomas Hobbes (1588–1679) agreed with Glaucon's theory of self-interest on all three counts: (1) Humans choose to live in a society with rules because they are concerned with their own safety and for no other reason; (2) humans are by nature self-interested, and any show of concern for others hides a true concern for ourselves; (3) we would be fools if we didn't look after ourselves. (We return to this point in the next section; you will find Hobbes's theory in the Primary Readings at the end of this chapter and his view of the selfish basis for pity in Box 4.4.)

Surely we all can remember events in our lives that show that we don't always act out of self-interest. You may remember the time you helped your best friend move across town. The time you sat up all night preparing your brother's taxes. The time you donated toys to the annual Christmas toy drive. The time you washed your parents' car. Did the dishes at Thanksgiving. Or perhaps even helped a stranger on the road or saved the life of an accident victim. Were all those good deeds really done for selfish reasons? The psychological egoist would say yes—you may not have been aware of your true motives, but selfish they were, somehow. You may have wanted to borrow your parents' car: hence, the car wash and the dishes. You helped your friend move because you were afraid of losing her friendship. You may have felt guilty for not helping with your brother's taxes the year before, so you did them this year. The toys? You wanted to feel good about yourself. The stranger on the road? You wanted to rack up a few points in the Big Book of Heaven. Helping the accident victim? You wanted to get your name in the paper.

What about Officer Walwyn Stuart and others who lost their lives at the World Trade Center and the Pentagon, or Todd Beamer and other passengers on Flight 93, fighting back against the terrorists, trying to help others by preventing their plane from crashing into another building? In the aftermath of September 11 there was very little doubt among the millions of us watching the attacks being replayed again and again on TV that those who perished saving lives were heroes—not movie heroes or sports heroes, but real-life heroes. Nevertheless, the psychological egoist would maintain that

Box 4.4   HOBBES AND THE FEELING OF PITY

Hobbes believed humans feel pity for others in distress because they fear the same may happen to themselves. We identify with the pain of others, and that makes us afraid for ourselves. Therefore, helping others may be a way to ward off bad events. In actual fact we have no pity for others for their sake—only for our own. (He is not the first thinker to have expressed this opinion; Aristotle said approximately the same thing, but without implying that we are selfish to the bone.) Hobbes was one of the first modern Western philosophers to ponder human psychology, and we might say that he put his finger on a sore spot: Sometimes we do sympathize with others because we imagine how awful it would be if the same thing were to happen to us. What exactly does Hobbes mean when he says we *identify* with others? It seems that we ask ourselves, If this happened to me, how would I feel? This does not necessarily lead to concern for ourselves but rather leads to a concern for others, precisely because we know how they feel. Furthermore, isn't it possible to feel pity for someone or something with which you don't identify so easily? We certainly can feel pity for someone of the other gender or someone of another race or culture, even if what happens to them wouldn't happen to us. But how about feeling pity for dolphins caught in gill nets? For animals caught in traps? For pets used in lab experiments? In the aftermath of the 2004 tsunami, stories of people being rescued were abundant, but in the midst of concerns for all the human suffering, people also found time and compassion for a couple of stranded dolphins: a humpback dolphin mother and her calf had been carried by the tsunami into a shallow lagoon, where they were spotted by a man looking for his missing wife and a rescue effort was mounted. After several futile attempts the female was netted and released back into the ocean. The calf was never found. To many of us it is amazing that people would spend time caring for animals when so many humans were suffering—for some of us it is a heart-warming sign that humans are better than our reputation; for others it is a dismal sign that humans are sentimental and scatterbrained. Be that as it may, it is hard to believe that in this case people cared only because they were afraid the catastrophe might happen to them. In a broad sense, perhaps we do identify with other creatures when their lives are in danger and feel that we ward off our own demise by saving their lives. In the final analysis, though, that idea is rather far-fetched, because if Hobbes is right and we fear "contamination" from the misery of others, wouldn't we rather turn our backs on them and flee rather than expose ourselves to their suffering? Given that we don't, perhaps there are forces at work other than selfishness. An easier explanation is that we simply, on occasion, care for the well-being of others.

as much as such acts may look like selfless acts of heroism, they can all be boiled down to some expression of our inherent selfishness: Perhaps these people wanted to be famous. Perhaps they wanted to make up for past sins of omission, or perhaps they just wanted to feel good about themselves. As far as the psychological egoist is concerned, everyone who engages in a seemingly heroic act is as selfish as one who doesn't, because we all are, in the final analysis, doing everything for ourselves.

   This theory, cynical as it may sound, had established itself firmly in the minds of many Westerners prior to September 11, and it is too soon to say whether the public's massive outpouring of sympathy and financial support for the families of the

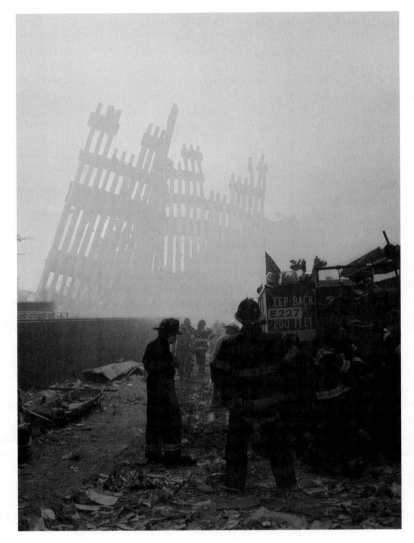

Psychological egoism claims that every act we do is for selfish reasons. For many people, September 11 put that notion to shame; an overwhelming number of stories documented police officers, firefighters, and civilians trying to help others escape the burning towers.

rescuers who perished has modified our modern cynicism in any major way; psychological egoism was an immensely popular theory throughout the twentieth century, a period abounding with its own stories of heroism, in both peace and wartime. So what is it that has proved so appealing about the theory? After all, it removes the halo from the head of every hero and every unselfish person in the history of humankind. In fact, that may be part of its appeal: We like to think, in this day and

Calvin and Hobbes

by Bill Watterson

One of the reasons psychological egoism has attained such popularity is that it appeals to a modern person's sense of honesty: In order not to fool ourselves into thinking we are better than we are, we should be honest and admit that we are selfish. Calvin, being a smart kid, not only uses this argument but also turns it to his advantage; in other words, he uses it as an excuse, which is one of the other reasons psychological egoism is popular. And let's face it: It is a very cynical slice of life

age, that we are honest about ourselves, and we don't want to be tricked into thinking that we are better than we are or that anyone else is either. (1) One reason, then, for this theory's popularity is its presumed *honesty*. Later in this section you'll find an example of this phenomenon in the story of Lincoln and the pigs.

Closely related to the notion of honesty is (2) our modern tendency toward *cynicism*. Somehow, we have a hard time believing good things about people, including ourselves. Refusing to take things at face value may be the mature thing to do, but it may also close our minds to the possibility that not all acts are selfish and not everybody is rotten at heart. (See Box 4.5 for a discussion of modern cynicism.) This possibility doesn't mean we shouldn't view the world with a healthy dose of skepticism and suspicion. Often, we really *are* taken advantage of, people *are* truly selfish and devious, and things *aren't* what they seem. But there is a difference between this kind of prudent skepticism and a universal cynicism that borders on paranoia. Such radical cynicism doesn't allow for the possibility of the existence of goodness and kindness.

A third reason that psychological egoism is so popular has to do with (3) *making excuses*. When psychological egoists say, "I can't help myself—it's my nature," they're saying they don't have to worry about remembering Aunt Molly's birthday or calling in on the cellphone to the radio station about the mattress they saw blocking the number-two lane on the freeway because humans are selfish *by nature,* and we are not capable of worrying about others—unless, of course, there is something in it for ourselves. But this is nothing but a bad excuse. Psychological egoists who take their own theory seriously never say we can't help being selfish to the bone—they just say there is some hidden selfish motive for whatever we do that we may not even be aware of.

Box 4.5   MODERN CYNICISM

There is much speculation about how cynicism began. It's not a new phenomenon. The ancient Greeks invented it: The Cynics, headed by Diogenes, did their best to undermine convention in order to break its hold on people's minds— one of the original "Question authority" movements. In later years, cynicism has questioned authority to the point at which misanthropy— automatically believing the worst about everybody—has become a form of authority in itself.

Modern cynicism has a precursor—or even a founder—in French philosopher and author Voltaire (1694–1778), whose sharp remarks about his contemporary France before the Revolution set the tone for the intellectual who rails against double standards and bigotry, trusts no one, including his or her government, and has a never-ending skepticism as far as human nature is concerned. Satire was one of the political weapons of choice in the Age of Reason. But in the last part of the nineteenth century, the Western world experienced a surge of optimism because many believed we were very close to solving all technological, scientific, and medical riddles. It was even assumed that we were too civilized to ever go to war again. You may remember from the section in Chapter 2 on war movies that enthusiasm for war by and large ended with World War I. Often our modern cynicism is regarded as having been born in the trenches of World War I, but there is an interesting precursor: the sinking of the *Titanic*. The 1997 award-sweeping film *Titanic* reminded us not only of the human tragedies involved but also of the hubris, the cocky assurance that human technology could conquer all obstacles. A ship so well built that it was unsinkable! As we know, it

wasn't, and the optimistic belief that now humans were the masters of the universe went to the bottom of the ocean with the great ship. It may not have been the very first blow to human self-assurance in the twentieth century, but it became the first serious crack in the hull of modern belief in technology.

Cynicism became a way of life in the twentieth century, fueled by the two world wars, the Great Depression, and the revelation of the horrors of the Holocaust. Children who lived through the tragedies and disappointments of the 1960s and 1970s, as well as their children, were all affected by the assassinations of John F. Kennedy, Robert Kennedy, and Martin Luther King, Jr., by the Korean and Vietnam wars, fuel shortages, and the Watergate and Iran-Contra scandals. And then there are the revelations from past decades such as the now infamous Tuskegee syphilis study, in which close to four hundred African American men from 1932 to 1972 unwittingly were reduced to the status of lab rats for government medical experiments. Other examples of the use of citizens for some larger purpose without their consent include the nuclear tests of the 1950s, which often involved soldiers and civilians who were given the impression that their lives were not in danger. Inuit people in Alaska were given radioactive medication as part of an experiment. In 1996, the *Los Angeles Times* revealed that in the 1950s the U.S. Army had sprayed chemicals and bacteria over large populations in New York and Washington and even over a school in Minneapolis. Years after the Vietnam War, it became apparent that soldiers had been exposed to a toxic exfoliant, Agent Orange. Gulf War Syndrome is

Psychological Egoism and the Concept of Free Will

It is time to take one step backwards and reassess one of the claims of psychological egoism: that we can't help what we're doing. When psychological egoists claim that we can't help being selfish because it is in our human nature, they are of course also say-still an unsolved riddle, attributed by some to chemical weapons in the area that the soldiers had not been warned about. So perhaps it is understandable that conspiracy rumors appear on a regular basis in response to important news stories; we just have to remind ourselves that while conspiracies do exist, there is a fine line between being a skeptical cynic and a paranoid cynic.

At the end of the second millennium it seemed as if the accumulated atrocities and disappointments of the twentieth century had brought us to a mind-set that left us perpetually skeptical, perpetually ready to believe the worst about politicians, religious figureheads, celebrities—and even ourselves. Cynicism had become a national pastime, with a brief moratorium after September 11, when there was bipartisan goodwill among politicians and news reporters. Now cynicism has returned, more voracious and more partisan than ever. One of the media events that best reflects the post-9/11 cynicism is probably the premiere of Michael Moore's *Fahrenheit 9/11*—a documentary to its fans, a propaganda film to its critics. A huge box-office success, the film created a firestorm of reactions, from very positive to very negative reviews. All in all, the American Left was cynical about the Bush administration's handling of the war in Iraq, and the American Right was cynical about the American Left. But politics is not the only arena for cynicism: The Catholic Church has become the target of criticism, and a fair amount of cynicism, for the way it has handled the scandal of child abuse committed by priests. An analysis by the John Jay College of Criminal Justice in 2004 estimated that 2.7 percent of priests have engaged in child molestation over the past fifty

years or more—and while 2.7 percent doesn't sound like much, it still amounts to 4,398 American priests, with multiple victims each. What has made so many people cynical, Catholics as well as non-Catholics, is not so much the molestation phenomenon itself, because there are child rapists in other churches too, as well as among teachers, Boy Scout leaders, and other groups, as the perceived lack of action or even concern by the Catholic Church. Most troubling was the active cover-up of these acts by bishops, who reassigned priests they knew to be child abusers to other dioceses without any forewarning to the community.

Perhaps the ultimate sign that cynicism is not only back in style, but even perhaps appropriately so, is the aftermath of the Christmas 2004 tsunami. With the deaths of more than 250,000 people in the floods, locals and tourists alike, the world responded with massive amounts of aid, as mentioned earlier in the chapter. However, the con artists instantly rose to the occasion, too: Scams were being run in person, by e-mail, and on the Internet; fake death messages were sent out; and in the flooded areas children orphaned by the tsunami were being abducted—the speculation is that they were sold into the thriving sex trade. So is cynicism an appropriate reaction to events and people that disappoint us? Appropriate or not, it is a sign of our times. But perhaps cynicism isn't altogether a bad thing—as it is sometimes said, a cynic is a disappointed idealist. You have a vision of how things ought to be, but you also have a considerable amount of skepticism. So somewhere between hope and skepticism you may be able to deal with the real world.

ing that we shouldn't be blamed for the selfish things we do (or be praised for the seemingly unselfish deeds either). This lines psychological egoism up with a famous—some would say, infamous—theory in philosophy: *hard determinism*. A hard determinist believes that since everything is an effect of a previous cause, then we should, in principle if not in reality, be able to predict events with complete accuracy—not only in nature but even in human lives and human decisions. This means that *according to hard determinism we have no free will* because everything we decide is a result of either our genetic heritage ("Nature") or our experience and environment ("Nurture"). In other words, it may *feel* as if we make free choices, but we really don't; everything is part of the great chain of cause and effect, even our thought processes and moral decisions This means that when people decide to break a moral rule or even the law, they can't help it and shouldn't be blamed, according to hard universalism. This line of thinking has spawned numerous discussions in ethics as well as in philosophy of law—because (1) we normally assume that people can be held morally accountable for what they do intentionally, and (2) our entire judicial system rests on the assumption that, in most cases, people should be held accountable if they break the law on purpose. Nevertheless, there are individual cases where people truly can't help doing what they're doing, morally and legally. You may want to think of a few such cases and discuss them.

In the sense that psychological egoism traces all human behavior back to self-preservation or self-love as the fundamental cause of all our decisions (such as Hobbes does)—in holding that we can't act otherwise and that we shouldn't be held accountable for being selfish—it can be called a deterministic theory. However, psychological egoism generally assumes that we can choose between several possible courses of action—but all are selfish actions nonetheless. And most psychological egoists would claim that we can be held accountable for choosing wrongly—because it would be in our selfish interest to avoid getting in trouble with the law, just as much as it might be selfishly gratifying to break it. This would speak against classifying psychological egoism as a hard determinist theory. In Chapter 7 you'll find a film about punishing people for the crimes they haven't committed yet (*Minority Report*), and in Chapter 10 we explore further the concept of having a free will in the philosophy of Jean-Paul Sartre and Henri Bergson, both antideterminists.

Shortcomings of Psychological Egoism

There is something beguiling about psychological egoism; once you begin to look at the world through the eyes of a psychological egoist, it is hard to see it any other way. In fact, no matter how hard we try to come up with an example that seems to run counter to the theory, the psychological egoist has a ready answer. This is due to several factors.

1. Falsification Is Not Possible Psychological egoism always looks for selfish motives and refuses to recognize any other kind. For any nonselfish motivation you can think of for doing what you did, the theory will tell you that there was another, ulterior motive behind it. It is inconceivable, according to the theory, that other motives might exist. This is in fact a flaw in the theory. A good theory is not one that can't be proven wrong but one that allows for the possibility of counterexamples.

The inability of a theory to allow for cases in which it doesn't apply is considered bad science and bad thinking. The principle of *falsification* was advanced by the philosopher Karl Popper (1902–1994) as a hallmark of a viable theory. It states that a good scientific theory must allow for the possibility that it might be wrong. If it declares itself right under any and all circumstances, it cannot be "falsified." So "falsification" doesn't mean that a theory has to be proven wrong but that it has to be engaged in rigorously testing itself—in other words, it has to consider the possibility that it might be wrong and test itself in any way possible. Popper says in his book *The Poverty of Historicism* (1957), "Just because it is our aim to establish theories as well as we can, we must test them as severely as we can; that is, we must try to find fault with them, we must try to falsify them. Only if we cannot falsify them in spite of our best efforts can we say that they have stood up to severe tests." Science itself doesn't always follow the principle of falsification; an example is the eighteenth-century debate about meteorites in which most scientists chose to side with their own theory that rocks couldn't fall from the sky, since outer space, they said, consists of a vacuum. The statements of reliable private citizens who claimed to have seen meteorites fall and land on the ground were consistently brushed aside by scientists as being lies or delusions because most scientists did not question their own theory: It was nonfalsifiable since it didn't allow for the possibility that it might be wrong. As we know, science later had to revise its notion of outer space (the theory was falsified): In 1803, scientists at a meeting at l'Aigle, France, actually observed meteorites falling.

Is the theory of evolution a good theory in the sense that it is falsifiable? Scientists today would say yes: The theory is based on empirical research that can be verified objectively (the fossil record), but it doesn't claim that it is correct no matter what happens; it claims that it is the most plausible theory of biology so far, but if new and different evidence should surface, then it is (presumably) open to revision.

Psychological egoism is not a good theory, according to Popper's principle, because it doesn't allow for the possibility that it might be wrong, but reinterprets all acts and motives so they fit the theory instead. That is not a theory, strictly speaking; it is a prejudice. It comes across as a strong theory precisely because there seems to be nothing that can defeat it; however, that is not a strength, scientifically speaking. A strong theory recognizes the reality of the problem of induction (see Chapter 3): Any empirical theory (that is, one based on evidence) can't be 100 percent certain.

In addition, the unfalsifiability of psychological egoism demonstrates the logical fallacy of *begging the question*. When an argument begs the question, it assumes that what it is supposed to prove is already true, so the "proof" does nothing but repeat the assumption (such as, "Marcia is right because Marcia is never wrong!"). Psychological egoism works in the same way: It assumes that all acts are selfish and therefore interprets all acts as selfish. So psychological egoism is not the scientific theory it claims to be.

2. Is Doing What We Want Always Selfish? Biologically, psychological egoists have a forceful argument: the survival instinct. It seems a fact that all animals, including humans, are equipped with some sort of instinct for self-preservation. We might ask ourselves, though, whether this instinct is always the strongest instinct in all relationships, animal as well as human. There are cases in which animals seem to sacrifice themselves for others, yet surely they don't have any underlying motives, such as the desire to be on TV or go to heaven. Nor is it likely that they would suffer from a guilt complex if they did not perform such deeds. There is, then, at least the possibility that some actions are not performed for the reason of self-preservation.

Is it true that we always do things for selfish reasons? Let us assume, for the sake of argument, that we do actually do what we want so that we may benefit from some long-term consequences. But is doing what we want in order to benefit ourselves always a "selfish" act? Abraham Lincoln seems to have agreed that it is. A famous story tells of him riding on a mud coach (a type of stagecoach) with a friend. Just as he is explaining that he believes everybody has selfish reasons for their actions, they pass by a mudhole where several piglets are drowning. The mother sow is making an awful noise, but she can't help them. Lincoln asks the driver to stop the coach, gets off, wades into the mudhole, brings the pigs out, and returns to the coach. His friend, remembering what Lincoln had just said, asks him, "Now, Abe, where does selfishness come into this little episode?" Lincoln answers, "Why, bless your soul, Ed, that was the very essence of selfishness. I should have had no peace of mind all day had I gone on and left that suffering old sow worrying over those pigs. I did it to get peace of mind, don't you see?"

So Lincoln saved the pigs in order to benefit himself (and here we thought he was just a nice man). That is, of course, the irony of the story: Lincoln is not known to us as a selfish person. But was his theory right? He may have been lying in claiming that he did his good deed for himself—or he may have been joking—but let us assume that he spoke the truth as he saw it—that he saved the pigs in order to gain peace of mind for himself. Was it still a "selfish" act? That depends on what you call selfish. Is doing things to benefit yourself always selfish, or does it perhaps depend on what it is you want to gain? Would there be a difference between saving a pig for its own sake and saving it because you want to eat it for dinner? Most people would say there is a substantial difference between the two. In other words, it is *what* you want that matters, not just the fact that you want something. If what you want is to save someone, that is surely different from wanting to hurt someone. Lincoln might, of course, interject that saving the pigs was still in his own self-interest, so it wasn't done for them but for himself—but is that true? Why would it have been in his self-interest to know that the pigs were safe if self-gratification was all he cared about? A selfish person hardly loses sleep over the misery of other human beings, let alone that of a sow. Let us suppose, then, that he did it just to feel "warm and fuzzy" inside, and let us conclude that people who help others because they enjoy it are as selfish as can be. Nevertheless, a person who enjoys helping others is not our usual image of a selfish person; rather, as James Rachels points out, that is exactly how we picture an *unselfish* person. (See Box 4.6 for further discussion of Lincoln's motivation.) So if we assume that it is the *objective* rather than the mere fact of our wanting something that makes our want selfish or unselfish, we have an answer to psychological egoism right there: If what made Lincoln feel good was the thought of the pigs being safe—for their own sake, not his—then his deed of saving them was not a selfish deed. If what made him feel good was that now he would somehow benefit from saving them other than by just feeling good, then it was selfish. And how about if it was both? Suppose he saw a certain advantage in people knowing that he was a good guy who cared about pigs (although that's certainly not part of the original story), but he also liked the thought of the pigs being safe? Then it is still a refutation of psychological egoism because there was an unselfish element in an otherwise selfish act. And here we have reached the level of common sense: Some acts are unselfish, some are selfish, and some are a mixed bag. In the Narratives section you will find a contemporary story about a woman who is accused of being selfish because she feels good about helping others, Phoebe from the television sitcom *Friends*.

Box 4.6   LINCOLN: HUMBLE MAN OR CLEVER JOKESTER?

We might ask how Lincoln could have been unaware of the distinction between caring and not caring that becomes apparent when we consider different kinds of behavior. For an intelligent man, his remarks seem unusually dim. It's possible, of course, that the pig story illustrates Lincoln's true nature: that of a very humble and honest man who does not wish to take credit for having done something good. The story makes him all the more endearing, if that is the case, for indeed we know him as Honest Abe. But there is another possibility—that he was joking. Lincoln had a fondness for jokes, and this may have been one of them. Knowing full well that he was doing a nice thing, he made use of *irony* by claiming that rescuing the piglets was nothing but a selfish act. Lincoln scholars may have to decide which version they like best. In any event, Lincoln was speaking as a psychological egoist, regardless of how unselfishly he acted, because he expressed the theory that everyone acts selfishly.

3. Problems of Language As we have seen, psychological egoism presents certain problems because it does not always describe the world in a way that allows us to recognize it. One of its flaws may actually be a problem of *language:* If Lincoln's act of saving the pigs is selfish, what do we then call acts that are *really* selfish? The British philosopher Mary Midgley is extremely critical of the theory of psychological egoism and points out that, since there is such a difference between what psychological egoists call normal selfish behavior (doing something nice for others so you can gain an advantage) and *really* selfish behavior (doing something hurtful to others so you can gain an advantage), it would be illogical to call both selfish. What is the logical consequence of that criticism? If psychological egoism insists that regardless of whether we want to help others or hurt them for our own gain, our desire to help or hurt them is a selfish want. In that case we may respond that we consider it less selfish to help others than to hurt them, and we may want to introduce some new terms: *less selfish* versus *more selfish,* terms that distinguish between acts done for yourself and acts done for others. This, however, is just another way of trying to distinguish selfish behavior from unselfish behavior. Psychological egoism seems to have overlooked the fact that we already have a concept for "less-selfish" behavior that is perfectly well understood: *unselfish.* Changing language to the extent that it goes against our common sense (by claiming that there is no such thing as *unselfish* but that it is acceptable to use the term *less selfish*) does not make psychological egoism correct. So, if the psychological egoist admits that there can be degrees of selfishness, we might reply that the least degree of selfishness is what the rest of us call *unselfish;* if the psychological egoist insists that all acts are self-serving in some way, critics of psychological egoism point to the linguistic phenomenon known as the *fallacy of the suppressed correlative.* The correlative of the word *selfish* is *unselfish,* just as the correlative of *light* is *dark;* other pairs are *hot/cold, tall/short,* and so on. It is a psychological as well as a linguistic fact that we understand one term because we understand the other: If everything were dark, we wouldn't understand the meaning of *light,* and neither would we understand the meaning of *dark,* because it is defined by its contrast to light; without the contrast there is no understanding. In other words, a concept without a correlative becomes meaningless. If all acts are selfish, *selfish* has no correlative, and the statement "All acts are selfish" has no meaning. In fact, we could not make such a statement at all if psychological egoism were correct; the concept of selfishness would not exist, since any nonselfish behavior would be unthinkable. So not only does psychological egoism go against common sense and preclude a complete understanding of the full range of human behavior; it also goes against the rules of language.

This may sound like a complex argument, but we actually use it frequently in everyday situations. Here are a few examples of suppressed correlatives, situations in which something becomes meaningless if it doesn't have any opposite: (1) If you use a highlighter in your textbook, you may have found yourself studying a difficult text and highlighting many sentences. After a while, when you look at the pages, you find that you've actually highlighted just about everything. The task of highlighting all of a sudden has become meaningless; now *everything* is highlighted (the highlighted areas have lost their contrast), and that is just the same as not having anything highlighted. (2) At Starbucks a small cup of coffee is called "tall," a medium is called "grande," and a large is called "venti" (Italian for "twenty"—ounces, presumably). Does the designation "tall" really mean anything anymore when it comes to coffees, or has the meaning been gutted by the disappearance of its opposite, "short"? (3) Sometimes I hear students plead (as a joke, I hope), "Why can't you just give us all A's?" (whether they are deserved or not). The answer is that (aside from the fact that it wouldn't be right), if everybody in the class or the school or the country got A's, the A would become meaningless since there would be no lower grade to serve as a contrast. If instructors bowed to the pressure to give only A's or B's, the whole idea of grading would be undermined. (4) There are situations that are supposed to have significance but are so common that the impact is nullified: Car alarms go off all the time, so the "alarm" effect is gone; people who curse all the time drain their words of any impact, so there is no way to emphasize a really bad situation; parents who yell at their children constantly have no voice impact left when the time comes for a yell to be effective; kids who "cry wolf" won't be believed in the end. And the psychological egoist who claims that everyone is selfish can't explain what *selfish* means if no behavior is recognized as unselfish.

Proponents of psychological egoism have responded that unselfishness doesn't actually exist, but you can still have the *concept* of unselfishness, which serves as the correlative of selfishness, even if it is imaginary; but critics of psychological egoism reply that the theory still does not make much sense. If it states that everybody is selfish to the bone, then it is a downright false theory. If it just says everybody has a selfish streak, then it is so trivial that it is not even interesting.

Ethical Egoism

We have already heard amazing stories about heroic acts of rescue on 9/11. As more survivors tell their stories, we'll probably hear more. A person such as Officer Stuart who lost his life helping commuters get out of the subway would be admired as a hero by most of us.

Calvin and Hobbes   by Bill Watterson

CALVIN AND HOBBES   © Watterson. Reprinted with permission of Universal Press Syndicate.
All rights reserved.

For many readers the idea that egoism might be a legitimate moral theory is surprising, but indeed
Calvin is right: "You ought to look out for Number One" is, in fact, a moral principle. However,
critics of ethical egoism point out that it is hardly an acceptable moral principle. (Since the philosopher Thomas Hobbes is mentioned in this chapter, you might like to know that Hobbes the tiger is
named after Thomas Hobbes.)

However, the ethical egoist would say that, in effect, he did the wrong thing. For
the ethical egoist there is only one rule: *Look after yourself.* The ethical egoist would
say you are throwing your life away.

Here we should make sure that we have our terms straight. This theory is called
ethical egoism simply because it is an ethical theory, a *normative* theory about how
we *ought* to behave (in contrast to psychological egoism, which claims to know how
we actually *do* behave). The theory implies that we ought to be selfish. Or, to put it
more gently, we ought to be *self-interested.* Calling the theory "ethical" does not suggest there might be a decent way to be selfish; it just means ethical egoism is a theory that advocates egoism as a moral rule. (Box 4.7 is a discussion of individual
ethical egoism.)

You Should Look After Yourself

Glaucon insisted that, if you don't take advantage of a situation, you are foolish.
Hobbes claimed that it makes good sense to look after yourself, and morality is a result of that self-interest: If I mistreat others, they may mistreat me, so I resolve to behave myself. This is a rather twisted version of the Golden Rule (Do unto others as
you would have them do unto you; see Box 4.8). It is twisted because it is peculiarly
slanted toward our own self-interest. The reason we should treat others the way we
would like to be treated is that it gives us a good chance of receiving just such treatment; we do it for ourselves, not for others. So the ethical egoist might certainly decide to help another human being in need—not for the sake of the other but to
ensure that "what goes around, comes around." The Golden Rule usually emphasizes

Box 4.7   INDIVIDUAL ETHICAL EGOISM

This version of *ethical egoism,* commonly adopted by small children and childish adults, holds that "everyone ought to do what I want," regardless of whether it is in the other person's interest. This view is rarely taken seriously as an ethical theory because it doesn't have any good arguments to support it except that it's what the person wants. We can't expect everyone else to follow our whims or even look after our interests; this is nothing but emotional tyranny. However, the ethical egoist attitude is not limited to children and childlike adults; people who throughout their lives have been used to having their way will sometimes display the same attitude. From royalty in times past to people of wealth and power in the present, certain individuals (although by no means the majority) will act as though others have responsibilities to them, but they feel exempt from having responsibilities to others.

A moral theory, if it is to be accepted today, has to involve an important element of acceptance. It has to be imaginable that most people, if not everyone, would be willing to adopt the theory for themselves. This phenomenon, which we shall discuss later, is known as *universalizability.* We can hardly imagine the world agreeing to serve our interests, because, after all, what makes us so special? However, it is a fact that some people choose to live their lives seeking to fulfill *someone else's* wishes or interests; such choices may be made by parents, spouses, grown children taking care of their parents, disciples following their guru or leader, and devout believers trying to live the way God wants them to live. If you are a parent or a political or religious leader, you may claim that "people should do what I want because it is good for them." In that case, you are moving out of the realm of egoism; the main interest is no longer yourself, but everyone; you just have the audacity to claim that you know better than anyone else how everyone's lives should be lived.

others, but for the ethical egoist it emphasizes the self. With ethical egoism we encounter a certain phenomenon for the first time in this book: an ethical theory that focuses on the *consequences* of one's actions. Any theory that looks solely to consequences of actions is known as a *consequentialist theory;* the consequences that ethical egoism stipulates are good consequences for the person taking the action. However, we can imagine other kinds of consequentialist theories, such as one that advocates good consequences for as many people as possible. Such a theory is discussed in Chapter 5.

Ethical egoists are themselves quite divided about whether the theory tells you to do *what you want* without regard for others or *what is good for you* without regard for others. The latter version seems to appeal to common sense because, in the long run, just looking for instant gratification is hardly going to make you happy or live longer. Saying that one ought to look after oneself need not, of course, mean that one should annoy others whenever possible, step on their toes, or deliberately neglect their interests. It simply suggests that one should do what will be of long-term benefit to oneself, such as exercising, eating healthy food, avoiding repetitive argumentative situations, and so forth. Even paying one's taxes might be added to the list. In addition, it suggests that other people's interests are of no importance. If you might advance your own interests by helping others, then by all means help others, but only if you

Box 4.8 THE GOLDEN RULE WITH VARIATIONS

Most people know the Golden Rule: Do unto others as you would have them do unto you, or treat others as you would like to be treated. It is often attributed to Jesus Christ; the Gospel of Matthew cites him as saying, "Therefore all things whatsoever ye would that men should do to you, do ye even so to them: for this is the law and the prophets" (7.12). However, others expressed similar thoughts long before the time of Jesus: The Chinese philosopher Confucius (551–479 B.C.E.) is known to have taught his students this version, taken from *The Doctrine of the Mean, The Four Books*: "What you do not like when done to yourself, do not do to others." This is sometimes called the "Silver Rule."

The rule teaches that in order to find a blueprint for treating others, we should imagine how we would or would not like to be treated. Ethical egoists don't read it that way, however; they read it as a rule for protecting yourself and being as comfortable as possible. The way to avoid trouble with others is to treat them as you'd want to be treated—the path of least resistance. The emphasis on *others* is not a given within the rule. This is the aspect of *prudence* connected with the Golden Rule. But as we see in Chapter 5, the Golden Rule is also used as a blueprint for general happiness, one's own as well as others'. In this case, it is concern for *the other person* that underlies the rule.

Recognizing the wisdom of the Golden Rule is perhaps the most important early stage in civilization because it implies that we see others as similar to ourselves and that we see ourselves as deserving no treatment that is better than what others get (although we would generally prefer it—we're not saints). However, the Golden Rule may not be the ultimate rule to live by because (as we discuss further in Chapter 11) what if others *don't want* to be treated as *you'd* like to be treated? Then, according to some thinkers, the "Platinum Rule" ought to kick in: Treat others as *they* want to be treated! Proponents of the Golden Rule say that this takes the universal appeal out of the rule. The spark of moral genius in the rule is precisely that we are *similar* in our human nature—not that we would all like to have things our way.

are the main beneficiary. It is fine to help your children get ahead in school, because you love them and this love is a gratifying emotion for you. But there is no reason to lend a hand to your neighbor's children unless you like them or you achieve gratification through your actions.

This interpretation—that the theory tells us to do whatever will benefit ourselves—results in a rewriting of the Golden Rule because, obviously, it is not always the case that you *will* get the same treatment from others that you give to them. Occasionally you might get away with not treating others decently, because they may never know that you are the source of the bad treatment they are receiving. Ethical egoism tells you that it is perfectly all right to treat others in a way that is to your advantage and not to theirs as long as you can be certain that you will get away with it. At the end of the chapter you'll find a Primary Reading as well as a Narrative by the American philosopher and novelist Ayn Rand, who is generally considered an ethical egoist. She wrote a book in defense of self-interest called *The Virtue of Selfishness,* from which the excerpt is taken, but she is better known for her novels *Anthem, The Fountainhead, We The Living,* and *Atlas Shrugged,* which is represented by an excerpt too. Rand advocated the idea that people have a right, even a duty, to look after themselves and seek their own happiness and that it is "moral cannibalism" to advocate altruistic theories where humans are supposed to feel obliged to help those who have no wish to help themselves—in Rand's words, "moochers and looters." Rand's philosophy was enormously popular some decades ago, and some people predict that there will be a Rand revival in the future.

Shortcomings of Ethical Egoism

Let us return now to Glaucon and his rings. He assumes that not only will the scoundrel take advantage of a ring that can make him invisible, but so will the decent man, and, furthermore, we would call them both fools if they didn't. A theory of psychological egoism, therefore, can also contain a normative element: ethical egoism (which tells us how we *ought* to behave). Of course, it is hard to see what the point is if we can't stop ourselves from doing what we do.

At the end of Glaucon's speech the reader expects Socrates to dispatch the theory of egoism with a quick blow. The answer, however, is a long time coming; as a matter of fact, Plato designed the rest of his *Republic* as a roundabout answer to Glaucon. In the end, Socrates' answer is, The unjust person can't be happy because happiness consists of a good harmony, a balance between the three parts of the soul: *reason, willpower (spirit),* and *desire.* Reason is supposed to dominate willpower, and willpower desire. If desire or willpower dominates the other two, we have a sick person, and a sick person can't be happy by definition, says Socrates. We will return to this theory later in this book.

In considering the question Why be just? we must consider justice in terms of the whole society, not just the individual. We can't argue for justice on the basis of individual situations but only in general terms. That makes the question Why be just? more reasonable because we don't look at individual cases but at an overall picture in which justice and well-being are interrelated. For Socrates and Plato, being just is part of "the good life," and true happiness cannot be attained without justice.

To the modern reader there is something curiously bland and evasive about these answers. Surely unjust persons can be disgustingly happy—they may seem to us to have sick souls, but they certainly don't act as if they are aware of it or suffer any ill effects from it. The answer to this—that being selfish is *just plain wrong in itself*—is not addressed by Socrates at all. For a modern person it seems reasonable to be "just" out of respect for the law or perhaps because that is the right thing to do, but Socrates mentions this only briefly; it is a concern that belongs to a much later time period than the one in which he lived. The highest virtue for the ancient Greeks was, on the whole, ensuring the well-being of the community, and this well-being remained the bottom line more than any abstract moral issue of right and wrong. Today we know this social theory as *communitarianism.* Because justice was best for the state in the final evaluation, justice was a value in itself. In the end, Socrates' answer evokes self-interest and urges us to discern truth from appearance: If you are unjust, your soul will suffer, and so will your community. Today communitarianism is alive and well in the United States—it is a political theory best illustrated by the African proverb "It takes a village to raise a child." In other words, individuals are part of the community and derive their identity from that community—and the

In *Madame Bovary* (MGM, 1942), Emma Bovary (Jennifer Jones, right) loves romantic novels and finds her own life unspeakably drab. She neglects her husband and her daughter, and in this scene she contemplates having an affair with the young man on the left, going shopping for new clothes, and buying new drapes and furniture—anything to make life a little more exciting. The story of *Madame Bovary* is outlined at the end of this chapter as an illustration of egoism.

community members share a responsibility toward each other. A professed contemporary communitarian is Senator Hillary Clinton.

Socrates' attitude may not impress persons seeking self-gratification (who are unlikely to be concerned about the effects of their actions on their souls or on the people around them), but it may have some impact on persons seeking long-term self-interest. It still rests on an empirical assumption, however: that sooner or later you must pay the piper—that is, atone for your wrongdoing. History, though, is full of "bad guys" who have gone to their graves rich and happy. The religious argument that you will go to hell or suffer a miserable next incarnation if you are concerned only with yourself is not really an argument against *egoism* because it still asks you to look after yourself, even to the point of using others for the purpose of ensuring a pleasant afterlife (treat others decently and you shall be saved).

The one type of argument against ethical egoism that has most appealed to scholars insists that ethical egoism is self-contradictory. If you are supposed to look after yourself and your colleague is supposed to look after herself, and if looking after yourself will mean stealing her files, then you and she will be working at cross-purposes: Your duty will be to steal her files from her, and her duty will be to protect her files. We can't have a moral theory that says one's duty should be something that conflicts with someone else's duty, so ethical egoism is therefore inconsistent.

Few ethical egoists find this argument convincing because they don't agree that we can't have a moral theory that gives a green light to different concepts of duty. Such a view assumes that ethical egoism benefits everyone, even when each person does only what is in his or her best interest. Occasionally, ethical egoism assumes just that: We should look after ourselves and mind our own business because meddling in other people's affairs is a violation of privacy; they will not like our charity, they will hate our superiority, and we won't know what is best for them anyway. So, along these lines, we should stay out of other people's affairs because it is best for everybody. The political theory resulting from this point of view is known as *laissez-faire,* the hands-off policy. Political theorists, however, are quick to point out that laissez-faire is by no means an egoistic theory, because it has everybody's best interests at heart. That is precisely what is wrong with the idea that we should adopt ethical egoism for the reason that it will be good for everybody: It may be true that if we all look after ourselves, we'll all be happier—but who is the beneficiary of this idea? Not "I," but "everybody," so this version is, in fact, no longer a moral theory of egoism but something else.

Another argument against ethical egoism is that it carries no weight as a solver of moral conflicts: If you and I disagree about the correct course of action, who is to say who is right? If you favor the course of action that is to your advantage and I favor the course of action that is to my advantage, then there is no common ground. But the ethical egoist generally answers in the same way as to the charge that ethical egoism is self-contradictory: It never claimed to be a theory of consensus in all approaches, merely in the basic approach—that everyone ought to look after him- or herself.

A better argument against the conceptual consistency of ethical egoism is this: Ethical egoism doesn't work in practice. Remember that the theory says all people ought to look out for themselves—not merely that *I* should look out for *myself.* But suppose you set out to look after your own self-interests and advocate that others do the same; within a short while you will realize that your rule is *not* going to be to your advantage, because others will be out there grabbing for themselves, and you will have fierce competition. You might decide that the smart thing to do is to advocate not that all people look out for themselves but that all people look after one another while keeping quiet about your own intention of breaking the rule whenever possible. This would be the prudent thing to do, and it probably would work quite well. The only problem is that this is not a moral theory because, for one thing, it carries a contradiction. It means you must claim to support one principle and act according to another one—in other words, it requires you to be dishonest. Also, a moral theory, in this day and age, has to be able to be extended to everybody; we can't uphold a theory that says it is okay for me to do something because I'm *me,* but not for you just because you're *not me*—that would be assuming that I should have privileges based on the mere fact that I'm *me.*

Logical attacks on ethical egoism have a persuasive power for some—as logical arguments rightly should have. However, perhaps the most forceful argument against ethical egoism involves an emotional component. Often, philosophers have been afraid to appeal to emotions because emotions have been considered irrelevant. But as philosophers such as Martha Nussbaum, Philippa Foot, Philip Hallie, and James Rachels point out, what is a moral sense without the involvement of our feelings? Feelings need not be irrational—they are often quite rational responses to our experiences (see Chapter 1). And what seems such an affront to most people is the apparent callousness of an ethical egoist: Other people's pain simply doesn't matter as a moral imperative.

One example may speak louder than theoretical speculations: the murder in 1998 of seven-year-old Sherrice Iverson by Jeremy Strohmeyer in a Nevada casino restroom. Strohmeyer's friend David Cash knew about the crime taking place, heard the screams, and may even have witnessed it. He never tried to stop his friend, nor did he alert casino security, nor did he turn in his friend afterward.

Psychologically, both Strohmeyer and Cash may have been warped and damaged, but Cash had quite a rational grip of the situation and a straightforward explanation for why he didn't step in. It is debatable whether Cash is an ethical egoist or a moral subjectivist. In an interview he said, "I'm not going to get upset over somebody else's life. I just worry about myself first. I'm not going to lose sleep over somebody else's problems." He seems to be recommending selfishness, not the tolerance of moral subjectivism's "to each his or her own." If so, is this the kind of practical expression of a moral theory that we should think is legitimate, just because it allows everyone else to be selfish too? Isn't this a case in which we are allowed to feel moral outrage over someone's inhumanity? Why, indeed, should we lose sleep over someone else's problems? *Because they are fellow human beings.*

Altruism: Ideal and Reciprocal

To return to the question of September 11: Were the rescuers—those who survived as well as those who died—selfish? Going back to our Lincoln discussion, we can say they were selfish only if they did what they did for purely self-serving reasons. Judging from the remarks of rescuers who survived, their own self-interests seemed to be very far from their minds. And how about the suicidal terrorists? Were they selfish or unselfish, or both? Judging from letters and statements from other terrorists and sympathizers from the same groups, their motivation was mixed: They believed the Koran promised them direct, immediate access to heaven, where they would live in bliss for eternity, attended by beautiful virgins—but they also believed they were doing a heroic deed for their people. The Western mind-set considers self-sacrifice to be noble. Then why do most of us not consider terrorist acts noble? Because self-sacrifice is usually regarded as an act wherein a person dies trying to help others, not one that involves deliberately killing innocent people. To discuss this issue further you may want to go directly to Chapter 13, where we address the question of terrorism—but you may also want to consider the concept of *group egoism:* extending your self-interest to the group you belong to, so that if you could help the group survive by giving up an advantage or even sacrificing yourself, then (theoretically) you'd be willing to do that. A group egoist would not consider members of other groups valuable, or as having claims as legitimate as those of one's own group. Suicide bombers do not have the interest of all at heart—just the interests of their own group—at the cost of others.

As an alternative to ethical egoism, *altruism* hardly seems preferable if we view it in its ideal, normative sense: *Everybody ought to give up his or her own self-interest for others*. In that case we might want to complain (as the philosopher and writer Ayn Rand did) that we have only one life to live, and why should we let the "moochers and leeches" drain our life away? If we let them take advantage of us, they surely will. Our lives are not things to be thrown away. Only a few philosophers and a few religions have ever held such an extreme altruistic theory. One person in the late twentieth century who did was the Lithuanian-French philosopher Emmanuel Levinas, whom you will meet in Chapter 10. For Levinas, the Other (another human being, the stranger) is always more important than you yourself are (which also means that you are important, as a stranger and an Other, to everyone else), and you should always put the needs of the Other ahead of your own. But Levinas is an exception among modern thinkers; usually there is a realistic recognition of the fact that humans are apt to ask what's in it for them. (See Box 4.9 for a discussion of psychological and ethical altruism.) Two stories in the Narratives section each explore the idea of utter selflessness: O. Henry's "The Gift of the Magi" and J. R. R. Tolkien's *Lord of the Rings*.

Ideal altruism seems to imply that there is something inherently *wrong* with acting to benefit oneself, and if that is the case, it will never become a widely accepted moral theory because it will work only for saints. According to the Australian philosopher Peter Singer, there is another way of viewing altruism, a much more realistic and rational way: Looking after the interests of others makes sense because, overall, everyone benefits from it. This moderate, limited version of altruism is sometimes called Golden Rule altruism (or reciprocal altruism): You are ready to place others' interests ahead of your own, especially in emergency situations, and you expect them to do the same for you. Philosophers are in disagreement over whether this position actually deserves the name of altruism. (David Hume's theory of fellow-feeling as an aspect of altruism is discussed in Box 4.10.)

In *The Expanding Circle* (1981), Singer suggests that egoism is, in fact, more costly than altruism. He presents a new version of a classic example, known as the prisoner's dilemma. Two early hunters are attacked by a saber-toothed cat. They obviously both want to flee, but (let us suppose) they also care for each other. If they both flee, one will be picked off and eaten. If one flees and one stays and fights, the fleeing one will live but the fighting one will die. If both stay and fight, there is a chance that they can fight off the cat. So it is actually in the interest of both of them to stay together, and all the more so if they care for each other. Singer's point is that evolution would favor such an arrangement, because trustworthy partners would be viewed as better than ones who leave you behind to get eaten, and they would be selected in future partnerships. If you are an egoist and you manage to get picked as a partner by an altruist, you will be the one who benefits from the situation (the altruist is sure to stay, and you'll be able to get away). This will work only a few times, however; after a while the altruist will be wise to you and your kind. In the end, then, it is in your own self-interest not to be too self-interested.

This argument actively defeats not only the everyday variety of ethical egoism that says you ought to do what you want—because in the end that will not improve

Box 4.9   PSYCHOLOGICAL AND ETHICAL ALTRUISM

The term *altruism* comes from the Latin *alter,* meaning "other." The version of altruism that we are discussing in this chapter is sometimes known as ethical altruism—not because there is a form of altruism that is *un*ethical, but simply because philosophers have seen a parallel to ethical egoism: "Everyone *ought* to disregard his or her own interests for the sake of others." In other words, ethical altruism is a normative theory, like its opposite, ethical egoism. But is there also a counterpart to psychological egoism, *psychological altruism*? I'll let you be the judge of that. As psychological egoism, a descriptive theory, claims that everyone is selfish at heart, psychological altruism would claim that everyone is unselfish at heart: "Everyone always disregards his or her own interests for the sake of others." Now who would hold such a theory? Not many, since it seems to fly in the face of the facts: We know very well that not everyone in this world is caring and unselfish. As a matter of fact, one might speculate that psychological altruism was invented by a philosopher with a sense of symmetry, just to have a matching pair of altruisms to compare the two forms of egoism with. But if psychological altruism is redefined in the following way, "There is something good and caring deep down in every human being," then the theory sounds quite familiar and plausible to many people. You may remember the phrase "ought implies can" used as an excuse by psychological egoism: "Don't tell me I ought to be unselfish, because I can't." The same idea works for psychological altruism: The person who is caring by nature might say to the ethical egoist, "Don't tell me I ought to be selfish, because I can't!"

The concoction of psychological altruism may not reflect any actual moral theory, but it does teach an interesting lesson in ethics: If we think psychological altruism is unrealistic and makes no sense, then we also have to criticize psychological egoism for the same reason because the theories are based on the same logic and are vulnerable to the same criticisms! My astute students at Mesa College pointed this little tidbit out, and I'm happy to share it with you.

your survival odds—but also the more sophisticated *rational ethical egoism* that requires us to think of what is to our advantage in the long run. If we look toward our own advantage exclusively, we may not be optimizing our chances, as the example of the hunters shows. Being capable of taking others' interests into consideration actually improves our own survival odds.

Why is this viewpoint not just another version of the ethical egoist's credo of looking after yourself? Because it involves someone else's interests too. It says that there is nothing wrong with keeping an eye out for yourself, so long as it doesn't happen at the expense of someone else's interests. In other words, the solution may not be myself *or* others, but myself *and* others. This idea, incorporated in the moral theory of *utilitarianism,* will be explored in the next chapter. The film *Return to Paradise,* featured in the Narratives section, explores the concept of how far altruism and egoism can take a person when it boils down to friendship obligations.

So what do biologists and psychologists at the cutting edge today think about the idea that humans are born selfish and become moral beings only through reluctant acculturation? It is not nearly as much in fashion as it used to be. The possibility that

Box 4.10   DAVID HUME: HUMANS ARE BENEVOLENT BY NATURE

David Hume, Scottish philosopher and historian. Hume believed that human beings are born with a fellow-feeling, a sense of compassion and empathy for others.

The Scottish philosopher David Hume (1711–1776) believed compassion is the one natural human feeling that holds us together in a society. For Hume, all of ethics can be reduced to the idea that reason acts as the handmaiden to our feelings; there is no such thing as an *objectively* moral act—nothing is good or bad in itself, not even murder. The good and bad lie in our *feelings* toward the act. For Hume, all morality rests ulti-

mately on our emotional responses, and there are no "moral facts" outside our own personal sensitivity. This theory says that whatever we would like to see happen we think of as morally good, and whatever we would hate to see happen we think of as morally evil. And what is it we would like to see happen? For Hume the answer is, whatever corresponds to our *natural feeling of concern for others.* Contrary to Hobbes, Hume believes that humans are equipped not only with self-love but also with love for others, and this emotion gives us our moral values. We simply react with sympathy to others through a built-in instinct—at least most people do. Even persons who are generally selfish will feel compassion toward others if there is nothing in the situation that directly concerns them personally. Having the virtues of compassion and benevolence is a natural thing to Hume, and if we are a little short on such virtues, it simply means that we lack a natural ability, as when we are nearsighted. Such people are an exception to the rule.

This means that Hume's theory, far from being merely a focus on how we feel about things, is actually an example of *soft universalism:* We may have many different ideas and feelings about right and wrong, good and bad, but as human beings, most of us share a bottom-line criterion for morality: a fellow-feeling, a natural concern for others.

---

human evolution has favored the less selfish individuals, as Singer's example claims, now seems quite plausible.

The Selfish-Gene Theory and Its Critics

A theory that arose in the 1970 and that has become popular to the extent that many people have taken its viewpoint as an established truth is the *selfish-gene* theory. This theory was introduced by Richard Dawkins in his book *The Selfish Gene* (1976) and supported by the famous sociobiologist Edward O. Wilson as a way of explaining, scientifically, why some animals as well as humans behave in an altruistic way. In the spirit of psychological egoism, it is not that humans and animals actually behave self-lessly, but that such behavior is an instinctive way to promote the survival, not of the individual, but of his or her genes. So why do humans help strangers, even if it some-times costs them their lives? Because we have an instinct built into us from ancient pre-hominid times that we must help our relatives live, so our DNA will live on in them; and our instincts haven't caught up to the fact that we usually aren't related to most people we encounter. Why would a baboon apparently sacrifice herself to leop-ards so that her "troop" can make a getaway? Because she is closely related to the troop, and her sacrifice ensures that her genes will survive. Why do dogs wake their owners up in the middle of the night to make sure they get out of the house that's on fire? Because they think their owners are the alpha dogs of their pack, and alpha dogs are related to the lower-status dogs, so their genes will survive. (At this point the crit-ics are beginning to raise their eyebrows in disbelief.) In October 2004 off the coast of New Zealand, a group of one adult lifeguard and three teens were herded together in a tight circle by a pod of dolphins—and they didn't understand why, until they saw a ten-foot white shark trying to approach them. The dolphins circled the humans for forty minutes until the shark got tired and swam off. The whole event was witnessed by another lifeguard in a boat and by people on the beach a hundred yards away. What would the selfish-gene theorist say to that? That the dolphins use the same ma-neuvers to protect their own young, and they can't tell the difference between a human in a wetsuit and dolphin babies. But few animal behaviorists would claim that dolphins, or any animal for that matter, can't tell the difference between humans and their own species, especially since they're excellent at telling the difference between their own babies and other dolphins' babies (because male dolphins will often try to kill the offspring of other male dolphins). So could we really be witnessing animals making *moral choices*? We will return to this question later.

As far as humans go, does the selfish-gene theory offer any kind of insight? Many philosophers believe it creates more problems than it solves: When humans behave altruistically toward strangers, it is often because of the very fact that they are strangers—we don't confuse them with relatives. On the contrary, we may deliber-ately *choose* to treat them *as if* they are relatives, which is something completely dif-ferent. The British philosopher Mary Midgley, whom you'll remember from an earlier section in this chapter, has been a vocal critic of the selfish gene theory as well as a critic of psychological egoism. Midgley suggests that a much simpler explanation ex-ists for our altruistic behavior than some selfish gene: It's the fact that we've all grown up in groups with other people, and in most cases the people who raised us loved us and cared about our well-being. And when we raise children, we care about them for their sake, too. So we have a built-in capacity for caring for our family—and in our human society we just extend that capacity to strangers, who become *honorary relatives* for a time. What makes this different from a version of the selfish-gene the-ory is that we extend our caring capacity to strangers not for *our* sake (to perpetuate our genes) but for *theirs* (because we care about how they feel).

An example may illustrate what Midgley means: In February 2002 a seven-year-old girl, Danielle van Dam, was abducted in the middle of the night from her bedroom in an upscale and supposedly safe San Diego neighborhood. Friends and neighbors of the parents immediately went about organizing a search, setting up a website, and distributing fliers. While everyone feared the worst—especially after a neighbor, after several weeks of investigation, was arrested and charged with kidnapping and murder in the case—the search effort continued. The San Diego district attorney commented that he had never heard of a volunteer effort that size in California: Some twenty-five hundred people came from all over San Diego, but also from Los Angeles, Oregon, Arizona, and Texas to participate in the search.

In the end it was indeed a group of volunteers who found the girl's body in a rural area. What made these strangers give up their time to look for a little girl they'd never met? Many said they were parents and if it were their child, they'd want someone to help look for him or her. But many also said that they just felt they had to. A television commentator perhaps said it best: Danielle had been adopted by all of San Diego, indeed, by the whole nation. Was it just because she was cute? Because she was white, perhaps? Because television played home videos of her? If so, what about all the abducted children who aren't cute, or white, or on video? Opinions may differ on that, but most volunteers simply saw her as a child taken from her own bed, supposedly the safest place on earth. She was, to them, their own honorary child for a while, and I think most of us who followed the story reacted not simply as Hobbes claims human nature dictates, out of fear the same thing might happen to our children, but out of a desire to extend to strangers emotions ordinarily reserved for family. Since Danielle's death other cases have been added to the phenomenon of public outpouring of emotion and care for strangers in need: the abduction of Elizabeth Smart in Salt Lake City; the murder of Laci Peterson in Modesto, California; and the abduction and murder of college student Dru Sjodin in North Dakota and eleven-year old Carly Brucia in Florida, to mention a few. In the introduction you read how such an interest may be rooted in some misdirected tribal form of human curiosity, but in Midgley's interpretation it becomes one of the finer emotions that we are capable of: caring about the welfare of strangers as if they are our own relatives, for a while.

In addition, studies of fifteen low-technology cultures around the world recently undertaken by the anthropologist Joe Henrich of UCLA, in close collaboration with economists from the United States and Switzerland, conclude that the story of the selfish gene doesn't hold up to scrutiny: Overall, in every group, humans are more generous than stingy, and the more socially interdependent the society, the more generous the individuals. Henrich concludes that neither egoism nor altruism is innate—the more social the culture, the less selfish the individuals.

Can Animals Have Morals?

But that leads us back to the question: If humans can truly behave in a somewhat/sometimes selfless manner, what about the higher animals? What about those dolphins saving the group of four swimmers in New Zealand? Throughout history there have been numerous similar examples. Is the most plausible explanation that they simply don't know what they're doing, or do they make what we would call a moral choice? Consider this story:

Some years ago a small boy fell into the Western Lowland gorilla pit at the Brookfield Zoo in Chicago. The female gorilla Binti Jua, herself a new mother, picked up the unconscious child and shielded him from the other gorillas. Then she carried him over to the doorway, where she was used to zoo personnel going in and out, and a rescue crew came and got the boy.

The story received nationwide attention. Why did Binti Jua show such seemingly "human" concern for the child? Many people were astonished to hear that a gorilla could show signs of compassion, let alone for someone not of her own species. A curator explained that she had been trained to bring her own baby to curators, and she was accustomed to being in close proximity with humans. So some concluded that Binti Jua did not act out of any rational or compassionate decision but simply on the basis of her training. Perhaps she was used to getting a reward for bringing her own baby and expected a reward for bringing the child. Other animal behaviorists who work with great apes didn't find Binti's action very remarkable: Gorillas and chimpanzees have a great capacity for compassion, they said, and will shield and defend an infant ape against aggressive adult apes. But Binti showed not just a compassion that went beyond her own species but good common sense in carrying the boy over to the place where humans would be most likely to come and get him. So is it possible for a great ape to act unselfishly? Binti may certainly have been expecting a reward, but she also exhibited a gentle concern for the boy himself, so in one gesture this gorilla demonstrated transspecies compassion and foresight that seem to go beyond instinct and training.

Science and philosophy have generally assumed that nonhuman animals live in a nonmoral universe of innocence, where what seems cruel to humans is just the natural response of self-preservation: They are beyond the categories of good and evil. But now comes thought-provoking new research, gathering results from years of observing monkeys, apes, dolphins, whales, elephants, and wolves. Contrary to what people have told each other for so long about nonmoral animals, it turns out that some form of moral code seems to prevail in all these groups of social animals, and "moral code" here doesn't just mean that each animal has an instinct for behaving within the group, because often an individual (usually a young animal) will misbehave and then be punished by the group (with beating or ostracism, but usually not death). After the punishment, there is usually a kiss-and-make-up phase. According to Frans de Waal of Emory University's Yerkes Primate Center, chimps share food with one another and are indignant when an individual who seldom shares his or her own food expects a share of someone else's. At the primate center, two young female apes came home late one day and held up dinner for all the other apes in the research group; the scientists kept them separate overnight for their safety, but the next day they were beaten up by the rest of the colony. That night they were the first to come home. So the origin of moral rules may have to be sought much farther back in time than the Pleistocene, when Singer's hunters decided whether to run or to fight the saber-toothed cat.

This also means that the psychological egoist's theory that we are "born" selfish needs to be rewritten because it is too vague a statement in light of new research. It is not impossible that each child (and each chimpanzee) is born completely selfish, exclusively focusing on what Freud calls the "pleasure principle," the pursuit of feeling good, and that we only begin to modify our selfish behavior when we realize we can't get away with it constantly (which was Hobbes's theory, and Glaucon's before him). But the child is not the same as the adult, and some thinkers claim that what I've outlined here is the *genetic fallacy*: confusing the origin of something with what it has become at a later stage. We don't ordinarily claim that children are moral agents, because psychologists tell us that children really don't know the difference between right and wrong before they are about seven or eight years old. So why should the amoral demeanor of a small child be held up as the natural morality of an adult? We don't claim that the talent of a gifted ballplayer, a star chef, a good parent, or a great teacher can be reduced to their skills and knowledge when they were four years old. Children experience *socialization,* and since humans are social beings by nature, the effects on the individual of living in society are part of what we are as human beings. With the right training, we develop intellectually and technically as we grow older; therefore, it should be apparent that we also develop morally. We may start out in life as selfish, but with socialization, most people end up being capable of taking other people's interests into account—not merely because it is the prudent thing to do but also because they develop an interest in other people's well-being. And that may be the secret behind the immense evolutionary success of human beings.

In his book *Good Natured: The Origins of Right and Wrong in Humans and Other Animals* (1996), Frans de Waal speculates that although humans are the only animals that can take delight in cruel treatment of others, both humans and great apes have the capacity for selfless caring for others. Echoing the thoughts of David Hume as well as Peter Singer and Charles Darwin himself, he writes:

> Human sympathy is not unlimited. It is offered most readily to one's own family and clan, less readily to other members of the community, and most reluctantly, if at all, to outsiders. The same is true of the succorant behavior of animals. The two share not only a cognitive and emotional basis, but similar constraints in their expression.
>
> Despite its fragility and selectivity, the capacity to care for others is the bedrock of our moral system. It is the only capacity that does not snugly fit the hedonic cage in which philosophers, psychologists, and biologists have tried to lock the human spirit. One of the principal functions of morality seems to be to protect and nurture this caring capacity, to guide its growth and expand its reach, so that it can effectively balance other human tendencies that need little encouragement.

Study Questions

1. What "other human tendencies" is Frans de Waal talking about? Do you agree with him that humans and some apes share the capacity for caring? Why or why not?

2. What are the most powerful arguments in favor of psychological egoism? What are the most damaging arguments against it?

3. Discuss the concept of ethical egoism in its most rational form: We ought to treat others the way we want to be treated to ensure our own safety and prosperity. What can be said for this approach? What can be said against it?

4. Discuss examples of heroic rescues from 9/11, including the story of the seeing-eye dog. Can they be sufficiently explained by psychological egoism? Why or why not?

Primary Readings and Narratives

The Primary Readings are the story of the Ring of Gyges from Plato's *Republic,* an excerpt from Erik Katz, "The Rings of Tolkien and Plato: Lessons in Power, Choice, and Morality," an excerpt from Thomas Hobbes's *Leviathan,* and an excerpt from Ayn Rand's philosophical essay "The Ethics of Emergencies." The first Narrative is a summary and excerpt from an episode of the TV show *Friends* about whether an unselfish act is possible. The second Narrative is a summary of the film *Return to Paradise,* whose plot is a variation on the prisoner's dilemma. The third Narrative is a summary and excerpt from Gustave Flaubert's classic novel *Madame Bovary,* about a woman who destroys the life of her family as well as her own. The fourth Narrative is an excerpt from *Atlas Shrugged,* about the rights of creative people to maintain their high standards and look out for themselves. Two more Narratives complete the chapter: O. Henry's "The Gift of the Magi," about the sacrifices of two young newlyweds, and J. R. R. Tolkien's *The Lord of the Rings*—here you'll find a summary of the main characters, with a focus on the themes of selfishness and sacrifice.

Primary Reading

Republic

PLATO

Book II. Excerpt.

You have already read a section of Plato's most famous Dialogue, *The Republic,* in Chapter 2. Here Socrates and Glaucon discuss the issue of justice and selfishness, illustrated by Glaucon's story of the Ring of Gyges. Glaucon is playing the devil's advocate, provoking Socrates into defending the concept of justice. Socrates is talking about the conversation to friends, so the narrator (the "I") is supposed to be Socrates himself (as written by Plato). Notice Socrates' answer at the end of this excerpt. Is he serious? Hardly; Socrates was famous for his wry, ironic answers, and this is one of them. The rest of *The Republic* is in a sense dedicated to proving Glaucon wrong.

Good, said Glaucon. Listen then, and I will begin with my first point: the nature and origin of justice.

What people say is that to do wrong is, in itself, a desirable thing; on the other hand, it is not at all desirable to suffer wrong, and the harm to the sufferer outweighs the advantage to the doer. Consequently, when men have had a taste of both, those who have not the power to seize the advantage and escape the harm decide that they would be better off if they made a compact neither to do wrong nor to suffer it. Hence they begin to make laws and covenants with one another; and whatever the law prescribed they called lawful and right. That is what right or justice is and how it came into existence; it stands half-way between the best thing of all—to do wrong with impunity—and the worst, which is to suffer wrong without the power to retaliate. So justice is accepted as a compromise, and valued, not as good in itself, but for lack of power to do wrong; no man worthy of the name, who had that power, would ever enter into such a compact with anyone; he would be mad if he did. That, Socrates, is the nature of justice according to this account, and such the circumstances in which it arose.

The next point is that men practise it against the grain, for lack of power to do wrong. How true that is, we shall best see if we imagine two men, one just, the other unjust, given full license to do whatever they like, and then follow them to observe where each will be led by his desires. We shall catch the just man taking the same road as the unjust; he will be moved by self-interest, the end which it is natural to every creature to pursue as good, until forcibly turned aside by law and custom to respect the principle of equality.

Now, the easiest way to give them that complete liberty of action would be to imagine them possessed of the talisman found by Gyges, the ancestor of the famous Lydian Croesus. The story tells how he was a shepherd in the King's service. One day there was a great storm, and the ground where his flock was feeding was rent by an earthquake. Astonished at the sight, he went down into the chasm and saw, among other wonders of which the story tells, a brazen horse, hollow, with windows in its sides. Peering in, he saw a dead body, which seemed to be of more than human size. It was naked save for a gold ring, which he took from the finger and made his way out. When the shepherds met, as they did every month, to send an account to the King of the state of his flocks, Gyges came wearing the ring. As he was sitting with the others, he happened to turn the bezel of the ring inside his hand. At once he became invisible, and his companions, to his surprise, began to speak of him as if he had left them. Then, as he was fingering the ring, he turned the bezel outwards and became visible again. With that, he set about testing the ring to see if it really had this power, and always with the same result: according as he turned the bezel inside or out he vanished and reappeared. After this discovery he contrived to be one of the messengers sent to the court. There he seduced the Queen, and with her help murdered the King and seized the throne.

Now suppose there were two such magic rings, and one were given to the just man, the other to the unjust. No one, it is commonly believed, would have such iron strength of mind as to stand fast in doing right or keep his hands off other men's goods, when he could go to the market-place and fearlessly help himself to anything he wanted, enter houses and sleep with any woman he chose, set prisoners free and kill men at his pleasure, and in a word go about among men with the powers of a god. He would behave no better than the other; both would take the same course. Surely this would be strong proof that men do right only under compulsion; no individual thinks of it as good for him personally, since he does wrong whenever he finds he has the power. Every man believes that wrong-doing pays him personally much better, and, according to this theory, that is the truth. Granted full license to do as he liked, people would think him a miserable fool if they found him refusing to wrong his neighbours or to touch their belongings, though in public they would keep up a pretence of praising his conduct, for fear of being wronged themselves. So much for that.

Finally, if we are really to judge between the two lives, the only way is to contrast the extremes of justice and injustice. We can best do that by imagining our two men to be perfect types, and crediting both to the full with the qualities they need for their respective ways of life. To begin with the unjust man: he must be like any consummate master of a craft, a physician or a captain, who, knowing just what his art can do, never tries to do more, and can always retrieve a false step. The unjust man, if he is to reach perfection, must be equally discreet in his criminal attempts, and he must not be found out, or we shall think him a bungler; for the highest pitch of injustice is to seem just when you are not. So we must endow our man with the full complement of injustice; we must allow him to have secured a spotless reputation for virtue while committing the blackest crimes; he must be able to retrieve any mistake, to defend himself with convincing eloquence if his misdeeds are denounced, and, when force is required, to bear down all opposition by his courage and strength and by his command of friends and money.

Now set beside this paragon the just man in his simplicity and nobleness, one who, in Aeschylus' words, "would be, not seem, the best." There must, indeed, be no such seeming; for if his character were apparent, his reputation would bring him honours and rewards, and then we should not know whether it was for their sake that he was just or for justice's sake alone. He must be stripped of everything but justice, and denied every advantage the other enjoyed. Doing no wrong, he must have the worst reputation for wrong-doing, to test whether his virtue is proof against all that comes of having a bad name; and under this lifelong imputation of wickedness, let him hold on his course of justice unwavering to the point of death. And so, when the two men have carried their justice and injustice to the last extreme, we may judge which is the happier.

My dear Glaucon, I exclaimed, how vigorously you scour these two characters clean for inspection, as if you were burnishing a couple of statues!

I am doing my best, he answered. Well, given two such characters, it is not hard, I fancy, to describe the sort of life that each of them may expect; and if the description sounds rather coarse, take it as coming from those who cry up the merits of injustice rather than from me. They will tell you that our just man will be thrown into prison, scourged and racked, will have his eyes burnt out, and, after every kind of torment, be impaled. That will teach him how much better it is to seem virtuous than to be so. [. . .]

With his reputation for virtue, [the unjust man] will hold offices of state, ally himself by marriage to any family he may choose, become a partner in any business, and, having no scruples about being dishonest, turn all these advantages to profit. If he is involved in a lawsuit, public or private, he will get the better of his opponents, grow rich on the proceeds, and be able to help his friends and harm his enemies. Finally, he can make sacrifices to the gods and dedicate offerings with due magnificence, and, being in a much better position than the just man to serve the gods as well as his chosen friends, he may reasonably hope to stand higher in the favour of heaven. So much better, they say, Socrates, is the life prepared for the unjust by gods and men.

Here Glaucon ended, and I was meditating a reply, when his brother Adeimantus exclaimed:

Surely, Socrates, you cannot suppose that that is all there is to be said.

Why, isn't it? said I.

Study Questions

1. How does Glaucon use the story of Gyges to express a theory of human nature?

2. Is Glaucon right? Why or why not?

3. Plato has Glaucon speculate about the terrible fate of the truly good man. How might Plato's readers interpret that? (Remember that this dialogue was written years after Socrates' death at the hands of the Athenian court.)

Primary Reading

The Rings of Tolkien and Plato:
Lessons in Power, Choice, and Morality

ERIK KATZ

Essay, 2003. Excerpt.

The Lord of the Rings and Philosophy is one in a series of books about films and television series and their philosophical content. The editors, Gregory Bassham and Eric Bronson, have collected sixteen essays exploring themes such as "The Ring," "The Quest for Happiness," and "Good and Evil in Middle-Earth." I have chosen some excerpts from the essay comparing the "Ring of Power" motif in Tolkien and Plato, relying on assurances from my students that the general plot of *The Lord of the Rings* is sufficiently familiar to the general movie-renting audience to eliminate the need for a summary of the story. Should you need a refresher, you'll find an overview of the most important characters in the Narratives section.

The Temptation of the One Ring

With this ancient challenge to the moral life as background, we can see how Tolkien's characters demonstrate various responses to the question posed by Plato: would a just person be corrupted by the possibility of almost unlimited power? Through these different responses, Tolkien shows us—not by philosophical argument, but by the thoughts and actions of "living" characters—why we should be moral beings, why we should live a virtuous life. But Tolkien's stories about the One Ring actually improve and augment Plato's argument, for Tolkien's Ring explicitly corrupts the souls of its possessors. The use of the One Ring corrupts the desires, interests, and beliefs of those who wield it. Plato *argues* that such corruption will occur, but Tolkien *shows* us this corruption through the thoughts and actions of his characters. Moreover, Tolkien also shows us the difficulties involved in living a life of virtue; there are burdens to be undertaken and sacrifices that must be made to fulfill the requirements of morality.

The character that most obviously illustrates Plato's argument that the unjust life leads to nothing but unhappiness is Gollum, who is invariably described as a miserable creature, afraid of everything, friendless, homeless, constantly seeking his "precious" Ring. Gollum is the mortal being who possessed the Ring for the longest period of time and he seems almost completely corrupted by the desire for it—every action he takes in the book, even guiding Frodo and Sam on their journey into Mordor, is designed to regain the Ring. It is during the long journey through the barren lands surrounding Mordor that we see the true disintegration of Gollum's personality, all caused by the desire of the Ring. Gollum constantly talks to himself, for his soul is split in two: one part is Sméagol, the hobbit he was before the Ring came into his possession, and one half is Gollum, the creature whose only desire is to possess the Ring again. The only reason that Gollom cooperates with Frodo and Sam is that the two halves (what Sam calls "Slinker and Stinker") have made a truce: "neither wanted the Enemy to get the Ring." Frodo recognizes the immense power that the thought of the Ring has on Gollum's mind. Earlier, he made Gollum swear on the Ring that he would be a faithful guide, but soon after, near the Black Gate of Mordor, Gollum was in "great distress" at the thought that Frodo would lose the Ring:

> "Don't take the Precious to Him! . . . Keep it, nice master, and be kind to Sméagol. Don't let Him have it. Or go away, go to nice places, and give it back to little Sméagol. . . . Sméagol will keep it safe; he will do lots of good, especially to nice hobbit."

This outburst by Gollum prompts Frodo to get to the heart of the matter, to describe to Gollum the peril he faces, the danger of losing his soul. Gollum swore a promise by what he calls the Precious. The Ring will not only hold Gollum to this promise, but will seek a way to twist it to Gollum's own undoing. "Already you are being twisted," Frodo tells Gollum. And then, with a strange prescience of the climax of the story, Frodo states that if the need arises, he would himself put on the Ring and command Gollum to cast himself into the fire.

Gollum is thus a clear example of the corruption of the soul and the loss of a meaningful life caused by the overwhelming desire for the Ring of Power. But Gollum is not a complete example of the problem posed by Plato, for we do not see the moment when he makes the choice to use the Ring. For Plato, as well as for Tolkien, the crucial moment in each character's story is the moment in which they are tempted to use the Ring. It is that moment of choice that determines a character's fate, that moment of choice that bears a remarkable similarity to Plato's story of the shepherd Gyges and his decision to use the ring of invisibility. Gollum's moment of choice occurred long before the opening pages of *The Lord of the Rings*—even long before the beginning of *The Hobbit*. Although Gandalf recounts the story—how Sméagol kills his friend Déagol to gain possession of the Ring—we do not live through Sméagol's original moral crisis and decision. In Gollum instead we see merely the final result of the life led in the pursuit of power, a life of misery and corruption.

Boromir is the character who most closely fits the model of Glaucon's moral argument concerning the shepherd Gyges—the virtuous man corrupted by the temptation of power. Tolkien depicts Boromir as a man of action—noble, good-hearted, and brave—who is bewildered by the complexities of the plan to destroy the One Ring. During the council of Elrond, Boromir asks why those assembled should not think that the Ring "has come into our hands to serve us in the very hour of need. . . . Wielding it the Free Lords of the Free may surely defeat the Enemy. . . . Let the Ring be your weapon . . . Take it and go forth to victory!" Boromir wants to use the One Ring for good purposes. He sees nothing wrong with using the Ring to satisfy the desires of the free peoples of Middle-earth (and of himself) to defeat the evil of Sauron.

Boromir's idea to use the Ring is rejected by Elrond—and the rest of the members of the Council—in terms that evoke Plato's argument in the *Republic:* "We cannot use the Ruling Ring. . . . It . . . is altogether evil. . . . The very desire of it corrupts the heart." Using the power of evil ultimately destroys the soul ("corrupts the heart").

Boromir seems to be persuaded, and throughout the journey south with the Fellowship he does not talk about wielding the Ring for the forces of good. But in the climax to *The Fellowship of the Ring,* Boromir is overcome by the temptation to use the Ring in the war against Mordor. He secretly follows Frodo into the woods near Amon Hen in order to convince him to bring the Ring to Gondor. Yet Boromir's words betray him, as he begins to envision himself as a great warrior in command of the Ring and of all the forces against Mordor. First, he argues that the Ring will save his people, but it soon becomes clear to Frodo that there are some selfish motives at work. "It is not yours save by unhappy chance," Boromir says. "It might have been mine. It should be mine. Give it to me!" Boromir attempts to take the Ring by force, but Frodo slips the Ring onto his finger, turns invisible, and escapes.

Boromir redeems his heroic nature by defending Merry and Pippin against the attacking orcs, and as he dies he confesses to Aragorn that he attempted to take the Ring from Frodo. The corruption caused by the Ring is thus not permanent, but perhaps only because Boromir ultimately had so little contact with the *Ring.* Nevertheless, Boromir is a perfect example of the immoralist's challenge that Glaucon proposes in Plato's dialogue: Boromir is the just man who finds a Ring of Power and is unable to resist the temptation to act with impunity, as if he were a god. The desire foe the power of the Ring so corrupts his soul that he accuses Frodo of being an evil ally of the Dark Lord.The ethical lesson is clear: A Ring of Power corrupts even the person who is brave, strong, and virtuous. . . .

Galadriel refuses the One Ring. She remains true to her principles, to her integrity as an individual, to herself—she will "remain Galadriel." Through her, Tolkien shows us that a strong and virtuous person can refuse the temptation of immense power, even at a great personal cost; for Galadriel knows that by refusing to accept the power of the Ring she will be helpless to maintain the elvish presence in Middle-earth. Galadriel thus represents one answer to the immoralist's challenge of Plato. She refuses to let the possibility of power corrupt her soul.

Boromir and Galadriel demonstrate two different responses to the problem posed by Plato concerning the relationship between power, personal choice, and morality. With these two characters, unlike Gollum, we see the actual moment of choice. But although the responses of Boromir and Galadriel are different, one aspect of the choices is the same: neither ever physically possesses the Ring. What of the characters that do choose to use the

Ring? Do their actions help us understand the relationship between power, corruption, and morality? Here we must turn to Tom Bombadil, Frodo, and Sam. . . .

Deep down in his heart, Sam knows who he is. As Galadriel knew to remain Galadriel and to reject the Ring, Sam knows that he can never be other than the plain commonsense hobbit, Samwise Gamgee, the small and caring gardener of the Shire. Fortified by his love for Frodo, he remains true to himself and rejects the power of the Ring. In Sam's rejection of the One Ring during his most extreme crisis we learn that the virtuous and strong-willed person can turn away from a life of evil, a life of almost unlimited power, by focusing on his or her true self.

It is clear that Tolkien is demonstrating to us the progressive forces of corruption of the possession and use of the One Ring, for even Frodo, the hero of the book, succumbs to its corruption in his failure to destroy the Ring. He begins with innocent and accidental uses of the Ring's power, but eventually gives over to its seductive power by making conscious and deliberate decisions to wear the Ring, and even, at last, not to destroy it. And as in Plato's argument, the key feature of corruption caused by the Ring is the corruption of the soul, the "heart," or the personality of the wielder of the Ring. To resist the Ring is to remain oneself, to be the person you are without any extraordinary powers. All who come in contact with the Ring (except, it appears, Bombadil) lose themselves (at least momentarily) in the desire to be greater than they are.

Study Questions

1. What are the similarities between the "Ring of Gyges" story and *Lord of the Rings,* according to this excerpt? If you are familiar with *Lord of the Rings,* would you agree? Why or why not? (The Narratives section has an overview of the main characters of the trilogy.)

2. Would you say that Frodo's quest to destroy the ring is an example of selfishness, selflessness, or a combination? Are there characters who are more selfish than Frodo, or less? Explain.

3. Who, according to Katz, is the closest parallel to Gyges in *The Lord of the Rings*? Do you agree? Why or why not?

4. Why is Sam's character so important, according to Katz?

Primary Reading

Leviathan

THOMAS HOBBES

1651. Excerpt.

Whereas Glaucon's arguments were the result of playing the devil's advocate, Thomas Hobbes came to the same conclusion in all seriousness some two thousand years later: Humans are selfish by nature, and society is our best way to protect ourselves from each other. Justice is a concept that is to be found in a society only once the rules have been laid down. Prior to the creation of society, in the "state of nature," where people live in a perpetual state of war against one another, life is "nasty, brutish, and short," and no rules apply except that of self-preservation. In order to improve our personal condition and for no other reason, we choose to live by the rules of society. Justice is indeed to Thomas Hobbes an invention based on self-preservation, nothing more.

Hereby it is manifest, that during the time men live without a common Power to keep them all in awe, they are in that condition which is called Warre; and such a warre, as is of every man against every man. For WARRE, consisteth not in Battell onely, or the act of fighting; but in a tract of time, wherein the Will to contend by Battell is sufficiently known: and therefore the notion of *Time,* is to be considered in the nature of Warre; as it is in the nature of Weather. For as the nature of Foule weather, lyeth not in a showre or two of rain; but in an inclination thereto of many dayes together; So the nature of War, consisteth not in actuall fighting; but in the known disposition thereto, during all the time there is no assurance to the contrary. All other time is PEACE.

Whatsoever therefore is consequent to a time of Warre, where every man is Enemy to every man; the same is consequent to the time, wherein men live without other security, than what their own strength, and their own invention shall furnish them withall. In such condition, there is no place for Industry; because the fruit thereof is uncertain: and consequently no Culture of the Earth; no Navigation, nor use of the commodities that may be imported by Sea; no commodious Building; no Instruments of moving, and removing such things as require much force; no Knowledge of the face of the Earth; no account of Time; no Arts; no Letters; no Society; and which is worst of all, continuall feare, and danger of violent death; And the life of man, solitary, poore, nasty, brutish, and short. . . .

To this warre of every man against every man, this also is consequent; that nothing can be Unjust. The notions of Right and Wrong, Justice and Injustice have there no place. Where there is no common Power, there is no Law: where no Law, no Injustice. Force, and Fraud, are in warre the two Cardinall vertues. Justice, and Injustice are none of the Faculties neither of the Body, nor Mind. If they were, they might be in a man that were alone in the world, as well as his Senses, and Passions. They are Qualities, that relate to men in Society, not in Solitude. . . .

The Passions that encline men to Peace, are Feare of Death; Desire of such things as are necessary to commodious living; and a Hope by their Industry to obtain them. And Reason suggesteth convenient Articles of Peace, upon which men may be drawn to agreement.

Study Questions

1. What does Hobbes mean by saying that when humans live in a state of war of everybody against everybody, there is neither justice nor injustice? What event creates justice and injustice?

2. Compare Glaucon's and Hobbes's ideas of justice.

3. Hobbes believes we are all selfish by nature; however, since right and wrong for Hobbes don't exist prior to the creation of society, is selfishness in itself a bad thing? Why or why not?

Primary Reading

The Ethics of Emergencies

AYN RAND

***The Virtue of Selfishness: A New Concept of Egoism*, 1964. Excerpt.**

Ayn Rand (1905–1982), an American writer and philosopher, emigrated to the United States from the Soviet Union at age twenty-one because of a deep disenchantment with the Communist ideology. Her viewpoints were controversial from the beginning of her career, and her theory of objectivism still generates debate. Today some members of the Libertarian Party claim intellectual kinship to Rand.

Many philosophers have been reluctant to recognize her as a fellow thinker and have preferred to label her a novelist. The reasons for this snub may be multiple, but the fact is that Rand had three counts against her: For one thing, American philosophers have until very recently been reluctant to think of philosophy and novels (and other stories) in the same sentence, as you'll remember from Chapters 1 and 2. So if Rand wrote novels, it would, for many philosophers, disqualify her as a fellow thinker. For another thing: She was a woman at a time where almost all philosophers were men, and it may simply have been a case of the problem of induction, a gender bias that most philosophers in the mid–twentieth century just weren't aware of having. She wasn't recognized as a thinker simply because of her gender. And the third factor? She was a political conservative in an intellectual environment of mostly liberal—and even hard left—thinkers. At a time where many American and European intellectuals flirted with Marxism, she was a ruthless critic of socialist theories, and this made her ideas unattractive to many philosophers. But among the reading public she became enormously popular, and her

Ayn Rand (1905–1982), the Russian-born American philosopher and writer, developed the theory of *objectivism,* which stresses the right of the individual to keep the fruits of his or her labors and not be held responsible for the welfare of others. She is today best known for her novels, although her philosophy is also gaining recognition as an original twentieth-century contribution.

ideas still retain some of their popularity. There is even talk of an Ayn Rand revival at the beginning of the twenty-first century.

The psychological results of altruism may be observed in the fact that a great many people approach the subject of ethics by asking such questions as: "Should one risk one's life to help a man who is: a) drowning, b) trapped in a fire, c) stepping in front of a speeding truck, d) hanging by his fingernails over an abyss?"

Consider the implications of that approach. If a man accepts the ethics of altruism, he suffers the following consequences (in proportion to the degree of his acceptance):

1.   Lack of self-esteem—since his first concern in the realm of values is not how to live his life, but how to sacrifice it.

2.   Lack of respect for others—since he regards mankind as a herd of doomed beggars crying for someone's help.

3.   A nightmare view of existence—since he believes that men are trapped in a "malevolent universe" where disasters are the constant and primary concern of their lives.

4.   And, in fact, a lethargic indifference to ethics, a hopelessly cynical amorality—since his questions involve situations which he is not likely ever to encounter, which bear no relation to the actual problems of his own life and thus leave him to live without any moral principles whatever.

By elevating the issue of helping others into the central and primary issue of ethics, altruism has destroyed the concept of any authentic benevolence or good will among men. It has indoctrinated men with the idea that to value another human being is an act of selflessness, thus implying that a man can have no personal interest in others—that *to value* another means *to sacrifice* oneself—that any love, respect or admiration a man may feel for others is not and cannot be a source of his own enjoyment, but is a threat to his existence, a sacrificial blank check signed over to his loved ones.

The men who accept that dichotomy but choose its other side, the ultimate products of altruism's dehumanizing influence, are those psychopaths who do not challenge altruism's basic premise, but proclaim their rebellion against self-sacrifice by announcing that they are totally indifferent to anything living and would not lift a finger to help a man or a dog left mangled by a hit-and-run driver (who is usually one of their own kind).

Most men do not accept or practice either side of altruism's viciously false dichotomy, but its result is a total intellectual chaos on the issue of proper human relationships and on such questions as the nature, purpose or extent of the help one may give to others. Today, a great many well-meaning, reasonable men do not know how to identify or conceptualize the moral principles that motivate their love, affection or good will, and can find no guidance in the field of ethics, which is dominated by the stale platitudes of altruism.

On the question of why man is not a sacrificial animal and why help to others is not his moral duty, I refer you to *Atlas Shrugged*. This present discussion is concerned with the principles by which one identifies and evaluates the instances involving a man's *nonsacrificial* help to others.

"Sacrifice" is the surrender of a greater value for the sake of a lesser one or of a non-value. Thus, altruism gauges a man's virtue by the degree to which he surrenders, renounces or betrays his values (since help to a stranger or an enemy is regarded as more virtuous, less "selfish," than help to those one loves). The rational principle of conduct is the exact opposite: always act in accordance with the hierarchy of your values, and never sacrifice a greater value to a lesser one.

This applies to all choices, including one's actions toward other men. It requires that one possess a defined hierarchy of *rational* values (values chosen and validated by a rational standard). Without such a hierarchy, neither rational conduct nor considered value judgments nor moral choices are possible.

Love and friendship are profoundly personal, selfish values: love is an expression and assertion of self-esteem, a response to one's own values in the person of another. One gains a profoundly personal selfish joy from the mere existence of the person one loves. It is one's own personal, selfish happiness that one seeks, earns and derives from love.

A "selfless," "disinterested" love is a contradiction in terms: it means that one is indifferent to that which one values.

Concern for the welfare of those one loves is a rational part of one's selfish interests. If a man who is passionately in love with his wife spends a fortune to cure her of a dangerous illness, it would be absurd to claim that he does it as a "sacrifice" for *her* sake, not his own, and that it makes no difference to *him,* personally and selfishly, whether she lives or dies.

Any action that a man undertakes for the benefit of those he loves is *not a sacrifice* if, in the hierarchy of his values, in the total context of the choices open to him, it achieves that which is of greatest *personal* (and rational) importance to *him*. In the above example, his wife's survival is of greater value to the husband than anything else that his money could buy, it is of greatest importance to his own happiness and, therefore, his action is not a sacrifice.

But suppose he let her die in order to spend his money on saving the lives of ten other women, none of whom meant anything to him—as the ethics of altruism would require. *That* would be a sacrifice. Here the difference between Objectivism and altruism can be seen most clearly: if sacrifice is the moral principle of action, then that husband *should* sacrifice his wife for the sake of ten other women. What distinguishes the wife from the ten others? Nothing but her value to the husband who has to make the choice—nothing but the fact that his happiness requires her survival.

The Objectivist ethics would tell him: your highest moral purpose is the achievement of your own happiness, your money is yours, use it to save your wife, *that* is your moral right and your rational, moral choice.

Consider the soul of the altruistic moralist who would be prepared to tell that husband the opposite. (And then ask yourself whether altruism is motivated by benevolence.)

The proper method of judging when or whether one should help another person is by reference to one's own rational self-interest and one's own hierarchy of values: the time, money or effort one gives or the risk one takes should be proportionate to the value of the person in relation to one's own happiness.

To illustrate this on the altruists' favorite example: the issue of saving a drowning person. If the person to be saved is a stranger, it is morally proper to save him only when the danger to one's own life is minimal; when the danger is great, it would be immoral to attempt it: only a lack of self-esteem could permit one to value one's life no higher than that of any random stranger. (And, conversely, if one is drowning, one cannot expect a stranger to risk his life for one's sake, remembering that one's life cannot be as valuable to him as his own.)

If the person to be saved is not a stranger, then the risk one should be willing to take is greater in proportion to the greatness of that person's value to oneself. If it is the man or woman one loves, then one can be willing to give one's own life to save him or her—for the selfish reason that life without the loved person could be unbearable.

Conversely, if a man is able to swim and to save his drowning wife, but becomes panicky, gives in to an unjustified, irrational fear and lets her drown, then spends his life in loneliness and misery—one would not call him "selfish"; one would condemn him morally for his treason to himself and to his own values, that is: his failure to fight for the preservation of a value crucial to his own happiness. Remember that values are that which one acts to gain and/or keep, and that one's own happiness has to be achieved by one's own effort. Since one's own happiness is the moral purpose of one's life, the man who fails to achieve it because of his own default—his failure to fight for it, is morally guilty.

Study Questions

1. Is Rand correct in saying that if you accept altruism, then you end up with a lack of self-esteem and a lack of respect for others?

2. Is Rand criticizing ideal or reciprocal altruism? Do you think that she would differentiate between the two? Would you?

3. Comment on the following quotation: "The proper method of judging when or whether one should help another person is by reference to one's own rational self-interest and one's own hierarchy of values: the time, money or effort one gives or the risk one takes should be proportionate to the value of the person in relation to one's own happiness." What might the social and political outcome be if this approach were implemented?

4. A suggestion: Reread this excerpt after you have studied Chapter 5, on utilitarianism, and speculate: How would Rand evaluate the theory that asks us to maximize happiness for the maximum number of people?

5. Go back to Chapter 3 and reread, in the excerpt from Ruth Benedict's paper "Anthropology and the Abnormal," the section about "unbridled and arrogant egoists" as being typical of Western civilization. What might Rand's comment be to that remark?

Narrative

The One Where Phoebe Hates PBS

MICHAEL CURTIS (TELEPLAY)
SHELLEY JENSEN (DIRECTOR)

An episode of **Friends, 1998–99. Summary.**

Can a television sitcom discuss moral problems in an even remotely significant way? I'll let you be the judge of that. If you've ever sat around the kitchen table after a party with friends discussing whether everyone is selfish, then you can relate to the main story line in this episode. Just a brief introduction to the characters: *Joey* is an aspiring actor who has a rather blatant tendency to think of himself first, and others second. *Phoebe* is a kindhearted and spiritual (some would say light-headed) poet/singer/masseuse who has her own private view of the world. She is the surrogate mother of triplets, given over to her half-brother and his wife who can't conceive. One morning while some of the friends (Phoebe, Chandler, Ross, and Monica) are having breakfast, Joey comes in, wearing a tuxedo. He has got a gig (he thinks), hosting a telethon for PBS, and he brags that he's doing a good deed for PBS while he himself is getting TV exposure. But Phoebe is appalled: for one thing, she thoroughly dislikes PBS because she had a bad experience with the network some years back. Her mother had just killed herself, and Phoebe was feeling sad, so she wrote to *Sesame Street* because she remembered them fondly from when she was a little kid. But nobody replied—they just sent her a key chain. And at the time she was homeless, living in a box, so she didn't even have any keys! Besides, she says, the only reason why Joey wants the gig is so he can get on TV, not because he wants to do something unselfish.

This gets the ball rolling: Now Joey accuses Phoebe of being selfish, herself, for having triplets for her brother—because it made her *feel good,* and, says Joey, that makes it selfish; we recognize the attitude of a convinced psychological egoist: everyone is selfish, and, in Joey's words, "there's no unselfish good deeds." Phoebe might just as well forget that, because that's like believing in Santa Claus. (Later on she casually asks him what he meant, and when she hears him say that Santa doesn't exist, we see the shock on her face.)

So Phoebe sets out to prove Joey wrong because, as she explains to Monica and her other friend Rachel, she just won't let her babies be raised in a world where Joey is right. Her first attempt involves sneaking over to an elderly neighbor and raking the leaves

The television sitcom *Friends* (1994–2004) may not seem like an obvious choice for a textbook about ethics, but real life is full of moral problems, and so are many of the *Friends* episodes, such as "The One Where Phoebe Hates PBS" where Phoebe (Lisa Kudrow, far left) and Joey (Matt LeBlanc, on her right) have a debate about selfishness. The other friends are, from left to right, Courtney Cox, David Schwimmer, Jennifer Aniston, and Matthew Perry.

from his doorstep. But he discovers her and treats her to cider and cookies, which makes her feel great. So, since her good deed made her feel good, it doesn't qualify as a selfless deed, according to Joey's definition.

Meanwhile, to his immense disappointment, Joey finds out that he isn't hosting the telethon after all; talk show host Gary Collins is; Joey is just going to answer phones, and it looks like he dressed in a tux for nothing. But one of the calls he receives is from Phoebe, who proudly announces that she has found a selfless, good deed: She went to Central Park and let a bee sting her, so it could look macho in front of its friends! And since she's hurting, it's not a selfish deed. But Joey shoots that down instantly: Since the bee probably died from stinging her, the bee didn't benefit (so it wasn't a good deed!).

Joey himself is doing a fine job of demonstrating what his true goal is: TV exposure, rather than helping PBS, thus proving Phoebe's point that he himself is just looking out for number one. He realizes that the place where he is answering calls isn't even within range of the television camera, so he tries to swap places with another volunteer, who is utterly unwilling to comply, to the point where they slug it out between the tables, in the background, while Gary Collins is talking about contributing to PBS's fine programming. So Joey's own quest of gaining an advantage for himself isn't doing too great. But now Phoebe makes one last attempt to prove that unselfishness exists.

She makes one more call to Joey, pledging $200 to PBS. She explains that even if she is still mad at them, she also knows that lots of children love their shows, so she is doing a good deed by supporting them, while it doesn't make her feel good at all: $200 is a lot of money, and she had plans for that sum: She was saving up to buy a hamster. Joey can't believe what he's hearing: A $200+ hamster? When they normally cost $10? Phoebe implies that it was a very special hamster (and we get the feeling that she was probably being taken for a ride, as often happens). So it looks like she has proved to Joey that selfless, good deeds do indeed exist! But here comes the twist: Because of Phoebe's pledge, the station has now surpassed the sum collected by pledges last year, and Gary Collins steps over to the volunteer who took the pledge—Joey! Who now gets his TV exposure: he is introduced by name standing there in his tux, with a big smile on his face. Phoebe is watching it on TV and is overjoyed that her pledge got Joey on TV—until she realizes what has happened! Her good deed, which was supposed to make her feel bad, now has made her feel good—which again proves Joey's point that all deeds are selfish! So she loses again.

Has Joey now been vindicated? Has Phoebe's failure in proving that she can do a "selfless, good deed" convinced us that psychological egoism is true? If things we do make us feel good afterwards, do they automatically fall into a "selfish" category, even if we didn't plan on feeling good, and the pleasure is an unintended aftereffect? Keep in mind the debate about whether Lincoln's act of saving the pigs was selfish or not. A truly selfish person would not feel good about having sacrificed something for others; as you've read, it could be a way to tell unselfish people from the selfish ones that they actually feel good after helping others.

Study Questions

1. Some would say that Phoebe's project was doomed from the start, due to the nature of her goal. What might that mean, and do you agree?

2. Discuss Phoebe's attempts at disproving Joey, relating them to the arguments against psychological egoism in the chapter text: the principle of falsification, the Lincoln story, and the fallacy of the suppressed correlative.

3. Is Joey selfish? Is Phoebe? Is everybody? Are you? Explain.

Narrative

Return to Paradise

WESLEY STRICK AND BRUCE ROBINSON (SCREENWRITERS)
JOSEPH RUBEN (DIRECTOR)

Film, 1998. Summary.

Peter Singer's story of the two hunters and the saber-toothed cat cited earlier in this chapter is a version of the so-called prisoner's dilemma: You and your friend are both political prisoners of a totalitarian regime, isolated from each other, and you are each told that the length of your sentence will depend on whether or not you confess: If you confess and your friend doesn't, you will get one year in prison and your friend will get ten years; if your friend confesses and you don't, he/she will get one year and you'll get ten. If neither of you confesses, you will each get two years. If both of you confess, you'll each get five years. So if your only goal is to limit your own sentence, logic demands that you confess, because you'll be ahead whether or not your friend also confesses. Since your friend is thinking along the same lines, chances are you'll both confess and both get five years. But if you're capable of thinking about each other's interests and can be certain that you can trust each other, then it's a win–win situation for both of you: If you both don't confess, you'll both get out after only two years. So the lesson of the prisoner's dilemma is that it can be of greater personal advantage to be less selfish than more selfish—just as in the hunter story. But it depends completely on whether we can trust each other—whether we dare take the chance that our friend will also put selfishness aside.

A film that explores the prisoner's dilemma with a chilling twist is *Return to Paradise,* based on the 1989 French movie *Force Majeure* by Pierre Jolivet. Here we have a prisoner who hopes that his two friends, enjoying their freedom, will submit to punishment for his sake, thus averting his own death sentence. The two friends must confront the conflict between their instinct for self-preservation and their sense of duty to help a friend. The film is thus a prisoner's dilemma story combined with an exploration of the nature of selfishness and altruism.

Sheriff, Tony, and Lewis are three young Americans having a good time in Malaysia, smoking dope, hanging out with the local young women, and enjoying the exotic scenery. On the way back from a trip to the market, they wreck a borrowed bicycle, and Sheriff heaves it over a precipice. A short time afterward, Sheriff and Tony go home to New York City, while Lewis stays on to help endangered orangutans. Before leaving, Sheriff and Tony give their stash of hashish to Lewis.

Two years later Sheriff is working as a limo driver in New York; Tony is working in construction and thinking about getting married. They haven't seen each other since leaving Panang. One night Sheriff has a fare, a young woman named Beth, who reveals that she is a lawyer for Lewis—he's been in the Panang jail ever since they left, for having in his possession more than the legal limit of 100 grams of hash. The excess amount was the stash given to him by his two friends. The man whose bicycle they wrecked came looking for it with the police, and they found the dope. Ten months ago Lewis received his sentence: death. All appeals have been exhausted, but only last week he mentioned his friends and the hashish story. So now the Malaysian authorities have the following suggestion: If Sheriff and Tony return to take their share of the responsibility, everybody gets three years in prison. If only one of them returns, he gets six years, and so does Lewis; if no one comes back to Panang, Lewis will be hanged—in eight days. Beth tells the same story to Tony, who is at once willing to consider going back but won't do it if Sheriff doesn't, because he is willing to lose only three years of his life, not six. Sheriff, on the other hand, sees no reason why he should even consider going—he doesn't think they can trust the deal, and it seems he just doesn't have the morals Beth assumes he has.

Beth is approached by a persistent journalist, who insists that she has a right to publish Lewis's story and that she can help him by drawing the world's attention to his case. Beth is terrified: In another case the Malaysian government reneged on a deal because of international publicity, and the prisoner was executed. She can't take such a chance but promises the reporter an exclusive if she will wait a few days.

Beth shows Sheriff a tape made by a physically and mentally worn-down Lewis, begging him and Tony to come and save his life. As the reality of Tony's impending execution dawns on Sheriff, he has a talk with his father, who is no help: He suggests that

In the film *Return to Paradise* (Polygram, 1998), two friends are faced with a moral problem: Should they voluntarily return to Malaysia to save another friend from a death sentence and share the blame for his illegal drug possession, even if it would entail prison time for both of them? Here attorney Beth Eastern (Anne Heche) is trying to convince Sheriff (Vince Vaughn) to return with her.

Sheriff go because Lewis is probably worth more as a person than Sheriff is. We realize he was being sarcastic. Why agonize over it, he says, when Sheriff isn't even considering going? So Sheriff tells Beth he won't go: "It isn't in me." Compelled by Sheriff's selfish attitude, Tony now promises to go, but Beth isn't certain of his commitment.

Sheriff and Beth have been developing an attraction for each other, and in a desperate mood they make love. The next morning he is still with her, now committed to helping her and his friend Lewis. Two days before Lewis's scheduled execution, all three of them are on the plane to Panang. The two friends have decided to give Lewis three years of their lives to save his.

Once in Panang, they go to see Lewis, but only one visitor is allowed. Sheriff finds Lewis hunched over, shivering, rocking back and forth, praying. Sheriff tries to comfort him and lift his spirits, and it seems to be working: As Sheriff is leaving, Lewis says to him, "I knew you'd come back—even if *you* didn't." Back with Tony and Beth, Sheriff expresses his concerns about Lewis's state of mind, and Beth lets slip that he's always been that way. How would she know, as his lawyer? It turns out she's not just his lawyer—she's his big sister.

With that revelation, the deal is off. Tony and Sheriff feel they can't trust her—she'd promise them anything just to get Lewis out. Fearing for their own lives, they take off for the airport. Tony boards the plane for New York—but Sheriff hesitates: He has realized it was his recklessness in throwing the bike away that put Lewis in this situation, so he must take responsibility for it. Tony leaves for New York, but Sheriff goes back to Panang, in time to walk into the courtroom where Lewis's sentence is about to be confirmed. The judge exclaims that his faith in humanity is half restored. Sheriff says they were young and stupid, but not evil; he is responsible and is willing to do what it takes to save his friend's life. The judge goes to his chambers to reassess the situation; he is expected to come out and pronounce a reprieve for Lewis and a six-year sentence for Sheriff.

But a commotion erupts as the media arrive at the courthouse. Apparently an American newspaper has published the persistent journalist's story, making the Malaysian system of justice look medieval and cruel. The judge emerges, livid: He won't have the Western media dictating the decisions of his court. The West might not understand his country's harsh drug sentences, he says, but Malaysian kids are safe from drugs, unlike kids in the West.

Will the judge stand by his word and give Lewis a lesser sentence because Sheriff came back? Or has the publication of the article endangered Lewis's life, as Beth predicted it would? The ending of this film is haunting and thought-provoking, and I would like for you to experience it yourself. Also, I'd like you to consider the following: If Lewis dies, has Sheriff's willingness to help him been for nothing?

Study Questions

1. Early in the film, Sheriff asks Beth whether *she* would go to prison for Lewis, if the question were put to her. Would *you* give three years of your life to save a friend? Would you give six? Explain.

2. Explore the changes in the characters of Tony and Sheriff. Which change is the greatest, and why?

3. What would a psychological egoist say to this story? What would an ethical egoist say?

4. Compare this story to the original prisoner's-dilemma scenario. What are the similarities, and what are the differences?

5. Is anyone being altruistic in this film? Does a person have to have no self-interest involved in order to be unselfish?

6. Go back to Chapter 2, reread the excerpt from Aristotle, and apply his theory of the perfect tragic plot to this film. Who is the ordinary man who makes a fatal error in judgment? Is Aristotle right that such plot lines are timeless?

Narrative

Madame Bovary

GUSTAVE FLAUBERT

Novel, 1857. Summary and Excerpt. Translated by Lowell Bair.
Film version in United States (1949) and in France (1991).

As a young girl in the country, Emma, the title character of *Madame Bovary,* devours sentimental novels and dreams about romantic love. She marries the first man ever to find her attractive, the decent and well-meaning but dull Dr. Charles Bovary. They have a little girl, but Emma finds no satisfaction in the tranquil life of a doctor's wife and a mother in a small French town. The fact that her husband is not even a mediocre doctor but a downright bad one doesn't help any. Emma falls in love with a wealthy neighbor and embarks on a path that leads to her ruin. She has an affair with the neighbor, and she begins an extravagant shopping spree by mail order, on credit. After a while she prepares to elope with her lover, only to find that he already has eloped—without her. Devastated, she falls ill, but she recuperates when she meets a former acquaintance, a young man who has been secretly in love with her for years. They have an affair, and Emma reembarks on her shopping venture, sending her daughter to live with strangers. Here we see how Emma entangles herself in a web of lies to be able to see her young lover Léon once a week in the nearby town of Rouen:

It was at about this time, toward the beginning of winter, that she apparently developed a great ardor for music.

One evening when Charles was listening to her, she started the same piece over again four times, growing more and more annoyed, while Charles, without noticing any difference, kept crying out, "Bravo! Very good! . . . You shouldn't stop! Keep going!"

"No! It's disgusting! My fingers are rusty."

The next day he asked her to "play him something again."

"All right, if you really want me to."

And he admitted that she had gotten a little out of practice. She struck wrong notes, fumbled and hesitated; then she stopped short and said, "No more! I ought to take lessons, but . . ." She bit her lip and added, "Twenty francs a lesson—it's too expensive."

"Yes, you're right, it is a little . . ." said Charles, laughing foolishly. "I think we might be able to find a teacher for less, though, because there are a lot of musicians who don't have a big reputation but are better than the celebrities."

"Well, find one of them," said Emma.

When he came home the next day he gave her a sly look and finally blurted out, "You're so opinionated sometimes! I went to Barfeuchères today, and Madame Liégeard told me that her three girls—they're all at La Miséricorde now—used to take lessons for two and a half francs an hour, and from a wonderful teacher, too!"

She shrugged her shoulders and left her instrument closed from then on.

But whenever she walked past it she would sigh (if Bovary happened to be there), "Ah, my poor piano!"

And when she had visitors she never failed to inform them that she had abandoned her music and could not go back to it now, for reasons beyond her control. Everyone pitied her. It was a shame! She had such talent! Some people even spoke to Bovary about it. . . .

And so Charles brought up the question of the piano again. Emma answered bitterly that it would be better to sell it. But that poor old piano had given his pride such satisfaction that to see it go would have been almost like watching Emma kill part of herself.

"If you want to . . ." he said. "After all, a lesson now and then wouldn't really make us go bankrupt."

"But lessons don't do any good," she replied, "unless you take them regularly."

It was thus that she obtained her husband's permission to go to the city once a week to see her lover. And by the end of the first month everyone found that she had made considerable progress. . . .

She was more charming than ever to her husband; she made him pistachio custards and played waltzes for him after dinner. He regarded himself as the luckiest of mortals, and she never worried about him until suddenly one evening he asked her, "It's Mademoiselle Lempereur who gives you lessons, isn't it?"

"Yes."

"Well, I saw her today," said Charles, "in Madame Liégeard's house. I talked to her about you: she doesn't know you."

It was like a thunderbolt. However, she answered in a natural tone, "She must have forgotten my name."

"Or maybe there are several piano teachers named Lempereur in Rouen," said the doctor.

"Maybe so." Then she quickly added, "Anyway, I have my receipts: here, look!"

She went to the writing desk, rummaged through all the drawers, mixed up all the papers and finally became so frantic that Charles strongly urged her not to go to so much trouble for those wretched receipts.

"Oh, I'll find them!" she said.

True enough, on the following Friday, as Charles was putting on one of his boots in the dark little room where he kept his clothes, he felt a piece of paper between the leather and his sock; he pulled it out and read: *"Received the sum of sixty-five francs, for three months of lessons, plus various supplies. Félicie Lempereur, Music Teacher."*

"How the devil did this get into my boot?"

"It probably fell down from that old box full of bills on the shelf," she replied.

From then on her whole life was a tissue of lies which she wrapped around her love like a veil, to hide it.

Lying became a need, a mania, a pleasure; so much so that if she said she had walked down the right side of a street the day before, it was almost certain that she had walked down the left.

Eventually the merchant who has been supplying her with clothes, jewelry, and furniture confronts Emma with her enormous debt and demands immediate payment in return for promising not to tell her husband of her affair. Emma, who is now desperate, begins selling off her own assets as well as Charles's property and his medical tools. In the end, forced to face her own degradation, she swallows poison and dies. Charles refuses to think evil of her and even when faced with the truth—Emma's love letters—sees only that she was a poor and desperate soul.

Study Questions

1. Can Emma's case be viewed as a case for psychological egoism?

2. Can Emma be considered an ethical egoist?

3. Emma gets her ideas about romantic passion from books. Does that mean that fiction can be morally dangerous?

4. Flaubert, the author, used to say *"Emma Bovary, c'est moi"* (Emma Bovary, that's me). Do you think he viewed his protagonist in an overall negative or positive way?

Narrative

Atlas Shrugged

AYN RAND

Novel, 1957. Summary and Excerpt.

In Greek mythology, Atlas is the god who holds up the earth on his shoulders—and when Atlas shrugs, the world shakes. Ayn Rand's book is about the shake-up of the world by those who form its economic foundation: the factory owners, the entrepreneurs, the railroad builders. It is not the workers but those who employ them who are the movers and the shakers of the world, and in Rand's opinion they have been abused by unions and "bleeding hearts" long enough. In this book she outlines her philosophy of objectivism "between the lines" of the novel, urging those people with creative powers to start thinking about themselves and taking pride in what they do, for without them the world literally will come to a halt. In *Atlas Shrugged,* the movers and shakers go on strike, led by the mythic figure of John Galt and joined by the railroad tycoon Dagny Taggart. The common folk who have no talent or will to keep themselves going must perish. This vision of ethical egoism sees the world as being divided between those who can think and create and those who are parasites on the creators; each person has a right to what he or she creates (and earns), and no one else has any right to any of it. The only duty we have is to look out for ourselves and not give our lives away to others who aren't willing to work for their own share. The following excerpt is from a conversation between Francisco d'Anconia, a copper tycoon and millionaire, and Henry Rearden, a steelworks owner and inventor who is beginning to understand that he has been letting people take advantage of him all his life:

> "If you want to see an abstract principle, such as moral action, in material form—there it is. Look at it, Mr. Rearden. Every girder of it, every pipe, wire and valve was put there by a choice in answer to the question: right or wrong? You had to choose right and you had to choose the best within your knowledge—the best for your purpose, which was to make steel—and then move on and extend the knowledge, and do better, and still better, with your purpose as your standard of value. You had to act on your own judgment, you had to have the capacity to judge, the courage to stand on the verdict of your mind, and the purest, the most ruthless consecration to the rule of doing right, of doing the best, the

utmost best possible to you. Nothing could have made you act against your judgment, and you would have rejected as wrong—as evil—any man who attempted to tell you that the best way to heat a furnace was to fill it with ice. Millions of men, an entire nation, were not able to deter you from producing Rearden Metal—because you had the knowledge of its superlative value and the power which such knowledge gives. But what I wonder about, Mr. Rearden, is why you live by one code of principles when you deal with nature and by another when you deal with men?"

Rearden's eyes were fixed on him so intently that the question came slowly, as if the effort to pronounce it were a distraction: "What do you mean?"

"Why don't you hold to the purpose of your life as clearly and rigidly as you hold to the purpose of your mills?"

"You have judged every brick within this place by its value to the goal of making steel. Have you been as strict about the goal which your work and your steel are serving? What do you wish to achieve by giving your life to the making of steel? By what standard of value do you judge your days? For instance, why did you spend ten years of exacting effort to produce Rearden Metal?"

Rearden looked away, the slight, slumping movement of his shoulders like a sigh of release and disappointment. "If you have to ask that, then you wouldn't understand."

"If I told you that I understand it, but you don't—would you throw me out of here?"

"I should have thrown you out of here anyway—so go ahead, tell me what you mean."

"Are you proud of the rail of the John Galt Line?"

"Yes."

"Why?"

"Because it's the best rail ever made."

"Why did you make it?"

"In order to make money."

"There were many easier ways to make money. Why did you choose the hardest?"

"You said it in your speech at Taggart's wedding: in order to exchange my best effort for the best effort of others."

"If that was your purpose, have you achieved it?"

A beat of time vanished in a heavy drop of silence. "No," said Rearden.

"Have you made any money?"

"No."

"When you strain your energy to its utmost in order to produce the best, do you expect to be rewarded for it or punished?" Rearden did not answer. "By every standard of decency, of honor, of justice known to you—are you convinced that you should have been rewarded for it?"

"Yes," said Rearden, his voice low.

"Then if you were punished, instead—what sort of code have you accepted?"

Rearden did not answer.

"It is generally assumed," said Francisco, "that living in a human society makes one's life much easier and safer than if one were left alone to struggle against nature on a desert island. Now wherever there is a man who needs or uses metal in any way—Rearden Metal has made his life easier for him. Has it made yours easier for you?"

"No," said Rearden, his voice low.

"Has it left your life as it was before you produced the Metal?"

"No—" said Rearden, the word breaking off as if he had cut short the thought that followed.

Francisco's voice lashed at him suddenly, as a command: "Say it!"

"It has made it harder," said Rearden tonelessly.

"When you felt proud of the rail of the John Galt Line," said Francisco, the measured rhythm of his voice giving a ruthless clarity to his words, "what sort of men did you think of? Did you want to see that Line used by your equals—by giants of productive energy, such as Ellis Wyatt, whom it would help to reach higher and still higher achievements of their own?"

"Yes," said Rearden eagerly.

"Did you want to see it used by men who could not equal the power of your mind, but who would equal your moral integrity—men such as Eddie Willers—who could never invent your Metal, but who would do their best, work as hard as you did, live by their own effort, and—riding on your rail—give a moment's silent thanks to the man who gave them more than they could give him?"

"Yes," said Rearden gently.

"Did you want to see it used by whining rotters who never rouse themselves to any effort, who do not possess the ability of a filing clerk, but demand the income of a company president, who drift from failure to failure and expect you to pay their bills, who hold their wishing to an equivalent of your work and their need as a higher claim to reward than your effort, who demand that you serve them, who demand that it be the aim of your life to serve them, who demand that your strength be the voiceless, rightless, unpaid, unrewarded slave of their impotence, who proclaim that you are born to serfdom by reason of your genius, while they are born to rule by the grace of incompetence, that yours is only to give, but theirs only to take, that yours is to produce, but theirs to consume, that you are not to be paid, neither in matter nor in spirit, neither by wealth nor by recognition nor by respect nor by gratitude—so that they would ride on your rail and sneer at you and curse you, since they owe you nothing, not even the effort of taking off their hats which you paid for? Would this be what you wanted? Would you feel proud of it?"

"I'd blast that rail first," said Rearden, his lips white.

Study Questions

1. What is it that d'Anconia accuses Rearden of?

2. Can you identify d'Anconia's political standpoint and the standpoint he argues against?

3. Why is this considered an example of ethical egoism? How does this excerpt relate to Rand's analysis of happiness as a moral purpose?

Narrative

The Gift of the Magi

O. HENRY (WILLIAM SYDNEY PORTER)

Short story, 1906. Summary and excerpt.

O. Henry's story of the two gifts may be familiar to you already. The narrative itself is not very long, and here you have an ultra-short version of it:

Della and Jim are a young, newlywed, turn-of-the-twentieth-century couple who are facing financially hard times. They would each like so very much to give each other a wonderful, meaningful gift for Christmas, but they have no money. They do, however, have a fine understanding of each other's hopes and dreams. Della knows how much Jim loves his gold watch, inherited from his father and his grandfather before him. And Jim knows the pride Della takes in her long, beautiful, brown hair, which reaches below her knees when she lets it down.

So, on Christmas Eve, Della comes up with a solution: She rushes down to a store where they sell hair products and offers her hair for sale. The woman in the store accepts her offer, cuts her hair off, and gives Della a tidy sum for it—enough for a handsome present for Jim. And she finds just the right thing: A gold chain for his gold watch.

Later that evening Jim comes home from work and stares at her short hair in tight curls (which was a highly unusual hairstyle, and even considered improper), but he isn't just surprised, he is devastated—for his Christmas present to her is a set of gorgeous, expensive tortoise-shell hair combs, a set she has wanted for a long time without ever hoping to own it. And with her short hair, they're now useless. Della assures him that her hair will grow back and gives him her present, the watch chain. But instead of happily bringing out his watch and attaching it, he tells her how he was able to afford the combs: by selling his gold watch.

O. Henry concludes his story with these words:

The magi, as you know, were wise men—wonderfully wise men—who brought gifts to the Babe in the manger. They invented the art of giving Christmas presents. Being wise, their gifts were no doubt wise ones, possibly bearing the privilege of exchange in case of duplication. And here I have lamely related to you the uneventful chronicle of two foolish children in a flat who most unwisely sacrificed for each other the greatest treasures of their house. But in a last word to the wise of these days let it be said that of all who give gifts these two were the wisest. Of all who give and receive gifts, such as they are wisest. Everywhere they are wisest. They are the magi.

Study Questions

1. Is this a story about failure to communicate, or of true love, or both? Explain.

2. What does this story tell us about love, and sacrifice, and gift-giving?

3. What does O. Henry want to express, with his reference to the Magi and the concluding words?

4. Can we apply the category of ideal altruism here? Reciprocal altruism? Psychological egoism? Ethical egoism? Explain.

Narrative

The Lord of the Rings

J. R. R. T O L K I E N

Trilogy of novels, 1939–55. Films: 1958, 2001–2003 (Trilogy). Overview of key characters.

In this particular case I'll take a chance and assume that most readers know the basics of the story—because that is all we need to include it as an example of selfishness versus altruism. As you have seen in the Primary Reading, "The Rings of Tolkien and Plato: Lessons in Power, Choice, and Morality," the theme of the Ring lends itself well to a comparison between Plato's story of the Ring of Gyges and Frodo's quest to save Middle Earth from Sauron's evil reign: In each story we have a ring of invisibility that yields great power, and each story speculates that most, if not all, ordinary people (humans, hobbits, or otherwise) will be tempted to use the power for their own benefit. This section is thus merely an overview of the key names and events in the trilogy, to jog your memory or to inspire you to read the books and watch the films. The films provide stunning visuals, but without the books you won't experience the entire richness of the story, the language element—and Tom Bombadil!

> **The Ring:** Forged by Sauron thousands of years earlier, as a tool of power and control. Inscribed on the Ring in the ancient language:
>
> *One Ring to rule them all, One Ring to find them,*
> *One Ring to bring them all and in the darkness bind them.*

The Fellowship of the Ring

Frodo Baggins: A young hobbit, Bilbo Baggins's nephew. After Bilbo's departure from the Shire, it falls to Frodo to try to keep the Ring out of the hands of Sauron's forces, because if Sauron regains the Ring, it will mean the end of the world for humans and hobbits. Frodo is a person without guile, and yet he is tempted to use the powers of the Ring. Through great personal sacrifice, Frodo and his helper Sam succeed in their mission, but not without Frodo giving in to the power of the Ring at the final moment.

Samwise Gangee (Sam): Frodo's friend and helper, perhaps the most selfless person in the trilogy. He has access to the Ring on several occasions, but all he is concerned with is helping Frodo and returning to his life in the Shire.

Boromir: A prince of the ruling House of Steward, he has sworn to protect Frodo and the Ring, but in the end he succumbs to the temptation of the Ring and tries to take it away from Frodo.

Gandalf: A wizard and a maiar—not a human being. He has great, but not unlimited powers and has fought Sauron for several thousand years. He helps Frodo whenever he can, even at the peril of his own life.

Aragorn, also known as Strider: A descendant of the ancient House of Isildur, he is the heir-at-law to the throne of Gondor, but travels incognito. His ancestor cut off Sauron's finger with the Ring attached to it, which limited Sauron's power, but the ring disappeared.

Gimli: A dwarf from a long line of dwarves with an illustrious mining tradition deep inside the mountains. The dwarves have a deep mistrust of the elves, but even so, Gimli and the elf Legolas become great friends.

Legolas: An immortal elf and a great archer. He chooses to help the humans and the hobbits, even while his people are leaving Middle-Earth, sailing west.

Merry and Pippin: Friends of Frodo. In the beginning they are mainly playful, irreverent youngsters, but they grow up to be courageous and inventive partners in the Fellowship.

Some Other Essential Characters

Gollum: The hobbit Smeagol found the Ring on his birthday and killed his friend Deagol over it. He kept it and was slowly affected by its evil powers to the extent that he doesn't even look like a Hobbit any more, but is now a creature whose instinct is focused exclusively on regaining the Ring. He does, however, appear more like a victim of the Ring's power than part of its evil force.

Sauron: The ultimate evil character, he was a shape-shifting sorcerer, but lost his bodily characteristics and is now disembodied. He forged the Ring of Power and has experimented with creating hybrid species who will do his bidding. His all-seeing eye can tell when Frodo wears the Ring.

Galadriel: The Queen of elves, who is offered the Ring by Frodo, because he feels he can no longer trust himself with it. She has a moment of weakness where she imagines herself all-powerful, but relinquishes the power and shuns its evil influence.

Bilbo Baggins: A hobbit who found the Ring in Gollum's cave in the book *The Hobbit*. Bilbo leaves the Shire early in the Trilogy and leaves the Ring with Frodo. Later, Frodo meets up with Bilbo again, and we see how the mere proximity to the Ring transforms Bilbo into a creature of greed and evil—we see how Gollum must have been transformed.

Tom Bombadil: A mysterious man of the woods who saves Frodo, Sam, Merry, and Pippin on several occasions. Not featured in the films. Tom even tries on the Ring, without any effect—he has his own ancient powers. Since Bombadil is not human, some readers have speculated that he may be Tolkien's version of the "Green Man," the ancient European wood spirit.

Study Questions

1. Who is being selfless, and who is selfish in this story?
2. Who is good, and who is evil? Is this the same question as the first question? or is it different? Explain.
3. Is Gollum an evil character? Why or why not?
4. If you were to compare Plato's shepherd Gyges with any of the characters, which one would it be? What are the similarities, and what are the differences?

Chapter Five

Using Your Reason,
Part 1: Utilitarianism

When deciding on a moral course of action, some of us find it is the potential consequences of our choice that determine what we decide to do. Others of us see those consequences as being of minor importance when we view them in light of the question of right and wrong. A student of mine, when asked to come up with a moral problem we could discuss in class, proposed this question to ponder: Imagine that your grandmother is dying; she is very religious, and she asks you to promise her that you will marry within the family faith. Your beloved is of another faith. Do you tell her the truth, or do you make a false promise? This profound (and I suspect, real-life) question makes us all wonder: If I think it is right to lie to Grandma, why is that? To make her last moments peaceful; what she doesn't know won't hurt her; why should I upset her by telling her the truth? Is that a good enough reason? And if I think lying to Grandma is wrong and refuse to do it, how do I justify making her last moments miserable? You will see that those of us who think lying to her is the only right choice because then she will die happy generally subscribe to the theory of *consequentialism,* in particular the theory of *utilitarianism,* the most widespread and popular form of consequentialism. If you think that lying is always wrong, even if it would make Grandma feel better, then hang in there until Chapter 6, where we discuss Kant's moral theory.

In the preceding chapter you encountered the philosopher Peter Singer, who claimed that we as humans are capable of caring for others as well as ourselves. Singer identifies himself as a utilitarian, as do numerous others today—philosophers as well as laypeople. Utilitarians see as their moral guideline a rule that encourages them to make life bearable for as many people as possible. Perhaps we can actively do something to make people's lives better, or perhaps the only thing we can do to make their lives better is to stay out of their way. Perhaps we can't strive to make people happy, but we can at least do our best to limit their misery. This way of thinking just seems the decent approach for many of us, and when we include ourselves among those who should receive a general increase of happiness and decrease of misery, then the rule seems attractive, simple, and reasonable. Small wonder this attitude has become the cornerstone of one of the most vital and influential moral theories in human history.

Utilitarians are hard universalists in the sense that they believe there is a single universal moral code, which is the only one possible, and everyone ought to realize it. It is the *principle of utility,* or the *greatest-happiness principle:* When choosing a course of action, always pick the one that will maximize happiness and minimize unhappiness for the greatest number of people. Whatever action conforms to this rule will be defined as a morally right action, and whatever action does not conform to this principle will be called a morally wrong action. In this way utilitarianism proposes a clear and simple moral criterion: Pleasure is good and pain is bad; therefore, whatever causes happiness and/or decreases pain is morally right, and whatever causes pain or unhappiness is morally wrong. In other words, utilitarianism is interested in the *consequences* of our actions: If they are good, the action is right; if bad, the action is wrong. This principle, utilitarians claim, will provide answers to all real-life dilemmas.

Are all theories that focus on the consequences of actions utilitarian? No. As we saw in Chapter 4, the consequences we look for may be happy consequences for ourselves alone, and in that case we show ourselves to be egoists. We may focus on the consequences of our actions because we believe that those consequences justify our actions (in other words, that the end justifies the means), but this does not necessarily imply that the consequences we hope for are good in the utilitarian sense that they maximize happiness for the maximum number of people. We might, for instance, agree with the Italian statesman Niccolò Machiavelli (1469–1527) that if the end is to maintain political power for oneself, one's king, or one's political party, this will justify any means one might use for that purpose, such as force, surveillance, or even deceit. Although this famous theory is indeed consequentialist, it does not qualify as utilitarian because it doesn't have the common good as its ultimate end.

Jeremy Bentham and the Hedonistic Calculus

It is often tempting to say that history moves in a certain direction. For example, eighteenth-century Europe and America saw a general movement toward greater recognition of human rights and social equality, of the value of the individual, of the scope of human capacities, and of the need for and right to education. During this period, known as the *Enlightenment,* rulers and scholars shared a staunch belief that human reason, *rationality,* held the key to the future—to the blossoming of the sciences as well as to social change. This period is, appropriately, also referred to as the *Age of Reason,* not so much because people were particularly rational at the time but because reason was the social, scientific, and philosophical *ideal.*

Perhaps, then, it is tempting to say that civilization moved toward an appreciation of human rationality, but it would be more appropriate to say that it was moved along by the thoughts of certain thinkers. Such a mover was the English jurist and philosopher Jeremy Bentham (1748–1832).

Bentham, author of *Introduction to the Principles of Morals and Legislation* (1789), set out to create not a new moral theory so much as a hands-on principle that could be used to remodel the British legal system. Indeed, it was not Bentham but another philosopher, David Hume, who invented the term *utilitarianism*. Hume believed that it is good for an action to have *utility* in the sense that it makes yourself and others happy, but he never developed this idea into a complete moral theory. Bentham, however, used the term to create a moral system for a new age.

In Bentham's England the feudal world had all but vanished. Society had stratified into an upper class, a middle class, and a working class, and the Industrial Revolution

Jeremy Bentham (1748–1832), English philosopher and jurist. With his friend James Mill he developed the theory of utilitarianism based on the principle of utility: Maximize happiness and minimize unhappiness for as many as possible. Bentham donated his body to medical research and his money to University College of London, with the provision that after research on his body was complete, it was to be preserved and displayed at university board meetings. This request is not as odd as it might sound: Bentham, a prominent person, hoped that by donating his body to science he would make a statement in support of the medical profession's need for cadavers for research. Most people at the time felt, however, that having one's deceased body cut up was a sacrilege, and so only the bodies of executed criminals were available. As a result, a thriving clandestine business arose, a trade in newly dead bodies stolen from their graves. In one case, the body snatchers didn't wait for corpses to be buried, but murdered sixteen people in one year and sold them to anatomists. By deciding to donate his body, Bentham took a stand against what he saw as superstition and attempted to put a stop to the practice of body snatching. And he may have thought further, What better way to undo superstitions about dead bodies than for his own to be on display at board meetings? He specified in his will that he was to become an *Auto-Icon,* an image of himself, and he even picked out the glass eyes to be placed in his head after his demise and carried them around in his pocket, according to legend. He had intended for his head to remain on the shoulders of his Auto-Icon, but after his death, the preservation process presumably went wrong, and a wax head was substituted. In this photo you see both the wax head (a good likeness), and Bentham's real head between his feet. He still sits in his mahogany case at the University College of London and is wheeled in at annual board meetings. He is recorded as "present, but not voting."

was just beginning. Conditions for the lowest class in the social hierarchy were appalling. Rights in the courts were, by and large, something that could be bought, which meant that those who had no means to buy them didn't have them. The world portrayed in the novels of Charles Dickens was developing; if you were in debt, you were taken to debtors' prison, where you stayed until your debt was paid. Whoever had funds could get out, but the poor faced spending the rest of their lives with their family inside debtors' prison. There were no child labor laws, and the exploitation of children in the workforce, which horrified Marx some decades later, was rampant in Bentham's day. Bentham saw it as terribly unfair and decided that the best way to redesign this system of unfair advantages would be to set up a simple moral rule that everyone could relate to, rich and poor alike.

Bentham said that what is good is what is pleasurable, and what is bad is what is painful. In other words, *hedonism* (pleasure seeking) is the basis for his moral theory, which is often called *hedonistic utilitarianism* (see Box 5.1). The ultimate value is happiness or pleasure—these things are *intrinsically* valuable. Anything that helps us achieve happiness or avoid pain is of *instrumental* value, and because we may do something pleasurable in order to achieve another pleasure, pleasure can have both intrinsic and instrumental value. (Box 5.2 explains this distinction in more detail.) In order for this basic rule to be useful in legislation, we need to let people decide for themselves wherein their pleasure lies and what they would rather avoid. Each person has a say in what pleasure and pain are, and each person's pleasure and pain count equally. We might illustrate this viewpoint by traveling back in our minds to nineteenth-century London. A well-to-do middle-class couple may feel that their greatest pleasure on a Saturday night is to don their fancy clothes, drive to Covent Garden in their shining coach, and go to the opera. The girl at Covent Garden who tries to sell them a bouquet of wilting violets as they pass by would probably not enjoy a trip to the opera as much as she would enjoy the bottle of gin she saves up for all week. Bentham would say she has as much right to relish her gin as the couple has a right to enjoy the opera. The girl can't tell the couple that gin is better, and they have no right to force their appreciation of the opera on her. For Bentham, what is good and bad for each person is a matter for each person to decide, and as such, his principle becomes a very *egalitarian* one. At the end of the chapter you'll find an excerpt from Bentham's *Introduction to the Principles of Morals and Legislation*, in which he outlines the principles of utility.

The Hedonistic Calculus

How exactly do we choose a course of action? Before we decide what to do, we must calculate the probable consequences of our actions. This is what has become known as Bentham's *hedonistic calculus* (also called the *hedonic calculus*). We must, he says, investigate all aspects of the proposed consequences: (1) Its *intensity*—how intense will the pleasure or pain be? (2) Its *duration*—how long will it last? (3) Its *certainty or uncertainty*—how sure can we be that it will follow from our action? (4) Its *propinquity or remoteness*—how far away is it, in time and space? (5) Its *fecundity*—how big are the chances that it will be followed by a similar pleasure or a similar pain? (6) Its *purity*—

Box 5.1   HEDONISM AND THE HEDONISTIC PARADOX

Often the Greek thinker Epicurus (341–270 B.C.E.) is credited with being the first philosopher to advocate a life in search of pleasure, hedonism. This, however, isn't quite accurate, because what Epicurus seems to have been after was a life free of pain—for if you are free of pain you have obtained peace of mind, *ataraxia,* the highest pleasure. But others have advocated that seeking pleasure and avoiding pain are human nature, and what humans ought to embark on in life is to accumulate good times. Jeremy Bentham believed all humans are hedonists. Everyone wants pleasure, so we search for it. Searching and finding are two different things, however, and the paradox of hedonism often prevents us from finding what we are looking for. Suppose we set out to achieve pleasure on the weekend. We go to the beach, we take a walk in the woods, we hang out at the mall, we go to the movies, but we're just not enjoying ourselves that much; pleasure has somehow eluded us, and we face Monday with the sense of a lost weekend, telling ourselves that next weekend we'll look harder. Our friend, on the contrary, had a great time; he went with us because he likes going to the beach, loves the woods, wanted to look for a pair of jeans at the mall, and had been looking forward to seeing a movie for weeks. He even enjoyed our company. Why did he have a good weekend while we felt unfulfilled? Because we were trying to have a good time, and he was doing things he liked to do and enjoying being with someone he liked. The plea-sure he got was, so to speak, a by-product of doing those things—it wasn't the main object of his activity. We, on the other hand, looked for pleasure without thinking about what we like to do that might give us pleasure, as if "pleasure" were a thing separate from everything else. The hedonistic paradox is this: If you look for pleasure, chances are you won't find it. (People who have been looking hard for someone to love can attest to this.) Pleasure comes to you when you are in the middle of something else and rarely when you are looking for it. Sometimes the "Don Juan syndrome" is cited as an example of the hedonistic paradox. A person (traditionally a man, but there is no reason it can't apply to women) who has a lot of sexual conquests very often feels compelled to move from partner to partner because he or she likes the pursuit but somehow tires of an established relationship. Why is this the case? It could be because such people are unwilling to commit themselves to a permanent relationship, but it also may be due to the paradox of hedonism: In each partner they see the promise of "pleasure," but somehow all they end up with is another conquest. If they had been setting their sights on building a relationship with their partners, they might have found out that pleasure comes from being with someone you care for, and you have to care in order to feel pleasure; you can't expect pleasure to appear if there is no genuine feeling—or so the theory says. . . .

how big are the chances that it will not be followed by the opposite sensation (pain after pleasure, for example)? (7) Its *extent*—how many people will be affected by our decision? After considering these questions, we must do the following:

> Sum up all the values of all the *pleasures* on the one side, and those of all the pains on the other. . . . Take the balance; which, on the side of *pleasure,* will give the general *good tendency* of the act, with respect to the total number or community of individuals concerned; if on the side of pain, the general *evil tendency,* with respect to the same community.

Box 5.2   INTRINSIC VERSUS INSTRUMENTAL VALUES

An *instrumental* value is one that can be used as an instrument or tool to get something else that we want. If you needed to get to class or work on time, a car might be the instrumental value that would get you there. If you didn't have a car, then money (or good credit) might be the instrumental value that would get you the car that would get you to school or to your workplace. How about going to school? If you're going to school in order to get a degree, then you might say that going to school is an instrumental value that will get your degree. And the degree? An instrumental value that will get you a good job. And the job? An instrumental value that will get what? More money. And what do you want with that? A better lifestyle, a better place to live, good health, and so

on. And why do you want a better lifestyle? Why do you want to be healthy? This is where the chain comes to an end, because we have reached something that is obvious: We want those things because we want them. Perhaps they "make us happy," but the bottom line is that we value them for their own sake, *intrinsically.* Some values can of course be both instrumental and intrinsic; the car may help you get to school, but also, you've wanted the car for a long time just because you like it. Exercising may make you healthy, but you also may actually enjoy it. And going to school is certainly a tool that can be used to get a degree, but some people appreciate training and knowledge for their own sake, not just because these goods can be used to get them somewhere in life.

What do we have here? A simple, democratic principle that seems to make no unreasonable demands of personal sacrifice, given that one's own pleasure and pain count just as much as anybody else's. Furthermore, in line with the scientific dreams of the Age of Reason, the proper moral conduct is calculated mathematically; values are reduced to a calculation of pleasure and pain, a method accessible to everyone with a basic understanding of arithmetic. By calculating pleasures and pains one can presumably get a truly rational solution to any moral as well as nonmoral (morally neutral) problem.

This sounds very good, and yet there is a problem—actually, there are several. For one thing, from where does Bentham get his numerical values? Ascertaining that our pleasure from eating a second piece of mud pie will be intense but will not last long and very likely will be followed by pain and remorse will not supply us with any numerical values to add or subtract: We have to make up the numerical values! This may not be as difficult as it seems, though. It is surprising how much people can agree on a value system, if they can just decide what should count as top and bottom value. If they agreed on a system that goes from −10 to +10, for example, most people would agree to assigning specific numerical values to the various consequences of eating that second piece of pie. What value would be assigned to the aspect of intensity? Not a 10, because that probably would apply only to the first piece, but perhaps an 8. The *duration* of the pleasure might get a measly 2 or 3, and the chance that it would be followed by pleasure or pain certainly would be way down in the negative numbers, perhaps −5 or worse. As for evaluating how many

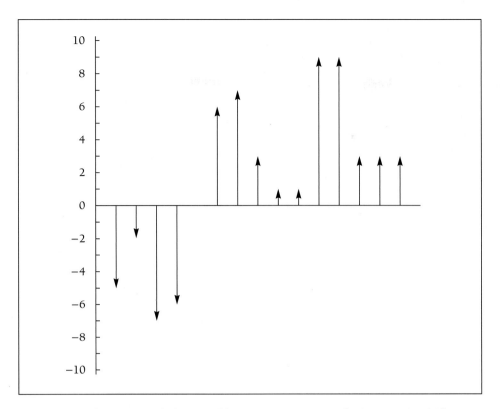

Sheer numbers: If we imagine the horizontal line representing a neutral position in terms of pain and pleasure, 0, the vertical line above 0 representing pleasure, and the line below 0 representing pain, we have a visual representation of the hedonistic calculus. Here all that matters is that the positive numbers outweigh the negative numbers. So if we have a scenario where many (humans or animals) are suffering but not much contentment is generated, the utilitarian would be against it. If only a few are suffering, and the many benefit from their suffering, it is the morally right course of action, according to utilitarianism.

people are affected by the decision, that could take into account friends and family who don't want you to gain weight or the person who owns the second piece of pie (which you stole), who will be deprived of it if you eat it. All such hypothetical situations can be ascribed a value if people can agree on a value system to use for all choices, from personal ones to far-reaching political decisions. (See Box 5.3 for a discussion of pleasure as an indicator of happiness.)

What this rating system adds up to is what most people would call the "pros and cons," those lists we sometimes make for ourselves when we are in severe doubt about what to do—what major field of study to choose, whether to go home for Thanksgiving or celebrate it with friends, whether to get married, whether to take a new job, and so on. The only difference is that in this system we assign numerical values to the pros and cons. Can such a list really help us make rational decisions? Bentham believed it was an infallible system for rational choice. A method that

Box 5.3   WHAT IS HAPPINESS?

One of the persistent problems in utilitarianism is the claim that the ultimate intrinsic value is happiness. We have already seen how the search for pleasure can lead to the hedonistic paradox (see Box 5.1), and this paradox is a problem for utilitarians as much as for anyone claiming that the ultimate reason we do things is to seek happiness. But is happiness the same as pleasure? Jeremy Bentham doesn't say, and indeed he doesn't care: For him, happiness is how *you* define it. John Stuart Mill defines happiness as distinct from both pleasure and contentment and views it as an intellectual achievement. Aristotle, who introduced the idea of happiness as a human goal to Western philosophy, also believed it was a result of rational activity and not a pursuit of pleasure. Few philosophers have chosen Bentham's path and al-

lowed for the possibility that happiness might have something to do with pleasure. An ancient story illustrates this tendency, not just within the Western tradition, to frown on the connection between happiness and physical comfort or indulgence: A Persian prince was told that in order to cure his unhappiness he had to wear the shirt of a happy man. The Persian prince now tried the shirts of lords, artists, merchants, soldiers, and fools, but it was to no avail. Happiness seemed to elude him. Finally he encountered a poor farmer singing behind his plow; the prince asked him if he was happy, and the farmer answered that he was. The prince then asked if he could have the farmer's shirt, and the farmer answered, "But I have no shirt!"

quantifies (makes measurable) the elusive qualities of life would certainly be useful, and several workplaces today are actually employing a form of hedonistic calculus in their hiring process: Applicants are rated according to their qualifications, and these qualifications are assigned numerical values (they are quantified); the person with the highest score presumably gets the job. Another area in which the calculus has had a rebirth is in the field of health care, where attempts are being made to create an objective measure for what is known as *quality of life* (see Chapter 7). One person's idea of quality of life may not be the same as another person's, however, and even in workplaces where such a hiring method is used, other, less rational, elements may play a part in the hiring process (such as the looks of the applicant or relation to the employer). People who have given Bentham's system a try in their own personal decision making often find that it may help in clarifying one's options, but the results are not always persuasive. You may end up with sixteen items on the con side and four on the pro side and still find yourself getting married or taking a new job simply because you want to so badly. There are parts of the human psyche that simply don't respond to rational arguments, and Bentham didn't have much appreciation for that. Interestingly enough, his godson and successor, John Stuart Mill, did have just such an appreciation, and we will look at his work shortly.

But suppose you actually make a detailed list of the consequences of your actions. How, exactly, do you decide on the values that you assign each consequence? In some cases it is easy, as for example when you compare school fees or driving distances. But if you want to decide whether to stay in school for the duration or quit and get a job and make fast money, how do you choose what things to put on your list? Critics of Bentham's approach say that if we assign a higher value to getting an education than to acquiring fast money, then it is because we are operating within a system that favors higher education; in other words, we are *biased,* and our choice of values reflects that bias. To put it another way, we rig the test even as we perform it. If we were operating within a system that favored making money—for instance, if we already had left school to make money—then our values would reflect that bias. The values, therefore, are truly arbitrary, depending on what we would like the outcome to be, and we can't trust the hedonistic calculus to give us an objective, mathematically certain picture of what to do. This does not mean such lists are useless; they can tell us much about ourselves and our own preferences and biases. However, they can do little more than that.

The Uncertain Future

Utilitarianism might still be able to offer a less presumptuous system, one designed to give guidance and material for reflection rather than objectively calculated solutions. Even with that kind of system, though, there are problems to be dealt with. One lies in the concept of *consequences* itself. Of course we can't claim that an action has any consequences before we actually have taken that action. The consequences we are evaluating are hypothetical; they have yet to occur. How can we decide once and for all whether an action is morally good if the consequences are still up in the air? We have to (1) make an educated guess and hope for the best, (2) act, and (3) wait to see the results. If we're lucky and wise, the results will be as positive as what we hoped for. But suppose they aren't? Before we learn the results, our good intentions are of course part of the plus side of the hedonistic calculus: If we intend to create beneficial consequences for as many as possible, it is a process that the utilitarian will approve of. But the true value of our action is not clear until the consequences are clear. You may intend to create much happiness, and your calculations may be educated, but your intentions may still be foiled by forces beyond your control. In that case, it is the *end result* that counts and not your fine intentions and calculations. How long do we have to wait until we know whether our actions were morally good or evil? It may take a long time before all the effects are known—maybe a hundred years or more. Critics of utilitarianism say it is just not reasonable to use a moral system that doesn't allow us to know whether what we did was morally right or wrong until some time in the far-off future. Furthermore, how will we ever be able to decide anything in the first place? Thousands—perhaps millions—of big and small consequences result from everything we do. Do we have to calculate them all? How can we ever make a quick decision if we have to go through such a complicated process every time?

Answers to such criticisms were provided by the philosopher and economist John Stuart Mill (1806–1873). For one thing, Mill says, we don't have to calculate every little effect of our action; we can rely on the common experience of humanity. Through the millennia, humans have had to make similar decisions all the time, and we can consider their successes and failures in deciding our own actions. (Because Mill had actually given up on calculating every action to an exact mathematical value, it was easier for him than for Bentham to allow for some uncertainty in future results.) What about having to wait a long time for future consequences to happen, in order to pass judgment on the morality of our action? Mill says all we have to do is wait a reasonable amount of time—a short wait for small actions, a longer wait for bigger actions. Mill relies on us to know intuitively what he means, and perhaps we do. But the problems inherent in utilitarianism are not solved with these suggestions, merely diffused a little.

The Moral Universe of Utilitarianism: Advantages and Problems of Sheer Numbers

Initially, the idea of creating as much pleasure as possible for as many as possible seems a positive one. If we read on in Bentham's writings, we even find that "the many" may not be limited to humans. Bentham's theory was so advanced for its time that it not only gave the right to seek pleasure and avoid pain to all humans, regardless of social standing, it also said that the criterion for who belongs in the moral universe is not who has the capability to speak or to reason but *who can suffer,* and surely suffering is not limited to human beings. (See Box 5.4 for a discussion of suffering and nonhuman animals.)

If we assume that the capacity to suffer (and feel pleasure) qualifies a living organism for inclusion in the moral universe, and if we believe that each individual's pleasure counts equally, we find ourselves with a dramatically expanded moral universe. Even today, the idea that all creatures who can suffer deserve to be treated with dignity does not meet with the approval of every policymaker. Moreover, if the decrease of suffering and the increase of happiness are all that counts for all these members of our moral universe, what does it mean for our decision if the happiness of some can be obtained only at the cost of the suffering of others? This is where we encounter the problem of *sheer numbers* in utilitarianism, because whatever creates more happiness for more individuals or decreases their pain is morally right *by definition.* If giving up animal-tested household products causes human housekeepers only minor inconvenience, then we have no excuse to keep using them, because major suffering is caused by such testing. However, if it could be shown that only a few animals would have to suffer (even if they would suffer horribly) so that an immense number of humans would find their housecleaning greatly eased, would it then be permissible to cause such suffering? Yes, if the pleasure gained from easy housecleaning in a large number of households could be added up and favorably compared to the immense suffering of only a very few nonhuman animals.

The argument for doing whatever benefits more living creatures, human or nonhuman, is usually advanced with regard to animal testing of medical procedures that could benefit humans. But because sheer numbers are all that matter in utilitarianism, the housecleaning example works too. Curing human ailments is not intrinsically "better" than helping humans clean their houses—what matters is the happiness that is created and the misery that is prevented. Suppose feline leukemia could be cured by subjecting ten humans to painful experiments. The humans would certainly suffer, but all cats would, from then on, be free of leukemia. For some, this type of example reveals the perversely narrow focus of utilitarianism; looking at pleasure and pain and

Box 5.4   WHO CAN SUFFER?

Jeremy Bentham's insistence that the moral universe be open to any creature who can suffer is still a controversial statement, and in Bentham's own day it was extremely radical. Of his influential contemporaries, only John Stuart Mill took up the idea that humans are not necessarily the only members of the moral realm; it was (and still is) standard procedure to view morality as something only humans can engage in or benefit from. Most arguments that exclude animals are based on the assumption that they can't speak or reason (which is why Bentham says this is irrelevant and asks, "Can they suffer?"). To most people, then and now, it is obvious that animals can suffer—all we have to do is observe an injured animal. But to some thinkers, this is not a foregone conclusion. An argument that used to be popular in theology was that humans suffer because Adam and Eve sinned against God in the Garden of Eden, and suffering was their, and their children's, punishment; since animals have not sinned against God, they can't suffer. A more influential argument in philosophy comes from René Descartes (1596–1650), otherwise known for opening up the gates of modern philosophy with his statement "I think, therefore I am." Descartes argued that only humans have minds; everything else in the world consists of matter only, including animals. If you have a mind, you can have awareness of suffering; if you have no mind, your body may be subjected to physical stress, but you won't

know it. The dog whose tail is caught in the door will yelp, but that is no sign of feeling pain, according to Descartes—that is the way the dog is constructed, like a clock with moving parts (in today's jargon, the dog is *programmed* to yelp). The dog itself has no mind and feels nothing. (Descartes actually was a dog owner; according to legend, his dog's name was Monsieur Grat.) When challenged by Margaret Cavendish, the Duchess of Newcastle, Descartes's answer was that if animals had minds, then oysters would have to have minds too, and he found that ridiculous. Margaret Cavendish was a writer with an interest in science. Like most contemporary readers, she knew that there is a considerable difference between the nervous systems of dogs and oysters, but Descartes's viewpoint has had immense influence on the treatment of animals to this day.

Modern biology generally assumes that mammals and many other animals can feel pain, precisely because there is such a similarity between their nervous systems and ours. In addition, the capacity for suffering seems to be an evolutionary advantage; a being that can feel pain is more likely to be cautious, to survive, and to propagate. At a conference in Chicago in 2000, animal researchers from a variety of fields concluded that there is no longer any reason to assume that animals can't feel, both physically *and* emotionally. You can read more about the issue of animals in Chapter 13.

adding them up are simply not enough. For others, examples like this one only confirm that all creatures matter, and no one's pain should be more or less important than anyone else's.

To focus on the problem, let's assume that we are faced with a situation in which some humans are sacrificed for the happiness and welfare of other humans. Suppose it is revealed that governments around the world have for years had a secret pact with aliens from outer space, whereby the governments have agreed to deny consistently that UFOs exist and to not interfere with occasional alien abductions of humans for

René Descartes (1596–1650), French philosopher, mathematician, and naturalist, known as the founder of modern philosophy; he is particularly famous for having said, "*Cogito, ergo sum,*" or, "I think, therefore I am." Descartes believed that a human consists of a body and a soul; thanks to the soul, humans can be self-aware and conscious of their bodies, including physical pleasures and pains. But since Descartes couldn't imagine that animals have souls, he had to conclude that animals couldn't be aware of their physical condition either, so the inevitable deductive conclusion was, for him, that animals can't feel pain.

medical experiments. In return, at the end of their experiments, the aliens will provide humanity with a cure for all viral diseases. For a great number of people this would be a trade well worth the suffering of the "specimens" involved—provided that they themselves would not be among the specimens. Indeed, some humans might even *volunteer* for the experiments, but let us assume, as a condition, that the human subjects are reluctant participants, and no volunteers are accepted. Although some people would gladly commit their fellow humans to death from suffering, others would insist that it is not right; somehow, these humans do not deserve such a fate, and the immense advantages to humankind forever do not really make up for it. In other words, some may have a moral sense that the price is too high, but utilitarianism can't acknowledge such a moral intuition because its only moral criterion is one of sheer numbers. For many, the morality of utilitarianism is counterintuitive when applied to some very poignant human situations.

The UFO example is (or at least it is intended to be) fictional. But the late twentieth century revealed to us a number of real-life, large-scale cases in which a number of people had unwittingly been made into guinea pigs for the sake of some greater cause. What if we could accomplish beneficial results for a large number of people or living beings at the cost of intolerable pain suffered by a few? Whether one sees immediate benefits to a population, such as security measures, or long-term benefits, such as medical knowledge, the price of pain and suffering, even death, was paid by human beings, not by choice but by force, for the sake of some higher goal. The Tuskegee syphilis experiment is a chilling example, but it doesn't end there. Other morally questionable governmental practices have been revealed; see Box 4.5 for some examples. Such experiments have reduced people to being mere tools in someone else's agenda. A classic utilitarian will answer that, depending on the greatness and nature of the goal, the sacrifice and suffering might well be worth the price. But John Stuart Mill added that, in the long run, a population abusing a minority will reap not good results but social unrest, so such practices should be discouraged (see the subsequent section on act and rule utilitarianism).

In *Runaway Jury,* Nick (John Cusack) and Marlee (Rachel Weisz) are having a serious talk, after Nick's apartment has been torched by the defense lawyer's goons: Is their venture to swing the jury for $10 million worth the risk? And are Nick and Marlee really just grifters, or are they crusaders for a cause?

Still, the salvation of humanity is a forceful argument. Let us suppose, however, that we are talking not about salvation from disease but about salvation from boredom. Television is already moving toward showing live or videotaped events involving human suffering and death; home movies are often the source of this footage, and this form of "entertainment" has become increasingly popular. Reality-based TV shows such as *Survivor* are flourishing. Is a future reality-based show with actual violence a possibility? Might viewers choose to watch real-time shows of criminals who are granted one television hour to run through a city or neighborhood, avoiding snipers and hoping to live through it all and win their freedom? The Romans watched Christians, slaves, criminals, prisoners of war, and wild animals fight each other, with much appreciation for the entertainment value of such events. If they had had the ability to televise the events, might we not assume that they would have done so, having recognized that "bread and circuses" (food and entertainment) would appease the unruly masses? According to the utilitarian calculation, a great number of people may be hugely entertained by the immense suffering of one or a few. How far are we allowed to let numbers run away with us in disregarding people's inherent right to fair treatment?

As you know, this would point out that under such circumstances, people start worrying about being victimized, and social unrest follows. Until that happens, though, utilitarians must conclude that there is justification in letting a large number of people enjoy the results of the suffering of a few (or even enjoy the suffering itself).

In the Narratives section you'll find several stories illustrating this problem of "sheer numbers": Wessel's satire "The Blacksmith and the Baker"; Ursula K. Le Guin's story about a child being tortured for the sake of communal happiness, "The Ones Who Walk Away from Omelas"; a selection from Dostoyevsky's *Brothers Karamazov;* and summaries of the films *Saving Private Ryan, Runaway Jury,* and *Extreme Measures.* Once we start identifying the utilitarian sheer-numbers problem as one of disregard for the rights of the individual for the sake of the well-being of the many, we tend to be critical of any decision that would favor the happiness of the majority over the rights of a minority, and perhaps rightfully so. However, there are compelling scenarios that make us reevaluate the simple math of Bentham's utilitarianism: When push comes to shove, and hard decisions have to be made in a split second, saving the many by sacrificing the few may be the decision most of us would agree with. Think back to that dreadful day of September 11, when four airplanes were hijacked with the presumed intent to cause as much damage as possible to people and institutions. Three planes hit their targets: the World Trade Center towers and the Pentagon. But as you'll recall, the fourth plane, Flight 93, did not reach its intended target, in all likelihood the Capitol, because of the heroic resolve of the passengers. But in the aftermath we also learned that had the passengers not acted, Flight 93 would probably not have reached its target anyway, because Air Force fighter jets were already poised to escort the plane down or, if necessary, shoot it down. This came as a shock to many Americans, in particular when the government announced that *any* plane on a collision course with a civilian or military structure would be regarded as a threat and would be shot down. Here we see the principle of utility at work in a desperate situation: Sacrifice the few on the plane rather than take a chance and risk the lives of the many on the ground and the security of our institutions. Some might say, "But those people on the plane were going to die when the plane hit the building anyway, so what difference did it make if they died sooner rather than later?" The difference is in the attitude regarding the few as expendable. Furthermore, it isn't a *given* that they would die anyway. So if we could limit terrible consequences for a large number of people by sacrificing a few innocent people, would the decision be acceptable, even if we happened to be among the unfortunate few ourselves? If we say "yes," where do we draw the line? How do we define "terrible consequences"? And, if we say "no," are we seriously advocating that it is better for the many to perish in the name of fairness than for the many to survive at the cost of the lives of the few?

The ante was upped in the spring of 2004 with the prisoner abuse scandal at the Abu Ghraib prison in Baghdad. Photos taken by American soldiers and reservists guarding Iraqi prisoners of war revealed that some guards had engaged in what looked like highly questionable practices, such as placing the prisoners in sexually explicit situations. Two questions arose, based on the suspicion that these American soldiers—male and female—hadn't acted entirely on their own: Who ordered the abuse? And why? As I write this, there are still no clear answers. While some voices in the United States pointed out that the press seemed to focus more on this abuse than on (1) the positive results of the war and (2) the fact that American hostages were being beheaded by terrorists, the media focus did bring one moral question to the forefront: Is torture of prisoners for the sake of information ever acceptable? This question goes to the heart of our debate in this chapter: If lives of our soldiers and civilians can be saved, should we engage in torture of prisoners who may have the knowledge to help us? The hedonistic calculus, of course, gives a clear answer—we just have to calculate the pains involved on one side and on the other. Generally, a follower of Bentham would approve of torture. It's just that we, as a civilized people, don't in general approve of even the thought of torturing other human beings, even if they are enemy combatants and even if our own lives could be saved in the process. The question raised by some today is, Is this the ultimate appropriate civilized attitude? Or is it unrealistic and squeamish? If Bentham's principle is brought to bear in such a situation, what is to stop us from using the same methods to achieve results that are less than life saving, such as for financial information or simply for entertainment? This is the slippery slope that utilitarians must face.

Some people have suggested a solution: Perhaps Bentham's mistake was to think the calculus was a cure-all, a method to be used in all situations. Because if we use it as the all-round problem solver, we do end up with a general permission to abuse a minority for the sake of the pleasure of the majority, regardless of what kind of pleasure it might be. However, suppose we view it as the ultimate *last resort*? When there are no other options to save lives, perhaps this is the only conceivable approach after all. If an airplane is headed toward the Capitol, and the pilot doesn't respond, or responds defiantly, perhaps the only sensible course is to shoot the plane down, sacrificing innocent civilians before more damage is done. Should we take this one step further? If the lives of millions are at stake, and one captured enemy has information that will save these lives, perhaps the only sensible act is to use whatever means are needed to make him or her talk. Since September 11 all Americans have been actors in the drama of the war on terrorism. Unpleasant changes in our lives have become the order of the day. But is this one of the changes we have to get used to? Critics point out that, from a utilitarian viewpoint, torture doesn't work: (1) It doesn't guarantee reliable informatoin and (2) it creates an increased risk that our POWs might be tortured. In Chapter 6 you'll encounter a theory that adamantly opposes such measures on principle, be they last-resort measures or the order of the day.

John Stuart Mill: Another Utilitarian Vision

Bentham was not alone in designing the theory of utilitarianism. He and his close friend James Mill worked out the specifics of the new moral system together. Mill's son John Stuart Mill was a very bright boy, and James Mill's ambition was to develop his son's talents and intelligence as much as possible and as fast as possible. The boy responded well, learned quickly, and was able to read Greek and Latin at an early age. Throughout his childhood he was groomed to become a scientist. He was tutored privately and performed marvelously until he came to a halt at the age of twenty, struck by a nervous breakdown. His crisis was quiet and polite, in accordance with his nature: He went on with his work, and few people close to him realized what was going on; but internally he stopped in his tracks and in a very modern

John Stuart Mill (1806–1873), English philosopher and econo-mist. Believing that utilitarianism was the only reasonable moral system, Mill nevertheless saw Jeremy Bentham's version as rather crude and created a more sophisticated version of the principle of utility, taking into consideration the qualitative differences be-tween pleasures.

sense decided to "get in touch with himself," for he had come to the realization that despite his intense studying, one part of his education was pitifully incomplete. He knew much about how to think, but he didn't know how to *feel;* as a child he had been emotionally deprived and had never been allowed to have playmates other than his siblings, and in terms of his emotional life he now felt totally inadequate. (If you remember from Chapter 2 the emphasis that was placed on feelings during the Age of Romanticism, you'll have an even better understanding of what Mill went through, because he was a young man of twenty when the Age of Romanticism was at its peak.) In the months before his breakdown, he had engaged in debates, pub-lished articles, helped edit a major work by Bentham, and was probably beginning to suffer from what we today call burnout—at the very least, he was overworked.

Later in life, Mill described his breakdown in his *Autobiography;* in modern ter-minology, he put a spin on it that reflected his rebellion against Jeremy Bentham:

> From the winter of 1821, when I first read Bentham . . . I had what might truly be called an object in life; to be a reformer of the world. My conception of my own life was entirely identified with this object. . . . But the time came when I awakened from this as from a dream. It was in the autumn of 1826. I was in a dull state of nerves, such as everybody is occasionally liable to; unsusceptible to enjoyment or pleasurable excitement. . . . In this frame of mind it occurred to me to put the question directly to myself: "Suppose that all your objects in life were realized; that all the changes in institutions and opinions which you are looking forward to, could be completely effected at this very instant: would this be a great joy and happiness to you?" And an irrepressible self-consciousness distinctly an-swered, "No!" At this my heart sank within me: the whole foundation on which my life was constructed fell down. . . . I seemed to have nothing left to live for. . . . If I had loved anyone sufficiently to make confiding my griefs a necessity, I should not have been in the condition I was.

What Mill read into his breakdown later in life was that his father's intellectual train-ing and Bentham's philosophy had let him down—the utilitarian greatest-happiness principle might lead to happiness for the many, but it didn't necessarily lead to happiness for the utilitarian. Mill, in his *Autobiography,* uses this term to ram a lesson home: You don't find happiness by looking for it but by enjoying life along the way as you focus on other things. "Ask yourself whether you are happy, and you cease to be so." In his crisis, Mill rediscovered the truth of the paradox of hedonism: The harder you look for happiness, the more likely it is to elude you. But what really happened to him psychologically may not have been clear to Mill at all. For one thing, he was over-worked, and winter was approaching. For another, he found himself a cerebral intel-lectual in the midst of the most feeling-oriented period so far in Western history. For a third, he was lonely and became depressed; he had what we've come to know as a severe case of "the blues." But the loneliness problem didn't last long. Neither did his disenchantment with utilitarianism—he just stopped looking for self-gratification in it and focused on the goal of improving the world.

Mill began exploring the world of feelings—music, poetry, literature—and later he went abroad to the European continent and traveled (as did the Romantic painters and poets). In a roundabout way, Mill's personal story illustrates Nussbaum's theory that emotions are not irrelevant for ethics (see Chapter 1). During this period he took time out to reexamine his life and his future, turned his back on the sciences, and decided to "go into his father's business" and become a social thinker. As a so-cial thinker he became one of the most influential persons of the nineteenth century, laying the foundation for many of the political ideas in the Western world on both the liberal and the conservative sides.

Mill's aim was to take his godfather and father's theory of utilitarianism and re-design it to fit a more sophisticated age. What had seemed overwhelmingly important to Bentham—a more just legal system—was no longer the primary goal, due to the re-alization that without proper education for the general population, true social equal-ity would not be obtained. Also, Mill realized that Bentham's version of utilitarianism had several flaws. For one thing, it was too simple; it relied on a very straightforward system of identifying good with pleasure and evil with pain, without specifying the na-ture of pleasure and pain. (Some say this was actually one of the strengths of early util-itarianism, but Mill saw it as a serious deficiency.) Bentham's version also assumed that people were so rational they would always follow the moral calculations. Mill pointed out, however, that even if people are clearly shown it would give them and others more overall pleasure to change their course of action, they are likely to continue doing what they are used to because people are creatures of habit; our emotions, rather than cool deliberation, often dictate what we do. We can't, therefore, rely on our rationality to the extreme degree that Bentham thought we could. (This doesn't mean, of course, that we can't *educate* children and adults to use their heads more profitably.) We will return to the education question later, but first we look at how Mill decided to redesign the theory of utilitarianism.

Mill was a more complex person than Bentham, and his theory reflects this com-plexity. For Mill the idea that humans seek pleasure and that moral goodness lies in obtaining that pleasure is only half the story—but it is the half that is most frequently misunderstood. What do people think when they hear this idea? That all that counts is easy gratification of any desire they may have—in other words, a "doctrine worthy only of swine," as Mill says, repeating the words of the critics of utilitarianism. And because people reject the notion of seeking only swinish pleasures, they reject utilitarianism as an unworthy theory. They get upset, said Mill, precisely because they are not pigs and want more out of life than a pig could ever want. People are simply not content with basic pleasures, and a good moral and social theory should reflect this. Furthermore, says Mill, all theories that have advocated happiness have been accused of talking about easy gratification, but that is an unfair criticism when applied to utilitarianism. Even Epicurus held that there are many things in life other than physical pleasures that can bring us happiness, and there is nothing in utilitarianism that says we have to define pleasure and happiness as mere gratification of physical desires.

Why was Mill so uneasy about being accused of seeking gratification of physical desires? Consider the changing times in which he lived. When Mill wrote his book *Utilitarianism* (1863), the British Empire was twenty-six years into the Victorian era. Queen Victoria had ascended the throne in 1837, and morals had subtly undergone a shift since Bentham's day; preoccupation with physical pleasures was, on the whole, frowned upon by the middle classes, more so than in the previous generation—it was not considered proper to display such indulgence. For many this signifies an age of hypocrisy, of double standards, but it would be unfair to accuse Mill of such double standards because several of his truly innovative social ideas stemmed from his indignation toward this preoccupation with the way other people choose to live. However, it may have been a sign of the times that Mill felt compelled to reassure his readers that they could be followers of utilitarianism without being labeled hedonists.

Some believe there is also a personal side to the story. In his early twenties, Mill, having earlier worried that he didn't have any knowledge of feelings, fell head over heels in love with a young married woman, Harriet Taylor, and the feeling was mutual. They maintained a relationship for almost twenty years, until her husband died, and then they finally got married. Their relationship had become an open secret over the years, even to Mr. Taylor. (Being honest people, they apparently told him of their feelings, but he was also assured that they had no intention of breaking up the Taylor marriage.) It has generally been assumed that they were sexually involved, but judging from their correspondence, it may well have been a platonic friendship until their wedding. Their letters testify to Mill's later version of utilitarianism: They both seem to agree that spiritual pleasures and intellectual companionship are more valuable than physical gratification. John Stuart Mill prepared his book *Utilitarianism* during the years of their marriage, but when it was published in 1863, Harriet was no longer alive. She died (probably of tuberculosis) less than ten years after they got married; however, Mill's moral and political writings were clearly inspired by their intellectual discussions over three decades. (See Box 5.5 for a discussion of Mill's views on women's rights.)

What, then, does Mill propose? That some pleasures are more valuable, "higher," than others. That on the whole, humans prefer to hold on to their dignity and strive for truly fulfilling experiences rather than settle for easy contentment. *It is better to be a human dissatisfied than a pig satisfied, better to be Socrates dissatisfied than a fool satisfied,* says Mill. Even if the great pleasures in life require some effort—for instance, one has to learn math in order to understand the joy of solving a mathematical problem—it is worth the effort, because the pleasure is greater than if you had just remained passive.

Harriet Hardy Taylor Mill (1807–1858) was a chief source of inspiration for her longtime friend and later husband John Stuart Mill. Her views on individual rights are reflected in Mill's book *On Liberty* (1859), published immediately after her death. They did not agree on everything, though: Mill believed that when a woman marries, she must give up working outside the home; Taylor believed that women have a right to employment regardless of their marital status and that no-fault divorce should be available. However, the spouses seemed to be in agreement on most other issues and found in each other what we today call a soul mate. Mill grieved deeply when she died and moved to a house close to the cemetery where she was laid to rest, so he could visit her grave often.

Now the question becomes, Who is to say which pleasures are the higher ones and which are the lower ones? We seem predisposed to assume that the physical pleasures are the lower ones, but need that be the case? Mill proposes a test: We must ask people who are familiar with both kinds of pleasure, and whatever they choose as the higher goal is the ultimate answer. Suppose we gather a group of people who sometimes order a pizza and beer and watch *Monday Night Football* or a reality show but also occasionally go out to a French restaurant before watching *Masterpiece Theatre* on PBS. We ask them which activity—pizza and football or French food and *Masterpiece Theatre*—is the higher pleasure. If the test works, we must accept it if the majority say that on the whole they think pizza and football is the higher pleasure. But will Mill accept that? This is the drawback of his test—it appears that he will not:

> Capacity for the nobler feelings is in most natures a very tender plant, easily killed, not only by hostile influences, but by mere want of sustenance; and in the majority of young persons it speedily dies away if the occupations to which their position in life has devoted them, and the society into which it has thrown them, are not favorable to keeping that higher capacity in exercise. Men lose their high aspirations as they lose their intellectual tastes, because they have not time or opportunity for indulging them; and they addict themselves to inferior pleasures not because they deliberately prefer them, but because they are either the only ones to which they have access or the only ones which they are any longer capable of enjoying.

What does this mean? It means if you vote for pizza and football as the overall winner, Mill will claim you have lost the capacity for enjoying gourmet French food and intellectual television (which demands some attention from your intellect). In other words, he has rigged his own test. This has caused some critics to voice the opinion that Mill is an intellectual snob, a "cultural imperialist" trying to impose his own standards on the general population. And the immediate victim of this procedure? The egalitarian principle that was the foundation of Bentham's version of utilitarianism—that one person equals one vote regarding what is pleasurable and what is painful—collapses under Mill's test. According to him, we have to go to the "authorities of happiness" to find out what it is that everybody ought to desire.

Box 5.5   MILL AND THE WOMEN'S CAUSE

John Stuart Mill is today recognized as the first influential male speaker for political equality between men and women in modern Western history. (In England, Mary Wollstonecraft published her *Vindication of the Rights of Women* in 1792, but already in 1673 the French author Poulain de la Barre, a student of Descartes, had published *De l'égalité des deux sexes,* in which he argued for total equality between men and women because of their equality in reasoning power. This book, however, was largely ignored for a long time.) Mill's book *The Subjection of Women* (1869) revealed to his readers the abyss of inequality separating the lives of men and women in what was then considered a modern society. His exposé of

this inequality was a strong contributing factor in women's obtaining the right to vote in England, as well as elsewhere in the Western world. In 1866 Mill, then a member of the British Parliament, had tried to get a measure passed that would establish gender equality in England. The measure failed, but Mill had succeeded in drawing attention to the issue. It is often mentioned in this context that Mill was inspired by his longtime friend and later wife, Harriet Taylor. Scholars now believe that Mill's fight for women's rights was not just a matter of subtle inspiration from Mrs. Taylor but a direct result of their long and detailed intellectual discussions, for Mrs. Taylor was an intellectual in her own right.

If we perform Mill's test and ask individuals who seem to know of many kinds of pleasure what they prefer, we may get responses that Mill would not have accepted, because some people may indeed favor physical pleasures over intellectual or spiritual ones; however, a recent study claimed (with no reference to Mill whatsoever) that people who have a spiritual side are happier overall than are people whose lives are completely focused on material pleasures. Now, it is questionable in itself whether it is at all possible to put together reliable statistics on this topic, but Mill would probably have welcomed the survey: It is not merely because higher, intellectual, or spiritual pleasures are somehow finer that he recommends them; it is because they presumably yield a higher form of happiness in the long run than do pleasures of easy gratification. (Box 5.6 explores Mill's attempt at proving that higher pleasures are more desirable and introduces the concept of the naturalistic fallacy.)

Be that as it may, the idea of a "spiritual life" is rather vague and intangible, so let us use an example that is more concrete: learning to play a musical instrument. Anyone who has attempted it knows that for the first few months it usually doesn't sound very good, practicing is hard work, and you'll be tempted to give up. But if you stick with it, there will probably come a day when you feel you can play what you want the way you want and even play with others, giving joy to yourself and your listeners. The same process occurs, of course, with many other skills that take hard work to learn but yield a lot of gratification when acquired: speaking a foreign language, for example, or painting with watercolors. So now Mill can step in and ask his question: If you had the choice, would you give up that skill, provided you could get all those hours of practice time back so you could spend them watching sitcoms? I doubt that a single one

Dilbert by Scott Adams

One of the deficiencies of utilitarianism is that if the final goal of any action is to feel good, it doesn't matter *what* makes us feel good. This *Dilbert* cartoon hits the nail on the head: If succeeding is supposed to make us feel good, but failure doesn't make us feel bad (because some believe that feeling good is important for people to maintain their self-esteem no matter how they do it), what is the incentive for success?

of us would say yes; identifying our artistic skill as the higher pleasure in spite of all the hours of hard work, tedium, and frustration leading up to it is no challenge at all. It seems that many of us, including Mill, and perhaps also Socrates, would indeed rather be temporarily dissatisfied if it meant we'd put the easy gratifications on hold for something higher and better down the road. But we'd still have to ask whether all skills that have taken an effort to acquire would qualify as "higher pleasures" according to Mill—as well as according to us: How about sports? Computer games? Or con artistry? At the end of the chapter, you can read a selection from *Utilitarianism* where Mill gives his version of a happy, meaningful life.

Mill's Political Vision: Equality and No Harm to Others

Did Mill achieve what he wanted? Certainly he wanted to redesign utilitarianism so that it reflected the complexity of a cultured population, but did he intend to set himself up as a cultural despot? It appears that what he wanted was something else entirely. Whereas Bentham wanted the girl who sold flowers at Covent Garden to be able to enjoy her gin in peace, Mill wants to *educate* her so that she won't *need* her gin anymore and will be able to experience the glorious pleasures enjoyed by the middle-class couple who have learned to appreciate the opera. What Mill had in mind, in other words, was probably not elitism, but the notion that the greater plea- sure can be derived from achievement. We feel a special fulfillment if we've worked hard on a math problem or a piece of music or a painting and we finally get it right. Mill thought this type of pleasure should be made available to everyone with a capacity for it. This Mill saw as equality of a higher order, based on general education. Once such education is attained, the choices of the educated person are his or hers

Box 5.6   THE NATURALISTIC FALLACY

John Stuart Mill acknowledges there is no proof that happiness is the ultimate value because no founding principles can be proved, yet he offers a proof by analogy. This proof has bothered philosophers ever since, because it actually does more harm than good to Mill's own system of thought. The analogy goes like this: The only way we can prove that something is visible is when we know people actually see it. Likewise, the only way we can prove that something is desirable is when we know people actually desire it. Everyone desires happiness, so happiness is therefore the ultimate goal. Why does this not work as an analogy? It doesn't work because being "visible" is not analogous to being "desirable." When we say that something is visible, we are describing what people actually see. But when we say that something is desirable, we are not describing what people desire. If a lot of people desire drugs, we do not therefore conclude that drugs are "desirable," because "desirable" means that something *should be* desired. The problem, however, goes deeper. Even if it were true that we could find out what is morally desirable by doing a nose count, why should we then have to conclude that because a lot of people desire something, there should be a moral requirement that we all desire it? In other words, we are stepping from "is" (from a descriptive statement that says something is desired) to "ought" (to a normative/prescriptive statement that says some-

thing ought to be desired), and as the philosopher David Hume pointed out, there is nothing in a descriptive statement that allows us to proceed from what people actually do to a rule that states what people ought to do. This step, known as the *naturalistic fallacy*, is commonly taken by thinkers, politicians, writers, and other people of influence, but it is nevertheless a dangerous step to take. We can't make a policy based solely on what is the case. For instance, if it were to turn out that women actually are better parents than men by nature, it still would not be fair to conclude that men ought not to be single fathers (or that all women ought to be mothers), because we can't pass from a simple statement of fact to a statement of policy. This does not mean we can't make policies based on fact; that would be preposterous. What we have to do is insert a value statement—our opinion about what is good or bad, right or wrong (a so-called hidden premise)—so we can go from a fact (such as "there are many teen pregnancies today") to the hidden premise ("We believe teen pregnancies are bad for teen girls, for their babies, and for society") and then to the conclusion ("We must try to lower the number of teen pregnancies"). In that case, someone who doesn't agree with our conclusion can still agree with the fact stated, but disagree with our hidden premise. Although this idea is occasionally contested by various thinkers, it remains one of philosophy's ground rules.

alone, and nobody has the right to interfere. However, until such a level is achieved, society has a right to gently inform its children and childlike adults about what they ought to prefer.

This sounds today like paternalism, and there is much in Mill's position that supports this point of view. In order to look more closely at Mill's ideas of what is best for people, we must take a look at what has become known as the *harm principle*.

Although the principle of utility provides a general guideline for personal as well as political action in terms of increasing happiness and decreasing unhappiness, it says very little about the circumstances under which one might justifiably become involved in changing other people's lives for the better. Mill had very specific ideas about the limitations of such involvement; in his essay *On Liberty* (1859), he examines the proper limits of government control. Because history has progressed from a time when rulers preyed upon their populations and the populations had to be protected from the rulers' despotic actions to a time when democratic rulers, in principle, *are* the people, the idea of absolute authority on the part of rulers should no longer be a danger to the people. But reality shows us that this is not the case, because we now must face the *tyranny of the majority*. In other words, those who now need protection are minorities (and here Mill thinks of political minorities) who may wish to conduct their lives in ways different from the ways of the majority and its idea of what is right and proper. As an answer to the question of how much the social majority is allowed to exert pressure on the minority, Mill proposes the harm principle:

> That principle is, that the sole end for which mankind are warranted, individually or collectively, in interfering with the liberty of action of any of their number, is self-protection. That the only purpose for which power can be rightfully exercised over any member of a civilized community, against his will, is to prevent harm to others. His own good, either physical or moral, is not a sufficient warrant. He cannot rightfully be compelled to do or forbear because it will be better for him to do so, because it will make him happier, because, in the opinions of others, to do so would be wise, or even right. These are good reasons for remonstrating with him, or reasoning with him, or persuading him, or entreating him, but not for compelling him, or visiting him with any evil in case he do otherwise. To justify that, the conduct from which it is desired to deter him must be calculated to produce evil to someone else. The only part of the conduct of anyone, for which he is amenable to society, is that which concerns others. In the part which merely concerns himself, his independence is, of right, absolute. Over himself, over his own body and mind, the individual is sovereign.

So how does this policy go with his statement four years later that higher pleasures are better for people than lower pleasures and that some people aren't capable of knowing what is good for them? Some Mill critics say that they don't go well together at all— that Mill is claiming in one text that people have a right to choose their own poison, and in the other that they haven't. But we can perhaps find a middle way: What Mill is saying in *On Liberty* is that people, if they so choose, should be allowed to follow their own tastes; what he is saying in *Utilitarianism* is that everybody should be allowed to be exposed to higher pleasures through education, so they might be able to make better choices—but he is not going to force anyone who is adult and in control of his or her mental faculties to submit to a life ruled by someone else's taste. At least this is a possible reading of Mill that brings the two viewpoints together. (See Box 5.7 for an application of the harm principle to the issue of the legalization of drugs.)

The harm principle has had extremely far-reaching consequences. Built in part on John Locke's theory of negative rights (see Chapter 7), that had had great influence not only in the United Kingdom, but also on the Constitution of the United States, Mill's theory helped define two political lines of thought that, paradoxically, are now at odds with each other. We usually refer to Mill's view as *classical liberalism* because of its emphasis

Box 5.7   THE HARM PRINCIPLE AND DRUG LEGALIZATION

John Stuart Mill's harm principle, that the only purpose of interfering with the life of someone is to prevent harm to others, has been applied in many social and political debates, with the general result that we see how ambiguous the principle really is. Examples are the euthanasia debate (see Chapter 7), the debate about "victimless crimes" such as (presumably) prostitution, and the discussion about the legalization of drugs.

A general utilitarian view of the legalization of drugs does not take a stand on whether drugs in themselves are "good" or "bad" but on whether more misery (or happiness) in the long run will be created through making them legally available than through prohibiting them. But remember that the harm principle sets limits to the "general-happiness principle" because it keeps us from interfering with people *for their own sake,* unless they are harming others. You can't force someone to try out someone else's model for happiness (and by now you have probably noticed that Mill's own theory of higher pleasures doesn't quite go well with his harm principle, because he believed people ought to be educated so they could enjoy the higher pleasures, even though they might not want to give up their lower pleasures).

Arguments in favor of drug legalization generally include these:

- The war on drugs isn't working—it is costly and clogs the jails with drug offenders; furthermore, drugs are still being brought across the borders.

- If drugs were legalized, they would be safer because they would be controlled by the state, and the black market would disappear. Drugs would become less expensive, and addicts wouldn't have to turn to crime in order to feed their habit.

- Heavy drug users could be helped by the state, and people who could manage their own drug use could be left to themselves;

after all, people who can manage their own drinking are not criminalized.

The harm principle obviously applies here: If a person does no one else harm by a moderate drug intake, then he or she should be allowed to continue using drugs. (This is the drug policy of the Libertarian Party.) This is where advocates of drug legalization usually seek Mill's support. But we should not draw hasty conclusions. If we take a closer look at the issue, do we still have a situation that involves only individuals who are mature enough to manage their own habits?

- The fact that the war on drugs isn't working is no reason to give it up. If jails are being inundated with drug offenders, the solution is not to decriminalize drug use but to educate children about drugs before they start using.

- Will crime go down? Will the black market disappear? Will drugs be safer? Only if you live in a fantasy world. Cigarettes are legal, but there is a huge black market for tobacco, smuggling is big business, and even with cheap drugs there will be some who can't afford them and will turn to crime. If drug legalization involves regulation (safer drugs), then there will surely arise a black market for unregulated drugs, which would begin the cycle again.

- Certainly it is a good idea for the state to help heavy users—individual states already do that. And it is also possible that many people could be completely responsible with a drug habit, just as many are responsible in their enjoyment of alcohol (which is, of course, a drug). But—and this is where the harm principle takes a turn—imagine all those people, young people in particular, who refrain from drugs simply because they are illegal. With drug legalization, that obstacle is removed; this means there will be many more people on the streets who are under the influence, endangering themselves *and* others in traffic, not to mention creating lifelong dependencies.

So opponents of drug legalization are saying that, overall, legalization will cause more harm than continued drug legislation. In addition, even though one individual may not be directly harming anyone else, he or she may serve as a role model of drug use for others less mature or responsible. Mill only considered direct harm to others a reason to interfere, not this kind of indirect harm. (But he would have considered drugs a "lower pleasure.") However, later critics as well as supporters of the harm principle have argued that the line between direct and indirect harm is often blurred. A bad role model may cause more obvious and direct harm to an impressionable child than to an adult who is supposed to be able to distinguish right from wrong. So the harm principle may be used to argue against drug legalization. The issue of medical use of drugs, such as marijuana, may be different, because drugs for medical use are already part of our culture. The question of legislating alcohol as a drug of course has similarities with the drug issue: Alcohol directly endangers not just the person under the influence, but others as well; MADD (Mothers Against Drunk Drivers) and other victims of alcohol-related accidents and their relatives can attest to that. But there is a difference: Most other drugs are taken strictly for their effect; alcohol is very often consumed not for its effect, but for its taste, and the intake need not reach a level where a person is a risk to others.

on personal liberty. The idea of civil liberties—the rights of citizens, within their right to privacy, to do what they want provided that they do no harm and to have their government ensure that as little harm and as much happiness as possible is created for as many people as possible—is also a cornerstone of *egalitarian liberalism*. But the notions of personal liberty and noninterference by the government have also become key in the political theory of *laissez-faire*, the hands-off approach that requires as little government interference as possible, primarily in private enterprise. The idea behind laissez-faire is that if we all look after our own business and no authorities make our business theirs, then we all are better off, which is today considered a *conservative* economic philosophy, expressed in its extreme form by the Libertarian Party.

The limitations of the right to privacy are more numerous than might be apparent at first glance. For one thing, what exactly does it mean that we are accountable to society only for our conduct that concerns others? What Mill had in mind certainly included the right of consenting adults to engage in sexual activity in the privacy of their own homes, regardless of how other people might feel about the issue. In such cases, only nosy neighbors might be "concerned," and for Mill their right to concern would be proportionate to the extent that they would be exposed to the activities of the couple in question. In other words, if it takes binoculars for you to become exposed to a situation (and hence become "concerned"), then put aside your binoculars and mind your own business.

But what about, say, a teenage girl who decides to put an end to her life because her boyfriend broke up with her? Might that fall within the harm principle? Is she harming only herself, so that society has no right to interfere? Here Mill might answer in several ways. First, she is harming not only herself but her family as well, who would grieve for her and feel guilty for not having stepped in. There is also the problem of role models. If other teens in the same situation learn about her suicide, they might think it would be a good idea to follow her example, and more harm would be caused. But when does indirect harm ever end? Doesn't it spread like rings in water? Mill himself would not allow for indirect harm, such as the harm caused by flawed role models, to be an obvious cause for the interference of authorities. To him, an adult should not be prevented from doing what he or she wants to do just because some other adult might imitate the action, but only if his or her action (such as a policeman being drunk on the job—Mill's own example) is a likely cause for direct harm to others. You may draw your own conclusions about current discussions concerning direct and indirect harm, such as the debate surrounding helmet laws. In the late 1990s an issue arose where the question of direct versus indirect harm became quite relevant: Militant anti-abortion groups created a website, "The Nuremberg Files," where names and addresses of doctors performing abortions were listed, with the presumed underlying intention that these doctors, labeled "baby butchers," should be targeted and harassed—perhaps even killed. An Oregon jury found the activists guilty of inciting violence and sentenced them to pay $107 million to Planned Parenthood. But in March 2001 the Ninth Circuit Court ruled that the website was protected by the First Amendment (freedom of speech). In October 2001 the appeals court nullified the earlier ruling and decided to rehear the case, presumably under the assumption that if someone takes it upon himself or herself to act on information supplied by the website, it is no longer a matter of free speech, but a direct call to violence. So would harm caused by the website be called indirect or direct harm, in your opinion? It is clear that Mill's interpretation of his own harm principle still engenders heated debate. As for our example of the suicidal teenage girl, Mill would most certainly add the following: This situation does not fall under the harm principle, because the girl is (1) not an adult and (2) not in a rational frame of mind:

> This doctrine is meant to apply only to human beings in the maturity of their faculties. We are not speaking of children, or of young persons below the age which the law may fix as that of manhood or womanhood. Those who are still in a state to require being taken care of by others, must be protected against their own actions as well as against external injury. For the same reason, we may leave out of consideration those backward states of society in which the [human] race itself may be considered as in its nonage. . . . Despotism is a legitimate mode of government in dealing with barbarians, provided the end be their improvement, and the means justified by actually effecting that end. Liberty, as a principle, has no application to any state of things anterior to the time when mankind have become capable of being improved by free and equal discussion. . . . But as soon as mankind have attained the capacity of being guided to their own improvement by conviction or persuasion (a period long since reached in all nations with whom we need here concern ourselves), compulsion . . . is no longer admissible as a means to their own good, and justifiably only for the security of others.

With this addition to the harm principle, Mill certainly makes it clear that children are excluded, but so is anyone who, in Mill's mind, belongs to a "backward" state of society. Again, we see evidence of Mill's complexity: He adamantly wants to protect civil liberties, but he is also paternalistic: Whoever is not an "adult" by his definition must be guided or coerced to comply with existing rules. Individuals as well as whole peoples who fall outside of the "adult" category must be governed by others until they reach sufficient maturity to take affairs into their own hands. Critics have seen this as a defense of not merely cultural but also political imperialism: There are peoples who are too primitive to rule themselves, so someone else has to do it for them and bring them up to Western standards. Who are these peoples? We may assume that they include the native-born peoples of old British colonies. Since Mill made his living not as a philosophy professor but as a Chief Examiner at India House, East India Company, which administered the colony of India (his father, James Mill, had worked for the Company and was the author of a lengthy work on the history of India), his knowledge of colony affairs came from the perspective of the colony power. This viewpoint, sometimes referred to as "the white man's burden," is very far from being acceptable in our era, but is it fair to accuse Mill of being an imperialist? Perhaps, especially if we take into account that Mill published his piece in 1859, and two years earlier the British Empire had been shocked by the so-called Sepoy mutiny in northern India, in which hundreds of British officers and their wives and children had been murdered by Indian infantry soldiers in the British-Indian army. This mutiny was the result of long-standing clashes and misunderstandings between the two cultural groups, after a hundred years of British dominion and (as many would describe it) exploitation. In the aftermath of the mutiny, India was taken over by the British Crown and ruled as a part of the empire. Mill was appalled at the mutiny but also at the takeover by the British government, and he retired, declining to take part in the new government. His chief aim seems to have been perpetuating not the British Empire but the utilitarian idea of maximizing happiness for the greatest number and minimizing pain and misery on a global scale. If Mill was biased toward the British way of life, it may be understandable: That way of life was in many ways the best the planet Earth had to offer in the nineteenth century for those with access to a good education. It was, in our terms, an extremely "civilized" culture, at least for the upper and middle classes. Perhaps, then, we can think of Mill not merely as an intellectual snob, but also as an educator who wanted to see everybody get the same good chances in life that he got and enjoy life as much as he did.

One final remark concerning Mill: Sometimes the present forces us to reevaluate things we thought were simply part of history—something we thought we understood pretty well. For at least half a century it has been considered right and appropriate (at least in this country) to criticize Mill for wanting to govern India until Indians were capable of governing themselves in a democratic fashion. Ethical relativism, being a strong cultural force in the twentieth century, has told us that each culture is right in its own way and that no culture has the right to superimpose its values on other cultures. But wait . . . in Chapter 3 we discussed the types of situations that have made so many people change their minds about ethical relativism. Should we just stand by while little girls are being circumcised? While people are being sold into slavery? Now suppose we add to the list: While people are being tortured and murdered by a dictator, while entire populations are being subject to genocide? What I am getting at is, of course, the war in Iraq. Even without considering the issue of the WMDs (weapons of mass destruction) or the connection between Saddam Hussein and al Qaeda, removing a dictator and creating a democracy became what the war in Iraq was all about. That puts us at a crossroads: On the one hand, we can stay with the earlier critical evaluation of Mill and say that no matter what the situation, a nation doesn't have the right to try to run another nation or change its regime to something that seems more right, or even just more acceptable or safer. On the other hand, if we agree with Mill that democracy is better than tyranny, and freedom of educated people is better than the superstition of illiteracy—then can we still claim that he is wrong? And if we think he has a point, how does that translate into the evaluation of the war in Iraq? For Mill and other British citizens, the Sepoy Mutiny can perhaps be understood as a kind of 9/11 experience. Even if he didn't approve of the way the British government handled the crisis, his conclusion was that nations who aren't "civilized" must be put under the civilizing influence of other nations until they have matured sufficiently to govern themselves. So if we view Mill's attitude through the lenses of our own 9/11 experience, and the subsequent wars in Afghanistan and—in particular—the war in Iraq, would you condemn his view, or would you instead reevaluate Mill's statement in light of the successful ouster of Saddam Hussein and the elected new Iraqi democratic government? Or do you see a third possibility, perhaps based on the situation in Iraq as it has evolved by the time you read this?

Act and Rule Utilitarianism

In the twentieth century it became clear to philosophers attracted to utilitarianism that there were severe problems inherent in the idea that a morally right act is an act that makes as many people as possible happy. One flaw is that, as we saw previously, it is conceivable many people will achieve much pleasure from the misery of a few others, and even in situations where people don't know that their happiness is achieved by the pain of others, this is still an uncomfortable thought. It is especially so if one believes in the Golden Rule (as John Stuart Mill did), which states that we should do for others what we would like done for ourselves and refrain from doing to others what we would not like done to ourselves. Mill himself was aware of the problem and allowed that in the long run a society in which a majority abuses a minority is not a good society. That still means we have to explain why the *first* cases of happiness occurring from the misery of others are wrong, even before they have established themselves as a pattern with increasingly bad consequences. In a sense, Mill tried to address the problem, suggesting that utilitarianism be taken as a general policy to be applied to general situations. He did not, however, develop the idea further within his own philosophy.

Others have taken up the challenge and suggested it is just that particular formulation of utilitarianism which creates the problem; given another formulation, the problem disappears. If we stay with the *classical* formulation, the principle of utility goes like this: *Always do whatever act will create the greatest happiness for the greatest number of people.* In this version we are stuck with the problems we saw earlier; for example, the torture of innocents may bring about great pleasure for a large group of people. The Russian author Dostoyevsky explored this thought in his novel *The Brothers Karamazov*: Suppose your happiness, and everyone else's, is bought by the suffering of an innocent child? (We look more closely at this idea in the Narratives section.) It is not hard to see this as a Christian metaphor, with Jesus' suffering as the condition of happiness for humans, but there is an important difference: Jesus was a volunteer; an innocent child is not. In any event, a utilitarian, by definition, would have to agree that if a great deal of suffering could be alleviated by putting an innocent person through hell, then doing so would be justified. Putting nonhuman animals or entire populations of humans through hell would also be justified. The glorious end (increased happiness for a majority) will in any event justify the means, even if the means violate these beings' right to life or to fair treatment.

Suppose we reformulate utilitarianism. Suppose we say, *Always do whatever type of act will create the greatest happiness for the greatest number of people.* What is the result? If we set up a one-time situation, such as the torture of an innocent person for the sake of others' well-being, it may work within the first formulation. But if we view it as a *type* of situation—one that is likely to recur again and again because we have now set up a *rule* for such types of situations—it becomes impermissible: The consequences of torturing a *lot* of innocent people will not bring about great happiness for anyone in the long run. Is this, perhaps, what Mill was trying to say? This new formulation is referred to as *rule utilitarianism,* and it is advocated by many modern utilitarians who wish to distance themselves from the uncomfortable implications of the classical theory, now referred to as *act utilitarianism.* If this new version is used, they say, we can focus on the good consequences of a certain type of act rather than on the singular act itself. It may work once for a student to cheat on a final, but cheating as a rule is not only dangerous (the student herself is likely to be found out) but also immoral to the rule utilitarian, because very bad consequences would occur if everyone were to cheat. Professors would get wise in no time, and nobody would graduate. Students and professors would be miserable. Society would miss out on a lot of well-educated college graduates. The Golden Rule is in this way fortified: Don't do something if you can't imagine it as a rule for everybody, because a rule not suited for everyone can have no good overall consequences.

Some critics have objected that not everything we do can be made into a rule with good consequences. After all, lots of the things we like to do are unique to us, and why should we assume that just because one person likes to collect movie memorabilia, the world would be happier if everyone collected movie memorabilia? This is not the way it is supposed to work, say the rule utilitarians. You have to specify that the rule is valid for people *under similar circumstances,* and you have to specify what *exceptions* you might want to make. It may be morally good to make sure you are home in time for dinner if you have a family to come home to but not if you are living by yourself. And the moral goodness of being there in time for dinner depends on there not being something of greater importance that you should see to. Such things might be a crisis at work, a medical emergency, extracurricular activities, walking the dog, seeing your lover, watching a television show all the way to the end, talking on the phone, or whatever you choose. They may not all qualify as good exceptions, but *you* should specify in your rule which ones are acceptable. Once you have created such a rule, the utilitarian ideal will work, say the rule utilitarians; it will make more people happy and fewer people unhappy in the long run. If it doesn't, then you just have to rework the rule until you get it right.

The problem with this approach is that it may be asking too much of people. Are we likely to ponder the consequences of whatever it is we want to do every time we are about to take action? Are we likely to envision everyone doing the same thing? Probably not. Even if it is wrong to make lots of private phone calls from a company phone, we think it won't make much difference if one person makes private calls as long as nobody else does. As long as most people comply, we can still get away with breaking the rule without creating bad consequences. Even so, we are in the wrong, because a healthy moral theory will not set "myself" up as an exception to the rule just because "I'm me and I deserve it." This, as philosopher James Rachels has pointed out, is as much a form of discrimination as racism and sexism are. We might call it "me-ism," but we already have a good word for it, *egoism,* and we already know that that is unacceptable.

This addition to utilitarianism, that one ought to look for rules that apply to everyone, is for many a major step in the right direction. Rule utilitarianism certainly was not, however, the first philosophy to ask, What if everybody did what you intend to do? Although just about every parent must have said that to her or his child at some time or other, the one person who is credited with putting it into a philosophical framework is the German philosopher Immanuel Kant. There is one important difference between the way Kant asks the question and the way it has later been developed by rule utilitarians, though. Rule utilitarianism asks, What will be the *consequences* of everybody doing what you intend to do? Kant asks, Could you wish for it to be a *universal law* that everyone does what you intend to do? We look more closely at this difference in the next chapter.

Study Questions

1. Explain the function of Bentham's hedonistic (hedonic) calculus and give an example of how to use it. Explain the advantages of using the calculus; explain the problems inherent in the concept of the calculus.

2. Explain John Stuart Mill's theory of higher and lower pleasures: What are the problems inherent in the theory? Overall, does Mill's idea of higher and lower pleasures make sense to you? Why or why not?

3. Evaluate Descartes's theory that only those beings with a mind can suffer and that only humans have minds. Explore the consequences for utilitarianism if we agree that animals (including human beings) have a capacity for suffering.

4. Explore Mill's harm principle: Do you find the principle attractive or problematic? Explain why. Discuss the application of the harm principle to the issue of drug legalization.

5. Are we more likely to accept the idea of utilitarianism in a time of crisis? If so, does that make the theory acceptable? Explain.

Primary Readings and Narratives

The two Primary Readings are Jeremy Bentham's definition of the principle of utility and John Stuart Mill's vision of true happiness. The Narratives based on literature include a Danish tale about utilitarianism in action and a pairing of excerpts from Dostoyevsky and Ursula K. Le Guin that look at the happiness of the many in light of the suffering of a few. A summary of the film *Saving Private Ryan* illustrates the wartime complexity of the utilitarian question of the few being sacrificed for the many, and another film summary, *Extreme Measures,* explores the moral question of performing medical experiments on a few unwanted homeless people in order to gain knowledge that will save the lives and mobility of thousands of others. Both films ask, in different ways, whether some individuals can be considered more valuable than others. And, finally, the film summary of *Runaway Jury* represents a pro-utilitarian view in the controversial story of a jury being manipulated to achieve what the main characters perceive as a moral victory.

Primary Reading

Of the Principle of Utility

JEREMY BENTHAM

From An Introduction to the Principles of Morals and Legislation, *1789. Excerpt.*

Jeremy Bentham's primary interests were legislative, and he wrote in a meticulous style suited to the language of the law. In this excerpt Bentham defines the principle of utility and outlines the consequences for individuals, for the community, and for moral concepts.

I. *Mankind governed by pain and pleasure.* Nature has placed mankind under the governance of two sovereign masters, *pain* and *pleasure.* It is for them alone to point out what we ought to do, as well as to determine what we shall do. On the one hand the standard of right and wrong, on the other the chain of causes and effects, are fastened to their throne. They govern us in all we do, in all we say, in all we think: every effort we can make to throw them off our subjection, will serve but to demonstrate and confirm it. In words a man may pretend to abjure their empire: but in reality he will remain subject to it all the while. The *principle of utility* recognises this subjection, and assumes it for the foundation of that system, the object of which is to rear the fabric of felicity by the hands of reason and of law. Systems which attempt to question it, deal in sounds instead of sense, in caprice instead of reason, in darkness instead of light.

But enough of metaphor and declamation: it is not by such means that moral science is to be improved.

II. *Principle of utility, what.* The principle of utility is the foundation of the present work: it will be proper therefore at the outset to give an explicit and determinate account of what is meant by it. By the principle of utility is meant that principle which approves or disapproves of every action whatsoever, according to the tendency which it appears to have to augment or diminish the happiness of the party whose interest is in question: or, what is the same thing in other words, to promote or to oppose that happiness. I say of every action whatsoever; and therefore not only of every action of a private individual, but of every measure of government.

III. *Utility, what.* By utility is meant that property in any object, whereby it tends to produce benefit, advantage, pleasure, good, or happiness, (all this in the present case comes to the same thing) or (what comes again to the same thing) to prevent the happening of mischief, pain, evil, or unhappiness to the party whose interest is considered: if that party be the community in general, then the happiness of the community: if a particular individual, then the happiness of that individual.

IV. *Interest of the community, what.* The interest of the community is one of the most general expressions that can occur in the phraseology of morals: no wonder that the meaning of it is often lost. When it has a meaning, it is this. The community is a fictitious *body,* composed of the individual persons who are considered as constituting as it were its *members.* The interest of the community then is, what?—the sum of the interests of the several members who compose it.

V. It is in vain to talk of the interest of the community, without understanding what is the interest of the individual. A thing is said to promote the interest, or to be *for* the interest, of an individual, when it tends to add to the sum total of his pleasures: or, what comes to the same thing, to diminish the sum total of his pains.

VI. *An action conformable to the principle of utility, what.* An action then may be said to be conformable to the principle of utility, or, for shortness sake, to utility, (meaning with respect to the community at large) when the tendency it has to augment the happiness of the community is greater than any it has to diminish it.

VII. *A measure of government conformable to the principle of utility, what.* A measure of government (which is but a particular kind of action, performed by a particular person or persons) may be said to be conformable to or dictated by the principle of utility, when in like manner the tendency which it has to augment the happiness of the community is greater than any which it has to diminish it.

VIII. *Laws or dictates of utility, what.* When an action, or in particular a measure of government, is supposed by a man to be conformable to the principle of utility, it may be convenient, for the purposes of discourse, to imagine a kind of law or dictate, called a law or dictate of utility: and to speak of the action in question, as being conformable to such law or dictate.

IX. *A partizan of the principle of utility, who.* A man may be said to be a partizan of the principle of utility, when the approbation or disapprobation he annexes to any action, or to any measure, is determined by and proportioned to the tendency which he conceives it to have to augment or to diminish the happiness of the community: or in other words, to its conformity or unconformity to the laws or dictates of utility.

X. *Ought, ought not, right and wrong, &c. how to be understood.* Of an action that is conformable to the principle of utility one may always say either that it is one that ought to be done, or at least that it is not one that ought not to be done. One may say also, that it is right it should be done; at least that it is not wrong it should be done: that it is a right action; at least that it is not a wrong action. When thus interpreted, the words *ought,* and *right* and *wrong,* and others of that stamp, have a meaning: when otherwise, they have none.

Study Questions

1. Identify the concept of moral right and wrong as defined by the principle of utility. Do you approve of such a definition? Why or why not?

2. How does Bentham identify the concept of "community"? Evaluate Bentham's statement in terms of possible political consequences. Do you agree with him? Why or why not?

3. In your opinion, is Bentham right in stating that pain and pleasure govern us in everything we do?

4. Some scholars see Bentham as one short step removed from ethical egoism. Why? Is that a fair assessment?

Primary Reading

Utilitarianism

JOHN STUART MILL

1863. Excerpt.

In this section Mill outlines the idea of a test of higher and lower pleasures according to the judgment of those who know and appreciate both kinds. He then speaks of the true nature of happiness, as he sees it: a feeling that has little to do with pleasure seeking and much to do with the joy of contributing to the common good.

It is quite compatible with the principle of utility to recognize the fact, that some *kinds* of pleasure are more desirable and more valuable than others. It would be absurd that while, in estimating all other things, quality is considered as well as quantity, the estimation of pleasures should be supposed to depend on quantity alone.

If I am asked what I mean by difference of quality in pleasures, or what makes one pleasure more valuable than another merely as a pleasure, except its being greater in amount, there is but one possible answer. Of two pleasures, if there be one to which all or almost all who have experience of both give a decided preference, irrespective of any feeling of moral obligation to prefer it, that is the more desirable pleasure. If one of the two is, by those who are competently acquainted with both, placed so far above the other that they prefer it, even though knowing it to be attended with a greater amount of discontent, and would not resign it for any quantity of the other pleasure which their nature is capable of, we are justified in ascribing to the preferred enjoyment a superiority in quality, so far outweighing quantity as to render it, in comparison, of small account.

Now it is an unquestionable fact that those who are equally acquainted with, and equally capable of appreciating and enjoying, both, do give a most marked preference to the manner of existence which employs their higher faculties. Few human creatures would consent to be changed into any of the lower animals, for a promise of the fullest allowance of a beast's pleasures; no intelligent human being would consent to be a fool, no instructed person would be an ignoramus, no person of feeling and conscience would be selfish and base, even though they should be persuaded that the fool, the dunce, or the rascal is better satisfied with his lot than they are with theirs. They would not resign what they possess more than he for the most complete satisfaction of all the desires which they have in common with him. If they ever fancy they would, it is only in cases of unhappiness so extreme, that to escape from it they would exchange their lot for almost any other, however undesirable in their own eyes. A being of higher faculties requires more to make him happy, is capable probably of more acute suffering, and certainly accessible to it at more points, than one of an inferior type; but in spite of these liabilities, he can never really wish to sink into what he feels to be a lower grade of existence. We may give what explanation we please of this unwillingness; we may attribute it to pride, a name which is given indiscriminately to some of the most and to some of the least estimable feelings of which mankind are capable; we may refer it to the love of liberty and personal independence, an appeal to which was with the Stoics one of the most effective means for the inculcation of it; to the love of power, or to the love of excitement, both of which do really enter into and contribute to it: but its most appropriate appellation is a sense of dignity, which all human beings possess in one form or other, and in some, though by no means in exact, proportion to their higher faculties, and which is so essential a part of the happiness of those in whom it is strong, that nothing which conflicts with it could be, otherwise than momentarily, an object of desire to them. Whoever supposes that this preference takes place at a sacrifice of happiness—that the superior being, in anything like equal circumstances, is not happier than the inferior—confounds the two very different ideas, of *happiness* and *content*. It is indisputable that the being whose capacities of enjoyment are low, has the greatest chance of having them fully satisfied; and a highly endowed being will always feel that any happiness which he can look for, as the world is constituted, is imperfect. But he can learn to bear its imperfections, if they are at all bearable; and they will not make him envy the being who is indeed unconscious of the imperfections, but only because he feels not at all the good which those imperfections qualify. It is better to be a human being dissatisfied than a pig satisfied; better to be Socrates dissatisfied than a fool satisfied. And if the fool, or the pig, are of a different opinion, it is because they only know their own side of the question. The other party to the comparison knows both sides. [. . .]

According to the "greatest happiness principle," [. . .] the ultimate end, with reference to and for the sake of which all other things are desirable (whether we are considering our own good or that of other people), is an existence exempt as far as possible from pain, and as rich as possible in enjoyments, both in point of quantity and quality; the test of quality, and the rule for measuring it against quantity, being the preference felt by those who in their opportunities of experience, to which must be added their habits of self-consciousness and self-observation, are best furnished with the means of comparison. This, being, according to the utilitarian opinion, the end of human action, is necessarily also the standard of morality; which may accordingly be defined, the rules and precepts for human conduct, by the observance of which an existence such as has been described might be, to the greatest extent possible, secured to all mankind; and not to them only, but, so far as the nature of things admits, to the whole sentient creation. [. . .]

[. . .] If by happiness be meant a continuity of highly pleasurable excitement, it is evident enough that this is impossible. A state of exalted pleasure lasts only moments, or in some cases, and with some intermissions, hours or days, and is the occasional brilliant flash of enjoyment, not its permanent and steady flame. Of this the philosophers who have taught that happiness is the end of life were as fully aware as those who taunt them. The happiness which they meant was not a life of rapture; but moments of such, in an existence made up of few and transitory pains, many and various pleasures, with a decided predominance of the active over the passive, and having as the foundation of the whole, not to expect more from life than it is capable of bestowing. A life thus composed, to those who have been fortunate enough to obtain it, has always appeared worthy of the name of happiness. And such an existence is even now the lot of many, during some considerable portion of their lives. The present wretched education, and wretched social arrangements, are the only real hindrance to its being attainable by almost all.

In a world in which there is so much to interest, so much to enjoy, and so much also to correct and improve, everyone who has [a] moderate amount of moral and intellectual requisites is capable of an existence which may be called enviable; and unless such a person, through bad laws or subjection to the will of others, is denied the liberty to use the sources of happiness within his reach, he will not fail to find this enviable existence, if he escape the positive evils of life, the great sources of physical and mental suffering—such as indigence, disease, and the unkindness, worthlessness, or premature loss of an affection. The main stress of the problem lies, therefore, in the contest with these calamities from which it is a rare good fortune entirely to escape; which, as things are now, cannot be obviated, and often cannot be in any material degree mitigated. Yet no one whose opinion deserves a moment's consideration can doubt that most of the great positive evils of the world are in themselves removable, and will, if human affairs continue to improve, be in the end reduced within narrow limits. [. . .]

As for vicissitudes of fortune, and other disappointments connected with worldly circumstances, these are principally the effect either of gross imprudence, of ill-regulated desires, or of bad or imperfect social institutions. All the grand sources, in short, of human suffering are in a great degree, many of them almost entirely, conquerable by human care and effort; and though their removal is grievously slow—though a long succession of generations will perish in the breach before the conquest is completed, and this world becomes all that, if will and knowledge were not wanting, it might easily be made—yet every mind sufficiently intelligent and generous to bear a part, however small and unconspicuous, in the endeavor, will draw a noble enjoyment from the contest itself, which he would not for any bribe in the form of selfish indulgence consent to be without.

And this leads to the true estimation of what is said by the objectors concerning the possibility, and the obligation, of learning to do without happiness. Unquestionably it is possible to do without happiness; it is done involuntarily by nineteen-twentieths of mankind, even in those parts of our present world which are least deep in barbarism; and it often has to be done voluntarily by the hero or the martyr, for the sake of something which he prizes more than his individual happiness. But this something, what is it, unless the happiness of others, or some of the requisites of happiness? It is noble to be capable of resigning entirely one's own portion of happiness, or chances of it: but, after all, this self-sacrifice must be for some end; it is not its own end; and if we are told that its end is not happiness, but virtue, which is better than happiness, I ask, would the sacrifice be made if the hero or martyr did not believe that it would earn for others immunity from similar sacrifices? Would it be made if he thought that his renunciation of happiness for himself would produce no fruit for any of his fellow creatures, but to make their lot like his, and place them also in the condition of persons who have renounced happiness? All honor to those who can abnegate for themselves the personal enjoyment of life, when by such renunciation they contribute worthily to increase the amount of happiness in the world; but he who does it, or professes to do it, for any other purpose, is no more deserving of admiration from the ascetic mounted on his pillar. He may be an inspiriting proof of what men *can* do, but assuredly not an example of what they *should*.

Study Questions

1. Do you agree with Mill that "A being of higher faculties requires more to make him happy [. . .] than one of an inferior type"?

2. What might be Ayn Rand's comment on the excerpt?

3. What does Mill mean by "the whole sentient creation"?

4. Comment on the meaning of this passage: "It is better to be a human being dissatisfied than a pig satisfied; better to be Socrates dissatisfied than a fool satisfied." What does Mill mean? Do you agree? Why or why not?

Narrative

The Blacksmith and the Baker

JOHANN HERMAN WESSEL

Poem, 1777. Loosely translated from Danish, from verse to prose. Summary and Excerpt.

Wessel is famous in his own country of Denmark for his satirical verses. This one may have been inspired by a real newspaper story or possibly by British fables.

Once upon a time there was a small town where the town blacksmith was a mean man. He had an enemy, and one day he and his enemy happened to meet at an inn. They proceeded to get drunk and exchange some nasty words. The blacksmith grew angry and

"The Blacksmith and the Baker," illustration by Nils Wiwel, 1895. Utilitarianism taken to an extreme: The baker is led away to be executed for what the blacksmith has done, because that is more useful to society. The policeman's belt reads "Honest and Faithful," and the building in the background is the old Copenhagen courthouse with the inscription "With Law Must Land Be Built."

knocked the other man out; the blow turned out to be fatal. The blacksmith was carted off to jail, and he confessed, hoping that his opponent would forgive him in Heaven. Before his sentence was pronounced, four upstanding citizens asked to see the judge, and the most eloquent of them spoke:

"Your Wisdom, we know you are thinking of the welfare of this town, but this welfare depends on getting our blacksmith back. His death won't wake up the dead man, and we'll never find such a good blacksmith ever again."

The judge said, "But a life has been taken and must be paid for by a life. . . ."

"We have in town an old and scrawny baker who'll go to the devil soon, and since we have two bakers, how about taking the oldest one? Then you still get a life for a life."

"Well," said the judge, "that is not a bad idea, I'll do what I can." And he leafed through his law books but found nothing that said you can't execute a baker instead of a blacksmith, so he pronounced this sentence:

"We know that blacksmith Jens has no excuse for what he has done, sending Anders Petersen off to eternity; but since we have but one blacksmith in this town I would be crazy if I wanted him dead; but we do have two bakers of bread . . . so the oldest one must pay for the murder."

The old baker wept pitifully when they took him away. The moral of the story: Be always prepared to die! It comes when you least expect it.

Study Questions

1. Do you think this is a fair picture of a utilitarian judge?

2. How might the utilitarian respond to this story?

3. Return to this story after reading Chapter 6 and consider: How might a Kantian respond?

Narrative

The Brothers Karamazov

FYODOR DOSTOYEVSKY

Novel, 1881. Film, 1958. Summary and Excerpt.

(This excerpt should be read in conjunction with the narrative "The Ones Who Walk Away from Omelas," which follows.)

The story of the brothers Karamazov, one of the most famous in Russian literature, is about four half-brothers and their father, an unpleasant, old, corrupt scoundrel. The brothers are very different in nature; the oldest son, Dmitri, is a rogue and a pleasure-seeker; the next son, Ivan, is intelligent and politically engaged; the third son, Alyosha, is gentle and honest; and the fourth son, Smerdyakov, was born outside of marriage and never recognized as a proper son. When a murder happens, each son in turn finds himself under suspicion.

Here, Ivan is telling Alyosha a story:

"It was in the darkest days of serfdom at the beginning of the century. . . . There was in those days a general of aristocratic connections, the owner of great estates, one of those men—somewhat exceptional, I believe, even then—who, retiring from the service into a life of leisure, are convinced that they've earned absolute power over the lives of their subjects. There were such men then. So our general, settled on his property of two thousand souls, lives in pomp, and dominates his poor neighbors as though they were dependents. He has kennels of hundreds of hounds and nearly a hundred dog-boys—all mounted, and in uniform. One day a serf boy, a little child of eight, threw a stone in play and hurt the paw of the general's favorite hound. 'Why is my favorite dog lame?' He is told that the boy threw a stone that hurt the dog's paw. 'So you did it.' The general looked the child up and down. 'Take him.' He was taken—taken from his mother and kept shut up all night. Early the next morning the general comes out on horseback, with the hounds, his dependents, dog-boys, and huntsmen, all mounted around him in full hunting parade. The servants are summoned for their edification, and in front of them all stands the mother of the child. The child is brought forward. It's a gloomy cold, foggy autumn day, a perfect day for hunting. The general orders the child to be undressed. The child is stripped naked. He shivers, numb with terror, not daring to cry. . . . 'Make him run,' commands the general. 'Run, run!' shout the dog-boys. The boy runs. . . . 'At him!' yells the general, and he sets the whole pack of hounds after the child. The hounds catch him, and tear him to pieces before his mother's eyes! . . . I believe the general was afterwards declared incapable of administering his estates. Well—what did he deserve? To be shot? To be shot for the satisfaction of our moral feelings? Speak, Alyosha!

"Tell me yourself, I challenge you—answer. Imagine that you are creating a fabric of human destiny with the object of making men happy in the end, giving them peace and rest at last. Imagine that you are doing this but that it is essential and inevitable to torture to death only one tiny creature—that child beating its breast with its fist, for instance—in order to found that edifice on its unavenged tears. Would you consent to be the architect on those conditions? Tell me. Tell the truth."

"No, I wouldn't consent," said Alyosha softly.

"And can you accept the idea that the men for whom you are building would agree to receive their happiness from the unatoned blood of a little victim? And accepting it would remain happy forever?"

"No, I can't admit it," said Alyosha suddenly, with flashing eyes.

Here Ivan and Alyosha are engaged in a discussion about the meaning of life: If God does not exist, then what? Then everything is permissible. But what if our highest moral aim is to make the majority happy? Do the means always justify the end? If the suffering of a child could somehow create general happiness and harmony, should its mother forgive those who caused it to suffer?

Study Questions

1. Answer Ivan's question: Would you agree to make humankind happy at the cost of a child's suffering? Explain how a utilitarian might answer, and then explain your own answer.

2. Should the mother ever forgive the general for murdering her son?

3. Return to this story after reading Chapter 6 and consider: How might a Kantian respond?

Narrative

The Ones Who Walk Away from Omelas

URSULA K. LE GUIN

Short story, 1973. Summary and Excerpt.

There is a festival in the city of Omelas. The weather is beautiful, the city looks its best, and people are happy and serene in their pretty clothes. This is a perfect place, with freedom of choice and no oppressive power enforcing the rules of religion, politics, or morality—and it works, because the people know they are responsible for their actions. This place is a Utopia, except for one thing: The happiness of the citizens is bought at a high price, with the full knowledge of every citizen.

> In a basement under one of the beautiful public buildings of Omelas, or perhaps in the cellar of one of its spacious private homes, there is a room. It has one locked door, and no window. A little light seeps in dustily between cracks in the boards, secondhand from a cobwebbed window somewhere across the cellar. In one corner of the little room a couple of mops, with stiff, clotted, foul-smelling heads, stand near a rusty bucket. . . . The room is about three paces long and two wide: a mere broom closet or disused tool room. In the room a child is sitting. It could be a boy or a girl. It looks about six, but actually is nearly ten. It is feeble-minded. Perhaps it was born defective, or perhaps it has become imbecile through fear, malnutrition, and neglect. It picks its nose and occasionally fumbles vaguely with its toes or genitals, as it sits hunched in the corner farthest from the bucket and the two mops. It is afraid of the mops. It finds them horrible. It shuts its eyes, but it knows the mops are still standing there; and the door is locked; and nobody will come. The door is always locked; and nobody ever comes, except that sometimes . . . the door rattles terribly and opens, and a person, or several people, are there. . . . The people at the door never say anything, but the child, who has not always lived in the tool room, and can remember sunlight and its mother's voice, sometimes speaks. "I will be good," it says. "Please let me out. I will be good!" They never answer.

All this is part of a greater plan. The child will never be let out—it will die within a short time—and presumably another child will take its place, for it is the suffering of this innocent being that makes the perfect life in Omelas possible. All the citizens know about it from the time they are adolescents, and they all must go and see the child so that they can understand the price of their happiness. They are disgusted and sympathetic for a while, but then they understand the master plan: the pain of one small individual in exchange for great communal happiness. Because the citizens know the immense suffering that gives them their beautiful life, they are particularly loving to each other and responsible for what they do. And what would they gain by setting the child free? The child is too far gone to be able to enjoy freedom, anyway, and what is one person's suffering compared to the realm of happiness that is achieved? So the people feel no guilt. However, a few young people and some adult visitors go to see the child, and something happens to them: They don't go home afterward, but keep on walking—through the city, through the fields, away from Omelas.

Study Questions

1. Where are they going, the ones who walk away? And why are they leaving?

2. How does Le Guin feel about the situation? Does she condone the suffering of the child, or is she arguing against it? Is the story realistic or symbolic?

3. How would an act utilitarian evaluate the story of Omelas? Would a rule utilitarian reach the same conclusion or a different one? Why?

4. Return to this story after reading Chapter 6 and develop a deontological critique of the people of Omelas (those who don't walk away).

5. In the film *Swordfish* a similar question is raised: "Would you kill a child to save the world?" However, in Omelas it is not a question of saving the world, just the happiness of all. In light of the discussion about "sheer numbers," would it make a difference to you if the torturous death of the child did indeed save the world and not just people's contentment? If yes, explain while focusing on where you would draw the line. If no, explain why not.

Narrative

Saving Private Ryan

ROBERT RODAT (SCREENWRITER)
STEVEN SPIELBERG (DIRECTOR)

Film, 1998. Summary and Excerpt of Screenplay.

Saving Private Ryan is a film that leaves very few viewers unmoved. Its level of stark realism in the opening and closing battle scenes marks it as too much of a true-to-life experience for some. Others argue, however, that these scenes can't be removed because without the experience of the bloody struggle on Omaha Beach, how can we appreciate the magnitude of the danger these eight young men will face *voluntarily* later in the film?

The movie is selected here as an illustration of the ideals of utilitarianism, and yet you may want to discuss whether the film is, in the end, pro-utilitarian or anti-utilitarian. Although I generally try to avoid giving away the ending of a story in discussing the moral issues, in *Saving Private Ryan* only a few things can remain secret because we need to know all the facts in order to determine whether the sacrifices were worth it.

The film throws us into a living hell: the landing on the beaches of Normandy on D-Day, June 6, 1944, the beginning of the end of the Nazi reign in Europe. In landing craft in a stormy sea, seasick, terrified young soldiers prepare for battle. Some of them never even set foot on dry land but are shot to pieces by machine gun fire from the bluffs; others drown as their equipment drags them under. Death is indiscriminate and terrible, whether it is quick or slow. Limbs are torn off, shocked soldiers revert to childhood and call for their mothers in mortal agony. A small group makes its way up under the bluff and, at a dreadful cost in lives, manages to take over a bunker from where the Germans were shooting down the beach. The aftermath is no less gruesome: There is no mercy shown to the defending German soldiers. Captain John Miller regroups his men and imposes both order and, eventually, a nominal return to decency among the survivors. Though an experienced veteran, the captain himself is deeply affected—he has developed an uncontrolled nervous twitching in his hand.

Meanwhile a mother in Iowa is told by the top military brass that she has lost three of her four sons in battle in different parts of the world. The one remaining son is James Ryan, a paratrooper behind enemy lines somewhere in Normandy. The chief of staff now sees it as imperative to bring Private Ryan home so his mother will not have lost all her sons, and he quotes a letter Abraham Lincoln wrote during the Civil War to a mother who had lost all of her five sons in battle. It is obvious to the chief of staff that some civilian sacrifices are just too great. But is it only the one last son who is so important—one son, one mother—or is there something deeper?

Captain Miller is given the order to find Private Ryan and bring him home. He selects a squad of men he can trust, seven young "veterans," survivors of the carnage on Omaha Beach. There is little comprehension among the squad as to why one soldier's life can be so important that eight men must risk their lives to save his. As they encounter enemy fire along the way and two of their group lose their lives, their job begins to take its toll, even on Captain Miller. He speculates that losing a soldier is supposed to mean that other soldiers' lives are saved:

Miller: Every time you kill one of your men, you tell yourself you just saved the lives of two, three, ten, a hundred others. You know how many men I've lost under my command?

Sarge: How many?

Miller: Ninety-four. So that must mean I've saved the lives of ten times that number. Maybe twenty, right? See, it's simple. It lets you always choose the mission over men.

Sarge: Except this time the mission is a man. . . .

Miller: And Ryan better be worth it. He better go home and cure some disease or invent a new longer-lasting lightbulb.

A captured German soldier who is the lone survivor of a group responsible for the death of one of Miller's men is about to be summarily executed by some of the enraged squad members. The nightmarish possibility of good soldiers murdering an unarmed prisoner out of revenge threatens to divide the group, but Miller again pulls everybody together by telling them a seemingly irrelevant fact: what he did for a living back home. He is beginning to feel that if he can save Private Ryan, he will have earned the right to return home to his wife and resume his life as a schoolteacher. But with every man he kills, the farther he gets from home and the person he once was. The prisoner is released. This is a decision that will come back to haunt Miller and his men.

Against enormous odds, the diminished squad does find Private Ryan, but the young man refuses to return to safety. Now that his brothers are gone, his fellow soldiers represent his "brothers," and they are holding a bridge, trying to prevent the Germans from using it in a counterattack on the beachhead. The men in Miller's troop have repeatedly questioned whether Ryan was worth saving and worth the lives of two good men, but his insistence on staying and fighting with his comrades gives Miller's men hope. Ryan seems to be a kid with character, and he wants to know the names of the men who died trying to rescue him. Leaving without Ryan would render their sacrifices meaningless, so Miller and his men decide to risk all and join forces with Ryan's little troop to hold the bridge, and, perhaps by saving the invasion, to restore meaningfulness to their members' sacrifices and earn the right to go home themselves.

Each soldier is prepared to fight to the end—we know that because Miller evokes the Battle of the Alamo, in which all the defenders perished. When the grueling battle is over, Ryan understands, in much the same way that Captain Miller felt saving Ryan would earn him the right to go home, that now he must earn the life that others have paid such an immense price to save.

This film is about duty and sacrifice; it is also about "sheer numbers": Eight men's lives are on the line to save one, whereas the losses of lives on Omaha Beach and on the other battlefields make the thought of one single life saved seem insignificant. So, according to the hedonistic calculus, was it worth the cost to save Private Ryan? In a narrow sense, no: The loss of most of the troop can't be balanced by one life, even if it makes his mother very happy. From a narrowly utilitarian point of view, the endeavor was a failure, a terrible waste of lives for the sake of one young man and his mother. But from a broader and deeper utilitarian perspective things change, and perhaps this is the most interesting perspective utilitarianism has to offer. Is Private Ryan just one young man? For the chief of staff he is much more: He is the very meaning of going to war. We fight so someone at home can live in freedom, and if there are no sons or daughters left at home, then the sacrifices are in vain. Private Ryan becomes a symbol of the future that must be saved, and, in the light of saving a world, the sacrifices made by Miller's men are not too great—in the balance of things, saving Private Ryan may make more sense than anything else the soldiers have been through. While the film shows the horrors of war with a certain amount of cynicism, it also has great faith in humanity.

In the film, Miller attains complete moral authority over his men. In real life, a similar situation arose: During the filming of *Saving Private Ryan,* the actors underwent a grueling week of boot camp training, and at some point in time, they all decided they had had enough—they were actors, not military men. But Tom Hanks (Captain Miller), who took part in the training program, talked to them and pointed out that they had their free will but also a responsibility to the story they were about to tell. So every man decided to stay and finish the training. The story is significant, because it shows that the command Miller had over this troop was a reflection of the professional authority and humanity of the actor portraying him.

Study Questions

1. Was saving James Ryan a meaningful or a meaningless order? Did Miller's men accomplish something worthwhile, or did they risk everything for nothing?

2. How might Ryan "earn" the rest of his life? What would you say would be sufficient as a "good life," considering that men died specifically to save him? Would saving Ryan have been less meaningful if it had turned out that he was not a good person? Why or why not?

3. Comment on the quotation from the film dialogue: What does Miller mean by saying that Ryan had better cure some disease or invent a better lightbulb?

4. In releasing the German soldier, Miller and his men respond to their deepest feelings of human decency. However, if you have seen the film, you know that it turns out to be a fateful decision: The German soldier returns. Is there such a thing as a *subjectively* morally right but an *objectively* morally wrong decision? How would a utilitarian respond? How would you respond?

5. Identify the utilitarian elements in the film. Is this a pro-utilitarian or an anti-utilitarian story? Explain your answer.

6. You may want to go back and reread the discussion in Chapter 2 about violence in films and Plato's and Aristotle's views on the value of drama. Given that the violence is extremely graphic in *Saving Private Ryan* but that it is also highly realistic, is this film likely to inspire more violence? Why or why not? Does this give us a hint about how to approach the debate about violence in movies and on TV? Is Aristotle right in saying that a good drama is better conveyed without what we today would call special effects?

𝒩arrative

Extreme Measures

TONY GILROY (SCREENWRITER)
MICHAEL APTED (DIRECTOR)

Film, 1997. Based on a novel by Michael Palma. Summary.

A young British emergency room doctor, Guy Luthan, is faced with a terrible moral and professional choice: In his emergency room, two patients need urgent care. One is a police officer who has been shot, and the other is the man who shot him, a troublemaker who pulled a gun on a bus. He was in turn shot by the cop. The officer is barely stabilized, whereas the gunman is in critical condition. There is only one surgery slot available. Whom should Guy choose? He needs to decide immediately. He sends the police officer into surgery and lets the gunman wait his turn. As it happens, they both survive, but a young nurse, Jodie, blames Guy for making an unprofessional moral choice: The gunman's medical needs were more urgent than the cop's. Guy explains, "I had to make a choice; on my right I see a cop with his wife in the corridor and pictures of his kids in his wallet, and on my left some guy who's taken out a gun on a city bus! I had ten seconds to make a choice, I had to make it—I hope I made the right one. I think I did, oh shit, maybe I didn't . . . I don't know."

This sets the scene for what could be just a run-of-the-mill hospital suspense story but which turns out to be an honest exploration of the principle of utility as a social, moral, and psychological justification.

The film *Extreme Measures* (Castle Rock, 1996) notes that sometimes we must make hard moral choices; the question is, What criterion should we use? Should we do what is right, regardless of the consequences, or should we try to obtain the best result for as many as possible with the least harm caused? This is the dilemma facing Dr. Guy Luthan (Hugh Grant), not only in his own career but also as the pawn in a greater plot orchestrated by a famous doctor: to use homeless people as guinea pigs. Here Guy has to choose whether to save the life of a police officer with a wife and kids or the gunman who shot the officer in cold blood.

Guy has just received a fellowship in neurology at New York University. This means much to him and his family, because his father in England, once a medical doctor, lost his license to practice after euthanizing an old friend—another moral choice with consequences.

Meanwhile, a patient is brought to Guy's emergency room from the street, half naked and in complete physical and mental breakdown. He has a hospital bracelet on, and, in a lucid moment before he dies, he says two things to Guy—the word *triphase* and the name of a friend. Not understanding the cause of death, Guy orders an autopsy, but the hospital loses track not only of the autopsy but also of the body itself. Guy feels that something is terribly wrong and pursues the dead man's records on his own. The man had been admitted to the hospital previously for a neurological examination. Other patients turn up in the computer with the same profile: homeless, without relatives, having lab work done, and all files on them deleted.

But Guy is in for another shock: His apartment has been burglarized, and the detectives investigating the burglary find a stash of drugs in his place. Guy is arrested. Since Guy doesn't do drugs, he realizes that the burglary was a ruse and that the drugs were planted to discredit him, to get him out of the way—by whom? Whoever it is, their plan succeeds;

Guy manages to raise bail, but once out of jail, he is suspended from his hospital position—his colleagues and supervisors assume that he is guilty. This also means that his fellowship to NYU will be lost because he will no longer be able to practice medicine—just like his father. Compelled to seek the truth, Guy locates a patient of his among the homeless and soon finds himself in a world underground in the subway system, where the homeless and destitute have made a world for themselves. Here he finds another piece of the puzzle: Doctors have been preying on the homeless, subjecting them to experiments leading to great suffering and death. But Guy himself is now being hunted in a prolonged chase, and just as he thinks he has found refuge with a friend, he is rendered unconscious.

Guy wakes up in a hospital bed—and to his horror, he finds himself paralyzed from the neck down. He is told that the blow he sustained to his spine severed it, and he will be a quadriplegic for life. Realizing the enormity of what has happened to him, Guy feels that, having no hope of recovery, he might as well be dead. The famous neurologist Dr. Myrick now pays him a visit, talking enigmatically about hope. What if there were hope for him after all? What would it be worth to him to return to his old life? What would he risk if a procedure were available? Guy answers, "Anything!" Myrick replies, "You'd better think about that."

Who is responsible for the burglary, the planted drugs, the disappearance of the homeless, and the attempt on Guy's life? The answer lies within Guy's own hospital environment. When Guy's paralysis miraculously wears off after 24 hours, he realizes he'd been drugged, and that it is Dr. Myrick, passionately engaged in helping victims of spinal cord injury, who has undertaken research into spinal cord regeneration by using homeless patients as guinea pigs for the good of humanity.

Guy now tries to escape from the hospital. This is a pivotal scene in the film, and I will not spoil the surprise twists for you. During a dramatic moment, Myrick tries to explain his actions to Guy: The homeless men he experimented on were useless beings—but now they are heroes, since their deaths have given hope to so many injured people. "Good doctors do the correct thing. Great doctors have the guts to do the right thing. . . . If you could cure cancer by killing one person, wouldn't you have to do it? Wouldn't it be the brave thing to do? One person, and it's gone tomorrow?" Guy replies that perhaps the homeless people he used weren't worth much, but they didn't choose to be heroes—he never asked for volunteers. To Guy, doctors can't do that—Myrick has been playing God.

One final confrontation remains—one that solves some issues but raises others. In the end, Guy is given all of Myrick's files from his research into spinal cord injuries . . . and Guy does not reject the files.

Study Questions

1. Discuss the opening scene. Did Guy make the right professional choice? The right moral choice? Should there be a difference? Explain your position.

2. Is Dr. Myrick's experimentation a noble quest in order to help humanity or a perverse abuse of human beings? Is there a third alternative? Explain your position.

3. Dr. Myrick asks Guy what he would be willing to do in order to regain his mobility at a time when Guy believes himself to be paralyzed for life. What does Guy answer, and why is this scene so important?

4. Guy accuses Myrick of playing God. Guy's own father lost his license to practice medicine because he euthanized a friend. Do you think there is a connection here, or is this a coincidence in the film?

5. In the end, Guy takes over Myrick's research papers. Is this gesture an acceptance of Myrick's utilitarian principles, or is there another possibility? By accepting the papers, have Guy's hands now been dirtied? Why or why not?

6. Is this a pro-utilitarian or an anti-utilitarian film? Explain.

7. The scene where Guy makes his decision in the ER and Myrick's explanation of his medical experiments are deliberately set up as parallels. What are the similarities, and what are the differences? Does the discussion in the chapter text about the hedonistic calculus as a *last resort* provide us with a tool for distinguishing between Guy and Myrich?

8. Scientists have announced that they believe great strides can be made toward curing paralysis through stem cell research. Given that the stem cells originated in a human embryo, do you think there is a difference between Myrick's experiments on homeless people for the sake of helping patients with paralysis and using stem cells from an embryo to accomplish the same thing? Explain similarities and differences.

Narrative

Runaway Jury

BRIAN KOPPELMAN (SCREENWRITER)
GARY FLEDER (DIRECTOR)

Film, 2003. Based on the novel by John Grisham. Summary.

This film is an exceptionally good illustration of the viewpoint that *the end justifies the means*—a utilitarian view, as long as the majority benefits from the consequences. Since this, in a way, applies to the film itself, it means that we have to include the ending in this summary, as much as I'm reluctant to do so.

Jacob Wood celebrates his young son's birthday and goes to work in his New Orleans office—only to be gunned down, together with other coworkers. The gunman then turns the gun on himself. Two years later, Wood's widow is taking Vicksburg Firearms, the manufacturers of the gun used in the massacre, to court in a civil trial, asking for damages, although it is clear that no laws were broken in the sale of the firearm. Within the context of the film, nobody has yet taken gun manufacturers to court and won; and at the beginning of the film, we learn that the lawyer for the plaintiff, Wendell Rohr, while being a practical man with legal savvy, is also an idealist: He confesses to Mrs. Wood that he wants to change the gun laws. He hires an enthusiastic young legal aide, not just because he knows the young man has a good legal background but also because he is impressed with his idealism: The young man believes in "a world without guns."

Meanwhile, the defense team is busy profiling potential jurors, tapping into their backgrounds and records, setting up a war room with electronics, illegal listening devices, video surveillance, and so forth; and we get the impression that they'll stop at nothing to win this case. They rig their defense counsel with a hidden video camera during the *voir dire* (the jury screening process) so that—unbeknownst to the judge—the high-powered jury consultant Rankin Fitch can okay or nix potential jurors from the war room. And Fitch is good—on his way from the airport he profiled the cab driver, accurately describing his home life. He proclaims that he hates Democrats and Baptists, and later he has a conversation with the gun manufacturer, who says, "Trials are too important to be left up to juries."

One of those potential jurors is a young man named Nick; he appears to be upset at the prospect of having to serve on a jury, but when he gets the summons, he says, cryptically, "Christmas comes early this year." And when he and his girlfriend contemplate their own giant display board of potential jurors, we realize that Nick wants to be on this jury very badly. During the *voir dire,* Fitch sees no problem with him, nobody objects, and he is in. Immediately, Nick begins a subtle manipulation of his fellow jurors; he suggests a blind juror as the jury foreman, he manages to get the judge to buy them all a fancy lunch, and he wins their sympathy by telling them about a friend who died in the Gulf War. Meanwhile, his girlfriend Marlee is carrying out her part of the plan: She has letters delivered to both the prosecution and the defense, offering to deliver a verdict through jury manipulation—for a price: "Jury for sale."

In the opening statement, Rohr tells the jury that gun violence happens because of accessibility of guns, and gun manufacturers must be held accountable. We don't hear the opening statement of the defense lawyer, but we do see Fitch on an outdoor shooting range with the gun manufacturer who has heard about the "Jury for Sale" note—and is worried, because he thought he already bought the jury, by hiring Fitch. Fitch suspects that Nick is involved, so he orders a henchman, Doyle, to break into Nick's place to find incriminating material—only to find that the incident has been videotaped by Nick. A power play ensues between Nick and Fitch: Nick gets a juror booted, and Fitch puts pressure on several jurors, threatening to reveal their personal secrets.

Nick and Marlee have a heart-to-heart talk in a church: A juror has tried to commit suicide because of the pressure, Nick's apartment has been torched by Fitch's people—is it worth it? What worries Nick is not the moral issue of their undertaking, though, but concerns for Marlee's safety.

Fitch's assistant Doyle has come up with amazing news: Nick has been compiling lists of juries from previous gun lawsuits, in 2000, 1999, and 1998, and has been close to being on a gun lawsuit jury once before, but under another name—an identity that evaporates into thin air, but leads to another name: Jeff Curr. In the meantime, Marlee has approached both Fitch and Rohr, offering to swing the jury their way for $10 million. When Rohr's key witness, a gun manufacturer employee, doesn't show up in court (because the defense got to him), Rohr is tempted to accept Marlee's offer. In a pivotal scene we see Rohr confronting Fitch in the men's room at the courthouse over the missing key witness. Fitch calls Rohr "a moral man, living in a world of moral relativity," and admits that he isn't fighting a battle for the Second Amendment (because he has taken on many cases, defending the gun industry), but to *win*—to do what he has been hired to do. Rohr points out that Fitch will lose, eventually, because he has nothing but contempt for people. And next time Rohr talks with Marlee, he rejects her offer—his moral compass is on track again.

In court, things aren't going well for Fitch, either. The gun manufacturer is put on the witness stand and loses his temper, so now Fitch wants to make a deal with Marlee. He and Nick have a secret meeting where they agree on the terms, and Fitch is content because he perceives that Nick is of his own kind—an "agnostic" about the law. In a twist to the story, Marlee raises the price to $15 million, because of an attack by one of Fitch's men; Fitch agrees and wires the money to Marlee. But Doyle has found out much more about Nick and Marlee—too late to do Fitch any good: Their real names are Jeff Curr and Gabby Grant, from Gardner, Indiana; Gabby's sister was gunned down in the school yard some years ago, in front of Jeff and Gabby, who were unable to do anything. Since then, however, they have been trying to make a difference and get guns banned, any which way they can. So the primary goal has never been the money, but justice for Marlee/Gabby's sister.

While this is going on, the jury is finally deliberating, out of reach of Fitch and Rohr, but with Nick in the thick of it. Most of the jurors are leaning toward not convicting the gun manufacturer, because that is in compliance with the law, but Nick is able to show that the primary spokesman for this view is against a conviction for self-serving reasons. And from here on, Nick asks the jurors to just consider the facts—although we hear no more about what goes on in the jury room, the result is a groundbreaking verdict for the plaintiff, $110 million to Mrs. Wood in damages. Fitch, who is out $15 million with a jury that didn't swing his way, is devastated. Later, in a bar he is confronted by Nick and Marlee, and now we hear the whole story: They weren't just trying to win a case against gun manufacturers, but were also trying to beat Fitch—because he was to blame for the gun manufacturers winning the case brought against them after Marlee's sister's death. And Nick explains that he didn't swing any votes, but just "let them vote their hearts" and prevented Fitch from stealing their votes. And now Fitch's career is ruined, because he attempted to buy the jury.

At the end, we see Marlee and Nick at a school yard near the court house, and we know they're thinking about justice for the dead sister. Rohr is leaving the courthouse, their eyes meet, and they smile; Rohr shrugs, smiles, gets into his car, and drives off.

Study Questions

1. Jury members who consider facts and render a verdict based on those facts are voting with their *heads,* not their *hearts.* What do you think of Nick's appealing to the jurors' emotions, rather than to their reason?

2. Evaluate the presentations of the plaintiff and defense teams: Rohr is a man of principle, and Fitch has no principles other than to win cases for his clients. How does this play into the gun control theme of the film? Does it matter to your evaluation of the film whether you are in favor of gun control or gun rights?

3. Just for the sake of readers who may not be familiar with the Second Amendment, here it is: "A well-regulated Militia being necessary to the security of a free State, the right of the people to keep and bear arms shall not be infringed." Throughout the film it is clear that the filmmakers want us to side with the plaintiff and gun control advocates. Hardly any time is given to a thorough representation of the Second Amendment. Does it matter to you that the film is not representing both views fairly? Why or why not?

4. One might say that two questions are being raised here: (1) Can juries be bought? And (2) Should they be bought? In other words, the film offers a *descriptive* and a *normative* angle. How does the film answer both questions? Do you agree? Why or why not?

5. According to the filmmakers, the "good guys" win, even if they use dirty tricks. Would you agree that a good end justifies dirty means? Does it matter how we identify a "good end"? Evaluate Rohr's reaction at the end: Does he approve of Marlee and Nick's scheme, or doesn't he?

6. Try to imagine the scenario being reversed: A juror who idealistically believes in the Second Amendment persuades the jury to think with their heads, not their hearts, and acquits the gun manufacturer. Would this scenario be more objectionable to you? Less objectionable? The same? Evaluate the influence of your political views on your sympathies in the film.

Chapter Six

Using Your Reason,
Part 2: Kant's Deontology

*O*n the whole, we might say that there are two major ways in which we can approach a problem. We might ask ourselves, What happens if I do X? In this case we're letting ourselves be guided by the future consequences of our actions. Or we might ask ourselves, Is X right or wrong in itself, regardless of the consequences? The first approach is utilitarian, provided that we are looking for good consequences for as many as possible. The version of the second approach that has had the most influence is Immanuel Kant's *duty theory*. (See Box 6.1 for a summary of Kant's life.)

Kant's moral theory is often referred to as *deontology* (the theory of moral obligation, from the Greek *deon,* "that which is obligatory"). Kant believed his theory was the very opposite of a consequentialist theory and his moral analysis was, in part, written to show how little a moral theory that worries about consequences has to do with true moral thinking. Let us look at an example to illustrate this fundamental difference.

The Good Will

Some years ago, newspapers reported an accident somewhere in the Pacific Northwest. A family had gone away for a short vacation and had left their keys with their neighbor so that he could water their plants and look after the place. On Sunday afternoon, a few hours before they were due to arrive home, the temperature was dropping, and the neighbor thought he would do them a favor and make sure they would come home to a nice, toasty house. He went in and turned on the furnace. You've guessed what happened: The house burned down and the family came home to a smoking ruin. This was the extent of the newspaper coverage, but suppose it had been reported by a classical utilitarian. Then the article might have ended something like this: "The neighbor will have to answer for the consequences of this terrible deed." Why? Because, given that only consequences count, the act of turning on the furnace was a terrible one, regardless of the man's good intentions. As it is sometimes said, the road to hell is paved with good intentions. In other words, only your deeds count, not what you intended by them.

Suppose, however, that a Kantian had written the article. Then it might have ended like this: "This good neighbor should be praised for his kind thought and good intentions regardless of the fact that the family lost their home; that consequence certainly can't be blamed on him, because all he intended to do was the right thing."

Box 6.1   KANT: HIS LIFE AND WORK

Some famous and influential people lead lives of adventure. The life of Immanuel Kant (1724–1804) seems to have been an *intellectual* adventure exclusively, for he did little that might in any other way be considered adventurous. He grew up in the town of Königsberg, East Prussia (a city on the Baltic Sea, now Kaliningrad in Russian territory). He was raised in an atmosphere of strict Protestant values by his devout mother and by his father, who made a meager living as a saddler. He entered Königsberg University, studied theology, graduated, and tutored for a while until he was offered a position at the university in his hometown. In 1770 he became a full professor in logic and metaphysics, and this was when the philosophical drama began, for Kant achieved influence not only in Western philosophy but also in science and social thinking—an influence that was never eclipsed by anyone else in the eighteenth century. He developed theories about astronomy that are still considered plausible (the so-called Kant-Laplace hypothesis has to a great extent been corroborated by the Hubbell Space Telescope); he laid out rules for a new social world of mutual respect for all citizens; he made contributions to philosophy of law and religion; he attempted to map the entire spectrum of human intelligence in his three major works, *Critique of*

Pure Reason (1781), *Critique of Practical Reason* (1788), and *Critique of Judgment* (1790), as well as in smaller works such as *Prolegomena to Every Future Metaphysics* (1783) and *Grounding for the Metaphysics of Morals* (1785). He continued working until late in life; one of his most influential works from that period is *The Metaphysics of Morals* (1797).

When Kant calls a book a "critique," he is not implying that he is merely writing a negative criticism of a subject; he is, rather, looking for the *condition of possibility* of that subject. In *Critique of Pure Reason* he asks, "What makes it possible for me to achieve knowledge?" (In other words, what is the condition of possibility of knowledge?) In *Critique of Practical Reason* he asks about the condition of possibility of moral thinking, and in *Critique of Judgment* he examines the condition of possibility for appreciating natural and artistic beauty. In all of these fields his insights helped shape new disciplines and redefine old disciplines. Kant was never an agitator for his ideas, though; on the contrary, he was famous for his extremely quiet and highly regulated routine. He remained single throughout his life, and his sole interest seems to have been his work. His students reported that he was in fact a good and popular teacher.

Let us continue speculating. Suppose the house didn't burn down, but instead provided a warm, cozy shelter for and saved the lives of the entire family, who (shall we say) had all come down with pneumonia. The utilitarian now would have to say that the act of lighting the furnace was a shining example of a morally good deed, but Kant would not change his mind: The neighbor's action was good because of his intention, and the consequences of the act don't make it any better or worse. It is not just any good intention, however, that makes an action morally good in Kant's view: One must have *a respect for the moral law* that is expressed in the intention. It isn't enough for the neighbor to be a kind man who wants his neighbors to be comfortable; he must imagine it to be a good thing for neighbors to act that way *in general*—not because it would make everyone comfortable and happy but strictly for the sake of the *principle* of doing the right thing. This is what Kant calls having a *good*

This painting shows the German philosopher Immanuel Kant, second from the left, dining with friends. Perhaps the most influential Western philosopher of "modern times" (the seventeenth century to the present), Kant was reportedly a popular guest at dinners and parties and equally popular with his students.

will. For Kant the presence of a good will is what makes an action morally good, regardless of its consequences. Therefore, even if you never accomplished what you intended, you are still morally praiseworthy provided you tried hard to do the right thing. In his book *Grounding for the Metaphysics of Morals* (1785; also commonly referred to as *Groundwork* or *Foundations*), Kant assures us that

> [e]ven if, by some especially unfortunate fate or by the niggardly provision of stepmotherly nature, this will should be wholly lacking in the power to accomplish its purpose;* if with the greatest effort it should yet achieve nothing, and only the good will should remain (not, to be sure, as a mere wish but as the summoning of all the means in our power), yet would

---

*To modern readers without much experience with older literature in English, the term *niggardly* generally gives pause because it bears an unfortunate resemblance to a racial epithet and people have in recent years been fired for using the word; however, the two words are unrelated in etymology and meaning, and there is no racial undertone in the word used by Kant's translators. The term means "avaricious" or "stingy." The original German word is *härglich*. But even though *niggardly* doesn't associate to bigotry and discrimination, how about the term *stepmotherly*? That is Kant's own term in translation.

it, like a jewel, still shine by its own light as something which has its full value in itself. Its usefulness or fruitlessness can neither augment nor diminish this value.

The Categorical Imperative

How do we know that our will is good? We put our intentions to a test. In *Grounding for the Metaphysics of Morals*, Kant says we must ask whether we can imagine our intentions as a general law for everybody. This means that our intentions have to *conform to a rational principle*. We have to think hard in order to determine whether we're about to do the right thing or not; it can't be determined just by some gut-level feeling. However, we don't have to wait to see the actual consequences in order to determine whether our intentions are good—all we have to do is determine whether we could imagine others doing to us what we intend doing to them. In other words, Kant proposes a variant of the Golden Rule—but it is a variant with certain specifics, as we shall see—and it illustrates that Kant is also a *hard universalist*, perhaps the hardest one ever to write a book on morals.

For Kant, humans usually know what they *ought* to do, and that is almost always the opposite of what they *want* to do: Our moral conflicts are generally between our duty and our inclination, and when we let our desires run rampant it is simply because we haven't come up with a way for our sense of duty to persuade us to do the right thing. Kant therefore proposes a test to determine the right thing to do. He refers to this test as the *categorical imperative*. But because it is a matter of doing the right thing not in terms of the outcome but in terms of the intentions, we must look more closely at these intentions.

Suppose a store owner is trying to decide whether to cheat her customers. She might tell herself, (1) "I will cheat them whenever I can get away with it" or "I will cheat them only on occasion so nobody can detect a pattern." We can all tell, intuitively, that this merchant's intentions aren't good, although they certainly might benefit her and give her some extra cash at the end of the week. In other words, the consequences may be good, yet we know that cheating the customers is not the right thing to do. (We'll get back to the reason in a while.) Suppose, though, that the owner decides not to cheat her customers because (2) she might be *found out,* and then she would lose their business and might have to close shop. This is certainly prudent, but it still is not a morally praiseworthy decision because she is doing it only to achieve good consequences. What if the store owner decides not to cheat her customers because (3) she *likes them too much* to ever do them any harm? She loves the little kids buying candy, the old ladies buying groceries, and everyone else, so how could she ever consider cheating them? This, says Kant, is very nice, but it still is not morally praiseworthy because the merchant is doing only what she feels like doing, and we can't be expected to praise her for just wanting to feel good. (If you want to reexamine this argument, go back to the section in Chapter 4 on psychological egoism, where a similar argument is analyzed in detail.) And indeed, what if some day she should stop loving her customers or just one of them? Then the reason for not cheating is gone; so, as a principle of right action, Kant cannot approve of motive 3, regardless of how much we generally approve of people who help others because they enjoy it.

The only morally praiseworthy reason for not wanting to cheat the customers would be if the store owner told herself, (4) "It wouldn't be right," regardless of consequences or warm and fuzzy feelings. Why wouldn't it be right? Because she certainly couldn't want everybody else to cheat their customers as a universal law.

If the store owner tells herself, "I will not cheat my customers because otherwise I'll lose them," then she is not doing a bad thing, of course. She is just doing a prudent thing, and Kant says our lives are full of such prudent decisions; they are dependent on each situation, and we have to determine in each case what would be the smart thing to do. Kant calls these decisions, which are *conditional,* because they depend on the situation and on one's own personal desires, *hypothetical imperatives—imperatives* because they are commands: *If* you don't want to lose your customers, *then* you should not cheat them. *If* you want to get your degree, *then* you should not miss your final exam. *If* you want to be good at baking biscuits, *then* you ought to bake them from scratch and not use a prepared mix. But suppose you're closing down your shop and moving to another town? Then you might not care about losing those customers. And suppose you decide to drop out of school—then who cares about that final exam? And if you and everyone you know hates biscuits, then why bother worrying about getting good at baking them? In other words, a hypothetical imperative is dependent on your interest in a certain outcome. If you don't want the outcome, the imperative is not binding. We make such decisions every day, and, as long as they are based merely on wanting some outcome, they are not morally relevant. (They can, of course, be morally bad, but, even if they have a good outcome, Kant would say that they are morally neutral.) What makes a decision morally praiseworthy is if the agent (the person acting) decides to do something because it might be applied to everyone as a *universal moral law.* In that case that person has used the categorical imperative.

What makes a categorical imperative *categorical* is that it is not dependent on anyone's desire to make it an imperative; it is binding not just in some situations and for some people, but always, for everyone. It is absolute. That is the very nature of the moral law: If it applies at all, it applies to everyone in the same situation. Although there are myriad hypothetical imperatives, there is only one categorical imperative, expressed in the most general terms possible: *Always act so that you can will that your maxim can become a universal law.* In ordinary language this means: Ask yourself what it is you want to do right now (such as making the house next door toasty for your neighbors, skipping classes on Friday, or lying to Grandma about dating someone outside your religion). Then imagine making that action into a rule (such as, Always make sure your neighbors come home to a toasty house; Always skip Friday classes; Always lie to Grandma to spare her pain). Now you've identified your *maxim,* or the principle or rule for your action. The next step is to ask yourself whether you could want that maxim to become a universal rule for everyone to follow. And, if you can't agree to that—if you don't think *everyone* should, under similar circumstances, light their neighbors' furnaces, skip classes, or lie to Grandma—then *you* shouldn't do it either.

It's that simple, and for Kant this realization was so breathtaking that it could be compared only to his awe of the universe on a starry night. Let us use Kant's own example to illustrate.

> [A man] in need finds himself forced to borrow money. He knows well that he won't be able to repay it, but he sees also that he will not get any loan unless he firmly promises to repay it within a fixed time. He wants to make such a promise, but he still has conscience enough to ask himself whether it is not permissible and is contrary to duty to get out of difficulty in this way. Suppose, however, that he decides to do so. The maxim of his action would then be expressed as follows: When I believe myself to be in need of money, I will borrow money and promise to pay it back, although I know that I can never do so. Now this principle of self-love or personal advantage may perhaps be quite compatible with one's entire future welfare, but the question is now whether it is right. I then transform the requirement of self-love into a universal law and put the question thus: how would things stand if my maxim were to become a universal law? He then sees at once that such a maxim could never hold as a universal law of nature and be consistent with itself, but must necessarily be self-contradictory. For the universality of a law which says that anyone believing himself to be in difficulty could promise whatever he pleases with the intention of not keeping it would make promising itself and the end to be attained thereby quite impossible, inasmuch as no one would believe what was promised him but would merely laugh at all such utterances as being vain pretenses.

Do we know why this man wants to borrow money? Perhaps he wants to buy a speedboat. Perhaps he wants to pay a hit man for a contract killing. Or he needs to pay the rent. Perhaps his child is ill, and he has to buy medication and pay the doctor's bill. We don't know. Is knowing his reason relevant? If we were utilitarians, it would be very relevant, because then we could judge the merit of the proposed consequences (saving his child generally has more utility than buying a boat or hiring a hit man). But Kant is no utilitarian, and the prospect of the man in the example wanting to do good with the borrowed money is no more relevant than the prospect of him wanting to buy a boat or even to hire a hit man. The main issue here is, Does the man have a good will? Would he refuse to follow a course of action if he couldn't agree to everyone else having the right to act the same way? At the end of the chapter you'll find an example from Kant's *Grounding* that illustrates what he means by having a good will.

Let us go over the structure of the proposed test of right and wrong conduct again: What is it you're thinking of doing? Imagine that as a *general rule* for action you'll follow every time the situation comes up. You have now expressed your *maxim.* Then imagine everybody else doing it too; by doing this you *universalize your maxim.* Then ask yourself, Could I want this? Could I still get away with it if everyone did it? The answer is no, you would *undermine your own intention,* because nobody would lend *you* any money if everyone were lying about paying it back. So it is not just the fact that banks would close and the financial world would be in chaos—it is the *logical outcome* of your universalized maxim that shows you that your intention was wrong. This means that it is your *duty* to refrain from following a self-contradictory maxim, simply because your reason tells you it can't be universalized. In Box 6.2 we take a closer look at the concept of duty as Kant saw it and

Box 6.2   WHAT IS DUTY?

The term *duty* has been linked forever with Kant's theory of the categorical imperative, but of course the word belongs to us all and isn't a Kantian invention. For most people, doing one's duty simply means doing what one is supposed to do, but doesn't really want to. But who determines what we are supposed to do? In most cultures this is determined by the social mores of the group, and by tradition. In philosophy we find a wide range of duty concepts, from the Greek notion of doing what custom requires, to various religious contexts where the rules are laid down by the priesthood and one's duty is to God rather than to people, to the utilitarian approach that makes it one's duty to create the greatest happiness for the greatest number. Kant's concept of duty has rightfully been singled out because he removes it from the religious tradition, the social mores, and the notion of happiness and ties it in exclusively with *reason*—with whether one could reasonably want an action to become a universal moral law. But at the same time that Kant lived, the German writer, poet, and politician whom you met in Chapter 2, Johann Wolfgang von Goethe, gave the notion of duty a twist which to this day inspires people: the concept of doing one's *nearest duty:*

Wrapped in our nearest duty is the key
Which shall unlock for us the Heavenly Gate:
Unveiled, the Heavenly Vision he shall see,
Who cometh not too early nor too late.

Like the star
That shines afar,
Without haste
And without rest,

Let each man wheel with steady sway
Round the task that rules the day,
And do his best.

What is your nearest duty? That depends on your individual situation and capability—but in a nutshell, if you have a relative who needs help, then help him, rather than engage yourself in causes that take your attention elsewhere. If your job or school requires you to complete a certain task, do that, and engage in other projects when you are done with it. For a child or a teenager, one's nearest duty could simply be doing homework, cleaning one's room, or standing by one's friend in school when others are picking on her. For an adult, it could be anything—raising your kids, doing that job around the house you promised, meeting the deadline at work, taking care of your parents, or going to war for your country—all depending on your other duties and capabilities. Then, once your nearest duty is done, you are free to engage in other causes that you may find inspirational.

---

as it was viewed by his countryman Goethe, who was a quarter of a century younger than Kant.

   The categorical imperative asks us in effect, Would you want others to treat you the way you're thinking of treating them? The association to the Golden Rule (see Box 4.8) is almost inevitable: How should we treat others? The way we would want to be treated. And yet Kant had harsh words for the old Golden Rule. He thought it was just a simplistic version of his own categorical imperative and that it could even be turned into a travesty: If you don't want to help others, just claim you don't want or need any help from them! But the bottom line is that the categorical imperative draws on that same fundamental realization that I called a spark of moral genius in the Golden Rule:

It sees self and others as fundamentally similar—not in the details of our lives but in the fact that we are human beings and should be treated fairly by each other.

Does this mean that the categorical imperative works only if *everyone* can accept your maxim as a universal law? Not in the sense that we have to take a poll before we decide to act; if everyone's actual approval were the final criterion, the principle would lose its appeal as an immediate test of where one's duty lies. There is an element of universal approval in Kant's idea, but it lies in the reflection of an *ideal* situation, not an *actual* one. If everyone put aside his or her personal interests and then used the categorical imperative, then everyone would, ideally, come up with the same conclusion about what is morally permissible. Kant, who belonged to an era of less doubt about what exactly rationality means, believed that if we all used the same rules of logic and disregarded our personal interests, then we all would come to the same results about moral as well as intellectual issues.

This immense faith in human rationality is an important factor in Kant's moral theory because it reflects his belief that humans are privileged beings. We can set up our own moral rules without having to seek guidance by going to the authorities; we need not be told how to live by the church or by the police or by the monarch or even by our parents. All we need is our good will and our reason, and with that we can set our own rules. If we choose a certain course of action because we have been told to—because we listen to other people's advice for some reason or other—we are merely doing what might be prudent and expedient, but if we listen to our own reason and have good will, then we are *autonomous lawmakers.*

Won't this approach result in a society where everyone looks after him- or herself and lives by multiple rules that may contradict one another? No, because if everyone has good will and applies the categorical imperative, then all will set the same, reasonable, unselfish rules for themselves because they would not wish to set a rule that would be impossible for others to follow.

In this way Kant believes he has shown us how to solve every dilemma, every problem where desire clashes with duty. When the categorical imperative is applied, we automatically disregard our own personal interests and look at the bigger picture, and this action is what is morally praiseworthy: to realize that something is right or wrong in itself. In the Narratives section you'll find a selection of stories that explore, each in its own way, the principle of doing the right thing regardless of the opinion of others or the consequences for oneself: Three films are placed together because of their similar plots: the classic Western *High Noon,* the sci-fi drama *Outland,* and the police drama *Cop Land* (both *Outland* and *Cop Land* are tributes to *High Noon,* so the similar plots are no coincidence). In addition, you can read a summary of the highly acclaimed film *The Insider,* about the difficult moral decisions made by a tobacco-industry whistleblower.

Criticism of the Categorical Imperative

Some people are immediately impressed by the idea that one's intentions count for more than the outcome of one's actions and that the question of right or wrong in itself is important; we can't consider only the consequences if it means violating the rights of others. Others claim that no matter how much you say you're not interested in consequences, they still end up being a consideration. Critics have raised five major points when finding fault with Kant's theory.

1. Consequences Count   Doesn't the categorical imperative actually imply concern for consequences? This is the criticism of John Stuart Mill, who had some sharp things to say about Kant's example of borrowing money and not keeping promises. If this was the best Kant could come up with to show that consequences don't count, he was not doing a very good job, said Mill, because what was he appealing to? By asking "What if everybody does what you want to do?" wasn't Kant worrying about *consequences*? What will happen if everyone borrows money and doesn't pay it back in spite of their promises? Then no one else can take advantage of promising falsely, either. In Mill's view, this is as much an appeal to consequences as regular utilitarianism is. This caused Mill to conclude that we all must include consequences in our moral theory, no matter how reluctant we are to recognize their importance. This appears to be a valid point against Kant. The only thing Kant might say in response to this (he never did, of course, since he was long dead by the time Mill criticized his point of view) is that his viewpoint does not look at actual consequences but at the logical implications of a universalized maxim: Will it or will it not undermine itself? Whether Mill has successfully criticized Kant or misunderstood him is still a topic of discussion among philosophers.

2. Conflict between Duties   Can we be so sure that the categorical imperative is always going to tell us what to do? Suppose we have a conflict between two things we have to do—and we don't particularly want to do either of them. Kant's system assumes that a moral conflict is one between duty and inclination—between what we have to do and what we want to do. In that case it is entirely possible we may be convinced to do the right thing by imagining our maxim as a universal rule for everyone. But suppose we have a conflict between two duties, such as having to take inventory at our workplace the night before we have a final exam for which we should be studying. Certainly we can't say we want to do one thing more than we want to do the other—anyone who has done both will probably agree that they are both rather unpleasant tasks. How might the categorical imperative help us decide what to do? All it can tell us is that failing to show up for the inventory would not be rational, but neither would skipping the final, because both are duties that everyone ought to fulfill under the same circumstances. The amount of help offered by the categorical imperative is at best limited to cases where duties are not in conflict. (Of course, in a situation where we have a conflict between duties, we already know of another approach that might answer the question of what to do: Bentham's hedonistic calculus. But most philosophers agree that you can't just mix and match theories according to your needs. In Chapter 11 we return to the question of combining the best of various moral theories.)

3. The Loophole   Might it not be possible to find a loophole in the imperative? Suppose the categorical imperative tells us that it would be irrational (and thus morally impermissible) for anyone to even think about robbing a bank if he needs money because we wouldn't want everyone in the same situation to take that course of action. But what exactly *is* the situation we're talking about? Suppose Joe is broke because he is out of work and has been for seven months. He is twenty years old and has a high school diploma. He worked at a video arcade, but now it is closed because of gang violence.

Joe likes to wear denim. His parents are divorced. He is dating a girl named Virginia who works at a supermarket and goes to the community college, and he needs money so that they can get married and rent a small apartment. Let's assume that Joe applies the categorical imperative and that his maxim is: Every time I (who am in a certain situation) am broke and cannot get a loan, I will rob a bank. Then he universalizes it: Every time someone who is twenty, and whose name is Joe, who has divorced parents, used to work in a video arcade, likes denim, and is dating a checkout girl named Virginia who goes to a community college—anytime he feels like robbing a bank because he is broke, it is all right for him to do so. Now is that rational? Will Joe's maxim undermine his intention because everyone else will do the same thing he is planning to do? No, because he has described his situation so that "everyone" is reduced to a group of very few people who are in his exact same situation. In fact, his description of "everyone" could apply to only one person: Joe himself. In that case it is perfectly logical for him to rob a bank, because he won't undermine his own intention. This is hardly the kind of ironclad philosophical proof of doing the right thing that we were looking for. This argument, which also works against rule utilitarianism, is of course not a valid excuse for doing the wrong thing, and Joe shouldn't run out and rob the bank because he thinks philosophers have shown it to be okay. It is, however, an attempt to show that if we work with a principle that is as general as the categorical imperative, we just can't expect it to answer all our moral questions without a doubt. Of course it isn't an example Kant himself would have appreciated. Kant would have complained that we are making the example too specific. But the fact remains that the categorical imperative needs some further clarification and definition to avoid the "escape clause" that the loophole provides. You may think this example is rather far-fetched, since it's pretty obvious that nobody designs a moral rule you can get away with breaking if it applies only to yourself. However, the story of Joe, be it ever so outlandish, is our own story, in all those situations where we ask for lenient treatment because "we're special." We know we're supposed to send our taxes in on time, and to show up for the final, and so forth, but it's been a hard year, we just had the flu, our family's falling apart, and we'd really like some special consideration. And, if the special circumstances apply only in our case, well, then, we've found a loophole. The example of Joe is just a little more extreme.

4. What Is Rationality?   Who is to say when something is irrational? This is an issue that might not have occurred to Kant. He, as a product of his times and a coproducer of the Age of Reason, believed that if we use our reason without looking to self-interest, then we will all come up with the same idea and result. Actually, Bentham believed the same thing, even though his moral vision was quite different from that of Kant. Today, after garnering a century of knowledge about the workings of the subconscious mind and realizing that people just aren't rational all or even most of the time, we are more inclined to believe that our individual idea of what is rational may depend greatly on who we are. If we use a very broad definition of rational, such as "realizing the shortest way to get to your goal and then pursuing it," we still may come up with different ideas about what is rational. Suppose not only that our Joe is broke but that he is also a political anarchist who believes that the sooner society breaks down, the better for all humanity and for himself in particular. Why then would it be particularly illogical for him to rob a bank, given that the downfall of society, including banks, is what he is longing for? And why should we refrain from lying to each other if what we want is to create social chaos and alienate our friends? Why refrain from hurting each other, if we are sadomasochists and believe it would be great to live in a world of mutual harmdoing? Although Joe is a fictional example, the real world provides examples of people who most of us believe to have acted irrationally although in their own minds they followed a sure rational path toward a goal. Consider Timothy McVeigh, the man responsible for the bombing of the Alfred P. Murrah Federal Building in Oklahoma City in 1995, which killed 167 men, women, and children. McVeigh was convicted of multiple murders of federal agents and was executed in June 2001. What kind of reasoning process did he go through in order to decide that taking human lives—the lives of strangers who had never done him any harm, the lives of toddlers and children—would somehow further a goal? If we ask whether he seriously considered the categorical imperative—Could he want others to do the same thing? Could he agree to a world in which someone did such things to him and his family?—then the Kantian tradition would probably claim that he could not, that his decision was irrational. But McVeigh already believed he did live in such a world, in which the *government* kills innocent people. (McVeigh was highly influenced by the federal raid on the Branch Davidian compound in Waco two years earlier.) In an interview he admitted that he thought his actions would start a revolution. So, if the rationality of one's decision depends on one's personal interpretation of the situation, how can the categorical imperative be a guarantee that we will all reach the same conclusion if only we use logic? Would using the categorical imperative have stopped Theodore Kaczynski, the Unabomber? For all his mental problems, Kaczynski is apparently an intelligent man and a scholar, and it is not improbable that he may have asked himself, Would you want your action to become a universal law? and answered Yes, I am doing the morally right thing.

Kant seems to assume that we all have the same general goals, which serve as a guarantee of the rationality of our actions. Change the goals, though, and the ideal of a reasonable course of action takes on a new meaning. (Box 6.3 further explores the issue of rationality.)

5. No Exceptions? Does it really seem right that we can never be morally correct in breaking a universal rule? In other words, can the categorical imperative always assure us that sticking to the rule is better than breaking it? Let us say that a killer is stalking a friend of yours, and the friend comes to your door and asks you to hide her. You tell her to go hide in the broom closet. (This is a slightly altered version of one of Kant's own examples.) The killer comes to your door and asks, "Where is she?" Most of us would feel a primary obligation to help our friend, but for Kant the primary obligation is to the truth. You are supposed to answer, "I cannot tell a lie— she is hiding in the broom closet." This is what is meant by an *absolutist* moral theory: A moral rule allows for no exceptions. But why? Most of us would assume that the life of our friend would at least be worth a white lie, but for Kant it is a matter of principle. Suppose you lie to the killer, but your friend sneaks out of the house, and the killer finds her; then it is your fault. If you had told the truth, your friend might still have escaped, and the killer could have been prevented from committing the murder (perhaps you could have trapped him in the broom closet). This far-fetched argument follows Kant's own reasoning for why we should always stick to the rule: because if we break a rule we must answer for the consequences, whereas

Box 6.3   WHAT IS RATIONALITY?

Philosophers often refer to conduct and arguments as being *rational* or *logical*. Since the Age of Reason (the Western Enlightenment) in the eighteenth century, the emphasis has been particularly strong, the assumption being that as long as you use your reason, you can't go wrong. If you do go wrong, the implication is that you have been applying faulty logic: One part of your conduct or your statement has been at odds with another part. For both Bentham and Kant, products of the Enlightenment, there is a staunch belief in the infallibility of properly applied reasoning. This belief was eroded considerably in the twentieth century, partly because of Freud's theories of the Unconscious as a powerful factor in our decision making but one fundamentally outside the control of our rational mind. In the last decades of the twentieth century, other criticisms were raised against the concept of rationality. If we choose a basic definition of rationality that says, "Decide on a goal and select the most direct method to achieve it," then critics of the philosophical emphasis on reason may point out that this method is above all a *Western* cultural ideal

and is not indicative of a worldwide method of conduct. Some cultures prefer *indirect* methods of achieving goals and consider direct methods rude. Some feminists point out that the direct method of rationality is a predominantly *male* approach, whereas many women prefer an indirect way of achieving a goal; in addition, they say, women make use of a special way of knowing: knowledge by emotion and intuition. Could it be true that men, having developed rational skills from millennia of being hunters, think in hunters' terms—going straight for the prey and killing it? And women, after millennia of being gatherers, think more in terms of picking and choosing and comparing? A comedian built this into his act in the 1990s, illustrating man the hunter going shopping at the mall, single-mindedly tracking down a shirt—and his wife, the gatherer, shopping around until all items have been compared. It was a pretty funny routine—and it may actually come close to an evolutionary truth. But many feminists, such as Alison Jaggar, argue that the highest kind of knowledge incorporates both traditional rational thinking and emotional think-

Is there a male and a female type of rationality? And does it reveal itself in our different styles of shopping? And if that might be the case, can a female shop the male way, and vice versa? Could there be other explanations for different shopping styles, rather than hard-wired gender nature?

ing—for both men and women. Although some rejoice in the possibility of there being several legitimate ways of being rational, some women thinkers worry that this view might turn back the clock and revive the old prejudice that "women can't think logically." And some advocates of traditional rationality as a universal philosophical method speculate that although it is possible that several different ways of conducting oneself rationally may exist, the rules of mathematics and logic are universal examples of applied rationality: The basic rules for pure, logical thinking are not culture- or gender-dependent.

if we stick to the rule, we have no such responsibility. If we tell the truth, and the killer goes straight for the broom closet and kills our friend, Kant insists that we bear no responsibility for her death. But why should we accept Kant's idea that consequences don't count as long as you are following the rule but that they do count when you are not? Philosophers tend to agree that you can't make such arbitrary choices of when consequences count and when they don't. At the end of the chapter, the second Primary Reading shows how serious Kant was about not accepting any exceptions to his moral principles: To the end of his days, in *The Metaphysics of Morals,* he insisted that even white lies are unacceptable.

If there are all these difficulties with the categorical imperative, why has it been such an influential moral factor? The reason is that it is the first moral theory to stress the idea of *universalizability:* realizing that the situation you are in is no different from that of other human beings. If something will bother you, it will probably bother others too, everything else being equal. If you allow yourself a day off, you should not gripe when others do the same thing. Most important, however, you should think about it before you allow yourself that day off and realize that it won't do as a universal rule. The problem is, on occasion we all encounter special situations when we might actually *need* a day off; perhaps we are sick or emotionally upset. Similarly, on the whole we should not kill, but in certain rare situations we may be called on to do just that, in war or in self-defense. On the whole we should not lie, but there may come a day when a killer is stalking a friend of ours, and we have a chance to save her. In that case we may need to lie. These are unusual situations, so why should Kant's generalizations apply to them? This issue has caused scholars to suggest that there really is nothing wrong with the format of the categorical imperative, provided that we are allowed to expand our maxim to include situations in which we might accept certain *exceptions* to our rule. As long as they don't expand to become a loophole, the universalization works just fine: We can universalize not killing, with the exception of self-defense and certain other specified cases. We can universalize not taking a day off from work unless we are sick or severely emotionally upset, as long as it doesn't happen very often. We can universalize not lying if it is understood that preventing harm to an innocent person would constitute an exception.

Rational Beings Are Ends in Themselves

In his book *Grounding for the Metaphysics of Morals,* Kant explores three major themes: the *categorical imperative,* the concept of *ends in themselves,* and the concept of a *kingdom of ends.* In a sense you might say that if we add the idea of people being ends in themselves to the idea of the categorical imperative, then the result will be a kingdom of ends. In the discussion that follows, we look at the ends-in-themselves concept as well as the kingdom of ends.

Persons Shouldn't Be Used as Tools

In *Grounding,* Kant suggests two different ways to express the categorical imperative. The first one we have just looked at; the other goes like this:

> Now I say that man, and in general every rational being, exists as an end in himself and not merely as a means to be arbitrarily used by this or that will. He must in all his actions, whether directed to himself or to other rational beings, always be regarded at the same time as an end.

What does it mean to be treated as an "end in himself"? Let us first look at the opposite approach: to be treated as a "means to an end only." What is a means to an end? It is a tool, an instrument to be used to achieve some goal; it is something that has *instrumental* value in the achievement of something of *intrinsic* value. If someone is used as a means to an end, she or he is treated as a tool for someone else's purpose, in a very broad sense. If someone is being sexually abused or kept as a slave, that person obviously is being treated as a means to an end, but so is the girl we befriend so we can get to know her brother. So is anyone who is being used for other people's purposes without regard for his or her intrinsic value and dignity as a human being, such as in the controversial film *Bumfights,* where young filmmakers persuaded homeless men to fight each other for the camera, for the sake of monetary gain. But Kant would condemn an act of using someone as a tool, even if the purpose is good—such as creating happiness for a large number of people. For Kant this is just another way of expressing the categorical imperative. What made him think this? For one thing, when you use the categorical imperative you are universalizing your maxim; and if you are refusing to treat others merely as means to an end, you are also universalizing a maxim, and a very fundamental one. Second, both maxims may be interpreted as expressions of the Golden Rule.

This statement about the immorality of treating other humans as means to an end was, for the eighteenth century, a tremendously important political and social statement. In Kant's era (although not in Kant's country) slavery was still a social factor; abuse of the lower classes by the upper classes was commonplace; Europe was just emerging from a time when monarchs and warlords could move their peasants and conscripted soldiers around like chess pieces with no regard for their lives and happiness. Then Kant clearly stated that it is not social status that determines one's standing in the moral universe, but one thing only: the capability to use reason. As one of the leading lights of the Age of Reason, Kant stated that any rational human being deserves respect. Rich and poor, young and old, all races and peoples—all are

For Better or For Worse® — by Lynn Johnston

Copyright © Lynn Johnston Prod., Inc. Dist. by United Features Syndicate, Inc.

Immanuel Kant says we should never treat another rational being as merely a means to an end; although extreme cases of reducing another person to an instrument for someone else's purpose, such as slavery or sexual abuse, are today recognized as morally unacceptable, we still have lots of everyday examples in which people treat one another as tools for their own agenda—as, for example, in this situation from the comic strip *For Better or For Worse.*

alike in having rationality as the one defining mark of their humanity, and none deserves to be treated without regard for that characteristic. Here it must be interjected, in case we get carried away with our praise, that Kant himself expressed doubt as to whether women were actually rational beings, or as rational as men; he may have had the same reservations about people of color (see Box 6.4), but we will be generous and look at the *implications* of Kant's theory for human rights, regardless of whether or not he himself saw as the goal that every human being deserves respect.

Why are rational beings intrinsically valuable? Because they can place a value on things. What is gold worth if nobody wants it? Nothing. Humans are value-givers; they assign a relative worth to things that interest them. However, as value-givers, humans always have an *absolute* value. They set the price, so to speak, yet cannot have a price set on them. We do, however, constantly talk about people being "worth money." A baseball player is worth a fortune, a Hollywood actress is worth millions. What does that mean? Have we set a price on humans after all? Not in the appropriate sense. It doesn't mean we can *buy* the Hollywood actress for a couple of million (well, we might, but in that case she is treating *herself* as a means to an end only, by selling her body). What we usually mean is that she has a lot of money. And the baseball player? He certainly can be "bought and sold," but hardly as a slave; he retains his autonomy and gets rich in the process. It is his talent and his services that are paid for. Under normal circumstances we don't refer to people as entities that can be bought for money, and if we do, we are usually implying that something bad is taking place (slavery and bribery, for instance). Thus people are value-givers because they can decide rationally what they want and what they don't want. This means that rational beings are *persons,* and the second formulation of the categorical imperative is focused on respect for persons: *Act in such a way that you treat humanity, whether in*

Box 6.4   KANT, THE ENLIGHTENMENT, AND RACISM

Over the years, Kant has been considered a primary source of the idea of human rights and equality because of his view that any rational being should be treated with dignity and never merely as a means to an end. This view has inspired Western thinkers, writers, and politicians to the point that we can actually say now that, even if the ideal has not yet been reached, the Western world is denouncing regimes that do not recognize all their citizens as equals, regardless of gender, income, race, ethnicity, religion, and nationality (see the United Nations Universal Declaration of Human Rights at the end of Chapter 7). But was this the goal Kant had in mind? It is rather discouraging to find out that it wasn't. Kant himself, as much as he has inspired today's quest for equality, had no philosophical goal of either gender or racial equality. Kant believed himself to be drawing on the cutting edge of biological research (he actually taught more classes in geography than in philosophy); in a rarely quoted text, "On the Different Races of Man" (1775), Kant voices the opinion that there are substantial differences in "natural dispositions" among what Kant sees as the four predominant human races of the world. For Kant and many other eighteenth-century Western thinkers, the European race was more intelligent than other races, and males were more intelligent than females. With no sound scientific evidence, some of the most important thinkers of the Western Enlightenment—which did usher in the first stages of global equality—decided that some humans were more advanced than others. This of course raises suspicion that Kant's "rational beings" may not have included all

humans, but primarily white males. However, ten years later Kant specified, in *Grounding*, that *all of humanity* should be treated like ends in themselves. It would be grossly unfair to assume that Kant thought only white males were "persons." But Kant's rule of "ends in themselves" only protects humans against abuse—it doesn't guarantee social equality.

Old heroes sometimes topple in the light of new research, and according to some critics this is what is happening to Kant: He may not be the champion of human rights we thought he was. We are even justified in calling him a racist, if we use today's view of racism as discrimination against individuals or groups of people solely based on their race. In my view, however, we should never forget that Kant was, for his day, indeed a champion of human rights. Europe was a place of serfdom, where peasants were treated as the property of the great landowners. Kant's writings did help set in motion the process that we all today have benefited from: the philosophical sea change that resulted in the concept of inalienable human rights. So Kant himself may have been locked in the racial bigotry of ignorance common for his day and age, but his ideas of a kingdom of ends in which *everyone* is treated with respect and dignity have today survived to become a Western political and philosophical ideal. He may fall short of the "minimum qualifications" considered necessary for an open-minded thinker today, but he did leave a legacy that can't be overestimated: the ideal of social and political dignity as a human birthright. That credit should not be taken away from him.

your own person or in the person of another, always at the same time as an end and never simply as means.

Notice that Kant is not talking about not mistreating just others. You have to respect yourself too, and not let others step on you. You have a right to set values of your own and not just be used by others as their key to success. But what exactly does it mean not to treat anybody *simply as means to an end*? We know that blatant abuse is wrong and that a subtler kind is no better. But what about using someone's services? When you buy your groceries, there usually is some person who bags your items. Truthfully, are you treating that person as a means to get your groceries bagged? Yes, indeed, but not *simply* as a means; he or she is getting paid, and you presumably don't treat these workers as though they were put on this earth just to bag your groceries. Everyday life consists of people using other people's services, and that is just the normal give-and-take of social life. The danger arises if we stop respecting people for what they do and reduce them in our minds to mere tools for our comfort or success. As long as the relationship is reciprocal (you pay for your groceries, and the bagger gets a paycheck), then there is no abuse taking place. Indeed, students use their professors as a means to an end (to get their degree), but the professors rarely feel abused, provided that they receive a salary. Likewise, the professors use students as a means to their ends (to receive that salary), but the professors surely don't imagine that the students were put on this earth to feed them or pay their mortgage. However, when people truly use others as tools for their own purpose and nothing else, from the phenomenon of "suicide by cop" to sexual abuse and terrorism, we are talking about treating others as a "means to an end only." In the Narratives section the film *Abandon Ship!*, based on a true story, illustrates the desperate circumstances of a shipwreck where the only way for some to survive is by sacrificing the lives of others—using them merely as a means to an end.

Many critics believe that John Stuart Mill was right when he pointed out that Kant, despite his own insistence that consequences are irrelevent for a good will, ended up including a reference to possible consequences in his categorical imperative in the universalization of the maxim: What happens if I do X? However, when we examine Kant's principle of never treating people simply as a means to an end, we have to conclude that this principle indeed does exclude any consideration of good or bad consequences: Nobody is supposed to reduce another, or themselves, to a mere tool or stepping-stone, regardless of whether it is for a good or a bad purpose, or whether it is based on mutual consent (which is why Kant was also against prostitution). So now we can return to the question raised in Chapter 5 about *torturing terrorists* to obtain vital information that may save lives. We saw that a utilitarian might agree that under specific circumstances it could be the right thing to do. For a Kantian, however, no amount of good consequences would justify the abuse of anyone, including serial killers, enemy POWs, or terrorists. Within a classical Kantian moral system, torture could never be allowed, even if it might save the life of your child, your spouse, your parents, or your country; it is better to suffer with common dignity and respect for other humans than it is to buy the safety and happiness of some with the suffering of others. That doesn't mean we can't punish criminals, including terrorists, with imprisonment or even execution, as we shall see in Chapter 7, but the purpose would be *justice* rather than creating good consequences.

Beings Who Are Things

Any rational being deserves respect. We assume that humans fall into that category, but what if there are rational beings who are not human? It is not unthinkable that humans might encounter extraterrestrials who are rational enough to know math, language, and space science; and how about the possibility of AI, Artificial Intelligence? Would Kant respect a thinking android or computer, or a rational alien, or would he advocate treating them like things? If these beings are *rational*, they qualify as full members of our moral universe, and humans have no right to treat them as tools to achieve knowledge or power. Aliens and androids would likewise have no right to cart humans off for medical experiments because all humans are generally rational beings.

There are beings on this earth who are not rational in Kant's sense of the word—animals, for example. In *Grounding* he presents his theory in this way:

> Beings whose existence depends not on our will but on nature have, nevertheless, if they are not rational beings, only a relative value as means and are therefore called things. On the other hand, rational beings are called persons inasmuch as their nature already marks them out as ends in themselves. . . .

This means that nonhuman animals don't belong in the moral universe at all; they are classified as *things* and can be used as a tool by a rational person because animals can't place a value on something—only humans can do that. And an animal is not worth anything in itself; it has value only if it is wanted for some purpose by a human. If nobody cares about cats, or spotted owls, then they have no value. Is it true, though, that animals can't place a value on things? Most people with firsthand knowledge of animals will report that pets are capable of valuing their owners above all and their food bowl second (or is it the other way around?). And animals in the wild place extreme importance on their territory and their young. Many people today categorize animal interests as just different in *degree* from human interests and not different in *kind* (Chapter 13). Although Kant and most of his contemporaries (with the exclusion of Bentham) believed that the moral universe is closed to nonhuman animals, it is just possible today that we not only might include animals as "creatures who deserve respect" but also might actively look for traces of *animal morality*. Might the self-sacrifice of a baboon to save her tribe from the leopard constitute a moral dimension? Is a gorilla morally good if she comes to the rescue of a child who has fallen into the gorilla enclosure at the zoo? Or are we just witnessing automatic instinctual responses? (See Box 6.5 for further discussion.)

Whatever we think now, the day could be near when dolphins, elephants, and the great apes are included in a category of rudimentary rational beings. For our purposes here, we simply should remember that for Kant it was not just a matter of being able to think—one must also be able to show that one has autonomy and can set up universal moral rules for oneself and others; and although certain animals may have some thought capacity, it is doubtful whether they ever can be considered *morally autonomous* in the Kantian sense of the term.

Numerous scholars have pointed out, however, that there is a serious problem with Kant's own classification of humans as rational beings, for suppose someone who is genetically human can't think rationally? There are many humans who aren't good at thinking or can't think at all because they are infants, toddlers, mentally disabled, or in a coma—or have Alzheimer's. Does this mean that all of these people aren't *persons* and should be classified as *things*? As some scholars have remarked,

Box 6.5   CAN ANIMALS THINK?

From the previous chapter you may remember that Descartes didn't believe animals had any mental activity because according to his theory they consisted of matter only. Kant does not deny that nonhuman animals have minds; he just does not believe them to be rational minds but rather instinctive—in his own words, "depending on nature" (*Grounding*). In *The Metaphysics of Morals* he explains further: Although animals and humans all have wills that propel them toward their goals, only humans have free choice; animals making choices about what to eat, with whom to mate, and where to sleep don't make use of moral laws, and so their choice is merely brutish (as some people's choices of the same type may be). But when a person makes a choice based on a rational principle of universalizability, then Kant calls it a free choice.

Today the issue of animal intelligence is still controversial. Some ethologists (animal behaviorists) continue to believe that human and nonhuman animal intelligence are different *in kind;* others now lean toward the assumption that they are different *in degree.* Close observations in experimental situations over years of research and coexistence with animals have led many modern biologists and behaviorists to conclude that at least certain animals, such as great apes, dolphins, and orcas (killer whales), have a rudimentary capacity for rational thinking and even for linguistic comprehension (as humans define language). In Chapter 13 we take a closer look at the issues of animal intelligence and animal rights.

there are animals who are more like persons (that is, rational beings) than newborn infants or severely mentally disabled humans are. Would Kant really say that such humans are no better than things? The trouble is that Kant never made provisions for any such subcategories of "persons" in *Grounding.* It is either-or.

There is no denying that problems arise if you divide the world into persons (with rights not to be abused by others) and things (that persons have a right to use). But twelve years after writing *Grounding,* in his long-awaited *The Metaphysics of Morals,* Kant addressed the question of an intermediate category: people who have absolute rights as ends in themselves but who also, for various reasons, "belong" to other persons. Kant calls it "the right to a person akin to a right to a thing"—such persons are legitimately treated *as if* they were possessions, although they cannot be owned as slaves. An example would be a small child: She is a person with the right to personal freedom; the child's parents can't destroy her, even if they brought her into the world; but the child does not have full self-determination either, because she is still regarded as a pseudo-possession of her parents until the day she is grown (if someone takes her, her parents can demand to have her back). The parents have a duty to raise the child properly, and the child has no duty to repay them. Similarly, servants of a household belong in the intermediate category of being pseudo-possessions: They are free persons, but because they have signed contracts they can't just take off whenever they feel like it, Kant says. On the other hand, they can't be bought and sold either, because then they would be slaves, and slavery is reducing someone to merely a means to an end. Some scholars believe that with this intermediate category between a person with full freedom and a thing with none, Kant has opened the door for the modern category sometimes called "partial rights": A being who is not a rational, human adult may be granted some rights but may still be regarded as under the guardianship of other humans. Vilifying Kant for poisoning philosophy toward the rights of partially rational beings hardly seems fair under these circumstances. But in *The Metaphysics of Morals* we also hear in no uncertain terms from Kant that animals are not rational and have no rights, because in order for us to have duties to other beings, they have to be capable of having obligations to us. (See Chapter 13 for a continuation of this debate.) Classifying an animal as a thing seemed reasonable to Kant, but, even so, he was concerned that some readers might take this as permission to treat animals any way they saw fit, including being cruel to them. Kant was very specific about condemning cruelty to animals; however, he took this stance not so much for the sake of the animals themselves but because someone who hurts animals might easily get used to it and begin to hurt people. It appears that Kant was more right than most of his readers could have known at the time; although Kant is not the first person to have claimed that cruelty to animals may lead to cruelty toward people (St. Thomas Aquinas had said the same thing in the thirteenth century), the depth of the connection only became apparent in the late twentieth century, when criminal profiling established that just about every serial killer questioned through the late 1990s turned out to have tortured small animals when he was a child. (This investigation focused on male serial killers, since there have been very few female serial murderers so far.) In addition, such individuals would also engage in setting fires and were chronic bed-wetters. This does not mean that a boy who wets his bed, sets fires, and tortures animals will invariably grow up to be a serial killer, but these behaviors are considered warning signs that should be attended to while the child is still young. The point Kant wanted to make, which criminal profiling has corroborated, is that desensitization to—or even enjoyment of—animal pain can lead to deliberately inflicting pain on human beings. In Kant's words (from *The Metaphysics of Morals*):

> It dulls his shared feeling of their pain and so weakens and gradually uproots a natural predisposition that is very serviceable to morality in one's relations with other men. Man is authorized to kill animals quickly (without pain) and to put them to work that does not strain them beyond their capacities (such work as man himself must submit to). But agonizing physical experiments for the sake of mere speculation, when the end could also be achieved without these, are to be abhorred.

It is interesting that Kant, having over the years acquired the reputation of being insensitive to the plight of animals, himself argued against causing needless pain to them. Contrary to Descartes, Kant never thought animals couldn't feel pain; he just thought that within the context of human moral issues it was only marginally relevant. Some issues are thus resolved in *The Metaphysics of Morals*, but not all issues. Even so, the idea that rational beings should never be treated merely as means to an end has been a powerful contribution to a world of equality and mutual respect because it is such a remarkable expansion of the moral universe described in previous moral theories, which tended to exclude social groups that somehow weren't considered quite as valuable as others. Furthermore, Kant placed the foundation of morality solidly with human rationality and not with the state or the church.

The Kingdom of Ends

This brings us to the third major theme in Kant's *Grounding,* the "kingdom of ends." Applying the categorical imperative is something all rational beings can do—and even if they can't do it exactly the way Kant uses it, the logic of it should be compelling for all people who can ask themselves, "Would I want everybody to do this?" Kant calls this *moral autonomy:* The only moral authority that can tell us to do something and not to do something else is our own reason. As we saw previously, if all people follow the same principle and disregard their own personal inclinations, then all will end up following the same good rules, because all have universalized their intention. In such a world, with everyone doing the right thing and nobody abusing anyone else, a new realm will have been created: the *kingdom of ends.* "Kingdom" poetically describes a community of people, and "ends" indicates that the people treat each other as ends only—as beings who have their own goals in life—never merely as means to other people's ends. Every time we show respect and consideration for one another, we make the kingdom of ends a little more real. In Kant's words from *Grounding,*

> By "kingdom" I understand a system of different rational beings through common laws. . . . For all rational beings stand under the law that each of them should treat himself and all others never merely as a means but always at the same time as an end in himself. Hereby arises a systematic union of rational beings through common objective laws, i.e., a kingdom that may be called a kingdom of ends (certainly only an ideal), inasmuch as these laws have in view the very relation of such beings to one another as ends and means.
>
> A rational being belongs to the kingdom of ends as a member when he legislates in it universal laws while also himself being subject to these laws. He belongs to it as sovereign, when as legislator he is himself subject to the will of no other. . . . In the kingdom of ends everything has either a price or a dignity. Whatever has a price can be replaced by something else as its equivalent; on the other hand, whatever is above all price, and therefore admits no equivalent, has a dignity.

Here we see how Kant combines the first part of his book, the categorical imperative, with the second part, the idea that nobody should be used merely as a means to an end. People who adhere to the method of the categorical imperative are autonomous lawmakers: They set laws for themselves that, when universalized, become acceptable to every other rational being. When we use that approach, we realize that we can't allow ourselves to treat others (or let others treat us) as merely a means to an end, but recognize that other people should be treated with respect because they are rational beings with dignity, *irreplaceable* beings. We all belong in the kingdom of ends, the realm of beings with dignity. But whatever doesn't qualify as rational has a price and can be replaced with a similar item. (This of course means that any human being has dignity and is irreplaceable, while your dog has no dignity and can be replaced.)

Some readers of Kant believe that he shows a more humane side in his theory of ends in themselves, and indeed we might take this idea and apply it to the problem of whether to lie to the killer who has come to murder your friend. The categorical imperative tells you to speak the truth always, because then you can't be blamed for the consequences. But is this really the same as saying we should treat others as ends in themselves? Perhaps there is a subtle difference; if we apply this rule to the killer who is stalking our friend, would we get the same result? Might we not be treating our friend as merely a means to an end if we refuse to lie for her, whether it is for the sake of principle or just so that we can't be blamed for the consequences? If we are sacrificing our friend for the sake of the truth, it might rightfully be said that in such a case we are treating her as a means to an end only. So even within Kant's own system there are irreconcilable differences. This should not cause us to want to discard his entire theory, however; since the nineteenth century, philosophers have tried to redesign Kant's ideas to fit a more perceptive (or, as Kant would say, more lenient) world. Some of these ideas are working quite well—for example, allowing for general exceptions to be built into the categorical imperative itself and allowing for animals to be considered more rational than Kant ever thought possible.

Study Questions

1. Evaluate the following statement: "Actions are morally good only if they are done because of a good will." Explain what Kant means by a "good will." Do you think the statement is correct or incorrect? Explain your position.

2. Analyze the following statement: "Man, and in general every rational being, should be treated as an end in himself, never merely as a means." What are the moral implications of this statement for humans, as well as nonhumans?

3. Explain Kant's position on lying: Is it always morally wrong to lie? What are the implications for the question raised in Chapter 5, "Should we lie to Grandma about something that will distress her?"

Primary Readings and Narratives

The first Primary Reading is an excerpt from Kant's famous *Grounding for the Metaphysics of Morals* in which he explains the structure of the categorical imperative. The second Primary Reading is an excerpt from Kant's less frequently quoted book, *The Metaphysics of Morals,* in which he explains why lying is wrong. The Narratives are all summaries: A set of three similar stories: *Outland* and *Cop Land* draw on the theme suggested by the original story, the famous Western *High Noon*, in which the town marshal chooses to face three gunmen alone after having been rejected by the community he is trying to defend. The film *Abandon Ship!* is a true story about a shipwrecked lifeboat with too many people on board. The film *The Insider* is about a tobacco-industry whistleblower.

Primary Reading

Grounding for the Metaphysics of Morals

IMMANUEL KANT

1785. Excerpt.

In this passage Kant introduces the categorical imperative and links it with the concept of the good will as an understanding of doing one's duty in accordance with reason.

Thus the moral worth of an action does not lie in the effect expected from it nor in any principle of action that needs to borrow its motive from this expected effect. For all these effects (agreeableness of one's condition and even the furtherance of other people's happiness) could have been brought about also through other causes and would not have required the will of a rational being, in which the highest and unconditioned good can alone be found. Therefore, the preeminent good which is called moral can consist in nothing but the representation of the law in itself, and such a representation can admittedly be found only in a rational being insofar as this representation, and not some expected effect, is the determining ground of the will. This good is already present in the person who acts according to this representation, and such good need not be awaited merely from the effect.

But what sort of law can that be the thought of which must determine the will without reference to any expected effect, so that the will can be called absolutely good without qualification? Since I have deprived the will of every impulse that might arise for it from obeying any particular law, there is nothing left to serve the will as principle except the universal conformity of its actions to law as such, i.e., I should never act except in such a way that I can also will that my maxim should become a universal law. Here mere conformity to law as such (without having as its basis any law determining particular actions) serves the will as principle and must so serve it if duty is not to be a vain delusion and a chimerical concept. The ordinary reason of mankind in its practical judgments agrees completely with this, and always has in view the aforementioned principle.

For example, take this question. When I am in distress, may I make a promise with the intention of not keeping it? I readily distinguish here the two meanings which the question may have; whether making a false promise conforms with prudence or with duty. Doubtless the former can often be the case. Indeed I clearly see that escape from some present difficulty by means of such a promise is not enough. In addition I must carefully consider whether from this lie there may later arise far greater inconvenience for me than from what I now try to escape. Furthermore, the consequences of my false promise are not easy to foresee, even with all my supposed cunning; loss of confidence in me might prove to be far more disadvantageous than the misfortune which I now try to avoid. The more prudent way might be to act according to a universal maxim and to make it a habit not to promise anything without intending to keep it. But that such a maxim is, nevertheless, always based on nothing but a fear of consequences becomes clear to me at once. To be truthful from duty is, however, quite different from being truthful from fear of disadvantageous consequences;

in the first case the concept of the action itself contains a law for me, while in the second I must first look around elsewhere to see what are the results for me that might be connected with the action. For to deviate from the principle of duty is quite certainly bad; but to abandon my maxim of prudence can often be very advantageous for me, though to abide by it is certainly safer. The most direct and infallible way, however, to answer the question as to whether a lying promise accords with duty is to ask myself whether I would really be content if my maxim (of extracting myself from difficulty by means of a false promise) were to hold as a universal law for myself as well as for others, and could I really say to myself that everyone may promise falsely when he finds himself in a difficulty from which he can find no other way to extricate himself. Then I immediately become aware that I can indeed will the lie but can not at all will a universal law to lie. For by such a law there would really be no promises at all, since in vain would my willing future actions be professed to other people who would not believe what I professed, or if they over-hastily did believe, then they would pay me back in like coin. Therefore, my maxim would necessarily destroy itself just as soon as it was made a universal law.

Therefore, I need no fear-reaching acuteness to discern what I have to do in order that my will may be morally good. Inexperienced in the course of the world and incapable of being prepared for all its contingencies, I only ask myself whether I can also will that my maxim should become a universal law. If not, then the maxim must be rejected, not because of any disadvantage accruing to me or even to others, but because it cannot be fitting as a principle in a possible legislation of universal law, and reason exacts from me immediate respect for such legislation. Indeed I have as yet no insight into the grounds of such respect (which the philosopher may investigate). But I at least understand that respect is an estimation of a worth that far outweighs any worth of what is recommended by inclination, and that the necessity of acting from pure respect for the practical law is what constitutes duty, to which every other motive must give way because duty is the condition of a will good in itself, whose worth is above all else.

Study Questions

1. What does Kant mean by a good will?

2. Explain the structure and purpose of the categorical imperative.

3. Can you think of a situation where it might actually be counterproductive to do a good or a harmless thing if everyone did the same thing? How might Kant respond?

Primary Reading

The Metaphysics of Morals

IMMANUEL KANT

Excerpt from Book I, Chapter II, 1797.

This book was actually printed separately in two parts but is considered one book today. The first part is *The Doctrine of Right,* and the second one is *The Doctrine of Virtue.* This section on lying from *The Doctrine of Virtue* illustrates Kant's talent for careful analysis of even an ordinary kind of experience in order to argue his points that you should not make choices you couldn't wish to become a universal law and that you should not make choices that diminish the dignity of others or yourself.

Man's Duty to Himself Merely as a Moral Being: This duty is opposed to the vices of *lying, avarice,* and *false humility* (servility).

On Lying: The greatest violation of man's duty to himself regarded merely as a moral being (the humanity in his own person) is the contrary of truthfulness, *lying (aliud lingua promptum, aliud pectore inclusum gerere).* ["To have one thing shut up in the heart and another ready on the tongue." Sallust, *The War with Catiline* X, 5.] In the doctrine of Right an intentional untruth is called a lie only if it violates another's right; but in ethics, where no authorization is derived from harmlessness, it is clear of itself that no intentional untruth in the expression of one's thoughts can refuse this harsh name. For the dishonor (being an object of moral contempt) that accompanies a lie also accompanies a liar like his shadow. A lie can be an external lie (*mendacium externum*) or also an internal lie. By an external lie a man makes himself an object of contempt in the eyes of others; by an internal lie he does what is still worse: He makes himself contemptible in his own eyes and violates the dignity of humanity in his own person. And so, since the harm that can come to other men from lying is not what distinguishes this vice (for if it were, the vice would consist only in violating one's duty to others), this harm is not taken into account here. Neither is the harm that a liar brings on himself; for then a lie, as a mere error in prudence, would conflict with the pragmatic maxim, not the moral maxim, and it could not be considered a violation of duty at all. By a lie a man throws away and, as it were, annihilates his dignity as a man. A man who does not himself believe what he tells another (even if the other is a merely ideal person) has even less worth than if he were a mere thing; for a thing, because it is something real and given, has the property of being serviceable so that another can put it to some use. But communication of one's thoughts to someone through words that yet (intentionally) contain the contrary of what the speaker thinks on the subject is an end that is directly opposed to the natural purposiveness of the speaker's capacity to communicate his thoughts, and is thus a renunciation by the speaker of his personality, and such a speaker is a mere deceptive appearance of a man, not a man himself. *Truthfulness* in one's declarations is also called *honesty* and, if the declarations are promises, *sincerity;* but, more generally, truthfulness is called rectitude.

Lying (in the ethical sense of the word), intentional untruth as such, need not be *harmful* to others in order to be repudiated; for it would then be a violation of the rights of others. It may be done merely out of frivolity or even good nature; the speaker may even intend to achieve a really good end by it. But his way of pursuing this end is, by its mere form, a crime of a man against his own person and a worthlessness that must make him contemptible in his own eyes.

It is easy to show that man is actually guilty of many inner lies, but it seems more difficult to explain how they are possible; for a lie requires a second person whom one intends to deceive, whereas to deceive oneself on purpose seems to contain a contradiction.

Man as a moral being (*homo noumenon*) cannot use himself as a natural being (*homo phaenomenon*) as a mere means (a speaking machine), as if his natural being were not bound to the inner end (of communicating thoughts), but is bound to the condition of using himself as a natural being in agreement with the declaration (*declaratio*) of his moral being and is under obligation to himself to *truthfulness*. Someone tells an inner lie, for example, if he professes belief in a future judge of the world, although he really finds no such belief within himself but persuades himself that it could do no harm and might even be useful to profess in his thoughts to one who scrutinizes hearts a belief in such a judge, in order to win His favor in case He should exist. Someone also lies if, having no doubt about the existence of this future judge, he still flatters himself that he inwardly reveres His law, though the only incentive he feels is fear of punishment.

Insincerity is mere lack of *conscientiousness,* that is, of purity in one's professions before one's inner judge, who is thought of as another person when conscientiousness is taken quite strictly; then if someone, from self-love, takes a wish for the deed because he has a really good end in mind, his inner lie, although it is indeed contrary to man's duty to himself, gets the name of a frailty, as when a lover's wish to find only good qualities in his beloved blinds him to her obvious faults. But such insincerity in his declarations, which man perpetrates upon himself, still deserves the strongest censure, since it is from such a rotten spot (falsity, which seems to be rooted in human nature itself) that the evil of untruthfulness spreads into man's relations with other men as well, once the highest principle of truthfulness has been violated.

Remark: It is noteworthy that the Bible dates the first crime, through which evil entered the world, not from *fratricide* (Cain's) but from the first *lie* (for even nature rises up against fratricide), and calls the author of all evil a liar from the beginning and the father of lies. However, reason can assign no further ground for man's propensity to *hypocrisy* (*esprit fourbe*), although this propensity must have been present before the lie; for an act of freedom cannot (like a natural effect) be deduced and explained in accordance with the natural law of the connection of effects with their causes, all of which are appearances.

Casuistical Questions: Can an untruth from mere politeness (e.g., the "your obedient servant" at the end of a letter) be considered a lie? No one is deceived by it. An author asks one of his readers, "How do you like my work?" One could merely seem to give an answer, by joking about the impropriety of such a question. But who has his wit always ready? The author will take the slightest hesitation in answering as an insult. May one, then, say what is expected of one?

If I say something untrue in more serious matters, having to do with what is mine or yours, must I answer for all the consequences it might have? For example, a householder has ordered his servant to say "not at home" if a certain man asks for him. The servant does this and, as a result, the master slips away and commits a serious crime, which would otherwise have been prevented by the guard sent to arrest him. Who (in accordance with ethical principles) is guilty in this case? Surely the servant, too, who violated a duty to himself by his lie, the results of which his own conscience imputes to him.

Study Questions

1. Why does a liar annihilate his or her own dignity? Is there a connection to the categorical imperative and/or the theory of respect for persons?

2. What is the difference between an external and an internal lie? Is one more acceptable than the other, according to Kant? And according to you?

3. Discuss Kant's own "study question," "Is the servant guilty?" Why? Compare this example to the example of the killer at the door.

Narrative

Three Deontological Films

High Noon

CARL FOREMAN (SCREENWRITER)
FRED ZINNEMAN (DIRECTOR)

Film, 1952. Summary.

This film may be the most famous Western of all time, and yet it is not a "true" Western. There is very little riding, no troops or Indians, no cattle, no cowboys—but much talk about the right thing to do. This film was made in the early days of McCarthyism in Hollywood, and Fred Zinneman (the director) has admitted that it is an allegory of the general attitude in 1952 Hollywood of turning your back on friends who were accused (mostly falsely) of "un-American" (Communist) activities and who might have needed help. When it was produced, it was not considered to have any potential as a classic but it has soared in public opinion ever since then. It is a Western—but a Western of a different sort—a Western about the problems of a budding civilization in the midst of an era of violence. The film also is very well crafted. The amount of time that elapses from the moment Marshal Will Kane realizes he will have to face four gunmen alone because the whole town worries about the consequences of siding with him to the moment the actual gunfight takes place is the exact amount of time you spend watching it in the theater or in front of your TV: an hour and a half.

The plot is simple. Five years before, Kane brought a killer, Frank Miller, to justice. Miller was sentenced to hang, but "up North they commuted it to life, and now he's free," as the judge says. He is coming in on the noon train to have it out with Kane. Word of his

In *High Noon* (United Artists, 1952) Will Kane (Gary Cooper, left) has just been married and has resigned as marshal of Hadleyville, but a killer he helped put in prison and three other gunmen are now looking for him. He tries to get the townspeople to stand by him the way they did when he captured the killer five years earlier, but now everybody turns their back on him, preferring not to get involved. In this scene a former friend, Herb (James Millican), is backing out of his promise to help Kane, having found out that nobody else is coming along.

intentions comes just as Kane is marrying his Quaker bride in a civil ceremony. He has already given up his job and is leaving town with his new wife when he turns around to face the gunmen coming in on the noon train. His wife, Amy, asks him why he is turning back—he doesn't have to play the hero for her, she says. He answers, "I haven't got time to tell you. . . . And if you think I like this, you're crazy."

In town, Kane tries to get his former deputies to join him, but everyone is afraid of Miller, except the deputy, who is the boyfriend of Helen Ramirez, Kane's former girlfriend. Helen is the only one who understands Kane's problem because, as a Mexican, she has always felt like an outcast herself—and besides, she used to be Frank Miller's girlfriend too. When Amy leaves Kane because she can't stand the threat of violence, she seeks out Helen because she thinks it is because of her that Kane is staying in town. Amy begs Helen to let him go, and when she hears that he isn't staying because of Helen, she asks, bewildered, what then is making her husband stay. Helen tells her, "If you don't know, I can't tell you." Helen's boyfriend, the deputy, finds Kane and tries to force him to leave town so that he can take over as town marshal. He also asks Kane why he is staying, and all Kane says is, "I don't know."

Desperate, Kane makes for the little church where the Sunday service is still going on, and we remember that an hour ago he was married in a civil ceremony. The service comes to a stop as he enters, and the minister asks him what could be so important since he didn't see fit to be married in church. Kane explains that his wife is a Quaker, and not a member of the town's Protestant congregation, and he knows he is not a churchgoing man, but he needs help. Some of the same men who were deputies with him when they arrested Miller are attending the service—don't they feel the call to duty? Democratically, the congregation plunges into a debate: Why is Kane still here if he is no longer marshal? Why hasn't he arrested the men at the depot? Why must private citizens pitch in every time law enforcement can't handle the situation? But Kane also has supporters who remember that he cleaned up the town and made it a place fit for civilized people. In the end, the mayor speaks: We owe Kane a great debt, he says, so we, the citizens, ought to take care of the situation—and Kane ought to get out of town so there will be no bloodshed. Because (and this is obviously the mayor's real concern) with bloodshed in the streets, investors from up North will shy away from putting money into the town. The support Kane was hoping for evaporates in light of financial concerns.

The "good citizens" want Kane to leave town so there will be no deterrence to progress. The former sheriff wants him to leave, saying that keeping the law is an ungrateful business. Everybody wants him to leave, and at the train depot Frank Miller's three gunmen are waiting for the train that will bring Frank. But Kane feels compelled to stay, even with nobody to side with him. The last man to abandon Kane is his friend Herb. When he realizes that it will be just him and Kane against Miller and his gang, he pleads with Kane, "I have a wife and kids—what about my kids?" And Kane responds, "Go home to your kids, Herb."

The train arrives, a gunfight ensues in the dusty streets of the town, and two of Frank's gunmen are killed. In the end, Amy comes to Kane's rescue and kills the third gunman; Kane kills Miller, and together he and Amy leave town—but not before Kane has thrown his marshal's star in the dust.

Study Questions

1. What makes Kane stay? Is he serious when he says, "I don't know"?

2. Is it fair of Kane to place Amy in a situation where she has to give up her own moral principles?

3. Why might we say that this is a "Kantian" Western?

4. How would a utilitarian judge Kane's feeling of conscience and duty?

5. Are the townspeople who refuse to help primarily deontologists, utilitarians, or ethical egoists?

The theme of the morally righteous loner has been repeated in two very different movies, one a sci-fi film and the other a cop film; in each case the focus is on the man who stands by his principles, working against the politics of his superiors and even the wishes of his community for the sake of the categorical imperative—although nobody ever mentions Kant on the silver screen. These two films are *Outland* and *Cop Land*.

Outland

PETER HYAMS (SCREENWRITER AND DIRECTOR)

Film, 1981. Summary.

Outland takes place in the near future on Io, one of Jupiter's moons, which has become a mining colony. Work is excruciatingly hard, and the workers are allowed to "play hard"; a number of deaths among veteran workers have been registered, all due to what seems like instant insanity involving violence, either toward others or toward themselves. In spite of warnings from the administration, Federal District Marshal William T. O'Niel sets out to investigate the deaths with no cooperation from the station's personnel except for the crusty female station physician. What does he find? That each of the dead workers had a drug in his system—a drug that allows the person to work beyond ordinary capacity for a while and then fatally attacks the brain. Marshal O'Niel concludes that this is not due to personal choice by the workers—this is a way for the administration to get as much labor out of each individual as possible with total disregard for his or her personal fate or well-being—in other words, the administration is treating these workers merely as a means to an end for the sake of profit. But O'Niel doesn't have long to ponder his findings: He learns that three hit men are arriving at the space station, sent by the administration to silence him. And as the arrival time for the shuttle nears, we see O'Niel preparing for the gun battle all by himself, abandoned by everyone except the doctor. Will he succeed in defending the principle of doing the right thing, in spite of the threat to his life? Watch this film and *High Noon*, and enjoy a sci-fi tribute to perhaps the most famous moral statement in any Western ever made!

See Study Questions following *Cop Land*.

Cop Land

JAMES MANGOLD (SCREENWRITER AND DIRECTOR)

Film, 1997. Summary.

Cop Land takes place not in the Old West of the past or in the outer space of the future but in the New Jersey of the present. "Cop Land" is the nickname for a small town across the Hudson River, Garrison, where many New York Police Department officers prefer to live and pretty much have the run of the town. There is very little crime, and the local nice-guy sheriff Freddy (who would really have liked to be an NYPD cop but is hearing impaired) is reduced to writing reports about garbage tampering. But then crime from the big city spills over into the small community: A young cop, "Superboy," fakes his own suicide after a traffic stop resulting in the shooting death of an unarmed man. While a spirited wake is held for Superboy, it dawns on Freddy that he is not dead at all—his friends and his uncle, a senior cop, are covering for him, to the point of killing off other cops who may be tempted to spill the beans. But as the existence of the "dead" cop is becoming hard to hide, Superboy himself becomes a target for his former friends, including his uncle: He is too hot to have around, and they try to eliminate him, because underlying this particular situation is a web of corruption and cover-ups that has gone on for years in Cop Land. The Internal Affairs office of NYPD appeals to Freddy to do his civic duty, to actually be a cop and report his findings, even if it involves informing on the police officers living in Cop Land. But the sheriff, who is not very bright, hesitates, not quite understanding where his loyalty ought to lie—with the people living in Cop Land whom he thinks he is hired to protect? Or to the truth? Freddy decides to do nothing—until he realizes that by not standing up for the good he is in effect letting evil run loose. And so he decides to fight evil all by himself, with obstacles from every direction: The Internal Affairs office has closed the case. Only one deputy remains by his side, but even he begins to talk about how his pregnant wife needs him, and Freddy sends him home. What does Freddy do? He finds Superboy and sets out to bring him in alive single-handedly, under fire from the police, as proof of the vast conspiracy permeating the seemingly quiet Cop Land. Does he succeed? Did Will Kane succeed? Did O'Niel succeed? Judge for yourself whether their success is complete. All three films are testimony to Kant's thought that doing the right thing, in spite of the danger and the apparent futility of the job, is worth it in itself, simply because it is the right thing to do—and because we wouldn't want to universalize sitting back and doing nothing or turning tail and running for the sake of personal convenience.

Study Questions

1. Compare *High Noon, Outland,* and *Cop Land:* What are the differences? What are the similarities?

2. Suppose Kane, O'Niel, and Freddy did not succeed in their lonely fight against evil forces, or suppose they had lost their nerve. Would it make any difference to Kant in evaluating the moral value of their actions? Would it make a difference to you? Why or why not?

3. When someone decides to act on principle against the wishes of the community, can we always assume that this person is doing the right thing? How would Kant decide? How would a utilitarian decide? How would you decide?

4. Evaluate Kane, O'Niel, and Freddy: How did each character do his duty? If you were faced with the same situation, would you act the same way? Explain.

Narrative

Abandon Ship!

RICHARD SALE (SCREENWRITER AND DIRECTOR)

Film, 1957. Summary.

Based on a true story, this film opens during the aftermath of an explosion on a luxury liner far from shore. The ship sank so quickly that no S.O.S. signal was sent, and no lifeboats were lowered. Now, some twenty survivors are clinging to the one lifeboat that was launched. It is the captain's dinghy, and it can hold fourteen people maximum. The captain is dying, and he transfers his authority to his first officer, Alec Holmes, admonishing him to "save as many as you can." Holmes is hopeful that help may arrive, but when he realizes that no S.O.S. has been sent, he knows that their only option is to row for the coast of Africa, fifteen hundred miles away. Kelly, an officer and a friend of Holmes, himself mortally wounded, tells Holmes that he won't be able to make it if he tries to keep everyone alive—he must "evict some tenants" in order to save others. When Holmes wants to break the tedium by having the survivors tell their stories, Kelly advises him not to get to know everyone too well—because Kelly knows that sooner or later, Holmes will have to choose who will live and who will die, and such a decision will be much harder if everyone has bonded. To set an example, Kelly throws himself overboard, because he would only be a hindrance to the survival of the "fittest." Holmes at first will hear nothing of this plan, but when a storm approaches, he realizes that he must choose between the death of them all and the death of those who already are hurt and can't pull their weight. When desperate passengers plead with him to at least draw lots, or save the women and children, or call for volunteers, he refuses to consider all approaches other than his own choice: The survivors must be able to row and bail and must be strong enough to stay alive. Under protest and at gunpoint, the others comply by forcing the wounded passengers and crewmen, who are wearing life preservers, overboard, setting them adrift in shark-infested waters. One professor remarks, "This is an interesting moral problem," and insists that it is barbarism—the civilized thing to do would be to choose to die together.

Another passenger, moved by seeing a young boy lose both his parents to Holmes's weeding-out process, breaks out a knife and tries to force Holmes to turn around and look for the ones that were adrift. Holmes kills the man in self-defense, but not before the man succeeds in wounding Holmes with his knife. Now the storm hits, and all through the night the remaining passengers and crew struggle to keep afloat. When dawn breaks, and the storm dies down, everyone on board has survived, and there is a general feeling of goodwill toward Holmes—but he is suffering severely from his knife wound. Now Holmes applies his rule to himself and slips overboard so as not to be a burden, but the others rescue him and bring him back on board. Just as the passengers are getting ready to thank him for his foresight and effort, a ship is spotted on the horizon. Miraculously, help has arrived, "too soon," as a feisty woman passenger remarks—too soon for everybody to have decided to support Holmes in his plan to force some of the passengers overboard. The people on the boat are rescued (it is hinted that some of the evicted passengers are rescued too), and

Facing a hard decision, Captain Holmes (Tyrone Power) surveys the situation after the shipwreck in *Abandon Ship!* (Columbia Pictures, 1957). Soon he must decide which passengers are fit to row to Africa and which must be thrown overboard, sacrificed so that the others have a chance to survive. The story of *Abandon Ship!* is an illustration of a clash between utilitarian and deontological views.

Holmes goes on trial for murder. The film concludes with the question, "If you had been on the jury, would you have found Holmes guilty or innocent?"

Study Questions

1. Can this film be seen as a defense of utilitarianism? Explain why or why not.

2. Do you agree that it would have been a more civilized thing for all of the passengers to die together?

3. Would you have convicted Holmes of murder? (In actual fact he was convicted, but he received a short sentence because of the unusual circumstances.)

4. How might Ayn Rand have evaluated Holmes's solution?

5. Can you think of another way of solving Holmes's problem?

6. What was Holmes's intention? Might a Kantian accept that as morally good?

Narrative

The Insider

ERIC ROTH AND MICHAEL MANN (SCREENWRITERS)
MICHAEL MANN (DIRECTOR)

Based on "The Man Who Knew Too Much," a magazine article by Marie Brenner.
Film, 1999. Summary.

This film is based on the true story of one man making the decision to go public against the tobacco companies with his expert knowledge of the addictive nature of nicotine. In the context of this chapter, the plot illustrates the story of two men's sense of duty, regardless of the consequences, acting just for the sake of a moral principle. In light of the upcoming Chapter 7 you may want to apply theories of respect for persons, and negative and positive rights (the negative right of free speech, and the positive right of receiving truthful information). But, in the context of Chapter 8, we might also view it as the story of a person of integrity choosing to fight for what is right, even if the outcome may cost him everything—a story paralleling that of Socrates. And, in the context of Chapter 13, we can choose to view it as a story of media responsibility: What is the bottom line for a television show doing investigative reporting—doing business or serving the public?

One day in the mid-1990s Jeffrey Wigand comes home from work early. His wife is horrified when she learns that he has been fired. They live in an expensive home and have lots of medical expenses: Their oldest daughter has asthma, and his wife can't work because someone has to look after the little girl in case she has an attack. Wigand was a corporate VP in charge of research and development at Brown & Williamson, the tobacco giant. He has a severance package, but the future looks grim. It is only as the story unfolds that we realize just how grim it is going to get. By coincidence, at the CBS studios in New York, the producer of *60 Minutes,* Lowell Bergman, is putting together a story about a tobacco study and calls Wigand. To his surprise Wigand won't talk to him—but he faxes him cryptic messages, indicating that he'd like to be able to talk, but has a confidentiality agreement with his former company. Later, Brown & Williamson executives let Wigand know that since they suspect he has broken the agreement, they want him to sign a new, expanded one—and if he doesn't, he'll lose all benefits. Now Wigand is furious—at B&W for threatening his family and at Bergman, whom he believes has leaked the story. Bergman flies down from New York to Wigand's home to persuade him that he, Bergman, can be trusted, and Wigand then tells him the story: At a congressional hearing on the tobacco industry and nicotine some years back, seven CEOs—the Seven Dwarfs, as Wigand calls them—from the tobacco industry testified that nicotine was not an addictive drug. But Wigand knows that to be false. So why was he working for the tobacco company? The pay was good, and there was good medical coverage, even if he perceived that integrity within the industry was a problem.

Mike Wallace, the investigative journalist for *60 Minutes* who early in the film has been introduced as a man of integrity himself, suggests a way for Wigand to be able to speak on his show: What if he was subpoenaed as a witness in a smoker's lawsuit in Mississippi?

In this scene from The Insider (Touchstone, 1999), Jeffrey Wigand (Russell Crowe) is being interviewed by Mike Wallace for 60 Minutes. When the actual interview between Wigand and Wallace aired in 1998, the impact was tremendous. Wigand told the inside story about nicotine that the tobacco companies didn't want us to know: that it is an addictive drug, and cigarettes are the delivery device for the drug. The film uses blurry images (such as the foreground in this picture) and mirror reflections with much effectiveness, perhaps symbolizing the contrast between truth and falsehood.

Then his statement would be on record, and in this way he could get around the confidentiality agreement. So Bergman links Wigand up with the lawyer for the plaintiffs in the Mississippi lawsuit. Meanwhile, the Wigands have had to move out of their beautiful home and into a more modest house. He begins a new career as a high school science teacher and forces himself to adjust to the situation, but his wife finds the transition hard. When they start to receive death threats, Wigand decides that it is time to go public.

He agrees to an interview with Wallace on *60 Minutes*. During the taping he reveals that the tobacco CEOs perjured themselves when they claimed nicotine isn't addictive: Cigarettes, he says, are "delivery devices for nicotine." In addition, he reveals that Brown & Williamson is enhancing nicotine chemically so it is absorbed more rapidly by the brain and that he got fired because he wouldn't keep quiet. Mike Wallace asks him if he wishes he hadn't blown the whistle. At times, Wigand says, but he'd do it again, because he thinks it was worth it. Now things start to happen quickly for Wigand, but in a way he hadn't imagined: Security guards are moving into his home because of the threats, and his wife is leaving him, taking their children with her. They keep the house, so he has to move into a hotel room. He testifies in the Mississippi lawsuit, specifically stating that nicotine is a drug, but his deposition is sealed, unavailable to the public. And the *60 Minutes* crew is in for a surprise: CBS executives lean on them to cut Wigand's interview, claiming the broadcasting company may be sued by the tobacco company for "tortious interference," a third party interfering in a contract situation, creating damages for the first party (the tobacco company).

Bergman is livid: Why should lawyers be able to determine the content of *60 Minutes,* a program of investigative journalism which has proved its integrity over and over again? Is the priority business or news? To Bergman's enormous disappointment, Wallace caves: In the twilight of his career, he has to consider his legacy, and sides with the corporate lawyers. And now the tobacco company embarks on a smear campaign against Wigand, digging up any old secret they can find, such as a dismissed shoplifting charge, so his word will be discredited. Jeffrey watches the cut, gutted interview air and becomes despondent. Both Bergman and Wigand have so much to lose: one his self-esteem and reputation for professional integrity, the other his family and perhaps his life. After a heated, then conciliatory, talk with Wigand, Bergman decides it is time for desperate measures: He leaks the story to the *New York Times.* When the story appears on the front page of the paper, Wallace changes his mind: He will air the original interview. The CBS executive tries to argue that this story will only last fifteen minutes and then people will forget it, but Wallace reminds him that it is fame that only lasts fifteen minutes—infamy lasts longer than that. So Jeffrey Wigand gets to tell his side of the story on national TV. After the airing, Lowell Bergman quits. What was broken doesn't get put back together again.

Study Questions

1. Apply Kant's concept of the good will to Wigand's decision, and next to Bergman's choice. What makes these decisions examples of a good will?

2. Use the categorical imperative to decide, with Wigand and Bergman, whether their actions are morally good.

3. Use Kant's second rule, that people should never be used merely as a means to an end, to evaluate Wigand and Bergman's actions.

4. If you were in Jeffrey Wigand's position, what do you think you would have done? Is Wigand doing his "nearest duty"? Is that important?

Chapter Seven

Personhood, Rights, and Justice

$\mathcal{T}$o Kant, any being who is capable of rational thinking qualifies as a person, and (according to Kant's *Grounding for the Metaphysics of Morals*) creatures incapable of rational thinking are classified as things. Today, the debate about what constitutes a person is still with us because the question has lost none of its urgency. At the time when Kant lived, human beings were often treated as things, tools, stepping-stones for the needs or convenience of others. This idea was a legitimate part of public policy in many places throughout the world, and the moral statement that a rational being should never be reduced to a mere tool for another's purpose became part of the worldwide quest for human rights—rights that still have not been universally implemented. This statement is historically important and should not be forgotten, even though many social thinkers today believe that Kant's fight for the recognition that all persons deserve respect must be expanded and that Kant himself didn't have a concept of universal human rights in mind.

In this chapter we discuss issues that reflect several of the theories already studied and that illustrate how such theories can be applied on a social scale in creating policies regarding the rights and duties of citizens. It is thus important that you have studied Chapters 5 and 6 in particular before you proceed.

What Is a Human Being?

If we focus on the rights of human animals, we have to address the question, What does it mean to be human? Are the criteria physical? Does a being have to look human in order to be human? How detailed must we get? A traditional answer is "a featherless biped"—in other words, a creature that walks upright on two legs but is not a bird—but these are hardly sufficient criteria. Nowadays, if we want to use physical criteria, we include not only physical appearance but also genetic information. But with this type of explanation we're faced with two problems: (1) genetically, there are creatures that are 98 percent identical to the human but are obviously not human: chimpanzees; (2) there are individuals born of human parents who may not have all the human physical characteristics—for instance, persons with multiple physical disabilities (not to mention *mental* disabilities). So is a being born of humans who happens to have some physical aberration—from missing limbs to minor abnormalities such as extra toes and fingers—human? For most people today, the answer is obviously yes, but this was not always so. A worldwide tradition in pretechnological societies has been to dispose of newborns with physical "handicaps" ranging from missing limbs to unwanted birthmarks, and not all of these disposals can be explained by saying that a tribe isn't able to feed those who can't feed themselves. Our culture doesn't follow that practice, but some of us do screen the fetus for severe disabilities and perform abortions if we believe that these disabilities will condemn the child to a less than dignified life. This is not a discussion of the pros and cons of abortion, any more than it is a discussion of infanticide, but it does point out that a good deal of policymaking in other cultures as well as our own depends on how we define "human being," including what a human being, and a human life, *should be like*—a normative concept.

The Expansion of the Concept "Human"

There was a time when people distinguished between friend and foe by calling friends humans and foes beasts, devils, or such. At the tribal level of human history, it has always been common to view the tribe across the river as not quite human, even if members of your tribe marry their sons or daughters. (In fact, the usual word that tribes use to designate themselves is their word for "human," "the people," or "us.") In any geographic area there are people who remain dubious about those from the "other side" because their habits are so different that it seems there must be something "strange" about their general humanity. From the time of the ancient Greeks until quite recently, a common assumption has been that women are not quite human. Interestingly enough, this idea has been held not only by many men but also by many women, who took the men's word for it. (Some still do.) At the nationalistic level, it still is common practice to view foreigners as less than human, not in a physical sense, but, rather, politically and morally. And the humanity of a people's wartime enemies almost always is denied, usually because it becomes easier to kill an enemy, either soldier or civilian, if you believe he or she really is not quite as human as you are. Thus the term *human* sometimes evolves into an honorary term reserved for those with whom we prefer to share our culture. Historically, the meaning of the term in the Western world expanded to include not only "our people" but also "all Europeans" and, with the advent of the Enlightenment, all free white males of any nationality. In the nineteenth century the term was expanded again to cover women as well as people born into slavery.

Persons and Rights

Many social thinkers prefer the term *person* to *human being* as a philosophical and political concept, partly in order to avoid the association with the human physical appearance. A person is someone who is capable of psychological and social interaction with others, capable of deciding on a course of action and being held responsible for that action. In other words, a person is considered a *moral agent*. (See Box 7.1 for a discussion of the abortion issue and the idea of the fetus as a person.) Being a person implies certain duties and privileges—in other words, it is a normative concept: what a person *ought to be and do* in order to be called a person. Personhood implies that one has certain social privileges and duties and that under extreme circumstances these can be revoked. What was a person to the Greeks? To the Romans? To medieval Europeans? To these groups a person was usually a male adult landowner or tribe member. Different societies have excluded some or all of

Box 7.1   IS A FETUS A PERSON?

The debate over whether abortion should be generally available often focuses on the question of whether the fetus is a person. In some cultures the fetus is not a person at all; even the newborn infant is not considered a person until after a waiting period that usually is imposed to see if the baby will live. The view adopted by the Catholic Church (but not by all churches or religious communities) is that the fetus is a person from conception. This has not always been Catholic dogma, however. The idea underlying this viewpoint is that the soul is present when the fetus *looks* human; thus, in earlier times, a fetus was not considered a person until well into the pregnancy. Saint Augustine specifically states that terminating a pregnancy before the fetus is able to *feel* anything should not be considered homicide, because until that point in time the soul is not present. However, in the late seventeenth century, a primitive microscope seemed to show that a tiny, fully formed person (a *homunculus*) could be seen in the spermatozoon, and so church policy considering the fetus a person from conception was established. The policy remained unchanged even with the advent of better microscopes, which conclusively refuted the previous theory, and when the existence of the ovum was established in 1847. One can of course choose to view the beginning of life as the beginning of personhood regardless of church policies and misunderstandings about microscopes. In that case the argument against abortion is generally that if it is wrong to kill a human being, a person, then it must also be wrong to kill a fetus who is either a person from conception or a potential person and should therefore have the same rights as a born person. Within the Catholic tradition one can circumvent the ban on killing a fetus through the principle of the *double effect,* which states that one mustn't take a life under normal circumstances, but that it is permissible under very special circumstances: (1) Death must be an *unintended* side

In the seventeenth century a young scientist reported that he saw a small person, a homunculus, inside a sperm cell while looking through a primitive microscope. Presumably, he saw something like this image. He was never able to duplicate the experiment; nevertheless, since then, the official Catholic policy is that a fetus is a person from conception.

effect of accomplishing something else (a primary effect), such as saving a life; (2) the primary effect must be *proportionately* very serious so as to outweigh the death; and (3) causing the death is *unavoidable* and the only way to accomplish the primary effect. Thus a pregnant woman who has cancer of the uterus will get permission from the church to have an abortion because it will be part of the necessary medical process to remove the uterus. The removal of the uterus will kill the fetus, but it is an unavoidable and unintended side effect of saving the woman's life. However, a pregnant woman whose pregnancy itself is in danger of killing her receives no such permission because killing the fetus would in this case be intentional—regardless of the woman's life being in danger. We will meet the double effect again in Box 7.5 on euthanasia, as well as in Chapter 13 in the discussion of the just-war concept.

What does it take for us to identify a fetus as a person? There are thinkers today who believe that we can surely call the fetus a human being, but we can't call it a person because it takes more to be a person than just having human genetic material. The philosopher Mary Ann Warren argues that a being has to have (1) consciousness and ability

(continued)

Box 7.1   IS A FETUS A PERSON? *(continued)*

to feel pain, (2) a developed capacity for reasoning, (3) self-motivated activity, (4) capacity to communicate messages of an indefinite variety of types, and (5) self-awareness in order to be considered a person; thus even the most developed fetus does not qualify. But neither do newborn babies, according to this viewpoint; so in order to avoid the specter of infanticide, Warren argues that as long as anyone in our culture objects to infanticide, then it should be outlawed—not for the sake of the infant (who is not a person yet) but for the sake of people's feelings in general.

A slightly less radical view is presented by another philosopher, Judith Jarvis Thomson, who argues for a woman's right to an abortion by saying that it does not matter whether the fetus is a person: What matters is that a woman has a *right to defend her body against intrusions*—even if the fetus should qualify for personhood. Thomson (who wrote her famous contribution to the abortion debate in 1971, just prior to *Roe v. Wade*) compares the pregnant woman to a person—any one of us—who wakes up in a hospital bed and finds herself (or himself) attached with intravenous tubes to someone in the next bed, a famous violinist. Suppose, Thomson says, you are told that the violinist can't be moved, or else he will die, so he must be sustained by you for the next nine months (or eighteen years). Do you have a right to unplug yourself? Yes, even if it would mean an innocent violinist's death. For

Thomson there is a small catch, however: You must have tried to take precautions not to be in that situation. Furthermore, if it is only a small sacrifice to you, then you have a moral duty to go through with it—but the violinist still doesn't have any right to demand your life and freedom.

Other positions put forth by abortion rights advocates, based on the view that the fetus may be a person, at least late in the pregnancy, argue that even so, the rights of the fetus as a person do not outweigh the rights of the woman as long as the fetus is not viable (can't survive outside the woman's body).

It is possible to approach the abortion issue from both a utilitarian and a deontological point of view, regardless of whether one is pro-choice or anti-abortion (pro-life). The utilitarian approach focuses on the *consequences* of abortion: The anti-abortion utilitarian will point to the many deaths of unborn children, and the utilitarian who is an abortion rights advocate will point to the back-alley deaths that occur when women seek illegal and unsanitary abortions. The deontological approach focuses on the issue of *rights*: The anti-abortion deontologist will argue that the fetus, as a person, is being used merely as a means to an end, its life and rights disregarded; the deontologist who is an abortion rights advocate will argue that the rights granted by the personhood and life of the woman outweigh the rights of the fetus, at least until viability (in the third trimester).

the following people from their concept of a person: slaves, women, children, foreigners, prisoners of war, and criminals. (See Box 7.2 for a discussion of the personhood of people on the fringes of society, such as prostitutes and drug addicts.) Usually the list of exclusion was extended to animals, plants, and inanimate objects, but other beings might well have been granted personhood, such as gods and goddesses, totems (ancestor animals), and dead ancestors.

Today we in the Western world assume that all humans are persons with inalienable rights. This is not a recognized truth all over the world, however (and even in our own society we may have doubts about our landlord, our professor, or the neighbor's noisy kids, though such feelings are usually rather tongue-in-cheek). A more serious problem of recent years is the reemergence of *racism,* which can be seen as a reduction of the human fellow-feeling, a return of the reluctance to call other humans "persons." Perhaps this reluctance was always there, at a primitive level, but lately it seems more persistent for any of various reasons: fears of each other or the economy, a need for scapegoats, and so forth. It is also possible that the new racism is in some cases not directed against persons of other races as much as persons of other *social strata.* In other words, much of what today is called racism may also have elements of class-oriented fears. Although racism seems to have been on the rise in the 1980s and 1990s, it is certainly not the only form of hostility and bigotry in modern society.

Questions about who counts as a person arise in a number of areas. We may think we treat everybody as persons with equal rights, but our society still experiences problems with sexism; and *ageism,* discrimination against the elderly (or for that matter, discrimination against the young) because of their age, is now recognized as a common problem. In the 1980s and early 1990s, AIDS and HIV patients experienced much discrimination, but new laws and an increased level of understanding have lessened that form of bigotry to some extent. Mentally disabled and mentally ill citizens still feel stigmatized, and so do physically disabled people, to the point that there is now a new word for discrimination against the disabled: *ableism.*

Is a *criminal* a person? For many people, the more callous the crime, the less human the criminal. Sometimes we even call murderers "animals," although few nonhuman animals have been known to display the methodical, deliberate preying on one's own species typical of human career criminals, serial rapists, and serial killers. In our attitudes toward such criminals, much of our view of what counts as human is revealed: We're not trying to describe their genetic makeup, we're expressing a moral condemnation of their actions and choices. Calling a criminal an animal is a normative statement, not a descriptive one: He has not lived up to our expectations of what a person ought to be and do, and so we view him as less than human. But genetically as well as legally, a serial killer such as Robert Yates (see Box 7.2) is still a person, and the very fact that we choose to hold him accountable in court is proof of that. Had he been an "animal," we wouldn't have taken him to court—he would have been put down immediately, like a vicious dog. However, criminals, even convicted ones, don't lose all their rights: Their personhood status is not revoked, at least not in our culture. They still have the right not to be tortured, for example, although they may have lost their right to liberty. Below we take a closer look at the animal issue as well as the concept of rights.

Children as a group have not until recently been considered "real people." Until recently, child abuse was not considered a felony. In previous times—in fact, as recently as the nineteenth century and, in some places, the twentieth century—the father of the household had the supreme right to treat his family (including his wife) any way he pleased. This might very well include physically punishing all the family members, even unto death. This right, *patria potestas,* is still in effect in certain societies in the

Box 7.2   IS A PROSTITUTE A PERSON?

In April 2000 a man named Robert L. Yates, Jr., was arrested for the murders of nine women in Spokane, Washington. In order to avoid the death penalty, he pleaded guilty to all nine murders, plus four others, including two that came as a complete surprise to the police. To this day it is speculated that we have yet to hear the end of the story, since there are many more women missing in the Pacific Northwest. He had been committing these murders since the mid-1990s but had been able to evade capture by blending into society with a seemingly normal existence as an ex–military man, a Seventh-Day Adventist, a helicopter pilot, a husband, and a father of five. Another factor that may well have helped him evade capture was the nature of his victims: He preyed on women whose lifestyles included drug addiction and prostitution.

While the detectives on the task force assigned to the serial killings in Spokane seemed highly committed to solving them, one can't help wondering (as many did) whether more funding might have been put into the investigation if the women had been college students, businesswomen, shopkeepers, or housewives rather than hookers and drug addicts. This is by no means an isolated phenomenon: From San Diego to Seattle to New York State we have had examples of serial killings of prostitutes that perhaps a few police detectives took very seriously, but that in no way stirred the general outrage of the community. A local radio talk show in Spokane received several calls from listeners who expressed the opinion that the prostitutes somehow were asking for it, living a criminal life on the fringes of society, and that somehow the serial killer was just "cleaning up." But the radio hosts took on the capture of the murderer as a righteous cause, keeping up the pressure in the community and

criticizing the apathy among citizens as well as what they saw as inadequate police work, even when the killings seemed to stop. The hosts raised questions such as "Are these women not human beings with the same rights as the rest of us? Don't they have families who mourn them? Don't they feel pain and anguish in their last moments at the mercy of a murderer? It may be illegal to be a prostitute and to use drugs, but it doesn't carry a death penalty."

Months before Yates was captured a billboard had been erected in downtown Spokane, with photos of sixteen victims and the plea "Help Us Find Our Killer." The billboard helped many citizens of the city realize that each murdered woman had had a life that was precious, each was a person who would have liked to stay alive. It is now part of the civic identity of Spokane that the sheriff's department managed to catch an elusive serial killer—a rare feat. But serious questions have been raised about the professional standards and efficiency of the task force, indicating that a more concerted police effort combined with more experience and willingness to reach out to the public might have resulted in finding Yates sooner, and thus saving lives.

Another result of the serial killer investigation was that the community in the end seemed to understand that the murdered women were fellow citizens too. A great many people, as well as the media, showed up in court to hear Yates's sentence—408 years in prison—and stood by the relatives of the victims as they cried out their grief and outrage at the murderer, one after the other, while he offered scripted apologies to each in turn as part of his plea bargain. In the text you will find a discussion of the appropriateness of anger felt by victims and survivors (resentment) and by the community (moral indignation). One

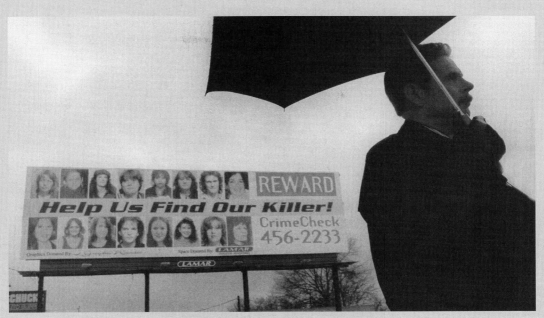

Copyright *Spokesman-Review,* Spokane

Years into the investigation of the serial murder of prostitutes, the Spokane sheriff's department appealed to the community for help, putting murder victims' faces on a billboard reading "Help Us Find Our Killer." The personalization of each woman may have inspired a change in attitude in the community toward the victims, from expendable outcasts to individuals with a right to live.

might say that on the day Yates was sentenced, the community did, at long last, stand up for the victims. Yates was later sentenced to death for two additional murders in Tacoma, Washington.

In the western part of the state, a similar situation unfolded in 2003–4: the capture, confession, and conviction of the notorious Green River Killer, Gary Ridgway. Ridgway had been killing prostitutes since the early 1980s in the Seattle-Tacoma area, and possibly elsewhere, and was captured due to excellent and foresighted police work. When confronted with incontrovertible evidence—his DNA linked to several of the victims—Ridgway confessed to forty-eight murders and thus avoided the death penalty. But in hour after hour of taped interrogations, he revealed to the police and the world that he didn't consider his victims as any different from trash: He killed them and threw them away. Interestingly, as with Robert Yates, the final chapter to Ridgway's long series of murders didn't generate much interest in the national press, and one is tempted to conclude that it has to do with the fact that their victims were "just" prostitutes.

world. The thought of protecting children against abuse, even abuse from their own parents, is actually quite a new idea in Western cultures; even in the recent past, child abuse cases were sometimes covered up or never reported. Starting in 2002, several Catholic priests were accused of having raped children in decades past. What angered many Americans (Catholics as well as non-Catholics) was not only the abuse, but the Catholic Church's apparent cover-up of the allegations and relocation of the priests to other regions. According to a study published in 2004 by the John Jay College of Criminal Justice, the percentage of Catholic clergy accused of molestations of children under eighteen between 1950 and 2002 is 2.7 percent, which may not sound like much—but the number translates into 4,398 priests and deacons, each presumably with multiple victims. While other religious groups report similar abuse cases against children and teens, there was widespread disappointment in the Catholic Church because of the perceived cover-ups, and also a widespread realization that the psychological damage done to these children is immeasurable. In the terminology of Kant, these children had been used merely as a means to an end. Today we recognize not only that children should be protected from abuse but also that children have interests and wishes that they are capable of expressing and that should be heard, such as which parent they wish to stay with after a divorce.

We are now at the point when the conscious interests of children (including everything from having enough food, shelter, love, and education to refusing to go to school in order to play video games or watch TV) must be balanced against what conscientious adults deem to be in the children's best interests, best *in spite of* themselves. In other words, we must remember that what children want is not necessarily good for them. The idea that children are minors who have neither the legal rights—nor the legal responsibilities—of adults is not about to disappear, even when their interests are taken into consideration. We tend to forget that when a group is excluded from having rights, it is usually also excluded from having responsibilities. In other words, such a group must be given legal protection so that its members, who are incapable of taking on civil responsibilities, will not be treated unjustly.

Historically, the idea of animals and children having responsibilities has shifted back and forth. Until the mid–nineteenth century, animals could be held legally responsible for their actions (although they had very few recognized rights); all through the European Middle Ages rats, roaches, and other pests were put on trial (usually in absentia) for the damage they caused to human lives and property. Even in the United States, animals were put on trial for hurting their masters or their own offspring, and they were "executed" if found guilty. Today, when an aggressive dog attacks a small child and is put to death, do we consider ourselves to be "executing" the dog? Some might argue that that is exactly what we are doing—we are punishing the dog for transgressing a human law. But legally we are simply disposing of the dog's owner's property not as a punishment against the dog but as a precaution in the public interest. Who *does* get punished? Not the dog, but the *owner,* who receives a fine or even a jail sentence. In San Francisco in 2002, a dog owner even received a second-degree murder sentence after her dogs attacked and killed a neighbor, but a judge later reduced the sentence to four years for manslaughter. Today we don't consider animals to be legally responsible for their actions, because we don't consider them to be moral agents. A dog who fails to wake up her owners when the house is on fire will not be blamed for it afterward, though her owners might be blamed for not training her properly. (In previous times, when animals were put on trial, the issue of whether they were moral agents still was not solved because it was commonly considered that they had no souls and thus had no free will. Were the people who put them on trial contradicting themselves? Yes. But so do we sometimes, and one of the objectives of discussing these issues is to get into the habit of thinking more consistently.)

The case of the legal responsibility of children parallels that of animals. It was only in the twentieth century that we in the Western world agreed not to hold minors responsible for criminal acts. The legendary German figure Till Eulenspiegel was a mischievous kid who played one too many tricks on decent citizens, and the decent citizens hanged him. The title character of Herman Melville's *Billy Budd* faced the same fate. Billy, a young sailor, was falsely accused of wrongdoing by a vicious officer. Because Billy had a problem articulating and could not speak up to defend himself, he acted out his frustration by striking the officer. Unfortunately, this resulted in the officer's death, and the captain, although aware of Billy's problem, had to follow the law of the sea: mandatory death for anyone who kills an officer. In the end, Billy had to submit to the traditional execution method by climbing up the rigging and slipping a noose around his own neck. Today a crime committed by a person under the age of eighteen must reveal an extraordinary amount of callousness and "evil intent" in order for the court to try the minor as an adult. This is because childhood is considered to be a state of mind and body that doesn't allow for the logical consistency we assume is available, most of the time, to adults; therefore children aren't held accountable for their actions to the degree that adults are.

The United States, however, has seen a shift lately in the attitude toward children who commit crimes. Although most child psychologists still agree that children below the age of seven or eight don't know enough about the difference between right and wrong to be held accountable, public demand is now growing for trying older child offenders as adults. What should the court do with a child who kills another child for his sneakers or his jacket? Or who takes a gun to school and kills a number of his classmates and teachers before being stopped? In some states, such as Arkansas, children cannot be tried as adults. In other states, it is the severity of the crime that determines whether the youth will be tried as an adult; we have lately seen teenagers being given hefty prison sentences (although the Supreme Court decided in 2005 that a child under eighteen can't be given the death penalty). The issue of when a child can be held criminally responsible for his or her actions is the focus of much current legal attention. For example, in 2000, thirteen-year-old Nathaniel Abraham was convicted of second-degree murder after being tried as an adult for a murder he committed at age eleven. He was *sentenced* as a juvenile, however, and was to be held in a juvenile detention facility until the age of twenty-one but had his prisoner status reduced in 2004 because of good behavior and will likely be able to reenter society shortly. An illustration of how times have changed since the 1970s is the case of Michael Skakel, indicted in 2000 for the 1975 murder of his fifteen-year-old neighbor, Martha Moxley. Skakel, a cousin of the Kennedy family by marriage, was himself fifteen years old at the time, and the state of Connecticut would, in

1975, have considered him a juvenile who could not therefore be tried as an adult. That law was changed a few years later, but Skakel's attorney argued, unsuccessfully, that Skakel, now very much an adult, should be tried as a juvenile. In 2002 he was tried as an adult and found guilty of murder.

In the past, the rights of women have followed a course similar to those of animals and children. Women had very few rights until the late-nineteenth century—no right to hold property, no right to vote, no right over their own person. This went hand in hand with the common assumption that women were not capable of moral consistency and thus were not responsible (mention of women and children in the same breath was no coincidence). This view often coincided with a male reverence for women and their supposedly higher moral standards, but such reverence was often combined with an assumption that women were idealists with no conception of the sordid dealings and practical demands of the real world.

When it applied to women, the practice of holding only those with rights legally responsible was not strictly adhered to. Many, many women were put on criminal trial. Even so, the general idea was that withholding rights from women *protected* them from the harsh world of reality, whose demands they weren't capable of answering. A similar kind of argument kept slaves from having rights throughout most slaveholding societies—rights were denied in order to provide "protection" for these people because they were "incapable." This did not preclude punishing slaves, of course, as anyone who has read *Huckleberry Finn* knows. In *On Liberty* (see Chapter 5), John Stuart Mill argues that the right to self-determination should extend universally, *provided* that the individuals in question have been educated properly, in the British sense, so that they know what to do with the self-determination. Until then, they are incapable of making responsible decisions and should be protected—children by their guardians and colonial inhabitants by the British. (Today, an animal rights activist might argue that we see the same pattern repeated with animals: We don't believe them to be fully developed moral agents, and so we protect them—by withholding rights from them.) An interesting concept evolves from these arguments; namely, that it is possible for someone to be considered a person, but a person with *limited* rights, duties, and privileges whose rights are assigned to a guardian. We will return to this idea in Chapter 13.

Science and Ethics in the New Millennium

As it stands now, we must agree that our culture has come a long way in terms of recognizing all postnatal humans as persons, at least in principle, although that principle sometimes seems to be overpowered by controversy. But what about the future? Genetically engineered children already walk among us, and there will be many more. Your children—and perhaps even you yourself—may be able to look forward to a longer, healthier life span due to genetic engineering. By the time you're reading this, there may be viable human clones among us too, legally or otherwise. Will these new members of our human family be considered persons, or will they encounter some new form of discrimination? In the Narratives section you'll find two stories that explore either end of this spectrum of possibilities: The film *Blade Runner* envisions a near future where genetically engineered "replicants" will be used as disposable people, slaves in the service of humans. The film *Gattaca* suggests a world, right around the corner, where genetic engineering has become mainstream, and it is those who have *not* been genetically "improved" at the embryo stage who will form the new underclass. Who will really be up, and who will be down, in such a "brave new world"?

We can ask ourselves two questions here: Given that a future involving a variety of options for genetic engineering and cloning is already upon us, (1) how should we deal with the scientific possibilities opening up for humanity? Should we be phobic about scientific developments and encourage bans and limits to scientific research? Or, should we encourage all such research under the assumption that somehow it may benefit us and that science has a right to seek knowledge for the sake of knowledge no matter the consequences? Or perhaps some position in between? (2) Should scientists themselves exercise some form of moral responsibility, taking into consideration that their results will be used in the future, perhaps to the detriment of humans and animals living in that future? In this section we take a look at one of the most burning issues today: the question of science and moral responsibility.

In 1968 a book came out in Germany which challenged the traditional scientific view that science is value-free, or morally neutral: the philosopher Jürgen Habermas's *Knowledge and Interest*. Scientists had claimed—some still do—that scientific research is done for the sake of knowledge itself, not for the social consequences it might bring. As such, scientists' professional integrity hinges on impeccable research; they have no responsibility to the community in terms of what problems—or even benefits—their research might lead to in the future. Habermas claimed that science might attempt to be objective but that an element of vested interest is always present. Society will fund only those projects it deems "valuable" for either further scientific progress, prestige, or profit. Political concerns, social biases, and fads within the scientific community often influence the funding of scientific research projects. Researchers often choose projects for similar reasons. Furthermore, the data selection (choosing research materials according to what the researcher finds relevant to the project) is influenced by the interests of the researcher—whether we like it or not. Habermas's point is that we may think science is conducted in a value-neutral way, but it is not. In addition, having seen what harm irresponsible scientists can cause to a society, wouldn't it be appropriate for scientists to conduct their research with a sense of obligation to the future? And for the community to monitor scientific research?

The question posed by the scientist Malcolm in *Jurassic Park* sums up the issue of "science without responsibility": Just because it is possible for science to create dinosaurs, does it mean that science *should* do it? After all, there is an underlying suspicion that some scientific research is done strictly to see whether it can be done.

Medical doctors of the past had their own share of moral problems: An army surgeon would have to decide which of the wounded soldiers he should operate on and which ones should be left to die. A nineteenth-century family doctor might have to choose between saving a young mother dying in childbirth or the infant being born. But today, technology allows medical procedures that would have been unimaginable a few generations ago. Life can be prolonged artificially; pregnancies can be terminated with comparative safety for the woman; genetic engineering can save babies from a life of illness while they are still in the womb; women can give birth after menopause; stem cell research promises to cure diseases; and the Human Genome Project, completed in 2000, suggests a future in which we will have mapped human DNA to the point of understanding and preventing a vast array of medical problems. In addition, the old science fiction dream (or nightmare) of creating children completely outside the womb of the mother now looks as if it might become a reality, with recent experiments at Cornell University involving an artificial womb. With the increased knowledge, however, comes an increase in moral problems.

In this new era of medical possibilities, there are few established rules to guide those making the decisions. For this reason, the medical profession has a vested interest in supporting the creation of a viable set of ethical procedures to follow in the gray areas of decision making. If healthy babies can one day be created in an artificial womb environment, what will that mean for the concept of *viability,* a concept that is essential to the abortion debate? Viability means that a fetus could, with medical assistance, survive outside the mother's body; at present, viability is set at the third trimester (so abortion becomes problematic at this time because the fetus will at that point be considered a person). But if viability can be extended backward into the second and even first trimester, does that mean that an early fetus thus becomes a person, not just in a religious sense, but in a legal sense as well? And what will that mean for the abortion debate? Further questions abound when we turn to DNA-related issues: When we finally have the complete ability to interfere purposefully with the human DNA code, how much is too much interference? Should we interfere strictly to prevent terminal diseases, or is it acceptable to interfere with nature in order to determine the shape of the baby's nose, for example? And given the limited resources of medicine, who should benefit from organ transplants—first come, first served? The young, the wealthy, the famous? Those who have waited the longest? Another element of the discussion of medical ethics is the attitude of society toward sick people—in particular, terminally ill people with communicable diseases. Should they remain part of society, or should they be locked away and forgotten? Do we as citizens act ethically toward contagious fellow citizens, or do we send them to leper colonies or other such places?

In the seventeenth and eighteenth centuries, the early years of modern science, the moral sensitivity that accompanied research seems to have differed from that which prevails today. The main concern of scientists then was how to proceed with research without violating the values believed to be expressed in the Bible. In modern times, scientists have occasionally diverged from the path of ethical behavior. In Nazi Germany the ultimate value was success for the Party and the realization of that abstract concept, "the Fatherland." Scientists in Nazi Germany engaged in painful, humiliating, and eventually fatal experiments on human subjects, primarily women and children. Even now, we occasionally learn that, since World War II, scientists have subjected people to experimental medical procedures or have withheld treatment from them— without their knowledge or consent. The Tuskegee Syphilis Study is one of the best known of these experiments. Less well known is the forced sterilization of about 7,500 people in Virginia from 1924 to 1979 based on the ideology of eugenics. California was also active in the eugenics project, sterilizing over 20,000 people.

Most scientists and laypeople today would agree that knowledge can come at a price in suffering that is too high; yet we have a credo that says science is value-free: Scientific research is supposed to be objective, and scientists are not to be swayed by personal ambitions and preference. But does that mean they are not supposed to be swayed by ethical values either?

Medical and general scientific researchers now have capabilities that could only be dreamed of in previous generations. We are only slowly developing a set of ethical rules by which to judge these capabilities, however. Genetic manipulation makes possible a future such as the one Aldous Huxley fantasized about in his *Brave New World,* one with a human race designed for special purposes. Agriculture has for several years been making use of genetic engineering to create disease-resistant crops. Milk and meat are being irradiated before they hit the stores. And perhaps the most controversial issue: *Transgenic* animals are being patented, such as pigs that have had human genes placed in them to facilitate organ transplants, and goats that have been genetically manipulated to contain spider silk proteins in their milk to be extracted and combined to produce materials of unprecedented strength. Although it may be to humankind's ultimate advantage to have access to these wonders, failure to contain such laboratory-generated genetic material, or failure to foresee the overall consequences of such genetic tinkering, could have disastrous results if no sense of ethics or social responsibility is instilled to guide the decision of researchers. After all, the infamous killer bees (which have now settled comfortably in the southwestern United States) are the result of a lab experiment gone out of control.

In Europe there is now a general mistrust of the entire idea of genetically engineered food products, from grain to farm animals. But what about genetically engineered humans?

In 2000 a little boy was born specifically in order to try to save the life of his older sister. Six-year-old Molly Nash had a congenital blood disease that would, in all probability, take her life before the age of ten. Doctors used "preimplantation genetic diagnosis" (PGD) to select an embryo in vitro that was both free of the disease and a good match as a blood cell donor. A month after the baby, Adam, was born, stem cells from his umbilical cord blood were transplanted into his sister. Molly was given the transplant while she held her little brother in her arms. Three months later she was allowed to return home from the hospital to her parents and her new brother, with her chances of survival improved to 85 percent.

Such are the possibilities opening up to us with genetic engineering. Then why are some people worried about the social consequences of this miracle cure? Because we, as a society, have not decided where we'd draw the line: Do we endeavor to create healthy babies, or should we go further, such as customizing babies according to their parents' specifications—or even to society's needs? Will babies be genetically engineered for sex, height, eye color, and skin color? And will those babies who have been genetically engineered be the new society's favorites, leaving the natural-born children behind as a new underclass? Molly and Adam Nash's doctor was quick to emphasize that the parents' use of PGD was acceptable because "they were not selecting in a eugenic sense," just looking for a donor baby. The doctors also outlined what they would consider unacceptable uses of the PGD technology, such as aborting selected implanted embryos just to collect tissue or putting the baby up for adoption after using its cord blood—in other words, using such babies merely as a means to an end, as Kant would say.

Although still controversial to many, stem cell research holds great promise as a means of repairing and replacing damaged organs. Stem cells are general cells, not yet specialized, and they apparently have the capacity to become any organ in the body, with the intervention of medical science. The controversy arises from the practice of harvesting and cloning stem cells from *embryos,* which involves taking the life of the embryo. If one is against abortion at any time during pregnancy because one considers the embryo a person from conception, one will also be against any form of stem cell research involving human embryos. However, contrary to what some people think, stem cells can't be harvested from aborted fetuses (yet) because they are too old; the stem cells have to be harvested within the first two weeks of fetal development at the zygote stage. In the summer of 2001, President George W. Bush laid down rules for future stem cell research so that no embryo would be conceived for the specific purpose of being used for stem cell research. Some seventy lines of stem cells are already in existence in various labs, however, and those have been made available for research. The question of what weighs heavier—existing humans whose lives are in peril, and who could be saved with stem cell research, or the lives of unborn fetuses—is something that divides entire intellectual and political communities today. Those who view early abortion as a reasonable option for women generally take little moral issue with the notion of zygotes being harvested and used for research; but for many who find the notion of taking the lives of fetuses objectionable, the stem cell question is particularly challenging—because even if one views the life of a fetus as intrinsically valuable, one also has to consider the importance of born humans who have lives, and people who love them, and who could be saved from a premature death with stem cell research.

A side effect of knowledge about a person's DNA profile was anticipated by new legislation a few years ago that prevents insurance companies and workplaces from discriminating against persons based on their DNA. An increased risk of cancer or early heart disease should not hurt a person's chances of employment or insurance— but it is not hard to imagine a future where such rules could be sidestepped.

Genetic engineering is closely related to another high-profile contemporary medical issue, *cloning.* A genetically engineered person is someone whose DNA has been manipulated before birth to avoid certain congenital problems or perhaps to enhance certain traits. A cloned person is someone who is, physiologically, a copy of another individual. The excitement and concerns about cloning began in 1994, with the announcement that researchers had successfully split a fertilized (but nonviable) human ovum into twins (which is what happens naturally to produce identical twins). But since then the cloning issue has taken off with a speed not even predicted by science fiction authors: In rapid succession, labs around the world have succeeded in cloning sheep, calves, goats, and mice, using a variety of techniques, including creating a copy of an adult individual using a cell from that individual with a technique pioneered by the creators of Dolly the sheep—raising the specter of genderless reproduction.

With the successful cloning of mice, scientists now seem ready to do any customized cloning their prospective customers may want as long as viable DNA is available—from duplicating your aging beloved mutt to creating custom-made pigs with human organs to resurrecting extinct woolly mammoths. The imagination is the only limit. In 2004 we had the first report of a successful cloning of a cat for commercial purposes: Not the first cat to be cloned, this little kitty was the first *made-to-order* clone. A woman had lost her 17-year-old cat and had had the cat cloned, to the tune of $50,000. The public reaction was not so much in response to the moral implications of the cloning itself as to the price tag: While some people found that it was a disgustingly high sum to spend on one's own selfish needs and pointed out that stray cats are looking for good homes, others found that people should be able to spend their money any way they see fit, be it on the re-creation of a beloved pet or buying luxury items. But we shouldn't forget that the pet-cloning venture has another side to it: We may be able to get our pets back in the flesh, so to speak, but we can't replicate their spirit or personality, because that would take duplication of the formative experiences of the original pet—meaning, we would need to replicate their childhood. Living beings don't consist just of their DNA but are also the sum of their experiences—and that goes for humans too. There are lessons to be learned about the entire notion of cloning: In order to get the "same" individual as its DNA donor, we would have to create a completely identical environment for the individual to grow up in—*nature* plus *nurture*. And even if that were accomplished, we would have to factor in what we might call *situation awareness,* what some would call *free will* (see Chapter 4), at least for humans: When a cloned child finds out he or she has been cloned, will he or she decide to be as similar as, or as different from, the original as possible? I would assume the latter, but you never know. This means that very little can in fact be predicted about how a clone might develop as an adult.

What we are talking about here is not the *therapeutic* cloning done from stem cells, the cloning that so many people hope will help cure illnesses of born humans, but the possibility of *reproductive* cloning, creating human beings as genetic copies of other human beings. In 2001 a lab in Massachusetts announced that it had cloned the first human embryo, consisting of six cells, after which the experiment was halted. That same year an Italian and an American doctor initiated attempts at cloning childless humans, but so far no scientifically verified results have been announced. The general assumption has been that scientists who attempt to clone humans for reproductive purposes are playing God and that there is no acceptable reason that anyone would want themselves cloned. Some have questioned the entire idea of human cloning from a religious point of view and have asked whether cloned children will have souls. Scientists have responded that if twins have individual souls (which is of course a matter of faith, not of science), then surely clones will have their own individual souls too. Other arguments against cloning include these:

- Overpopulation threatens the planet as it is, so why add more people artificially?
- Why create people who, as copies of someone else, will have to struggle to find their identity?

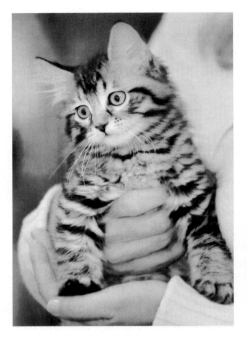

This little bundle of joy, "Little Nicky," cost his owner Julie $50,000. He was cloned from "Nicky," who had passed away, by the company Genetic Savings and Clone. They now hope to be able to clone dogs too. Does it matter what the price tag is, if we feel that we get a beloved pet back? And does it matter if the clone does not have exactly the same personality as the original?

- Clones might be considered expendable people, a new slave population—or perhaps so valuable that they would become a preferred population group. In other words, cloning might lead to a new form of discrimination.

- Animal cloning has led to individuals with abnormal physical traits being born. Aren't we risking the same thing making human clones?

These are good questions, but before we become too "scientophobic," we should reconsider the issue. What does reproductive cloning entail? Some imagine that a cloned embryo can be frozen and later "activated" for spare parts. Others focus on human cloning as the answer to being childless. But why would anyone want to have himself or herself cloned? Why not opt for adopting an already existing child who needs a home? Well, for some people the whole point is to have a child who is *related* to them, and cloning would provide that (but here we should note that the clone would be a blood relative, a twin, of just one of the parents, not both). The reasons people want babies are complex: Some people want children so they can love them and raise them to be good citizens; others want an additional hand on the farm, an heir to their name, a tax write-off, or a status symbol to parade in front of their friends. We have yet to set up legal rules for what reasons are *good* reasons to have children (although we already have an idea of which reasons count as *morally* good reasons). Excluding some prospective parents from parenthood because they'd like a kid who looks like themselves will exclude a whole lot more people than those lined up to be cloned. Some say, If it can be done, it will be done, so why make an issue of it? Supply and demand will rule! A viable alternative approach probably lies somewhere in the middle: The day will indeed come when we have human clones, from occasional individuals created to carry on the family name or be the bearer of the cherished face of a departed loved one to the nightmare scenario of mass-produced "worker ants." We need to think carefully about the implications of this technology for society and about the need for legislation. We have to consider the difference between a cloned child who would be loved and cared for by its parents and one who might be used or enslaved for society's purposes. Perhaps the bottom line, as with any planning involving a child, is whether that child can reasonably expect a stable, loving home—not the circumstances of the child's conception. There is a wide variety of issues for legislators and ethicists to consider in the twenty-first century.

Questions of Rights

We have already referred to the concept of rights several times; now we are going to take a closer look at what it entails. In Western culture today it is generally assumed that all people have rights; the nature and extension of these rights is continually being disputed, however. In the seventeenth century some European thinkers began to advocate the idea of *natural rights,* and this idea became very important in the eighteenth century with its many social revolutions. A natural right was defined as a right one was born with as a human being (or as a male human being, as it was most often argued). Sometimes the concept of natural rights is intended as descriptive (as in, "We are actually born with rights"), and sometimes its intention is normative ("We ought to have such rights because we are human"). The utilitarian Jeremy Bentham had his doubts about the concept of natural rights. His response to the Declaration of the Rights of Man (1789) of the French Revolution—and implicitly also to the American Declaration of Independence (1776)—was that all men are obviously *not* born free, and they are *not* born or do not remain equal in rights. (Nor should they—someone has to give the orders, he says. We can't have associations between equal members, such as equality in marriage—Bentham believed that would never work out!) People are not born with rights because the concept of rights is a human invention and does not occur in nature. One might wish it did, he says, but it doesn't. So for Bentham, the concept of natural rights is "nonsense upon stilts." That doesn't mean we can't operate with the concept of rights though; we must just recognize it as a legal principle (not a natural one) and identify its goal as being the creation of as happy a society as possible—in other words, maximizing happiness for the maximum number of people (the basic utilitarian principle).

You may remember John Stuart Mill's insistence that there ought to be such a thing as a personal right to be left alone if you are not harming anybody else (the "harm principle"). As in so many other areas, Mill is here redefining utilitarianism from within, but he still remains a utilitarian; his ultimate reason for setting limits on government involvement in people's private affairs is the overall happiness of the population. There is no such thing as a concept of "rights" or "justice" for its own sake in utilitarianism, even in Mill's version: The ultimate goal is still the general happiness, not an abstract principle of justice. We have to go to another theory in order to find a defense of the concept of rights for their own sake, not for what good so-cial consequences may come of enforcing them: to Kant's deontology. As you have read in Chapter 6, he insists that human beings are ends in themselves and may not be treated merely as a means to an end. This means that even if treating a person as a means to an end might be useful for the majority in a society, it is still not per-missible to do so. Good overall consequences for a majority do not provide a suffi-cient reason to do away with the rule that every person deserves respect. The question of whether decisions affecting many people in a society should be made on the basis of social utility or individual rights is still very much part of the contem-porary debate, as we shall see.

What Is Equality?

When we try to define equality, we sometimes feel as much confusion as Saint Augus-tine did in trying to define time: "When you don't ask me, I know what it is; when you ask me, I don't know." We tend to think equality has something to do with treating everybody the same way—but since everybody is not the same, or even similar, how can that be fair? And we know that equality and fairness are supposed to be linked. There are actually several definitions of equality:

1. **Fundamental equality** is the concept we know from the American Declara-tion of Independence and the French Declaration of the Rights of Man and of the Citizen. The American Declaration reads, "We hold these truths to be self-evident, that all men are created equal, that they are endowed by their Creator with certain unalienable Rights, that among these are Life, Liberty, and the pursuit of Happiness." The French Declaration begins, "All men are by nature free and equal in respect of their rights." However, these declarations do not say that people *are* factually equal—such as equally tall, strong, pretty, or smart—just that people *should be treated as* equals by their government and their legal system: no special privileges, just an en-titlement to respect and consideration as human beings.

2. **Social equality** refers to the idea of people being equal within a social setting, such as politics or the economy. Today, most Western political theories are in tune with the idea of fundamental equality, but what exactly social equality (and indeed "people") can mean is variable: The French Revolution did not see women as socially or politi-cally equal with men, and neither did the American Declaration of Independence, al-though Thomas Jefferson himself has been quoted as being opposed to viewing women as second-class citizens or as property. People of color were generally not considered in-cluded in the social equality of the Declaration of Independence either, although Jeffer-son seemed to have had some second thoughts about that too. Social equality today is generally obtained through such formal rights as the right to vote and to stand for pub-lic office; however, that doesn't mean that everyone's social status or income is supposed to be equal.

3. **Equal treatment for equals** is an ancient idea, in glaring contradiction to the fundamental equality principle; we find it in Aristotle's *Politics*. Justice means treating people of the same, usually social, group in the same way. But since we don't know from the definition what it would take to be considered an "equal," it is generally as-

sumed to be an elitist principle with no underlying intent to recognize equality as a fundamental human right.

Sometimes an alternative definition is proposed: *Treat equals equally and unequals unequally.* At first sight this looks like principle (3), equal treatment for equals, but there is a potential difference. It may look like a principle of elitism and bigotry, but who are "equals"? And who are "unequals"? Instead of pointing to a social or political group or saying that "equals" means "everybody," let's say that "equals" in this definition are people who are in a similar situation under similar circumstances. Imagine the freeway at rush hour: We are all out there in our cars, either moving at high speeds or simply stuck. We don't know each other, but we all deserve respect and decent treatment from each other, no more and no less. Now imagine a person trying to change lanes so he can reach the next exit, because he has some kind of emergency— a flat tire, a sick passenger perhaps. He signals, and you let him go in front of you. Because of his situation he is in fact an "unequal," in special need of assistance. Now imagine that someone else up ahead is impatient and wants to get off the freeway, so she cuts in front of someone else and causes him to brake hard, resulting in a couple of fender benders that include your car. Now that person has also become an "unequal" and deserves special, "unequal" treatment that others don't get unless they have transgressed: punishment. So the principle states that under ordinary circumstances we are just "equals" and deserve the usual decent treatment and respect. When someone has special needs, he or she becomes an "unequal" who needs assistance in order to reach the level of those who are "equals." And when someone breaks the rules, he or she also becomes an unequal and deserves special punishment (see the later section on criminal justice). The principle of *treating equals equally and unequals unequally* is in harmony with the fundamental equality principle, but it is more elaborate because it recognizes that we sometimes have special needs or sometimes transgress and so sometimes deserve special treatment. The principle supports affirmative action, if people who have experienced the effects of discrimination are considered to be "unequals" in the sense that the "playing field" is not yet level and that some "players" need special assistance before everyone on the field will actually have equal opportunities.

One thing the principle of equality usually does not imply is *sameness.* What would it be like if we were required to treat others and to be treated in exactly the same way, even if we are physically different? Kurt Vonnegut's short story "Harrison Bergeron" (1970) is a scathing parody of a future society in which it is politically incorrect (years before the term became popular) to be smarter, stronger, or more beautiful than anyone else. In Bergeron's future the smart people wear caps with buzzers that prevent them from thinking a thought through; the beautiful people wear bags over their heads so the less-than-pretty people won't feel bad. Dancers are weighed down with lead so ungraceful people won't feel left out, and strong people wear lots of bags of lead so they won't have an advantage over the weaker ones. Vonnegut doesn't write about how the truly disabled might feel about such artificial disabling or about what constitutes "normal" sameness, but the story does effectively question the identification of sameness and equality.

Dworkin: Rights Can't Be Traded for Benefits

A contemporary thinker who uses Kant's approach to the issue of rights is the American philosopher Ronald Dworkin. For Dworkin the importance of rights becomes apparent precisely at the moment when social considerations might justify the violation of those rights; we may think that our rights are protected by the Constitution, but there is such a thing as a constitutional amendment. Could we imagine a situation so serious that horrible social consequences will ensue if certain rights are not set aside for the common good? In other words, when push comes to shove, should we adopt a utilitarian view that social benefits outweigh the rights of the individual, or should we, along with Kant, hold the rights of the individual higher than social benefits? Dworkin asks us to consider an example: the right to free speech. Suppose someone, angered by some personal or collective experience, gets up and speaks in public, in an emotional manner, advocating violence as a way to secure political equality. Suppose the emotional speech starts a riot, and suppose people get hurt or even killed. Many would say that if such a situation can be prevented by making such a type of speech illegal, then that is the course we have to take. Dworkin would not. He argues that we can use one of two models for our political thinking about rights:

1. The first model says we have to find a balance between the rights of the individual and the demands of society. If the government *infringes* on a right, it does the individual wrong; but if it *inflates* a right, it does the community wrong (by depriving it of some benefit, such as safe streets). So we should steer a middle course and take each situation on a case-by-case basis. Well-behaved discussion groups can have more freedom of speech than unruly demonstrators because there is more social risk involved in the demonstration. This model of balancing the public interest against personal claims sounds reasonable, but it is not, says Dworkin. If we adopt the model, he asserts, we will have given up on two very important ideas: One is the idea of human dignity (Kant would say, Don't treat people merely as means), and the other is the idea of political equality (if one person has a certain freedom, then all persons should have that freedom, regardless of the effect on the general good). In Dworkin's words (from his book *Taking Rights Seriously*):

> So if rights make sense at all, then the invasion of a relatively important right must be a very serious matter. It means treating a man as less than a man, or as less worthy of concern than other men . . . then it must be wrong to say that inflating rights is as serious as invading them.

So we can't balance individual rights against social goods; what we *can* do is balance individual rights against each other when the claims collide, because then each individual still retains his or her dignity. But the best proof that the first model doesn't work, says Dworkin, is that it is *not* applied in actual cases in which the stakes for the individual are the highest: in criminal processes. Social benefits don't determine the outcome of a trial. The adage says, It is better that many guilty people go free than that one innocent person be punished, and this is Dworkin's choice for his second model.

2. The second model says that invading a right is far worse than inflating it. If people are prevented from expressing themselves freely and in any way they like,

Box 7.3 DWORKIN'S MODEL AND THE SECOND AMENDMENT

Dworkin's discussion involving his two models is directed specifically toward the First Amendment, which includes the right to free speech. His first model says we have to find a balance between the right of the individual and the needs of the community, and his second model (which he favors) says that invading or restricting a right for the sake of the needs of the community is wrong and should be done only in very rare cases. In the chapter text you find an analysis of the second model and freedom of speech—but how might Dworkin's model work if we apply it to the Second Amendment, the right to bear arms? The Second Amendment says that "A well-regulated Militia being necessary to the security of a free State, the right of the people to keep and bear Arms shall not be infringed." This amendment has been considered controversial for decades; for many liberals the right to bear arms is (1) outdated, (2) dangerous, and (3) a misinterpretation of the Bill of Rights, which, according to some interpreters, says only that militia members should have the right to be armed. For many moderates and conservatives, there is no doubt, however,

that the amendment addresses individuals ("the people") and their right to bear arms, not just militia members. Furthermore, many supporters of the Second Amendment quote Aristotle: "Both oligarch and tyrant mistrust the people, and therefore deprive them of their arms." Regardless of what Dworkin might say about the right to gun ownership per se, how would his principle apply to the Second Amendment? If we apply the *first model*, balancing the right to own guns with the need of the community for security, Dworkin would have to conclude that individual rights shouldn't be balanced against social goods—individual rights can only be balanced against other individual rights. His *second model* would state it in even stronger terms: Someone's right to bear arms should not be abridged just because someone else might choose to harm others because of that right. Would this example of Dworkin's principle used on another amendment make you agree with his principle all the more, or less? You may want to revisit the Narrative *Runaway Jury* in Chapter 5 for an expanded debate about the issue.

then that is an assault on human personality, and all the more so if the subject of a speech is morally important to the speaker. The only time that the government might actually be allowed to step in would be if the consequences of such a speech would very certainly be grave. But when is anyone that certain? According to Dworkin the risk involved is speculative; someone's right to free speech should not be abridged just because someone else might harm others as a result of that speech. This is the only way to protect the rights of individuals and in particular the rights of the few against the many. For a discussion of Dworkin's model and the second amendment, see Box 7.3.

Dworkin seems to imply that freedom of speech (which might lead to violence) is typically used to defend the idea of human dignity; in other words, most decent people might agree with the content of the speech, if not with its emotional character. That may not always be the case. You might want to consider Dworkin's second model in the scenario of an inflammatory racist hate speech being delivered on your campus. Would you say that the right of the speaker to express a personal opinion is more important than the harmful effects on the group being targeted for hatred or even the harmful effects on the audience being stirred up? Lately we have seen several examples not only of hate speech but of supremacist demonstrations (one being a Ku Klux Klan demonstration in the aftermath of the murder of an African American hitchhiker in Jasper, Texas). Although such demonstrations have drawn scant participation and hardly any spectators, the risk of riots and mayhem is still very much a factor, with the possibility of lives lost in the process. According to Dworkin's second model, such demonstrations should be allowed to take place because the rights of demonstrators should not be invaded (the First Amendment allows not only freedom of *speech* but also freedom of *assembly*). But the Constitution grants no right to create a public disturbance. So critics of Dworkin's second model suggest a middle course: Certainly we have freedom of speech and freedom of assembly—but that doesn't entail an automatic police permit to march in a demonstration. So let those who want to exercise their freedom of speech assemble someplace, in a hall or on a street corner, but limit the possibility of harm to the public if the issue is volatile. The tendency in our society is increasingly to move toward protection of the public rather than protection of the individual's right to freedom of speech, assembly, or movement. Some years ago judges were generally reluctant to issue restraining orders against domestic abusers because of their right to freedom of movement; today such restraining orders are much more common. You might want to argue about rights within this scenario from the viewpoints of Dworkin and John Stuart Mill. Box 7.4 further explores the concept of civil rights versus the security of citizens.

Negative Rights

Some social thinkers believe that although we do and should have rights, those rights should only be of a certain kind: *negative rights,* so called because they specify what ought *not* to be done to you (they are rights of noninterference). John Locke (1632–1704), a philosopher within the British tradition, is the author of the idea that people have natural rights against the government—the rights are natural because even outside of society, says Locke, people would agree that these rights are reasonable, but they are easier to enforce within a society. These rights are the right *to life, to liberty,* and *to property.* In his *Second Treatise on Government* (1690) Locke specifies that "The State of Nature has a law of Nature to govern it, which obliges everyone, and Reason, which is that law, teaches all mankind who will but consult it, that being all equal and independent, no one ought to harm another in his life, liberty, health or possessions." So even before a society is formed with all its rules and laws, says Locke, there is a law of nature guiding our rational thinking toward realizing that everyone is equal by birth, and everyone should be able to live their life in liberty without the interference of anyone else. In many ways Locke's philosophy was an inspiration to the Framers of the United States. Ayn Rand (see Chapter 4) expressed the conviction that the United States was the first moral society in history because it set limits on the power of the state and respected the concept of the rights of the individual. In an essay, "Man's Rights," from *The Virtue of Selfishness* (1965), she says, "All previous systems had regarded man as a sacrificial means to the ends of others, and society as an end in itself. The United States regarded man

Box 7.4   CIVIL LIBERTIES VERSUS SECURITY

In the fall of 2001, as a step in the war against terrorism, Congress passed the U.S.A. Patriot Act of 2001, directed at preventing future terrorism through increased powers of wiretapping, including "roving wiretaps" that zero in on a person rather than a telephone number, and intercepting e-mails, faxes, and so on. The purpose is to find and arrest any terrorist, foreign or domestic, who might threaten the security of U.S. citizens at home and abroad. In the wake of September 11 such measures seemed welcome and reasonable to many, but there were also voices who warned that we might come to regret this decision.

Interestingly, these voices have come from both the Left and the Right within American politics: Liberals see these measures as a threat to political dissidents in an era of conservative government. Conservatives see them as a danger to individual freedom—especially under some possible future liberal administration. And both point out that it in effect undermines the Fourth Amendment of the Bill of Rights, the search-and-seizure amendment, which says officers have to demonstrate *probable cause* (that a crime has been/is being committed) before entering and searching the premises of a citizen without that citizen's permission. The Patriot Act was intended to be in effect for four years, until 2005. However, extending the act had already been suggested in 2004.

In addition, September 11 inspired sweeping measures to try foreign terrorists in military tribunals, so as to keep the proceedings—and especially the evidence—secret and thus out of reach of other terrorists. And the threat of bioterrorism seems to call for further measures of protection (as illustrated by the film *Outbreak,* summarized in the Narratives section).

How far are we willing to go in giving up our civil liberties, and even our constitutional rights, in order to obtain security? What are we willing to do? In the days following September 11 many Americans would have said, "Anything, just so

we're safe," but others have reminded us that having an open, free society carries with it some inherent risks. If we put up too many safeguards to protect our society, we may lose our freedoms in the process. Benjamin Franklin wrote, "They that can give up essential liberty to obtain a little temporary safety deserve neither liberty nor safety." It is not unusual, however, for a country to enact strict legal measures in wartime that then will be lifted when the war is over.

What puts this into perspective is that prior to September 11 there was already a tendency in American politics (supported by eight years of a Democratic presidency) to "trade rights for benefits," as Ronald Dworkin would put it. In 1994 a seven-year-old New Jersey girl named Megan Kanka was killed, and her murderer was suspected to be a known child molester. In the aftermath, the question was asked, Could her death have been prevented if the whereabouts of the released child molester had been made public beforehand? In that case the community would have known to keep their children away from him. The law requiring such notification, known as Megan's Law, was passed by Congress in 1997, although individual states had earlier passed similar laws. In January 1999 it took effect across the United States. The addresses of sex offenders who are released from prison will be on file at the local police stations for the community to inquire into and make public. In some communities, the names and addresses of sex offenders are regularly released by community leaders or radio stations and posted on the Internet. In other communities, citizens have a more difficult time getting access to the information.

From the point of view of the community, this is tremendous progress in protecting the lives and well-being of our children; from the point of view of the sex offender, though, this is hardly good news. So what? we might say—who cares what sex offenders think of our attempts to foil

(continued)

Box 7.4   CIVIL LIBERTIES VERSUS SECURITY (*continued*)

their future exploits? The trouble is that our conception of civil liberties doesn't quite correspond to this idea of protection of the community. The sex offenders have served their time, paid their debt to society, and in most other cases this means they can start over again—with a criminal record but with the past behind them. They may have lost some rights (such as the right to vote and to own weapons), but presumably they retain the right not to be assumed guilty before they have done anything. Megan's Law casts this freedom into doubt: The past crimes of sex offenders will never be put behind them, and, as such, the punishment never seems to come to an end. To some

philosophers of law, this is terribly unfair, but others point out that the crimes such offenders have committed never come to an end either—the victims of sexual molestation (if they survive it) will have to live with the memory always. Even so, this is not an argument in favor of Megan's Law, because punishment is not intended to match the pain intensity caused by the crime—how would that be possible? To the legal complaint that having one's name posted in the community prolongs the punishment, the court replied that the surveillance and posting of names is the community exercising its right to self-protection—it is not part of the punishment.

as an end in himself, and society as a means to the peaceful, orderly, *voluntary* coexistence of individuals."

So what are these individual rights? There is only one fundamental right, says Rand: the right to your own life and to act free of coercion. In that sense it is a positive right. But as for your neighbors, they have negative rights against you: the right not to have their right to life and liberty violated. How do we maintain our life? By our own effort, Rand says; this means you have the right to make money or own property without having it taken away. So the right to property is also a negative right. Are these rights absolute? Do you always have a right to your life, liberty, and property? Not if you have violated someone else's right to life, liberty, or property. In such a case your rights have been forfeited; so the limit of your own liberty is the liberty of the other person. But does this mean you have a right to be kept alive if you can't provide for yourself? Do you have a right to be given property and to be provided with the means to enjoy your liberty? No, says Rand. If you can't fend for yourself, then society has no obligation to help you (but others may want to, because they are caring people). There is no such thing as a right to a job, home, or fair wages—nor a right to be made happy, only the right to not be interfered with if you don't bother others in your own pursuit of happiness. (See Box 7.5 for a discussion of the right to die: euthanasia.)

The American philosopher John Hospers expresses the same sentiments in defending the political viewpoint of libertarianism in his book *The Libertarian Alternative* (1974):

Each man has the right to life: any attempt by others to take it away from him, or even to injure him, violates this right, through the use of coercion against him. Each man has a right to liberty: to conduct his life in accordance with the alternatives open to him without coercive action by others. And every man has the right to property: to work to sustain his life (and the lives of whichever others he chooses to sustain, such as his family) and to retain the fruits of his labor.

Both Rand and Hospers emphasize the right to life; does this mean they are part of the right-to-life movement? If we identify the right to life as an anti-abortion viewpoint, then it is not the same as the libertarian negative right because libertarians are generally concerned with the right of people who are already born not to have their lives taken away. The Libertarian Party platform of 1994 specified a pro-choice stand, as a logical consequence of its view that the right to liberty includes the right for women to choose for themselves; however, the platform also specified that libertarians are against public funding of abortion clinics because forcing others to pay for abortions violates the right to property.

Accordingly, the right to life is simply a right not to have your life interfered with. What if you are not capable of working to sustain your life? Then you have a problem, because Rand and Hospers do not believe you have a right to receive other people's property without their consent. In practical terms, this means you should have planned ahead while you were able to work and saved up or taken out insurance; for those who never have been and never will be able to work, libertarianism advocates private charity, not government interference, because the only role for the government, say both Hospers and Rand, is to protect the negative rights of the citizens against violation. Anything else is, in the colorful language that Hospers echoes from Rand, "moral cannibalism." You may remember the excerpt in Chapter 4 from Rand's *Atlas Shrugged* in which she speaks of the right of the capable person not to have to support the lives of "whining rotters"—those she elsewhere calls "moochers and leeches" and "moral cannibals." Critics of this philosophy—and there are many—sometimes invoke the Golden Rule and ask of the libertarian, Is this the way *you* would want to be treated if stricken with a personal catastrophe that you could not have prepared for? Should the goods of this world be reserved for those who are strong, healthy, and capable of securing them for themselves, or should weaker individuals who lack such abilities also have a right to share in the goods in a civilized society?

Positive Rights

Views in opposition to libertarianism can be found in several areas of modern social thinking. The most extreme alternative would be provided by Marxism (rather quiet at the moment), which holds, on the basis of the ideal of social equality, that everyone in society has the right to have his or her life sustained, "to receive according to need, and to give according to ability." This makes the right to live and have your life sustained a *positive right* (a right to receive something from somebody, usually the government). As has often been pointed out, the politics of communism exclude the negative rights just described: It rarely recognizes any right as not to be interfered with by the government.

Box 7.5   EUTHANASIA AS A RIGHT?

Negative rights are traditionally defined as the right to life, liberty, and property. The right to die is usually not part of the discussion. We shall here take a look at the concept of the right to die and its relation to negative and positive rights.

First of all, what is euthanasia? Literally, it is Greek for "good death." There are four major distinctions: *voluntary* and *involuntary* euthanasia and *active* and *passive* euthanasia. "Voluntary" implies that the patient requests euthanasia. "Involuntary" has two meanings: (1) The patient clearly doesn't want to die, but is killed anyway (this is the kind of "euthanasia" performed by doctors in the death camps of Hitler's Holocaust); (2) the patient is incapable of communicating his or her wish, leaving the decision to the family (this is also sometimes called *nonvoluntary* euthanasia to distinguish it from outright killing). "Active" euthanasia refers to the patient's life being taken directly, by means such as drugs or the use of a weapon; "passive" euthanasia usually refers to the withholding of treatment from the patient that would otherwise have kept the patient alive longer. At the time of writing, Oregon is the only state that allows active voluntary euthanasia, under specifically defined circumstances (and this law is in conflict with federal law, according to former U.S. Attorney General John Ashcroft). Passive voluntary euthanasia is common: The patient wishes life-prolonging treatment to end. Active involuntary euthanasia is not a legal option, whether it means killing someone who doesn't want to die or assisting someone whose family requests assisted suicide for them. Passive involuntary euthanasia is common, if we take "involuntary" to mean "nonvoluntary": The family requests a stop to life-prolonging measures.

When Dr. Jack Kevorkian began his work of either helping suffering people end their lives or killing misguided patients (depending on which view you hold), the idea of doctor-assisted suicide was still considered a radical one by most Americans. In 1999, Kevorkian stood trial for the third time. Acquitted of assisting suicide on two previous occasions, this time he was convicted of second-degree murder. The main reason Kevorkian had been acquitted twice was, in fact, the principle of the double effect, which you know from Box 7.1: His lawyer argued that his primary intent had been to alleviate the patients' suffering (allowing them to inject themselves with a large dose of painkiller), with death as an unintentional and unavoidable side effect. Some of us may think that such an argument was a bit of a stretch, since by Kevorkian's own admission the fatal outcome was intentional, but legally it made a difference between a direct and an indirect action. Also, when Kevorkian was eventually convicted it was partly because the double effect argument couldn't be used: He had himself administered the lethal dose to a patient who subsequently died.

The key arguments in favor of active voluntary euthanasia (which is what the debate usually focuses on) are that (1) it should be the right of individuals to decide the manner and time of their own death; (2) it should be a person's right to avoid otherwise inevitable suffering (in other words, the right to death with dignity); (3) we help others we love when their lives are at an end and they are facing severe pain—our pets—so we should be able to do the same for our human loved ones; (4) we might want to have that option ourselves someday.

The most common counterarguments are that (1) it is not up to patients or doctors to play God: There is a time to die for everyone, and we shouldn't interfere; (2) it goes against the Hippocratic oath, by which doctors are sworn to heal, not to take lives; (3) having opened up the possibility of doctors assisting in people's death, the step from voluntary to involuntary euthanasia (the kind where the patient has not given his or her consent) is only as short as the doctor's and family's conscience; (4) financial pressures might be brought to bear on a terminally ill family member whose insurance is about to run out.

Could the right to die be considered a *negative* right? Yes, if one's body is considered property, then we may argue that we have a right to do with our bodies what we please, provided it doesn't infringe on other people's rights. But it doesn't entail that we have a right to *assisted suicide,* which is the issue. Could the right to die be considered a *positive* right? This is more probable. We may argue that the right to death with dignity is an entitlement all people have, similar to the right to food, shelter, clothing, work, education, and so forth. However, it would be hard to compel others, such as doctors, to help in *taking* lives as a professional duty; nor does a woman's right to seek abortion mean that a doctor is obliged to perform the abortion.

Socialist viewpoints (which are generally not as radical as communist ones in terms of government control) also support positive rights (entitlements) such as the right to work, to have shelter, and possibly also to have health care, education, clothing, and food.

According to the German political philosopher Karl Marx (1818–1883), the communist state will take care of the needs of the individual: The individual has a positive right to have his or her needs met. But *needs* is an amorphous term. What does it mean to have your needs met? Marx had in mind the basics: food, shelter, clothing, meaningful work, education, and health care. The needs of your family, however, might stretch the definition of basic needs. Wanting and needing are, after all, not the same. What about feeling you *need* an extra VCR so you can tape two news shows at a time and be really well informed? What about braces for your daughter's teeth? What about a copy of the Phonics Game for your son? You may argue that the kids really *need* those things to secure their future, but who is to judge? And who is to pay for them? Those who have the ability to work.

In Marx's vision of the communist state—the final stage of political development after feudalism and capitalism—the world will have changed. The capitalist concept of profit will have disappeared because profit is the "surplus value" that the factory owner adds to the product on top of the wages paid to the factory worker—in Marx's view, value stolen from the worker and created on the worker's time and through the worker's effort. In the world of communism, people no longer go to work in order to make wages or make a profit—they go to work because they have certain abilities that they put into the service of the state. And since they are allowed (ideally!) to work with whatever their talents dictate, they are not bored: The compensation for hard work is the joy of having meaningful work in itself. So society can require a person to work for the good of the community to the extent that he or she is able to do it (willingness is simply assumed). In compensation, the workers will be paid in goods according to their needs. In the early stages of the new world, Marx envisioned a monetary system, but within the completed communist system, money would be abolished. In *Atlas Shrugged,* Ayn Rand (who fled the Soviet Union for the

United States) creates a wicked parody of the fate of a factory run on communist principles. The workers with needs soon outnumbered those who were able to put in long hours of work. Those workers with bright ideas and abilities were put on overtime without compensation, so that very soon they were out of ideas and discovered that they were able to put in only a feeble amount of work. But everybody was quick to think up new needs. . . .

The concept of positive rights need not take on such extreme proportions. Most liberal philosophies (see the next section) include the view that negative rights are not of much use if one's health or the country's economy prevent one from making a living. What good is the right to vote, to express yourself freely, and to hold office if you are so sick or destitute that you can't feed your kids or give them a safe place to grow up? In order to enjoy negative rights, one must be assured of having basic needs met. Welfare for a limited number of years is intended to tide a person over until he or she is able to work full-time again (although we have yet to see whether the current welfare system is an incentive toward personal responsibility in taking charge of one's life or whether it leaves people stranded because they can't find work). As mentioned previously, affirmative action, in recent years under scrutiny (and presumably abolished in California's public sector after Proposition 209 passed in 1996), is intended to help overcome the inequalities of the past. Education itself is often considered a positive right, something the state must provide to its citizens in some basic form, such as public schools. We'll return to the topic of affirmative action. The first Primary Reading at the end of the chapter is the United Nation's Declaration of Human Rights. You may want to study it specifically for its emphasis on negative as well as positive rights—rights of noninterference as well as entitlements.

Distributive Justice

In modern social philosophy we talk about two kinds of justice. One is the kind that is upheld by the law; it is generally referred to as *criminal justice,* and we will return to it at the end of this chapter. The other kind is *distributive justice,* theories of how to distribute the goods of society fairly. This distinction dates all the way back to Aristotle, who says in his *Nicomachean Ethics* that "A just thing . . . will be (1) that which is in accordance with the law, (2) that which is fair; and the unjust thing will be (1) that which is contrary to law, (2) that which is unfair."

For some social thinkers in the past, distributive justice depended on who could grab how much and hold on to it, but in modern times a clear understanding has emerged among social philosophers that in order for society to be a functioning system, it must offer both some recognition of needs and some way to meet those needs.

Rawls: Justice as Fairness

One of the most influential arguments against exclusively negative rights and in favor of positive rights—an argument that is also directed against a utilitarian view of rights as merely a means to happiness for the majority (*social utility*)—comes from the American philosopher John Rawls (1921–2002). This is usually identified as a *liberal* argument, not in the sense of Mill's *classical* liberalism (which comes close to today's libertarianism), but in the sense of the modern *egalitarian* liberalism, which believes that everyone should have equal access to social goods, in some way or other. A liberal generally believes in some positive rights as well as some negative rights: You need the right to life and liberty (such as freedom of speech), but without positive rights you may not be able to enjoy those negative rights, so you also have a basic right to be taken care of by society if you can't take care of yourself.

In order to envision a society that is as fair toward everyone as possible, Rawls suggests a thought experiment: Imagine, he says, that we are about to make rules for a brand-new society and that we are all in on it. (This is one of the most modern versions of the old *social contract theory* that you'll remember from Chapter 4.) Then, he says, imagine that you don't know who or what you'll be when the rules take effect; you may be rich, you may be poor, young or old, male or female, of another race. You pretend you are ignorant of your position in the future; you have now lowered a *veil of ignorance* over your mind's eye. This Rawls calls the *original position* because it is from this position that we should imagine making rules for all of society. If you don't know who or what you will be, you will want to make certain that whatever rules you help make about fair distribution of the goods of society (such as jobs, food, shelter, child care, health care) don't place you at the bottom of the pile. If you end up being poor and ill, your new rules should be as fair to you as to anyone else; if you end up being rich, you would want fairness too. This is, of course, a form of rational self-interest—but in the bigger picture it transforms itself into an understanding of other people's needs. In Rawls's own words, from his influential work *A Theory of Justice* (1971),

> Thus we are to imagine that those who engage in social cooperation choose together, in one joint act, the principles which are to assign basic rights and duties and to determine the division of social benefits. . . . This original position is not, of course, thought of as an actual historical state of affairs, much less as a primitive condition of culture. It is understood as a purely hypothetical situation characterized so as to lead to a certain conception of justice. Among the essential features of this situation is that no one knows his place in society, his class position or social status, nor does any one know his fortune in the distribution of natural assets and abilities, his intelligence, strength, and the like. . . . The principles of justice are chosen behind a veil of ignorance. This ensures that no one is advantaged or disadvantaged in the choice of principles by the outcome of natural chance or the contingency of social circumstances.

An example may help illustrate this (it is not an image that Rawls uses, but he might): Think of a birthday party for a little girl. There is a big birthday cake, and she would like to cut a big piece for herself before any of the guests get some of it. But her parents tell her, "You may cut the cake, but you get to choose last!" She is a smart girl; what will this force her to do? Cut pieces as evenly as possible, because a tiny piece is likely to be rejected by her guests and thus be the last one remaining for her. In a sense she is in the original position, creating a system of fair distribution for the future.

This analogy works well for the original position, but real life is different. The needs (or wants) of the party guests were for a piece of cake, but in real life some may need more food, shelter, and health care than others, and some have talents that others don't have. So a completely fair distribution of goods would be one in which, as a result, no one is in need of the bare essentials. Justice, then, consists in equal liberty (having the same rights and duties as everyone else) for persons within a society. This doesn't mean that everyone should be treated the same way. As a matter of fact, some inequality is permissible, says Rawls, provided that the end result is *everyone* in society benefits from that inequality (and not just some majority, as in utilitarianism). In the Primary Readings you'll find an excerpt from John Rawls's influential essay "Justice as Fairness."

Wolgast and Friedman: Reactions to Abstract Individualism

Rawls's viewpoint has helped immensely in identifying goals within liberal politics; as you can imagine, he has critics among nonliberals, but he also has them even among thinkers who are generally in favor of social equality involving fair distribution of goods. Here we look at viewpoints from two American philosophers, Elizabeth Wolgast and Marilyn Friedman; each in her own way points to a lack in Rawls's approach: the understanding that humans are not just "social atoms," separate individuals who might imagine themselves to be someone else entirely, but persons already existing in a web of interrelationships.

The idea of individualism has a long and important history, says Elizabeth Wolgast, and it has helped make this country what we perceive it to be: a place for individual achievement as a result of competition. It began with René Descartes daring to assert that humans all have the capacity to reason and are equal in their intelligence. Since everyone has this capacity, there is no need for any religious or political authority: We can figure things out for ourselves. This is the beginning of the egalitarianism, as well as the anti-authoritarianism, of Western individualism, says Wolgast, the source of a "do-it-yourself science and theology" that lets everyone play a part. Other thinkers, such as Thomas Hobbes and John Locke, emphasized the right of the individual as a "self-motivated unit" to decide his or her own social destiny, at least in extreme circumstances. One of the modern thinkers who has the most influence in supporting this idea of the individual as a separate unit is John Rawls. If we imagine a society in which everyone is an equal atom, then those atoms are interchangeable, and so ideally each person should be treated the same. But since we are not the same, a policy of justice should take that into consideration, and this is what Rawls's original position policy is all about. This is ingenious as an abstract ideal, but what about real life? asks Wolgast. This model of thinking, beginning with Descartes and culminating with Rawls, presupposes that all human relationships are entered into by separate "atomic" individuals as if they are entering into a contract, as if they weren't in any binding relationships already. According to Wolgast in *The Grammar of Justice* (1987):

> The atomistic model has important virtues. It founds the values of the community on private values; it encourages criticism of government and requires any government to answer to its original justification; it limits government's powers, as they may threaten to interfere with the needs of atomistic units. . . . But it leaves a great deal out. . . . In it one cannot picture human connections or responsibilities. We cannot locate friendliness or sympathy in it any more than we can imagine one molecule or atom moving aside for or assisting

Elizabeth Wolgast (b. 1929), a philosophy professor emerita at California State University, Hayward, is the author of *The Grammar of Justice* (1987) and several other books and papers. She argues that Rawls's famous theory views people as separate individuals without any recognition of the community ties that bind these individuals. As an alternative she argues for a return to communitarianism, the view that an individual is partly understood through his or her ties to the community.

another; to do so would make a joke of the model. . . . we need to loosen the hold that the atomistic picture has on our thinking, and recognize the importance that theory has on our judgments and our moral condition.

What is Wolgast saying? She is siding with the much older political theory of *communitarianism,* which stems from the ancient Greek tradition. For the Greek thinkers, and Aristotle in particular, an individual does not understand himself or herself as a separate entity but as a social being. We understand ourselves, and others understand us, through the connections we have to our community. A society is not just a collection of individuals but part of the very purpose of the life of an individual. We are all someone's daughter or son; we have parents and children and siblings; we have friendships and trade relations and other community ties; and stripped of those we are nobody (which is why, to many Greeks, banishment from the community was a horrible threat, as we shall see in the next chapter). As Wolgast says, "the whole makes the part comprehensible." This is the view that has been popularized with the title of Hillary Rodham Clinton's book *It Takes a Village* (to raise a child, an African proverb). So Rawls's thought experiment is bound to have limits in this real world because we are not simply atomic units, individuals alone in the universe. We have responsibilities to our community, and a good theory of justice must take such community ties into account. (See Box 7.6 for a discussion of bioethics and the needs of the individual versus the needs of the community.)

Marilyn Friedman agrees with much of Wolgast's criticism of the "abstract individualism" of Western modern philosophy and social thinking. She points out that many women thinkers in particular are now critical of this approach because they don't see themselves or people who depend on them and on whom they depend as utterly separate individuals but rather as a network or a group of individuals relying on one another. And the solution of communitarianism is tempting and reasonable, says Friedman in a paper from 1989, "Feminism and Modern Friendship: Dislocating the Community"—but we should be careful, because it may take us places we don't want to go. What do we mean by "community"? Very often what is meant is the *family,* the *neighborhood,* and the *nation;* communitarianism teaches that the traditions and demands of

Box 7.6   BIOETHICS: HUMANS ARE NOT COMMODITIES

One area in which utilitarian and deontological approaches clash is in the moral debate about access to health care. We all want policies to live up to the ideals of equality as well as of justice, but we also know that some people's needs are greater than others'. Since resources seem to be dwindling, it is a question of how to distribute such social goods in a manner that is "fair." In the health care debate the question is becoming urgent because whatever ethical viewpoint we adopt as the basis for our policies will determine the way in which people with health problems are going to be treated in the future. The utilitarian viewpoint of creating as much happiness for as many as possible was a genuine improvement over the lack of concern for ordinary people that was common in the public policies of Bentham's day, but in Chapter 5 we saw some problems that have arisen from the principle of utility: The majority may be happy, but what if the price of their happiness is the misery of a minority?

Kant's rule that we should never treat a rational being as merely a means to an end has become an antidote to the utilitarian disregard for the minority. In the health care debate the discussion is forming along these same lines: The utilitarian view points to the limited resources of society and the overall capacity for pain and pleasure of the individual and suggests that resources should be directed toward people whose quality of life will be improved in the long run, rather than toward people whose quality of life might not improve dramatically. Bentham's idea of quantifying a qualitative experience (putting numbers on feelings) is in the forefront again, because that may help doctors decide which patient to help: a thirty-five-year-old person or a ninety-three-year-old person (under the assumption that society can't afford to help both). Since the thirty-five-year-old may enjoy life and contribute to society for many years, resources should probably go there instead of to a person

close to the end of life whose quality of life might not be improved much; where the concept "quality of life" used to refer to extreme situations in which a person was suffering so much that life was no longer enjoyable, it has now come to mean an overall "global" evaluation of a person's life, a concept that has become known as Quality Adjusted Life Years (QALY). Some utilitarian doctors argue that it is the overall QALY calculation that will tell where funding is going to go, and this means that the care of elderly or terminal patients (which has a low QALY yield) will receive less priority than will the care of younger patients whose lives may be saved.

Some doctors and philosophers are disturbed by this development, because they see it as a complete disregard for the respect for *all* individuals (regardless of their age) that Kant argued for and that Rawls is working for in his theory of the original position (in which everyone must have at least minimal care and security, no matter who he or she is). As a modern equivalent of Kant's idea, these philosophers suggest the concept *irreplaceability*. In his essay "Social Justice," the Danish philosopher Peter Kemp writes,

> The irretrievable loss of another is one of the most universal human experiences. If I smash a plate I can buy another one. If my house burns down I can build another one in the same style as the old one. Everything we appreciate solely in material terms can be replaced. But another human being can never be replaced. . . . The death of another (which also occurs when e.g. a marriage or friendship breaks down irreversibly) is the fundamental reality from which the irreplaceable ethic springs.

According to the ethics of irreplaceability, each person, no matter how old or how isolated and lonely, is unique and should be respected as a person, never to be sold out to the happiness of the majority. This also means that individuals can't be reduced to a resource for society—their bodies as incubators or their organs for transplants—without their consent. The discipline of bioethics is continually struggling to create policy suggestions for all the areas in which human needs may collide, such as the abortion issue, genetic profiling, euthanasia, and organ transplants; but the underlying philosophy is that human beings and their bodies are not commodities to be used for someone else's purpose, even if that purpose may be the greater good.

our community are highly important and should be a defining factor in each person's sense of self. But if we look at such communities in a historical sense, we find that most often they have been very oppressive toward women; so if we choose communitarianism over Rawls's idea of people as social atoms, aren't we risking going backward and accepting traditions dictating, for instance, that women are the property of their husbands, that children have no rights, or that men have no place in the kitchen or nursery? Traditions may be a wonderful legacy for a community, but not all traditions are necessarily so. And suppose some of the old traditions were to blame for divisions and resentment among people today; ought we not be morally obligated to overcome those traditions? We can't just celebrate our community attachments uncritically, as some modern communitarians suggest, says Friedman. And how can we get to a point at which we can allow ourselves to be critical? By not throwing out the concept of the modern self without affiliations (what Wolgast called a "social atom"), a self who has learned to be critical of society's claims that we have social and moral obligations.

Furthermore, communitarians seem to believe that we are always a part of a community from the beginning; we have not chosen it, and yet we have responsibilities as members. But, says Friedman, that is true only when we are young; an adult person can generally choose many of his or her community affiliations. Does she want to belong to a union? Does he want to move to this or that neighborhood? Does she want to emigrate? Does he want to join a new church? We choose affiliations based on our personal needs, wishes, and critical sense, and they don't even have to be live-in communities. Today it's possible to belong to communities that don't really have a location, such as chat rooms on the Internet (when Friedman wrote her paper, the Internet was still in the future). So Friedman concludes (in "Feminism and Modern Friendship") that looking to community ties in order to expand traditional abstract individualism is a good idea, but it should not be done uncritically: We must develop communitarian thought beyond its complacent regard for the communities in which we once found ourselves toward (and beyond) an awareness of the crucial importance of "dislocated" communities, communities of choice.

Forward- and Backward-Looking Justice

In the debate about the nature and goals of justice it may seem confusing that legal experts sometimes talk about improving things in the *future* and sometimes talk

Marilyn Friedman (b. 1945), a philosophy professor at Washington University, St. Louis, is the author of *What Are Friends For? Feminist Perspectives on Personal Relationships and Moral Theory* (1993) and several papers on philosophy, ethics, and feminism. In "Feminism and Modern Friendship: Dislocating the Community" (1989) she argues that although Rawls's abstract individualism is not sufficient to explain social ethics, neither is classical communitarianism, because it tends to be oppressive to women. An appreciation for the individual as well as for new types of community relationships is needed.

about making up for mistakes and evils of the *past,* as if the two approaches might exclude each other. And to some legal minds they effectively do, because the issue of justice can be defined in two ways: as *forward-looking* and as *backward-looking.* One concept focuses on future consequences; the other is a rights-based concept centered on responding to conditions in the past. Here it is essential that you have studied Chapters 5 and 6, because this section relies heavily on your understanding of the goals of utilitarianism and other consequentialist theories, as opposed to the ideals of a Kantian viewpoint.

A forward-looking view of justice sees the purpose of justice as creating a fair system of distribution of social goods in the future. (Social thinkers use "social goods" to mean access to opportunities such as jobs as well as material things available to citizens in a community.) Regardless of what in the past has brought us to where we are today, our focus must be on creating consequences as good as possible for as many as we can—for everyone, if possible—in the future. A utilitarian would concentrate on creating a functional society of equality and access to opportunities for the majority, under the assumption that that's the best we can do. Of course, a utilitarian might also consider instituting social *inequalities,* provided that the overall outcome is considered beneficial for the many.

A backward-looking view of justice requires us to look to conditions in the past and ask, What has brought us to where we are today in terms of inequality and unfair distribution of social goods, and how can we make amends? In the backward-looking view it is essential that we identify both the root causes of today's inequalities and the people in the past who have been affected by them, as well as their descendants and those still living today. Whether compensation for past wrongs done to these people will actually accomplish a system of fair distribution of goods in the future is not relevant—the main concern is to rectify the past wrongs.

An interesting hybrid form is John Rawls's theory of the original position. The Rawlsian focus would be on creating a fair system for *everyone,* using the original position to create rules of distribution of social goods so that no one falls through the cracks. As you'll remember, the original position is a thought experiment requiring that we forget about who we are and have been in the past, in order to imagine a fair and just society of the future where everyone is equal, and no one will be sacrificed for the convenience of anyone else. As such it is future-oriented, forward-looking. But Rawls himself is not a consequentialist; rather, he is a follower of Kant's philosophy that nobody should be used as merely a means to other people's ends, even if it might create good consequences. So Rawls's theory of justice in effect looks forward, drawing on a concept of rights and fairness, not on good social consequences as such. Later we look at Rawls's own theory of combining forward-looking and backward-looking theories of punishment.

In the field of *affirmative action* the views of forward- and backward-looking justice have determined the way many issues have been raised and solved. While the entire concept of affirmative action—a term coined by President Lyndon B. Johnson in the 1960s in connection with the Civil Rights Act—is now undergoing scrutiny by politicians, the media, and citizens for its overall results and possibly negative impact on public jobs and education, the goal of affirmative action ("preferential treatment," as it is referred to by critics) was to level the playing field for disadvantaged citizens. But exactly who the disadvantaged citizens are, and how the playing field is to be leveled, depends on whether one adopts a forward-looking or a backward-looking view.

A *forward-looking* approach identifies those in society who, at this point, seem disenfranchised, and those who in the near future may be in danger of being caught up in a socially disadvantaged situation, and will focus on making access to public jobs and education easier for that group, regardless of why the situation has arisen or whether the beneficiaries or their ancestors were discriminated against in the past. Thus it is the present needs of disenfranchised individuals and groups that would determine the measure of help required, not their experience with discrimination in the past. A forward-looking view has to determine how far into the future such programs will have to exist in order to level the playing field—forever, or a few generations—because there will always be needy individuals.

A *backward-looking* view will focus on the history of disenfranchised groups and seek some form of compensation or restitution to those groups—living members or their descendants—based on the past experiences of group members regardless of whether everyone in that group today has in fact experienced discrimination in his or her lifetime. A backward-looking view will also have to determine how far into the past one must go in order to rectify old wrongs—should it be limited to living memory, meaning about a hundred years at the most, or should it go back several more generations? Regarding the question of compensation to African Americans for past injustices caused by slavery, the issue is extremely relevant: Assuming that one finds the idea of reparations at all reasonable (which many don't), a living memory criterion would include compensation not for slavery itself, but for the consequences of slavery. And a broader criterion would have to seek compensation not just from descendants of American slave owners, but also from descendants of Arab slave traders, and so on. At the end of the chapter, you'll find an excerpt from Dr. Martin Luther King, Jr's "Letter from Birmingham Jail" on the concept of just and unjust laws. Also in the Narratives section, you'll read about the film *Mississippi Burning*, based on the true story of the murders of three young civil rights activists in

Philadelphia, Mississippi, on June 21, 1964. In 2005 a separatist Baptist minister and Ku Klux Klan member, seventy-nine-year-old Ray Killen, was arrested and charged with engineering these murders, one of the most infamous events of the civil rights movement of the 1960s. Consider how the criminal charges against Ray Killen, forty-one years after the murders, are an example of a backward-looking view.

The very different approaches of forward- and backward-looking justice can be found not only within the realm of what we call distributive justice, the distribution of social goods, but also as an important part of what we refer to as *criminal justice*.

Criminal Justice

As a society, we believe that law-abiding persons should be treated equally, *ceteris paribus*. The Latin expression means "everything else being equal," so if you just go about your business, you deserve the same decent treatment by the government that anyone else deserves, no more and no less. But sometimes everything else is not equal: You may come from a historically deprived group, and legislation may state that such persons deserve special benefits (such as affirmative action). Or you may have experienced personal hardship that couldn't be anticipated and may need special help, perhaps in the form of welfare (all depending on which government system is in effect and what kind of rights its legislators may believe in: negative rights, positive rights, both, or none). Or you may have actually benefited society in some way, so the government believes you should be rewarded (some governments will pay families bonuses or give them tax breaks for having children, for example). But suppose you have broken the law? Then, according to criminal justice, the government is entitled to treat you differently from the rest of the population—by depriving you of benefits and sometimes also of certain rights, by punishing you for the crime committed. You may recognize the principle of treating equals equally and unequals unequally.

The concept of punishment is as old as human history, but only in the past two hundred years has it acquired the face we see today. In past eras around the world, punishment often involved banishment (temporary or permanent), financial restitution to the victims or their families, or loss of body parts—or even execution. The principle of "an eye for an eye," today referred to as the law of retaliation, or *lex talionis*, has been in effect for the past four thousand years, since the Code of Hammurabi.

Incarceration was rarely considered a form of punishment in former times, but could be a method of keeping dangerous people under control—either political figures who had worn out their welcome or who had a high enough profile that they could be held for ransom, such as the twelfth-century British king Richard the Lion-Hearted. In seventeenth-century Denmark the old king's daughter Leonore Christine was locked up for twenty-two years in a castle tower because her husband was a traitor, and the new king's queen thoroughly disliked her. The Tower of London and the dungeons of medieval castles served similar purposes, at a time when due process was a concept of the future. Torture, often a feature of these "holding facilities," would have several functions, among them obtaining information from the prisoner and punishing a crime. This was often undertaken privately rather than by the authorities. The fact that people were kept locked up was not in itself considered part of the punishment but rather a means of facilitating the torture. The custom of incarceration as a form of punishment dates back only a few hundred years; the idea of keeping people in prison to punish them for their crimes has in itself undergone changes, from the notion that people should be kept in solitary confinement so they could contemplate the magnitude of their crimes and thus become rehabilitated to simply keeping criminals out of circulation as a way to protect the public.

While most people today think punishment (in some form) is an appropriate response to crime, the viewpoint has been advanced, particularly in the last half of the twentieth century, that punishment is a demeaning and inhumane approach. The question was raised, Who are we, law-abiding citizens, to pass judgment on people who have perhaps been deprived of the chances in life that have resulted in our being law-abiding? And who is to say that punishment will actually deter them from further criminal activity? Rather than punish people for what they have done, we ought to educate them and supply them with the chance they may never have had before to become a good citizen. In other words, the purpose of incarcerating criminals or subjecting them to other restraints has been viewed not as *punishment,* but as *therapeutic rehabilitation.* This fundamental philosophical difference between viewing punishment as something deserved and viewing it as something superimposed by a power structure that, somehow, has helped create the problem has led to the distinction between *retributive* and *restorative* justice. In defense of *restorative* justice, Pat Nolan of the Justice Fellowship says,

> If all we do is focus on the broken law, then all you can do is enforce the power of the government, the fist of government, and lock people up, to punish them. If, on the other hand, you look at crime as "victim harming," the solution should bring repair to the harm done to the victim. And when you repair the harm done to the victim through restitution and reparation, generally the victim becomes very forward looking and doesn't want to harm and further punish the offender, but says, "I don't want you to do this again." "What can we do to make you not do this again?" "How can we change your life?" Transformation becomes important.

Nolan served fifteen years in the California State Assembly—and twenty-five months in a federal prison on racketeering charges. So perhaps he has an insider's understanding of the issue. He believes the solution lies in religion and in teaching morals. Those who focus on restorative justice emphasize that the balance in society is not restored by locking perpetrators up or executing them. The balance can only be restored if their criminal propensities can be transformed.

Proponents of restorative justice such as Howard Zehr, professor of sociology, often point out the differences between their view and retributive justice: Retributive justice sees a crime as a violation of rules and relationships, while restorative justice sees it as harm caused to people; retributive justice sees the state as the victim, while restorative justice sees people as victims. Retributive justice focuses on the past, while restorative justice focuses on the future. The courtroom is a battle situation for retributive justice, while for restorative justice the model is a dialogue. And for retributive justice, the debt is paid through punishment, while for restorative justice the debt is paid by "making it right."

The most influential, and perhaps also the most comprehensive defense of retributive justice to this day may have been supplied by Immanuel Kant. For Kant, justice *must* focus on the past, because that is how we identify the criminal and the severity of the crime; it must be seen as a violation of rules because it is by the rationality of rules that we justify our moral system—but Kant would not conclude that only rules and not people are victims. On the contrary. Respecting the inherent dignity of another human being—victim as well as criminal—is the foundation of his retributive justice. Among contemporary supporters are the philosopher Igor Primoratz and the author Robert James Bidinotto. Below we look at Kant's argument in favor of *retributivism*.

So even though most social thinkers believe there should be an institution of punishment within society, there is widespread disagreement on not only *what kind of punishment* people should reasonably be subjected to but also *why* they should be punished. It should not be hard for you to guess at some of the major disagreements.

Five Common Approaches to Punishment

Among all the different reasons people might give for punishment to be an option for society, five appear most often. Four of them are classics in the law books; the fifth one, although popular, is not considered legitimate by most legal experts.

Deterrence   It is often argued that punishment, provided it is swift and strict, is a good deterrent against crime. It may make the criminal change his or her mind about breaking the law again (specific deterrence) and it may make others think twice before turning to crime (general deterrence). Statistics indicate that in places where severe forms of punishment are the norm, such as Singapore, where disturbing the peace is punished by caning and political dissidence can lead to the death penalty, streets are noticeably safer than in free, Western-style societies. We must of course ask ourselves what price we are willing to pay for safe streets—a question we explored in Box. 7.4. It appears that here in the United States, crimes against property may be deterred by the knowledge of likely punishment. Who knows how many people refrain from stealing cars only because they know they'll face prison time if they're caught? It has been reported that some juvenile criminals deliberately scale down their criminal activity when they reach the age of eighteen because they know their punishment will be harsher—meaning that the concept of punishment *can* have a deterrent effect. But violent crimes seem not to be deterred much by the threat of punishment. California's controversial three-strikes law, which sends felons to jail for twenty-five years to life when they're convicted of a third serious crime, may serve as a deterrent in cases where two strikes are already on a person's record—but other factors may be at work too, such as shifts in the economy.

Rehabilitation   Some social thinkers see the purpose of punishment as making a better person out of the criminal (see the previous section); having undergone some form of appropriate punishment (generally incarceration), the criminal will have learned not to turn to crime again. This viewpoint generally presupposes prison programs that offer the inmate alternatives to a life of crime.

Incapacitation If punishment keeps the criminal off the streets, the public is safe and a social good has been achieved. But the proponents of the incapacitation, or protecting the public, approach don't specify *how* a wrongdoer should be incapacitated. Locking someone up is usually considered sufficient for protecting the public, but in the case of an individual who is a flight risk, conditions may have to be tightened, such as placing him or her in a high-security prison. A convicted rapist may be required to submit to chemical castration (although that does not address the problem of violence and aggression underlying the rape), so he is incapacitated in terms of his offense but may still be released into society. The ultimate incapacitation is of course executing the criminal, which eliminates the chance that he or she will prey on innocent people again. We return to this issue in Chapter 13.

These three approaches to punishment have one important thing in common: They all focus on the future social consequences of punishment; in other words, they are *forward-looking*. If there are no future benefits to be had from punishing someone, then a forward-looking theory will not recommend punishment. Because the primary forward-looking social theory today is utilitarianism, these three approaches are often labeled utilitarian.

By now you may wonder why these viewpoints don't address what for many is the best reason for punishing someone: the fact that he or she is *guilty of a crime*. But that is in effect a separate reason for punishment; because utilitarianism approves of punishment only if there is social good involved, it is theoretically possible that the overall benefits of punishing some guilty person are minimal, whereas the benefits of punishing someone who is *not* guilty may be considerable—instantly punishing a scapegoat may have a deterrent effect that far outweighs that of catching and convicting the real perpetrator some time in the future (and it may even deter the perpetrator from doing it again). In addition, setting an example by punishing someone with disproportionate harshness is a utilitarian possibility. If, however, we think that it ought to be of some importance whether a person is actually guilty and that we should take the magnitude of the crime into consideration, we must look to the fourth theory.

Retribution A person should be punished because he or she has committed a crime, and the punishment should be in proportion to that crime. Social utility does not enter into the picture. The most influential thinker advocating retribution as the only proper reason for punishment is Kant. The principle he applies is *lex talionis*, the law of retaliation. Kant would not approve of the three forward-looking approaches because they allow us to use a person *merely as a means* to achieve social utility. When we use a person to set an example, others may be deterred from committing a crime; the goal of incapacitation is to keep the public safe; rehabilitation does indeed make a better person out of the criminal, but who decides how the criminal ought to be? We, society. So even here Kant implies that society is using people for its own purpose. The only acceptable reason for punishment is to show the criminal the respect any person deserves: It is to assume that he or she decided freely to commit the crime. With freedom comes responsibility, so if we want the freedom of never being treated merely as means to an end, we must also accept the responsibility that goes with it. If we transgress, we should be punished for our transgressions.

As I mentioned earlier, these four reasons might be found in a legal text on retributive justice. But if you ask a person without any legal training why a criminal should be punished, she or he might answer in the following way: "Well, it just makes us feel better to see the murderer (or rapist, or burglar) get punished."

In the weeks following September 11, when the grief and shock for many people were followed by a furious anger, the question of vengeance came up. The nineteen suicidal terrorists who hijacked the airplanes could obviously not be punished further, so now attention was directed to their accomplices—the people who had trained them and planned the attacks and the nations that gave them shelter. Some moderate voices feared that America's anger might turn into a clamor for blind vengeance, resulting in the deaths of more civilians. And some did indeed want vengeance, pure and simple. But for others, the issue was clear: It was not vengeance they wanted, but *justice*. Initially the government's name for the war on terrorism was "Operation Infinite Justice," until some American Muslims protested that only Allah can be associated with infinite justice. The name was then changed to "Operation Enduring Freedom." In Chapter 13 we return to the issue of vengeance and justice in the sections on the concept of a just war and on the death penalty. For now it will suffice to outline the fundamental difference between a vengeance approach and a justice approach, as some scholars see it.

Vengeance   Vengeance and retribution have something in common: They are both *backward-looking* theories, looking to the past (asking, "Who did this?") in order to punish the guilty. Like retribution, the approach based on vengeance seeks to punish the criminal because of the crime committed, but according to most retributivists there are three major differences between retribution and vengeance:

1. Retribution is based on *logic,* whereas vengeance is an *emotional* response: It is possible for people bent on vengeance to take their anger out on individuals other than the guilty person.

2. Retribution is a *public* act, done with the authority of the government, whereas vengeance is a *private* enterprise, undertaken by private citizens (vigilantes).

3. Retribution wants punishment to be proportionate to the crime, but vengeance may go beyond that and exceed the damage done by the criminal.

Generally, people who are in favor of the death penalty, but who are critical of utilitarianism, emphasize that there is a big philosophical difference between revenge and retribution, since they see retribution as legally and morally acceptable, but vengeance as unacceptable. A small minority of scholars who are in favor of the death penalty claim that revenge is indeed the overriding emotion behind the support for capital punishment and that it is also an appropriate reason. However, a growing number of scholars and other critics of the death penalty voice the opinion that as much as we think we can find reasons why revenge and retribution are different, it comes down to the same thing: a wish to get back at the criminal, to even the score. In Chapter 13 we take a closer look at the death-penalty debate.

We have now considered three forward-looking and two backward-looking arguments for punishment, although the last one (vengeance) is rarely considered legitimate by philosophers of law. But are forward- and backward-looking theories always destined to be opposite? We know that utilitarians and Kantians don't agree on the basic moral motivations, but in real life most of us believe that sometimes people ought to be punished because it will deter others from doing the same thing; sometimes we want the wrongdoer incapacitated; and sometimes we think a first-time offender can be saved from a life of crime and rehabilitated with the proper form of punishment. And sometimes we think a criminal should be punished by the book simply because the crime warrants it and for no other reason. If we as individuals can hold such different views, does it mean we are just inconsistent, or does it mean we have some deeper, if inarticulated, understanding of the issue?

John Rawls has a suggestion that may shed some light on this phenomenon. In his paper "Two Concepts of Rules" (1955) he says utilitarians and retributivists are both right—but in different ways. In *individual* court cases we appeal to retributivism: A burglar goes to prison because he has committed a crime, and the crime determines the length of the sentence. But why do we send people to prison *in general*? To make society a better place—which is the point utilitarianism makes. So the *judge's* reason for sending a person to prison is retributivist, but the *legislator's* reason for making laws is utilitarian. The danger, as Rawls sees it, is that this definition might allow the utilitarian to make laws that might sacrifice the innocent for the sake of social benefits for the many—the problem of "sheer numbers" which you encountered in Chapter 5. Thus the application of utilitarianism must be very careful; in other words, a system of checks and balances is needed. In the Narratives section you'll find a summary of the film *Minority Report,* where future crimes are punished before they take place—one might call it the ultimate forward-looking criminal justice system, but would we really label such a system "just"?

Is Anger Ever Appropriate?

A utilitarian, forward-looking penologist (someone interested in theory of punishment) usually sees no difference between retribution and vengeance: *Retributivism* is just a fancy word for the emotional demand for revenge. A retributivist will argue that the difference between vengeance and retribution is that vengeance is based on an emotion, anger, whereas retributivism is based on a wish for a proportional, logical response. This would imply that if we feel anger toward a perpetrator, whether as victims or as other members of society, we are merely being emotional and should set aside those emotions for the sake of logic.

In *For Capital Punishment: Crime and the Morality of the Death Penalty* (1979), Walter Berns argues that anger has a deep connection with justice that modern penology hasn't understood. Berns says,

> If men are not saddened when someone else suffers, or angry when someone else suffers unjustly, the implication is that they do not care for anyone other than themselves or that they lack some quality that befits a man. . . . Punishment arises out of the demand for justice, and justice is demanded by angry, morally indignant men; its purpose is to satisfy that

moral indignation and thereby promote the law-abidingness that, it is assumed, accompanies it.

(In 1979 gender-neutral language hadn't yet become the norm in academic publications, but I assume Berns is talking about morally indignant men *and* women.) If we are not angry, says Berns, it is because we are selfish utilitarians who are concerned only with *compensations,* but you can't compensate victims for the loss of their physical integrity due to rape or for the loss of their life. (As Kant and the Danish philosopher Peter Kemp would say, people are irreplaceable.) Not all crimes can be balanced by compensation, but without righteous moral indignation we won't have an understanding of that.

The British philosopher P. F. Strawson argues, in his paper "Freedom and Resentment" (1982), that it is normal and appropriate to react emotionally to other people's actions toward us. We feel *resentment* if we are directly harmed, and we feel *moral indignation* if our involvement is indirect. To this the philosopher of law Diane Whiteley adds in her paper "The Victim and the Justification of Punishment" (1998, excerpted in the Primary Readings at the end of the chapter) that we must also take human *empathy* into account, because it is "by virtue of human beings possessing the three natural capacities of moral understanding, self-evaluation, and empathy that they have the capability to be moral agents." This means the demand for justice and punishment becomes society's communication of the victim's resentment and the community's moral indignation. In this way, the community stands up for the victim and shows the person respect. If there is no (or too lenient) punishment, the community sends out two messages: that it feels no "retributive sentiment" (or, as Berns would say, anger) toward the criminal and no respect for the victim. And a victim who feels no resentment and doesn't insist on punishment has too little self-esteem. A battered spouse who doesn't want her (or his) spouse punished may have internalized the spouse's claim that she has deserved being beaten. And the community that feels no moral indignation over a crime being committed against one of its members fails to stand up for that member and fails to show the respect for the victim that she deserves.

But, says Whiteley, this is not merely a blindly emotional response (you'll remember Martha Nussbaum in Chapter 1 arguing that emotions can have their own inherent logic and can be rational responses to situations). Provided that the victim's resentment is directed toward the right person, and for the right reason, it is an appropriate sentiment, and the community's moral indignation is an endorsement of the victim's resentment as well as a condemnation of the criminal act that has attempted to deprive the victim of moral value (because if you value someone you don't commit a crime against him or her—committing a crime against someone is reducing her or him to merely a means to an end of instrumental value only). Resentment and indignation are proper elements in the process of justice and punishment if they lead, not to pure revenge, but to retribution based on a natural fellow feeling within a community.

In the aftermath of September 11, the debate arose whether it was appropriate to seek revenge on the people ultimately responsible for the terrorist attacks, and whether rage was a destructive emotion that would lead to vengeance rather than justice. From Whiteley's analysis (although it was of course written before 9/11) we might draw the conclusion that a *lack* of moral indignation and resentment against the terrorists would have been morally wrong—and that such an anger doesn't have to lead to bloody revenge but can be channeled into an appropriate societal response that takes the dignity of the victims into account.

However, there is a big difference between regarding an emotion such as anger as relevant and allowing emotions to decide for us. As you know, Nussbaum argues in favor of viewing emotions as morally relevant, but not morally all-important: Reason has to play the main part in our moral decisions. Some social commentators have pointed out that in recent years, emotions seem to have become more legitimate as a deciding factor in public situations whereas previously reason would have the final word, increasing the danger that we may lose the calming influence of rationality—the influence that Plato and Kant so staunchly defended (as indeed most philosophers always have). Case in point: The trial of Scott Peterson in Modesto, California, accused and found guilty of murdering his pregnant wife Laci Peterson on Christmas Eve 2002 and dumping her in the San Francisco Bay, where her body and that of her unborn baby Conner floated ashore months later. This case gripped the nation for two years. While the guilt phase of a trial is supposed to lay out the facts, the penalty phase allows family members and others to make emotional "victim impact statements" for the jury to consider. During the penalty phase, emotions ran high, as is customary, when Laci's mother talked on the witness stand about her grief and anger at her daughter's murderer. After the jury came back with a death penalty recommendation in December 2004—a surprise to most pundits because Peterson did not have a prior criminal record—individual jurors explained that Scott Peterson's *lack of emotion* during the trial was the primary reason for their recommendation. Some commentators asked, Is this allowing emotions to go too far within the legal system? I'll let you be the judge of that.

Study Questions

1. What are Dworkin's two models? Explain, and apply his second model to the issue of protecting a country against terrorism.

2. What does it mean that science is supposed to be value-free? Do you agree? Why or why not? Apply the theory of value-free science to contemporary issues such as cloning and genetic engineering.

3. Explain the three principles of equality. Which one do you find most reasonable? Why?

4. Explain the concepts of negative and positive rights, and identify supporters of each theory.

5. What is the "original position"? Explain the pros and cons of Rawls's theory.

6. Explain forward-looking and backward-looking justice and apply both to the issue of affirmative action.

7. Explain forward-looking and backward-looking theories of punishment. Which approach seems the most reasonable to you? Why?

8. Can anger ever be justified as a reason for punishment? Explain, referring to Berns and Whiteley.

Primary Readings and Narratives

The Primary Readings are the United Nations Universal Declaration of Human Rights; an excerpt from John Rawls's "Justice as Fairness"; an excerpt from Martin Luther King's "Letter from Birmingham Jail"; and an excerpt from Diane Whiteley's "The Victim and the Justification of Punishment." The first Narrative is a summary of the film *Blade Runner,* a science fiction story about future exploitation of artificial humans; the second is a summary of the film *Gattaca,* about genetic engineering creating a human super-race as well as an underclass. The third Narrative is a summary of the 1988 film *Mississippi Burning,* about the murders of three civil rights activists in 1964. The fourth is a summary of the film *Outbreak,* a fictional story of government response to an Ebola-type epidemic in the United States. The fifth is a summary of the film *Minority Report,* envisioning a future where crimes can be predicted and "punished" before they occur.

Primary Reading

The United Nations Universal Declaration of Human Rights

1948.

Now, Therefore, The General Assembly proclaims

This universal declaration of human rights as a common standard of achievement for all peoples and all nations, to the end that every individual and every organ of society, keeping this Declaration constantly in mind, shall strive by teaching and education to promote respect for these rights and freedoms and by progressive measures, national and international, to secure their universal and effective recognition and observance, both among the peoples of Member States themselves and among the peoples of territories under their jurisdiction.

Article 1: All human beings are born free and equal in dignity and rights. They are endowed with reason and conscience and should act towards one another in a spirit of brotherhood.

Article 2: Everyone is entitled to all the rights and freedoms set forth in the Declaration without distinction of any kind, such as race, colour, sex, language, religion, political or other opinion, national or social origin, property, birth or other status.

Furthermore, no distinction shall be made on the basis of the political, jurisdictional or international status of the country or territory to which a person belongs, whether it be independent, trust, non-self-governing or under any other limitation of sovereignty.

Article 3: Everyone has the right to life, liberty and security of person.

Article 4: No one shall be held in slavery or servitude; slavery and the slave trade shall be prohibited in all their forms.

Article 5: No one shall be subjected to torture or to cruel, inhuman or degrading treatment or punishment.

Article 6: Everyone has the right to recognition everywhere as a person before the law.

Article 7: All are equal before the law and are entitled without any discrimination to equal protection of the law. All are entitled to equal protection against any discrimination in violation of this Declaration and against any incitement to such discrimination.

Article 8: Everyone has the right to an effective remedy by the competent national tribunals for acts violating the fundamental rights granted him by the constitution or by law.

Article 9: No one shall be subjected to arbitrary arrest, detention or exile.

Article 10: Everyone is entitled in full equality to a fair and public hearing by an independent and impartial tribunal, in the determination of his rights and obligations of any criminal charge against him.

Article 11:
1. Everyone charged with a penal offence has the right to be presumed innocent until proved guilty according to law in the public trial at which he has had all the guarantees necessary for his defense.
2. No one shall be held guilty of any penal offence on account of any act or omission which did not constitute a penal offence, under national or international law, at the time when it was committed. Nor shall a heavier penalty be imposed than the one that was applicable at the time the penal offence was committed.

Article 12: No one shall be subjected to arbitrary interference with his privacy, family, home or correspondence, nor to attacks upon his honour and reputation. Everyone has the right to the protection of the law against such interference or attacks.

Article 13:
1. Everyone has the right to freedom of movement and residence within the borders of each state.
2. Everyone has the right to leave any country, including his own, and to return to his country.

Article 14:
1. Everyone has the right to seek and to enjoy in other countries asylum from persecution.
2. This right may not be invoked in the case of prosecutions genuinely arising from non-political crimes or from acts contrary to the purposes and principles of the United Nations.

Article 15:
1. Everyone has the right to a nationality.
2. No one shall be arbitrarily deprived of his nationality nor denied the right to change his nationality.

Article 16:

1. Men and women of full age, without any limitation due to race, nationality or religion, have the right to marry and to found a family. They are entitled to equal rights as to marriage, during marriage and at its dissolution.
2. Marriage shall be entered into only with the free and full consent of the intended spouses.
3. The family is the natural and fundamental group unit of society and is entitled to protection by society and the State.

Article 17:

1. Everyone has the right to own property alone as well as in association with others.
2. No one shall be arbitrarily deprived of his property.

Article 18: Everyone has the right to freedom of thought, conscience and religion; this right includes freedom to change his religion or belief, and freedom either alone or in community with others and in public or private, to manifest his religion or belief in teaching, practice, worship and observance.

Article 19: Everyone has the right to freedom of opinion and expression; this right includes freedom to hold opinions without interference and to seek, receive and impart information and ideas through any media and regardless of frontiers.

Article 20:

1. Everyone has the right to freedom of peaceful assembly and association.
2. No one may be compelled to belong to an association.

Article 21:

1. Everyone has the right to take part in the government of his country, directly or through freely chosen representatives.
2. Everyone has the right of equal access to public service in his country.
3. The will of the people shall be the basis of the authority of government; this will shall be expressed in periodic and genuine elections which shall be by universal and equal suffrage and shall be held by secret vote or by equivalent free voting procedures.

Article 22: Everyone, as a member of society, has the right to social security and is entitled to realization, through national effort and international cooperation and in accordance with the organization and resources of each State, of the economic, social and cultural rights indispensable for his dignity and the free development of his personality.

Article 23:

1. Everyone has the right to work, to free choice of employment, to just and favourable conditions of work and to protection against unemployment.
2. Everyone, without any discrimination, has the right to equal pay for equal work.
3. Everyone who works has the right to just and favourable remuneration ensuring for himself and his family an existence worthy of human dignity, and supplemented, if necessary, by other means of social protection.
4. Everyone has the right to form and to join trade unions for the protection of his interests.

Article 24: Everyone has the right to rest and leisure, including reasonable limitation of working hours and periodic holidays with pay.

Article 25:

1. Everyone has the right to a standard living adequate for the health and well-being of himself and his family, including food, clothing, housing and medical care and necessary social services, and the right to security in the event of unemployment, sickness, disability, widowhood, old age or other lack of livelihood in circumstances beyond his control.
2. Motherhood and childhood are entitled to special care and assistance. All children, whether born in or out of wedlock, shall enjoy the same social protection.

Article 26:

1. Everyone has the right to education. Education shall be free, at least in the elementary and fundamental stages. Elementary education shall be compulsory. Technical and professional education shall be made generally available and higher education shall be equally accessible to all on the basis of merit.
2. Education shall be directed to the full development of the human personality and to the strengthening of respect for human rights and fundamental freedoms. It shall promote understanding, tolerance and friendship among all nations, racial or religious groups, and shall further the activities of the United Nations for the maintenance of peace.
3. Parents have a prior right to choose the kind of education that shall be given to their children.

Article 27:

1. Everyone has the right freely to participate in the cultural life of the community, to enjoy the arts and to share in scientific advancement and its benefits.
2. Everyone has the right to the protection of the moral and material interests resulting from any scientific, literary or artistic production of which he is the author.

Article 28: Everyone is entitled to a social and international order in which the rights and freedoms set forth in this Declaration can be fully realized.

Article 29:

1. Everyone has duties to the community in which alone the free and full development of his personality is possible.
2. In the exercise of his rights and freedoms, everyone shall be subject only to such limitations as are determined by law solely for the purpose of securing due recognition and respect for the rights and freedoms of others and of meeting the just requirements of morality, public order and the general welfare in a democratic society.
3. These rights and freedoms may in no case be exercised contrary to the purposes and principles of the United Nations.

Article 30: Nothing in this Declaration may be interpreted as implying for any State, group or person any right to engage in any activity or to perform any act aimed at the destruction of any of the rights and freedoms set forth herein.

Study Questions

1. Find examples of negative and positive rights, and explain the difference.

2. Evaluate these articles from a libertarian approach and from Rawls's approach.

3. In your opinion, are there any rights that should be on the list but aren't included? Are there any rights you disagree with? Explain.

Primary Reading

Justice as Fairness

JOHN RAWLS

Excerpt from a 1958 essay.

John Rawls is generally considered the most influential American social thinker in the twentieth century. Influenced by Kant's philosophy of never using another person simply as a means to an end, Rawls outlines a theory of justice based on the ideas that utilitarianism is unacceptable, and that it is possible to agree on basic principles of justice if we agree to see each other as equals. In this excerpt from his famous paper written years before his even more famous book, *A Theory of Justice* (1971), Rawls outlines the conditions where inequality might be acceptable in a society of equals.

The conception of justice which I want to develop may be stated in the form of two principles as follows: first, each person participating in a practice, or affected by it, has an equal right to the most extensive liberty compatible with a like liberty for all; and second, inequalities are arbitrary unless it is reasonable to expect that they will work out for everyone's advantage, and provided the positions and offices to which they attach, or from which they may be gained, are open to all. These principles express justice as a complex of three ideas: liberty, equality, and reward for services contributing to the common good.

The term "person" is to be construed variously depending on the circumstances. On some occasions it will mean human individuals, but on others it may refer to nations, provinces, business firms, churches, teams, and so on. The principles of justice apply in all these instances, although there is a certain logical priority to the case of human individuals. As I shall use the term "person," it will be ambiguous in the manner indicated.

The first principle holds, of course, only if other things are equal: that is, while there must always be a justification for departing from the initial position of equal liberty (which is defined by the pattern of rights and duties, powers and liabilities, established by a practice), and the burden of proof is placed on him who would depart from it, nevertheless, there can be, and often there is, a justification for doing so. Now, that similar particular cases, as defined by a practice, should be treated similarly as they arise, is part of the very concept of a practice; it is involved in the notion of an activity in accordance with rules. The first principle expresses an analogous conception, but as applied to the structure of practices themselves. It holds, for example, that there is a presumption against the distinctions and classifications made by legal systems and other practices to the extent that they infringe on the original and equal liberty of the persons participating in them. The second principle defines how this presumption may be rebutted.

It might be argued at this point that justice requires only an equal liberty. If, however, a greater liberty were possible for all without loss or conflict, then it would be irrational to settle on a lesser liberty. There is no reason for circumscribing rights unless their exercise would be incompatible, or would render the practice defining them less effective. Therefore no serious distortion of the concept of justice is likely to follow them including within it the concept of the greatest equal liberty.

The second principle defines what sorts of inequalities are permissible; it specifies how the presumption laid down by the first principle may be put aside. Now by inequalities it is best to understand not *any* differences between offices and positions, but differences in the benefits and burdens attached to them either directly or indirectly, such as prestige and wealth, or liability to taxation and compulsory services. Players in a game do not protest against there being different positions, such as batter, pitcher, catcher, and the like, nor to there being various privileges and powers as specified by the rules; nor do the citizens of a country object to there being the different offices of government such as president, senator, governor, judge, and so on, each with their special rights and duties. It is not differences of this kind that are normally thought of as inequalities, but differences in the resulting distribution established by a practice, or made possible by it, of the things men strive to attain or avoid. Thus they may complain about the pattern of honors and rewards set up by a practice (*e.g.* the privileges and salaries of government officials) or they may object to the distribution of power and wealth which results from the various ways in which men avail themselves of the opportunities allowed by it (*e.g.* the concentration of wealth which may develop in a free price system allowing large entrepreneurial or speculative gains).

It should be noted that the second principle holds that an inequality is allowed only if there is reason to believe that the practice with the inequality, or resulting in it, will work for the advantage of *every* party engaging in it. Here it is important to stress that *every* party must gain from the inequality. Since the principle applies to practices, it implies that the representative man in every office or position defined by a practice, when he views it as a going concern, must find it reasonable to prefer his condition and prospects with the inequality to what they would be under the practice without it. The principle excludes, therefore, the justification of inequalities on the grounds that the disadvantages of those in one position are outweighed by the greater advantages of those in another position. This rather simple restriction is the main modification I wish to make in the utilitarian principle as usually understood. When coupled with the notion of a practice, it is a restriction of consequence, and one which some utilitarians, for example Hume and Mill, have used in their discussions of justice without realizing apparently its significance, or at least without calling attention to it. Why it is a significant modification of principle, changing one's conception of justice entirely, the whole of my argument will show.

Further, it is also necessary that the various offices to which special benefits or burdens attach are open to all. It may be, for example, to the common advantage, as just defined, to attach special benefits to certain offices. Perhaps by doing so the requisite talent can be attracted to them and encouraged to give its best efforts. But any offices having special benefits must be won in a fair competition in which contestants are judged on their merits. If some offices were not open, those excluded would normally be justified in feeling unjustly treated, even if they benefited from the greater efforts of those who were allowed to compete for them. Now if one can assume that offices are open, it is necessary only to consider the design of practices themselves and how they jointly, as a system, work together. It will be a mistake to focus attention on the varying relative positions of particular persons, who may be known to us by their proper names, and to require that each such change, as a once for all transaction viewed in isolation, must be in itself just. It is the system of practices which is to be judged, and judged from a general point of view: unless one is prepared to criticize it from the standpoint of a representative man holding some particular office, one has no complaint against it.

Study Questions

1. Describe Rawls's two principles in your own words.
2. Can you think of a policy involving inequality that Rawls might approve of?
3. Judging from this excerpt, what would you think Rawls's position on affirmative action might be? Explain.

Primary Reading

A Letter from Birmingham Jail

MARTIN LUTHER KING, JR.

Excerpt from an essay written April 16, 1963.

This open letter was written by the civil rights leader Martin Luther King, Jr., in response to a published statement from eight clergymen from Alabama who had criticized King's activities as "unwise and untimely." As president of the Southern Christian Leadership Conference, King had taken part in a nonviolent protest against racial segregation in Birmingham, and he and others had subsequently been jailed for "parading without a permit." King notes in the published version of his letter that he began writing his response to the clergymen in the margin of the newspaper where the statement had appeared and continued on scraps of paper because that was all he had available in his jail cell.

You express a great deal of anxiety over our willingness to break laws. This is certainly a legitimate concern. Since we so diligently urge people to obey the Supreme Court's decision of 1954 outlawing segregation in the public schools, at first glance it may seem rather paradoxical for us consciously to break laws. One may well ask: "How can you advocate breaking some laws and obeying others?" The answer lies in the fact that there are two types of laws: just and unjust. I would be the first to advocate obeying just laws.

One has not only a legal but a moral responsibility to obey just laws. Conversely, one has a moral responsibility to disobey unjust laws. I would agree with St. Augustine that "an unjust law is no law at all."

Now, what is the difference between the two? How does one determine whether a law is just or unjust? A just law is a man-made code that squares with the moral law or the law of God. An unjust law is a code that is out of harmony with the moral law. To put it in the terms of St. Thomas Aquinas: An unjust law is a human law that is not rooted in eternal law and natural law. Any law that uplifts human personality is just. Any law that degrades human personality is unjust. All segregation statutes are unjust because segregation distorts the soul and damages the personality. It gives the segregator a false sense of superiority and the segregated a false sense of inferiority. Segregation, to use the terminology of the Jewish philosopher Martin Buber, substitutes an "I-it" relationship for an "I-thou" relationship and ends up relegating persons to the status of things. Hence segregation is not only politically, economically and sociologically unsound, it is morally wrong and awful. Paul Tillich has said that sin is separation. Is not segregation an existential expression of man's tragic separation, his awful estrangement, his terrible sinfulness? Thus it is that I can urge men to obey the 1954 decision of the Supreme Court, for it is morally right; and I can urge them to disobey segregation ordinances, for they are morally wrong.

Let us consider a more concrete example of just and unjust laws. An unjust law is a code that a numerical or power majority group compels a minority group to obey but does not make binding on itself. This is *difference* made legal. By the same token, a just law is a code that a majority compels a minority to follow and that it is willing to follow itself. This is *sameness* made legal.

Let me give another explanation. A law is unjust if it is inflicted on a minority that, as a result of being denied the right to vote, had no part in enacting or devising the law. Who can say that the legislature of Alabama which set up that state's segregation laws was democratically elected? Throughout Alabama all sorts of devious methods are used to prevent Negroes from becoming registered voters, and there are some counties in which, even though Negroes constitute a majority of the population, not a single Negro is registered. Can any law enacted under such circumstances be considered democratically structured?

Sometimes a law is just on its face and unjust in its application. For instance, I have been arrested on a charge of parading without a permit. Now, there is nothing wrong in having an ordinance which requires a permit for a parade. But such an ordinance becomes unjust when it is used to maintain segregation and to deny citizens the First Amendment privilege of peaceful assembly and protest.

I hope you are able to see the distinction I am trying to point out. In no sense do I advocate evading or defying the law, as would the rabid segregationist. That would lead to anarchy. One who breaks an unjust law must do so openly, lovingly, and with a willingness to accept the penalty. I submit that an individual who breaks a law that conscience tells him is unjust, and who willingly accepts the penalty of imprisonment in order to arouse the conscience of the community over its injustice, is in reality expressing the highest respect for law.

Study Questions

1. How does King justify advocating breaking some laws and obeying others? Would you agree with him? Why or why not?

2. What, according to King, is unsound about segregation? Explain. Would that also apply to a group of people who would *voluntarily* segregate themselves from other groups?

3. How does King reconcile the breaking of an unjust law with respect for the law? Do you agree? Why or why not?

4. Is King's ideal of nonviolent resistance to unjust laws a concept that has mainly historical interest, or might it have something to say to people of the twenty-first century? Explain.

Primary Reading

The Victim and the Justification of Punishment

DIANE WHITELEY

Excerpt from a 1998 article.

Diane Whiteley is a scholar associated with the administration at Simon Fraser University in British Columbia. In this paper, published in the John Jay College of Criminal Justice's journal *Criminal Justice Ethics,* she argues that the focus of justice has been insufficiently directed toward the concerns of the victim and too much toward the wrongdoer and the community. In addition, she argues that if we as a community don't feel moral indignation over what the criminal has done, we are letting the victim down.

The victim's resentment is a moral sentiment. But what is a moral sentiment? To begin with, it is worth pointing out that a moral sentiment may judged justified or not. I offer some examples of unjustified moral sentiments presently. A justified moral sentiment is an "intelligent" emotion in the sense that it conveys a "considered" emotional reaction— one which is based on reasons and takes account of the circumstances. Significantly, a moral sentiment is directed at another person. Resentment, for example, would not arise on injury by a natural disaster or an animal—at least not appropriately. It is experienced on being harmed by a person.

A moral sentiment is not a mere passion such as vengefulness which is characterized by inappropriate intensity or a failure duly to consider facts and circumstances. It can be evaluated, judged appropriate or not, and controlled. It is not a simple feeling—a pleasant or unpleasant sensation such as a pounding heart or queasy stomach. While there is no denying that a moral sentiment may have a physiological component, it is, in part, a cognitive state of belief. It is *about* something, a way of seeing and engaging with the world. In short, it is a complex emotion that involves a belief, an evaluation, and a relation to action.

The victim's resentment is, in fact, a paradigmatic moral sentiment. Its cognitive content consists in a belief that the wrongdoer did the crime. But resentment also involves the victim's corresponding evaluation of the wrongdoer. It is an attitude towards him that stems from viewing him in the light of the belief that he did the harm and related beliefs about his moral qualities. The wrongdoer is evaluated as uncaring of the victim's value. The victim infers that he is capable of respecting her dignity but failed to do so. As Murphy points out, the reason we deeply resent moral injuries done to us

> is not simply that they hurt us in some tangible or sensible way; it is because such injuries are also *messages*—symbolic communications. They are ways a wrongdoer has of saying to us, "I count but you do not," "I can use you for my purposes," . . . Intentional wrongdoing *insults* us and attempts (sometimes successfully) to *degrade* us.

Resentment has, in addition, an affective component. It arouses in the victim desires or feelings directed at the wrongdoer. Those desires motivate the victim to act in ways characteristic of the emotion. The attitude that arises in the resenter is one of defiance in which she denies to herself and others the presumption, fostered by the wrongdoer's action, that she is low in value. This psychological reaction is analogous to one's physical reaction of striking out in self-defense at an assault. It motivates the victim to get back at the wrongdoer by *expressing* her resentment. Failure to express it may signify acceptance of the wrongdoer's evaluation. And acceptance would indicate that she suffers some psychological pathology such as a severe lack of self-esteem.

For example, a woman who suffers from the "battered woman syndrome" is a victim who does not react with resentment when she is beaten by another person. Instead, she accepts the batterer's assessment that she deserves to be beaten. She should resent the beatings. The fact that we judge her lack of resentment to be pathological indicates that experiencing resentment is an appropriate reaction to the deliberate harm of another.

As a moral sentiment involving a belief, an evaluation, and an affective component, the victim's resentment can be judged as justified or not. It is unjustified if the belief about the wrongdoer is false. For example, resentment toward the accused thief, Smith, would be unjustified if Smith did not, in fact, snatch the victim's purse but was mistakenly apprehended because he was in the vicinity and fit the description of the real thief. The resentment would be unjustified were the victim's evaluation of the wrongdoer incorrect. If Jones snatched the purse because he was coerced into doing so by a gang that was threatening his life, the victim's evaluation of Jones as uncaring of her value would be incorrect and unjustified. Finally, the affective component of the resentment may be inappropriate. If, on having her purse snatched, the victim's resentment were so intense that she would express it by cutting the thief's hands off so that he could never steal again, we would judge her resentment unjustified because it was too intense.

Even if the resentment is justified, however, the question remains as to whether it should be communicated through the social institution. Before addressing that question, it will be helpful to consider the moral psychology of the remaining stakeholder, the community.

The members of the community react to a harm in which they are not personally involved with a certain disinterest. Their experience of moral indignation involves sympathy for the victim but tends to be less intense than resentment. Like resentment, however, moral indignation rests on and reflects the moral demand for some degree of goodwill.

Moral indignation is a complex emotion. It is similar to resentment in that it involves a belief, a related evaluation, and an affective component. In addition, however, it has a normative dimension. It is grounded in *approval* of the victim's resentment. It reflects sympathy for the victim from an impersonal standpoint. As such, it is not a mere *feeling* of sympathy arising out of sentimentality. It involves a reflective evaluation of the victim's resentment which results in a judgment to endorse it. The cognitive content of the moral indignation is the belief that the wrongdoer did the crime. The related evaluation is that the wrongdoer is uncaring, to some degree, of the victim's value. The affective component, which is normally less intense than that of resentment, involves sympathy for the victim and a desire to get back at the wrongdoer on the victim's behalf.

The fact that moral indignation involves a judgment to endorse the victim's resentment entails that it may be modified or even withdrawn when the facts of the case are examined. Feinberg points out that at a criminal trial the absolution of the accuser often hangs as much in balance as the guilt of the accused. In the case of date rape, for example, the victim's motives and actions may be examined and questioned equally with those of the accused. The upshot is that, in our system in which the value of fairness is given a high priority, the community withholds its expression of moral indignation until the wrongdoer is pronounced guilty.

In sentencing, the community has the opportunity to express its moral indignation. The expression is intended to send a message. The community intends that the wrongdoer and public recognize that the punishment means denunciation, among other things. In crimes such as robbery, assault, rape, or murder the wrongdoer fails to meet the demand for goodwill. In extreme cases such as violent, brutal murder, her actions express outright malevolence. But in all cases a criminal act shows that the wrongdoer views the victim as having no or reduced moral value. If the community were to fail to express censure, it would be acquiescing in the wrongdoer's devaluation of the victim. Jean Hampton suggests that the community's response involves "a *kind* of fear and defiance." On her view, the community *fears* that by not opposing the wrongdoer's challenge to its values, it invites further challenges. Therefore, it *defies* the challenge. I think Hampton's analysis is correct for our existing justice system. But if the system were changed to accommodate the victim's concerns by giving him a role, the community's response could also reflect sympathy for him, the sympathy inherent in moral indignation. The sentence would involve denunciation of the wrongdoer to be sure, but it would also be a way of standing up for the person devalued by the crime. In other words, the community would acknowledge the victim as one of its audiences.

From the community's perspective, as already mentioned, punishment conveys a variety of messages, not just moral indignation. I have focused on the retributive sentiment of moral indignation because of its connection to the victim's resentment.

This examination of moral psychologies makes it clear that, when the wrongdoer commits the crime, it is not just her relationship with society as a whole that is affected. The victim, too, has a substantial and justifiable stake in what happens to her. In other words, the recognition that the victim's resentment may be justified and that it needs to be expressed provides at least a *prima facie* reason to include the victim as a stakeholder in the social institution and as an audience for the communication. From the victim's perspective, an appropriate, public acknowledgment and communication of his justified resentment through the justice system would serve a number of purposes. It would convey publicly his resentment. It would communicate his demand for a minimum degree of respect from the wrongdoer and others. Finally, it would signify to the victim that the community is willing to stand up for him and reject his devaluation.

In the next section, I proceed with the second step in the argument about whether the victim's concerns are pertinent to the justification of punishment. I argue that the victim's personal, justified reaction should be acknowledged as a justifying reason for punishment by giving him a role in the social institution.

Study Questions

1. What is, to Whiteley, a "justified moral sentiment," and what makes a victim's resentment of the wrongdoer justified?

2. How should the community react toward a wrongdoer?

3. Why, to Whiteley, is it appropriate to include the emotion of moral indignation in the concept of punishment? Do you agree? Why or why not?

4. What does Whiteley mean by saying that moral sentiments can have a cognitive content? Why is this important for her theory of justification of punishment?

5. Does Whiteley's inclusion of emotions with a cognitive element in the justification of punishment lead to the acceptance of revenge? Why or why not?

Narrative

Blade Runner

HAMPTON FANCHER AND DAVID PEOPLES (SCREENWRITERS)
RIDLEY SCOTT (DIRECTOR)

Based on the novel Do Androids Dream of Electric Sheep?
by Philip K. Dick. Film, 1982. Summary.

At its premiere the critics weren't impressed with *Blade Runner;* it was too weird for most moviegoers' taste at the time. Over the years, though, the film has achieved cult status among film lovers for its film noir style and prophetic theme of asking, Who counts as a person? What looked like cultural mishmash in 1982 is now recognized as an accurate depiction of life in the inner cities—not only in the far-distant future, but even today.

This is the Los Angeles portrayed in the movie: dirty, perpetually rainy because of pollution, and populated with people from all cultures, all of whom are looking out for themselves. The language of the streets is a mix of Japanese, German, and English. Giant blimps cruise the skies advertising "a new life off-planet," away from the hopelessness of earth life. There are almost no nonhuman animals left on earth, so humans are manufacturing mechanical pets—robotic owls and ostriches and snakes and what have you. In addition they are manufacturing artificial humans, "replicants," to take on hazardous and difficult work off-world. The latest series of replicants is particularly advanced. Stronger and more intelligent than humans, they already have become a danger to them: They are rebelling and have already killed some humans. Private detective Deckard is assigned the job of hunting them down and destroying them. He meets with their manufacturer, who tells him that these beings have a built-in self-destruct mechanism; four years is the maximum life span. Deckard has no sympathy for these beings; as far as he is concerned, they are mere things to be terminated. A young woman, Rachael, is staying at the house of the manufacturer. Deckard is attracted to her, and his view on replicants begins to change when he realizes that she is a replicant, although she herself is unaware of it. She is an experimental model, and her "brain" contains implants of someone else's childhood memories, which make her seem more human and make her believe she is human. Given the existence of such extraordinary features, who can say for sure who is a replicant and who isn't? Might Deckard himself also be one?

Arriving on earth without a clue where to go, but with a strong sense that an injustice must be corrected, the replicants slowly find their way to their manufacturer, to hold him accountable for creating lives without rights, and of such brief duration. But before they come face to face with the manufacturer, they find his chief designer, Sebastian, who lives by himself in an abandoned building. Sebastian is a genius, but he is also a lonely man, and he has created friends for himself—robots of all sizes and shapes that greet him when he comes home. Ironically, Sebastian has no problem seeing the replicants as people—he treats his own robots as people. In another ironic twist, Sebastian suffers from an illness that is causing him to age rapidly. His days are numbered just as surely as those of the replicants are. But as much as Sebastian is able to relate to the plight of the replicants, to them he is a means to an end: getting to the manufacturer. And when they reach the man who is responsible for creating them for a life of slavery, they show him no mercy.

Eventually, Deckard catches up with the runaway replicants one by one. Their leader, Batty, the strongest and most intelligent of all of them, engages Deckard in a fight to the death. (The replicant's death is approaching anyway, because his four years are almost up.) In the fight, when Deckard is close to losing his own life, he realizes that what the replicant wants is what all humans want—just a little more time to live, to sense, and to breathe. Dying, Batty speaks of his life: "I've seen things you people wouldn't believe . . . attack ships on fire off the shoulder of Orion. . . . I've watched c-beams glitter in the dark near the Tanhauser Gate. All those moments . . . they'll be lost, in time . . . like tears in rain. . . ."

Study Questions

1. What statement does *Blade Runner* make about humanity and human rights, if any?

2. Are the runaway replicants persons? Is Rachael? Is Deckard? Is the manufacturer? What makes someone a person?

3. What might Kant's position be concerning the rights of the replicants—or the rights of any future self-aware artificial intelligence? (See Chapter 6 for Kant's distinction between a person and a thing.)

The replicant Batty (Rutger Hauer) and Deckard (Harrison Ford) struggle in the dramatic conclusion of *Blade Runner* (Warner Bros., 1982). Batty, dying because of a built-in self-destruct mechanism, shows that even with only four years of life, an artificial intelligent being can, in a sense, develop a soul. And Deckard is left wondering about the nature of his own humanity.

Narrative

Gattaca

ANDREW NICCOL (SCREENWRITER AND DIRECTOR)

1997 film. Summary.

The ancestor of all mad-scientist stories surely must be the tale of Frankenstein's monster. Invented by nineteen-year-old Mary Wollstonecraft Shelley as a contribution to a ghost story contest among friends in 1816 and pronounced a classic by Sir Walter Scott, it is the haunting account of a scientist who wants to control nature and create artificial life. Mary Shelley's monster is not the hulking idiot of the movies but an intelligent creature who is malicious because he is lonely; there is no one like him, and he has no purpose, since his creator, Dr. Frankenstein, denounces him. Shelley's subtitle for the story, *The Modern Prometheus,* gives another clue as to who the monster is. Prometheus was a figure from Greek myth credited with creating humans out of clay and giving them fire from the gods' hearth. Perhaps we all are Frankenstein monsters, abandoned by our creator, who didn't know quite what he was doing in the first place?

One might say that the film *Gattaca* is an offspring of Shelley's story, but here the scientists are benevolent, and the "monsters" have become the norm. The monstrous one is now the person who has *not* been genetically engineered.

Gattaca is a science fiction film (and an unusual one at that, since there are very few special effects or futuristic inventions). The science fiction element is almost exclusively one of a thought experiment, a mind game: What if . . . ? What if babies could be designed in the lab, eradicating birth defects, nearsightedness, high cancer risk, and so forth? Wouldn't that be wonderful? Perhaps not. Exploring the possible human future of genetic engineering (reminiscent of Huxley's *Brave New World*), *Gattaca* tells the story of a near-future society in which each child is the dream child of its parents, the best combination of their genes—if the child is legitimately conceived in the lab, that is. Children conceived the natural way are considered flawed and will never rise above being manual laborers.

Vincent Freeman is such a child, the firstborn son of young parents. He is born with myopia and a high probability of heart failure before the age of thirty; even so, as a young adult he outpaces his younger brother, a more socially acceptable individual conceived in a petri dish with all the good genes. At the beginning of the film we witness Vincent's parents' visit to the clinic where they and the doctor discuss the future genetic characteristics of Vincent's brother-to-be, as yet an embryo. We see how reluctant the parents are at first, being resigned to following custom and merely having the embryo screened for diseases, but the doctor persuades them that life is hard enough as it is, so why not give him all the advantages that are possible? "He will still be you—only the best of you." But growing up, the one with the ambitious goals is not the perfect boy conceived in the lab, Anton, but his imperfect older brother. Vincent dreams of becoming an astronaut and leaving for the outer solar system, but as a natural-born individual he has no chance—legally. So he embarks on acquiring an illegal identity, not just a new name and history but new DNA, an entirely new genetic profile. An identity broker sets him up with a genetically perfect individual, Jerome

Gattaca (Columbia Pictures, 1997) posits a future world where respectable persons are conceived and genetically designed in vitro; only slobs and destitute people have children the natural way. Here Vincent/Jerome (Ethan Hawke) and Irene (Uma Thurman) are hiding from the police, and his false identity is in danger of being revealed.

Eugene ("good genes"), who has no use for perfection. Jerome is disabled after a suicide attempt that was never registered, so Vincent pays him "rental" on his identity and moves in with him. The transformation involves surgery to add height to Vincent's legs, but otherwise the two young men are fairly similar. Vincent, now "Jerome," acquires a dream job at the Gattaca complex, where future space programs are planned and astronauts trained, by submitting urine and blood samples from Eugene. Every morning Eugene prepares samples of more blood, urine, hair and skin cells, and so forth for Vincent to use for the ongoing tests so that no trace will reveal the identity of the impostor. In the process, Vincent and Eugene become close friends.

Everything is working smoothly, and Vincent/Jerome is valued at work for his high intelligence, his physical stamina, and his flawless genetic code. He meets a young female coworker, Irene, who also longs for the stars but has a heart disease probability that restricts her future as an astronaut. Vincent tries to make her realize that such preset probabilities are nothing but that, probabilities. They are not set in stone. He himself is overdue for his heart attack. He has apparently overcome all social obstacles handed to him by his low birth, but an unforeseen event happens: A Gattaca executive hostile to the current space program is found murdered. Although there is no evidence linking him to the murder, one of Vincent's eyelashes is found near the scene of the crime. The police run a genetic analysis on it and come up with Vincent's original identity; but since he as "Jerome" has a different genetic profile, nobody makes the connection. Even so, he fears he will be found out on the threshold of his dream: He has been slated for the next launch to Titan. As the police detectives move closer to his personal life and his girlfriend herself is beginning to suspect that "Jerome" is not what he seems to be, his audacious attempt at breaking out of the social hierarchy seems to be failing and his true identity seems about to be revealed.

Will Vincent go to prison for the murder, or will he go to Titan after all? Will his heart hold out? Will Irene guess his identity? What happens to Eugene? Who killed the executive? And where is Vincent's brother? The ending of this interesting film offers many surprises.

Study Questions

1. What elements in the *Gattaca* plot do you think might become a reality in the future? Should we welcome them or fight them? Is there a third alternative? Explain your position.

2. The film addresses first and foremost the discrimination against Vincent and others who are being excluded from having a happy, productive life because of their genes. But there is also an underlying angle: a criticism of the *predictable* future society in which there are no surprises because they have been bred out of the population. What is your opinion? Does society need genetic "surprises," unforeseeable genius and generosity as one side of the coin and unpredictable criminal pathology as the other? Or are we better off with the vast majority of the population falling into a predictable norm?

3. Do the characters' names add something to the story? Explain.

4. When the film came out, very few people caught on to the significance of the title. Now that the Human Genome Project has been completed, it may not seem so mysterious to us. GATC are the initials of materials in the DNA code: guanine, adenine, thymine, and cytosine. What do you think the moviemakers wanted to say by calling the film, and Vincent's workplace, *Gattaca*?

5. The *Gattaca* DVD has outtakes (missing scenes), some of which add interesting elements to the story. The scene with Vincent's parents in the lab, discussing the future characteristics of Anton, is longer and gives us an understanding of their switch from skepticism to enthusiasm when they hear that they can determine the boy's height and even a musical talent! But the addition of the talent turns out to be too expensive, so they settle for having a strong, smart, healthy, tall kid. This is the only time we hear that acquiring good genes is also a matter of money. In a future where genetic engineering is the order of the day, do you think the scenario of *Gattaca* is realistic? Does the outtake make a difference to the story? Should it have been left in?

Narrative

Mississippi Burning

CHRIS GEROLMO (SCREENWRITER)
ALAN PARKER (DIRECTOR)

Film, 1988. Summary.

On June 21, 1964, three young civil rights activists were murdered in Philadelphia, Mississippi, an event that has haunted and divided the community to this day. Michael Schwerner, James Chaney, and Andrew Goodman—one black and two white men—had come to the small Mississippi community to register black voters. They were reported as missing and later were found murdered. The Ku Klux Klan was implicated. Some Klan members were brought to trial and found guilty, while others were acquitted. This film is a fictionalized story based on the actual events, and at the end of the summary you can read about an additional feature added to the story in 2005.

It is the early 1960s, in Jessup County, Mississippi, a time of racial segregation—made clear in the opening shot: one modern water cooler for whites and another, older model for blacks. Into this community come three young activists to ensure that black Americans will be able to exercise their right to vote, but in the dead of night their car is chased and overtaken by men in three vehicles, one of them a police car. They force the young men out of the car and shoot them. When the news spreads in the following days that the young men are missing, riots break out, and two FBI agents arrive in town: Rupert Anderson, himself a former sheriff from a small town in Mississippi, and Allan Ward, a go-by-the-book FBI man. Right away we sense that the two men are very different, with clashing personalities and outlooks. When paying a visit to the office of Sheriff Stuckey, Anderson treats the hostile officers like good ol' boys up to a point—and then we realize that he can get very confrontational. Ward, on the other hand, goes by Bureau regulations. The sheriff's story is that the three young men were arrested for speeding, released, and drove off.

The difference between Ward and Anderson is accentuated when they try to have lunch in the local restaurant: The hostess tells them there are no tables available, but Ward sees empty seats in the section for "Coloreds only." He heads straight for a seat next to a young black man and starts questioning him about what he may have heard regarding the activists. The young man is frightened and doesn't respond to Ward. Everyone is shocked, blacks and whites alike; and Anderson appears to be embarrassed that Ward is not only causing a scene but also approaching the issue in the wrong way. Later we see the indirect consequences of Ward's approach: The young black man is thrown from a car onto Main Street, beaten up as a warning.

In the meantime, we learn more about the antagonism between Anderson and Ward. Anderson says he believes the activists are being used politically, by cynical people, but for Ward it is a matter of doing what you believe in and sometimes risking death in order to do the right thing. When Ward speculates about where all this hatred comes from, Anderson tells him a story: When he was a kid in the South, his father was a poor man, but their black neighbor Monroe was a little better off because he got himself a mule. Shortly thereafter, somebody poisoned the mule, and Anderson's father later admitted to being the poisoner. For Anderson the culprit is poverty, not race. He wants to handle the situation his way, but Ward wants a whole investigative FBI team to become involved, and so they take over the movie theater for their operations. Anderson, though, follows his own nose, and goes to the barber shop, where he finds the sheriff and the mayor. Still acting like a small-town Southern sheriff, he engages the mayor in a conversation about the situation. The mayor tells him the blacks in the community ("the nigras") were happy until the civil rights activists showed up. He believes that there are two cultures in the South, a black and a white culture, and that any effort of the federal government to effect change is an intrusion.

Next, Anderson heads to the beauty salon, to get the women's point of view. The salon is managed by Deputy Pell's wife Mary. She is uneasy about the situation, and we sense that she knows a lot more than she's saying, about the Klan as well as the disappearances.

The missing activists' car is found in the river on the Choctaw Indian Reservation, but there are no bodies. However, it now seems certain that the boys are dead, so Ward arranges for a full-scale dredging operation, to no avail. But the Klan responds with burnings of churches and homes in the black community. Ward and Anderson know that Sheriff Stuckey has an alibi, but they find Deputy Pell's alibi questionable, so they pay him a visit. While Ward confronts Pell with the allegation that he holds a high position in the Klan, Anderson seeks out Mary in the kitchen; and on several subsequent occasions, he makes a point of chatting her up, bringing her flowers, and just exchanging small talk, gaining her trust. And Mary is very different from her husband—we see her having a genuinely good time talking with a local black woman and her baby, people her husband has nothing but scorn for.

In the meantime, the national news media have descended on Jessup County, interviewing white locals. Most of the people interviewed think the whole thing is the fault of the civil rights activists, that Martin Luther King is a communist, and that the three young activists were asking for whatever they got. Some are convinced it's a hoax—a publicity stunt. A Klansmember, Clayton Townley, makes no bones about it: A white supremacist, he doesn't accept Jews, Catholics, or communists, and he wants "to protect

Anglo-Saxon democracy and the American way." At the same time a KKK leader rallies the white community against racially mixed relationships, the "mongrelization" of America. Things are escalating, and Anderson now shows his true colors: As much as he comes across as a "redneck," his loyalties are to the FBI, and he single-handedly confronts Pell and his henchman Frank when they claim that no blacks will be allowed to vote. Moreover, he is discovering a new ally in Mary, who lets him know about an upcoming Klan meeting.

Ward and Anderson stake out the "meeting," which turns out to be a manhunt: A young black man is released from prison, then hunted down by the sheriff's men and driven away. The two FBI agents try to follow but lose sight of the sheriff's cars; later that night, they find the young man lying in the woods, alive but castrated. They failed to stop the sheriff's men, but now they suspect that the civil rights activists met their end the same way: released and then hunted down by the Klan.

When the farm belonging to the family of the young man who was Ward's first unwitting contact is torched, things come to a breaking point. The young man, Eric, rescues his mother and siblings, then witnesses their cows burn to death. His father is captured when he tries to defend his home and then lynched. Eric manages to release the rope before his father chokes to death, and the next day Ward and Anderson help them leave the county for Detroit, where they have family.

This development disturbs Mary immensely, and during a quiet moment with Anderson where Pell is at one of his "meetings," she tells him how things are: Hatred, she says, isn't something you're born with—it is taught, every day, by your surroundings. And she wants it to stop—so she tells Anderson what she knows: Her husband shot the civil rights activists, and she knows where they are buried.

Now that the bodies are retrieved, Anderson and Ward have a heated argument about methods—Anderson's questioning of Mary has resulted in Pell's beating her to within an inch of her life. In a surprising change of attitude, Ward decides to back Anderson: They have the authority, and they'll do it his way. They need someone to talk—and they find somebody who will talk to protect himself. It is the mayor. In a stunning reversal of events, the mayor is kidnapped, by a hooded man. Gagged and bound, the mayor is offered a choice by his captor, who turns out to be a black man—an FBI agent with special talents: Either he talks, or he will be castrated, the same way KKK members have castrated black men. And the mayor talks.

Now Ward and Anderson know who was involved, but since the mayor's story was extracted under duress, they can't use it in court. Instead, they manipulate Pell and his men, making them think each one has been talking to the FBI, and one of them gives up the others. A series of arrests and trials follow, but we also have a feeling that some of the culprits are never going to be held accountable.

Anderson pays a visit to Mary, whose house has been ransacked, and apologizes for having essentially ruined her life. But she explains that she'll stay on, because there are enough people in town who see things her way. Finally, at the burned-out church, black and white citizens gather together for a service.

The film was met with mixed reviews: Some reviewers found that it was a fine, well-crafted, moving story, while others thought it was a manipulative misrepresentation:

Blacks were reduced to one-dimensional victims; Klan members were portrayed as degenerates; FBI Director J. Edgar Hoover was portrayed as a civil rights supporter, whereas he, in fact, kept extensive files on Dr. Martin Luther King, Jr.; and FBI agents were depicted as people with questionable ethics. Yet other movie critics pointed out that films are not supposed to be historically accurate social documentaries, but well-told narratives with their own message and their own reality. This film is, of course, not a documentary—it is fictionalized, with invented characters.

But history is writing another chapter to the story as I am writing this: In January 2005, a 79-year-old man was arrested after a county grand jury indictment for being the mastermind behind the deaths of Schwerner, Chaney, and Goodman: Edgar Ray Killen, an alleged Ku Klux Klan leader and a Baptist preacher. Killen was tried on federal charges in 1967 but released after one juror refused to convict him (others were convicted, and some were acquitted); he is a known separatist and has been quoted as saying that God didn't create blacks and whites equal.

Study Questions

1. Do you agree with Anderson's approach? With Ward's? Or perhaps with another viewpoint expressed in the film? Explain.

2. Is this film an example of forward-looking or backward-looking justice? Explain.

3. Is this film a fair representation of the FBI? Of the civil rights movement? Of the locals in the small Mississippi county? Some reviewers called the film itself unethical. Can you imagine why?

4. What is the message of this film? Explain. Could there be several messages? Discuss.

5. Go back to the Reading by Dr. Martin Luther King, Jr., in this chapter, and the Narrative in Chapter 3, *Do the Right Thing,* and assess the current situation in the area of the United States that you know best: What are race relations like today, as far as you can discern? Is there general goodwill and understanding, are there underlying animosities and hidden racism, or is there an open racial conflict? What would you consider progress in race relations in this country?

Narrative

Outbreak

LAURENCE DWORET AND ROBERT ROY POOL (SCREENWRITERS)
WOLFGANG PETERSEN (DIRECTOR)

Film, 1995. Summary.

It is 1967 in Motaba, Zaire; a camp of mercenaries is struck by a deadly and unknown virus that is 100 percent lethal. Doctors from an American military unit come in, investigate, draw blood samples—and leave. The next thing we know, the camp is annihilated by a bomb blast.

We move on to the present day and are introduced to Colonel Sam Daniels and his ex-wife Robby Keough, both medical scientists at a military center for disease control, cleared to work with pathogens at the most contagious levels. Sam has to go to Zaire to investigate an outbreak of what looks like a new virus, 100 percent lethal, which kills its victims within three to four days.

In the lab, Sam and his superior officer General Billy Ford investigate the virus; Sam wonders why Ford does not seem surprised by this virus and does not wish any measures taken to prevent it from entering the country. But behind Sam's back Ford is in touch with his own superior officer, General Donald McClintock, and now we learn that the new virus is the same as the one from 1967, that Ford knows of an antidote, and that McClintock was responsible for the bombing of the mercenary camp in order to contain the virus—and perhaps also for another reason. To prevent Sam from finding out, they assign him to another case . . . but when news comes in of a viral outbreak in Boston and in Cedar Creek, California, Sam defies orders and goes to Cedar Creek. Here he encounters Robby, who has been assigned to do research on the outbreak.

How did these outbreaks occur? We are told the story in flashes: A monkey is caught by animal dealers in Zaire, brought illegally to San Francisco on board a ship, placed temporarily in an animal research facility, and taken from there by an animal trader, Jimbo Scott, to a pet store in Cedar Creek. The pet store owner doesn't want the monkey (wrong gender), especially after the monkey scratches him. So Jimbo takes the monkey out in the woods and releases it. Meanwhile, the pet store owner gets very sick; the lab assistant at the hospital dealing with his blood test gets sick and infects an entire movie theater full of people; Jimbo gets sick while flying home to Boston and infects his wife. Within three to four days, everybody infected dies from symptoms much like those associated with the Ebola virus: bleeding from all orifices. In Boston the only ones infected were Jimbo and his wife, but the infection is rampant in Cedar Creek because a mutation has occurred: The California strain is now airborne. And so the army moves into Cedar Creek and isolates the town. No one goes in or out. Sick family members are rounded up and taken to a camp from which nobody is expected to return. Ford tries to use the old antidote here (and this tips Sam off to the fact that Ford knew about this virus all along), but it doesn't work because the virus has mutated.

This crisis reaches to the level of the president of the United States. How fast can the disease spread? Within days the entire country could be infected. What must be done to help the people of Cedar Creek and to save the lives of other Americans, perhaps the world? The solution, reached with much hesitation and soul-searching, is "Clean Sweep": an eradication of the town of Cedar Creek in the same manner the mercenary camp was bombed in 1967. In McClintock's words, "Our procedure must be viewed objectively. Be compassionate, but be compassionate globally." As the president's aide remarks, the firebombing of Cedar Creek is unconstitutional because nobody should be deprived of life, liberty, or property without due process—so if the decision is made to go ahead, everyone should know what price is being paid for the safety of the world. Ford and McClintock have their own conversation where Ford points out that you can't treat the people of Cedar Creek like that—they are Americans. McClintock replies that the rest of America may be dying; the people of Cedar Creek should be regarded as casualties of war.

The film *Outbreak* (Warner Brothers, 1995), a medical thriller, pits concern for the safety of the many against the rights of the few: In a situation where a contagious, fatal disease is spreading, is it acceptable to adopt a utilitarian policy of isolating and "terminating" the infected? Here Casey (Kevin Spacey), Sam (Dustin Hoffman), Walter (Cuba Gooding, Jr.), and Robby (René Russo) are searching for records that might help pinpoint the origin of the fast-spreading Ebola-like virus.

Back at the isolated town, Robby is infected by accident, and Sam confronts Ford: Why was the antidote not given in time, before the mutation happened? Because, as Sam guesses, there was an ulterior motive: The virus presented the perfect biological weapon and had to be protected, so the antidote was withheld. Ford defends the decision as a matter of national security: "At the time it was felt that we could afford a certain amount of losses." And now Ford reveals that Clean Sweep will take place in twenty-four hours.

With the help of young Major Salt, Sam commandeers a helicopter: Quick action must be taken. They now know that the virus came into the country with a monkey as a host. They break into a local television newscast with a warning and a picture of the monkey. This has immediate results: a mother knows her daughter has been playing with a monkey in the woods, not far from Cedar Creek. Sam and Salt capture the monkey and send immediate word to Ford, but to their horror they find out that McClintock has no intention of calling off Clean Sweep, even if serum can now be made from the monkey to save the people of Cedar Creek and Robby. He still wants to protect the virus as a future biological weapon. The pilots of Clean Sweep are in the air, and McClintock is telling them to do their duty. Sam gets on the intercom and pleads with them to reconsider; he tells them the entire story, but they don't respond. In a last-ditch effort, Sam tries to make Ford stop the bombing, but all Ford can do is send an indirect message to Sam by telling him that he must "get out of the way," because the mission will have to be aborted if his chopper is in the flight path of the incoming bomber. . . .

Will Sam and Salt succeed in stopping the firebombing of Cedar Creek? Will McClintock win? Will Robby live? Will she and Sam get together again? I'm not going to tell!

Study Questions

1. How would an act utilitarian evaluate McClintock's decisions? Would a rule utilitarian respond any differently? What would a Kantian say? Explain.

2. Can Ford's actions as co-conspirator acting on the orders of his superior officer be defended? Why or why not?

3. Use Ronald Dworkin's two models on the scenario. What would Dworkin conclude about "Clean Sweep"?

4. After September 11, the country underwent yet another series of traumatic events: Numerous pieces of mail on the East Coast had been tainted with anthrax spores, causing the deaths of five people, affecting practically the entire nation with postal delays, and adding to the fears of an already traumatized population. (At the time of this writing the culprit has yet to be identified.) In the wake of the anthrax attacks came speculations that terrorists might be preparing for other biological attacks on U.S. citizens. In a worst-case scenario, such a bioterror assault might spread like the virus in *Outbreak*. Would the government be entitled to protect the rest of the citizens by isolating and perhaps hastening the deaths of the infected ones? Why or why not? Is there any kind of scenario that, in your opinion, would allow for such drastic measures?

Narrative

Minority Report

SCOTT FRANK (SCREENWRITER)
STEVEN SPIELBERG (DIRECTOR)

Based on short story by Philip K. Dick. Film, 2002. Summary.

It is the year 2054 in Washington, D.C. For six years, local crime has been virtually abolished, thanks to the new Department of Pre-Crime: Crimes, especially murder, can now be predicted with, presumably, 100 percent accuracy, thanks to three individuals—the precogs, young people with precognition. They "see," in their mind's eye, future crimes; thanks to an elaborate brain-monitoring system, the police officers working for Pre-Crime can share the vision, arrest the "culprit" before the crime is done, and neutralize him or her permanently in a state of suspension. It is a society of total surveillance; eye scanners identify everyone in their everyday activities.

John Anderton, the chief of detectives who is the primary reader of the jumble of precog visions, is himself the victim of a crime, committed just months before the Department of Pre-Crime was established: His young son was abducted from a public pool while he himself was playing a game with his boy, holding his breath under water. The whereabouts of the abductor is unknown, as is the fate of his son. Because of the stresses following the abduction, John and his wife divorced, and John is a frequent buyer of illegal drugs to soothe his own guilt and nightmares.

The elderly director of the Pre-Crime Department, Lamar Burgess, appears to view John as something of a son, or protégé, and cautions him that much is riding on the Pre-Crime project: If approved by voters nationally in the near future, the project will go national. Crime will then be a thing of the past. A federal agent shows up at the department, ostensibly to get a tour, but soon he reveals that he is looking for flaws in the system, to test it before it goes national. He and John have a brief conversation where John proudly explains the principle of Pre-Crime: Thanks to the precogs, crimes can now be prevented before they happen, and the guilty will be isolated. The agent asks how they can be held responsible since they haven't yet done anything? For John, these pre-criminals are guilty because the future is certain—for the federal agent they are not, precisely because they are prevented from committing the crime.

When the agent forces his way into the "temple" where the three precogs lie suspended in a sensory deprivation tank, the precog Agatha grabs John, in an unprecedented move—because nobody but the caretaker is supposed to talk to the precogs, for fear of contamination. She asks him, "Do you see?" and he sees her vision of a woman being drowned.

John doesn't know it yet, but this shared vision is about to become his undoing. Shortly afterward there is another murder prediction by the precogs: John is himself named as a future murderer, the killer of a man he's never heard of, Leo Crow. Knowing that protests of innocence are futile, John takes off, running away from the SWAT team who are already on to him. After shaking them off, he seeks out the recluse elderly inventor of the precog program, Iris Hineman, to find out the truth: Can the precogs be wrong? And Iris tells him about the occasional discrepancy—the "minority report" phenomenon: When the vision of one precog differs from the rest, the report is destroyed—it only exists inside the precog's memory.

To avoid the ubiquitous eye scanners, John now gets his eyes removed, and has another person's eyes transplanted—but he keeps his own eyes in a bag. Narrowly avoiding the Pre-Crime team, he makes his way back to the lab where he succeeds in abducting Agatha: It was her vision that showed him the man he supposedly is to kill, and he needs her to guide him to the place. But first they stop at a virtual reality facility where John has a recording made of Agatha's vision, with her cooperation—she wants him to see what she sees, because it is important to her: a woman being drowned by a man in black. The vision is cut short because the Pre-Crime team is on to John and Agatha, but through her ability to see the near future they make it to a tenement building where John recognizes elements from her vision, including the name and picture of the man he is about to kill, on the building roster: Leo Crow. They enter his apartment, which is empty—except for a pile of photos piled up on the unmade bed. And among the photos John discovers a picture of his little boy, in the company of the man from the apartment and the vision. Now John knows that this is not a minority report—the vision is true, and he really is going to kill this man for abducting his son. As Crow steps into the room, the vision comes to life: John threatens him with his gun, while Agatha is frozen in dread, but all the while she whispers to him that *he has a choice*—the future isn't predetermined, *because he already knows it, so he can choose to do otherwise.* And as his watch moves toward zero, the time where the crime will be committed, we expect him to shoot Crow; but zero arrives, and John still hasn't fired his shot—he truly has a choice. And he reads Crow his rights, formally arresting him. But now Crow speaks—he is horrified that John hasn't killed him, because that's what he was promised: that in return for being killed, his family would be taken care of. And John realizes that the whole thing was a set-up—the man is not responsible for his son's disappearance, but is just somebody who got paid to put the pictures on the bed and then be killed. But who set the whole thing up? Crow doesn't know—and as John struggles to understand, Crow grabs his gun and pulls the trigger, making the vision come true as he falls out the broken window to his death.

Desperate, John flees with Agatha to his former home by the sea, where his ex-wife Lara is now living. While they're fleeing, the federal agent who was looking for a flaw in the Pre-Crime system is now at Crow's crime scene—and realizes that it was a set-up. Puzzled, he goes to John's boss and mentor Lamar Burgess and shares his suspicion that someone is manipulating the system. Burgess readily agrees with him—and shoots him point blank. As he dies, Burgess points out that since one of the precogs is missing, there is no precog record of this murder—it will be pinned on John too.

At her seaside home, Lara sees John and Agatha coming and calls Burgess so John can get the help he needs. But instead the Pre-Crime team arrives, and this time he is arrested and placed under mind control just like the many pre-criminals he himself has placed under arrest. However, before the team arrives, Agatha lets John and Lara share the alternate reality of the life their son would have lived; and he and Agatha share the story of the drowned woman with Lara—because John has realized that Agatha is the woman's daughter, and someone manipulated the precog system so they could get away with murder and keep Agatha a precog.

John is now taken away to spend the rest of his life in a tank, removed from the rest of the human race—in a state of semi-consciousness, for all intents and purposes dead to the world. That's what happens to the pre-criminals. Lara, in her grief, goes to find comfort with Burgess—but when he, with a slip of the tongue, reveals that he knows the story about Agatha's mother, Lara realizes the truth: that it is Burgess who is responsible for John's downfall. But why? Because John understood that the system had been manipulated to cover the murder of Agatha's mother—and the person responsible for that murder was Burgess himself.

And now John's future is in the hands of Lara. What will she do? Is there a life for John after the tank? What will happen to Burgess? And what about the Pre-Crime program? Suffice it to say that John will confront Burgess with his newfound wisdom: that once you know the future, you have a choice . . .

Study Questions

1. What if our society in the near future will be able to predict criminal behavior with near certainty? What should be done to the would-be criminals? Can we justify punishing people for something they haven't done yet?

2. Identify the Pre-Crime approach to justice in this film as being either forward-looking or backward-looking. Does it make any difference? Explain.

3. In Chapter 4 you read about the concept of *free will*. Apply this concept to *Minority Report:* Does John Anderton have freedom of the will, the ability to make free choices despite the influences of this heredity or his environment? Does anybody? What does it matter for the criminal justice system whether or not we have the capacity to choose our actions freely? Explain.

Part 3

How
Should
I Be?

THEORIES OF VIRTUE

Chapter Eight

Socrates, Plato, and the Good Life

Throughout most of Western civilization and most of the history of ethics, scholars have tried to answer the question, What should I do? Part 2 of this book explored this quest. Theories that consider what proper human conduct is are often referred to as *ethics of conduct*.

There is a more ancient approach to ethics, and in the past few decades this older approach has experienced a revival. This form of ethics asks the fundamental question How should I be? It focuses on the development of certain personal qualities, of a certain behavior pattern—in other words, on the development of what we call *character*. Because its foundation is in ancient Greek theories involving the question of how to be a virtuous person, this approach usually is referred to as *virtue ethics*.

What Is Virtue?

The concept of virtue (Greek: *aretē*) is complex. For one thing, it carries certain associations, which it has acquired over the centuries; thus, in English, we may think of virtue as a basically positive concept—a virtuous person is someone you can trust. We also may experience, however, a certain negative reaction to it; sometimes, a virtuous person is thought of as being rather dull and perhaps even sanctimonious (being called a "Goody Two-Shoes" is not a compliment). In everyday language, "virtue" often refers to sexual abstinence, and that can of course be a positive concept as well as a negative one, depending on one's viewpoint. A book titled *Raising Maidens of Virtue* was published in 2004, advocating raising teenage girls according to biblical principles of purity, modesty, cleanliness, and other traditional virtues.

However, the ancient Greek concept of *aretē* differs considerably from what we today associate with "virtue." For one thing, it has its origin in the name of the Greek god Ares, the god of war, and must originally have meant having warrior-like qualities (and here we can add that the term *virtue* in itself comes from Latin, and its origin is *vir*, or "male"!). But regardless of origins in deep Antiquity, the associations a Greek-speaking person at the time of Socrates and Plato would have with the word *aretē* would not have any negative connotations, because the word *aretē* signifies a different kind of person altogether: not a person of untainted thoughts and behavior, but a person who does what he or she does best and does it excellently, on a regular basis. We still have a trace of the ancient meaning of *aretē* in the word *virtuosity*. Originally, a virtuous person was a *virtuoso* at everything he or she did, due to proper choices and good habits but, above all, because such a person had succeeded in developing a good character.

What Is Character?

Today we often take a deterministic view of the concept of character. It is something we are born with, something we can't help. If we try to go against our character, it will surface in the end. This viewpoint may or may not be correct, but in any event it is shaped by modern schools of thought in philosophy and psychology. Not everyone shares this view; it often is pointed out that we may be born with a certain character, but our character can be molded to a certain extent when we are young, and it certainly can be *tested* throughout our lives. This point of view comes closer to the prevailing attitude toward virtue among Greek philosophers: Character is indeed something we are born with, but it is also something that can and must be shaped. We are not the victims of our character, and if we let ourselves be victimized by our own unruly temperaments, then we are to blame.

The Case for Virtue Ethics

What happened to virtue ethics, and why has it been revived by scholars of ethics recently? By and large, what happened was Christianity—with its emphasis on following God's rules and conducting oneself according to the will of God. The ancient world had taught for many centuries that virtue is a matter of shaping one's character, the implication being that once one has succeeded, one can justifiably be proud of what one has become—one can take a legitimate pride in being a self-made virtuous person. (We shall see how this is an important part of Aristotle's virtue theory in the next chapter.) But in Christian thinking, one can accomplish nothing without the help and grace of God—meaning that one just can't take credit for having become a good person, for the credit or glory goes exclusively to God, *Soli Dei Gloria*. A chasm appeared between the teachings of the classical tradition and the moral and philosophical viewpoints of the rising religion. Disagreements exceeded verbal argumentation and turned violent for the first time in Christian history (but unfortunately not for the last time). See Box 8.1 for some examples of this violence. One result, nonviolent but with important symbolic consequences, was the closure of both Plato's and Aristotle's schools in Athens by the Roman emperor Justinian in 529 C.E., after these schools had been in existence for over 800 years. (In comparison, the oldest European university was founded in Bologna, Italy, in 1088. The University of Paris opened in 1160, and Oxford University in 1190. Harvard University was founded in 1636, and Columbia University in 1754). Later in this chapter and in the next chapter we return to the significance of the closing of Plato's and Aristotle's old schools.

To *do the right thing* became the main imperative of Christian ethics; however, the concepts of virtue and vice became main elements. Within the Christian tradition and within every aspect of our Western outlook on life that has been shaped by this tradition, the idea of virtue is central, but scholars of ethics point out that it is not so much the question of *shaping your own character* that is important in this tradition as it is recognizing the *frailty of human character in general* and believing that with the help of God one may be able to choose the right thing to do.

Box 8.1 VICTIMS OF RELIGIOUS FANATICISM

Since 2001 we have heard much about fundamentalist Muslim terrorism and fanaticism, and devastating results of this fanaticism have been felt around the world, from 9/11 in the United States, to the bombings in Bali and elsewhere, to the beheadings of foreign civilians in Iraq and Pakistan. As most people are aware, this does not mean that all Muslims are violent fanatics. What most people don't know is that in the early days of Christianity, small groups of Christian fanatics set out to strike terror in the hearts of non-Christians, because these groups refused to accept the values of the traditional pagan Greco-Roman world. Two such examples of what could be called fundamentalist Christian terrorism took place in the Egyptian city of Alexandria. In the year 415 C.E. a mob of fanatical Christian monks, possibly inspired by the Bishop of Alexandria, attacked and murdered one of the first women philosophers on record, Hypatia, leader of the Neoplatonic Institute in Alexandria. As far as we know, Hypatia lectured on Plato, Aristotle, and Pythagoras, and thus the Christians associated her with paganism. As she was riding through town in her chariot during one of the many religious riots, the mob dragged her out of her cart, tore off her clothes, and flayed her alive with clamshells. Hypatia had done her research in the great library at Alexandria (or what was left of it), which was founded by one of Alexander the Great's generals, Ptolemy I, who became the founder of an Egyptian dynasty (fourth century B.C.E.). The library was expanded over the centuries and probably contained most of the works of Greek philosophy, literature, and science, either in the original or copied by hand. During the reign of Queen Cleopatra, one of Ptolemy's descendants (around 30 B.C.E.), a part of the library was burned down by the Roman army, possibly by mistake. When another section of the library went up in flames in 391 C.E. (along with a pagan temple), there was no doubt that the destruction was caused by Christian extremist fundamentalists. It is, of course, important to note that these small groups of fanatics were an exception. Most Christians in the Roman Empire were not extremist, nor did they advocate terror, any more than they do today. In 380 Emperor Theodosius had made Christianity the official religion of Rome; Emperor Constantine had converted already in 312 C.E., and at the Church Council in Nicea in 325 the Christian bishops had established what were to count as official Christian sacred writings of the Old and the New Testament.

One last word about the library in Alexandria: Its ultimate destruction came at the hands of Islamic fundamentalist invaders in 646 C.E. Scholars estimate that science suffered a setback of perhaps a millennium from the loss of the library; humanity's loss in works of art—philosophy, literature, drama, and artifacts—cannot be measured. And there is a further lesson, that religious fanaticism is not the monopoly or invention of one religion, past or present.

From the time of the Renaissance to well into the twentieth century, questions of ethics were less a matter of doing the right thing to please God and more a matter of doing the right thing because it led to general happiness—because it was prudent or because it was logical. However, present-day scholars interested in virtue ethics have put forth the following argument: You may choose to do the "right thing" to please God or to escape unpleasant consequences or to make some majority happy or to satisfy your inner need for logic—but you may still be a less than admirable person. You

Hypatia (370–415 C.E.), the leader of the Neoplatonic Institute in Alexandria and one of the first female philosophers that we know of, was driving through the streets of town in her chariot when she was intercepted, tortured, and killed by Christian extremists.

may give to charity, pay your taxes on time, remember your nieces' and nephews' birthdays, hold the door for physically challenged people, and still be a morose and mean person. As we saw in the chapter on psychological egoism, you may be doing all the "correct" things just to get a passport to heaven or to be praised by others or to make sure they owe you a favor. So "doing the right thing" doesn't guarantee that you are a good person with a good *character*. However, if you strive to develop a good character—to be courageous or protective or tolerant or compassionate—then, on the basis of this character trait, you will *automatically* make the right decisions about what to do, what course of action to take. In other words, virtue ethics is considered to be more fundamental than ethics of conduct, yielding better results.

In today's discussions on ethics, opinions are divided as to the merits of virtue versus conduct; however, no virtue theory is complete without recognition of the importance of conduct. We can have a marvelous "character," but if it never translates into action or conduct, it is not of much use—and how do we develop a good character in the first place if not through *doing* something right? Also, one of the most conduct-oriented ethical theories, Kant's deontology, has the question of character embedded in it. For Kant, a good character in the form of a *good will,* a fundamental respect for other people, and respect for the nature of the moral law itself is essential to the moral decision process. Indeed, one-half of the book he wrote late in life, *The Metaphysics of*

Morals, focuses on a doctrine of virtue (in Chapter 6 you read the section concerning *lying*), and what he used to call the good will is here renamed a *virtuous disposition*. The question of whether we should choose ethics of conduct or virtue ethics is a bifurcation fallacy or a false dilemma (see Chapter 1); we can certainly decide that there is room for both approaches.

In this and the next chapter we look at the classical virtue theories of Plato and Aristotle. We then move on to some examples of modern virtue theory.

The Good Teacher

The saying goes that a good teacher is one who makes herself or himself superfluous. In other words, a good teacher lets you become your own authority; she or he does not keep you at the psychological level of a student forever. As a matter of fact, great personalities who have had considerable influence on their followers often have failed in this respect. For a teacher it is hard to let go and consider the job done (whether one is a professor or a parent), and for a student it is often tempting to absorb the authority of the teacher, because life is hard enough as it is without having to make your own decisions about everything all the time. This is what the good teacher or parent prepares the student for, however—autonomy, not dependence.

The teacher-student relationship between Socrates and Plato would probably not have become so famous if Plato had remained merely a student, a shadow of the master. Indeed, we have Socrates' own words (at least through the pen of Plato) that the good teacher does not impose his ideas on the student but rather serves as a midwife for the student's own dormant intellect. In many ways Socrates has become a philosophical ideal. As we shall see, he stood by his own ideals in the face of adversity and danger; he believed in the intellectual capacities of everyone; he strove to awaken people's sense of critical thinking rather than give them a set of rules to live by, and, above all, he believed that "the unexamined life is not worth living."

Socrates, Man of Athens

What do we know of Socrates? There is no doubt that he lived—he is not a figment of Plato's imagination, as much as Plato may have made use of poetic license in his writings. Aristophanes, the author of comedies in Athens, refers to Socrates in his play *The Clouds* (albeit in a rather unflattering way). The fact is that we don't have any writings by Socrates himself, for his form of communication was the discussion, the live conversation—what has become known as the *dialogue*. From this word is derived the term for Socrates' special way of teaching, the *dialectic method* (sometimes also called the *Socratic method*). A method of teaching that uses conversation only, no written texts, is not exactly designed to affect posterity, but posterity has nevertheless been immensely affected by our indirect access to Socrates through the writings—the *Dialogues*—of Plato.

What we know of Socrates is that he lived in Athens from approximately 470 to 399 B.C.E. The son of a sculptor and a midwife, he was married to Xantippe and had children. He was one of several teachers of philosophy, science, and rhetoric in Athens at a time when internal politics were volatile (aristocrats versus democrats) and when Greece, which had experienced a golden age of cultural achievements in the wake of the Persian wars, was actually on the verge of decline. The single most important political element of the time was the city-state, the *polis* (the origin of the word *politics*). With the peculiar features of the Greek countryside—the inland features of tall mountains and the seaside features of islands—the stage had been set for centuries for a specific power structure: small, independent, powerful realms warring and/or trading with one another. Two of the main areas were Athens and Sparta. Each area, a state in itself, considered itself to be geographically Greek but politically specific to its particular *polis*. Thus it meant more to an Athenian to be a citizen of Athens than it meant to be Greek. Being a free citizen of a particular *polis* carried with it an inordinate pride. Today some might condemn such a pride as being overly nationalistic or even chauvinistic (in the original sense of the word); for a Greek of the time it was a reasonable feeling. When Socrates was younger, he had been a soldier in the Athenian infantry and had distinguished himself as a courageous man. The loyalty to Athens that was expected of him then was something he lived up to his entire life; indeed, when he returned from the war, he stayed put in his hometown.

In one of Plato's dialogues, *Phaedrus,* Socrates and a friend, Phaedrus, have ventured outside the city walls, and Socrates carries on about the beauty of nature, the trees and the flowers, to such a degree that Phaedrus remarks that Socrates acts like a tourist. Socrates agrees, because he never ventures outside of Athens, not even to go to the Olympic Games. The city of Athens is everything to him. It is the life among people, the communication, the discussions, the company of friends that are important to him, not nature, as beautiful as it may be: "My appetite is for learning. Trees and countryside have no desire to teach me anything; it's only the men in the city that do."

It is not unusual to hear a big-city person say the same thing today—that New York or Paris or Rio has everything they could ever want. Most of us think such people are missing out on a few things, but Socrates' attitude becomes crucial to our understanding of his conduct toward the end of his life.

The Death of Socrates and the Works of Plato

Many cultures take the position that someone's life cannot be judged until it is over, that the ending helps define—sometimes even determine—how we think of the life spent. This may seem terribly unfair, for few of us are in full control of our lives, and we would prefer not to have our accomplishments judged primarily by circumstances beyond our control. In the case of Socrates, though, it seems fitting that his life is judged in the light of his death, for in the face of adversity, in the ultimate "situation beyond his control," he seems to have remained in full control of *himself.* This is another reason that Socrates has become not just the philosopher's ideal but also a human role model—because he did not lose his head but instead faced injustice with courage and rationality.

After what in antiquity passed for a long life (he was nearing age seventy), Socrates found himself in a difficult political situation, brought about by several factors. First, Socrates had great influence among the young men of Athens—those young men who might be of political influence in the future—and many were the sons of noblemen.

Jump Start by Robb Armstrong

JUMP START reprinted by permission of United Feature Syndicate, Inc.

The words of Socrates sometimes turn up in popular culture, such as in this comic strip about a young police officer and his family. Here his mother, an erudite woman, quotes Plato. Another introduction to Socrates from the realm of popular culture is the film *Bill and Ted's Excellent Adventure,* although Bill and Ted persist in pronouncing his name wrong.

Second, Socrates conducted his classes in public (this was customary at the time in Athens, prior to the formalization of classes, schools, and academy life), and his method was well known to his students, as well as to any city council member who might cross the agora (the public square) while Socrates was teaching. Socrates used a certain method of *irony* to get his point across, and this often involved engaging politicians in a discussion under the pretext of ignorance in order to trick the speaker into revealing his own ignorance or prejudice. His students adored him for it, because this was the ultimate "questioning of authority." The fact that Socrates himself may have been serious in a roundabout way about claiming his ignorance was something his listeners may not have realized. Socrates did not adhere to any one conception of reality unless it could be tested by reason; in other words, he would not profess to "know" anything for certain before investigating it and discussing it. This attitude, which was essentially one of humility rather than arrogance, seems to have been lost on his enemies, and over the years he acquired a considerable number of such enemies. Third, the most elusive factor but perhaps also the most important one: Athens was changing; what had been a place of comparatively free exchange of ideas, the undisputed center of the intellectual Western world, was becoming a place in which people expressed themselves more cautiously. Old laws against impiety were now more thoroughly enforced, and people were being banished for offenses against the state. The reason was complete exhaustion after thirty-seven years of war with Sparta, political upheavals, and an ensuing suspicion of dissidents. Most important, in Socrates' case, he had expressed reservations concerning the democratic government (not "democratic" in any modern political or partisan sense of the word, but a form of government in which male citizens of the city-state had a political voice, as opposed to the oligarchic form of government by the few). For most of Socrates' life Athens had had a democratic constitution, but during a brief, troubled time after Athens lost the long Peloponnesian War to Sparta, a group of aristocrats seized power and overthrew the constitution. The leader of this group of "Thirty Tyrants," Critias, had been a former member of Socrates' circle, and although Socrates himself fell into disfavor with the tyrants, scholars speculate that some of his enemies had old scores to settle, even though the new Athenian democratic government had given amnesty to all involved in the affair after the fall of the tyrants. Another of Socrates' earlier associates, Alcibiades, had been responsible for a major naval expedition that went terribly wrong: He deserted, and the expedition was destroyed. These connections may also have contributed to the downfall of Socrates.

Eventually his enemies took action. There was no way of getting rid of Socrates by political means, so they resorted to what appears to be a standard charge: that Socrates was "offending the gods and corrupting the youth." Socrates was tried and convicted by a jury of 500 male citizens of Athens. The Athenian court would vote once for conviction or acquittal, and once again if the verdict was guilty, in what we today would call the "penalty phase," determining the punishment. Socrates himself gave two speeches, one in his defense, and one concerning his punishment. His speech during the penalty phase featured an in-your-face suggestion that the proper punishment would be not death, but a *reward* for services to the state, much like a sports hero: to be feted by the city of Athens.

The verdict was determined by a simple majority, not by a unanimous vote. The jury was almost split down the middle as to Socrates' guilt: Some speculate that if Socrates had had another 30 votes in his favor, he would have been acquitted. It seems that 280 voted for conviction, while 220 voted for acquittal, and a tie vote—half the difference between 280 and 220—would have been resolved in favor of the accused. But the votes in favor of the death penalty after Socrates' "reward" speech were considerably higher than for his conviction—which means that some people who had thought him innocent were now so outraged at his behavior that they voted for capital punishment.

It seems possible that his enemies did not intend to get rid of Socrates by actually executing him. The standard reaction to such charges by accused citizens was to leave the city and go elsewhere within the Greek realm, and there were many places to choose from, because this realm extended from Italy well into the Middle East. But because Socrates chose to stand trial, arguing that by leaving he would be admitting guilt, his fate appeared sealed. Even so, to the last minute there were powers working to free him; his friends, many of whom were of considerable influence, conspired to spring him from jail and bring him to exile in safety. In Plato's dialogue *Crito* we hear how Socrates' good friend Crito pleads with him to listen to his friends and take their offer of escape and life, because "otherwise people will say we didn't do enough to help you." Socrates answers:

> In questions of just and unjust, fair and foul, good and evil, which are the subjects of our present consultation, ought we to follow the opinion of the many and to fear them; or the opinion of the one man who has understanding? . . . Then, my friend, we must not regard what the many say of us: but what he, the one man who has understanding of just and unjust, will say, and what the truth will say.

When Crito suggests that Socrates ought to escape because he has been convicted by unjust laws, Socrates replies that two wrongs don't make a right, and the laws of

The Death of Socrates (1787) by Jacques-Louis David shows Socrates still exploring issues of life and death with his friends, even though he will soon drink the cup of poison prepared for his execution by the distraught jailer.

Athens have supported him throughout his life; even though unjust, they are still the laws of Athens. If he, Socrates, had been a less faithful citizen of Athens, he might choose to leave, but because he never left the city, he believes he has to live by his own rule of respecting the laws and the rules of reason and virtue and not turn his back on them.

So Socrates, the citizen of Athens, could not envision a life away from the city, even when the alternative was death.

Could Socrates have done a better job defending himself? Given that only a narrow majority of the 500 jury members found him guilty, it seems clear it wouldn't have taken much for that small majority to change their minds. In Plato's dialogue the *Apology* (an excerpt of which appears as a Primary Reading at the end of this chapter), Socrates isn't exactly expressing himself cautiously or diplomatically in his address to his judges. He is assuming they will use rational judgment and see his point of view; he doesn't seem to understand the considerable animosity many feel toward him. The end result is of course a conviction. Since we can see in retrospect that another style of argumentation, or even just being slightly apologetic, might have saved his life, many have speculated that perhaps he didn't try too hard because he *wanted* to die and make a point. This theory goes all the way back to Plato's contemporary Xenophon, who thought Socrates deliberately antagonized the jury to get

During the time of Socrates (fifth century B.C.E.) the Greek cultural realm stretched from Italy in the west to Asia Minor in the east; although people would consider themselves citizens of the Greek culture, their most important affiliation was with the city-state (*polis*) in which they were born.

a conviction. Others are convinced that he didn't and claim that he was arguing in a style completely true to his personality and outlook on life, that he fought for his life in court, in his own way, until the very end.

In the Narratives section you will find another historical figure, Sir Thomas More (*A Man for All Seasons*), who apparently made the same choice: that standing up for the truth is more important than staying alive. But that doesn't mean he, or Socrates, *wanted* to die. You might say they chose integrity over personal concerns, and that is probably what makes the Socratic example so compelling.

Since we're speculating, let's take it one step further: What might have happened if the jury had been convinced of Socrates' innocence—or if Socrates had been convinced by Crito and had allowed himself to escape? If Socrates hadn't been executed, chances are Plato wouldn't have become a writer or a philosopher, for he wouldn't have felt compelled to preserve Socrates' name for posterity and give him philosophical immortality. And without Plato's writings we would have no Platonism, no school influencing antiquity for nine hundred years and beyond, into Christianity. And without Plato's school the young man from Stagira who came to the big city of Athens to get an education—Aristotle—might never have become a philosopher. And without Aristotle's philosophy? Universities would probably be structured differently, sciences would have other categories, ethics would be different, and elements of Christianity would be absent. Our world might look substantially different today if Socrates had died a natural death.

Was Socrates guilty? His accusers may have believed so, although we may find it hard to imagine why. Did he offend any gods? He seems to have been a religious man; he often made the traditional sacrifices to the gods, and Plato has him referring to gods or "the god" often in his dialogues. But Socrates also referred to what he called his *daimon* (spirit), a little voice inside him telling him what to do. It is hard to know whether he was just talking about his conscience or whether he believed in some guardian spirit, but it may have seemed to his accusers that he was trying to introduce new gods. Did he corrupt the youth of Athens? Well, yes, if you believe that teaching young people to think for themselves, to use their reason in search of the truth, is corrupting them. In his speech in his own defense (see *Apology* in the Primary Reading section) Socrates asked those young people to come forth if they felt they had been corrupted; of course, none of the young people of his own circle did.

Plato tells us about the last, dignified minutes of Socrates' life, thereby giving history and philosophy the legacy of someone who chose to die for a rational principle. The scene is vividly described in the dialogue *Phaedo*. Plato writes that he himself wasn't present because of illness, and the story of Socrates' death is told by another student, Phaedo, but others have speculated that Plato may have already left Athens as a precaution, fearing reprisals against Socrates' supporters. In the end, Socrates' friends and students are gathered to say good-bye. They are on the verge of breaking down, while Socrates does his best to keep their spirits up. Even the jailer who brings in the poison apologizes to the old philosopher for having to cause him harm and hopes Socrates will not hold it against him. Socrates assures him that he will not and swallows the poison, an extract of hemlock. He continues talking, but the end approaches quickly. He lies down and pulls a blanket over himself, covering himself completely. But then—it must have been a dramatic moment for his friends—he removes the cover from his face for a final statement. And what are the last words coming from the Master's mouth? None of the wisdom they were used to hearing him speak, such as "The unexamined life is not worth living." No, he says to his old friend Crito, "I owe a rooster to Asclepius—will you remember to pay the debt?" Crito promises that he will, and within minutes Socrates is dead. The meaning of this request has been discussed by philosophers ever since. Was Socrates driven by the memory of an unpaid debt, or was he talking in symbolic terms? Asclepius was a common Greek name but also the name of the god of healing. Did he want his friends to sacrifice the rooster to the god because Asclepius had "cured" him—that is, released his soul from the prison of the body? We can only guess.

The effect of Socrates' death on Plato was profound. Born in about 427 B.C.E., Plato had been Socrates' student, in an informal sense, for thirteen years, and the death of his teacher caused him to take leave of Athens for a lengthy period, during which he traveled to Egypt and Sicily, among other places. Eventually he returned to Athens, and some time before 367 B.C.E. he founded his own school of philosophy, the Academy (Plato's own home—which he opened up to his students—named after the Greek hero Academus). This school appears to have been the beginning of a more formalized teaching institution, with regular lectures and several professors associated with the school. It remained open until 529 C.E., when it was closed by Christians. As Plato took on the mantle of his teacher, he began to reconstruct Socrates' intellectual legacy

Plato (427?–347 B.C.E.) was the son of Ariston and Perictione. They named their son Aristocles, but he became known as Plato, literally "broad." Some people speculate that it meant "broad forehead," referring to his wide knowledge, but others trace the term back to—wrestling! Plato was a wrestler in his youth, and his nickname traveled with him into his career as a philosopher. It seems to have indicated that he had broad shoulders. His father died when Plato was a young boy. His mother Perictione was apparently a philosopher in her own right, although women in ancient Greece had virtually no independence.

by writing the *Dialogues*. These books remain some of the most influential writings in philosophy, but they also are works of literature, as brilliant as any drama written in antiquity. That Plato from the very first dialogues reveals himself to be a great storyteller is all the more interesting, for, as you may remember from Chapter 2, he himself was not in favor of the arts, because he believed they spoke to people's emotions and made them forget the cool balance of reason. And, yet, Plato's own writings are works of art in themselves. Socrates and his friends and students come alive. We understand their way of talking, and we gain insight into their thinking, which, on occasion, is rather alien to our own day and age. The early dialogues of Plato give a picture of Socrates that is very fresh and probably quite accurate. However, scholars believe that in later dialogues Socrates changes into something that is more Plato's image of an ideal philosopher than Socrates himself. Indeed, in the last dialogues, Socrates appears as Plato's mouthpiece for his own advanced theories on metaphysics—theories that Socrates probably never held himself. This may mean that Socrates was indeed a good teacher who did not hinder Plato from "graduating" intellectually. It also means that through this lifelong tribute to Socrates, Plato showed that you can kill a thinker but not his thoughts; so in a sense Plato made certain that Socrates, long dead at the hands of the Athenian judges, lived on to affect the history of thought well after his accusers had turned to dust.

The Good Life

Socrates' statement to Crito that some things are more important than life itself, such as being true to your principles, no matter how others may feel about it, holds the key to what Socrates seems to have considered the "good life" or a life worth living. This would be a life in which one is not ruled by the opinion of others or even by one's own opinions, those ideas of ours that may or may not have some basis in the truth but that we haven't bothered to examine closely. If we stop for a minute and examine such opinions, we will probably discover that they constitute the basis for the majority of our viewpoints: We think we live in a great country, or perhaps we think we live in a deceitful, oppressive country. We think that chicken soup is good for colds. We may think that what scientists say must be true as long as they are wearing white lab coats. Perhaps we think that people who believe in UFOs are nuts, or we think that UFOs abduct humans from time to time. We hear actors weighing in on politics, and if they are our favorite actors, perhaps we value their opinion—but how exactly do actors get to be experts on politics? Some are indeed very well informed (and some actors also happen to be politicians); others just have *opinions*. And it is the opinion issue that interested and irritated Socrates. We think a lot of things, and if we allow ourselves to examine these opinions, we will usually find that they are based on very flimsy evidence. Of course, on occasion we feel strongly about something precisely because we *have* examined it, but, in that case, Socrates would say, we are not talking about opinion (*doxa*) anymore—we are talking about knowledge (*epistēmē*). This, for Socrates, was the test of truth: Can it stand up to unprejudiced scrutiny? If so, it must override any sort of opinion we may have, even though it may hurt the feelings of others, because if they see the truth, they, too, will understand, for *only ignorance leads to wrongdoing*. For Socrates as well as for Plato this is a truth in itself: No one is willfully evil, provided that he or she understands the truth about the situation. And if a person still chooses the wrong course of action, it must be because his or her understanding is faulty.

For a modern person the response to this seems inevitable: What if there is more than one way of looking at the situation? In other words, what if there is more than one truth? We are so used to assuming there is more than one way of looking at something that we sometimes assume there is no truth at all. This, however, is very far from the intellectual attitude of Socrates. For Socrates, as well as for Plato, each situation has its Truth, and each thing can be described in one way that best captures its true nature, its essence. This does not mean that this was a common attitude among Greek thinkers. In Socrates' own time, contact with other cultures had brought about a certain amount of cultural relativism, and Greece was sufficiently heterogeneous to foster a tolerance of different customs. Accordingly, for many of Socrates' contemporaries, such as the Sophists, relativism became the accepted answer to the search for absolute truth. For Socrates the theory that virtue might be a question of personal preference or relative to one's own time and culture was the epitome of misunderstanding, and much of the Socratic quest for the true nature, the essence, of a thing or a concept is a countermeasure to the prevailing relativism of the Greek intelligentsia. This also implies a fundamental Socratic principle: that truth should not be confused with appearance. The external appearance of something—a person, or a situation—is not necessarily the same as its true nature. Just as *doxa* must be discarded for *epistēmē*, appearance must yield to knowledge of the inner truth. In the Narratives section you'll find a film which, even if it is a comedy about cartoon characters, illustrates this principle that a later time has called "not judging a book by its cover": *Shrek*. Later in the chapter we return to the idea that the truth is somehow not to be judged by our senses but by our rational mind: Plato's theory of Forms.

Virtue for Socrates means to question the meaning of life and to keep one's integrity while searching, to not be swayed by one's physical longings or fear of unpleasant situations or concern for comfort. This ideal is attainable because the Truth can be found—in fact, it can be found by *anyone* who has as a guide a teacher with integrity. In other words, Socrates says we can't hope to attain virtue without the use of our *reason*. Later on (in particular during the Middle Ages), the link between virtue and reason was weakened, but, for Plato and Socrates, as well as for Greek antiquity as such, the connection was obvious. Using our reason will make us realize what virtue is and will actually make us virtuous.

The good life, therefore, is not a pleasant life in which we seek gratification for the sake of having a good time. The good life is strenuous but gratifying in its own way, because one knows that one seeks and sees the Truth, and one is in control of oneself. In the Narratives section there is a summary and an excerpt of a science fiction story from the time of the Cold War, "The Store of the Worlds," about recognizing and appreciating the good life, even if it is just our everyday life.

The Virtuous Person

Let us now focus on what makes a person good. You may remember that Plato's brother Glaucon told a story about the Ring of Gyges, stating that if you had the chance to get away with something and you didn't, you had to be stupid. For Socrates this matter was of grave importance, and this was his answer: A person who does something unjust to others is either ignorant or sick. If we inform that person that he is being unjust, he may realize his ignorance and improve himself. But there is the chance that he will laugh in our face. In that case, Socrates said, he is simply not well—he is out of balance. (When I say "Socrates says . . ." it is the same as saying "Plato says . . . ," because the words assigned to Socrates in the dialogues are, as far as we know, the opinions of Plato, at least in most cases.) Glaucon's argument that an unjust person is happier than a just person carries no weight with Socrates, because an unjust person can't be happy at all; only a well-balanced person can be happy. But what is a well-balanced person?

Everybody has desires, and sometimes these desires can be very strong. We may want something to drink when we are thirsty, something to eat when we are hungry; we have desires for sex, for power, and for many other things. We also have desires to get away from things, as when we move away from a fire we're too close to. These needs and wants Plato calls *appetites,* and these are what we must control if we are to achieve the good life. Appetites may rule a person's life, but that is not good, because the things we desire aren't necessarily the things that are good for us. (As a matter of fact, Plato is not just talking truisms here; there are many philosophers who believe that what is natural for humans is good for them!) So sometimes we pull away from what we want because we realize that it will be bad for us. This power that pulls us back is our *rational element,* our *reason.*

There is a third element at play; Plato calls it *spirit.* Sometimes he calls it *willpower.* We feel it when we sometimes let our appetites win out over our reason; afterward we feel disgusted with ourselves, and this anger directed at ourselves is our spirit. When we fall off our diet, our reason may have lost the battle, but our spirit will be angry at our weakness and will keep bothering us. What, then, should a person do? Establish a good working relationship between reason and spirit; let reason be clear about what it wants to do, and then train the spirit to help control the appetites. Reason and spirit will, side by side, keep the body healthy and the soul balanced. In his dialogue *Phaedrus* Plato describes the three-sided relationship by the following metaphor: A charioteer has two horses to pull his chariot; suppose one is well-behaved, whereas the other is wild and unruly. He is stuck with both and can't choose another horse, so he must make the well-behaved horse help him control the unruly horse and subdue it. So which roles do these figures play? The charioteer is Reason, the well-behaved horse is Willpower, and the wild horse is Appetites. Notice that a "balanced" individual to Plato does not have one-third of each element—he or she has total control by reason and willpower over appetites. When reason rules, the person is *wise;* when spirit controls the appetites, that person is also *brave* (because it takes courage to say "no" to temptation and "yes" to a painful experience); and when the appetites are completely controlled, the person is *temperate.* Such a person is well balanced and would not dream of being unjust to anybody; on the contrary, he or she would be the very picture of *justice,* and justice is the virtue that describes the well-balanced human being who is wise, brave, and temperate. Only this kind of person can be happy in the true sense of the word; Glaucon's idea that an unjust person is happier than a just person can be discarded, because such a person is off balance. (For another thinker's view of the tripartite soul, see Box 8.2.)

Plato was not just interested in the virtuous individual; further on in his famous dialogue *the Republic,* he speculates that a well-balanced person can be compared with a society in harmony with itself; as appetites must be controlled by reason and willpower, so, too, must parts of the population be controlled by other parts. Who corresponds to *reason*? Wise rulers, says Plato, "philosopher-kings" who would rather not rule; they will get the job done without fuss and with reason as their principle of guidance. Who corresponds to *willpower* in a state? The "auxiliaries," soldiers and law enforcement. And what about all the rest of the population—merchants, businesspeople, educators, entertainers, private citizens? They correspond to the *appetites* and must be thoroughly controlled. If they are not—such as in a democracy—then that society is off balance and sick. This restrictive social plan did not correspond to democratic Athenian society at all, and Plato has been vilified by democratically minded thinkers ever since. See Box 8.3 for Plato's idea of a well-balanced society.

Among modern Plato scholars there is some disagreement about Plato's intentions in his social theory of the ideal state. Its radical principles include not only a strict hierarchy but also rules about marriage and children among the philosopher-kings. For one thing, Plato advocates that anyone would be eligible as a guardian (a ruler or a soldier), depending on his or her talent and regardless of *gender;* to his contemporaries (and even to some of our contemporaries) the idea of a woman ruler (or president) is outlandish or even outrageous, but Plato apparently found it a completely reasonable thought. Most people today, however, find his rules about childbearing among the guardians too extreme and certainly both outlandish and outrageous: For the sake of eugenics (creating a superior breed of people by mating selected men and women), guardians would be paired off and mated during their childbearing years, but the children would be removed from the mothers and raised in common

Box 8.2   THE TRIPARTITE SOUL: PLATO AND FREUD

Plato

Elements of the Soul		Virtues
Reason	— corresponds to —	Wisdom
Willpower	— corresponds to —	Courage
Appetites	— corresponds to —	Temperance

Freud

Theory of the Psyche

Superego

Ego

Id

If an individual has succeeded in mastering his or her appetites by using reason to guide willpower, then a fourth virtue comes into play: *justice.* In that case Plato would say we have encountered a truly virtuous individual: a just person, a person of internal balance and integrity.

In the early twentieth century Sigmund Freud suggested a theory about the human psyche that has some parallels to Plato's theory: Freud's psyche comprises the Id (the Unconscious), the Ego (the conscious self), and the Superego (the codes and rules we have been taught). Can the Id be compared to appetites? Yes, as long as we remember that, for Freud, the Id can't be accessed, whereas Plato believed a person could understand his or her own appetites. As for the Ego and the Superego, they don't match Plato's schema too well: The Ego is part reason but also part willpower; the Superego has elements in common with both, too. The similarity between Plato's theory of the soul and Freud's theory of the psyche is not a coincidence: Freud was a great admirer of Plato's dialogues.

so that no parent would know his or her own child. Plato envisioned such a plan to allow personal preferences and affiliations to be held to a minimum so that the guardians could focus on what was good for the state.

These radical thoughts have caused some Plato scholars to say that Plato may not have meant one word of his political theory—it was all tongue-in-cheek, a big joke on his students told at a dinner party. Women in government! He couldn't possibly have been serious. However, at least two things speak for taking Plato seriously: For one thing, late in life he left his teaching position in Athens to return to Syracuse, presumably in order to tutor the young tyrant Dionysius II. Apparently Plato used his own principles as outlined in the *Republic* to try to groom Dionysius into a guardian, without much success. Even though Plato's family had intended for him to go into politics, it is obvious that Plato was much more a scholar and a writer than a successful politician. For another thing, Plato's student Aristotle had no doubt that Plato was serious, and who could be a better judge than a contemporary source who had heard Plato discuss his theories?

There is little evidence that Socrates himself ever had such political visions; his main interests seem to have been getting individuals to improve their thinking and become better persons. Examining the concept of virtue, he would begin with a concept, a word of common usage, such as *justice* or *piety,* and ask his partners in the dialogue to define it, under the assumption there would be one, and only one, description that would be the true one. At some point in the Platonic dialogues we begin to lose the sense that it is Socrates talking, for a theory develops that is Plato's own: the theory of Forms.

Plato's Theory of Forms

When we ask about a person's view of reality, we generally want to know whether that person is religious or an atheist, pessimistic or optimistic about other people and events, interested in a historical perspective or mainly looking to the present and the future, and so on. Philosophically speaking, however, a person's view of reality is what we call *metaphysics*. What exactly is the nature of reality as such? In philosophy the answer will be one of three major types: Reality is made up of things that can be measured (*materialism*); or Reality is totally spiritual, all in the mind (*idealism*); or Reality consists of part matter, part mind (*dualism*). (These three theories of metaphysics are described in Box 8.4.) What, exactly, was Socrates' philosophical view of reality? The early dialogues indicate that he seems to have believed in an immortal soul that leaves the body at death, which would make him a dualist. In later dialogues, though, Plato chooses to let Socrates speak for a theory—which was obviously Plato's own—that says reality is very much different from what our common sense tells us. What we see and hear and feel around us is really a shadowy projection of "true reality." Our senses can't experience it, but our mind can, because this true reality is related to our mind: It is one of the Ideas, or *Forms*.

What exactly is a Form? Today it is hard to grasp Plato's concept, but for the Greek mind of Plato's own day it was not so alien. In early times the Greeks saw each good thing as represented by some divinity; there was a goddess for justice, another for victory. There were the Muses, lesser goddesses representing each form of art. The Olympic gods each had their own areas of protection. At the time of Plato many intellectuals, including Plato himself, had left traditional Greek religion behind. Some of the ancient tendency to personify abstract ideas, though, may have survived in his Forms. A Form is at once the ideal abstraction and sole source of each thing that resembles it. Let us look at an example. There are all kinds of *beds* today—double beds, twin beds, bunk beds, futons, waterbeds, hammocks. Plato would ask, What makes these things beds? We, today, would approach the question in a functionalistic manner and say something about them all being things to sleep on. Plato would say they are all beds because they all participate in the Form of Bed, a kind of ideal "bedness" that they not only have in common as a *concept* but that also actually *exists* above and beyond each singular bed. It is this quality that gives the bed its share of reality, as a

Box 8.3   A WELL-BALANCED PERSON IN A WELL-BALANCED SOCIETY

On page 389 you'll find a graphic illustrating Plato's notion of a well-balanced soul—not Plato's own illustration, mind you, but a shortcut that to me gathers some of Plato's key ideas: The well-balanced person's reason rules; it is aided by his or her spirit or willpower; and the person's desires are controlled at all times. Here we expand it to cover Plato's theory of the ideal society, Plato's Republic (and it is because of Plato's social theory that I thought of using the pyramid as an illustration in the first place, since Plato says that society is simply the structure of the soul, in a large format). So, following the pyramid structure of the ideal balanced soul, we have the ideal balanced society ruled by philosopher-kings (reason) at the top, a small but powerful group. Next we have the auxiliaries, meaning the soldiers and law enforcement, helping the philosopher-kings keep law

and order, and protecting everybody from unrest and enemy onslaughts (compare willpower or spirit). And at the bottom? "The people," what Plato calls merchants and tradesmen, meaning everybody who doesn't get to be in law enforcement or the military, or in government (appetites or desires). *That would mean most of us.* And following the parallel of the individual pyramid, the people never have a say about anything at all that goes beyond their own personal and professional lives—but they are not oppressed (supposedly), since the government is looking out for their interests and the interests of society as a whole (just as reason looks out for the interests of the entire body). This social model is what has caused critics—fairly or unfairly—to call Plato a supporter of totalitarianism, and the *Republic* the first blueprint for a totalitarian society.

sort of dim copy of the true Bed Form. This realm of Forms is true reality, and the entire world in which we move around is only a dim copy of the ideal Form. Where exactly *is* this world of Forms? It is nowhere that you can see and touch, because then it would just be another example of a copy. It has to be "out of this world," in a realm that our body does not have access to but that our mind does. So it is through our intellect that we can touch true reality, and only through our intellect. This is why Plato has Socrates tell Phaedrus that trees and countryside can't teach him anything— because there is nothing to be learned from the senses except confusion. The only true lesson in reality is achieved by letting the mind, the intellect, contemplate the Forms, because the world we see changes constantly, but the world of Forms never changes. The Forms are eternal, and for Plato (and for many other philosophers), the more enduring something is, the more real it is.

But how did Plato conceive of such a theory? And how does he propose to persuade us that he is right? One example answers both questions: Think of a circle; now think of a perfect circle. Have you ever drawn one? No. Have you ever seen one? No. Can you imagine one? Yes. Can you describe one mathematically (if you have the training)? Yes. If you have never experienced it, then how can you imagine it and describe it? Because your mind understands that the perfect circle really exists—not just as a mathematical formula, but in a higher, mental realm of reality. From this higher realm the perfect Form of a circle (and all the other Forms) lend

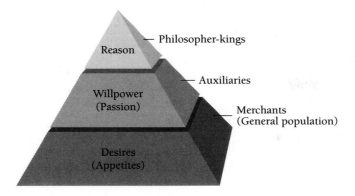

Plato himself never suggested that one might illustrate his theory of the balanced soul and the good state with a pyramid, but the image works, for several reasons. Plato imagines his ideal society to be a hierarchy of power, with the philosopher-kings on top, the auxiliaries in the middle, and the general population at the bottom. The pyramid shape lends itself naturally to this kind of social structure. But Plato also insists that the ideal society has the same structure as the ideal soul. So when the pyramid illustrates the mind of a just person, the configuration looks like this: At the top of the pyramid we have Reason—the smallest part of our mind, but the most important one. Reason has to dominate and seek the aid of Willpower (sometimes called Passion) in order to control the Desires (Appetites). This creates a very balanced person who will not be swayed by his or her emotions—just as a pyramid is a very stable structure. Imagine placing the pyramid on its tip—then you'll have the image of a person who is out of balance, because his or her reason is ruled by desires. You may want to revisit Chapters 2 and 4, and apply the pyramid image to Plato's reluctance to go to the theater for fear of losing control and to Socrates' argument against Glaucon that a person who lets desires control him is sick, and a sick person can't be a happy person.

their reality to imperfect circles and other things in our tangible world; if the Form of a circle didn't exist, then you wouldn't have a notion that a circle could be perfect! Today we would say we understand the perfect circle because we can describe it mathematically, but that doesn't mean it exists somewhere else. (See Box 8.5 for a discussion of how we can know Forms.)

Because the world of Forms is purely spiritual and immaterial, some philosophers choose to call Plato an idealist; however, more prefer to call him a dualist, because the world of matter is not "nonexistent" but merely of a lesser, shadowy existence than the world of Forms.

Does everything have a Form? Concepts such as justice, love, and beauty have their natural place in the realm of Forms; they may be on this earth incompletely, but their Forms are flawless. Cats and dogs obviously have Forms; things of nature have a perfect Form in the spiritual realm, which gives them reality. Manufactured objects have Forms too, so in the realm of Forms there is a Form of a chair, a knife, a cradle, and a winding staircase. What about a Form of something that has not "always" been—like a computer, a video game, or a microwave oven? Here we are moving into an uncomfortable area of Plato's theory, because even if microwave ovens are a new invention, presumably their Form has always existed. But what about Forms for dirt, mud, and diseases? Plato gives us the impression that the Forms are perfect and somehow closer to goodness than things on this earth; however, it is hard to envision perfect dirt, mud, and diseases, even though the theory of Forms certainly implies

Box 8.4   THREE THEORIES OF METAPHYSICS

In philosophy we encounter three major theories of the nature of reality, or of metaphysics: *materialism, idealism,* and *dualism.* Through the ages people have leaned toward one or the other, and today the prevailing theory in the Western world is overwhelmingly materialistic. This does not mean people are overwhelmingly interested in accumulating riches, although this may be the case. Metaphysical materialism has nothing to do with greed; it merely means you think reality consists of things that are *material*—they or their effects can be *measured* in some sense. This category includes everything from food to briefcases to brainwaves. It follows that a materialist doesn't believe in the reality of things supposedly immaterial, such as souls or spirits. Typical philosophical materialists are Thomas Hobbes, Karl Marx, and Paul and Patricia Churchland.

Idealism is the theory that only spiritual things have true existence and that the material world is somehow just an illusion. Again, this has very little to do with the colloquial use of the word, which we associate with a person with high ideals. Few people in philosophy define themselves as idealists today, but this theory had a certain influence in earlier times. Bishop George Berkeley was an idealist, and so was the German philosopher G. W. F. Hegel. The Hindu belief that the world we see is a mere illusion, *maya,* is also an example of idealism.

The theory of *dualism* combines materialism and idealism in that a dualist believes reality consists of a matter-side and a spirit-side—in other words, that although the body is material, the soul/spirit/mind is immaterial and perhaps immortal. Although this theory seems to appeal to our common sense, it poses several logical problems, which philosophy has not been able to solve, for how exactly does the mind affect the body if the mind is immaterial and the body is material? René Descartes is the most famous of the dualists, but Plato also is often counted among them, although some might prefer to call him an idealist because of his theory of Forms.

---

they exist. (A generation later, Plato's student Aristotle was to criticize the theory of Forms for assuming that every phenomenon has a Form. Aristotle asserted that some phenomena are merely a "lack" or deficiency of something. A doughnut hole doesn't have a Form—it is just the empty middle of a doughnut.)

The Form of the Good and Plato's Influence on Christianity

For Plato the world of Forms represents an orderly reality, nothing like the jumble of sensory experience. Forms are ordered according to their importance and according to their dependence on other Forms. Certainly worms and dirt have Forms, but they are very low in the hierarchy; at the highest level are abstract concepts such as justice, virtue, and beauty. At the very top of the hierarchy Plato sees the Form of the Good as the most important Form and also as the Form from which everything else derives.

Is the Form of the Good a god, in the final analysis? Followers of Plato around the fourth and fifth centuries C.E., the *Neoplatonists,* leaned toward that theory, but it is hard to say whether Plato himself had specifically religious veneration for his Forms; it is certain that he had intellectual respect and veneration for them and for the Form of the Good in particular.

Box 8.5   THE THEORY OF ANAMNESIS

How do we know about the Forms if we can't learn about them by observing the world around us? Plato believed that we remember the Forms from the time before we were born, because during this time the soul's home was the realm of the Forms themselves. At birth the soul forgets its previous life, but, with the aid of a philosopher "in the know," we can be reminded of the nature of true reality. This is one of the functions of Socrates in the literature of Plato: to cause his students to remember their lost knowledge. The process is known as *anamnesis,* a reremembering, or, literally, a nonforgetting. In Plato's dialogue *Meno,* Socrates shows that this knowledge is accessible to everyone, as he helps a young slave-boy "remember" truths of math and logic that he has never learned in this life.

Plato, furthermore, believed in *reincarnation* (transmigration of souls). Reincarnation was not a common belief among the ancient Greeks, who seem to have believed in a dreary, dark Hades to which all souls were destined to go, regardless of whether they had been good or bad in life. But Plato apparently saw it differently: Toward the end of the *Republic,* Socrates tells an evocative story of the soul's long journey after death, called "The Myth of Er." He claims that the soul must undergo several cycles of life before it is purified sufficiently to go back to the Forms to stay forever. We know that Plato was influenced by Pythagoras, who believed in reincarnation; but some scholars also speculate that Plato may have been under the direct or indirect influence of Hindu theories of karma and reincarnation, which had existed in India for at least five hundred years prior to Plato's own time. However, other scholars point out that Hinduism hadn't yet spread beyond isolated groups in India.

The Form of the Good allows us to understand a little better what Plato means by saying that evil acts stem from ignorance, because, according to the theory of Forms, if a person realizes the existence of the Forms and in particular the highest Form of them all, the Good, it will be impossible for that person to deliberately choose to do wrong; the choice of wrongdoing can come only from ignorance of the Good. The choice to follow the Good is not an easy one, though, even when we have knowledge of it, because we have desires that pull us in other directions. Besides, Plato says the first time we hear about the Forms, the theory sounds so peculiar that we refuse to accept our own recollection of it. Plato tells a story to illustrate this, "The Myth of the Cave." (See the excerpt from Plato's *Republic* with the story of the cave at the end of this chapter.) In a large cave a group of prisoners are kept chained to their seats so they can look only in one direction, toward a huge wall. Behind them there is a fire that casts shadows on the wall. The prisoners, having never seen anything else, believe these shadows are all the reality there is. One prisoner gains his freedom and now sees the cave, the fire, and the world outside the cave for what they really are—but will the others believe him when he returns?

As the cave is our everyday world of the senses, and as we are the prisoners who see only two-dimensional shadows instead of a multidimensional reality, we have the same problems the prisoners have when one prisoner stands up and claims that he or she has "seen the light" and knows that reality is totally different from what we think. How do we respond to such "prophets"? We ignore them or ridicule them or silence

Dilbert by Scott Adams

© 1998 DILBERT reprinted by permission of United Feature Syndicate, Inc.

The influence of Plato's "Myth of the Cave" can be detected in this *Dilbert* strip that asks, What is reality? In the *Dilbert* universe we can be sure it is our worst nightmare.

them and continue to live on in our illusion. And what is the duty of the philosopher who has seen "the light" of true reality, the Good and the other Forms, according to Plato? To return to the cave, even if it would be wonderful to remain in the light of the Truth and forget about the world of shadows. The philosopher's duty is to go back and tell the others, and this, Plato believed, was what he himself was doing with his dialogues. For Plato, Truth was not something relative that differed for each person; it was an absolute reality beyond the deceptive world of the senses, a reality that never changes and that we, when we shed the chains of our physical existence—either intellectually or through death, will be able to see and be in the presence of. (For a contemporary Cave allegory with a twist, go to the Narratives section and read the summary of the film *The Truman Show*. Truman Burbank lives in a Cave of his own, unbeknownst to himself, but on live television to the rest of the world.)

Plato's momentous influence on Western thinking is not measured by how many people took his theory of Forms to heart. As a matter of fact, not many scholars followed Plato's metaphysics to the letter; however, his idea of a never-changing realm of goodness, light, and justice to which our soul can have access made its way into Christianity, along with the Platonic disdain for the physical world as an obstruction to this access. Many early Christian thinkers had been trained in the Platonic and Neoplatonic schools of thought (which were probably taught by Hypatia in Alexandria, for one, before she was murdered), and the view of true reality as something that is not of this world came naturally to them; controlling the desires of the body and focusing on the afterlife are elements that Platonic philosophy and early Christian thinking have in common. Saint Augustine (354–430 C.E.), for example, had had a thorough pagan spiritual education prior to his conversion to Christianity at age thirty-two. He had studied Manichaeism, the then-popular Persian philosophical religion that taught the powers of light and the powers of darkness are locked in battle until the final day and

In Plato's "Myth of the Cave," a group of prisoners are placed so they can only see on the wall of the cave reflections of objects carried back and forth in front of a fire behind them. Since this is all they see, they assume it to be reality. Had Plato been acquainted with movie theaters, he might have chosen the movie screen as a metaphor for the shadow world of the senses.

the powers of light will not win unless we humans help them in their fight for goodness. He had studied Neoplatonism, a philosophy developed by the thinker Plotinus on the basis of Plato's philosophy, which taught that this tangible, material world is unimportant compared to the world of the spirit and even that the material world is godless and should be shunned. This intellectual and religious legacy that Augustine brought with him subtly changed the direction of Christianity forever, according to historians. It is, of course, the ultimate irony that Plato's Academy in Athens was closed in 529 by the Christian emperor Justinian, as you read earlier in this chapter, presumably to stop the pagan influence of the ancient school or simply as a symbolic gesture that Antiquity had come to an end—but the most influential of all Christian thinkers in the early centuries of Christianity, Augustine, was already well acquainted with the philosophical principles of Plato's metaphysics by the time he converted to Christianity. In the writings of Augustine, Christianity became a religion which, even more than previously, looked to the afterlife as the true reason for human existence and shunned earthly concerns and earthly pleasures. This disregard for the physical world and our physical existence has been heavily criticized since the end of the nineteenth century by scholars such as Nietzsche (see Chapter 10), who believe that it shows an abysmal

Box 8.6   DIVINE COMMAND THEORY AND NATURAL LAW

In Plato's dialogue *Euthyphro* Socrates is engaged in a discussion of religion and morals with a young man and asks a question that sums up one of the most persistent problems in the entire debate about religion and values then and now (because the question just won't go away): Socrates asks, Is something right because the gods command it, or do the gods command it because it is right? At the end of this chapter you'll find an excerpt from Euthyphro.

If you answer that a moral law is made right by a *divine command,* it implies that the divinity commanding the moral issue is omnipotent (all-powerful) and creates moral right and wrong, and it implies that without the divinity there would be no right or wrong; many people feel just this way about their God and their moral law. But here comes the problem: If God creates moral right and wrong, what is to prevent him (or her) from declaring that lying is morally right, or cheating, or murder? Remember that God is omnipotent (according to this *divine command theory*), and if God should decree that cheating is morally good, then it would instantly appear to us that cheating is, of course, morally good. This has the unfortunate effect of rendering the moral law *arbitrary*—it depends on God's tastes or whims. So suppose you answer that God, in his (her) wisdom, doesn't have whims and would never make cheating morally right, because cheat-

ing is simply wrong in itself. Then you have, in a manner of speaking, played into Socrates' hands, because that is his next point: If God calls murder, cheating, and lying morally wrong, then it must be because he in his wisdom realizes that they *are* morally wrong. But that means God is not seen as all-powerful anymore: The moral power of reasoning is not under his command, but it is a *natural law* of reason that even God must conform to. This argument has the advantage of making morality accessible by our reason, and it makes God's reason accessible for a believer simply because humans and God presumably share the same kind of rationality; but the concept of God as the inventor and creator of morality has gone out the window. (Here we are looking at the debate strictly from *within* a religious viewpoint; natural law does not have to lead to atheism or agnosticism, but it does lead to a view of God's power as limited by reason.)

Thomas Aquinas incorporated natural law into Catholic theology and moral thinking; this makes God's commands accessible through individual reason. The concept of natural law is more complex than that, however; it also entails a theory of what is natural for human beings, such as procreation, self-preservation, social existence, and intellectual curiosity about God. We revisit the concept of natural law in Chapter 9.

contempt for what Nietzsche saw as the only true reality there is: the ever-changing reality of our physical existence on this earth.

Study Questions

1. What are the elements that constitute a person, according to Plato? What is the proper relationship between these elements? (In other words, what is a virtuous person?)

2. You read that Socrates' last words referred to paying a debt to Asclepius. What do you think he meant?

3. Explain Plato's theory of Forms, using his story of the cave as an illustration. Is Plato's theory of reality (metaphysics) materialistic, idealistic, or dualistic? Explain.

4. Imagine that you were assigned to be Socrates' legal counsel. What would you advise him to do or say in order to escape a death sentence? Do you think it might make a difference? Why or why not?

Primary Readings and Narratives

The two Primary Readings are an excerpt from Plato's dialogue *Euthyphro,* about the question of loyalty and morals, and one from his *Apology,* his version of Socrates' speech in his own defense. The first two Narratives have Socratic themes: a summary of the film *A Man for All Seasons,* whose title character finds himself falsely accused by advisers to King Henry VIII and defends himself in a manner reminiscent of Socrates, and an excerpt from Plato's *Republic,* "The Myth of the Cave," in which people have been imprisoned all their lives so that the only reality they know is the shadows on the wall. The third Narrative is a summary of the film *The Truman Show,* a story that questions the nature of reality; and in the fourth we encounter the question of what constitutes a good life in the short story "The Store of the Worlds." The fifth narrative is a summary of the film *Shrek*—perhaps not an obvious choice as an illustration of Socratic thinking, but an eloquent defense of Socrates' argument that it is the inner truth that counts, not the world of appearances.

Primary Reading

Euthyphro

PLATO

Dialogue excerpt, fourth century B.C.E. Translated by R. F. Allen.

The dialogue *Euthyphro,* one of Plato's early works, probably depicts Socrates fairly realistically. It is particularly famous for its question *Is something right because it is favored by the gods, or do the gods favor it because it is right?* (See Box 8.6 for a discussion of this question.) This excerpt has been chosen partly for this famous question but also for the interesting exchange between Socrates and Euthyphro about the proper course of action when someone close to you is in trouble with the law or has done something wrong: Do you denounce the person for the sake of pure justice? Or do you stand by him or her in a display of friendship and loyalty? According to our moral standards of today, the idea of justice generally overrides the idea of loyalty, but, as you will see, Socrates (and Greeks in general in his day and age) thought differently. Loyalty to family and friends was an important virtue, and standing by your kin was considered a sacred duty.

Euthyphro: Perhaps you will settle your case satisfactorily, as I think I will mine.

Socrates: What about that, Euthyphro? Are you plaintiff or defendant?

Euthyphro: Plaintiff.

Socrates: Against whom?

Euthyphro: Someone I am again thought mad to prosecute.

Socrates: Really? He has taken flight?

Euthyphro: Far from flying. As a matter of fact, he is well along in years.

Socrates: Who is he?

Euthyphro: My father.

Socrates: Your own father, dear friend?

Euthyphro: Yes, indeed.

Socrates: But what is the charge? What is the reason for the suit?

Euthyphro: Murder, Socrates.

Socrates: Heracles! Surely, Euthyphro, the majority of people must be ignorant of what is right. Not just anyone would undertake a thing like that. It must require someone quite far gone in wisdom.

Euthyphro: By Zeus, very far indeed, Socrates.

Socrates: Was the man your father killed a relative? But, of course, he must have been—you would not be prosecuting him for murder in behalf of a stranger.

Euthyphro: It is laughable, Socrates, your thinking it makes a difference whether the man was a relative or not; the only thing to watch out for is whether his slayer was justified. If so, let him off. If not, prosecute him, even if he shares your health and table. For if you knowingly associate with a man like that and do not cleanse your-self, and him, by bringing action at law, the pollution is equal for you both. Now as a matter of fact, the dead man was a day-laborer of mine, and when we were farm-ing in Naxos he worked for us for hire. Well, he got drunk and flew into a rage with one of our slaves and cut his throat. So my father bound him hand and foot, threw him in a ditch, and sent a man here to Athens to consult the religious adviser as to what should be done. In the meantime, my father paid no attention to the man he had bound; he neglected him because he was a murderer and it made no difference if he died. Which is just what he did. He died of hunger and cold and his bonds before the messenger got back. But even so, my father and the rest of my rel-atives are angry at me for prosecuting him for murder in behalf of a murderer. For he did not kill him, they claim, and even if he did, still, the fellow was a murderer, and it is wrong to be concerned in behalf of a man like that—and anyway, it is un-holy for a son to prosecute his father for murder. They little know, Socrates, how things stand in religious matters regarding the holy and the unholy.

Socrates: But in the name of Zeus, Euthyphro, do you think you know so accurately how matters stand respecting divine law, and things holy and unholy, that with the facts as you declare, you can prosecute your father without fear that it is you, on the contrary, who are doing an unholy thing?

Euthyphro: I would not be much use, Socrates, nor would Euthyphro differ in any way from the majority of men, if I did not know all such things with strict accuracy.

Socrates: Well then, my gifted friend, I had best become your pupil. Before the action with Meletus begins I will challenge him on these very grounds. I will say that even in former times I was much concerned to learn about religious matters, but that now, in view of his claiming that I am guilty of loose speech and innovation in these things, I have become your pupil. "And if, Meletus," I shall say, "if you agree that Euthyphro is wise in such things, then accept the fact that I worship correctly and drop the case. But if you do not agree, then obtain permission to indict this my teacher in my place, for corrupting the old — me and his own father — by teaching me, and by correcting and punishing him." And if I can not persuade him to drop charges, or indict you in place of me, might I not then say the same thing in court I said in my challenge?

Euthyphro: By Zeus, if he tried to indict me, I would find his weak spot, I think, and the discussion in court would contain him long before it concerned me.

Socrates: I realize that, my friend. That is why I want to become your pupil. I know that this fellow Meletus, and no doubt other people too, pretend not even to notice you; but he saw through me so keenly and easily that he indicted me for impiety. So now in Zeus's name, tell me what you confidently claimed just now that you knew: what sort of thing do you say the pious and impious are, both with respect to murder and other things as well? Or is not the holy, itself by itself, the same in every action? And the unholy, in turn, the opposite of all the holy — is it not like itself, and does not everything which is to be unholy have a certain single character with respect to unholiness?

Euthyphro: No doubt, Socrates.

Socrates: Then tell me, what do you say the holy is? And what is the unholy? . . . For consider: is the holy loved by the gods because it is holy? Or is it holy because it is loved by the gods?

Euthyphro: I do not know what you mean, Socrates.

Study Questions

1. In your opinion, is something morally right because God commands it, or does God command it because it is morally right? What is the difference? (The question seems to assume that you have a religion, but it is entirely possible to approach the question theoretically: If there is a god, then does something become morally right because the god commands it, or does the god command it because it is morally right?)

2. If a close relative or a friend of yours had committed a felony, would you volunteer as a witness for the prosecution? Why or why not? What would Euthyphro advise? What would Socrates advise? Are there alternatives?

3. You may remember from Chapter 4 that in 1998, a college student from California, Jeremy Strohmeyer, raped and strangled seven-year-old Sherrice Iverson in a restroom in a Nevada casino. His friend David Cash knew about the crime taking place and may have witnessed it. Strohmeyer is serving a life sentence, but the State of Nevada wasn't

able to prosecute Cash for his silence because he had broken no law. Cash explained that he didn't want to be the one to turn Strohmeyer in because they were best friends. He was displaying the virtue of loyalty to a friend. Can this virtue be carried too far? Should he have turned Strohmeyer in? Prior to that, should he have attempted to stop the rape and murder? Are there other alternatives? Strohmeyer himself later implied that Cash was not a good friend because he could have stopped Strohmeyer but didn't. How do you view the demands and limits of the virtue of friendship?

Primary Reading

Apology

PLATO

Dialogue excerpt, fourth century B.C.E., translated by R. G. Bury.

In the *Apology*, one of Plato's dialogues, Socrates argues in his own defense while on trial. This is not a typical "dialogue" since Socrates does most of the talking, but we know he has listeners because he begs for their attention and asks them not to heckle him. Is this a true retelling of what Socrates actually said, or is Plato here (as often elsewhere) making things up? Scholars have speculated that Plato, being present at the trial, must surely have remembered every word of this traumatic, horrible event; however, the account was probably not written until some years later, perhaps as much as ten years, so we must assume that Plato tells it not only the way he remembers it but also the way he believes it *ought* to sound. Since Plato's account of the trial is not the only one in existence, we can assume that the general gist of Socrates' defense was the way Plato presented it.

I have said enough in my defense against the first class of my accusers; I turn to the second class. They are headed by Meletus, that good man and true lover of his country, as he calls himself. Against these, too, I must try to make a defense. Let their indictment be read; it runs like this: "Socrates is a doer of evil who corrupts the youth, and who does not believe in the gods of the state, but has other new divinities of his own." Such is the charge; now let us examine the particular counts. He says that I am a doer of evil and corrupt the youth; but I say, men of Athens, that Meletus is a doer of evil, since he pretends to be in earnest when he is only joking, and is so eager to bring men to trial from a pretended zeal and interest about matters in which he really never had the smallest interest. And the truth of this I will try to prove to you.

Come here, Meletus, and let me ask you a question. You think a great deal about the improvement of youth?

Yes, I do.

Tell the judges, then, who is their improver; for you must know, since you care so much.* You say you have discovered their corrupter, and are citing and accusing me before them. Speak then, and tell the judges who their improver is. Observe, Meletus, that you are silent and have nothing to say. But is not this disgraceful, and a clear proof of what I say, that you have never cared about this? Speak up, friend, and tell us who their improver is.

The laws.

But that, my good sir, is not my meaning. I want to know who the person is who, in the first place, knows the laws.

The judges, Socrates, who are present in court.

What, do you mean to say, Meletus, that they are able to instruct and improve youth?

Certainly they are.

What, all of them, or some only and not others?

All of them.

By the goddess Hera, that is good news! There are plenty of improvers, then. And what do you say of the audience—do they improve them?

Yes, they do.

And the members of the Council?

Yes, they improve them.

But perhaps the members of the Assembly corrupt them? Or do they too improve them?

They improve them.

Then every Athenian improves and elevates them except me; and I alone am their corrupter? Is that what you affirm?

That is what I stoutly affirm.

I am very unfortunate if you are right. But suppose I ask you a question. How about horses? Does one man do them harm and all the world good? Is not the exact opposite the truth? One man is able to do them good, or at least not many; the trainer of horses does them good, and others who have anything to do with them rather injure them. Is that not true, Meletus, of horses or of any other animals? Surely it is; whether you and Anytus say yes or no. Happy indeed would be the condition of youth if they had one corrupter only, and all the rest of the world were their improvers. But you, Meletus, have sufficiently shown that you never had a thought about the young; your carelessness is seen in your not caring about the very things you bring against me. Now, Meletus, I will ask you another question—by Zeus I will. Which is better, to live among bad citizens or among good ones? Answer, friend, I say; the question can be easily answered. Do not the good do their neighbors good, and the bad do them evil?

Certainly.

And is there anyone who would rather be injured than benefited by those who live with him? Answer, my good friend, the law requires you to answer—does anyone like to be injured?

Certainly not.

---

*A play on Meletus's name, which means "one who cares" in Greek. [Ed.]

And when you accuse me of corrupting the youth, do you allege that I corrupt them intentionally or unintentionally?

Intentionally, I say.

But you have just admitted that the good do their neighbors good, and evil do them evil. Now, is that a truth which your superior wisdom has recognized so early in life, and am I at my age in such darkness and ignorance that I do not know that if one of my associates is corrupted by me, I am very likely to be harmed by him? Yet I corrupt him, and intentionally too? So you say, although neither I nor any other human being is ever likely to be convinced by you. Either I do not corrupt them, or I corrupt them unintentionally; and in either case you lie. If my offense is unintentional, the law has no cognizance of unintentional offenses; you should have taken me aside privately and warned and admonished me. For if I had been better advised, I would have stopped doing what I only did unintentionally—no doubt I would; but you had nothing to say to me and refused to teach me. Instead you bring me up in court, which is a place not of instruction, but of punishment. It will be very clear to you, Athenians, as I said, that Meletus has no care at all, great or small, about the matter. But still I would like to know, Meletus, how you think I corrupt the young. I suppose you mean, according to your indictment, that I teach them not to acknowledge the gods the state acknowledges, but some other new divinities instead. These are the lessons by which I corrupt the youth, you say.

Yes, that I say emphatically. . . .

I have said enough in answer to the charge of Meletus; any elaborate defense is unnecessary. But I know only too well how many are the enmities I have incurred, and this is what will be my destruction if I am destroyed—not Meletus or Anytus, but the envy and detraction of the world, which has been the death of many good men, and will probably be the death of many more; there is no danger of my being the last of them.

Someone will say, "Are you not ashamed, Socrates, of a course of life which is likely to cause your death?" To him I may fairly answer: There you are mistaken; a man who is good for anything should not calculate the chances of living or dying; he should only consider whether in doing anything he is doing right or wrong—acting the part of a good or a bad man. . . . Wherever a man's place is, whether he has chosen it or has been placed in it by his commander, there he should remain in the hour of danger; he should not think of death or of anything but disgrace. For so it is, men of Athens, in truth.

Strange indeed would be my conduct, men of Athens, if I who, when I was ordered by the generals you chose to command me at Potidaea and Amphipolis and Delium, remained where they placed me, like any other man, facing death, and if now, when I believe the god orders me to fulfill the philosopher's mission of searching into myself and other men, I were to desert my post through fear of death or any other fear. That would indeed be strange, and I might justly be arraigned in court for denying the existence of the gods, if I disobeyed the oracle because I feared death, fancying that I was wise when I was not. For the fear of death is indeed the pretense of wisdom and not real wisdom, being a pretense of knowing the unknown; for no one knows whether death, which men in their fear think is the greatest evil, may not be the greatest good. Is not this ignorance disgraceful, the ignorance which is the conceit that man knows what he does not know? In this respect only I believe I differ from men in general, and may perhaps claim to be wiser than they are—that whereas I know but little of the world below, I do not suppose that I know; but I do know that injustice and disobedience to a better, whether god or man, is evil and dishonorable, and I will never fear or avoid a possible good rather than a certain evil. Therefore if you let me go now, and are not convinced by Anytus, who said that since I had been prosecuted I must be put to death (for otherwise I should never have been prosecuted at all), and that if I escape now, your sons will all be utterly ruined by listening to my words—if you say to me, "Socrates, this time we will not listen to Anytus and we will let you go, but upon one condition, that you do not inquire and speculate in this way any more, and that if you are caught doing so again you will die"—if this was the condition on which you let me go, I would reply: Men of Athens, I honor and love you; but I will obey the god rather than you. And while I have life and strength I will never cease from the practice and teaching of philosophy, exhorting anyone I meet and saying to him in my manner, "You, my friend, a citizen of the great and mighty and wise city of Athens, are you not ashamed of heaping up the greatest amount of money and honor and reputation, and caring so little about wisdom and truth and the greatest improvement of the soul, which you never regard or heed at all?" And if the person with whom I am arguing says, "Yes, but I do care," then I will not leave him or let him go at once, but will interrogate and examine him, and if I think he has no virtue in him, but only says he has, I will reproach him for undervaluing the greater and overvaluing the less. And I will repeat the same words to everyone I meet, young and old, citizen and alien, but especially the citizens, since they are my brothers. For this is the command of the god; and I believe no greater good has ever happened in the state than my service to the god. For I do nothing but go about persuading you all, old and young alike, not to think of your persons or properties, but first and chiefly to care about the greatest improvement of the soul. I tell you that virtue is not given by money, but that from virtue comes money and every other good of man, public as well as private. This is my teaching, and if this is the doctrine which corrupts the youth, I am a mischievous person. But if anyone says this is not my teaching, he is speaking an untruth. Therefore, men of Athens, I say to you, do as Anytus bids or not as Anytus bids, and either acquit me or not; but whichever you do, understand that I will never alter my ways, not even if I have to die many times.

Men of Athens, do not interrupt, but hear me; there was an understanding between us that you would hear me to the end. I have something more to say, at which you may be inclined to cry out; but I believe that to hear me will be good for you, and therefore I beg you not to cry out. I would have you know that if you kill such a one as I am, you will injure yourselves more than me. Nothing will injure me, not Meletus or Anytus—they cannot, for a bad man is not permitted to injure one better than himself. I do not deny that Anytus may perhaps kill me, or drive me into exile, or deprive me of civil rights; and he may imagine, and others may imagine, that he is inflicting a great injury on me; but there I do not agree. For he does himself a much greater injury by doing what he is doing now—unjustly taking away the life of another.

Study Questions

1. What does Socrates mean by saying, "The fear of death is indeed the pretense of wisdom and not real wisdom"?

2. What does he mean by saying that if the Athenians put him to death, they will hurt themselves more than him?

3. It has been speculated by philosophers that Socrates in his heart really wanted to die, and for that reason he said things in his argument for his defense that would irritate the jury of 500 citizens (who voted guilty with only a small majority); however, newer research points toward Socrates being serious about defending himself. In your opinion, based on this excerpt, should Socrates have argued for his defense in some other way?

4. Socrates has been called a martyr to the principle of seeking the Truth. Could you imagine any principle so important to you that you would be willing to give up your life for it? Alternatively, can you think of any circumstances that to you would override even the most important principle?

Narrative

A Man for All Seasons

ROBERT BOLT (SCREENWRITER)
FRED ZINNEMAN (DIRECTOR)

Based on a 1960 play by Robert Bolt. Film, 1966. Summary.

This film, which won multiple Academy Awards, including best picture, best director, and best actor, portrays a real event in England's history. It is the sixteenth century; Henry VIII is king, and he has a problem: His wife Catherine, whom the pope gave him dispensation to marry because she was his brother's widow (and as such, a relative), has not borne him any sons, and since he is concerned with the line of succession, he is looking around for another queen. The problem is that, since England is Catholic, the king has no legal access to divorce, unless clever lawyers can find a loophole in his marriage. Churchmen, government officials, and legal experts, concerned with their own future, put together a strategy: to declare the marriage annulled on the grounds that the pope had no authority to grant the permission to marry in the first place. However, there is one legal expert who refuses to go along with the scheme: Sir Thomas More, a man whom the king considers a friend. Hoping to win him over, King Henry appoints him chancellor and shows up in person at More's estate on the River Thames in order to persuade him, but he leaves in anger when it becomes clear that More considers the word of the pope to have a higher authority. Why is it so important for the king to get More on his side, when he has the support of everyone else? Because, as the king himself remarks, More is an honest man who would not choose convenience over his conscience, and receiving More's blessing would make the plan legitimate to the king. But More refuses to budge, even though he knows that incurring the king's wrath can be a dangerous thing; indeed, this is the beginning of the end for More, as his erudite daughter Margaret soon realizes.

In the 1966 film *A Man for All Seasons* we meet Sir Thomas More (Paul Scofield), a lawyer associated with the court of King Henry VIII. In this true story, More becomes a victim of his own high moral standards: The king wants More's support in annulling his marriage, but More's professional integrity won't allow him to give it. In this scene paralleling Socrates' speech in his own defense (see the *Apology*), More argues for his viewpoint and his life, well knowing that he is already condemned.

When Henry VIII institutes the Reformation and outlaws Catholicism so he can divorce Catherine and marry his new love, Anne (who herself will be executed to make way for another queen a few years later), More withdraws from his position as chancellor in silence, never uttering a word in public or private about the king's activities. A brilliant lawyer, More is trying to protect himself and his family by following both his conscience and the law to the letter, believing that his silence will be a shield, but he discovers that his silence does not protect him, as it should according to the law. As the king's man Thomas Cromwell remarks, More is an innocent and does not envision the schemes being prepared by his adversaries. A young man, Richard, who used to be part of the circle around More but believed he could find glory and fortune by attaching himself to Cromwell instead, now serves as an informant on More. But there is truly nothing to report: More is a man of integrity, the only lawyer in London who has not accepted bribes on a regular basis, says More's friend, the Duke of Norfolk. Since More refuses to sign a new oath of allegiance to the king and to accept the new rules of succession according to the Protestant Church of England, he is called in for a hearing, where his sharp legal mind outwits Cromwell; but from now on he is considered an enemy of the court, and being his friend becomes dangerous. Norfolk tries to persuade him to do as everyone else, do the convenient thing to save himself and his career, but following one's principles is more important to More than life and safety. To save his friend Norfolk from the danger and embarrassment of their friendship, he provokes a quarrel that leaves Norfolk hurt and angry, so that he turns his back on More.

Soon More finds himself a prisoner in the Tower of London, the last stage in the lives of many political prisoners; through several seasons he languishes in the damp cell without being allowed to see his family, under constant pressure from Cromwell to either sign the oath or speak up against it. We see how his posture has deteriorated; his hair is gray, and his face shows the hardship of imprisonment. One day he is surprised and overjoyed to see his family—his wife Alice, his daughter, and her husband—but when he realizes that they have been ordered to come just to put pressure on him, he understands that he will not be seeing them again and that staying in England will endanger their lives; he makes them promise that they will flee the country, by different routes, on the same day, and very soon.

His daughter asks him why he can't just sign the oath to save himself—speak it with his mouth and speak against it in his heart—and More answers,

> What is an oath, then, but words we say to God? Listen, Meg, when a man takes an oath, he is holding his own self in his own hands, like water—and if he opens his fingers then, he needn't hope to find himself again.

But Margaret is not satisfied; to her, it is not her father's fault if the state is three-quarters bad, and if he elects to suffer for it, then he elects himself a hero. More replies:

> That's very neat. If we lived in a state where virtue was profitable, common sense would make us saints, but since we see that avarice, anger, pride and stupidity commonly profit far beyond charity, modesty, justice and thought, perhaps we must stand fast a little, even at the risk of being heroes.

More knows that his daughter will understand, but his wife Alice is tormented by the suffering he is putting her through—she says she is afraid that when he is gone, she is going to hate him for what he has done to them; and, for once, at this moment, Thomas More begins to lose his composure. It means so much to him that his wife understand why he may be going to his death. He begs her to say she does, for without her understanding he might not be able to endure what is going to happen to him. And now she looks at him, embraces him, and tells him she understands that he is a good man and that he must do what his conscience tells him to do. Sad but relieved, he hugs his daughter and his wife one last time.

At last More stands trial; he has often told his family as well as his adversaries that there can be no trial because they have nothing on him; silence can be used only to signify tacit consent and not dissent. But now there is a witness: A man in fancy clothes, a rich and powerful man, approaches the bench. It is Richard, the young man who sold out to Cromwell, More's former friend who now holds a high public office, a position received in return for the perjury he is about to commit. He swears that he has heard More speak his mind, against the king and the new Church of England. Cromwell asks the questions, and his instructions to the jury consist of saying that the jury hardly need deliberate. Thus we know that they, too, must have been "instructed" prior to the trial. And indeed the verdict is "guilty." Almost deprived of his right to speak, More now rises, a condemned man, and breaks his silence, arguing that he is being executed for not agreeing to the king's divorce, which he certainly was against, because it nullified the authority of the pope. Cromwell decries this as treason; and soon after, on a sunny day in summer, More is executed by beheading.

Study Questions

1. Find similarities between Socrates and Thomas More; are there any significant differences?

2. What does More mean by saying, "When a man takes an oath, he is holding his own self in his own hands, like water—and if he opens his fingers then, he needn't hope to find himself again"?

3. If you were in More's position, what might you have chosen to do? If you had been in the position of More's daughter or wife, would you have understood and accepted his actions? Why or why not?

4. Virtue ethics, as you know, focuses not on what to do but on how to be; the film shows More as a man of honesty and integrity, two very important virtues. But would it be possible to criticize More for having failed the test of the virtues of family loyalty and flexibility? Why or why not? (This question actually reveals one of the problems with virtue ethics: What do we do about conflicting virtues?)

Narrative

The Myth of the Cave

PLATO

Excerpt from the* Republic, *fourth century* B.C.E., *translated by Francis MacDonald Cornford.

There is no better fictional narrative that illustrates Plato's theory of Forms than the Myth, Fable, or Allegory of the Cave itself. Here you have it in its entirety; the two persons talking are Socrates, telling the story, and Plato's brother Glaucon, listening.

> Next, said I, here is a parable to illustrate the degrees in which our nature may be enlightened or unenlightened. Imagine the condition of men living in a sort of cavernous chamber underground, with an entrance open to the light and a long passage all down the cave. Here they have been from childhood, chained by the leg and also by the neck, so that they cannot move and can see only what is in front of them, because the chains will not let them turn their heads. At some distance higher up is the light of a fire burning behind them; and between the prisoners and the fire is a track with a parapet built along it, like the screen at a puppet-show, which hides the performers while they show their puppets over the top.

I see, said he.

Now behind this parapet imagine persons carrying along various artificial objects, including figures of men and animals in wood or stone or other materials, which project above the parapet. Naturally, some of these persons will be talking, others silent.

It is a strange picture, he said, and a strange sort of prisoners.

Like ourselves, I replied; for in the first place prisoners so confined would have seen nothing of themselves or of one another, except the shadows thrown by the fire-light on the wall of the Cave facing them, would they?

Not if all their lives they had been prevented from moving their heads.

And they would have seen as little of the objects carried past.

Of course.

Now, if they could talk to one another, would they not suppose that their words referred only to those passing shadows which they saw?

Necessarily.

And suppose their prison had an echo from the wall facing them? When one of the people crossing behind them spoke, they could only suppose that the sound came from the shadow passing before their eyes.

No doubt.

In every way, then, such prisoners would recognize as reality nothing but the shadows of those artificial objects.

Inevitably.

Now consider what would happen if their release from the chains and the healing of their unwisdom should come about in this way. Suppose one of them was set free and forced suddenly to stand up, turn his head, and walk with eyes lifted to the light; all these movements would be painful, and he would be too dazzled to make out the objects whose shadows he had been used to see. What do you think he would say, if someone told him that what he had formerly seen was meaningless illusion, but now, being somewhat nearer to reality and turned towards more real objects, he was getting a truer view? Suppose further that he were shown the various objects being carried by and were made to say, in reply to questions, what each of them was. Would he not be perplexed and believe the objects now shown him to be not so real as what he formerly saw?

Yes, not nearly so real.

And if he were forced to look at the fire-light itself, would not his eyes ache, so that he would try to escape and turn back to the things which he could see distinctly, convinced that they really were clearer than these other objects now being shown to him?

Yes.

And suppose someone were to drag him away forcibly up the steep and rugged ascent and not let him go until he had hauled him out into the sunlight, would he not suffer pain and vexation at such treatment, and, when he had come out into the light, find his eyes so full of its radiance that he could not see a single one of the things that he was now told were real?

Certainly he would not see them all at once.

He would need, then, to grow accustomed before he could see things in that upper world. At first it would be easiest to make out shadows, and then the images of men and things reflected in water, and later on the things themselves. After that, it would be easier to watch the heavenly bodies and the sky itself by night, looking at the light of the moon and stars rather than the Sun and the Sun's light in the day-time.

Yes, surely.

Last of all, he would be able to look at the Sun and contemplate its nature, not as it appears when reflected in water or any alien medium, but as it is in itself in its own domain.

No doubt.

And now he would begin to draw the conclusion that it is the Sun that produces the seasons and the course of the year and controls everything in the visible world, and moreover is in a way the cause of all that he and his companions used to see.

Clearly he would come at last to that conclusion.

Then if he called to mind his fellow prisoners and what passed for wisdom in his former dwelling-place, he would surely think himself happy in the change and be sorry for them. They may have had a practice of honouring and commending one another, with prizes for the man who had the keenest eye for the passing shadows and the best memory for the order in which they followed or accompanied one another, so that he could make a good guess as to which was going to come next. Would our released prisoner be likely to covet those prizes or to envy the men exalted to honour and power in the Cave? Would he not feel like Homer's Achilles, that he would far sooner "be on earth as a hired servant in the house of a landless man" or endure anything rather than go back to his old beliefs and live in the old way?

Yes, he would prefer any fate to such a life.

Now imagine what would happen if he went down again to take his former seat in the Cave. Coming suddenly out of the sunlight, his eyes would be filled with darkness. He might be required once more to deliver his opinion on those shadows, in competition with the prisoners who had never been released, while his eyesight was still dim and unsteady; and it might take some time to become used to the darkness. They would laugh at him and say that he had gone up only to come back with his sight ruined; it was worth no one's while even to attempt the ascent. If they could lay hands on the man who was trying to set them free and lead them up, they would kill him.

Yes, they would.

Study Questions

1. To recapitulate: This is an allegory of what Plato sees as reality. What does it mean? Who are the prisoners? Where is the cave? What does it mean to see the sun?

2. What did Plato have in mind when he let Socrates speak the final sentences?

3. In what way might this worldview correspond to elements in the worldview of the Christian tradition? Are there significant differences?

4. Can you think of a modern story (film or novel) that speculates about the nature of reality? (Does it ask questions such as, Is reality the way we see it? What are we on this earth for? and Is there life after death?) Does it agree or disagree with Plato's version?

Narrative

The Truman Show

ANDREW NICCOL (SCREENWRITER)
PETER WEIR (DIRECTOR)

Film, 1998. Summary.

This film is one of those stories we can interpret in a number of ways. That it is a satire on the entertainment industry and its mixing of reality and fiction is the easy interpretation, but some also see it as an allegory about the freedom of the human spirit in a world that is overly regulated. It could also be one man's fantasy of being the center of the universe. But in essence *The Truman Show* is about seeking and finding true reality beyond the illusion that presents itself as everyday life, and as such it becomes a story with a Socratic twist, a parallel to Plato's "Myth of the Cave."

Truman Burbank is a young insurance salesman who lives with his wife, a nurse, in the small, pleasant island community of Seahaven, the kind of place where everybody knows everyone else—at least they all know Truman. It's a friendly town, and Truman has never been anywhere else. When he was a boy his father drowned during an outing in their sailboat: Surprised by a storm, Truman's dad fell overboard and disappeared in the waves. This traumatic experience gave Truman a fear of deep water, so the mere thought of going on the ferry to the mainland, or driving across the bridge, makes him anxious. Nevertheless, he has travel dreams: He wants to go to Fiji. As a boy he wanted to be an explorer, but his teacher was quick to tell him that all the places have already been discovered, so why would he want to go anywhere? His best friend since childhood does his best to discourage Truman's longing for exotic places, and Truman's wife points out that they can't afford to just take off, they have obligations and must meet house payments and so on. In fact, everyone seems to be trying to make Truman stay in Seahaven.

When he was in high school, he fell in love with Sylvia, a beautiful, elusive girl who seemed to have something important on her mind, but somehow they were always prevented from seeing each other—until a fateful evening at the library when they were able to sneak out and make a run for it to the beach. But within minutes a vehicle showed up, presumably driven by her father, who snatched Sylvia away from him. She wasn't normal, he said, and shouted that they were moving to Fiji. So we understand the reason Truman wants to go to Fiji isn't just to see a faraway place—it is to look for Sylvia. Before her father took her away, she tried to convey to Truman that something was wrong—but he didn't understand what she meant.

Now, years later, he is beginning to feel that something *is* wrong. His wife is constantly telling him about new household products with unnatural enthusiasm, as if she is acting in a commercial. In his car on the way to work the radio malfunctions, and he hears a voice describing the route he is taking. He walks into a building at the spur of the moment and tries to enter the elevator, only to find that there is no back wall to the elevator—he can see clear through to a backstage area where people are having lunch. But first and foremost, it is the chance encounter in the street with a homeless person who looks

Truman (a *true man*, as opposed to all the other characters in the show) is on television 24/7, but he doesn't know it. The world is real to him, while everyone else knows it is a soundstage, a world of fakery. The only thing that isn't faked in the show is Truman himself and his emotional reactions. Once he realizes his world is not real, will he try to seek true reality, or be content with illusions and safety? Compare the question asked by Socrates in the Myth of the Cave: What is the philosopher supposed to do, once he realizes he has been stuck in a cave of illusions all his life?

awfully familiar to him. He turns, takes a second look—and realizes that it is Dad, returned from the dead! But at that moment, strangers turn up and whisk the older man away on a bus.

This is the turning point for Truman: Is somebody trying to prevent him from talking to his father? Increasingly, he has the feeling that his entire reality is somehow staged and that people are not what they seem. And as viewers we know that he is right: Everything *is* staged except for Truman and his reactions, because Truman is the hero of *The Truman Show,* a live, twenty-four-hours-a-day television series broadcast to the entire world. This was the secret that Sylvia was trying to tell him but never quite managed to convey.

It is a hugely popular show. Truman has been on TV from the day he was born, without having the slightest idea that his reality isn't normal. And in a way it is "normal"—an idealized normality that doesn't exist for anyone else. His mother is an actor, his wife is an actor, even his best friend whom he has known since childhood—everyone is in on it except Truman. *The Truman Show* is the brainchild of the brilliant director Christoph, who watches over everything on the set high above Seahaven, in a control booth disguised as a perennially visible full moon. The control booth makes the sun rise and set electronically, changes the weather, and cues everyone on the set through earphones. The words of friendship spoken by his best friend are lines fed to the friend by

Christoph. In a rare interview the great director is asked why Truman has never questioned his reality, and he answers that we all believe the reality that is presented to us.

But Truman's gullibility is coming to an end: When he realizes that the travel agent has no intention of selling him a ticket to Fiji, he packs his suitcase and heads for the bus depot, and buys a ticket to Chicago. But the bus isn't going anywhere—the bus driver is an actor who can't get the bus started—and Christoph isn't about to let Truman leave. There is nowhere to go; the set is enclosed. But Truman doesn't give up. One night, as the TV crew relaxes because they think he is asleep, what they're really watching is a dummy under a blanket, with a tape recorder producing snoring sounds. Truman has sneaked out. For the first time in his life he is not on camera.

Christoph mobilizes the entire island: All the actors are now engaged in looking for Truman, but he is nowhere to be found—until they think to look for him in the unthinkable place: on the water, in a sailboat, headed for—Fiji? All over the world, viewers watch with bated breath. Will Truman succeed in his quest? Will he escape his confining, designed world? Even Sylvia is watching, praying that Truman will make it. Christoph does what he can to thwart Truman, even ordering his reluctant engineers to whip up a nearly fatal storm. In spite of his deep-seated fear of water, Truman hangs in there and outlasts Christoph's rage. He continues on his way toward the horizon—which comes up sooner than expected: All of a sudden the bow of his boat goes right through the sky, a beautifully painted backdrop. He has been sailing around in a huge tank on the soundstage.

Immediately ahead is a flight of stairs, leading up to a door. Truman steps off the boat, walks to the stairs along the edge of the world, and ascends to the door. And now Christoph, desperate, addresses him over the speaker system, a disembodied loving voice coming from above. He tells Truman about how long he has been observing him as a boy and a young man, all the kinds of experiences a parent would remember— and how well he knows him and his fears. Nothing bad can ever happen to him in Seahaven—the real world is a dangerous place. The door is open to the dark, mysterious real world. Is Truman going to go through it and disappear? or will he act true to his conditioning and go back?

Study Questions

1. What are the similarities between Plato's "Myth of the Cave" and *The Truman Show,* and what are the differences? In Plato's myth the perfect world is outside the cave. Where is it in the film? You may also want to explore the concept of one person being deluded versus humanity as such being deluded. Is this exclusively Truman's story, or are we all "Trumans," stuck on the soundstage as in Plato's cave?

2. What is the significance of Truman's first name? What does it mean in the context of the story?

3. If you could choose, would you rather have a pleasant life based on a lie, or a difficult, unpredictable life founded on a true perception of the world?

Narrative

The Store of the Worlds

ROBERT SHECKLEY

Short story, 1959. Summary and Excerpt.

What is a "good life"? For many people today it means a life of no financial worries, of material goods and successful pursuit of pleasures. Socrates believed that a good life must involve intellectual and moral awareness: "The unexamined life is not worth living," he said. In order to live a full and fruitful life, one should stay aware and alert, not take things for granted, question authority, acquire knowledge, and certainly also make a point of enjoying oneself. For Socrates a good life would be one spent thinking; analyzing; trying to be a fair, just, and decent human being; and not letting the moments of life go to waste.

This little story written at the height of the Cold War, with its constant fear of sudden global nuclear annihilation, offers a version of what a good life is that may come as a surprise to you. And then again, perhaps not. For Mr. Wayne's fantasy of a perfect life doesn't involve fame or fortune, just the chance to enjoy more of an ordinary life that is gone forever. In the wake of September 11, I think many of us understand the moral of this little story—as does anyone who has come face-to-face with the loss of the daily life he or she has taken for granted.

Mr. Wayne is on a clandestine errand: Making certain he hasn't been followed, he slips into a small, obscure shack, clutching a parcel. Inside the primitive shack is the man he has come to see, Mr. Tompkins. Mr. Tompkins's activity is illegal, and yet word has spread about it; Wayne would like to know more. Tompkins explains.

> What happens is this, you pay me my fee. I give you an injection which knocks you out. Then, with the aid of certain gadgets which I have in the back of the store, I liberate your mind. . . . Your mind, liberated from its body, is able to choose from the countless probability-worlds which the Earth casts off in every second of its existence.

In every second of Earth's existence, Tompkins explains, alternate realities have been created: All the ways things could have happened, but didn't, in our own reality. You can spend a year in any alternate reality you choose! But the fee is high: Just about everything you own, plus ten years off your life. It will have the complete feel of reality, and the method of choosing will not even be conscious; your choice will be guided by your deepest unconscious desires. Tompkins is still working on a way to make it permanent, but so far he can manage only a year, and that is so strenuous to the body that the customer loses ten years of lifetime.

Mr. Wayne is fascinated, and tempted, but the price frightens him, so he asks if he can think it over. All the way home on the train to Long Island he ponders. But when he arrives home, he has other things to think about: His wife Janet needs to discuss household problems with him, his son wants help with his hobby, and his young daughter wants to tell about her day in kindergarten. Janet notices that he seems preoccupied, but he has no intention of telling her that he went to see the weirdo at the Store of the Worlds.

Next day his attention is completely absorbed by things at the office: Middle East events cause a panic on Wall Street, so he has to put all thoughts of the Store on the back burner. On weekends he goes sailing with his son; his daughter catches the measles; the boy wants to know about atomic bombs and hydrogen bombs and cobalt bombs and all the other kinds, and Wayne explains to the best of his ability. Sometimes on summer nights he and Janet go sailing on Long Island Sound, and it is cool and lovely. Occasionally he thinks about the Store; but autumn comes, and there are other everyday things to deal with. In mid-winter there is a fire in the bedroom, and the repairs put all luxuries out of his reach. Working at the office, worrying about the political tensions around the world, taking care of his son when he comes down with the mumps—all of a sudden it is spring again—a whole year has passed. . . .

"Well?" said Tompkins. "Are you all right?"

"Yes, quite all right," Mr. Wayne said. He got up from the chair and rubbed his forehead.

"Do you want a refund?" Tompkins asked.

"No. The experience was quite satisfactory."

"They always are," Tompkins said. . . . "Well, what was yours?"

"A world of the recent past," Mr. Wayne said.

"A lot of them are. Did you find out about your secret desire? Was it murder? Or a South Seas island?"

"I'd rather not discuss it," Mr. Wayne said, pleasantly but firmly.

"A lot of people won't discuss it with me," Tompkins said sulkily. "I'll be damned if I know why."

"Because—well, I think the world of one's secret desire feels sacred, somehow. No offence . . . Do you think you'll ever be able to make it permanent? The world of one's choice, I mean?"

The old man shrugged his shoulders. "I'm trying. If I succeed, you'll hear about it. Everyone will."

"Yes, I suppose so." Mr. Wayne undid his parcel and laid its contents on the table. The parcel contained a pair of army boots, a knife, two coils of copper wire, and three small cans of corned beef.

Tompkins's eyes glittered for a moment. "Quite satisfactory," he said. "Thank you."

"Good-bye," said Mr. Wayne. "And thank *you*."

Mr. Wayne left the shop and hurried down to the end of the lane of grey rubble. Beyond it, as far as he could see, lay flat fields of rubble, brown and grey and black. Those fields, stretching to every horizon, were made of the twisted corpses of cities, the shattered remnants of trees, and the fine white ash that once was human flesh and bone.

"Well," Mr. Wayne said to himself, "at least we gave as good as we got."

That year in the past had cost him everything he owned, and ten years of life thrown in for good measure. Had it been a dream? It was still worth it! But now he had to put away all thought of Janet and the children. That was finished, unless Tompkins perfected his process. Now he had to think about his own survival.

With the aid of his wrist geiger he found a deactivated lane through the rubble. He'd better get back to the shelter before dark, before the rats came out. If he didn't hurry he'd miss the evening potato ration.

Study Questions

1. What was the world of Mr. Wayne's secret desire? What might the author want to convey with this story? Does it seem more relevant to you because of 9/11? Why or why not?

2. How might Socrates comment on this story? Has Mr. Wayne examined his life, thus making it worth living?

3. Describe what you would call "a good life."

4. Today we are close to having access to Mr. Tompkins's invention through computerized *virtual reality;* given the choice of alternate realities, which would you choose to spend a year in? Would you consider the lesson of "The Store of the Worlds"?

5. Is this a didactic story? Why or why not?

Narrative

Shrek

TED ELLIOTT (SCREENWRITER)
ANDREW ADAMSON AND VICKY JENSON (DIRECTORS)

Based on the book by William Steig. Film, 2001. Summary

To put a green ogre in the company of Socrates and Plato may seem sacrilegious to some, but as it happens, the film *Shrek* nicely illustrates one of the key lessons of Socrates: that you can't judge something by its appearance. Socrates himself was by no means a handsome man, according to the Greek ideal of beauty in his own day, but we have all learned to see the beauty of Socrates as something internal rather than external. And here comes Shrek, who teaches the same lesson to children and adults, many of whom will never get anywhere near a textbook featuring Socrates, let alone Plato's *Dialogues.* Contrary to most of the story summaries in this book, I have to reveal certain aspects of the ending, because otherwise the Socratic lesson isn't clear, and I apologize if I've revealed more than you'd like to know!

Down in the swamp lives an ogre, a great green monster; he has the countryside terrified of him because he is mean and, above all, antisocial. As we get to know Shrek (whose name in German, *Schrek,* means *terror*), we come to understand that his seclusion isn't just because he wants it that way—he is convinced that because of his meanness and ugliness nobody will want to hang out with him. He needs no one, and nobody needs him. But fate has a job for Shrek: rescuing the Princess Fiona from her captivity in the tower guarded by the dragon, so she can marry her Prince Charming. The fairy tale demands that the prince himself rescue her, but he is a bit too comfortable and fastidious, so through blackmail, threatening to destroy Shrek's home in the swamp, he hires

Throughout Plato's *Dialogues* Socrates emphasizes that we shouldn't judge anything by its appearance—that we must look for the inner essence of things. This is, of course, a timeless lesson that can be taught in different ways to each new generation. In the *Shrek* films we learn that we shouldn't judge an Ogre by his frightening looks or bad reputation—or a beautiful princess by her daytime appearance—because beauty can be an inner quality. Here Fiona and Shrek are feeling a mutual attraction, even if Shrek at this point doesn't know Fiona's secret: that she, too, is part Ogre.

Shrek to be the knight in shining armor, by proxy. But no knight is complete without a squire, and an unlikely one presents himself: the talking donkey, Donkey. Now Donkey wants desperately to spend time with his new friend Shrek (he fantasizes about spending the night and making waffles in the morning), because he is even more lonely than the ogre, but Shrek is not interested.

Outsmarting the dragon, Shrek rescues the princess, who is as beautiful as her legend has foretold. But she is an impatient, haughty woman and can't quite believe that her Prince Charming has sent someone in his place—that just isn't done. She's supposed to love her rescuer, and he is not supposed to be working for someone else.

Together, the three make their way back to Prince Charming's kingdom, and on the journey we get to know the princess better. She and Shrek are developing a mutual liking for each other, and in a private moment, as the sun sets, we learn her secret: During the daytime she is a human beauty, but at night she is transformed into the shape of— an ogre, a chubby green woman. The transformation from one to the other is a punishment her parents tried to hide by placing her in the tower, and now she has to hide from her rescuers until she meets the prince because, as legend has it, love's first kiss will transform her into her true shape. Shrek has no inkling of her dual nature—but Donkey

sneaks a peek and learns her dark secret. Now you'd think that if Fiona is a part-time ogre, she and Shrek could find common ground. Not so, because Shrek overhears her bemoan her ugliness and thinks she's talking about him. So for the rest of the journey they are alienated.

When Fiona is introduced to the prince, she is terribly disappointed—Prince Charming is a conceited little man with grandiose notions of himself. But she's convinced that he is her Prince Charming, and she will find rescue and redemption through him, so she follows him to the castle and engages in wedding preparations. Shrek goes home and sulks—and has to face an additional problem, because his swamp has been taken over by squatters, other fairy tale beings who have been evicted from their traditional homes by the prince.

But it wouldn't be a fairy tale if it didn't have a happy ending: Shrek realizes that he can't just stand by and watch her get married, and she realizes that she's already met her true love, and it's not Prince Charming—it's Shrek. So Shrek invades the wedding and kisses her at the altar. Love's first kiss—which will transform her into her true form! And the transformation happens, miraculously. Before us stand—two ogres. Her true shape is the shape of the ogre, the dimply, chubby, sweet green woman, perfectly suited for Shrek, if you believe that couples have to be of the same physical type . . . and they have a wedding party, and everybody lives happily until the sequel. And even Donkey finds love—because the dragon, who is female, has fallen in love with him.

Now why is this a Socratic story? Shrek's true nature can't be gleaned from his threatening appearance—he is the Beast to Fiona's Beauty. But Fiona herself has a true nature that is hidden under her beauty, and it may be an ogrish nature, but she is neither threatening nor beastly. Her true nature lends understanding and grace to Shrek himself, and we learn that both of them have a sweetness that is on the inside, rather than the outside. It is the inner truth that counts, not the world of appearances.

Study Questions

1. Find other stories with a similar message: It is the inner beauty and truth that count, not the external appearance. Evaluate the message: Is it always true? Why or why not?

2. Fiona is transformed from a slim, haughty beauty to a chubby, lovable ogress. Does this transformation contain an underlying discrimination against overweight people, or does it work in the opposite direction—an acceptance of people for their inner worth, regardless of their shape?

3. If you have seen *Shrek 2* (2004), you may want to weigh in on the further story: Is it still a Socratic journey to find the inner truth, or has the theme changed? *Shrek 2's* theme is, above all, the choices we make for love. What might love's choices have to do with seeing the inner truth?

Chapter Nine

Aristotle's Virtue Theory

*A*fter Plato's death in 347 B.C.E., leadership of the Academy fell to his nephew, Speusippus. History believes that another man had expected to take over, and with good reason, for he was by far the best student ever to be associated with the Academy. This man was Aristotle, who had studied for twenty years with Plato. Scholars now think that because of the amount of traveling Plato did, Aristotle may never have been especially close to his teacher; it seems certain that the closeness between Socrates and Plato was never repeated between Plato and Aristotle.

Because Aristotle was not a native-born Athenian but was born in Stagira in northern Greece (in 384 B.C.E.), he did not have the rights of Athenians and had no recourse when he was not chosen as the new leader of the school. He left Athens, presumably in anger. He traveled to Asia Minor, got married, and began his studies in biology. In 343 he went to Macedonia, where he became a tutor for the young prince, the son of King Philip. (In three short years, this boy would become the regent of Macedonia and later of an immense realm covering most of the classical world. He would come to be known as Alexander the Great.) Exactly what Aristotle's status was at court is a matter of speculation—some scholars think that his tutoring of Alexander was actually a minor job compared to the real purpose of his stay, which may have been completely political: King Philip hoped to get Aristotle elected as head of Plato's Academy even if he'd already been passed over for Plato's nephew Speusippus, because Speusippus was anti-Macedonian, and Philip apparently had expansionist ambitions and needed a pro-Macedonian leader of the most powerful school in the Greek culture. But when Speusippus died, Aristotle was passed over a second time, and King Philip focused on going to war with Athens instead. So Aristotle packed up and left for his home in Stagira, but his connection with the Macedonian court was by no means over: When Philip died suddenly, and Alexander became king, Alexander found use for his old teacher and sent him to Athens in 335 to open up a school of his own, in competition with Plato's school. There is some speculation that even at this point, Aristotle had hoped to become leader of the Academy, for he traveled to Athens with a huge amount of teaching material and an entire staff to run the school, but it never happened. Instead, Aristotle started teaching at the site of the public horse track, known as the Lyceum after Apollo Lykeion, and for twelve years—not a particularly long span, as academic careers go—he taught students and wrote books about issues that were of interest to him in philosophy, science, and what we today would call social and political science.

Empirical Knowledge and the Realm of the Senses

Making claims about someone's influence on history can be a risky business because such claims tend to be exaggerated. In Aristotle's case, however, it is quite safe to say that he is one of the persons in antiquity who has had the most influence on Western thinking and that even in modern times few people have rivaled his overall historical importance. As Plato left his legacy in Western philosophy and theology, Aristotle opened up the possibility of scientific, logical, empirical thinking—in philosophy as well as in the natural sciences.

It is no wonder that Plato made no contribution in this area. He wouldn't have been interested in natural science, because its object is the world of the senses, far removed from the Forms. Although Aristotle was a student of Plato and did believe in the general reality of Plato's Forms, he believed that Forms are *not* separate from material things; as a matter of fact, Aristotle believed the Forms have no existence outside their objects. If we're enjoying the view of a waterfall cascading off a cliff face, we are at the same time, Aristotle believed, directly experiencing the Forms of cliff, of waterfall, and of falling. If we're in love with someone and think the person is beautiful, we are experiencing the Form of beauty right there in the person's face. And if we are studying a tree or a fossil, the Form that gives us knowledge about the history of that tree or fossil is right there. In other words, knowledge can be sought and found directly from the world of the senses. Compared to Socrates' remark in *Phaedrus* (which you may remember from the previous chapter) that he never ventured outside the city because trees and countryside could not teach him anything, Aristotle would most definitely look to those trees for knowledge.

This turn in Aristotle's thinking—from Forms being separate to being inseparable from the thing or experience—is what made it possible for him to think in terms of empirical research (gathering evidence, making hypotheses, and testing theories on the basis of experience). Legend holds that Alexander the Great, on his exploits deep into Persia and Afghanistan, had samples of flora and fauna collected and sent to his old teacher. Aristotle would have been delighted to receive such samples and would have studied them carefully, because he believed in the possibility of empirical knowledge.

Aristotle the Scientist

Aristotle was instrumental in founding the sciences—not the exact disciplines as we know them today, but sciences in the sense that the concepts of *logic* and *observation* were combined. The extent of his influence, however, goes beyond that. It is hard for us to imagine that there was an era when a human being actually could "know everything," in the sense of having access to all available knowledge at the time, and yet it seems that Aristotle was such a person. He was the author of what we know as classical logic; he laid down the foundations of the classifications in biology; he developed theories of astronomy; he was interested in politics, rhetoric (the art of

Aristotle (384–322 B.C.E.), Greek philosopher and naturalist, here shown teaching the young Alexander. If one were to pick one scholar as the most influential in Western cultural history, it would have to be Aristotle. Not only did he leave influential writings in a multitude of fields such as biology, metaphysics, logic, ethics, drama, and politics, he also introduced the concept of empirical science to the ancient world. It is said about Aristotle that he knew everything there was to know at the time, and that may well be an accurate description.

verbal persuasion), and drama; he wrote books on the proper structure of tragedy and of comedy; he developed theories of the nature of the soul, of God, and of other metaphysical questions. Indeed, the term *metaphysics* derives from Aristotle: He supposedly wrote a book on physics and then another book without a title about the nature of reality. Because it came after the book on physics, his followers called it the "book after physics," *ta meta ta physica.*

His book about ethics may prove to have the most enduring influence of them all. But he also wrote about the justification of slavery and the nature of woman as a lower being. Aristotle thus presents ideas in his writings that are deeply offensive

During the Renaissance, Raphael painted this vision of Plato's Academy, titled *The School in Athens*—not a true representation of daily life in the school, but rather a highly symbolic image of two schools of thought. Two figures are approaching the steps in the center: Plato and Aristotle. Plato, the older man, is on the left. On the left side of the painting are some of Plato's students; but most are historical figures, including some from Raphael's own day, who have subscribed to the Platonic way of thought. Plato is pointing upward to the world of Forms, his image of true reality, whereas the younger man next to him, Aristotle, is stretching out his hand toward us, palm downward. He seems to say that it is in this world we can find true knowledge, not in any intellectual realm removed from the senses. On the right we find the Aristotelians of history, the scientists. And on the far right, Raphael has chosen to place himself, peeking straight out at us.

to most modern Western readers, but philosophers usually choose to read his more controversial writings as historical documents rather than as blueprints for how to live our lives. In many ways Aristotle was not what we call a critical thinker; indeed, Socrates would not necessarily have approved of him, for he often refrains from analyzing a viewpoint (such as the status and nature of women) but rather limits himself to mentioning it. He seems to assume that some things are obvious; most people who lived during his time probably agreed with him.

A great many of Aristotle's writings are lost to us. Aristotle, like Plato, wrote dialogues, and the Roman orator Cicero held them in high regard, but only some fragments remain. For the most part, they're lecture notes and course summaries that he

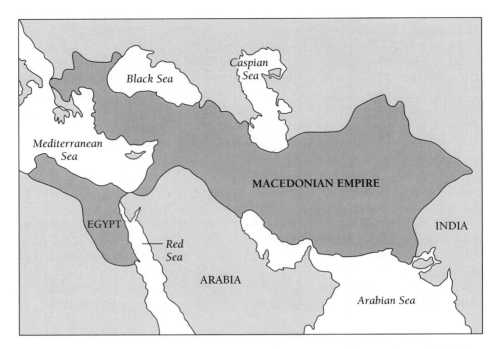

The realm conquered by Alexander the Great (356–323 B.C.E.) was immense by the standards of the time period and even of today; however, it was short-lived. On Alexander's death his generals divided the spoils and had to deal with local insurrections. Nevertheless, the memory of Alexander was kept alive in cultures as far apart as Egypt and northern India; in the mountainous reaches of Afghanistan, Pakistan, and northern India the name "Sikander" (Alexander) became a legend: For example, the Afghan city of Kandahar, which figured in the U.S. war on terrorism, is named after Alexander. In Egypt a dynasty was founded by his general Ptolemy, and a city was named after him which centuries later would become the new center of civilization, the city of Alexandria.

used in his classes; some were written for general audiences and some for more advanced students. Some of the works are supplemented by notes taken by his students.

Aristotle and Virtue

Virtue and Excellence

In the first part of Chapter 8 we saw that the Greek conception of virtue was slightly different from our colloquial use of the word. Although calling someone virtuous may for some imply a certain amount of contempt, no such meaning was implied by the ancient Greeks. If you were virtuous, you would not be considered dull or withdrawn from life because being virtuous meant, above all, that you managed your skills and your opportunities well. To be virtuous meant to act with *excellence*—we might even say with *virtuosity,* because this term retains some of what the Greeks associated with virtue.

Nowhere is that more apparent than in Aristotle's philosophy: You might say that virtue lies in the difference between doing something and doing it well. To Aristotle, everything on this earth has its own virtue, meaning that if it "performs" the way it is supposed to by its nature, then it is virtuous. For one thing, this means that virtue is not reserved for humans; for another thing, it means that everything that exists, including humans, has a purpose. There is virtue to a sharp knife, a comfortable chair, a tree that grows straight, and a healthy, swift animal. For young, growing entities such as saplings and babies one might talk about *potential virtue*.

Teleology: The Concept of Purpose

One concept that is essential for understanding Aristotle's ideas on virtue comes from his metaphysics: the concept of *teleology*. In Greek, *telos* means goal or purpose, and a teleological theory or viewpoint assumes that something has a purpose or that the end result of some action is all-important. Examples of teleological theories exist even today; we encounter them often in everyday discussions about "the meaning of life." Modern science, however, has preferred to leave the question of the purpose of the universe behind. Plato also believed in the purpose of things, but Aristotle built his teleology into a complete metaphysical theory of "causes." (For Aristotle's four causes, see Box 9.1.)

For Aristotle, everything that exists has a purpose, built into the fabric of reality from the very beginning. The idea of a purpose seems reasonable when we look at manufactured objects, because these objects must surely have started with an idea, a purpose, in the mind of their maker. When we wallpaper our bathroom we do it for a purpose: to make the place nicer or perhaps to get a better price for our house. If a cutler makes a knife, its purpose is to cut well, not just to make a dent. When you bake muffins you intend them to be edible, whether they turn out that way or not. But can't we have human actions without a purpose? Aristotle would say no, especially if we are creating an object; its purpose is a given thing.

What about nature-made objects? Does a tree have a purpose? a wolf? an ant? a river? Today we would hesitate before saying "yes," because after all, who are we to make such assumptions? If we say the purpose of a tree is to give us shade, or apples, we are assuming that it is here for us humans and not just for its own sake in the order of things. Even if we say the wolf's purpose is to cull the herd of caribou, we still hesitate to say that someone "designed" it that way, with a purpose in mind. Today, if we tend to use the term *purpose* or *function* to describe how things work in nature, we should probably remind ourselves once in a while that, scientifically, we are referring to how things work within the ecosystem, without implying that there is an underlying designed purpose to nature. (Aristotle himself was not particularly interested in the relations between things in nature, such as an ecosystem, but was more concerned with the separate characteristics of natural phenomena.) There may well be such a purpose, as well as a designer, but scientists today generally believe that such assumptions fall outside the scope of science. Few scientists, regardless of how they feel privately, would willingly mix up personal religious opinions and professional theories. Aristotle, however, had no such compunction about making statements that

Box 9.1   THE FOUR CAUSES

For Aristotle every event has four causes, or four factors that work on it and bring it into being. These are the *material cause,* or the "stuff" the thing is made of; the *efficient cause,* the force that has brought it into being; the *formal cause,* the shape or idea (the Form) of the thing; and the *final cause,* the purpose of the thing. Consider this illustration (for which I give credit to one of my students):

• Material cause: flour, water, and so on

• Efficient cause: me, the baker

• Formal cause: the idea of muffins

• Final cause: to be eaten!

The material cause and the efficient cause are fairly straightforward from a modern point of view: We have a general idea what Aristotle means when he says the material cause of a thing is the actual physical material that makes it what it is. But what about the efficient creative force? For a muffin, the creative force is the baker; for a wolf, it would be the wolf's parents; for a river, it would be mountain springs and precipitation. (Later religious traditions inspired by Aristotle have chosen to read God as the creative, efficient force.)

But the formal and final causes are less intuitive. In the formal cause we see the last surviving element of Plato's theory of Forms in Aristotle's philosophy, but the Form is not outside the object in some intellectual realm; it is right there in the object itself. (Consider the painting by Raphael on p. 419: Aristotle is pointing downward, almost as if saying, "*This world* is where you find true reality.") A successful muffin displays the perfect Form of muffin, whereas a misshapen muffin is only a weak representation of the muffin Form.

For Aristotle, the final cause was by far the most important cause from a philosophical point of view, because it allows us to understand the purpose of a thing—in other words, its essential qualities and nature. We do not understand the nature of a thing—natural or manufactured—until we understand its purpose. It follows that Aristotle believed everything has a purpose given to it by nature; if the object realizes its potential, it has fulfilled its purpose and is a success. A sharp knife, a fast rabbit, and a smart human being would be examples of potential purpose actualized because each has become what it was supposed to be.

reflected anthropocentrism (the view that everything happens for the sake of humans) or speculations about the general structure of the universe (for he believed he understood it). For Aristotle, everything in nature does have a purpose, although it may not be easy to determine just what that purpose is. How *do* we go about determining what the purpose is? We investigate what the thing in question *does best.* Whatever this is will be the special characteristic of that thing. If the thing performs its purpose or function well, then it is *virtuous.*

The Human Purpose

For Aristotle, there is no question that a specifically human purpose in life exists. Each limb and organ of the body has a purpose, he says—the eye for seeing, the hands for grasping—so we must conclude that the person, as a whole, has a purpose above and beyond the sum of the body parts. (For Aristotle this was an obvious conclusion; today we are not so quick to conclude anything about purposes. See Box 9.2.)

Box 9.2 TELEOLOGICAL EXPLANATIONS

We use teleological explanations quite often even today, although generally they are not acceptable as a scientific form of explanation. If we were to explain why giraffes have long necks, we might say something like "So they can reach tall branches." Saying "so they can" implies that somehow giraffes are designed for that purpose or else that they have stretched and stretched over the ages until they can finally reach those branches. (There actually was such a theory in the nineteenth century, prior to Charles Darwin. Its proponent was Jean Lamarck, and the theory is referred to as "inheritance of acquired characteristics.") Even though we all know that giraffes do eat leaves off of tall branches, it would not suit modern science to assume that that is their *purpose*. Darwin, with his theory of *natural selection*, proposed a new point of view: that giraffes don't come equipped with a purpose, nor does any other creature, but we all adapt to circumstances, and those who adapt the best survive and have offspring. We therefore must imagine the ancestors of giraffes as being rather short-necked, with some born with longer necks as a result of mutation. Because the ones with long necks could reach the leaves that the others couldn't reach, they were successful during times of hardship when many of the others perished. They gave birth to long-necked offspring, who gave birth to offspring with even longer necks, and so on. This is a *causal explanation*; it looks to reasons in the past to explain why something is the way it is today, instead of looking toward some future goal.

The idea that humans are born for a reason and with a purpose is irresistible even to many modern minds. We ask ourselves, "What is the reason for my being here on this earth?" "Why was I born?" We hope to find some answer in the future—some great deed we will do, a work of art we will create, the children we plan to raise, the influence we will exert on our profession, or the money and fame we plan to acquire. Some believe their greatest moment has come and gone, like an astronaut who has been on the moon—how do you top that? Such people may spend the rest of their lives searching for a new purpose.

Our belief in destiny, in one form or another, influences our perception of the purpose of our lives. But this is only half of Aristotle's concept of *telos*, because it applies only on a *personal* level. Aristotle is talking not only about the person becoming what he or she is supposed to become but also about the human being *as such* becoming what human beings are supposed to become. In other words, Aristotle believed not only that a telos exists for an individual but also that it exists for a species. How do we know what the purpose of an individual as a member of a species is? We investigate what that creature or thing does best—perhaps better than any other creature or thing. The purpose of a bird must involve flying, although there are flightless birds. The purpose of a knife must involve cutting, although there are movie prop knives that don't cut a thing. The purpose of a rock? To do whatever it does best: lie there. (This is true Aristotle, not a joke.) And the purpose of a human? To *reason*. We can't evaluate a person without taking into consideration the greater purpose of being human, which is to *reason well*:

Now if the function of man is an activity of soul which follows or implies a rational principle . . . [and we state the function of man to be a certain kind of life, and this to be an activity or actions of the soul implying a rational principle . . . and if any action is well performed when it is performed in accordance with the appropriate excellence: if this is the case,] human good turns out to be activity of soul in accordance with virtue, and if there are more than one virtue, in accordance with the best and most complete.

But we must add "in a complete life." For one swallow does not make a summer, nor does one day; and so too one day, or a short time, does not make a man blessed or happy.

Scholars are usually generous here in labeling reasoning the purpose of *humans*—for in Aristotle's terminology it is the "purpose of *man*." As we go deeper into Aristotle's works it becomes apparent that he is not using the word inclusively, to cover males and females, as was to become the intellectual habit in the eighteenth, nineteenth, and most of the twentieth centuries: He means *males*. For Aristotle, men are the creatures who have the true capacity for reasoning; women have their own purpose (such as childbearing) and their own virtues. In this, Aristotle seems to have joined forces with the public opinion of the times, although not with the opinion of his own teacher, Plato, who believed that the role of women depended on what they were well suited for, individually. (See Box 9.3 for what others have said about the human purpose.)

The purpose for man, Aristotle would say, is to think rationally, on a regular basis, throughout his life, as a matter of habit—in other words, to develop a rational *character*. And this, according to Aristotle, is the same as *moral goodness*.

For modern thinkers this is a surprising twist: that moral goodness can be linked with being good *at something* rather than just being good, period. Moral goodness seems for us to have more to do with not causing harm, with keeping promises, with upholding the values of our culture, and so on. For Aristotle, though, there is no difference between fulfilling one's purpose, being virtuous, doing something with excellence, and being morally good. It all has to do with his theory of *how* one goes about being virtuous.

Aristotle recognizes two forms of virtue, *intellectual* and *moral*. When our soul is trying to control our desires, we engage our moral virtues. But when our soul concentrates on intellectual and spiritual matters, we engage our intellectual virtues: When we think about objects of this world that are subject to change and try to make appropriate decisions, we engage our practical wisdom, our *phronesis*. But when we think about higher matters—the eternal questions of philosophy—we use our theoretical wisdom, our *sophia* (*philosophy* is a combination of *philo* = "love of" and *sophia* = "wisdom"). One may excel in other virtues, but the highest virtue of them all is *sophia*, actualizing the uniquely human potential for abstract thought. So the intellectual virtues involve being able to learn well, think straight, and act accordingly. The moral virtues also involve the use of the intellect, because the only way humans can strive for perfection is to engage their intellect in developing a keen sense of the needs of the moment.

The Golden Mean

Ancient Greece gave us the concept of moderation, or the "Golden Mean." Over the entrance to the temple of Apollo at Delphi were inscribed "Know Thyself" and

Box 9.3 IS THERE A HUMAN PURPOSE?

Aristotle inspired an entire school of thought long after he was dead. The Catholic Church came upon his writings some fifteen hundred years after his death, and Saint Thomas Aquinas incorporated several of Aristotle's ideas into his Christian philosophy in the thirteenth century, including the idea that humans have a purpose. For Aquinas this purpose included life, procrea-tion, and the pursuit of knowledge of God (see Box 8.6 on natural law). Other thinkers are not so certain that humans have a purpose; Jean-Paul Sartre (1905–1980) believed there is no such thing as human nature and that anyone who says there is is only looking for an identity to hide behind so that he or she won't have to make difficult choices (see Chapter 10).

"Nothing in Excess." Socrates incorporated the idea of moderation in his teachings, as did several other thinkers, but above all it is at the heart of Aristotle's idea of virtue: an action or feeling responding to a particular situation at the right time, in the right way, in the right amount, for the right reason—not too much and not too little. By using the Golden Mean, Aristotle believes he describes the "good for man"—where a human can excel, what a human is meant to do, and where a human will find happiness. We will return to the subject of happiness shortly.

In his *Nicomachean Ethics,* named for his son Nichomachus, Aristotle compares the Golden Mean with an artistic masterpiece; people recognize that you can't add anything to it or take anything from it, because either excess (too much) or deficiency (too little) would destroy the masterpiece. The mean, however, preserves it. This may remind some readers of a joke among artists: "How many artists does it take to make a great painting? Two—one to paint it, and the other to hit the painter over the head when the painting is done." Why the bash on the head? Because there comes a time, if the work is good enough, when more paint would be too much, and sometimes the artist doesn't recognize that moment. Aristotle would reply that the *virtuous* artist will know this moment—indeed, this is precisely what constitutes a great artist. If this is the case for art, then it must apply to moral goodness: We are morally good if we are capable of choosing the proper response to every situation in life, not too much and not too little:

> Virtue, then, is a state of character concerned with choice, lying in a mean, i.e., the mean relative to us, this being determined by a rational principle by which the man of practical wisdom would determine it. Now it is a mean between two vices, that which depends on excess and that which depends on defect; and again it is a mean because the vices respectively fall short of or exceed what is right in both passions and actions, while virtue finds and chooses that which is intermediate.

Aristotle tells us that every action or feeling must be done in the right amount. In many ways this is quite modern and a very down-to-earth approach to our daily problems. We all have to make big and little decisions every day: How much gratitude should I show when someone does a favor for me or gives me a present I didn't expect?

How much is the right amount of curiosity to express about my friend's personal life? (I don't want to appear to be snooping, and I don't want to appear cold either.) How much should I study for my final? (I know when I've studied too little, but what exactly is studying too much?) How long should I leave the roast in the oven in order for it to be done to perfection when the kids like it gray and my spouse likes it bloody? How much love should I feel, and show, in a new relationship? We face these types of problems every day, and we rarely find good answers to them. In this sense Aristotle shows a feeling for what we might call the "human condition," common human concerns that remain the same throughout the ages. Very few philosophers have done as much as he to try to give people some actual advice about these mundane matters. Thus, even though Aristotle's ideas derive from an ancient, alien world of slavery and other policies that are unacceptable to us today, there are features of his works that make his writings relevant for modern times and modern people. At the end of the chapter you'll find two excerpts from Aristotle's *Nicomachean Ethics,* where he explores the golden mean as well as the virtue of courage.

Does Aristotle actually tell us what to do? Not really. He warns us that we each are prone to go toward one extreme or the other and that we must beware of such tendencies, but the only help we can find on the road to virtue is the idea that we must try and try again.

There are three questions one might want to ask. The first is, As this is supposed to be a theory of *character,* why does it seem to talk about actions and conduct and what to *do*? The answer is that for Aristotle, this *is* a question of character because he is not so much interested in our response to singular situations as he is in our response in general. If we perform a considerate or courageous act only once, he would not call us considerate or courageous; the act must be done on a regular basis, as an expression of the kind of person we strive to be. In other words, we have to acquire some good habits. This means we can't hope to be virtuous overnight—it takes time to mold ourselves into morally good people, just as it takes time to learn to play a musical instrument well. The second question one might ask is, What does this have to do with the specific human virtue of rational thinking? The answer lies in the fact that the way we find out what the mean is in every situation is through reasoning, and the more times we have done it and acted correctly as a result, the better we can build up this habit of responding correctly. Now let's ask the third question: Does this mean we are supposed to do *everything* in the right amount, not too much and not too little? It is easy to imagine eating in the right amount and exercising in the right amount, but what about acts like stealing? Lying? Or committing murder? Must we conclude that we can steal and lie and murder too much but also too little? That we will be virtuous if we steal, lie, and murder in the right amount? Hardly, and Aristotle was aware of this loophole; he tells us that some acts are just wrong by themselves and cannot be done in the right amount. Similarly, some acts are right in themselves and cannot be done too often. One such thing is justice: You can't be "too just," because being just already means being as fair as you can be.

How exactly do we find the mean? After all, it is not an absolute mean; we cannot identify the exact midpoint between the extremes the way we would measure

An application of Aristotle's theory of virtue: Three women on a bridge see a drowning child being swept along by the waters. One woman is rash and jumps in without looking; the other is too cautious and frets so much that the time for action is past. But the third one reacts "just right": She has developed a courageous character; she chooses an appropriate action and acts at the right time to save the child.

the exact amount of calories allowed in a diet. It is far more complex than that, and Aristotle warns us that there are many ways to go wrong but only one way to "hit the bull's-eye" in each situation. It takes a full commitment, involving the entire personality, over a lifetime of training. In his lectures Aristotle appears to have used a chart of virtues. Let us look at a few of them.

If someone is in danger, that person can react in three ways: with too little courage (in which case he is a coward), with the right amount of courage, or with too much courage (in which case he is being foolhardy). Courage was for Aristotle a very important virtue, and you'll find his analysis of courage in the Primary Readings. Box 9.4 applies the virtue of courage as well as the vices of cowardice and foolhardiness to a specific situation, and two stories in the Narratives section focus on courage as a virtue: the ancient Icelandic *Njal's Saga* and the film based on Joseph Conrad's novel *Lord Jim*. In addition, the theme of courage is explored as a contemporary virtue in Chapter 11.

Let's consider the act of pleasure seeking. If you overdo it, you are intemperate— but suppose you are not capable of enjoying pleasures at all? That is not a virtue, and Aristotle doesn't know what to call such a person except "unimpressionable." The virtue is to know in what amount to enjoy one's pleasures; that Aristotle calls *temperance*. Thus

Box 9.4   THE RIGHT DECISION AT THE RIGHT TIME

Imagine three women on a bridge: Heidi, Jill, and Jessica. Below them a dark river is rushing along, sweeping a little boy toward them, carrying him to certain doom. Heidi looks down at the swirling water and imagines all the things that could go wrong if she were to attempt a rescue: the submerged rocks, how heavy her shoes and jeans will get if she jumps in, the fact that she just got over a bad cold, and the fact that she doesn't swim well. Besides, she remembers, she has to make it to the library before closing time. While she has been doing all this thinking, Jill has already jumped in the river to save the boy. She jumped without thinking, however, and hit her head on one of the submerged rocks and knocked herself out. Jessica sees the boy, and fast as lightning she calculates the swiftness of the river, the position of the rocks, her own swimming prowess—and she runs down the little staircase to the riverbed, throws in the life preserver that is hanging on the wall, saves the boy, and pulls ashore the unconscious Jill for good measure. Or maybe she sheds her shoes and jumps in and saves the boy. Or shouts to some men who are out fishing and asks them to give her a hand. The main thing is that she *thinks,* and then *acts,* at the right time, in the proper amount. That is courage to Aristotle. Jill acted rashly. Heidi may have had the right intentions, but she did not act on them. You must act on your intentions and succeed in order to be called virtuous.

But what if some time in the future, by some odd coincidence, Heidi finds herself in the same situation again? A bridge, a drowning child—or some other situation where she might be in a position to help by making the right split-second decision. Her previous failure might help her do better this time around. Aristotle believes we become virtuous through doing virtuous acts; and, if Heidi has learned anything from watching Jessica, then she, too, might do the right thing this time. (But she has to remember that no two situations are exactly alike. In another situation acting exactly as Jessica did could be to act either rashly or too timidly.) Similarly, Jill might have learned from the situation; next time around she might be too timid, but eventually she, too, might get it right. Now Jessica: Can we rely on her to always make the right choice from now on? Most of us would not have such lofty expectations and would forgive her for a future mistake, but for Aristotle it was clear: When you have ascended to the level of a virtuous person, then your future actions will generally also be virtuous, because you have developed virtuous habits. One brave deed does not make a person brave (as one swallow does not make a summer). If Jessica slips and makes a wrong judgment call, then she is not so virtuous after all.

for Aristotle there is no virtue in staying away from pleasures, for "temperance" does not mean "abstinence." The key is to enjoy them *in moderation.*

Suppose we look at the art of spending money. For Aristotle there is a virtuous way to spend money too. If you spend too much you are prodigal, and if you spend too little you are a miser. Spending just the right amount at the right time on the right people for the right reason makes you *liberal.*

For the Greek mind, for the man of the polis, *pride* is a natural virtue, and so it is for Aristotle. You can, however, overestimate your honor and become vain, or you can underestimate it and become humble. The virtuous way to estimate yourself and your accomplishments is through *proper pride.* (See Box 9.5 for a discussion of the

Box 9.5   THE CLASH BETWEEN CLASSICAL
AND CHRISTIAN VIRTUES

For a modern Western person the idea that it is legitimate to take pride in an accomplishment is not strange; we understand why Aristotle says we should not humiliate ourselves by making ourselves less than we are. But his idea that we have a right to feel proud about things that aren't our own doing, like being born of a certain class and race, is more problematic. To the traditional Christian mind, in fact, the entire idea of legitimate pride is a grave misconception. As much as Aristotle became an inspiration to medieval Chris-

tianity, there is a marked discrepancy between most of Aristotle's virtues and the Catholic lists of the cardinal virtues and the cardinal sins. For the Christian it is a cardinal sin to feel pride because our accomplishments come through the grace of God and are not our own doing. This is expressed in the Latin words *Soli Dei Gloria,* the honor (glory) is God's alone. The cardinal virtues are justice, prudence, temperance, fortitude, faith, hope, and charity. The cardinal sins are pride, lust, envy, anger, covetousness, gluttony, and sloth.

differences between Aristotle's virtues, such as pride, and the traditional Christian list of cardinal virtues and vices.)

Is there a virtuous way to feel *angry?* Absolutely—by having a good temper or, as we might say today, being even-tempered. Being hot-tempered is a vice, but so is being meek. If you have been wronged, Aristotle believes, you ought to be angry in proportion to the offense against you.

Let us now consider the virtue of *truthfulness.* We probably would agree with Aristotle that this is a good thing, but what is his idea of a deficiency of truthfulness? Not *lying,* as we might expect, but *irony,* or as it is often translated, "mock-modesty" (in other words, downplaying the situation). Aristotle obviously would not have enjoyed Socrates' ironical bantering. The excess of truthfulness? Bragging. To the modern reader the excess of truthfulness might be something different, such as being *rude* by telling someone, "You sure gained weight over the holidays!" But for Aristotle it is not a matter of not harming others by lying or by being rude but a matter of assessing the situation properly, neither underplaying nor overplaying the truth. Here we touch on a hidden element of Aristotle's virtue theory: *Who is the theory intended for?* Not necessarily young people who need to get their lives straightened out. It is, instead, directed at future politicians. The young noblemen and sons of wealthy landowners who had the leisure time to go to school were expected to become the pillars of Athenian society. What Aristotle is teaching them is, in many ways, to be good public figures. That is why it is necessary to know how much money to spend, in large sums. That is why it is important to know the extent of your pride and your anger. Of course, Aristotle's virtues are also applicable to other people, but some of them—such as the virtues of wit or humor—carry a direct message to those young men who plan to enter public life. Most of us probably would like our partners to have a sense of humor. But imagine how important it is for a public figure not to be

Box 9.6   VARIATIONS ON ARISTOTLE'S THEME
OF THE GOLDEN MEAN

Virtues on Aristotle's list include magnificence (spending large sums of money correctly), friendliness, modesty, and righteous indignation (a sense of justice). And Aristotle's approach can be applied to many situations we find ourselves in on an everyday basis; you might want to discuss this additional list of virtues and vices and add your own suggestions.

ADDITIONAL VIRTUES AND VICES

EXCESS (VICE)	MEAN (VIRTUE)	DEFICIT (VICE)
Loyalty without critical eye	Loyalty	Disloyalty
Passivity	Patience	Impatience
Judgment lacking; intrusion	Compassion	Absence of feelings
Sense of being perpetually indebted	Gratitude	Absence of any gratitude
Being too serious	Responsibility	Irresponsibility
Stubbornness	Perseverance	Unreliability
Rudeness	Honesty	Deceit; deception
Rigid adherence to rules	Rules set with exceptions	Leniency
Anxiety over everything	Awareness of real concerns	Obliviousness
Speeding	Maintaining speed limit	Driving too slowly
Excessive studying; workaholism	Sufficient studying to pass test	Insufficient studying; laziness

And so on and so forth! Can you think of a vice (one not mentioned by Aristotle) that has no mean? Can you think of a virtue that has no excess?

In Chapter 7 you read about a theory that it is right and appropriate for a victim of a crime to feel *resentment* toward the perpetrator, as well as for the community to feel *moral indignation* on behalf of the victim. Since Aristotle believes there is a Golden Mean for the feeling of anger—somewhere between being prone to rage versus being cold or meek—and he also believes that *righteous indignation* is a virtue, his thinking is in harmony with this theory. Where, within the virtuous middle range, might the proper resentment/ indignation response be for a person hit by a computer virus? For a rape victim? For a community targeted by bioterrorism?

a boor, not to be a buffoon, and to have a ready wit. Aristotle recognized this fact. (See Box 9.6 for additional discussion of virtues.)

There are, then, three dispositions: two vices, one on either side, and virtue in the middle. How do we find the virtue? It may be difficult, depending on our own personal failings. If we have a hard time controlling our temper, we might try for a while to be so cool that nothing makes us angry, just to get out of the habit of being irascible; in other words, we might shoot *past* the target of good temper until we feel we can control ourselves and find the mean. If we tend to overindulge in desserts, we might try to lay off sweet things completely for a while. This is not the ideal situation, but Aristotle advises us to experiment until we get it right. Besides, if we find ourselves at one extreme, it is hard for us to see the difference between the other extreme and the virtue: A chocolate lover finds the chocolate hater and the person who has just a few bites of chocolate each week equally dull and unsympathetic. Indeed, some extremes are closer to the mean, the virtue, than others. Being a coward is probably more opposed to being courageous than to being foolhardy. So if you don't know what path to choose, at least stay away from the extreme that is more opposed to the mean than the other extreme. We all have to watch out for our own personal failings, and we also have to watch out for temptations, because if we let ourselves indulge in too many pleasures we lose our sense of moderation and proportion. These matters are not easy, and Aristotle knew that we must judge each situation separately. At the end of the chapter you'll find the ancient Greek story of the "Flight of Icarus," which illustrates that virtue lies in following a middle course between too much and too little—not because it ensures a bland, average existence, but because it ensures survival.

Does Aristotle then propose a set of guidelines for what virtue is that can be applied in all situations? Nothing beyond the general range of the Golden Mean and an appeal to intuition, reasoning, and good habits. In other words, the virtuous person will know how to be virtuous! This has caused some ethicists to call Aristotle an ethical relativist, because virtue is, in a sense, relative to the situation. But labeling Aristotle an ethical relativist is wrong. He never states that morals are completely culture-dependent or that each social group determines what counts as its moral code. On the contrary, Aristotle is quite adamant about virtues having a rock-bottom value for each situation; it is just that situations may differ, and one may be called upon to do more in one context than in another. If we want to apply a modern term to Aristotle, we might dare to call him a soft universalist (albeit with values typical for his day and age): Our responses to situations must remain flexible, and we each have our own ideals and failings, but the right, virtuous response reveals itself in being appropriate to the situation and falls within a range that is recognized by other people of virtue.

Is there such a thing as a perfectly virtuous person for Aristotle? Yes, it appears that he thought it was possible. Furthermore, he seems to have believed that if you are virtuous in one respect but fail miserably in another, then you have lost out completely. If you deviate only slightly, though, you are still a virtuous person—a person who is good at being human and at realizing the human potential.

In the Narratives section I have included two stories that each illustrate Aristotle's idea that we become virtuous by doing virtuous things and thus developing good habits: The way to become courageous is to do courageous things, the way to become compassionate is to do compassionate things, and pretty soon it will become part of your character. One Narrative is Isaac Bashevis Singer's story, "A Piece of Advice," about a cantankerous old man who becomes a decent human being by doing decent things, and the other is a remarkably similar story about another cantankerous old man who becomes a decent human being by doing decent things: the film *As Good As It Gets.*

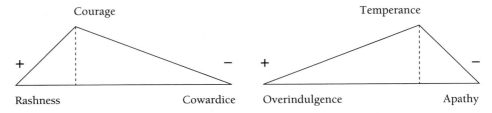

Courage   Temperance

+   −   +   −

Rashness   Cowardice   Overindulgence   Apathy

For Aristotle the mean between the extremes is not an absolute middle; in other words, depending on the situation, the persons involved, and the virtue itself, the mean may be closer to one extreme than the other, and Aristotle advises us to stay away from the vice that is the furthest from the mean. If you imagine yourself at one of the extremes, you also can imagine that it might be hard to tell exactly where the mean is; that is why Aristotle says we must find it through trial and error. A mean that might be viewed as closer to the vice of excess than to deficiency would be *courage*, which can be said to be closer to rashness than to cowardice; a virtue that is closer to the vice of deficiency than the vice of excess might be *temperance*.

Happiness

Being virtuous makes you happy—this is Aristotle's sole reason for designing the development of a virtuous character. But if the goal is happiness, why does he warn us about indulging in too many pleasures? Because pleasure and happiness are not identical, as most ancient thinkers would agree. We have to ask what exactly Aristotle means by happiness.

Happiness is what's "good for man," according to Aristotle. For most of us a good life means a happy life, but a good person means a moral person. For Aristotle there was no conflict. We can be happy only if we're good, but in what way? The highest realizable goods are to live well, to be happy, to do well; what is good for man can't be something that harms him, and indulgence in too many pleasures can certainly be harmful. A further requirement of true happiness is that it must be steadfast; if we rely too much on pleasures, we'll find that they cease to give us a thrill after a while, so pleasure can't be the same as happiness. Nor can fame or fortune, because those things are certainly ephemeral—we can lose both overnight. So what is the thing that can be ours forever, that nobody can take away, and that is not harmful but beneficial to us as human beings? Good reasoning, or, as the ancient Greeks would put it, *contemplation*. This can be ours forever, and, as anyone who has struggled with an intellectual problem and solved it knows, it can even be exhilarating. For Aristotle, then, the ultimately happy life is the life of the thinker. But Aristotle is a realist too—he adds that, although the truly happy life may be a life of contemplation, it doesn't hurt to have friends, money, and good looks!

What about happiness as a reward for good behavior, in the afterlife? For Plato, the goal of a human life seemed to be a comprehension of the world of Forms and ultimately a reunification with that world in an afterlife. Aristotle seems to have had a different view of spirituality: As far as we can tell, he had no belief in an afterlife. In his theory of the soul he states that the soul is the *form* of a human while the body is one's *matter,* but form cannot exist separate from matter, so when the body dies, the soul ceases to exist in any personal way, even if (as he also says) the form of a human being may be immortal. In any event, whatever we are while we are alive will cease to exist when we die; therefore, happiness for Aristotle is exclusively a phenomenon for the living and must be achieved in this world for a person's life to have fulfilled its purpose. While Plato's metaphysics (as we have seen in Chapter 8) could easily be incorporated into a religion that focused on life after death, Aristotle's metaphysics offers no "pie in the sky." Thus it is all the more extraordinary that Aristotle's philosophy became one of the great pillars of support for Christianity as it evolved in the High Middle Ages.

Was Aristotle himself happy in his lifetime? It appears that during his twelve years in Athens running his own school, he enjoyed contemplation, he had money, and he had friends. (Whether he was good-looking we just don't know, since no images of Aristotle have been preserved, but he reputedly liked to dress in the latest styles.) But with the death of his former student Alexander the Great in 323 B.C.E. at the age of thirty-two, it all came to an abrupt end. The anti-Macedonian feelings that were mounting in the realm controlled by Alexander's troops (including the city-state of Athens) no longer could be kept in check, and because Aristotle was considered pro-Macedonian, the Athenian city council decided to get rid of him. Ironically, their method was to charge him with the same offense that had been leveled against Socrates, of offending the gods. But whereas Socrates chose to stay and die for his principles, Aristotle packed up and left Athens for good, so that "Athens wouldn't sin twice against philosophy." He took off for his country estate in Chalcis—a place he had inherited from his mother—but he died the year after of a stomach ailment.

Here we might want to ask ourselves, According to his own system of seeking the mean between extremes, did Aristotle in the end display courageous behavior, or was his behavior "deficient"? It is tempting to compare his choice with Socrates', and many would probably say that the comparison does not come out in Aristotle's favor. But here we should remember that the relationship Socrates had with the city of Athens was vastly different from that of Aristotle with the city-state; it had been Socrates' hometown, he had been concerned for its welfare all his life, and he had fought for it as a soldier. Aristotle was, for all intents and purposes, a foreigner, a "migrant worker" in the philosophy trade. He may have felt a certain loyalty to Athens from having spent over thirty years of his life in the city, but there was general discrimination against noncitizens, and Aristotle can't have been immune to that. He himself might have said that leaving was the perfectly rational, virtuous thing to do: the right action at the right time, for the right reason, not too much and not too little.

Aristotle's Influence on Aquinas

Today, Aristotle looms as one of the most influential persons in human history, but several times after his death it seemed as if his writings were destined to be totally forgotten. After his death, his books were collected by the new leader of the Lyceum, Theophrastus, who had been a student of Aristotle's; and subsequent generations of leaders hid the books to preserve them from theft and other threats—especially since the Lyceum was temporarily closed when foreign philosophers were kicked out of

Athens around 300 B.C.E. The Lyceum did reopen and stayed open until its official closure by Emperor Justinian in 529 C.E., but it was never the great success story that Plato's Academy had become. Aristotle's own books were damaged in storage and would have been lost, had it not been for an avid book collector, Apellicon, who simply appropriated them along with other classic writings and brought them to Rome in 100 B.C.E. Here they were copied, starting a new Aristotle fad among Roman philosophers, but even that was to fade away: When the Lyceum was finally closed by the Roman emperor along with Plato's Academy, the scholars working at Aristotle's school feared for their safety and fled to Persia with copies of Aristotle's books. Back in the Roman cultures around the Mediterranean, Aristotle's works were largely forgotten, and even the location of the Lyceum was lost, until its rediscovery in 1997 by archaeologists. Primarily in Alexandria, it was the Platonic spirit that survived to put its mark on the new world religion. In the Middle East, though, Aristotle's works were studied continually. As the scientific spirit declined in the West, Arabic scholars kept Aristotelian research alive until the advent of another new world religion, Islam, in which Aristotle's philosophy has remained influential. It was not until well into the next millennium that an interest in Aristotle was rekindled in the Christian world. Eventually his theories found their way back into Western philosophy through the works of Saint Thomas Aquinas (1225–1274). In the late Middle Ages and through the Renaissance, Aristotle eclipsed Plato as a philosopher and was known in European intellectual circles (as he had been for centuries in the Arabic world) as "The Philosopher." So for a man who for all intents and purposes didn't have an established career by the time he was 38, whose life's unfulfilled ambition apparently had been to become leader of Plato's school, and who eventually lost his job because of political persecution, Aristotle's posthumous career is nothing short of remarkable: His influence on philosophy itself is immeasurable; his theories of science laid the groundwork for the basic scientific concepts in the Western tradition after the so-called Dark Ages of the early Medieval period; his entire system of classification of sciences and humanities became, to a great extent, the inspiration for the structuring of the first universities in Europe in the high Middle Ages and Renaissance; he provided inspiration for Islamic interpretations of the Koran; and some of his ideas became the cornerstone of the theology of Catholicism, through the works of Aquinas.

It was Aristotle's concept of teleology that became particularly fascinating for Aquinas: If everything has a purpose, then surely it was designed by God. And if we humans, with our free will, decide to follow God's purpose for us, then it must mean we are following God's will, and we are doing right; on the other hand, if we decide to go against God's purpose, we are doing wrong. So what is God's purpose for us? Aquinas identified four specific goals that together made up what has become known as Aquinas's *natural law:* (1) We are obliged to preserve our own lives. (2) We are obliged to procreate within marriage. (3) We are obliged to live as good citizens among other people. (4) We are obliged to seek knowledge, primarily about God and his creation. These four rules are natural to us because we have been designed that way, says Aquinas. It doesn't mean these rules can't be broken—people commit suicide, people have babies outside of wedlock or take measures to avoid getting pregnant, some people care little about living in harmony with others, and some show no interest in seeking knowledge about God. However, they are going against God's will—a will that, for Aquinas, is knowable and understandable to humans, because this will is rational, and humans have been endowed with reason so we can understand God's rules. So if we decide not to follow our built-in purpose, it is because of a sinful willpower. (Aquinas's natural law is not to be confused with the *laws of nature* we are familiar with from science. Such scientific laws are descriptive, while Aquinas's natural law is normative: You can't break the law of gravity, but you can break the law of procreation.)

What happens to people who break these rules of the natural law? Aquinas is convinced that they will not get away with it—they might in this life, but certainly not in the next. That is why there is also *divine law,* for those offenses that God knows about but other humans haven't discovered. On this earthly plane there is also of course *human law,* so that criminal offenses that are discovered can be punished. And the entire universe is run by God according to eternal rules, the *eternal law.*

You may recognize some of Aquinas's views on natural law as contemporary Catholic doctrine. For example, it is Aquinas's rule of self-preservation that forbids suicide, and his rule of procreation that forbids abortion, contraception, and homosexual relationships (because all procreation must take place naturally between married couples, without hindrance, and in no other way). This was not always so: Aquinas's teachings were for centuries considered controversial by the Church, and not until a Church council in 1914 was it decided that they would from then on be considered official Catholic doctrine. So we can say that Aristotle long after his death not only made an everlasting mark on Western science and philosophy, as well as Middle Eastern philosophy, but also to this day has been influential within Christianity.

Some Objections to Greek Virtue Theory

As mentioned earlier, the particular brand of ethical theory known as virtue ethics that we find in the Greek tradition by and large disappeared from view with the rise of modern philosophy. This was not merely because the texts were forgotten; this was a concerted effort by scholars to find a better approach to ethics, because as the centuries passed it was becoming clear, for a number of reasons, that the Greek theories of virtue had several shortcomings. For one thing, Thomas Aquinas found it difficult to reconcile Aristotle's virtues not just with Christian virtues but also with the Christian respect for *God's laws.* In the Christian approach to morals, following commandments is far more important than striving toward virtues, and belief in the human ability to shape one's own character autonomously is considered to be a sin of pride. You become what you ought to be by God's grace, not merely by your own effort.

Philosophy, after parting ways with theology in the sixteenth and seventeenth centuries, began to look critically at virtue ethics from a secular point of view, for, as we have seen, Aristotle was talking about the virtues of a ruling class, virtues that could not be disputed by someone with a different point of view. The modern, political vision of equality does not enter into the Aristotelian moral theory, and from both a

Christian and a social viewpoint an egalitarian approach had become indispensable for an acceptable moral theory by the eighteenth century. For those scholars believing in "natural rights" for all people, it was necessary to set up a moral theory that everyone could follow regardless of status, birth, or intelligence, and such a theory could be based only on laws that were clear and reasonable. Virtues were criticized as being too vague and logically problematic, because what happens if two virtuous people disagree about what to do? How can one persuade the other? There is no recourse to reason in that case except to declare one person less virtuous than the other, so virtue ethics is not a tool in itself for solving conflicts. Such a problem does not arise if you have a clear set of moral and civil laws to refer to. This is what is needed if we regard each other as equals—not a theory with a static view of what makes a person virtuous. The rejection of virtue theory in favor of a rule- or duty-oriented moral theory was, therefore, considered a step forward in moral egalitarianism.

There is a more fundamental problem embedded in classical virtue theory: its basis in *teleology*. It was natural for Plato and Aristotle to assume that as human actions had a purpose, so did humans themselves have a purpose, and that purpose was to let their rationality shine because that was what human nature was all about. And because this is the human purpose, what is good for humans must begin and end with rationality. But that gives rise to a series of questions: (1) Must what is good for someone always be linked with what he or she does best? Suppose a man is excellent at forging paintings. Does that mean his life should include this as a purpose, in order to make him happy? Aristotle and Plato would reject this on the basis that forging paintings is bad in itself, but that is surely a lame answer because it assumes that we know beforehand which purposes are acceptable and which aren't. However, even if we stick to the idea of rationality, it is not all that obvious that this is the human purpose. (2) Why must we talk about a human "purpose" at all? Science as well as philosophy today do not, as a rule, talk about purposes of nature, including human nature. A purpose requires that *someone* has that purpose; individuals may have purposes, but we hesitate to claim that nature has a purpose or even that there is a higher power with a purpose. This is outside the realm of science and also that of contemporary moral philosophy. (3) Even if humans are very good at being rational, they are not excellent at it, at least not everybody, and even the select few geniuses can't be rational all the time. We are instead good at *being able* to act rationally some of the time, and with these qualifications it is hard to claim that rationality is our overriding purpose. And (4) Why should there be just one purpose for humans? A knife can be used to cut, to throw, to clean your nails (don't try this at home), to hang on the wall, and any number of other things. A tree surely has more functions than to supply humans with shade and fruit—it provides oxygen, its leaves fertilize the ground, it provides a home for birds and squirrels and maggots, it supplies a subject for an art class to paint—and makes more trees. Why should we assume that each thing or species has one function that defines it? Humans surely have a multitude of functions. It is doubtful, then, whether a theory of virtue should, indeed, involve the question of function or purpose at all. Contemporary theories of virtue tend to steer clear of this ancient, problematic issue, as we will see shortly.

Study Questions

1. Explain Aristotle's theory of the four causes.

2. What is Aristotle's Golden Mean? Does it imply that the virtuous person is an average person of average talents and intelligence?

3. Explain Aristotle's theory of virtue in detail, using at least three examples. At least two of the examples must be Aristotle's own.

4. In the end, Aristotle was accused of the same crimes as Socrates, but, unlike Socrates, Aristotle chose exile. Evaluate Aristotle's choice: Was he himself displaying courage? Was he a coward? Was he rash? How do you think Aristotle would have defended his course of action?

Primary Readings and Narratives

The two Primary Readings are excerpts from Aristotle's *Nicomachean Ethics.* The first is from Book II, in which Aristotle explains the doctrine of the Golden Mean. The second is from Book III, in which he elaborates on the virtue of courage. The first Narrative is the ancient Greek myth of the flight of Icarus, illustrating Aristotle's theory that the virtuous person always seeks the middle way, avoiding the extremes of excess and deficiency: Flying on wings made of feathers and wax, Icarus disregarded his father's advice to take a middle course. The next Narrative explores the theme of courage; it is an excerpt from *Njal's Saga,* the Icelandic epic that takes place in the late Viking Age. In the excerpt, Njal, his wife Bergthora, and their little grandson face death with stoic courage, choosing to perish together. This is followed by the novel and film *Lord Jim.* The fourth Narrative is an excerpt from a twentieth-century short story by Isaac Bashevis Singer, "A Piece of Advice," in which a nasty, temperamental man learns virtue by developing the habit of pleasant behavior. In a parallel story, another nasty man experiences a character transformation by doing nice things for others: the Academy-Award-winning film *As Good As It Gets.* In both cases, each man becomes less selfish by pursuing better habits *for their own sake.*

Primary Reading

Nicomachean Ethics

ARISTOTLE

Excerpt from Book II, fourth century B.C.E. ***Translated by W. D. Ross.***

This excerpt contains some of Aristotle's most famous writings on virtue: he explains the relationship between virtue and conduct in Chapter 4, and in Chapter 6 he outlines the general theory of the Golden Mean. The excerpt from Chapter 7 gives us most of Aristotle's own list of virtues as examples of the relationship between the mean flanked by two extremes, too much and too little.

4   The question might be asked, what we mean by saying that we must become just by doing just acts, and temperate by doing temperate acts; for if men do just and temperate acts, they are already just and temperate, exactly as, if they do what is in accordance with the laws of grammar and of music, they are grammarians and musicians.

Or is this not true even of the arts? It is possible to do something that is in accordance with the laws of grammar, either by chance or at the suggestion of another. A man will be a grammarian, then, only when he has both done something grammatical and done it grammatically; and this means doing it in accordance with the grammatical knowledge in himself.

Again, the case of the arts and that of the virtues are not similar; for the products of the arts have their goodness in themselves, so that it is enough that they should have a certain character, but if the acts that are in accordance with the virtues have themselves a certain character it does not follow that they are done justly or temperately. The agent also must be in a certain condition when he does them; in the first place he must have knowledge, secondly he must choose the acts, and choose them for their own sakes, and thirdly his action must proceed from a firm and unchangeable character. These are not reckoned in as conditions of the possession of the arts, except the bare knowledge; but as a condition of the possession of the virtues knowledge has little or no weight, while the other conditions count not for a little but for everything, i.e. the very conditions which result from often doing just and temperate acts.

Actions, then, are called just and temperate when they are such as the just or the temperate man would do; but it is not the man who does these that is just and temperate, but the man who also does them as just and temperate men do them. It is well said, then, that it is by doing just acts that the just man is produced, and by doing temperate acts the temperate man; without doing these no one would have even a prospect of becoming good.

But most people do not do these, but take refuge in theory and think they are being philosophers and will become good in this way, behaving somewhat like patients who listen attentively to their doctors, but do none of the things they are ordered to do. As the latter will not be made well in body by such a course of treatment, the former will not be made well in soul by such a course of philosophy.

6   Virtue, then, is a state of character concerned with choice, lying in a mean, i.e. the mean relative to us, this being determined by a rational principle, and by that principle by which the man of practical wisdom would determine it. Now it is a mean between two vices, that which depends on excess and that which depends on defect; and again it is a mean because the vices respectively fall short of or exceed what is right in both passions and actions, while virtue both finds and chooses that which is intermediate. Hence in respect of its substance and the definition which states its essence virtue is a mean, with regard to what is best and right an extreme.

But not every action nor every passion admits of a mean; for some have names that already imply badness, e. g. spite, shamelessness, envy, and in the case of actions adultery, theft, murder; for all of these and suchlike things imply by their names that they are themselves bad, and not the excesses or deficiencies of them. It is not possible, then, ever to be right with regard to them; one must always be wrong. Nor does goodness or badness with regard to such things depend on committing adultery with the right woman, at the right time, and in the right way, but simply to do any of them is to go wrong. It would be equally absurd, then, to expect that in unjust, cowardly, and voluptuous action there should be a mean, an excess, and a deficiency; for at that rate there would be a mean of excess and of deficiency, an excess of excess, and a deficiency of deficiency. But as there is no excess and deficiency of temperance and courage because what is intermediate is in a sense an extreme, so too of the actions we have mentioned there is no mean nor any excess and deficiency, but however they are done they are wrong; for in general there is neither a mean of excess and deficiency, nor excess and deficiency of a mean.

7   We must, however, not only make this general statement, but also apply it to the individual facts. For among statements about conduct those which are general apply more widely, but those which are particular are more genuine, since conduct has to do with individual cases, and our statements must harmonize with the facts in these cases. We may take these cases from our table. With regard to feelings of fear and confidence courage is the mean; of the people who exceed, he who exceeds in fearlessness has no name (many of the states have no name), while the man who exceeds in confidence is rash, and he who exceeds in fear and falls short in confidence is a coward. With regard to pleasures and pains—not all of them, and not so much with regard to the pains—the mean is temperance, the excess self-indulgence. Persons deficient with regard to the pleasures are not often found; hence such persons also have received no name. But let us call them 'insensible'.

   With regard to giving and taking of money the mean is liberality, the excess and the defect prodigality and meanness. In these actions people exceed and fall short in contrary ways; the prodigal exceeds in spending and falls short in taking, while the mean man exceeds in taking and falls short in spending. (At present we are giving a mere outline or summary, and are satisfied with this; later these states will be more exactly determined.) With regard to money there are also other dispositions—a mean, magnificence (for the magnificent man differs from the liberal man; the former deals with large sums, the latter with small ones), an excess, tastelessness and vulgarity, and a deficiency, niggardliness; these differ from the states opposed to liberality, and the mode of their difference will be stated later.

   With regard to honour and dishonour the mean is proper pride, the excess is known as a sort of 'empty vanity', and the deficiency is undue humility; and as we said liberality was related to magnificence, differing from it by dealing with small sums, so there is a state similarly related to proper pride, being concerned with small honours while that is concerned with great. For it is possible to desire honour as one ought, and more than one ought, and less, and the man who exceeds in his desires is called ambitious, the man who falls short unambitious, while the intermediate person has no name. The dispositions also are nameless, except that that of the ambitious man is called ambition. Hence the people who are at the extremes lay claim to the middle place; and we ourselves sometimes call the intermediate person ambitious and sometimes unambitious, and sometimes praise the ambitious man and sometimes the unambitious. The reason of our doing this will be stated in what follows; but now let us speak of the remaining states according to the method which has been indicated.

With regard to anger also there is an excess, a deficiency, and a mean. Although they can scarcely be said to have names, yet since we call the intermediate person good-tempered let us call the mean good temper; of the persons at the extremes let the one who exceeds be called irascible, and his vice irascibility, and the man who falls short an inirascible sort of person, and the deficiency inirascibility.

There are also three other means, which have a certain likeness to one another, but differ from one another: for they are all concerned with intercourse in words and actions, but differ in that one is concerned with truth in this sphere, the other two with pleasantness; and of this one kind is exhibited in giving amusement, the other in all the circumstances of life. We must therefore speak of these too, that we may the better see that in all things the mean is praiseworthy, and the extremes neither praiseworthy nor right, but worthy of blame. Now most of these states also have no names, but we must try, as in the other cases, to invent names ourselves so that we may be clear and easy to follow. With regard to truth, then, the intermediate is a truthful sort of person and the mean may be called truthfulness, while the pretence which exaggerates is boastfulness and the person characterized by it a boaster, and that which understates is mock modesty and the person characterized by it mock-modest. With regard to pleasantness in the giving of amusement the intermediate person is ready-witted and the disposition ready wit, the excess is buffoonery and the person characterized by it a buffoon, while the man who falls short is a sort of boor and his state is boorishness. With regard to the remaining kind of pleasantness, that which is exhibited in life in general, the man who is pleasant in the right way is friendly and the mean is friendliness, while the man who exceeds is an obsequious person if he has no end in view, a flatterer if he is aiming at his own advantage, and the man who falls short and is unpleasant in all circumstances is a quarrelsome and surly sort of person.

Study Questions

1. According to Aristotle, can we become virtuous just by doing the right thing? Can a person be virtuous without doing the right thing?

2. Examine the virtue of proper pride. The modern equivalent of humility might be called low self-esteem. Do you think there is such a vice as too much self-esteem? Why is pride considered a sin by the Catholic tradition?

3. Set Aristotle's list of virtues and vices up in a schema with "too little" to one side, virtue (the mean) in the middle, and "too much" to the other side. Are there virtues missing that you think ought to be essential to a virtue ethics? If yes, which ones?

Primary Reading

Nicomachean Ethics

ARISTOTLE

Excerpt from Book III. **Translated by W. D. Ross.**

You may remember that the first virtue on Aristotle's list was *courage,* and we shall look at the theme of courage for the next few pages. Here Aristotle goes into detail examining what he considers true courage.

That it is a mean with regard to feelings of fear and confidence has already been made evident; and plainly the things we fear are terrible things, and these are, to speak without qualification, evils; for which reason people even define fear as expectation of evil. Now we fear all evils, e. g. disgrace, poverty, disease, friendlessness, death, but the brave man is not thought to be concerned with all; for to fear some things is even right and noble, and it is base not to fear them—e. g. disgrace; he who fears this is good and modest, and he who does not is shameless. He is, however, by some people called brave, by a transference of the word to a new meaning; for he has in him something which is like the brave man, since the brave man also is a fearless person. Poverty and disease we perhaps ought not to fear, nor in general the things that do not proceed from vice and are not due to a man himself. But not even the man who is fearless of these is brave. Yet we apply the word to him also in virtue of a similarity; for some who in the dangers of war are cowards are liberal and are confident in face of the loss of money. Nor is a man a coward if he fears insult to his wife and children or envy or anything of the kind; nor brave if he is confident when he is about to be flogged. With what sort of terrible things, then, is the brave man concerned? Surely with the greatest; for no one is more likely than he to stand his ground against what is awe-inspiring. Now death is the most terrible of all things; for it is the end, and nothing is thought to be any longer either good or bad for the dead. But the brave man would not seem to be concerned even with death in all circumstances, e. g. at sea or in disease. In what circumstances, then? Surely in the noblest. Now such deaths are those in battle; for these take place in the greatest and noblest danger. And these are correspondingly honoured in city-states and at the courts of monarchs. Properly, then, he will be called brave who is fearless in face of a noble death, and of all emergencies that involve death; and the emergencies of war are in the highest degree of this kind. Yet at sea also, and in disease; the brave man is fearless, but not in the same way as the seamen; for he has given up hope of safety, and is disliking the thought of death in this shape, while they are hopeful because of their experience. At the same time, we show courage in situations where there is the opportunity of showing prowess or where death is noble; but in these forms of death neither of these conditions is fulfilled.

What is terrible is not the same for all men; but we say there are things terrible even beyond human strength. These, then, are terrible to every one—at least to every one sensible man; but the terrible things that are not beyond human strength differ in magnitude and degree, and so too do the things that inspire confidence. Now the brave man is as dauntless as man may be. Therefore, while he will fear even the things that are not beyond human strength, he will face them as he ought and as the rule directs, for honour's sake; for this is the end of virtue. But it is possible to fear these more, or less, and again to fear things that are not terrible as if they were. Of the faults that are committed one consists in fearing what one should not, another in fearing as we should not, another in fearing when we should not, and so on; and so too with respect to the things that inspire confidence. The man, then, who faces and who fears the right things and from the right motive, in the right way and at the right time, and who feels confidence under the corresponding conditions, is brave; for the brave man feels and acts according to the merits of the case and in whatever way the rule directs. Now the end of every activity is conformity to the corresponding state of character. This is true, therefore, of the brave man as well as of others. But courage is noble. Therefore the end also is noble; for each thing is defined by its end. Therefore it is for a noble end that the brave man endures and acts as courage directs.

Of those who go to excess he who exceeds in fearlessness has no name (we have said previously that many states of character have no names), but he would be a sort of madman or insensible person if he feared nothing, neither earthquakes nor the waves, as they say the Celts do not; while the man who exceeds in confidence about what really is terrible is rash. The rash man, however, is also thought to be boastful and only a pretender to courage; at all events, as the brave man is with regard to what is terrible, so the rash man wishes to *appear;* and so he imitates him in situations where he can. Hence also most of them are a mixture of rashness and cowardice; for, while in these situations they display confidence, they do not hold their ground against what is really terrible. The man who exceeds in fear is a coward; for he fears both what he ought not and as he ought not, and all the similar characterizations attach to him. He is lacking also in confidence; but he is more conspicuous for his excess of fear in painful situations. The coward, then, is a despairing sort of person; for he fears everything. The brave man, on the other hand, has the opposite disposition; for confidence is the mark of a hopeful disposition. The coward, the rash man, and the brave man, then, are concerned with the same objects but are differently disposed towards them; for the first two exceed and fall short, while the third holds the middle, which is the right, position; and rash men are precipitate, and wish for dangers beforehand but draw back when they are in them, while brave men are keen in the moment of action, but quiet beforehand.

As we have said, then, courage is a mean with respect to things that inspire confidence or fear, in the circumstances that have been stated; and it chooses or endures things because it is noble to do so, or because it is base not to do so. But to die to escape from poverty or love or anything painful is not the mark of a brave man, but rather of a coward; for it is softness to fly from what is troublesome, and such a man endures death not because it is noble but to fly from evil.

Study Questions

1. Aristotle is often assumed to have said that "a brave man is never afraid." Is this a fair statement?

2. What, according to Aristotle, is the most courageous behavior? Do you agree with him?

3. Would Aristotle consider Socrates' choice to stand trial a brave decision? Why or why not?

4. After September 11 a debate arose in the media about whether hijacking a plane and deliberately flying it into a building, causing death and anguish to civilians, was a "cowardly act." In many people's opinion the terrorist actions were the very picture of cowardice, using innocent poeple as weapons against other innocent people. A dissenting view came from television talk-show host Bill Maher, who suggested that deliberately flying an airplane into a building was not cowardly (and for that remark his show was eventually cancelled). Media magnate Ted Turner chimed in, calling the hijackers "brave" but "a little nuts." In your view, were the terrorists brave or cowardly? Is there a third possibility? For a solution you might want to turn to Chapter 10 and the section on Philippa Foot, who suggests that a virtue without good intentions is no virtue at all.

5. In Chapter 11 you'll find an expanded discussion of courage, distinguishing between physical and moral courage. Apply Aristotle's Theory of the Golden Mean to both kinds.

Narrative

The Flight of Icarus

Ancient Greek Myth.

This myth illustrates an element in Aristotle's virtue theory that most Greeks were familiar with because it corresponds to the classic Greek ideal of moderation, or what the Greeks called *sophrosyne;* in the *Nicomachean Ethics* we know it as the mean between extremes, not too much and not too little. The story of Icarus, part of Greek mythology, has been used often as a symbol in Western literature over the past several hundred years.

Wanted for the murder of his nephew, the great artisan Daedalus hid out on Crete, where he built King Minos a labyrinth to house the monster Minotaur (a creature with a bull's head and a man's body). Here Daedalus lived for years, fell in love with one of Minos's slaves, and had a son by her, Icarus. When Icarus was a young man, Daedalus decided to leave Crete. But Minos did not want to lose his master craftsman and so locked Daedalus and his son up in the labyrinth; they escaped with the help of Minos's wife. It was difficult to get off the island, because Minos kept all his ships under military guard, but Daedalus had an idea: He fashioned a pair of feather wings for himself and another pair for Icarus. The quill feathers were threaded together, but the smaller feathers were held together with wax. Daedalus was quite emotional when he told Icarus how to use the wings on the perilous journey, admonishing his son not to fly too high to avoid having the wax be melted by the sun and not to fly too low so that ocean water wouldn't soak his feathers. Then he told his son, "Follow me!" and they set out across the ocean toward the northeast. They had already traveled a considerable

Pieter Bruegel the Elder, *The Fall of Icarus* (c. 1558). The inventor Daedalus made wings of feathers and wax for himself and his son Icarus, so they could escape from Crete, but Icarus flew too close to the sun, and the wax melted. If you look closely, you can see the legs of poor Icarus in the water (right-hand corner). Bruegel was so fascinated by this story that he painted it twice, both times with the farmer in the foreground. This is the original painting; the second is nearly identical except that Daedalus is shown flying above the cliffs. The Roman poet Ovid, who retold the story, specifically mentioned in his *Metamorphoses* that the fall was witnessed by a plowman, a shepherd, and a fisherman, and that is why Bruegel put them in his painting. What do you think the significance might be of the artist's having placed the tragedy of Icarus off to the side?

distance when Icarus, for whatever reason, disobeyed his father. He began rising toward the sun, enjoying the air currents and the sweep of his great wings.

When Daedalus looked back to see if his son was still following close behind him, there was nobody—but far below, on the waves, floated the feathers of Icarus' wings. He had risen too close to the sun, and the wax on his wings had melted, plummeting him toward the water below; Icarus had drowned. His father circled around and around until the body of his son rose from the waters; then he picked it up and carried it to a nearby island where he buried it.

Study Questions

1. Is this story meant to be taken literally? Why or why not?

2. Bruegel's painting shows the fall of Icarus, but you have to look hard to find him. Why do you think the artist didn't make Icarus the focal point of the painting?

3. In Western literature the story of Icarus has often been used as a metaphor for overextending yourself, or being overconfident. It has been taken as a warning not to

reach above your station in life, to "know your place." Is this lesson exactly the same as the original story teaches? (What would Aristotle say? What lesson might a parent be trying to teach his or her child when telling this story?)

4. Is this a didactic story? Why or why not?

Narrative

Njal's Saga

Prose epic, ca. 1280. Author unknown. Summary and Excerpt.

This story is set in the latter part of the Viking Age (700–1000 C.E.). It isn't a story of Vikings, however, but of their relatives, who stayed in Iceland to farm the land. The area was settled by the Norsemen (mostly Danes and Norwegians) in about 800, and by the time *Njal's Saga* was written it was a land of great unrest; blood feuds and various intrigues led to the Danish takeover of the country, which for four hundred years had been independent. *Njal's Saga* is one of many *sagas,* which are historical epics about past life in Iceland.

Nordic mythology teaches that the world as well as the gods eventually will perish in a natural disaster. Thus the Norsemen (the farmers as well as the Vikings) held to the belief in a gloomy fate looming ahead. Even though Christianity was by that time the official religion, the old view of life being ruled by fate still had a hold on people's minds.

This very brief outline cannot explain the complex plot of the saga and can only hint at the inevitable tragic ending. Njal, his wife, Bergthora, and their four sons are carrying on a blood feud with neighbors, not because either party is evil but because over the years events have led in that direction. Through misunderstandings and gossip, the enmity between Njal's family and their neighbors grows, even though Njal does his best to avert it by talking sense to everybody. His negotiations backfire, though, and things get worse. At the *Alting* (the place of arbitration) it becomes clear that all hope of peace is lost, and Njal goes home and prepares for a siege. His adversary, Flosi, arrives with a hundred men, and Njal asks his sons to help him defend the house from inside. The enemy are quick to take advantage of the situation and set fire to the farmhouse.

> There was an old woman at Bergthorsknoll called Sæunn. She knew a lot about many things and had second sight. She was very old by this time, and the Njalssons called her senile because she talked so much; but what she predicted often came true. One day she snatched up a cudgel and made her way round the house to a pile of chickweed that lay there, and started beating it and cursing it for the wretched thing that it was. Skarp-Hedin [one of Njal's sons] laughed at this, and asked her why she was so angry with the chickweed.
>
> The old woman replied, "This chickweed will be used as the kindling when they burn Njal and my foster child Bergthora inside the house. Quickly, take it away and throw it into some water or burn it."

"No," said Skarp-Hedin "for if that is what is ordained, something else will be found to kindle the fire even if the chickweed is not here."

The old woman kept nagging them all summer to take the chickweed indoors, but they never got round to doing it. . . .

Months later, Flosi has now shown up with his force of 100 men, and Njal has fortified himself and his household inside the farmhouse. Now the chickweed which figured in Sæunn's predictions becomes a weapon:

. . . They [Flosi and his men] brought the chickweed up and set fire to it, and before those inside knew what was happening, the ceiling of the room was ablaze from end to end. . . .

Njal said to them, "Be of good heart and speak no words of fear, for this is just a passing storm and it will be long before another like it comes. Put your faith in the mercy of God, for He will not let us burn both in this world and the next."

. . . Now the whole house began to blaze. Njal went to the door and said, "Is Flosi near enough to hear my words?"

Flosi said that he could hear him.

Njal said, "Would you consider making an agreement with my sons, or letting any-one leave the house?"

"I will make no terms with your sons," replied Flosi. "We shall settle matters now, once and for all, and we are not leaving until every one of them is dead. But I shall allow the women and children and servants to come out. . . ."

. . . Flosi said to Bergthora, "You come out, Bergthora, for under no circumstances do I want you to burn."

Bergthora replied, "I was given to Njal in marriage when young, and I have promised him that we would share the same fate."

Then they both went back inside.

"What shall we do now?" asked Bergthora.

"Let us go to our bed," said Njal, "and lie down."

Then Bergthora said to little Thord [their grandson], Kari's son, "You are to be taken out. You are not to burn."

The boy replied, "But that's not what you promised, grandmother. You said that we would never be parted; and so it shall be, for I would much prefer to die beside you both."

She carried the boy to the bed. Njal said to his steward, "Take note where we lay our-selves down and how we dispose ourselves, for I shall not move from here however much the smoke or flames distress me. Then you can know where to look for our remains."

The steward said he would.

An ox had recently been slaughtered, and the hide was lying nearby. Njal told the steward to spread the hide over them, and he promised to do so.

Njal and Bergthora lay down on the bed and put the boy between them. Then they crossed themselves and the boy, and commended their souls to God. These were the last words they were heard to speak. The steward took the hide and spread it over them, and then left the house. . . .

Study Questions

1. Do you think Njal, Bergthora, and the little boy display courage, or are they just giving up?

2. Would removing the chickweed have prevented the arson?

3. For the old Norsemen and -women, the name and reputation you left behind when you died was all-important. How do you think Njal and Bergthora were regarded after they died?

4. Would Aristotle recognize their final act as courageous? Why or why not?

Narrative

Lord Jim

JOSEPH CONRAD

Film by Richard Brooks (director and screenwriter), 1965. Summary. Based on the novel by Joseph Conrad, 1900.

Lord Jim is one of the finest fictional explorations of a human soul trying to do the right thing, at the right time, for the right reason. The film based on Joseph Conrad's classic novel tells the story of a young man named Jim who dreams of doing great deeds. As a newly appointed officer in the British Mercantile Marine, he spends quiet moments on board his ship fantasizing about saving damsels in distress and suppressing mutinies. After having been stranded in a Southeast Asian harbor due to a broken leg, Jim takes a job as chief mate to a crew of drunken, raucous white sailors with an equally unpleasant captain on the rusty old *Patna,* which is transporting a group of Muslim pilgrims to Mecca. Once at sea, a storm approaches, and Jim inspects the ship's hull. It is so rusty it is on the verge of breaking up. Back on deck Jim sees that the crew is lowering a lifeboat into the water— just one, for themselves. No measures are being taken to save the hundreds of pilgrims on the ship. Jim insists to the others that he is staying on board, but, at the last minute, as the storm hits, he comes face to face with his fear of death, which causes him to push aside all dreams of heroic deeds, and he jumps into the lifeboat after all.

Believing that the *Patna* is lost already, the men in the lifeboat set course for shore. When they arrive, they see that someone got there ahead of them; in the harbor lies the *Patna* herself, safe and sound. She was salvaged and towed to shore by another crew, and all the pilgrims are safe. Jim is relieved that no one was lost, but his dreams of valor have been shattered—he is tormented by guilt. There is an inquest, and Jim decides to tell all, to the dismay of his superiors, who believe that dirty linen should not be aired in public. His testimony so affects the prosecutor that the prosecutor later kills himself, leaving a note saying that if fear can break even one of us, how can anyone believe himself to be safe and honorable? Jim's officer's papers are canceled. Everywhere he goes from now on, the memory of the *Patna* will haunt him; somebody will recognize him or mention the scandal, and he will have to go somewhere else, to another port and another odd job.

Is Jim a coward? Were all the dreams of noble deeds just fantasies? He doesn't know. Months later, in some harbor in Southeast Asia, Jim is now a common dockside worker. One day, while transferring goods from shore to ship, he finds himself in a new, dangerous

To stay or to jump? Jim (Peter O'Toole) is about to make the decision that will ruin his life: During a storm, he abandons ship and the many passengers who had put their trust in him, in *Lord Jim* (Columbia Pictures, 1965).

situation: A worker with a grudge against the shipping company lights a fuse that threatens to blow up the ammo being freighted to the ship, and he calls out to all hands to jump, before it blows. But Jim, on hearing the yell "Jump!," stands fast. The only man remaining on board, he puts out the fire and becomes a hero. The administrator of the shipping line, Stein, offers him a job, which Jim later accepts because he wants to get out of town. The job entails taking the guns and ammunition up river to the village of Patusan to help the local people fight against a tyrant. He becomes the hero of the people, respected and trusted. They call him *Tuan Jim,* Lord Jim. He now believes that he finally has proved himself, but in fact the real test is yet to come. A band of pirates land in Patusan, and with the help of a traitor from the village they trick Jim into believing that they have good intentions. They are white, they promise they will sail away without harming any of the villagers, and Jim chooses to believe them; he lets them go without disarming them, trusting their word. He vows to the chief of the village that if anyone is harmed because of his decision, he will forfeit his own life. As it turns out, the chief's own son is killed in a fight between the pirates and the villagers. The villagers expect Jim to flee to save his life, and Stein tries to make Jim leave the village with the native woman he loves, but this time Jim stands fast; he explains to Stein, "I have been a so-called coward and a so-called hero, and there is not the thickness of a sheet of paper between them. Maybe cowards and heroes are just ordinary men who, for a split second do something out of the ordinary." In the morning Jim goes to the chief, who is mad with grief over his son, and offers him his life. Does the chief kill Jim? Read the book or watch the film.

Study Questions

1. Is Jim a coward, or is he courageous? Is it possible to be both?

2. Do you think we all are like Jim in the sense that we all have a moral breaking point which, when we reach it, reveals the frailty of our character?

3. How would Aristotle rate Jim? Is he in the end a virtuous person?

4. Although the virtue of *honor* is not on Aristotle's list, it was an important concept in his day. Today it may not seem terribly important to many in the Western world, but in the time period of Lord Jim, the concept of personal honor was at least as important as when Aristotle was alive. Do you agree with the author (Joseph Conrad) that it is more honorable for Jim to confess his failings during the inquest than to keep quiet and follow the lead of his superiors? Is Jim an honorable man? Why or why not?

5. Compare the plot of *Lord Jim* with Aristotle's prescription for the perfect tragic plot: Something horrible happens to an ordinary man, not because of some vice or depravity of his character but because of a great error in judgment. Does this fit Jim? If so, is Aristotle right that we feel pity and fear because we understand what he is going through—that we might react the same way?

𝒩*arrative*

A Piece of Advice

ISAAC BASHEVIS SINGER

Translated by Martha Glicklich and Joel Blocker. Short story, 1958. Summary and Excerpt.

This story takes place in a pre–World War II Polish-Jewish village; Singer (1904–1991), who won the Nobel Prize in literature in 1978 for his "impassioned narrative art," drew on his Polish-Jewish background for most of his stories.

Baruch lives with his wife's family in the village of Rachev; it is a much grander household than his own childhood home was because his father-in-law is a wealthy man and likes to live in style. The father-in-law is a good man in many ways, and a learned man, but he has one major fault: He has a terrible temper. Unwilling to forgive and forget, he harbors resentments over any little offense. One time Baruch borrowed a pen from him and forgot to return it, and this sent his father-in-law into such a fit of rage that he struck Baruch in the face. This upset the family terribly because a father-in-law does not have that kind of authority over his son-in-law, but Baruch, being an easygoing young man, was quite willing to forgive the older man. The differences between the two men are noticeable: The older man is fastidious, and Baruch is lazy; his father-in-law is always sharp and on top of things, while Baruch is terribly forgetful and sometimes can't even find his way home because he doesn't pay attention to where he is. But after the incident with the pen Baruch's father-in-law approaches him—a rare event—and asks his advice on how to control his anger, for he has alienated all his business partners. Baruch suggests that they go to see the Rabbi of Kuzmir, a neighboring town. At first the older man scoffs at the thought, but later he agrees to go.

They arrive in Kuzmir on a Friday afternoon (at the beginning of the Sabbath) after a long journey through the winter snows, and Baruch's father-in-law goes to talk with Rabbi Chazkele; for three-quarters of an hour he is alone with the rabbi, and then he emerges, irate, calling the rabbi a fool, an ignoramus, to the embarrassment of his son-in-law. What was the rabbi's advice that so infuriated Baruch's father-in-law? That he must become a flatterer. For a week he must flatter everyone he meets, going through the motions of saying nice but insincere things to all of them regardless of who they might be. And that, to the father-in-law, is worse than murder. But Baruch suspects there must be a deeper meaning to the odd piece of advice. The older man wants to go home immediately, but since it is the evening of the Sabbath they can't leave for home (because one does not travel on the Sabbath, between sunset on Friday and sunset on Saturday). So they stay in Kuzmir to celebrate the Sabbath and listen to the prayers of Rabbi Chazkele. Both Baruch and his father-in-law are deeply moved by the rabbi's chanting, and by his words.

> The rabbi commented on the law. And what he said was connected with what he had told my father-in-law at their meeting. "What should a Jew do if he is not a pious man?" the rabbi asked. And answered: "Let him play the pious man. The Almighty does not require good intentions. The deed is what counts. It is what you do that matters. Are you angry perhaps? Go ahead and be angry, but speak gentle words and be friendly at the same time. Are you afraid of being a dissembler? So what if you pretend to be something you aren't? For whose sake are you lying? For your Father in Heaven. His Holy Name, blessed be He, knows the intention and the intention behind the intention, and it is this that is the main thing."
>
> How can one convey the rabbi's lesson? Pearls fell from his mouth and each word burned like fire and penetrated the heart. It wasn't so much the words themselves, but his gestures and his tone. The evil spirit, the rabbi said, cannot be conquered by sheer will. It is known that the evil one has no body, and works mainly through the power of speech. Do not lend him a mouth—that is the way to conquer him. Take, for example, Balaam, the son of Beor. He wanted to curse the children of Israel but forced himself to bless them instead, and because of this, his name is mentioned in the Bible. When one doesn't lend the evil one a tongue, he must remain mute.
>
> Why should I ramble on? My father-in-law attended all three Sabbath meals. And when, on the Sabbath night, he went to the rabbi to take leave of him, he stayed in his study for a whole hour.
>
> On the way home, I said, "Well, father-in-law?" And he answered: "Your rabbi is a great man."
>
> The road back to Rachev was full of dangers. Though it was still midwinter, the ice on the Vistula had cracked—iceblocks were floating downstream the way they do at Passover time. In the midst of all the cold, thunder and lightning struck. No doubt about it, only Satan could be responsible for this! We were forced to put up at an inn until

Tuesday—and there were many Misoagids staying there. No one could travel further. A real blizzard was raging outside. The howling in the chimney made you shiver.

Misoagids are always the same. These were no exception. They began to heap ridicule upon Hasids—but my father-in-law maintained silence. They tried to provoke him but he refused to join in. They took him to task: "What about this one? What about that one?" He put them off good-naturedly with many tricks. "What change has come over you?" they asked. If they had known that he was coming from Rabbi Chazkele, they would have devoured him.

What more can I tell you? My father-in-law did what the rabbi had prescribed. He stopped snapping at people. His eyes glowed with anger but his speech was soft. And if at times he lifted his pipe about to strike someone, he always stopped himself and spoke with humility. It wasn't long before the people of Rachev realized that my father-in-law was a changed man. He made peace with his enemies. He would stop any little brat in the street and give him a pinch on the cheek. And if the water carrier splashed water entering our house, though I knew this just about drove my father-in-law crazy, he never showed it. "How are you, Reb Yontle?" he would say. "Are you cold, eh?" One could feel that he did this only with great effort. That's what made it noble.

In time, his anger disappeared completely. He began to visit Rabbi Chazkele three times a year. He became a kindly man, so good-natured it was unbelievable. But that is what a habit is like—if you break it, it becomes the opposite. One can turn the worst sin into a good deed. The main thing is to act, not to ponder. He even began to visit the ritual bath. And when he grew old, he acquired disciples of his own. This was after the death of Rabbi Chazkele. My father-in-law always used to say, "If you can't be a good Jew, act the good Jew, because if you act something, you *are* it. Otherwise why does any man try to act at all? Take, for example, the drunk in the tavern. Why doesn't he try to act differently?"

The rabbi once said: "Why is 'Thou Shalt Not Covet' the very last of the Ten Commandments? Because one must first avoid doing the wrong things. Then, later on, one will not desire to do them. If one stopped and waited until all the passions ceased, one could never attain holiness."

And so it is with all things. If you are not happy, act the happy man. Happiness will come later. So also with faith. If you are in despair, act as though you believed. Faith will come afterwards.

Study Questions

1. Is this an example of virtue ethics or ethics of conduct? Explain your answer.

2. Do you think someone can become a better person by constantly doing the right thing, even if his or her inclination is to do something else entirely? What might Aristotle say?

3. Comment on this quote: "One could feel that he did this only with great effort. That's what made it noble." What might Kant say to this? After you've read Chapter 10, return to this question and discuss what Philippa Foot might answer.

Narrative

As Good As It Gets

MARK ANDRUS AND JAMES L. BROOKS (SCREENWRITERS)
JAMES L. BROOKS (DIRECTOR)

Film, 1998. Summary.

Melvin Udall is a famous writer of romance novels. He is also a terrible person; he is an "equal opportunity offender," having epithets and other insults ready for anyone who crosses his path—blacks, Jews, foreigners, women, homosexuals, anyone at all. His gay neighbor's little dog irritates him, so he stuffs the dog down the disposal chute. Melvin is utterly obnoxious and self-centered. When eating at his favorite restaurant, he will only sit at one specific table and be served by one specific waitress, Carol; he even insults other customers so that they will leave and he can claim "his" table. In addition, he won't use the restaurant's silverware but carries a sealed plastic set. We begin to realize that Melvin is not just obnoxious, but also sick; he suffers from obsessive-compulsive disorder. But the disorder in itself doesn't excuse or explain away Melvin's selfishness and rudeness.

Melvin wants to continue his life with as few variations as possible: being careful not to step on cracks while walking from his Manhattan apartment to the restaurant and back; having no physical contact with anyone; eating at the restaurant, being served by and exchanging casual remarks with Carol; and spending his time alone and uninterrupted, writing his best-selling novels about people who experience the grand passion of their lives. But around him, things begin to change dramatically: His gay neighbor, Simon, an artist, is attacked and left for dead by one of his models and his pals. While Simon is in the hospital with terrible injuries, his good friend, an art dealer named Frank who is black, calls on Melvin to lend a helping hand. He figures Melvin owes Simon. They have exchanged words previously, when Simon had tried to confront Melvin about his dog (who came back safe from the chute experience) and Melvin closed the door in Simon's face. Frank then confronts Melvin and threatens him into behaving decently to Simon. Melvin is terrified of him, and when Frank insists that Melvin take the dog for a while, Melvin has no choice but to comply. And with this little change, a crack has opened in Melvin's armor.

As the weeks go by, Melvin doesn't just get used to the dog but dotes on him, feeding him bacon from the restaurant. When Simon gets back from the hospital, bruised and broke, he is devastated to find that his terrible neighbor is now his dog's favorite.

Other things change: One day Carol is no longer at work, and Melvin, being obsessive about who serves him, finds out why: Her little son Spence, who has asthma, has been getting worse. So Melvin makes a point of visiting her to try to persuade her to go back to work. Realizing the gravity of her son's condition, he arranges for a physician to make house calls to do for Spence what Carol's HMO hadn't done—make him better—thus freeing Carol to return to the restaurant and serve his meals. Carol tries to thank Melvin by writing him a long letter, but Melvin doesn't know how to accept gratitude and refuses to read it.

How do Aristotle, Isaac Bashevis Singer, and the movie *As Good As It Gets* (TriStar, 1998) propose transforming a cantankerous, mean-hearted, and selfish person into a kind and caring human being? By making him do things that a kind and caring person would, thus developing kind and caring habits. In this scene Melvin (Jack Nicholson) and Carol (Helen Hunt) share a tender, tentative moment in the midst of helping a mutual friend, although Melvin's transformation is not yet complete.

Frank talks Melvin into driving Simon to Baltimore to see his estranged parents; Simon is about to lose his apartment and needs financial help. Melvin doesn't want to travel alone with Simon and asks Carol to come along. The threesome embark on a strange journey that results in Simon becoming able to paint again and to get his confidence back, Melvin admitting to himself that he is in love with Carol, and Carol disliking Melvin more than ever, because she had been close to falling in love with him until he began acting in his old selfish, insensitive way. Upon their return to New York, Simon and Carol have become the best of friends—and Melvin reveals that he has arranged for Simon to share his big apartment. Now what remains is for Melvin to convince Carol that she loves him and that life with him will be good.

This story almost has the character of a fable—the mean boy who became a good boy, the lost young woman who found love, the friendless man who found a friend in his enemy—but all of it is saturated with humor and sarcasm, so very little sentimentality is allowed to linger. But what is the connection to virtue ethics? Here is a man of despicable character, rude and selfish, who is changed—by what? *By changing his habits.* By doing things differently, he becomes a different person. Compare this to the story by Isaac Bashevis Singer, and remember Aristotle's advice that "it is by doing just acts that the just man is produced."

Study Questions

1. Is Melvin a believable character? Is it likely that an insensitive, selfish person could become a better person by doing good deeds, even though they are done reluctantly and without good intentions?

2. Is Carol being too suspicious? How would you describe her character, referring to Aristotle's concept of the Golden Mean?

3. Compare Melvin and Baruch's father-in-law in Singer's story. What are the similarities? What are the differences?

4. Is it good enough to become a different and better person by having a change of habits forced on you, or is it better if you choose to change your habits yourself? Reread the first Primary Reading, Aristotle's *Nicomachean Ethics,* and explain what Aristotle would say. What do you yourself think? Has your character ever improved by being forced into a situation?

Chapter Ten

Contemporary Perspectives

*J*n the introduction to Chapter 8, I mentioned that the idea of a good character as one of the key elements in a moral theory was eclipsed by the general notion that all that matters is *doing the right thing*. With the advent of Christianity, virtue ethics was rejected in favor of an *ethics of conduct*—asking the kind of questions introduced in Part 2 of this book. As we saw earlier, this was in part a result of a greater social awareness: There is more fairness in asking everybody to follow rules of conduct than there is in trying to make people adapt to vague principles of how to be, and there is a greater chance of developing rational arguments for your position regarding rules of conduct than there is of getting others to agree to your viewpoint concerning what is virtuous. In recent years, though, philosophers have turned their attention to the ancient thoughts about character building, and virtue theory is now experiencing a revival. (See Box 10.1 for a brief overview of virtue ethics and character.) This trend has been hotly contested by scholars such as J. B. Schneewind, who believe the original reasons for adopting ethics of conduct are still valid.

The revival of virtue theory has been primarily a British and American phenomenon, and we will look at some of the proponents of this new way of approaching ethics. In continental philosophy (European philosophy excluding the British tradition), there was a separate renewal of interest in Aristotle and his virtue theory in the twentieth century, but in a sense a version of virtue theory has been in effect in continental philosophy ever since the nineteenth century, and we will take a look at this tradition too. Because virtue theory is now associated with the new British/American theory, we will call its continental counterpart the "Quest for Authenticity."

Ethics and the Morality of Virtue

As we have seen, there is a subtle difference between morality and ethics, and in the debate about virtue this difference becomes very clear. In an *ethics of virtue* the issue is to ask yourself what kind of person you want to be, to find good reasons to back up your view and to listen to possible counterarguments, and then to set forth to shape your own character, all the while being ready to justify your choice of virtue rationally or to change your mind. An ethics of virtue doesn't specify what *kind* of virtue you should strive for, although it is usually assumed that it will be something benevolent or at least nothing harmful. The important thing is that you realize you *can* mold your character into what you believe is right. The question of whether your chosen virtue really is a morally good choice is not necessarily part of the issue.

Box 10.1   CAN WE CHANGE OUR SPOTS?

Opponents of virtue ethics often claim that in order for people to be praised for what they do, or blamed for it, it must be assumed that they are *responsible* for their actions. But are we responsible for our character and disposition? Virtue theory asks us to look primarily at people's character. Suppose we ask someone to give to charity, and she doesn't have a generous disposition. Can we then blame her for her lack of virtue? If we can't, then virtue ethics is useless as a moral theory. It may praise people for dispositions that they already have, but it doesn't tell us how to im-prove ourselves. Virtue theory's response to this is that certain people have certain dispositions, and in that respect some are more fortunate than others, morally speaking; some people are just naturally thoughtful and generous, or courageous, or truthful. The rest of us have to work on these things. Just because we lack a good disposition doesn't mean we can't work on improving it, and just because we have a tendency toward a certain disposition doesn't mean we can't work on controlling it.

However, a *morality of virtue* focuses precisely on this issue: Which virtue is desirable to strive for, and which is no virtue at all? Parents of young children generally know that telling stories can be an excellent way to teach moral virtues, but lately politicians as well as educators have also taken notice. The politician and writer William H. Bennett has published several collections of stories with morals—didactic stories—meant to be read to young children; the best known of these collections is simply titled *The Book of Virtues* and contains stories from the Western cultural heritage, as well as from other cultures, all with a short added moral explanation. (Box 10.2 discusses stories that warn against following nonvirtuous role models.)

In the last half of the twentieth century, virtue ethics made another entrance on the stage of British and American philosophy. For some thinkers it was an absolute necessity to make the switch from an ethics of conduct to virtue ethics because, as virtue ethicists say, you can do the right thing and still be an unpleasant person; however, if you work on your character, you will become a good person *and* do the right thing without even having to think about it. For others, virtue ethics has become a much-needed supplement to an ethics of conduct. Some see virtue ethics as a way for people to explore the issue of a good character; others view it as a way to teach what a good character should be all about.

The Political Aspect of Conduct Versus Character

In the last decade of the twentieth century the political debate in the United States became polarized in a new way—which actually turned out to be a polished and updated version of the older polarization between *conduct* and *character.* Republican politicians brought up the issue of character: Is the candidate trustworthy? Does he or she have integrity? Does he or she keep promises? In short, is the candidate a virtuous person—in his or her private life as well? Democratic politicians responded by pointing to the public policies of the candidate: What has he or she accomplished politically so far?

Box 10.2   NEGATIVE ROLE MODELS

Virtue theory usually focuses on heroes and saints who are to be emulated, but little attention is given to those characters who perhaps teach a deeper moral lesson: the negative role models. Whether we look to real-life figures or fictional characters, moral lessons can be learned by observing the destiny of "bad guys," provided that they don't get away with their misdeeds. (Twisted souls can of course learn a lesson from the evildoer who does get away with it, but that is another matter.) From childhood we hear of people who did something they were not supposed to do and suffered the consequences. Most of these stories are issued as a warning: Don't "cry wolf," because in the end nobody will believe you. Look what happened to Adam and Eve, who ate the fruit of the one tree they were not supposed to touch. Look what happened to the girl who stepped on a loaf of bread so she wouldn't get her feet wet. She was pulled down into the depths of hell (in a Hans Christian Andersen story). When we grow up we learn the lesson of politicians who turned out to be crooked, of televangelists who didn't practice what they preached, of rich and famous people who have serious drug problems. Movies and novels also bombard us with negative models: Darth Vader (*Star Wars*) sells out to the Dark Side, so we learn to beware of people who have lost their integrity. Charles Foster Kane

(*Citizen Kane*) forgets his humanity and dies lonely, his heart longing for the time when he was a small boy. The Count of Monte Cristo loses his own humanity through an obsession with revenge. Madame Bovary loses control of her life because she fantasizes too much. And Smeagol loses not only his self but even his identity as a hobbit when he becomes Gollum through allowing the Ring to take over his spirit (*The Lord of the Rings*). Through exposure to such characters we get a warning; we live their lives vicariously and find that bitterness lies at the end. Films such as *Money for Nothing, A Simple Plan, Goodfellas,* and *Fargo* show us that the life of selfish pursuits carries its own punishment. There are, however, works that fail to bring home the moral lesson because they are either too pompous or simply misinformed. Such a film is *Reefer Madness,* which is now a cult classic depicting the life of crime and madness that results from smoking marijuana. Another antidrug film but with a far superior story and impact is *Requiem for a Dream.* It realistically describes the downward spiral of drug addictions, in this case from diet pills as well as heroin. (If you remember your fallacies from Chapter 1, you'll be able to identify *Reefer Madness* as an example of the slippery slope fallacy, while *Requiem* depicts an actual, chilling slippery slope.)

What social policies does the candidate support, and with what success rate has he or she had them implemented? This is not just an interesting revival of the philosophical question of conduct versus character; this goes to the heart of how we view the importance of values. Do we think the question of personal character and integrity is the most important form of ethics—perhaps even the only form of ethics? Or do we believe that the personal standards of someone who serves the public are less important than his or her social conscience and efforts to change things for the better? For some politicians, the entire question of character has in itself become a matter of a person's outlook on social policies rather than a question of personal values: A person of good character is a person who supports certain social policies. The complete polarization of opinion as to what counts as moral values in politics came to a head in 1998 with

Zits by Jerry Scott and Jim Borgman

© 1997 ZITS Partnership. Reprinted with permission of King Features Syndicate.

Virtue ethics recommends that we emulate role models; however, in this culture we also encourage individuality and the characteristics that make people unique and natural. Immanuel Kant warns about holding siblings up as role models, because this may create resentment rather than inspiration to be good. In *Zits*, the teen Jeremy is inundated with conflicting advice to be like someone else but also to be himself—is it any wonder he is confused?

the debate surrounding the impeachment of President Bill Clinton. The situation was illustrated by the comment of a Democratic politician who said he couldn't judge the *private* morals of the president but that the president had the highest *public* morals of anyone he had ever met. During the first term of the George W. Bush presidency the debate shifted, and during the 2004 election campaign some Democrats chose to focus on the character of Democratic leaders rather than their voting record, while some Republicans pointed to the importance of the anti-terrorism policy of President Bush, rather than bringing up the character issue. Regardless of how one feels about national politics, it is philosophically interesting that the revived debate between ethics of conduct and virtue ethics is not always a partisan story—the virtue concept is not in itself a Republican issue, and the policy issue is not by nature Democratic—it all depends on the political needs of the moment.

As with so many of the moral issues we have looked at, an extreme either/or turns out to be a *false dichotomy*—a false either/or with other possible alternatives. If we assume that character is important, why should we assume that a person's stand on social issues is less important? And if we assume that social views count, then why shouldn't character count as well? A person can have a perfectly squeaky-clean character and yet be completely ineffective as a decision maker or negotiator or even have little grasp of or interest in social policies and the needs of society. And a highly effective politician, well liked and radiating understanding of social and economic problems in the population, can turn out to have a personal life that is in shambles because of a lack of character. At times, though, it does seem all-important that a political leader have character and integrity—even if there is disagreement about his or her policies.

The emerging pattern shows that each group focuses on what it considers most important: On the whole, conservatives focus on character and liberals focus on a variety of social policies, such as the right to abortion, affirmative action, gun control, school lunches, welfare, and other causes related to the general question of what to do.

Have Virtue, and Then Go Ahead: Mayo, Foot, and Sommers

Bernard Mayo

In 1958 the American philosopher Bernard Mayo suggested that Western ethics had reached a dead end, for it had lost contact with ordinary life. People don't live by great principles of what to do ("Do your duty" or "Make humanity happy"); instead, they measure themselves according to their moral qualities or deficiencies on an everyday basis. Novelists have not forgotten this, says Mayo, because the books we read tell of people who try hard to be a certain way—who sometimes succeed and sometimes fail—and we, the readers, feel that we have learned something.

An ethics of conduct is not excluded from virtue ethics, says Mayo—it just takes second place, because whatever we *do* is included in our general standard of virtue: We pay our taxes or help animals that are injured in traffic because we believe in the virtues of being a good citizen and fellow traveler on Planet Earth. In other words, if we have a set of virtues we believe we should live by, we will usually do the right thing as a consequence. However, an ethics of conduct without virtue may not be benevolent at all; it is entirely possible to "do your duty" and still be a bad person— you do it for gain or to spite someone (a good example of such a person is Dickens's Ebenezer Scrooge in *A Christmas Carol,* who may appear to be a pillar of society, but only because it is profitable to him). You can do something courageous without actually being courageous, says Mayo (although Aristotle would insist that if you do it often enough you actually *become* courageous, and utilitarians would insist that it doesn't matter why you do something, as long as it has good results).

So how should we choose our actions in an everyday situation? Mayo says we shouldn't look for specific advice in a moral theory (Do such and such); we should, instead, adopt general advice (Be brave/lenient/patient). This will ensure that we have the "unity of character" a moral system of principles can't give us. Mayo advises us to select a role model, either an ideal person or an actual one. Be just, be a good American—or be like Socrates or Buddha or choose a contemporary role model such as Jane Goodall or Maya Angelou. There are heroes and saints throughout history we can choose from, not necessarily because of what they have done, but because of the kind of people they were.

So when Mayo suggests that we learn from factual *exemplars* such as Martin Luther King, Jr., Mother Teresa, or perhaps our parents, he is not saying we should emulate their actual doings but rather that we should live in their "spirit" and respond to everyday situations with the strength that a good character can give. This is a much more realistic approach to morality than is reflected in the high ideals of principles and duty that an ethics of conduct has held up for people. People have felt inadequate because nobody can live up to such ideals, says Mayo, but everyone can try to be like someone they admire. Critics of this enthusiasm for role models have pointed out that just emulating someone you admire doesn't in itself solve your moral dilemmas: (1) What if your idea of a role model doesn't correspond to what other people consider models of decent behavior? This is one of the traditional problems with virtue ethics: Who gets the final word about what is to count as virtue? It provides no easy method for solving moral disputes. (2) What if your role model turns out not to be so perfect after all? If he or she is still alive, you have to assume that anyone can make a wrong turn, even someone you have chosen to emulate. Are you supposed to keep a critical distance or just follow your model every step of the way? And even if your role model is a historical figure (who can't make any new mistakes), there is always the risk that new material will surface, showing another and less virtuous side to that person. Are you then supposed to drop your hero or find ways to defend him or her? (3) The most serious complaint may be the one that comes from several philosophers (from different time periods) who find fault with the very idea that one can be virtuous by just imitating someone else (Mayo, of course, didn't invent that idea; he just made it part of a modern philosophy of virtue). One is Kant, and you can find his thought-provoking criticism in Box 10.3. Another is the French philosopher Jean-Paul Sartre, who insisted that we ought to take responsibility for every single thing we do in order to be true to ourselves and become authentic human beings. Taking such responsibility precludes settling for just copying what others do, because that approach would give us a false sense of who we are and a false sense of security—by making us believe we can go through life and be good persons just by imitating others. In Sartre's terminology, we would then be living a life of inauthenticity.

Philippa Foot

Opponents of virtue theory ask how we can call beneficial human traits "virtues" when some humans are *born* with such traits and others don't have them at all. In other words, human responsibility for these dispositions doesn't enter into the picture at all. Good health and an excellent memory are great to have, but can we blame those who are sick and forgetful for not being virtuous?

The British philosopher Philippa Foot counters this argument in her book *Virtues and Vices* (1978) by stressing that virtues aren't merely dispositions we either have or don't have. A virtue is not just a beneficial disposition but a matter of our *intentions*. If we couple our willpower with our disposition in order to achieve some goal that is beneficial, then we are virtuous. So having a virtue is not the same as having a skill; it is having the proper intention to do something good—and being able to follow it up with an appropriate action.

For Foot, virtues are not just something we are equipped with. Rather, we are equipped with some tendency to go astray, and virtue is our capacity to *correct* that tendency. Human nature makes us want to run and hide when there is danger; that is why there is the virtue of courage. And we may want to indulge in more pleasure

Bernard Mayo points out that Kant rejected the idea of imitating others as a moral rule and called it "fatal to morality." Kant deplored holding up an example of an ideal, rather than striving for the ideal itself. Mayo thinks striving for the ideal itself is too much to ask of ordinary people. If we read Kant's *Lectures on Ethics* we find an interesting argument for why it is not a good idea to point to *people* as worth emulating: If I try to compare myself with someone else who is better than I am, I can either try to be as good or I can try to diminish that other person; this second choice is actually much easier than trying to be as good as the other person, and it invariably leads to *jealousy.* So when parents hold up one sibling for the other to emulate, they are paving the way for sibling rivalry; the one who is being set up as a paragon will be resented by the other one. Kant suggests that we should recommend goodness as such and not proffer individuals to be emulated, because we all have a tendency to be jealous of people we think we can't measure up to. So the Kantian rejection of role models is not merely an abstract preference for an ideal but a realistic appreciation of family relationships and petty grudges. It may even serve as a valid psychological explanation for why some people have a profound dislike for so-called heroes and make consistent efforts to diminish the deeds of all persons regarded as role models by society. Such an attitude may just be another reaction against being told that someone else is a better person than you are.

than is good for us; that is why there is the virtue of temperance. Foot points out that virtue theories seem to assume human nature is by and large sensual and fearful, but there actually may be other character deficiencies that are more prevalent and more interesting to try to correct through virtue—such as the desire to be put upon and dissatisfied or the unwillingness to accept good things as they come along.

But what about people who are *naturally* virtuous? The philosophical tradition has had a tendency to judge them rather oddly. Suppose we have two people who make the decision to lend a hand to someone in need. Person A likes to do things for others and jumps at the chance to be helpful. Person B really couldn't care less about other people but knows that benevolence is a virtue, so he makes an effort to help in spite of his natural inclination. For Kant the person who makes an effort to overcome his or her inclination is a *morally better person* than the one to whom virtue comes easily. But surely there is something strange about that judgment, because in real life we appreciate the naturally benevolent person so much more than the surly one who grudgingly tries to be good for the sake of a principle. As a matter of fact, those are the people we *love,* because they *like* to do things for the sake of other people. Many schools of thought agree that it takes a greater effort to overcome than to follow your inclination, so it must be more morally worthy. Aristotle, however, believed that the person who takes pleasure in doing a virtuous action is the one who is truly virtuous.

Foot sides here with Aristotle: The person who likes to do good, or to whom it comes easily, is a morally better person than the one who succeeds through struggle. Why? Because the fact that there is a struggle is a sign that the person is *lacking in virtue* in the first place. Not that the successful struggler isn't good, or virtuous, but the one who did it with no effort is just a little bit better, because the virtue was already there to begin with. Foot's own example, in *Virtues and Vices*, is honesty:

> For one man it is hard to refrain from stealing and for another man it is not: which shows the greater virtue in acting as he should? . . . The fact that a man is *tempted* to steal is something about him that shows a certain lack of honesty: of the thoroughly honest man we say that it "never entered his head," meaning that it was never a real possibility for him.

In addition, Foot offers a solution to another problem plaguing virtue ethics: Can we say that someone who is committing an evil act is somehow doing it with virtue? Say that a criminal has to remain cool, calm, and collected in order to open a safe or has to muster courage in order to fulfill a contract and kill someone. Is this person virtuous in the sense of having self-control or courage? Foot borrows an argument from the one ethicist who is most often identified with an ethics of conduct, even though his work also includes the topic of virtue—Kant: *An act or a disposition can't be called good if it isn't backed by a good will.* Foot interprets it this way: If the act is morally wrong, or, rather, if the *intentions* behind the act are bad, then cool-headedness and courage *cease to be virtues.* Virtue is not something static; it is a dynamic power that appears when the intention is to do something good. The "virtue" value is simply switched off when the good intention is absent. And here we have an answer to the study question raised at the end of Chapter 9, after Aristotle's text on courage: *Can a terrorist be courageous?* Should we acknowledge that the September 11 hijackers were somehow brave, in spite of their evil intentions? Foot would probably say no: A virtue is nullified if it is done with an evil intention. The hijackers may have experienced some kind of spiritual fortitude, but it doesn't deserve the name *courage* if we view courage as a virtue. And saying that their intention may have been to do something good for somebody other than the victims doesn't count, in any moral theory: not in the religion of Islam, which forbids the killing of innocents; nor in Christianity and Judaism, which forbid the same thing; nor in utilitarianism, which sees the immensity of the massacre and psychological turmoil that followed throughout the world as unjustified by any local cause the hijackers may have had; nor in Kant's theory, which says we should never use any other person merely as a means to an end; nor in virtue theory, which, as we can now see, holds that it is *motivation* that determines whether or not a character trait can be called virtuous.

We find parallels in other situations in which there may not be any evil or criminal element. Hope, for example, is generally supposed to be a virtue, but if someone is being unrealistic and daydreams about wish fulfillment, hope is no longer a virtue. And temperance may be a virtue, but not if a person is simply afraid to throw herself into the stream of life. In that case it is a shield and not a virtue.

Critics of Foot's positive attitude toward the person who is naturally good with few selfish inclinations often point to Kant's argument against the storekeeper who decides not to cheat customers (similar to the version of the argument you know from Chapter 6): To say you like your customers so much that you would never cheat them is not enough, because what if you stopped liking your customers? Similarly, the person who has never been tempted because susceptibility to temptation is not in her or his nature may seem a higher moral person to Foot; but perhaps it is just because that person has never come across temptation before, and in that case it is easy enough to be virtuous. True virtue, say Kant's followers, shows itself precisely in the face of temptation—and not in its absence. However, when we have the choice between a store where they have a strict policy against cheating but the personnel are cold and grumpy and the store where they've known us for years and ask us how we're doing, don't we prefer to shop at the friendly place rather than at the unfriendly, but morally correct, place? Kant may think we should choose the unfriendly place, but Foot disagrees: We prefer friendliness, not principles. But what makes being friendly morally superior to being principled, in Foot's view? Remember, Kant rejected the storekeeper's third option because someone who wouldn't cheat his or her customers because of a sunny disposition toward them is really just doing what he or she wants, out of self-gratification, not out of principles. Of course it is possible to be of a sunny disposition *and* be principled, but that is not the issue here. The issue is whether a sunny disposition is enough to make someone a moral person or whether having a character that isn't tempted is morally superior to being a person who encounters temptation and fights it. Foot says yes: The storekeeper who wouldn't dream of cheating her customers is a better person than the one who has had a moment's temptation and rejected it, because temptation simply wasn't a factor. Foot's assumption is that it takes a weak character to be tempted. But, realistically, perhaps all that was missing was exposure and opportunity. So perhaps Kant has a point after all.

Christina Hoff Sommers

Which, then, are the virtues to which we should pay attention? Foot leaves the question open to an extent, because people tend to differ about what exactly is good for others and desirable as a human trait. Another ethicist, however, prefers to be more direct; her aim is not so much to defend virtue ethics as such but to focus on specific virtues and moral failings in our Western world. Christina Hoff Sommers tells of the woes an ethics professor of her acquaintance would experience at the end of a term. In spite of the multisubject textbooks they had read and the spirited discussions they had engaged in, the professor's students somehow got the impression that there are no moral truths. Everything they had studied about ethics had been presented in terms of rules that can be argued against and social dilemmas that have no clear solutions. More than half of the students cheated on their ethics finals. The irony of cheating on an ethics test probably did not even occur to these students.

What is lacking in our ethics classes? asks Sommers. It can't be good intentions on the part of instructors, because since the 1960s teachers have been very careful to present the material from all sides and to avoid moral indoctrination. (Even this text, as you have noticed, contains sporadic mention of the difference between doing ethics and *moralizing*.) Somehow, though, students come away with the notion that because everything can be argued against, moral values are a matter of taste. The teacher may prefer her students not to cheat, but that is simply her preference; if the student's preference is for cheating as a moral value ("Cheat but don't get caught"), then so be it. The moral lesson is learned by the student, and the chance for our society to hand down

Christina Hoff Sommers (b. 1950), American philosopher, co-editor of *Vice and Virtue in Everyday Life* (1985), and author of *Who Stole Feminism?* (1994) and *The War Against Boys* (2000), argues for a return to virtue ethics in order for people in modern society to regain a sense of responsibility rather than leave it to social institutions to make decisions on moral issues.

lessons of moral decency and respect for others has been lost because of a general fear of imposing one's personal values on others.

What does Sommers think should be done? She suggests that instead of teaching courses on the big issues such as abortion, euthanasia, and capital punishment, we should talk about the little, everyday, enormously important things, such as honesty, friendship, consideration, respect. These are virtues that, if not learned at a young age, may never be achieved in our society. Sommers mentions that, in ethics courses of the nineteenth century, students were taught how to be good rather than how to discuss moral issues. When asked to name some moral values that can't be disputed, Sommers answered,

> It is wrong to mistreat a child, to humiliate someone, to torment an animal. To think only of yourself, to steal, to lie, to break promises. And on the positive side: it is right to be considerate and respectful of others, to be charitable and generous.

For Sommers it is not enough to investigate virtue ethics—one must practice it and teach it to others. In this way virtue *theory* becomes virtue *practice*. If we study virtue theory in school, chances are we will find it natural to seek to develop our own virtues. Sommers believes a good way to learn about virtues is to use the same method that both Bernard Mayo and philosopher Alasdair MacIntyre (see Box 10.4) advise: to read stories in which someone does something decent for others, either humans or animals. Through stories we "get the picture" better than we get it from philosophical dilemmas or case studies. Literary classics can tell us more about friendship and obligation than a textbook in moral problems can. For Sommers, there are basic human virtues that aren't a matter of historical relativism, fads, or discussion, and the better we all learn them, the better we'll like living in our world with each other. These virtues are part of most people's moral heritage, and there is nothing oppressive about teaching the common virtues of decency, civility, honesty, and fairness.

Too often we tend to think that certain issues are someone else's problem; the state will take care of it, whether it is pollution, homelessness, or the loneliness of elderly people. For Sommers this is part of a virtue ethics for grown-ups: *Don't as-*

Here is another stab at doing philosophy from Calvin, who is voicing rare scruples about cheating on an ethics test (scruples which apparently were not shared by the students of Christina Hoff Sommers's colleague). Is Hobbes right that "simply acknowledging the issue is a moral victory"?

sume that it is someone else's responsibility. Don't hide from contemporary problems—take them on and contribute to their solution. Do your part to limit pollution. Think of how you can help homeless people. Go visit someone you know who is elderly and lonely. Virtues like these will benefit us all and are the kind we must learn to focus on if we are to make a success out of being humans living together.

This vision of personal virtues is probably the most direct call to a resurgence of moral values that has been produced so far within the field of philosophy. Sommers, however, is arguing not for a revival of religious values but for a strengthening of basic concepts of personal responsibility and respect for other beings. Her claim is that few ethicists dare to stand by values and pronounce them good in themselves these days for fear of being accused of indoctrinating their students. For Sommers the list of values cited above is absolute: They can't be disputed. Herein lies one answer to why Sommers today remains one of the most controversial of American contemporary philosophers (another answer can be found in Chapter 13: her approach to feminism): In the intellectual climate of the 1990s, it was considered not only customary but even proper to view values as something more or less relative, to one's culture and to one's personal life experience; we've explored the issue in Chapter 3.

Box 10.4   MacINTYRE AND THE VIRTUES

The American philosopher Alasdair MacIntyre believes that our moral values would be enriched if we followed the examples of older cultures and let *tradition* be part of these values. We don't exist in a cultural vacuum, he says, and we would understand ourselves better if we'd allow a historical perspective to be part of our system of values. This doesn't mean that everything our ancestors did and thought should become a virtue for us, but a look back to the values of those who came before us adds a depth to our modern life that makes it easier to understand ourselves. And how do we understand ourselves best? As the tellers of stories of history, of fiction, and of our own lives. We understand ourselves in terms of the story we would tell of our own life, and by doing this we are defining our *character.* So virtue and character development are essential to being a moral person and doing what is morally good. But virtues

are not static abilities for MacIntyre any more than they are for Philippa Foot. Virtues are linked with our aspirations; they make us better at *becoming* what we want to be. It is not so much that we have a vision of the good life; rather, we have an idea of what we want to accomplish (what MacIntyre calls "internal goods"), and virtues help us accomplish these goals. Whatever our goal, we usually will be more successful at reaching it if we are conscientious and trustworthy in striving for it. Whatever profession we try to excel in, we will succeed more easily if we try to be courageous and honest and maintain our integrity. With all the demands we face and all the different roles we have to play—in our jobs, sexual relationships, relations to family and friends—staying loyal and trustworthy helps us to function as one whole person rather than as a compilation of disjointed roles.

As you have heard, the entire intellectual juggernaut of academic instruction had, since the 1970s, been moving away from the very notion of "indoctrination," of instructors telling their students what to think about values. For Sommers, however, the end result has not been what was presumably intended—an enhanced individual moral responsibility—but rather the opposite: no sense of responsibility at all, since morals are perceived to be relative. So Sommers digs deeper into who we are as humans and finds a common ground of values.

But is she right? Can we just pronounce the virtues of decency, civility, honesty, and so forth the ultimate values without any further discussion? For many of her colleagues and readers, this is an unacceptable return to what we in this book have called *hard universalism.* Perhaps Sommers is right that most people would agree her values are good, and perhaps not. For many, what Sommers is doing is just old-fashioned moralizing (and some applaud that effort, but others don't). In effect, this isn't just Sommers's problem—it is a problem inherent in all genuine virtue ethics, as you'll remember from the previous chapter: When there is a dispute about virtues, among virtuous people, who gets to be right? How do we determine exactly what virtue is, if virtue is its own answer? How can college students be convinced that cheating is a bad thing? How can teens be convinced that sharing copyrighted material via the Internet is wrong? It can't be done by simply teaching them that honesty is a virtue; this might work for young children, but adolescents and adults need *reasons.* Reasons and reasoning are the key here. A moral story such as Charles Dickens's *A Tale of Two Cities* may tell us that self-sacrifice is a "far, far better thing" to practice than anything else, and it may make sense to me, but in your ears it may just sound like propaganda. What we need is to add rational argumentation to virtue ethics: give good reasons why something is a virtue, and a value. The stand-off between Sommers and many of her colleagues might, in this respect, be deflected by seeking an answer in what we've called *soft universalism* and in an approach you're familiar with from elsewhere in this book: looking for the common ground, plus finding good reasons why something is, or should be, a virtue.

The Quest for Authenticity: Kierkegaard, Heidegger, Sartre, and Levinas

Within what is called "contemporary continental philosophy"—by and large European philosophy after World War I—one school of thought holds there is only one way to live properly and only one virtue to strive for: that of *authenticity.* This school of thought is *existentialism.* Although existentialism developed primarily at the hands of Jean-Paul Sartre as a response to the experience of meaninglessness in the day-to-day struggle of World War II, it has its roots in the writings of the Danish philosopher Søren Aabye Kierkegaard. In this section we take a look at Kierkegaard, Martin Heidegger, and Sartre, and in addition we will look at a philosopher, also coming out of the existential tradition, who in more recent years has emerged as a forceful voice for ethics as fundamental to human existence: Emmanuel Levinas. Whereas Kierkegaard's form of authenticity is ultimately conceived as a relationship between *oneself and God,* Heidegger's authenticity deals with one's relationship to *one's own form of existence,* and Sartre's authenticity deals with *one's relationship to oneself as a person making moral choices,* Levinas focuses on the relationship between *oneself and the Other*—our fellow human beings.

Kierkegaard's Religious Authenticity

During his lifetime (1813–1855), Kierkegaard was known locally, in Copenhagen, as a man of leisure who had a theology degree and spent his time writing convoluted and irritating attacks on the Danish establishment, including officials of the Lutheran church. Few people understood his points because he was rarely straightforward in his writings and hid his true opinions under layers of pseudonyms and irony. The idea that there might be a great mind at work, developing what was to become one of the most important lines of thought in the twentieth century, was obvious to no one at the time, in Denmark or elsewhere. As a matter of fact, Kierkegaard was working against the general spirit of the times, which was focused politically on the development of socialism and scientifically on the ramifications of Darwinism. People weren't ready to listen to ideas such as the value of personal commitment, the psychological dread that accompanies the prospect of total human freedom of the will, the relativity of truth, and the value of the individual. As it happened, though, such ideas were to become key issues for French and German existential philosophers a couple of generations after Kierkegaard's death.

Søren Kierkegaard (1813–1855), Danish philosopher, writer, and theologian, believed that there are three major stages in human spiritual development: the aesthetic stage, the ethical stage, and the religious stage. Not everyone goes through all stages, but true selfhood and personal authenticity can't happen until one has put one's complete faith in God.

There are two major, very different ways of approaching the strange writings of Søren Kierkegaard. You can dismiss him as a man who had a difficult childhood and as a consequence developed an overinflated ego with no sense of proportion as to the importance of events. In other words, you can view his writings as simply the product of an overheated brain that pondered the "great mystery" of Søren Kierkegaard's life and times. Or you can view his writings as words that speak to all humanity from a uniquely insightful point of view, which just happens to have its roots in events in Kierkegaard's own life. Among current scholars this second approach has become the prevailing one.

What was so eventful about Kierkegaard's life? Nothing much, compared to the lives of other famous people; but, contrary to most people, Kierkegaard analyzed everything that happened to him for all it was worth and with an eerie insight. He was born into a family of devout Lutherans (Lutheranism is the state religion in Denmark and has been since the Protestant Reformation) and was the youngest boy born to comparatively old parents. Several of his older siblings died young, and for some reason both Søren and his father believed that Søren would not live long either. His father's opinion had an extreme influence on the boy—an influence that Kierkegaard later analyzed to perfection, years before Freud described conflict and bonding between fathers and sons.

When his father was young and a shepherd in rural Denmark, he was overcome by hunger and cold one bleak day on the moors, and he stood up on a rock and cursed God for letting a child suffer like that. Shortly after this incident his parents sent him to Copenhagen as an apprentice, and his hard life was over. This was a psychological shock to him, because he had expected punishment from God for cursing him, and he waited for the punishment most of his life. He grew rich while others lost their money, and for that reason he expected God to punish him even more severely. The first tragic thing that happened to him was that he lost his young wife; however, two months later he married their maid, who was already pregnant at the time.

When Søren's older siblings died, his father thought that God's punishment had struck again, but otherwise his luck held while his guilt grew. It is possible that he then got the idea of letting his youngest son somehow make amends for him—take on the burden and strive for a reconciliation with God. In the Lutheran tradition there is no such thing as making a confession to your minister in order to "get things off your chest"—you alone must face your responsibility and handle your relationship with God. This means that you have direct access to God at any time, in your heart; you have a direct relationship to God. Your faith is a personal matter, and for Kierkegaard in particular the concept of faith was to become extremely personal.

Søren turned out to be an extraordinarily bright child, and his father devoted much time to his education, in particular to the development of his imagination. The two made a habit of taking walks—in their living room. Søren would choose where they were going—to the beach, to the castle in the woods, down Main Street—and his father would then describe in minute detail what they "saw." It was intellectually and emotionally exhausting for the boy, and scholars have ridiculed the father for his fancy, but today it is recognized by many that the combination of imagination and intellectual discipline is just about the best trait a parent can develop in a child, although one might say that this was a rather extreme way of going about it. At the end of this chapter you can read an excerpt from Kierkegaard's *Johannes Climacus* where he describes his father's vivid imagination.

Kierkegaard was a young adult when his father died, and he understood full well the immense influence his father had had on him. He wrote the following in *Stages on Life's Way* (1845), though he didn't let on that he was writing about himself:

> There was once a father and a son. A son is like a mirror in which the father beholds himself, and for the son the father too is like a mirror in which he beholds himself in the time to come. . . . the father believed he was to blame for the son's melancholy, and the son believed that he was the occasion of the father's sorrow—but they never exchanged a word on this subject.

> Then the father died, and the son saw much, experienced much, and was tried in manifold temptations; but infinitely inventive as love is, longing and the sense of loss taught him, not indeed to wrest from the silence of eternity a communication, but to imitate the father's voice so perfectly that he was content with the likeness . . . for the father was the only one who had understood him, and yet he did not know in fact whether he had understood him; and the father was the only confidant he had had, but the confidence was of such a sort that it remained the same whether the father lived or died.

So Kierkegaard *internalized* the voice of his father; as Freud would say, he made his father's voice his own *Superego*. This had the practical effect of prompting Kierkegaard finally to get his degree in theology (which his father had wanted him to do, but which he hadn't really wanted himself). Kierkegaard also internalized his father's guilt and rather gloomy outlook on life. (See Box 10.5 for another event that may have been influenced by his father.) Kierkegaard believed that everyone, even a child, has an intimate knowledge of what anguish feels like; he believed that you feel dread or anguish when you look to the future—you dread it because you realize you must make choices. This feeling, which has become known by the Danish/German word, *Angst,* is comparable, Kierkegaard says, to realizing that you're far out on the ocean and you have to swim or sink, act or die, and there is no way out. The choice

Edvard Munch, *The Scream* (1893). This image, which exists in more than fifty original versions, is the epitome of the feeling of angst. Munch described in his diary the moment that inspired him to do this work: "I was walking along the road with two friends—the sun was setting—all of a sudden the sky turned crimson—my friends walked on, and I froze, shaking with anguish—and I felt that through nature was passing a vast, endless scream." (Ulrich Bischoff, *Edvard Munch 1863–1944*, Köln: Benedikt Taschen GmbH & Co, 1989. Translated by Nina Rosenstand.)

is yours, but it is a hard choice, because living is a hard job. Suppose you refuse to make your own decisions and say, "Society will help me," or "The church will help me," or "My uncle will help me"? Then you have given up your chance to become a real person, to become *authentic,* because you don't accomplish anything spiritual unless you accomplish it yourself, by making the experience your own. Each person is an individual, but only through a process of individuation—choosing to make one's own decisions and take responsibility for them in the eyes of God—can a person achieve selfhood and become a true human individual. The truth you experience when you have reached this point is *your truth alone,* because only you took that particular path in life. Other people can't take a shortcut by borrowing "your truth"—they must find the way themselves. We can't, then, gain any deep insights about life from books or from teachers. They can point us in the right direction, but they can't spoon-feed us any truths. In the Primary Readings you'll find a short excerpt from *Either/Or* where Kierkegaard describes the nature of making hard choices.

This attitude is reflected in Kierkegaard's cryptic and disturbing assertion that *truth is subjective,* an idea that has been vehemently disputed by scientists and philosophers alike. Some philosophers believe Kierkegaard meant there is no objective knowledge at all; we can never verify statements such as "2 + 2 = 4," "The moon circles the earth," and "It rained in Boston on April 6, 2002," because all such statements are, presumably, just a matter of subjective opinion, or what we call *cognitive relativism.* This would mean that we could never set any objective standard for knowledge. Although other philosophers, such as Friedrich Nietzsche, have actually worked toward such a radical viewpoint, Kierkegaard is not among them. He never says that *knowledge* is subjective, and to understand what he means we have to look more closely at what he says. His actual words are *"Subjectivity is Truth,"* and Kierkegaard scholars believe this to mean the following: There is no such thing as "Truth" with a capital *T* that we can just scoop up and call our own. The "meaning of life" is not something we can look up in a book or learn from anybody else, because *it just isn't there unless we find it ourselves.* There is no *objective* truth about life, only a *personal* truth, which will be a little bit different for each individual. It will not be vastly different, though, because when we reach the level at which we are truly personal, we will find that it corresponds to other people's experiences of individuation too. In other words, the personal experience becomes a *universal* one—but only if you have gone through it yourself. This is the ultimate meaning of life and the ultimate virtue: to become an authentic human being by finding your own meaning. If you settle for accepting other people's view of life, you are no better than the evil magician Noureddin (or Jaffar, in the Disney movie version) in the story of Aladdin; he has no personal magic or talent himself, so he tries to steal it from the one who has, Aladdin.

For Kierkegaard himself, truth is a religious truth: One must take on the concept of sin and responsibility and seek God's forgiveness directly, as an individual. But this is hard for most people to do because we are born with quite another character. Typically humans are born into the *aesthetic stage:* the stage of sensuous enjoyment. Children obviously have a very strong interest in the joys of their senses, but if this persists into adulthood it can result in unhealthy character development, symbolized by the Don Juan type who loves to pursue the girl, but loses interest

Box 10.5   A KIND OF LOVE AND MARRIAGE
THAT WASN'T: REGINE OLSEN

An event of great importance in Søren Kierkegaard's life occurred when he fell deeply in love for the first and only time. The woman's name was Regine Olsen, and she was the daughter of a minister. Regine and Søren became engaged, and he engaged himself in a new intellectual scrutiny: What was this feeling? Was it constant or a fluke? What might go wrong? Was it right for him to try to do something "universal" that everybody did, like get married and have children, or would it somehow interfere with his father's plans for him to be a sacrifice to God? Regine, a kind and loving woman, was utterly puzzled at Søren's reluctance to accept that they were just young people in love. When they were together he was in a good mood and was confident about their future together, but, when he was alone, the doubts started closing in on him. It appears that he felt he was not quite worthy of her, for some reason—perhaps because in years past he had visited a brothel, or perhaps because he couldn't quite explain his father's influence on him to her. Mostly, though, it was the shock of the physical attraction he felt toward her that distracted him, he thought, from becoming truly spiritual. During this period he began to understand one aspect of the Don Juan character: He realized that he loved Regine the most *when he was not with her* but was fantasizing about her. Once they were together his ardor cooled considerably. Eventually he decided that it was better for both of them if they broke up, but because nineteenth-century mores demanded that the woman, not the man, break off the engagement if her character were to remain stainless, he had to try to force Regine to break the engagement. This he did by being as nasty to her as he could, even though he still loved her. He embarked on a program he himself had devised, alternating between playing the fool and the cynic; once when she asked him if he never intended to marry, he answered as nastily

Regine Olsen, Søren Kierkegaard's fiancée, a gentle Copenhagen woman who did her best to understand the intellectual scruples of her boyfriend, who could not reconcile his devotion to God with the idea of physical attraction to a woman and a subsequent bourgeois marriage. This photo was taken a few years after Kierkegaard finally broke up with her. (Photo of Regine Schlegel [*née* Olsen] courtesy of The Royal Library, Copenhagen.)

as he could, "Yes, in ten years when I've sown all my wild oats; then I'll need a young girl to rejuvenate me." For a long time he persisted in being rude to her, and she continued to forgive him, because she was very much in love with him. In the end he himself broke up with her, however, and she appears to have talked about killing herself. Kierkegaard wanted her to despise him, and a short time later she actually became engaged to a friend of theirs. After that, Kierkegaard never tired of talking about woman's fickle, stupid, and untrustworthy nature.

once he has seduced her. She wants to get married, and he wants *out*. He leaves, only to fall in love with and pursue some other girl, and on it goes. Today we would say this is a person who *can't commit*. Kierkegaard makes the same basic observation but explains that this happens because the Don Juan type is steeped in sensuous enjoyment, which sours on itself: Too much of the same is not a good thing, but a person who is stuck in the aesthetic stage doesn't have any sense of what is morally right or wrong. Such knowledge usually comes as people mature and enter the *ethical stage* (although some people are stuck in the aesthetic stage forever).

In the ethical stage people realize that there are laws and conventions, and they believe that the way to become a good person is to follow these conventions. A fictional character from nineteenth-century middle-class Copenhagen becomes Kierkegaard's prototype for the ethical stage: Judge William, the righteous man who tries to be a good judge and a good husband and father. Scholars don't quite agree on how to evaluate this good and kind man, because the fact is that we are rarely certain when Kierkegaard is being serious and when he is being sarcastic. Kierkegaard also cites Socrates (whom he greatly admired) as an example of an ethical person. Although Socrates is commonly recognized as a truly courageous and virtuous man who strove to live (and die) the right way, Judge William doesn't come across as a heroic person; we even get the impression that he is actually a pompous, self-righteous, bourgeois bore who has his attention fixed on "doing the right thing" merely because society expects it of him. So it seems Kierkegaard wants to tell us that it isn't enough to follow the rules and become what everyone else thinks you ought to be; that way you exist only in the judgment of others. You have to take on responsibility for judging yourself, and the way you do that is by making a *leap of faith* into the *religious stage*. It isn't enough to judge your own life in terms of what makes sense according to society's rules and rational concepts of morality; what you must do in order to become an authentic person is leave the standards of society behind, including your love for reason and for things to make sense, and choose to trust in God, like Abraham, who made that same choice when he brought his son Isaac to be sacrificed, even though it didn't make sense to him. Reason and the rules of society can't tell you if the insight you reach as a religious person is the truth.

So why is Socrates not a perfect person? Why did he stay within the ethical stage and make no leap of faith to the religious stage, according to Kierkegaard? Because the leap was not available to him, since he didn't belong to the Judeo-Christian tradition. Socrates is an example of how far you can reach if you stay within the boundaries of reason. However, in the religious stage there is no objective measure of meaning. At this stage you take responsibility for yourself, but at the same time you give up your fate and place it in the hands of God. Finally you can become a true human being, a complete individual and person, because only in the religious stage can you realize what it means to say that "Subjectivity is Truth."

Heidegger's Intellectual Authenticity

Martin Heidegger is an enigmatic and controversial philosopher. He is enigmatic because he aims to make people break through the old boundaries of thinking by

Martin Heidegger (1889–1976), German philosopher and poet and a member of the National Socialist Party, believed authentic life is a life open to the possibility of different meanings. The feeling of *Angst* can help jolt us out of our complacency and help us see the world from an intellectually flexible point of view.

inventing new words and categories for them to think with. This means there is no easy way to read Heidegger; you must acquaint yourself with an entirely new vocabulary of key concepts and get used to a new way of looking at reality. In spite of his rather inaccessible style, though, Heidegger has become something of a cult figure in modern European philosophy. He is controversial because he was a member of the Nazi Party during World War II (see Box 10.6).

Heidegger sees human beings as not essentially distinct from the world they inhabit, in the same sense that traditional epistemology does: There is no "subject" on the inside of a person and no "object" of experience on the outside. Rather, humans are thrown into the world at birth, and they interact with it and in a sense "live" it. There is no such thing as a person who is distinct from his or her world of experience—we *are* our world of experience. This idea of interaction with the world from the beginning of life is one that Heidegger took over from his teacher and mentor Edmund Husserl, but he adds his own twist to it: What makes humans special is not that they are on the inside and the world is on the outside, but that they experience their *existence* differently than all other beings do. Humans *are there* for themselves; they are aware of their existence and of certain essential facts about that existence, such as their own mortality. So Heidegger calls humans "Being-there" (*Dasein*) rather than "humans." Things, on the other hand, don't know they exist, and to Heidegger neither do animals; an animal may know it is hungry, or in pain, or in heat, but it doesn't know its days are numbered, and that makes the difference. Our humanity consists primarily of our continuous awareness of death, our "Being-toward-death" (*Sein-zum-Tode*). On occasion we let ourselves get distracted, because this awareness is quite a burden on our minds, and we let ourselves forget. We become absorbed in our jobs, our feelings, the gossip we hear, the nonsense around us. According to Heidegger, we often refer to what "They" say, as if the opinion of those anonymous others has some obvious authority. We bow to what "They" say and believe we are safe from harm and responsibility if we can get absorbed by this ubiquitous "They" (*Das Man*) and don't have to think on our own. In other words, we try to take on the safe and nonthinking existence-form of things—we objectify ourselves.

Box 10.6   HEIDEGGER AND THE NAZI CONNECTION

At the time of Hitler's takeover of Germany in 1933, Martin Heidegger's philosophy professor, Edmund Husserl, was head of the philosophy department at the University of Freiburg. Husserl was already a famous philosopher, having developed the theory of *phenomenology,* a philosophical theory of human experience. Its main thesis is that there is no such thing as a consciousness that is empty at first and then proceeds to order and analyze the objects of sense experience; instead, our mind is already engaged in the process of experiencing the world from day one. We can't separate the concepts of the experiencing mind and the experience of the mind, and, because it is impossible for philosophy to say anything about a nonexperiencing mind and the unexperienced object-world, phenomenology sees its primary task as describing, as clearly as possible, the phenomenon of experience itself. Husserl had been the essential inspiration for many of Heidegger's writings; in fact, he had taken Heidegger under his wing when Heidegger was a young scholar. Husserl was Jewish, though, which meant that he was targeted for persecution by the new Nazi leaders. He was fired from his university position and eventually died as a result of Nazi harassment. Heidegger, his former student and protégé, profited from these events by taking over Husserl's position as department chair; indeed, it seems that he never raised any protest against the treatment of his old professor. At this time Heidegger joined the Nazi Party for, as he explained later, purely professional reasons: He couldn't have kept his university position without becoming a party member. This appears to be stretching the truth, for Heidegger never did anything at all to distance himself from the Nazi ideology during the war years. Today people are divided in their views on Heidegger; some feel that because of his Nazi association, his philosophy is tainted and must somehow contain elements of Nazi thinking. Others believe that Heidegger was essentially apolitical, although he was not very graceful about it; they think his philosophy should be viewed independent of his personal life.

This does not make an authentic life, however, and in any event it is doomed to failure because we can't forget so completely. Humans just can't become things, because we are the ones who understand the relationship between ourselves and things. When we do the dishes we understand what plates are for, what glasses are for, and why they must be cleaned. We understand the entire "doing dishes" situation. When we prepare a presentation on our computer we understand what a report is, what a computer is, and why the two have anything to do with ourselves, even if we may not understand what the report is for or how the computer works. In the end, humans are different because we can ask, What is it for? and understand the interconnections of the world we live in. We are asking, thinking creatures, and in order to regain our awareness of that fact, we must face our true nature. We may pretend to be nothing but victims of circumstances (I have to do the dishes; there is no other choice), but we also can choose to realize that we interact with our world and affect it. In *Being and Time* (1927), Heidegger calls this phenomenon (in his exasperating style) "An-already-thrown-into-the-world-kind-of-Being who is existing-in-relationship-to-existing-entities-within-that-world" (*Sich-vorweg-schon-sein-in* [*der-Welt*] *als Sein-bei* [*innerwelt-lich begegendem Seindenen*]). But he also describes it, in a slightly more down-to-earth fashion, as the structure of *care*. "Being-theres" always "care" about something, Heidegger says. This doesn't mean humans care *for* others, or *for* things—it merely means we are always *engaged* in something (the state of being engaged in something Heidegger called care—*Sorge*). Sometimes this involves caring for others, but mostly it involves engaging in our own existence: We fret, we worry, we look forward to something, we're concerned, we're content, we're disappointed about something—our health, our promotion, our family's well-being, our new kittens, or the exciting experiences we anticipate on our next vacation. We are always engaged in some part of our reality, unless we get caught up in another and deeper element of human nature: a *mood,* such as dread or anguish—Angst.

Heidegger's concept of *Angst* is related to Kierkegaard's: It does not involve fear of something in particular; it is, rather, the unpleasant and sometimes terrifying insecurity of not knowing where you stand in life and eventually having to make a choice—perhaps with little or no information about your options. For Kierkegaard this experience is related to a religious awakening, but for Heidegger the awakening is metaphysical: You realize that all your concerns and all the rules you live by are *relative,* in the deepest sense; you realize that you have viewed the world a certain way, within a certain frame, and now for some reason the frame is breaking up. A woman may feel angst if she loses her tenured job at a university, not just because she is worried about how she will provide for her family but because her world-view—her professional identity and sense of security—has been undermined. A young man may feel angst if he learns he has an incurable disease—not just because he is afraid to die but because "this isn't supposed to happen" to a young person. Children may feel angst if they are drawn into a divorce battle between their parents. A hitherto religious person may feel angst if he or she begins to doubt the existence of God, because this is the breakup of the ultimate framework. And humans may feel angst when they realize that their worldview is somehow not a God-given truth.

People whose attitude toward the world is *inauthentic* may experience the most fundamental form of angst. Heidegger himself states that if a Being-there is open to the possibility of different meanings in his or her reality, then he or she is living an authentic life. If, however, a Being-there does not want to accept the possibility that something may have a different meaning than he or she has believed up until now, then he or she is inauthentic. A typical trait of those who are inauthentic is that they become absorbed in just reacting to the things in their world—in driving the car, loading the laundry into the dryer, working on the computer, shopping, watching TV. Such persons think the predigested opinions of others or of the media are sufficient for getting by; they let themselves become absorbed in "The They," *das Man.*

But what does authenticity mean? Is it a call to "get in touch with yourself" by pulling away from the world? Or is it just a banal reminder to "stay open-minded"? Even worse, is it a built-in feature of being human, something we can't escape? Some Heidegger scholars see it not just as a call to reexamine yourself or to avoid hardening of the brain cells; to them authenticity is a fundamentally different attitude from one by which we allow the readily available worldviews of others to rule our lives. Being authentic means, for Heidegger, that you stop being absorbed by your doings and retain an attitude that "things may mean something else than what I expect."

Only through this kind of intellectual flexibility can we even begin to think about making judgments about anything else, be they facts or people. So authenticity is, in a sense, remaining "open-minded," but it also involves performing a greater task by constantly forcing yourself to realize that reality is in flux, that things change, including yourself, and that you are part of a world of changing relationships. And *this* causes angst, because this means you have to give up your anchors and security zones as a matter of principle. In the end, angst becomes a liberating element that can give us a new and perhaps better understanding of ourselves and the world, but it is hard to deal with while we are in the midst of it.

Sartre's Ethical Authenticity

For some people angst is simply an existential fact, something we have to live with all our days. Jean-Paul Sartre is one of those persons. Sartre is the best known of the French existentialists of the mid–twentieth century; others include Albert Camus, Gabriel Marcel, and Simone de Beauvoir.

Sartre studied phenomenology (the discipline of the phenomenon of human consciousness and experience) in Berlin during the years between the two world wars, and he was well acquainted with the theories of Edmund Husserl and Martin Heidegger. During World War II Sartre was held by the Nazis as a prisoner of war, but he escaped and joined forces with the French Resistance movement. These experiences in many ways influenced his outlook on politics and on life in general: His political views were socialist and at times even Marxist, to a certain degree. Always politically active, Sartre may well be considered the most influential philosopher in twentieth-century Europe and possibly elsewhere—perhaps not as much because of his philosophical or literary writings (for Sartre was also a dramatist and novelist) as because of his intellectual inspiration. The existential movement may not have reflected a completely faithful version of the Sartrean philosophy, but it is certain that in his own century Sartre inspired the most extensive philosophical movement ever to reach people outside the academic world—the movement of existentialism.

Although existentialism as a fad in the 1950s became stereotyped as the interest of morose young people who dressed in black, chain-smoked late at night in small cafés, and read poems to each other about the absurdity of life, Sartre's existentialism had a whole other and more substantial content. Partly inspired by his experiences during the war, Sartre came to believe that there is no God, and, because there is no God, there are no absolute moral rules either. The concept that God's nonexistence makes everything permissible was not new at the time; it was well known to Western readers of Dostoyevsky and his novel *The Brothers Karamazov* as well as to readers of Friedrich Nietzsche. (See Box 10.7 for a discussion of Nietzsche's contributions to existentialism.) But it was given a new twist by Sartre. Instead of saying, as many other atheists did, that we can find our values in our own human context and rationality, Sartre held that without the existence of a God, there are no values, in the sense that there are no *objective* values. There is no master plan and, accordingly, nothing in the world *makes sense;* all events happen at random, and *life is absurd.* So what do we do? Give a shrug, and set about to make merry while we

French philosopher and writer Jean-Paul Sartre (1905–1980) was recognized as the most influential thinker in the existentialist movement. His best-known works of philosophy are the lecture "Existentialism as Humanism" (1945) and the much larger, much more intellectually challenging *Being and Nothingness* (1943).

can? No, we must realize that because no values exist outside ourselves, we, as individuals in a community, become the *source* of values. And the process by which we create values is the process of *choice.*

When a person realizes that he or she has to make a choice and that the choice will have far-reaching consequences, that person may be gripped by *anguish*—Sartre uses the image of a general having to choose whether to send his soldiers to their death. It is not a decision that can be made lightly by a person of conscience, and such a person may worry about it a great deal, precisely because he doesn't know beforehand whether he will make the right decision. If he realizes the enormity of the situation and still makes his choice as best he can, shouldering whatever consequences may develop, he is living with *authenticity.* However, suppose the general says to himself, "I *have* to send the soldiers out, for the sake of my country/my reputation/the book I want to write." Then he is acting inauthentically: He is assuming that he *has no choice.* But for Sartre we always have a choice. Even the soldier who is ordered to kill civilians still has a choice, although he may claim he will be executed if he doesn't follow orders and thus has no choice. For Sartre there are some things that are worse than death, such as killing innocent civilians. So claiming that one's actions are somehow *determined* by the situation is inauthenticity or, as Sartre calls it, *bad faith.* Bad faith can be displayed in another way too: Suppose the general is so distraught at having to make a choice that he says, "I just won't choose—I'll lock myself in the bathroom and wait until it is over." In that case, Sartre would say, the general is deluding himself, because he is already making a choice—*the choice not to choose*—and thus he is in even less control of the consequences of his choice than if he actually had chosen a course of action. In our hearts we know this, and Sartre maintains we can never deceive ourselves 100 percent. There will always be a part of us that knows we are not like animals or inert things that can't make choices, simply because we are human beings, and human beings make choices, at least from time to time. (See Box 10.8 for Henri Bergson's view of choice—and the ethical choices he made.) Animals and things can exist without making choices, but humans can't, because humans are aware of their own existence and their own mortality; they have a relationship to themselves (they exist

Box 10.7   NIETZSCHE AND EXISTENTIALISM

The German philosopher Friedrich Nietzsche (1844–1900), one of the truly controversial figures in Western philosophy, is often credited with being one of the contributors to the French existentialism of the twentieth century. Sartre's view that life is absurd because there is no God has an early counterpart in Nietzsche's statement that "God is dead"; by this Nietzsche did not mean that Christ had died, or that there is no God, but that faith in God was waning if not gone altogether, and as a result the guarantees of stable, universal values provided by a faith in God had disappeared. For Nietzsche there are no absolute values in the absence of God; there are no values at all except those we as humans decide on. Whereas, for Sartre, the values we must decide on are the values that make us into beings who take responsibility for our lives as well as for the lives of others who look to us for guidance, Nietzsche suggested that the old Christian value system of loving one's neighbor and turning the other cheek must be scrapped, because it is the morality of a weak person, a "slave" who fears his "master," the strong-willed, self-made individual.

For Nietzsche, the "slave-morality" began in ancient times when slaves hated and feared their masters and resented anyone who wielded power over them. Whereas the values of the master would include pride, courage, and loyalty to one's clan, the values of the slave population included a fellowship with other slaves against the master. Because pride and courage are "master"-values, the slave prizes equality and meekness. Nietzsche speculates that when slavery was finally abolished in the ancient world, the former slaves took their value system with them and made it into social and religious ideals: social equality, resentment against anyone who stands above the crowd, and turning the other cheek in meekness. Nietzsche sees the slave-morality as a form of spiritual slavery to majority opinion. In its place, he advocates

a new "master-morality" in which values reflect respect for one's equal but disdain for weaker individuals; the person who is strong enough to create his own values in the face of absurdity has the right to forge ahead and make whatever life he wants for himself. (The use of the gender-specific *he* and *himself* here is deliberate: Nietzsche saw the powerful individual as male and displayed a generally misogynist approach to women in his writings.) For Nietzsche this meant a liberation from the hypocrisy of the late nineteenth century, in which, as he saw it, Europe was suffering from the fear of excelling, of anybody being stronger or more clever than a neighbor; he saw it as an opportunity for a gifted individual (an "Overman") to seize the day and create a life worth living. (Sometimes Nietzsche's term *Übermensch* is translated as "Superman," but many Nietzsche scholars tend to avoid that translation, since it so easily, and wrongly, associates to the familiar flying figure in a red cape. Instead the more direct translation, *Overman,* is used.) Nietzsche abhorred political despotism and would never have wanted his idea of the Overman to be transformed into an ideology of a "master race" because he saw the Overman as an individual, not a member of a group. But this is what happened when certain German politicians of the early twentieth century did a deliberately selective reading of his works. Early Nazi thinkers saw Nietzsche's ideas of the Overman as legitimizing the idea that some people (meaning some *races*) are nobler and more valuable than others, and many of Nietzsche's thoughts were worked into Nazi ideology. This association with the Nazis tainted Nietzsche's writings for many readers in the second half of the twentieth century, although he himself would probably have greatly disapproved of what Nazi thinkers got out of his philosophy.

Nietzsche's thoughts on the Overman are generally referred to as a *transvaluation of values:*
(continued)

Box 10.7   NIETZSCHE AND EXISTENTIALISM (*continued*)

Through rejecting the herd mentality of the majority, the individual can reach an authentic set of values for himself. French existentialism has a clear line to Nietzsche's idea that life is absurd because God is dead, and there are no absolute values, but they part ways on the question of how to decide on a value system; there is no connection between French existentialism and Nietzsche's ideas of the right of the gifted individual to create his own values without taking other people into consideration.

"for themselves," *pour soi*), whereas animals and things merely float through existence (they exist "in themselves," *en soi*). In *Being and Nothingness* (1943), Sartre says:

> Thus there are no *accidents* in a life; a community event which suddenly bursts forth and involves me in it does not come from the outside. If I am mobilized in a war, this war is *my* war; it is in my image and I deserve it. I deserve it first because I could always get out of it by suicide or by desertion; these ultimate possibilities are those which must always be present for us when there is a question of envisaging a situation. For lack of getting out of it, I have *chosen* it. This can be due to inertia, to cowardice in the face of public opinion, or because I prefer certain other values to the value of the refusal to join in the war (the good opinion of my relatives, the honor of my family, etc.). Any way you look at it, it is a matter of choice. . . . If therefore I have preferred war to death or dishonor, everything takes place as if I bore the entire responsibility for this war.

How does bad faith manifest itself? Sartre's famous example involves a young woman on a date. The woman's date makes a subtle move on her—he grasps her hand—and she doesn't quite know what to do. She doesn't want to offend him or to appear to be prudish, but she really doesn't know whether she wants to have a relationship with him either. So she does nothing. She somehow manages to "detach" herself from the situation, as if her body really doesn't concern her, and, while he moves in on her, her hand seems not to belong to her at all. She looks at his face and pretends that she has no hand, no body, no sexuality at all. This, says Sartre, is bad faith: The woman thinks she can turn herself into a thing by acting thinglike, but it is an illusion, because through it all she knows that sooner or later she has to say yes or no. What should she do in order to be authentic? She should realize that she has to make up her mind, even if she can't foresee whether she will want to have a relationship or not. Making up her mind will then create a new situation for her to react to, even though it is essentially unforeseeable. This openness to the unforeseen is part of being authentic. When we make a choice, Sartre says, we are taking on the greatest of responsibilities, for we are choosing not only for ourselves and our lives but for everyone else too. Whatever choice we make sends out the message to everyone else that "this is okay to do." Therefore, through our choices we become role models for others. If we choose to pay our taxes, others will notice and believe that it is the right thing to do. If we choose to sell drugs to little children, somebody out there will see

Box 10.8   HENRI BERGSON: LET YOUR TRUE SELF EMERGE

The French philosopher Henri Bergson (1859–1941) is not considered an ethicist per se, but his theories of consciousness and time perception involve an unusual concept of authenticity. For Bergson, humans live most of their lives subject to the demands of circumstances and customs and to the internalized opinions of others. Once in a while, however, their true selves break through. We can't live our lives without a certain amount of custom and regard for immediate circumstances, but if we are to remain true to what we really are, we need to listen to the murmurs of our own self that are hiding behind the facade of our civilized lives. And how do we know there is such a true self? We all have agonized over some decision, weighing the pros and the cons, coming up with the most logical answer or the one that will please us or seems to be the morally right thing to do. Then, sometimes, to our own surprise, we end up doing something else entirely. Afterward, when we are asked why, we answer that we just "had to do it"—we "couldn't help ourselves." This, says Bergson, is our true self emerging. It may happen to a person who has decided to marry someone, received all the gifts, ordered all the catering, and is standing at the altar—the person says NO! when she meant to say yes. If you experience, in the midst of your everyday life, a sense that all of a sudden there is *something you must do before it is too late,* such as running away with the circus, learning the art of fencing, going to Paris, or having a baby, this, says Bergson, is your true self trying to get your attention, and this is true authenticity—all the rest is a veneer. There are two major problems with

Bergson's view. The first is that we have no assurance that this "deeper self" is actually a *good* self; the urge that comes over us may be to kill or betray someone. So it is doubtful that Bergsonian authenticity can actually be called a "virtue." The second problem is that Bergson thought this deeper self was proof that we have freedom of the will, but the whole point is that we have *no control* over what that self wants, and this is hardly what we normally mean by having a free will. Bergson's philosophy became immensely influential for just about all the French thinkers of the twentieth century, either as an inspiration or in creating a critical reaction. Sartre himself was greatly influenced by Bergson, and so was Emmanuel Levinas.

As a private person Bergson seems to have been a man of much integrity; in 1917 he went to the United States in order to fulfill a moral duty, as he saw it—to put an end to World War I. He also was utterly devoted to his daughter, who was hearing-impaired. In 1941 he lined up in the rain to be registered as a Jew by the Nazis during the Paris occupation; he contracted pneumonia, and it caused his death. He had wished to convert to Catholicism, but in view of Hitler's persecution of the Jews he decided to remain a member of the Jewish faith as a gesture of solidarity. These are the deeds of what we would call a person of moral virtue, so let us suppose we asked Bergson whether he did these things as a conscious, free decision. We might have received the answer that other people of moral virtue have given in similar situations: I did what I did because I could not do otherwise.

it and think it is a good idea. (Interestingly, doing something just because someone else is doing it is not enough for Sartre; as we saw in the section on Mayo's theory of role models, true authenticity must come from personal choices and not from just following role models.) Whatever we choose, even if we think it will concern only ourselves, actually will concern all of humanity, because we are endorsing our action as a general virtue. This is why choices can be so fraught with anxiety—and for Sartre this anxiety never goes away. We must live with it, and with the burden of the choice, forever. We are free to choose, but we are not free to refrain from choosing. In other words, *we are condemned to be free.*

This emphasis on human freedom is one of the strongest in the history of philosophy and one of the most radical, demanding theories of freedom of the will. You'll remember from Chapter 4 (and also from the film *Minority Report* in Chapter 7) that historically, there has been a dispute between supporters of the idea of *free will* and supporters of what we call *hard determinism,* the theory that everything in human life as well as in nature is determined by causal factors: heredity and environment, or nature and nurture. Sartre is one of the strongest critics of the theory of hard determinism, claiming that every kind of explanation of human actions that refers to outside forces or some kind of inner compulsion—in other words, any view that that we have no choice—is bunk, a bad excuse, or—in the terminology of existentialism—bad faith. Free will is our only "nature" as human beings; it is in a sense our fate to have no fate, to always be faced with multiple possibilities and the need to make choices, without having control over their consequences—and live with the resulting anguish. That, to Sartre, is living as an authentic human being.

So can we at least find comfort in the company of other people, close friends, lovers, or relatives who also have to face hard choices? For Sartre this presents no real solution; the presence of the Other—another person, different from myself—only reminds me of my absolute responsibility to make choices. And besides, the very presence of the Other is problematic in itself: When another person looks at me, and our eyes meet, he or she is always trying to dominate me, as I am trying to dominate him or her. For Sartre every human relationship is a game of dominance using the gaze as a tool of power, and this is especially the case for relationships between lovers. Essentially, we are alone with our choices and responsibilities. In the Narratives section you'll find three stories, each of which in its own way is a wonderful illustration of exactly what Sartre is talking about. One is the Woody Allen film *Hannah and Her Sisters,* in which a man faces his own mortality, not with fear, but with angst; next is Sartre's own famous stage play *No Exit*—for Sartre was also a writer of plays and novels—where three people face each other in hell for eternity, with each other's constant company as the only incessant torment; and finally you have the film *A Few Good Men,* where the theme is the ultimate existential responsibility to make free, responsible choices that can serve, as Sartre would say, as an example for others to follow and not succumb to the excuse that "I was just obeying orders."

But how can we make a choice if the world is absurd and all of our actions are meaningless? When we first experience the absurdity of existence we may feel nauseated, dizzy from the idea that reality has no core or meaning. But then we realize we must create a meaning; we must choose for something to matter to us. For Sartre the social conditions of France became a theme that mattered to him, but you might choose something else—your family, your job, or your Barbie doll collection. Any kind of life project will create values, as long as you realize that the world is still absurd in spite of your project! If you think you are "safe" with your family or your job or your doll collection—if you think you've created a rock-solid meaning for your life—then you've fallen back into bad faith. This is the case with the waiter (another of Sartre's examples) who wants so badly to become the perfect waiter that he takes on a "waiter identity" that provides answers to everything: how to speak, what to say, how to walk, where to go. The waiter has not chosen a project; he has turned himself into a thing, an "in itself" that doesn't have to choose anymore. Living authentically means living in anguish, always on the edge—confronting the absurdity of life and courageously making choices in the face of meaninglessness. When something you care about appears, then you will know what to do. The French philosopher and novelist Simone de Beauvoir, Sartre's significant other and his collaborator on the subject of existentialism, puts it like this: "Any man who has known real loves, real revolts, real desires, and real will knows quite well that he has no need of any outside guarantee to be sure of his goals."

Suppose you decide you'll do something about your life *tomorrow*. That *next year* you'll write that novel. Or go back to college. Suppose you decide you *should have* married someone else, had children, gone to see the Pyramids, or become a movie actor. Then there is not much hope for your authenticity, says Sartre, because your virtue lies only in what you accomplish, not in choices you make about things you are *planning* to do. If you never start that book, you have no right to claim you are a promising writer. If you never tried to become an actor, then you can't complain that you're a great undiscovered talent. We are not authentically anything but what we *do,* and we are hiding from reality if we think we are more than that. Like Aristotle, Sartre links the value of our virtue with the success of our conduct: Intentions may be good, but they aren't enough. (For an exploration of the issue of personal identity as it relates to authenticity, see Box 10.9).

Levinas and the Face of the Other

Emmanuel Levinas (1905–1995) was born the same year as Sartre, but whereas Sartre became a philosopher of the mid–twentieth century, Levinas was a late bloomer and became one of the leading voices of French philosophy only in the last decades of the twentieth century. His most important works are *Totality and Infinity* (1961; translated into English, 1969) and *Otherwise Than Being or Beyond Essence* (1974; translated into English, 1981). In many ways his experience parallels that of Sartre. He, too, became interested in the philosophies of Husserl and Heidegger in Germany; indeed, his interest preceded Sartre's by more than a decade, and it was Levinas, not Sartre, who introduced these ideas to the French public with books on Husserl and Heidegger. (According to Simone de Beauvoir, Sartre, when reading Levinas's book on Husserl, exclaimed, "This is the philosophy I wanted to write!"—although Sartre afterward claimed he could do it better.) Like Sartre, Levinas was a prisoner of war during World War II, doing forced labor for the Nazis; also like Sartre, he developed a highly personal philosophy based on his early interest in German phenomenology. Both became recognized as distinguished scholars within the field of philosophy. But here the similarities end. Sartre was French by birth, whereas Levinas—born a Lithuanian—became

Box. 10.9   PERSONAL IDENTITY AS AN ETHICAL ISSUE

The question of *Who am I?* is something you may encounter in a philosophy class focusing on metaphysics, or theory of knowledge (epistemology), but you don't find it that often within a discussion about ethics. The assumption is, presumably, that once we start worrying about how to behave with *others,* we're already fairly sure who *we* are. But that is of course not necessarily the case, and even if we are familiar with ourselves, there is more to the sense of self than just a descriptive level: we shouldn't forget the normative level. William Shakespeare says, in *Hamlet,*

> This above all: to thine own self be true,
> And it must follow, as night the day,
> Thou can'st not then be false to any man.

Here Shakespeare assumes that we're fairly familiar with who we are, but that this awareness also carries a moral virtue, and a duty: to have integrity and be true to ourselves—the best in ourselves, that is. (Presumably it doesn't imply that once you know your weaknesses, you should cultivate them!) Understanding who we are *so that* we can become better persons is an idea that dates back to Socrates—he interpreted the inscription "Know Thyself" at the Apollo temple in Delphi as meaning just that: introspection with self-improvement as a result. Let us take a look at three examples:

For the existentialists such as Sartre the concept of *authenticity* captures the moral value of knowing oneself; it isn't merely a question of being comfortable with who you are, or even of constantly questioning yourself and your role in life; more importantly, you must be able to act out of a sense of integrity, and with absence of bad faith, in everything you do.

For American psychologists the idea of knowing oneself has been labeled as having *ego integrity* ever since the influential German-born analyst Erik Erikson (1902–1994) coined the term. Erikson, who also identified and named the phenomenon *identity crisis,* saw ego integrity as having inner harmony and balance of the mind; you don't dwell on what might have been, or how others have done you wrong, but accept things you have no control over.

For the thinker who is interested in storytelling, such as the French philosopher Paul Ricoeur (born 1913), the quest for personal identity becomes a quest *for self-comprehension through telling one's own story.* Finding one's narrative self doesn't mean that we remember everything and then put it into words, or that we tell everything exactly like it was, but that we find our *character arc* (see Chapter 2) in the process of connecting the dots in our life—seeing a pattern in the events leading up to the present time.

In all these cases we are talking about a normative approach to personal identity: First we must understand who we are, and then this understanding must make a difference in the rest of our lives. In this way the quest for personal identity becomes a moral journey.

French by choice. Whereas Sartre's Catholic belief in God came to an end, Levinas never lost his Jewish faith. Whereas Sartre developed his existential philosophy based on the fundamental anguish of the choice—an essentially lonely enterprise—Levinas sees the bottom line of all human existence as the encounter with the Other, not in a competition for dominance, as Sartre sometimes would express it, but in coming face-to-face with another human being and realizing that the Other is alive, looking at *you,* speaking to *you,* needing *you* to recognize him or her as someone

The Lithuanian-French philosopher Emmanuel Levinas (1905–1995) believed that ethics is the deepest and most primary human experience: We see the other person looking at us and we hear him or her talking to us, and we understand that this is someone whose life is precious and irreplaceable. The Other commands us not to kill, and we feel obliged to place his or her needs above our own.

who is fundamentally different from you and fundamentally vulnerable. Levinas maintains that "ethics precedes ontology": Understanding the needs of the Other and *my* own responsibility for the needs of the Other comes before any philosophy about existence. That is why Levinas has described ethics as "First Philosophy": This is the foundation and the beginning point, which we are normally not even aware of but where we encounter what is really important in life: the face of the Other.

As we have seen, many modern theories of ethics state that everyone ought to be treated as *equal*. Bentham talks about how each person has one vote in terms of his or her pain and pleasure; Kant claims that all persons should be viewed as ends in themselves; Rawls points out that justice consists of treating all persons with fairness regardless of who they are. The Golden Rule is in effect even in philosophical systems that are otherwise opposed to each other. For Levinas there is nothing wrong with the political quest for equality, but this quest is not fundamental to ethics; what is fundamental is another experience altogether. When I meet another human being, another face, the ethical reaching out to that person consists in realizing precisely that we are *not* equal. Levinas is not saying I am "better" than the Other. On the contrary, the Other counts more than I: The Other, no matter who he or she is, is a person in need, always "poor" and asking for my help and understanding; first and foremost the Other is telling me, "You must not kill." As Levinas says in a dialogue with Richard Kearney:

> The approach to the face is the most basic mode of responsibility. As such, the face of the other is verticality and uprightness; it spells a relation of rectitude. The face is not in front of me (*en face de moi*) but above me; it is the other before death, looking through and exposing death. Secondly, the face is the other who asks me not to let him die alone, as if to do so were to become an accomplice in his death. Thus the face says to me: you shall not kill. . . . In ethics, the other's right to exist has primacy over my own, a primacy epitomized in the ethical edict: you shall not kill, you shall not jeopardize the life of the other. The ethical rapport is asymmetrical in that it subordinates my existence to the other.

Of course, this is not really a description of most actual encounters between people; fortunately, we rarely find ourselves in situations in which we are begging for our lives. But for Levinas this encounter is the underlying foundation beneath all human encounters: The face is naked, the eyes are pleading, the voice speaks. For Levinas, the true ethical moment happens when we are being addressed by the Other. In response, it is not enough to say, "Well, he or she is just the same as I am, we are all humans." That, to Levinas, is not going far enough, or it is going too far: That would be making us all into some collective form of being, some anonymous humanity. Instead, we are supposed to say, "He/she is completely different from what I am, so his/her life is my responsibility." This is the unequal, asymmetrical situation, the *alterity* (otherness) of the Other, which makes the other human individual our responsibility. In particular it is the Other's voice that calls to us, more so than looking into his or her eyes. Sartre's existential philosophy has often alluded to the power of the *gaze,* the eyes trying to dominate the other person's, but Levinas sees the typical encounter between humans as not only a visual but also an aural experience: You hear the voice speak to *you,* and you respond by being there for the other person. And when you respond with your whole being in acceptance that the Other is there, demanding attention, then you become special to the Other, you become *irreplaceable.* For Levinas, humans in an ethical relationship with each other recognize the Other as irreplaceable, "non-substitutable." The loss of the Other can't be made up for by finding another. (Box 10.10 explains how Levinas would look at the story of Abraham and Isaac in terms of the face of the Other.)

So is this the way things actually are between people, or is it the way Levinas thinks they ought to be? In other words, is he being descriptive or normative? Elegantly, Levinas answers that the encounter is something that happens before we even think in such categories: The encounter with the Other is not merely an actual situation but the framework within which human encounters take place, so it is the way we actually meet, deep down before we start speculating about existence and responsibility and all the rest, but it is also in a sense the way one ought to meet each individual person—because (sadly) not everyone sees other people as unique individuals who are supposed to be held higher than one holds oneself; some people even see others as "merely a means to an end."

The ultimate disregard for the Other is to Levinas represented by the Nazi Holocaust (in which he lost his entire Lithuanian family). The Holocaust represents the utter evil of putting people through torture and to death not for their convictions but for their ancestry. The fact that Heidegger had been involved with the Nazi Party made Levinas say, in later years, that "one can forgive many Germans, but there are some Germans it is difficult to forgive. It is difficult to forgive Heidegger." And, yet, the dreadful event of the Nazi death camps, where, in Levinas's words, God was not present but the devil was, in some roundabout way did not destroy his belief in God; he says,

Before the twentieth century, all religion begins with the promise. It begins with the "Happy End." It is the promise of heaven. Well then, doesn't a phenomenon like Auschwitz invite you, on the contrary, to think the moral law independent of the Happy End? That

Box 10.10   KIERKEGAARD, LEVINAS, AND ABRAHAM

You may remember a section in Chapter 2 dealing with the biblical story of Abraham about to sacrifice his son Isaac to God. To briefly recapitulate: Abraham believes that God has told him to sacrifice his and Sarah's only son, so he takes young Isaac up on the mountain, letting Isaac carry the firewood; Isaac is wondering where the sacrificial lamb is, but Abraham explains that God will provide. On the top of the hill, they build the sacrificial altar, and Abraham straps his son down and is ready to slaughter him when the voice of God intervenes and rewards Abraham for his faith in God's command. Kierkegaard (whom you now know better than you did in Chapter 2) said that Abraham's attempt to sacrifice his son violated the ethics of the community, but believing that he served God's purpose took Abraham to a higher stage—to the religious stage, which he had to ascend to by a leap of faith—bringing him into direct contact with God. Levinas, on the other hand, believes that Kierkegaard misunderstood the entire situation: The important moment is not that Abraham disregards his beloved son for God's sake, but that Abraham through the voice of Isaac himself is called back from the brink, back to the ethical demands of life and fatherhood; in a sense, Isaac's face intervenes on his own behalf. Levinas says that for Kierkegaard ethics is the rigid rules of the community that have to be overcome in order to be religious. For Levinas, however, ethics is the Other's voice speaking to one. Essentially, Levinas sees Abraham as someone who almost made a monumental mistake, but he sees Kierkegaard as having made the mistake of believing that the leap of faith was a matter between the individual and God alone and that to get there one had to leave behind the world of the others with their rules and morals. For Levinas, ethics, and in a sense also faith itself, takes place between one person and the Other.

is the question. . . . It is easier to tell myself to believe without promise than it is to ask it of the other. That is the idea of asymmetry. I can demand of myself that which I cannot demand of the other.

Interview with Wright, Hughes, and Ainley, in Bernasconi and Wood (1988)

So ethics becomes the highest form of religious faith: Without the relief of a promise of heaven, we must be there for the Other, serve the Other for no reward at all. According to Levinas, "Faith is not a question of the existence or non-existence of God. It is believing that love without reward is valuable."

With his philosophy that we look to the Other as someone we must give our love to but who doesn't have to return it (an ethic that is sometimes used to describe the relationship between parent and child), Levinas's ethics stands as a complete renewal within the European tradition of autonomy, finding personal integrity in a relationship of the individual not to oneself but to someone else. In this he comes closest of all the modern European philosophers to an ethics of virtue, seeing the ultimate virtue as the willingness to serve the Other; as a thinker within the modern tradition of authenticity, he regards the asymmetrical relationship to the Other as the truly authentic relationship. Levinas's philosophy, which today perhaps more than any other philosophy stands for kindness and sacrifice of one's self for the sake of others, is nevertheless not without controversy.

Some critics see his thinking as a kind of throwback to a time when ethics were expressed in personal, even religious, terms, and further, in terms of male and female. And for some critics this throwback is a serious weakness. In a disarmingly innocent way, in his early writings Levinas insisted that the Other is, essentially, feminine (something that Sartre, by the way, has also been criticized for asserting): "The feminine is other for the masculine being not only because of a different nature but also inasmuch as alterity is in some way its nature."

In later years he modified his position, but it still generates discussion. Levinas's critics see this as just another statement in the long line of sexist philosophies in which a male point of view pronounces women to be "deviant" or "different" or "really kind of strange," and which assumes that women accept this as an objective truth. Seen in the light of this old tradition, it is small wonder that many women philosophers, most notably Simone de Beauvoir (see Chapter 12), have accused Levinas of being reactionary, deliberately taking a man's point of view, seeing himself as the Absolute and the woman as the Other.

But even if Levinas could be said to hold the opinion that woman is completely different from man, it does not mean he thinks woman is inferior to man; on the contrary, according to his theory of the Other, if anything is absolute, it is precisely the Other. In his later years, Levinas would talk about the feminine virtues of the home, of the welcoming feminine touch, the quality of "discretion" of the feminine face as opposed to the male face with its authority and self-assertion, but always in positive terms (however, whether you regard "feminine" as inferior or superior, it is still sexism to a *classical* feminist). A feminist philosopher, Tina Chanter, suggests that Levinas is in fact praising the feminine qualities as true *human* qualities; "feminine" does not mean biologically female to Levinas, says Chanter, and "masculine" doesn't mean "male"; rather, each term stands for features in all of us. This interpretation (in some ways similar to the gender philosophy of the psychoanalyst Carl Jung) may give another dimension to Levinas's controversial words about the Other as feminine. In the Primary Readings you will find an excerpt from an interview with Levinas in which he talks about the "face of the Other."

Study Questions

1. Evaluate the question of character versus conduct in politics. Which do you think is of the highest importance for a person running for (or elected to) office to have: personal integrity? or a view on government that you agree with? Is there an alternative? Explain.

2. Discuss the question of character versus conduct in personal matters: Philippa Foot claims, with Aristotle, that a person who has a good character is slightly better than a person who has to control himself or herself. Kant would say the opposite. Explain these viewpoints. Which do you agree with more and why?

3. Bernard Mayo wants us to emulate role models. Can you think of a person—a historical figure, a living person, or a fictional character—whom you

would like to emulate? Explain who and why. What are some of the problems involved with the idea of emulating role models?

4. Kierkegaard believes that being ethical is not the ultimate ideal mode of existence—one must also have religious faith. Explore his viewpoint: What does he think faith can give that ethics cannot? Do you agree? Can we be ethical without faith? Can we have religious faith without ethics? Explain.

5. For Sartre, any explanation that deflects one's complete responsibility is an example of bad faith. Do you agree? Are there cases where people should not be held accountable for what they have done? or cases where it is legitimate to say, "I had no choice"? Explain.

6. Levinas is reluctant to include animals as beings with "faces." Do you agree that ethics can be extended to animals only as a secondary move patterned after ethics toward humans? Or should ethics toward animals be a primary form of ethics? Can Levinas's own theory be redesigned to include animals?

Primary Readings and Narratives

The first two Primary Readings are short excerpts from the writings of Søren Kierkegaard, one from *Johannes Climacus* and one from *Either/Or*, Volume II. The third Primary Reading is an excerpt from an interview with Emmanuel Levinas, conducted by three graduate students, Tamra Wright, Peter Hughes, and Alison Ainley, and published as "The Paradox of Morality: An Interview with Emmanuel Levinas." All three Narratives explore, in one way or another, the existential themes of choice, angst, authenticity, and responsibility. The first is a summary of an episode from Woody Allen's film *Hannah and Her Sisters* about a hypochondriac in the throes of existential angst. The second is a summary of Jean-Paul Sartre's classic play *No Exit* about three souls condemned to live in each other's company forever, in hell. The third is a summary of the film *A Few Good Men,* which raises the moral question of whether "I was just carrying out an order" is ever an acceptable excuse.

Primary Reading

Johannes Climacus

SØREN KIERKEGAARD

Written 1842–1843, first published 1912. Excerpt translated by Nina Rosenstand.

Kierkegaard used to speak through many aliases, and some we are not supposed to take seriously; Johannes Climacus became one of his most serious and personal aliases, and here we read about Johannes's childhood, which exactly resembles Kierkegaard's own.

His father was a very strict man, apparently dry and prosaic, but under this coat of coarse weave he hid a glowing imagination which not even his advanced years managed to conceal. When Johannes on occasion would ask permission to go out, he was most often refused; however, on one occasion his father offered, as a form of compensation, to take a walking tour up and down the floor. This was at first glance a poor substitute, and yet this turned out to be like the coarse coat: It hid something else entirely. The suggestion was accepted, and the decision where to go was left entirely to Johannes. So they left by the gate, walked to a nearby castle in the woods, to the beach, or up and down the streets, anywhere Johannes wanted, because for his father nothing was impossible. While they were walking up and down the floor, his father would describe everything they saw; they said hello to people passing by, coaches rolled noisily past, drowning out his father's voice; the fruits of the vendor woman looked more inviting than ever. He related everything so accurately, so vividly; he described so immediately in the most minute detail things that were familiar to Johannes, and whatever Johannes didn't know he described in such elaborate and educational manner that he, after having walked with his father for half an hour, was just as tired as if he had been outside an entire day. . . . For Johannes it was as if his father was the Good Lord, and he himself was his favorite who was allowed to come up with silly ideas to his heart's content; for he was never turned down, his father was never perturbed, everything was included and happened to Johannes's satisfaction.

Primary Reading

Either/Or

SØREN KIERKEGAARD

Excerpt from Volume II, 1843. Translated by Nina Rosenstand.

In this text, written shortly after Kierkegaard broke up with Regine Olsen, he speaks with the voice of Judge Williams, admonishing a friend who refuses to make choices (about getting married, in particular). In his friend's words, "Get married, and you'll regret it. Don't get married and you'll regret it." Williams responds,

The choice itself is decisive for the content of one's personality. . . . If you imagine a first mate on his ship at the moment when it has to make a turn, then he might say, I can do either this or that. However, if he is not a poor navigator, he will also be aware that the ship is all the while moving ahead at its regular speed, and that he thus only has an instant where it is immaterial whether he does one thing or the other. So it is with a human being: Should he forget to take account of the speed, there comes at last a moment when it is no longer a question of an either-or, not because he has chosen, but because he has refrained from choosing—which is the same as saying, because others have chosen for him, because he has lost his own self.

Study Questions

1. Do you approve of Kierkegaard's father's teaching technique? Explain. Are there similarities between his technique and virtual reality? Are there differences?

2. Who do you think Kierkegaard identifies most with, the friend who doesn't want to choose? or Williams? Or perhaps both?

3. Compare the second excerpt with Sartre's theory of the existential choice.

Primary Reading

The Paradox of Morality: An Interview with Emmanuel Levinas

Interview conducted in 1986 by Tamra Wright, Peter Hughes, and Alison Ainley. Excerpt.

Three graduate students from the University of Warwick interviewed Levinas after taking a seminar on one of his books, *Totality and Infinity.* In the section on Levinas you read about one of the controversial points in his philosophy, his remarks about the feminine. Here you have a hint of another controversy: Levinas's statements about the face of another human being as the fundamental ethical experience; does this imply that we can't have an ethical relationship to a nonhuman—an animal, for instance?

Is the face a simple or a complex phenomenon? Would it be correct to define it as that aspect of a human being which escapes all efforts at comprehension and totalization, or are there other characteristics of this phenomenon which must be included in any definition or description of the face?

The face is a fundamental event. Among the many modes of approach and diverse ways of relating to being, the action of the face is special and, for this reason, it is very difficult to give it an exact phenomenological description. The phenomenology of the face is very often negative.

What seems essential to me is, for example, the manner in which Heidegger understood the *Zeug*—that which comes to hand, the instrument, the thing. He understood it as irreducible prototype. The face is similar in that it is not at all a representation, it is not a given of knowledge, nor is it a thing which comes to hand. It is an irreducible means of access, and it is in ethical terms that it can be spoken of. I have said that in my analysis of the face it is a demand; a demand, not a question. The face is a hand in search of recompense, an open hand. That is, it needs something. It is going to ask you for something. I don't know whether one can say that it is complex or simple. It is, in any case, a new way of speaking of the face.

When I said that the face is authority, that there is authority in the face, this may undoubtedly seem contradictory: it is a request and it is an authority. You have a question later on in which you ask me how it could be that if there is a commandment in the face, one can do the opposite of what the face demands. The face is not a force. It is an authority. Authority is often without force. Your question seems to be based on the idea that God commands and demands. He is extremely powerful. If you try not doing what he tells you, he will punish you. That is a very recent notion. On the contrary, the first form, the unforgettable form, in my opinion, is that, in the last analysis, he can not do anything at all. He is not a force but an authority. . . .

Is it necessary to have the potential for language in order to be a "face" in the ethical sense?

I think that the beginning of language is in the face. In a certain way, in its silence, it calls you. Your reaction to the face is a response. Not just a response, but a responsibility. These two words [*réponse, responsabilité*] are closely related. Language does not begin with the signs that one gives, with words. Language is above all the fact of being addressed . . . which means the saying much more than the said.

In the word "comprehension" we understand the fact of taking [*prendre*] and of comprehending [*comprendre*], that is, the fact of englobing, of appropriating. There are these elements in all knowledge [*savoir*], all familiarity [*connaissance*], all comprehension; there is always the fact of making something one's own. But there is something which remains outside, and that is alterity. Alterity is not at all the fact that there is a difference, that facing me there is someone who has a different nose than mine, different colour eyes, another character. It is not difference, but alterity. It is alterity, the unencompassable, the transcendent. It is the beginning of transcendence. You are not transcendent by virtue of a certain different trait.

In totalization there is certainly the fact of inclusion, of adding up. Men can be synthesized. Men can easily be treated as objects. We speak to the other who is not encompassed, who, on the contrary, is the one who offers his face to you.

The analysis can go further. I'm not saying that it is completed. The idea that is very important to me is frailty, the idea of being in a certain sense much less than a thing. One can kill, annihilate. It is easier to annihilate than to possess the other.

For me, these two starting points are essential: the idea of extreme frailty, of demand, that the other is poor. It is worse than weakness, the superlative of weakness. He is so weak that he demands. This, of course, is the beginning of the analysis, because the way in which we behave concretely is different. It is more complex. In particular because, what seems to me very important, is that there are not only two of us in the world. But I think that everything begins as if we were only two. It is important to recognize that the idea of justice always supposes that there is a third. But, initially, in principle, I am concerned about justice because the other has a face. . . .

If animals do not have faces in an ethical sense, do we have obligations towards them? And if so, where do they come from?

It is clear that, without considering animals as human beings, the ethical extends to all living beings. We do not want to make an animal suffer needlessly and so on. But the prototype of this is human ethics. Vegetarianism, for example, arises from the transference to animals of the idea of suffering. The animal suffers. It is because we, as human, know what suffering is that we can have this obligation.

The widespread thesis that the ethical is biological amounts to saying that, ultimately, the human is only the last stage of the evolution of the animal. I would say, on the contrary, that in relation to the animal, the human is a new phenomenon. And that leads me to your question. You ask at what moment one becomes a face. I do not know at what moment the human appears, but what I want to emphasize is that the human breaks with pure being, which is always a persistence in being. This is my principal thesis. A being is something that is attached to being, to its own being. That is Darwin's idea. The being of animals is a struggle for life. A struggle for life without ethics. It is a question of might. Heidegger says at the beginning of *Being and Time* that *Dasein* is a being who in his being is concerned for this being itself. That's Darwin's idea: the living being struggles for life. The aim of being is being itself. However, with the appearance of the human—and this is my entire philosophy—there is something more important than my life, and that is the life of the other. That is unreasonable. Man is an unreasonable animal. Most of the time my life is dearer to me, most of the time one looks after oneself. But we cannot admire saintliness. Not the sacred, but saintliness: that is, the person who in his being is more attached to the being of the other than to his own. I believe that it is in saintliness that the human begins; not in the accomplishment of saintliness, but in the value. It is the first value, an undeniable value. Even when someone says something bad about saintliness, it is in the name of saintliness that he says it.

Study Questions

1. What does Levinas mean by saying, "The face is a hand in search of recompense, an open hand. That is, it needs something. It is going to ask you for something"?

2. Do you agree with Levinas that "there is something more important than my life, and that is the life of the other"? Why or why not?

3. Do you agree with Levinas that the prototype for all ethics, including ethical treatment of animals, is human ethics, based on the experience of the human face? Why or why not?

Narrative

Hannah and Her Sisters

WOODY ALLEN (SCREENWRITER AND DIRECTOR)

Film, 1986. Summary.

Can a comedy deal seriously with issues such as angst and the absurdity of life? Absolutely, at least when the director is Woody Allen. We will look primarily at the character played by Allen—Mickey, a hypochondriac who is always running to doctors believing he has some form of terminal illness. While his friends engage in stealthy extramarital affairs and other self-realization projects, Mickey finds that he is experiencing some dizziness and has lost some hearing in one ear, so he goes to see his doctor. He fully expects the doctor to shrug it off as an imagined disease as usual, but this time the doctor suggests X rays, because, although it might be just a minor problem, it also might be a brain tumor.

Mickey is plunged into the abyss of despair; he tries to make deals with God. He can't believe it is happening, and yet he believes it. On the X ray there is an ominous spot, and the doctor schedules a CAT scan. The idea of death, as often as he has played around with it, now seems both real and unfathomable: "You're in the middle of New York City, this is your town, you're surrounded by people and traffic and restaurants—how can you just one day—vanish?"

Finally, in the doctor's office, the doctor has all the charts and X rays out and shows him with clinical exactitude where the tumor is, saying there is nothing that anyone can do about it. The hypochondriac's worst nightmare is coming true.

And yet—a split second later—we find that he has just *imagined* the doctor speaking the words of doom; now the doctor comes in and says what Mickey was hoping to hear, that they can't find out why he has a minor hearing loss, but it is not a tumor. Mickey should be revived and elated, right? At first he is, but the close call has profoundly disturbed his equilibrium; he comes to the realization that life is absurd and meaningless because it can be threatened, and regarded, so casually. If we can be gone in an instant, what's the point of living? he asks. His release from *fear* has actually deepened his existential angst, for now he sees that there are no guarantees, no master plan, and no ready-made meaning for him to hold on to. If life is going to come to an end anyway, why bother doing anything? Nothing is worthwhile anymore; the hypochondriac has become a *nihilist*.

If only he could believe in God. . . . Mickey seeks help from religious experts, from Catholic priests to Hare Krishna converts (much to his Jewish mother's chagrin—couldn't he just give his own religion a try?). And yet one day Mickey is feeling better. He meets an old acquaintance, his ex-wife's nutty sister, and tells her the story: Recently he had reached the bottom of the abyss and was toying with the idea of killing himself. He actually held a rifle to his head, pondering the question of life and death, when the gun went off, shattering a window! He had held the trigger so tightly that it just went off, but because of his sweaty palms it slipped out of his hands. In a state of total confusion he went out, walked the streets of New York, and ended up in a revival movie theater where they were showing an old Marx Brothers comedy. Here he recaptured the meaning of life: "What if the worst is true—there is no God and you only go around once. Don't you want to be part of the experience?"

So Mickey finds meaning in absurdity, and he finds marriage and children with his ex-wife's nutty sister.

Study Questions

1. Do you think such an experience as Mickey's is common?

2. Has Mickey learned Sartre's lesson about living with absurdity, or hasn't he?

3. How would Sartre suggest that Mickey solve his problem of existential angst? Would Erik Erikson have a suggestion? What might Levinas suggest, if anything?

Narrative

No Exit

JEAN-PAUL SARTRE

Play, 1966. Summary.

For Sartre there is no life after death, for there is no God to send the soul to one realm or the other. But as a dramatist and a novelist Sartre played with the idea of hell nevertheless. In the drama *No Exit* three characters find themselves in a locked room with no windows: a middle-aged man, Garcin; a young woman, Estelle; and a lesbian woman, Inez. They all know that they are dead and in hell, and they are highly surprised that there is no torture chamber—merely a room decorated in bad taste. They don't know each other, but they are forced to spend an unforeseeable amount of time together in this room, interrupted only occasionally by a prison guard, the "valet." For a while they can "glimpse" the life of the living, but that soon fades, and all they have is each other. Each pretends to wonder what the others have done to be sent to hell, but, as Inez says, they are all "murderers." Estelle killed her baby, Inez killed her lover's husband (or at least drove him to his death), and Garcin killed the spirit in his wife by his cruelty to her. What tortures Garcin most, though, is that he is a deserter. He, who always thought he would live and die bravely, never had a chance to prove himself, he says—he died too soon. But Inez corrects him:

> One always dies too soon—or too late. And yet one's whole life is complete at that moment, with a line drawn neatly under it, ready for the summing up. You are—your life, and nothing else.

Estelle is beginning to find Garcin attractive (she is used to men fawning over her). Inez is falling in love with Estelle, and Garcin is himself attracted to Estelle but prefers that each of them stay in their own corner rather than hurt each other. But the stage is set, and they can't help interacting. All three try to manipulate each other; they team up, two against the third one. They constantly scrutinize each other (for in hell you have no eyelids you can close). They need each other for comfort and support, but they have no trust in each other. They realize that there is no need for torture instruments and devils—they are each other's torturers. The room and the other two people in it *are* hell for them: Their punishment is spending an eternity with each other in a hostile triangle. In the end Garcin succeeds in opening the locked door to their room, but now all three are reluctant to leave, because for each that would mean the other two had won the dominance game. All three stay to torment each other, forever.

On the symbolic level Sartre is—probably—not talking about any real life after death, but about the human condition. He is saying we make life a hell for each other, because we are so very good at manipulating each other, and every human relationship, even that between lovers, has at its core a battle for power and dominance. Sartre concludes with one of his most famous lines: "Hell is—other people."

Study Questions

1. Would you agree with Sartre that "Hell is other people"?

2. Do you think Garcin, Estelle, and Inez might apply Sartre's own principles of existentialism to cope with their life in hell? How?

 Narrative

 A Few Good Men

AARON SORKIN (SCREENWRITER)
ROB REINER (DIRECTOR)

Based on the play by Sorkin. Film, 1992. Summary.

On the U.S. Marine base in Cuba, a young private, Santiago, is attacked in the middle of the night, bound and gagged and left in his room. An hour later he dies of what looks like poisoning: The rag used to gag him may have been soaked with a chemical. Two fellow marines, Corporal Dawson and Private Downey, are arrested for murder.

A Navy officer, the young lawyer Joanne Galloway, is interested in the case and requests that the Marines be transferred to Washington, D.C., for trial; she suspects that the case involves a so-called Code Red, an order given by a superior to discipline a subordinate soldier. Her request to become their counsel is denied, however, and another young Navy lawyer, Dan Kaffee, gets the case because of his outstanding record for plea bargaining. Joanne and Dan experience instantaneous dislike for each other; she thinks he is callous, and he thinks she is stuck-up. Dan goes to see the two Marines in the holding facility and comes face-to-face with another worldview: the Marine code. Although Dan himself is part of the armed forces, he regards his job as a career choice, not a lifestyle, but both young Marines see their Marine identity as a chosen way of life according to the code: Unit, Corps, God, and Country. While they show Dan all the respect their training requires (which he doesn't want), they have little respect for him as a person.

Joanne, unwilling to be left out, persuades a relative of one of the young Marines that he needs separate counsel and becomes his lawyer. Together, she, Dan, and Dan's aide now go to Guantanamo Bay in Cuba to question Santiago's superior officers. Information has surfaced that Santiago had been sending out numerous requests to be transferred to another post; his most recent request included a proposition to an officer who outranks the highest-ranking officer at Guantanamo, Colonel Jessep. If he is transferred, he said, he will testify about an illegal shooting incident between a Marine and a Cuban soldier across the fence between the base and Cuban territory. For this reason and because, as Dawson explains, Santiago didn't follow the chain of command but went directly to Jessep's superiors with his complaint, the lawyers assume that Santiago was harassed and killed.

On the base Dan and Joanne view Santiago's quarters, with his bloodstained bed, his closet full of clothes, and other personal items; they talk with Santiago's officers, who in-

The 1992 film *A Few Good Men* (Castle Rock) asks the question Is following orders ever a suffi-cient excuse? Paralleling the existential demand that each person take responsibility for his or her actions, the film shows soldiers coming to grips with demands of personal moral integrity that run counter to their training and their code. Here we see a clash between lawyer styles: Joanne Gal-loway (Demi Moore) confronts Daniel Kaffee (Tom Cruise) outside Navy headquarters early in the film, before they reach a stage of cooperation and mutual respect.

sist that strict orders had been given to the Marines not to lay a hand on Santiago. In ad-dition, Jessep tells them that Santiago was about to be transferred that same morning, but regretfully the transfer came too late to save him. Dan seems satisfied with the explana-tions, but Joanne (who outranks him) insists on asking Jessep some tough questions about Code Red. Highly irritated, Jessep informs her that on the record he discourages the illegal code, but off the record it is an invaluable training instrument for disciplining soldiers who are out of line, who don't know how to be a member of the unit.

   Back in Washington, Dan and Joanne now confront Downey and Dawson and ask them if they were given a Code Red order, and they admit that Kendrick, one of Jessep's officers, gave the order to them in private after telling the other Marines not to touch San-tiago. A lawyer friend of Dan's, the Marine prosecutor in the case, suggests a deal: Have Downey and Dawson plead guilty and get two years; if they plead innocent, the whole ma-chinery of justice will be used against them, and they will be locked up for life. Dan takes the deal to the Marines and is astounded when they refuse, but Dawson and Downey don't think they have done anything wrong: They have followed orders and acted like Marines ought to act, and if they plead guilty, they will have acted without honor. And furthermore, what would they do after spending time in jail? What kind of life would be available to them? Dan is now exasperated; he decides to withdraw from the case and get the Marines another lawyer. Sam, Dan's associate, is repulsed at the Marines' attitude and asks Joanne why she likes them so much; she answers, "Because they stand on a wall, and they say, 'Nothing is going to hurt you tonight, not on my watch.'"

Next day the trial begins, but Dan, to the surprise of his friends, enters a not-guilty plea instead of requesting another defense lawyer. Dan succeeds in showing that Santiago's death may have been due to a heart condition, not to poisoning, but otherwise the defense has very little material.

Out of the blue a missing person resurfaces: Colonel Jessep's second-in-command, Lieutenant Colonel Markinson, who has been incommunicado, contacts Dan in secret. He knows the truth about Santiago, and he considers himself to blame for not speaking up and preventing the tragedy from happening. Jessep never ordered any transfer, because he wanted Santiago "trained," and Markinson suspects that Jessep himself ordered the Code Red. Dan and Joanne quickly put Markinson in a hotel with a guard to protect him, as a key witness, but it does them no good: When Markinson learns that Dan plans to put him on the stand, he writes a letter to Santiago's family, apologizing for not having been strong enough to save their son's life, puts on his dress uniform, and shoots himself. Without Markinson as a witness, and with the surprise revelation that Downey never even heard any Code Red order from anyone but his corporal, Dawson, Dan is ready to give up. That evening, drunk and depressed, he has a flash of insight: Santiago's room hadn't been touched when they saw it at the base, and all his clothes and personal items were there, with no evidence of packing. Even so, without Markinson their only recourse is to put Jessep on the stand. They hope that they can play upon Jessep's anger at civilians and other non-Marines and make him confess to ordering the Code Red.

Jessep arrives in court, full of disdain for Dan, the Navy, and the entire situation. Dan does his best to provoke Jessep and involve him in contradictions: If Jessep gives an order (such as "Don't touch Santiago") will it then be followed? Jessep insists that following orders is a matter of life and death in the Marines. But then, says Dan, why would Santiago need to be transferred? He wouldn't be in any danger if the order was to leave him alone. Jessep's anger is mounting, and he blows up in Dan's face, yelling that the Marines stand on the wall, protecting him and others, because they know how to take orders. And Dan, seizing the moment, asks the question: Did Jessep order the Code Red? Proudly and defiantly, Jessep yells back that as civilians, "You can't handle the truth"—the truth being that indeed he did; silence envelops the courtroom, and Jessep is the only one who doesn't understand that a major event has taken place. When he is being restrained and arrested by the MPs he still doesn't understand that his admission at once let the Marines off the hook for murder and declared his own guilt. The verdict is soon reached: Dawson and Downey are found not guilty of murder and conspiracy—but guilty of conduct unbecoming a Marine, with a dishonorable discharge. The lawyers are relieved, but Private Downey understands nothing. Why are they being punished, when they had been good Marines and had followed orders? Dawson, on the other hand, understands completely, and says to Downey that they are Marines and are supposed to fight for the weak, for those who can't fight for themselves. They should have fought for Santiago.

Study Questions

1. The film assumes that Marines don't have the right to question the orders of a commanding officer; this, in fact, is not true. Any soldier has a duty to disobey an order that goes against regulations. In your opinion, should a soldier have the right to question the orders of his or her commanding officer? If no, why not? If yes, under what kind of circumstances?

2. Identify the elements of the film that Sartre would call examples of "bad faith."

3. Identify the elements of the film that Levinas might call the encounter with the Other.

4. As Sam, Dan's associate, remarks, the defense that "I was just following orders" didn't work at the Nazi trials after World War II, and it didn't work for the officer accused of the My Lai massacre of civilians in Vietnam. Can you imagine a situation in which a person's defense that he or she was following orders would be acceptable? Why or why not?

5. Is this film fair to members of the Marine Corps? Why or why not? In light of the responsibilities resting on the shoulders of the U.S. military, and in particular after the shocking realizations of September 11, perhaps it would be appropriate to reconsider Colonel Jessep's words, "You can't handle the truth." Perhaps we should ask ourselves whether we can handle the truth if we find out that American lives have been saved by military personnel using approaches that aren't considered acceptable in peacetime, or in civilian life, such as harsh interrogation techniques (and let us assume that these techniques are still according to regulations). Could Jessep have a point? Civilians don't "get it"? In Chapter 13 we return to the question of wartime ethics.

Chapter Eleven

Case Studies in Virtue

*T*his chapter presents three classical virtues—*courage, compassion,* and *gratitude*—for closer examination. We look at how they have been perceived by some philosophers of the past and present and how they may affect our lives. Why these virtues? Why not also loyalty, honesty, honor, and other virtues held dear by various traditions? Just for the simple reason that the topics of courage, compassion, and gratitude have provoked some fascinating contributions to the study of ethics and I would like to share these with you. And there is another simple reason: We have to limit our discussion to just a few samples. However, if you should feel inspired to continue the debate with other virtues as topics, I would wholeheartedly encourage it!

Courage: What Is It? and Who Has It?

During the Great Depression in 1933 President Franklin D. Roosevelt reassured the nation when he said, "The only thing we have to fear is fear itself." Those words helped millions of Americans, not only through the Depression, but also through the trying times of World War II, to find courage to carry on, but is it true that fear and courage exclude each other? You'll remember that the first virtue Aristotle had on his list was courage—the proper "Golden Mean" response to danger. But in the *Primary Readings* for Chapter 9 you also saw that even Aristotle believed that courage is not synonymous with the absence of fear—that would be foolhardiness. Rather, it is an appropriate response to fear, at the right time, and the right place, and for the right reason. Just to recap: Aristotle says (see pp. 441–442), "Properly, then, he will be called brave who is fearless in face of a noble death, and of all emergencies that involve death; and the emergencies of war are in the highest degree of this kind. Yet at sea also, and in disease; the brave man is fearless. . . . The man, then, who faces and who fears the right things and from the right motive, in the right way and at the right time, and who feels confidence under the corresponding conditions, is brave." As you can tell from the excerpt, Aristotle himself does not say that the brave man has no fear, but that properly managed fear distinguishes a courageous person.

Of course, fear can be paralyzing when we are faced with a difficult choice and a dangerous task, but many a brave man or woman has decided to do the courageous thing precisely because of being afraid, not just in spite of being afraid. In many ways, courage has been the exemplary virtue for many philosophers, often in a rather abstract sense, because they were most often speculating about other people's response to dangerous situations. Interestingly, we know that Socrates indeed had the reputation for being a courageous man in battle when he was a young soldier in the war against Sparta, but courage in battle just isn't one of Socrates' primary themes. Perhaps that is in itself significant: Those who are courageous generally don't talk about it. In this section we explore some of the many faces of courage. Courage in battle may seem like the most obvious example, and perhaps this is where the most extreme forms of courage manifest themselves; but not all defiant acts under fire qualify for the term *courageous*—some are pure instinct, some are done because one fears a worse consequence (such as being tried for desertion), and some are done for the sake of some future advantage (medals, a political career, and so forth). But even outside of the battle situation, we of course encounter courageous people—"ordinary people in extraordinary situations," as they are often described.

What is courage, and why is it a virtue? You already know that Kant says a quality such as bravery is not virtuous unless it is backed by a good will (Chapter 6). This means we can't just declare somebody who is brave a virtuous person—it takes more than simple fearlessness. In Chapter 10 you saw Philippa Foot add her opinion to what makes an admirable character trait a virtue—not the character trait alone, but the intent behind it.

In 2003–4 the confluence of several things led to a renewed debate about courage, especially courage in war. For one thing, the war in Iraq had elevated a number of people to the forefront of the news: Some of them lived through their ordeal, others did not. Private Jessica Lynch, the female prisoner of war who was rescued from her Iraqi captors and lived to set the record straight, was at first hailed as a truly courageous woman warrior who fought until her gun was empty. She was not a combat soldier but had received very basic combat training before being sent on a maintenance mission with her crew: They took a wrong turn and were captured by Iraqi soldiers. As firefight ensued, most of her group died, and the survivors were taken to a hospital. Exactly what happened next is unclear; the other female POW, Lori Piestewa, died from her injuries, but Jessica survived. When the Marines came through the hospital looking for her and announcing that they were American soldiers, she said the words that have become famous: "I'm an American soldier too!" Was she abused and tortured while in captivity? She had no clear memory of it. But from her own mouth we have learned that she never fired a shot, and her survival was more or less a matter of luck; she even feels that it is inappropriate that she was given the Bronze Star for "meritorious service in combat." Many people who are in favor of the idea of women in combat pointed out that her courage was as great as any male soldier's and clear proof that women can function well in battle. Others said that she was an excellent example of why women should *not* be in combat—not necessarily because they can't handle it, but because their presence will make their fellow male soldiers focus on their safety rather than on the object of their mission. Returning home, Jessica steered clear of the entire debate about women in combat, went on TV, and declared that what she did was nothing special—that all the glory should go to the Marines who rescued her. Now was she courageous in battle? We don't know—there are stories of soldiers doing far more heroic things. But was she courageous in standing up and revising her media image, playing down her role? Here we have a good example of two different kinds of courage, which often are related—*physical* and *moral courage*—and we'll talk about them in the coming text. Jessica's war experience probably can't be taken as either

During the early days of the war in Iraq, in March 2003, a U.S. army maintenance crew took a wrong turn and was ambushed by Iraqi forces. Eleven crew members died, and seven were captured. Private Jessica Lynch, one of the captured, was rescued on April 1 by U.S. special operations forces from the hospital where she had been kept prisoner. The story told by the Pentagon and the media was that she had fought valiantly and had been mistreated during her captivity. Afterwards, a different picture emerged: Jessica's gun had jammed, and she hadn't fired any shots—and she had no recollection of what happened at the hospital. In subsequent interviews she graciously refused to be called a hero and pointed out that the real heroes were the soldiers who rescued her.

proof or disproof of the appropriateness of women in combat, but she does serve as a good example of an individual who shows courage in claiming that she did nothing extraordinary—which is extraordinary in itself. In Chapter 12 we return to the issue of women in combat.

Other stories coming out of Iraq, through the embedded journalists and soldiers interviewed by them, have been giving us a picture of what courage is. But as chance would have it, 2004 was also the sixtieth anniversary of D-Day, the American and British invasion of Normandy that turned the tide in World War II and signified the beginning of the end of Hitler's regime. What became sadly apparent during the commemorative events in France, as well as the celebration at the new World War II memorial in Washington, D.C., was that the surviving World War II veterans were thinning in the ranks. Mostly in their eighties and nineties, these vets, called "the Greatest Generation," and their extraordinary experiences will soon be, literally, history; and many felt that it was high time their stories were recorded if they hadn't already been, and their courage and sacrifice celebrated. A swell of books and magazines were published, focusing on the D-Day stories in particular, the excruciating fight just to get off the landing beaches alive under heavy enemy fire. (In the *Narratives* section you will find the story of such a real-life individual, slightly fictionalized, in one of the episodes from the acclaimed HBO series *Band of Brothers*.) One of the books that came out in 2004 did not focus on either the war in Iraq or D-Day, but on the concept of courage in general: John McCain's *Why Courage Matters*. For Senator McCain, himself a Vietnam War veteran and a POW, the notion of courage has been "defined down": We tend to confuse courage with fortitude, discipline, righteousness, or virtue; we call athletes courageous when they play a good game, we call people courageous if they just do their job—but real courage takes more. What is virtue without courage? he asks. We need courage to keep being virtuous even when our virtue is being tested. In McCain's words, "We can admire virtue and abhor corruption sincerely, but without courage we are corruptible."

Such courageous people are not just the heroes of famous battles or political struggles, but also ordinary people who do their best, following their convictions even to the point of losing everything, including their lives, says McCain. One such person is Angela Dawson, a mother who decided to stay with her children in their neighborhood and fight the drug dealers—a decision that cost both her and her chil-

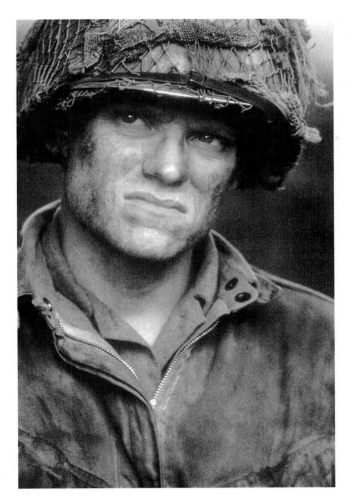

In thirteen episodes the acclaimed HBO television series *Band of Brothers* follows E Company from D-Day (June 6, 1944) to the end of World War II in Europe (May 1945). One of the frequent themes explored is courage, of both the physical and the moral variety. In the episode summarized in the Narratives section, "Carentan," you'll meet this man, Private Albert Blithe (Marc Warren), who must face his paralyzing fear of combat.

dren their lives, because the dealers burned her house down, trapping her and the kids inside; other names include the Navajo chief Manuelito; John Lewis, a disciple of Dr. Martin Luther King, Jr.; Hannah Senesh, the young Jewish woman who worked to establish a Jewish homeland; Aung San Suu Kui, the oft-imprisoned political activist in Burma (Myanmar), and many others. McCain tells their stories, and lets us see wherein their courage lies. Echoing Aristotle, he emphasizes that courage comes from doing courageous things—but in one important respect McCain and Aristotle differ: Consider the case of Angela Dawson. She certainly had the courage to stand by her convictions and stand up to the drug dealers, but the result was that her home was torched, and she and her kids were burned alive. Did she have courage? It would certainly seem so. But what would Aristotle say? She had too much of it—she was being foolhardy, stubbornly risking her own life and the lives of her children. Aristotle might have said that Dawson misjudged the situation, and because of that (although it is a harsh thing to say) she was not virtuous. So McCain's theory that courage is the foundation of virtue perhaps needs to take into account Aristotle's theory of the Golden Mean—we can often discern when someone has too little courage, but can we also discern when they have too much? Aristotle's criterion was, Did they succeed? Then they were virtuous. And how did they succeed? By using their *reason* in determining when something is too much and when it is too little. These are two different views of what courage means, and it is up to us to decide if they speak to us, if we prefer one over the other, or if we think it would make sense to modify one with aspects of the other.

Another aspect is the concept of *hero* in itself; we approached it briefly above, in the section about Private Jessica Lynch: Is anyone who displays courage a hero? Does it matter what the end result of a courageous deed is, or is it the display of courage that counts? Some critics have pointed out that we are much too quick to pronounce somebody a hero these days—the word has been inflated. If someone such as Private Lynch has displayed courage but hasn't done much more than simply survive an ordeal, the media will often slap a "hero" label on the person. But that label is offensive to people who set their standards for heroism higher: Saving the lives of others, with courageous disregard for one's own safety, is a suitable criterion for some. In that case, Officer Walwyn Stuart (Chapter 4) would be a hero. For others, a true hero is someone who rises above what he or she has been hired or trained to do and performs an extraordinary deed that helps others—"ordinary people doing extraordinary things." In that case, some of the locals and tourists staying behind to help find survivors and victims of the 2004 tsunami would qualify as heroes, as would those civilians who chose to stay behind and help strangers rebuild their lives. Mostly we tend to assume that courage is part of the picture—unless we choose to think that celebrities are heroes just because they are celebrities, or good at their job, like the so-called sports heroes or movie heroes. In your view, is it true that we have inflated the concept of hero? Can you be heroic without courage? What would be your definition of a hero?

Physical and Moral Courage

Your adrenaline is pumping, your heart rate is accelerated, you may even experience tunnel vision and a sense that time has slowed down. But it isn't a movie—it's you, in a dangerous situation, making split-second decisions. You do what you are trained to do, perhaps what seems the logical thing to do, or perhaps you just act out of instinct. Then, if you're lucky, you'll live to talk about it. So now people are calling you a hero—but you didn't feel that you were doing anything heroic; you just responded to the needs of the moment. Do you recognize the situation? If you do, I salute you. Most of us don't, but we have all heard of people who, after having done something that looks extraordinarily heroic, deny having done anything special. As a matter of fact, when is the last time you heard such a person stand up afterwards and say, "Yeah, I'm a hero!"? So the title of hero, and the admiration of bravery, is usually something that is bestowed upon an individual by *others*. As we have seen in Chapter 4, we really can't look into the hearts of people and see their true motivation for the deeds they do. As long as it looks like an unselfish act, and involves physical danger, we're generous with our praise and call it courage.

Indeed it may be courage. It could also be luck, or a misinterpretation of motive—in the film *Hero* (1992) a small-time con artist enters a crashed airplane, and in his quest for loot he manages to save every passenger on board. But disregarding physical danger for the sake of others' life, liberty, property, or simply happiness is generally identified as courage. What we shouldn't forget is that this is only one of many types of courage: the *physical* kind. While most of us will perhaps never be in a situation where we can prove to ourselves and the world that we can be physically brave, the other type of courage works in the shadows, is rarely recognized, and is perhaps so common that most of us don't even realize when we've had a courageous moment of the *moral* kind: the kind where you stand by your friend when it would be more convenient to distance yourself from him or her; the kind where you don't allow the powerful clique at school to exclude a newcomer, or someone who is a little different from them; the kind where you stand up to your boss because you know you're right, even if you may lose that job. A whistleblower such as Erin Brokovich certainly must have had physical courage, but the very thought of blowing the whistle takes moral courage to begin with. Moral courage may not result in the spectacular saving of lives, yet we recognize it in particular when it is *absent*. We may understand, and forgive, friends who failed us when we really needed them, but we rarely forget. And if we have failed a friend in her or his moment of need—if we are decent human beings, this will come back to haunt us even long after our friend has assured us that it was okay, that he or she understands. McCain believes there isn't much difference between physical and moral courage when push comes to shove, and it may certainly be true that the person who has one kind also is likely to have the other; but even so, there is one big difference that we should take into account: Physical courage is *visible,* while moral courage often is not—it is often lived through without a sense of accomplishment, or reward, or even acknowledgment. In the *Primary Readings* section we take a look at McCain's suggestion for how to teach our kids moral courage, by teaching them to do their "nearest duty."

A controversial topic within the discussion of courage is the topic of suicide. Is a person who decides to commit suicide courageous or a coward? Or perhaps those categories don't apply at all. In Box 11.1 you'll find a discussion of the subject.

Let us suppose that we now have a better understanding of courage. It involves taking action, or just standing up for something or someone you believe in, when doing so may involve a risk to yourself, your job, your well-being, even your life—instead of remaining silent because it is easier or less risky, or because speaking up might be considered politically incorrect by some. It involves doing the right thing when it is difficult, not when it is easy. (In the Narratives section, the story of Tom Horn illustrates a certain kind of courage: choosing to protect your friends even to the point where it may cost your life.) But here we run into a new problem: When do we know

Box 11.1   IS SUICIDE COURAGEOUS OR COWARDLY?

The issue of suicide has come up on occasion in this book; in Chapter 2 you read about young Werther, who killed himself out of unrequited love, and in Chapter 5 we used suicide as an example in the debate about John Stuart Mill's harm principle. Shocking to most of us, statistics show that suicide is the second greatest killer of American college students, more than all illnesses and birth defects *combined,* and takes a back seat only to accidents. So within a college environment, the debate does tend to gravitate toward the subject from time to time, and the issue sometimes comes up: Is committing suicide a courageous act, or is it cowardly? The question assumes there is one clear answer. If we grant that suicide can sometimes be attempted by sane people, then we can apply the issue of virtue and vice, of morally right and wrong (because we wouldn't use moral condemnation on mentally ill people who don't have a choice in their actions), and then the question of courage versus cowardice will have to do with the how and the why. Much of our attitude toward suicide is rooted in religion; Catholicism sees suicide as a deadly sin, condemning a soul to eternal damnation. Buddhism views suicide as a personal failure to deal with one's karma—a failure that will have negative results in the next life. But some moral systems, whether religious or secular, such as those in Imperial Japan and Imperial Rome, have had great respect for the suicide solution. It is hard to rise above the ethics of one's culture and upbringing in this regard, but if we can for a moment forget the issue of whether or not suicide is plain wrong, we can focus on the courage/cowardice issue.

What if a person allows himself or herself to die, or downright commits suicide so that others may live? Self-sacrifice is usually not even labeled suicide in our language, so that gives us a clue: There is supposedly something *selfish* in suicide. The question is, How much? And of what nature? If a person commits "suicide by cop," by forcing a situation where a police officer has no choice but to shoot, the selfishness extends beyond that person's own wants and usually is met by heavy condemnation because it also inflicts misery on others (the police officer will face a hearing, might lose his or her badge, and will have to live with killing another person to the end of his or her life). If people kill themselves because they can't face the shame of some personal situation being disclosed, the world usually pities them for their mental agony but would have admired them more if they had stayed alive to face the music—so there is some sense that suicide is an "easy way out." Generally, the only type of suicide that is met with a kind of silent acceptance or even admiration in this culture (where euthanasia is illegal in all but one state) is the decision by a terminally ill person to cheat the reaper and take matters into his or her own hands, shortening the time of torment. However, all these cases surely require a definite amount of personal guts, just to stand up and go through with it. So is there courage in the suicidal act? Undoubtedly, in the decision and act itself—but might there be more bravery in staying alive? This may be a very individual judgment call, but our willingness to call the act of suicide both brave and cowardly shows not only that we have mixed feelings about it but also that we may be referring to different aspects of the act: We judge the immediate decision to die, but we also judge the decision to avoid the future.

whether our "cause" is actually morally righteous? Can we just trust our moral intuition? As you'll see below, Hitler's right-hand man, Heinrich Himmler, thought he was doing the right thing by setting the "Final Solution" in motion—the mass extermination of the German Jews—and he found it a very hard thing to do. Did that make it right? Of course not. Below you'll see what virtue can be added to "courage" to make it less likely that courage is misspent: compassion. In addition, we'll look at the role of reason and reexamine why emotions may be morally relevant, but why we also need reason to moderate and give direction to the moral feelings.

Compassion: Are We Born with It?

A story that is familiar to most people raised in the Christian tradition is the parable of the Good Samaritan: A victim of a robbery and an assault is passed over by several so-called upstanding citizens and is finally helped by someone who is moved by his plight: the Good Samaritan. You'll find the story in the Narratives section. It is generally recognized that people *are capable of* showing compassion—the debate usually centers on *why*: You'll remember Thomas Hobbes's view that humans are by nature self-centered and that compassion is something humans show toward others in distress because they are afraid the same calamity might happen to them. In other words, when people show sympathy and pity toward one another either it is to make sure that others will help them if the same thing should happen to them, or else it is a kind of superstition, a warding off of the fate of others. There are scholars who think Hobbes's viewpoint was fostered by the political unrest of the seventeenth century, which might well have caused a thinker to focus on his own survival and to believe that self-love is the primary driving force.

In the eighteenth century, the Age of Reason, two philosophical giants shared a different idea. Both the Scottish philosopher David Hume and the Swiss philosopher Jean-Jacques Rousseau believed that humans are naturally compassionate toward one another. Hume held that even a selfish person will feel benevolence toward strangers whenever his self-interest is not involved. Rousseau claimed that the more we are corrupted by civilization, the more we tend to forget our natural inclination to help others and sympathize with them, because it is not an aberration of nature that makes people selfish—it is *civilization* itself. Rousseau certainly agreed that there are people who show compassion only because they are afraid something might happen to them and because they have only their own interests at heart, but this is not a natural thing, he said; it is caused by human culture. If we would seek only the natural capacities in ourselves, we would find the natural virtue of compassion still intact. The best way to reestablish contact with our original nature is to educate children as freely as possible so that they don't become infected with the evils of civilization.

Philosophers in the Western tradition were not the only ones to speculate about human nature and compassion; in the third century B.C.E. the Chinese philosopher Mencius (see below) claimed, as Rousseau would some two thousand years later, that humans are compassionate and benevolent by nature but have been corrupted by the circumstances of everyday life. One story from the tradition of India is the compassion of King Yudisthira, and you'll find it in the Narratives section.

Philip Hallie: The Case of Le Chambon

Could Rousseau have been right that civilization is the cause of evildoing, or does "civilized" mean "compassionate"? An answer has been given indirectly by the American philosopher Philip Hallie (1922–1994), whom I once had the privilege of meeting. Hallie was an unusual philosopher, as today's philosophers go, because he was never afraid to talk about his own feelings and the feelings of others. You cannot understand evil unless you understand how it feels to those who are being victimized, he said, and you cannot understand goodness unless you ask those to whom goodness has been shown. Having been a U.S. soldier in World War II, Hallie had seen his share of bloodshed and cruelty, including the revelations of the Holocaust death camps. Deeply depressed about the apparent inability to fight evil without becoming as violent as one's enemy, Hallie was profoundly moved by learning about a concrete example of compassion that occurred in the midst of a civilization under the heel of barbarism. In the southern part of France there is a small village called Le Chambon-sur-Lignon, where the population has had a long history of being persecuted for their Huguenot faith. During World War II the people of the village came to the aid of Jewish refugees from all over France in a rescue effort that was matched only by the massive efforts of Danish citizens to save the Danish Jews by smuggling them across the water to neutral Sweden. The people of Le Chambon saved about six thousand lives (more than twice the number of their own population). The majority were Jewish children whose parents had already gone to the extermination camps. This took place all during the German occupation of France, even when southern France ceased to be a "free zone" governed by French collaborators.

As a contrast to the compassion of the French villagers, Hallie points to the sadism displayed during the Nazi reign. The Nazis regularly humiliated their prisoners; during marches prisoners were not allowed to go to the bathroom and had to perform their physical functions while on the march. Hallie describes this as an "excremental assault" and calls it an example of *institutionalized cruelty.* Hallie defines this type of cruelty as not only physical but also psychological. When a person's or a people's self-respect and dignity are attacked on a regular basis, the victims often begin to believe that somehow this cruelty is *justified* and that they really are no better than dirt. This is especially true when one population group commits this offense against another group. Thus cruelty becomes a social institution, endorsed by the victimizer and tolerated by the victim. Such instances of institutionalized cruelty can be seen not only in oppressive wartime situations but also in race relations throughout the course of history, in relations between the sexes, and in certain parent–child relations. The general pattern is a demeaning and belittling of one group by another, so that soon such behavior becomes routine.

Why does institutionalized cruelty occur? Because one group is more powerful than the other, either in terms of physical strength (it is bigger, is more numerous, or has more weapons) or in terms of economic, educational, or political clout (as when one group can hold property, get an education, and vote, and the other group can't). Power can even be verbal, as when one group has the monopoly of using slurs against the other.

How can it be helped? By changing the power balance, says Hallie. This, of course, is hard—it is hard to acquire the right to vote, to own property, to get an equal education. It is hard to build up physical strength. And it is hard to reverse the trend of slurs and other insults. Even if all this is achieved, though, the insidious effect of institutionalized cruelty is not over when the cruelty ceases, because *it leaves scars*. The prisoners who were liberated from Nazi extermination camps were never truly "free" again; they carried their scars with them forever. And just being "kind" to a victim doesn't help—it only serves as a reminder of how far he has sunk. What truly helps is a gesture similar to what the people of Le Chambon did for the Jewish refugees in the face of the Nazi occupation.

Hallie heard of Le Chambon and went there to talk to the people; most of them didn't think they had done anything exceptional. What these people did for the refugees was to show them compassion in the form of *hospitality*. They showed the refugees that they were equal to the villagers themselves, that they deserved to live in the villagers' own homes while their escape across the mountains to Switzerland was being planned. This, says Hallie, is the only effective antidote to institutionalized cruelty: hospitality offered as an act of compassion, in a way that makes it clear to the victims that their dignity is intact.

The story of Le Chambon has a twist that makes it even more exceptional. How did the rescue effort succeed in an occupied country with Nazi soldiers everywhere? It wasn't that the villagers were tremendously discreet—no group can hide six thousand people who pass through over a five-year period. It was because of the courage of the town minister, André Trocmé, and his masterly organization of the smuggling operation that Nazi curiosity was deflected for the longest time. Trocmé's cousin Daniel Trocmé was arrested and executed by the Nazis, but this did not stop the rescue effort, because the villagers had an ally in a very unlikely person: the Nazi overseer of the village, Major Julius Schmäling. Schmäling's task was to keep the peace in the region—meaning, in Hallie's words, "to keep the French quiet while Germany raped the country and went about its business of trying to conquer the world." And Schmäling did keep the peace, but not through terror. Instead, he chose to ignore the steady stream of refugees and did not report the incidents to his superiors. One victim of the Nazis whom Schmäling could not save was one of the two doctors of Le Chambon, Le Forestier, who himself was not engaged in the underground movement. But one day he gave a ride to two hitchhikers from the underground, who hid their weapons in his Red Cross ambulance. When the ambulance was later searched by Nazi soldiers, the weapons were found and Le Forestier arrested. Intervention by Schmäling led the doctor's family to believe that he would only be sent to a work camp in Germany as a doctor, but in actual fact the Nazis intercepted the train taking the doctor to Germany. They took him off the train and executed him the following day with about 110 other people. The Trocmés found out the truth from Schmäling years after the war and realized that Schmäling, ever since that day, had agonized about the one life he hadn't been able to save.

In his posthumously published book *Tales of Good and Evil, Help and Harm* (1997), Hallie writes about the complex character of Schmäling: He and his wife tried for the longest time to avoid membership in the Nazi Party, but when it was finally imminent, Schmäling joined the army so that he wouldn't have to be a party member. Originally a schoolteacher in Munich, he had told his students that decency has no price, no market value, but as an overseer he was very efficient; otherwise he couldn't have stayed on the job. So that makes him a morally ambiguous man, says Hallie. "He served a government that systematically persecuted defenseless people, but he would not persecute

Box 11.2   IS IT BETTER TO CRY OVER YOUR VICTIM
THAN NOT TO FEEL SORRY?

In a celebrated paper the philosopher Jonathan Bennett claims that it is better to be a person guilty of wrongdoing who has compassion than it is to be an innocent person who has no compassion. An example of the first kind of person is Heinrich Himmler, who, as head of the Nazi SS (an elite guard unit), developed stomach troubles because of what he felt he had to do. The seventeenth-century American minister Jonathan Edwards was the other type of person; although he presumably served the needs of his flock, he believed everybody deserved to go to hell. Philip Hallie responds to Bennett's point of view by referring to an incident in Lewis Carroll's *Alice in Wonderland*. The Walrus and the Carpenter lure some little oysters to take a nice walk with them along the beach. After a while they all sit down on a rock, and the Carpenter and the Walrus begin to eat the oysters. The Walrus feels sorry for them and weeps, but he eats them nevertheless. The Carpenter couldn't care less about the oysters and is just concerned with eating them. Hallie asks, Are we really supposed to believe that the Walrus is a better creature than the Carpenter because he has sympathy for his victims? The Walrus ate as many oysters as he could stuff into his mouth behind his handkerchief. Likewise, Himmler killed more than 13 million people even though he was "feeling sorry" for them. For Hallie sympathy is no redeeming quality at all if it isn't accompanied by compassionate action.

them himself." And this refusal to persecute the weak did not go unnoticed by the people of Le Chambon: After the liberation of Paris in 1944, when Nazi officers were held accountable for their atrocities in trials all over France, Schmäling's trial was most unusual. As he walked up the aisle toward the judge, everyone rose to pay tribute to this man who had saved so many at the risk of his own life. When asked why he had not reported the Jewish children hiding in the village, he responded, "I could not stand by and watch innocent blood be shed." Schmäling spent some time in prison in France but later returned to Germany, where he lived in modest circumstances until his death in 1973. (See Box 11.2 for Hallie's views on one of the major Nazi leaders.)

To Hallie, virtue is this: the compassion one shows in reaching out to save others at the risk of one's own life. It it not necessarily the result of logical thinking—it may be an act of the heart. For Hallie there are degrees of moral behavior, though. If you just refrain from doing harm, you are following the *negative command,* "Do not cause harm." That is commendable, but there is a stronger command, a *positive command:* "Help others in need." It is much harder to follow a positive moral rule than a negative one, which just requires you to do nothing. The people of Le Chambon followed the harder path of the positive rule. In your opinion, what did Major Schmäling do? Did he follow the negative rule of no harmdoing, or did he, under the circumstances, also follow a positive rule of actively helping? At the end of this chapter we look at a powerful story of compassion similar to that of Le Chambon, Steven Spielberg's film *Schindler's List,* and in the Primary Readings, you'll find an excerpt from Hallie's *Tales of Good and Evil, Help and Harm.*

Richard Taylor: Compassion Is All You Need

In Chapters 3 through 7 we looked at a number of rules and principles regarding the nature of moral goodness and the proper conduct of human beings. Even in this section on virtue, most of the theories we have discussed involve using *reason* to evaluate the proper moral action. But in Chapter 1 you encountered a suggestion which, in the last decades of the twentieth century, seemed extremely controversial but which has gained considerable interest and acceptance lately among philosophers: the notion that reason isn't everything when it comes to moral evaluations and decisions, that *moral feelings* are highly important too. You'll remember Martha Nussbaum's claim that emotions can have a reasonable side that makes them indispensable to moral decision making. In his own way, Philip Hallie considers the virtue of compassion as an *emotion* that is essential for the moral makeup of a decent human being. However, neither Hallie nor Nussbaum suggests that we can dispense with reason. Such a radical view isn't held by many, but some thinkers do believe that the way to do the right thing and have virtue is very simple: We do the right thing *when our heart is in the right place;* moral goodness is simply a gut feeling that we all have, a conscience that speaks without words, an empathy that leads us to reach out in compassion to others. If we don't have that, we have no morality at all. For Richard Taylor, an American philosopher, reason has *no* role to play in making the right moral choice. Taylor belongs to a school of thought that says moral principles are, in effect, useless, because we can always find exceptions. You will remember that this was one of the issues we discussed in Chapter 6. But Taylor doesn't believe the alternative is a moral nihilism. On the contrary—in his book *Good and Evil* (2000) Taylor says:

> Moral principles are nothing but conventions, but they have the real and enormous value to life that conventions in general possess. They help us to get where we want to go. Without them social life would be impossible, and hence any kind of life that is distinctively human. Their justification is, therefore, a practical one and has nothing to do with moral considerations in the abstract. The moment such a principle ceases to have that value, the moment its application produces more evil than good, then it ceases to have any significance at all and ought to be scorned.

So if rational principles aren't the basis of ethics, then what is? It is the virtue of compassion, a phenomenon of the heart, not the brain. The eternal focus in ethics on reason needs an antidote, and Taylor finds it in an analysis of *malice versus compassion.*

Imagine a series of atrocities. A child pins a bug to a tree just to watch it squirm. Boys set fire to an old cat and delight in its painful death. Soldiers make a baby girl giggle before they shoot her, and force an old man to dig his own grave before they beat him to death. What is so awful about these stories? It is not just that these victimizers did not live by the categorical imperative, says Taylor (referring to Kant). It is not that they didn't try to maximize general happiness for everyone involved (referring to utilitarianism). It is not that they were ignorant (Socrates) or didn't follow the Golden Mean (Aristotle). The horror we feel—and for Taylor it is the *same kind of horror* in all three cases—stems from the fact that these incidents are simply malicious. The acts are horrible not because the consequences are so terrible (the death of one bug, one cat, and two war victims may not have widespread effects) but because the intent was to cause suffering for the sake of someone else's pleasure or entertainment. These are not crimes against *reason* but crimes against *compassion*.

True moral value, then, lies in compassion, Taylor believes, and he illustrates this with three more tales. A boy comes up to an attic to steal something and rescues some pigeons that are trapped there, despite his father's strict command to leave the birds alone. When his father returns home he gives the boy a beating. A white sheriff beats up a black rioter during the race riots of the 1960s and then, breaking down in tears, cleans the man up and takes him home, after which he goes and gets drunk. An American soldier who is trapped on an island with a Japanese soldier during World War II finally finds the Japanese asleep but is not able to kill him. In each of these cases, Taylor says, these people had been taught moral principles that told them to do one thing ("Obey your father"; "Uphold the law through violence"; "Kill the enemy"), but their heart told them something else, and *their heart told them right.* According to Taylor,

> There are no heroes in these stories. . . . Goodness of heart, tenderness toward things that can suffer, and the loving kindness that contradicts all reason and sense of duty and sometimes denies even the urge to life itself that governs us all are seldom heroic. But who can fail to see, in these mixtures of good and evil, the one thing that really does shine like a jewel, by its own light?

In the end we can't trust our reason, but we can trust our heart; compassion is all we need in order to be moral human beings, compassion toward all living things. Even people who do the right thing can't be called moral if they don't have compassion—in other words, if they don't have the right intention.

This is a much more radical view than Hallie's because it tells us to *disregard* our reason. Let us look at how that might work in practice. Taylor assumes that we all have this compassion in us—he appeals to our *moral intuition.* But what about the boys who set fire to the cat? Where was their natural compassion? And what about soldiers who kill defenseless civilians? Obviously, not everyone has this compassion, not even the people in Taylor's own examples. What can we do about people who have no compassion? Well, we can try to tell them stories about malice and compassion, but chances are that they will think it is a great idea to set fire to a cat and that the boy in the attic should have left the pigeons trapped. How can we appeal to people who are not responsive to compassion? If we were to ask Kant, Mill, Aristotle, or just about any moral thinker, he or she would say we must try to appeal to their *reason.* If we all had compassion there might not be any need for reason, but as we have seen, not everyone has it, and not everyone has it at the right time, at the right place, and for the right people. Therefore we must have something that might convince people who are lacking in compassion, and this is where reason has to come in. What arguments can we use? We might say, "How would you like it if someone did that to you?" In other words, we might appeal to their logical sense of universalizability and invoke the Golden Rule. Or we might say, "If you do this you will get caught and punished." In this way we appeal to their sense of logic and causality; they can't possibly get away with any wrongdoing. If these two arguments don't convince them to do right, we might just lock them up—protect them from themselves, and us from them—until

Huck and Jim on the raft, from Mark Twain's *The Adventures of Huckleberry Finn*. While Jim is expressing his gratitude to Huck, Huck is torn between what his heart tells him—to help Jim—and what his head tells him—to turn Jim in.

they display enough rationality to understand our arguments. Reason, then, is not a substitute for moral feeling (compassion), but it becomes the necessary argument when the moral feeling is absent or deficient. A moral theory that leaves room for only compassion is powerless when it comes to enforcing moral values and virtues.

There is one more problem with Taylor's idea that compassion is all we need, and to illustrate it we will turn to Mark Twain's novel *Huckleberry Finn*. In the story Huck, a young boy, helps Jim, a slave, escape from his owner, Miss Watson. Jonathan Bennett analyzes this famous literary incident—and Bennett is a philosopher who believes in reason as an important part of ethics. He concludes that Huck certainly did the right thing in helping Jim, but it still wasn't good enough because he did it for the wrong reason. Let's review what happens in the story. Huck wants to help his friend Jim, but he realizes that by doing so he will be going against the morals of the town, which require him to return stolen property, which is what a runaway slave is. Because nobody has ever told Huck that owning people is wrong, he has no principle of equality to hold up against what Bennett calls the "bad morality" of the nineteenth-century town. So in the end Huck ends up lying to protect Jim without understanding exactly why, and he resolves not to adhere to any moral principles from then on because they are too hard to figure out. Bennett's conclusion is that Huck did the right thing, but for the wrong reason; he should have set up a new principle of his own, such as "It is wrong to own people" or merely "Jim is my friend, and one should help one's friends." This way Huck's sympathy for Jim would have been supported by his *reason,* and he would not have had to give up on morality because it was too puzzling.

To this we might add something: Mark Twain himself probably wouldn't have shared Bennett's conclusion, because for Twain Huck is a hero who does the right thing for the best of reasons—because he has compassion for a fellow human being (a human being whom many educated readers of Twain's own day and age might have chosen to turn in). Huck has virtue, even if he doesn't think very well. So Twain and Taylor would be in agreement there. But that doesn't make Huck's attitude any better, philosophically speaking, because it is just a stroke of luck that Jim is a good guy and worthy of Huck's compassion. Suppose the story had featured not the runaway slave Jim but a runaway chain-gang prisoner, Fred the axe murderer? Huck still might have felt compassion for this poor, frightened man and decided to help him go down the river and get rid of his irons. But later that night, Fred might have repaid Huck by killing him and an entire farm family farther down the river in order to get money and take possession of Huck's raft. This, tragically, is the fate of many a Good Samaritan. What Huck lacked was not compassion but *reason* to shape it, reason to help him choose when to act and when not to act—because surely not all people are deserving of our compassion to the extent that we should help them escape what society has determined is their rightful punishment. We may sympathize with mass murderers and understand that they had a terrible childhood, but that doesn't mean we should excuse their actions and help them go free.

This example serves another purpose too. Not only does it show that we can't dispense with reason; it also shows that there is something else missing in virtue theory: If we focus solely on building a good character and developing the right virtues, such as loyalty, compassion, and courage, we still have to decide *what to do* once we've developed the virtues. We may have a wonderfully virtuous character but still be stuck with deciding between several mutually exclusive courses of action. Huck might ask himself (once he has decided to be loyal to Jim) what exactly is the best way to enact that loyalty: Is it to take Jim up north where nobody can own slaves, or is it to hide him until his owner stops looking for him? Might it be to help him escape with his family, hire him a lawyer, or what? Philosophers who object to virtue theory complain that even if we are virtuous, we still may not have a clue as to what to do in specific situations. A possible answer is that virtue ethics need not necessarily stand alone; even Aristotle talks about finding the right course for one's *actions,* not just for one's character. But if virtue ethics needs some rules of conduct in order to be a complete theory, then surely an ethics of conduct would do well to include elements from virtue ethics. We will take another look at the possibility of a combination of theories at the end of this chapter.

Gratitude: How Much and When?

The Russian writer Ivan Turgenev tells the following story in his *Prose Poems* (1883): Once upon a time there was a party in heaven, and the Most High had invited all the virtues. Big and small virtues arrived, and everybody was having a good time, but the Most High noticed that two beautiful virtues didn't seem to know each other, so He went over and introduced them: "Gratitude, meet Charity; Charity, meet Gratitude." The two virtues were very surprised, because this was their very first encounter since the creation of the world. . . . Gratitude as a virtue usually implies that it is something that is *owed* to someone. The question is, Are we obliged to feel or show gratitude just because someone expects it, or are there guidelines for when we should express gratitude?

For one thing, gratitude is a feeling, like love (see Box 11.3). Either you feel love or you don't, and nobody can make you feel it if you don't. (This is something that is known by anyone who has experienced unrequited love.) Similarly, we can't make people feel grateful toward us for something we have done for them; indeed, the more we point out how grateful they should be, the more distant and uncooperative they may become. So perhaps we should not talk about making people *feel* gratitude; perhaps we should talk instead about encouraging them to *show* it. Even if you don't *feel* grateful for the socks you got for Christmas, it would be virtuous to *show* gratitude to the person who gave them to you. Not everyone agrees with this viewpoint—I knew a European pedagogue who taught his children that they never had to say thank you or show gratitude for presents given to them, because they had not asked for those presents and to show gratitude without feeling was, in his view, hypocrisy. He may have been right, but life must have been hard for these children when they realized that few others play by the same rules as their father. There are limits to how far you can place yourself and your family outside the mainstream of your culture without getting your nose bloodied from time to time.

We Owe Our Parents Everything: Confucius, Mencius, and Lin Yutang

Most of the topics we have discussed in this book are part of the Western philosophical legacy, but other cultures around the world have their own philosophical traditions and moral values. Here we take a look at the moral philosophies of Confucius and his student Mencius and carry the theme into the twentieth century with the Chinese philosopher Lin Yutang. The subject is gratitude, and the natural recipients of our gratitude are the elderly.

Chinese culture was already ancient in 551 B.C.E. when Confucius was born. When he died in 479 B.C.E., his thoughts on the *superior man* had already changed life and politics in his country, and they were to remain influential, even during periods of opposition, until the twentieth century in China. For centuries the common Chinese attitude toward virtue and right conduct had been to ask the advice of the spirits through divination. However, a certain practical vision had by and large replaced this view by the time of Confucius—a realization that human endeavor was more effective than spiritual guidance. The more important questions became What exactly is a good person? and What is the best kind of human endeavor? The question was important, because whoever was best—a "man of virtue"—was considered to be the person best equipped to rule the country. Prior to Confucius, such a man was presumed to be a nobleman, but Confucius redefined the man of virtue, the superior man, as someone who is wise, courageous, and humane; someone who thinks well and acts accordingly;

Box 11.3   LOVE AS A VIRTUE

When we talk about love as a virtue, we usually are not talking about passionate love. Passionate love does involve virtue; the passionate lover should not be self-effacing or too domineering, for example. However, that is not the issue here. The issue is love that we can *expect* of someone, and we usually can't expect to receive passionate love on demand. During the marriage ritual, when we promise to love and cherish each other, are we promising our partner that we will be passionately in love with him or her forever? Some undoubtedly see it this way, and they often are in for terrible disappointment if the passionate love of their relationship turns out not to last forever. Of course there are fortunate couples who remain passionately in love over the years or whose passion develops into even deeper feelings, but this is not something every couple can count on. The promise to love each other is rather a promise to *show* love, to show that you care about the other person's welfare and happiness and are 100 percent loyal to that person. This we *can* promise to do, even if passion might not last. So love can be a virtue between people who love each other. The Christian virtue of love does not imply any marital promises but is rather an impersonal reverence for other people. Because it also does not involve romantic passion, it can be a requirement in an ethical system too.

someone who models his behavior after virtuous men of the past; and someone who understands that life is a long learning process. The man of virtue exhibits his humanity by being benevolent, and he seeks not profit or revenge, but righteousness. Right conduct may show itself in rectifying what is wrong or in particular in rectifying *names,* or titles (in other words, using the proper words to address others, in particular one's superiors). Studying proper conduct and developing proper character are the same as studying *the Way* (*Dao,* or *Tao*). The Way means the way to proper conduct and proper character—wisdom—and only through studying the Way do people become superior. How do we practice the Way? By developing good habits and continual good thinking. The evils to watch out for are, in particular, greed, aggressiveness, pride, and resentment. It truly is possible to become a superior man, according to Confucius, because people can be transformed by learning. Once we have learned enough about the Way to recognize it, we will know that there is virtue in *moderation.* (Like the Greeks, Confucius believed in the virtuous nature of the *mean* between the extremes of deficiency and excess; see Box 11.4.)

Confucianism is closer to virtue ethics than to an ethics of conduct, although proper conduct is also part of Confucius's philosophy. For the Confucian philosopher, ethics is not a matter of rigid definitions of what to do or how to be but a matter of virtues and behaviors that depend on circumstances. In order to know whether an action is appropriate, you must know how it affects others and whether it might be conducive or detrimental to the harmony of society. Virtue, *te,* consists of both personal character formation and good use of power by a government with good intentions. A person or a government that has achieved *te* is living according to *tao* (*dao*) and has also attained the basic virtues of *jen, li,* and *yi.* As with the term *tao,* there are no easy

Box 11.4   CONFUCIUS AND ARISTOTLE

There are some extraordinary parallels between the virtue theory of Confucius and that of Aristotle; both men greatly influenced posterity, each in his own way. For both thinkers, good habits are the proper way to develop a good character. Both Confucius and Aristotle emphasized the link between good thinking and subsequent action, and both believed that the virtuous human being is one who recognizes the *mean*, the middle state of moderation. But there are also considerable differences. For Confucius the superior man is one who shuns pride and strives for humility; Aristotle would have considered such a man to have insufficient self-appreciation. Confucius also seems to have reached out to a more inclusive moral universe than Aristotle did, and this has caused some scholars to compare him to Christian thinkers. Confucius is known to have expressed a version of the Golden Rule: Don't do to others what you wouldn't want them to do to you, sometimes called the "Silver Rule." (See Box 4.9.) We don't find this attitude in Aristotle's writings, because the general idea of *moral equality,* which is essential for the Golden Rule, is absent in Aristotle's code of ethics. Confucius's superior man also must appreciate *cooperation*—both between people and between people and Nature—whereas Aristotle stressed the hierarchy of rule. Both men, however, envisioned a state that is run according to the model of a well-functioning family, with the ruler as paterfamilias at the head, deciding what is best for his family.

Western translations for these concepts: *Jen* means having a caring attitude toward others, including nonhuman beings; *li* means understanding and performing rituals correctly, but *li* is empty without *jen* (just knowing how to perform ceremonies correctly is meaningless if you don't have a caring approach); and *yi* is the understanding of what is proper and appropriate, not just in terms of etiquette but also in terms of whether something is reasonable and rational. So in order to have *li* (the understanding of rituals) you have to have *jen* (caring), but you must definitely also have *yi* (reasoned judgment) so you know what rituals are important and why. The classical Chinese society was burdened with many elaborate rituals and ceremonies, and Confucius allowed for one's critical sense to cut through and determine what was essential and practical and what was not, depending on the circumstances.

Confucius's ideas of the virtuous man and the well-run state became so influential that they were adopted as state religion in China for a period of several hundred years (618–907 C.E.) in spite of the fact that Confucius didn't concern himself with religious questions. He believed that because we know very little about death and any life after death, we must focus our effort on this life and our relationships with other human beings. (Box 11.5 explains some differences between Confucianism and Taoism.)

Mencius (371–289 B.C.E.) followed in Confucius's footsteps but took Confucianism one step further. He believed not only that humans can learn to be good but also that they are good from the beginning; they just have been corrupted by life and circumstances. Mencius thought the proper method of finding our way back to our lost goodness is to look inside ourselves and recapture our nature—our conscience and our intuition. If we pay proper attention to our own good nature, it will grow and take

Box 11.5   TAOISM

The Chinese philosopher Lao-Tzu was a contemporary of Confucius. The two men knew each other and disagreed politely on several essential points, the most important one being the usefulness of social action. For Confucius the superior man must try to effect change, to make life better for others. For Lao-Tzu this is a useless endeavor, because humans can't effect changes. Nature is a complex duality of opposite forces working together, the forces of yin and yang, he believed. These forces work according to a pattern that can't be observed by most humans, and things happen in their own time. The best humans can do is to contemplate this fact. This is the only access to the Way, or Tao: By doing nothing, by letting nature take its course, we are not obstructing this course; we are emptying our minds of the constant question What should I do next? And by letting our minds become still and perfectly empty, we are opening ourselves to the truth of the Way. The Tao of Lao-Tzu is far more mystical than that of Confucius, which is why his ideas have acquired their own label, Taoism. Virtue and proper conduct meld together in the concept of "doing nothing," or rather "not overdoing it," *wu wei*, which entails unselfishness and mental tranquility. Interestingly enough, this doesn't mean that you deliberately should refrain from doing things like taking a box of matches out of the hands of a three-year-old; indeed, not to do so would be a selfish, willful act. You *should* take the matches away from the child but without congratulating yourself that you've saved her life; after all, she may head straight for your medicine cabinet next. Do what you have to do, but don't think you can make a difference; eventually this will give you peace of mind. This is the hard lesson of Taoism.

over. Only through ourselves can we find the right way, and this process requires a certain amount of suffering. When we suffer, our character is developed. Mencius doubts that someone who has led an easy life can be truly virtuous. The virtues we are supposed to develop through suffering are independence, excellence, mental alertness, courage, and quietude of spirit. When we have reached such a mental equilibrium, we can help others achieve the same, because benevolence is the prime virtue.

The following admonishments are quoted from *The Book of Mencius*, a collection of sayings probably compiled by his followers. This excerpt shows that for Mencius the development of one's character is fundamentally the most important moral task. Although one has duties (which is why there are rules for *conduct,* which one ought to follow), one is not able to fulfill these duties without being *virtuous*—in other words, without having retained one's moral character:

> What is the most important duty? One's duty towards one's parents. What is the most important thing to watch over? One's own character. I have heard of a man who, not having allowed his character to be morally lost, is able to discharge his duties towards his parents; but I have not heard of one morally lost who is able to do so. There are many duties one should discharge, but the fulfillment of one's duty towards one's parents is the most basic. There are many things one should watch over, but watching over one's character is the most basic. . . . Benevolence is the heart of man, and rightness his road. Sad it is indeed when a man gives up the right road instead of following it and allows his heart to

stray without enough sense to go after it. When his chickens and dogs stray, he has sense enough to go after them, but not when his heart strays. The sole concern of learning is to go after this strayed heart.

The tradition of Confucius and Mencius continued into twentieth-century China and is noticeable to this day. A modern voice of this tradition is Lin Yutang (1895–1976). Aside from Mao Zedong, Lin Yutang may be the most influential of all twentieth-century Chinese writers in the West. He traveled extensively in the United States but never lost touch with his Chinese heritage and values. Even more than by Confucius, Lin Yutang was inspired by Mencius. Lin Yutang himself believed that Western philosophers were too fixated on the idea of reason and had forgotten what the ancient Greek thinkers saw as the most important element of their philosophy: human happiness. In his 1937 book *The Importance of Living,* he mentions with much modesty that he is uneducated in philosophy. His knowledge of both Chinese and Western philosophy is considerable, however. What is the importance of living? Knowing when to take things seriously and when to laugh at the solemnity of life; being so fortunate and living so long that one can become a serious intellectual and then return to a higher level of simple thinking and simple ways.

In several books Lin Yutang attempted to bridge the gap between East and West, especially at a time during the first half of the twentieth century when there wasn't much understanding between the two worlds. Writing about family values in a transitional period during which Chinese values were changing (the later Communist takeover forced a transfer of authority to the people as the feudal system was dissolved), Lin Yutang saw the greatest difference between East and West not in the area of politics or gender issues but in the way we treat our elderly—our parents in particular.

Whereas a Western man might think most about helping women and children, a Chinese man would think primarily about helping his parents and other elderly people. This is not because the elderly are thought of as being helpless; it is because they are *respected.* In the Chinese tradition, the older you are, the more respect you deserve. Lin Yutang describes this in *The Importance of Living:*

> In China, the first question a person asks the other on an official call, after asking about his name and surname, is "What is your glorious age?" If the person replies apologetically that he is twenty-three or twenty-eight, the other party generally comforts him by saying that he still has a glorious future and that one day he may become old. But if the person replies that he is thirty-five or thirty-eight, the other party immediately exclaims with deep respect, "Good luck!"; enthusiasm grows in proportion as the gentleman is able to report a higher and higher age, and if the person is anywhere over fifty, the inquirer immediately drops his voice in humility and respect.

Just as people under twenty-one in our culture may lie about their age in order to get into clubs that serve liquor, Chinese young people may pretend to be older in order to gain respect. But in the West there is a point at which most people don't want to seem older than they are; in fact, they might like to appear *younger* than they are. The Chinese traditionally want to appear *older* throughout their lives, because it is to their advantage. Lin Yutang saw the quest for youth in American culture as alien and

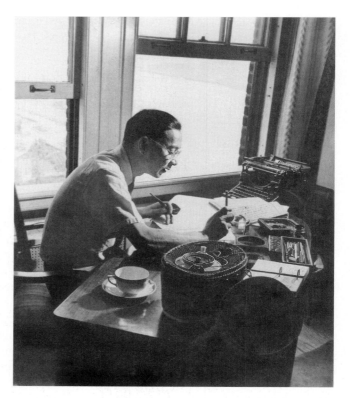

Lin Yutang (1895–1976), the author of *The Importance of Living* (1937) and *The Wisdom of China and India* (1955), may be the modern Chinese thinker best known in the Western world. He worked hard to create a cross-cultural understanding between East and West, but he himself believed that some traditional Eastern values, such as respect for the elderly, are fundamentally different from modern Western values.

frightening—and he was writing in the 1930s, when American teens still attempted to dress and act as "adults." Today, in the exaggerated youth cult that is part of the baby boomer legacy, the phenomenon has become even more extreme. As respect grows with age in the Chinese traditional culture, it seems to *diminish* with age in the West: Somehow we perceive ourselves and others as less powerful, beautiful, and valuable as we reach the far side of fifty or even forty. Lin Yutang quotes an American grandmother who says that it was the birth of her first grandchild that "hurt," because it seemed to be a reminder of the loss of youth. (Box 11.6 discusses our attitude toward aging and how it affects retirement.)

American parents are afraid to make demands on their children, says Lin Yutang. Parents are afraid of becoming a burden, of meddling in their children's affairs, of being nosy. But in whose affairs would we meddle if not in the affairs of those who are closest to us? he asks. Parents do have a right to make demands of their children, he says; they do have a right to be cared for by their children. This is because *their children owe*

Box 11.6 SELF-WORTH AND RETIREMENT

Lin Yutang chastises the West for its "throwaway" attitude toward the older generation. He praises respect and love for one's parents and grandparents as virtues that have to be learned. The West, however, has not always discarded its citizens at the onset of old age. In earlier farming communities in particular, elders not only were respected but were considered an important part of the community because of their *usefulness.* Perhaps they couldn't knead bread or plow the field anymore, but they still could look after the children and share their wisdom. In some parts of the Western world we still can find this type of relationship within a community. But as most people would agree, this is not the case in the larger cities of the West, where it is not customary for grandparents to live with their children. The general attitude seems to be that showing signs of aging is somehow a flaw. A British writer once wrote of Americans that they think death is optional—that if you die you must have done something wrong, like not having taken enough vitamins.

It would appear that part of our problem with accepting the aging process is that as Westerners we have developed the attitude that when we stop being *productive,* we stop being *valuable* as human beings. When a person retires, this feel-

ing often is reinforced, because the person is all of a sudden excluded from part of his or her habitual environment—the workplace. Especially during the early and middle years of the twentieth century, when people would stay in their jobs for over forty years, retirement forced a reevaluation of the person's identity, and all too often the retiree felt that he or she had been *reduced* in value, had been deemed useless by society. This may be one reason it is not uncommon for people to fall ill and even die a short time after retirement, even if they had initially looked forward to it.

There are signs that this trend may change; there is a growing awareness that older people are still people, and because nowadays people usually don't stay at the same job as long as they did in previous generations they may depend less on their jobs for their sense of identity. Also, many retirees reenter the workforce part-time, either because they want to or, sadly, because they can't afford not to. Soon the oldest members of the baby boomer generation will be reaching retirement; perhaps they will refuse to be "thrown away." We may see more emphasis on the autonomy, competence, and worthiness of the retired or older person in the future.

it to them. We owe a never-ending *debt of gratitude* to our parents for raising us, for being there when we were teething, for changing those diapers and taking care of us when we were sick, and just for feeding and clothing us. (See Box 11.7 for further views.) Among Chinese who immigrated to the United States, for example, the guilt over not being with their parents in China is enormous, even if they have brothers and sisters who can perform the duty in their homeland.

According to the Chinese conception of virtue, letting his parents grow old and die without his support is the gravest sin a man can commit. This is true for a woman too, but less so, because it is the duty of the firstborn boy to take care of his parents. Who is the daughter supposed to take care of? Her *husband's* parents. Herein lies the secret as to why it is so important for Chinese families to have male offspring—even today, when restrictions call for only one child per family. The state may take care of you in your retirement, but even so, life is not complete without a son to lean on in

Box 11.7   THE DUTY TO TAKE CARE OF ONE'S PARENTS

For Lin Yutang, the duty to take care of one's parents is a quintessential feature of Chinese culture; as a legacy of Confucian virtue theory, which stresses respect for older people and caring for one's parents, it is a powerful cultural tradition even in today's China. However, the duty to care for aging parents is a near-universal moral rule, except in the less family-oriented lives of many modern city-dwellers. In more traditional cultures it is usually the oldest son who is expected to take care of his parents, as in China, but other traditions exist: In Chapter 12 you will encounter *Like Water for Chocolate* and its criticism of the family tradition of the youngest daughter's stay-

ing unmarried in order to take care of her mother; it is, in fact, a widespread tradition in several parts of the world that the daughter, and often the youngest daughter, inherits the obligation of taking care of her aging parents. Whether we might call it a new tradition or simply the demands of circumstances, in our society it is quite often the daughter living closest to her aging parents who takes on the task of caring for them; this frequently places a particular strain on such middle-aged female caregivers, since they, in today's world, also are likely to work full-time outside the home and, in addition, may be in the process of raising teenage children.

your old age. The pressure to have male babies is so intense that occasionally female babies are killed at birth so that the parents can try again to have a male child, or the birth of a girl is simply kept a secret: a difficult choice, since pregnancies are monitored by the state and abortions forced on women who already have one child. An alternative is paying a hefty fine for the second child. If parents choose to keep a little girl, the response from friends and colleagues is quite different than it would be if they had a boy. A boy is cause for celebration; a baby girl may prompt friends and colleagues to send cards of condolence to the parents. Despite attempt to revise the policy, it appears that the Chinese government is committed to the one-child-per-family rule for now, but the rule has now been in place for sufficient time that long-term consequences are emerging: There are simply not enough young girls in China now to "go around" and become sexual partners and wives in the next generation—and a shortage of women may have far-reaching consequences. Already now we hear of female babies being purchased from neighboring countries or downright stolen—and the specter of a culture with a large number of "surplus" young males raises more questions: How will these young men cope, and what will the Chinese state do for its bachelor citizens?

So far, the system has provided for its elderly citizens. Much to the shame of traditional Chinese, there are now some nursing homes for the elderly in the villages of China, but they are presumably more humane than the "human storage tanks" we have in our Western civilization because the elderly are still part of the community, and the problems of the village are presented to them in their capacity as advisers. In this manner the traditional respect for the older people is maintained, at least on a symbolic level, even though the family patterns have been disrupted.

We Owe Our Parents Nothing: Jane English

A young American philosopher, Jane English (1947–1978), proposed a solution to the constant and very common squabbles between parents and their grown children. It seems rather radical: She suggests that we owe our parents nothing. This idea is not as harsh as it appears, however. English thinks the main problem between grown children and parents is the common *parental* attitude that their children somehow are indebted to them. This *"debt-metaphor"* can be expressed in a number of ways, such as, "We are paying for your schooling, so you owe it to us to study what we would like you to study"; "We've clothed you and fed you, so the least you could do is come home for Christmas"; or "I was in labor with you for thirty-six hours, so you could at least clean up your room once in a while." The basic formula is, "You owe us gratitude and obedience because of what we have done for you." For English this attitude undermines all filial love, because the obvious answer a kid can give is "I didn't ask to be born." And there is not much chance of fruitful communication after that. (As one of my students remarked, a parent can always fire back with "And you weren't wanted, either," but that would surely be the end of any parent-child friendship.)

So what should parents do? English said they should realize that there are appropriate ways of using the debt-metaphor and that applying it to a parent-child relationship is not one of them. An appropriate way to use the debt-metaphor is shown in the following example given by English in her essay "What Do Grown Children Owe Their Parents?":

> New to the neighborhood, Max barely knows his neighbor, Nina, but he asks her if she will take in his mail while he is gone for a month's vacation. She agrees. If, subsequently, Nina asks Max to do the same for her, it seems that Max has a moral obligation to agree (greater than the one he would have had if Nina had not done the same for him), unless for some reason it would be a burden far out of proportion to the one Nina bore for him.

English labels what Nina does for Max a "favor"—and favors incur *debts*. But once you have paid your debt—once Max has taken Nina's mail in—then the debt is discharged, and the matter is over. This is *reciprocity,* and it means that you must do something of a similar nature for the person you are in debt to. But what if Nina never goes out of town, so Max never has an opportunity to take in her mail and pay off the debt? Then he might mow her lawn, give her rides to work, or walk her dog. If she has no lawn or dog and likes to drive to work, then he might figure out something else to do for her, and chances are that they might become friends in the process. In that case another type of relationship kicks in, one that no longer is based on a reciprocal system of favors and debts. Instead, the relationship is based on a system of duties relating to *friendship.* (See Box 11.8 for further discussion.)

In friendship, according to English, the debt-metaphor ceases to be appropriate, because friends shouldn't think they owe each other anything. Although debts are discharged when a favor is reciprocated, friendships don't work that way; just because you do something for your friend who has done something for you doesn't make you both "even." Friendships aren't supposed to be "tit for tat," and if they are, then the

PEANUTS
BY SCHULZ

The philosopher Jane English suggests that parents adopt a conversational tone toward their adult children that avoids laying guilt on the child as a method of persuasion—because the child can always answer back, "I didn't ask to be born." Here is a classic *Peanuts* strip illustrating the issue from an unusual angle: Lucy and Linus are engaged in a discussion about whether we actually ever ask to be born!

people involved aren't real friends. Friendship means that you are there for each other when needed and that you do things for each other because you *like* each other, not because you *owe* each other. The fact that there can be no debts doesn't mean that there are no obligations, however; on the contrary, friendship carries with it the never-ending obligation to be there for each other, at least while the friendship lasts. It implies a mutual sense of duty toward each other. With friendship, instead of reciprocity, there is *mutuality*.

Let us speculate a bit beyond what English herself writes: Suppose you borrow fifty dollars from a friend, and then you have a falling-out with her. Because there are no debts in a friendship and because obligations last only as long as the friendship does, you don't have to pay back the money, right? Wrong, because owing money is a true debt in our society and money must be paid back regardless of whether it is owed to friends or strangers. Similarly, you have to fulfill your part of a contract, regardless of whether it is with a friend, business partner, or stranger. Such transactions come under the proper use of the debt-metaphor and persist beyond the extent of friendships. (In fact, they often are the cause of the breakup of friendships.)

Box 11.8 DATING, DEBT, AND FRIENDSHIP

Many of the problems of dating stem from a difference in attitude, says Jane English. One person thinks of the date in terms of a friendship, and the other one sees it as a debt-metaphor situation. Suppose Alfred takes Beatrice out for dinner and a movie, and at the end of the evening Alfred expects "something" in return for his investment. Alfred has chosen to view the situation as a favor-debt situation; he sees Beatrice as being indebted to him. Beatrice, however, is upset, because she viewed the situation as a friendship situation, with no favors and debts. In essence, Beatrice doesn't owe Alfred a thing, because Alfred's gesture was not presented as a "quid pro quo" situation to begin with but as an overture to friendship. The situation would have been more complex had Beatrice *agreed with Alfred* in the beginning that the dinner and movie were to be a "business arrangement" to be "paid off" later in the evening. A survey from some years back showed that, shockingly, a majority of California high school students, females as well as males, feel that dating is in fact a favor-debt situation. In that case we must say that if both participants agree, then so be

it. There is, however, a good old word for when someone sells physical favors for material goods; that word is *prostitution*. In such a situation the one who is "bought" becomes merely a means to an end.

What can you do if you want to make sure to avoid a favor-debt situation on a date? For one thing, you can insist on going Dutch. Both of you probably make the same kind of money these days, so why should one of you pay for the other? Remember, nobody should expect payment for doing someone an unsolicited favor (if the people involved aren't friends), and nobody should expect payment for doing any kind of favor if the people involved are friends. So either way you shouldn't expect anything of your date, and you shouldn't feel pressured by your date to repay anything. Be careful not to abuse this rule, though. One girl commented that "it's great to be able to be taken to a dinner and a movie and not have to do anything in return!" With this attitude, she reduces her date to becoming merely the means to an end, and that's not the idea.

English believes we often fall into the trap of regarding friendship duties as debts. Most couples find themselves saying things like, "We've been over to Frank and Claire's four times now, so we owe them a dinner." For English this is a gross misunderstanding of what friendship is all about. You can go visit Claire and Frank a hundred times, and you still don't owe them a thing because they aren't doing you a "favor"; they ask you over because they like you. To most readers this may seem a trifle idealistic; after the twentieth dinner, Claire and Frank surely will think something is wrong and won't ask you over again. But English's idea is that you will be there if they need you and that you should contribute to the friendship in *some way or other*—she doesn't say how much you should contribute or in what way; how you contribute is up to you.

English says the relationship between parents and grown children should be modeled after the friendship pattern and not after the debt-metaphor pattern. Parents don't do their children a favor by raising them, and, accordingly, children don't owe any debt to them. But this doesn't mean grown children don't have *obligations* to their parents—they have the same obligations as they have to their friends. Those obligations are limitless as long as the relationship lasts; they cease when the relationship

Box 11.9   WHAT ABOUT RELATIVES?

Jane English's main concern is for parents and grown children to realize that their relationship ought to be like that between good friends, and in such a relationship there are limitless obligations. But do we have any obligations to people who aren't yet our friends (we may hardly know them) but aren't strangers, either, because they are more distant relatives? Should they rank as friends or strangers? English has no category for them, and yet many people are concerned about how much we can and should rely on the support of relatives other than those in our immediate family. When they come to visit, should we give up our bedroom to them? Can I, as a student, ask my mother's cousin in Paris if I can stay with her for a year while I study at the Sorbonne? How can we tell our aunt and uncle from Sweden/Los Angeles/Idaho/Mexico that it really is not convenient for them to stay six weeks in our apartment? Am I obliged to find a lawyer for my half-brother who is in trouble? And so on. Many

times we might *choose* to help, just as we might help a stranger, but often the old line "Blood is thicker than water" makes us feel that we do have a specific *duty* to our extended family. One solution might be to think of this duty as a "duty to do small favors"—like finding your relatives a good, cheap hotel or showing them around town and taking them out a few times—but not as a duty to provide very large favors, like letting them have the run of your home for six weeks. Instead of finding a lawyer for your half-brother who is in trouble, you might provide him with the number of a good legal agency but let him choose a lawyer himself and let him be financially responsible. By doing these small favors, a small debt to reciprocate now rests with the relative. If this debt is discharged to everyone's satisfaction—through reciprocal hospitality or perhaps through an annual Christmas card—you can all proceed to becoming friends.

ends. No reciprocity can be evoked, such as "You fed and clothed me for eighteen years, so I'll take care of you for the next eighteen but not a minute longer." *Mutuality,* however, is expected at all times. (What is expected in terms of other relatives is discussed in Box 11.9.)

What is the basis for a good parent-child relationship, then? Above all, love and friendship. If these are present, all that must be considered are (1) the need of the parents and (2) the ability and resources of the grown child. The parents may be sick and in need, and their son may love them, but he also may be out of work and unable to help with the medical bills. In that case, helping to pay the bills would *not* be part of his obligations, but other things would, such as providing cheerful company, taking the trash out, or making other contributions.

Suppose the parents need help, but there is *no friendship* between the parents and the child. Then, essentially, the grown child is not obliged to help, especially if the end of the friendship (if in fact it ever existed) was the parents' choice. One might imagine that this would be the time for the parents to approach their estranged child and ask for a favor in the hope of reestablishing the friendship. English seems to assume that all the parents have to do is announce that they are sorry and would like to be friends again—but what if they follow this approach with immediate requests for support? Then their son or daughter might soon get the idea that there is a calculated reason behind this renewal of friendship. (This works both ways, of course; if the son or daughter has left home in anger and later decides that he or she needs help from home, an approach of remorse and offers of renewal of friendship followed by requests for support will look equally suspicious to the parents.)

For a solution we might want to turn to the American philosopher Fred Berger (whose theory we discuss in more detail shortly). In assessing the extent of the gratitude you ought to show others for acts of kindness toward you, Berger says you should look for the *motivation*. Were these acts of kindness done for your sake? for the doer's? or both? If done for your sake alone, you should show gratitude; if done for the doer's own sake, you have no obligation; if done partly for your sake and partly for the doer's own sake, you should show some gratitude, but there is no need to go overboard. In a similar manner, we might ask, why are the parents approaching their grown child (or the children their parents)? Is it because of a genuine wish to reestablish contact, is it solely because they want assistance, or is the truth somewhere in between? If the approached party can determine the motivation with reasonable accuracy, then he or she can decide how to react.

What should parents say if they very much would like their grown child to take a certain course of action but realize that he or she does not owe it to them to do so? Not "You owe us" but something like "We love you, and we think you'd be happier if you did x." Or, suggests English, "If you love us, you'll do x." But is this second example a very good one? To most people this alternative would set off a tremendous guilt trip, because it plays on the notion that if you don't comply, you don't love your parents. Few people are able to follow their parents' advice all the time, no matter how much love and friendship there may be between them. One alternative approach, which was suggested by one of my students, is for the parents to explain the whole situation: "Because of our past experience, we believe it is best for you, but it's your choice."

Jane English never lived to develop her theory further; she died at the age of thirty-one while on a mountaineering expedition in Switzerland. In her short life she published several other thought-provoking papers, and one might wonder how this bright person might have felt about the same issue had she lived to become a parent of grown children.

Friendship Duties and Gratitude

English supplies some guidelines for how we should consider *friendship* as a virtue that applies to the relationship between parents and grown children; Lin Yutang believes the virtue that should be applied to such relationships is *gratitude*. But what about both friendship and gratitude in other types of relationships, like those between friends, or lovers, or neighbors? How far do our duties of friendship go? Are we obliged to help our friends in every way? to help them cheat on their tax returns? to lie to their spouse about where they were last night? to hide them from the police? to buy them drugs? The answer is of course no—even if they would do those things for us. Friendship may be a virtue, but it doesn't entail giving up one's other moral standards merely for the sake of friendship; besides, your friend is hardly displaying the virtue of friendship toward you, since by helping him or her you may be considered "aiding and abetting"

Box 11.10   DOES THE GOLDEN RULE ALWAYS WORK?

The Golden Rule has been mentioned several times in this text, and it is certainly one of the most widespread rules of ethics in existence, finding expression in religions and moral teachings throughout recorded history. But is it always the best solution to do unto others as you would have them do unto you? Suppose a friend wants you to put her up for a few weeks. She tells you she has been involved in a hit-and-run accident, and now she wants to hide from the police. You are reluctant to let her stay, but she assures you that she would do the same for you or even that you would want her to do the same for you if you were in trouble. But that may not be the case; you may see the situation in quite a different light. If you were in trouble you might need a friend, but you might not ask that friend to hide you; chances are you wouldn't have left the scene of the accident in the first place. (Staying at the scene is of course the only ethical course of action—besides, it's the law.) Your friend's perception of what she wants done for her is not the same as what you might want a friend to do for you. In everyday life we find lots of examples of this type of situation: Maria gives Cheryl a bread machine for Christmas because that's what Maria would like to get. But she didn't think to find out whether Cheryl might also like one, and in fact Cheryl doesn't like kitchen gifts. Even an episode of the television series *The Simpsons* has dealt with the phenomenon: Homer Simpson shops for a present for his wife Marge and ends up giving her—a bowling ball, because that's what *he* wants! Often, such misplaced acts of kindness are caused by a self-centered attitude or a lack of perception, but they also may happen due to a fundamental difference in the approach to life. In her book *That's Not What I Meant,* the linguist Deborah Tannen describes a classic situation of misapplied Golden Rule approaches between partners who have different visions of correct behavior (or what Tannen calls different "styles"):

> Maxwell wants to be left alone, and Samantha wants attention. So she gives him attention, and he leaves her alone. The adage "Do unto others as you would have others do unto you" may be the source of a lot of anguish and misunderstanding if the doer and the done unto have different styles.

It appears that if we are to act on the Golden Rule, we have to make certain that the others really want to "be done unto."

someone in trouble with the law. A good friend doesn't ask that of another. But this doesn't mean you can't do *something* for your friends when they are in trouble, like be there for them to talk to or find them an appropriate counselor. (Box 11.10 discusses how the Golden Rule applies to such issues.)

A more mundane but equally tricky situation arises when someone does something nice for us that we didn't ask for and then expects something in return. Jane English states that such "unsolicited favors" do not create any debt, so we don't have to reciprocate. However, the situation may be more complex than that: The favor extended may be in an emergency situation in which a person is not capable of requesting help (such as someone picking up a wallet a person has dropped and returning it, or giving someone first aid after an accident). Jane English doesn't address such issues. And what if a person doing an unsolicited favor for a stranger is truly trying to be nice?

In that case, doing nothing in return seems rude, even if we didn't ask for the favor. Here Fred Berger answers that certainly we have an obligation, and that obligation is to *show gratitude*. A simple thank-you, verbal or written, may be all it takes. In some situations the person who did us an unsolicited favor (offered to give us a ride or gave us a present) may *insist* that we show gratitude and reciprocate by doing business with them, going out with them, or even having sex with them. In that case, Berger says, we have to look at the giver's *intentions*: Did he give us something or do us a favor just so that we would be indebted to him? In that case, we don't owe the person anything, not even gratitude, because he did it for *himself,* not for us.

So how do we know when we owe people gratitude? Certainly we owe it when we have *asked* them to do us a favor. As far as unsolicited favors go, though, we should express gratitude when we can be reasonably certain that (1) they did it for our own sake—because they like and respect us, as Kant would say, as *ends in ourselves,* not because they viewed us as the *means to an end.* We also should make certain that (2) they did help us *on purpose* and didn't just blunder into the situation. Moreover, we have to ascertain that (3) they did it *voluntarily,* that no one else forced them to do it. In Berger's words, gratitude should be a response to benevolence, not benefits, and this applies to all relationships, even those between parents and children. We should express gratitude in proportion to the things that are done for our sake (to be sure, not everything parents do is done for the sake of the child). If something is done for other reasons, our duty to show gratitude diminishes proportionately. And, says Berger, when we do show gratitude to people who have done something for us, we show that we appreciate *them* as intrinsically valuable persons—as ends in themselves and not just as instruments for our well-being.

Suppose the people who do things for us like us and respect us but still hope to get something out of being nice to us? You'll recall that we discussed the issue of selfishness vs. altruism in Chapter 4, and we can apply that lesson here. We shouldn't disqualify others from deserving our gratitude just because they were hoping for some little advantage themselves; it is when we were considered solely a means to an end that our duty to show gratitude disappears.

Suppose you have good reason to feel grateful for something someone has done. Let's assume you are a poor student and your neighbors have seven kids. They cook up a huge dinner every night, and at the end of the month, when you are broke, they always invite you over for dinner. They say, "We have to cook anyway, so come on over." And you do, month after month. You keep waiting for the moment when the family may need your invaluable assistance with something, but the time never comes. So you keep eating their food and feeling like a moocher. What can you do? Well, you might do the dishes once in a while or help babysit. In other words, you can contribute to the mutuality of a friendship even if you aren't specifically asked to do so.

Let's return to the question How much gratitude should I feel? The answer, says Berger, lies in Aristotle's theory of virtue: just enough—not too much and not too little. As vague as it is, this is still the guideline most people instinctively use when they try to figure out how to respond to an act of kindness. We know that enslaving ourselves for the rest of our natural lives, giving up our firstborn, and other such measures

Box 11.11   A SHORT VIEW OF VICES

No case study of virtues would be complete without sneaking a peek at the forbidden zone: the vices. In his list of virtues, Aristotle himself devotes much attention to the extremes of deficiency and excess, because without knowing when there is too much or too little of something, how do we know when there is just enough? Some people use this as an excuse for exploring the vices before settling for being virtuous, but virtue theory doesn't assume that such explorations are necessary; just knowing the limits of virtue may be sufficient. For our three virtues in this chapter the corresponding vices, in an Aristotelian approach, would be as follows:

- For *courage:* The vices of excess and deficiency are familiar to you from Chapter 9: foolhardiness and cowardice.

- For *compassion:* The vice of excess might be for a person to be intrusive and nosy or lack an understanding of when others should be pitied; the vice of deficiency would be for a person to be coldhearted and unfeeling.

- For *gratitude:* The vice of excess might be to feel perpetually indebted; the vice of deficiency would, of course, be ingratitude.

As you will remember from our discussion about negative role models, the fascination for how *not* to be is at least as deep as our interest in being a good person. Vices keep inspiring authors from all parts of the world, and two of the most commonly used vices in works of fiction are *jealousy* and the *thirst for revenge.*

Jealousy should be distinguished from envy, which is wanting what another person has or is; by jealousy we usually mean sexual jealousy: the feeling of gnawing anger and hurt at the thought (or prospect, or fact) of the one we love in an amorous situation with someone else. For some people any kind of jealousy is a vice, because it reduces the one we love to a piece of *property,* which we think we can own; others see it as a healthy expression of love, provided that it is not carried to excess through perpetual suspicion.

Thirst for revenge would for Aristotle probably be excessive, but the idea of revenge itself would not be a vice for the ancient Greek mind: It would rather be appropriate under specific circumstances of settling an offense; otherwise, one might seem meek and weak-hearted (and in this the ancient Greeks and the Vikings would have seen completely eye to eye). For the Christian tradition, however, revenge is supposed to be a matter for God to carry out; the old saying from the Bible is "Vengeance is mine, saith the Lord" (Rom. 12:19). As you may remember from Chapter 7, vengeance is not acceptable as a reason for punishment in the modern legal system. Retribution is supposedly a different phenomenon, a socially sanctioned action based on logic rather than emotion and designed to mete out justice in proportion to the crime. Revenge can easily spill over into a blood feud, resulting in the killing of innocents.

would be too much. We also know that being rude and doing or saying nothing to show our appreciation is too little. (For vices of too much and too little, see Box 11.11.) But where exactly lies the right amount? This is, as with all the Aristotelian virtues, a case-by-case matter. Sometimes the right amount consists of a thank-you note, a bottle of wine, or a batch of chocolate-chip cookies. Sometimes it is house-sitting for six months, and sometimes it is going across country to give someone a helping hand. If we manage to hit the bull's-eye and find the right response, perhaps Aristotle is right, and we are on the way to becoming virtuous. In the Narratives section, the film *Pay It Forward* suggests that gratitude should be handed on, as a favor to someone else, who then in turn shows her or his gratitude by doing something for someone else—"paying it forward."

How to Receive Gratitude?

One aspect of the question of gratitude rarely touched on by philosophers is a matter that, in everyday life, is almost as important as the questions of when to be grateful and how much gratitude to show, and that is the virtue of gracefully *accepting gratitude*. Just as it takes skill to be a good giver, so it takes skill to be a good receiver, regardless of whether we talk about gifts, favors, or reciprocation. What if you are the person who did someone else a favor without expecting anything in return? In other words, you treated that someone as an end in himself or herself, and the mere fact that you were able to help is enough reward for you. But now the other person wants to thank you and do something for you in return. What do you do? Saying you don't want any thanks may be telling the other person how you feel, but it may not be enough, because the other person may feel he or she *needs* to reciprocate; so you must be able to sometimes allow the other to do so, with the implicit understanding that it is not going to lead to a game of one-upmanship with returned favors. Sometimes a simple "You're welcome" is enough, while sometimes the proper way to accept gratitude may be to gracefully accept a favor or a gift in return, even if you did not do the original favor in order to get rewarded. And here Aristotle comes in handy again: Your guideline as to how big a favor you can accept in return for a favor should be the extent of the original favor ("just right"). At the end of the chapter we will look at *Grand Canyon,* a film that explores just this kind of situation: showing and accepting gratitude.

Virtue and Conduct: A Combination?

In Chapters 3–7 we explored the most influential theories of what has become known as ethics of conduct, and in Chapters 8–11 we have looked at classical and contemporary versions of virtue ethics. The majority of ethicists over the years have perceived their task as defining in the simplest terms possible, and with as few rules as possible, a moral theory that would have universal application, one that would be valid in all situations. As we have seen, no theory so far can be said to work equally well in all situations; all theories, when put to the test, show some flaws or problems. For all its positive elements, ethical relativism allows for a tolerance that objects to nothing, not even crimes against humanity; egoism, while recognizing the right of the individual to look after his or her own interests, fails to recognize that humans may actually be interested in serving the interests of others; utilitarianism, while seeking general happiness for all sentient beings, seems to allow for the few to be used, and even sacrificed, for the sake of the many; Kantian deontology wants to do the right thing but is so focused on duty that it may overlook bad consequences of doing one's duty—consequences that otherwise could have been avoided. And virtue ethics, which is intended as an alternative to these theories of conduct, hasn't quite solved the problem of when and how to use one's reason and rational argumentation in terms of defining moral standards, and it hasn't succeeded in coming up with a theory of action in which the general ideas of virtue can be brought into play in particular situations or in solving disagreements between people who consider themselves virtuous. For those who look for a good answer to moral problems, this can be more than discouraging, and some might even decide, like Huck Finn, that moral speculations are too confusing and it's better just to follow their gut feelings. But this would be taking the easy way out, and actually it is not a very satisfying solution. On occasion we all may have to justify an action, and "It seemed like a good idea at the time" is not an adequate answer. Furthermore, we may decide that ethicists haven't come up with a complete solution to moral problems, but that doesn't mean we don't have to keep on trying to solve them on an individual basis. Just because the experts haven't given us all the solutions on a silver platter doesn't mean we're exempt from seeking solutions on our own. There *are* alternative answers.

Most of the theories we have looked at originated in time periods when it was assumed that humans would someday know all the answers to everything. It also was assumed, from a scientific viewpoint, that a simple explanation was better and more pleasing than a complex one. To a great extent that is still true: A theory gains in strength if unnecessary elements are cut away (this phenomenon is often referred to as *Occam's razor,* from the British medieval philosopher William of Occam). But the late twentieth century also taught us that simple solutions may not always be available, or even desirable, because there may be many possible ways of looking at each situation. (A case in point is Deborah Tannen's example of different "styles" of behavior described in Box 11.10.) So we are not focused on seeking simple answers to complex issues in ethics any longer.

I often hear students remark, Why do all these philosophers have to be so single-minded about everything? Why can't their theories allow for nuances? It is a good question—but it is a question that is possible only because we have become a culture that allows for nuances and different perspectives. (Many theories do, in fact, allow for nuances, but it is unfortunately in the nature of introductory courses that some of those nuances tend to fall by the wayside in the effort to express a theory as clearly, and as briefly, as possible.) This culture probably wouldn't have arrived at such an openness had it not been for the progression in moral theory (the phenomenon the Australian philosopher Peter Singer referred to as "the expanding circle," as you may remember from Chapter 4). Elements in theories that may now seem too narrow and absolutist at some point in time expanded or broke a narrower and more rigid system of values. It seems that we are now ready for something of a more complex nature: an expansion that allows for assuming the possibility that we can have certain basic values in common and at the same time allows for a relativistic tolerance of other values. We may be looking for what was introduced in Part 2 as *soft universalism:* the theory that deep down, we can agree on certain core values that are based on our common humanity. However, this is not going to be easy, because we have to agree on *which* values are supposed to be the ones we have in common, and here our different cultural upbringing and ethnic diversity may come into play.

Some philosophers have been trying for a long time to redesign the traditional theories (such as utilitarianism, deontology, or virtue theory) to make them more logical, more responsive to present-day sensitivities, or more tolerant of exceptions. But we can choose another path: seeking the best advice from a multitude of theories. The approach of Fred Berger to the question of compassion is an example of this approach: He uses both Aristotle's theory of the mean between extremes and Kant's theory of ends in themselves in order to explore the subject of compassion. In other words, he allows for several different theories to be used at the same time, letting them work together to achieve a functional solution. This is a very pragmatic approach, and some might even call it a very American approach, because Americans are (presumably) typically interested in whether or not something *works.*

This approach may work if we don't expect too much. Letting the vast spectrum of ethical viewpoints and traditions become available as options will certainly be no easy road, primarily because we can't just decide to take the best elements of all theories and lump them together in the hope that they may work. For one thing, they may well contradict each other; for another, if we choose a theory for its advantages, we're stuck with its disadvantages too. We can't just decide to add deontology to utilitarianism, for example, and assume that a smooth theory will emerge; we may have doubled our range of solutions, but we have also doubled our problems.

It is, however, probably the only viable solution for a future theory of ethics. We need theories of conduct, and we need theories of virtue, from more than just a few cultural groups; besides, most of us already use an approach that combines theories on a day-by-day basis. Sometimes we consider consequences as vitally important (especially in matters of life and death); sometimes we think keeping promises and other obligations is more important than worrying about consequences; sometimes we feel we're entitled to look after ourselves and our own interests; and sometimes we are focused on developing a good character—based on compassion, courage, or another virtue. Often we do combine these views in specific situations. But we have to be able to decide when one viewpoint or aspect is more appropriate than another, and we have to try to avoid contradicting ourselves by putting together principles that are in obvious opposition to each other. You can't claim at the same time that consequences don't count and that consequences are all-important. What you *can* claim is that there are times when consequences are supremely important (such as calling and waiting for the ambulance to come for your neighbor who keeled over with a heart attack, even if you have to break your movie date in order to do that), and at other times a principle may be more important than certain consequences (such as a jury turning in a guilty verdict based on clear evidence, even if it may result in rioting). So despite the reluctance of many ethicists to mix and match moral theories, we do it on an everyday basis, and we can train ourselves to do it better by making sure we don't just make loopholes for ourselves, but genuinely try to address and evaluate the various aspects of real-life ethics as they arise in real situations: duty theory, consequentialism, virtue ethics, respect for other moral traditions—and, on occasion, some legitimate self-interest (provided that it doesn't seriously disregard the interests of others).

For many ethicists today the answer lies in what is called *ethical pluralism,* multiple ethical viewpoints coexisting on our planet and within the same culture. At least this was the viewpoint of many prior to September 11; some still see ethical pluralism as being the only civilized way for all of us to live together, while others have taken a second look at our Western ideals and traditions and found them to be worth supporting and offering to the world as a sensible moral code. Where does soft universalism stand, in a post-9/11 context? That depends greatly on what we call ethical pluralism. If it simply means that our culture consists of disparate and mutually exclusive viewpoints—individuals and groups not conversing, isolating themselves within their group identities, whether they be religious, political, or just based on different ethnic traditions—then soft universalism and ethical pluralism have little in common. But if an ethical pluralist can support the idea of a diverse society that wishes to create an environment with mutual respect and interest in sharing the responsibilities and joys of the community, then soft universalism can lend a hand, with its credo that we can show respect for a variety of moral viewpoints, as long as we agree that we can find some common values underlying the differences. Because, contrary to ethical relativism, moral subjectivism, and ethical pluralism (sometimes simply lumped together as "moral relativism" by its critics), soft universalism recognizes that there are, or ought to be, basic moral truths such as respect for others and a love of freedom—moral ideals which our nation and the Western civilization in general are based on, even though those ideals have not always been held in equally high regard by everybody. So a soft universalist will be able to profess pride in the traditions and values that promote such a respect for other human beings and an ideal of individual freedom while at the same time recognizing the value of diversity—as long as it is a diversity that accepts the notion of a common ground in shared democratic values. Is that less "tolerant" than ethical relativism? Yes, it is, and I suppose it is one of the philosophical legacies of 9/11 that the thinker who wants to be at peace with the world and accept diversity is more willing to draw the line at what he or she is willing to accept.

In the end, the view of soft universalism is that those common values are founded in our common humanity, in the fact that we live in groups and bond with other human beings but are also competitive individuals within our groups. So the challenge of soft universalism is to provide justification for why certain values are to be considered common ground. It must set up a system of justification for which moral values should be considered valid at all times (such as the United Nations' list of human rights, for example), which values should be considered a matter of cultural preference and tradition, and which values should be considered globally unacceptable (such as "Some people are born to be free, and others are born to be slaves" or "People of a different religion/race/gender should be considered as having no rights"). Given that there are, in these times, schools around the world where young boys learn to hate everything Western and prepare for a life dedicated to destroying Western values and human beings, a system of ethics for the twenty-first century must look for the common ground we share as human beings, while balancing on the razor's edge of respecting others' traditions and at the same time cherishing and holding on to the best elements of our own. Ethical relativism doesn't have the capacity to do this, and neither does hard universalism. Whether soft universalism can provide genuine solutions to the problems of our highly complex world remains to be seen, but, as the philosopher Dwight Furrow would say, we have to try.

Diversity, Politics, and Common Ground?

It is time to gather a few threads that have been spun at various times in this edition: In Chapter 1 you read about the division experienced by much of the nation during and after the 2004 presidential election, with the country dividing itself into "red" and "blue" states and counties. You may want to revisit the map of voters, county by county. A British paper asked on November 3, the day after the election, "How can 50 million people (meaning the people voting for President Bush) be so stupid?" In the heated media debate right after the election former Democratic vice-presidential candidate Geraldine Ferraro said on Fox News that if all the "blue" states got together and seceded, "nothing" would be left, because "all the talent is on the sides," meaning the two coasts. Such statements echoed the feelings of many "blue state" voters and was terribly offensive to many "red state" voters. It illustrates a certain attitude toward people who do not share one's moral and political views: that they must be *ignorant or stupid or willfully evil.* This attitude can be found among liberals and conservatives alike, and if we subscribe to that attitude, it entails that people whose views differ drastically (or even moderately) from "ours" essentially have no right to think what they think, because they are by definition wrong. *We* are the reasonable, sensible people, and those who disagree with us must be taught the error of their ways—retrained, perhaps even rehabilitated. They must be taught to see the light. If they resist, they are people of bad faith. But is this really the world of democracy, diversity, and tolerance that most people believe the United States is supposed to exemplify? As much as one may believe that one's own attitude is the enlightened one and that the others just refuse to face the facts, then this can evolve into a dogmatic attitude, whether it is from the right or the left.

We have focused on *diversity* in this culture for a couple of decades now: People of different ethnic and racial backgrounds have found a place and changed what we now see as mainstream America. Women have found a place in public life and changed the face of the nation. People of different sexual orientations have, likewise, been included as part of the mainstream. But some of us tend to forget that diversity is not just a matter of race, ethnicity, and gender, but also a matter of *convictions.* An environment that welcomes diversity must also include moral and political diversity. This means that a traditional, conservative environment must learn to accept that liberal members in its midst are liberal because they believe their own values are good and rational—not just because they are too stupid or narrow-minded or immoral to accept other values. And liberals, likewise, must rise above the notion that a conservative is someone who has not revised, or refuses to revise, his or her traditional opinions about values and politics. They must realize that "conservative" is not a derogatory term, and a conservative is not someone who is ignorant, stupid, or evil, but whose choice of values can develop with as much rationality and critical soul-searching as the development of liberal values. This means we must get to a point where we *respect the fact that other people may have different convictions*—but we don't necessarily have to *respect* those convictions! I am allowed to try to change your view, and you can try to change mine. But in recognizing your right to have a different opinion, and in your recognition of mine, we will live up to the quintessential American attitude, voiced by Patrick

Henry in the eighteenth century: *"I may disagree with what you have to say, but I will fight to the death for your right to say it."* And thus we will share the fundamental value of this democracy: That people have a right to think what they want and speak their mind about it, and when decisions have to be made, *we will take a vote.* Whoever wins gets to determine the policies—and those who didn't win still have the right to their conviction and to try to change the course of the future in a democratic way. We don't all have to agree that late-term abortions should be banned or that same-sex marriage should be allowed. But we should be able to acknowledge that those who don't agree with us on the issues we care about are, in general, not evil scoundrels, but people who also have good will and who also are trying to create the best nation possible—as long as their agenda does not allow deliberate harm of others. So within the setting of a democracy, we all must agree to draw the line somewhere: We don't want to have a thought police, but we can't allow the enactment of political and moral views that entail some people being less than persons. The core value of respect for others' humanity and human dignity is the bottom line.

In Chapter 3, I speculated that the issue of finding common ground in our American culture might have a lot to do with whether we perceive an outside threat, or whether we choose to focus on internal differences. Suppose we look at the issue in light of the previous discussion about soft universalism. How do we distinguish this proposed moral and political diversity from moral relativism? Precisely through this realization that we must choose and agree on some core values. We shouldn't ask for tolerance of all political and moral views. Some views seem offensive, or ludicrous, to me, and I will not hesitate to say so if someone asks me. But I am suggesting giving people the benefit of the assumption that they, too, make rational decisions based on their worldview, and that is what soft universalism entails: a respect for a diversity that respects our common humanity.

Study Questions

1. Was American POW Jessica Lynch a courageous soldier? Explain. Do you think John McCain would call her courageous? Define McCain's concept of courage. Do you agree with him?

2. What does Philip Hallie mean by negative and positive commands? Explain. Do you agree with him that positive commands are harder to live up to than negative commands?

3. Evaluate Richard Taylor's view that morality is a matter not of rational principles but of having your heart in the right place. Explore the pros and cons of such a view.

4. Evaluate the respect for the elderly as expressed in the philosophies of Confucius, Mencius, and Lin Yutang. Are such values completely alien to Western culture? Do you think modern Western culture would be improved by incorporating such ideas? Why or why not?

5. Contrast the conclusions of Jane English and Lin Yutang concerning the parent–grown child relationship.

6. Discuss the issue of dating: Is it a favor/debt or a friendship situation? Is there a way of resolving the problem of different expectations for dating partners in the twenty-first century?

Primary Readings and Narratives

The first Primary Reading is an excerpt from John McCain's *Why Courage Matters;* the second is an excerpt from Philip Hallie's *Tales of Good and Evil, Help and Harm.* The third Primary Reading, an excerpt from Lin Yutang's essay "On Growing Old Gracefully," discusses traditional ideas of gratitude within the family; the summaries of the films *Eat Drink Man Woman* and *Grand Canyon* illustrate how this virtue can be practiced in modern life. Prior to these two films we have summaries of two other films illustrating the virtue of courage: an episode from the television series *Band of Brothers,* "Carentan," and the film *Tom Horn,* with an added excerpt from Tom Horn's autobiography.

To illustrate the virtue of compassion, praised as the true universal virtue by Western as well as non-Western thinkers, I have chosen the parable of the Good Samaritan, the Hindu tale "King Yudisthira and the Dog," and the film *Schindler's List.* These stories explore not only when one should show compassion but also whom one should show compassion toward—in other words, who counts as a member of one's moral universe.

Reading

Why Courage Matters: The Way to a Braver Life

JOHN McCAIN

Excerpt, 2004

In this excerpt Senator John McCain suggests that we teach our children about moral courage by teaching them to "do their nearest duty." McCain didn't invent this notion, nor does he claim to. He cites the Unitarian social reformer James Freeman Clarke, who in his turn cited Johann Wolfgang von Goethe, whom you'll remember from Chapter 2. Also, in Chapter 6, Box 6.2, you read the poem by Goethe that calls doing one's nearest duty the key that "unlocks the Heavenly Gate."

First we must answer the question "So what?" What do we need courage for anymore? Not to quiet our anxieties caused by September 11. A sense of proportion and a little righteous anger ought to suffice for that job. So what do we need it for?

We need it because without courage all virtue is fragile: admired, sought, professed, but held cheaply and surrendered without a fight. Courage is what Winston Churchill called "the first of human qualities . . . because it guarantees all the others." That's what we mean by the courage of convictions. Not that our convictions possess an innate courage, but that if we lack the courage to hold them, not just when they accord with the convictions of others but against threatening opposition, in the moment of their testing, they're superficial, vain things that add nothing to our self-respect or our society's respect for the virtues we profess. We can admire virtue and abhor corruption sincerely, but without courage we are corruptible.[. . .]

Most of us see the need for moral courage. Most of us accept social norms: that it's right to be honest, to respect the rights of others, to have compassion. But accepting the appropriateness of these qualities, wanting them, and teaching our children to want them aren't the same as actually possessing them. Accepting their validity isn't moral courage. How honest are we if we tell the truth most of the time and stay silent only when telling the truth might get us fired or earn us a broken nose? We need moral courage to be honest all the time. It's the enforcing virtue, the one that makes all the others possible. And it really isn't different from physical courage, except sometimes in degree and sometimes in the occasions when it encounters risk. If you don't have the courage to keep your virtue when facing unwanted consequences, you're not virtuous.[. . .]

We do not begin life fearing losses suffered by others. We are born selfish and struggle against it all our lives. We are concerned with our self-regard, although we might recognize it is dependent on the approval of our family. Later, the circle of those whose good opinion we require widens to encompass our friends. When does the moment occur when concern for our dignity enlarges to encompass the dignity of others? I think the transformation must begin when our desire to be loved becomes love for the object of our desire. And it progresses when our desire to emulate the behavior of our beloved, to ensure their love, becomes a love for the virtues that constitute their character. In that moment our conscience is born, our capacity to see that what's right for us is right for others. "If a man be brave," wrote the Unitarian social reformer James Freeman Clarke, "let him obey his conscience."

Clarke had borrowed from Goethe his life's motto: "Do your nearest duty." It's not always as easy as it sounds, to see your nearest duty or to want to see it. It's even harder to anticipate when our children will recognize their nearest duty. It's as hard for us to recognize sometimes as it is for them. We may not want to recognize it because we fear for them more than they fear for themselves, and their nearest duty might contain risks to their immediate happiness or worse. We can pay attention to them as they recount their day at school or on the playground, and identify in the routine occurrences of their experience an occasion where a duty would have appeared to a good person, with the choice to risk something or not to do it. But we don't always want to, even if we know that what they risk isn't something of lasting value.

We want our children to be popular almost as much as our children want to be popular. Popularity offers temporary security, enhances confidence, eases the petty disappointments of youth, and can be confused for love. But it's not love. It has no moral quality. It's a condition that might be hard to attain for some but doesn't represent an achievement of lasting significance. Its effects aren't as determinative of the quality of life as you might think when you're young and crave it. But still our children want to be popular, and we want them to be. If they are not, if they have suffered some embarrassment, some reduction in their circumstances in the constant ups and downs of childhood society, we'll try to comfort and encourage them by observing how transitory and ultimately insignificant a thing is popularity. But they'll feel the loss of it just the same, as will we. We hurt for them, and while we might know the hurt will pass, we would not want them to risk it again unnecessarily.

Teaching them virtue in the abstract, without recommending it in a specific situation, is not such a demanding thing. We don't experience empathetic apprehension and pain by urging them to be always honest, always fair, always respectful, the virtues that will alert them of their duty. We don't usually imagine their possession of those virtues provoking much more than the admiration of adults, their teachers, our neighbors and friends. If we're honest, we have in the backs of our minds as we impart these lessons to our children our own pride, our regard for our children as a reflection of our parenting. We want them to be honest and respectful because they and we will be admired for it. It's the allure of popularity that afflicts adults no less than children.

So it can be quite hard to help our children recognize their nearest duty if by so doing they risk social embarrassment or alienation from the peers whose friendship they most desire. But for kids, those are the most common risks of doing your nearest duty. In fact, they are the most common risks we adults face in our settled, mostly tranquil country.

What do you do when, in the course of your children's recitation of the day's events, they mention how bad they felt when their friend, the most popular girl or boy in the crowd, was cruel to a child with few friends, made the child cry from embarrassment and loneliness? We tell them that it's right to feel bad about it, as we should about any cruelty inflicted on the innocent. But don't we hesitate to tell them what they should do beyond empathizing with the victim? Maybe we recommend that they seek out the child and offer their companionship, even though we recognize such an act of decency might risk some opprobrium from the person who caused the injury. But do we recommend our children confront that popular boy or girl whose friendship they enjoy and tell them they think less of them for their unkindness? We might, but usually not without hesitation, dreading the impact it might have on our children's happiness. It's hard to tell children to recognize their nearest duty and to make the choice to accept it, when we know they may suffer for it.

When the pangs of our conscience confront our dread of the consequences for our loved ones who answer the call of theirs, it's our own courage we must summon as much as theirs. We have to believe in the truths we utter to our children when they are the ones who have been hurt, treated unkindly for no reason. We have to believe that there really is no great significance to being popular. We have to believe that if we love and are loved, by our family, by our true friends, and from that love we become good, the loss of popularity will hurt no longer than a bee sting. People who have only popularity to recommend themselves to our memory are soon forgotten. People with virtue, who do their nearest duty as their conscience instructs, are remembered. They are remembered as a source of happiness, not someone who resents another's.

We cannot explain virtue just in the abstract to them and hope that somehow they'll be okay. We have to help them recognize virtue's opposite and to feel an outrage that incites us to action and to accept the consequences. Keep the consequences in perspective, know that they are not the worst things in life, but accept them; accept them and resolve to provoke them again when virtue demands.

Study Questions

1. What does McCain mean by saying "without courage all virtue is fragile"?
2. Explain the concept of moral courage using an example. Is it different from physical courage?
3. What does McCain mean by "doing one's nearest duty"? Do you agree? Why or why not?

Primary Reading

Tales of Good and Evil, Help and Harm

PHILIP HALLIE

Excerpt, 1997.

In this chapter, you read about Philip Hallie's encounter with people in Le Chambon who saved six thousand Jews from Nazi death camps. Here Hallie speculates that doing good is morally superior to refraining from doing evil.

Most of the old ethical theories and commandments present ethics as a friend of life and an enemy of death. And so those theories and commandments praise help and condemn harm. They celebrate the spreading of life with two sorts of ethical rules or ideals: negative and positive. The negative rules are scattered throughout the Bible and other ethical documents, but Moses brought the most memorable ones down to the West from Mount Sinai: Thou shalt not murder, thou shalt not betray. . . . These rules say no to the deliberate extinction of life and joy. On the other hand, positive rules are also spread across many ethical documents. For instance, the Bible enjoins us to be our brother's keeper. These rules say yes to the protection and spreading of life.

The naysaying ethic forbids our doing certain harmful things, and the yeasaying one urges us to help those whose lives are diminished or threatened. To follow the negative ideals you must have clean hands; but to follow the positive ones you can be less hygienic—you can dirty your hands doing something helpful. If you would be your brother's keeper you must go out of your way. The negative ethic is the ethic of decency, of restraint. It is terrible to violate it—to be a murderer or a liar—but obey it and you could be a dead person. A corpse does not kill and does not betray. Moreover, you could obey the no ethic by being silent, and it was the silent majority in Germany and in the world who fed the torturers and the murderers with their silence. The murderers and the torturers drank the silence like wine, and it made them drunk with power.

On the other hand, the yes ethic demands action. You must be alive if you would meet its demands; sometimes you must even put your life on the line. You must go out of your way, sometimes very *far* out of your way. In combat I had to become a killer in order to help stop Germany in its tracks. I had to violate the no ethic in order to help stop the many tortures and murders that Nazi Germany was perpetrating in Central Europe.

. . . My experience had led me to believe that human beings are doomed either to be clean-handed and helpless or murderous and helpful. I knew no one who was both clean and noble.

But in that story about the village of Le Chambon I found people who were both. Here were people in this slaughterhouse of a world who avoided hating and hurting life and at the same time prevented murder. . . .

. . . .

If evil has to do with the twisting and diminution of human life, then the government [Schmäling] ably served was evil. In a mountainous part of France where there were many French guerrilla fighters, he helped keep the French from stabbing his fellow Germans in the back and hindering the cruel march of Nazism. He helped an evil cause ably, and importantly.

But if goodness has to do with the spreading of human life, and the prevention of hatred and cruelty and murder, then he was surely good. Good and evil have much to do with perspectives, points of view. If you want to know whether cruelty is happening and just how painful it is, do not ask the torturer. Do not ask someone like Obergruppenführer [Lieutenant General] Otto Ohlendorff, the head of the special troops assigned to kill unarmed civilians in Eastern Europe. The victimizer does not feel the blows, the victim feels them. Do not ask a sword about wounds; look to the person on whose flesh the sword falls. Victimizers can be blinded by simple insensitivity, by a great cause, by a great hatred, or by a hundred self-serving "reasons." Victims too can be desensitized, but usually they are the best witnesses to their pain. They feel it in their flesh and in their deepest humiliations and horrors.

And if you want to know about goodness, do not ask only the doers of good. They may be doing what they do out of habitual helpfulness or for some abstract cause. They may not realize exactly how they are helping the people they have helped: They may not be looking deeply into the eyes and minds of the beneficiaries of their good deeds.

But usually the beneficiaries of those deeds know. Usually they have this knowledge in their flesh and in their passions. And usually if they do not have this knowledge, goodness is not happening, the joy of living is not being enhanced and widened for them. Do-gooders can in fact do great harm. The points of view of victims and beneficiaries are vital to an understanding of evil and of good.

Study Questions

1. What is the difference between naysaying ethics and yeasaying ethics? Explain. What does this have to do with the story of the people of Le Chambon?

2. What does Hallie mean by saying, "To follow the negative ideals you must have clean hands; but to follow the positive ones you can be less hygienic—you can dirty your hands doing something helpful"? Explain, and evaluate Hallie's viewpoint: Is he right?

3. What is Hallie's final verdict on Schmäling? Was he good or evil? Explain.

Primary Reading

On Growing Old Gracefully

LIN YUTANG

The Importance of Living, 1937.

In this excerpt Lin Yutang talks about the duty of the adult male toward his parents and about the process of aging, which, to him, ought to be a stage characterized by both happiness and wisdom.

Every one realizes . . . that orphanages and old age pensions are poor substitutes for the home. The feeling is that the home alone can provide anything resembling a satisfactory arrangement for the old and the young. But for the young, it is to be taken for granted that not much need be said, since there is natural paternal affection. "Water flows downwards and not upwards," the Chinese always say, and therefore the affection for parents and grandparents is something that stands more in need of being taught by culture. A natural man loves his children, but a cultured man loves his parents. In the end, the teaching of love and respect for old people became a generally accepted principle, and if we are to believe some of the writers, the desire to have the privilege of serving their parents in their old age actually became a consuming passion. The greatest regret a Chinese gentleman could have was the eternally lost opportunity of serving his old parents with medicine and soup on their deathbed, or not to be present when they died. For a high official in his fifties or sixties not to be able to invite his parents to come from their native village and stay with his family at the capital, "seeing them to bed every night and greeting them every morning," was to commit a moral sin of which he should be ashamed and for which he had constantly to offer excuses and explanations to his friends and colleagues. This regret was expressed in two lines by a man who returned too late to his home, when his parents had already died:

> The tree desires repose, but the wind will not stop;
> The son desires to serve, but his parents are already gone.

. . . It seems a linguistic misfortune that hale and hearty old men in America tell people that they are "young," or are told that they are "young" when really what is meant is that they are healthy. To enjoy health in old age, or to be "old and healthy," is the greatest of human luck, but to call it "healthy and young" is but to detract from that glamour and impute imperfection to what is really perfect. After all, there is nothing more beautiful in this world than a healthy wise old man, with "ruddy cheeks and white hair," talking in a soothing voice about life as one who knows it. The Chinese realize this, and have always pictured an old man with "ruddy cheeks and white hair" as *the symbol of ultimate earthly happiness.* Many Americans must have seen Chinese pictures of the God of Longevity, with his high forehead, his ruddy face, his white beard—and how he smiles! The picture is so vivid. He runs his fingers through the thin flowing beard coming down to the breast and gently strokes it in peace and contentment, dignified because he is surrounded with respect, self-assured because no one ever questions his wisdom, and kind because he has seen so much of human sorrow. To persons of great vitality, we also pay the compliment of saying that "the older they grow, the more vigorous they are." . . .

I have no doubt that the fact that the old men of America still insist on being so busy and active can be directly traced to individualism carried to a foolish extent. It is their pride and their love of independence and their shame of being dependent upon their children. But among the many human rights the American people have provided for in their Constitution, they have strangely forgotten about the right to be fed by their children, for it is a right and an obligation growing out of service. How can any one deny that parents who have toiled for their children in their youth, have lost many a good night's sleep when they were ill, have washed their diapers long before they could talk and have spent about a quarter of a century bringing them up and fitting them for life, have the right to be fed by them and loved and respected when they are old? Can one not forget the individual and his pride of self in a general scheme of home life in which men are justly taken care of by their parents and, having in turn taken care of their children, are also justly taken care of by the latter? The Chinese have not got the sense of individual independence because the whole conception of life is based upon mutual help within the home; hence there is no shame attached to the circumstance of one's being served by his children in the sunset of one's life. Rather it is considered good luck to have children who can take care of one. One lives for nothing else in China.

Study Questions

1. Explain the quote: "Water runs downwards and not upwards." What does this have to do with the relationship between parents and children?

2. Evaluate Lin Yutang's view of gratitude toward parents: Is it dependent on parental love? Why or why not? Is that an important issue?

3. When evaluating two opposing viewpoints in this chapter, Lin Yutang's and Jane English's, whose approach do you find more appealing? Explain why.

Narrative

Band of Brothers, Third Episode, "Carentan"

TOM HANKS AND STEVEN SPIELBERG (PRODUCERS)

Television series, 2001. ***Summary***

The highly acclaimed HBO television series *Band of Brothers* is, in effect, a sequel to the film *Saving Private Ryan* (Chapter 5)—not in the sense that we encounter the same characters, but because we move within the same time frame and subject: American soldiers on D-Day, June 6, 1944, and further into the final year of World War II. *Saving Private Ryan* star Tom Hanks and director Steven Spielberg wanted to explore in more depth the war experiences of real American soldiers on D-Day and afterwards. In the series we follow "Easy" (E) Company's campaigns, with each episode's prologue delivered by real survivors from that unit. In this narrative I've chosen to focus on a story that is part of, but by no means all of, the third episode: the story of Private Albert Blithe. I intend for it to illustrate the concept of *physical courage,* but that is an issue you may want to discuss afterwards.

It is the day after D-Day and the soldiers of Easy Company, having parachuted through a storm of anti-aircraft fire, are still scattered around the Normandy countryside. Some soldiers were shot before they hit the ground, others head toward their objectives despite the loss of most of their equipment. As these stragglers from many different units encounter one another, they form impromptu teams to engage the enemy while they try to locate their brethren. Except Private Albert Blithe. When some E Company wanderers come across Blithe, we sense that something is dreadfully wrong with him—not physically, but psychologically. He stares up at the sky, as if he's a young bird fallen from its nest looking back up at the peaceful, safe haven from which it tumbled. His gaze is fixed, he barely hears his buddies' questions, and yet there is nothing wrong with him physically.

After rejoining E Company, and surviving a firefight with German soldiers in the streets of the town of Carentan, and after seeing fellow soldiers drop dead from bullets or have limbs torn from their bodies, Blithe sinks to the ground—not wounded, but struck blind by fear and the horrors he has seen. His superior officer, Lieutenant Winters, assures him that he will be sent back to England and treats him with kindness and understanding, even though there doesn't seem to be anything physically wrong with his eyes. Winters' compassionate words are enough to bring Blithe around; his vision apparently returns, and he rejoins his platoon. It is during a quiet moment with another officer that Blithe confesses what is troubling him. We learn that after he hit the ground on D-Day, he hid in a ditch and fell asleep, rather than seek out his comrades and pursue the enemy. He feels his own fear is greater than his brain can handle. At this crucial time in his universe of terror, the brave Lieutenant Speirs (who later in the series performs acts of unfathomable courage) offers Blithe a piece of advice: You hid, he says, not because of fear, but because you still had hope—hope of survival. That hope will paralyze your actions. The only way to do your job and be a soldier is to tell yourself you're already dead.

Another battle ensues: German tanks roll over American soldiers, gunfire is cutting down the soldiers of Easy, bullets whiz and splat around the screaming Private Blithe. But now something happens to him: He raises his rifle, and as if to shoot back at the madness assaulting him, he finds the trigger and fires (and we sense that this is the first time he has fired his gun in battle) and blindly fires again, and again. At the end of the battle when he spies a German soldier on the skyline, he stands up, and without regard for his own safety, *carefully* aims this time, shoots, and sees his enemy fall. Standing over his vanquished foe, Blithe notices the man he killed is wearing an *Edelweiss*—an alpine flower that denotes its wearer as a great warrior. He takes the Edelweiss and affixes it to his own tunic. From somewhere deep within himself, Private Albert Blithe has found courage in battle. Later when a necessary and dangerous mission calls for volunteers, he is the first to step up. But this act of selfless courage is his undoing: He is shot in the neck; and though he is saved by a medic, we learn at the end of the episode that he never recovered from his wounds, and died in 1948, three years after the end of the war. The last we see of Albert Blithe, he is lying in his hospital bed, eyes staring upward, toward the peaceful sky from which he tumbled.

Study Questions

1. What happened to Blithe? Did he lose his fear? Is loss of fear necessary to find courage?

2. Does Lieutenant Speirs's advice seem wise to you? Why or why not? Does such a piece of advice apply only in battle, or is it relevant in other dangerous situations too? Is there a downside to such a piece of advice? Explain.

3. If you are a veteran, you may want to share your reaction to this story with the class or in an essay: Does it ring true? Why or why not? If you have seen the entire *Band of Brothers* series, you may want to put this episode into the greater context of the series.

4. Imagine what John McCain might say to the story of Blithe. Was Blithe courageous? Why or why not?

Narrative

The Life of Tom Horn

TOM HORN

Autobiography, 1903. Summary and excerpt.

Tom Horn

THOMAS McGUANE AND BUD SHRAKE (SCREENWRITERS)
WILLIAM WIARD (DIRECTOR)

Film, 1980. Summary.

This example of moral as well as physical courage will be considered controversial by some historians because it involves a man who was executed for murder: the American army scout, cattle detective, author, and frontier legend Tom Horn. It rests on the theory, suggested by several historians, that he was "framed," and that the state of Wyoming executed an innocent man. While in jail, awaiting the appeal of his death sentence, Horn writes the story of his life. It is presented the way he would want to be remembered, probably not 100 percent accurately, but written with a sense of professional duty as well as a great deal of humor. Horn's life seems to fall into two phases, and historians have had a hard time reconciling them, because in his early forties he was a convicted child killer; but in his twenties Horn distinguished himself as a very courageous and resourceful man. He was an on-again, off-again scout and interpreter for the U.S. Army in Arizona during the Apache wars of the 1880s. He had lived in Mexico and among the Apaches and spoke German, Spanish, and several Apache dialects aside from his native English; and in his autobiography he displays an understanding of both Mexican and Apache customs and outlook that is light-years ahead of his "monocultural" employers. Chief Geronimo saw him as a friend of the Apaches. Even so, his loyalties were with his employers, in particular his boss, the famed scout Al Sieber. On one occasion in particular, he stood his ground in battle with the Apaches, and through his steadfast example he saved both Sieber and the troops who would otherwise have been overwhelmed by the Indians. Horn was not known to be a modest man, yet he describes the following situation in his autobiography with modesty as often characteristic of physically courageous people:

I received a long complimentary letter from the Department Commander, General Wilcox, along in the fall or early winter, telling me I was an excellent man, and that he had taken proper steps to have a medal presented to me for bringing old Sergeant Murray out of the fight after he was wounded . . . describing how I, under heavy fire, took one man and gained a high commanding point over the troops and kept them from getting demoralized and annihilated, by yelling to the soldiers to keep cool and to send up another man or two. . . That was the first time I learned I had done anything very great. . . .

. . . Of course I brought old Sergeant Murray out of the fight, but I had taken him in also, and I could not very well leave the old man alone. . . . I was afraid that Sieber would get killed, for I could have run away myself easily enough, but Sieber kept with the soldiers and he and some men were carrying Hentig, who was dead. I could not run away and leave Sieber. He would not leave the soldiers, and when I saw that, I knew I would have to fight the Indians away till they all got out. . . I never thought of saving the rest of the command.

. . . So the whole letter, while highly complimentary, was simply based on some account of these affairs as reported to him by some army officer, and in reality there was nothing extraordinary about it.

By the way, that was the last I ever heard of that medal.

Eventually, the army had no further use for Tom's services, and he took on other careers, such as serving as an agent for the Pinkerton detective agency. Eventually he drifted north into Wyoming. At this point I'll let the summary of the film *Tom Horn* tell the rest of the story. Although the film isn't completely historically accurate, it captures the spirit and the essence of the last years of Tom Horn's life:

A scruffy trail-worn cowboy rides into a frontier town in Wyoming, and immediately gets into a saloon fight because he'd rather drink to Geronimo—there's a man he respects—than to a bragging prizefighter. The cowboy, who introduces himself as Tom Horn, is outnumbered, and takes a terrible beating—but his presence is noted in town, and he is approached by a local rancher, John Coble. Would Tom be interested in a job? It would be completely free rein, no questions asked, as long as he gets results. The ranchers are plagued by rustlers, stealing cattle and changing their brands (which, in the Old West, was a hanging offense). So they would like Tom to stop the rustlers—cold. That means if they can't get scared off the land, Tom is to eliminate them. Coble emphasizes, though, that this conversation has to be confidential. "We've never had this talk," he says, because Tom's job will take him outside the boundaries of due process, something the "civilized" ranchers wouldn't want to have associated with their good name. Tom accepts the job, and agrees to keep silent about his employers; and to a man steeped in the Old West's code of honor, his word is his bond. In Tom's world of the frontier, where peace officers are few and far between, it is not unusual even for people with good intentions to take the law into their own hands to protect themselves and their property. Tom is introduced to the other ranchers at an outdoor picnic. Here he encounters the New West, the West of the future where wealthy ranchers have live lobsters brought in from Maine (Tom looks at the strange sea creatures and declares, "I never ate a bug that big before!"), and civilization and the new century are just around the corner. Many people are eager to put the old violent days of the West behind them. One person who professes her love for the Old West and its ways is the local schoolteacher, Glendolene Kimmell, and there is a sense of immediate sympathy and attraction between the two.

Tom goes about his business as a cattle detective, tracking rustlers, scaring them off if he can, and otherwise doing what he believes he is hired to do—killing them—on the direct orders of the Cattlemen's Association: It's better to avoid bringing the rustlers to trial. And he is a very efficient employee. Coble has already assured him that he and the Association are behind him 100 percent (to which Tom says, "I'll have to take your word for it" and Coble answers, "You've got it"). Ironically, as he succeeds in his job, and the ranchers see fewer cattle thieves, his presence is becoming an embarrassment to the men who hired him; his ways are not of the new century, regardless of the fact that he is now making their modern way of life possible. And Tom knows way too much about who hired him. In short, it would be better if Tom were gone. One of the men of the new century, Marshall Joe Belle, has political ambitions, and he and the Association see eye to eye. And a conspiracy is formed to get rid of Tom.

Tom has a personal problem: He drinks, periodically, and when he drinks, he brags. Shortly after Jimmy Nolt (in real life: Willie Nickell), the fourteen-year old son of a sheep farmer, is murdered by a sniper, Tom finds himself in a saloon, getting drunk. He doesn't find it suspicious that Belle wants to talk with him in private and asks him questions about the Nolt murder. At some point Tom declares that if he had shot the boy, it would have been "the best shot and the dirtiest trick I'd ever done." But when he is arrested and charged with the murder, he realizes that it was a setup: Hiding behind the door was a stenographer who took down his "confession." In the transcript it says, "It was the best shot and the dirtiest trick I've ever done."

And so the system of injustice rolls on. John Coble hires a lawyer for Tom, but for some reason, his defense is uninspired The prosecution's theory is allowed to stand unchallenged, paving the way for Tom's conviction as well as Marshall Belle's career in politics; and Tom offers nothing in his own defense. Coble has already pleaded with him not to speak up—and he doesn't. Never giving up the names of those who hired him, including Coble, he just sits in the makeshift outdoor courtroom tent and stares at the mountains that are lost to him forever, while the prosecution paints him as a murderer whose blood lust has driven him to kill poor squatters all over the territory. So Tom is found guilty of murder, and the sentence is death by hanging. On November 20, 1903, he is walked to the scaffold and hanged according to a new, modern mechanical method involving water running into a trough, lifting a lever and springing the trap door. And so, just as they avoided sullying their hands in eliminating the rustlers, by using Tom, the men of the New West have now eliminated an embarrassing reminder of their own violent past.

In this film, Tom may have met his unjust end without flinching, but that is not why I chose his character as an example of courage. It is because of what he knew and didn't say when it might have saved his life. What about the ranchers who hired him? They faded away, never acknowledging that he was on their payroll or following their instructions. John Coble himself was present at the trial but offered no support for Tom other than hiring a useless lawyer. So it appears that out of loyalty toward Coble, and a sense of professional honor, Tom never spoke up for himself or gave up the names of his employers. Perhaps we can even apply the words of John McCain in *Why Courage Matters:* "Enduring an inescapable fate stoically is admirable, but it is not the same thing as

Was Tom Horn a cold-blooded child killer or a scapegoat who met his fate with moral courage? The film *Tom Horn* presents Tom as a victim of financial and political interests in the new twentieth century, staying true to nineteenth-century values of honor and friendship. Here Tom (Steve McQueen) is being prepared for his execution. According to witnesses, the real Tom Horn kept his composure throughout the process and even displayed a dry sense of humor.

courage. Suffering stoically a terrible fate that you could have escaped, but that your convictions, your sense of honor, compelled you to accept, is."

Is this the true story of the real Tom Horn? Some think it is pure fiction and that Horn was simply a bloodthirsty killer, but an increasing number of researchers believe that Tom was indeed a wronged man, sacrificed by the interests of the Cattlemen's Association. In real life Tom sat in his jail cell for one whole year, waiting for the Supreme Court to look at his appeal, which was eventually denied. He wrote numerous letters to John Coble and to lawyers, and judges, pointing out errors in the trial, to no avail—and he never did mention his employers. Glendolene wrote an eloquent tribute to Tom after his death, where she describes him as being crushed between two civilizations, the old and the new. And Coble? After Tom's death he published Tom's book, with a moving preface. But by then it was too late to do something for Tom, and a few years later, Coble, now destitute and ill, and perhaps haunted by thoughts of things undone, shot himself to death in the back room of a local saloon.

Study Questions

1. Was Tom Horn brave in keeping silent about his employers? or was he simply foolish? How far would you go to protect the identity of someone you considered a friend? Or an employer?

2. What did Glendolene mean by saying that Tom was crushed between two civilizations, the old and the new?

3. The film presents Tom as an innocent man, framed and sacrificed by others' interests and ambitions. Would it make a difference in terms of evaluating his courage if he really was guilty of killing the boy? What might Phillipa Foot (Chapter 10) say? What might Aristotle say?

4. Would you say the quote by McCain fits Tom? Why or why not? Can you think of other examples of someone in history or in fiction who—because of his or her convictions—accepts a terrible fate he or she could have escaped?

Narrative

The Parable of the Good Samaritan

From the New Testament, Luke 10:30–37, King James Version.

For readers with a Christian background, the story of the Good Samaritan is the archetypal story of compassion. The Good Samaritan is one of the parables of Jesus of Nazareth, and it is intended to be taken as an allegory.

> A certain man went down from Jerusalem to Jericho, and fell among thieves, which stripped him of his raiment, and wounded him, and departed, leaving him half dead. And by chance there came down a certain priest that way: and when he saw him, he passed by on the other side. And likewise a Levite, when he was at the place, came and looked on him, and passed by on the other side. But a certain Samaritan, as he journeyed, came where he was: and when he saw him, he had compassion on him. And went to him, and bound up his wounds, pouring in oil and wine, and set him on his own beast, and brought him to an inn, and took care of him. And on the morrow when he departed, he took out two pence, and gave them to the host, and said unto him, Take care of him; and whatsoever thou spendest more, when I come again, I will repay thee. Which now of these three, thinkest thou, was neighbor unto him that fell among the thieves? And he said, He that shewed mercy on him. Then said Jesus unto him, Go and do thou likewise.

To the modern reader, the story illustrates that the Good Samaritan is the one who is truly good because he acts with compassion while others, who are supposed to know the

Arrival of the Good Samaritan at the Inn (1866) by Gustave Doré. The Good Samaritan has rescued a victim of a highway assault and here is taking him to be cared for. The Samaritan pays for the victim's keep and treatment out of his own pocket and lets the innkeeper know that if the costs add up to more, he will pay for that, too.

difference between right and wrong, do nothing. For contemporaries of Jesus, however, the story may have meant something slightly different. A Samaritan was, for the Jews of Israel, a social outcast; the Samaritans were a population politically and ethnically distinct from the Hebrews, and people from Samaria were not held in high regard. The Jews, then, would have seen Jesus' purpose in telling the story as not so much instructing us to be compassionate as instructing us to recognize who our *neighbor* is (our neighbor is any person who acts with compassion toward us). The lesson is, "Even" a Samaritan can be our neighbor. But of course the overriding lesson is to "go and do likewise."

Study Questions

1. Explain what Jesus seems to mean by using the term *neighbor*. Is this story meaningful for Christians only, or might it also appeal to people of other faiths, agnostics, and atheists? Explain.

2. What might an ethical egoist say about this story? Why? Would you have a critical response, or would you agree? Why?

3. A university study conducted years ago tested people's willingness to stop and help someone in distress. A group of students were told to go to a lecture about the parable of the Good Samaritan, and on their way they encountered a man who appeared to be in severe pain. Apparently the topic of the lecture didn't make any difference: Many of those students who thought they were early for the talk stopped to help, whereas few of the students who thought they were late stopped. Do you think it would make a difference to you, if you found yourself having to choose between helping or hurrying on, whether you remembered this story?

Narrative

King Yudisthira and the Dog

Summary. A story from the epic Indian poem the Mahabharata, fourth century C.E.

When King Yudisthira, a son of the god Dharma, was an old man and felt that he had served his people well, he decided to withdraw from the world. With his four brothers and his beloved wife Drapaudi he set out on foot toward the high Mount Meru to seek entrance to the gates of the City of Heaven. Soon they discovered that a dog was following them.

The mountain was steep, and the road was very long; on the way the old king saw one brother die, and then another, and another, until he had lost all four brothers. In the end even Drapaudi lost her life. But the dog was still with him, following him quietly and faithfully all the way to the gates of heaven.

There they were met by the god Indra, who welcomed the old king and was about to let him in; but the king had a question first: What about his wife and his brothers? Indra assured him that they had already arrived in heaven and were waiting for him. But the king's next request was more problematic, because he insisted that the faithful dog deserved to be let in the gates with him. Indra was taken aback and refused to consider the possibility of granting a dog immortality, especially since dogs were considered unclean. He asked the king if it could really be that he would be willing to give up his immortal bliss for the sake of an animal? Yes, said Yudisthira, because he had always lived according to three vows: never to desert someone who is frightened and who seeks his protection, or who is destitute, or who is too weak to protect his own life. "And now there is a fourth," said Yudisthira: never to abandon someone who shows devotion to you. Never abandon a friend. And he bent down to pat the dog, but suddenly, right before his eyes, the dog was changing, and growing, and taking on the shape of a god. And there, before him, stood Dharma in all his splendor, the god of Justice and Righteousness—and of course, Yudisthira's own father?

Indra smiled and said to Yudisthira, "You have shown compassion for another creature instead of choosing to spend eternity with the gods. Compassion for the humble is the highest virtue of all, and you shall be honored in heaven." And so the king entered heaven accompanied by Dharma and was met by his wife and his four brothers.

Study Questions

1. Evaluate the moral lesson: Is it a virtue to give up a lifelong goal or benefit for the sake of another? Why or why not?

2. It has sometimes been speculated by various writers that "all dogs go to heaven": that if there is such a thing as heaven, then pets, in their innocence and loyalty, deserve to get there more than most people do. Mark Twain, who was a cat lover, once said he believed that the pets we have loved and lost are patiently waiting for us at the gates of heaven. How do you feel about the idea that *if* there is another life beyond this one, then pets belong there too? Explain.

3. Do you think Yudisthira might have preferred to keep the dog rather than have him transformed into the god Dharma even if it was his father?

4. A *Twilight Zone* episode from 1962, "The Hunt," tells the same story, but with a twist. Old Mr. Simpson and his dog find themselves dead and arrive at a gate; the gatekeeper says that it is the entrance to heaven and that the old man is welcome, but dogs aren't allowed. The dog growls, and Simpson in anger turns his back on heaven, taking his dog down the road again—but farther down the road he meets an angel sent to find him and bring him and his dog to the real heaven. The gate he had just visited was actually the entrance to hell. Simpson asks the angel why hell doesn't allow any dogs, and the angel answers, "You see, Mr. Simpson, a man, well he'll walk right into hell with both eyes open—but even the devil can't fool a dog!"

   Compare the two versions: Are there significant differences? Which one appeals more to you? Why?

Narrative

Schindler's List

STEVEN ZAILLIAN (SCREENWRITER)

STEVEN SPIELBERG (DIRECTOR)

Film, 1993. Based on the 1982 book by Thomas Keneally.

All the story summaries in this book come with a strong suggestion: that you experience the stories in their original version because the summaries are only intended to highlight certain moral problems and can in no way do justice to the experience of reading the book or watching the film. This is especially true of the award-sweeping *Schindler's List,* based on a true story from Poland in World War II. The historical fact of the Holocaust is (or ought to be) familiar to everyone, but even if we think we know what happened, the experience of *hearing and seeing* people suffering (even in a Hollywood version) is more powerful than any words can convey. For the sake of the moral of the story I have to tell you the entire story line, but I have of course omitted a great many details.

The year is 1939; the place is Kraków, Poland; the Nazi army has by now taken Poland, and Polish Jews are being moved to the 600-year-old Kraków ghetto. Deprived of the right to make a living, the Jews are trying to adjust. A German Gentile, Oskar Schindler, approaches the *Judenrat* (the Jewish Council) with a suggestion: Their investments and his business sense could make the start of a new factory. But Itzhak Stern, a member of the council, turns him down. We see Schindler getting cozy with top Nazi officials, showing himself to be a high roller and making friends, all for the sake of future business connections.

Two years later the overcrowded ghetto becomes a prison for Kraków's Jewish population; everybody of Jewish heritage is moved into the old city, and Schindler profits from the situation: He takes over the beautiful apartment belonging to a Jewish businessman. And now he again approaches the council with his suggestion; this time they are desperate for food and other goods unavailable to them, so investors agree to help Schindler set up his factory, making enamelware crockery. Stern becomes his production manager and immediately sees a way to help people in the ghetto by hiring them as skilled workers for the factory, people who have never done manual labor before—a rabbi, a musician, a history professor—because if they can't prove that they can contribute to the war effort, they will be deported.

Schindler sends for his wife from his hometown and proudly tells her that he is about to get rich—that all his previous failed business ventures lacked an essential ingredient that is now present: war. He is selling his crockery to his Nazi friends and making money hand over fist.

When Stern leaves his identification papers behind and is stopped without them, the Nazis are quick to put him on a train to Auschwitz. As the train pulls out, Schindler turns up and saves him by threatening the young Nazi officers with an end to their careers; Stern is grateful, but it is clear that Schindler didn't do it for Stern's sake. He says, "What if I'd got here five minutes later? Then where would I be?"

Philip Hallie talks about the *institutionalized cruelty* of Nazi Germany and of the antidote of hospitality provided by the people of Le Chambon; another example of an antidote against the Nazi horrors is the true story of Oskar Schindler, told by Steven Spielberg in his 1993 film *Schindler's List* (Universal Pictures). By hiring Jews as workers in his factory, Schindler was able to cheat the Nazi extermination machinery of more than 1,100 men, women, and children. Here Schindler (Liam Neeson) argues desperately with an SS guard at the Auschwitz death camp that the children of his workers are also needed at his factory because their small hands can polish the inside of artillery shell casings.

For the others being sent to Auschwitz there is no salvation; we see their suitcases opened by Nazi officials, the contents placed on shelves, their jewelry collected—and their gold teeth as well.

A new commander arrives at Plazov, the nearby labor camp: He is Amon Goeth, a ruthless and barely sane man who delights in shooting people at the slightest provocation or merely as target practice. On his order the Nazi storm troopers commence the liquidation of the Kraków ghetto: Everybody is rounded up and either shot on the spot or moved to Plazov. From a hilltop overlooking the ghetto, Schindler watches the horror of the mass murder. From afar he notices a little girl in a red coat (*Schindler's List* is a black-and-white film; the girl's coat is one of only a few items of color); we see his reaction when he understands that the girl will not survive.

Back in his factory, Schindler is all alone; the workers are gone. So he goes to Goeth to get his workers back, complaining that he is losing money. Goeth demands a cut of his profit and lets him have his workers back, all except Stern.

Up until now profit may have been the true drive behind Schindler's actions, but when he is approached by a young woman begging him to take in her parents as "workers" so they won't be killed, he agrees (after first refusing). We begin to see a change in him; he is beginning to see his Jewish workers, the "Schindler Jews," as people. Goeth is in no such frame of mind, though—he tells his maid, one of the young Jewish women, that he likes her, even if "she is not a person in the strictest sense of the word." When he is tempted to kiss the frightened young woman, he accuses her of almost seducing him and cuts her up with a piece of broken glass.

More prisoners are arriving at Plazov, and Goeth wants to make room for them; his method is to sort the healthy from the unhealthy, and so he forces the entire camp to take off their clothes and run around in a circle, naked, under the eyes of the camp doctors. Anyone looking less than completely fit is taken aside and shot. When the survivors are allowed to dress, they are elated—but their joy is short-lived: In the meantime, the Nazis have rounded up the children and are now taking them away to be exterminated. A few children manage to hide, some of them inside the latrine.

After a period of more heartbreaks, Stern tells Schindler that he has been put in charge of the final "evacuation" to Auschwitz, with himself on the last train. Schindler is resigned to going home with his money and calling it quits, but as he is packing up all his money, he thinks of a use for it: He approaches Goeth and asks if he can *buy* his workers' lives, to have them transferred to another camp in order to set up a new factory. Goeth drives a hard bargain and agrees; now Schindler and Stern together must make a list of names of people to be saved: as many names as Schindler can afford. In the end, the list includes more than 1,100 Jews, and Stern tells him, "The list is life"—all around it is death. So the Schindler Jews are taken to the safe haven of Schindler's hometown in Czechoslovakia; but only the men and boys arrive. The train with the women and the girls has been sidetracked, through a clerical error—to Auschwitz.

By bribing the overseer at Auschwitz with diamonds, Schindler buys his women workers back but has to put up a fight to save their daughters. Finally the families are reunited, and for the remaining seven months of the war the factory produces useless artillery shells, for Schindler does not want to contribute to the killing. By the time the war ends, Schindler has no more money; he has spent his entire fortune saving 1,100 people. Saying good-bye to his Jewish friends (he is now considered a war criminal and must flee), he breaks down, thinking that he might have saved just a few more people if he had sold his car and his jewelry, but Stern and the others give him a letter, signed by everyone, and a gold ring with a quote from the Talmud: "Whoever saves one life saves an entire world." They collected the gold by extracting their own gold teeth and melting them down.

Study Questions

1. Explain the quote from the Talmud: "Whoever saves one life saves an entire world."

2. How does the compassion shown by Schindler compare with the virtue of hospitality shown by the people of Le Chambon (see the discussion of Philip Hallie)?

3. Does the fact that Schindler originally hired the Kraków Jews for profit detract from his efforts to save them? Why or why not? (Here you might use Berger's criteria for gratitude.)

4. Compare the scene in which the prisoners are forced to run naked in front of the Nazi officers with Hallie's theory of institutionalized cruelty.

Narrative

Eat Drink Man Woman

HUI-LING WANG, JAMES SCHAMUS,
AND ANG LEE (SCREENWRITERS)
ANG LEE (DIRECTOR)

Film, 1994.

I chose this film for its conflict between the old Confucian virtue of gratitude toward parents (in particular the virtue of children's sacrificing their happiness for the sake of their parents) and the virtue of seeking and creating happiness wherever you can find it.

The master chef Chu is preparing one of his fantastic meals—not at the restaurant where he has been working for many years, but at his home in Taipei, Taiwan. Everything is prepared with serious dedication, even though Chu has a problem: He has lost his sense of taste. His three grown daughters, whom he is cooking for, don't hesitate to point out if there is something amiss with the recipes; quarreling is not unusual in their home, and before she died, their mother used to quarrel with their father herself. It seems that the only way Chu knows how to express himself is through cooking, and it is through his efforts with his meals that we realize how much he cares for his daughters, especially the middle daughter, Jia-Chien.

Jia-Chien is a modern young woman: She is an airline executive, she has a once-in-a-while lover, and she is preparing to move out of her childhood home. We learn that she grew up in her father's restaurant kitchen and learned all the elaborate recipes, but her father wanted her to get a "real job," so she had to give up her dreams of becoming a great chef. The youngest daughter, Jia-Ning, is working as a waitress and trying very hard to steal her best friend's boyfriend away from her. The oldest daughter, Jia-Jen, a math teacher, has had a sad life: Nine years ago her boyfriend, a young student of chemistry, broke up with her and went to the United States, and she has never been able to get over it. Now she has converted to Christianity and believes she must resign herself to staying single in order to take care of their father.

Chu may love his daughters, but he does not understand them. After work at the restaurant (where he salvaged a botched dinner for important customers), he and his old friend, Old Wen, get drunk together and talk about life. Wen says, "Eat, drink, man, woman—food and sex—basic desires—can't avoid them!" Chu complains, "All my life, every day, all I do. . . . is that all there is? Is this the good life?" And Old Wen replies, "We're still alive, still cooking, thank God."

Dinners in the Chu household are the times when family announcements are made, and Jia-Chien announces that she is moving out, thus stealing her father's thunder, for he had an announcement to make too, but we don't get to hear it. And it looks as if things are going well for her: She is about to be promoted to a position in Amsterdam. A new colleague is introduced to her at work, a young man who has lived for years in the United States, and she finds herself attracted to him but is horrified when she realizes that he is her sister's former boyfriend, the man who broke her heart. She is even

The film *Eat Drink Man Woman* (Central Motion Pictures, 1994) explores updated versions of Confucian values in a modern Taiwanese family: When the oldest daughter believes that her father needs her, she gives up any idea of marriage (at least for a while); when, later, the middle daughter suspects that her father is ill, she gives up a career opportunity to stay with him. Here the middle daughter (Chien-Lien Wu) and her father (Sihung Lung) share a moment of understanding over an excellent dinner for two.

more horrified when she confronts him with the old story and learns that he has no idea who her sister is—the girl he used to date was her sister's best friend, Jin-Rong. So now Jia-Chien knows that her sister made the whole thing up.

Jin-Rong herself married someone else and is now getting divorced from him. They live close by Mr. Chu's house. She has a little daughter, Shan-Shan, and Mr. Chu finds himself becoming protective toward the little girl; he watches her get on the bus to school, a tiny child disappearing among pushy big adults, and we can tell that his heart goes out to her. Since her mother is not a good cook, he begins to prepare a lunchbox with elaborate little dishes for Shan-Shan; he takes Jin-Rong's food home and eats it (it is not very good). It soon turns out that Jin-Rong has found out, but she is not angry—she is very grateful that Mr. Chu cares about her little girl. Changes are happening in Jin-Rong's household, too: Her mother is returning after having lived in the United States for many years. Mrs. Liang smokes, gossips, and loves to visit with Mr. Chu, and Chu's daughters soon believe they know what is happening: perhaps a permanent arrangement between their father and Mrs. Liang?

Old Wen collapses at work and is taken to the hospital, where Jia-Chien visits with him. Here he tells her that her father represses his emotions but that he loves her and is very proud of her. The next time she goes to visit Old Wen he has left for home, but further down the hallway she sees a familiar figure: her father, walking into the cardiovascular unit. At this moment her attitude toward her father changes: She believes he is keeping up a brave front, but that his days are numbered, and when Old Wen dies on his first day back at work the reality of her father's age and the brevity of life overwhelms her. So when her promotion to the Amsterdam office comes through, she turns it down, to the surprise of her coworkers: She thinks her father needs her more.

Family developments continue, all announced during dinners: Jia-Ning has become pregnant and moves in with her new boyfriend; Jia-Jen falls in love with the new coach at her school and marries him in secret; and that leaves Chu and Jia-Chien alone in the big old house, except for visits from Mrs. Liang, her daughter, Jin-Rong, and little Shan-Shan. But now Chu has an announcement to make, and he prepares a most elaborate dinner for everybody: the daughters and the two new husbands, Jin-Rong, her daughter and her mother. During the dinner he toasts his daughters, one toast after another, because he is trying to gather enough courage to say what must be said. The daughters, as well as Mrs. Liang, believe they know what he is going to say. Most believe that he will announce his engagement to Mrs. Liang; Jia-Chien believes the bad news about his health will finally come out. But Chu has something else on his mind. Proudly (and a bit drunkenly) he proclaims that he has sold the old house, shows Mrs. Liang his new health certificate to prove he is in great shape, and asks, formally, for her daughter's, Jin-Rong's, hand in marriage. Jin-Rong, the same age as his oldest daughter, Jia-Jen, sits modestly by his side, facing the incredulous family, and Mrs. Liang falls off her chair in a fainting spell. That was not the news she had expected. The evening ends in general emotional upheaval.

A few months later: Jin-Rong is pregnant and happy in their new house. Chu comes to visit the almost-empty old house for the last time and have a last meal there—but this time it is Jia-Chien who is cooking: Using her skills to prepare a meal the way her father has taught her, she proves that she really is a marvelous cook. And as they sit there, the two of them together, her father gently criticizing her food, he realizes that he can *taste* her soup—that his palate is functioning again and that for the first time in years he can taste food.

Study Questions

1. How does the filmmaker use food as a symbol in this film? (You might compare it with *Like Water for Chocolate* (Chapter 12), which also uses food symbolically.)

2. Describe the Confucian traditions in the film, and contrast them with the modern elements.

3. If you believed that your aging mother or father needed you, would you give up a promotion/transfer you had wanted in order to become a caregiver and stay at home for the remainder of your parent's life? Why or why not? How would Lin Yutang respond? How would Jane English respond?

Narrative

Pay It Forward

LESLIE DIXON (SCREENWRITER)
MIMI LEDER (DIRECTOR)

Film, 2000. Based on the book by Catherine Ryan Hyde. Summary.

This film can be viewed within several contexts in this book: One context is the virtue of gratitude, which is why it is placed in this chapter, but you could equally well view it in light of Chapter 4 and the discussions about selfishness and altruism.

On a rainy winter night, there is a hostage situation in Los Angeles. A young journalist's car is totaled by the fleeing hostage taker's SUV, and he is now stranded in the rain, at night, in L.A. Out of the mist comes a man who hands the journalist the keys to his Jaguar. It's his to keep, says the stranger—"Call it generosity among strangers."

Cut to Las Vegas, four months earlier. It is the first day of school, and social studies teacher Eugene Simonet is giving his usual class introduction to the seventh grade. Simonet's face is disfigured after what looks like a burn accident, and he obviously has a chip on his shoulder. He asks the kids, Are they interested in the world? One of these days the world will be in their face, he says, and they may want to try to change it. So he gives them an assignment—the same he gives every year: "Think of an idea to change the world, and put it into action." An eleven-year old boy, Trevor, takes the idea to heart. On his way home he sees a homeless young man trying to eat garbage. The next thing we see is Trevor having dinner at home—cereal and milk—with the homeless man. Trevor's project is beginning to take shape, the *Pay it Forward* project. But his mother Arlene, who is a waitress in a casino, comes across the homeless guy Jerry in her garage and is not enthusiastic; frightened and skeptical, she questions Trevor, who tells her it is an assignment. She goes to his school to confront Simonet. The meeting doesn't go off well: Simonet is standoffish, and she resents him for being condescending. Arlene, divorced from Trevor's father, is an alcoholic. She comes home one day to find the homeless man, Jerry, in her garage—repairing her truck so she can sell it. He is already paying Trevor's good deed forward: Trevor gave him money so he could get cleaned up, and he found a job—and he'll try to kick his drug habit. Now Trevor explains his project in class: If we each help three strangers, and they in turn have to help three other strangers, then we will see a very rapid change for the better in the world. But each act of helping has to be

From the film *Pay It Forward:* For a short while, Trevor (Haley Joel Osment) is happy: He has brought his mother Arlene (Helen Hunt) and his favorite teacher Eugene Simonet (Kevin Spacey) together, and it looks as if things might be working out. But Trevor's violent, alcoholic father Ricky returns, and Arlene decides to give him another chance.

a major, difficult thing, or otherwise it doesn't count. Simonet is impressed—it is the first new idea he has heard in his years of teaching.

Trevor experiences two setbacks—Jerry has a relapse back into drugs, so now Trevor has to find someone else to help. He focuses on a small school friend who suffers from asthma and who is regularly tortured by two older boys; but when push comes to shove, Trevor can't make himself intervene. And the third person he has decided to help? Simonet. He wants him to date his mother, both for the teacher's sake and for Arlene's—because Arlene is an alcoholic and needs someone stable in her life, and if someone is there, then Trevor's father might not try to come back. We hear that Trevor's father Ricky has beaten up Arlene on several occasions, and we understand that Trevor is afraid the old pattern is going to repeat itself, in a never-ending circle of alcohol and violence. So now Trevor plays matchmaker for his mom and Eugene Simonet. Slowly the two warm up to each other and begin to understand that they are not trapped in roles where they are unloved and unwanted. For a short while they seem like a happy couple, and all three act like a content, normal nuclear family—until the return of Ricky puts an end to their happiness. Arlene decides to give Ricky another chance, and when Eugene blames her for exposing Trevor to danger, we finally hear the story behind Eugene's disfigurement: His own father was a violent alcoholic, and when Eugene was 16, he confronted his father—who beat him senseless, dragged him into the garage, doused him with gasoline, and set fire to him.

In the meantime, we hear more about the journalist who was given a Jaguar by a complete stranger. Intrigued, he has tracked down the owner and made him reveal why he gave away his car. He was "paying it forward"—after an immense gesture extended to him by a very unlikely character: He was in the emergency room with his daughter, who was suffering from an asthma attack, and the nurse wasn't paying attention to her. An injured man, a young black gangbanger, took charge and forced the nurse to help the gasping girl, firing his gun to make a point. The gunman went to prison, but the girl's life was saved. And the gunman told the father that he must pay the favor forward, to three people—so the journalist stuck in the rain was one.

The journalist seeks out the young black man in prison and gets him to tell his story by arranging an early parole date. The young man explains that he was running away from rival gang members in Vegas when an old white lady gave him a ride and saved his life—she was a bag lady, living out of her car, and she told him to pay it forward. So now the journalist must look for the old lady in Las Vegas, because he recognizes a good story when he sees one.

We meet Jerry one more time; he has left Las Vegas and gone up to the Pacific Northwest, without being able to kick his drug habit. Absorbed in his own misery, he crosses a bridge—and sees a woman about to jump to her death. He manages to talk her down and realizes that he is now paying it forward—Trevor's project is indeed spreading.

The journalist manages to find the bag lady, who tells her story. Her daughter had sought her out in one of the places where she'd normally drink herself into a stupor and spend the night, simply to tell her that she had forgiven her—for terrible things done to her when she was a child, by her mother's boyfriends while her mother was drunk. She will even let her mother visit with her son again, if the old lady can stay sober; and she has decided to forgive her mother because of an invention her son has made, which he calls "pay it forward." The daughter is, of course, Arlene, Trevor's mother. So now the journalist finally meets Trevor, the source of the project that is spreading like wildfire—to Los Angeles, San Francisco, Phoenix, and the Northwest. On his twelfth birthday he is interviewed by the journalist at the school. Trevor is not impressed with himself; he doesn't think he has succeeded, but he does tell the journalist that you have to try to make changes—that some people are so afraid of change, even for the better, that they just give up. Hearing these words, Eugene realizes that he is one of those people, and he and Arlene fall into each other's arms. And that night, Trevor's interview will be broadcast on national TV, and everyone will hear about the Pay It Forward project.

After the interview Trevor is about to leave the school and sees his friend, the asthmatic boy, again being attacked by the two older boys. Trevor wants so badly to make the world better, to make a difference—will he be able to help his friend this time? Will he be able to enjoy the changes he has indeed set in motion and have a real family life with his mother and Eugene? I will not reveal the ending of the film—you will have to watch it yourself.

Study Questions

1. What might Fred Berger say about showing one's gratitude by paying it forward? Would that be an appropriate reaction? Why or why not? What would Jane English say?

2. Could you undertake a project such as "Pay it Forward"? Whom would you choose to help? Remember the help must be big, and difficult for you, if it is to count. And what if someone chooses to do something special for you, as a "Pay it Forward" project—would you feel obliged to continue the project?

3. If you do a big favor for someone, would you be content with him or her paying it forward, or would you like a show of gratitude that is directed toward yourself?

4. From a realistic (some would say, cynical) point of view, is this a wise behavior model to follow? In 2003 a young girl was abducted and killed by a homeless man the family had invited home for dinner, and the same year Elizabeth Smart was abducted by a street person her father had hired as a handyman to help him out—but Elizabeth was rescued and returned safely nine months later. Is it advisable to do favors for strangers, as Trevor does? Are we being too cynical if we think of worst-case scenarios?

5. Compare this story of helping strangers to *How to Be Good* in Chapter 1. Which story do you find most compelling? Why?

Narrative

Grand Canyon

LAWRENCE KASDAN AND MEG KASDAN (SCREENWRITERS)
LAWRENCE KASDAN (DIRECTOR)

Film, 1991. Summary.

This film provides a discussion of the idea of gratitude toward strangers: how much, when, and why?

Mack and Claire are a white middle-aged couple living in Los Angeles. On his way home from a game one night, Mack tries to get around the traffic and finds himself in a run-down neighborhood with broken windows and other evidence of gang violence. And here his car dies on him. From a phone booth he calls a service station, acutely aware that he is on dangerous and unfamiliar turf, and runs back to his car, where a group of armed young black males approach him and threaten him. What exactly they want is something Mack does not find out (it could be his car, his wallet, or perhaps his life), because like an angel from heaven a savior arrives: the towtruck driver, Simon (a black man). Soft-spoken and polite, he persuades the gang to leave. He then hooks Mack's car to his truck and takes Mack to his garage. Outside, after Mack has called home, he has a curbside talk with Simon about the dangers of modern life, and Simon tells him about an experience he had when visiting the Grand Canyon: It is so big, so old, and so impersonal that one's ego shrinks to nothing; he felt like "a gnat landing on the ass of a cow." For Simon the world is a cold place to live in, and one can't count on one's luck.

Mack returns home, grateful for being safe and alive. Simon returns to his sister's home on a street with heavy gang activity.

The 1991 film *Grand Canyon* (Twentieth Century Fox) is a story about the harsh realities of living in Los Angeles (or any other big city) and about learning to recognize and accept that good things as well as bad happen to us, even if they may not follow a logical pattern. One theme running through the film is the question of gratitude—how to show it and how to acknowledge it. Simon (Danny Glover, right) has just rescued Mack (Kevin Kline) from a gang encounter, and here they are exchanging views of life.

In the following days several things happen that are out of the ordinary for Mack and Claire: Mack's friend Davis, a self-centered producer of violent films, who has commented to Mack that all people feel fear and attempt to hide their fear, is shot by a mugger and has to undergo extensive surgery. In the hospital bed he experiences an epiphany and denounces all future contributions to the world of violence. From now on he will make only positive films dealing with the life energy. Claire, who visits him, is elated, because she has been a harsh critic of his for years, and, besides, she is undergoing her own transformation: On her usual jogging route through their pleasant neighborhood, she discovers a baby girl, hidden under some bushes; driven by some compelling force—perhaps the life energy that Davis talked of—she takes the baby home and keeps her for nine hours without notifying the police. When Mack comes home he is taken aback by her displaying such a lack of judgment, and they turn the baby over to the authorities, but Claire insists that if the baby is not claimed, she wants to adopt her. This is not Mack's idea of a rational move, since he himself is happy that their son is a teenager and no longer a baby. Claire tries to explain that perhaps it is not good to be so rational all the time; perhaps things happen for a reason, and we must see them through. Meanwhile, she is having nightmares about homeless people, about seeing her husband and son leave, and about losing sight of the baby in the bushes.

But Mack himself is not being all that rational either, and his own attitude has come as a surprise to him: He finds himself thinking constantly about Simon and what Simon did for him and finds himself compelled to look Simon up. He invites Simon for breakfast and learns more about his life, his deaf daughter, and his sister's predicament. And Mack, to a puzzled Simon's slight embarrassment, offers to find his sister an apartment in a new neighborhood. Simon declines politely, saying that he doesn't deserve any thanks, but now we hear why Mack has been so preoccupied with Simon's helping hand. Some time ago Mack was walking on the "Miracle Mile" in L.A., deep in his own thoughts. He was about to step off the curb to cross the street when a hand grabbed him from behind and held him back, and instantly a large vehicle sped by where he would have been standing. The woman who had stopped him just walked on, and all he could think of doing was to say, "Thank you." Since then he has been thinking about it, and knowing that his life was saved that day, he feels terrible for not having done more in appreciation. So now he wants to make sure that he shows appreciation to Simon, but Simon wants none of it. He thinks that Mack was just lucky, and sometimes people are not so lucky; if you live long enough, he says, something terrible is bound to happen to you. So he wants no favors in return, and when Mack asks him why, he says, "Sometimes it's hard, even dangerous, reaching in and mucking around with other people's lives—sometimes there's a reason for them doing what they're doing." But later, when the sister is approached by an insurance salesman who wants her to take out policies on her children's lives, she decides to move, and Mack helps her find a place in a safer neighborhood.

And now Mack is on a roll: Somehow feeling that he can do even more for Simon, he sets him up on a blind date with an African American coworker, Jane. Against their expectations, they find themselves falling in love and credit Mack with having a deep understanding of both of them, or perhaps, as Simon says, "We are the only two black people he knows!"

Not everything is working out smoothly: Simon's teen nephew feels uncomfortable in the new neighborhood, which is predominantly white, especially since he is pulled over by the police merely for running through the streets; Claire has problems convincing Mack that her wish to adopt the little girl is not just because their son is growing up and she is approaching middle age. And Davis "recovers" from his phase of planning nonviolent films; he explains to Mack that movies don't create violent situations, but just imitate them, and besides, since there is now a chasm, a "Grand Canyon," between the haves and the have-nots, creating more and more violence, film producers have a duty to show it like it is until the chasm is gone.

How will it end? Will Claire get to adopt her baby girl? Will Simon and Jane continue seeing each other? Will Simon and Mack become friends? See for yourself; suffice it to say that the film serves as a fine illustration not only of the problem of gratitude but also of the issue of whether reason or emotion should be the determining factor in one's moral deliberations and life choices.

Study Questions

1. How would you evaluate Mack's attempt to show his gratitude? Is he doing too much (butting in) or too little, or is he achieving the mean? What would Fred Berger say?

2. Is Simon a good "receiver" of gratitude? Why or why not?

3. Even though this film is used as an example of gratitude, it also works to illustrate the discussion about reason versus emotion (or moral intuition). Do you agree with Claire that we should not strive to be completely logical all the time, or would you agree with Mack's viewpoint, that we must remain rational in order to have some control over our lives? Is there a middle way? What would Richard Taylor say? What would Jonathan Bennett say? What might Martha Nussbaum (Chapter 1) say? Could this be a gender issue? Why or why not?

4. What does the metaphor of the Grand Canyon mean in this film?

5. Do you think (with Claire and Simon) that there may be a reason for the things that happen to us? Explain.

6. Is this a "Pay It Forward" kind of film? Why or why not?

Chapter Twelve

Different Gender, Different Ethics?

*I*n this book we have examined prominent theories regarding ethics of conduct and virtue ethics, and their applications. As you have seen, both men and women have contributed to these theories, especially since the middle of the twentieth century. But in addition, there is a special branch of ethics dealing with the question of *gender,* and we generally label it *feminist ethics,* even if there is a great variety of opinions within this branch. Feminist ethics asks two separate, but related, questions: (1) Is there a morally correct way for society to approach the issue of gender equality? and (2) Is ethics gender-specific—meaning, is there an approach to ethics that is typical for women, and another for men? In this chapter we look at both issues.

If you ask a woman in the Western world today whether she is a feminist, chances are she will say no; if you ask her whether she believes that women and men should have equal opportunities, that women should not be discriminated against based on their gender, and that women and men should get equal pay for equal work, chances are she will say yes, and so will most men. This, according to classical feminism, qualifies anyone who agrees as a feminist, because these are the goals of classical feminism. But the word has today been weighed down by additional connotations to the extent that many people don't want to be associated with the idea of feminism; the term *feminazis,* coined by talk show host Rush Limbaugh, hasn't helped any. Are feminists the same as feminazis? Not according to Limbaugh himself, who says he reserves the term "feminazis" for those he considers radicals. But the label "feminism" has caused some people to assume that all feminists somehow want to rule the world. If you believe that we should end sex discrimination and help create a friendly, cooperative working environment as well as private partnership for men and women based on equality, however, you are in fact a feminist, regardless of whether you are male or female according to many contemporary feminists.

Feminism and Virtue Theory

Originally, feminism was associated with acquiring political and social rights for women: the right to work, to own property, to vote, to get a divorce, and other rights considered irrelevant for women by most thinkers with political influence until well into the nineteenth century. Later in the chapter we take a brief look at that development. During its struggle for political equality, feminism rarely regarded itself as a separate moral theory; the male-dominated (often called *patriarchal* by feminists) world would often point to women's sensibilities as those of a higher moral view (think of the role of the schoolmarm in Western movies, exercising her civilizing influence), but because that was usually coupled with an assumption that women were unfit for life in the rough and heartless real world of men, early feminists usually placed little emphasis on this notion. However, a connection not just to ethics as such but to virtue theory as well has become apparent in the past decades.

For modern virtue theory the important question is, How should I be? In other words, What is the character I should strive for? The moral rules of "doing unto others," of "universalizing one's maxim," of "maximizing happiness for as many as possible," and of "treating everyone with impartial fairness" take second place to virtues such as loyalty to family and friends, generosity, compassion, and courage. A moral vice may, under such circumstances, very well turn out to be related to a famous rule of moral conduct: If you act only when you can imagine others being allowed to do the same thing (Kant's categorical imperative), then your child or friend may die while you wonder about allowing all others to defend their child or friend. If you insist on treating everyone with impartial fairness (John Rawls's "original position"), you have an equal obligation to a starving person on the other side of the world and to your niece down the street; you have no right to prefer helping your niece. Virtue ethics, however, discards that approach as a breach of loyalty and family responsibility and insists that you *should* help your niece before you spread yourself thin helping strangers. And you can be accused of the same vice if you are trying to make strangers happy (the principle of utility) at the expense of the needs of your family.

This is where the connection to modern feminism comes in. You have already read, in Chapter 7, that Rawls was criticized for assuming we can pretend to be just strangers to each other in order to achieve fairness. In this chapter we will take a look at the modern feminist theory that is the basis for that criticism, a theory which suggests that women and men tend to view the entire field of ethics from different viewpoints. Whereas men (who have written most of the theories about ethics, law, and justice so far) tend to think of morality in terms of *rules of conduct,* justice, and fairness, says the theory, women tend to think of morality in terms of relationships, of staying friends, and of caring for those who are close to you or for whom you have accepted responsibility. In other words, women tend to think in terms of the *virtues* of caring, loyalty, and compassion. This theory is advanced by the psychologist Carol Gilligan, and we look at her ideas in further detail later. But first we must take a look at the idea of gender equality: What is it? do we have it now? and what has been done to achieve it?

What Is Gender Equality?

The purpose of feminism throughout its history, with a few exceptions (such as the 1960s women's organization SCUM, Society for Cutting Up Men, which may or may not have been meant as a joke), has been to achieve equality for the sexes. Today many refer to this goal as *gender equality* (see Box 12.1 for an explanation of sex versus gender). You know from Chapter 7 that the principle of equality does not imply that everyone is the same, but that everyone should be treated as equals unless special circumstances apply. But what exactly does that entail when applied to the two sexes? Below we look at the concepts of cultural as well as biological equality.

Box 12.1   SEX OR GENDER?

By consensus, the term that is most commonly used today when people talk about sexual differences that go beyond mere biological functions is *gender.* Although this used to be a strictly grammatical term, it now is used instead of the biological term *sexual* as a sociopolitical term.

Gender and Language

Throughout the Enlightenment and on into the twenty-first century it has been customary to use words of the masculine gender to refer to both males and females. For many of us it is surprising to learn that the term *man* in some political statements, such as the American Declaration of Independence ("All men are created equal"), may not have been intended to cover women or people of color—an issue that is being discussed among constitutional scholars today.

It is not true, of course, that the term *men* can *always* be used to include women; it doesn't make any sense to say, for instance, that half of all men have ovaries and half don't. Today, the use of the terms *he* and *men* to include women is considered by many to be discriminatory. And despite the fact that very few men or women ever intended discrimination by using the word *he* for a man or a woman and *man* for all humankind, we now are moving away from what is known as "gender-specific" language toward "gender-neutral" language, because many believe that even when used with the best intentions, gender-specific terms subconsciously tell us that being male is somehow more important than being female and that certain social roles are best performed by men. The real reason for being sensitive about gender and language is, of course, to achieve gender equality. (Box 12.2 provides a discussion of issues involved in gender-neutral language.)

Textbooks and cultural documents are continually being reworded to accommodate our new sensitivity toward gender and language. The Catholic Church has officially endorsed the use of non-gender-specific language in religious documents and biblical translations. Gender-specific words such as *mailman, chairman, housewife,* and *maid* are being changed to *mail carrier, chairperson, homemaker,* and *maintenance assistant* in order to signify that these terms cover both genders. Writers and speakers alike are instructed to avoid the use of *he* as a generic term and instead use *he or she, they, one,* or *you.* College students are urged to avoid gender-specific language in their term papers. Perhaps you think this is a subject of little importance—that it is merely a matter of semantic misunderstanding. But consider this. If you are male and you hear a statement such as, "Now is the time for every man to stand up for what he believes in," there is a good chance you will feel somehow compelled to think hard about what you believe in. If you are female, you *may* feel the same way, but chances are you will feel, subconsciously, that somehow this statement does not apply to you; you may even think, "Yes, it is about time *they* pulled *themselves* together!" If even a few women feel excluded when they read or hear language that uses the masculine gender—excluded

Box 12.2 THE ISSUE IS MANHOLE COVERS

People often seem to feel that we are getting too radical in our elimination of gender-specific terms. It may make sense to do away with words such as *chairman* and *fireman* and use *chairperson* and *firefighter* instead, but what about all the words in the English language that just happen to include a gender-specific term but for which there is no graceful substitute? Will *freshman* now be *freshperson*? Do we have to say *personhole* cover instead of *manhole* cover? How about *manpower*? And *manned space missions*? (And, jokesters might ask, how about *man*-ipulate? and *his*-tory?) Other languages present similar challenges, but some languages have less of a problem finding a common word for humanity. German has a specific term for "human being"—*Der Mensch*—which is different from the terms for man and woman but which still includes a gender-specific term (*Mensch,* which is masculine in gender). In Danish the word for "human being" is a gender-neutral term, *Et Menneske*. And in Sweden, the term for "human being" is *En Människa*, a grammatically feminine word! To make matters even more interesting, there is a word in ancient Icelandic, *man,* that means slave/maid/mistress! Apparently that word has no connection with the ancient Germanic word for man (*Madr*), which is the source for the term *man* in English.

So, getting back to the manhole covers, what should we do? Change some words and not others? Leave *manhole covers* alone, but change *manned mission* to *crewed mission*? Change them all? Leave them all the way they are? Two things are at stake here: the self-esteem of half the English-speaking population versus the comfort of those used to an established language. We can choose between four major courses of action: (1) Forcibly change language to some degree (and we have seen that this can be done within a generation). (2) Wait until a new gender-neutral terminology evolves by itself, in response to the changing times. (3) Make a distinction between sexist and nonsexist terms and change only the blatantly sexist ones. (4) Insist on keeping the traditional terms. What would you suggest?

either in the sense of feeling left out or in the sense of not having to get involved—then that is enough reason to make some changes in the way we phrase things.

Is Biology Destiny?

When we ask whether or not sexual equality exists, we really are asking one of two questions: (1) Does cultural and social equality exist? or (2) Does biological equality? The first question is relative to the historical time period: Today we have reason to say that we have not reached total equality yet, but we hope to do so in the future. (In the past, in Western society, the answer would have been a flat no.) But if we ask the second question, we have to ask a follow-up question: What do we mean by "biological equality"? Do we mean that men and women are the same? Or similar? That they will do similar things in similar situations? Or perhaps that they have a similar genetic makeup, even if there are cultural differences?

The bottom line is the difference between a descriptive and a normative approach. A descriptive theory of equality compares capabilities and pronounces people to be "similar" or "dissimilar." A normative theory of equality may or may not look at the "facts" presented by the descriptive theory but states that people *ought* to be treated a certain way—(1) the same, or (2) similarly under similar conditions, or (3) differently. And if a normative theory asserts that equality is a good thing, it will present a theory for how to achieve it.

Sexual equality, as an idea, is a complex issue (the same is true of racial equality). We must ask, Is sexual equality a biological fact? What does that mean? And is that important for an ethical policy? Let us look at what it means first. Are men and women biologically equal? We all know that, physically, most men are taller and stronger than most women, but that doesn't mean individual women can't be taller and stronger than individual men. In nature there is such a thing as *sexual dimorphism,* meaning that the two sexes of a species look very different, with one sex usually being much bigger than the other. (A consequence of dimorphism is usually that the bigger sex dominates the smaller sex and that one individual of the bigger sex can have many mates of the smaller sex, but not vice versa. Where the sexes are of the same size there are usually lifelong monogamous relationships and equal partnerships.) So do humans have sexual dimorphism? Not nearly to the extreme that gorillas do but slightly more than bonobo chimpanzees do; gorilla society is male-dominated, but bonobo chimpanzees, our closest relatives on this earth, have a gender-equal society with a tendency toward matriarchy. Biologically, there is no reason to assume that it is natural for one human gender to dominate the other, but neither can we conclude that we have an obvious natural tendency to be completely equal partners.

But are we then biologically equal when it comes to the *intellect*? The viewpoints on male and female intelligence are diverse, stretching from the old assumption that men are logical and women are not, to the assumption shared by many modern people that if we are intellectually different at all it is merely a subtle difference, to the view that women's intellectual style is superior to that of men. What exactly would intellectual equality mean? That we reach the same results when faced with the same problem? or that we reach the same results *the same way* when faced with the same problem? Recent studies of the human brain have revealed that men and women actually use their brains differently when dealing with the same math problems, but they generally reach the same results in the same amount of time.

But whether we talk about physical or intellectual equality, some philosophers would call out a warning: Looking for actual equality is one thing, and perhaps a positive one, but if we intend our policy of gender equality to rest on a foundation of what we think is *actual, biological equality,* then we may be in trouble, because what if scientists someday prove that biologically we really are not the same at all? Then our reason for gender equality has disappeared, and we may slide back into some form of gender discrimination against women or against men. Better to forget about looking for actual similarities and concentrate on making a policy based on *what we would like to see happen:* In other words, instead of using *descriptive* means to make us politically equal, let us use normative means, spelling out how we ought to treat each other. Remember from Chapter 5 that if we try to go from fact to policy, from an "is" to an "ought," then we are committing the *naturalistic fallacy,* basing a policy on mere fact without adding a moral premise. But that doesn't mean we can't take biology into consideration when we establish policies. The idea of sexual, or rather *gender,* equality is so important to us now that we have antidiscrimination laws against "sexism." In other words, we believe that regardless of whether equality between the genders is a natural fact, it should be a cultural and sociological institution.

Women's Historical Role in the Public Sphere

Gender equality is, of course, a novel idea in terms of Western history. Until the mid-nineteenth century it was common practice in Western culture to assume that male and female natures were essentially different in their functions, aspirations, and potential, and that male nature was somehow more *normal* than female nature. It was not thought of as necessarily *better,* for, as I mentioned earlier, many men seemed to believe that women had higher moral standards; but it was considered more important in the sense that male nature was more representative of the human species than female nature was. What was this assumption based on? Today we might say *prejudice,* but it can't be dismissed as easily as that, because for a great many thinkers, objectivity was an important ideal. They tried to describe things as they saw them, not as they believed things ought to be, nor as they might appear to an undiscerning eye. And what they saw was that few women had any role to play in public life: There were few women politicians, few women artists, few women scientists. But why were there so few women in public life? The answer is tentative; not all the facts are in yet. It seems obvious, though, that a person's contribution to what we call public life is greatly dependent on that person feeling called or welcome as a contributor. If no one expects or wants you to become a good politician or mathematician or sculptor, you might not think of trying. Encouragement and expectation are major factors in such choices. On the other hand, if it appears that you are *destined* for a certain task, you might not question that either. For most women (until the arrival of dependable birth control), motherhood, several times over, was their destiny. And for those familiar with the demands of large families, it does not come as news that the person in charge of the *private sphere,* the home, has precious little time for anything else, unless she can afford domestic help. Indeed, throughout history—Western history as well as world history—most cultural contributions by individual women were made by those who did not play the role of homemaker.

An interesting question is why women's contributions to the private sphere are rarely discussed. It's certainly true that when women could not own property, vote, or hold a job without the permission of a guardian, many women still had considerable power within the four walls of their home. They managed the bookkeeping and purchases, planned and prepared meals for the household, educated the children, and kept things running on the farm—a full-time job in itself. Why were these management skills not considered important? In an odd way, they were; it is probably our modern-day prejudice to think that they weren't. A young woman chosen as a spouse was expected to have these skills, and "woman's work" was a vitally important social factor. But in terms of the public sphere, women had no place and were not considered potential contributors until almost the end of the nineteenth century. (This assertion, of course, refers to women from middle- and upper-middle-class backgrounds; many working-class women have, for as long as there has been a working class, generally participated in the

Box 12.3   WOMEN IN COMBAT?

Should women be soldiers? Whether you agree or not, the fact is that women are in the armed forces, and have been, in some capacity, since before World War I, starting with the creation of the Army Nurse Corps in 1901 and the Navy Nurse Corps in 1908. It wasn't until 1948, however, that women got permanent status in the armed forces with President Truman's signing of the Women's Armed Services Integration Act. In 1967 president Johnson made it theoretically possible for women to advance to the top. Today women constitute nearly 15 percent of the U.S. Army, but only 6 percent of the Marine Corps. The issue today is not whether women should be soldiers, but whether they should be allowed in combat.

The debate is, of course, more complex than a box can do justice to, but at least we can outline the main arguments:

Those in favor of allowing women in combat argue that

- It is a natural progression toward complete gender equality in a modern society.
- Qualified women can be as effective, and as brave, as their male counterparts.
- Many women want to serve their country in combat; and if they qualify, it would be unfair to exclude them.

- Since combat experience is necessary for officers' advancement within the military, it is discriminatory to exclude women officers—it maintains a glass ceiling.

Those against allowing women in combat argue that

- Women simply aren't "qualified," except for perhaps a very few. The training criteria for a combat soldier include carrying a heavy backpack plus weapon during a forced march, and the vast majority of even very motivated women just can't do that. And if standards are lowered so more women qualify, the effectiveness of the forces will be diminished, and soldiers put in unnecessarily dangerous situations.

- It is dangerous for the male soldiers to have female comrades-in-arms: Because of a natural chivalry and an instinct to protect, the male soldiers will be more focused on protecting their female colleagues and may become distracted from their battle training.

- Women POWs are in greater danger of being raped than male POWs, and threats or violence against the female POWs could become an element in the enemy's interrogation techniques, wearing down the resistance of the male POWs.

public sphere, simply because they have had no choice. If a widow with small children didn't enter the workforce, her children might starve to death—and she too.) Even today, many people accept the idea that the public sphere is the vital one—perhaps because work in the public sphere is *paid for* and work in the private sphere generally is not. However, asking the question whether women's work has been valued may in itself be choosing the viewpoint of the public sphere in which men have traditionally determined values; women have traditionally always valued one another's work, learned from it, criticized it, improved it, and shared it. From a traditional woman's point of view, the question of public (male) recognition for her work may not be the most important question: What might matter more is receiving recognition and appreciation for her work from her peers in the community, other women.

In March 2003 several women soldiers were among the prisoners of war in Iraq: You have already read about Jessica Lynch in Chapter 11; her close friend and comrade in arms, Private Lori Piestewa (right), a Hopi Indian, was killed in the ambush where Jessica was injured and taken prisoner. In the same ambush, Private Shoshana Johnson (left) became the first female black prisoner of war in U.S. war history. She, along with several male soldiers, was captured during the U.S. advance on Baghdad; but with the collapse of the Iraqi government, their captors vanished, and they were rescued by the advancing U.S. forces.

you read about Private Jessica Lynch's ordeal and rescue as a POW during the war in Iraq. Two other women were captured in the same incident during the early weeks of the war: Private Lori Piestewa, Lynch's friend, and Private Shoshana Johnson, also an army maintenance soldier. Johnson made it back injured, but alive, while Piestewa died from her wounds. None of these three women had been trained for combat except for a few hours of basic weapons training: They were all members of a maintenance unit, but even so, they found themselves in a confrontation with the enemy. There is little doubt that they acted as soldiers with backbone and courage, and some advocates of women in combat have argued that their fortitude proves that women can be good combat soldiers. Others have pointed out that their ordeal proves what a thoroughly bad idea it is for military women to be present, not only in combat, but anywhere near the front lines. Has the story of these three women changed, or perhaps solidified, your view about allowing women to be trained for combat?

- It is simply uncivilized to have women in combat.

In your view, which arguments carry the most weight? Can you think of additional arguments for or against women in combat? In Chapter 11

Another factor must be mentioned here. In early times having women remain outside the public sphere was thought by most men (and women too) to be a way of *protecting* women; they were spared the unpleasantness and insecurity of the world of affairs. This is the viewpoint of the Arab fundamentalist culture, where much the same pattern prevails today. Some critics believe it can be interpreted as a way of treating women as *property* (namely the property of their fathers and husbands)—as an investment in the next generation and as a working resource.

This pattern of women being excluded from the public sphere may seem so ancient that we believe it has always existed. However, a theory advanced by many feminist scholars today is that the subjection of women to men (which we know as a historical fact going back at least three thousand years) may not have been the ancient order of things. You may remember that John Stuart Mill was an early advocate of women's rights (see Chapter 5 and p. 578). In his book *The Subjection of Women* (1869) he says that we don't know what it would be like for women not to be subjected to men because they always have been. But he may well have been wrong, because archaeological evidence (artifacts and written documents) now points to the possibility of women having had far more influence in early Middle Eastern and African cultures than we used to think. In what is now Turkey there appear to have been civilizations more than ten thousand years ago who revered a mother goddess of fertility; in Greek and Middle Eastern legends we find ancient myths of a creator goddess and powerful priestesses and queens. Similarly, African legends suggest a strong memory of a mother goddess and of women who had much social power in their communities. Whether we should call these ancient cultures *matriarchal* is open to question because we have no evidence that they were *ruled* by women, but there is tentative evidence that until some gradual cultural change toward patriarchy happened around thirty-five hundred years ago, women in the Old World had higher social standing than they did later. Part of this social standing may have derived from the local religions' belief in a creator goddess rather than a creator god.

Further challenges to the universality of patriarchy have come from other parts of the world: In the American Indian tradition, women were considered respected, full members of the community with rights to have their own opinions and to choose a husband and divorce him. Furthermore, in Eastern tribes it was not uncommon for the chief to be a woman. However, according to American Indian historian Paula Gunn Allen, the European settlers rarely reported this fact, and history books have most often referred to these chiefs as being male. At various times and places in human history, women seem to have had considerably more social influence than they have had in the Western world of the past several thousand years except for the past four decades.

A place where goddess worship may have lasted longer than most other places, and where women may have had comparatively more influence, was Ireland prior to the advent of Christianity with Saint Patrick in 435. And for centuries after Christianity took hold, the high public standing of women that was a legacy of the goddess religion remained a factor in Ireland. Saint Brigit of Kildare (453–525) was raised by the pagan Druid priesthood but was attracted to Christianity. She was ordained as a bishop by mistake, instead of as a nun, as a result of the wrong oath being administered. It initiated a new tradition, and from then on until the Vikings arrived several hundred years later, women in Ireland could become bishops. Irish bishops generally had a more gender-egalitarian view of women than the rest of Europe did, and when in 900 a European bishops' council convened to decide whether women had souls, the yes votes won—by one vote. That vote came from an Irish bishop.

In the European convents of the early Middle Ages, women received an education that allowed them to become medical practitioners, illustrators, composers, and writers, aside from having clerical powers equal to the male clergy of the monasteries. One such woman was Hildegard of Bingen (1098–1179), a German abbess. She was given to the Church at the age of eight and began having visions at an early age. She wrote a number of books on God's plan for humanity, two about her visions, and another two on science and nature. She composed liturgical songs, and wrote what is recognized as the first morality play about the battle between good and evil, *Ordo Virtuem*. She founded her own convent, Rupertsberg, where her music was performed. Toward the end of her life she offered her writings to the new University of Paris, only to suffer the indignity of having them rejected on the grounds that she was a woman.

In the twelfth to fourteenth centuries, women lost ground within the Catholic Church. New policies deprived abbesses of their right to hear confessions, and convents that had functioned as hospitals and social safety nets for the community were closed down or transformed into isolated cloisters. No secular schools had been founded yet, and young women were now barred from a religious education. The reason may seem strangely arbitrary to a modern person: In order to be accepted as a student, receive an education, and communicate with God, the young acolyte's head had to be shaved into a tonsure. But according to Scriptures (in particular Paul's first letter to the Corithians), women not only weren't allowed to shave their heads but were also supposed to hide their hair under a veil when in the presence of God. And since you can't have a tonsure, and thus be eligible for a religious education, while having a full head of hair and wearing a veil, the tonsure policy kept women out of schools.

First-, Second-, and Third-Wave Feminism

We often hear feminism referred to as "first wave," "second wave," and "third wave." These chronological terms form a time line for awareness of women's social situation. The first wave generally refers to the feminist movement in Europe and the United States from its early beginnings in the seventeenth century to the accomplishment of its most urgent goal, the right for women to vote. In 1869 women in Wyoming gained the right to vote, but general suffrage for women wasn't obtained in the United States until 1920. In the meantime, New Zealand women had been included as voters in 1893; in 1902 Australia followed suit. Norway joined the list in 1913, and Denmark in 1915. So, too, did Canada, England, Germany, and Austria after World War I, in 1918. Sweden gave women the right to vote in 1921, but it wasn't until 1944 that French women could go to the polls, and Mexico followed in 1947. Switzerland waited until 1971, and in 1994 black women gained full suffrage in South Africa. What began as furtive discussions four hundred years ago has still not reached full global implementation.

Early Feminism in France and England

A very early speaker for the rights of women was the French thinker Poulain de la Barre, who in 1673 argued that men and women are fundamentally similar because they have the same powers of reasoning. Poulain believed women should have access to all occupations in society, even as generals in the army and leaders of Parliament. Few people paid much attention to Poulain, however; he remained both unique and unknown as a seventeenth-century feminist. During the French Revolution (begun in 1789) things changed considerably in France. Women began to let their voices be heard in the pre-Revolution debate: Olympe de Gouges wrote "The Rights of Women" in 1791, in which she argued for complete equality between men and women, including rights to vote, to

English philosopher Mary Wollstonecraft (1759–1797), wrote *A Vindication of the Rights of Women,* which was much ridiculed at the time by male scholars but would have a lasting influence. Wollstonecraft died in childbirth, giving life to a second Mary Wollstonecraft, who, under her married name Shelley, was to give life to another kind of creature with the story of Frankenstein and his monster.

own property, to serve in the military, and to hold office. During the Revolution she wrote over 30 pamphlets and considered herself a revolutionary, but since she was against the killing of the royal family, she was targeted as an anti-revolutionary and beheaded during the Reign of Terror in 1793 at the age of 48. Another high-profile woman was Madame Zepherine d'Epinay, who believed that women and men have the same nature and the same constitution and will display different virtues and vices only if they are brought up that way; any differentiation is due to social pressure, nothing else. Her ideas inspired the philosopher the marquis de Condorcet, who in 1792 suggested that education should be available to women because both men and women were, primarily, members of the human race. Condorcet's opponent, Talleyrand, who was inspired by the social critic Jean-Jacques Rousseau, managed to put a stop to these ideas, which, it seems, were too radical even for the revolutionaries. Thus the view of Rousseau, which had become popular in the late eighteenth century—that men should live in a democracy of equals but that their women belonged at home as intelligent but subordinate partners to their spouses—became the official view of the gender issue in France of the early nineteenth century.

In eighteenth-century England there were voices—male as well as female—that argued for the possibility of a different order. The British philosopher Mary Wollstonecraft (1759–1797) was one of the few women of the eighteenth century who directly addressed women's situation. (See Box 12.4 for a short list of other women ethicists before the twentieth century.) In *A Vindication of the Rights of Women* (1792) she suggests not only that it is unfair to women to socialize them to be uneducated, unthinking creatures who are only eager to please but also that it is unfair to men, because although a man may fall in love with that kind of woman, he certainly won't want to live with her. After all, what will the two have in common once the seduction is over and they are married? No, Wollstonecraft wrote, women should have the same opportunities as men. If they don't measure up, men will have reason to claim superiority; but to apply two different value systems—one that says what is proper for men and one that says what is proper for women—is to make a mockery out of the concept of virtue itself:

Box 12.4   WOMEN MORAL PHILOSOPHERS

Carol Gilligan is right in saying that the famous and influential moral theories within the Western philosophical tradition have until recently all been expressed by male thinkers. This does not mean, however, that there have been no women moral thinkers in Western history aside from Mary Wollstonecraft and Harriet Taylor Mill; here is a small selection from a list of more than thirty names in the *Encyclopedia of Ethics* of women ethicists (Western as well as Eastern) from the earliest years of philosophy to the nineteenth century. I don't wish to imply that women's contributions to ethics until the twentieth century can be contained in a box. However, most of these names are not generally well known, and prior to the twentieth century women thinkers had very little influence in philosophy. This list demonstrates that there were women who could and did think and write during times when women were discouraged or even banned from taking part in intellectual life. In all probability there were many more thinking and writing women than history has recorded.

Phintys of Sparta (c. 420 B.C.E.) held that it was not unfitting for women to philosophize and that courage, justice, and wisdom were common to women as well as men; in the tradition of Greek moral thinking (which you will recognize from Aristotle, who was not born yet when Phintys wrote her book, *On the Moderation of Women*), she recommends moderation in all things as a virtue for women.

Makrina of Neocaesaria (c. 300 C.E.) so impressed her brother, the Bishop of Nyssa, that he cited her moral philosophy in his own writings. Makrina was familiar with Plato's philosophy and taught that women were created in God's image and had rational souls; with a rational soul, one is capable of becoming morally virtuous and thus eligible for entry into heaven after death, she believed.

Murasaki Shikibu (978–c. 1031) was a Japanese courtier who, in her novel *Genji Monogatari* (*The Tale of Genji*), which is considered the first real novel, led her main character, the woman Ukifune, to a realization of freedom and moral responsibility in the face of existential dread. Today this story is seen as an early exploration of the key themes of existentialism as they were later defined in the Western world of the twentieth century.

Christine de Pizan (1365–1431) wrote a book, *Cité des Dames* (*The City of Women*), in which she envisioned women living in a community to protect themselves from physical and moral harm. She argued that oppression of women was counterproductive to the improvement of society and that women should strive to avoid activities that dull their intellect, since they were limited by certain social roles.

Marie le Jars de Gournay (1565–1645) was the editor of Montaigne's *Essays* and wrote in a work of her own, *Egalité des Hommes et des Femmes* (*Equality Between Men and Women*), that women are equal to men in their capacity for moral reasoning and action. She believed that sexual differences are related exclusively to reproduction and have otherwise no bearing on male or female nature.

Mary Astell (1666–1731) worked on a synthesis of the traditions of Locke and Descartes and believed that reason ought to govern our passions. The only way to accomplish that, she said, was to have universal education for women as well as for men.

Antoinette Brown Blackwell (1825–1921) was the first ordained American woman. She was a prolific writer of philosophy and theology and maintained that women and men make moral judgments differently; in a forerunner of Gilligan's argument about an ethic of justice and an ethic of care, Blackwell claimed that women bring compassion to justice and caring to the concept of rights.

> I wish to persuade women to endeavour to acquire strength, both of mind and body, and to convince them that the soft phrases, susceptibility of heart, delicacy of sentiment, and refinement of taste, are almost synonymous with epithets of weakness, and that those beings who are only the objects of pity and that kind of love, which has been termed its sister, will soon become objects of contempt. . . . Besides, the woman who strengthens her body and exercises her mind will, by managing her family and practicing various virtues, become the friend, and not the humble dependent of her husband.

In the nineteenth century John Stuart Mill, inspired by his longtime intellectual friend (and later wife) Harriet Taylor, wrote about how women's as well as men's characters are molded by society:

> All women are brought up from the earliest years in the belief that their ideal of character is the very opposite to that of men; not self-will, and government by self-control, but submission, and yielding to the control of others. All the moralities tell them that it is the duty of women, and all the current sentimentalities that it is their nature, to live for others.

Under different social circumstances, Mill says, we would see women acting no longer as the full-time slaves of their husbands but as independent individuals with original intellectual ideas to contribute to society. If women are capable of fulfilling social functions, they should be free to do so. If it is impossible for a woman to do certain things because of her nature, then what need is there to prohibit her from doing them? The old saying "'ought' implies 'can'" applies: You can't tell someone she ought (or ought not) to do something unless she is actually able to do it. Mill does believe that male and female qualities in general are not the same—that men and women are usually good at different things—but that from a moral point of view these qualities should be considered equally important. So what might Mill say about the current controversy as to whether women soldiers should be allowed in combat? Probably that most women would prefer not to and would not qualify but that those who want to and who do qualify should be allowed to do so. At the end of the chapter you can read Harriet Taylor Mill's own argument for why women should be allowed in the workforce.

Feminism in America

The philosophy and goals of the first wave of feminism in the United States were straightforward: rights for women to self-determination; rights to inherit and own property, even in marriage (as opposed to the ownership of one's inherited or earned property passing to one's husband); rights to raise one's children; and above all the right to vote. The philosophy of the second wave is more complex, because during this period women had achieved the right to vote but not gender equality in any real measure—not in education nor in the job market, politics, or the private sphere. The goals of many second-wave feminists became equal pay for equal work, equal job and education opportunities, and an end to the treatment of women as though they were children without the ability to take care of themselves. The third wave is the hardest to define philosophically. Many young people believe that the second wave has paved the way for true equality, and they expect relationships between men and women to reflect this political equality. Some third-wave feminists want to attack the problem of gender discrimination radically; others believe that the work has been accomplished and that men and women are now free to explore whatever gender roles suit them. Here we take a look at some highlights of the first, second, and third waves.

Challenges to the Euro-American patriarchal system by individual women, as well as women's groups, happened sporadically through the 1700s and the first half of the 1800s, but the first Women's Rights Convention in Seneca Falls, New York, in 1848 is generally regarded as the beginning of the American women's movement. Led by Lucretia Mott and Elizabeth Cady Stanton, the convention resulted in a Declaration of Sentiments that stated "all men and women are created equal." Stanton later became the first woman candidate for Congress (1866), although women would not get the right to vote for another fifty-four years. The former slave Sojourner Truth gave speeches to white women's groups and others in which she stressed both the importance of women's rights and the urgency of the abolition of slavery. During the Civil War white women in the North organized to seek fair treatment for women workers, as well as abolition. Susan B. Anthony collected signatures for passage of the Thirteenth Amendment to abolish slavery. She also worked hard for an amendment to give women suffrage (the right to vote) and was tried and convicted for voting illegally. She and Elizabeth Cady Stanton formed the National Woman Suffrage Association in 1869. In 1869 women in Wyoming gained the right to vote, fifty years before they did in the rest of the nation. In 1893 the National Council of Jewish Women was formed, as was the National Association for Colored Women in the following year.

From the end of the 1800s to the early 1900s, many women were engaged in the temperance movement, working to get alcohol banned. The primary reasoning behind the temperance movement was that alcohol destroyed families by making drunks out of the breadwinners: fathers and husbands. These efforts often went hand in hand with the suffrage movement. Interestingly, the anti-alcohol movement succeeded before the suffrage movement did; Prohibition began in 1917 with the Eighteenth Amendment, three years before women achieved the right to vote.

We shouldn't forget that during those last few years of the first wave, what was on most people's minds was the Great War, World War I. The involvement of the United States from 1917 to 1918 not only meant anguish for women who saw their sons, fathers, husbands, and boyfriends go to war, but also had a homefront effect. Women all over the Western world took on men's jobs, partly to support themselves and their families but also to meet the needs of society. This was a major revelation both to women and to the political powers (although the same effect had happened to a lesser degree during the Civil War), because it conclusively proved that women could hold technical and intellectual jobs previously thought of as "male." One direct result of this was the Nineteenth Amendment of 1920, which granted women the right to vote.

After 1920 the women's movement quieted down, as though the effort of securing the right to vote had used up all its energy. The Great Depression of the 1930s created huge obstacles for women who wanted to work outside the home because they were resented for taking jobs away from unemployed men. Even so, individual women campaigned for greater equality and freedom for women, and groups such as the National Council of Negro Women were founded. In Hollywood, movies were made depicting the problems of women in the workforce. The films in which Katharine Hepburn and Spencer Tracy starred together in the 1930s and 1940s, such as *Adam's Rib,* often showed both the funny and the serious aspects of men and women getting used to each other as working partners.

World War II repeated the phenomenon of women taking jobs in the male workplace to feed their families and serve their country. "Rosie the Riveter," a fictional woman working in the fighter plane industry, became a symbol for the new woman (the movie *Swing Shift* tells the story of this time period very well). But after World War II there was a gigantic push to get women out of the job market and back in the home in order to open up jobs for returning servicemen. Indeed, many of the ideals of gender equality were all but forgotten with the birth of the baby boom generation. In the Narratives section you'll find a summary of a film that illustrates the ideological clash between a young, idealistic, classical feminist teaching art history and her young female students at Wellesley College in the 1950s: *Mona Lisa Smile.*

The second wave of feminism in the United States was ushered in with the 1963 publication of Betty Friedan's book *The Feminine Mystique.* (In France, a similar reaction followed the publication of Simone de Beauvoir's *The Second Sex* in 1949.) The following year, the Civil Rights Act, which prohibited discrimination in employment because of race, also banned sex discrimination. In the 1960s the challenges to traditionally male institutions and occupations increased: The National Organization for Women (NOW) was organized in 1966, the concept of "women's liberation" became part of the culture of the 1960s and 1970s, and formal charges of sex discrimination in workplaces reached the courts. In 1972 the Equal Rights Amendment was passed by the House of Representatives but was later defeated in the Senate. What many feminists consider the landmark achievement of the era was the Supreme Court's *Roe v. Wade* decision in 1973 that women have the freedom to choose abortion in the first trimester. (In the second and third trimesters, states may impose special limitations.)

For most feminists of the second wave, the primary goal was the creation of an equal-opportunity society without discrimination because of one's sex—a society in which women, as well as men, would be able to freely choose their way of life. For many feminists of this period, such a society seemed possible only if the structures of patriarchy were toppled, and those structures were often perceived as not just male dominated but also middle-class dominated. In other words, for many feminists of the second wave, women's liberation was also a political battle against the *capitalist economy,* and many second-wave feminists have identified themselves as Marxists.

Many feminists of the 1960s and 1970s focused on the traditional upbringing of boys and girls and speculated that bringing up children to think of themselves as *persons* rather than as either "boys" or "girls" would lead to the elimination of many male and female stereotypes within a few generations. Men would be accustomed to doing work around the house without feeling they were being emasculated or that they were "helping" rather than contributing their fair share; women would feel at home and welcome in the public sphere and comfortable about choosing a life without children and/or marriage. For politically engaged feminists regardless of party affiliation, a primary goal was to get women elected to office—a rarity in the 1960s and 1970s.

For all the second-wave feminists, though, a common goal was complete and discrimination-free access for women to any education or profession they might be interested in and qualified for. Most second-wave feminists went through years of battling traditions in education, in the workplace, and even within their own families to change the perception that there were things women shouldn't do and places women shouldn't go. Part of the battle was against the traditional assumption that women were more fragile and less intelligent than men. This is why a second-wave feminist, to this day, may balk at having the door held for her or her chair pulled out at the table by a man. These small protests, which sometimes puzzle third-wave feminists (that is, many college students today), should be seen in their proper perspective. If a man holds the door for a woman today, it is generally seen as a gesture of courtesy. However, in the long tradition challenged by second-wave feminists, holding the door meant for them that men found women in need of help because of their second-class status. These were hard-fought battles, and the fact that the perception of what women can do has changed so dramatically testifies to the fact that they are also hard-earned victories.

Some identify the beginning of the third wave of feminism with the publication of Carol Gilligan's *In A Different Voice* (1982); others find the publication of Susan Faludi's *Backlash: The Undeclared War Against American Women* (1991) to be the defining moment. Many point to the Senate hearings of 1991 in which Supreme Court nominee Clarence Thomas was accused of sexual harassment by law professor Anita Hill, formerly Thomas's aide. (Box 12.5 discusses the topic of sexual harassment.) The hearings launched sexual harassment into mainstream American culture as a social and legal concept, and the American public noted that (1) The committee hearing the charges was an all-male roster; it lacked any female perspective. (2) An overwhelming number of women came forth with similar experiences of having been harassed sexually by teachers, professors, bosses, and other male persons of authority—something that had not been publicly discussed prior to the hearings. As a result of the hearings, a large number of women decided to run for office in the 1992 election—1992 incidentally having been designated "the Year of the Woman" by the United Nations—and both the House and the Senate saw such an increase in women members that restrooms for women had to be installed.

Whereas the aim of the first wave of feminism was the achievement of suffrage and the second wave focused on a discrimination-free society, there is no defining idea (as yet) behind third-wave feminism. Some third-wavers believe that equality really has been achieved and that it is now up to individual women and men to learn to get along even better. Others believe the work has just begun. Radical feminists of the 1990s have striven to identify the roots of the sex-discrimination problem and believe that although patchwork improvements have been made, the patriarchy is still in place and must be addressed or uprooted. Other third-wavers have decided to focus on specific issues rather than on the big picture and engage themselves in feminist environmentalism, easier access to child care for working women, combating economic and racial discrimination along with sexual discrimination, and so forth.

There is no sharp line between second- and third-wave feminism. Generally, it is a generational reference. Feminists who were young in the 1950s, 1960s, and 1970s are

Box 12.5   WHAT IS SEXUAL HARASSMENT?

Since the 1970s sexual discrimination has been unacceptable in most Western cultures, but it is only within the past few decades that *sexual harassment* has been identified as a related but separate problem. Unfortunately there is little clarity about what exactly sexual harassment means. Does it mean that someone at your workplace or your school corners you and touches you? Or cracks sexist or obscene jokes in your presence? Does it mean that someone compliments you on your looks? Or that someone from your workplace or your school asks you out? What seems like sexual harassment to one person may not look like it to another, and that is why there are now guidelines for the perplexed. According to the California Fair Employment and Housing Act, sexual harassment consists of

- Unwanted sexual advances
- Offering employment benefits in exchange for sexual favors
- Making or threatening reprisals after a negative response to sexual advances
- Visual conduct: leering, making sexual gestures, displaying of sexually suggestive objects or pictures, cartoons, or posters
- Verbal conduct: making or using derogatory comments, epithets, slurs, and jokes
- Verbal sexual advances or propositions
- Verbal abuse of a sexual nature; graphic verbal commentaries about an individual's body; sexually degrading words used to describe an individual; suggestive or obscene letters, notes, or invitations
- Physical conduct: touching, assault, impeding or blocking movements

From this list it is obvious that cornering and touching an employee is sexual harassment, regardless of whether the cornered person is male or female. But what about asking someone out? That should depend on whether the advance is considered sexual and whether or not it is wanted, and that would certainly be a case-by-case judgment. And could complimenting someone on her, or his, looks be construed as "verbal abuse"? Under certain circumstances it might, and this is what frustrates so many people, mostly men who are used to showing friendliness by complimenting female employees. In order to determine whether or not sexual harassment has taken place, review boards often ask the person making the complaint if he or she perceived the situation as being one of sexual harassment; it is thus the *perception* of the victimized person that will stand in many cases, not the *intention* of the perceived victimizer.

In order to avoid all such situations some simple rules of the road are suggested: If you are in a superior position, at school or in the workplace, don't go out with someone in a position that you may be able to influence, because it can be seen as a "benefit/reprisal" situation of pressure, with the other person's job or grades on the line. In addition, others may view your date as now having an unfair advantage in terms of grades or the job. Some schools are moving toward banning all relationships between instructors and students, as some workplaces are banning relationships between coworkers, to avoid misunderstandings, ill will after relationships end, and (let's be realistic) lawsuits—because, as the guidelines based on the Fair Employment and Housing Act read, "If harassment occurs, an employer may be liable even if management was not aware of the harassment."

thought to belong to the second wave; feminists from the 1980s, 1990s, and the early twenty-first century are thought to belong to the third wave. But of course any individual can decide at any time to address any particular feminist issue. An older woman who has been living a life as a traditional homemaker without being touched or troubled by issues of sex discrimination may, perhaps because of widowhood, be thrown late in life into awareness of sex discrimination for the first time, and thus effectively become a second-wave feminist decades after other women of her own generation did.

Facets of Feminism Today

Today the idea of gender equality has several facets. Feminists generally agree that there should be gender equality, but they don't necessarily agree on what is female and male human nature, nor on what exactly our policies should be in order to combat gender discrimination. The philosophies of feminism are in a process of development, responding to the pressures of the past and present and the challenges of the future. One facet is *classical feminism,* which calls for men and women to be considered as *persons* first and gendered beings second. Another is *difference feminism,* which holds that women and men possess fundamentally different qualities and that both genders should learn from each other. A facet of feminism that sometimes has received bad press is *radical feminism;* although some radical feminists indeed seem to be militant or extremist, the main point of radical feminism is not to mount the barricades but to seek out and expose the *root* of the problem of gender discrimination ("root" is *radix* in Latin; hence, radical feminism). And then there is a breakout form of feminism severely criticized by many feminists that labels itself *equity feminism:* An equity feminist holds that the battle for equality has been won, that we should not think of women as victims of patriarchy any longer, and that we can now adopt any kind of gender roles we like because gender discrimination is by and large a thing of the past. (Box 12.6 discusses equity feminism.)

Classical Feminism: Beauvoir and Androgyny

For those taking the view that men and women should be considered as persons first, gender differences are primarily cultural. Biological differences are significant only in terms of procreation, they say; apart from birthing and breastfeeding infants, which can be done only by women, the sexual differences are irrelevant. Culture has shaped men and women, and a cultural change could therefore allow for another type of gender: the *androgynous* type.

In her groundbreaking work *The Second Sex,* Simone de Beauvoir, one of the most powerful voices for equal education and equal opportunities in the twentieth century, accuses the philosophical tradition of seeing man as the "typical" human being, so woman thus becomes "atypical." For man, woman becomes "the Other," an alien being who helps man define himself through her alienness, and with whom he communicates on an everyday basis but who never becomes "one of the boys." Woman, who has been placed in this situation for millennia, has also come to believe she is atypical. The female anatomy is seen as a psychologically determining factor, whereas the male

SALLY FORTH *by GREG HOWARD and CRAIG MacINTOSH*

© 1997 Greg Howard. Reprinted by permission of King Features Syndicate.

Classical feminism taught that if gender differences are perpetuated, it is to the detriment of women's freedom. One of the traditions discarded by classical feminists was chivalry: men holding doors for women, pulling out chairs, and so on. The underlying assumption, said classical feminism, was that women are too weak or stupid to do things themselves, so chivalry was, in effect, demeaning to women. Now, in the age of third-wave feminism, opinion is divided as to traditional male chivalry. What do you think—can men be chivalrous to women without being sexists? Should women also hold doors for men? Would that be a veiled comment on a man's weakness?

anatomy is not. In other words, women do what they do because they are women; men do what they do because they are normal. But this is a *cultural* fact, not a natural one, says Beauvoir. And the only way a woman can become *authentic* is to shed her role as "deviant" and become a true human being by rejecting the traditional female role. Society can assist in this process by treating little boys and girls the same—by giving them the same education and the same subsequent opportunities. Here we must remember that Beauvoir was engaged in issues other than feminism; she was, with her partner Jean-Paul Sartre, one of the strongest voices in the philosophical existentialist movement of the mid–twentieth century (see Chapter 10). Existentialism posits that there is no human nature; any attempt at claiming we *have to* do or be something is nothing but a poor excuse for not wanting to make a choice: *bad faith*. If we carry this over into Beauvoir's theory of feminism, we understand what she means when she says that a woman must shed her culturally given role as the second sex: There is no female human nature any more than there is any human nature in general; we must fight the cultural traps of gender roles and their assumption that this is how we have to be, because that is nothing but a poor excuse for not making our own choices. (However, if we should *want to* make the choice of traditional gender roles, Beauvoir would have little patience with us, since she believed the choice of gender freedom is best made if the traditional option of stay-at-home-mom is not available to women. Many contemporary feminists find that this hardly constitutes true freedom of choice.)

It is against the background of the traditional male philosophical approach to the gender question that Beauvoir criticizes Emmanuel Levinas and his view of the Other as essentially feminine (see Chapter 10). To Beauvoir, this is nothing but old-fashioned reactionary male-oriented thinking, because for a classical feminist like her, the attitude

Box 12.6   CHRISTINA HOFF SOMMERS'S EQUITY FEMINISM

In a highly controversial book, *Who Stole Feminism?* (1994), Christina Hoff Sommers (see Chapter 10) argues that feminism has been split into two movements: the "equity feminists," wanting equal opportunity for women and men, and the "gender feminists," "resenter feminists," or "feminist radicals," who, as Sommers sees it, have male-bashing as their main agenda. Sommers sees herself as an equity feminist. She also uses the terms "new feminists" and "gynocentric feminism" to describe the type of feminism she believes has done the movement a grave disservice by creating an atmosphere of general mistrust of men and of women who work with, support, or admire them. Here Sommers doesn't align herself exactly with any of the facets of feminism that we have discussed; although radical feminism comes closest to what she calls gender feminism, Sommers also finds that difference feminism has elements of misandry in that women's approaches are considered superior to those of men. And classical feminism, although being the form of feminism that probably comes closest to what Sommers calls equity feminism, also has elements of gender feminism for Sommers: Simone de Beauvoir, she says, had no intention of letting women choose gender roles freely but wanted to dictate the proper upbringing and life choices for women. Among contemporary gender feminists, Sommers counts Susan Faludi, Marilyn French, Carolyn Heilbrun, and Catharine MacKinnon. Sommers writes:

> Once I get into the habit of regarding women as a subjugated gender, I'm primed to be alarmed, angry, and resentful of men as oppressors of women. I am also prepared to believe the words about them and the harm they cause to women. I may even be ready to fabricate atrocities. . . . Resenter feminists like Faludi, French, Heilbrun and MacKinnon speak of backlash, siege, and an undeclared war against women. But the condition they describe is mythic—with no foundation in the facts of contemporary American life.

Since women now have their political and personal freedom, says Sommers, they should be making use of it, instead of judging the authenticity of each other's attitudes:

> But women are no longer disenfranchised, and their preferences are being taken into account. Nor are they now taught that they are subordinate or that a subordinate role for them is fitting and proper. . . . Since women today can no longer be regarded as the victims of an undemocratic indoctrination, we must regard their preferences as "authentic." Any other attitude toward American women is unacceptably patronizing and profoundly illiberal.

The feminists Sommers criticizes generally respond that Sommers herself has misunderstood the goals and nature of feminism; while the overt oppression of previous times is over, it has now become covert and internalized, and it lives in the hearts of the critics of feminism, women as well as men. Although opportunities have opened to women, many women still grow up believing that the masculine cultural world is their only option; it takes a long time for such wounds to heal, and they don't heal without active interference. For that reason, and for their own sake, women must be shown that equality is still far away. So when Sommers says women have the right to choose a life in which they work at home, raising children, or work in a male-dominated environment or when she says they have the right to enjoy romance literature in which men are strong and women are seduced, then Sommers must herself have internalized the traditional male view of what a woman's proper place is, according to some critics.

Sommers responds by claiming that gender feminism simply does not represent the viewpoint of most women today—women who are politically aware and concerned with gender

(continued)

Box 12.6   CHRISTINA HOFF SOMMERS'S EQUITY FEMINISM   *(continued)*

equality—in other words, feminists. Most women today, says Sommers, have access to the professions of their choice and want to lead lives in which they have friendly relations with male coworkers and loving relations with male partners. Many want families, and some even want to live the traditional life of a homemaker, and they are not interested in being represented by women who tell them they have a false consciousness. As a fellow equity feminist, Sommers cites the author and fellow philosopher Iris Murdoch, who believed in a "culture of humanity," not in a "new female ghetto" of misandric feminism.

of seeing the sexes as fundamentally different also means that one is generally dominating the other; when Levinas praises feminine qualities as the nurturing and welcoming element in both men and women, the classical feminist still sees this as discrimination (against men as well as against women) because it persists in stereotyping the typically feminine as nurturing.

Until women begin to think of themselves as a group, Beauvoir says, they will believe that they are abnormal human beings. And as long as men and women receive different educations and different treatment from society, woman will not feel responsible for the state of the world but will regard herself as men regard her—as an overgrown child. Of course women are weak, Beauvoir says. Of course they don't use male logic (here we must remember that she is talking about uneducated women before World War II). Of course they are religious to the point of superstition. Of course they have no sense of history, and of course they accept authority. Of course they cry a lot over little things. They may even be lazy, sensual, servile, frivolous, utilitarian, materialistic, and hysterical. They may, in short, be all that some male thinkers thought they were. *But why are women all these things?* Because they have no power except by subterfuge. They have no education, so they have never been taught about the cause and effect of history and the relative powers of authority. They are caught up in a never-ending stream of housework, which causes them to be practically oriented. They nag because they realize they have no power to change their situation. They are sensual because they are bored. In *The Second Sex* Beauvoir says, "The truth is that when a woman is engaged in an enterprise worthy of a human being, she is quite able to show herself as active, effective, taciturn—and as ascetic—as a man." (See Box 12.7 for Beauvoir's influence on modern philosophy.) At the end of the chapter you can read an excerpt from this book as well as a summary of one of Beauvoir's short stories, "The Woman Destroyed."

So if we change our culture, we will change what has for so long been considered female nature—and with it, probably also male nature. We will create people who are responsible human beings above all and who will respect each other for that reason. This philosophy was adopted by many late-twentieth-century feminists, including Germaine Greer, Gloria Steinem, and Joyce Trebilcot.

Box 12.7   THE OTHER: SIMONE DE BEAUVOIR

Simone de Beauvoir (1908–1986), a feminist and existentialist, was long considered a minor thinker by the philosophical community. One reason was that she was Jean-Paul Sartre's "significant other," and her books, such as *The Second Sex,* show considerable influence from Sartre's ideas. However, most philosophers now recognize that many of the fundamental ideas of existentialism came about through discussions between Sartre and Beauvoir, and many ideas first published by Sartre may well have originated during these discussions. There is even some suspicion that Sartre occasionally may have published ideas by Beauvoir under his own name. True or not, this new attitude reveals a changing perspective on women in philosophy. In the twenty-first century, Beauvoir's influence in the area of gender inequality has turned out to be just as viable as Sartre's philosophy. Beauvoir is primarily interested in the existence of woman as a cultural phenomenon; she analyzes woman's subjugation in a man's world—a situation that was far more common in the mid-twentieth century than now. She hopes that instead of a world where woman is considered deviant and man normal, we will have a society of *human beings,* not just males and females, and people will interact with each other equally as productive, authentic beings. Beauvoir has come under heavy criticism from some fem-

inists for not realizing that she herself regards man as the norm and wants women to be treated and to act like men, rather than rejoice in their inherent female nature. It appears that Beauvoir herself decided to live a child-free life in order to escape the female stereotype.

The quest for *androgynism* has taken on several shapes. A moderate, modern viewpoint advocates a common upbringing for all children, one that avoids using pink for girls and blue for boys and makes use of toys that don't perpetuate typical male/female roles. Proponents of this viewpoint advocate a general change in language from gender-specific terms to gender-neutral terms.

Two versions of androgynism as a political goal have been advocated, and Joyce Trebilcot analyzes both. One proposes a society in which men and women *share* all the best characteristics of the traditional gender roles, and if a woman *doesn't* want to hold a job (typically a male role) or if a man prefers *not* to care for his sick children (typically a female role), then society must teach them the necessity of sharing these duties. This version is sometimes referred to as *monoandrogynism*. The other version, *polyandrogynism*, suggests that gender roles be left as open as possible, with no demand that the duties be shared. If a man wants to fulfill the traditional male role, he is free to do so. If a woman wants to live the life of a traditional male, she can. If a man wants to stay home and care for the kids, fine. If a woman wants to do the same thing, so be it. Both theories assume that gender roles are cultural artifacts; however, polyandrogynism allows for the possibility that people just might be biologically different from one another. Trebilcot herself opts for polyandrogynism.

An ultraradical version of androgynism assumes that there are profound biological differences between men and women and suggests that we eradicate them. Thus, if women are the only humans capable of giving birth, we must *change human biology* so that this becomes an option for men also.

The question is, Can we choose our gender at all? Obviously we can't choose our *sex* (not without going through major surgery, anyway). But the term *gender* also encompasses our *social roles* as male and female. Can we, then, decide which social role we wish to adapt—which gender we wish to be—or do biological factors exist that prevent people from exercising gender choice? In other words, is our gender determined by our biology to a greater extent than people who advocate androgyny realize?

Psychologists of the 1960s and 1970s generally assumed that sex roles were purely a matter of upbringing, or *nurture*. The theory of *psychosexual neutrality*, inspired by the theory of behaviorism, which arose earlier in the century, held that a child can be molded into being male or female, but is born neither except by virtue of the genitals; if a person seems stereotypically male, it is because of his upbringing, and not a biological fact. This theory also suggests that if we'd like our children to be less stereotypically male or female than tradition expects, we just have to give them a more unisex upbringing. But the theory of psychosexual neutrality has come under severe criticism within the past few years: Cases that had been reported as successful molding of children born with ambiguous genitalia (formerly called hermaphrodites, they're now referred to as *intersexual* children) are now under scrutiny for simply having assigned a sex to the child and assuming that upbringing and hormone treatment would take care of the rest.

A disturbing story is that of David Reimer, who lost his penis to a botched circumcision as an infant in the late 1960s and was raised as a girl, Brenda. In spite of the parents' well-meaning efforts to convince Brenda that she was a girl, she never felt comfortable, and upon discovering the truth at the age of fourteen, promptly discarded the female persona for that of David. He had reconstructive surgery and married a woman whose children he adopted. But the stresses of his abnormal childhood proved to be too much for David, and after being divorced he took his own life in 2004. The case of Brenda/David as well as cases of intersexual children do seem to point toward *nature* as being more important in forming a person's sexual identity than *nurture* is. (See Box 12.8 for a discussion of homosexuality and gender choice.) But we shouldn't discount the influence of nurture completely: The manner in which we express our sexuality and whether or not we become "typically" male or female may well be a matter of our upbringing, at least to some extent.

CATHY © 1997 Cathy Guisewite. Reprinted with permission of Universal Press Syndicate. All rights reserved.

The psychologist John Gray theorizes in his best-selling self-help book *Men Are from Mars, Women Are from Venus* that men and women have very different approaches and expectations. Difference feminism agrees. Classical feminism, on the other hand, assumes that if we minimize gender differences in a child's upbringing, a new generation of people who are persons first and gendered beings second will appear. Here is a classical feminist, Cathy, with a classical feminist dilemma: how to buy for children without perpetuating gender stereotypes. Does cartoonist Cathy Guisewite touch on a real problem? If so, what can be done about it?

Box 12.8   CAN GAYS CHOOSE NOT TO BE GAY?

In talking about the possibility of choosing gender roles, it is reasonable to discuss the issue of homosexuality and the gay lifestyle. There is still considerable political and moral opposition to homosexuals in Western societies, in some more than in others. In some societies homosexuals can now marry; in others homosexuality is still illegal. Why is there a traditional opposition to homosexuality in Christian countries? It is because of several traditional Christian assumptions, such as (1) homosexuality is a *moral choice,* and one that goes against nature (nature calls for procreation), so homosexuality is morally wrong; and (2) homosexuals are primarily seducers of adolescents, who will then become homosexual. In the early 1990s scientists reached the *tentative* conclusion (based on brain autopsies) that male homosexuality is not a matter of choice but of biology. In that case both of the above objections would be invalid, because (1) gay men don't choose their lifestyle or sexual orientation but are born with it (so it is *natural* for them); and (2) boys can't be seduced to become homosexuals; they either are born that way or not. (Besides, being gay does not imply that one is primarily interested in young boys.) But there is as yet no extensive research about lesbianism, nor about bisexualism. The advantage for homosexuals of a conclusive result pointing to biological factors is obvious: There could be no more reason for discrimination based on the belief that homosexuality is an "immoral choice." But such a finding might open the door for new areas of discrimination: Might we see parents take their young children to the doctor to have them "screened" for homosexuality, and if they test positive, ask to

have them "cured"? In this way homosexuality would be labeled a *defect,* a disease. Some homosexuals might say they would prefer to be heterosexual if that were possible, but certainly not all would. Joyce Trebilcot would say that in a polyandrogynous society the question of what your sexual orientation ought to be would never come up in the first place.

In 2004 the issue of same-sex marriage became headline news in several states around the country, as well as in Europe. In several European countries gay civil marriages had already been legal for years, but in some European communities the issue became one of allowing gays to have church weddings. In the United States the focus was on civil marriages versus civil unions; while many states allow what are called civil unions, same-sex partnerships that are recognized by employers, insurance companies, and health care officials, some mayors and judges around the country thought it only fair to extend the possibility of a civil marriage to gay couples. In San Francisco it became a media event, with gay celebrities getting hitched in front of the cameras. Later that year, the California Supreme Court nullified the marriages as being against state law, but in 2005 a judge found the ruling unconstitutional. The issue remains politically volatile: While there seems to be a growing acceptance of the concept of civil unions by the American public, the majority of voters find the idea of same-sex marriage unacceptable: In the 2004 election eleven states decided on constitutional amendments that defined marriage as an institution between a man and a woman, and in most cases the amendment won by a large margin.

Difference Feminism: Gilligan and the Ethic of Care

The idea that nature will prevail over nurture has given a boost to the theory of *difference feminism,* which emerged in the 1980s to claim that women and men should be viewed as equal, but fundamentally different. By the beginning of the 1980s women had been in the workforce long enough for people to begin to evaluate the situation, and although some women felt good about working in what used to be a "man's world" and conforming to its standards (to a greater or lesser degree), others felt that somehow those standards were damaging to their female identity. Few provisions for child care existed, there was little understanding of family demands, and the overriding atmosphere was one of competition and isolation rather than cooperation and teamwork. For these women, survival in the male-dominated public sphere was possible only if they were willing to give up some of their female values. Difference feminism proposed that the feminist agenda could include not just equal opportunity and equal pay for men and women but an acknowledgment that many women want something different than men do and some of women's capabilities lie in areas other than those of most men.

Interestingly enough, this was not the first time such ideas have been advanced—Western history, and certainly the history of philosophy, is rich with statements about the nature of women being different from that of men. Some famous examples include Aristotle, who believed that women were deformed men; Kant, who found it thoroughly improper for a woman to display any interest in intellectual or technological pursuits, even if she might be good at them; Rousseau, who saw a woman as a man's helpmate and little else; and Nietzsche, who admired women for being more "natural" than men but vilified them for being inconsistent. Theories such as these all state that women and men have different abilities and thus different places in society. However, these theories were not advanced with any notion of gender equality. John Stuart Mill was the first influential philosopher to suggest that although men and women have different capacities, they should nevertheless be given equal opportunities and equal respect for their abilities. It is this concept toward which the new feminism looks.

In general, the values we've celebrated for so long as good human behavior have been predominantly male values, say the new feminists, because the male person has been considered the "real" person, whereas women have been thought of as slightly deviant. The man is the typical human being. In older textbooks on human development, the earlier forms of hominids, such as *Homo habilis* and *Neandertal,* have usually been depicted as males ("Neandertal man"). Only recently in textbooks and articles have humans been symbolized by both male and female figures. Even recent theories of psychology seem to use boys and men as their research material rather than girls and women, and the medical community must now face the problems resulting from years of conducting research with primarily male subjects. The statistics regarding women and certain diseases (heart disease, for example) are unreliable, and the administration of medicine to women is often decided on the basis of research on male subjects. This is not just a matter of a slanted ideology; it is a very practical problem. Women have for a long time been judged by the standards of men, as though women were what Aristotle claimed so long ago—deficient males. Difference feminism wants to replace the image of one of the genders being more "normal" than the other with an image of both genders, with all their unique characteristics, being equally representative of the human race. This shift involves upgrading the female tasks of motherhood, housekeeping, caring for family members, and so on, tasks that for some people seemed to fall by the wayside in the first rush to get women into the workforce. Typical female virtues that arise from concentrating on these tasks are generosity, caring, harmony, reconciliation, and maintenance of close relationships. The virtues that typically have been considered male are justice, rights, fairness, competition, independence, and adherence to the rules.

Psychologist Carol Gilligan has been a major inspiration in the gender debate. Her book *In a Different Voice* (1982) analyzes reactions of boys and girls, men and women, and concludes that there is a basic difference in the *moral attitudes* of males and females. In one of her analyses she uses an experiment by a well-known contemporary psychologist, Lawrence Kohlberg; it is called the *Heinz dilemma*. An interviewer using Kohlberg's method asked two eleven-year-old children, Jake and Amy, to evaluate the following situation: Heinz's wife is desperately ill, and Heinz can't afford medication for her. Should Heinz steal the medication? Jake has no doubts; he says yes, Heinz should steal the medication, because his wife's life is more important than the rule of not stealing. Amy, though, is not so sure. She says no, he shouldn't steal the medication, because what if he got caught? Then he would have to go to jail, and who would look after his sick wife? Perhaps he could ask the pharmacist to let him have the medication and pay later. The interviewer concluded that Jake had a clear understanding of the situation: It would be just that the wife should receive the medication, because her rights would override the law of not stealing. The interviewer thought that Amy's comprehension of the situation was fuzzy at best. Jake understood what it was all about: rights and justice.

Gilligan rereads Amy's answer and comes up with another conclusion entirely: Although Jake answered the question *Should Heinz steal the drug or not?* Amy heard it differently: *Should Heinz steal the drug, or should he do something else?* In effect, the children were answering different questions, and Amy's response makes as much sense as Jake's. But Amy is not concerned with the issues of rights and justice as much as she is with what will happen to Heinz and his wife; she even takes the humaneness of the pharmacist into consideration. In other words, she thinks in terms of *caring*. She acknowledges that there are laws, but she also believes people can be reasoned with. The interviewer, Gilligan says, didn't hear this in Amy's answer because he was looking for the "justice" answer. Gilligan concludes that boys and men tend to focus on an *ethic of justice*, while girls and women look toward an *ethic of care*.

Gilligan's influence on modern thinking about gender issues has been enormous, although other philosophers, psychologists, and linguists have also approached them in similar ways, and some of them long before Gilligan's book came out. Perhaps the first person to suggest that women tend to think in terms of caring while men think in terms of justice was not a philosopher, or a psychologist, but a playwright: the Norwegian Henrik Ibsen, in his monumentally influential play *A Doll's House* from 1879. You can read an excerpt from this play in the Narratives section. Also, you may remember the debate in Chapter 7 about justice, in which John Rawls suggested that we adopt "the original position," pretending that we don't know who we are when our policy takes effect; you may also remember the responses from Wolgast and Friedman that we can't just assume we are strangers who don't know each other, because part of being a social person is precisely that we have caring relationships with others and don't just exist in some abstract legal universe. This is, in essence, similar to Gilligan's

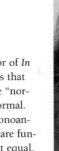

Carol Gilligan (b. 1936), American psychologist and author of *In a Different Voice*. Like Simone de Beauvoir, Gilligan believes that throughout Western history men have been considered the "normal" gender and women have been viewed as not-quite-normal. However, unlike Beauvoir, Gilligan does not argue for a monoandrogynous society, believing instead that men and women are fundamentally different in their approach to life—different but equal.

criticism of a traditional ethic of justice as being the traditional male approach to moral questions and emphasizes that we can't just pretend we don't have our own gender. In the Primary Readings you'll find an excerpt from Gilligan's *In a Different Voice*. In the Narratives section you can read the summary of a film that explores the notion that women are, or should be, caring and nurturing: *Like Water for Chocolate*.

Does this mean Gilligan is claiming that all women are always caring? That is a matter of interpretation. Some readers see her theory as a description of what we might call the "female condition": Because of either nature or upbringing or both, most women *are* caring human beings. Others see this as a preposterous statement. Not all women are caring, and few women, even if they are generally caring persons, are caring all the time. Gilligan's theory of the ethics of care does not have to be read as a description of how women really act, though; with its emphasis on values it is a theory about how most women believe they *ought to act*. It is a theory of women's normative values—we might call it a theory about the *caring imperative*—not a theory about some inevitable female nature.

What does the Gilligan theory add up to? For many women it means that their experiences of attachment and their focus on relationships are normal and good and not "overly dependent," "clinging," or "immature"; it means an upgrading of what we consider traditional female values. The point of Gilligan's book is to prompt the mature woman to understand rights and the mature man to understand caring, so we all can work and live together in harmony. Her hopes may not be realized for decades to come, however, for although some may argue that they know some very caring men and some very justice-oriented women, it seems Gilligan is right in claiming that most women in the United States grow up believing that caring is what is most important, and most men grow up believing that individual rights and justice are the ultimate ethical values.

There are risks involved in Gilligan's theory. Some think we may end up elevating female values far above male values. In that case we will have reversed an unfair system but created another unfair system by declaring women "normal" and men "slightly deviant." A more pressing problem is the following: If we say it is in a woman's nature to be understanding and caring, we may be forcing her right back into the private sphere from which she just emerged. Men (and also women) may say, Well, if most women aren't able to understand "justice," then we can't use them in the real world, and they'd better go home and do what nature intended them to do: have babies and care for their man. Similarly, if a job calls for "caring" qualities, employers may be reluctant to hire a man, because men are not "naturals" at caring. So instead of giving people more opportunities, Gilligan may actually be setting up new categories that could result in policies that exclude women from "men's work" and men from "women's work." It is not enough to say that the qualities of one gender are not supposed to outweigh the qualities of the other, because we all know that even with the best intentions, we tend to rank one set of differences higher than the other. We may all be equal, but remember George Orwell's *Animal Farm*? In this novel, which is a metaphor for political despotism, Orwell warns against some being considered "more equal than others." Critics have claimed that what Gilligan is doing is throwing a monkey wrench into the philosophy of gender equality, and her "ethic of care" theory may result in statements such as this: "We need a new executive with a good head for legal rules—but we can't hire a woman, of course, even though she seems otherwise qualified, because science says that women have a lousy sense of justice." In short, there is a danger that a psychological theory of gender may shift from describing what seems to be the case to prescribing a set of rules about who ought to do what.

Although her theory of the ethic of care may raise problems in the future, there is no doubt that Gilligan has touched on something a vast number of women have been able to relate to. I'll let this anecdote illustrate her talent for seizing the situation: Some years ago she gave the keynote address at an ethics conference at the University of San Diego. Gilligan, who is a petite woman, arrived at the podium in the great lecture hall—and completely disappeared behind the imposing lectern, designed in a more traditional age for taller male scholars. No provisions had been made for shorter speakers. Causing a storm of applause, she reappeared on the other side of the lectern and grabbed the microphone, calmly commenting, "There is obviously still work to be done!"

Recently Gilligan and other feminists engaged in a written debate in the *Atlantic Monthly* with Christina Hoff Sommers (see Box 12.6 and Chapter 10) who by then had acquired a solid reputation among some feminists as being no feminist at all. Sommers had just published a book, *The War Against Boys,* in which she claimed that because of what she calls gender feminism, young boys are now facing a hard time in school. Contrary to the standard wisdom that girls are overlooked in the classroom in favor of the more assertive boys, Sommers says it is in fact the girls who nowadays are getting all the attention from the teachers and are being held up as role models as smarter and better behaved than the boys. This makes boys lose self-esteem. Sommers's claims caused consternation and disbelief among readers of the *Atlantic Monthly,* where her views were first published. But she has also found an audience who agree that conditions in schools have changed dramatically over the past decades to the benefit of girls, and we need to look at the possibility that in some cases it may have come at a price: the shortchanging of boys. Since her book came out in 2000, her claims have, to a great extent been substantiated.

Radical Feminism: Uprooting Sexism

The term *radical* alone is often enough to make some people tune out. We are used to the term meaning "extremism." For some, a radical feminist is a stereotypical male-basher. But we must be cautious here, because much depends on how we interpret the term *radical*. If we read it as "extremist feminism," then it will generally be used by anti-feminists to describe anything they disagree with as being too extreme. The feminists themselves who are tagged with the label may think of themselves as mainstream. It is thus a relative concept and often used in a disparaging sense, meaning any feminism that goes further than you're willing to accept ("Equal pay for equal work" could sound like radical feminism to some traditionalists). To be sure, there are feminists who think in more sweeping terms than others. Some see sexual intercourse with men as inherently humiliating for women. And there are misandric feminists who assume that all men are incapable of wanting or working for gender equality, just as there are misogynist men who think ill of all women. But most of those who today call themselves radical feminists have a different agenda: They take the term *radical* in its original Latin meaning, going to the *root* (*radix*) of the matter. Such radical feminists ask, How did gender discrimination arise? What were the structures that kept it in place? And do we still have elements of those structures today? The answers are generally: *It arose in patriarchy;* those structures have kept gender discrimination alive to this day. A child is still considered to be of the father's family more than of the mother's; yet a mother is still considered to be the primary caregiver of a child taken ill at school, even though the father's profession might be less demanding than hers and his workplace closer to the child's school. A woman is still expected to take her career less seriously than a man is, and some continue to consider a woman's career contributions as less important than a man's. Sexual liberty is still considered more acceptable for boys and men than for girls and women. Commercials persist in depicting women in the kitchen and men at the workbench. Little girls' toys are still in the pink section in the toy stores, and little boys' toys are still action figures from a world with practically no equal women participants. The radical feminist doesn't necessarily want boys to play with dolls or girls to play Mortal Kombat, but she or he wants us to understand *where these choices are coming from* and to decide to discard any tradition that sees women as lesser beings than men.

A famous radical feminist, Andrea Dworkin (1946–2005), wrote in her book *Right-Wing Women: The Politics of Domesticated Females* (1983):

> To achieve a single standard of human freedom and one absolute standard of human dignity, the sex-class system has to be dismembered. The reason is pragmatic, not philosophical: Nothing less will work. However much everyone wants to do less, less will not free women. Liberal men and women ask, Why can't we just be ourselves, all human beings, begin now and not dwell in past injustices, wouldn't that subvert the sex-class system, change it from the inside out? The answer is no. The sex-class system has a structure; it has deep roots in religion and culture; it is fundamental to the economy; sexuality is its creature; to be 'just human beings' in it, women have to hide what happens to them as women because they are women—happenings like forced sex and forced reproduction, happenings that continue as long as the sex-class system operates. The liberation of women requires

facing the real condition of women in order to change it. 'We're all just people' is a stance that prohibits recognition of the systematic cruelties visited upon women because of sex oppression.

Dworkin says that one of the toughest challenges to women is to realize that all women have a common condition, even women you don't like, women you don't want to be compared to. The common condition is that women are, in Dworkin's words, "subordinate to men, sexually colonized in a sexual system of dominance and submission, denied rights on the basis of sex, historically chattel, generally considered biologically inferior, confined to sex and reproduction: this is the general description of the social environment in which all women live."

The goal of radical feminism is thus to raise the individual awareness of what the patriarchal tradition has done to us, men as well as women. We must try to undo the social and psychological damage done by centuries of male-dominated culture—by making women aware of how much in their personal and professional lives has been dominated and designed by men. Radical feminism sees women's minds as by and large shaped by men's accomplishments and thinking, and unless women learn to focus on women's talents and accomplishments, they/we will always have a "false consciousness": We think we understand, but all we have to work with are mind tools and concepts invented by men. Another radical feminist, Gerda Lerner, says that women have until recently been excluded from the "power of naming and defining." Men have defined the problems deemed worthy of attention, as well as the vocabulary with which they should be described. Being able to put a name to a problem is part of solving it, and if women are deprived of naming their own problems, the problems remain unrecognized. For that reason, sex discrimination isn't uprooted simply by listening to the private wishes and professional ideas of women, because these wishes and ideas may be favored by the male tradition we all grew up within. Radical feminism insists that both women and men must be educated to see this tradition as one of oppression and be encouraged to create a new one based on a female perspective.

The Bridge Builders: Tannen and Gurian

For many people, regardless of whether or not they call themselves feminist, the gender debate in the late-twentieth/early-twenty-first century has become too divisive: The classical feminist view seems to fly in the face of the fact that gender appears to be a true natural characteristic, not something that we can change through upbringing and education. The difference feminist view, on the other hand, seems to solidify some old stereotypes that many are happy to have escaped, and radical feminists haven't been making many friends among women and men who enjoy and believe in traditional gender relations. But a few researchers have weighed in with an alternative approach—one that sounds promising if you happen to lean toward soft universalism, like your author. Two names in particular deserve to be mentioned: The linguist Deborah Tannen and the neuropsychologist Michael Gurian. I have chosen to call them bridge builders, because for both researchers the primary goal is to make it possible for women and men to *understand* each other, not to become like each other or to compete against each other. Deborah Tannen gained national attention with her second popular book, *You Just Don't Understand,* based on her research into differences in conversation styles between women and men, and girls and boys, and through a subsequent series of works, both scholarly and popular, exploring why we tend to misunderstand each other and what we can do to bridge the gap between us. In the Primary Readings section you'll find an excerpt from her book on men and women communicating in the workplace, *Talking from 9 to 5,* a section about male and female fears of sexual harassment.

Tannen's theory is that while many differences in our conversational styles may be due to hard-wiring (nature), some of it has to do with our environment (nurture), and she thus places herself in between classical and difference feminism, although she does point out that cross-culturally, all over the planet, some male-female behavioral differences seem to be universal. For Tannen, we are sufficiently similar that we can learn to understand where our significant other—or colleague or boss—of the other gender is coming from, so we can learn to see life through the eyes of our partner and make mutual adjustments to take his or her expectations into consideration. You'll perhaps remember reading about Tannen and the Golden Rule in Chapter 11—this is one of her suggestions: If a man prefers to relax and not have to say anything when he comes home, and his wife or girlfriend is yearning to talk about her day and hear about his, when she comes home, it is no good if we torture each other by one being noncommunicative and the other being overly communicative. What we must do is try to see it from the other's perspective: If you're a woman who wants to talk, give him a little quiet time! If you're a man who just wants peace and quiet, put yourself in her place and be interested in what she has to say about her day, and don't try to solve her problems! She just wants to share her day with you, not get a twelve-step program.

Michael Gurian is a psychotherapist who has staked out a slightly different territory: In a series of very popular works that can be described as self-help books, he has outlined not only the psychological characteristics and needs of boys and girls, but also the neurobiological science behind their behavior. In his book *What Could He Be Thinking? How a Man's Mind Really Works* (2003), he explores what he considers typical male brain patterns, presented for female readers in particular to help in making relationships less rocky and providing a basis for a mutual understanding. While many books written by difference feminists explore the natural differences between women and men, Gurian's book is an exception because he, like Tannen, seeks to emphasize *understanding* the differences. In addition, Gurian contributes to the gender debate with a concept that is uniquely his own: *Bridge brains.* Neurologically, says Gurian, there are "typical" masculine men and "typical" feminine women. But in addition, there are women who are comfortable thinking and acting in ways that some would describe as more masculine than feminine, and men who act and think in more feminine than masculine ways. Sometimes such bridge brains are gay or lesbian, but often the bridge brains are heterosexual—they're just really good at understanding the other gender, because neurologically, their brains are less typically male or female. While some have criticized Gurian for being a traditionalist, his books, like Tannen's, have provided much practical relief and insight to readers who have been turned off by the divisiveness of twentieth-century feminism as well as the oppressiveness of the traditional gender roles. The final word has by no means been said about male and female human nature, and about what roles we ought to play in the dance of human relationships, but there is something to be said for people who try to make the dance smoother for the rest of us, rather than more complicated.

Study Questions

1. Give a brief account of the similarities and differences between classical, difference, radical, and equity feminism. Can these facets overlap? Explain.

2. Can a third-wave feminist be a classical feminist? Can a first-wave feminist be a difference feminist? Can a second-wave feminist be a radical feminist? Explain.

3. Which brand of feminism do you think is the most relevant today? Are you a feminist? If yes, why? If no, why not?

4. Outline the advantages and problems associated with difference feminism.

Primary Readings and Narratives

The first Primary Reading is an excerpt from Harriet Taylor Mill's "Enfranchisement of Women," and the second is from Simone de Beauvoir's *The Second Sex*. The third is an excerpt from Carol Gilligan's *In a Different Voice*. The fourth is an excerpt from the linguist Deborah Tannen's *Talking from 9 to 5* in which she explores the phenomenon of sexual harassment from a male and female point of view. The first Narrative is a summary and excerpt from the classic play by Henrik Ibsen, *A Doll's House,* in which a nineteenth-century housewife, treated as a beloved but mischievous child by her husband, proves to be very much an adult person. The second Narrative is a summary of Laura Esquivel's novel *Like Water for Chocolate,* in which we get to know the women in the De la Garza family. The third Narrative is a summary of and excerpts from Beauvoir's short story "The Woman Destroyed," in which the title character's husband leaves her for another woman. The final Narrative is a summary of the film *Mona Lisa Smile,* about a young art professor at Wellesley in the 1950s.

 Primary Reading

Enfranchisement of Women

HARRIET TAYLOR MILL

Excerpt, 1851.

You have read about Harriet Taylor Mill in Chapter 5, as being John Stuart Mill's soul mate and intellectual partner, and in this chapter you have read about their collaboration on the philosophy of women's rights in mid-nineteenth-century Great Britain. Here you have an excerpt from Harriet Taylor Mill's text, written in 1851—sixteen years before John Stuart Mill's own book about women's rights, *The Subjection of Women,* was published. In 1851 Harriet and John were also finally married, two years after the death of Harriet's husband and after a relationship of twenty-one years. Until Harriet's untimely death from tuberculosis in 1858, she and John went on collaborating about other projects such as an analysis of domestic violence, property rights, and the work that was to become John Stuart Mill's first book after her death: *On Liberty.*

In this excerpt H. T. Mill dismisses three standard nineteenth-century arguments against women in the workforce: that allowing women in the workforce would (1) go against the duties of motherhood, (2) be unfair competition to men, and (3) mean an unsuitable hardening of the female character.

Concerning the fitness, then, of women for politics, there can be no question: but the dispute is more likely to turn upon the fitness of politics for women. When the reasons alleged for excluding women from active life in all its higher departments, are stripped of their garb of declamatory phrases, and reduced to the simple expression of a meaning, they seem to be mainly three: the incompatibility of active life with maternity, and with the care of a household; secondly, its alleged hardening effect on the character; and thirdly, the inexpediency of making an addition to the already excessive pressure of competition in every kind of professional or lucrative employment.

The first, the maternity argument, is usually laid most stress upon: although (it needs hardly be said) this reason, if it be one, can apply only to mothers. It is neither necessary nor just to make imperative on women that they shall be either mothers or nothing; or that if they have been mothers once, they shall be nothing else during the whole remainder of their lives. Neither women nor men need any law to exclude them from an occupation, if they have undertaken another which is incompatible with it. No one proposes to exclude the male sex from Parliament because a man may be a soldier or sailor in active service, or a merchant whose business requires all his time and energies. Nine-tenths of the occupations of men exclude them *de facto* from public life, as effectually as if they were excluded by law; but that is no reason for making laws to exclude even the nine-tenths, much less the remaining tenth. The reason of the case is the same for women as for men. There is no need to make provision by law that a woman shall not carry on the active details of a household, or of the education of children, and at the same time practise a profession or be elected to parliament. Where incompatibility is real, it will take care of itself: but there is gross injustice in making the incompatibility a pretence for the exclusion of those in whose case it does not exist. And these, if they were free to choose, would be a very large proportion The maternity argument deserts its supporters in the case of single women, a large and increasing class of the population; a fact which, it is not irrelevant to remark, by tending to diminish the excessive competition of numbers, is calculated to assist greatly the prosperity of all. There is no inherent reason or necessity that all women should voluntarily choose to devote their lives to one animal function and it consequences. Numbers of women are wives and mothers only because there is no other career open to them, no other occupation for their feelings or their activities. Every improvement in their education, and enlargement of their faculties—everything which renders them more qualified for any other mode of life, increases the number of those to whom it is an injury and an oppression to be denied the choice. To say that women must be excluded from active life because maternity disqualifies them for it, is in fact to say, that every other career should be forbidden them in order that maternity may be their only resource.

But secondly, it is urged, that to give the same freedom of occupation to women as to men, would be an injurious addition to the crowd of competitors, by whom the avenues to almost all kinds of employment are choked up, and its remuneration depressed. This argument, it is to be observed, does not reach the political question. It gives no excuse for withholding from women the rights of citizenship. The suffrage, the jury-box, admission to the legislature and to office, it does not touch. It bears only on the industrial branch of the subject. Allowing it, then, in an economical point of view, its full force; assuming that to lay open to women the employments now monopolized by men, would tend, like the breaking down of other monopolies, to lower the rate of remuneration in those employments; let us consider what is the amount of this evil consequence, and what the compensation for it. The worst ever asserted, much worse than is at all likely to be realized, is that if women competed with men, a man and a woman could not together earn more than is now earned by the man alone. Let us make this supposition, the most unfavourable supposition possible, the joint income of the two would be the same as before, while the woman would be raised from the position of a servant to that of a partner. Even if every woman, as matters now stand, had a claim on some man for support, how infinitely preferable is it that part of the income should be of the woman's earning, even if the aggregate sum were but little increased by it, rather than that she should be compelled to stand aside in order that men may be the sole earners, and the sole dispensers of what is earned. Even under the present laws respecting the property of women,[1] a woman who contributes materially to the support of the family, cannot be treated in the same contemptuously tyrannical manner as one who, however she may toil as a domestic drudge, is a dependent on the man for subsistence. . . . But so long as competition is the general law of human life, it is tyranny to shut out one-half of the competitors. All who have attained the age of self-government, have an equal claim to be permitted to sell whatever kind of useful labour they are capable of, for the price which it will bring.

The third objection to the admission of women to political or professional life, its alleged hardening tendency, belongs to an age now past, and is scarcely to be comprehended by people of the present time. There are still, however, persons who say that the world and its avocations render men selfish and unfeeling; that the struggles, rivalries, and collisions of business and of politics make them harsh and unamiable; that if half the species must unavoidably be given up to these things, it is the more necessary that the other half should be kept free from them; that to preserve women from the bad influences of the world, is the only chance of preventing men from being wholly given up to them.

There would have been plausibility in this argument when the world was still in the age of violence; when life was full of physical conflict, and every man had to redress his

---

[1] The truly horrible effects of the present state of the law among the lowest of the working population, is exhibited in those cases of hideous maltreatment of their wives by working men, with which every newspaper, every police report, teems. Wretches unfit to have the smallest authority over any living thing, have a helpless woman for their household slave. These excesses could not exist if women both earned, and had the right to possess, a part of the income of the family.

injuries or those of others, by the sword or by the strength of his arm. Women, like priests, by being exempted from such responsibilities, and from some part of the accompanying dangers, may have been enabled to exercise a beneficial influence. But in the present condition of human life, we do not know where those hardening influences are to be found, to which men are subject and from which women are at present exempt. Individuals now-a-days are seldom called upon to fight hand to hand, even with peaceful weapons; personal enmities and rivalries count for little in worldly transactions; the general pressure of circumstances, not the adverse will of individuals, is the obstacle men now have to make head against. That pressure, when excessive, breaks the spirit, and cramps and sours the feelings, but not less of women than of men, since they suffer certainly not less from its evils. There are still quarrels and dislikes, but the sources of them are changed. The feudal chief once found his bitterest enemy in his powerful neighbour, the minister or courtier in his rival for place: but opposition of interest in active life, as a cause of personal animosity, is out of date; the enmities of the present day arise not from great things but small, from what people say of one another, more than from what they do; and if there are hated, malice, and all uncharitableness, they are to be found among women fully as much as among men. In the present state of civilization, the notion of guarding women from the hardening influences of the world, could only be realized by secluding them from society altogether. The common duties of common life, as at present constituted, are incompatible with any other softness in women than weakness. Surely weak minds in weak bodies must ere long cease to be even supposed to be either attractive or amiable.

But, in truth, none of these arguments and considerations touch the foundations of the subject. The real question is, whether it is right and expedient that one-half of the human race should pass through life in a state of forced subordination to the other half. If the best state of human society is that of being divided into two parts, one consisting of persons with a will and a substantive existence, the other of humble companions to these persons, attached, each of them to one, for the purpose of bringing up *his* children, and making *his* home pleasant to him; if this is the place assigned to women, it is but kindness to educate them for this; to make them believe that the greatest good fortune which can befall them, is to be chosen by some man for his purpose; and that every other career which the world deems happy or honourable, is closed to them by the law, not of social institutions, but of nature and destiny.

When, however, we ask why the existence of one-half the species should be merely ancillary to that of the other—why each woman should be a mere appendage to a man, allowed to have no interests of her own, that there may be nothing to compete in her mind with his interests and his pleasure; the only reason which can be given is, that men like it. It is agreeable to them that men should live for their own sake, women for the sake of men; and the qualities and conduct in subjects which are agreeable to rulers, they succeed for a long time in making the subjects themselves consider as their appropriate virtues. . . . Under a nominal recognition of a moral code common to both, in practice in self-will and self-assertion form the type of what are designated as manly virtues, while abnegation of self, patience, resignation, and submission to power, unless when resistance is commanded by other interests than their own, have been stamped by general consent as pre-eminently the duties and graces required of women. The meaning being merely, that power makes itself the centre of moral obligation, and that a man likes to have his own will, but does not like that his domestic companion should have a will different from his.

Study Questions

1. What are Harriet Taylor Mill's counterarguments to the three standard arguments against women in the workforce? Are they convincing to you? Why or why not?

2. Might the three arguments (motherhood, unfair competition, and hardening of the character) be valid in any conceivable modern context? Explain why or why not.

3. Apply H. T. Mill's arguments to the idea of women in combat. Do you see the same arguments supporting the idea? or is there a difference? Explain.

4. Comment on H. T. Mill's statement that the only reason women have been ancillary (subordinate) to men is that men like it; is that a fair statement within the context of the nineteenth century, as far as you can tell? Would it be a fair statement in the twenty-first century?

Primary Reading

The Second Sex

SIMONE DE BEAUVOIR

Excerpt, 1949.

In this excerpt, Beauvoir demonstrates her commitment to what we have called classical feminism: If boys and girls were raised as human beings rather than two different species, sexism would no longer exist. The "castration complex" and the "Oedipus complex" are references to Sigmund Freud's psychoanalytic theories that little girls feel inferior to boys because they have no penis (and believe they have been deprived of one). Here you should remember that the style of child-rearing Beauvoir criticizes is, for most educated people in the Western world, a thing of the past. Her critical assessment of the traditional upbringing of boys and girls has been a powerful factor in changing that tradition.

A world where men and women would be equal is easy to visualize, for that precisely is what the Soviet Revolution *promised*: women raised and trained exactly like men were to work under the same conditions and for the same wages. Erotic liberty was to be recognized by custom, but the sexual act was not to be considered a "service" to be paid for; woman was to be *obliged* to provide herself with other ways of earning a living; marriage was to be based on a free agreement that the spouses could break at will; maternity was to be voluntary, which meant that contraception and abortion were to be authorized and that, on the other hand, all mothers and their children were to have exactly the same rights, in or out of marriage; pregnancy leaves were to be paid for by the State, which would assume charge of the children, signifying not that they would be *taken away* from their parents, but that they would not be *abandoned* to them.

But is it enough to change laws, institutions, customs, public opinion, and the whole social context, for men and women to become truly equal? "Women will always be women," say the skeptics. Other seers prophesy that in casting off their femininity they will not succeed in changing themselves into men and they will become monsters. This would be to admit that the woman of today is a creation of nature; it must be repeated once more that in human society nothing is natural and that woman, like much else, is a product elaborated by civilization. The intervention of others in her destiny is fundamental: if this action took a different direction, it would produce a quite different result. Woman is determined not by her hormones or by mysterious instincts, but by the manner in which her body and her relation to the world are modified through the action of others than herself. The abyss that separates the adolescent boy and girl has been deliberately opened out between them since earliest childhood; later on, woman could not be other than what she *was made,* and that past was bound to shadow her for life. If we appreciate its influence, we see clearly that her destiny is not predetermined for all eternity.

We must not believe, certainly, that a change in woman's economic condition alone is enough to transform her, though this factor has been and remains the basic factor in her evolution; but until it has brought about the moral, social, cultural, and other consequences that it promises and requires, the new woman cannot appear. At this moment they have been realized nowhere, in Russia no more than in France or the United States; and this explains why the woman of today is torn between the past and the future. She appears most often as a "true woman" disguised as a man, and she feels herself as ill at ease in her flesh as in her masculine garb. She must shed her old skin and cut her own new clothes. This she could do only through a social evolution. No single educator could fashion a *female human being* today who would be the exact homologue of the *male human being;* if she is raised like a boy, the young girl feels she is an oddity and thereby she is given a new kind of sex specification. Stendhal [a nineteenth-century French novelist] understood this when he said: "The forest must be planted all at once." But if we imagine, on the contrary, a society in which the equality of the sexes would be concretely realized, this equality would find new expression in each individual.

If the little girl were brought up from the first with the same demands and rewards, the same severity and the same freedom, as her brothers, taking part in the same studies, the same games, promised the same future, surrounded with women and men who seemed to her undoubted equals, the meanings of the castration complex and of the Oedipus complex would be profoundly modified. Assuming on the same basis as the father the material and moral responsibility of the couple, the mother would enjoy the same lasting prestige; the child would perceive around her an androgynous world and not a masculine world. Were she emotionally more attracted to her father—which is not even sure—her love for him would be tinged with a will to emulation and not a feeling of powerlessness; she would not be oriented toward passivity. Authorized to test her powers in work and sports, competing actively with the boys, she would not find the absence of the penis—compensated by the promise of a child—enough to give rise to an inferiority complex; correlatively, the boy would not have a superiority complex if it were not instilled into him and if he looked up to women with as much respect as to men. The little girl would not seek sterile compensation in narcissism and dreaming, she would not take her fate for granted; she would be interested in what she was *doing,* she would throw herself without reserve into undertakings. . . .

I shall be told that all this is utopian fancy, because woman cannot be "made over" unless society has first made her really the equal of man. Conservatives have never failed in such circumstances to refer to that vicious circle; history, however, does not revolve. If a caste is kept in a state of inferiority, no doubt it remains inferior; but liberty can break the circle. Let the Negroes vote and they become worthy of having the vote; let woman be given responsibilities and she is able to assume them. The fact is that oppressors cannot be expected to make a move of gratuitous generosity; but at one time the revolt of the oppressed, at another time even the very evolution of the privileged caste itself, creates new situations; thus men have been led, in their own interest, to give partial emancipation to women: it remains only for women to continue their ascent, and the successes they are obtaining are an encouragement for them to do so. It seems almost certain that sooner or later they will arrive at complete economic and social equality, which will bring about an inner metamorphosis.

However this may be, there will be some to object that if such a world is possible it is not desirable. When woman is "the same" as her male, life will lose its salt and spice. This argument, also, has lost its novelty: those interested in perpetuating present conditions are always in tears about the marvelous past that is about to disappear, without having so much as a smile for the young future. It is quite true that doing away with the slave trade meant death to the great plantations, magnificent with azaleas and camellias, it meant ruin to the whole refined Southern civilization. The attics of time have received its rare odd laces along with the clear pure voices of the Sistine *castrati,* and there is a certain "feminine charm" that is also on the way to the same dusty repository. I agree that he would be a barbarian indeed who failed to appreciate exquisite flowers, rare lace, the crystal clear voice of the eunuch, and feminine charm.

When the "charming woman" shows herself in all her splendor, she is a much more exalting object than the "idiotic paintings, overdoors, scenery, showman's garish signs, popular chromos," that excited [French poet Arthur] Rimbaud; adorned with the most modern artifices, beautified according to the newest techniques, she comes down from the remoteness of the ages, from Thebes, from Crete, from Chichén-Itzá; and she is also the totem set up deep in the African jungle; she is a helicopter and she is a bird; and there is this, the greatest wonder of all: under her tinted hair the forest murmur becomes a thought, and words issue from her breasts. Men stretch forth avid hands toward the marvel, but when they grasp it it is gone; the wife, the mistress, speak like everybody else through their mouths: their words are worth just what they are worth; their breasts also. Does such a fugitive miracle—and one so rare—justify us in perpetuating a situation that is baneful for both sexes? One can appreciate them at their true value; if these treasures cost blood or misery, they must be sacrificed.

Study Questions

1. Identify the characteristic elements of classical feminism in this excerpt.

2. Comment on Beauvoir's remark that one can appreciate the beauty of flowers, the charm of women, and "appreciate them at their true value; if these treasures cost blood and misery, they must be sacrificed."

3. What does Beauvoir mean by saying, "Let the Negroes vote and they become worthy of having the vote; let woman be given responsibilities and she is able to assume them"?

4. Evaluate the criticism that the gender-free model of upbringing Beauvoir envisions for boys and girls is really just patterned after the traditional upbringing of boys; does Beauvoir want women to become men in order to achieve social and political freedom?

Primary Reading

In a Different Voice

CAROL GILLIGAN

Excerpt, 1982.

In this excerpt, Gilligan refers to the psychoanalyst Erik Erikson, whom you encountered briefly in Chapter 10. Erikson's theory of development focuses on the importance of the adolescent boy's separating himself from his parents to achieve a personal identity before he can experience any intimacy. For the adolescent girl it is different, says Erikson; she doesn't experience the same kind of separation. However, it is the boy's development that becomes the typical individual development for Erikson, according to Gilligan. In this excerpt she also refers to how fairy tales may give similar portrayals of male and female psychology. Gilligan here introduces the experience of the ethic of care from the woman's point of view.

Erikson's description of male identity as forged in relation to the world and of female identity as awakened in a relationship of intimacy with another person is hardly new. In the fairy tales that [psychoanalyst] Bruno Bettelheim describes [in *The Uses of Enchantment*] an identical portrayal appears. The dynamics of male adolescence are illustrated archetypically by the conflict between father and son in "The Three Languages." Here a son, considered hopelessly stupid by his father, is given one last chance at education and sent for a year to study with a master. But when he returns, all he has learned is "what the dogs bark." After two further attempts of this sort, the father gives up in disgust and orders his servants to take the child into the forest and kill him. But the servants, those perpetual rescuers of disowned and abandoned children, take pity on the child and decide simply to leave him in the forest. From there, his wanderings take him to a land beset by furious dogs whose barking permits nobody to rest and who periodically devour one of the inhabitants. Now it turns out that our hero has learned just the right thing: he can talk with the dogs and is able to quiet them, thus restoring peace to the land. Since the other knowledge he acquires serves him equally well, he emerges triumphant from his adolescent confrontation with his father, a giant of the life-cycle conception.

    In contrast, the dynamics of female adolescence are depicted through the telling of a very different story. In the world of the fairy tale, the girl's first bleeding is followed by a period of intense passivity in which nothing seems to be happening. Yet in the deep sleeps of Snow White and Sleeping Beauty, Bettelheim sees that inner concentration which he considers to be the necessary counterpart to the activity of adventure. Since the adolescent heroines awake from their sleep, not to conquer the world, but to marry the prince, their identity is inwardly and interpersonally defined. For women, in Bettelheim's as in Erikson's account, identity and intimacy are intricately conjoined. The sex differences depicted in the world of fairy tales, like the fantasy of the woman warrior in Maxine Hong Kingston's recent autobiographical novel [*The Woman Warrior,* 1977] which echoes the old stories of Troilus and Cressida and Tancred and Corinda, indicate repeatedly that active adventure is a male activity, and that if a woman is to embark on such endeavors, she must at least dress like a man. [. . .]

"It is obvious," Virginia Woolf says, "that the values of women differ very often from the values which have been made by the other sex." Yet, she adds, "it is the masculine values that prevail." As a result, women come to question the normality of their feelings and to alter their judgments in deference to the opinion of others. In the nineteenth-century novels written by women, Woolf sees at work "a mind which was slightly pulled from the straight and made to alter its clear vision in deference to external authority." The same deference to the values and opinions of others can be seen in the judgments of twentieth-century women. The difficulty women experience in finding or speaking publicly in their own voices emerges repeatedly in the form of qualification and self-doubt, but also in intimations of a divided judgment, a public assessment and private assessment which are fundamentally at odds.

Yet the deference and confusion that Woolf criticizes in women derive from the values she sees as their strength. Women's deference is rooted not only in their social subordination but also in the substance of their moral concern. Sensitivity to the needs of others and the assumption of responsibility for taking care lead women to attend to voices other than their own and to include in their judgment other points of view. Women's moral weakness, manifest in an apparent diffusion and confusion of judgment, is thus inseparable from women's moral strength, an overriding concern with relationships and responsibilities. The reluctance to judge may itself be indicative of the care and concern for others that infuse the psychology of women's development and are responsible for what is generally seen as problematic in its nature.

Thus women not only define themselves in a context of human relationship but also judge themselves in terms of their ability to care. Women's place in man's life cycle has been that of nurturer, caretaker, and helpmate, the weaver of those networks of relationships on which she in turn relies. But while women have thus taken care of men, men have, in their theories of psychological development, as in their economic arrangements, tended to assume or devalue that care. When the focus on individuation and individual achievement extends into adulthood and maturity is equated with personal autonomy, concern with relationships appears as a weakness of women rather than as a human strength. [. . .]

The discovery now being celebrated by men in mid-life of the importance of intimacy, relationships, and care is something that women have known from the beginning. However, because that knowledge in women has been considered "intuitive" or "instinctive," a function of anatomy coupled with destiny, psychologists have neglected to describe its development. In my research, I have found that women's moral development centers on the elaboration of that knowledge and thus delineates a critical line of psychological development in the lives of both of the sexes.

Study Questions

1. Examine "The Three Languages," the first fairy tale cited in the excerpt, and compare it to "Snow White" and "Sleeping Beauty" (which I assume you are familiar with). Explain how each can be said to contain a view of the male and female psyche. You may want to read the section on fairy tales in Chapter 2 again.

2. How does this excerpt on women's moral values relate to virtue theory?

3. Evaluate Gilligan's statement that "Women's deference is rooted not only in their social subordination but also in the substance of their moral concern. Sensitivity to the needs of others and the assumption of the responsibility for taking care lead women to attend to voices other than their own and to include in their judgment other points of view." How do you think Levinas (Chapter 10) would comment on this statement? What do you think Christina Hoff Sommers might say? And what is your own opinion?

Primary Reading

Talking from 9 to 5

DEBORAH TANNEN

Excerpt, 1994.

Deborah Tannen's book *Talking from 9 to 5* followed on the heels of her immensely popular *You Just Don't Understand* (1990), a book about male and female forms of communication within personal relationships. Drawing on her linguistic research into speech patterns and conversational styles, Tannen concludes that, as men and women, we have different expectations of each other, based on the friendships we developed as children: Girls are used to games in intimate groups. Boys are used to a hierarchy of playmates. Girls will engage in "troubles talk," sharing their problems with their best friend in a seemingly equal environment. Boys tend to hide their problems except in the company of special close friends, for fear of appearing to be one-down, lower in the hierarchy. And that's why men don't ask for directions, she says! In *Talking from 9 to 5,* Tannen explores the conversational styles in the workplace. Here she claims that fear of sexual harassment is shared by both men and women, but on different grounds, and to a different degree.

Men Can Be Harassed Too — But It's Different

When the Clarence Thomas hearings took place, I was asked to appear on radio and television to talk about the role of language in sexual harassment. I had previously spent the major part of a year appearing on such shows and writing articles on the topic of women's and men's conversational styles and had rarely gotten a negative response. Nearly everyone seemed to appreciate my even-handed approach: Women's and men's styles are equally valid; each has its own logic; problems occur because of the differences in style. But when I made public statements about sexual harassment, I had to say that things were different for women and men. I received several letters of complaint from men who felt I was slighting them. "Men can be sexually harassed too," they accurately protested. Michael Crichton's novel *Disclosure* dramatizes this. But it also shows that, although the situation can occur, its fundamental elements are different from those that underlie harassment of women by men.

Maureen Dowd summarizes the premise of *Disclosure* in a book review:

> Meredith Johnson, the cool, beautiful blond who is the new boss at Digital Communications in Seattle, summons one of her division managers, Tom Sanders, to her office for their first business meeting.
>
> She has a chilled bottle of chardonnay waiting. Her skirt is riding up her thigh. She kicks off her heels and wiggles her toes. She crosses and uncrosses her legs several times, explaining that she doesn't wear stockings because she likes "the bare feeling." She half parts her full lips and looks dreamily at him through preternaturally long lashes. She tells him that he has "a nice hard tush." She asks for a neck massage.

Dowd comments about the Crichton book, "Here is the novel Hollywood has been waiting for: Sharon Stone as Bob Packwood." But compare her description of the novel's action with a description of Bob Packwood's behavior, according to an account in *The New York Times Magazine:*

> While running for reelection in 1980, Bob Packwood was eager to meet his campaign chairwoman for Lane County, Ore. The Senator invited Gena Hutton to dinner at the motel where he was staying in Eugene for a get-acquainted meeting. Hutton, a 35-year-old divorced mother of two, had brought along pictures of her children and even her cats.
>
> Then it was time to go and Packwood offered to walk her to her car. "As I started to put the key in the car door," Hutton recalls, "he just reeled me around and grabbed me and pulled me close to him." For an instant, she thought he was offering a good-night hug. But then the Senator planted a full kiss on her lips, wriggling his tongue into her mouth.

Packwood's behavior toward Hutton was aggressive. He grabbed her, pulled her toward him, and pushed his tongue into her mouth. In contrast, the woman in the Crichton novel, although clearly abusing her power, is seductive: She doesn't begin by lunging at Tom, but by luring him to her. Rather than forcibly pulling him toward her and doing things to him, she invites him to move toward her and do things to her. ("She asks for a neck massage.")

Later in Dowd's summary, Meredith is described as physically attacking Tom: "She pushes him onto the couch and pinions him there." But this physical assault comes after the seductive behavior previously described, not out of the blue as in the alleged Packwood example. And if Tom Sanders does not push Meredith Johnson off him, it is not because he is not big and strong enough to fight her off, but because he is unwilling to ruin his career by hitting his boss. Gena Hutton, in contrast, was smaller in stature and weaker in strength than Bob Packwood, as is usually the case when a woman and a man have an encounter. Hutton did not accept Packwood's invitation to enter his motel room, but if she had, and if he had wanted to, he would probably have been physically capable of throwing her down and "pinioning" her, and she would probably have been physically incapable of fighting him off.

Behaviors associated with the sexes in our culture are differently apportioned. Men's sexual behavior is expected to be aggressive, women's seductive. Imagine the scene of the Crichton novel with the genders reversed:

> Tom Sanders, the cool, beautiful blonde who is the new boss at Digital Communications in Seattle, summons one of his division managers, Meredith Johnson, to his office for their first business meeting.
>
> He has a chilled bottle of chardonnay waiting. His trousers are riding up his calves. He kicks off his shoes and wiggles his toes. He crosses and uncrosses his legs several times, explaining that he doesn't wear socks because he likes "the bare feeling." He half parts his full lips and looks dreamily at her through preternaturally long lashes. He tells her that she has "a nice hard tush." He asks for a neck massage.

It would not be surprising if Meredith Johnson, observing Tom Sanders behaving this way, would burst out laughing or determine he had come unhinged. Even the initial description, "cool, beautiful blonde," is incongruous when applied to a man, because it is only with women that physical attractiveness is the key feature, which is why the word "beautiful" has come to be associated with women—except, perhaps, to describe a young man from the perspective of someone who might be drawn to him. A description of a male boss would more likely be in terms of his size and appearance of power.

Woman As Witch

It might seem puzzling, at first, that Michael Crichton's character Meredith, a woman boss who sexually harasses a man who works for her, is portrayed as young and beautiful. Dowd suggests it is Crichton's way of finessing the irony that "while women think power is sexy in men, men often find power threatening in women." In other words, had the "carnivorous supervisor" been a large, physically overpowering older woman, the image of her making sexual advances toward Tom would have been less titillating for readers, a problem that would not have arisen if the genders were reversed.

But there is another reason, I think, for the way Meredith is portrayed. And it too comes down to cultural stereotypes and collective memory. A cultural icon deeply associated with female characters in folk tales and popular culture is the witch. In her book *Reflections on Gender and Science,* Evelyn Fox Keller quotes a character in a play published in 1659, Walter Charleton's *Ephesian Matron,* who is railing against witches in the form of woman: "You are the true *Hiena's,* that allure us with the fairness of your skins; and when folly hath brought us within your reach, you leap upon us and devour us."

It is the fear of being devoured by a woman he is attracted to, fear inspired by the very attraction he feels, that can stir such atavistic anxiety in a man. The fear results from the loss of control entailed by attraction. In other words, it is precisely the beautiful, alluring woman who is terrifying to men (especially when she is "cool," impervious to losing control as a result of sexual attraction herself), in a way that a large, physically threatening woman would not be. Although such a woman might frighten an individual man in a real-life encounter, the thought of a large, unattractive woman trying to seduce a man would not strike terror in most men's hearts but would be more likely to make them laugh; rather than tapping into deep fears, it would simply seem incongruous and therefore funny.

The woman as witch is also, I think, at the heart of another popular literary work about sexual harassment written by a man: David Mamet's play *Oleanna.* In it, a college student named Carol destroys a professor named John by falsely accusing him of sexual harassment and then rape. The action takes place in the professor's office. In the first act, Carol is insecure and self-effacing, confessing that she is unable to follow the course material and terrified of failing. "I can't understand," she wails. "I sit in class, in the back, and I smile, but I don't know what anyone's talking about. I'm just stupid." The professor is touched. He fears it is his fault, not hers, that she doesn't understand, so he tries to make amends. He reassures her: He'll tutor her privately; she will get an "A." At the end of the act, in his attempt to comfort her, he puts his arm around her shoulders. In Act II, we learn that Carol has filed a sexual-harassment suit against John, just when his tenure (the key to a professor's career) is hanging in the balance.

It is easy to imagine a real-life situation in which a professor might put his arm around a student to comfort her, and she might take offense, though hard to imagine her going so far as to file a complaint. Later in the play, however, Carol ups the ante and threatens to accuse him of rape. The action that follows leaves the realm of reality and enters the world of nightmare. In Act II, Carol is transformed. She is articulate, self-assured, and on the attack. Now it is she who is standing, lecturing, interrupting, and he who is sitting, helpless, speechless.

When I first saw this play, I found Carol's transformation from Act I to Act II baffling. I could only regard it as incompetent playwriting. But the description of witches makes it comprehensible. The play captures what it is about the issue of sexual harassment that so frightens men. Like a witch, a woman can lure a man with the fairness of her skin and a pretense of weakness, then leap upon him and destroy him. (This is the same deep fear that is embodied in the story of Samson and Delilah.) The professor in Mamet's play explains that he has always felt that authorities were out to get him: parents who told him he didn't understand and made him feel stupid, bosses, and now the tenure committee. The play shows that the ability to yell "sexual harassment" gives women students that kind of power over him, since any one of them could, in theory, fabricate a charge and destroy him.

This is why women and men seem so often to be holding on to different legs of this elephant. The aspect of sexual harassment that taps into women's fears is the specter of assault, verbal or physical, by a man from whose clutches they cannot easily escape. This aspect is likely to be dismissed by many men. Indeed, some men find it insulting because they hear the statement "the *possibility* of violence against women is ubiquitous" as an (obviously unfounded) accusation that all men are rapists. The aspect that holds power for most men is the possibility of a false charge, a possibility that many women dismiss as unlikely to happen, since bringing charges is so damaging to the accuser. For their part, many women are insulted by men's concern, which they hear as an accusation that women are manipulative liars. In fact, it is far more common for women to be physically assaulted or sexually harassed than for them to bring false charges, but these realities do not change the power each fear holds for the individuals who identify with one party or the other.

I believe that most men do not wish to use their status and position to hurt and exploit women. But many good men worry, What would I do if someone brought a false charge against me? Not realizing that those who are guilty of serious sexual harassment are doing things they would not think of doing, they ask themselves, "What kind of remark have I made, in innocence, that could be misconstrued?" Again, the relative infrequency with which women make false charges is not relevant here; it suffices that the possibility is theoretically real, and there have been enough such cases to dramatize the possibility. In other words, each group tends to dismiss the other's deep fears as unlikely to occur. Their own fears, however, thrive on the awareness of possibility.

Study Questions

1. Compare the *Disclosure* summary with Tannen's spoof. What makes the difference, and why is the spoof funny? What does that tell us about the phenomenon of sexual harassment?

2. What is it men are afraid of, according to Tannen? What is it women are afraid of? Is she right? Explain.

3. Comment on the reference to the play *Oleanna* (also a film, 1994, directed by the playwright, David Mamet). Is the story told from the professor's or the student's point of view? How might that make a difference? How might a student view the issue of sexual harassment? How might a professor view it?

Narrative

A Doll's House

HENRIK IBSEN

Play, 1879. Summary and Excerpt. Translated by William Archer. Two British film versions exist, both from 1973; one stars Claire Bloom and Anthony Hopkins; the other stars Jane Fonda and David Warner.

By the time the Norwegian playwright Henrik Ibsen wrote *A Doll's House,* isolated voices had been speaking out for the liberation of women for over a hundred years, but there was not a single country in the Western world where women had yet achieved the right to vote. When Ibsen's play was performed on the stages of Europe, the final act turned out to be a bombshell; Ibsen allows us to see Nora's situation from her own point of view and shows us that this viewpoint is heroic in its own way. In her quest to be regarded as a mature human being, Nora sent signals to men and women all over the Western world and made a considerable impact on the gender debate in Scandinavia at the end of the nineteenth and the beginning of the twentieth century. The story has been considered so compelling that the play is still performed today.

Some contemporary readers may prefer to look for literature about the condition of women written by *women,* not by *men.* But, for one thing, Ibsen's play has had historical importance in helping men as well as women see the traditional woman's role as a political question; for another thing, good writers gifted with clear powers of observation and an imaginative genius, such as Ibsen, are often quite capable of seeing a situation from the other gender's point of view.

The conflict between the feminine virtue of caring and the masculine focus on justice may seem new to many readers of Carol Gilligan, but in these excerpts you can see the outlines of that very same debate, anticipated by Ibsen more than a century ago.

Nora and Torvald Helmer are a happily married middle-class couple with three young children. Helmer regards his lively wife as another child, always happy and singing; his pet names for her are his songbird, his lark, his little squirrel. He accuses her of being a spendthrift, of always asking for more pocket money, but he forgives her because she is so sweet and amusing. And even to her friends she seems like a carefree, coddled woman with no worries other than choosing what clothes to wear for parties. But things are not what they seem on the surface. An old friend of Nora's comes to visit, and Nora tells her a deep secret of which she is very proud: Some years ago Helmer was very ill, and the doctor recommended an expensive trip to Italy as a cure. Helmer believes that Nora's father lent them the money, and he is now dead, so he can't tell. But Nora paid for the trip all by herself, with no income or fortune of her own: She took out a private loan, with high interest, and that is why she has been asking Helmer for so much pocket money, buying only the cheapest things for herself, and paying the loan off, always on time, with interest. And it won't be long now before the loan will be paid off: Helmer is being promoted to bank manager, and their finances will improve.

But disaster waits in the wings: An employee at the bank, Krogstad, turns up and begs her to ask her husband to let him keep his job. Why might he lose it? Because he has a criminal record; he has forged papers. And why would he come to Nora? Because Nora knows him well—he is the man who lent her the money for the trip to Italy. He threatens to tell Helmer, but what is worse, he has done some research. Nora's father cosigned the loan, as security—but the signature is dated days after her father died. The conclusion is obvious: Nora forged her father's signature, and now Krogstad threatens her with the law and tells her that his crime was no worse than her own.

> *Krogstad:* May I ask you one more question? Why did you not send the paper to your father?
>
> *Nora:* It was impossible. Father was ill. If I had asked him for his signature, I should have had to tell him why I wanted the money; but he was so ill I really could not tell him that my husband's life was in danger. It was impossible.
>
> *Krogstad:* Then it would have been better to have given up your tour.
>
> *Nora:* No, I couldn't do that; my husband's life depended on that journey. I couldn't give it up.
>
> *Krogstad:* And did it never occur to you that you were playing me false?
>
> *Nora:* That was nothing to me. I didn't care in the least about you. I couldn't endure you for all the cruel difficulties you made, although you knew how ill my husband was.

Krogstad: Mrs. Helmer, you evidently do not realise what you have been guilty of. But I can assure you it was nothing more and nothing worse that made me an outcast from society.

Nora: You! You want me to believe that you did a brave thing to save your wife's life?

Krogstad: The law takes no account of motives.

Nora: Then it must be a very bad law.

Krogstad: Bad or not, if I produce this document in court, you will be condemned according to law.

Nora: I don't believe that. Do you mean to tell me that a daughter has no right to spare her dying father trouble and anxiety?—that a wife has no right to save her husband's life? I don't know much about the law, but I'm sure you'll find, somewhere or another, that that is allowed. And you don't know that—you, a lawyer! You must be a bad one, Mr. Krogstad.

Krogstad: Possibly. But business—such business as ours—I do understand. You believe that? Very well; now do as you please. But this I may tell you, that if I am flung into the gutter a second time, you shall keep me company.

[*Bows and goes out through hall.*]

Nora: [*Stands a while thinking, then tosses her head.*] Oh nonsense! He wants to frighten me. I'm not so foolish as that. [*Begins folding the children's clothes. Pauses.*] But—? No, it's impossible! Why, I did it for love!

Later, Helmer talks to her about what a despicable man Krogstad is, and how vile his crime. Shortly after, Helmer fires Krogstad, in spite of Nora's pleas, and Krogstad shows up again. Now he wants more: Unless Nora makes Helmer reinstate him and give him a promotion, he will reveal all. And if Nora should think of drastic solutions, such as killing herself, her husband will still be told everything. Now Krogstad wants Helmer to know, so he can blackmail the two of them, instead of only her, and he leaves a letter for Helmer, telling him everything. Nora is desperate and tries to distract Helmer when he comes home by dancing for him, and she makes him promise that he will not open the letter until the next day. Meanwhile, she pleads with her friend and confidante to go to Krogstad and persuade him to stop his threats.

The following night Nora and Helmer are at a dance, and Nora dances as if it is her last night on this earth. Coming home, there is still the letter waiting for them, and Nora, deep in despair, is waiting, too: for a miracle, for without it she is going to kill herself.

But Helmer reads the letter, and is horrified: the woman he loved, a liar and a criminal! He blames her weakness of character and her father's bad influence and sees himself as a ruined man. He insists that Nora can no longer see her children—they must be protected from her evil influence. Nora threatens suicide, but Helmer scoffs at it: How is that going to help *him* and *his* ruin? And now it dawns on Nora that her motivation for forging her father's signature is utterly lost on Helmer; the miracle she was hoping for, and dreading, is far from happening.

But now comes the salvation: Nora's friend has succeeded in persuading Krogstad to drop the matter (through a personal sacrifice which Nora knows nothing about).

Krogstad returns Nora's I.O.U. with an apologetic letter, and Helmer is ecstatic, exclaiming that now he is saved. And, magnanimously, he now sees Nora as a poor, misguided soul who has not understood what she has done, and he forgives her. All she needs now is his guidance, he says—from now on he'll be her will and her conscience, and everything will be as before.

Meanwhile Nora, stone-faced, has changed out of her masquerade dress and into her ordinary clothes. For her, the masquerade is over, and although he doesn't know it yet, it is, too, for him. She asks him to sit down, for she has much to talk over with him.

Helmer: You alarm me, Nora. I don't understand you.

Nora: No, that is just it. You don't understand me; and I have never understood you—till tonight. No, don't interrupt. Only listen to what I say. — We must come to a final settlement, Torvald.

Helmer: How do you mean?

Nora: [*After a short silence.*] Does not one thing strike you as we sit here?

Helmer: What should strike me?

Nora: We have been married eight years. Does it not strike you that this is the first time we two, you and I, man and wife, have talked together seriously?

Helmer: Seriously! What do you call seriously?

Nora: During eight whole years, and more—ever since the day we first met—we have never exchanged one serious word about serious things.

Helmer: Was I always to trouble you with the cares you could not help me to bear?

Nora: I am not talking of cares. I say that we have never yet set ourselves seriously to get to the bottom of anything.

Helmer: Why, my dearest Nora, what have you to do with serious things?

Nora: There we have it! You have never understood me. — I have had great injustice done me, Torvald; first by father, and then by you.

Helmer: What! By your father and me? — By us, who have loved you more than all the world?

Nora: [*Shaking her head.*] You have never loved me. You only thought it amusing to be in love with me.

Helmer: Why, Nora, what a thing to say!

Nora: Yes, it is so, Torvald. While I was at home with father, he used to tell me all his opinions, and I held the same opinions. If I had others I said nothing about them, because he wouldn't have liked it. He used to call me his doll-child, and played with me as I played with my dolls. Then I came to live in your house—

Helmer: What an expression to use about our marriage!

Nora: [*Undisturbed.*] I mean I passed from father's hands into yours. You arranged everything according to your taste; and I got the same tastes as you; or I pretended to—I don't know which—both ways, perhaps; sometimes one and sometimes the other. When I look back on it now, I seem to have been living here like a beggar, from hand to mouth. I lived by performing tricks for you, Torvald. But you would have it so. You and father have done me a great wrong. It is your fault that my life has come to nothing.

Helmer: Why, Nora, how unreasonable and ungrateful you are! Have you not been happy here?

Nora: No, never. I thought I was; but I never was.

Helmer: Not—not happy!

Nora: No; only merry. And you have always been so kind to me. But our house has been nothing but a play-room. Here I have been your doll-wife, just as at home I used to be papa's doll-child. And the children, in their turn, have been my dolls. I thought it fun when you played with me, just as the children did when I played with them. That has been our marriage, Torvald.

. . . .

Helmer: To forsake your home, your husband, and your children! And you don't consider what the world will say.

Nora: I can pay no heed to that. I only know that I must do it.

Helmer: This is monstrous! Can you forsake your holiest duties in this way?

Nora: What do you consider my holiest duties?

Helmer: Do I need to tell you that? Your duties to your husband and your children.

Nora: I have other duties equally sacred.

Helmer: Impossible! What duties do you mean?

Nora: My duties towards myself.

Helmer: Before all else you are a wife and a mother.

Nora: That I no longer believe. I believe that before all else I am a human being, just as much as you are—or at least that I should try to become one. I know that most people agree with you, Torvald, and that they say so in books. But henceforth I can't be satisfied with what most people say, and what is in books. I must think things out for myself, and try to get clear about them.

. . . .

Nora: I have waited so patiently all these eight years; for of course I saw clearly enough that miracles don't happen every day. When this crushing blow threatened me, I said to myself so confidently, "Now comes the miracle!" When Krogstad's letter lay in the box, it never for a moment occurred to me that you would think of submitting to that man's conditions. I was convinced that you would say to him, "Make it known to all the world"; and that then—

Helmer: Well? When I had given my own wife's name up to disgrace and shame—?

Nora: Then I firmly believed that you would come forward, take everything upon yourself, and say, "I am the guilty one."

Helmer: Nora—!

Nora: You mean I would never have accepted such a sacrifice? No, certainly not. But what would my assertions have been worth in opposition to yours?—That was the miracle that I hoped for and dreaded. And it was to hinder that that I wanted to die.

Helmer: I would gladly work for you day and night, Nora—bear sorrow and want for your sake. But no man sacrifices his honour, even for one he loves.

Nora: Millions of women have done so.

So, in the end, Torvald is the one who understands nothing; he promises to love her, to do anything if she will only stay with him. But she sees him now as a stranger and prepares to leave. In her final words to him she says that in order to get together again, they would both have to change so much that "communion between them shall be a marriage." And Nora leaves, closing the door behind her.

Study Questions

1. What does Nora mean by the final line in this excerpt?

2. If you were in Nora's position, would your reaction be similar or different? Why? If you were in Helmer's position, would your reaction be similar or different? Why?

3. Examine the excerpts and find evidence of virtue ethics as opposed to an ethics of justice.

4. Ibsen refers to his characters as "Nora" and "Helmer" rather than "Nora" and "Torvald." What kind of effect might that have on the reader of the play? Do you think it is intentional?

5. You'll remember Flaubert's *Madame Bovary,* summarized in Chapter 4; Flaubert told of a vain and selfish woman who ruined her own and her husband's life by racking up debts for her own amusement. *A Doll's House,* from approximately the same time period and the same social world, is a story of another woman who also goes into debt. Compare the two stories: Are there significant similarities? Are there significant differences?

Narrative

Like Water for Chocolate

LAURA ESQUIVEL

Novel, 1989. Summary. Film version by Alfonso Arau (director) and Laura Esquivel (screenwriter), 1992.

One might get the impression that feminism claims all women are always caring and always in complete understanding with each other; but as we discussed earlier, not all women are caring or nurturing beings. Neither is it the case that women have a secret understanding that makes them friends or sisters; occasional enmity between women is a fact of life. However, as both classical and difference feminism claim, certain conditions shared by just about all women—such as a common biology and family roles—can be seen as laying down some ground rules for women's relationships with each other. One of these conditions is being raised in a male-dominated world; for difference feminists, the *caring imperative* is one of the ground rules. On the basis of these common conditions and rules, women should be able to understand each other to a great extent. A story that illustrates how common conditions make it possible to reach an understanding is the Mexican novel *Like Water for Chocolate.* In this story, which became a critically acclaimed film that won Academy Awards, Laura Esquivel tells of a matriarchal family consisting of the mother, three sisters, and the helpful ghost of a cook and of their relationships to each other and to the men in their lives. There are twelve chapters in the novel, one for each month of the year, and each with its own recipe attached to it, because this is a story of food and of cooking, of "mood meals" and how the intense emotions of a good cook can transform the lives of those eating her food.

Mama Elena and her daughters, Gertrudis, Rosaura, and Tita, live on a ranch in Mexico. The story takes place during the Mexican revolution in the early twentieth century, and the troops of rebel leader Pancho Villa play a part in the lives of the women.

Mama Elena is a strict woman who rules her household with an iron fist; "I've never needed a man for anything," she says. "All by myself, I've done all right with my ranch and my daughters." But there is little love between her and her youngest daughter, Tita, who feels that their cook, Nacha, is more of a mother to her. Together they spend their time in the kitchen, and Tita's toys are the pans and the stove and the traditional Mexican and pre-Columbian recipes of Nacha, who has Indian blood. Tita loves Nacha and the kitchen, but she also has another love: Pedro, a young man she has seen in the village. It was love at first glance for both of them, and now he has asked her mother for her hand in marriage; but that can never be, says Mama Elena, because Tita must, according to the family tradition, never marry or have children. As the youngest daughter, she must consecrate her life to taking care of her mother. And Tita asks, Who came up with this idea? And who will then take care of Tita when she grows old? And what about women who marry and can't have children? But all questions must be buried, because Mama Elena's rule is absolute. However, Mama Elena has an idea: If Pedro wants to get married, then Tita's sister Rosaura is available. The household is horrified (a maid says, "You can't just switch them, like tacos and enchiladas"), but nobody is more surprised than Tita when Pedro agrees to the marriage. She believed he would love her forever . . . but he explains to her, during a clandestine meeting, that this was the only way he could be with her forever, as part of the family.

During the wedding banquet something strange happens. Tita is dry-eyed, because she cried all her tears the day before when preparing the wedding cake, supported by Nacha. Tita's tears fell into the meringue icing, and when Nacha tasted it, she was seized by the most terrible longing. She remembered her fiancé of long ago, whom Doña Elena wouldn't allow her to marry, and she started crying so hard that she couldn't attend the wedding banquet the next day. As the wedding guests taste the cake, they, too, are gripped with longing; and furthermore they begin to throw up, so it is not the wedding Rosaura had dreamed of. And next morning they find Nacha dead, clutching a picture of her fiancé.

Life goes on at the ranch; Pedro has moved in, and Tita has become the head cook. To bring herself out of her grief for Nacha, Tita makes an ancient recipe based on rose petals—roses she received from Pedro, which she clutched so hard that they were stained with her blood. Again the meal has a profound effect: Pedro loves it, Rosaura doesn't want to eat it, but Gertrudis experiences an instant rush of sexual heat, which makes her perspire rose-scented sweat; a young man she likes, a soldier in Villa's army, is called from afar by the scent and carries her away to a new life.

After a while, Rosaura has her first baby, Roberto; nobody is in the house at the time but Tita, who takes charge of the delivery, and from then on the boy seems as close to her as if he were her own son. When Rosaura has no milk, milk miraculously wells up in Tita's breasts; always the nurturer, Tita is capable of feeding everybody, including her little nephew.

Someone else has now been introduced to the house: the doctor tending Rosaura, Dr. John Brown, an American physician. A widower, he falls in love with Tita and is appalled when he hears about the family tradition. In the course of events he does experience a close relationship with Tita, but in a way other than he had imagined: When Elena sends Rosaura, Pedro, and their baby to live in San Antonio, Tita loses all interest in life; and when the news that the little boy is dead reaches the ranch, Tita goes mad with grief and accuses her mother of having killed the boy, because she deprived him of Tita's care. Tita takes refuge in the pigeon coop in a state of madness, and Dr. Brown is called to remove her to an asylum; instead he takes her to his home and nurses her back to mental health. He is not alone, though. In a small room in the house Tita finds company, a silent old Indian woman who reminds her of Nacha and who shows her curative herbs and rekindles her interest in life. Soon she realizes that the woman is John Brown's long-dead grandmother, a Kikapu Indian called Morning Light. John, who does not see her, tells Tita of a theory his grandmother held: Each of us is born with a box of matches inside us, but we can't strike them by ourselves; we need oxygen (like the breath of a person you love) and a candle (like a beautiful experience). When the match is lit, we feel an intense emotion, which fades slowly until the next match is struck. This fire is the food for our soul. If you don't find out in time what sets off your explosions, the matches will dampen and you will never feel a spark. But you must take care not to light them all at the same time, because then you will be so dazzled that your soul will escape to its divine origin; your body will die.

Tita, feeling better, is visited by the maid from the ranch with oxtail soup from home, and Tita swears she will never return; but things have a way of happening: Arriving home, the maid is raped in a raid, and Elena, trying to defend her property, is shot and paralyzed from the waist down. Now Tita has to go home to take care of her mother. But everything Tita serves her tastes bitter to her, even if it tastes fine to the others, so Elena believes she is being poisoned. In order to counteract the poison she secretly swallows great amounts of emetics, which end up killing her. Cleaning up after her, Tita finds an old box with an old secret: Elena herself had been the victim of parental authority. She was never allowed to marry the man she loved, the son of a Mexican man and an African American woman. Gertrudis is actually this man's child, and only Rosaura and Tita are the daughters of the man Elena was forced to marry.

Rosaura and Pedro now have a little girl, Esperanza (and later we learn that she will be the mother of the storyteller); Tita hopes her sister will not perpetuate the family tradition, but Rosaura insists that Esperanza must never marry and will stay home to take care of her when she is old. Rosaura herself is becoming a nasty, smelly woman, and Pedro and Tita find secret opportunities for making love; but Tita is haunted by the ghost of Mama Elena, who is nagging her constantly. A turning point occurs when Gertrudis, now a general in the rebel army, comes to visit in the company of her beloved, and gives Tita the courage to confront Rosaura. In a terrible exchange of words they reveal what they think of each other, and that is the end of their friendship. Tita and Esperanza, on the other hand, grow very close to each other, like Nacha and Tita, in the old kitchen. (Eventually Tita will leave her book of recipes to her niece, and that is how Esperanza's child, the storyteller, can share them with us.)

John asks Tita to marry him, even though he knows she still loves Pedro; but Rosaura dies suddenly (we guess that she dies from just being so nasty that she has poisoned herself with evil), and Pedro is free. Will Tita and Pedro finally find happiness together? Or will Tita marry John? I suggest you read the book or watch the film and find out for yourself; and remember Morning Light's theory of the matches: If you don't strike them one by one, they may all go off at one time.

And the secret of the title, a mystery to moviegoers? Like water for making chocolate, when it feels as if life conspires against you, you're at the point of boiling!

Study Questions

1. Can this story be interpreted as a feminist narrative? If no, why not? If yes, which kind of feminism? You may want to consider the different roles played by Tita the nurturer and Gertrudis the warrior; what are the roles of Elena and Rosaura?

2. Evaluate the custom of the youngest daughter's being obliged to stay single in order to care for her aging parents. Can the custom be defended? Why or why not?

3. Do any of the characters exhibit an "ethic of care"? Explain your answer.

4. An existentialist such as Simone de Beauvoir might call the custom of the youngest (or eldest) daughter remaining single so she can take care of her parents an example of *bad faith*. What does that mean? Do you agree?

Narrative

The Woman Destroyed

SIMONE DE BEAUVOIR

Short story, 1967. Summary and Excerpt. Translated by Patrick O'Brian.

As you know from Chapter 10, Jean-Paul Sartre was not only a philosopher but also a novelist and playwright. The fact that his longtime partner Simone de Beauvoir also wrote fiction is not quite as well known. Here we look at passages from her short story "The Woman Destroyed," about Monique, who has been married to Maurice for more than twenty years. Their two daughters are grown and no longer live at home, and Monique is under the impression that now she and Maurice will continue with the pleasant life they've established and which has become a habit. So it is a dreadful shock to her to discover that he has been having an affair with an acquaintance of theirs, Noëllie, for quite some time.

In these excerpts you will see Monique swing between extremes of blaming Noëllie, her husband, and herself for the situation that has developed. Maurice doesn't deny the relationship, and initially he doesn't want to lose either woman. He wants to have his cake and eat it too.

Maurice will see anything I say against Noëllie as the effect of my jealousy. It would be better to say nothing. But I really do find her profoundly disagreeable. She reminds me of my sister—the same confidence, the same glibness, the same phonily offhand elegance. It seems that men like this mixture of coquetry and hardness. When I was sixteen and she was eighteen Maryse swiped all my boyfriends. So much so that I was in a dreadful state of nerves when I introduced Maurice to her. I had a ghastly nightmare in which he fell in love with her. He was indignant. "She is so superficial! So bogus! Paste diamonds, rhinestones! You—you're the real jewel." Authentic: that was the word everyone was using in those days. He said I was authentic. At all events I was the one he loved, and I was not envious of my sister anymore; I was happy to be the person I was. But then how can he think a great deal of Noëllie, who is of the same kind as Maryse? He is altogether gone from me if he likes being with someone I dislike so very much—and whom he ought to dislike if he were faithful to our code. Certainly he has altered. He lets himself be taken in by false values that we used to despise. Or he is simply completely mistaken about Noëllie. I wish the scales would drop from his eyes soon. My patience is beginning to run out. [. . .]

"I don't want any sharing: you must make your choice."

He had the overwhelmed look of a man who is saying to himself, *Here we are! It had to happen. How can I get myself out of this one?* He adopted his most coaxing voice. "Please, darling. Don't ask me to break with Noëllie. Not now."

"Yes, now. This business is dragging on too much. I have borne it too long by far." I looked at him challengingly. "Come now, which do you like best? Her or me?"

"You, of course," he said in a toneless voice. And he added, "But I like Noëllie too."

I saw red. "Admit the truth, then! She's the one you like best! All right! Go to her! Get out of here. Get out at once. Take your things and go."

I pulled his suitcase out of the wardrobe, I flung clothes into it higgledy-piggledy, I unhooked coat hangers. He took my arm: "Stop!" I went on. I wanted him to go; I really wanted it—it was sincere. Sincere because I did not believe in it. It was like a dreadful psychodrama in which they play at truth. It is the truth, but it is being acted. I shouted, "Go and join that bitch, that schemer, that dirty little shady lawyer."

He took me by the wrists. "Take back what you have said."

"No. She's a filthy thing. She got you by flattery. You prefer her to me out of vanity. You're sacrificing our love to your vanity."

Again he said, "Shut up." But I went on. I poured out everything I thought about Noëllie and him. Yes: I have a confused recollection of it. I said that he was letting himself be taken in like a pitiful fool, that he was turning into a pretentious, on-the-make vulgarian, that he was no longer the man I had loved, that once upon a time he had possessed a heart and given himself up to others—now he was hard and selfish and concerned only with his career.

"Who's selfish?" he cried. And he shouted me down. I was the one who was selfish—I who had not hesitated to make him give up a resident post, who would have liked to confine him to a small-time career all his life long so as to keep him at home, I who was jealous of his work—a castrating woman. [. . .]

Evening

I had an inspiration this morning: the whole thing is my fault. My worst mistake has been not grasping that *time goes by.* It was going by and there I was, set in the attitude of the ideal wife of an ideal husband. Instead of bringing our sexual relationship to life again I brooded happily over memories of our former nights together. I imagined I had kept my thirty-year-old face and body instead of taking care of myself, doing gymnastics and going to a beauty parlor. I let my intelligence wither away: I no longer cultivated my mind—*later,* I said, *when the children have gone.* (Perhaps my father's death was not without bearing on this way of letting things slide. Something snapped. I stopped time from that moment on.) Yes: the young student Maurice married felt passionately about what was happening in the world, about books and ideas; she was very unlike the woman of today, whose world lies between the four walls of this apartment. It is true enough that I tended to shut Maurice in. I thought his home was enough for him: I thought I owned him entirely. Generally speaking I took everything for granted; and that must have irritated him intensely—Maurice who changes and who calls things in question. Being irritating—no one can ever get away with that. I should never have been obstinate about our promise of faithfulness, either. If I had given Maurice back his freedom—and made use of mine, too, perhaps—Noëllie would not have profited by the glamour of clandestinity. I should have coped with the situation at once. Is there still time? [. . .]

It is only now that I realize how much value I had for myself, fundamentally. But Maurice has murdered all the words by which I might try to justify it: he has repudiated the standards by which I measured others and myself; I had never dreamed of challenging them—that is to say of challenging myself. And now what I wonder is this: what right had I to say that the inner life was preferable to a merely social life, contemplation to trifling amusements, and self-sacrifice to ambition? My only life had been to create happiness around me. I have not made Maurice happy. And my daughters are not happy either. So what then? I no longer know anything. Not only do I not know what kind of a person I am, but also I do not know what kind of a person I ought to be. Black and white merge into one another, the world is an amorphous mass, and I no longer have any clear outlines. How is it possible to live without believing in anything or in myself?

Study Questions

1. In your opinion, does Beauvoir want us to identify with Monique, or criticize her attitude, or perhaps a little bit of both? Identify the passages that support your view.

2. Compare these excerpts to the text excerpt from *The Second Sex* (p. 602). How might Beauvoir analyze Monique's situation and attitude from the viewpoint of her own classical feminism?

3. Monique seems to think she has no moral right to hold on to her husband. Do you agree? Why or why not?

Narrative

Mona Lisa Smile

LAWRENCE KONNER AND MARK ROSENTHAL (SCREENWRITERS)
MIKE NEWELL (DIRECTOR)

Film, 2003. Summary.

It is 1953, the beginning of the fall semester at Wellesley College, a women's college in Massachusetts with many proud traditions. The semester starts with a ritual: A young student (who later, with an ironic twist, turns out to be one of the main characters, Joanie) knocks on the massive wooden doors of the college. The school president asks, "Who knocks at the door of learning?" The student answers that she is everywoman, and the president replies that anyone who seeks knowledge and wants to dedicate her life to knowledge is welcome. The professors at Wellesley are competent men and women, and the standards for teaching are high, but as the film progresses, we realize that the main reason most of the girls are receiving a very expensive, highly respected education is not to dedicate their life to knowledge, but mainly to learn what a well-mannered high-society wife needs to know. Few students actually end up using their degree.

Into this school of traditions comes a young progressive art professor and graduate student from California on a one-year probation hire: Katherine Watson. She has idealistic notions about opening the eyes of other young women eager to learn, but her first "History of Art 100" class is a disaster: She is lecturing from the textbook, but all the students have already read the book and end up ignoring her and leaving for independent studies. It seems that Katherine's stay at Wellesley is going to be difficult: The alumni and professors find her proposed thesis on Picasso much too avant-garde, and a professor scolds her for losing control of her first class. She rooms with another teacher who teaches classes in etiquette, and promptly tells Katherine that she would have been married except for her fiancé's dying in World War II. We get the impression that getting married is the ultimate ideal for everyone, professors and students alike—except for Katherine's other roommate, the school nurse Amanda Armstrong, a woman with a strong personality and a good sense of humor but with a tragedy in her life: Her "companion" has just died—and so we know that Amanda is a lesbian. She warns Katherine that too much independence will frighten the establishment at Wellesley.

Next class Katherine is better prepared: Instead of following the official syllabus, she introduces her own and starts showing the students modern art, to shock them into a realization that art appreciation doesn't come out of a book, but is a lived experience: The question What is Art? is more important than the answer. But immediately she is up against the traditionalists among her students, above all Betty, daughter of a socialite, who is about to have all her dreams fulfilled and get married. Betty is "popular" because she wields power, but not well-liked; she is always putting the less popular, less attractive girls down and does her best to undermine not only Katherine but also the nurse Amanda, who has been distributing illegal contraception to the students. Writing a tell-all column in the school paper about the birth control issue, Betty effectively gets Amanda fired. But in her

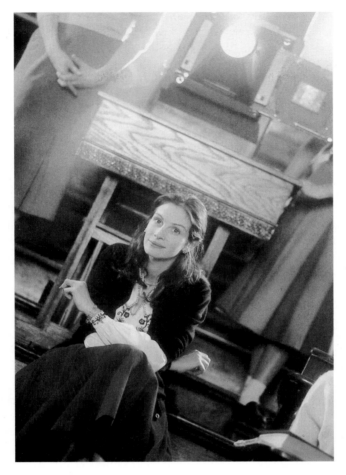

From the film *Mona Lisa Smile*: Katherine Watson (Julia Roberts) does her best to teach her students at Wellesley College to appreciate modern art. At the same time, she tries to convince them not to let their education, and their intellect, go to waste.

own life Betty is under the strict influence of her mother, who arranges all wedding preparations, including telling Betty how to manipulate her future husband.

Other students begin to awaken to Katherine's persuasively fresh outlook: Joanie, Betty's friend, begins to see things Katherine's way; and above all, the free-spirited Giselle takes her art lessons to heart and begins to see Katherine as a role model. Giselle is looking for love, dates her handsome Italian language professor Bill Dunbar for a while, and isn't ready to accept that the relationship is over. Dunbar himself tells fascinating stories of when he was a soldier in Italy in World War II, in his classes as well as on dates, and Katherine herself begins to take a liking to him.

Joanie has a heart-to-heart talk with Katherine and reveals that she would like to go to Yale Law School, but doesn't consider it an option since she's getting married to Tommy. Katherine insists that she can do both and helps her submit an application to Yale, in secret. To Joanie's enormous surprise, she is accepted. In the meantime, Betty marries Spencer in a lavish wedding where the "movers and shakers" of the community are invited, and Betty stops taking classes so she can go on her honeymoon and set up her new home.

Right before the Christmas break President Carr lets Katherine know that her job indeed is in peril—if she doesn't change her ways and lecture less on modern art, she will not get her contract renewed.

During the break, Joanie and her boyfriend are visiting Betty and Spencer in their new home, and Betty shows off her washer and dryer, her home, and "everything she ever dreamed of." When she hears Joanie has been accepted to Yale, she can't believe Joanie would even consider it—she is so close to having her dreams fulfilled, and now she's about to throw it all away! But perhaps Betty's life isn't so perfect after all: Spencer gets a call from New York and has to leave on business right after dinner, and Betty is stuck with her dinner guests and a bunch of unanswered questions.

Katherine gets a Christmas surprise: Paul, her boyfriend from California, shows up and proposes to her. He's so miserable without her that he's willing to move back East to be with her. So now it looks as if she really can have both too—but that same evening she realizes that she really doesn't want a marriage with Paul at all—especially since she inadvertently calls him *Bill*, and we know it's professor Dunbar who is on her mind.

Betty returns to classes in the new semester and expects to pick up where she left off so she can graduate. This procedure seems to be acceptable to everyone at Wellesley, but Katherine comes down hard on her: If she doesn't catch up, she will be failed—and Betty responds that Katherine's position is by no means certain. The power struggle between the two is in full bloom. After the girls hear Katherine's view that marriage is not a necessity, Betty writes a scathing column where she denounces Katherine as subversive. Katherine responds by running a series of commercial ads in art class, showing women as housewives, in girdles, with their intellect being wasted, and goes to President Carr, telling her she resigns—Wellesley is not a real college, she says; it's just a glorified finishing school. They're not educating future leaders—but their wives! Carr responds angrily that 100 years ago women couldn't even get an education, so they've come a long way.

Bill Dunbar convinces Katherine to give Wellesley another chance because they need someone like her, and she and Bill start dating—but before long she finds out, through encountering an old war buddy of Bill's, that he was never in Italy, but merely at the Language Institute in Long Island. All his stories were lies, and she breaks up with him in disappointment. He tells her that she is disappointed in everybody—but perhaps she should not expect people to change according to her way, but according to their own.

Joanie herself voices the same opinion when Katherine finds out that she and Tommy eloped and got married, and now she'll follow him to Washington instead of going to Yale. To Katherine's desperate plea for her to continue with her education, Joanie says, "You're the one who said I could do anything I wanted—this is what I want." She says she would regret not having a husband and a family more than she'll regret not going to law school.

Meanwhile, of all the students who have come under Katherine's influence, it is Betty who has the greatest change of heart: In an important scene she looks at a photo of Leonardo's

Mona Lisa, and says, "Mona Lisa is smiling, but is she happy?" When her husband turns out to be a philanderer, and her mother tells her to put up with it and keep quiet about it, she stands up to her mother and demands a divorce. At the graduation ceremony, Betty announces that she is going to move to Greenwich Village with Giselle and become a law student.

Will Katherine be invited back to teach at Wellesley? Will she accept such an invitation? Will she patch it up with Bill? I'll leave that for you to experience for yourself, but I will tell you that the story of Katherine Watson is told, in retrospect, by her best student, Betty, in her final column for the school paper before she graduates and embarks on a career of her own.

Study Questions

1. Would you say this film is told from the perspective of a predominantly classical feminist, a difference feminist, a radical feminist, or an equity feminist? Explain.

2. What would Simone de Beauvoir say to Joanie's decision to be a homemaker rather than go to law school? What would Christina Hoff Sommers say? What do you think of her decision?

3. What do the screenwriters want us to conclude about traditional values, marriage, and same-sex relationships, judging from this film? Do you agree?

4. Try to retell the story from Wellesley President Carr's point of view, pointing out the problems of having a "subversive" teacher undermine the good conservative values of the school. Is Katherine more right than President Carr? Why or why not?

5. The mission statement of Wellesley College is, according to its website, "to provide an excellent liberal arts education for women who will make a difference in the world." It was founded in 1870 and remains a highly prestigious school to this day. You may want to do some research of your own and determine whether the film accurately portrays the school in 1953 and whether the school today differs from that depicted in *Mona Lisa Smile*.

Chapter Thirteen

Applied Ethics: A Sampler

*T*his final chapter is a result of several reader requests for more detailed discussions of issues involving applied ethics, drawing on the previous chapters on ethics of conduct and virtue ethics. In general, this book is designed not to cover the field of applied ethics as such, but rather to discuss theories of ethics using stories as examples, and occasionally to explore issues in applied ethics. This chapter does reflect issues I spend extra time on in my own classes: *media ethics, animal rights,* and *the death penalty.* In addition, because of September 11, the war in Afghanistan, and the war in Iraq, we have talked at length about the *Just War* concept, and chances are you may be interested in discussing this subject too. As such, Chapter 13 is intended to complement Chapter 7, with its focus on rights and justice, and Chapter 11, with its focus on three virtues.

Of course there are many areas within applied ethics that space concerns prevent me from addressing in further detail, such as abortion, euthanasia, gun control, and free speech on the Internet. I hope you will feel inspired to discuss these and other subjects further on your own, drawing on the theories you have been introduced to in this book.

Media Ethics

The media seem to be showing an increasing interest in reporting issues of moral controversy. This certainly reflects their perennial interest in "good copy" (news that sells papers or commercial air time); if people weren't interested in hearing about such matters, it wouldn't be good copy. Most frequently these stories of moral controversy involve transgressions by the rich and famous. In recent years, though, general reporting of differences of opinion about what's right and wrong has become more common. Issues such as abortion and euthanasia are high on the list of media topics, and whenever candidates vie for office, their opinions on such matters, as well as on matters of gender and racial politics, are closely examined.

The question of moral standards in the news profession itself is an especially important one: Is it ethical, for example, for a journalist to make public a matter of national security? And does the public always have a "right to know"? Journalists who gain access to sensitive material and publish it may be said not only to report the news but also to create conditions for more "news" to report. In other words, they may play an active role in situations that they supposedly are merely reporting.

The Right to Know

The public's "right to know" has become questionable in the aftermath of hugely publicized court cases and human tragedies of the 1990s. After examining the effects of televised high-profile trials, some now question the wisdom of allowing cameras in the courtroom because their presence may actually affect the trial, at least turning it into a circus, as it did in O. J. Simpson's criminal trial in 1995. And does the public really have a "right" to see TV close-ups of relatives grieving over grisly photos of murder scenes? Sensationalism in the mainstream media seems to have become the order of the day. Decades ago, the tabloid ("yellow") press was where you'd find subjects with salacious content, and not much evidence of journalistic concern for verifying facts. But according to some media commentators, the line between mainstream and tabloid media has blurred, to the extent that people have been demonized in the "court of public opinion" with the help of the mainstream media, relying primarily on leaks and rumors. And once the story has hit the press, the genie can't be put back in the bottle. Hasty accusations of wrongdoing published by the media, although later proven to be untrue, may hang over a person's head for years, perhaps for life. When the media decided to go with the story that Richard Jewell, the suspect in the 1996 bombing of Olympic Park in Atlanta, had a history of aberrant behavior, the story was disseminated nationwide. When he was later exonerated (and took the media to court for libel), it wasn't front-page news. And most of us just happen to remember sensational headlines on front pages rather than the follow-ups on page 13. At the end of the chapter, you'll find an excerpt from "Ethics as a Vehicle for Media Quality" in which Andrew Belsey and Ruth Chadwick explore the concept of virtue in journalism.

One moral problem for the media is sensationalism; another is stretching the truth, or downright *lying*. And lately, the credibility of certain news media (if not all of them) has been damaged by instances such as these: In June 1998 a *Boston Globe* columnist, Patricia Smith, was forced to resign because she had invented characters in her columns—which were supposed to depict real people and real events. Another *Globe* journalist, Mike Barnicle, was also forced to resign after using borrowed material without mentioning the source. Within the same month, CNN and *Time* magazine were quick to break a news story that U.S. forces used nerve gas to kill defectors from the United States during the Vietnam War. Shortly after, CNN and *Time* had to issue retractions and apologies and have since been sued for defamation: There was no corroborating evidence to support the story. In Great Britain's *Daily Mirror* newspaper in 2004, fake photos of Iraqi prisoner abuse appeared, and the story had to be retracted. Perhaps one of the most shocking stories was the revelation that Jayson Blair, *New York Times* correspondent, had plagiarized stories from other journalists, or simply made things up as he went along, despite warnings to his superiors from other journalists that Blair's stories weren't legitimate. At *USAToday,* reporter Jack Kelley resigned after having been caught doing the same thing. In the aftermath of each case, a few editors' heads rolled, figuratively speaking. Perhaps the highest-profile media scandal in recent years happened a mere two months before the 2004 presidential election: CBS's anchor Dan Rather aired documents, allegedly from 1973, stating problems with President Bush's National Guard service, written by his superior officer. When Internet bloggers and typewriting experts began to point out that the documents looked like a forgery, because they contained superscript, proportional spacing, and other modern computer features that few typewriters in 1973 had the capacity for, the scandal accelerated. In addition, according to the officer's family, the documents didn't correspond to what they knew of the situation, but their statements weren't included in the CBS *60 Minutes* show. Dan Rather later admitted, under the pressure of experts, the media, and disturbed Democrats as well as Republicans, that he had not been careful enough in airing the documents—that indeed CBS had been taken. Rather added that the information was, essentially correct, but without tangible evidence, such a statement is merely opinion. The fallout was primarily along party lines: Democrats found that it was the information that ought to count and not the manner in which it was obtained, while Republicans saw a credibility gap, not only in Rather's career, but also in CBS's political approach in general. Shortly after the election Rather retired as anchor of the *CBS Evening News*. A couple of months later, CBS sent pink slips to several of the CBS employees who had been associated with the fiasco; Rather, however remained employed by CBS as a contributor to *60 Minutes*.

A sobering statistic: Numerous studies in the late 1990s and early 2000s, including a Gallup Poll, show that we are losing in terms of media: According to Gallup, in terms of trustworthiness and ethical standards, we rate journalists below politicians and just above used-car salesmen.

The linguist and author Deborah Tannen (see also Chapters 11 and 12) suggests in her 1998 book *The Argument Culture* that the media have become argument-crazy: Every issue must be presented with an opposing point of view in order to get a "good fight" going, even when people agree about the subject and no real opposing point of view exists. This means that controversial stories get front-page coverage and that if there is no controversy, the media will look for an opposing point of view until someone is willing to supply it. This is what is sometimes called the *adversarial* method. Although this method is excellent at exploring truly opposed, equally challenging viewpoints, it is no help as a problem solver if it invents problems for the sake of stirring up debate. Tannen suggests that although the press is not supposed to take on the docile role of a *lapdog*, it seems to have given up its role as the nation's *watchdog* for a much less attentive but louder role as an *attack dog*, picking fights for the fun of it. Interestingly, Tannen's book was virtually ignored by the conflict-oriented television talk-show circuit.

Media Ethics in Wartime

Whatever we may have thought of the public's right to know, and the media's right to find out, under those conditions that we regarded as "normal" before September 11, a wartime media ethics has a different makeup—although not fundamentally different. The idea that the public has a right to know certain things, even in wartime, is at the very heart of the notion of freedom of the press—which of course is a constitutional right, embedded in the First Amendment; on the other side of the issue, however, looms the concept of national security.

An extreme illustration of the clash between the media and wartime interests is the secret U.S. troop landing on the beach in Somalia in 1998 under cover of darkness—secret until huge floodlights illuminated the entire scene, welcoming the troops to Africa: CNN and other television crews were on the shore already, functioning as a welcoming committee. The world did indeed get to see a live military beach landing, but the American troops lost the element of surprise. For many, the

In the film *15 Minutes,* a television station acquires a videotape depicting the murder of a popular police detective. A tabloid-TV journalist (Kelsey Grammer) makes the decision to air the video as an exclusive, because, as he says, "If it bleeds, it leads." In the scene depicted here, the journalist has acquired yet another tape, this one showing the killer's confession. Do you think a TV station would deliberately air a murder? In an accelerated, sensationalist news environment, might the scenario of *15 Minutes* become possible—here or abroad?

conflict between the people's "right to know" and legitimate military concerns came into sharp focus at that moment, especially since CNN and now also Fox News are networks that are watched globally—by foe as well as by friend.

The press may have had a hard time adjusting to wartime conditions in the 1990s, but since 9/11 the concept of reporting on wartime conditions has become part of daily life for the American media. This also means that new solutions have been tried, and new problems have shown up. On the first day of what has become known as the war on terrorism, 9/11, television stations first showed footage of people jumping to their deaths from the burning towers, but after a while, all networks stopped showing the footage. At the time it was done to minimize the shock and also out of sensitivity toward the families of the victims. In retrospect one might ask, should we perhaps have been allowed to see these dreadful images as often as we've seen the actual towers fall? Would it not have brought it home to us that individuals went through agony and perished? As the war in Iraq progressed, and kidnapped individuals were executed on video by al Qaeda, the debate shifted to whether the newsmedia should show these videos, so we could witness the cruelty of the enemy firsthand and remain angry and motivated, or whether it was the right decision and the higher moral ground not to give the cruelty of terrorism any direct air time. Box 13.1 discusses the subject of terror videos on television.

Box 13.1   HOW FAR WOULD—AND SHOULD—TELEVISION GO?

How far are the media willing to go to secure an exclusive story—or to provide unique footage? And how far is too far? In the chapter text you read that the news media stopped showing footage of people jumping from the burning World Trade towers. Over time, live TV has inadvertently shown unexpected deaths, such as the shooting of Lee Harvey Oswald in 1963, the police shooting of a tank hijacker in San Diego in the 1990s, and a man jumping to his death from a bridge in Los Angeles after having held up traffic for hours; but such deaths rarely are rebroadcast on the evening news. Does that mean we are not likely to see violent deaths broadcast, live or canned, on network or cable TV in the future? CBS, on *60 Minutes,* chose to air a videotape of the assisted-suicide death of one of Dr. Jack Kevorkian's patients. When *Wall Street Journal* reporter Danny Pearl was executed by terrorists in Pakistan in 2002 and the process videotaped by those same terrorists, CBS aired part of his interrogation, but not his death itself—it was, however, posted to the Internet on several websites. And this now seems to have become a standard procedure: In Iraq, after the major battles of 2003, al Qaeda (and possibly also Iraqi insurgents) has kidnapped and executed numerous civilians who were in Iraq as part of the reconstruction effort: The first one to be executed was Nick Berg, an American citizen who had gone to Iraq of his own accord, presumably to help out as well as make some money for himself. Berg's headless body was found after his disappearance, and a videotape was posted to an al Qaeda website with Berg in an orange jumpsuit being interrogated by masked men and then having his head cut off by those same men. While the news media stopped at showing the execution itself, or chose to run the gruesome soundtrack but not the video, numerous websites posted the whole video. Since then, many other civilians, including citizens of Italy and Nepal, have been executed in Iraq, usually by being beheaded. And this is where opinions are beginning to differ: Before, and immediately after 9/11, proper media ethics included not showing violent deaths or other shocking scenes, for the sake of the individuals involved and their loved ones. In the Narratives section you'll find the film *15 Minutes,* where the following scenario is suggested: What if the videotaped murder of a famous, popular person is being offered to the networks? Will they take the high road and refuse to air it, or will they air it, because if they don't, someone else will? The moral of *15 Minutes* is that airing it would be the wrong, and greedy, thing to do—but what if we are talking about footage of terrorists killing American citizens? For some, that makes no difference—showing the footage plays into the hands of the terrorists and furthers their agenda. But for others this represents a different situation: If we don't actually see how vicious and evil these terrorists are, we may think they can be reasoned with and negotiated with—so the media, by protecting us from shocking footage, may actually be preventing us from judging the situation correctly. In your view, does the airing of such violent footage have any merit, or should it be avoided?

A dramatic shift in the role of the media happened at the beginning of the war in Iraq in 2003, when we were introduced to the concept of "embedded journalists," reporters from TV stations, newspapers, and magazines traveling with the military as they moved toward Baghdad and other key cities. In previous wars, the press have usually stayed behind the lines, except for a few individuals who have chosen to go it alone and report from the front lines, but the war in Iraq has probably changed wartime journalism forever. Skeptical voices warned that having journalists along would (1) endanger the journalists, (2) impede the progress of the armies because the soldiers would have to take the safety of the civilians into consideration, (3) present a problem if journalists were taken prisoner, (4) make "believers" and military supporters out of the journalists rather than objective observers, or the opposite, (5) add a live note of criticism and pessimism to a campaign from the inside. And yet the presence of reporters as American and British troops moved through the desert became what many consider a media success story: Individual reporters gave their personal take on the situation, without any wholesale left- or right-wing bias, and perhaps best of all, we (think we) saw the real conditions our soldiers had to deal with on an everyday basis and heard from the soldiers themselves in mini-interviews throughout the day and night. One particularly controversial incident was the filming by an NBC reporter, Kevin Sites, of a Marine shooting a wounded Iraqi insurgent during the battle of Fallujah in November 2004. Aside from the heated debate about whether it was justifiable to shoot a wounded combatant under the assumption that he might still be a threat (by detonating a grenade, for example), part of the media discussion centered on Sites himself: Was it appropriate for an embedded journalist to broadcast footage that made United States soldiers look bad? Especially since the video showed up instantly on Middle Eastern anti-American television stations and websites? Was Sites just reporting objectively, doing exactly what an embedded journalist is supposed to do, or did he have an agenda? Such questions are inevitable when embedded reporters are free to report what they see. So, was having embedded journalists the right media approach to the war? Some of the dire predictions didn't come to pass, but that doesn't mean it is an ideal approach in future conflicts. And we shouldn't think that we, the audience at home, had complete access to all information, or all events, or even that we have a right to such access. But as it was, it provided instant information that many Americans felt we needed during a controversial war.

But how about the home front? How have the media been reporting about homeland threats since 9/11? In 2001–2 the nation was worried about the anthrax scare: letters being sent around to prominent politicians as well as to private individuals, laced with anthrax. The nation was terrified, and yet the losses, and the risks, were fairly limited and local. But the media reported any possibility of anthrax attack with much gusto, which made many Americans ask themselves whether the story was perhaps being blown out of proportion by twenty-four-hour news networks scrambling to find stories to fill their programming. Such an approach may help create an atmosphere of fear and thus help the culprits achieve their goal of terror. Since 2002 we have seen the terror alert level raised, and lowered, time and again, with rumors being spread by the media, under the policy that it's better that we be informed about the rumors rather than surprised by an actual attack. But exactly how much is too much? When is the media providing vital information, and when is it "crying wolf"?

At a town meeting hosted in San Diego by Peter Jennings of ABC News, members of the press were asked about the choices they make when bringing such stories to the forefront, and several journalists responded that they just report the facts; they don't invent them or doctor them—but that can surely be dismissed as a media myth: Before journalists report the facts, they select which facts to report (having decided what counts as a fact), and they choose *how* and *when* to report them. A debate about media ethics must be based on an understanding of that process.

How much a journalist should report and an editor release, and when, of course depends on the situation. Aristotle's theory of the Golden Mean provides a good starting point for solving the media ethics problem. For each situation there is one correct answer, somewhere within the middle range. Sometimes the media need to freely share information, as unpleasant as it may be, in the interest of the public's right to make decisions based on informed consent. At other times the proper amount of coverage called for is the bare minimum, either because no more information is available at the time (and excessive speculation may hurt more than help the public), or because the dissemination of the information might threaten the security of the country. Crying wolf is poor journalistic ethics, but so are apathy and indifference. It is a brilliant journalist or editor who knows the difference in each single instance.

Theory of a Just War

World War II has been referred to as "the last good war," meaning the last one that had identifiable good and evil sides. But even World War II was, in the beginning, not considered clear-cut at all to many Americans; even after the Japanese attack on Pearl Harbor (December 7, 1941), some argued that more violence was not a proper response to violence. In addition, victories over the Nazis and imperial Japan during the war didn't come without their cost in civilian lives.

For many Americans—young as well as older people—during the Vietnam War, the very idea that a war could be "just" was an oxymoron. During the late sixties and early seventies the war in Vietnam was widely perceived as an *unjust war* since the principles being fought for were unclear or downright objectionable to many, involving mainly politics. Conscription was in effect, and many of the young men drafted against their will saw the war they were being asked to fight as not being a matter of national self-defense. Some veterans returning from the war, such as John Kerry, raised critical voices against the war. Conscientious objectors found the entire idea of a just war self-contradictory.

When the United States and its allies engaged in the Gulf War against Iraq, liberating occupied Kuwait, some people who, two decades before, had stood against the idea of the Vietnam War had mixed emotions: Liberating another country from an occupational force seemed a noble enough cause, but then there was the question of oil and the availability of it for an oil-dependent nation. The suspicion remained for many that the underlying motivation for U.S. involvement was tainted with self-interest. Of course, it is a good question exactly why it is supposed to be suspect for a country to pursue its own interests; it becomes questionable only when that self-interest prevents other countries from pursuing *their* own interests. (You'll remember the harm principle from Chapter 5; you'll also remember from Chapter 4 and Chapter 11 that an action that is motivated not just by self-interest but also by concern for others cannot be labeled as straight egoism.)

NON SEQUITUR

Much of the criticism of the press in the past few years, and especially in the wake of September 11, is that it has become a fearmonger because a good dose of anxiety ("Anthrax found in a post office! More news at 11!") keeps people glued to their television sets or makes them buy more papers and magazines. Is that a fair criticism? Do the media just report the news, or do they also select what news to report and when and how to report it? Where do we draw the line between the media giving out information, including warnings and alerts, and whipping up panic?

The U.S. military response to the terrorist attacks of September 11 changed a lot of things, including some people's perception of what constitutes a just war. Here was an attack on American soil, against civilians, directed from outside the United States by forces who had already expressed their wish to "kill all Americans," an attack that was (as most Americans saw it) unprovoked and utterly unjustifiable. British prime minister Tony Blair declared on September 12, 2001, that regardless of whatever grievances and grudges anyone might have against the United States, nothing could justify those acts of aggression. Later that same fall, U.S. Secretary of State Colin Powell expressed the same idea: In his view, no amount of anger or frustration could be justifications for acts of terrorism.

Another change in our outlook was the entire concept of war in itself, which traditionally had been applied to a conflict between *nations*. Now the concept of war has been expanded to include warfare against terrorists without a nation backing them up—a rightful expansion according to some, but illegitimate according to others, because in their view terrorism should be dealt with as a criminal act, not an act of war. Regardless of one's viewpoint, the notion that the war on terrorism will continue for many years to come has become part of twenty-first century life. One of the difficulties in the discussion of war and terrorism is that the definition of a terrorist is itself in dispute, and Box 13.2 explores that issue further.

For several months after September 11, an extraordinary feeling of bipartisanship permeated the American political scene; but with the war in Afghanistan in 2002, there were already signs that the unity between right and left, between Republicans and Democrats, couldn't hold. There was a sense of united purpose in sending troops

Box 13.2   TERRORIST OR FREEDOM FIGHTER?

A terrorist is someone who terrorizes others in order to obtain a goal, usually of a political nature, and usually by means of violence or threat of violence. That's the easy definition. Terrorism has been used as a political weapon by political subgroups in the West particularly since the 1970s, when left-wing terrorist groups emerged in Germany and the United States, with stated goals of overthrowing the government. In the last decades we have also seen right-wing terrorists, such as abortion clinic bombers and snipers; left-wing terrorism has branched off into *eco-terrorism,* terrorist attacks on behalf of the environment. Generally, most people in democratic cultures frown on the use of fear and violence as a means of making a political point, and this attitude was only strengthened by the 9/11 attacks. But after 9/11 a saying was quite often heard in political discussions: "One person's terrorist is another person's freedom fighter." Does this expression merit consideration? Given the fact that Osama bin Laden, the supposed mastermind behind 9/11, received support from the United States back in the days when he was fighting in Afghanistan with underground Afghani troops against the Soviet occupational forces, the question is legitimate. Perhaps all that matters is from whose perspective one sees it. When we approve of their fight, they become freedom fighters, and when we disapprove, they're terrorists. But we don't have to accept this relativistic definition if we can decide on a distinction. Some, including myself, suggest that you can be a freedom fighter with a political goal, and even use violence and fear to obtain your goal, as long as your target is an occupational or other oppressive force within a country you call your own, and violence is not directed deliberately against civilians. An additional important element is the ultimate goal: If your goal is increased freedom for your people to achieve self-determination, then you can indeed be called a freedom fighter. But if your goal is to achieve power without any intention of establishing a democracy, the term "freedom" fighter

to Afghanistan, because that was where the al Qaeda training camps were, where Osama bin Laden had been operating for years, and where the Taliban, the absolute governing power, had allowed al Qaeda to operate; but even so, there were voices who warned against going to war for any reason. One such voice was the novelist Barbara Kingsolver, whom you met in Chapter 3, expressing a pacifist viewpoint. Her op-ed piece, "No Glory in Unjust War on the Weak," appeared in the *Los Angeles Times* in October 2001:

> I am somebody's mother, so I will say that right now. The issue is, people are getting hurt [in the war on terrorism]. We need to take a moment's time out to review the monstrous waste of an endless cycle of retaliation. The biggest weapons don't win this one, guys. When there are people on Earth willing to give up their lives in hatred and use our own domestic airplanes as bombs, it's clear that we can't out-technologize them. You can't beat cancer by killing every cell in the body—or you could, I guess, but the point would be lost. This is a war of who can hate the most. There is no limit to that escalation. It will only end when we have the guts to say it really doesn't matter who started it, and begin to try and understand, then alter the forces that generate hatred.

would be a travesty. (And of course you can be a freedom fighter without resorting to violence at all. Gandhi was such a freedom fighter, and so was Martin Luther King, Jr. I doubt that anyone today would call them terrorists, although their nonviolent, passive-resistance policy did strike fear in the hearts of opponents.) A terrorist directs his or her acts of violence not only against military and/or occupational forces, but against civilians. The only way a terrorist can claim to be a freedom fighter is to claim that there are no innocents among his or her targets, which was indeed a claim made by bin Laden on video in the fall of 2001, but it was a claim that most Americans found hard to accept, since we distinguish between military and civilian targets and victims, and there were no military victims anywhere except at the Pentagon on 9/11. An argument sometimes used by people targeting what most of us would call civilians is that if you don't actively rebel against your government, then you are an accomplice in its transgressions, so you are not a civilian. But the 9/11 attacks didn't follow that definition either, since there were children (who don't make political decisions) among the victims—and apparently there was no attempt to weed them out or ascertain whether any adults on board the planes or at the World Trade Center harbored ill feelings toward the U.S. government (and should thus have been excluded as targets).

Of course, there is still some leeway in the interpretation of what qualifies as an occupational or oppressive force—some would say that the American and British forces in Iraq themselves took on the role of occupiers, while others regard us as liberators—but not nearly as much when it comes to a definition of civilians. In the Primary Readings the philosopher Jan Narveson explains what he thinks characterizes a terrorist, and the philospher David Rodin discusses the concept of terrorism in a post-9/11 world.

In contrast, and coincidentally in the same issue of the same paper, commentator Marc Cooper, identifying himself as a liberal, stated,

> The left must recognize that these forces [the terrorists] cannot be neutralized by nonviolent moral suasion or international law alone. As some of the left have argued, the WTC attacks demand a "just response" that includes limited, targeted, and effective military action aimed at lessening the threat of future terrorist attacks and restoring a sense of domestic security. For those who are squeamish about taking out Osama bin Laden's network and its Taliban defenders, let them reflect on just how much further American politics will slide to the right if there are a half-dozen more major terror attacks here at home.

After the war in Afghanistan—which continued with Taliban groups and warlords engaging our troops in skirmishes even after a new Afghan government was in place—the fragile unity was further fragmented until, with the war in Iraq, we were left with what you read about in Chapter 1: a "50-50 nation," a nation divided, even from county to county, between supporters of the war and the administration of President George W. Bush and opponents of the war and of the administration. In order not to fall into the divisive anti-military sentiment of the Vietnam era, both critics and sup-

Box 13.3   PATRIOTISM: TOO MUCH, TOO LITTLE,
OR JUST THE RIGHT AMOUNT?

In the wake of September 11, we saw flags go up by the thousands in just about every neighborhood in the country—in windows, displayed on walls and car bumpers, and flown from flagpoles and car antennae. To some, this was one of the few upsides of 9/11: that people discovered, or rediscovered, a love of their country. To others, it was an oppressive display of excessive nationalism, what used to be called *jingoism.* In my classes we discussed the issue at length, and a viewpoint emerged among my students that the news media hadn't explored: that many put flags up not because they hadn't loved their country before and all of a sudden discovered they did, or that they wanted to shove their patriotism in others' faces, but simply because *it made them feel better* at a time when we all felt the ground shaking under us. Sometimes emotional gestures should be seen in their own context rather than as exclusively political symbols. Some of us held on to our parents, spouses, and children, to our pets, even to stuffed animals. Some of us held on to our flag. In the days that followed, some TV networks took the line that wearing a flag pin was a personal statement, undermining the professional objectivity of their journalists, and banned flags in the newsrooms;

other news media supported the view that the flag is a national symbol, appropriate as a display in wartime, and not just a personal political statement, and hung the Stars and Stripes, or allowed their reporters to decide whether or not to wear flag pins.

But what exactly is patriotism, and when is it too much, too little, or just the right amount? In the 1970s the opinion was voiced among philosophers that patriotism is like racism and sexism: It is an unfounded preference for one's own country just because it is one's own country, just as sexism is a preference for one's own sex and a disregard for the other sex, and racism is a preference for one's own race and a disregard for other races. One of the visions of Marxism, for example, is people shedding their national affiliations and boundaries and becoming international, because the plight of workers is presumably the same everywhere. The final words of the original French song and rallying cry for Communism from 1871, *The Internationale,* are "The Internationale unites the human race." Less radical views of patriotism have been suggested, based on the criticism that it makes no sense to say we aren't allowed to love our country more than other countries—just as it would make no sense

porters of the war have been united in supporting our troops, however. In Box 13.3 we take a look at the phenomenon of patriotism.

For many, the war in Iraq has not met the criteria of a just war, while for others it qualifies. Below we take a closer look at what constitutes a "just war," and you may want to use whatever knowledge you have of the war in Iraq and come up with your own evaluation.

So is there such a thing as a just war? For a *pacifist,* the answer is no: Nothing on this earth—no attack on our loved ones, no danger to our life or our country—warrants raising our hand or using weapons of any kind against another human being. If you're a pacifist, say critics, you can't make an exception such as "I don't believe in war, but I'd of course want to defend my family," for two reasons: (1) If you have proclaimed that you reject the idea that force can solve a problem, then it doesn't matter to say we shouldn't love our own family more than we love strangers. In a paper from 1989, "In Defense of 'Moderate Patriotism,'" Steven Nathanson (whom you will also meet in the section on the death penalty) argues against critics of patriotism that "Patriotism is a virtue as long as the actions it encourages are not themselves immoral. . . . That a morally acceptable form of patriotism is possible can be seen by comparing patriotism to love or family loyalty. People may (and, one hopes, typically do) have a special interest and concern for their parents, spouses, and children. They really do care more about those 'near and dear' than about strangers. Yet, so long as this concern is not an exclusive concern, there is nothing the matter with it." In other words, it is acceptable to be a patriot as long as one is mainly expressing a love for one's country and homeland and isn't implying that one's country is always automatically right—in other words, this view rejects the notion of "My country, right or wrong," but allows for a personal sense of affiliation and love for one's roots. Part of the American tradition is the right to question authority—to ask good questions and expect them to be answered. One might say that it is a matter of pride in one's tradition, of patriotism, to keep asking good questions. Something that is deeply American and an ingrained feature in both the political Left and the Right is to want the United States to be the best that it can be, because we love this country and wish it well. What has been disturbing to many in the first three years after 9/11 is that the debate over who is a better patriot has become shrill at times: There is an assumption among the Left that they are not *allowed* to voice a critical opinion of the war in Iraq or the Bush administration—that the Right has monopolized patriotism itself. Conversely, there is a sense among the Right that the Left is speaking with a voice of treason, criticizing the administration at a time when displaying disagreement in the nation makes us more vulnerable to enemy attacks and plays into the hands of the terrorists. For some, love of country means loving what it *could be,* while for others, it means loving what it *has been,* and *is.* Wherever we find ourselves in this troubled spectrum, it is good to remind ourselves that conservatives don't have a monopoly on patriotism, and neither do liberals.

if we talk about it on a grand or a small scale: Force is impermissible, period. (2) If you believe that it is okay for you to resort to force in order to save your family from harm, what about those who don't have family members to save *them* from harm? That is traditionally the state's role: to protect its citizens from enemies, both domestic and foreign. When it is engaged in protection against harm caused by a foreign force, we call it war. And if you find it acceptable for an individual to protect his or her family from harm, then, logically, you should accept that the state takes on a similar action to protect its citizens.

So, according to the critics, the only consistent viewpoint for a pacifist is to reject the notion of using force to defend one's family against harm. Other forms of defense are acceptable, such as calling 911 (but if you don't approve of violence, you can't allow the police to use violence to save your family, either). Or you can put yourself in harm's way and use passive resistance, hoping that harm to your family will be deflected onto you, or that the harm-doer will think twice. In the 1930s and 1940s, Mohandas K. Gandhi (1869–1948), known by the reverent title of Mahatma, headed a movement to make the British pull out of their colony of India and give it its independence. His method, passive resistance, provided an alternative for countless people—in India as well as elsewhere—who would like to express their disapproval of an idea or a policy without resorting to violence. Gandhi's approach helped bring about Indian independence in 1946, but in 1948 he himself became a victim of violence, being gunned down by an assassin. Martin Luther King, Jr., met with the same fate in 1968 after being a life-long admirer of Gandhi's philosophy of passive resistance and advocating the same method in his civil rights movement. King's commitment continues to inspire people who seek to create political change without resorting to any form of violence.

But critics of pacifism point out: (1) If you put yourself in harm's way to save your family without personal use of force and lose your life, and your act of sacrifice doesn't save your family, nothing has been gained. (2) You may have the right to refuse to use any form of force or violence yourself, but if you have responsibility for others, such as small children, your right does not extend to them, because they are under your protection, morally and legally.

If you are not a pacifist and believe in the concept of a just war, the alternative isn't simply to be a "hawk," a "war-monger," or a belligerent, violent person. On the contrary: The doctrine of just war is based on the assumption that the ideal condition is peace; war is seen as the last resort to restore peace. Once that is a given, several other conditions must be in place in order to call a war just (*jus ad bellum*). These rules were worked out in the late Middle Ages by the so-called Schoolmen or scholastics, building on Roman law and early Christian thinkers such as Augustine and Ambrose, and they have become the foundation for military ethics in the West ever since. Here we look at an overview of these rules, as they are taught in military ethics courses:

- **Last resort** As stated above, a war can be just only if all other ways of restoring peace have been exhausted, such as negotiations, economic sanctions, etc.

- **Just cause** If going to war is the only way a country can defend its values and lives of innocent citizens against aggression and restoring peace, then the cause is considered just. In modern-day terms, identified by Michael Waltzer in his influential book *Just and Unjust Wars* (1977), this boils down to a response to an aggression and a defense of rights.

- **Legitimate, competent authority** War can be declared only by a competent governmental authority. A clarification may be necessary here: A "competent authority" doesn't refer to the leader's intelligence or lack thereof, but exclusively to whether or not the leader is the legitimate representative of the people and whether he or she has the constitutional authority to declare war. Some overenthusiastic general can't start a war on his or her own.

- **Comparative justice** The values and rights that are being defended must be so important that their defense outweighs the horrors of war.

- **Right intention** The intention must be to defend the rights in question, and not have some ulterior motive as gaining territory or enhancing business.

- **Probability of success** There has to be a reasonable assumption that the war will accomplish its goal, and there has to be:

- **Proportionality of ends** The costs of the war must not exceed the presumed benefits. Some victories are too costly, as any utilitarian will tell you. The term for such a victory is *Pyrrhic,* from Pyrrhus, the king of Epirus who won a battle against the Romans in 279 B.C.E., but sustained such huge losses that it put the value of the victory in doubt.

These are the rules that have to be in place when war is declared; in addition, there are rules that must be followed while conducting the war, "justice in war" (*jus in bello*). Over the past few centuries there has been a tendency to emphasize justice in war rather than just war, because the "just cause" concept is hard to define: After all, any nation (or terrorist group) can claim that its values are at risk and then march off to war. Instead, scholars have focused on limiting the damage done by war through these two rules:

- **Proportionality of means** While some harm will of course be caused, one should avoid causing unnecessary damage.

- **Discrimination** The term *discrimination* here means discerning, or "discriminating" between combatants and noncombatants. This rule was added to Just War theory in the Middle Ages; prior to those days Western thinking did not discriminate between soldiers and civilians (as some would argue that certain non-Western cultures are still not doing). Since everyone knows that wars usually involve civilian casualties, especially modern wars, the last rule doesn't exclude the loss of innocent non-combatants altogether, but they can't be *deliberately* targeted. Having some civilian casualties—on the enemy side, but also on one's own side—is considered acceptable as long as the overall result furthers the goal of peace. This falls under the principle of the *double effect,* which you read about in Chapter 7, a principle based on Catholic theology: An action which is prohibited under normal circumstances can be permitted if part of the outcome is (1) unintended, (2) doesn't exceed the goal in magnitude, and (3) unavoidable in order to accomplish its goal.

Even if two warring nations do follow these rules (which of course is not a given), there are still plenty of gray areas where one group can interpret the rules differently than another. And just wars can involve unjust acts. Some would cite the internment of Japanese Americans during World War II as an example of an unjust action during a just war.

So was the war in Iraq a just war? Some will answer flat out no, others say yes, and some will say that we simply haven't been presented with all the facts yet. Let us look at the seven criteria for a just war: The critics point out that (1) the war can't be described as a *last-resort effort,* since the U.N. inspectors hadn't completed their search for the so-called WMDs, the weapons of mass destruction. The war supporters have countered that the accumulated results of twelve years of trying to make Saddam Hussein comply with the restrictions following the Gulf War of 1991, and finally reaching a point where everything had been tried, meant there was no further reason to try again. The critics have said that (2) it was not a *just cause,* because the WMDs simply were not there, and Iraq was not a threat to us after all. The war supporters have answered that various intelligence sources claiming that WMDs existed had either misled the government or had been misinterpreted. Furthermore, WMDs had indeed been used on previous occasions, such as the extermination attempt on the Kurds, so it was a given that Saddam Hussein had possessed them earlier, and they might still be found—and, further still, there were other reasons for going to war, such as liberating 20 million people from tyranny. (3) The critics have claimed that President Bush was not a *legitimate authority* since his 2000 election was determined by the Supreme Court, not by the voters; the supporters of the Bush administration have answered that, aside from the election result's being constitutionally valid, eventually, after recounting all the Florida votes that were in dispute in the 2000 election, it turned out that Bush indeed had won by a small majority. (4) For the critics, the war did not represent *comparative justice,* since, in their eyes, our values and way of life were not genuinely threatened by Iraq, but rather by al Qaeda, and no connection between al Qaeda and Saddam Hussein had been established—and besides, for all intents and purposes, it looked as if the hunt for bin Laden had been given up, or at least put on the back burner, for the sake of the war in Iraq. The supporters have said that had Hussein had the power to attack us in the future, he would have done so, and it was right not to sit back and wait for that to happen—and, furthermore, the very fact that al Qaeda showed up in Iraq during the war was proof enough that a connection indeed was there—and that the search for bin Laden never stopped during the war in Iraq, but rather continued quietly. (5) According to the critics, the *right intentions* have not been shown, given that Iraq is rich in oil and provides the United States with business opportunities; supporters point out that defense of our country, prevention of future wars, liberation of a country from abuse and tyranny, and establishing a democracy in the Middle East for the sake of stability and freedom are all very powerful, right intentions. (6) And how about the *probability of success?* Critics have been very vocal, pointing out that the United States and its allies have had no exit strategy, meaning that once the war was won, there was no blueprint for "winning the peace," and chaos ensued, placing a burden on Iraqi families as well as on the families of fallen U.S. soldiers. Supporters, on the other hand, have pointed out that success has already been achieved: The tyrant is gone, 20 million people are free to pursue their chosen destiny, Iraq is no longer a threat to the United States, there are no more political murders, and Iraq had its first truly democratic election in 2005. (7) And *proportionality of ends?* This is something that posterity will have to judge—as it will have to judge the entire war against terrorism in general. Will the war in Iraq have proved to be too costly? The critics say yes, the loss of American lives—by the early 2005 numbering more than 1,300 men and women—was too high a price to pay. And the monetary sums being poured into the reconstruction of Iraq, at a time when the homeland economy hadn't been doing well, were just over the top. For supporters, however, the issue must be seen in a larger perspective: Losses of American soldiers now, numbering in the thousands, are still light compared to World War II and Vietnam losses and must be seen in contrast to potential greater losses of military and civilian lives down the line if Iraq's killing machine hadn't been stopped. And since the so-called "Iraqi insurgents" are driven not only by Saddam loyalists but primarily by al Qaeda, it appears that we are indeed fighting the war against terror in Iraq. So whether we find that the critics or the supporters of the war in Iraq have the best arguments, the debate illustrates that even if we have rules of just war, they are by no means unambiguous, and they can serve only as guidelines, not as a clear and easy check list.

When we look to discussions of a just war and terrorism by contemporary philosophers, most papers and books written before 9/11 have one thing in common: They imagine a future enemy to be a nation with an identifiable government, rarely a shadowy association of international terrorists. At the end of the chapter you will find a selection of text excerpts on the subject predating 9/11, and one written after the terrorist attacks. In war-torn eighteenth-century Prussia, Kant wrote one of his last works, "Perpetual Peace." With a clarity that wasn't apparent to readers until after World War II, Kant envisioned the slippery slope of escalating wars of the future leading to a war of mutual extermination and admonished that the only way civilization will survive is for all governments to become republican (that is, a democracy instead of various forms of dictatorship that regard their citizens as merely a means to an end). You will remember the concept of the *kingdom of ends* from Chapter 6, and this is what Kant was dreaming of: a world where people respect one another and their laws, where no nation abuses its own citizens, where nations will join together in a federation of free states, and where strangers are considered people too. While some might say Kant's vision is both a trifle naive and incomplete, one might hope there is a profound truth to his observation that truly democratic countries, where each citizen knows he or she has constitutionally protected rights, are less likely to generate wars of aggression—or have individuals embark on terrorist ploys against their own government or other nations—than countries where the individual has few or no rights and feels like a pawn in the political games of others. An active global effort toward democracy might thus go a long way toward preventing future terrorist actions as well as future wars. The American philosopher John Rawls, whom you know from Chapter 7, focused in his final book, *The Law of Peoples* on some of the same issues, and you'll find an excerpt in the Primary Readings.

Animal Welfare and Animal Rights

In Chapters 5 and 6 we touched on the issue of animals as candidates for moral respect. Chapter 5 introduced you to Descartes's idea that animals cannot feel pain because they have no minds and Bentham's and Mill's view that since animals obviously can feel pain and experience pleasure, consideration for animals should be included in whatever moral decisions we make that might affect them. Today, research by animal behaviorists has established that nonhuman animals are capable of feeling physical pain. In addition, animal studies in the wild as well as under more controlled conditions in animal behavior labs support the old anecdotal assumption that animals can also feel emotions; and the criticism, raised repeatedly throughout the twentieth century, that animal researchers are just "anthropomorphizing" their subjects is rarely heard now. Animal researchers and writers are increasingly affirming the observations of David Hume and Charles Darwin that if animals act as if they feel emotions similar to fear, joy, and sadness, then it is the simplest and most likely

Box 13.4   RATIONAL ANIMALS?

The question of animal intelligence has been a challenge ever since Aristotle claimed that animals can think in a practical sense, but only humans can think rationally and abstractly. What does it take to think rationally? You'll remember that our working definition of rationality in Chapter 6 was the ability to identify a goal and take the shortest route to it (and that definition itself was questionable). For Kant the true test of a rational being is whether he or she can understand the categorical imperative: Could you allow yourself to do something you wouldn't accept as a universal law? Most of us, however, have a less strict view of what it is to think rationally. If someone solves a problem through trial and error, we usually view it as a rational method, but it is even better if someone can envision a solution to a problem without having encountered the problem before, and solve it on the first try simply by having thought about it abstractly.

Most of us are probably willing to accept that nonhuman animals have some sort of mental activity whereby they associate time and place, link past fears and joys with present persons and places, and anticipate events in the near future, such as dinner. But can nonhuman animals solve abstract problems and even conceive of a kind of categorical imperative? Throughout the twentieth century this question was so controversial that most scholars steered clear of it for fear of ridicule; in 1900 a horse in Germany, Clever Hans, believed by his owner and numerous scientists to be able to do math because he could thump out the correct answers to math questions when asked, was revealed to be "simply" a good reader of human body language, and research into animal intelligence carried the stigma of Clever Hans with it well into the last half of the twentieth century. But since new research into animal intelligence was made public during the 1980s and 1990s, many researchers have been less reluctant to consider nonhuman animals as having a rudimentary capacity for rational thinking and even for language comprehension. Close observation and interaction with dolphins, orca whales, monkeys, pigs, and even birds have led to a new appreciation of the possibility of nonhuman animal reasoning. In particular, research into the behavior and language capacity of nonhuman great apes (bonobo chimpanzees, chimpanzees, gorillas, and to a lesser extent orangutans) has made it conceivable that the great apes have a grasp of abstract rational thinking as well as trial-and-error thinking.

Of the great apes, the bonobo chimpanzee Kanzi may be the most famous example of nonhuman animal intelligence today, although his sister Panbanisha now seems to surpass him in linguistic talent. They both live at the Georgia State University Language Research Center under the tutelage of psychologist Sue Savage-Rumbaugh. Having taught himself how to use a lexigram (an electronic "talking" board with symbols for English words) by watching the humans try, unsuccessfully, to teach his mother its use, Kanzi answers questions or tells his human friends what he wants, including watching videos where humans in ape costumes are featured. Panbanisha has been raised in the human-language environment and has learned to use the lexigram as well. Kanzi's feats include understanding new sentences and reacting accordingly (such as "Put the key in the refrigerator"), as well as displaying logical thinking, going through a series of actions to achieve a goal (such as cutting a string to get into a box with a key that opens another box with a treat). Panbanisha has shown an interest in copying the words she sees on the computer screen and has reportedly taken up writing words in English on the floor with chalk. In addition, Panbanisha now serves as an interpreter for her and Kanzi's mother, who never learned the use of the lexigram.

The bonobo chimpanzee Kanzi is today perhaps the most outstanding, and controversial, example of a nonhuman being using and understanding language and demonstrating rational thought—at the approximate level of a human child of three (and occasionally even older). Never having been trained to understand human language or use a lexigram (a talking board with symbols signifying nouns, verbs, and names), Kanzi picked up both skills as an infant from watching his mother in training. Here, at sixteen years of age, Kanzi is working with his lexigram, answering questions for Sue Savage-Rumbaugh at Georgia State University's Language Research Center.

Would Kant recognize these behaviors as evidence of rational thinking and welcome Kanzi and Panbanisha as persons instead of things? That would depend on whether it is possible for the apes to grasp the concept of universalization: Might they understand the idea of "Don't do that—how would you like it if we did that to you?" Kanzi's and Panbanisha's language comprehension is now presumably at the level of a three-year-old human child's. If we are ready to recognize a small child as having some grasp of rational thought and as understanding the preceding sentence, and are willing to call a three-year-old child a person, why not be as open-minded about the personhood of an ape if he or she is on the approximate same intellectual level? For some thinkers, the entire ape language experiment hinges on whether it's merely some smart animals "aping" human behavior for rewards, or whether apes can really communicate freely (within limits) in a human language. Since one of the first apes who learned American Sign Language, Washoe, taught her son the ASL signs and communicated with him using signs even when they thought themselves to be

(continued)

Box 13.4   RATIONAL ANIMALS?   *(continued)*

unobserved by humans, and Panbanisha is now teaching her young son how to use the lexigram, the answer seems to be yes.

But what about the apes who haven't learned human language? Might they still have rational thought activity? In other words, is it possible to think without language? In the Primary Readings you'll find a text by Savage-Rumbaugh, who argues that thinking without words is a natural phenomenon among apes as well as among humans.

explanation that they do in fact feel such similar emotions—although we will have a hard time showing exactly how similar, until the day when we can hook up animals (and people) to monitors and read their minds electronically and chemically, or in fact talk to the animals themselves and ask them, as some ape researchers are already doing. (The question of animal *intelligence* is considered in Box 13.4.)

The Utilitarian Approach

Within the utilitarian philosophy the recognition that animals can feel pain—physically, and even emotionally—obviously doesn't mean we as humans are not allowed to cause animals pain or distress, any more than it means we are not allowed to cause other humans pain: When great results can be obtained for a majority (of humans and/or animals), then causing pain to sentient creatures is morally acceptable and even commendable. For this reason, classical utilitarians such as Bentham and Mill and most utilitarians today rarely use the term "animal rights." Rather, modern utilitarians talk about "animal welfare." As you'll remember from Chapter 7, Bentham thought the notion of human rights was "nonsense upon stilts," and obviously a utilitarian would view animal rights in the same light, inasmuch as a utilitarian doesn't believe it serves any good purpose to talk about rights that are absolute and can never be infringed on, if the protection of such rights would be detrimental to the majority in a society.

John Stuart Mill does talk about rights, in particular the rights to security, liberty, and justice, but you will also remember from Chapter 7 that he says, "particular cases may occur in which some other social duty is so important, as to overrule any one of the general maxims of justice." A utilitarian believes we should take animal pain and pleasure into consideration whenever there are no overriding concerns that would justify causing pain for the sake of achieving good consequences for the many. As we saw in Chapter 5, a typical utilitarian response to animal experiments would be to frown on the use of animals in research on household products or cosmetics, because the contentment or protection each individual human would gain from the pain of animal experiments—a safer hairspray, a milder detergent—does not outweigh that pain, especially since humans can choose to avoid products that make your eyes sting and dry out your hands. However, when the focus shifts to medical experiments possibly resulting in the cure for terminal or debilitating illnesses, many utilitarians change their minds: The beneficial outcome of such research, which uses a limited number of animals, could be so overwhelming that there is no excuse not to perform such experiments. (You will recognize the problem from the film *Extreme Measures,* summarized in Chapter 5, even though the film addresses the problem of *human* test subjects.)

The Kantian Approach

As you will remember from Chapter 6, Kant excludes animals from moral consideration as ends in themselves because, to him, they are not rational creatures. Rational creatures are capable of understanding moral rules and, above all, moral duties and responsibilities. Kantians believe that only those who are capable of entering into a mutual relationship involving moral responsibilities are eligible for rights, and since animals are not perceived as having such capabilities, the deontological tradition reserves rights for humans. So what happens to human beings who, for some reason, are not capable of taking on duties and responsibilities? Some modern Kantians, such as the philosopher Carl Cohen, choose to solve that problem by saying that as long as most people are capable of rational thinking and understanding duties, then respect should also be extended to the few who aren't. However, even if it may appear as though an animal is capable of understanding its "duties," what this understanding really amounts to is training based on rewards or punishment—not a true understanding of moral duties—so from a Kantian point of view, animals are by their very nature excluded from having rights. This is what Cohen and others refer to as *contractarianism:* If your mind is capable of comprehending the obligations involved in a contract—written or oral—then you are a rational being and should be treated with respect. A creature that doesn't understand the implications of a contract can't have duties and consequently can't have any rights either. This doesn't mean we can't or shouldn't choose to be kind to animals, because there is no excuse for causing needless suffering, but although we may take on the responsibility of caring for an animal, our pet has no moral claim on us.

Rights and Interests

From the viewpoint that having rights entails having an understanding of duties, the path to animal rights ought to remain blocked. However, there is an alternative viewpoint linking rights not with *duties,* but with *interests.* You were introduced to the ideas of Australian philosopher Peter Singer in Chapter 4, and you may remember the title of one of his books, *The Expanding Circle.* The circle Singer would like to see expanded is our moral universe: Who counts as a morally important being? Singer sees our view of who counts as having expanded from the family or the tribe to nations and to all humans. Singer and others would now like to see this circle expanded further to include the great apes and possibly other intelligent, social species, such as whales, dolphins, and wolves, in what is called "the community of equals," as stated in the Declaration on Great Apes. The argument used by many thinkers advocating rights for animals is that if a living being is capable of having interests, then these beings should have at least some moral standing (they should be taken into our moral universe). But what does it mean to have an interest? It may seem as if our cars have an interest in regular maintenance, because otherwise they break down. But presumably our cars don't suffer when they break down (only we, the owners, do). So the capacity for suffering and the interest in not suffering must be included in the basic description of a being with moral standing. But is an interest something that some individual really wants, or is it something that is good for that individual? And if interests imply rights, does it mean that individuals with interests have a right to have the interest fulfilled? For Singer it is the capacity for interests that makes an individual eligible for rights, but that capacity doesn't mean those individuals have a right to have their wishes (or even their needs) fulfilled; however, they have a right to have their needs taken into consideration as morally relevant. In concrete terms, Singer's suggestions for "rights for the great apes" would include the right not to be tortured, not to be deprived of their freedom, and not to be killed, but it would not include any right to a steady supply of jellybeans (if that's what some individual ape might prefer). Some critics have remarked that it is unusual for a utilitarian philosopher such as Singer to use a concept such as *rights* instead of *welfare,* since traditionally any right for a utilitarian must be superseded by overriding social concerns. But Singer's philosophy of the ethical treatment of animals comes as close to the concept of rights as is possible for a utilitarian, since he believes the possibility that these rights would ever be overridden by other concerns is remote. For Singer, harming an animal would be permissible only in extreme cases such as saving all of humanity.

Other thinkers sharing Singer's view that beings with interests should have rights include Joel Feinberg and Steve Sapontzis. For Feinberg it is obvious that individual animals have interests, perhaps more interests than some humans who are severely mentally impaired, so individual animals should have rights. However, an entire species can't have "interests," so Feinberg doesn't favor the rights of endangered *species,* only those of *individuals,* nonhuman or human. But, says Feinberg, if the criterion for being a member of the moral universe is that you can make moral claims against someone else, then animals already have such rights, because they can be represented in court by humans protecting their interests.

Sapontzis looks at the issue from both a utilitarian and a Kantian point of view: If we agree that animals probably have an overall narrower range of interests than humans, that is still not a sufficient reason to disregard such interests. In "The Moral Significance of Interests," he writes: "It certainly does not follow on utilitarian grounds that because an individual has a narrower range of interests he may be treated as a tool for the gratification of the interests of a being with a wider range of interests. If that did follow, renaissance men could eat specialists and peasants for dinner." Utilitarians aren't obliged to treat humans and animals in *the same* way, just to take their interests into equal consideration (so there won't be a question of giving animals the right to vote or to a good, well-rounded education, as some critics are fond of speculating).

What if we apply Kantianism to the issue of animal interests? Sapontzis points to the wealth of new research in animal intelligence, as well as to our common experiences with animals: It is about time, he says, that we put the debate over whether animals are rational behind us; of course they are—not to the degree of human rationality, but rational nevertheless. They may not be able to use the categorical imperative, but they are courageous, loyal, and devoted, and if we want to extend moral worth to humans with the same qualities, then we must let many animals into the moral fold too. As Sapontzis says, "Anyone still inclined to believe that only humans are rational should adopt a dog and get to know him personally."

What if you still think that granting rights to animals is too big a step, since humans, after all, have such a wide range of moral interactions that animals may never comprehend or participate in? You may consider a solution suggested by the philosopher Mary Ann Warren: *partial rights*. Because many animals do have the same rudimentary intellectual capabilities as small children and the same (or an even greater) capacity for suffering, they should have some moral standing; but since human capacities for both reasoning and suffering are more extensive, they may override the rights of animals. Animals can probably never be morally autonomous the way humans can, but moral autonomy need not be the only criterion for having rights. It is, however, an important factor. So Warren suggests that humans should be the only beings granted full, equal rights (at least until we find other morally autonomous creatures), but nonhuman animals can be the bearers of partial rights, to be superseded by human rights only in extreme cases.

The Death Penalty

When the question of punishing criminals comes up today, it is usually related to the issue of sentencing children as adults or that of the death penalty. The issue of trying children in adult court was examined briefly in Chapter 7, and here we explore the issue of capital punishment. In order to get the most out of the debate it is recommended that you have the punishment discussion from Chapter 7 fresh in your mind, particularly the five categories of punishment: deterrence, rehabilitation, incapacitation, retribution, and vengeance.

Two Philosophers on Capital Punishment

Most philosophers up until the twentieth century have had no compunction about arguing in favor of the death penalty. Two voices coming from two different traditions have been particularly influential, and you are familiar with both of them: John Locke, in seventeenth-century England, stated that humans have rights even before the social contract, in the state of nature. These are the three negative rights, to *life, liberty, and property*. But since there is no government in the state of nature to enforce these rights, one must take on that task oneself. Therefore, if a person has infringed on your rights, you are free to punish the perpetrator (if you can catch him or her, that is). And, says Locke, if someone in the state of nature has taken a life, then he has given up his own right to life and can be hunted down and killed like a wild animal. Locke believes such action will have two effects: (1) *deterrence*—those who see how a killer is treated will think twice about doing the same thing—and (2) *retribution,* restoring the balance that was disrupted by the murder. So Locke uses both a forward-looking and a backward-looking argument in favor of killing a killer.

THE WIZARD OF ID　　　　　　　　　　　　　　　　**Brant parker and Johnny hart**

By permission of Johnny Hart and Creators Syndicate, Inc.

With a particularly dark sense of humor, this *Wizard of Id* strip deals with capital punishment—a topic that isn't usually a source of laughter. The strip creates a perverted application of a utilitarian principle of punishment: As long as punishment has good consequences (such as deterrence or rehabilitation), then the issue of guilt or innocence is of minor importance.

The other familiar voice in favor of the death penalty is Immanuel Kant, speaking to us from eighteenth-century Prussia. Kant argues that capital punishment is a rational response to a capital crime—and he argues exclusively in favor of *retribution:* If we execute a criminal in order to obtain some good social consequences such as safe streets, then we are in effect using the killer as merely a means to an end—we are using him or her as a stepping-stone to safe streets. Indeed, executing an *innocent* person would probably have the same kind of deterrent effect. Instead, Kant insists that there should be one reason, and one reason only, for punishing a person: because of his or her *guilt.* And in order for us to proceed according to the principle of *lex talionis,* we should punish the guilty in proportion to the crime, not with an eye toward any further social consequences. This means the only proper punishment for murder is death—even if good social consequences might actually come out of imprisoning the killer for life or letting him or her go free after a period of rehabilitation.

We see how seriously Kant takes this principle by his example: If a society decides to disband but still has people waiting on death row, then the last action of that society should be to execute its convicted murderers, even if there will be no society afterward to enjoy the safer streets. Furthermore, it is only right and proper to execute a murderer for his crime—and in a sense it is showing the convicted killer the utmost *respect* as a human being: Instead of using him for some social purpose (such as deterrence), or trying to rehabilitate him under the assumption that he didn't know what he was doing, we give him credit for actually having made up his own mind to commit a crime—and then we hold him accountable for it.

It wasn't until the nineteenth century that strong voices began to speak up against capital punishment as such, and not merely in opposition to executions for lesser crimes such as burglary. In the twentieth century opposition to the death penalty became known as *abolitionism* (whereas "abolition" in the nineteenth century referred to abolishing slavery in America).

Today's Capital Punishment Criteria

From 1968 to 1976, there was a moratorium on the death penalty in the United States, but since 1976 individual states have been able to decide whether they want to make certain crimes punishable by death, as long as their laws meet guidelines established by the U.S. Supreme Court. In the fall of 2004 thirty-eight states allowed capital punishment, while twelve states didn't. Out of the thiry-eight states, New York had declared its death penalty statute unconstitutional in the summer of 2004, and local governments all over the United States, as well as a number of professional organizations such as the American Bar Association have called for a new moratorium on capital punishment.

What crimes are today punishable by death in the thirty-eight states that allow capital punishment? Theoretically, treason is, but the death penalty is evoked only under rare circumstances, as with the execution of Julius and Ethel Rosenberg for espionage in 1953—still a controversial judicial decision, especially since 2001, when a witness for the prosecution admitted that he lied on the stand. In previous decades, murder, even if committed in a state of rage or panic, might lead to the gas chamber or the electric chair, but today one or more "special circumstances" have to apply, depending on the state legislation. In California, for example, some of the special circumstances are killing more than one person; raping and killing a person; stalking a victim before killing him or her; killing a police officer, a judge, or a jury member; killing with poison; and killing while carjacking. Richard Allen Davis, who abducted, sexually assaulted, and killed twelve-year-old Polly Klaas in Petaluma, California, in 1993, is on death row: He pleaded not guilty but was convicted. Brandon Wilson, who killed nine-year-old Matthew Checci in 1998 in Oceanside, California, after following him into a restroom (stalking), is now on death row. These are cases in which the California law of special circumstances applies. In other death penalty states, other rules may apply. In the state of Washington, for example, a killer of multiple victims must be shown to have had a "common scheme" in killing them, such as robbery. The simple fact of there being more than one victim isn't enough in itself to warrant the death penalty; Washington legislators have been debating changing the law in the wake of the capture of several serial killers.

Abolitionist Arguments

Abolitionists make the following general arguments:

1. The death penalty is an uncivilized, cruel, and unusual form of punishment, depriving the criminal of the ultimate right: the right to life. Abolitionists often cite the fact that among Western nations, the United States is the only country that still executes its citizens, and abolitionist nations around the world usually refuse to extradite a murderer to the United States if he or she may be executed. Proponents of the death penalty, called *retentionists* because they want to *retain* the penalty, reply that of all Western nations, the United States is the only country in which serial killers operate on a regular basis and that the homicide rate is generally higher than in other Western nations, so special measures have to be taken.

2. Executing a murderer is no better than stooping to the level of the murderer, making murder state-sanctioned. Retentionists reply that this is a false analogy: The murderer kills innocent people, whereas the state executes someone who has been found guilty.

3. As it is administered today, at least in certain states, the death penalty shows patterns of discrimination: The poor, the uneducated, and African American men are more likely to receive the death penalty than are people from other population groups, regardless of the crime rate. Retentionists reply that this is not an argument against the death penalty as such, only against the way it has been administered—which admittedly has been discriminatory. But such slanted approaches can be avoided in the future, and according to a recent report from the Justice Department such approaches are virtually a thing of the past, at least in federal cases. Be that as it may, the general perception among abolitionists as well as many retentionists is that the discrimination issue is still far from having been resolved.

4. Mistakes have been made and innocent people executed—twenty-three known innocents in this country in the twentieth century. A person wrongly incarcerated cannot have the years he or she spent behind bars restored, but he or she can be compensated financially. An innocent person who has been executed can't be compensated in any way, because everything has been taken from him or her. To many, this argument is the strongest abolitionist point, leading to the adage that it is better that many guilty go free than that one innocent person be punished. In the Primary Readings you'll find an excerpt from Mark Fuhrman's *Death and Justice* (2003), in which he argues that since mistakes *can't* be avoided, it is better to abolish the death penalty.

5. An aspect that is rarely brought forth, but that may be very important, is the influence of politics. As Mark Fuhrman mentions in his book *Death and Justice*, as long as the death penalty is a factor in local and state politics, there is a danger of its being abused, to secure votes and look "tough on crime." Because judges, sheriffs, and district attorneys are *elected* in many states and have to run election campaigns, their stance on the death penalty and their history of convictions will be part of those campaigns. Deliberately or inadvertently, isn't there a risk that this external factor may slant the view of what is "the worst of the worst" among criminals—those cases deserving the death penalty? Fuhrman cites examples in Oklahoma to that effect: While Bob Macy was District Attorney, executions were at an all-time high, with twenty-one executions in 2001 alone. When there is even the slightest suspicion that such a factor may play into seeking the death penalty, there is reason for caution.

6. Some abolitionists argue that you can choose to be a retentionist only if you are ignorant, sadistic, or emotional, and that once you bothered to examine exactly what goes on at an execution, and to distance yourself from your emotional response to the victims, then you would become an abolitionist. (These arguments are set forth in the abolitionist book *Who Owns Death? Capital Punishment, the American Conscience, and the End of Executions* [2000] by Robert Jay Lifton and Greg Mitchell.) Retentionists answer that even botched executions are no argument against the death penalty as such, only against incompetence; that most retentionists don't *like* the thought of putting people to death and regard capital punishment as a necessary evil; and relat-

ing to the suffering of the victims is extremely relevant to the entire issue of punishment. You'll remember the argument from Berns, Strawson, and Whiteley in Chapter 7 that if we are incapable of feeling some form of morally righteous indignation and anger on behalf of the victim—and all the more so on behalf of a murder victim—then we have in effect lost respect and empathy for other human beings.

Retentionist Arguments

Retentionists make the following arguments:

1. Only capital punishment can fit the severity of the crime of murder, and a person who murders has forfeited his or her own right to life. In other words, the issue for many retentionists is *justice,* and the only adequate justice they see for a capital crime is one of retribution. The murderer deserves to die; the victim's family deserves closure; and society deserves to have the books balanced: Commit a crime, and you will pay for it in proportion to the crime. Abolitionists reply that the whole issue of proportionality ("an eye for an eye") has been distorted by retentionists. Only in murder cases do they invoke the principle—does anyone ever talk about "an eye for an eye" when the issue is burglary? Does the court go in and take something from the home of the thief as punishment? Or how about carjacking, embezzlement, or prostitution? How do you punish someone proportionately to that? In the Primary Readings you'll find an excerpt by Stephen Nathanson arguing against the proportionality principle, and Tom Sorell argues in his paper, "Two Ideals and the Death Penalty" that, carefully applied, the death penalty is a just and proper form of punishment.

2. The only way to protect the public effectively from future killings is to eliminate the murderer (the argument of *incapacitation*). An abolitionist may argue that keeping a murderer in prison for life without the possibility of parole is just as effective, but the retentionist will answer that the prison has not yet been built that is 100 percent escape-proof. Even science fiction contains escape scenarios from asteroid penal colonies! And even if prisons were escape-proof, we may still have gubernatorial decisions pardoning murderers. A serial killer of children may appear to be completely rehabilitated in prison and given a pardon, but recidivism in these cases is very high. Here an abolitionist may point to the slippery slope, implying that perhaps any criminal who can't be rehabilitated should be executed regardless of his or her crime. Or perhaps we should even try to anticipate what criminal tendencies a first-time offender has and execute him or her on the basis of what he or she will probably do later on! But though some retentionists would welcome a broadening of capital punishment to cover rapes and child molestation, no serious philosophers of law argue that a person should be punishable for something he or she has not done yet, and most retentionists reserve capital punishment for murders with special circumstances.

3. Some retentionists argue that a conviction followed by execution is a deterrent (whereas almost everyone agrees that the longer the time lag between conviction and execution, the less deterrent effect the execution has). It will certainly be a specific deterrent for that criminal, because he or she is not going to commit murder again! In the general sense of the word, others will be deterred by the threat of sure and swift punishment. Some retentionists cite swift justice as a formidable deterrent

in countries where civil liberties are not on the main political agenda: If you know you will have your hand amputated if you steal, are you really going to take the chance? But other retentionists claim that civil liberties and rights are too high a price to pay for safe streets. The effectiveness of general deterrence is undecided statistically: Some statistics show some deterrence factor after an execution; other statistics actually portray the crime rate as going up after executions. (Deterrence seems to be a fact in noncapital crimes. However, it is hotly debated whether the "three strikes and you're out" law in California and similar laws in other states have had any deterrent effect.) Abolitionists sometimes point out that if a person has killed once and knows that he or she is likely to get caught, convicted, and executed, then what is to deter the murderer from killing again, perhaps witnesses? They can suffer the penalty only once. And retentionists answer back by saying that a murderer in prison for life might well (and often does) go on murdering in prison, knowing that there can be no stricter penalty than the one he or she is already suffering, so the only way to prevent further killings is to retain and use the death penalty. In the Primary Readings, John Douglas argues in favor of specific deterrence, in an excerpt from his and Mark Olshaker's book *Journey into Darkness*.

The five reasons for punishment discussed in Chapter 7 all have a role in the death penalty debate. As we just saw, *deterrence* can be used as a retentionist argument. The effect is usually assumed to be that others are deterred from committing the same crime; the intention is less to deter the criminal from doing it again (specific deterrence). (See *The Wizard of Id* on page 648, a spoof of a retentionist utilitarian argument: The wrong man may be executed, but the real killer learns a valuable lesson.) *Incapacitation* can likewise be a retentionist argument, but what about *rehabilitation*? Rehabilitation is not relevant here, for obviously an executed person doesn't learn not to commit the same crime again. *Retribution,* on the other hand, is highly relevant, for a retributivist will usually argue that the death penalty is the ultimate form of justice: It fits the crime, provided that society can be certain it has caught and convicted the guilty person. *Vengeance,* the supposedly nonlegitimate reason for punishment, is generally the most prevailing retentionist view among laypeople, who often argue that a murderer ought to die because he or she ought to suffer the way the victim suffered and that the suffering of the murderer will make society feel better. An abolitionist will generally argue that a life term can be as effective a deterrent as death, that a life term also incapacitates a murderer, and that there is always a chance that a murderer can be rehabilitated. Few retributivists are abolitionists, but it is possible to argue that a life term is the proportionate punishment for a murder, so we can have proportionality and still have respect for life, even the life of a murderer; vengeance is never an option for an abolitionist, who generally sees the death penalty as an expression of primitive social revenge.

It has been customary among scholars to view this insistence on how we *feel* as a primitive trait, but before we reject all references to emotions in the death penalty debate outright, we should remember that several philosophers have recently argued that emotions are not altogether irrelevant in our moral decision process. Martha Nussbaum (Chapter 1) argues that emotions can have their own logic; Richard Taylor (Chapter 11) says that the fundamental morality of compassion comes from the heart, not the brain; Walter Berns (Chapter 7) says a society that punishes without feeling anger toward the criminal doesn't care for its victims; Diane Whiteley (Chapter 7) argues that a proper understanding of justice includes a sense of moral indignation over harm done to a victim. No thinkers today argue that punishment should take place along exclusively emotional lines, because in that case we'd probably quickly see the punishment exceed the severity of the crime, but maybe justice should not be completely separated from emotions either. Should we be seeking a Golden Mean between impartial justice that punishes according to a set scale with neither rage nor compassion and a system of justice that allows a measure of emotion to enter into the picture, as an outlet for society's righteous anger against an identified and justly convicted perpetrator, as well as an opening for mercy when an unusual set of circumstances warrants it? Or is that a dangerous step toward legitimatizing revenge? In the Narratives Section you'll find two stories dealing with the death penalty; one is Larry Niven's," science fiction short story, "The Jigsaw Man," and the other is the 2003 film *The Life of David Gale.*

The DNA Issue

Recently, a number of people serving life sentences or waiting on death row have been exonerated and released as the result of DNA testing. According to the Death Penalty Information Center, an abolitionist website, 115 death row inmates had been freed between 1973 and the fall of 2004. It should be pointed out, however, that of these 115, only 14 have been exonerated because of DNA testing—the rest have been freed because of other factors. These reversals have prompted both retentionists and abolitionists to question the procedures that convicted these people in the first place. In Idaho, Charles Fain was on death row eighteen years for raping and killing a nine-year-old girl. When DNA analyses cleared him in 2001, he magnanimously said that he had no hard feelings, but was just looking forward to resuming his life after years of incarceration. It appears that the small town where he had been convicted had conveniently pounced on him as a newcomer to the area, even though he had an alibi. And in Oklahoma City it was revealed in 2001 that a forensic chemist whose testimony had contributed to 23 people being sent to death row and 11 already executed, had lied on the stand on at least six occasions. Given such cases, one doesn't have to be an abolitionist to wonder how many other executions may have involved a less-than-fair trial. But a retentionist will state that such cases still don't provide a compelling argument against the death penalty as such, only against the way it has been administered, and retentionists as well as abolitionists are generally in favor of introducing mandatory DNA testing of suspects in a wide array of criminal cases so the risk of convicting an innocent person can be minimized.

However, not all crime scenes contain DNA from the perpetrator; only if the criminal leaves blood, saliva, hair with follicles, body tissue, or semen at the crime scene can DNA be used to rule out other suspects and point to one suspect in particular. And it is equally important to realize that DNA is not the only important evidence that can convict a criminal. Eyewitnesses *can* be reliable and, contrary to the popular conception, circumstantial evidence can sometimes be extremely strong.

When Gary Ridgway was apprehended in December 2001 in Seattle and charged with the Green River serial killings of the early 1980s, most people who had followed the case were astonished that an arrest had actually been made. The case had dragged on so long, with several suspects but not enough evidence, that only a few dedicated police detectives were still on the case. But these clear-thinking officers had collected a saliva sample from one of the suspects years earlier on the off chance that science at some time in the future could do something with it, and in the late 1990s the DNA technology was available. When the Washington State lab got around to testing the sample in 2001, the perseverance of the detectives paid off: There was a DNA match between semen found on three Green River victims and the saliva sample. Confronted with an overwhelming amount of evidence and a possible death sentence, Ridgway confessed to 48 murders after a long series of chilling interviews with the police, where he talked, in extremely callous terms, about the individual victims and their deaths. The confession was part of a plea bargain, and thus Ridgway exchanged a trial and a near-certain death sentence for life imprisonment without the possibility of parole. In San Diego a DNA match was found between semen on two little boys murdered in the 1980s and a man who was already serving a sentence for rape and assault, but who was free at the time of their deaths, and now he has been sentenced to death for their murder. It seems that with the new, faster DNA tests there is no legal or moral downside: Innocent people are being set free, and killers are being matched up with their victims even decades after their murders. In addition, it isn't just the criminal's DNA left at the crime scene that can help convict him or her—the victim's DNA speaks loudly too. If the victim's blood, for example, has been found in the suspect's home or on his or her clothes, it provides important evidence, such as in the case of seven-year-old Danielle van Dam, abducted from her San Diego home in the middle of the night and murdered in the spring of 2002. Her blood found in David Westerfield's motorhome and on his clothes gave the judge reasonable cause to order him to stand trial. He was found guilty in August 2002 and sentenced to death.

You may have wondered why it is that police and lawyers talk about DNA matches as being one in 5, 6, or even 10 billion, since there are "only" 6 billion humans on the planet these days. How can there be a match between a suspect and another nonexistent person? The fact of the matter is that talking about matches of one to several billion is just another way of saying that the DNA points *exclusively* to the accused. The roundabout way of saying it is, in effect, a consequence of a scientific problem you are well acquainted with from Chapter 3, the problem of induction. Since DNA research is an empirical science, a good scientist can't make statements about anything being 100 percent certain, but referring to the actual statistical possibility of another person being born with the exact same DNA (which would be, presumably, 10 billion to one), you can make a statement in court that translates into common English as a complete and indisputable identification of a criminal, even better than with a fingerprint.

If the American criminal justice system in the future *can* eliminate most of the doubt as to someone's guilt or innocence through DNA analysis, would that also eliminate the abolitionist argument that the death penalty sometimes kills innocents? In cases where no DNA evidence exists, there would still be a danger of an innocent person being executed. And it is the principle of the state taking a life that the abolitionist is protesting more than anything. But for reluctant retentionists the increased certainty of guilt might pave the way for a *greater* confidence in the justification of capital punishment. Proposals of mandatory DNA tests for all criminals and even a DNA profile for all children born in the United States might go a long way to help solve crimes and avoid wrongful convictions.

Even with these new scientific safeguards against convicting the wrong person, however, there appears to be a growing unease in the United States about the very nature of the death penalty, at least at the legislative level. Case in point: In 2000 the state of Illinois declared a moratorium on the death penalty, and in the spring of 2002 a fourteen-member panel recommended a major reform of capital punishment in the state, including a statewide DNA database, an independent forensic lab, videotaping of interrogations, and a ban on executing mentally retarded murderers. The bipartisan commission stopped short of recommending an end to capital punishment, but a narrow majority on the panel concluded that since no system can guarantee that no innocent person is ever sentenced to death, the death penalty should be abolished in the state of Illinois. The concept of having all criminals tested for DNA has won bipartisan support in Washington, and in October 2004 the Advancing Justice through DNA Technology Act was signed into law by President Bush after having passed the House and Senate, making funding available for states to help pay for postconviction DNA testing. In addition, the Supreme Court banned executions of teens under the age of eighteen in 2005. Could this be the beginning of the end of the death penalty in America? Many people think so.

Stories and Issues: A Final Word

In this chapter we have examined four issues within the field of applied ethics. Of course there are many more issues with a moral dimension that concern us in today's world, such as euthanasia, abortion, and gun control. I hope that you will make use of the theories we have explored throughout this book to embark on discussions of some of these other issues as well, since you now have the theoretical background to weigh in with more than how you *feel* about an issue. As we have seen numerous times in this book, feelings about moral issues need not be irrelevant, but feelings can't take the place of rational arguments—primarily because an appeal to feelings rarely solves conflicts, but an appeal to logic might. In addition, I hope you will approach the world of stories with an enhanced appreciation for issues raised in television shows, in movies, and in literature, be it stories about cloning and genetic engineering, media ethics and responsibilities, human relations involving compassion and gratitude, or perhaps stories of courage in wartime and peacetime. In this book we've used summaries and excerpts of such stories to illustrate and explore some intricate moral issues, and I hope you've felt inspired to seek out and experience the original stories in their entirety by yourself, because a summary or even an excerpt doesn't do a good story justice. My hope is that as the access to a moral theory has perhaps been made easier or more relevant by a movie or a novel, so, too, might a good background knowledge of moral theories enhance your enjoyment of a fictional story. I know it has for me. There are lots of issues out there, nationally and globally, and lots of stories about them. Enjoy the exploration!

Study Questions

1. If you were a journalist, how might you describe the proper balance between the public's right to know and the need for national security? Would it make a difference if you were not a journalist but a member of law enforcement? Or a schoolteacher? Or a military person?

2. In your view, can a war be just? Explain in detail, referring to the text.

3. What is patriotism? Can we apply Aristotle's concept of the Golden Mean and talk about too much, the right amount, and too little patriotism? Explain.

4. Should animals have rights? If no, explain why not. If yes, explain whether your view is based on their ability to suffer, their ability to think, both, or neither.

5. Which, in your view, is the strongest argument in favor of the death penalty? Which is the strongest argument against it? In your view, should we retain or abolish capital punishment? Explain.

Primary Readings and Narratives

The first Reading is an excerpt from "Ethics as a Vehicle for Media Quality" by Andrew Belsey and Ruth Chadwick, exploring the concept of a "virtuous journalist." Because of the national and global focus on terrorism and the concept of just war, we have excerpts from three primary texts covering that issue. The first is from John Rawls's book *The Law of Peoples,* in which he explores the theory of a just war; the second is from Jan Narveson's essay "Morality and Violence: War, Revolution, Terrorism," and the third excerpt from David Rodin's "Terrorism Without Intention" focuses on the legitimate treatment of terrorists and a general definition of terrorism. An excerpt from Sue Savage-Rumbaugh's book *Kanzi: The Ape at the Brink of the Human Mind* explores ape rationality. An issue that I pay particular attention to in my own classes is the death penalty, and four texts round off the Primary Readings section. Two texts are by philosophers, one an abolitionist, and the other a retentionist: Stephen Nathanson's *An Eye for an Eye,* and Tom Sorell, "Two Ideals and the Death Penalty." Two texts are from authors with a law-enforcement background, one a retentionist: John Douglas's *Journey into Darkness,* and the other an abolitionist: Mark Fuhrman's *Death and Justice, an Exposé of Oklahoma's Death Row Machine.* The Narratives are the film *15 Minutes,* about media ethics; the short story "The Jigsaw Man" about a utilitarian rationale for capital punishment; and the film *The Life of David Gale,* about an abolitionist activist on death row for murder.

Primary Reading

Ethics as a Vehicle for Media Quality

ANDREW BELSEY AND RUTH CHADWICK

Excerpt, 1995.

In this paper Belsey and Chadwick argue that if the media have too many legal restrictions, journalists are going to be distracted by trying to get around them, rather than behaving with professional ethics. The fewer legal constraints a journalist has, the higher his or her ethical standards will have to be, according to the authors, because a legal right to publish is not equivalent to a moral right to publish. The authors use the concept of a "virtuous journalist," linking the notion of journalism to virtue ethics. Virtues mentioned are fairness, integrity, objectivity, trustworthiness, and accuracy, among others. In addition, the authors suggest that an ethical code of practice would be useful. Such a code of practice would involve both "dos" and "don'ts" of the profession.

The Ethical Route to Media Quality

No legal framework guarantees ethical behavior in any area of life, though the law does provide an arena in which some forms of behavior are encouraged and some discouraged. There will be (dis)incentives in the form of sanctions and penalties, but ultimately a society depends on the sense of morality and responsibility of its members. This is how it ought to be in a democracy. Similarly, neither the negative nor the positive aspects of the legal route will guarantee media quality. Unless media professionals have a sense of morality and responsibility too, the quality will be lacking. But in relation to the media there is an important interplay between law and ethics. To put the point simply: too many legal prohibitions and restrictions force journalists to concentrate on what they can get away with in legal terms, and thus distract their attention away from matters of ethics. This has a distorting and a trivializing effect on the output of the media, to the detriment of quality. Conversely, giving legal rights and freedoms to journalist places them under an obligation to pay attention to the ethical issues of their profession. As Klaidman and Beauchamp put it in their influential discussion of media ethics, "freedom from legal constraints is a special privilege that demands increased awareness of moral obligation."

This is because a legal right to publish does not mean that it is morally right to publish. Even when the law is satisfied there are still ethical questions in areas such as obscenity, character assassination, privacy, confidentiality, deception, sexism, and homophobia. Journalists need to select from the mass of possible information what should be included and what should not, and judgments about what is important, significant, trivial, or tasteless are, basically, ethical judgments. Similarly, judgments about presentation are also ethical, inasmuch as they raise issues of sensitivity and taste on the one hand, and sensationalism and vulgarity on the other. All these ethical issues can be summed up in the concept of professional competence, as this requires not just a command of technical skills but also the ability to deploy moral qualities (Klaidman and Beauchamp, 1987, 12). Thus, for example, a commitment to truth-telling, often put forward as constitutive of journalism (and therefore basic to journalistic competence), requires honesty, integrity, tenaciousness, and no doubt other ethical qualities, too, on the part of the journalist.

One interesting and important way of spelling out further what is involved in this ethical notion of competence in the media is by referring to Klaidman and Beauchamp's prescription for journalism in terms of virtue and the virtues: every journalist the "virtuous journalist" (Klaidman and Beauchamp, 1987). The virtuous journalist will display a commitment to many virtues, including fairness, accuracy, honesty, integrity, objectivity, benevolence, sensitivity trustworthiness, accountability, and humor. More important, though, than a list of specific virtues is virtue: the virtuous journalist is one who has a virtuous character, one who therefore has a disposition to act virtuously not only in familiar but also in novel situations. It is in this sense that the competent journalist is the virtuous journalist and is also the journalist with a commitment to quality.

In such a way, then, can ethics be a vehicle for media quality. As before, it is a vehicle which can travel the ethical route in two ways, a positive aspect emphasizing the ethical requirements for maintaining quality in the media (the virtues, like truth-telling), and a negative aspect emphasizing the prohibitions (the corresponding vices, such as lying).

The Ethical Route via a Code of Practice?

The ethical route to media quality requires a commitment by individual journalists and other media practitioners to certain ethical principles and standards—a commitment which can be conveniently expressed by the notion of the "virtuous journalist." But should this commitment be further demonstrated by adherence to an ethical "code of practice," incorporating the various principals and standards?

While not essential, such an approach has advantages. It joins journalism with other occupations that have promulgated codes of practice, and is one of the moves which demonstrate an aspiration to move beyond mere occupation to professional status. Adherence to a code brings journalists together as professionals recognizing common aims and interests and accepting responsibilities to the public. Adherence to a code thus shows a collective public commitment to acknowledged ethical principles and standards, rather than a purely solitary conscientiousness about ethical matters. Putting ethical principles and standards into a published code is a convenience, announcing to both professionals and the public that there is a commitment to quality and to the standards of behavior and practice necessary to achieve quality.

An ethical code of practice will have both positive and negative aspects, detailing what is required and what is prohibited. Both aspects clearly have a contribution to make to media quality. A code of practice for the media, for example, could require journalists to be honest and accurate in all matters, to be impartial and objective in reporting news, to publish corrections, to offer a right of reply, to protect the identity of confidential sources. It could also, presumably, prohibit deception, harassment, invasions of privacy, doorstepping the victims of traumatic events, exploiting children, buying the stories of criminals. It is noticeable that these prohibitions tend to be much more specific than the positive requirements.

However, a code of practice could be seen as having functions other than just listing the requirements and prohibitions. First, a code could have a disciplinary function, linking breaches of requirements and prohibitions with sanctions. A code could also have an educative function, in that it would teach what was expected of a journalist and would both state and encourage the standards of competence and the underlying thinking that constitute journalism as professional practice. Related to this a code could also have a "utopian" function, which would be a statement of the ideals and aspirations of the profession, going beyond a list of requirements and prohibitions. In the case of a code of the media, such ideals could go back to First Amendment aspirations, linking press freedom with the requirements of democracy.

Study Questions:

1. What is a *virtuous journalist,* according to the authors? And what do they mean by an "ethical code of practice"?

2. According to this excerpt, is it legitimate for a journalist to have a political agenda in his or her writings? Explain why or why not.

3. Evaluate the case of Jayson Blair (*New York Times*) according to this text. Why were his actions a breach of journalistic ethics?

4. Evaluate the case of Dan Rather (CBS, *60 Minutes*) according to this text. Did Rather go against the rules of ethical journalism? Explain why or why not.

Primary Reading

The Law of Peoples

JOHN RAWLS

Excerpt, 1999.

John Rawls, whom you met in Chapter 7 as well as in this chapter, hopes in his *Law of Peoples* to outline a *realistic utopia* according to the principles of justice, recognizing that peoples should view each other as free and independent. He sees five kinds of domestic societies: *Reasonable, liberal peoples* and *decent peoples* ("nonliberal societies whose basic institutions meet certain specified conditions of political right and justice") together form the category of *well-ordered peoples;* then there are *outlaw states; societies burdened by unfavorable conditions;* and *societies of benevolent absolutisms* (societies that recognize human rights but don't allow their citizens a political voice). Here Rawls explores the right of well-ordered peoples to go to war.

Role of Nonideal Theory

To this point we have been concerned with ideal theory. In extending a liberal conception of justice, we have developed an ideal conception of a Law of Peoples for the Society of well-ordered Peoples, that is, liberal and decent peoples. That conception is to guide these well-ordered peoples in their conduct toward one another and in their designing common institutions for their mutual benefit. It is also to guide them in how to deal with non-well-ordered peoples. Before our discussion of the Law of Peoples is complete, we must therefore consider, though we cannot do so wholly adequately, the questions arising from the highly nonideal conditions of our world with its great injustices and widespread social evils. On the assumption that there exist in the world some relatively well-ordered peoples, we ask in nonideal theory how these peoples should act toward non-well-ordered peoples. We take as a basic characteristic of well-ordered peoples that they wish to live in a world in which all peoples accept and follow the (ideal of the) Law of Peoples.

Nonideal theory asks how this long-term goal might be achieved, or worked toward, usually in gradual steps. It looks for policies and courses of action that are morally permissible and politically possible as well as likely to be effective. So conceived, nonideal theory presupposes that ideal theory is already on hand. For until the ideal is identified, at least in outline—and that is all we should expect—nonideal theory lacks an objective, an aim, by reference to which its queries can be answered. Though the specific conditions of our world at any time—the status quo—do not determine the ideal conception of the Society of Peoples, those conditions do affect the specific answers to questions of nonideal theory. For these are questions of transition, of how to work from a world containing outlaw states and societies suffering from unfavorable conditions to a world in which all societies come to accept and follow the Law of Peoples.

There are [. . .] two kinds of nonideal theory. One kind deals with conditions of noncompliance, that is, with conditions in which certain regimes refuse to comply with a reasonable Law of Peoples; these regimes think a sufficient reason to engage in war is that war advances, or might advance, the regime's rational (not reasonable) interests. These regimes I call *outlaw states*. The other kind of nonideal theory deals with unfavorable conditions, that is, with the conditions of societies whose historical, social, and economic circumstances make their achieving a well-ordered regime, whether liberal or decent, difficult if not impossible. These societies I call *burdened societies.*[1]

I begin with noncompliance theory, and recall that the fifth initial principle of equality of the Law of Peoples gives well-ordered peoples a right to war in self-defense but not, as in the traditional account of sovereignty, a right to war in the rational pursuit of a state's rational interests; these alone are not a sufficient reason. Well-ordered peoples, both liberal and decent, do not initiate war against one another; they go to war only when they sincerely and reasonably believe that their safety and security are seriously endangered by the expansionist policies of outlaw states. In what follows, I work out the content of the principles of the Law of Peoples for the conduct of war.

---

[1]There are also other possibilities. Some states are not well-ordered and violate human rights, but are not aggressive and do not harbor plans to attack their neighbors. They do not suffer from unfavorable conditions, but simply have a state policy that violates the human rights of certain minorities among them. They are therefore outlaw states because they violate what are recognized as rights by the Society of reasonably just and decent Peoples, and they may be subject to some kind of intervention in severe cases.

Well-Ordered Peoples' Right to War

No state has a right to war in the pursuit of its *rational,* as opposed to its *reasonable,* interests. The Law of Peoples does, however, assign to all well-ordered peoples (both liberal and decent), and indeed to any society that follows and honors a reasonably just Law of Peoples, the right to war in self-defense.[2] Although all well-ordered societies have this right, they may interpret their actions in a different way depending on how they think of their ends and purposes. I will note some of these differences.

When a liberal society engages in war in self-defense, it does so to protect and preserve the basic freedoms of its citizens and its constitutionally democratic political institutions. Indeed, a liberal society cannot justly require its citizens to fight in order to gain economic wealth or to acquire natural resources, much less to win power and empire.[3] (When a society pursues these interests, it no longer honors the Law of Peoples, and it becomes an outlaw state.) To trespass on citizens' liberty by conscription, or other such practices in raising armed forces, may only be done on a liberal political conception for the sake of liberty itself, that is, as necessary to defend liberal democratic institutions and civil society's many religious and nonreligious traditions and forms of life.[4]

The special significance of liberal constitutional government is that through its democratic politics, and by following the idea of public reason, citizens can express their conception of their society and take actions appropriate to its defense. That is, ideally, citizens work out a *truly* political opinion, and not simply an opinion about what would best advance their own particular interests, of whatever kind, as members of civil society. Such (truly political) citizens develop an opinion of the rights and wrongs of political right and justice, and of what the well-being of different parts of society requires. As in *Political Liberalism,* each citizen is regarded as having what I have called "the two moral powers"—a capacity for a sense of justice and a capacity for a conception of the good. It is also assumed that each citizen has, at any time, a conception of the good compatible with a comprehensive religious, philosophical, or moral doctrine. These capacities enable citizens to fulfill their role as citizens and underwrite their political and civic autonomy. The principles of justice protect citizens' higher-order interests; these are guaranteed within the framework of the liberal constitution and the basic structure of society. These institutions establish a reasonably just setting within which the background culture[5] of civil society may flourish.

Decent peoples also have a right to war in self-defense. They would describe what they are defending differently from the way a liberal people would; but decent peoples also have something worth defending. For example, the rulers of the imagined decent people, Kazanistan, could rightly defend their decent hierarchical Muslim society. They allow and respect members of different faiths within their society, and they respect the

---

[2]The right to war normally includes the right to help to defend one's allies.

[3]Of course, so-called liberal societies sometimes do this, but that only shows they may act wrongly.

[4]See *A Theory of Justice,* sec. 58, pp. 380ff.

[5]See *Political Liberalism,* p. 14.

political institutions of other societies, including non-Muslim and liberal societies. They also respect and honor human rights; their basic structure contains a decent consultation hierarchy; and they accept and abide by a (reasonable) Law of Peoples.

The fifth kind of society listed earlier—a *benevolent absolutism*—would also appear to have the right to war in self-defense. While a benevolent absolutism does respect and honor human rights, it is not a well-ordered society, since it does not give its members a meaningful role in making political decisions. But *any* society that is nonaggressive and that honors human rights has the right of self-defense. Its level of spiritual life and culture may not be high in our eyes, but it always has the right to defend itself against invasion of its territory.

Study Questions

1. What are the two kinds of nonideal theories, and what is Rawls's purpose in introducing the concept?

2. When do well-ordered peoples have a right to go to war, according to Rawls? Would you agree? Why or why not?

3. What are "the two moral powers"? What roles do they play in society, and how do they complement each other?

Primary Reading

Morality and Violence: War, Revolution, Terrorism

JAN NARVESON

Essay published in the anthology Matters of Life and Death, *1993. Excerpt.*

Jan Narveson, a libertarian philosopher, explores the nature and function of terrorism in this essay written years before September 11, 2001, but well within the modern era of terrorist acts. He asks the question whether terrorism is ever justified, and whether terrorists deserve to air their grievances and be heard.

In recent times, the use of political terrorism has been much too prominent for comfort. As the term suggests, terrorism has a major psychological dimension. Hooded figures appear out of nowhere, spraying an airport with bullets from automatic weapons; car bombs go off; civilian hostages are taken. These things do physical damage, indeed; but their main purpose is to frighten us, thus (so the terrorist reasons) to compel us or our leaders to accept a political program or act that we would not otherwise accept. "Terror" arises because the terrorist is intentionally indiscriminate: anyone can be targeted, and even those not targeted can easily be in the way of an assassin, especially one whose modus operandi is the time bomb or other means lacking immediate control. The fact that damage to the inno-cent might well ensue doesn't worry the terrorist at all—but it *does* worry *us*.

Terrorism is, then, a sort of war, waged on behalf of political causes; but unlike ordi-nary wars, which are "up front," this war is in the shadows. And it is so because those fo-menting it are too weak to wage open warfare, where it is clear who the combatants are. So terrorism is (quite reasonably) seen as underhanded, "sneaky," disreputable.

This characterization calls for an important distinction between two very different contexts of employment of terror. On the one hand we have "insurgent" terrorism, that used by groups on the *outside* of official political power, as exemplified by the Red Army in Germany and Italy, the Irish Republican Army, several Palestinian organizations, and so on. On the other hand we have "state" terrorism, employed by those very officials themselves: the Stalinist regime with its "Gulag Archipelago," the dread SS troops of the Nazis, the Czarist secret police, assassination squads in some Latin American countries. What these two kinds of terrorism have in common is their shadowy, extralegal (or in the case of state terrorism, often spuriously legal) character, so that victims can't predict what will happen to them nor appeal to regular sources of redress. But they differ dras-tically in the extent of their effects.

Of the two, state terrorism is the overwhelmingly greater in the extent of evils done. Millions of victims fell to Eastern European Communism, Nazism, and other evil regimes, as against thousands at the hands of "insurgents." Condemnation of state terrorism is easy. There is no question about whether to disapprove of regimes that resort to such meth-ods to secure themselves in power and defend their policies: they are simply evil, ghastly monstrosities masquerading as real governments devoted, however fuzzily, to the good of their people. For that reason we will talk only of insurgent terrorism from here on, hoping that we will have sufficiently averted the risk of leaving the reader with the im-pression that this is the only sort there is.

Insurgent terrorists are characteristically weak. If they could command real armies with a serious chance of winning, they would engage the forces of the state in open battle. As it is, they can do little real damage—the number of victims of this kind of terrorism is comparatively small. (Even in Ireland, the total number of deaths from terrorism doesn't nearly equal the rate from auto accidents, say.) This type of terrorist is, then, in a kind of strategic dilemma. Can he create enough fear to win the concessions he aims for? But there is a problem. He cannot do anything else, being too weak. And a rare outburst will not do the trick. On the other hand, a really substantial campaign of terror, if he can manage that, will have at least two drawbacks from his point of view: first, it will put the established order's counterterrorism facilities in high gear, which could easily be fatal to the Movement. Second, if terrorism becomes the order of the day, people become calloused and blasé, as in Lebanon: the terrorist no longer inspires the sort of terror by which alone he can hope to be effective. Terrorists become a terrible nuisance, but that is all.

The trouble in this regard is that the terrorist trades on what is in fact an irrational ten-dency in human nature—the tendency to magnify unexpected and "mysterious" evils out of their true proportion. And the cure is a dose of rationality, plus a modicum of courage. The life expectancy of the average citizen is very little reduced by terrorism, whereas the expected evil if we accede to the terrorists' demands is great. The statesman, therefore, won't be cowed, but will soldier on.

There are other problems inherent in the use of terrorist methods as well. To forward their cause, terrorists must publicize the fact that it was they who threw the bomb, or whatever. But such publicity sets people on the road to tracking them down and destroying them, for terrorist groups are never strong enough to resist real armies or well-organized and well-armed police. Besides, those who resort to terrorist tactics inspire hatred, which is hardly a propitious environment for an aspirant to political power. If we know what these evil people can do when they are weak, what could we expect if they were strong? Our motivation to make sure they do not become so is redoubled with every victim.

Is terrorism ever justified? Are there any circumstances and any causes which would allow moral resort to such tactics? One is tempted to answer in the negative. Unfortunately, terrorism has been disconcertingly effective in the past: in Ireland, earlier in this century; in Israel in the late 1940s; and on many other occasions. And while we may take the view that no possible end could justify such evil means, this may be just lack of perspective. The German officers' plot to assassinate Hitler in 1944 was of the same general kind of terrorism, but few of us think it was morally unjustified.

Insofar as terrorism has worked, why has it? For two rather different reasons, I believe. On the one hand, those in charge have concluded that they're better off knuckling under to the threats than attempting further to resist them. On the other, and I believe more importantly, those in charge have concluded that their own position is untenable. Sometimes what they conclude is that it is *morally* untenable. The terrorists are seen, after all, to be supporting the just cause.

Clearly that should not happen. Terrorism is prima facie unjust, as is all violence. If people resort to using terrorist methods, why do they do so? It must be because they see no chance of their proposals being adopted by the powers that be if they confine themselves to more civilized methods. But if their proposals are just, they should be acceptable to people, and hence popular. Either those proposals are not so good after all, or the state against whom the terrorist methods are being used is unjustly subjugating its populace. In the latter case, if terrorist methods are used in a selective manner, against the officials of the regime rather than the general populace, there may be some expectation of success, since the populace may be presumed to sympathize with the aims of the terrorists. The efforts of officials to track down the terrorists and root them out will be thwarted by a populace not inclined to cooperate with them. A government that rules only by force can perhaps be brought down by determined persons using such tactics. The cost of doing so is high, of course. But there may be literally no other way, in which case the question is whether the result is worth the cost. Many of those killed will surely be innocent even if they are officials of the regime, not to mention others who are not connected with nor sympathetic to it. One who throws bombs and the like has a lot to answer for, and the answers had better be good ones. But it is difficult to argue that the use of terrorist tactics cannot possibly be morally justified, for the same reason that military means cannot be ruled out when all else (or at least, enough else) fails. Thus, we have noted the existence of terror inspired in a populace by its own government: people snatched from their beds and dragged off to the gulag, or tortured and shot in miserable dungeons, opposition members disappearing without a trace. Governments that rule by these methods are, one may plausibly argue, the most purely and absolutely evil of all human agencies on earth. Such regimes do not deserve the support of their people or of anyone else, and almost any sort of rebellion that has any chance of success against them is likely to be justified. Indeed, the fact that a regime is seen as a *terrorist regime* in that sense, ruling exclusively by force, is itself a principal cause of counterterrorism by insurgents. The least we can do is be aware of, and publicize as much as possible, the facts about such regimes, hoping to inspire some kind of redress by whatever means—and be thankful that democratic governments, whatever their other vices, are at least largely free of such tactics. (We should also not complacently think that they are entirely free of them, nor that the relatively civilized impositions of democratic governments on their citizens are of no account.)

In conclusion, we cannot condemn terrorists absolutely, without giving their cause a hearing. Indeed, the impossibility of *getting* a sufficient hearing by standard means is probably one of the main causes of the resort to terrorism. And if our hearing finds that they have a point, then we must do something about it; else we leave the terrorists in the situation of saying, "Well, that's our point: we *must* act like this, for otherwise we just continue to suffer." But beyond that? Clearly we must not knuckle under to the terrorists' threats simply because they are threats. To do that is to give way to greater evils to come.

Study Questions

1. Define the two types of terrorism according to Narveson's guidelines. Do the terrorist attacks of September 11 fall within either category? Explain.

2. What, to Narveson, is it in particular that terrorists trade on? And what is the antidote? In light of September 11, do you agree? Why or why not?

3. What should a civilized nation do to combat terrorism, according to Narveson? How does that compare to the war on terrorism? Do you agree with Narveson? Why or why not?

4. Narveson argues that we should not altogether refuse to listen to the grievances of terrorists. In light of September 11, do you agree? Why or why not? In your view, are there any grievances that would legitimate the deliberate targeting of civilians? Explain.

Primary Reading

Terrorism Without Intention

DAVID RODIN

Excerpt, 2004.

In the first couple of years after September 11, many books and articles were written in defense of as well as in criticism of the war on terror, but philosophers have been conspicuously absent from the debate, except for occasional op-ed pieces in newspapers. In 2004 that changed, primarily with the publication of the special issue of the journal *Ethics* in July 2004. This volume contains papers from a symposium on war, terrorism, and justice held at Georgia State University in April 2003. From this special issue I have selected an excerpt from David Rodin's "Terrorism Without Intention." In this paper, Rodin argues that terrorism ought to be defined as "the deliberate, negligent, or reckless use of force against noncombatants, by state or nonstate actors for ideological ends and in the absence of a substantively just legal process." With this highly controversial definition Rodin attacks tactical bombing as a kind of terrorist act, because civilian casualties are unavoidable, and claims there is no moral difference between that kind of bombing and terrorist bombing.

If we are to be engaged in a "war on terrorism," then we had better get clear about what terrorism is. Until we achieve a clear and coherent understanding of what the morally relevant features of terrorism are, we cannot hope to develop an appropriate moral response to the "war on terrorism" now being prosecuted by the United States and its allies—its proper aims, scope, limitations, and potential exceptional permissions.

In this article, I present a unified way of understanding the moral significance of terrorism. I begin by briefly identifying four different strategies for defining terrorism. I then introduce a definition of terrorism which locates its moral significance in the object of attack—terrorism is given its distinctive moral character by the fact that it uses force against those who should not have force used against them. In the idiom of the just war theory, it uses force against noncombatants. . .

Consider a domestic example. If the only way I can flee an assailant is to kill or impose a significant risk of death upon an innocent bystander, such action would certainly be proportionate on any reasonable interpretation of proportionality. But most people would view such action as wrong, and the reason for this is that there is no relevant moral fact about the bystander which could justify inflicting this (admittedly proportionate) harm upon him or her. In the same way, the conclusion that much collateral damage caused by military operations is negligent or reckless is not motivated only by the thought that the force is disproportionate (though it may well be that also). It is rather motivated by the thought that it is inflicted upon those who should not have force inflicted upon them—those who because they are noncombatants have no liability to have force (not even proportionate force) used against them. Proportionality, therefore, is not the appropriate locus for the kind of moral issue I have been raising.

One may accept all of this, however, and still have reservations about extending the definition of the term "terrorism" to include unintentional, albeit reckless and negligent, use of force against noncombatants. One might feel that to do so would be an act of disreputable persuasive redefinition akin to arguments that seek to define inequality and poverty as forms of violence. But in reality, very little turns on the purely terminological question of the usage of the word "terrorism." The important issue is whether one accepts the substantive argument put forward in this article: that the unintentional killing of some noncombatants in the course of military operations is morally culpable to the same degree and for the same reasons that typical acts of terrorism and culpable.

If one does accepts this conclusion, then I think there are two entirely reasonable ways to settle the terminological question. The first is to restrict the definition of terrorism to the intentional (in the narrow sense of directly intended) use of force against noncombatants and to categorize the reckless and negligent use of force against noncombatants as a separate class of offense. This has the virtue of mirroring the distinction made in criminal law between murder, which requires the mens rea of intention, and the lesser offense of manslaughter, for which recklessness or negligence suffices (in the United States the distinction is between first- and second-degree murder). This is not an intrinsically objectionable way of settling the terminological question, however the manslaughter/murder distinction has been criticized by legal scholars as unhelpful and ad hoc. Indeed, murder is one of the few criminal offenses for which recklessness is not a sufficient mens rea. What is more, we have no term in our moral vocabulary for the reckless, as opposed to intentional, use of force against noncombatants for ideological reasons. An artificial term would need to be introduced (perhaps "reckless terrorism" or "terrorist manslaughter") which may have difficulty in gaining general currency.

The second response, reflected in my moral definition, is to hold that the crucial point about terrorism is not the direct intention of the agent but the wrongfulness of the act. Many acts which would generally be considered as sufficient for terrorism such as assault, battery, or the threat of the use of force, are lesser offenses than reckless manslaughter. It is difficult to see why such intentional acts should be included in the definition of terrorism, while the more serious offense of reckless manslaughter is excluded. Following this line of logic, my moral definition of terrorism makes reference to the "deliberate, reckless, or negligent" use of force against noncombatants. I believe that this definition best articulates what is morally most important about the phenomenon of terrorism.

Conclusion

What conclusions for policy can be drawn from this moral analysis of terrorism? There are, I think, two broad and tentative lines of thought which emerge and which concern the *jus ad bellum* and the *jus in bello* of any engagement with terrorist adversaries. The first is that we should be extremely cautious about extending the rules of *jus ad bellum* so as to include terrorism as a just cause for war. What has come to be called "the Bush doctrine" asserts that countries have the right to use force (and indeed to engage in preemptive war) if they believe they may be subject to a tangible terrorist threat. But if my analysis is correct, it is apparent that terrorism in the morally relevant sense is a relatively broad military and political practice which is frequently utilized by states, including the United States and her allies. This has been obviously true in cases such as the terror bombing of Germany and Japan during the Second world War. But, as I have here suggested, terrorism in the sense of the reckless use of force against noncombatants has also been an issue in several recent conflicts including NATO's bombing campaign against the Federal Republic of Yugoslavia in 1999, Operation Enduring Freedom in Afghanistan, the war in Iraq, and, perhaps most clearly, Israel's military response to the Palestinian intifada. Viewing terrorism as itself a just cause for war would therefore result in a dangerous and unwelcome extension of the right to resort to force, one which would expose a number of Western powers themselves to the use of military force.

Second, in terms of the *jus in bellow,* it seems intuitively correct that any engagement which has as part of its goal the elimination of terrorist threats and which is called a "war on terror" should not, if it is to be legitimate, use terrorist tactics itself. At a minimum this will require much greater care to eliminate noncombatant casualties than has been demonstrated by Western powers in recent operations. So-called smart targetable munitions have the potential to revolutionize the humanitarian aspects of war. But aerial bombardments in Iraq, Afghanistan, and Kosovo have all resulted in very significant noncombatant casualties, and Western powers continue to use substantially indiscriminate weapons such as cluster munitions and land mines. Moreover, the increased ability to target accurately means that we must pay greater attention to the nature of targets selected. The increasing tendency to target "dual use" facilities such as power stations, transport, and media infrastructure is particularly worrying in this context, for destroying such targets has the potential to cause very significant noncombatant deaths for months and even years after the conflict has ended. If the war against terrorism is to avoid being a terrorist war, then such practices must be seriously reconsidered.

Study Questions

1. Comment on Rodin's example. In his view it is not acceptable to endanger the life of an innocent bystander in order to escape an assailant. He uses this example to create a parallel to "collateral damage" caused by military operations: There is no good reason to endanger the lives of innocent civilians, even to protect others. In other words, Rodin argues against the principle of proportionality in just war theory. Do you agree? What if the only way you can protect your child from being killed is to endanger an innocent stranger's life? Assume that if you refuse, claiming you don't have that right, your child will most likely be killed. Do you have a right to endanger your child's life for the sake of a stranger, or do you have a duty to save your child? Is this a fair parallel in the context of collateral damage?

2. Rodin introduces a new term for unintentional terrorism, "terrorist manslaughter," to distinguish it from intentional terrorism and to create a parallel to the legal term *manslaughter*. Even so, he contends that it isn't the intention that counts, but the wrongfulness of the act, so unintentional terrorism is morally reprehensible too. Would you agree? Why or why not?

3. Rodin asserts that terrorism can't be a just cause for war; do you agree? What alternatives does he offer in combating terrorism? Can you think of alternatives?

4. Comment on this quote from Rodin's paper: "Any engagement which has as part of its goal the elimination of terrorist threats and which is called a 'war on terror' should not, if it is to be legitimate, use terrorist tactics itself." What does Rodin regard as terrorist tactics? If you are a veteran, evaluate his view in light of your military training. Regardless of whether you have had military training or not, evaluate his standpoint from (a) an anti-war stance, and (b) a pro-war stance.

Primary Reading

Kanzi: The Ape at the Brink of the Human Mind

SUE SAVAGE-RUMBAUGH AND ROGER LEWIN

1994. Excerpt.

Sue Savage-Rumbaugh's work with Kanzi at Georgia State University's Language Research Center during the first fourteen years of his life is documented in the book *Kanzi*. He was born in 1980 and has by now surpassed many of the linguistic skills described in the book, as has his sister Panbanisha. In this excerpt Savage-Rumbaugh argues that because behavioral science has forced animal behaviorists to avoid anthropomorphic language at all costs (language comparing animals to humans), important insight into the obvious similarities between apes and humans in terms of thought and feeling has been overlooked.

The physical world that surrounds us is of a different order from the animal world. The greater the degree of development of the nervous system, the more these two worlds differ in kind. The purpose of complex nervous systems is to permit flexible actions, unique to each situation. To the extent that organisms take in environmental information and make decisions about future actions, they become increasingly different from inanimate matter and require different paradigms for their study.

Once organisms have developed nervous systems sufficiently complex to postulate presumed goals and/or intentions for other living creatures, a world based on the moment-by-moment interpretations of the intent of others will arise. That is, it will be the presumed intent behind the behavior, rather than the specific actions themselves, that will mold the response of the observer. Certainly, humans and apes have entered the world of interpreted intent, and I suspect that a number of other animals have done so as well.

Some students of animal behavior have sought to escape the limitations posed by the laboratory by engaging in fieldwork. They rightly argue that by observing an animal in its natural habitat, one does not arbitrarily constrain the range of options available to it. The view that the behavior of animals is fundamentally different from that of man nonetheless manages to hold sway, even among those who do field observations. This is, in part, because a special language has been devised to describe and label behaviors of animals in nature. This devised language carefully avoids using any terms that we would apply to similar human behaviors. The taboo against using terms reserved for humans to describe the behavior of animals becomes most apparent when we observe apes. If a chimpanzee frowns and presses his lips together in a display of anger, either feigned or real, fieldworkers do not say he was mad; they say he displayed a bulged lips face. When he smiles and hugs another animal after a fisticuffs, they say he displayed an open-mouth bared-teeth grin and an arm around. Field researchers are admonished to speak in this manner in order to avoid the bugbear of anthropomorphism—the act of attributing human emotions to animals.

Consequently, out of fear that we might see a humanlike emotion where it does not exist, we design ways of speaking that permit us to talk about animal behavior without attributing any humanlike emotion to the animals whatsoever. We therefore approach the study of the animal mind with the unwritten assumption that it would be an error of the greatest magnitude if we were to conclude wrongly, in any circumstance, that an animal (even one that shares 99 percent of our DNA) felt as we do when angry or happy. Thus, even when we observe the animal in nature, the way we are taught as scientists to ask our questions, to structure our data, and to discuss what we see, constrains the conclusions we permit ourselves to find.

What if we were to assume at least partial continuity of emotional expression and intelligence between animals and man and thus permit ourselves to talk about animal behavior in a new light? We might risk the error of sometimes attributing capacities that did not exist, but we would surely find humanlike capacities that do exist but are currently hidden from us by the blinders we press over our eyes. Would the error of sometimes erroneously attributing capacities that did not exist be greater than that of never discovering any emotional or intellectual capacities that were continuous with our own? I think not. At the very least, if one scientist made a mistake and attributed some capacity to an animal that was far beyond its true ability, another scientist would come along and correct this mistake. As the situation currently stands, we don't even have the right to make the mistake. We should be able to ask questions about how animals perceive their worlds, their roles in those worlds, and what kinds of events or relationships alter these perceptions. It seems to me that this is what a science of animal behavior should be about.

I am not the first to suggest that we need to look at animal behavior through a different lens. Donald Griffin has been urging us to do so since the 1970s. Why are so many behavioral scientists still unable to break out of their constraints? The problem lies in part in the omniscience we attribute to the human mind, an omniscience that we believe is made possible by the gift of language. Even students of behavior who would not deny minds to animals nonetheless maintain there is no way of gaining access to the animal mind; consequently, they believe the issue is, like that of religious experience, beyond science. I suggest that we expand our ways of doing science to encompass such questions.

The essence of the difference between the human and the animal mind is often claimed to be that man can reflect upon his actions while animals, lacking words, cannot. Crucial to this view is the underlying and unspoken premise that language is the only possible means of reflection. Without language how can we ask an animal what it is thinking? And without language how can it tell us? And if it cannot tell us, how can we legitimately assume that it is thinking?

Once, while riding in the car through the woods with Kanzi's sister Panbanisha, I noted she appeared to be very quiet and pensive. I was moved to ask her what she was thinking—a question I generally avoid since I have no means of validating the answer, nor even of determining if an ape understands the question. Occasionally, when I have posed this question in the past, I have generally been ignored. However, at this moment Panbanisha looked literally lost in thought, and so I dared. She seemed to reflect upon the question a few seconds and then answered [via lexigram] "Kanzi." I was very surprised, as she almost never uses Kanzi's name. I replied, "Oh, you are thinking about Kanzi, are you?" and she vocalized in agreement, "Whuh, whuh, whuh."

Similarly, one time I was riding in a car with Heather, one of the [human] children in our project, through the very same area of woods. Heather was two years of age and just beginning to form sentences. She, like Panbanisha, typically ignored questions like "What are you thinking about?" But, like Panbanisha, at this moment she appeared lost in thought and so I dared to inquire. She replied "Mommy." I asked, "Do you wish your Mommy was here?" and she nodded her head.

I cannot be certain that either Panbanisha or Heather was really thinking. Currently there is no way to establish scientific consensus regarding the inner thoughts of another person. Yet it seems that credence should be given to the fact that both Heather and Panbanisha, on occasions when they appeared pensive, elected to answer the question. On other occasions, when they were engaged in other activities, the question was ignored as though it were nonsensical. These observations suggest that it is possible that children and apes think in a reflexive sense, even before they are competent language users. Could it be that they think in some way other than with words?

Thought, or the manipulation of one's mental model of the world, surely must take place in the absence of language, utilizing neurological machinery that services the channels of perception through which the world is viewed. It requires but a moment's reflection to recognize that humans engaged in complex nonverbal activities—such as in dance, music, sculpting, and athletic skills—depend on wordless thought. To suggest otherwise "is a notion that only a college professor or other professional wordsmith could have ever taken seriously."

Mary Midgley, the British philosopher of science, puts the issue more generally: "If language were really the only source of conceptual order, all animals except man would live in a totally disordered world. They could not be said to vary in intelligence, since they could not have the use of anything that could reasonably be called intelligence at all. . . . The truth seems to be that—even for humans—a great deal of the order in the world is pre-verbally determined, being the gift of faculties we share with other animals." Nonhuman animals quite evidently live in ordered worlds, an outcome of their own cognitive processes. Without such mental ordering, the management of the myriad interactions among other members of a community and the efficient exploitation of a diverse resource base would be nearly impossible. There is no question that language enhances thought processes, permitting a more intricate and powerful manipulation of mental worlds. But this is surely an extension of faculties already in place, not the establishment of something novel. Spoken language, and the thoughts it mediates, is built on the same neurological foundation that underlies thinking in nonhuman animals.

Study Questions

1. Why has behavioral science enforced an avoidance of "anthropomorphic language" in descriptions of animal behavior? What has the effect been, according to Savage-Rumbaugh?

2. What is Savage-Rumbaugh trying to tell us with her stories of Panbanisha and Heather? Do you think she is right in her assessment of their inner life?

3. In your view, can apes think without words? Can you? If so, what might that entail for our future treatment of apes and other intelligent nonhuman animals? What might Immanuel Kant say to this discussion?

Primary Reading

An Eye for an Eye? The Morality of Punishing by Death

STEPHEN NATHANSON

Excerpt. 1987.

Stephen Nathanson, a philosophy professor at Northeastern University, argues for abolitionism. He sees the death penalty as an affront to the humanity of everyone, including the criminal, and a state-sanctioned way to continue the cycle of violence.

According to the *lex talionis* or principle of "an eye for an eye" we ought to treat people as they have treated others. What people deserve as recipients of rewards or punishment is determined by what they do as agents. [. . .] Applied strictly, it would require that we rape rapists, torture torturers and burn arsonists whose acts have led to deaths. [. . .] This is not its only defect. In many other cases, the principle tells us nothing at all about how to punish [. . .] what would we decide to do to embezzlers, spies, drunken drivers, airline hijackers, drug users, prostitutes, air polluters, or persons who practice medicine without a license? If one reflects on this question, it becomes clear that there is simply no answer to it. We could not in fact design a system of punishment simply on the basis of the "eye for an eye" principle.

In order to justify using the "eye for an eye" principle to answer our question about murder and the death penalty, we would first have to show that it worked for a whole range of cases, giving acceptable answers to questions about amounts of punishment. Then, having established it as a satisfactory general principle, we could apply it to the case of murder. It turns out, however, that when we try to apply the principle generally, we find that it either gives wrong answers or no answers at all. Indeed, I suspect that the principle of "an eye for an eye" is no longer even a principle. Instead, it is simply a metaphorical disguise for expressing belief in the death penalty. People who cite it do not take it seriously. They do not believe in a kidnapping for a kidnapping, a theft for a theft, and so on. Perhaps "an eye for an eye" once was a genuine principle, but now it is merely a slogan. Therefore, it gives us no guidance in deciding whether murderers deserve to die.

In reply to these objections, one might defend the principle by saying that it does not require that punishment be strictly identical with crimes. Rather, it requires only that a punishment produce an amount of suffering in the criminal which is equal to the amount suffered by the victim. [. . .] Unfortunately, this reply really does not solve the problem. [. . .] Just how much suffering is produced by an airline hijacker or a spy? And how do we apply the principle to prostitutes or drug users, who may not produce any suffering at all? We have rough ideas about how serious various crimes are, but this may not correlate with any clear sense of just how much harm is done.

Furthermore, the same problem arises in determining how much suffering a particular punishment would produce for a particular criminal. People vary in their tolerance of pain and in the amount of unhappiness that a fine or jail sentence would cause them. Recluses would be less disturbed by banishment than extroverts. Nature lovers will suffer more in prison than people who are indifferent to natural beauty. A literal application of the principle [of "an eye for an eye"] would require that we tailor punishments to individual sensitivities, yet this is at best impractical. [. . .]

What is the symbolic message that we would convey by deciding to renounce the death penalty and to abolish its use?

I think that there are two primary messages. The first is the most frequently emphasized and it is usually expressed in terms of the sanctity of human life, although I think we could better express it in terms of human dignity. One way we express our respect for the dignity of human beings is by abstaining from depriving them of their lives, even if they have done terrible deeds. In defense of human well-being, we may punish people for their crimes, but we ought not to deprive them of everything, which is what the death penalty does.

[. . .] But, one might ask, hasn't the murderer forfeited whatever rights he might have had to our respect? Hasn't he, by his deeds, given up any rights that he had to decent treatment? Aren't we morally free to kill him if we wish? [. . .] Certainly, when people murder or commit other crimes, they do forfeit some of the rights that are possessed by the law-abiding. They lose a certain right to be left alone. It becomes permissible to bring them to trial and, if they are convicted, to impose an appropriate—even a dreadful—punishment on them.

Nonetheless, they do not forfeit all their rights. [. . .] No matter how terrible a person's deeds, we may not punish him in a cruel and unusual way. We may not torture him, for example. His right not to be tortured has not been forfeited. Why do these limits hold? Because this person remains a human being, and we think there is something in him that we must continue to respect in spite of his terrible acts. [. . .]

[The second symbolic message:] We want to avoid the cycle of violence that can come from retaliation and counter-retaliation. Violence is a contagion that arouses hatred and anger, and if unchecked, it simply leads to still more violence. The state can convey the message that the contagion must be stopped, and the most effective principle for stopping it is the idea that only defensive violence is justifiable. Since the death penalty is not an instance of defensive violence, it ought to be renounced.

Study Questions

1. Is Nathanson right that the death penalty is not an instance of defensive violence? Why or why not?

2. Nathanson doesn't believe in the idea of proportional justice (an eye for an eye) as a defense of the death penalty. Can you think of a defense of the death penalty (a retentionist argument) that doesn't imply the principle of an eye for an eye?

3. Nathanson wants to abolish the death penalty to send symbolic messages of respect for humans and stop the cycle of violence. Can you think of a symbolic message implied in the retentionist position?

Primary Reading

Journey into Darkness

JOHN DOUGLAS AND MARK OLSHAKER

Excerpt. 1997.

John Douglas is not a professional philosopher, although his years as a profiler for the FBI have prompted him to philosophize about the nature of crime and punishment. Here he argues for a limited use of the death penalty, reserved for extreme cases, from the perspective of the victims and their families rather than from that of the rights of the criminal. In other words, Douglas is a retentionist.

Capital punishment is one of those issues like abortion. Not many of us are ever going to change anyone's opinion about it, one way or the other. If you are against the death penalty on moral grounds, I think a case can be made for putting away the worst of these monsters for life with no possibility they will ever be let out or paroled. But we know that there is no such thing. And frankly, in certain cases, I don't think it's enough.

As [special agent and profiler] Steve Mardigian put it, "The tremendous devastation against victims warrants that we do something appropriately serious. In my view, we have no reason to keep people capable of inflicting this kind of horror alive."

Some would argue that capital punishment is "legalized murder" and therefore an immoral act on the part of society. My personal feeling is that these offenders have made a choice to remove themselves from society and therefore it is a moral statement to say that society will not tolerate the perpetrator of this kind of horrible act in its midst.

Asserting that capital punishment is legalized murder does a tremendous injury, in my opinion, to the very concept of right and wrong, in that it trivializes the crucial distinction between the victim of the crime and its perpetrator—the innocent life and the one who chose for his own vile reasons to take that innocent life.

If you ask me if I'm personally prepared to throw the switch that would legally end the life on earth of [serial killers] Sedley Alley, Larry Gene Bell, Paul Bernardo, Lawrence Bittaker, or others of their ilk, my answer would be a resounding "Yes!" And for those who talk of forgiveness, I'll tell them I am sympathetic to the concept, but at the same time I do not feel I am authorized to forgive; it's not my place.

Had Sedley Alley *merely* (and I use this word with some trepidation) raped, beaten, and tortured Suzanne Collins, but left her alive and her mental faculties intact, then she, and only she, would have been in a position to forgive him if she so chose. And as far as I'm concerned, she remains the only one capable of forgiving him, but because of what actually did happen, she can only do so now *after* his jury-imposed sentence has been carried out. [. . .]

Now, on the subject of deterrence, I admit that there can be little doubt that as presently administered in the United States, the death penalty is not a general deterrent to murder in many, if not most, situations. Common sense should tell us that if you're a young urban criminal making your living off the drug trade where there are huge amounts of money at stake and your business competition is out there trying to kill you every day, the dim prospect of a possible death sentence and execution somewhere at the end of a fifteen year procedural morass—that is, if you get caught, if you don't plea bargain, if you draw a tough judge and a tough jury, if you don't get reversed, if they don't change the law, et cetera, et cetera—isn't much of a deterrent, or a risk, for that matter, compared to the occupational hazards you face on the street every day of your working life. So let's be realistic about that aspect of this argument.

If the death penalty were applied more evenly and uniformly, and if the period of time from sentence to execution were reduced to a reasonable matter of months rather than a protracted period of years or even the decades that people like the Collinses have had to endure, then perhaps it would become more useful in dissuading would-be offenders in certain types of murders. But frankly, this theoretical speculation doesn't concern me all that much. Meted out fairly and consistently, perhaps the death penalty could become a general deterrent; I'm not certain and I wouldn't be optimistic about it.

But of one thing I am certain: it is, by God, a specific deterrent. No one who has been executed has ever taken another innocent life. And until such time as we really mean it as a society when we say "imprisonment for life," I, and the families of countless victims, would sleep better at night knowing there is no chance that the worst of these killers will ever again be able to prey on others. Even then, I personally believe that if you choose to take another human life, you ought to be prepared to pay with your own. [. . .]

Then there's the argument that rather than killing these guys, we should keep them alive "for study." I'm not sure what people mean by this; I don't think they know, themselves. I suppose they mean that if we study enough of them long enough, we'll figure out why they kill and what we can do to stop them.

Now as it happens, my colleagues at Quantico and I are among the few professionals who actually have studied these people. If anyone has a stake, therefore, in keeping them alive for intellectual reasons, it's us. And here's my response to that: If they're willing to talk to me at all, there is plenty of time during the protracted appeals process. If they're only willing to talk—as Ted Bundy ultimately was—as a bargaining chip for staying alive longer, then what they tell me is going to be tainted and self-serving anyway. When you tell me we should keep someone like Bundy alive to study, I say, "Fine, keep him alive six hours longer; that's all I need." I really don't think we're going to get much more beyond that. [. . .]

But no responsible discussion of the death penalty can fail to include reflection on the fact that our legal system is imperfect and there is always the chance that the wrong man will be convicted. Inevitably, in any consideration of capital punishment, we must confront the example of David Vasquez. And much as we may hate to admit it, his copping of an Alford plea might have saved his life. [Douglas explains the Alford plea as "not a guilty plea but acknowledging that the prosecution has sufficient evidence to try and convict the defendant of a more serious crime."]

The fact that this was a rare, odd type of case in which the [innocent] defendant actually confessed, not once, but three times, should not give us too much comfort or reassurance. At the same time, I don't think this is a valid argument for scrapping the death penalty altogether.

What I think it is a valid argument for is the insistence on an overwhelming amount and degree of proof. And while some might argue that you can never be absolutely sure, I think in the kinds of cases I'm talking about, you can be sure enough that innocent people like Vasquez will not go wrongly to their deaths.

The types of offenders I most want to see face the ultimate penalty are the repeat, predatory, sexually motivated killers. By the time we catch them there is generally a mountain of solid, behaviorally consistent, forensic evidence against them. As with Cleophus Prince, if he did one of the murders, he did all of them. If there isn't a sufficiently formidable mountain of evidence, then don't execute. But if there is, as there was against Bell, as there is against Alley and Bernardo and Bittaker and so many others, then do what needs to be done. [. . .]

So how do you prioritize all our concerns and all the things we might wish the criminal justice system to be? To me, it's innocent potential victims first, victims of violent crime and their families second, and defendants and their families last. First and foremost, I'll do anything I can to see to it that someone does not become the victim of someone who has already committed a similar crime. Failing that, I want to bring victims and their families to the forefront of the system, to give them the due that is rightly theirs. And then I want to make sure that defendants get a fair trial and convicted felons receive appropriate sentences for their crimes. None of these need be mutually exclusive.

Does this mean I think we need a police state? Of course not. It means simply what it says—that we need to keep our priorities straight if we hope to be a just and civilized society.

Study Questions

1. The debate about the death penalty is often polarized into a "criminal's rights" view versus a "victim's rights" view. Do these two viewpoints have to be opposed, or can you think of some common ground?

2. Douglas argues that the death penalty should be reserved for the kind of murderer who isn't likely to change, such as serial killers and child molester/killers. Would you agree that (1) there are people who are essentially unredeemable? (2) the best way for society to deal with them is killing them? Why or why not?

3. Does Douglas's view reflect the theory of retribution? Deterrence? Incapacitation? Revenge?

4. Often abolitionists argue that executions are nothing but state-sanctioned murder, that the right to life ought to be considered inalienable, and that the state stoops to the level of the murderer by taking the life of a citizen. How does Douglas respond? What is your opinion?

Primary Reading

Two Ideals and the Death Penalty

TOM SORELL

2002. Excerpt.

In 2002 the John Jay College of Criminal Justice's biannual journal *Criminal Justice Ethics* had a special symposium on the death penalty. In his paper British philosopher Tom Sorell argues in favor of the death penalty, stating that in principle capital punishment is justified for aggravated murder. Within a just society, and with safeguards in place, it would be wrong not to have access to capital punishment, because of the concept of *responsible agency*. For Sorell, the death penalty is a kind of punishment that is appropriate not only in an ideal society, but also within the real world, what Sorell calls the "worldly ideal." An explanatory note: The ICCPR which Sorell refers to is the International Covenant on Civil and Political Rights.

I now return to the question of whether there is a tension between the ideal of a just state, when it is taken to be the sort of state that protects and promotes the rights mentioned in the ICCPR, and the ideal of taking responsibility. The rights outlined in the Universal Declaration of Human Rights, the ICCPR and the International Covenant on Economic, Social and Cultural Rights were first declared against the background of the then recent experience of state-directed atrocities by the Nazis and the systematic denials of individual freedoms by countries in the Soviet bloc. No one believed that these injustices would immediately be eradicated or that they would even be significantly reduced throughout the world in a short time. The human rights instruments at best indicated a trajectory of improvement from what, in some parts of the world, were very low levels of access to fair trials, elections or legislative bodies at the time those instruments were formulated. The idea of taking responsibility has different degrees of force depending on where on that trajectory a state's courts, punishments, and penal institutions can be located. A state that imposes the death penalty for a greater range of crimes than the ICCPR allows, say for theft or corruption, does not encourage the criminal to take responsibility. In such a state, the wrongdoer has more of an excuse for not confessing to his crime than someone who faces a year or two of imprisonment in a humane and modern prison system. The same goes for someone who is liable to be stoned to death for adultery or who can have his hand amputated for theft. The more disproportionate the punishment, the more unequal the treatment is in the courts, or the less attention that is paid to evidence, the more the evasion of responsibility by wrongdoers is counterbalanced and excused by the injustice present in the social response to wrongdoing. On the other hand, in a state whose institutions and protections are high on the development trajectory indicated by the ICCPR, and thus close to the ideal, the scope for justifiable evasion of responsibility would seem to be correspondingly small.

What about evasion of responsibility for a crime that attracts the death penalty? Is this, too, unjustifiable in a state with good legal protections for the accused? A prior question is whether a state whose institutions and protections are close to ideal can impose the death penalty at all. If the answer is "Yes," then the evasion of responsibility, even for capital crimes, is hard to justify. A natural interpretation of the ICCPR is the following: as long as the death penalty is reserved for the most severe crimes, is not imposed on minors, and can be commuted, its existence is not by itself a violation of rights or sufficient to constitute a legal regime as unjust. Given general legal protections, The ICCPR seems to be saying, a state can apply the death penalty sparingly without failing to satisfy the ideal of a just state. On the other hand, in view of the 1989 protocol to the ICCPR calling for the abolition of the death penalty, which identifies the abolition of the death penalty as a means of protecting the right to life, things are not so clear.

I believe that the argument justifying the abolition of the death penalty by appeal to the right to life, as is found in the 1889 protocol, is unstable in cases in which the death penalty is reserved for aggravated murder, and the only other grounds for supposing that the death penalty and the just state to be incompatible are weak. The death penalty *can* be applied by a just state. The fact that a state can be just and apply the death penalty does not, of course, mean that the death penalty cannot be applied in error, but the fact that it can be applied in error does not by itself justify the abolition of the death penalty in cases in which the burden of proof is high. Possible miscarriages of justice do not justify the abolition of the death penalty across the board, for they do not justify those who are guilty of capital crimes evading responsibility for their crimes in legal systems that protect human rights. On the contrary, the ideal of taking responsibility justifies nothing less than cooperation with the prosecuting authorities in such states. It justifies confessions, and it justifies willing submission to proportionate punishment, including, for the worst crimes, capital punishment.

I begin my argument for this with the reasoning implicit in the 1989 protocol that calls for the abolition for the death penalty. The preamble to the protocol asserts twice that the abolition of the death penalty takes further the enhancement of the right to life guaranteed by Article 6 of the ICCPR. But what exactly is this right to life? It is not an absolute right to life, one that rules out, for example, killing in self-defense or killing in war. Again, the protocol itself permits death as a penalty for a serious crime of a military nature committed in wartime. At most, the right to life recognized by the ICCPR is a right to life for those who are blamelessly going about their business in accordance with other rights that are supposed to be extended to members of civil society. According to the ICCPR, the right to life can lapse when the life is that of someone who takes away life. It seems consistent with the ICCPR for threats to the existence of civil society or the right to life of individuals to be countered with threats of proportionate punishment on the part of states. If death is a proportionate response to certain kinds of murder, large scale terrorism, or serious military crimes in wartime, then it may be threatened; and if it may justly be threatened, then it may justly be carried out on those who are genuinely guilty. Safeguards against error in the identification of the guilty are of course also required by justice, but not safeguards against self-identification *by* the guilty where punishments are proportionate to crimes.

Unless the death penalty is always disproportionately severe, no matter *what* the crime to which it is applied, or unless Hobbes is right and one has the right to do *anything* one can to save one's life (something I have already disputed), there is something wrong with evading responsibility, even in cases in which taking responsibility means death. Part of what is wrong with the evasion of responsibility for capital crime is the same as what is wrong with the evasion of responsibility for *any* crime. But the more serious crime, the greater the wrong of evading responsibility for it. Serious crimes taint a whole life and sometimes a whole era, and for the guilty person to proceed as if nothing has happened, or as if nothing much has happened, or as if it is all right for *him* to have committed a crime because he got away with it against great odds, is a denial of the difference between big and small wrong-doing. Since the more things *look* like small wrongdoing the less things look wrong at all, denying the difference between big and small wrongdoing is a way of eroding the category or wrongdoing itself. Therefore it is important to maintain scales of wrongdoing. This does not mean refusing to revise them, but it does place the burden of proof on those who revalue downwards the seriousness of serious crime.

Proportionality, which is rightly insisted upon as a condition of just punishment, cannot operate in the absence of such scales. And proportionality cannot be a norm that only the authorities are expected to respect; it has to constrain the thinking and action of ordinary agents as well. One does not have to be an angel to meet this condition. A thief who avoids guns because he draws the line at armed robbery and does not want to get involved in murder reflects in his behavior the relative seriousness of armed robbery and murder. A computer hacker who penetrates the security codes of a major corporation but would not dream of infecting a hospital's computer system with a virus represents a similar type of case. The argument that someone should not be allowed to get away with, or get away lightly with, serious wrongdoing, is as much an argument from proportionality as the argument that death should not be the penalty for tax evasion or perjury. And the proportionality reflected in certain kinds of criminal behavior show that proportionality is a value accessible to the immoral as well as to the moral. Just as you do not need to be an angel to do your best to avoid killing and kidnapping in your criminal activities, you do not need to be an angel to recognize that people who kill and kidnap and act as if nothing has happened are sometimes far lower in the hierarchy of non-angels than you are.

This line of thought has a bearing on miscarriages of justice. I said at the beginning that in the case of the most severe penalties, the greatest precautions need to be taken against their wrongful imposition. But the duty to avoid miscarriages of justice is not only a duty on states. It is a duty on everyone. It is a duty on those who have evidence that clears the innocent person to make that evidence public. But it is also a duty on the guilty to take responsibility. In saying this, I am not, of course, making an *appeal* to the guilty to take the rap. I am trying to point to an ideal that shows that guilt and the evasion of responsibility have weight in our thinking about the abolition of the death penalty, and that those things are left out in arguments against the death penalty from the ideal of the just state. I am not claiming that things will be morally better on balance if all the guilty are caught and punished and a few of those executed along the way are innocent. It *may* be better for the guilty to go free than for the innocent to be punished. It may, accordingly, be better for those guilty of horrible crimes to go free than for an innocent person to be executed for one of them. But there is still something wrong with the guilty going unpunished, and there is something wrong, too, with those who are guilty of horrible crimes being punished as if their crimes were minor. Part of the source for these thoughts is the ideal of responsible agency, and a theory or a rhetoric that ignores this ideal is defective as a theory of or rhetoric about the death penalty.

Study Questions

1. Sorell argues that the death penalty is the only true way to achieve a just punishment for extreme crimes. Would you agree with him? Why or why not? What would Nathanson say?

2. In Sorell's opinion it is possible to create a sufficiently safe judicial system so that no innocent person is sentenced to death. Do you agree? Return to this question after reading Fuhrman's text (next) and reevaluate Sorell's argument.

3. If you are in favor of the death penalty, which crimes would you make eligible for execution, and why? What would Sorell say?

Primary Reading

Death and Justice: An Exposé of Oklahoma's Death Row Machine

MARK FUHRMAN

2003. Excerpt.

An earlier Reading offered a retentionist argument by ex-FBI profiler John Douglas. Law-enforcement officers are traditionally retentionists; they see horrific crimes committed, they witness the suffering of the victims and, in murder cases, the victims' loved ones, who in turn become victims too. They are closer to the experience of pain and loss due to crime than most people in academia, who view such issues perhaps with much interest and sympathy, but generally from a remove and abstractly. It is a natural, and widespread, reaction among police officers that the only appropriate punishment for murder is death—not because they are particularly bloodthirsty, but because they see, with their own eyes, what murder does to human beings, and they view the death penalty as the only real form of justice. For this reason *Death and Justice* is a highly unusual and thought-provoking book: Mark Fuhrman, a former LAPD homicide detective and now an author of true-crime books as well as a talk-show host and television commentator, undertook an investigation of the death penalty expecting to see his retentionist views confirmed, but the opposite happened: During the course of his investigation he found himself changing his mind about the justification of the death penalty. His focus was on death penalty cases in Oklahoma City, where the District Attorney, Bob Macy, was such a firm believer in capital punishment that he chose to overlook (and perhaps even encouraged) shoddy work and evidence mishandling by the forensic scientist Joyce Gilchrist. Due to Macy's zealousness and Gilchrist's less-than-professional work, doubt was raised about the guilt of people on Oklahoma's death row as well as people who have already been executed; and Fuhrman cites example after example of Oklahoma prisoners whose cases have been reexamined. Some have been exonerated and released, some are awaiting new trials, and some have had their death sentences changed to life without parole.

Because of his research, Fuhrman changed his mind—going from being a retentionist to being an abolitionist—not because he is against the death penalty in principle, but because, as he says, in the real world you simply can't have a judicial system where district attorneys and judges are political players running for election and reelection and still have a guarantee of a fair trial at the state level, because some of these officials will take a "tough-on-crime" stance for the sake of their own political future. Interestingly, Fuhrman believes a *federal* death penalty should still be an option for the worst crimes such as terrorism and serial murders. In addition to his misgivings about the practical feasibility of a fair legal system that includes capital punishment, his book concludes with a reexamination of the notions of justice and revenge.

I used to believe in the death penalty. It was an article of faith for a cop. During my twenty years on the force, I saw so much death, pain, and misery that I never questioned whether or not capital punishment was just. There were some people who deserved to die. That's what I thought, and so did my fellow cops.

We often expressed our support for the death penalty with crude terms and lofty rationalizations. We never used the word *revenge*. Instead, we called it justice, but it was cloaked in hate and anger. When we talked about the death penalty it was always with contempt for the suspect. "Fry the fucker," we'd say, "drop the pill on that asshole." That was the way we talked and the way we felt. I was empowered by my peers and that led to a feeling of self-righteousness. I had a closed mind about the issue and refused to accept any facts that might shake my worldview. There was no good reason, that I saw, to be against the death penalty, unless you wanted criminals to get away with murder. It seemed absolutely right and justified. [. . .]

When I started working on this book, I thought that since death penalty cases carry the highest punishment, they would be investigated more thoroughly and professionally. I quickly realized that the opposite is true. Catastrophic errors occur in many death penalty cases, because of the pressure to make a strong case and get a capital conviction.

Death penalty cases are all high-profile. Maybe you don't see them on the evening news, but within that jurisdiction, even in Oklahoma County, where they were so commonplace, a death penalty case creates the same pressure and scrutiny, the same temptations to cheat or cover up that I saw in the Simpson trial.

Once a prosecutor announces the death penalty will be sought, anything less than a capital conviction is seen as a failure. If Bob Macy hadn't asked for the death penalty in these cases, Joyce Gilchrist and the rest of the OCPD wouldn't have felt so much pressure to not only solve the case but also ensure a capital conviction. That pressure was self-reinforcing among those involved in a death penalty case. It gathered a momentum that swept everybody along with it. No one could afford to go against the flow.

The first place where a death penalty case goes wrong is with the detective. His investigation is the foundation on which the prosecution is built. It is up to him whether the crime is investigated thoroughly, professionally, and responsibly. It would be easier if the detectives were simply incompetent, yet certain efforts to hide the mistakes and holes in their cases indicate that they were competent enough to know when they were wrong.

Cops are supposed to follow the rules. That's what makes us different from criminals. What I saw in Oklahoma was that the more law enforcement felt superior to criminals, the more they started to act like them.

The problem isn't just Okalahoma County or Bob Macy or Joyce Gilchrist. It's the death penalty itself. Capital punishment is driven by two emotions—revenge and ambition. The public says it wants revenge for horrible crimes. But they want that revenge secondhand, carried out discreetly by clinical professionals in a small room very far away. The mob cries for blood—they just don't want to actually see it. And so they are never satisfied with, or sickened by, the revenge that is carried out for them. They never learn that revenge has no end; it just completes the circle of violence. The loss that the family of a murder victim feels is not made any less painful by the execution of their loved one's killer. If there ever is any closure for the family of murder victims, it should be based on forgiveness, not revenge. [. . .]

If we didn't feel guilty about the death penalty, we wouldn't have to erect such a complex mechanism in order to achieve it. Lately, that guilt has expressed itself in concern that innocent people are being convicted and possibly executed. From the reinstatement of the death penalty in 1977 to the time I am writing this, of the one hundred people released from death row, only eight of those cases involved DNA evidence.

Statewide, Oklahoma has one wrongful conviction for approximately every forty death sentences passed since 1973. These are cases of demonstrated innocence, not cases overturned because of reversible error. Of the seven innocents released from McAlester's death row, two of them, Clifford Henry Bowen and Robert Lee Miller, had been prosecuted by Bob Macy. [. . .]

"What if an innocent person is executed?" I asked Bob Macy. "Is that sacrifice worth keeping the death penalty?"

"I'd have to say yes," Macy replied.

I don't agree with Macy. I think that one innocent man's life is worth losing the death penalty. I'll go one step further. I think the nearly eleven years that Robert Lee Miller spent in prison are reason enough to lose the death penalty.

When you work in law enforcement, it's us versus them. Good guys and bad guys. You erect a wall between yourself and the criminals. Sometimes during my police career I let down that wall and developed a rapport, even an understanding, with a suspect. This often happened during interrogations. For a moment, I would see the suspect as a man. I would have empathy for him. That made it difficult to do my job, so the wall went back up again.

In order to execute people, we have to demonize them, deny their humanity, and mark them with the stigma of evil so great that there is no choice but to kill them. The system is built to minimize any feelings of empathy or responsibility. There is a sense of inevitability in death penalty cases that gradually achieves momentum until nothing, not even the United States Supreme Court, can stop an execution.

Justice is supposed to be blind, but we all know it's not and never will be. We want it to be perfect and flawless, unlike any other human endeavor.

"As long as the criminal justice system is administered by human beings," Jim Fowler said, "We should not have a punishment that is one hundred percent irrevocable."

Throughout my research and writing of this book, I wanted to have it both ways. I wanted to support the death penalty. When I found problems with it, I wanted them to be identified and fixed. I soon came to realize that the problem was the death penalty it-self. We have tried tinkering with the system, when the Supreme Court overturned the death penalty nationwide in *Furman v. Georgia* and then established guidelines for state legislatures in *Gregg v. Georgia*. It took only a few years before prosecutors like Bob Macy were arguing that almost every murder was "heinous, atrocious and cruel" and therefore satisfied the aggravators that the Oklahoma legislature had established in accordance with the Supreme Court's decisions. Bob Macy used the vagueness of the Oklahoma statutes and court precedent concerning the death penalty to create a system in which almost any murder, from domestic violence to armed robbery to a drive-by shooting, was de-serving of the death penalty.

Every murder is "heinous, atrocious and cruel." By executing the innocent we have committed an act just as "heinous, atrocious and cruel" ourselves.

In my career as a detective, both as a police officer and an author, I have always fol-lowed the evidence, wherever it led. My investigation of the death penalty in Oklahoma County has brought me to this conclusion: death penalty cases are not investigated or prosecuted at a level that can guarantee justice, or even that the accused is actually guilty.

I no longer believe in the death penalty. I no longer have faith that it is administered fairly or justly. I fear that innocent people have been executed.

That's why I am calling for the abolition of the death penalty. Not only in Oklahoma but in every state. The federal government should reserve the right to execute only those guilty of treason, terrorism, and political assassination. In these circumstances, we as a na-tion would be executing the criminal, and it would no longer be up to individuals like Bob Macy and Joyce Gilchrist. These federal executions should be televised and broad-cast on the Internet. If we don't have the stomach to watch executions, we shouldn't be performing them.

I could make all sorts of arguments about deterrence, cost-effectiveness, wrongful convictions, politics, philosophy, and so on. But it boils down to this—the death penalty brings out the worst in all of us: hatred, anger, vengeance, ambition, cruelty, and deceit.

This book has been a journey. I had to reach deep down within myself to come to this conclusion and the words to express it. I was wrong about the death penalty. I chose revenge instead of justice. And I was not alone. Instead of being an individual, I was just another ugly face in the crowd, chanting for death. Now I recognize the need to change not just our laws but ourselves.

Murder creates a pain that can't be forgotten or ignored. Our efforts to bring justice to those responsible should not make that pain any worse. In seeking the death penalty, horrible mistakes were made that cannot be undone. However, once we admit these mis-takes, we have taken the first step toward reconciling and working together to ensure those mistakes don't happen again. Then we can begin to right the terrible wrongs that have been committed, not just against death row inmates but against our system of jus-tice and therefore all of us.

Study Questions

1. Do you think Fuhrman is right in his assessment that death penalty proponents may think they want justice, but what they really want is revenge?

2. Would you agree with Bob Macy that executing an innocent person is a price worth paying for retaining the death penalty? Why or why not?

3. Would you agree with Fuhrman that it is not possible to have a judicial system that allows for the death penalty and at the same time elects judges, sheriffs, and district attorneys through a process that makes them vulnerable to political pressures?

4. Compare Fuhrman's and Sorell's stance on the death penalty: Taking both texts into consideration, do you think the death penalty can be applied justly?

5. As an interesting aside, executions in Oklahoma City have gone down from twenty-one in 2001 to fourteen in 2003, and six in 2004. In comparison, Texas executed twenty-three people, and Ohio came in second with seven executions in 2004. Fuhrman's book came out in 2003. Do you think a book such as *Death and Justice* might be able to influence the attitude toward the death penalty within a state's judicial system?

Narrative

15 Minutes

JOHN HERZFELD (SCREENWRITER AND DIRECTOR)

Film, 2001. Summary.

The American avant-garde artist Andy Warhol once said that in the future, everyone will be famous for fifteen minutes. He was referring to the mass-media hunger for news, feeding on brief stories about individual lives. You've seen this quote in Chapter 7, in *The Insider.*

Movie reviewers weren't very kind to the film bearing the promising title *15 Minutes,* and it wasn't much of a box office success either, but I find that it is far better than its reputation, especially in raising the question of media responsibility. As you read in Box 13.1, opinions differ on how far a TV network might go in terms of securing an exclusive story. Would they choose to air a videotaped murder? *15 Minutes* speculates that some tabloid show might do just that, for the sake of ratings.

In addition, the theme of what might happen when a fascination for Hollywood and the movies goes bad links this film up with our discussion about Hollywood influence in Chapter 2.

Two men go through immigration in New York; one, Oleg, is a Russian with a Hollywood fixation. He explains to the immigration officer that he has come to America because he saw *It's a Wonderful Life.* The other is Emil, a Czech, who has acquaintances in New York who owe him money. On the way to visit Emil's acquaintances Oleg steals a video camera. When they reach their destination and it turns out that his friend can't pay Emil what he owes him, Emil kills him and his wife with a kitchen knife. Meanwhile, Oleg is filming the event in detail, the first step toward fulfilling his dream of becoming an American film director.

Emil, having no intention of letting a couple of murders stop him, seeks to cover up the crime by setting fire to the apartment—but someone is watching from an adjacent bathroom: a woman. She flees down the stairs but has left her purse behind. So Emil and Oleg set out to find her.

Meanwhile, we encounter the host of a New York tabloid show, Robert Hawkins. His producer is trying to tone down the violent style of his show, but Hawkins is adamant: If they don't run a violent story, someone else will—and besides, what is a better lead story? "If it bleeds, it leads," he says.

A frequent guest on his show is popular New York police detective Eddie Fleming. His face is on the cover of magazines, and he is quite aware of his own celebrity status—but not merely because he enjoys the attention. He explains that if his fame can buy him just a little extra goodwill from the public so more crimes can be solved, then that's what he'll use it for. He may be narcissistic, but he is also a pro.

The apartment where Emil committed the murders and set the fire is now burned out, and the New York Fire Department takes control of the scene. A young arson inspector, Jordy Warsaw, finds to his dismay that NYPD and star detective Fleming are already there. At first Fleming thinks it is an accident, but he bows to the younger man's expertise when he shows him evidence of its being arson, and thus a murder scene.

In the meantime, Oleg and Emil are watching TV in a cheap hotel room and see Hawkins interview a serial killer who has been deemed temporarily insane. Emil's reaction: "I love America—nobody is responsible for what they do!" In an attempt to find the female witness, they call an escort service, dialing a number they found on a card in her purse. The woman who shows up from the escort service isn't the witness—but they murder her when she won't give out the escort service's address. (And Oleg films the entire incident.) Later, when the police and Fleming investigate this new crime scene, they find that she has been murdered with the same knife that was used in the arson murders.

Fleming, at home, hears a noise outside, investigates, and sees nothing—but in the meantime Emil and Oleg make their way into his apartment, attack him, and tie him to a chair with duct tape while Oleg films it all. Emil, with the logic of a madman, explains his plan to Fleming: They will kill someone famous and film it—which will prove they're crazy, because who else but crazy men would film their crimes? Then a judge will sentence them to a mental hospital instead of prison, but in the hospital they will reveal that they are sane, and because of the American double-jeopardy law (you cannot be tried for the same crime twice), they will be set free, sell their film to Hollywood, and become rich.

Fleming, knowing himself to be in a desperate predicament, fights back every way he can, using the chair he is strapped into as a weapon, but in the end it does him no good: While Oleg films everything, Fleming is knifed by Emil and dies.

Now Hawkins is approached by Emil and Oleg. They have a story worth a lot of money: a tape of Fleming's death. Will he buy it? And will he air it? Indeed, Hawkins shows up at the arranged place and buys the tape. Oleg films the exchange of the tape and the briefcase full of cash. When Hawkins arrives back at the TV station, Fleming's police colleagues try to talk sense to him and beg him for the tape, but it is too late: Minutes later, it is being broadcast all over New York and beyond, with Hawkins's introduction stating that he, as a journalist, feels obliged to show it.

As Oleg and Emil are watching the broadcast in a restaurant, their fellow patrons are horrified by what they see on the giant TV in the middle of their dinner, and when they hear the two men quarreling over the movie rights, they recognize them from the televised tape. In short order Emil is caught; Oleg disappears into the crowd.

Several twists and turns of the plot lead us to a final resurfacing of Oleg. Enraged that Emil, having found a lawyer who will argue that he was legally insane and that Oleg planned the whole thing, is found incompetent and indeed will escape punishment, Oleg has a trump card: the tape where Emil tells Fleming of his plan, effectively proving that he was legally sane and responsible for his crimes. What does Oleg do with this tape? Will he succeed in becoming a famous American film director? Will Hawkins have a change of heart about what constitutes media ethics? I will leave that for you to experience on your own.

Study Questions

1. In your opinion, was Hawkins acting responsibly as a journalist when he chose to air Fleming's death scene? Why or why not? Remember that Hawkins says, "If it bleeds, it leads," but that he also says it is his duty as a journalist to show the tape. If you answered no, then what, in your view, might be the responsible action of a journalist faced with Hawkins's moral choice?

2. Oleg is obsessed with American movies, to the point that he wants to make his own. However, he also seems to think that Hollywood has given an accurate portrayal of American society. Hollywood films shown around the world may indeed give people a skewed view of life in America—but do you think there are many such as Oleg who believe this view is true? If so, what can be done about it?

3. Do you think it possible that a "reality show" such as *Survivor* might air scenes where its participants are injured or perhaps killed? Why or why not? Should they? Why or why not?

4. Emil is misinformed about the rules of double jeopardy: If a legally insane convict recovers his sanity, he can be tried as a sane person. But in order for someone to be judged insane, he or she has to be unaware of the difference between right and wrong. Might Emil, in a real-life situation, be found legally insane? Explain why or why not.

5. What does the title refer to in the context of the film?

Narrative

The Jigsaw Man

LARRY NIVEN

Short story, 1967. Summary.

This science-fiction story explores a topic that seemed far-fetched in 1967 to most readers, illegal trade in organs. But reality seems to be catching up: For years Chinese dissidents who had escaped to the West told stories about the Chinese organ trade, but it wasn't until 2000 that the rumors were corroborated: Chinese prisons tailor executions of death row inmates according to the organs needed. Kidneys are especially popular; Chinese recipients pay less for them than foreign customers do, and such customers have been traced world-wide, including transplant recipients in the United States. Stories in the West about people turning up with kidneys missing may be an "urban legend," but a five-year-old Russian boy was close to being sold for parts by his grandmother in 2000, for $90,000. Niven not only speculates about the future but also seems to express a viewpoint on capital punishment: Young Lew is in jail, awaiting his trial. He knows that the outcome will be a sentence of death. They have evidence enough to convict him, and many people are being convicted and executed these days. We are in the late part of the twenty-first century (in Larry Niven's "Known Space," a future history of Earth and the universe).

In jail, Lew is confronted with a grisly story: Two fellow inmates tell about their crime of organlegging. Organs for transplant are in high demand among wealthy people, and high prices are paid for illegally acquired organs. How does one acquire organs illegally? One kidnaps healthy people, murders them, and sells their organs. One of Lew's cellmates is the bodysnatcher; the other is the doctor performing the organ extractions. They are both scheduled for execution.

Are there no legal organ transplants in this future society? Of course there are. By this time a method has been developed to keep organs fresh indefinitely, and worthy recipients are always waiting for life-saving organs, but there are more people needing organs than there are organs made available through accidents. As a result, an alternative method has been in use for almost a century (since the 1990s): On death row are people whose death, some say, doesn't do society any good, so they are made to "atone" for what evil they did in life by having their organs serve others when they die. Organ harvesting of condemned murderers is part of the system of punishment now, so Lew's two cellmates know what awaits them: an injection, instant freezing, death, and organ extraction. However, society needs more organs than the murderers on death row can supply. So, while kidnapping was already punishable by death in some states, now other crimes have joined the list.

Suddenly there is activity in the cell: The two cellmates are pressing themselves up against the bars and invite Lew to join them: They are about to commit suicide in a way that will make the organ banks reject them. The doctor has a hollowed-out space in his leg with a bomb implanted, and in a gruesome display of blood and gore the two inmates are blown to pieces—but so is the outside wall! Lew manages to squeeze out the hole in the wall, but he is very far off the ground, up close to the roof of the building. Driven by fear, he manages to swing himself upward toward the roof, and he lands on a pedwalk moving from the jail to the adjoining building. From there he jumps to a ledge and breaks through a window, into an office. While looking for something he can use to make himself less conspicuous—a change of clothes, shaving gear, anything—he notices what building he is in. A hospital. The hospital where criminals are executed and their organs removed. He has landed in the organ bank. Moving from room to room, he tries to find a way out, but he is being tracked, and beams of tranquilizer sounds are hitting him. Desperately he looks around and realizes that he is in the room of organ tanks. Refusing to die for what he considers nothing, he grabs a chair and starts smashing tanks, and he keeps smashing tanks until he blacks out.

Final scene: Lew is in court, hearing prosecutor and defense argue about his case; to his amazement, nobody mentions the organ tanks. They have plenty on him as it is; extra charges are considered only as a backup. Lew knows that he will lose his life, but at least he also knows that he has put up a fight. And now we learn what Lew is accused of, with plenty of ironclad evidence: "The state will prove that the said Warren Lewis Knowles did, in the space of two years, willfully drive through a total of six red traffic lights. During that same period the same Warren Lewis Knowles exceeded local speed limits no less than ten times, once by as much as fifteen miles per hour."

Study Questions

1. How does this story illustrate the type of argument called a "slippery slope"?

2. In your view, can the harvesting of organs from executed criminals be justified? If so, how? If not, why not?

3. Is this story a criticism of a forward-looking reason for punishment or a backward-looking one? Explain.

4. How would a utilitarian respond to this story? How would a deontologist respond? Explain in detail.

Narrative

The Life of David Gale

CHARLES RANDOLPH (SCREENWRITER),
ALAN PARKER (DIRECTOR)

Film. 2003. Summary.

This film is viewed as a powerful argument against the death penalty—and yet, because of the surprise ending, it is not a one-dimensional abolitionist argument, but rather an exploration of people's commitment to a cause. For that reason I am summarizing the entire story, including the ending—because the moral of this story lies in seeing the beginning in light of the end.

In the film *The Life of David Gale,* David Gale (Kevin Spacey) is a philosophy professor who likes to challenge his students. He is a firm believer in the abolition of the death penalty and constructs a way to influence the debate significantly. Here, in the beginning of the film, he is lecturing on the philosophy of controversial French psychoanalyst Jacques Lacan. Study question 5 explores the Lacan angle of the film.

An investigative reporter at a magazine gets a dream assignment: an exclusive interview with a death row inmate, just days before his execution for murder. The prisoner, David Gale, has selected the young reporter because of her reputation: She has spent a week in jail because she would not give up her source for one of her stories. So Gale knows that the reporter, Bitsey Bloom, has tenacity and integrity. Gale himself has spent six years on death row in Huntsville, Texas, for the rape and murder of Constance Harraway. He has now exhausted his appeals and has only three days left before he will be put to death. He used to be a professor of philosophy at the University of Austin and—what's more significant—he used to be a high-profile death penalty abolitionist, a member of "Death Watch," who debated capital punishment on TV with the governor of Texas. And now, having kept silent for six years, he wants to tell his story. When Bitsey first sits down in front of David Gale, with guards monitoring the interview, he says to her that someone on death row is no longer a person, just a crime—and he wants to be remembered for his life, not just for his death. He has claimed innocence from the beginning, but we also sense that he has no hope that his life will be spared—he is resigned to die. And in three days of interviews we get his story in flashbacks, as he tells it (and as viewers, we should remember that since he tells the story it is the version he wants us to believe is true).

First we see Gale as a philosophy professor, lecturing on the French twentieth-century psychoanalyst Lacan, summarizing one of Lacan's theories: that we can't have our fantasy and still want it—that our desires must remain unfulfilled in order for us to still want them—and so to be fully human is to live by ideals and ideas, not through wishes. And, "In the end, the only way we can measure the value of our lives is to value the lives of others." Only later do we, the viewers, realize that this is the blueprint for Gale's entire purpose in life.

A pretty female student, Berlin, approaches him after class—she is failing the class and will do "anything" to pass. Gale whispers to her, suggestively, that he'll give her a very good grade if she will . . . study hard. That same evening, things take an ugly turn: David is at a party for students and professors. His young son is at home with a sitter, and his wife is in Spain, apparently with a lover. At the party, Berlin shows up, and Gale learns that she has been dropped because of failing grades—she puts up a brave front and makes it clear to Gale that since she is no longer a student, they are now free to have an affair. Gale is drunk, and they end up having rough sex in the bathroom. Next day he relates this folly to his good friend Constance Harraway, a fellow professor, and Death Watch member—and the later murder victim. Constance is appalled that David would be so stupid, but she has more important things to focus on: The TV debate with the governor is coming up, David hasn't done his homework, and what they need is an example of an innocent man or woman who has in effect been executed—and they can't come up with evidence to that effect. She says that finding an innocent man on death row will only show that the system works—they need an *executed* innocent man to force a moratorium on capital punishment in Texas. During the debate Gale loses his cool and is caught by the governor because he can't come up with evidence that an innocent person has been executed in Texas. But the day is about to get a lot worse: Outside the studio David Gale is arrested for rape—Berlin has accused him of sexual assault. As David relates the story to Bitsey, we hear that the charges are eventually dropped, and Berlin sends him a postcard in which she writes how sorry she is for the whole thing. But even so, the consequences are devastating: He loses his job; his wife leaves him and takes his son along to Spain; he loses his house and starts drinking heavily. At some point, in a flashback, we see him reduced to being a drunk on a downtown street, ranting about the Greek philosophers he used to teach in his classes—Socrates was ugly, Plato was fat, and Aristotle was a prissy dresser! And yet, because of a chance he might get custody of his son, he cleans up his act, goes to AA meetings, and gets a blue-collar job—and he keeps on being an abolitionist. But eventually he is even kicked out of Death Watch—he is a liability. The final blow is when he learns that Constance is dying from leukemia.

Bitsey has become engaged in David's story in spite of herself—she prides herself on being objective. Two days earlier she believed that David was guilty and deserved death, but strange things start happening after she and an intern go to Constance's house, which has been turned into a ghoulish museum. A gothic girl shows them around, and Bitsey sees the layout of the kitchen and the chalk marks on the floor where the body was found. Later that night she finds a tape placed in her hotel room, with the actual death scene: Constance, naked on the floor, quietly dying, handcuffed, with duct tape over her mouth and a plastic bag tied around her neck—and according to court reports, with the key to the cuffs in her stomach, swallowed before her death. Bitsey is now convinced that Gale has been framed, to make abolitionists look crazy—but we also hear from the intern that Gale apparently could have received a life sentence had his lawyer not messed up. Even so, Gale stood by him and didn't request another lawyer.

The interview series with Gale continues. On the last day of Constance's life, she and David talk philosophically about death: She is not resigned to go, but she is so tired and frightened—and she regrets not having had more sex than she's had. In his own way David loves her, and they make love—which is why Constance had his semen in her when she was found. A close friend of Constance's and a fellow Death Watch abolitionist, Dusty (who wears a cowboy hat) has shown up from time to time, and he is also there now. And then there is a gap in Gale's story—he meanders around town, sleeps in his car, and is arrested, for the rape and murder of Constance.

What happened that night? Can Bitsey find out before Gale's execution the next day? She is determined to help, but he tells her that she is not there to save him, but to save his son's memory of his father. And sometimes, maybe death is a gift . . .

Now Bitsey is on a mission. She goes back to Constance's house with the intern and puts heself in the spot of the victim, to perform an experiment—she cuffs herself and places a bag over her head. Sure enough, after a minute she begins to struggle; it is not a quiet agony. When she is freed, she has found the clue: Constance did it herself, David didn't kill her. But why make it look like a murder? Because Death Watch needs an *executed innocent* person to further their cause! And to Bitsey, Dusty is the only possible suspect. She and the intern lure Dusty away from his home and ransack his place—and find a videotape, addressed to Bitsey herself. This videotape has the whole death scene on it, with Dusty stepping into the frame after Constance's death—but Bitsey wasn't meant to see it until *after* David's execution.

Desperate, Bitsey tries to reach the prison before David's execution; does she make it in time? Outside the prison the crowd is howling, "ugly faces screaming for revenge," to quote a previous Reading. But David is executed right on schedule—Bitsey doesn't manage to save him. Devastated, she believes this to be the end, as we, the audience, do. But there is an epilogue: As the nation watches, Constance's death tape implications hit the news; it becomes clear that an innocent man has been executed—and the debate about a Texas moratorium on the death penalty has begun. As a commentator says, in death David Gale achieved what he worked for in life. But was this the death of a martyr? In the mail Betsey receives yet another tape—the original, with the final scene. We see who steps up to the camcorder to shut it off, and that man is David Gale himself.

Study Questions

1. What does it mean for our understanding of the whole story that David himself removed the tape? Look for clues in the summary to the ending of the film.

2. Is David a hero, or is he a deceitful conspirator? Can one be both? Is there another possibility? Does the final scene of the tape undercut David's own intentions of sacrificing himself? And what do you think about Constance's decision to participate in her own death, to make a moral point?

3. Is this a film about the death penalty, about believing in a cause, about making one's life count, or perhaps a bit of all of these elements? In the end, is it an abolitionist film? Who, in effect, are we supposed to root for?

4. From Chapter 5 you'll remember the theory of utilitarianism. Would it be fair to say that David Gale believes in the idea that the end (ending capital punishment) justifies the means (faking a murder)? Does that make him a utilitarian?

5. The reference to the French psychoanalyst Jacques Lacan may have intrigued you. It is indeed not just a passing reference, but adds a deeper meaning to the film, according to Rose Pacatte, the director of the Pauline Center for Media Studies. In an essay, "Sex, Lies, and Videotape: What Is the Value of a Human Life," she writes,

> If you are familiar with linguistic theory (not as boring as it sounds—honest!), then the script for *The Life of David Gale* takes on deeper levels of meaning and shows an intelligence that goes beyond ordinary entertainment. Why so? Because the reference to Lacan makes the film become an invitation to viewers to examine the structures of language, meanings and values that the powers in our nation, such as government, the news media and the Church, use to communicate. Whether we think that capital punishment "makes sense" or not, it behooves us to examine how we reached that conclusion. Thought and language are inextricably entwined with how we live within our culture. As Alan Parker [the director] hoped, his film offers us a "space" to examine and "deconstruct" the place of the human person in society, especially in relation to capital punishment, and just how "free" we really are.

Is Pacatte right? Is the film an invitation for us to reexamine our thoughts and language about who we are as persons? If you are familiar with Lacan, you may want to engage in a discussion about this.

Selected Bibliography

Works of Nonfiction

Ammitzbøll, Marianne. *Den skjulte skat.* Copenhagen: Olivia, 1995.

Andersen, Pauli. "Celleklumper eller mennesker." *Berlingske Tidende,* November 26, 2001.

Aristotle. *Nichomachean Ethics.* In *Introduction to Aristotle,* edited by Richard McKeon, translated by W. D. Ross. New York: Random House, 1947.

———. *Poetics.* In *Introduction to Aristotle,* edited by Richard McKeon, translated by Ingram Bywater. New York: Random House, 1947.

Arrison, Sonia. "New Anti-Terrorism Law Goes Too Far." Op-ed, *San Diego Union-Tribune,* October 31, 2001.

Austin, Jonathan D. "U.N. Report: Women's Unequal Treatment Hurts Economies." CNN.com, September 20, 2000.

Badinter, Elisabeth. *The Unopposite Sex.* Translated by Barbara Wright. New York: Harper & Row, 1989.

Beauvoir, Simone de. *The Second Sex.* Translated by H. M. Parshley. New York: Knopf, 1952.

———. *The Ethics of Ambiguity.* Translated by Bernard Frechtman. New York: Philosophical Library, 1948.

Bedau, Hugo A., ed. *Justice and Equality.* Englewood Cliffs, N.J.: Prentice-Hall, 1971.

Belenky, Mary Field, et al. *Women's Ways of Knowing.* New York: Basic Books, 1986.

Belsey, Andrew, and Chadwick, Ruth "Ethics as a Vehicle for Media Quality." In *The Media and Morality,* edited by Robert M. Baird, William E. Loges, and Stuart E. Rosenbaum. New York: Prometheus Books, 1999.

Benedict, Ruth. "Anthropology and the Abnormal." *Journal of General Psychology* 10 (1934).

Bentham, Jeremy. *Principles of Morals and Legislation.* In *The Utilitarians.* New York: Anchor Books, 1973.

———. *The Works of Jeremy Bentham,* vol. 2. Edited by John Bowring. Edinburgh, 1838–43.

Berger, Fred. "Gratitude." In *Vice and Virtue in Everyday Life,* edited by Christina Hoff Sommers and Fred Sommers. Fort Worth: Harcourt Brace Jovanovich, 1985.

Bergson, Henri. *Time and Free Will.* Translated by F. L. Pogson. New York: Harper, 1960.

Bernasconi, Robert, and Wood, David, eds. *The Provocation of Levinas.* New York: Routledge, 1988.

Bok, Sisela. *Strategy for Peace.* New York: Random House, 1989.

Bonevac, Daniel, ed. *Today's Moral Issues.* Mountain View, Calif.: Mayfield, 1992.

Bonevac, Daniel, et al., eds. *Beyond the Western Tradition.* Mountain View, Calif.: Mayfield, 1992.

Booth, Wayne C. *The Company We Keep.* Berkeley: University of California Press, 1988.

———. "Why Ethical Criticism Fell on Hard Times." In *Ethics: Symposium on Morality and Literature* 98, no. 2 (January 1988). Chicago: University of Chicago Press.

Boss, Judith A. *Ethics for Life.* Mountain View, Calif.: Mayfield, 1998.

"Boy Sentenced to Watch *Saving Private Ryan.*" Associated Press, August 20, 1998.

Brickhouse, Thomas B., and Smith, Nicholas D. *Socrates on Trial.* Princeton, N.J.: Princeton University Press, 1989.

The Cambridge Companion to John Stuart Mill. Edited by John Skorupski. New York: Cambridge University Press, 1998.

Carmody, Denise Lardner, and Carmody, John Tully. *How to Live Well: Ethics in the World Religions.* Belmont, Calif.: Wadsworth, 1988.

Chan, W., ed. *A Source Book in Chinese Philosophy.* Princeton, N.J.: Princeton University Press, 1963.

Cohen, Carl. "The Case for the Use of Animals in Biomedical Research." *New England Journal of Medicine* 315 (October 2, 1986).

Confucius. *The Analects.* New York: Dover, 1995.

Cooper, Marc. "Liberals Stuck in Scold Mode." Op-ed, *Los Angeles Times,* October 14, 2001.

Coren, Stanley. *The Intelligence of Dogs.* New York: Macmillan, 1994.

Donn, Jeff. "Company Says It Cloned Human Embryo." Associated Press, November 25, 2001.

Douglas, John, and Olshaker, Mark. *Journey into Darkness.* New York: Pocket Star Books, 1997.

———. *Obsession.* New York: Scribner, 1998.

Dworkin, Andrea. *Right-Wing Women.* New York: Perigree, 1993.

Dworkin, Ronald. *Taking Rights Seriously.* Cambridge, Mass.: Harvard University Press, 1977.

"Editor Sacked over Fake Photos." *The Globe and Mail.* May 15, 2004.

Ehrenburg, Ilya. "Bøger." In *Evige Tanker,* edited by Anker Kierkeby. Copenhagen: Westmans Forlag, 1951.

The Elder Edda. A selection translated from the Icelandic by Paul B. Taylor and W. H. Auden. London: Faber and Faber, 1973.

Encyclopedia of Ethics. Edited by Lawrence C. Becker and Charlotte B. Becker. New York: Garland, 1992.

English, Jane. "What Do Grown Children Owe Their Parents?" In *Having Children: Philosophical and Legal Reflections on Parenthood,* edited by Onora O'Neill and

William Ruddick. New York: Oxford University Press, 1979.

Erikson, Erik. *Childhood and Society.* New York: Norton, 1964.

Ethics as First Philosophy: The Significance of Emmanuel Levinas. Edited by Adriaan T. Peperzak. New York: Routledge, 1995.

Ethics for Military Leaders I—II. Edited by Aine Donovan, Donald E. Johnson, George R. Lucas, Jr., Paul E. Rousch, and Nancy Sherman. American Heritage Christian Publishing, 1997.

Feinberg, Joel. "Psychological Egoism." In *Ethical Theory,* edited by Louis P. Pojman. Belmont, Calif.: Wadsworth, 1989.

———. "The Rights of Animals and Unborn Generations." In *Philosophy and Environmental Crisis,* edited by William T. Blackstone. Athens: University of Georgia Press, 1974.

Fitzsimmons, Mike. Editorial on anti-terrorism law. KXLY, October 30, 2001.

Foot, Philippa. *Virtues and Vices.* Berkeley: University of California Press, 1978.

Freeman, Derek. *The Fateful Hoaxing of Margaret Mead.* Boulder, Colo.: Westview Press, 1999.

Friedman, Marilyn. "Feminism and Modern Friendship: Dislocating the Community." *Ethics* 99 (1989), University of Chicago Press.

Fuhrman, Mark. *Death and Justice: An Exposé of Oklahoma's Death Row Machine.* New York: HarperCollins 2003.

———. *Murder in Spokane.* New York: Harper-Collins, 2001.

Furrow, Dwight. "Of Cave Dwellers and Spirits: The Trouble with Moral Absolutes." In *Moral Soundings: Readings on the Crisis of Values in Contemporary Life,* edited by Dwight Furrow. New York: Rowman & Littlefield, 2004.

Genovese, E. N. *Mythology: Texts and Contexts.* Redding, Calif.: C.A.T. Publishing, 1991.

Gilligan, Carol. *In a Different Voice.* Cambridge, Mass.: Harvard University Press, 1982.

Glenn, Linda MacDonald, "Ethical Issues in Genetic Engineering and Transgenics." June 2004. Retrieved January 13, 2005, from http://actionbioscience.org/biotech/glenn.html.

Gonzales, John Moreno, "Shacks, Tidy Yards and Tight-Lipped Neighbors Surround the Long-Time Home of a Suspect in the Killings of 3 Civil Rights Workers 40 Years Ago." Newsday.com, Jan. 10, 2005.

Graves, Robert. *The Greek Myths.* 2 vols. Penguin, 1960.

Gross, Hyman. *A Theory of Criminal Justice.* New York: Oxford University Press, 1979.

Guillo, Karen. "Study Finds No Death Penalty Bias." Associated Press, June 7, 2001.

Gyekye, Kwame. *An Essay on African Philosophical Thought: The Akan Conceptual Scheme.* New York: Cambridge University Press, 1987.

Hallie, Philip. "From Cruelty to Goodness." In *Vice and Virtue in Everyday Life,* edited by Christina Hoff Sommers and Fred Sommers. Fort Worth: Harcourt Brace Jovanovich, 1985, 1989.

———. *Tales of Good and Evil, Help and Harm.* New York: HarperCollins, 1997.

Harris, C. E., Jr. *Applying Moral Theories.* Belmont, Calif.: Wadsworth, 1986.

Heidegger, Martin. *Being and Time.* Translated by John Macquarrie and Edward Robinson. New York: Harper & Row, 1962.

Herodotus. *The Histories.* Translated by Aubrey de Sélencourt. New York: Penguin Books, 1996.

Hertel, Hans. *Verdens litteraturs historie,* vols. 1–7. Copenhagen: Gyldendal, 1985–93.

Hinman, Lawrence. *Ethics, A Pluralistic Approach.* Austin: Harcourt Brace, 1993.

Hobbes, Thomas. *English Works.* Vol. 3. Edited by Sir W. Molesworth. London: J. Bohn, 1840.

Hohlenberg, Johannes. *Søren Kierkegaard.* Copenhagen: Aschehoug Dansk Forlag, 1963.

Horn, Tom. *The Life of Tom Horn, Government Scout and Interpreter.* 1904. Reprinted by Triton Press, 1988.

Hume, David. *An Enquiry Concerning the Principles of Morals.* In *Enquiries Concerning Human Understanding and Concerning the Principles of Morals,* 3rd ed., edited by L. A. Selby-Bigge, revised by P. H. Nidditch. Oxford: Clarendon, 1975.

Illustreret Videnskab Nr. 3, March 1994. Copenhagen: Bonnier.

Jalbert, Shana. "U.S. Must Address Real Problems, Forget Military Might, Turner Says." *Brown* (University) *Daily Herald,* February 12, 2002.

Kalin, Jesse. "In Defense of Egoism." In *Ethical Theory,* edited by Louis P. Pojman. Belmont, Calif.: Wadsworth, 1989.

Kant, Immanuel. *Grounding for the Metaphysics of Morals.* Translated by James W. Ellington. Indianapolis: Hackett, 1981.

———. *The Metaphysics of Morals.* Introduction, translation, and notes by Mary Gregor. Cambridge: Cambridge University Press, 1991.

———. "On the Distinction of the Beautiful and Sublime in the Interrelation of the Two Sexes." In *Philosophy of Woman,* edited by Mary Briody Mahowald. Indianapolis: Hackett, 1983.

Kaplan, Alice. "The Trouble with Memoir." *Chronicle of Higher Education,* December 5, 1997.

Katz, Eric. "The Rings of Tolkien and Plato: Lessons in Power, Choice, and Morality." In *The Lord of the Rings and Philosophy: One Book to Rule them All,* edited by Gregory Bassman and Eric Bronson. Chicago: Open Court, 2003.

Kearney, Richard. *Dialogues with Contemporary Continental Thinkers: The Phenomenological Heritage.* Manchester: Manchester University Press, 1984.

Kemp, Peter. "Etik og narrativitetens tre niveau'er." *Psyke & Logos,* Copenhagen, no. 1, vol. 17.

———. "Social Justice." In *The Good Society: Essays on the Welfare System at a Time of Change,* edited by Egon Clausen. Copenhagen: Ministry of Social Affairs, 1995.

———. *Das Unersetzliche: Eine Technologie-Ethik.* Berlin: Wichen-Verlag, 1992.

Kemp, Peter, Lebech, Mette, and Rendtorff, Jacob. *Den bioetiske vending.* Copenhagen: Spektrum/Forum Publishers, 1997.

Kierkeby, Anker, ed. *Evige Tanker.* Copenhagen: Westmans Forlag, 1951.

Kierkegaard, Søren. *Enten-Eller. Anden Deel.* Copenhagen: H. Hagerup's Forlag, 1950.

———. *Johannes Climacus* (written 1842–43, first published 1912). Copenhagen: Gyldendal, 1967.

Kingsolver, Barbara. "No Glory in Unjust War on the Weak." Op-ed, *Los Angeles Times,* October 14, 2001.

Kittay, Eva Feder, and Meyers, Diana T., eds. *Women and Moral Theory.* Savage, Md.: Rowman & Littlefield, 1987.

Körner, Stephan. *Kant.* Harmondsworth, England: Penguin, 1955.

Kravets, David. "Court to Revisit Ruling on Abortion Opponent." *San Diego Union-Tribune,* October 4, 2001.

Kurtz, Stanley. "Free Speech and an Orthodoxy of Dissent." *Chronicle of Higher Education,* October 26, 2001.

Leake, Jonathan. "Scientists Teach Chimpanzee to Speak English." *The Sunday Times,* UK, July 25, 1999.

Le Guin, Ursula K. "It Was a Dark and Stormy Night." In *On Narrative,* edited by J. I. Mitchell. Chicago: University of Chicago Press, 1981.

Lerner, Gerda. *The Creation of Feminist Consciousness.* New York: Oxford University Press, 1993.

———. *The Creation of Patriarchy.* New York: Oxford University Press, 1986.

Levin, Richard. *The Question of Socrates.* New York: Harcourt, Brace & World, 1961.

Levinas, Emmanuel. *Ethics and Infinity: Conversations with Philippe Nemo.* Pittsburgh: Duquesne University Press, 1985.

Lifton, Robert Jay, and Mitchell, Greg. *Who Owns Death? Capital Punishment, the American Conscience, and the End of Executions.* New York: Morrow, 2000.

Lin Yutang. *The Importance of Living.* London: Heinemann, 1937.

Lloyd, *Genevieve. The Man of Reason.* Minneapolis: University of Minnesota Press, 1984.

Louv, Richard. "Line Between Reality and Science Fiction Has Been Eroding." *San Diego Union-Tribune,* October 28, 2001.

———. "War on Terrorism Calls for Re-evaluation of Military Ethics." *San Diego Union-Tribune,* October 21, 2001.

MacIntyre, Alasdair. *After Virtue.* Notre Dame, Ind.: University of Notre Dame Press, 1981, 1984.

Mackie, J. L. *Ethics: Inventing Right and Wrong.* New York: Penguin, 1977.

Mahowald, Mary Briody, ed. *Philosophy of Woman.* Indianapolis: Hackett, 1983.

Malinowski, Bronislaw. "Myth in Primitive Psychology." In *Magic, Science, and Religion.* Garden City, N.Y.: Doubleday Anchor, 1954.

Maltin, Leonard. *Leonard Maltin's TV Movies and Video Guide.* New York: Signet, 1996.

Mappes, Thomas A., & Zembaty, Jane S., eds. *Social Ethics.* 4th ed. New York: McGraw-Hill, 1992.

Mayo, Bernard. "Virtue or Duty?" In *Vice and Virtue in Everyday Life,* edited by Christina Hoff Sommers and Fred Sommers. Fort Worth: Harcourt Brace Jovanovich, 1985, 1989.

McCormick, Patrick T. "Adult Punishment Doesn't Fit the Underage Criminal." *Spokesman-Review,* September 4, 2001.

McLemee, Scott. "What Makes Martha Nussbaum Run?" *Chronicle of Higher Education,* October 5, 2001.

Medlin, Brian. "Ultimate Principles and Ethical Thought." In *Ethical Theory,* edited by Louis P. Pojman. Belmont, Calif.: Wadsworth, 1989.

Mencius. Translated by D. C. Lau. Harmondsworth, England: Penguin, 1970.

Mill, Harriet Taylor. "Enfranchisement of Women," in *Philosophy of Woman,* 3rd ed., edited by Mary Mahowald. Indianapolis: Hackett, 1994.

Mill, John Stuart. *Autobiography.* New York: Columbia University Press, 1924.

———. *On Liberty.* In *The Utilitarians.* New York: Anchor Books, 1973.

———. *The Subjection of Women.* Cambridge, Mass.: MIT Press, 1970.

———. *Utilitarianism.* In *The Utilitarians.* New York: Anchor Books, 1973.

Mitchell, J. I., ed. *On Narrative.* Chicago: University of Chicago Press, 1981.

Mitrovich, George, and Winters, Timothy. "Separated by a Hyphen." Op-ed, *San Diego Union-Tribune,* October 11, 2001.

"Moderates, Liberals Hear Call to Morality Debate." *Los Angeles Times,* Nov.10, 2004.

Morality in Criminal Justice. Edited by Daryl Close and Nicholas Meier. Belmont, Calif.: Wadsworth, 1995.

Morlin, Bill, and White, Jeanette. *Bad Trick: The Hunt for Spokane's Serial Killer.* Spokane, Wash.: New Media Ventures, 2001.

Mulhauser, Dana. "National Group Rallies Students Who Question Campus Feminism." *Chronicle of Higher Education,* October 5, 2001.

Narveson, Jan. "Morality and Violence: War, Revolution, Terrorism." In *Matters of Life and Death,* 3rd ed., edited by Tom Regan. New York: McGraw-Hill, 1993.

Nathanson, Stephen. *An Eye for an Eye? The Morality of Punishing by Death.* Savage, Md.: Rowman & Littlefield, 1987.

———. "In Defense of 'Moderate Patriotism,'" *Ethics,* vol. 99 (April 1989).

"News Media's Credibility Crumbling." *Insight Magazine/World Net Daily,* May 8, 2004.

Nietzsche, Friedrich. *Beyond Good and Evil.* Translated by Helen Zimmern. Riverside, N.J.: Macmillan, 1911.

———. *On the Genealogy of Morals.* Translated by Walter Kaufmann and R. J. Hollingdale. New York: Random House, 1969.

Nussbaum, Martha. *Love's Knowledge.* New York: Oxford University Press, 1990.

———. *Hiding from Humanity: Disgust, Shame, and the Law.* Princeton: Princeton University Press, 2004.

"N.Y. Times Uncovers Dozens of Faked Stories by Reporter." *Washington Post,* May 11, 2003.

O'Brian, William. *The Conduct of Just and Unjust War.* Westport, CT. Praeger Publishers, 1981.

Oden, Thomas C., ed. *Parables of Kierkegaard.* Princeton, N.J.: Princeton University Press, 1978.

Packe, Michael St. John. *The Life of John Stuart Mill.* New York: Capricorn, 1954.

Parekh, Bhikhu. "The Concept of Multicultural Education." In *Today's Moral Problems,* edited by Daniel Bonevac. Mountain View, Calif.: Mayfield, 1992.

Park, Michael Y. "Army Looks to Hollywood for Scenarios." Foxnews.com, October 8, 2001.

Plato. *Apology.* In *Dialogues of Plato.* Translated by Benjamin Jowett. New York: Washington Square Press, 1968.

———. *Euthyphro.* In *The Dialogues of Plato,* with an introduction by Erich Segal, translated by R. E. Allen. New York: Bantam Books, 1986.

———. *Plato's Phaedrus.* Translated by W. C. Helmbold and W. G. Rabinowitz. New York: The Liberal Arts Press, 1956.

———. *The Republic.* Translated by G. R. U. Grube. Indianapolis: Hackett, 1974.

———. *The Republic of Plato.* Translated by Francis MacDonald Cornford. London: Oxford University Press, 1945.

Pojman, Louis P., ed. *Ethical Theory.* Belmont, Calif.: Wadsworth, 1989.

Punishment and the Death Penalty: The Current Debate. Edited by Robert M. Baird and Stuart E. Rosenbaum. New York: Prometheus, 1995.

Race and the Enlightenment: A Reader. Edited by Emmanuel Chukwudi Eze. Oxford: Blackwell, 1997.

Rachels, James. *The Elements of Moral Philosophy.* New York: Random House, 1986, 1999.

Rand, Ayn. "The Ethics of Emergencies," "Man's Rights." In *The Virtue of Selfishness.* New York: Penguin, 1964.

Rawls, John. "Justice As Fairness." *Philosophical Review* 67 (April 1958).

———. *The Law of Peoples.* Cambridge, Mass.: Harvard University Press, 2001.

———. "Two Concepts of Rules." *Philosophical Review* 1–13, 1955.

Rendtorff, Jacob Dahl, and Kemp, Peter. *Basic Ethical Principles in European Bioethics and Biolaw.* Vol. 1, *Autonomy, Dignity, Integrity and Vulnerability.* Copenhagen: Centre for Ethics and Law, and Barcelona: Institut Borja de Bioètica, 2000.

Rescher, Nicholas. *Distributive Justice.* Indianapolis: Bobbs-Merrill, 1966.

Ricoeur, Paul. *Interpretation Theory.* Fort Worth: Texas Christian University Press, 1976.

———. "Narrative Time." In *On Narrative,* edited by J. I. Mitchell. Chicago: University of Chicago Press, 1981.

———. *Time and Narrative.* 3 vols. Chicago: University of Chicago Press, 1985–1989.

Rodin, David. "Terrorism Without Intention." In *Ethics: Symposium on Terrorism, War, and Justice,* vol. 114 (July 2004).

Rosenstand, Nina. "Arven fra Bergson: En Virknings-historie." In *Den Skapende Varighet,* edited by Hans Kolstad. Oslo, Norway: H. Aschehoug & Co., 1993.

———. "Everyone Needs a Stone: Alternative Views of Nature." In *The Environmental Ethics and Policy Book,* 2nd ed., edited by Donald VanDeVeer and Christine Pierce. Belmont, Calif.: Wadsworth, 1998.

———. *The Human Condition: An Introduction to Philosophy of Human Nature.* New York: McGraw-Hill, 2002.

———. "Med en anden stemme: Carol Gilligans etik." In *Kvindespind—Kønsfilosofiske Essays,* edited by Mette Boch et al. Aarhus, Denmark: Forlaget Philosophia, 1987.

———. *Mytebegrebet.* Copenhagen: Gads Forlag, 1981.

———. "Myths and Morals: Images of Conduct, Character, and Personhood in the Native American Tradition." In *Tribal Mythologies,* edited by Helmut Wautischer. Aldershot: Ashgate, 1998.

Rousch, Paul E. "Justification for Resort to Force" in *Ethics for Military Leaders,* edited by Aine Donovan, David E. Johnson, George R. Lucas, Jr., Paul E. Rousch, and Nancy Sherman. American Heritage Christian Publishing, 1997.

"Russian Grandmother 'Wanted to Sell Child for Organs.'" CNN.com, November 28, 2000.

Ruth, Sheila, ed. *Issues in Feminism.* Mountain View, Calif.: Mayfield, 1998.

Sapontzis, Steve F. "The Moral Significance of Interests." *Environmental Ethics,* Winter 1982.

Sartre, Jean-Paul. Excerpt from *Being and Nothingness.* In *Reality, Man and Existence: Essential Works of Existentialism,* edited by H. J. Blackham. New York: Bantam, 1965.

———. *Existentialism Is a Humanism.* Translated by P. Mairet. New York: The Philosophical Library, 1949.

Savage-Rumbaugh, Sue, and Lewin, Roger. *Kanzi: The Ape at the Brink of the Human Mind.* New York: Wiley, 1994.

Saving Private Ryan: The Men. The Mission. The Movie. Edited by Linda Sunshine. New York: Newmarket Press, 1998.

Schmidt, Kaare. *Film-historie, kunst, industri.* Copenhagen: Gyldendal, 1995.

Schneewind, J. B. "The Misfortunes of Virtue." *Ethics* 101, October 1990. Chicago: University of Chicago Press, 1990.

"Sexual Harassment Is Forbidden by Law." San Diego State University pamphlet, November 1994.

Shapiro, Laura. "Guns and Dolls." *Newsweek,* May 28, 1990.

Shaw, William H. *Morality and Moral Controversies.* Englewood Cliffs, N.J.: Prentice-Hall, 1981.

Singer, Peter. *The Expanding Circle.* Farrar, Straus and Giroux, 1981.

Sommers, Christina Hoff. "Teaching the Virtues." *Imprimis.* Hillsdale College, Michigan, November 1991.

————. *Who Stole Feminism?* New York: Simon & Schuster, 1994.

Sommers, Christina Hoff, and Sommers, Fred, eds. *Vice and Virtue in Everyday Life.* Fort Worth: Harcourt Brace Jovanovich, 1985, 1989.

Srinivasan, Kalpana. "Feds Accuse Entertainment Industry." Associated Press, September 11, 2000.

Steifels, Peter. "Emmanuel Levinas, 90, French Ethical Philosopher." Obituary, *New York Times,* December 27, 1995.

Steindorf, Sara. "A Novel Approach to Work." *Christian Science Monitor,* January 29, 2002.

Stone, I. F. *The Trial of Socrates.* New York: Doubleday, 1988.

Stone, Oliver, and Sklar, Zachary. *JFK: The Book of the Film.* New York: Applause Books, 1992.

"Study of Monkeys Hints at a Thinking Ability Without Language." New York Times News Service, October 24, 1998.

"Sudanese Criticize Governor's Decree on Women." CNN.com, September 6, 2000.

Tannen, Deborah. *The Argument Culture.* New York: Random House, 1998.

————. *Talking from 9 to 5.* New York: William Morrow and company, Inc., 1994.

————. *That's Not What I Meant!* New York: Ballantine, 1986.

————. *You Just Don't Understand.* New York: Morrow, 1990.

Taylor, Mark C. *Journeys to Selfhood: Hegel & Kierkegaard.* Berkeley: University of California Press, 1980.

Taylor, Paul W. *Principles of Ethics: An Introduction.* Belmont, Calif.: Wadsworth, 1975.

Taylor, Richard. *Good and Evil.* New York: Prometheus, 2000.

Trebilcot, Joyce. "Two Forms of Androgynism." *Journal of Social Philosophy,* January 1977.

"USA TODAY Editor Resigns After Reporter's Misdeeds." *USAToday,* Apr. 20, 2004.

Waal, Frans B. M. de. "Do Humans Alone 'Feel Your Pain'?" *Chronicle of Higher Education,* October 26, 2001.

————. *Good Natured: The Origins of Right and Wrong in Humans and Other Animals.* Cambridge, Mass.: Harvard University Press, 1996.

Warren, Mary Ann. "Human and Animal Rights Compared." In *Environmental Philosophy: A Collection of Readings,* edited by Robert Elliot and Arran Gare. State College: Pennsylvania State University Press, 1983.

Weiss, Rick. "Test-Tube Baby Born to Save Ill Sister." *Washington Post,* October 3, 2000.

Wesley, John. "Reel Therapy." *Psychology Today,* February 2000.

Wilgoren, Jodi. "Death Knell for the Death Penalty?" New York Times News Service, April 15, 2002.

Williams, Ian. "China Sells Organs of Slain Convicts." *Observer* (UK), December 10, 2000.

Williams, Bernard. *Morality: An Introduction.* New York: Harper & Row, 1972.

Wolgast, Elizabeth. *The Grammar of Justice.* Ithaca, N.Y.: Cornell University Press, 1987.

Wollstonecraft, Mary. *A Vindication of the Rights of Women.* Excerpt in *Philosophy of Woman,* edited by Mary Briody Mahowald. Indianapolis: Hackett, 1983.

Wright, Tamra, Hughes, Peter, and Ainley, Alison. "The Paradox of Morality: An Interview with Emmanuel Levinas." In *The Provocation of Levinas,* edited by Robert Bernasconi and David Wood. New York: Routledge, 1988.

Zack, Naomi. *Thinking About Race.* Belmont, Calif.: Wadsworth, 1998.

Works of Literature

Andersen, Hans Christian. *Eventyr og Historier.* 16 vols. Odense, Denmark: Skandinavisk Bogforlag, Flensteds Forlag.

Beauvoir, Simone de. *The Woman Destroyed.* Translated by Patrick O'Brian. New York: Putnam, 1969.

Bennett, William J. *The Book of Virtues.* New York: Simon & Schuster, 1993.

Conrad, Joseph. *Lord Jim: A Tale.* New York: Bantam, 1981.

Dostoyevsky, Fyodor. *The Brothers Karamazov.* New York: Signet Classic, New American Library, 1957.

Esquivel, Laura. *Like Water for Chocolate.* Translated by Carol and Thomas Christensen. New York: Doubleday, 1992.

Euripides, *Medea.* In *Classical Mythology: Images and Insights,* by Stephen L. Harris and Gloria Plazner. Translated by Moses Hadas. Mountain View, Calif., Mayfield, 1995.

Flaubert, Gustave. *Madame Bovary.* Translated by Lowell Lair. New York: Bantam, 1981.

Goethe, Johan Wolfgang von. *The Sorrows of Young Werther.* Translated by Elizabeth Mayer and Louise Bogan. New York: Vintage Books, 1973.

Graves, Robert. *The Greek Myths*. 2 vols. Harmondsworth, England: Penguin, 1960.

Grimm's Complete Fairy Tales. Garden City, N.Y.: Doubleday.

Henry, O. "Gift of the Magi." Retrieved January 13, 2005, from http://www.auburn.edu/~vestmon/Gift_of_the_Magi.html.

Hornby, Nick. *How to Be Good*. New York: Riverhead Books, 2002.

Huxley, Aldous. *Brave New World*. New York: Bantam, 1958.

Ibsen, Henrik. *A Doll's House*. In *The Collected Works of Henrik Ibsen*, vol. 7: *A Doll's House, Ghosts*. Introductions and translations by William Archer. New York: Scribner, 1906.

Jewkes, W. T., ed. *Man the Myth-Maker*. New York: Harcourt Brace Jovanovich, 1973.

Kafka, Franz. *The Basic Kafka*. New York: Simon & Schuster, 1979.

Kingsolver, Barbara. *The Poisonwood Bible*. New York: HarperTorch, 1998.

Lee, Spike, with Lisa Jones. *Do the Right Thing*. New York: Simon & Schuster, 1989.

Le Guin, Ursula K. "The Ones Who Walk Away from Omelas." In *The Wind's Twelve Quarters*. New York: Harper & Row, 1981.

Matheson, Richard. "Mantage." In *Shock I*. New York: Berkeley, 1961.

Niven, Larry. "The Jigsaw Man." In *Tales of Known Space: The Universe of Larry Niven*. New York: Ballantine, 1975.

Njal's Saga. Translated by Magnus Magnusson and Hermann Palsson. Baltimore: Penguin, 1960.

Poe, Edgar Allan. *Complete Tales and Poems*. New York: Barnes & Noble Books, 1992.

Rand, Ayn. *Atlas Shrugged*. New York: Signet, 1957.

Sartre, Jean-Paul. *No Exit*. New York: Random House, 1989.

Shelley, Mary. *Frankenstein*. New York: Bantam, 1981.

Singer, Isaac Bashevis. "A Piece of Advice." From *The Spinoza of Market Street*. Translated from Yiddish into English by Martha Glicklich and Joel Blocker. New York: Fawcett Crest, 1958.

Tarantino, Quentin. *Pulp Fiction, A Quentin Tarantino Screenplay*. New York: Hyperion, 1994.

Tepper, Sheri S. *Sideshow*. New York: Bantam Books, 1993.

Walker, Alice. *Possessing the Secret of Joy*. New York: Simon & Schuster, 1993.

Wessel, Johann Herman. "Smeden og Bageren." In *De gamle huskevers*. Edited by Fritz Haack. Copenhagen: Forlaget Sesam, 1980.

Zicree, Marc Scott. *The Twilight Zone Companion*. New York: Bantam, 1982.

Selected Website Sources

AP falsification incident
http://www.worldnetdaily.com/news/article.asp?ARTICLE_ID=40331

Ape language research
http://www.gsu.edu/~wwwlrc/

Aristotle's biography
http://www.gradesaver.com/ClassicNotes/Authors/about_aristotle.html
http://www-history.mcs.st-andrews.ac.uk/Mathematicians/Aristotle.html

Aristotle's Lyceum
http://www.newadvent.org/cathen/01713a.htm

Atlantic Monthly websites, Christina Hoff Sommers debate
http://www.theatlantic.com

Barbara Kingsolver
http://www.english.eku.edu/SERVICES/KYLIT/KINGSLVR.HTM

California's Three Strikes Law
http://www.rand.org/publications/RB/RB4009/RB4009.word.html

CBS document scandal
http://www.southerndigest.com/vnews/displays.v/ART/2004/09/14/41472eba1033d
http://www.azcentral.com/news/articles/0910bush-memos10.html

Charles Dickens
http://www.worldwideschool.org/library/books/lit/charlesdickens/ATaleofTwoCities/Chap1.html

Christianity's development in the Roman Empire
http://www.roman-empire.net/religion/religion.html

CSI: Crime Scene Investigation series
http://www.cbs.com/primetime/csi/main.shtml

Criminal justice ethics
http://www.lib.jjay.cuny.edu/cje/html/cje.html

Death penalty facts
http://www.deathpenaltyinfo.org/

Dolphins saved after tsunami
http://www.seattlepi.nwsource.com/national/apasia_story.asp?category=1104&slug=Tsunami%20Dolphins

Ed Koch on Michael Moore's Farenheit 9/11
http://www.newsmax.com/archives/articles/2004/6/28/190852.shtml

Ethical wills
http://www.csmonitor.com/2004/0707/p11s02-lifp.html

Ethics Updates, edited by Lawrence Hinman
http://ethics.acusd.edu/index.html

Fired because of use of word
http://www.adversity.net/special/niggardly.htm

Gandhi
http://www.mkgandhi.org/

The Great Ape Project
http://www.greatapeproject.org

Herrad of Hohenbourg
http://home.infionline.net/~ddisse/herrad.html

Ibn Fadlan
http://www.luth.se/luth/present/sweden/history/viking_age/Viking_age4.html

Illinois death penalty report
  http://www.cnn.com/2002/LAW/04/15/death.penalty.
  report/index.html

Immanuel Kant's "Perpetual Peace"
  http://www.mtholyoke.edu/acad/intrel/kant/kant1.htm

Jeremy Bentham's Auto-Icon
  http://www.ucl.ac.uk/Bentham-Project/info/jb.htm

Jerome Krause, on A Shark's Tale
  http://www.prnewswire.com/cgi-bin/stories.pl?
  ACCT=104&STORY=/www/story/09-27-2004/
  0002258979&EDATE=

John Jay College of Criminal Justice study of child abuse by
  priests
  http://www.jjay.cuny.edu/churchstudy/main.asp

King Yudisthira
  http://www.bestfriends.com/allthegoodnews/magazine/
  BFMjan03.pdf

Life of David Gale, Analysis
  http://www.daughtersofstpaul.com/mediastudies/
  reviews/filmdavidgale.html

Linda MacDonald Glenn
  http://www.actionbioscience.org/biotech/glenn.html

Lord of the Rings, list of characters
  http://www.lord-of-the-rings.org/books.html

Martin Luther King's "A Letter from (a) Birmingham Jail"
  http://almaz.com/nobel/peace/MLK-jail.html

Michael Gurian
  http://www.michaelgurian.com/

Mississippi Burning reviews
  http://www.cinepad.com/reviews/mississippi.htm
  http://www.law.umkc.edu/faculty/projects/ftrials/
  price&bowers/movie.html

The Molly and Adam Nash story
  http://www.amednews.com/2001/prse0115

"Movies with a Message"
  http://www.jsonline.com/onwisconsin/movies/
  oct04/266611.asp

Nathaniel Abraham
  http://www.wsws.org/articles/2000/jan2000/
  abra-j14. shtml

O. Henry, "The Gift of the Magi"
  http://www.auburn.edu/~vestmon/Gift_of_the_Magi.
  html

Oldest European universities
  http://www.unbf.ca/psychology/likely/scholastics/
  universities.html

Olympe de Gouges
  http://www.pinn.net/~sunshine/march99/gouges2.html

The Primates Home Page
  http://www.dwebsoft.com/PrimatesWeb/

Retributive and restorative justice
  http://www.georgetown.edu/centers/woodstock/
  report/r-fea61a.htm

Robert Yates investigation files
  http://www.krem.com

The Society for the Study of Ethics and Animals
  http://mail/Rochester.edu/~nobs/ssea.html

Spokane serial killer
  http://www.kxly.com/default.asp

"Truth Falls Victim to Politics"
  http://www.spokesmanreview.com/opinion/topstory.
  asp?ID=32295

Tuskegee syphilis study
  http://www.med.virginia.edu/hs-library/historical/
  apology/

U.S. Constitution
  http://www.nwbuildnet.com/nwbn/
  usconstitutionsearch.html

"Who's a terrorist and who isn't?" AP article, 10/03/01
  http://www.msnbc.com/news/636814.asp

Women in the armed forces
  http://www.womensmemorial.org/
  historyandcollections/history/learnmoreques.htm

Women's suffrage
  http://www.rochester.edu/SBA/history.html

Women's suffrage, global
  http://www.womenshistory.about.com/library/
  weekly/aa091600a.htm

Credits

view with Emmanuel Levinas" from *The Provocation of Levinas*, edited by Robert Bernasconi and David Wood. Copyright © 1988 by Routledge. Reprinted with permission.

Lin Yutang, "On Growing Old Gracefully" excerpted from *The Importance of Living*. Copyright © 1995 by Lin Yutang and Hsiang Ju Lin. Reprinted with the permission of William Morrow, a division of HarperCollins Publishers, Inc.

John McCain, excerpts from *Why Courage Matters: The Way to a Braver Life*. Copyright © 2004 by John McCain and Marshall Salter. Reprinted with the permission of Random House, Inc.

Harriet Taylor Mill, excerpts from "Enfranchisement of Women" from *Philosophy of Woman: An Anthology of Classic and Current Concepts, Third Edition,* edited by Mary Brody Mahowald. Copyright © 1994 by Hackett Publishing Company. Reprinted with the permission of Hackett Publishing Company, Inc. All rights reserved.

Jan Narveson, excerpt from "Morality and Violence: War, Revolution, and Terrorism" from *Matters of Life and Death: New Introductory Essays in Moral Philosophy*, edited by Tom L. Beauchamp and Tom Regan. Reprinted with the permission of The McGraw-Hill Companies.

Stephen Nathanson, excerpt from *An Eye for an Eye? The Morality of Punishing by Death*. Copyright © 1987 by Rowman & Littlefield. Reprinted with permission. Reprinted with the permission of the publishers.

Martha Nussbaum, excerpt from *Love's Knowledge: Essays on Philosophy and Literature*. Copyright © 1990, 1992 by Martha C. Nussbaum. Reprinted with the permission of Oxford University Press, Inc.

Bhikhu Parekh, from "The Concept of Multicultural Education" from *Multicultural Education: The Interminable Debate*, edited by Shohan Modgil et al. Copyright © 1986 by Falmer Press. Reprinted with the permission of Routledge.

Plato, excerpts from Books II and X and excerpts from "The Myth of the Cave" from *The Republic*, translated by Francis MacDonald Cornford. All reprinted with the permission of Oxford University Press, Ltd. Plato, excerpts from "Euthyphro," translated by R.F. Allen, in Erich Segal, *The Dialogues of Plato*. Copyright © 1984 by Yale University. Reprinted with the permission of Bantam Books, a division of Random House, Inc.

Tristine Rainer, from *Your Life as Story*. Copyright © 1997 by Tristine Rainer. Reprinted with the permission of Jeremy P. Tarcher, an imprint of Penguin Group (USA) Inc.

Ayn Rand, excerpts from "The Ethics of Emergencies" from *The Virtue of Selfishness: A New Concept of Egoism*. Copyright © 1961, 1964 by Ayn Rand. Excerpt from *Atlas Shrugged*. Copyright © 1957 by Ayn Rand, renewed (1985 by Eugene Winick, Paul Gitlin and Leonard Peikoff. All reprinted with the permission of Dutton Dignet, a division of Penguin Group (USA) Inc.

John Rawls, excerpts from "Justice as Fairness" from *A Theory of Justice*. Copyright © 1971 by the President and Fellows of Harvard College. Excerpts from *The Law of Peoples*. Copyright © 1999 by the President and Fellows of Harvard College. All reprinted with the permission of The Belknap Press of Harvard University Press.

David Rodin, (excerpts from "Terrorism without Intention" from *Ethics* 114 (July 2004). Copyright © 2004 by The University of Chicago. Reprinted with the permission of the author and The University of Chicago Press.

Sue Savage-Rumbaugh and Roger Lewin, from *Kanzi: The Ape at the Brink of the Human Mind*. Copyright © 1994 by Sue Savage-Rumbaugh and Roger Lewin. Reprinted with the permission of John Wiley & Sons, Inc.

Isaac Bashevis Singer, from "A Piece of Advice," translated by Martha Glicklich and Joel Blocker, from *The Spinoza of Market Street*. Copyright © 1961, renewed 1989 by Isaac Bashevis Singer. Reprinted with the permission of Farrar, Straus & Giroux, LLC.

Tom Sorell, excerpts from "Two Ideals and the Death Penalty," *Criminal Justice Ethics* 23, no. 2. Reprinted with the permission of The Institute for Criminal Justice Ethics, 555 West 57th Street, Suite 601, New York, NY 10019-1029.

Deborah Tannen, excerpt from *Talking from 9 to 5*. Copyright © 1994 by Deborah Tannen. Reprinted with the permission of William Morrow, a division of HarperCollins Publishers, Inc.

Sheri S. Tepper, excerpts from *Sideshow*. Copyright © 1992 by Sheri S. Tepper. Reprinted with the permission of Bantam Books, a division of Random House, Inc.

United Nations General Assembly, "The United Nations Universal Declaration of Human Rights" (1948). Reprinted with the permission of the United Nations

Diane Whiteley, excerpt from "The Victim and the Justification of Punishment" from *Criminal Justice Ethics* (Summer/Fall 1998). Reprinted with the permission of The Institute for Criminal Justice Ethics, 555 West 57th Street, Suite 601, New York, NY 10019-1029.

Photo Credits

Page 19: Photo by T. Scott Niendorf. Courtesy Martha Nussbaum; **46**: The Granger Collection; **84**: © Bettmann/CORBIS; **114**: © Bettmann/CORBIS; **127**: Courtesy James Rachels; **143**: © AP/Wide World Photos; **149**: © AP/Wide World Photos; **162**: © Bettmann/CORBIS; **164**: © Fabian Falcon/Stock Boston; **182**: © Bettmann/CORBIS; **196**: UPI/Bettmann/CORBIS; **215**: © Photography and Illustration Centre/University College London; **224**: © Bettmann/CORBIS; **228**: The Granger Collection; **305**: The Spokesman Review, Spokane WA; **314**: © AP/Wide World Photos; **329**: Courtesy Elizabeth Wolgast; **332**: Courtesy Marilyn Friedman; **379**: The Metropolitan Museum of Art, Catherine Lorillard Wolfe Collection, Wolfe Fund 1931. (31.45); **382**: © Bettmann/CORBIS; **418**: © Bettmann/CORBIS; **419**: © Bettmann/CORBIS; **444**: © Scala/Art Resource, NY; **464**: Courtesy Christina Hoff Sommers; **468**: © Bettmann/CORBIS; **470**: © ARS, NY, photo: Erich Lessing/Art Resource, NY; **472**: Courtesy of the Royal Library; **474**: © Bettmann/CORBIS; **478**: © Bettmann/CORBIS; **485**: Ulf Andersen/Agence Enguerand; **502**: © CORBIS; **520, 550**: The Granger Collection; **573**: (left to right) © Stefan Zaklin/Getty Images, © Getty Images; **576**: The Granger Collection; **587**: © Bettmann/CORBIS; **593**: © Bettmann/CORBIS; **643**: Courtesy the Savage-Rumbaugh, Language Research Center, Georgia State University

Glossary

abolitionism: Today: the viewpoint that the death penalty ought to be abolished. *See* retentionism.

absolution: Forgiveness; usually God's forgiveness.

absolutism: The ethical theory that there is a universal set of moral rules that can and should be followed by everybody.

absurdity: The existentialist concept that life is meaningless because there is no God to determine right and wrong (or because we can't know what God's values are, if God happens to exist).

acculturation: Cultural development.

act utilitarianism: The classical version of utilitarianism that focuses on the consequences of a single act.

ad hominem argument: A logical fallacy (a formally faulty argument) that assumes that because a person is who he or she is, his or her viewpoint must be wrong.

ad misericordiam fallacy: Appeal to pity.

agnosticism: The view that God is unknown or that it cannot be known whether or not there is a God.

altruism: Concern for the interests of others. Extreme (ideal) altruism: concern for the interests of others while disregarding one's own interests. Moderate altruism (also known as Golden Rule altruism or reciprocal altruism): taking others' interests into account while being concerned for one's own interests as well.

ambiguity: Quality exhibited in an expression or statement that can be interpreted in different ways.

anamnesis: Greek: re-remembering. Plato's theory of remembering the truth about the Forms, forgotten at birth.

androgynism: Male and female nature in the same individual, either in terms of sex (biological) or gender (cultural).

android: An artificial intelligence; a robot made to resemble a human being. Literally: manlike. There is no accepted word for a female android, but the equivalent would be *gyneoid.*

angst: Existentialist term for anxiety or anguish, a feeling of dread without any identifiable cause. Most frequently felt when one has to make important decisions. Different from *fear,* where the object of the emotion is known.

anthropocentrism: Viewing everything from an exclusively human perspective.

anthropology: The study of humans. Physical anthropology: the study of human biology and biological prehistory. Cultural anthropology: the study of human cultures.

anthropomorphism: Literally: making into a human shape. Projecting human characteristics into the behavior of other animals.

antiquity: Usually refers to the historical time period in ancient cultures around the Mediterranean after the invention of writing (about 6000 years ago) and prior to the early Middle Ages (approx. 500 C.E.).

anxiety: *See* angst.

approximation: To approach something with as much accuracy as the conditions allow.

arbitrary: Coincidental, without meaning or consistency.

artificial womb: Medical environment allowing a fetus to grow to maturity outside a mother's womb.

asceticism: Denying oneself physical pleasures and indulgence.

ataraxia: Epicurus's highest form of pleasure, having peace of mind due to freedom from pain.

atheism: The conviction that there is no God.

authenticity: Being true to yourself, having personal integrity. Existentialism: not succumbing to the idea that you have no free choice. *See* bad faith.

auto-icon: An image of oneself that consists of oneself. Bentham's term for his own planned future position as a stuffed corpse on display.

autonomy: Independence; a state achieved by those who are self-governing. Autonomous lawmaker: Kant's term for a person using the categorical imperative without regard for personal interest, arriving at something he or she would want to become a universal law. Moral autonomy: being capable of and allowed to make moral decisions on your own.

backward-looking justice: Correcting past wrongs.

bad faith: Existentialist term for the belief that you have no choice; the belief that you can transform yourself into a thing with no will or emotions.

begging the question: A logical fallacy whereby a person who is supposed to prove something assumes from the start that it is a fact.

Being-there: Heidegger's term for human beings, or at least for beings who are self-aware.

benevolence: Interest in the well-being or comfort of others.

bibliotherapy: Using books, usually stories of fiction, in therapy sessions to facilitate patients' understanding of themselves and their situation and options.

bipartisan: "Of two parties," politically neutral or objective.

blog, blogger: From *weblog,* personal websites devoted to opinion and observations, often political.

care: (1) Heidegger's concept of human existence, involving a *Care-structure,* being engaged in living; (2) Gilligan's concept of ethics as it is typically viewed by women— an *ethics of care* rather than an *ethics of justice.*

catalyst: A person or agent that causes something to happen.

categorical imperative: Kant's term for an absolute moral rule that is justified because of its logic: If you can wish for your maxim to become a universal law, your maxim qualifies as a categorical imperative.

catharsis, cathartic: Cleansing. *See* Aristotle's theory of drama, Chapter 2.

causality, causal explanation: The chain of cause and effect. Aristotle's theory of causation: material cause (the material aspect of a thing), efficient cause (the maker of a thing), formal cause (the idea of a thing), and final cause (the purpose of a thing).

character arc: A concept used in screenwriting and narrative theory. A character in the story undergoes a certain development leading to a conclusion.

chauvinism: Originally: excessive feeling of nationalism, from the Frenchman Chauvin. Today it usually means male chauvinism (sexism from a male point of view).

classical feminism: The feminist view that women and men ought to be considered persons first and gendered beings second.

cloning: Creating a genetic copy of another individual, either through a process where multiple twins are created, or a process where a cell nucleus is taken from the original individual, implanted in an emptied ovum, and allowed to develop into an embryo. If the embryo is terminated within ten to fourteen days, *stem cells* may be harvested. If an embryo can survive and be carried to term, a cloned individual is the result. Cloning will not result in a perfect copy of another individual, physically or mentally, because of the variety of circumstances surrounding the growth process that can't be duplicated.

cognitive, cognition: The faculty of knowing, examining something rationally.

collateral damage: Unintentional and unavoidable civilian casualties during a war.

communitarianism: A moral and political theory that the individual receives his or her identity from his or her community and can flourish only within the community. The theory is found in the ancient Greek tradition but is also evident in traditional African tribal cultures. Modern communitarians mentioned in this book include Alasdair MacIntyre and Elizabeth Wolgast. In addition, Hillary Rodham Clinton has declared herself a communitarian with the publication of her book, *It Takes a Village.*

conceptualize: Make a vague notion into a concept with a clear definition that can be used in a description or an argument.

condition of possibility: What makes something possible, or what makes it come into being.

consequentialism: A theory that focuses exclusively on the consequences of an action. Utilitarianism is the best-known consequentialist theory, but ethical egoism also qualifies as an example of consequentialism.

Continental philosophy: Philosophical traditions from the European continent (excluding British traditions).

contractarianism: The theory that only humans can have rights, because only humans can enter into agreements (contracts) and recognize duties springing from those agreements.

correlative: A term or a concept that is understood in its relation to other concepts. The fallacy of the suppressed correlative: If terms are correlative, like *hot/cold,* and *tall/short,* they help define each other. If one is suppressed, the other ceases to have any meaning.

counterfable/countermyth: A story/fable/myth told deliberately to prove another story, type of story, or idea wrong.

criminal justice: Punishment of people found guilty of crimes.

criterion: A test, rule, or measure for distinguishing between true and false, relevant and irrelevant. A standard for a correct judgment. Plural: *criteria.*

Crusades, the: Military expeditions undertaken by European Christians from the eleventh through the thirteenth centuries to recover the Holy Land from the Muslims.

cultural diversity: The recognition of a variety of ethnic and racial groups within a given region (all the way from a neighborhood to planet Earth).

cultural imperialism: A critical term for the attitude of imposing one's cultural accomplishments and moral convictions on other cultures.

cultural relativism: The theory that different societies or cultures have different moral codes. A descriptive theory.

culture war: Ideological disagreement between liberal and conservative values.

cynicism: Distrust in evidence of virtue or disinterested motives. Pessimism. Originally a Greek school of thought believing that virtue, not pleasure or intellect, was the ultimate goal of life. Deteriorated into the idea of self-righteousness.

debt-metaphor: English's term for using the terms *owing* and *debt* in situations where they may or may not be appropriate. Appropriate use: a situation in which favors are owed. Inappropriate use: a situation of friendship or family relationship.

deduction: The scientific and philosophical method of identifying an item of absolute truth (an axiom) and using this as a premise to deduce specific cases that are also absolutely true.

deontology: Duty-theory. An ethical theory that disregards the importance of consequences and focuses only on the rightness or wrongness of the act itself.

descriptive: Describing a phenomenon without making an evaluative or judgmental statement. Opposite of normative.

deterrence: A concept of criminal justice: punishing criminals with the intent to deter them (*specific* deterrence) or others (*general* deterrence) from committing the same crime.

dialectic method: Socrates' method of guiding his students to their own realization of the truth through a conversation, a dialogue. Also called the Socratic method.

dichotomy: An "either-or" statement. A false dichotomy: an either-or statement that ignores other possibilities.

didactic: Done or told for the purpose of teaching a lesson.

difference feminism: The feminist view that women and men are fundamentally different, morally and psychologically.

dilemma: The situation of having to choose between two courses of action that either exclude each other or are equally unpleasant.

distributive justice: Fair distribution of social goods.

divine command theory: A theological theory that God has created the laws of morality; in other words, something is right because God commands it. Opposed to *natural law theory,* which claims that God commands something because it is right. *See* also natural law.

double effect: A principle primarily found within Catholic ethics: An action that is otherwise prohibited can be permitted, provided that it is an *unintended* side effect to some other, necessary action; that the effect of the primary action is *proportionately very serious,* and the effect of the secondary action is *unavoidable.* The principle is used to justify rare cases of euthanasia and abortion, among others.

dualism: The metaphysical theory that reality consists of matter and mind. Also used as a term for any theory of opposite forces.

egalitarian: A theory that advocates social equality.

Ego: Freud's term for the human experience of the self. *See also* Superego and Id.

ego integrity: Erikson's term for mental equilibrium, accepting one's past, and not playing the "what if" game with oneself.

elitism: The belief that a certain advantage (for instance, knowledge, education, or wealth) should be reserved for a small part of the population, an elite.

embedded journalist: A journalist who travels with a military force.

empiricism: The philosophical school of thought that claims humans are born without knowledge, that the mind is an empty slate (*tabula rasa*) at birth, and that all knowledge comes through the senses.

end in oneself: Kant's term for a person. Persons (rational beings) should be regarded as dignified beings who have their own goals in life; they should not be used as a means to an end only. *See* means to an end, merely.

end justifies the means, the: The statement of a consequentialist: Only the consequences count, not how they are brought about.

enfranchisement: Having rights, and thus political power (*disenfranchisement* means having those powers taken away).

Enlightenment, the: In the European and American cultural tradition, the eighteenth century saw a new focusing on the rights of the individual, the importance of education, and the objectivity of science. Also called the *Age of Reason* or the Western Enlightenment; rationality was considered the ultimate cultural goal by scientists, philosophers, and many politicians.

epistemology: Theory of knowledge. One of the main branches of traditional philosophy.

equilibrium: In this book: A well-balanced mind, capable of fair judgment.

equity feminism: The feminist view that the battle for equality has been won and that further insistence on women's inequality only serves to make women into victims.

essence: A thing's inner nature. "Essence precedes existence": the traditional philosophical conception of reality, including human nature; the theory that there is a design or purpose that nature must follow.

ethical egoism: The theory that everybody ought to be egoistic/selfish/self-interested.

ethical pluralism: Several moral systems working simultaneously within one culture.

ethical relativism: The theory that there is no universal moral code and that whatever the majority of any given society or culture considers morally right is morally right for that culture. A normative theory. *See also* cultural relativism.

ethical will: Personal legacy letter summarizing one's values and life lessons.

ethicist: A person professionally or vocationally involved with the theory and application of ethics.

ethics: The study, questioning, and justification of moral rules.

ethics of conduct: The study of moral rules pertaining to decisions about what course of action to take or "what to do."

ethics of virtue: The study of moral rules pertaining to the building of character or "how to be."

ethos: The moral rules and attitudes of a culture.

eudaimonia: Greek: well-spirited, contentment, happiness. Aristotle's term for the ultimate human goal.

Eurocentric: A critical term meaning that American culture is overly focused on its European roots. Possibly a misnomer, since Americans rarely focus on European traditions, politics, and history, but rather on the European *legacy* for mainstream American culture.

euthanasia: Mercy killing; doctor-assisted suicide. Literally: "good death," from Greek. Voluntary euthanasia: requested by the patient. Involuntary euthanasia: (a) The patient is killed against her or his will; (b) The patient cannot communicate his or her wish, so the decision is made by the family (also called nonvoluntary euthanasia). Active euthanasia: helping someone to die at his

or her request. Passive euthanasia: withholding treatment that will not help a terminally ill patient.

evidence: A ground or reason for certainty in knowledge. Usually empirical evidence; facts gathered in support of a theory.

exemplar: A model, an example for others to follow.

existence precedes essence: Existentialist belief that humans aren't determined by any essence (human nature) but exist prior to any decision about what and how they ought to be.

existentialism: A Continental school of thought that believes all humans have freedom of the will to determine their own life.

extrinsic value: *See* instrumental value.

fable: A short narrative with a moral, introducing persons, animals, or inanimate things as speakers and actors.

fallacy: A flaw in one's reasoning; an argument that does not follow the rules of logic.

falsification, principle of: The concept that a valid theory must test itself and allow for the possibility of situations in which the theory doesn't apply. In a sense, part of the verification process of a theory is being able to hypothetically falsify it.

fatalism: The theory that life is determined by a higher power and that our will can't change our destiny.

faux pas: French: a misstep, a social blunder.

fecundity: Being fruitful, having good consequences.

first-wave feminism: Feminism from the eighteenth century until approximately 1920. *See* second- and third-wave feminism.

forensic: Related to the use of scientific or medical procedures to investigate a death.

Forms, theory of: Plato's metaphysical theory of a higher reality that gives meaning and existence to the world we experience through our senses. This higher reality is accessible through the mind. Example: a perfect circle; it doesn't exist in the world of the senses, but it does exist in the intelligible world of Forms.

fortitude: Strength of mind and courage in the face of adversity.

forward-looking justice: Creating good future social consequences. *See also* consequentialism.

free will: The notion that we can make choices that are not completely determined by our heredity and our environment.

fundamentalism: A religious approach to reality that interprets the dogmas and sacred scriptures of the tradition literally.

gender-neutral: Not gender-specific. Usually used when referring to language. Examples: Scientists must do their research well. Nurses should take good care of their patients.

gender-specific: Applying to one sex only. Examples of gender-specific language: A scientist must do *his* research well. A nurse must take good care of *her* patients.

genetic engineering: Scientific manipulation of the DNA code of an individual (human, animal, or plant), usually to enhance certain desired characteristics or eliminate congenital diseases.

genetic fallacy, the: Assuming that something can be fully explained by pointing to its original/first condition.

genocide: The murder of all or most of a population.

genre: A literary type of story (or film), such as horror, western, or science fiction.

Golden Mean, the: The Greek idea of moderation. Aristotle's concept of virtue as a relative mean between the extremes of excess and deficiency.

good will: For Kant, having good will means having good intentions in terms of respecting a moral law that is rational and deserves to be a universal law.

greatest-happiness principle, the: *See* utility.

hard determinism: The theory that everything can, in principle, be predicted and understood with 100 percent accuracy, because everything is an effect of a previous cause.

hard universalism: *See* absolutism.

harm principle, the: John Stuart Mill's idea that one should not interfere with other people's lives unless those people are doing harm to others.

hedonism: Pleasure-seeking. The paradox of hedonism: The more you look for pleasure, the more it seems to elude you. Hedonistic calculus: Bentham's pros-and-cons system, in which pleasures are added and pains subtracted to find the most utilitarian course of action.

heterogeneous: Consisting of dissimilar or diverse elements.

hierarchy: A structure of higher and lower elements, ordered according to their relative importance.

homogeneous: Consisting of similar elements.

human condition, the: What it means to be a human being, usually in terms of inevitable facts: having physical and spiritual needs, being a social creature, and being subject to illness and aging.

hyphenated: A political term for the distinction between one's national or ethnic ancestry and one's American identity, such as *Swedish-American.* To be "hyphenated" indicates for some people that one's loyalties are divided. Today it is common to omit the hyphen, as in *Swedish American.*

hypothetical imperative: A command that is binding only if one is interested in a certain result. An "if-then" situation.

Id: Freud's term for the Unconscious, the part of the mind that the conscious self (the Ego) has no access to but that influences the Ego.

idealism: The metaphysical theory that reality consists of mind only, not matter.

immutability: Something that remains stable and can't be changed.

inalienable: Incapable of being taken or given away.

incapacitation: A concept of criminal justice: punishing a criminal with the intent of making the public safe from his or her criminal activity. May refer to incarceration as well as other forms of punishment, including capital punishment.

incredulity: Skepticism; refusal to believe something.

induction: The scientific and philosophical method of collecting empirical evidence and formulating a general theory based on those specific facts. The problem of induction: Because one never knows if one has collected enough evidence, one can never achieve 100 percent certainty through induction.

institutionalized cruelty: Hallie's term for cruelty (psychological or physical) that has become so established, it seems natural to both victimizer and victim.

instrumental value: To have value for the sake of what further value it might bring. Also known as extrinsic value; good as a means to an end. *See* means to an end.

intersexual: A person with both male and female genitalia.

intrinsic value: To have value in itself without regard to what it might bring of further value. Good in itself, good as an "end in itself." *See* end in oneself.

intuition: Usually, an experience of understanding that is independent of one's reasoning. Can also mean the moment of understanding, an "Aha" experience. Moral intuition: a gut-level feeling of right and wrong.

ipso facto: By the fact itself.

irony: Ridicule through exaggeration, praise, or understatement.

jus ad bellum: Just war: a war conducted in self-defense according to set rules.

jus in bello: Justice in war. Rules for proper conduct of war.

kingdom of ends: Kant's term for a society of autonomous lawmakers who all use the categorical imperative and show each other mutual respect.

leap of faith: Kierkegaard's concept of the necessary step from the ethical to the religious stage. It involves throwing yourself at the mercy of God and discarding all messages from your rational mind or your self-interested emotions.

lex talionis: The law of retaliation; an eye for an eye. A retributivist argument for punishment.

liberalism: A political theory that supports gradual reforms through parliamentary procedures and civil liberties.

libertarianism: (1) A theory of government that holds the individual has a right to life, liberty, and property; that nobody should interfere with these rights (negative rights); and that the government's role should be restricted to protecting these rights. (2) A theory that humans have free will independent of mechanistic causality.

Magi, the: The Three Kings, or Wise Men, who came to worship Jesus in the manger, bearing gifts of gold, frankincense, and myrrh.

master morality: Nietzsche's view of the morality of strong individuals in ancient times; includes respect for the enemy, loyalty to friends and kin, and scorn for weaker individuals. Leads to the concept of the Overman (Superman), the strong individual who has gone beyond the moral rules and sets his own standards of good and evil.

materialism: The metaphysical theory that reality consists of matter only, not mind.

matriarchy, matriarchal: A society in which women have great social influence and the words of older women within the family carry much weight. Sometimes taken to mean a society ruled by women.

maxim: Kant's term for the rule or principle of an action.

means to an end: Something used to achieve another goal, an end. *See* instrumental value.

means to an end, merely: Kant's term for using others as a stepping-stone for one's own purpose.

mental state: Any mind activity or mental image.

metaethics: The approach to ethics that refrains from making normative statements but focuses on the meaning of terms and statements and investigates the sources of normative statements.

metaphor: An image or an illustration that describes something in terms of something different. A figurative image such as "My boyfriend is a tiger."

metaphysics: The philosophical study of the nature of reality or of being.

misanthropy: Misgivings about, hatred of, or lack of trust in the goodness of human nature.

misogyny: Misgivings about, hatred of, or lack of trust in female human nature. There is no traditional equivalent term for mistrusting male human nature, but such a term might be *misandry.*

monism: A type of metaphysics that holds that there is one element of reality only, such as materialism or idealism.

monoculturalism: As opposed to multiculturalism. The concept of a dominant culture, viewing its history and cultural practices as the only significant contributions to the culture in question.

moral agent: A person capable of reflecting on a moral problem and acting on his or her decision.

moral cannibalism: Ayn Rand's description of any moral theory that advocates altruism.

morality, morals: The moral rules and attitudes that we live by, or are expected to live by.

mores: The moral customs and rules of a given culture.

multiculturalism: The policy of recognizing cultural diversity to the extent where all cultures within a given region are fairly represented in terms of public life and education. Sometimes includes gender as cultural diversity. *See also* cultural diversity, pluralism, and particularism.

myth: A story or a collection of stories that give identity, guidance, and meaning to a culture. Usually these are stories of gods and heroes, but they may involve ordinary people, too. In common language myth has come to mean "falsehood" or "illusion," but this is not the original meaning.

narrative: A story with a plot. Narrative structure: perceiving events as having a logical progression from a beginning through a middle to an ending.

narrative time: The time frame within which a story takes place. The experience of sharing this time frame as one reads or watches the story unfold.

natural law: A view introduced to the Catholic Church by Thomas Aquinas that what is natural for humans (in other words, what God has intended) is good for humans. What is natural for humans includes: preservation of life, procreation, socialization, and pursuit of knowledge of God.

natural rights: The assumption that humans (and perhaps also nonhumans) are born with certain inalienable rights.

naturalistic fallacy: The assumption that one can conclude from what is natural/a fact ("what is") what should be a rule or a policy ("what ought to be"). Not all philosophers think this is a fallacy.

negative command: Hallie's term for a moral command involving a prohibition, such as "Don't lie" or "Don't cause harm." *See* positive command.

negative rights: Rights not to be interfered with; usually includes the right to life, liberty, and property. Originally an element in John Locke's political philosophy; has become a defining element of modern Libertarian philosophy.

neo-classicism: A style of art and architecture in the seventeenth and eighteenth centuries that revived classical Greek and Roman forms. Also, any spiritual and philosophical movement that tries to recover the classical ideals of moderation and order.

nihilism: From the Latin *nihil*, nothing. The attitude of believing in nothing. Moral nihilism: the conviction that there are no moral truths.

normative: Evaluating and/or setting norms or standards. Opposite of descriptive.

objectification: Making an object, a thing, out of someone: disregarding their human dignity. Also reification, making a thing out of someone.

objective: The kind of knowledge that is supported by evidence and that has independent existence apart from experience or thought.

ontology: A philosophical discipline investigating the nature of existence.

original sin: The Christian belief that the disobedience of Adam and Eve is inherited by all humans from birth, so all humans are born sinful.

Other, the: A philosophical concept meaning either something that is completely different from yourself and all your experiences or someone who is different from you and is thus hard to understand.

Overman, or Superman: Nietzsche's term for the individual who has recognized his will to power and created his own system of values based on an affirmation of life.

pacifism: The belief that war and violence are morally wrong, regardless of the circumstances.

parable: A short narrative told to make a moral or religious point.

particularism: The branch of multiculturalism that believes people not belonging to the dominant culture should retrieve their self-esteem by learning about the traditions and accomplishments of their own cultural group rather than those of the dominant group or any other group. Also called exclusive multiculturalism.

paterfamilias: The male head of the household.

patriarchy: A society ruled by men, or a society in which men have great social influence.

philanthropy: Greek: loving humans. Doing good deeds, being charitable.

philology: The study of language, its structure and history.

phronesis: Aristotle's term for practical wisdom, our everyday decision-making process.

pleasure principle: Freud's term for the oldest layer of the human mind, which caters selfishly to our own pleasure. For most people it is superseded by the reality principle, at least most of the time.

pluralism: The branch of multiculturalism that believes racial and ethnic discrimination in a population of cultural diversity can be abolished by a shared orientation in each other's cultural traditions and history. Also called inclusive multiculturalism. Also: any theory or culture that includes several different viewpoints.

positive command: Hallie's term for a moral command to actively do something rather than merely refraining from doing something wrong (a negative command). Example: "Help another being in distress."

positive rights: Rights of entitlement. The theory that each individual has a right to the basic means of subsistence against the state, such as food, shelter, clothing, education, welfare, health services.

preconceived notion: An idea that is formed prior to actual knowledge or experience and that you don't think of questioning.

prerational: Before the use of reason; instinctive; belonging to human nature prior to the development of reason.

prescriptive: *See* normative.

presocial: Before the existence of society.

principle of utility: *See* utility.

procreation: Having offspring, giving birth.

protagonist: The hero of the story.

psychological altruism: The theory that everyone is always unselfish.

psychological egoism: The theory that everyone is selfish, self-interested.

psychosexual neutrality: The behaviorist theory that human sexuality is a matter of upbringing (nurture) rather than a hardwiring of the brain (nature).

radical feminism: The feminist view that the root cause of male dominance of women and discrimination against women must be examined.

rational being: Anyone who has intelligence and the capacity to use it. Usually stands for human beings, but may exclude some humans and include some nonhuman beings.

rationalism: The philosophical school of thought that claims humans are born with some knowledge, or some capacity for knowledge, such as logic and mathematics. Opposite of empiricism.

reality principle: Freud's term for the knowledge that we can't always have things our own way.

reductio ad absurdum: A form of argument in which you reduce your opponent's viewpoint to its absurd consequences.

rehabilitation: A concept of criminal justice: punishing a criminal with the intent of making him or her a better socialized person at the end of the term of punishment.

reification: *See* objectification.

relevance: Direct application to a situation; pertinence.

Renaissance: Literally: rebirth. The European cultural revival of the arts and sciences in the fourteenth through sixteenth centuries. This period marked the end of the Middle Ages.

replicant: Term used in the film *Blade Runner* for androids. *See* android.

reproductive cloning: Creating an individual (human) as a genetic copy of another (human) individual.

restorative justice: Rehabilitation of criminals, and restitution to the victims.

retentionism: The viewpoint that the death penalty ought to be retained (kept as an option).

retribution: A concept of criminal justice: the logical dispensing or receiving of punishment in proportion to the crime. Sometimes known as "an eye for an eye," *lex talionis.* To be distinguished from vengeance, which is an emotional response that may exceed the severity of the crime.

retributive justice: Punishment of criminals in proportion to their crime.

revisionism: Advocacy of revision of former values and viewpoints. Today: refers mostly to a cynical revision of heroic values of the past.

rhetoric: The art of verbal persuasion.

Romanticism, the Romantic Movement: A movement among artists, philosophers, and social critics in the late eighteenth and nineteenth centuries, partly based on the idea that emotion is a legitimate form of expression and can give access to higher truths without necessarily involving the intellect.

rule utilitarianism: The branch of utilitarianism that focuses on the consequences of a type of action done repeatedly, and not just a single act. *See* act utilitarianism.

satire: The use of sarcasm in a criticism of conditions one doesn't approve of.

second-wave feminism: Feminism in the United States and Europe from the mid-1950s on. Some consider second-wave feminism to have ended by the mid-1980s; others see it as continuing.

selfish gene: The twentieth-century theory that humans as well as animals have a disposition that favors themselves, but also the survival of their genes. Occasionally, animals (or humans) will sacrifice themselves so that their closely related relatives or offspring may survive.

Silver Rule, the: Do not do to others what you would not like them to do to you. A negative version of the Golden Rule, Do unto others as you would have them do unto you.

skepticism: The philosophical approach that we cannot obtain absolutely certain knowledge. In practice it is an approach of not believing anything until there is sufficient evidence to prove it.

slave morality: Nietzsche's concept of the morality of the "herd," people who in his view resent strong individuals and claim that meekness is a virtue.

slippery slope argument: A version of the *reductio ad absurdum* argument; you reduce your opponent's view to unacceptable or ridiculous consequences, which your opponent will presumably have to accept or else abandon his or her theory. Your opponent's argument must "slide down the slope" of logic. A way to defeat the slippery slope argument is to "draw the line" and defend your viewpoint on the basis that there is a difference between the "top of the slope" and the "bottom of the slope."

social contract: A type of social theory, popular in the seventeenth and eighteenth centuries, that assumes humans in the early stages of society got together and agreed on terms for creating a society.

soft universalism: The ethical theory that although humans may not agree on all moral rules or all customs, there are a few bottom-line rules we can agree on, despite our different ways of expressing them.

sophia: Greek: wisdom. Aristotle's term for theoretical wisdom, the highest intellectual virtue.

spatial: Associated with space.

straw man (straw dummy) argument: A logical fallacy that consists of attacking and disproving a theory invented for the occasion.

subjective opinion: One that is not supported by evidence, or is dependent on the mind and experience of the person.

subjectivism: Ethical theory that claims that your moral belief is right simply because you believe it; there are no intersubjective (shared) moral standards.

Superego: Freud's concept of the human conscience, the internalized rules of our parents and our society.

teleology: A theory of purpose. A teleological theory such as Aristotle's may assume that everything has a purpose. Also used to designate theories interested in the outcome of an action, that is, consequentialist theories.

temperance: In virtue theory this means moderation. In a modern context it may mean abstinence from alcohol.

temporal: Associated with time. Temporal being: a being living in time and understanding himself or herself in terms of a past, a present, and a future.

theology: The study of God and God's nature and attributes.

therapeutic cloning: Cloning of stem cells for the purpose of curing illness.

third-wave feminism: Feminism from the mid-1980s to the present day.

totalitarianism: A form of government that views the state as all-important and the lives of its citizens as disposable.

transgenic: Genetic engineering of an animal or a plant (or, theoretically, a human) with some genes from another species.

universal law: Kant's term for a moral rule that can be imagined as applying to everybody in the same situation and accepted by other rational beings.

universalizability: A maxim that is acceptable as a universal law.

universalization: The process by which one asks oneself whether one's maxim could become a universal law: "What if everybody did this?"

unrequited: Unreturned, nonreciprocal.

utilitarianism: The theory that one ought to maximize the happiness and minimize the unhappiness of as many people (or sentient beings) as possible.

utility: Fitness for some purpose, especially for creating happiness and/or minimizing pain and suffering. Principle of utility: To create as much happiness and minimize suffering as much as possible for as many as possible. Also: the greatest-happiness principle.

Utopia: Literally, no place. Sir Thomas More's term for a nonexistent world, usually used as a term for a world too good to be true. Utopia can also mean "good place." A bad place is known as "Dystopia."

vengeance: Revenge. When used as a concept of criminal justice: an emotional response to punishment.

viability: The time in a pregnancy where a fetus could survive outside the mother's body.

vicariously: To experience something through the experiences of others.

Voir dire: The questioning of potential jurors during jury selection.

Way, the: Chinese: Tao (Dao). The morally and philosophically correct path to follow.

yin and yang: The two cosmic principles of Taoism, opposing forces that keep the universe in balance.

Index

Page numbers in **boldface** refer to primary readings and narratives. Page numbers in *italics* refer to illustrations.